Lecture Notes in Computer Science   10861

Commenced Publication in 1973
Founding and Former Series Editors:
Gerhard Goos, Juris Hartmanis, and Jan van Leeuwen

More information about this series at http://www.springer.com/series/7407

Yong Shi · Haohuan Fu
Yingjie Tian · Valeria V. Krzhizhanovskaya
Michael Harold Lees · Jack Dongarra
Peter M. A. Sloot (Eds.)

Computational Science – ICCS 2018

18th International Conference
Wuxi, China, June 11–13, 2018
Proceedings, Part II

 Springer

Editors

Yong Shi
Chinese Academy of Sciences
Beijing
China

Haohuan Fu
National Supercomputing Center in Wuxi
Wuxi
China

Yingjie Tian
Chinese Academy of Sciences
Beijing
China

Valeria V. Krzhizhanovskaya (iD)
University of Amsterdam
Amsterdam
The Netherlands

Michael Harold Lees
University of Amsterdam
Amsterdam
The Netherlands

Jack Dongarra
University of Tennessee
Knoxville, TN
USA

Peter M. A. Sloot (iD)
University of Amsterdam
Amsterdam
The Netherlands

ISSN 0302-9743   ISSN 1611-3349 (electronic)
Lecture Notes in Computer Science
ISBN 978-3-319-93700-7   ISBN 978-3-319-93701-4 (eBook)
https://doi.org/10.1007/978-3-319-93701-4

Library of Congress Control Number: 2018947305

LNCS Sublibrary: SL1 – Theoretical Computer Science and General Issues

Printed on acid-free paper

This Springer imprint is published by the registered company Springer International Publishing AG
part of Springer Nature
The registered company address is: Gewerbestrasse 11, 6330 Cham, Switzerland

Preface

Welcome to the proceedings of the 18th Annual International Conference on Computational Science (ICCS: https://www.iccs-meeting.org/iccs2018/), held during June 11–13, 2018, in Wuxi, China. Located in the Jiangsu province, Wuxi is bordered by Changzhou to the west and Suzhou to the east. The city meets the Yangtze River in the north and is bathed by Lake Tai to the south. Wuxi is home to many parks, gardens, temples, and the fastest supercomputer in the world, the Sunway TaihuLight. ICCS 2018 was jointly organized by the University of Chinese Academy of Sciences, the National Supercomputing Center in Wuxi, the University of Amsterdam, NTU Singapore, and the University of Tennessee.

The International Conference on Computational Science is an annual conference that brings together researchers and scientists from mathematics and computer science as basic computing disciplines, researchers from various application areas who are pioneering computational methods in sciences such as physics, chemistry, life sciences, and engineering, as well as in arts and humanitarian fields, to discuss problems and solutions in the area, to identify new issues, and to shape future directions for research.

Since its inception in 2001, ICCS has attracted increasingly higher quality and numbers of attendees and papers, and this year was no an exception, with over 350 expected participants. The proceedings series have become a major intellectual resource for computational science researchers, defining and advancing the state of the art in this field.

ICCS 2018 in Wuxi, China, was the 18th in this series of highly successful conferences. For the previous 17 meetings, see: http://www.iccs-meeting.org/iccs2018/previous-iccs/.

The theme for ICCS 2018 was "Science at the Intersection of Data, Modelling and Computation," to highlight the role of computation as a fundamental method of scientific inquiry and technological discovery tackling problems across scientific domains and creating synergies between disciplines. This conference was a unique event focusing on recent developments in: scalable scientific algorithms; advanced software tools; computational grids; advanced numerical methods; and novel application areas. These innovative novel models, algorithms, and tools drive new science through efficient application in areas such as physical systems, computational and systems biology, environmental systems, finance, and others.

ICCS is well known for its excellent line up of keynote speakers. The keynotes for 2018 were:

- Charlie Catlett, Argonne National Laboratory|University of Chicago, USA
- Xiaofei Chen, Southern University of Science and Technology, China
- Liesbet Geris, University of Liège|KU Leuven, Belgium
- Sarika Jalan, Indian Institute of Technology Indore, India
- Petros Koumoutsakos, ETH Zürich, Switzerland
- Xuejun Yang, National University of Defense Technology, China

This year we had 405 submissions (180 submissions to the main track and 225 to the workshops). In the main track, 51 full papers were accepted (28%). In the workshops, 97 full papers (43%). A high acceptance rate in the workshops is explained by the nature of these thematic sessions, where many experts in a particular field are personally invited by workshop organizers to participate in their sessions.

ICCS relies strongly on the vital contributions of our workshop organizers to attract high-quality papers in many subject areas. We would like to thank all committee members for the main track and workshops for their contribution toward ensuring a high standard for the accepted papers. We would also like to thank Springer, Elsevier, Intellegibilis, Beijing Vastitude Technology Co., Ltd. and Inspur for their support. Finally, we very much appreciate all the local Organizing Committee members for their hard work to prepare this conference.

We are proud to note that ICCS is an ERA 2010 A-ranked conference series.

June 2018

Yong Shi
Haohuan Fu
Yingjie Tian
Valeria V. Krzhizhanovskaya
Michael Lees
Jack Dongarra
Peter M. A. Sloot
The ICCS 2018 Organizers

Organization

Local Organizing Committee

Co-chairs

Yingjie Tian	University of Chinese Academy of Sciences, China
Lin Gan	National Supercomputing Center in Wuxi, China

Members

Jiming Wu	National Supercomputing Center in Wuxi, China
Lingying Wu	National Supercomputing Center in Wuxi, China
Jinzhe Yang	National Supercomputing Center in Wuxi, China
Bingwei Chen	National Supercomputing Center in Wuxi, China
Yuanchun Zheng	University of Chinese Academy of Sciences, China
Minglong Lei	University of Chinese Academy of Sciences, China
Jia Wu	Macquarie University, Australia
Zhengsong Chen	University of Chinese Academy of Sciences, China
Limeng Cui	University of Chinese Academy of Sciences, China
Jiabin Liu	University of Chinese Academy of Sciences, China
Biao Li	University of Chinese Academy of Sciences, China
Yunlong Mi	University of Chinese Academy of Sciences, China
Wei Dai	University of Chinese Academy of Sciences, China

Workshops and Organizers

Advances in High-Performance Computational Earth Sciences: Applications and Frameworks – IHPCES 2018
Xing Cai, Kohei Fujita, Takashi Shimokawabe

Agent-Based Simulations, Adaptive Algorithms, and Solvers – ABS-AAS 2018
Robert Schaefer, Maciej Paszynski, Victor Calo, David Pardo

Applications of Matrix Methods in Artificial Intelligence and Machine Learning – AMAIML 2018
Kourosh Modarresi

Architecture, Languages, Compilation, and Hardware Support for Emerging Manycore Systems – ALCHEMY 2018
Loïc Cudennec, Stéphane Louise

Biomedical and Bioinformatics Challenges for Computer Science – BBC 2018
Giuseppe Agapito, Mario Cannataro, Mauro Castelli, Riccardo Dondi, Rodrigo Weber dos Santos, Italo Zoppis

Computational Finance and Business Intelligence – CFBI 2018
Shouyang Wang, Yong Shi, Yingjie Tian

Computational Optimization, Modelling, and Simulation – COMS 2018
Xin-She Yang, Slawomir Koziel, Leifur Leifsson, T. O. Ting

Data-Driven Computational Sciences – DDCS 2018
Craig Douglas, Abani Patra, Ana Cortés, Robert Lodder

Data, Modeling, and Computation in IoT and Smart Systems – DMC-IoT 2018
Julien Bourgeois, Vaidy Sunderam, Hicham Lakhlef

Mathematical Methods and Algorithms for Extreme Scale – MATH-EX 2018
Vassil Alexandrov

Multiscale Modelling and Simulation – MMS 2018
Derek Groen, Lin Gan, Valeria Krzhizhanovskaya, Alfons Hoekstra

Simulations of Flow and Transport: Modeling, Algorithms, and Computation – SOFTMAC 2018
Shuyu Sun, Jianguo (James) Liu, Jingfa Li

Solving Problems with Uncertainties – SPU 2018
Vassil Alexandrov

Teaching Computational Science – WTCS 2018
Angela B. Shiflet, Alfredo Tirado-Ramos, Nia Alexandrov

Tools for Program Development and Analysis in Computational Science – TOOLS 2018
Karl Fürlinger, Arndt Bode, Andreas Knüpfer, Dieter Kranzlmüller, Jens Volkert, Roland Wismüller

Urgent Computing – UC 2018
Marian Bubak, Alexander Boukhanovsky

Program Committee

Ahmad Abdelfattah	Ioannis Anagnostou	Adam Belloum
David Abramson	Michael Antolovich	Abdelhak Bentaleb
Giuseppe Agapito	Hartwig Anzt	Stefano Beretta
Ram Akella	Hideo Aochi	Daniel Berrar
Elisabete Alberdi	Tomasz Arodz	Sanjukta Bhowmick
Marco Aldinucci	Tomàs Artés Vivancos	Anna Bilyatdinova
Nia Alexandrov	Victor Azizi Tarksalooyeh	Guillaume Blin
Vassil Alexandrov	Ebrahim Bagheri	Nasri Bo
Saad Alowayyed	Bartosz Balis	Marcel Boersma
Ilkay Altintas	Krzysztof Banas	Bartosz Bosak
Stanislaw	Jörn Behrens	Kris Bubendorfer
Ambroszkiewicz	Adrian Bekasiewicz	Jérémy Buisson

Aleksander Byrski
Wentong Cai
Xing Cai
Mario Cannataro
Yongcan Cao
Pedro Cardoso
Mauro Castelli
Eduardo Cesar
Imen Chakroun
Huangxin Chen
Mingyang Chen
Zhensong Chen
Siew Ann Cheong
Lock-Yue Chew
Ana Cortes
Enrique
  Costa-Montenegro
Carlos Cotta
Jean-Francois Couchot
Helene Coullon
Attila Csikász-Nagy
Loïc Cudennec
Javier Cuenca
Yifeng Cui
Ben Czaja
Pawel Czarnul
Wei Dai
Lisandro Dalcin
Bhaskar Dasgupta
Susumu Date
Quanling Deng
Xiaolong Deng
Minh Ngoc Dinh
Riccardo Dondi
Tingxing Dong
Ruggero Donida Labati
Craig C. Douglas
Rafal Drezewski
Jian Du
Vitor Duarte
Witold Dzwinel
Nahid Emad
Christian Engelmann
Daniel Etiemble

Christos
  Filelis-Papadopoulos
Karl Frinkle
Haohuan Fu
Karl Fuerlinger
Kohei Fujita
Wlodzimierz Funika
Takashi Furumura
David Gal
Lin Gan
Robin Gandhi
Frédéric Gava
Alex Gerbessiotis
Carlos Gershenson
Domingo Gimenez
Frank Giraldo
Ivo Gonçalves
Yuriy Gorbachev
Pawel Gorecki
George Gravvanis
Derek Groen
Lutz Gross
Kun Guo
Xiaohu Guo
Piotr Gurgul
Panagiotis Hadjidoukas
Azzam Haidar
Dongxu Han
Raheel Hassan
Jurjen Rienk Helmus
Bogumila Hnatkowska
Alfons Hoekstra
Paul Hofmann
Sergey Ivanov
Hideya Iwasaki
Takeshi Iwashita
Jiří Jaroš
Marco Javarone
Chao Jin
Hai Jin
Zhong Jin
Jingheng
David Johnson
Anshul Joshi

Jaap Kaandorp
Viacheslav Kalashnikov
George Kampis
Drona Kandhai
Aneta Karaivanova
Vlad Karbovskii
Andrey Karsakov
Takahiro Katagiri
Wayne Kelly
Deepak Khazanchi
Alexandra Klimova
Ivan Kondov
Vladimir Korkhov
Jari Kortelainen
Ilias Kotsireas
Jisheng Kou
Sergey Kovalchuk
Slawomir Koziel
Valeria Krzhizhanovskaya
Massimo La Rosa
Hicham Lakhlef
Roberto Lam
Anna-Lena Lamprecht
Rubin Landau
Johannes Langguth
Vianney Lapotre
Jysoo Lee
Michael Lees
Minglong Lei
Leifur Leifsson
Roy Lettieri
Andrew Lewis
Biao Li
Dewei Li
Jingfa Li
Kai Li
Peijia Li
Wei Li
I-Jong Lin
Hong Liu
Hui Liu
James Liu
Jiabin Liu
Piyang Liu

Weifeng Liu
Weiguo Liu
Marcelo Lobosco
Robert Lodder
Wen Long
Stephane Louise
Frederic Loulergue
Paul Lu
Sheraton M. V.
Scott MacLachlan
Maciej Malawski
Michalska Malgorzatka
Vania
  Marangozova-Martin
Tomas Margalef
Tiziana Margaria
Svetozar Margenov
Osni Marques
Pawel Matuszyk
Valerie Maxville
Rahul Mazumder
Valentin Melnikov
Ivan Merelli
Doudou Messoud
Yunlong Mi
Jianyu Miao
John Michopoulos
Sergey Mityagin
K. Modarresi
Kourosh Modarresi
Jânio Monteiro
Paulo Moura Oliveira
Ignacio Muga
Hiromichi Nagao
Kengo Nakajima
Denis Nasonov
Philippe Navaux
Hoang Nguyen
Mai Nguyen
Anna Nikishova
Lingfeng Niu
Mawloud Omar
Kenji Ono
Raymond Padmos

Marcin Paprzycki
David Pardo
Anna Paszynska
Maciej Paszynski
Abani Patra
Dana Petcu
Eric Petit
Serge Petiton
Gauthier Picard
Daniela Piccioni
Yuri Pirola
Antoniu Pop
Ela Pustulka-Hunt
Vladimir Puzyrev
Alexander Pyayt
Pei Quan
Rick Quax
Waldemar Rachowicz
Lukasz Rauch
Alistair Rendell
Sophie Robert
J. M. F Rodrigues
Daniel Rodriguez
Albert Romkes
James A. Ross
Debraj Roy
Philip Rutten
Katarzyna Rycerz
Alberto Sanchez
Rodrigo Santos
Hitoshi Sato
Robert Schaefer
Olaf Schenk
Ulf D. Schiller
Bertil Schmidt
Hichem Sedjelmaci
Martha Johanna
  Sepulveda
Yong Shi
Angela Shiflet
Takashi Shimokawabe
Tan Singyee
Robert Sinkovits
Vishnu Sivadasan

Peter Sloot
Renata Slota
Grażyna Ślusarczyk
Sucha Smanchat
Maciej Smołka
Bartlomiej Sniezynski
Sumit Sourabh
Achim Streit
Barbara Strug
Bongwon Suh
Shuyu Sun
Martin Swain
Ryszard Tadeusiewicz
Daisuke Takahashi
Jingjing Tang
Osamu Tatebe
Andrei Tchernykh
Cedric Tedeschi
Joao Teixeira
Yonatan Afework
  Tesfahunegn
Andrew Thelen
Xin Tian
Yingjie Tian
T. O. Ting
Alfredo Tirado-Ramos
Stanimire Tomov
Ka Wai Tsang
Britt van Rooij
Raja Velu
Antonio M. Vidal
David Walker
Jianwu Wang
Peng Wang
Yi Wang
Josef Weinbub
Mei Wen
Mark Wijzenbroek
Maciej Woźniak
Guoqiang Wu
Jia Wu
Qing Wu
Huilin Xing
Wei Xue

Contents – Part II

**Track of Architecture, Languages, Compilation and Hardware
Support for Emerging ManYcore Systems**

**Track of Biomedical and Bioinformatics Challenges
for Computer Science**

Track of Data, Modeling, and Computation in IoT and Smart Systems

Track of Advances in High-Performance Computational Earth Sciences: Applications and Frameworks

Development of Scalable Three-Dimensional Elasto-Plastic Nonlinear Wave Propagation Analysis Method for Earthquake Damage Estimation of Soft Grounds

Atsushi Yoshiyuki$^{(\boxtimes)}$, Kohei Fujita, Tsuyoshi Ichimura, Muneo Hori,
and Lalith Wijerathne

Earthquake Research Institute and Department of Civil Engineering,
The University of Tokyo, Bunkyō, Japan
{y-atsu,fujita,ichimura,hori,lalith}@eri.u-tokyo.ac.jp

Abstract. In soft complex grounds, earthquakes cause damages with large deformation such as landslides and subsidence. Use of elasto-plastic models as the constitutive equation of soils is suitable for evaluation of nonlinear wave propagation with large ground deformation. However, there is no example of elasto-plastic nonlinear wave propagation analysis method capable of simulating a large-scale soil deformation problem. In this study, we developed a scalable elasto-plastic nonlinear wave propagation analysis program based on three-dimensional nonlinear finite-element method. The program attains 86.2% strong scaling efficiency from 240 CPU cores to 3840 CPU cores of PRIMEHPC FX10 based Oakleaf-FX [1], with 8.85 TFLOPS (15.6% of peak) performance on 3840 CPU cores. We verified the elasto-plastic nonlinear wave propagation program through convergence analysis, and conducted an analysis with large deformation for an actual soft ground modeled using 47,813,250 degrees-of-freedom.

1 Introduction

Large earthquakes often cause severe damage in cut-and-fill land developed for housing. It is said that earthquake waves are amplified locally by impedance contrast between the cut layer and fill layer, which causes damage. To evaluate this wave amplification, 3D wave propagation analysis with high spatial resolution considering nonlinearity of soil properties is required. Finite-element methods (FEM) are suitable for solving problems with complex geometry, and nonlinear constitutive relations can be implemented. However, large-scale finite-element analysis is computational expensive to assure convergence of the numerical solution.

Efficient use of high performance computers is effective for solving this problem [2,3]. For example, Ichimura et al. [4] developed a fast and scalable 3D

© Springer International Publishing AG, part of Springer Nature 2018
Y. Shi et al. (Eds.): ICCS 2018, LNCS 10861, pp. 3–16, 2018.
https://doi.org/10.1007/978-3-319-93701-4_1

nonlinear wave propagation analysis method based on nonlinear FEM, and was selected as a Gordon Bell Prize Finalist in SC14. Here, computational methods for speeding up the iterative solver was developed, which enabled large-scale analysis on distributed-shared memory parallel supercomputers such as the K computer [5]. In this method, a simple nonlinear model (Ramberg-Osgood model [6] with the Masing rule [7]) was used for the constitutive equation of soils, and the program was used for estimating earthquake damage at sites with complex grounds [8]. However, this simple constitutive equation is insufficient for simulating permanent ground displacement; 3D elasto-plastic constitutive equations are required to conduct reliable nonlinear wave propagation analysis for soft grounds. On the other hand, existing elasto-plastic nonlinear wave propagation analysis programs based on nonlinear FEM for seismic response of soils are not designed for high performance computers, and thus they cannot be used for large scale analyses.

In this study, we develop a scalable 3D elasto-plastic nonlinear wave propagation analysis method based on the highly efficient FEM solver described in [4]. Here, we incorporate a standard 3D elasto-plastic constitutive equation for soft soils (i.e., super-subloading surface Sekiguchi-Ohta EC model [9–11]) into this FEM solver. The FEM solver is also extended to conduct self-weight analysis, which is essential for conducting elasto-plastic analysis. This enables large-scale 3D elasto-plastic nonlinear wave propagation analysis, which is required for assuring numerical convergence when computing seismic response of soft grounds.

The rest of the paper is organized as follows. In Sect. 2, we describe the target equation and the developed nonlinear wave propagation analysis method. In Sect. 3, we verify the method through a convergence test, apply the method to an actual site, and measure the computational performance of the method. Section 4 concludes the paper.

2   Methodology

Previous wave propagation analysis based on nonlinear FEM [4] used the Ramberg-Osgood model and Masing rule for the constitutive equation of soils. Instead, we apply an elasto-plastic model (super-subloading surface Sekiguchi-Ohta EC model) to this FEM solver for analyzing large ground deformation. In elasto-plastic nonlinear wave propagation analysis, we first find an initial stress state by conducting initial stress analysis considering gravitational forces, and then conduct nonlinear wave propagation analysis by inputting seismic waves. Since the previous FEM implementation was not able to carry out initial stress analysis and nonlinear wave propagation analysis successively, we extended the solver. In this section, we first describe the target wave propagation problem with the super-subloading surface Sekiguchi-Ohta EC model, and then we describe the developed scalable elasto-plastic nonlinear wave propagation analysis method.

2.1 Target Problem

We use the following equation obtained by discretizing the nonlinear wave equation in the spatial domain by FEM and the time domain by the Newmark-β method:

$$\left(\frac{4}{dt^2}\mathbf{M} + \frac{2}{dt}\mathbf{C}^n + \mathbf{K}^n \right) \delta\mathbf{u}^n$$

$$= \mathbf{f}^n - \mathbf{q}^{n-1} + \mathbf{C}^n\mathbf{v}^{n-1} + \mathbf{M}\left(\mathbf{a}^{n-1} + \frac{4}{dt}\mathbf{v}^{n-1} \right), \qquad (1)$$

with

$$\begin{cases} \mathbf{q}^n = \mathbf{q}^{n-1} + \mathbf{K}^n\delta\mathbf{u}^n, \\ \mathbf{u}^n = \mathbf{u}^{n-1} + \delta\mathbf{u}^n, \\ \mathbf{v}^n = -\mathbf{v}^{n-1} + \frac{2}{dt}\delta\mathbf{u}^n, \\ \mathbf{a}^n = -\mathbf{a}^{n-1} - \frac{4}{dt}\mathbf{v}^{n-1} + \frac{4}{dt^2}\delta\mathbf{u}^n. \end{cases} \qquad (2)$$

Here, $\delta\mathbf{u}, \mathbf{u}, \mathbf{v}, \mathbf{a}$, and $\mathbf{f}$ are vectors describing incremental displacement, displacement, velocity, acceleration, and external force, respectively. $\mathbf{M}, \mathbf{C}$, and $\mathbf{K}$ are the mass, damping, and stiffness matrices. dt, and n are the time step increment and the time step number, respectively. In the case that nonlinearity occurs, $\mathbf{C}, \mathbf{K}$ change every time steps. Rayleigh damping is used for the damping matrix $\mathbf{C}$, where the element damping matrix $\mathbf{C}_e^n$ is calculated using the element mass matrix $\mathbf{M}_e$ and the element stiffness matrix $\mathbf{K}_e^n$ as follows:

$$\mathbf{C}_e^n = \alpha^*\mathbf{M}_e + \beta^*\mathbf{K}_e^n,$$

The coefficients α^* and β^* are determined by solving the following least-squares equation,

$$\text{minimize}\left[\int_{f_{\min}}^{f_{\max}} \left(h^n - \frac{1}{2}\left(\frac{\alpha^*}{2\pi f} + 2\pi f\beta^* \right) \right)^2 \mathrm{d}f \right].$$

where $f_{\max}$ and $f_{\min}$ are the maximum and minimum target frequencies and h^n is the damping ratio at time step n. Small elements are locally generated when modeling complex geometry with solid elements, and therefore satisfying the Courant condition when using explicit time integration methods (e.g., central difference method) leads to small time increments and considerable computational cost. Thus, the Newmark-β method is used for time integration with $\beta = 1/4, \delta = 1/2$ (β and δ are parameters of the Newmark-β method). By applying Semi-infinite absorbing boundary conditions to the bottom and side boundaries of the simulation domain, we take dissipation character and semi-infinite character into consideration.

Next we summarize the super-subloading surface Sekiguchi-Ohta EC model [9–11], which is one of the 3D elasto-plastic constitutive equations used in nonlinear wave propagation analysis of soils. The super-subloading surface Sekiguchi-Ohta EC model is described using subloading and superloading surfaces summarized in Fig. 1. The subloading surface is a yield surface defined inside of the normal yield surface. It is similar in shape to the normal yield surface and a current stress state is always on it. We can take into account plastic deformation in the normal yield surface and reproduce smooth change from elastic state to plastic state by introducing the subloading surface. On the other hand, the superloading surface is a yield surface defined outside of the normal yield surface. It is similar in shape to the normal yield surface and the subloading surface. Relative contraction of the superloading surface (i.e., the expansion of the normal yield surface) describes the decay of the structure as plastic deformation proceeds. At the end, the superloading surface and the normal yield surface become identical. Similarity ratios of the subloading surface to the superloading surface, of the normal yield surface to the superloading surface are denoted by R, R^*, respectively ($0 < R \leq 1, 0 < R^* \leq 1$). $1/R$ is overconsolidation ratio and R is the index of degree of structure. As plastic deformation proceeds, the subloading surface expands and the superloading surface relatively contracts. The expansion speed $\dot{R}$ and contraction speed $\dot{R}^*$ are calculated as in Fig. 1. $D, \dot{\epsilon}^p$ are the coefficient of dilatancy, the plastic volumetric strain speed and m, a, b, c are the degradation parameters of overconsolidated state and structures state, respectively. Using this R and R^*, a yield function of the subloading surface is described as $f(\boldsymbol{\sigma}', \epsilon_v{}^p)$ in Fig. 1. Here, $M, n_E, \boldsymbol{\sigma}', \boldsymbol{\sigma}_0'$ are the critical state parameter, the fitting parameter, the effective stress tensor, the effective initial stress tensor and η^*, p', q are the stress parameter proposed by Sekiguchi and Ohta, the effective mean stress, the deviatoric stress. The following stress-strain relationship is obtained by solving the simultaneous equations in Fig. 1.

$$
\begin{aligned}
\dot{\sigma}' &= \left(\mathbf{C}^e - \frac{\mathbf{C}^e : \frac{\partial f}{\partial \boldsymbol{\sigma}'} \otimes \frac{\partial f}{\partial \boldsymbol{\sigma}'} : \mathbf{C}^e}{\frac{\partial f}{\partial \boldsymbol{\sigma}'} : \mathbf{C}^e : \frac{\partial f}{\partial \boldsymbol{\sigma}'} - \frac{\partial f}{\partial \epsilon_v{}^p} \frac{\partial f}{\partial p'} + \frac{m}{D} (\ln R) \frac{\partial f}{\partial R} \left\| \frac{\partial f}{\partial \boldsymbol{\sigma}'} \right\| - a (R^*)^b (1 - R^*)^c \frac{\partial f}{\partial R^*} \left\| \frac{\partial f}{\partial \boldsymbol{\sigma}'} \right\|} \right) : \dot{\epsilon}, \\
&= \mathbf{C}^{ep} : \dot{\epsilon},
\end{aligned}
\tag{3}
$$

where,

$$
C^e_{ijkl} = \left(K - \frac{2}{3} G \right) \delta_{ij} \delta_{kl} + G \left(\delta_{ik} \delta_{jl} + \delta_{il} \delta_{jk} \right),
$$

$$
K = \frac{\Lambda}{MD(1 - \Lambda)} p', G = \frac{3(1 - 2\nu')}{2(1 + \nu')} K,
$$

$\mathbf{C}^e(C^e_{ijkl}), \mathbf{C}^{ep}$ are the elasticity tensor, the elasto-plasticity tensor and K, G, Λ, ν' are the bulk modulus, the shear modulus, the irreversibility ratio, the effective Poisson's ratio, respectively.

2.2   Fast and Scalable Elasto-Plastic Nonlinear Analysis Method

In this subsection, we first summarize the solver algorithm in [4] following Algorithm 1. By changing the $\mathbf{K}$ matrix in Algorithm 1 according to the change in the constitutive model, we can expect high computational efficiency when conducting elasto-plastic analyses. In the latter part of the subsection, we describe the initial stress analysis and nonlinear wave propagation analysis procedure.

The majority of the cost in conducting finite-element analysis is in solving the linear equation in Eq. (1). The solver in [4] enables fast and scalable solving

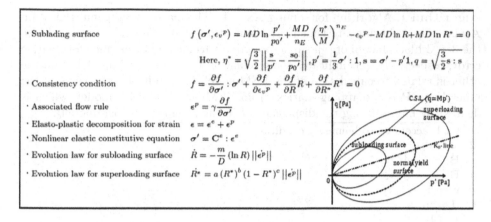

- Subloading surface

$$f\left(\sigma', \epsilon_v{}^P\right) = MD \ln \frac{p'}{p_0'} + \frac{MD}{n_E} \left(\frac{\eta^*}{M}\right)^{n_E} - \epsilon_v{}^P - MD \ln R + MD \ln R^* = 0$$

$$\text{Here, } \eta^* = \sqrt{\frac{3}{2}} \left\| \frac{s}{p'} - \frac{s_0}{p_0'} \right\|, \; p' = \frac{1}{3}\sigma' : 1, s = \sigma' - p'1, q = \sqrt{\frac{3}{2}s : s}$$

- Consistency condition $\quad f = \dfrac{\partial f}{\partial \sigma'} : \sigma' + \dfrac{\partial f}{\partial \epsilon_v{}^P} + \dfrac{\partial f}{\partial R}R + \dfrac{\partial f}{\partial R^*}R^* = 0$

- Associated flow rule $\quad \epsilon^P = \gamma \dfrac{\partial f}{\partial \sigma'}$

- Elasto-plastic decomposition for strain $\quad \epsilon = \epsilon^e + \epsilon^P$

- Nonlinear elastic constitutive equation $\quad \sigma' = \mathbf{C}^e : \epsilon^e$

- Evolution law for subloading surface $\quad \dot{R} = -\dfrac{m}{D}(\ln R)\|\dot{\epsilon}^P\|$

- Evolution law for superloading surface $\quad \dot{R}^* = a\,(R^*)^b\,(1-R^*)^c\,\|\dot{\epsilon}^P\|$

Fig. 1. Governing equation of stress-strain relation and relation of yield surfaces

of Eq. (1) by using adaptive conjugate gradient (CG) method with multi-grid preconditioning, mixed precision arithmetics, and fast matrix-vector multiplication based on the Element-by-Element method [12,13]. Instead of storing a fixed preconditioning matrix, the preconditioning equation is solved roughly using an another CG solver. In Algorithm 1, outer loop means the iterative calculation of the CG method solving $\mathbf{Ax} = \mathbf{b}$, and the inner loop means the computation of preconditioning equation (solving $\mathbf{z} = \mathbf{A}^{-1}\mathbf{r}$ by CG method). Since the preconditioning equation needs only be solved roughly, single-precision arithmetic is used in the preconditioner, while double precision arithmetic is used in the outer loop. Furthermore, the multi-grid method is used in the preconditioner to improve convergence in the inner loop itself. Here, a two-step grid with second-order tetrahedral mesh (FEMmodel) and first-order tetrahedral mesh (FEMmodel$_c$) is used. Specifically, an initial solution of $\mathbf{z} = \mathbf{A}^{-1}\mathbf{r}$ is estimated by computing $\mathbf{z}_c = \mathbf{A}_c^{-1}\mathbf{r}_c$, which reduces the number of iterations in solving $\mathbf{z} = \mathbf{A}^{-1}\mathbf{r}$. In order to reduce memory footprint, memory transfer sizes, and improve load balance, a matrix-free method is used to compute matrix-vector products instead of storing the global matrix on memory. This algorithm is implemented using MPI/OpenMP for computation on distributed-shared memory computers.

We enable initial stress analysis and nonlinear wave propagation analysis successively by changing the right hand side of Eq. (1). The calculation algorithm for each time step of the elasto-plastic nonlinear wave propagation analysis is shown in Algorithm 2. Here, the same algorithm is used for both the initial stress analysis and the wave propagation analysis. In the following, we describe initial stress analysis and nonlinear wave propagation analysis after initial stress analysis.

In this study, we use self-weight analysis as initial stress analysis. Gravity is considered by calculating the external force vector in Eq. (1) as

$$\mathbf{f}^n = \mathbf{f}^n + \int \rho g \mathbf{N} \mathrm{d}V, \tag{4}$$

Algorithm 1. Algorithm for solving $\mathbf{Ax} = \mathbf{b}$. The matrix-vector multiplication $\mathbf{Ay}$ is computed using an Element-by-Element method. $diag[\ ]$, $(\bar{\ })$ and ϵ indicate the 3×3 block Jacobi of $[\ ]$, single-precision variable, and tolerance for relative error, respectively. $(\ )_c$ indicates the calculation related to FEMmodel$_c$, and the other is related to calculation of the FEMmodel. $(\ )^{in}$ indicates the value in the inner loop. $\bar{\mathbf{P}}$ is a mapping matrix, from FEMmodel$_c$ to FEMmodel, which is defined by interpolating the displacement in each element of FEMmodel$_c$.

```
 1: set b according to boundary condition
 2: x ⇐ 0
 3: B̄ ⇐ diag[A]
 4: B̄c ⇐ diag[Ac]
 5: r ⇐ b
 6: β ⇐ 0
 7: i ⇐ 1
 8: (*outer loop start*)
 9: while ||r||²/||b||² ≥ ε do
10:    (*inner loop start*)
11:    r̄ ⇐ r
12:    z̄ ⇐ B⁻¹r
13:    r̄c ⇐ P̄ᵀr̄
14:    z̄c ⇐ P̄ᵀz̄
15:    z̄c ⇐ Āc⁻¹r̄c (*Inner coarse loop: solved on FEMmodelc with εcⁱⁿ and initial
          solution z̄c*)
16:    z̄ ⇐ P̄z̄c
17:    z̄ ⇐ Ā⁻¹r̄ (*Inner fine loop: solved on FEMmodel with εⁱⁿ and initial solution
          z̄*)
18:    z ⇐ z̄
19:    (*inner loop end*)
20:    if i > 1 then
21:        β ⇐ (z,q)/ρ
22:    end if
23:    p ⇐ z + βp
24:    q ⇐ Ap
25:    ρ ⇐ (z,r)
26:    α ⇐ ρ/(p,q)
27:    q ⇐ -αq
28:    r ⇐ r + q
29:    x ⇐ x + αp
30:    i ⇐ i + 1
31: end while
32: (*outer loop end*)
```

where ρ, g, and $\mathbf{N}$ are density, gravitational acceleration and the shape function, respectively. We apply the Dirichlet boundary condition by fixing vertical displacement at bottom nodes of the model.

During nonlinear wave propagation analysis, waves are inputted from the bottom of the model. Thus, instead of using Dirichlet boundary conditions at

Algorithm 2. Algorithm for elasto-plastic nonlinear wave propagation analysis in each time step. $\mathbf{D}, \varepsilon, \sigma$ and ϵ indicate the constitutive tensor, strain, stress and tolerance for error, respectively. $(\ )^{n}{}_{(i)}$ indicates the value during i-th iteration in the n-th time step.

1: calculate $\mathbf{K}^{n}$, $\mathbf{C}^{n}$ by using $\mathbf{D}^{n}$
2: calculate $\delta\mathbf{u}^{n}{}_{(1)}$ by solving Eq. (1) taking Eq. (4) and Eq. (5) into account
3: update each value by Eq. (2)
4: $i \Leftarrow 1$
5: $\delta\mathbf{u}^{n}{}_{(0)} \Leftarrow \infty$
6: (*iteration start*)
7: **while** $\max |\delta u^{n}{}_{(i)} - \delta u^{n}{}_{(i-1)}| \geq \epsilon$ **do**
8:     calculate $\varepsilon^{n}{}_{(i)}$ by using $\delta\mathbf{u}^{n}{}_{(i)}$
9:     $\delta\varepsilon^{n}{}_{(i)} \Leftarrow \varepsilon^{n}{}_{(i)} - \varepsilon^{n-1}$
10:     calculate $\delta\sigma^{n}{}_{(i)}$ and $\mathbf{D}^{n}{}_{(i)}$
11:     re-evaluate $\mathbf{K}^{n}$, $\mathbf{C}^{n}$ by using $\mathbf{D}^{n}{}_{(i)}$
12:     re-calculate $\delta\mathbf{u}^{n}{}_{(i+1)}$ by solving Eq. (1)
13:     re-update each value by Eq. (2)
14:     $i \Leftarrow i + 1$
15: **end while**
16: (*iteration end*)
17: $\sigma^{n} \Leftarrow \sigma^{n-1} + \delta\sigma^{n}{}_{(i-1)}$
18: $\mathbf{D}^{n+1} \Leftarrow \mathbf{D}^{n}{}_{(i-1)}$

---

the bottom of the model, we balance gravitational forces by adding reaction force to the bottom of the model obtained at the last step of initial stress analysis (step t_0). Here, the reaction force

$$- \mathbf{f}^{t_0} + \mathbf{q}^{t_0 - 1}, \tag{5}$$

is added to the bottom nodes of the model in Eq. (1). Here, $\mathbf{f}^{n}$ is calculated as in Eq. (4).

3   Numerical Experiments

3.1   Verification of Proposed Method

As we cannot obtain analytical solutions for elasto-plastic nonlinear wave propagation analysis, we cannot verify the developed program by comparing numerical solutions with analytical solutions. However, we can compare 1D numerical analysis results with the same elasto-plastic constitutive models with 3D numerical analysis results on a horizontally stratified soil structure to verify the consistency between the 1D and 3D analyses as well as the numerical convergence with fine discretization of the analyses. As we use the results of the 1D analysis (stress and velocity) with the same elasto-plastic models as the boundary condition at base and side faces of the 3D model for 3D analyses, we can check the consistency between the 3D and 1D analyses and their numerical convergence by checking the uniformity of 3D analysis results in the $x - y$ plane.

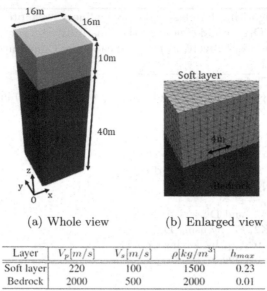

(a) Whole view   (b) Enlarged view

Layer	$V_p[m/s]$	$V_s[m/s]$	$\rho[kg/m^3]$	h_{max}
Soft layer	220	100	1500	0.23
Bedrock	2000	500	2000	0.01

(c) Ground property. V_p, V_s and h_{max} are the P-wave velocity,
the S-wave velocity and the maximum damping ratio.

M	D	Λ	ν	n_E	m	$\sigma_{v_i}[kPa]$	$\sigma_{v_0}[kPa]$	K_i	K_0	R^*	a	b	c
1.2	0.021	0.95	0.37	1.2	10.0	73.5	195.0	0.92	0.58	1.0	1.0	1.0	1.0

(d) Elasto-plastic property of soft layer

Fig. 2. Horizontally layered model and ground property

We conducted numerical tests on a horizontally stratified ground structure
with soft layer of 10 m thickness on top of bedrock of 40 m thickness. The size
of the 3D model was $0 \leq x \leq 16$ m, $0 \leq y \leq 16$ m, $0 \leq z \leq 50$ m (Fig. 2). The
ground properties of each layer and elasto-plastic parameters of the soft layer are
described in Fig. 2. Here, K_i and K_0 are the coefficient of initial earth pressure at
rest and the coefficient of earth pressure at rest, respectively. We used $h_{max} \times 0.01$
for Rayleigh damping of the soft layer. Following previous studies [8], we chose
element size ds such that it satisfies

$$ds \leq \frac{V_s}{\chi f_{\max}}. \tag{6}$$

Here, $f_{\max}$ and χ are the maximum target frequency and the number of elements per wavelength, respectively. χ is set to $\chi > 10$ for nonlinear layers and
$\chi > 5$ for linear layers for numerical convergence of the solution. Taking the
above conditions into account, we considered two models whose minimum element size is 1 m and 2 m, respectively, and the maximum element size is 8 m
in both 1D analysis and 3D analysis. We used the seismic wave observed at
the Kobe Marine Meteorological Observatory during the Great Hanshin Earth-

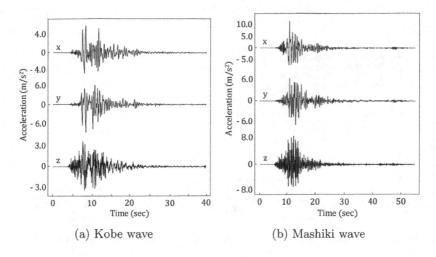

(a) Kobe wave   (b) Mashiki wave

Fig. 3. Input wave

quake in 1995 (Fig. 3, Kobe wave). We pull back this wave to the bedrock and input it to the bottom of the 3D model. Since the major components of the response is influenced by waves below 2.5 Hz, we conduct analysis targeting frequency range between 0.1 and 2.5 Hz. We first conduct self-weight analysis with $dt = 0.001\,\mathrm{s} \times 700{,}000$ time steps, and then conduct nonlinear wave propagation analysis with $dt = 0.001\,\mathrm{s} \times 40{,}000$ time steps using the Kobe wave. Instead of loading the full gravitational force at the initial step, we increased the gravitational force by 0.000002 times every time step until 500,000 time steps for both the 1D and 3D analyses. For the 3D analysis, we used the Oakleaf-FX system at the University of Tokyo consisting of 4,800 computing nodes each with single 16 core SPARC64 IXfx CPUs (Fujitsu's PRIMEHPC FX10 massively parallel supercomputer with a peak performance of 1.13 PFLOPS). For the model with minimum element size of 1 m, the degrees-of-freedom was 85,839, and the 3D analysis took 20,619 s using 576 CPU cores (72 MPI processes × 8 OpenMP threads). For the model with minimum element size of 2 m, the degrees-of-freedom was 14,427, and the 3D analysis took 12,278 s by using 64 CPU cores (8 MPI processes × 8 OpenMP threads).

Results of the 1D and 3D analyses are shown in Figs. 4 and 5. From Fig. 4, we can see that the time history of displacement on ground surface for each analysis are almost identical. Figure 5 shows the displacement distribution at surface of the 3D analysis. We can see that the difference of displacement values at each point is converged within about 0.75%. Although not shown, the maximum difference was about 2% for the case with element size of 2 m. We can see that the 3D analysis results converge to the 1D analysis results by using sufficiently small elements (in this case, 1 m elements).

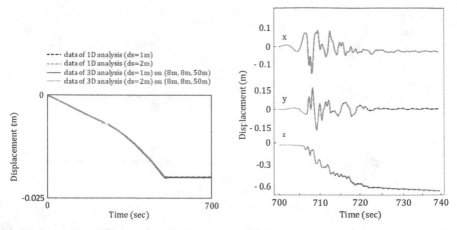

(a) During self-weight analysis (z direction) (b) During wave propagation analysis

Fig. 4. Displacement time history at surface for horizontally stratified ground model

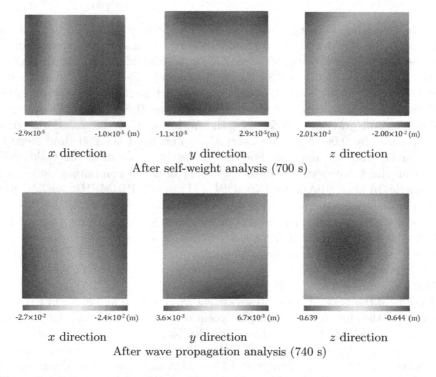

Fig. 5. Displacement on surface for horizontally stratified ground model ($ds = 1$ m)

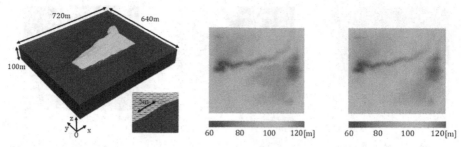

(a) Whole view & Enlarged view   (b) Contour of ground surface   (c) Contour of bedrock

Layer	$V_p[m/s]$	$V_s[m/s]$	$\rho[kg/m^3]$	h_{max}
Soft layer	90	48	1330	0.23
Bedrock	2000	500	2000	0.01

(e) Ground property

M	D	A	ν	n_E	m	σ_{v_i}[kPa]	σ_{v_0}[kPa]	K_i	K_0	R^*	a	b	c
0.98	0.064	0.873	0.3	1.2	10.0	65.0	195.0	0.92	0.58	1.0	1.0	1.0	1.0

(f) Elasto-plastic property of soft layer

Fig. 6. Geometry and ground property of application problem

3.2   Application Example

The Kumamoto earthquake occurring successively on September 14 and 16, 2016 caused heavy damage such as landslides and house collapse. At a residential area in the Minamiaso village with large-scale embankment, houses near the valley collapsed due to landslide and some cracks occurred in the east-west direction [14]. In addition, ground subsidence occurred at a residential area little far from the valley. Targeting this residential area, we conducted elasto-plastic nonlinear wave propagation analysis using the developed program.

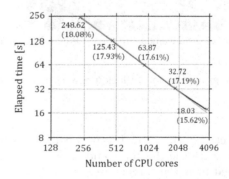

Fig. 7. Strong scaling measured for solving 25 time steps of application problem. Numbers in brackets indicate floating-point performance efficiency to hardware peak.

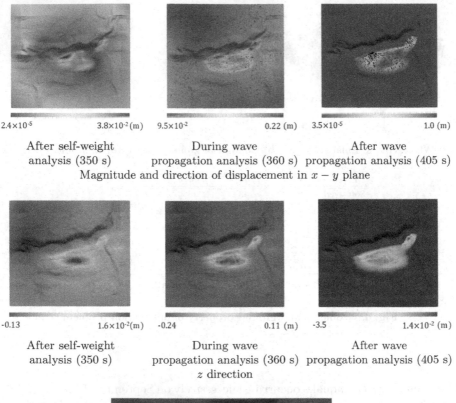

2.4×10⁻⁵   3.8×10⁻²(m)   9.5×10⁻²   0.22 (m)   3.5×10⁻⁵   1.0 (m)

After self-weight   During wave   After wave
analysis (350 s)   propagation analysis (360 s) propagation analysis (405 s)
       Magnitude and direction of displacement in $x - y$ plane

-0.13   1.6×10⁻²(m)   -0.24   0.11 (m)   -3.5   1.4×10⁻² (m)

After self-weight   During wave   After wave
analysis (350 s)   propagation analysis (360 s) propagation analysis (405 s)
                              z direction

Magnitude and direction of displacement in $x - y$ plane after 350 s (Enlarged view)

Fig. 8. Displacement on ground surface. Black arrow indicates the displacement direction in $x - y$ plane.

The FEM model used is shown in Fig. 6. There is no borehole logs in the target area, so we estimate the thickness and shape of the soft layer based on borehole logs measured near the target area. The elevation was based on the digital elevation map of the Geospatial Information Authority of Japan. Finally, we assume the ground consists of two layers. The size of the model was $0 \leq x \leq 720\,\mathrm{m}, 0 \leq y \leq 640\,\mathrm{m}, 0 \leq z \leq$ about 100 m. The ground properties of each layer shown in Fig. 6 were set based on [15]. Here we used $h_{max} \times 0.01$ as the Rayleigh damping of the soft layer. Based on the results of Sect. 3.1, we set the minimum element size to 1 m, and the maximum element size to 16 m. The model consisted of 47,813,250 degrees-of-freedom, 15,937,750 nodes, and 11,204,117 tetrahedral elements. We pulled the seismic wave observed at the KiK-net [16] station KMMH16 during the Kumamoto earthquake (Fig. 3, Mashiki wave) to the bedrock and computed the response targeting frequency range between 0.1 and 2.5 Hz. We first conducted self-weight analysis with $dt = 0.001 \times 350,000$ time steps and then conducted wave propagation analysis with $dt = 0.001 \times 55,000$ time steps. Here we increased the self-weight by 0.000004 times every time step until full loading at 250,000 time steps.

In order to check the computational performance of the developed program, we measured strong scaling on this model using the first 25 time steps. As shown in Fig. 7, the program attained 86.2% strong scaling efficiency from 240 CPU cores (30 MPI processes × 8 OpenMP threads) to 3840 CPU cores (480 MPI processes × 8 OpenMP threads). This enabled 8.85 TFLOPS (15.6% of peak) when using 3840 CPU cores of Oakleaf-FX (480 MPI processes × 8 OpenMP threads), leading to feasible analysis time of 31 h 13 min (112,388 s) for conducting the whole initial stress and wave propagation analysis. This high peak performance could be attained by the method using matrix free matrix-vector multiplication, single-precision arithmetic and so on indicated in Sect. 2.2.

The magnitude of the displacement in the x, y directions and the displacement distribution in the z direction on ground surface are shown in Fig. 8. From this figure, we can see permanent displacement towards the north valley at part of the soft layer after wave propagation analysis. We can also see large subsidence at the center of the soft layer. These results are effects caused by using the elasto-plastic model into the 3D analysis. By setting more suitable parameters to the soft soil based on site measurements, we can expect improvement of analysis results following the actual phenomenon.

4   Concluding Remarks

In this study, we developed a scalable 3D elasto-plastic nonlinear wave propagation analysis method. We showed its capability of conducting large-scale nonlinear wave propagation analysis with large deformation through a verification analysis, scaling test, and application to the embankment of the Minamiaso village. The program attained high performance on Oakleaf-FX, with 8.85 TFLOPS (15.6% of peak) on 3840 CPU cores. In the future, we plan to apply this method to the seismic response analysis for roads in mountain region and bridges which are prone to seismic damage.

Acknowledgment. We thank Dr. Takemine Yamada, Dr. Shintaro Ohno and Dr. Ichizo Kobayashi from Kajima Corporation for comments concerning the soil constitutive model.

References

1. FUJITSU Supercomputer PRIMEHPC FX10. http://www.fujitsu.com/jp/products/computing/servers/supercomputer/primehpc-fx10/
2. Dupros, F., Martin, F.D., Foerster, E., Komatitsch, D., Roman, J.: High-performance finite-element simulations of seismic wave propagation in three-dimensional nonlinear inelastic geological media. Parallel Comput. **36**(5–6), 308–325 (2010)
3. Elgamal, A., Lu, J., Yan, L.: Large scale computational simulation in geotechnical earthquake engineering. In: The 12th International Conference of International Association for Computer Methods and Advances in Geomechanics, pp. 2782–2791 (2008)
4. Ichimura, T., Fujita, K., Tanaka, S., Hori, M., Lalith, M., Shizawa, Y., Kobayashi, H.: Physics-based urban earthquake simulation enhanced by 10.7 BlnDOF × 30 K time-step unstructured FE non-linear seismic wave simulation. In: SC 2014: International Conference for High Performance Computing, Networking, Storage and Analysis, pp. 15–26 (2014). https://doi.org/10.1109/SC.2014.7
5. What is K? http://www.aics.riken.jp/en/k-computer/about/
6. Idriss, I.M., Singh, R.D., Dobry, R.: Nonlinear behavior of soft clays during cyclic loading. J. Geotech. Eng. Div. **104**, 1427–1447 (1978)
7. Masing, G.: Eigenspannungen und Verfestigung beim Messing. In: Proceedings of the 2nd International Congress of Applied Mechanics, pp. 332–335 (1926)
8. Ichimura, T., Fujita, K., Hori, M., Sakanoue, T., Hamanaka, R.: Three-dimensional nonlinear seismic ground response analysis of local site effects for estimating seismic behavior of buried pipelines. J. Press. Vessel Technol. **136**(4), 041702 (2014). https://doi.org/10.1115/1.4026208
9. Ohno, S., Iizuka, A., Ohta, H.: Two categories of new constitutive model derived from non-linear description of soil contractancy. J. Appl. Mech. **9**, 407–414 (2006)
10. Ohno, S., Takeyama, T., Pipatpongsa, T., Ohta, H., Iizuka, A.: Analysis of embankment by nonlinear contractancy description. In: 13th Asian Regional Conference, Kolkata (2007)
11. Asaoka, A., Nakano, M., Noda, T., Kaneda, K.: Delayed compression/consolidation of natural clay due to degradation of soil structure. Soils Found. **40**(3), 75–85 (2000)
12. Gene, H.G., Qiang, Y.: Inexact preconditioned conjugate gradient method with inner-outer iteration. SIAM J. Sci. Comput. **21**(4), 1305–1320 (1999)
13. Barrett, R., et al.: Templates for the Solution of Linear Systems: Building Blocks for Iterative Methods. SIAM, Philadelphia (1994)
14. Hashimoto, T., Tobita, T., Ueda, K.: The report of the damage by Kumamoto earthquake in Mashiki-machi, Nishihara-mura and Minamiaso-mura. Disaster Prev. Res. Inst. Ann. **59**(B), 125–134 (2016)
15. Takagi, S., Tanaka, K., Tanaka, I., Kawano, H., Satou, T., Tanoue, Y., Shirai, Y., Hasegawa, S.: Engineering properties of volcanic soils in central Kyusyu area with special reference to suitability of the soils as a fill material. In: 39th Japan National Conference on Geotechnical Engineering (2004)
16. NIED: Strong-motion Seismograph Networks (K-NET, KiK-net). http://www.kyoshin.bosai.go.jp/

A New Matrix-Free Approach
for Large-Scale Geodynamic Simulations
and its Performance

Simon Bauer[1], Markus Huber[2], Marcus Mohr[1(✉)] [iD], Ulrich Rüde[3,4],
and Barbara Wohlmuth[2]

[1] Department of Earth and Environmental Sciences,
Ludwig-Maximilians-Universität München, Munich, Germany
{simon.bauer,marcus.mohr}@lmu.de
[2] Institute for Numerical Mathematics (M2), Technische Universität München,
Munich, Germany
[3] Department of Computer Science 10, FAU Erlangen-Nürnberg,
Erlangen, Germany
[4] Parallel Algorithms Project, CERFACS, Toulouse, France

Abstract. We report on a two-scale approach for efficient matrix-free
finite element simulations. The proposed method is based on surrogate
element matrices constructed by low-order polynomial approximations.
It is applied to a Stokes-type PDE system with variable viscosity as is a
key component in mantle convection models. We set the ground for a rigorous performance analysis inspired by the concept of parallel textbook
multigrid efficiency and study the weak scaling behavior on SuperMUC,
a peta-scale supercomputer system. For a complex geodynamical model,
we achieve a parallel efficiency of 95% on up to 47 250 compute cores.
Our largest simulation uses a trillion ($\mathcal{O}(10^{12})$) degrees of freedom for a
global mesh resolution of 1.7 km.

Keywords: Two-scale PDE discretization
Massively parallel multigrid · Matrix-free on-the-fly assembly
Large scale geophysical application

1 Introduction

The surface of our planet is shaped by processes deep beneath our feet. Phenomena like earthquakes, plate tectonics, crustal evolution up to the geodynamo are
governed by forces in the Earth's mantle that transport heat from the interior of
our planet to the surface in a planetwide solid-state convection. For this reason,
the study of the dynamics of the mantle is critical to our understanding of how
the entire planet works.

There is a constant demand for ever more realistic models. In the case of
mantle convection models (MCMs), this includes, e.g., compressible flow formulations, strongly non-linear rheologies, i.e., models in which the fluid viscosity

© Springer International Publishing AG, part of Springer Nature 2018
Y. Shi et al. (Eds.): ICCS 2018, LNCS 10861, pp. 17–30, 2018.
https://doi.org/10.1007/978-3-319-93701-4_2

depends not only on pressure and temperature, but also on the flow velocity, the inclusion of phase transitions or the tracking of chemical composition. A discussion of current challenges is, e.g., given in [15]. Another trend is the growing use of MCMs to perform inverse computations via adjoint techniques in order to link uncertain geodynamic modeling parameters to geologic observables and, thus, improve our understanding of mantle processes, see e.g. [7]. These advanced models require efficient software frameworks that allow for high spatial resolutions and combine sophisticated numerical algorithms with excellent parallel efficiency on supercomputers to provide fast time-to-solution. See [11,15,21] for recent developments.

We will focus here on the most compute-intensive part of any MCM, which is the solution of the generalized Stokes problem, where $\mathbf{f}$ represents the buoyancy forces, $\mathbf{u}$ velocity, p pressure, T temperature and $\nu(\mathbf{u},T)$ is the viscosity of the mantle.

$$- \operatorname{div} \left[\frac{1}{2}\nu \left(\nabla \mathbf{u} + (\nabla \mathbf{u})^{\top} \right) \right] + \nabla p = \mathbf{f}, \quad \operatorname{div} \mathbf{u} = 0. \tag{1}$$

Problem (1) needs to be solved repeatedly as part of the time-stepping and/or as part of a non-linear iteration, if ν depends on $\mathbf{u}$. Note that in (1) we assume an incompressible fluid, as the best way to treat the compressibility of the mantle is an open question, [15], outside the scope of this contribution.

Most current global convection codes are based on finite element (FE) discretizations, cf. [8,15,21]. While traditional FE implementations are based on the assembly of a global system matrix, there is a trend to employ matrix-free techniques, [2,4,17,19]. This is motivated by the fact that storing the global matrix increases the memory consumption by an order of magnitude or more even when sparse matrix formats are used. This limits the resolution and results in a much increased memory traffic when the sparse matrix must be re-read from memory repeatedly. Since the cost for data movement has become a limiting factor for all high performance supercomputer architectures both in terms of compute time and energy consumption, techniques for reducing memory footprint and traffic must receive increased attention in the design of modern numerical methods.

In this contribution, we report on the prototype of a new mantle convection framework that is implemented based on Hierarchical Hybrid Grids (HHG) [1,4,11,14]. HHG employs an unstructured mesh for geometry resolution which is then refined in a regular fashion. The resulting mesh hierarchy is well suited to implement matrix-free geometric multigrid methods. Multigrid techniques play an important role in any large-scale Stokes solver, most commonly as preconditioner for the momentum operator in a Krylov solver, or as inner solver in a Schur complement approach. We employ a geometric Uzawa-type multigrid solver that treats the full Stokes system all-at-once [12]. We present a new approach that allows to assemble the resulting FE stencils in the case of curved geometries and variable viscosity on-the-fly as a core component of matrix-free multigrid solvers. It is based on a polynomial approximation of the local element matrices, extending our work in [2].

We will carry out a systematic performance analysis of our HHG-based implementation and investigate parallel performance with respect to run-time, memory consumption and parallel efficiency of this new numerical approach for a real-world geophysical application. It will be investigated and tuned on the SuperMUC peta-scale system of the Leibniz Supercomputing Center (LRZ).

2 Software Framework and Discretization

Here we consider the thick spherical shell $\Omega = \{\mathbf{x} \in \mathbb{R}^3 : r_{\text{cmb}} < \|\mathbf{x}\|_2 < r_{\text{srf}}\}$, where r_{cmb} and r_{srf} correspond to the inner and outer mantle boundary, and $\| \cdot \|_2$ denotes the Euclidean norm of a vector. By taking the Earth radius as reference unit, we set $r_{\text{cmb}} = 0.55$ and $r_{\text{srf}} = 1$. We discretize Ω by an initial tetrahedral mesh $\mathcal{T}_0$ using a standard icosahedral meshing approach for spherical shells, see e.g. [8]. From this we construct a family of semistructured meshes $\mathcal{T} := \{\mathcal{T}_\ell, \ell = 0, \ldots, L\}$ by uniform refinement up to level $L \in \mathbb{N}_0$. For the finite element discretization of the Stokes system (1), we employ standard conforming linear finite element spaces for velocity and pressure on $\mathcal{T}$. While this P^1–P^1 pairing is of computational interest, it is known to be unstable. We use the pressure stabilization Petrov-Galerkin (PSPG) method [6] as stabilization technique. Using standard nodal basis functions for the finite element spaces, we obtain on each level ℓ of the hierarchy a linear system of algebraic equations

$$\mathcal{L}_\ell \begin{pmatrix} \mathbf{u}_\ell \\ \mathbf{p}_\ell \end{pmatrix} := \begin{pmatrix} A_\ell & G_\ell \\ D_\ell & -C_\ell \end{pmatrix} \begin{pmatrix} \mathbf{u}_\ell \\ \mathbf{p}_\ell \end{pmatrix} = \begin{pmatrix} \mathbf{f}_\ell \\ \mathbf{g}_\ell \end{pmatrix}, \quad \ell = 0, \ldots, L, \tag{2}$$

where $\mathbf{u}_\ell \in \mathbb{R}^{n_{\mathbf{u};\ell}}$ and $\mathbf{p}_\ell \in \mathbb{R}^{n_{\mathbf{p};\ell}}$. The dimensions of the velocity and the pressure space are denoted by $n_{\mathbf{u};\ell}$ and $n_{\mathbf{p};\ell}$. For our considerations below, it is advantageous to re-write (2) by sorting the vector of unknowns with respect to the different types of degrees of freedom to expose the scalar building blocks of (2)

$$\mathcal{L}_\ell = \begin{pmatrix} A_\ell^{11} & A_\ell^{12} & A_\ell^{13} & G_\ell^1 \\ A_\ell^{21} & A_\ell^{22} & A_\ell^{23} & G_\ell^2 \\ A_\ell^{31} & A_\ell^{32} & A_\ell^{33} & G_\ell^3 \\ D_\ell^1 & D_\ell^2 & D_\ell^3 & -C_\ell \end{pmatrix}, \quad \begin{pmatrix} \mathbf{u}_\ell \\ \mathbf{p}_\ell \end{pmatrix} = \begin{pmatrix} \mathbf{u}_\ell^1 \\ \mathbf{u}_\ell^2 \\ \mathbf{u}_\ell^3 \\ \mathbf{p}_\ell \end{pmatrix}. \tag{3}$$

In this representation, the upper left 3×3 substructure of blocks corresponds to A_ℓ and is related to the divergence of the strain tensor in (1). The submatrix D_ℓ, resulting from the discretization of the divergence operator in the continuity equation, has a 1×3 block-structure, while G_ℓ, coming from the pressure gradient in (1), has a 3×1 block-structure and our discretization yields $D_\ell = G_\ell^\top$. The stabilization C_ℓ term acts only on the pressure and, therefore, gives a 1×1 block. It can be viewed as a discrete Laplacian operator acting on the pressure with Neumann boundary condition. Note that, while it is obvious that A_ℓ depends on the viscosity ν, it is also necessary to include ν^{-1} in the stabilization C_ℓ.

The mesh hierarchy $\mathcal{T}$ allows to construct an efficient geometric all-at-once Uzawa multigrid method [12]. For solving the linear system (2), we apply multigrid V-cycles with three pre- and post-smoothing steps on level L and on each coarser level two extra smoothing steps are added. Using a Uzawa type smoother then guarantees mesh-independent convergence, and we denote this type of multigrid as $V_{\mathrm{var}}(3,3)$. As the multigrid method acts both on velocity and pressure, the problem that needs to be solved on the bottom of the V-cycle is also of the form (2). For this, we employ the preconditioned minimal residual method (PMINRES). Our preconditioner has a block structure, where we apply a Jacobi preconditioned conjugate gradient method to the velocity part and perform a lumped mass matrix scaling on the pressure.

The HHG framework is a carefully designed and implemented high performance finite element multigrid software package [3,12] which has already demonstrated its usability for geodynamical simulations [1,22]. Conceptually, refinement of the input mesh T_0, which we call *macro mesh*, generates new nodes on edges, faces and within the volume of the tetrahedra of the input mesh. In HHG, these nodal values are organized by their geometric classification into a system of container data-structures called *primitives*. The nodal values in the interior of each macro tetrahedron are stored in a volume primitive, and similarly the values on macro edges, faces and vertices in their respective primitives. In this way, each nodal value is uniquely assigned to one primitive. Note that, only starting with refinement level two, we get nodes to store in the volume primitives. We use T_2 as coarsest level in our multigrid solver. HHG's approach of splitting nodes between primitives of different geometric dimensionality naturally integrates with distributed-memory parallelism. Primitives are enriched by the nodal values of neighboring primitives in the form of ghost layer data-structures and kept up-to-date by MPI-communication in case of off-process dependencies, [3,4].

The structured refinement of the input mesh, employed in HHG, results in the same types of tetrahedra being adjacent to each node within a certain primitive type and, thus, identical coupling patterns for these nodes. For constant ν on each macro tetrahedron, the discretization results also in the weights of these coupling being constant when proceeding from one node of a primitive to the next. This allows to use a constant stencil for all nodes in each volume primitive in a matrix-free approach, resulting in a significantly improved performance of computationally-intensive matrix-vector multiplications. In view of the system matrix in (3), we can identify the non-zero entries of each row of each block by a stencil and denote it by

$$s_{ij}^{A;m,n} = (A_\ell^{mn})_{ij}, \quad s_{ij}^{D;m} = (D_\ell^m)_{ij}, \quad s_{ij}^{G;m} = (G_\ell^m)_{ij}, \quad s_{ij}^C = (C_\ell)_{ij},$$

for row index i and column index j and $m,n \in \{1,2,3\}$. Within each volume primitive each stencil reduces to 15 non-zero entries. In the following, we will denote a stencil weight by s_{ij}, if there is no ambiguity. The full 15pt stencil at node i will be written as $s_{i,:}$.

3   Efficient On-the-Fly Stencil Assembly

While the hybrid approach of HHG exhibits superior performance, its geometry approximation on curved domains such as the spherical shell, is limited in the sense that no refined nodes reside on the actual boundary. To account for this, in our implementation the fine grid nodes can be projected outwards onto the spherical surface. Also all interior nodes are projected to form concentric spherical layers. In a matrix-free framework, this comes at the cost that the FE stencils have to be repeatedly re-assembled on-the-fly.

We briefly describe the assembly procedure. For brevity, we show this only for A_ℓ^{11} from (3); the other entries are computed analogously. For linear FE the stencil weight s_{ij} can be computed by

$$s_{ij} = \sum_{t \in \mathcal{N}(i,j)} J_t^{-\top} \nabla \hat{\phi}_{i_{\mathrm{loc}}} \cdot J_t^{-\top} \nabla \hat{\phi}_{j_{\mathrm{loc}}} |\det(J_t)| \int_t \nu \, d\mathbf{x} = \sum_{t \in \mathcal{N}(i,j)} E_{i_{\mathrm{loc}}, j_{\mathrm{loc}}}^t \bar{\nu}_t \quad (4)$$

where J_t is the Jacobian of the mapping from the reference element $\hat{t}$, $\mathcal{N}(i,j)$ the set of elements with common nodes i and j, $E^t \in \mathbb{R}^{4 \times 4}$ the local element matrix on t, i_{loc} the element local index of the global node i, and $\hat{\phi}_{i_{\mathrm{loc}}}$ the associated shape function. We can use a vertex based quadrature rule for the integral over ν by summing over the four vertices of t with weights $1/4$. This fits naturally to the HHG memory layout where the coefficients ν_i are stored point-wise. Also techniques for elimination of common sub-expressions can be employed, see [14].

A traditional matrix-free implementation requires to repeatedly evaluate (4) on-the-fly. For the full 15pt stencil $s_{i,:}$, this involves the computation of E^t on each of the 24 elements adjacent to node i. Even though we use optimized code generated by the FEniCS Form Compiler [18] for this task, it constitutes the most expensive part in the stencil assembly procedure and severely reduces overall performance. We term this approach IFEM and it will serve as our baseline for comparison. We remark that our implementation is node- and not element-centric. A benefit of this is, e.g., that the central stencil weight, essential for point-smoothers, is directly available. A disadvantage is that it performs redundant operations as it does not take into account the fact that each element matrix is shared by four nodes. We could slightly reduce the operation count by computing only the i-th row of the matrix when dealing with node i. However, this still involves the Jacobian of the reference mapping which gives the largest contribution to the number of operations.

In order to recover the performance of the original HHG implementation also on curved domains we recently proposed an alternative approach in [2] for block-wise constant ν. It replaces the expensive evaluation of (4) with approximating the values of s_{ij} by a low-order polynomial. The polynomial coefficients are computed via a least-squares fit in a setup phase and stored. Hence we denote the technique as LSQP. Later, whenever the stencil $s_{i,:}$ is needed, one has to evaluate 15 polynomials at node i, one for each stencil weight. In [2] quadratic polynomials gave the best compromise between accuracy and runtime performance provided that the coarse scale mesh was fine enough. Furthermore, we showed that this approximation does not violate the optimal approximation order of the L^2-discretization error for linear finite elements, provided that the pairing of refinement depth L and macro mesh size H is selected carefully. Results for the Laplace operator [2, Table 4.1] indicated that for eight levels of refinement the converted macro resolution of the spherical shell should be at least around 800 km. For the experiments carried out in Sect. 5, this is satisfied except for the smallest run, though even there we find good results, see Table 2.

For our PDE problem (2), we have to deal with two additional challenges. Firstly, instead of a scalar PDE operator as used in [2] we have a system of PDEs. Secondly, we have to incorporate the non-constant viscosity in the elliptic operators A_ℓ and C_ℓ. Conceptually, our discrete PDE system (3) consists of 4×4 operator blocks coupling the three velocity components and the pressure. Our implementation allows to individually replace any of 16 suboperators by a LSQP approximation. Here, we only report on the most compute time saving approach, which is to replace all of the suboperators by the surrogates. We do this on all levels $\mathcal{T}_\ell$, apart from the coarsest one $\ell = 2$. We remark that the polynomials are evaluated at the nodal centers which leads to a small asymmetry in the operators. In [2] we found this relative asymmetry to be in $\mathcal{O}(h)$. This does not impact the algebraic convergence of the multigrid solver. However, it leads to a small issue on the coarsest level. There LSQP uses the same matrix $\mathcal{L}_2$ as IFEM. That matrix is symmetric positive semi-definite with a trivial kernel. Due to the asymmetry in our LSQP approach the restricted residual can include contributions from that kernel, which we fix by a simple projection of the right-hand side onto $\mathrm{Im}(\mathcal{L}_2)$ to avoid problems with our PMINRES solver.

How to accommodate variable viscosity is a more intricate problem. In addition to the geometry variation, which can be approximated by quadratic polynomials as shown in [2], we also get variations due to the non-constant viscosity. If these are smooth enough, LSQP still yields good results. For more complex viscosity models, like in Sect. 5, with strong lateral variations a low order polynomial approximation may lead to poor results. Also in time-dependent and/or non-linear simulations where viscosity changes together with temperature and/or velocity, we would need to regularly recompute the polynomial coefficients. We, therefore, choose another approach. Recall that the most expensive part in (4) is the computation of the 24 element matrices. Instead of directly approximating s_{ij}, one can also approximate the contributions of E^t by quadratic polynomials. That is we substitute the expensive $E^t_{i_{\mathrm{loc}}, j_{\mathrm{loc}}}$ by an inexpensive polynomial approximation $\widetilde{E}^t_{i_{\mathrm{loc}}, j_{\mathrm{loc}}}$ in (4). The polynomial approximation then solely depends on the geometry and is independent of the coefficients. Thus, it works for all kinds of coefficients. To distinguish between the two variants, we denote the original one as $\mathrm{LSQP_S}$ and the new modified one as $\mathrm{LSQP_E}$. Note that due to the linearity of the least-squares fit w.r.t. the input data, $\mathrm{LSQP_E}$ yields the same stencil weights as $\mathrm{LSQP_S}$ in case of blockwise constant coefficients.

Each element matrix E^t contributes four values to one stencil $s_{i,:}$. Thus, in total the $\mathrm{LSQP_E}$ version requires to define $4 \cdot 24$ quadratic polynomials per macro element. For the full system (2) with general ν, we approximate the stencils of A_ℓ and C_ℓ via $\mathrm{LSQP_E}$, while for G_ℓ and $G_\ell^\top$ the faster $\mathrm{LSQP_S}$ version is used.

4 Towards a Rigorous Performance Analysis

The LSQP$_S$ approach was shown in [2] to be significantly faster than the traditional IFEM implementation. A more fundamental performance study must employ an absolute metric that does not rely on just quantifying the speed-up with respect to an arbitrary baseline implementation. To account for the real algorithmic efficiency and scalability of the implementation in relation to the relevant hardware limitations, we follow [14] where the notion of *textbook multigrid efficiency* [5] was extended to analyze massively parallel implementations. This metric is known as *parallel textbook multigrid efficiency* (parTME) and relies on detailed hardware performance models. While this goes beyond the scope of our current contribution, this section will provide first results and lay the foundation for further investigations.

The parTME metric is based on an architecture-aware characterization of a work unit (WU), where one WU is defined as one operator application of the full system. Here, we restrict ourselves to one scalar suboperator of (3). Conceptually, the extension to the full system is straightforward. The operator application can be expressed in terms of stencil based nodal updates $u_i \leftarrow \sum_{j=1}^{15} s_{ij} u_j$. The number of such updates performed per unit time is measured as *lattice updates per second* (Lup/s). This quantifies the primary performance capability of a given computer system with respect to a discretized system. A careful quantification of the Lup/s with an analytic white box performance model will often exhibit significant code optimization potential, as shown in [14]. Equally important, it provides absolute numbers of what performance can be expected from given hardware. This is crucial for a systematic performance engineering methodology. Our target micro-architecture is the eight-core Intel Sandy Bridge (SNB) Xeon E5-2680 processor with clock frequency 2.7 GHz as used in SuperMUC Phase 1. This processor delivers a peak performance of 21.6 double precision GFlops per core, and 172.8 GFlops per chip. However, this is under the assumptions that the code vectorizes perfectly for the Sandy Bridge AVX architecture, that the multiply-add instructions can be exploited optimally, and that no delays occur due to slow access to data in the different layers of the memory hierarchy.

We start with a classic cost count per update to derive an upper bound for the maximal achievable Lup/s. Here, we will compare the versions IFEM, LSQP$_S$ and LSQP$_E$ that are extensions of (CC) and (VC) for domains with curved boundaries.

First, we briefly recapitulate the cost for (CC) and (VC) and refer to [14] for details. On a blockwise regular mesh with constant coefficients, also the stencils are blockwise constant. Thus, for (CC) only one single 15pt stencil is required per block. This can be easily stored and loaded without overhead. Therefore, the cost for one stencil based update is 14 add/15 mult. For variable coefficients, the stencils have to be assembled on-the-fly. This requires the additional evaluation of (4). In the (VC) implementation, one can exploit the fact that on a polyhedral domain there exist only six different congruency classes of local elements. Thus, again per block its contributions to (4) can be pre-computed.

Table 1. Maximal and measured performance on one Intel SNB core

Kernel	Domain	Coefficients	Add/Mult	$p_{\text{core}}^{\max}$	Measured
CC	Polyhedral	Blockwise constant	14/15	720 MLup/s	176 MLup/s
VC	Polyhedral	Variable	136/111	79.4 MLup/s	39.5 MLup/s
IFEM	Curved	Variable	1480/1911	5.7 MLup/s	0.7 MLup/s
LSQP_S	Curved	Moderately variable	44/45	245 MLup/s	71.7 MLup/s
LSQP_E	Curved	Variable	328/303	33.0 MLup/s	11.3 MLup/s

Now, we turn to curved domains. The LSQP_S approach is the extension of (CC) with the additional cost of 15 evaluations of a quadratic polynomial, one for each stencil component. For the evaluation, we use the scheme described in [2] that allows to evaluate a quadratic polynomial with 2 multiply-add operations. We note that LSQP_S can also be seen as an extension of (VC) for moderately variable coefficients. For problems with strongly variable coefficients, we propose either to use IFEM or the LSQP_E approach. Different from (VC), the contributions of the 24 neighboring element matrices must be re-computed on-the-fly. For IFEM, we count 56 additions and 75 multiplications per element matrix. The advantage of LSQP_E is obvious, since only 4 polynomial evaluations, one for each of the four contributions are required per element matrix. Again, this can be achieved with 8 multiply-add operations. In Table 1, we report the total number of operations for the different algorithms. Based on the operation count, the processor peak performance provides an upper limit on the achievable performance. In Table 1 we show these upper bounds as well as the measured values. For (CC) and (VC) the values are taken from [14]. For the measurements, we employed the Intel C/C++ Compiler 17.0 with flags *-O3 -march = native -xHost*.

Table 1 clearly shows that the peak rates are far from being obtained. For the simpler kernels (CC) and (VC), we carefully analyzed the performance discrepancy using the roofline and Execution-Cache-Memory models, see [14] and the references therein. Reasons why the peak rates are not achieved, are the limitations in bandwidth, but also bottlenecks that occur in the instruction stream and CPU-internal memory transfers between the cache layers. A full analysis for the advanced kernels is outside the scope of this contribution, but will be essential in the future to exhibit the possible optimization potential. But even the simple Flop count and the measured throughput values indicate the success of LSQP_S and LSQP_E in terms of reducing operation count as compared to a conventional implementation, such as IFEM. Similarly, the MLup/s show a substantial improvement. Both together, and the comparison with (CC) and (VC) indicate that there may be further room for improvement.

5   Accuracy and Weak Scaling Results

In this section, we analyze the accuracy and scaling behavior of our implementation for a geophysical application. Our largest simulation run will be with a global resolution of the Earth's mantle of $\sim$1.7 km.

System: We run our simulations on SuperMUC Phase1, a TOP500 machine at the LRZ, Garching, Germany. It is an IBM iDataPlex DX360M4 system equipped with eight-core SNB processors, cf. Sect. 4. Per core around 1.5 GB of memory are available to applications. Two sockets or 16 cores form one compute node, and 512 nodes are grouped into one island. The nodes are connected via an Infiniband FDR10 network. In total, there are 147 456 cores distributed on 18 islands with a total peak performance of 3.2 PFlop/s. We used the Intel compiler with options as in Sect. 4 and the Intel 2017.0 MPI library.

Setup: The icosahedral meshing approach for the spherical shell does not allow for an arbitrary number of macro elements in the initial mesh and the smallest feasible number of macros would be 60 already. Also we are interested in the scaling behavior from typical to large scale scenarios. Thus, we perform experiments starting on one island and scaling up to eight islands. We try to get as close as possible to using the full number of nodes on each island, while keeping the tangential to radial aspect ratio of the macro elements close to 1:1.

Inside a node, we assign two macro elements to each MPI process running on a single core. As the memory consumption of our application is on average about 1.7 GB per core, we utilize only 12 of the 16 available cores per node. These 12 cores are equally distributed on the two sockets by setting $I\_MPI\_PIN\_PROCESSOR\_LIST = 0\text{-}5,8\text{-}13$. A deep hierarchy with 8 levels of refinement is used. This yields problem sizes with $1.3 \cdot 10^{11}$ DoFs on 5 580 cores (one island), $2.7 \cdot 10^{11}$ DoFs on 12 000 cores (two islands), $4.8 \cdot 10^{11}$ DoFs on 21 600 cores (four islands) and $1.1 \cdot 10^{12}$ DoFs on 47 250 cores (eight islands).

Geophysical Model: In order to have a realistic Stokes-type problem (1) as it appears in applications, we consider the following model. On the top of the mantle we prescribe non-homogeneous Dirichlet boundary conditions, composed of a no-outflow component and tangential components given by present day plate velocity data from [20]. On the core-mantle boundary vanishing tangential shear stress resulting in a free-slip condition is enforced.

In terms of viscosity, we employ a similar model as used in [9]. The viscosity is the product of a smooth function depending on the temperature and the radial position and a discontinuous function reflecting a viscosity jump in radial direction due to an asthenospheric layer, a mechanically weak zone where the viscosity is several orders of magnitude smaller than in the lower mantle. The concrete thickness of the asthenosphere is unknown and subject to active research, see e.g. [22]. Here, we choose the model from [22] with a thickness of 660 km as this depth is one of two transition zones of seismic wave velocities. The viscosity model in non-dimensional form is given by

$$\nu(\mathbf{x}, T) = \exp\left(2.99\frac{1 - \|\mathbf{x}\|_2}{1 - r_{\text{cmb}}} - 4.61T\right)\begin{cases} 1/10 \cdot 6.371^3 d_a^3 & \text{for } \|\mathbf{x}\|_2 > 1 - d_a, \\ 1 & \text{else.} \end{cases}$$

where $d_a = 660/R$ with the Earth radius $R = 6371$ (km). Finally, we used present day temperature and density fields to compute the buoyancy term $\mathbf{f}$ and the viscosity, see [7].

Table 2. Results for one island scenario with $1.3 \cdot 10^{11}$ degrees of freedom: differences in the velocities inside the mantle obtained with IFEM and LSQP for different refinement levels (left); characteristic velocities in cm/a for level 8 (right).

level	discr. L_2	max-norm	charac. velocities	IFEM	LSQP	difference
4	$2.81 \cdot 10^{-4}$	$2.58 \cdot 10^{-2}$	avg. (whole mantle)	5.92	5.92	$5.60 \cdot 10^{-5}$
5	$4.05 \cdot 10^{-4}$	$4.84 \cdot 10^{-2}$	avg. (asthenosphere)	10.23	10.23	$1.10 \cdot 10^{-4}$
6	$5.19 \cdot 10^{-4}$	$6.70 \cdot 10^{-2}$	avg. (lower mantle)	4.48	4.48	$1.12 \cdot 10^{-4}$
7	$5.75 \cdot 10^{-4}$	$7.89 \cdot 10^{-2}$	max. (asthenosphere)	55.49	55.49	$2.61 \cdot 10^{-4}$
8	$6.83 \cdot 10^{-4}$	$8.58 \cdot 10^{-2}$	max. (lower mantle)	27.46	27.46	$6.33 \cdot 10^{-4}$

Accuracy: Before considering the run-time and scaling behavior of our new LSQP approach, we demonstrate its applicability by providing in Table 2 a comparison to results obtained with IFEM. We observe that the differences are sufficiently small in relation to typical mantle velocities and the uncertainties in the parameters that enter the model. The fact that the differences slightly grow with level reflects the two-scale nature of LSQP, as the finite element error decreases with mesh size h of the finest level, while the matrix approximation error is fixed by the mesh size H of the coarsest level, see also [2].

Memory Consumption: One important aspect in large scale simulations is memory consumption. Ideally, it should stay constant in weak scaling runs, as the number of DoFs per process remains the same. However, this is not always the case, especially in large scale simulations, due to buffer sizes that scale with the number of MPI ranks, see [10] for some examples.

To determine how strongly this affects our application, we measure the memory consumption per MPI process using the Intel MPI Performance Snapshot (mps) tool [16]. In Fig. 1 (left), we report the mean and maximum memory usage over all MPI processes. For each process, we assigned two volume primitives. The difference between the mean and maximum value comes from the different numbers of lower dimensional primitives attached to one process.

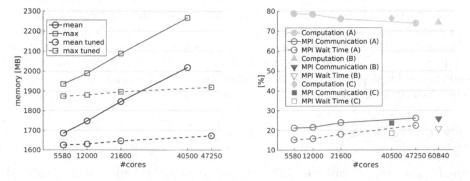

Fig. 1. Left: mean and max memory usage over all MPI processes. Right: percentage of computation versus communication (non-overlapping).

Table 3. Default and tuned Intel MPI DAPL settings (p = total no. of MPI processes.)

Environment variable	Default	Tuned
I_MPI_DAPL_UD_SEND_BUFFER_NUM	$16 + 4p$	8208
I_MPI_DAPL_UD_RECV_BUFFER_NUM	$16 + 4p$	8208
I_MPI_DAPL_UD_ACK_SEND_POOL_SIZE	256	8704
I_MPI_DAPL_UD_ACK_RECV_POOL_SIZE	$512 + 4p$	8704
I_MPI_DAPL_UD_RNDV_EP_NUM	4	2

For the default MPI buffer settings, we observe a significant linear increase in the memory usage caused by MPI. As a result the eight islands case runs out of memory. We therefore reduced the number of cores per node for this run to 10 resulting in configuration (B) (Table 4). Alternatively, one could decrease the number of MPI ranks for the same problem size and core count by using hybrid MPI/OpenMPI parallelism as done in [11]. This does, however, also not attack the root of the problem. For this, we need to deal with the MPI library instead.

On an Infiniband cluster the Intel MPI library uses the Shared Memory (SHM) transport mechanism for intra-node communication, while for inter-node communication it uses the Direct Access Programming Library (DAPL). While the UD (User Datagramm) version of DAPL is already much more memory conservative than the RC (Reliable Connection) version, the default buffer pool sizes still scale with the number of MPI processes, [10]. This can be seen from the default configuration values in Table 3. As suggested in [10], we set the internal DAPL UD buffer sizes to the fixed values given in Table 3, leading to a significant decrease of the memory consumption. The latter, now, shows almost perfect weak scalability and allows to go to extreme scales. Compared to the all-to-all communication scenarios shown in [10], we even see a much better scaling behavior up to 47 250 MPI ranks. We also do not notice any performance loss.

Computation vs. Communication: Current supercomputers provide tremendous computing capacities. This makes computations relatively cheap compared to communication that gets more expensive, the more processes are used. So, often communication is the bottleneck in high-performance codes.

To investigate the ratio of both, we again employ the Intel mps tool to measure the time for computation, i.e., mean time per process spent in the application code versus time for MPI communication. The latter is the time spent

Table 4. Configurations used in our experiments; default is to use configuration (A).

Configuration	Macro elements per core	Cores per node	# Cores (8 islands)	# DoFs (8 islands)
A	2	12	47 250	$1.1 \cdot 10^{12}$
B	2	10	40 500	$9.1 \cdot 10^{11}$
C	1	16	60 840	$6.8 \cdot 10^{11}$

inside the MPI library. This tool also reports the MPI imbalance, i.e., the mean unproductive wait time per process spent in the MPI library calls, when a process is waiting for data. This time is part of the reported MPI communication time. Here, a high percentage of computation is favorable, while the MPI imbalance should be small. Note that we do not overlap computation and communication. Using overlapping communication does not improve the performance significantly [13].

Besides our default configuration (A) and configuration (B), we consider a third case (C) for the eight islands run. Here, we increase the number of cores per node to the maximum of 16. This increases the total number of MPI processes to 60 840. To make this feasible, we assign one single macro element per rank. This can be seen as the most critical run in terms of communication as it involves the largest number of MPI processes.

The results are shown in Fig. 1 (right), where all initialization times are excluded. We find only a slight increase of communication during weak scaling. And even for the extreme cases the amount of communication is only about 25%. However, we also observe a relatively high MPI imbalance of around 20%. This is partly due to the imbalance of lower dimensional primitives and could be improved by a load balancing scheme that takes the cost of face primitives into account. Changing the number of macro elements per MPI process (C), or varying the number of cores per node (A, B) does hardly affect the results.

Parallel Efficiency: Finally, we report in Table 5 the time-to-solution. For these runs, we switch off any profiling. The iteration is stopped when the residual is reduced by 10^5 starting with a zero initial guess. For our geophysical application such a stopping criterion is more than sufficient. The high viscosity jump in our application makes the problem particularly difficult for the coarse grid (c.g.) solver. Choosing the right stopping criterion is essential for the Uzawa multigrid (UMG) convergence rate, while tuning it becomes quite tricky. It turned out that a criterion based on a maximal iteration count is favorable compared to a tolerance based criterion. In Table 5, we also report the best values we came up with. We remark that for the two islands case we could not find an acceptable number of c.g. iterations that reduced the UMG V-cycles below 10. For this run,

Table 5. Weak scaling results for geophysical application: Runtime w/ and w/o coarse grid solver (c.g.) and no. of UMG iterations. Values in brackets show no. of c.g. iterations (preconditioner/Minres). Parallel efficiency is shown for timings w/ and w/o c.g. *Timings and parallel efficiency are scaled to 7 UMG iterations.

Islands	Cores	DoFs	Global resolution	UMG V-cycles	Time-to-solution	Time-to-sol. w/o c.g	Parallel efficiency
1	5 580	$1.3 \cdot 10^{11}$	3.4 km	7 (50/150)	1347 s	1151 s	1.00/1.00
2	12 000	$2.7 \cdot 10^{11}$	2.8 km	10* (100/150)	1493 s	1183 s	0.90/0.97
4	21 600	$4.8 \cdot 10^{11}$	2.3 km	7 (50/250)	1468 s	1201 s	0.92/0.96
8	47 250	$1.1 \cdot 10^{12}$	1.7 km	8* (50/350)	1609 s	1209 s	0.83/0.95

the element aspect ratio deviates most from 1:1. For all other simulations, the UMG iterations are stable around 7. Note that for the largest simulation the residual reduction was $9.9 \cdot 10^4$ after 7 iterations, so the stopping criterion was only slightly missed. For a fair comparison of runtimes, we scaled all timings to 7 iterations. On up to eight islands, we find a parallel efficiency of 83%. Taking into account that it includes the c.g. solver with its non-optimal complexity, this is an excellent value. Examining the time-to-solution with the c.g. solver excluded, we find an almost perfect parallel efficiency on up 47 250 cores of 95%. Compared to the IFEM reference implementation, we observe for the smallest run a speed-up of a factor larger than 20. In order to save core-h, and thus energy, we did not perform such a comparison for the larger scenarios.

6 Outlook

We extended our LSQP approach to systems of PDEs with variable coefficients and demonstrated that it is suitable for large scale geophysical applications. A systematic performance analysis demonstrates the new matrix-free techniques lead to substantial improvements compared to conventional implementations and they indicate that there is potential for further improvement. In future work, we will expand our study by detailed performance models for a rigorous performance classification and optimization.

Acknowledgments. This work was partly supported by the German Research Foundation through the Priority Programme 1648 "Software for Exascale Computing" (SPPEXA) and WO671/11-1. The authors gratefully acknowledge the Gauss Centre for Supercomputing (GCS) for providing computing time on the supercomputer Super-MUC at LRZ. Special thanks go to the members of LRZ for the organization and their assistance at the "LRZ scaling workshop: Emergent applications". Most scaling results where obtained during this workshop.

References

1. Bauer, S., et al.: Hybrid parallel multigrid methods for geodynamical simulations. In: Bungartz, H.-J., Neumann, P., Nagel, W.E. (eds.) Software for Exascale Computing - SPPEXA 2013–2015. LNCSE, vol. 113, pp. 211–235. Springer, Cham (2016). https://doi.org/10.1007/978-3-319-40528-5_10
2. Bauer, S., Mohr, M., Rüde, U., Weismüller, J., Wittmann, M., Wohlmuth, B.: A two-scale approach for efficient on-the-fly operator assembly in massively parallel high performance multigrid codes. Appl. Numer. Math. **122**, 14–38 (2017)
3. Bergen, B., Gradl, T., Rüde, U., Hülsemann, F.: A massively parallel multigrid method for finite elements. Comput. Sci. Eng. **8**(6), 56–62 (2006)
4. Bergen, B., Hülsemann, F.: Hierarchical hybrid grids: data structures and core algorithms for multigrid. Numer. Linear Algebra Appl. **11**, 279–291 (2004)
5. Brandt, A.: Barriers to achieving textbook multigrid efficiency (TME) in CFD. Institute for Computer Applications in Science and Engineering, NASA Langley Research Center (1998)

6. Brezzi, F., Douglas, J.: Stabilized mixed methods for the Stokes problem. Numer. Math. **53**(1), 225–235 (1988)
7. Colli, L., Ghelichkhan, S., Bunge, H.P., Oeser, J.: Retrodictions of Mid Paleogene mantle flow and dynamic topography in the Atlantic region from compressible high resolution adjoint mantle convection models: sensitivity to deep mantle viscosity and tomographic input model. Gondwana Res. **53**, 252–272 (2018)
8. Davies, D.R., Davies, J.H., Bollada, P.C., Hassan, O., Morgan, K., Nithiarasu, P.: A hierarchical mesh refinement technique for global 3-D spherical mantle convection modelling. Geosci. Model Dev. **6**(4), 1095–1107 (2013)
9. Davies, D.R., Goes, S., Davies, J., Schuberth, B., Bunge, H.P., Ritsema, J.: Reconciling dynamic and seismic models of earth's lower mantle: the dominant role of thermal heterogeneity. Earth Planet. Sci. Lett. **353–354**, 253–269 (2012)
10. Durnov, D., Steyer, M.: Intel MPI Memory Consumption. The Parallel Universe 21 (2015)
11. Gmeiner, B., Rüde, U., Stengel, H., Waluga, C., Wohlmuth, B.: Performance and scalability of hierarchical hybrid multigrid solvers for Stokes systems. SIAM J. Sci. Comput. **37**(2), C143–C168 (2015)
12. Gmeiner, B., Huber, M., John, L., Rüde, U., Wohlmuth, B.: A quantitative performance study for Stokes solvers at the extreme scale. J. Comput. Sci. **17**(Part 3), 509–521 (2016)
13. Gmeiner, B., Köstler, H., Stürmer, M., Rüde, U.: Parallel multigrid on hierarchical hybrid grids: a performance study on current high performance computing clusters. Concurr. Comput.: Pract. Exp. **26**(1), 217–240 (2014)
14. Gmeiner, B., Rüde, U., Stengel, H., Waluga, C., Wohlmuth, B.: Towards textbook efficiency for parallel multigrid. Numer. Math. Theor. Meth. Appl. **8**(01), 22–46 (2015)
15. Heister, T., Dannberg, J., Gassmöller, R., Bangerth, W.: High accuracy mantle convection simulation through modern numerical methods - II: realistic models and problems. Geophys. J. Int. **210**(2), 833–851 (2017)
16. Intel Corp.: MPI Performance Snapshot, version: 2017.0.4 (2017). https://software.intel.com/en-us/node/701419
17. Kronbichler, M., Kormann, K.: A generic interface for parallel cell-based finite element operator application. Comput. Fluids **63**, 135–147 (2012)
18. Logg, A., Ølgaard, K.B., Rognes, M.E., Wells, G.N.: FFC: the FEniCS form compiler. In: Logg, A., Mardal, K.A., Wells, G. (eds.) Automated solution of differential equations by the finite element method. LNCSE, vol. 84, pp. 227–238. Springer, Heidelberg (2012). https://doi.org/10.1007/978-3-642-23099-8_11
19. May, D.A., Brown, J., Pourhiet, L.L.: A scalable, matrix-free multigrid preconditioner for finite element discretizations of heterogeneous Stokes flow. Comput. Methods Appl. Mech. Eng. **290**, 496–523 (2015)
20. Müller, R.D., Sdrolias, M., Gaina, C., Roest, W.R.: Age, spreading rates, and spreading asymmetry of the world's ocean crust. Geochem. Geophys. Geosyst. **9**(4), 1525–2027 (2008)
21. Rudi, J., Malossi, A.C.I., Isaac, T., Stadler, G., Gurnis, M., Staar, P.W.J., Ineichen, Y., Bekas, C., Curioni, A., Ghattas, O.: An extreme-scale implicit solver for complex PDEs: highly heterogeneous flow in earth's mantle. In: Proceedings of the International Conference for High Performance Computing, Networking, Storage and Analysis, SC 2015, pp. 5:1–5:12. ACM (2015)
22. Weismüller, J., Gmeiner, B., Ghelichkhan, S., Huber, M., John, L., Wohlmuth, B., Rüde, U., Bunge, H.P.: Fast asthenosphere motion in high-resolution global mantle flow models. Geophys. Res. Lett. **42**(18), 7429–7435 (2015). https://doi.org/10.1002/2015GL063727

Viscoelastic Crustal Deformation Computation Method with Reduced Random Memory Accesses for GPU-Based Computers

Takuma Yamaguchi[1(✉)], Kohei Fujita[1,2], Tsuyoshi Ichimura[1,2], Anne Glerum[3], Ylona van Dinther[4], Takane Hori[5], Olaf Schenk[6], Muneo Hori[1,2], and Lalith Wijerathne[1,2]

[1] Department of Civil Engineering, Earthquake Research Institute, The University of Tokyo, Bunkyo, Tokyo, Japan
{yamaguchi,fujita,ichimura,hori,lalith}@eri.u-tokyo.ac.jp
[2] Advanced Institute for Computational Science, RIKEN, Kobe, Japan
[3] Helmholtz-Centre Potsdam, GFZ German Research Centre for Geosciences, Potsdam, Germany
acglerum@gfz-potsdam.de
[4] Institute of Geophysics, ETH Zurich, Zurich, Switzerland
ylona.vandinther@erdw.ethz.ch
[5] Research and Development Center for Earthquake and Tsunami, Japan Agency for Marine-Earth Science and Technology, Yokosuka, Japan
horit@jamstec.go.jp
[6] Faculty of Informatics, Università della Svizzera italiana, Lugano, Switzerland
olaf.schenk@usi.ch

Abstract. The computation of crustal deformation following a given fault slip is important for understanding earthquake generation processes and reduction of damage. In crustal deformation analysis, reflecting the complex geometry and material heterogeneity of the crust is important, and use of large-scale unstructured finite-element method is suitable. However, since the computation area is large, its computation cost has been a bottleneck. In this study, we develop a fast unstructured finite-element solver for GPU-based large-scale computers. By computing several times steps together, we reduce random access, together with the use of predictors suitable for viscoelastic analysis to reduce the total computational cost. The developed solver enabled 2.79 times speedup from the conventional solver. We show an application example of the developed method through a viscoelastic deformation analysis of the Eastern Mediterranean crust and mantle following a hypothetical M 9 earthquake in Greece by using a 2,403,562,056 degree-of-freedom finite-element model.

Keywords: CUDA · Finite element analysis
Conjugate gradient method

© Springer International Publishing AG, part of Springer Nature 2018
Y. Shi et al. (Eds.): ICCS 2018, LNCS 10861, pp. 31–43, 2018.
https://doi.org/10.1007/978-3-319-93701-4_3

1   Introduction

One of the targets of solid earth science is the prediction of the place, magnitude, and time of earthquakes. One approach to this target is to estimate earthquake occurrence probability by comparing the current plate conditions with plate conditions when past earthquakes have occurred [9]. In this process, inverse analysis is required to estimate the current inter-plate displacement distribution using the crustal deformation data observed at the surface. In order to realize this inverse analysis, forward analysis methods computing elastic and viscoelastic crustal deformation for a given inter-plate slip distribution are under development.

In previous crustal deformation analyses, simplified models such as horizontally stratified layers were used [8]. However, recent studies point out that the simplification of crustal geometry has significant effects on the response [11]. Recently, 3D crust property data as well as crustal deformation data measured at observation stations are being accumulated. Thus, 3D crustal deformation analyses reflecting these data in full resolution are being anticipated.

The 3D finite-element method is capable of modeling 3D geometry and material heterogeneity of the crust. However, modeling the available 1 Km resolution crust property data fully into 3D finite-element crustal deformation analysis leads to large computational problems with more than 10^9 degrees-of-freedom. Thus, acceleration of this analysis using high-performance computers is required. Targeting the elastic crustal deformation analysis problem, we have been developing unstructured finite-element solvers suitable for GPU-based high-performance computers by developing algorithms considering the underlying hardware [7]. When compared with elastic analysis, viscoelastic analysis requires solving many time steps and thus its computational cost becomes even larger; therefore we target further acceleration of this solver in this paper.

Due to its high floating point performance, GPUs generally have relatively low memory bandwidth. Furthermore, data transfer performance is further decreased when memory access is not coalesced. Finite-element analysis mainly consists of memory bandwidth bound kernels, and the most computationally expensive sparse matrix-vector product kernel has many random memory accesses. Thus, it is not straight forward to utilize the high arithmetic capability of GPUs in finite-element solvers. Reduction of data transfer and random access is important to improve computational efficiency. In this study, we accelerate the previous GPU solver by introducing algorithms that reduce data transfer by reduction of solver iterations, and reduce random access of the major computational kernels. Here we use a multi-time step method together with a predictor to obtain the initial solution of the iterative solver. We improve the convergency of the iterative solver by adapting the predictor to the characteristic of solutions for the viscoelastic problem. In addition, by using several vectors for computation, we can reduce random memory access in the major sparse matrix-vector kernel and improve performance.

Section 2 explains the developed method. Section 3 shows the performance of the developed method on Piz Daint [4], which is a P100 GPU based supercomputer system. Section 4 shows an application example using the developed method. Section 5 summarizes the paper and gives future prospects.

2 Methodology

We target elastic and viscoelastic crustal deformation to a given fault slip. Following [8], the governing equation is

$$\sigma_{ij,j} + f_i = 0, \tag{1}$$

with

$$\dot{\sigma} = \lambda \dot{\epsilon}_{kk} \delta_{ij} + 2\mu \dot{\epsilon}_{ij} - \frac{\mu}{\eta} \left(\sigma_{ij} - \frac{1}{3} \sigma_{kk} \delta_{ij} \right), \tag{2}$$

$$\epsilon_{ij} = \frac{1}{2}(u_{i,j} + u_{j,i}), \tag{3}$$

where σ_{ij} and f_i are the stress tensor and outer force. $(\dot{\ }), (\ )_{,i}, \delta_{ij}, \eta, \epsilon_{ij}$, and u_i are the first derivative in time, spatial derivative in the i-th direction, Kronecker delta, viscosity coefficient, strain tensor, and displacement, respectively. λ and μ are Lame's constants. Discretization of this equation by the finite-element method leads to solving a large system of linear equations. For a solver, (i) good convergency and (ii) small computational cost in each kernel are basically required to reduce the time-to-solution. The proposed method considering these requirements is based on viscoelastic analysis by [10], which can be described as follows (Algorithms 1 and 2).

An adaptive preconditioned conjugate gradient solver with Element-by-Element method [13], multi-grid method, and mixed-precision arithmetic is used in Algorithm 2. Most of the computational cost is in the inner loop of Algorithm 2. It can be computed in single precision, and we can reduce computational cost and data transfer size; thereby we can expect it to be suitable for GPU systems. In addition, we introduce the multi-grid method and use a coarse model to estimate the initial solution for the preconditioning part. This procedure reduces the whole computation cost in the preconditioner as the coarse model has less degrees-of-freedom compared to the target model. Below, we call line 7 of Algorithm 2(a) as the inner coarse loop and line 9 of Algorithm 2(a) as the inner fine loop. First-order tetrahedral elements are used in the inner coarse loop and second-order tetrahedral elements are used in the inner fine loop, respectively. The most computational costly kernel is the Element-by-Element kernel which computes sparse matrix-vector products. The Element-by-Element kernel computes the product of the element stiffness matrix and vectors element wise, and adds the results for all elements to compute a global matrix vector product. As element matrices are computed on the fly, the data transfer size from memory can be reduced significantly. This leads to circumventing the memory bandwidth bottleneck, and thus is suitable for recent architectures including GPUs, which have low memory bandwidth compared with its arithmetic capability. In summary, our base solver [1] computes much part of computation in single precision, reduces the amount of data transfer and computation, and avoids memory bound computation in sparse matrix-vector multiplication. They are desirable conditions for GPU computation to exhibit higher performance. On the other hand,

1 Compute $\mathbf{f}^1$ by split-node technique
2 Solve $\mathbf{K}\mathbf{u}^1 = \mathbf{f}^1$
3 $\{\sigma^j\}_{j=1}^4 \Leftarrow \mathbf{D}\mathbf{B}\mathbf{u}^1$
4 $\{\delta\mathbf{u}_j\}_{j=1}^4 \Leftarrow \mathbf{0}$
5 $i \Leftarrow 2$
6 **while** $i \leq N_t$ **do**
7   **If** $6 \leq i \leq 8$ **then**
8   Compute initial guess solution by 2nd-order Adams-Bashforth
        method $\delta\mathbf{u}^{i+3} \Leftarrow \mathbf{u}^i - 3\mathbf{u}^{i+1} + 2\mathbf{u}^{i+2}$
9   **end**
10   **if** $i \geq 9$ **then**
11   Compute initial guess solution by linear predictor
        $\delta\mathbf{u}^{i+3} \Leftarrow (-17\delta\mathbf{u}^{i-7} - 10\delta\mathbf{u}^{i-6} - 3\delta\mathbf{u}^{i-5} + 4\delta\mathbf{u}^{i-4} + 11\delta\mathbf{u}^{i-3} +$
        $18\delta\mathbf{u}^{i-2} + 25\delta\mathbf{u}^{i-1})/28$
12   **end**
13   **while** $\|\mathbf{K}^v \delta\mathbf{u}^i - \mathbf{f}^i\| > \epsilon$ **do**
14      $\{\mathbf{f}^j\}_{j=i}^{i+3} \Leftarrow \sum_k \int_{\Omega_e^k} \mathbf{B}^T(dt\mathbf{D}^v\{\boldsymbol{\beta}^j\}_{j=i}^{i+3} - \{\sigma^j\}_{j=i}^{i+3})d\Omega_e + \mathbf{f}^0$
15   Solve $\mathbf{K}^v\{\delta\mathbf{u}^j\}_{j=i}^{i+3} = \{\mathbf{f}^j\}_{j=i}^{i+3}$ using **Algorithm 2**
16      $\{\sigma^j\}_{j=i+1}^{i+3} \Leftarrow \{\sigma^j\}_{j=i}^{i+2} + \mathbf{D}^v(\mathbf{B}\{\delta\mathbf{u}^j\}_{j=i}^{i+2} - dt\{\boldsymbol{\beta}^j\}_{j=i}^{i+2})$
17   **end**
18    $\mathbf{u}^i \Leftarrow \mathbf{u}^{i-1} + \delta\mathbf{u}^i$
19    $\sigma^{i+4} \Leftarrow \sigma^{i+3} + \mathbf{D}^v(\mathbf{B}\delta\mathbf{u}^{i+3} - dt\beta^{i+3})$
20    $i \Leftarrow i+1$
21 **end**

Algorithm 1. Coseismic/postseismic crustal deformation computation against given fault displacement. $(\ )^n$ is the variables in the nth timestep. dt is time increment and $\boldsymbol{\beta}^n = \mathbf{D}^{-1}\mathbf{A}\sigma^n$, where $\sigma^n = (\sigma_{11}^n, \sigma_{22}^n, \sigma_{33}^n, \sigma_{12}^n, \sigma_{23}^n, \sigma_{13}^n)^T$. $\mathbf{B}$ is the displacement-strain transformation matrix and $\mathbf{D}$ and $\mathbf{A}$ are 6×6 matrices indicating material properties. $\mathbf{D}^v = (\mathbf{D}^{-1} + \alpha dt\boldsymbol{\beta}')$, where α is a controlling parameter and $\boldsymbol{\beta}'$ is the Jacobian matrix of $\boldsymbol{\beta}$.

the key kernel in the solver, Element-by-Element kernel, requires many random data accesses when adding up element wise results. This data access becomes the bottleneck in the solver. In this paper, we aim to improve the performance of the Element-by-Element kernel. We add two techniques described in following subsections, into our baseline solver.

2.1 Parallel Computation of Multiple Time Steps

In the developed method, we solve four time steps in the analysis in parallel. [6] describes its approach to obtain the accurate predictor using multiple time steps for linear wave propagation simulation. This paper extends the algorithm to viscoelastic analyses. As the stress of the step before needs to be obtained before

(b) Inner loop

1 $\bar{\mathbf{e}} \Leftarrow \sum \overline{\mathbf{K}}_e \bar{\mathbf{u}}_e$

(a) Outer loop

2 $\bar{\mathbf{e}} \Leftarrow \bar{\mathbf{r}} - \bar{\mathbf{e}}$

1 $\mathbf{r} \Leftarrow \sum \mathbf{K}_e \mathbf{u}_e$

3 $\bar{\beta} \Leftarrow 0$

2 $\mathbf{r} \Leftarrow \mathbf{f} - \mathbf{r}$

4 $i \Leftarrow 1$

3 $\beta \Leftarrow 0$

while $\|\bar{\mathbf{e}}_1\|^2 / \|\bar{\mathbf{r}}_1\|^2 > \bar{\epsilon}$

4 $\bar{\mathbf{u}} \Leftarrow \overline{\mathbf{M}}^{-1} \mathbf{r}$

and $N > i$ do

5 $\bar{\mathbf{r}}_c \Leftarrow \overline{\mathbf{P}}^T \mathbf{r}$

5    $\bar{\mathbf{z}} \Leftarrow \overline{\mathbf{M}}^{-1} \bar{\mathbf{e}}$

6 $\bar{\mathbf{u}}_c \Leftarrow \overline{\mathbf{P}}^T \bar{\mathbf{u}}$

6    $\bar{\rho}_a \Leftarrow (\bar{\mathbf{z}}, \bar{\mathbf{e}})$

if $i > 1$ then

7 Solve $\bar{\mathbf{u}}_c = \overline{\mathbf{K}}_c^{-1} \bar{\mathbf{r}}_c$ in (b) with $\bar{\epsilon}_c^{in}$ and N_c

7    $\big| \quad \bar{\beta} \Leftarrow \bar{\rho}_a / \bar{\rho}_b$

8 $\bar{\mathbf{u}} \Leftarrow \overline{\mathbf{P}} \bar{\mathbf{u}}_c$

end

9 Solve $\bar{\mathbf{u}} = \overline{\mathbf{K}}^{-1} \bar{\mathbf{r}}$ in (b) with $\bar{\epsilon}^{in}$ and N

8    $\bar{\mathbf{p}} \Leftarrow \bar{\mathbf{z}} + \bar{\beta} \bar{\mathbf{p}}$

10 $\mathbf{u} \Leftarrow \bar{\mathbf{u}}$

9    $\bar{\mathbf{q}} \Leftarrow \sum \overline{\mathbf{K}}_e \bar{\mathbf{P}}_e$

11 $\mathbf{p} \Leftarrow \mathbf{z} + \beta \mathbf{p}$

10    $\bar{\gamma} \Leftarrow (\bar{\mathbf{p}}, \bar{\mathbf{q}})$

12 $\mathbf{q} \Leftarrow \sum \mathbf{K}_e \mathbf{p}_e$

11    $\bar{\alpha} \Leftarrow \bar{\rho}_a / \bar{\gamma}$

13 $\rho \Leftarrow (\mathbf{z}, \mathbf{r})$

12    $\bar{\rho}_b \Leftarrow \bar{\rho}_a$

14 $\gamma \Leftarrow (\mathbf{p}, \mathbf{q})$

13    $\bar{\mathbf{e}} \Leftarrow \bar{\mathbf{e}} - \bar{\alpha} \bar{\mathbf{q}}$

15 $\alpha \Leftarrow \rho / \gamma$

14    $\bar{\mathbf{u}} \Leftarrow \bar{\mathbf{u}} + \bar{\alpha} \bar{\mathbf{p}}$

16 $\mathbf{r} \Leftarrow \mathbf{r} - \alpha \mathbf{q}$

15    $i \Leftarrow i + 1$

17 $\mathbf{u} \Leftarrow \mathbf{u} + \alpha \mathbf{p}$

end

Algorithm 2. The iterative solver to obtain a solution $\mathbf{u}$. $(\ )_c$ are variables in first-order tetrahedral model, while others are in second-order tetrahedral model. $(\ ^-\ )$ represents single-precision variables, while the others are double-precision variables. The input variables are $\mathbf{K}, \overline{\mathbf{K}}, \overline{\mathbf{K}}_c, \overline{\mathbf{P}}, \mathbf{u}, \mathbf{f}, \bar{\epsilon}_c^{in}, N_c, \bar{\epsilon}^{in}$, and N. The other variables are temporal. $\overline{\mathbf{P}}$ is a mapping matrix from the coarse model to the target model. This algorithm computes four vectors at the same time, so coefficients have the size of four and vectors have the size of $4 \times$ DOF. All computation steps in this solver, except MPI synchronization and coefficient computation, are performed in GPUs.

solving the next step, only one time step can be solved exactly. In Algorithm 1, we focus on solving the equation on i-th timestep. Here we compute until the error of the i-th time step (displacement) becomes smaller than prescribed threshold ϵ as described in lines 13 to 17 of Algorithm 1. The next three time steps, $i+1, i+2$, and $i + 3$-th time steps, are solved using the solutions of the steps before to estimate the solution. The estimated solution of the step before is used to update the stress state and outer force vector, which is corresponding to lines 18 and 19 in Algorithm 1. By using this method, we can obtain estimated solutions for improving the convergency of the solver. In this method, four vectors for $i, i + 1, i + 2$, and $i + 3$-th time steps can be computed simultaneously. In the Element-by-Element kernel, the matrix is read only once for four vectors; thus we can improve the computation efficiency. In addition, four values corresponding

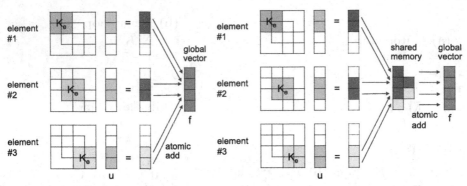

(a) Original scheme. Element-wise results are added to the global vector directly using atomic operations.

(b) Proposed scheme. Element-wise results are firstly summarized using shared memory, and then nodal values are added to the global vector.

Fig. 1. Rough scheme for reduction in Element-by-Element kernel to compute $\mathbf{f} \Leftarrow \sum \mathbf{K}_e \mathbf{u}_e$.

to the four time steps will be consecutive in memory address space. Therefore we can reduce random memory accesses and computation time compared to conducting the Element-by-Element kernel of one vector for four times. That is, the arithmetic count per iteration increases by approximately four times, but the decrease in the number of iterations and the improvement of computational efficiency of the Element-by-Element kernel are expected to reduce the time-to-solution.

In order to improve convergency, it is important to estimate the initial solution of the fourth time step accurately. We can use a typical predictor such as the Adams-Bashforth method, however we developed more accurate predictor considering that solutions for viscoelastic analysis smoothly change in each time step, as described in lines 7 to 12 in Algorithm 1. For predicting the 9th step and on, we use a linear predictor. In this linear predictor, a linear regression based on the accurately computed 7 time steps are used to predict the future time step. As regressions based on higher order polynomials or exponential base functions may lead to jumps in the prediction, we will not use them in this study.

2.2   Reduction of Atomic Access

The algorithm introduced in previous subsection is assumed to circumvent the bottleneck of the performance of Element-by-Element kernel. On the other hand, implementation in the previous study [7] requires to add up element wise results directly to the global vector using atomic function, as shown in Fig. 1a. Considering that each node can be shared by multiple elements, performance may decrease due to the race condition; thereby we need to modify its algorithm to improve the efficiency of the Element-by-Element kernel. We use a buffering method to reduce the number of accesses to the global vector. Regarding

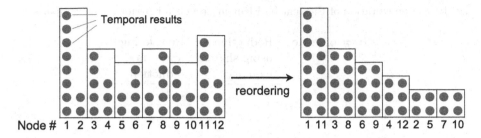

Fig. 2. Reordering of reduction table. Temporal results are aligned in corresponding node number. In this figure, we assume there are two threads per warp and 12 nodes in the thread block for simplicity. Load balance in warp is improved by reordering.

NVIDIA GPU, we can utilize a shared memory, in which values can be referred among threads in the same `Block`. The computation procedure is as below and also described in Fig. 1b.

1. Group elements in to blocks, and store element wise results into a shared memory
2. Add up nodal values in shared memory using a precomputed table
3. Add up nodal values to global vector.

We can expect the performance improvement as the number of atomic operations to the global vector can be reduced and summation of temporal results is mainly performed in preliminary reduction in a shared memory, which has wider bandwidth. In this scheme, the setting of block size is assumed to have some impact on its performance. By allocating more elements in a `Block`, we can improve the number of reduction of nodal values in shared memory. However, the total number of threads is constrained by the shared memory size. In addition, we need to synchronize threads in a `Block` when switching from element wise matrix-vector multiplication to data addition part, using large number of threads in a `Block` leads to an increase in synchronization cost. Under these circumstances, we allocate 128 threads (32 elements × four time steps) per `Block`.

In GPU computation, SIMT composing of 32 threads is used [12]. When the number of computation differs between the 32 threads, it is expected to lead to decrease in performance. In reduction phase, we need to assign threads per node. However, since the number of connected elements differs significantly between nodes, we can expect large load imbalance among the 32 threads. Thus we sort the nodes according to the number of elements to be added up as described in Fig. 2. This leads to good load balance among the 32 threads, leading to higher computational efficiency.

This method on shared memory requires implementation by CUDA. We also use CUDA for inner product computation to improve the memory access pattern and thus improve efficiency. On the other hand, other computations such as vector addition and subtraction are very simple computation; thus each thread uses almost the same number of registers whether we use CUDA or OpenACC.

Table 1. Configuration of Element-by-Element kernels for performance comparison

Case	# of vectors	Reduction using shared memory	Reordering of nodes in reduction
A	1	x	-
B	4	x	-
C	4	o	x
D	4	o	o

Also it is not necessary to use functions specialized for NVIDIA GPUs such as shared memory or warp function. For these reasons, the computations result in memory bandwidth bound and there is little difference between implementation by CUDA and by OpenACC. Thus we use CUDA for these performance sensitive kernels, and use OpenACC for the other parts. The CUDA part is called via a wrapper function.

3 Performance Measurement

We measure performance of the developed method on hybrid nodes of Piz Daint[1].

3.1 Performance Measurement of the Element-by-Element Kernel

We use one P100 GPU on Piz Daint to measure performance of the Element-by-Element kernels. The target finite-element problem consists of 959,128 tetrahedral elements, with 4,004,319 degrees-of-freedom in second-order tetrahedral mesh and 522,639 degrees-of-freedom in first-order tetrahedral mesh. Here we compare four versions of the kernels summarized in Table 1. Case A corresponds to the conventional Element-by-Element kernel, and Case D corresponds to the proposed kernel.

Figure 3 shows the normalized elapsed time per vector of the kernels in inner fine and coarse loops. We can see that the use of four vectors, reduction, and reordering significantly improves performance. In order to assess the time spent for data access, we also indicate the time measured for the Element-by-Element kernel without computing the element wise matrix-vector products. We can see that the data access is dominant in the Element-by-Element kernel on P100 GPUs, and that the elapsed time of the kernel has decreased with the decrease in memory access by reduction. When compared to the performance in second-order tetrahedral mesh, the performance in first-order tetrahedral mesh was further

[1] Piz Daint comprises of 1,431 × multicore compute node (Two Intel Xeon E5-2695 v4) and 5,320 × hybrid compute node (Intel Xeon E5-2690 v3 + NVIDIA Tesla P100) connected by Cray Aries routing and communications ASIC, and Dragonfly network topology.

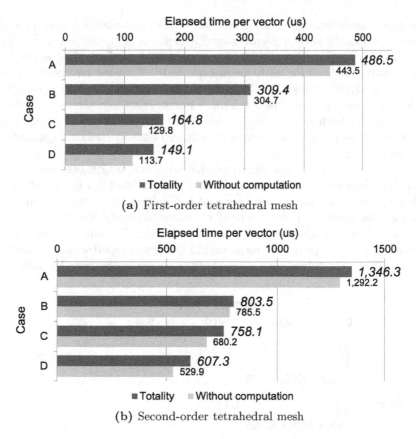

Fig. 3. Elapsed time per Element-by-Element kernel call. Elapsed times are divided by four when using four vectors.

improved by reduction using shared memory. This effect can be confirmed by the number of call for atomic add to the global vector: In second-order tetrahedral mesh, atomic addition is performed 115,095,360 times in Case B and 43,189,848 times in Case D; thereby the number of calls is reduced by about 37%. For the first-order tetrahedral mesh, atomic addition is performed 46,038,144 times in Case B and 10,786,920 times in Case D; thus the number of calls is reduced by about 23%. In total, we can see that the computational performance of the developed kernel (Case D) has improved by 3.3 times in first-order tetrahedral mesh and 2.2 times in second-order tetrahedral mesh when comparing with the conventional kernel (Case A).

3.2 Comparison of Solver Performance

We compare the developed solver with the previous viscoelastic solver in [10] using GPUs in Piz Daint. This solver is originally designed for CPU-based supercomputers and we port this to GPU computation environment and for performance measurement. The solver uses CRS-based matrix-vector products, however, we modify this to Element-by-Element method, because it would be more clear to confirm the effects of our proposed method. The same tolerances of solvers is used for both methods, $\epsilon = 10^{-8}$ is used for the outer loop, $(\bar{\epsilon}_c^{in}, N_c) = (0.1, 300)$ is used for the inner coarse loop, and $(\bar{\epsilon}^{in}, N) = (0.2, 30)$ is used for the inner fine loop. These tolerance numbers are selected to minimize the elapsed time for both solvers. We use time step increment $dt = 2592000$ s with $N_t = 300$ time steps, and measure performance of the viscoelastic computation part (time step 2 to 300).

A model with 41,725,739 degrees-of-freedom and 30,720,000 second-order tetrahedral elements is computed using 32 Piz Daint nodes. Figure 4 shows the number of iterations and elapsed time of the solvers. By using the multistep predictor, the number of iterations of the most computationally costly inner coarse loop has decreased by 2.3 times. In addition, Element-by-Element kernel performance is improved as measured in the previous subsection. These two modifications to the solver have decreased the total elapsed time by 2.79 times.

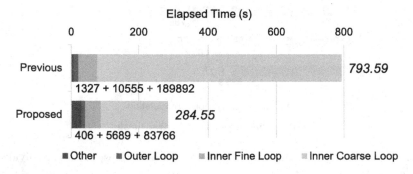

Fig. 4. Performance comparison of the entire solver. The numbers of iteration for outer loop, inner fine loop, and inner coarse loop are described below each bar.

4   Application Example

We apply the developed solver to a viscoelastic deformation problem following a hypothetical earthquake on the Hellenic arc subduction interface, which affects deformation measured in Greece and across the Eastern Mediterranean. We selected this Hellenic region, because recent analysis of time-scale bridging numerical models suggests that the large amount of sediments subducting could mean that a larger than anticipated M 9 earthquake might be able to occur in this highly populated region [3]. To model the complete viscoelastic response of the system we simulate a large depth range, including the Earth's crust, lithosphere and complete mantle down to the core boundary. The target domain is of size 3,686 km × 3,686 km × 2,857 km. Geometry data of layered structure is given in spatial resolution of 1 km [2].

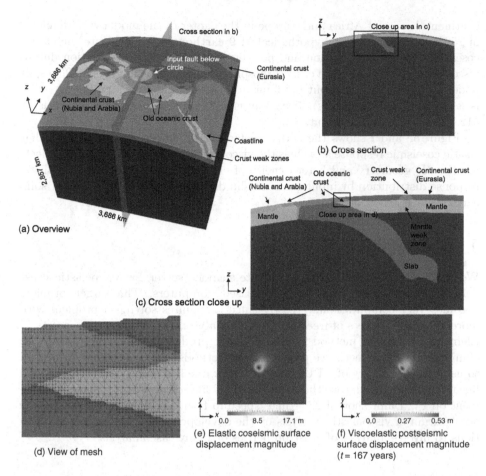

Fig. 5. Finite-element mesh for application problem. The 10 layered crust is modeled using 0.9 km resolution mesh. Elastic coseismic and viscoelastic postseismic displacements. (a) Overview of finite-element mesh with position of input fault and position of cross section. (b) Cross section of finite element mesh. (c) Close up area in the cross section. (d) Close up view of mesh. (e) Elastic coseismic response and (f) viscoelastic postseismic response.

To fully reflect the geometry data into the analysis model, we set resolution of finite-element model to 0.9 km (second-order tetrahedral element size is 1.8 km). As this becomes a large scale problem, we use a parallel mesh generator capable of robust meshing of large complex shaped multiple material problems [5,6]. This leads to a finite-element model of 589,422,093 second-order tetrahedral elements, 801,187,352 nodes, and 2,403,562,056 degrees-of-freedom shown in Fig. 5a–d. We can see that the layered structure geometry is reflected into the model. We input a hypothetical fault slip in the direction of the subduction, that is, slip with $(dx, dy, dz) = (25, 25, -10)$ m, at the subduction interface separating the continental crust of Africa and Europe in the center of the model with diameter of 250 km. Following this hypothetical M 9 earthquake we compute the elastic coseismic surface deformation and postseismic viscoelastic deformation due to viscoelastic relaxation of the crust, lithosphere and mantle. Following [10], a split node method is used to input the fault dislocation, and time step increment dt is set to 30 days (2,592,000 s). The analysis of 2,000 time steps took 4587 s using 512 P100 GPUs on Piz Daint.

Figure 5e and f shows the surface deformation snapshots. We can see that elastic coseismic response as well as the viscoelastic response is computed reflecting the 3D geometry and heterogeneity of crust. We can expect more realistic response distribution by inputting fault slip distributions following current solid earth science knowledge.

5 Conclusion

We developed a fast unstructured finite-element solver for viscoelastic crust deformation analysis targeting GPU-based computers. The target problem becomes very computationally costly since it requires solving a problem with more than 10^9 degrees-of-freedom. In this analysis, the random data access in Element-by-Element method in matrix-vector products was the bottleneck. To eliminate this bottleneck, we proposed two methods: one is a reduction method to use shared memory of GPUs, and the other one is a multi-step predictor and linear predictor to improve the convergency of the solver. Performance measurement on Piz Daint showed 2.79 times speedup from the previous solver. By the acceleration of viscoelastic analysis by the developed solver, we expect applications to inverse analysis of crust properties or many case analysis.

References

1. Agata, R., Ichimura, T., Hirahara, K., Hyodo, M., Hori, T., Hori, M.: Robust and portable capacity computing method for many finite element analyses of a high-fidelity crustal structure model aimed for coseismic slip estimation. Comput. Geosci. **94**, 121–130 (2016)
2. Bird, P.: An updated digital model of plate boundaries. Geochem. Geophys. Geosyst. 4(3), 1027 (2003)
3. Brizzi, S., van Zelst, I., van Dinther, Y., Funiciello, F., Corbi, F.: How long-term dynamics of sediment subduction controls short-term dynamics of seismicity. In: American Geophysical Union (2017)
4. Piz Daint. https://www.cscs.ch/computers/piz-daint/
5. Fujita, K., Katsushima, K., Ichimura, T., Hori, M., Maddegedara, L.: Octree-based multiple-material parallel unstructured mesh generation method for seismic response analysis of soil-structure systems. Procedia Comput. Sci. **80**, 1624–1634 (2016). 2016 International Conference on Computational Science, ICCS 2016, 6–8 June 2016, San Diego, California, USA

6. Fujita, K., Katsushima, K., Ichimura, T., Horikoshi, M., Nakajima, K., Hori, M., Maddegedara, L.: Wave propagation simulation of complex multi-material problems with fast low-order unstructured finite-element meshing and analysis. In: Proceedings of the International Conference on High Performance Computing in Asia-Pacific Region, HPC Asia 2018, pp. 24–35. ACM, New York (2018)

7. Fujita, K., Yamaguchi, T., Ichimura, T., Hori, M., Maddegedara, L.: Acceleration of element-by-element kernel in unstructured implicit low-order finite-element earthquake simulation using OpenACC on Pascal GPUs. In: Proceedings of the Third International Workshop on Accelerator Programming Using Directives, pp. 1–12. IEEE Press (2016)

8. Fukahata, Y., Matsu'ura, M.: Quasi-static internal deformation due to a dislocation source in a multilayered elastic/viscoelastic half-space and an equivalence theorem. Geophys. J. Int. **166**(1), 418–434 (2006)

9. Hori, T., Hyodo, M., Miyazaki, S., Kaneda, Y.: Numerical forecasting of the time interval between successive M8 earthquakes along the Nankai Trough, Southwest Japan, using ocean bottom cable network data. Mar. Geophys. Res. **35**(3), 285–294 (2014)

10. Ichimura, T., Agata, R., Hori, T., Hirahara, K., Hashimoto, C., Hori, M., Fukahata, Y.: An elastic/viscoelastic finite element analysis method for crustal deformation using a 3-D island-scale high-fidelity model. Geophys. J. Int. **206**(1), 114–129 (2016)

11. Masterlark, T.: Finite element model predictions of static deformation from dislocation sources in a subduction zone: sensitivities to homogeneous, isotropic, poisson-solid, and half-space assumptions. J. Geophys. Res. Solid Earth **108**(B11) (2003)

12. Nickolls, J., Buck, I., Garland, M., Skadron, K.: Scalable parallel programming with CUDA. Queue **6**(2), 40–53 (2008)

13. Winget, J.M., Hughes, T.J.R.: Solution algorithms for nonlinear transient heat conduction analysis employing element-by-element iterative strategies. Comput. Methods Appl. Mech. Eng. **52**(1–3), 711–815 (1985)

An Event Detection Framework
for Virtual Observation System:
Anomaly Identification for an ACME
Land Simulation

Zhuo Yao[1], Dali Wang[1,2(✉)], Yifan Wang[1], and Fengming Yuan[2]

[1] Department of Electric Engineering and Computer Science,
University of Tennessee, Knoxville, TN 37996, USA
[2] Environmental Science Department, Oak Ridge National Laboratory,
Oak Ridge, TN 37831, USA
`wangd@ornl.gov`

Abstract. Based on previous work on in-situ data transfer infrastructure and compiler-based software analysis, we have designed a virtual observation system for real time computer simulations. This paper presents an event detection framework for a virtual observation system. By using signal processing and detection approaches to the memory-based data streams, this framework can be reconfigured to capture high-frequency events and low-frequency events. These approaches used in the framework can dramatically reduce the data transfer needed for in-situ data analysis (between distributed computing nodes or between the CPU/GPU nodes). In the paper, we also use a terrestrial ecosystem system simulation within the Earth System Model to demonstrate the practical values of this effort.

1 Introduction

Considerable effort has been made to develop accurate and efficient climate and Earth system simulations in the last two decades. Climate change analysis with both domain knowledge and observational datasets has drawn more and more attention since it seeks to assess whether extreme climate events are consistent with internal climate variability only, or are consistent with the expected response to different combinations of external forces and internal variability [10,12]. However, detecting extreme events in large datasets is a major challenge in climate science research. Current algorithms for detecting extreme events are founded upon scientific experience in defining events based on subjective thresholds of relevant physical variables [7]. dos Santos et al. proposes an approach to detect phenological changes through compact images [11]. Spampinato et al. propose an automatic event detection system based on the Makov Model [3]. Nissen and Ulbrich propose a technique for the identification of heavy precipitation events, but only by means of threshold identifications, which is not suitable for

Y. Shi et al. (Eds.): ICCS 2018, LNCS 10861, pp. 44–55, 2018.
https://doi.org/10.1007/978-3-319-93701-4_4

big database [7]. Gao et al. detect the occurrence of heavy precipitation events by using composites to identify distinct large-scale atmospheric conditions [9]. Zscheischler et al. present a methodological framework, also using thresholds, to detect spatiotemporally contiguous extremes and the likely pathways of climate anomalies [17]. Shirvani et al. develop and investigate a temperature detection model to detect climate change, but it is limited to a single domain [14]. The common theme in all of the above event detection methods is that it only considers post simulation data analysis. When analyses are performed in post-simulation mode, some or all of the data is transferred to different processors, either on the same machine or all together on different computing resources all together [4]. However, in reality, the data streams in climate simulations are enormous, which makes the data transfer over network unaffordable. In addition, with such enormous data streams, the memory and the calculating power of the remote machine would be rapidly exceeded. Furthermore, researchers can take action immediately based on the detected events while the system simulation is running and benefit most from the performance of graphics processing unit (GPU). We propose an unsupervised event detection approach that does not require human-labelled data as was required by [1,3]. This is an advantage since it is not clear how many labels are needed to understand events in a huge database. Instead of human labeling, we expect the infrastructure to learn bench patterns through long-term experiment datasets under an unknown background. For all these reasons, we propose an event detection framework for the virtual observation system (VOS) that provides run-time observation capability and in-situ data analysis. Our detection method enables our processing framework to detect events efficiently since the complexity of the output space is reduced. In this paper, we begin by introducing the VOS framework and then describe the functionalities of its components. Secondly, we explain how to apply signal-processing theory to reduce data and capture high and low frequency anomalies. Finally, we use the framework to identify anomalies and events then verify the detected events using observed datasets in Accelerated Climate Modeling for Energy (ACME) simulation.

2   Event Detection for Virtual Observation System

2.1   Virtual Observation System and Design Considerations

Over the past few decades, climate scientists and researchers have made tremendous progress in designing and building a robust hierarchy framework to simulate the fully coupled Earth system. This simulation can advance our understanding of climate evolution and climate extreme events at multiple scales. Significant examples of event information about extreme climate phenomena include floods [8], precise water availability, storms probability, sea level, the frequency and duration of drought, and the intensity and duration of the extreme heat. Understanding the role of climate extremes is of major interest for global change assessments; in addition, such phenomena have enduring and extensive influence on national economies. In detecting events in such a large dataset within the extreme-scale computing context, I/O constraints can be a great challenge. Scientists typically tolerate only minimal impact on simulation performance, which places significant restrictions on the analysis. In-situ analysis typically shares primary computing resources with simulation and thereby encounters fewer resource limitations because the entirety of the simulation data is locally available. Therefore, a potential solution is to change the data analysis pipeline from post-process centric to a concurrent approach based on in-situ processing. Moreover, a GPU has a massively parallel architecture consisting of thousands of smaller, more efficient cores designed for handling multiple tasks simultaneously which accelerate analytics. The simulation only analyze variables status in real time. Instead, scientists and researchers want to know what elements increase/decrease abnormal immediately, therefore they would decide what action to take when what type of event happens. A previous paper [15] presented a virtually observed system (VOS) that provides interactive observation and run-time analysis capability through high-performance data transport and in-situ data process method during system simulation.

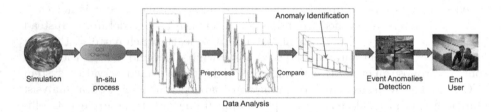

Fig. 1. VOS overview.

Figure 1 illustrates how the VOS works. The VOS framework has three components: the first one is a compiler-based parser, which analyses target modules' internal data structure and inserts the data stream's statement to the original model code. The second component is the communication service using CCI (common communication interface), an API that is portable, efficient, and robust to meet the needs of network-intensive applications [2]. Once the instrumented scientific code starts to simulate, the VOS turns on the CCI channel to listen and interact with the simulation. The CCI channel employs a Remote Memory Access method to send remote buffers to the data analysis component in GPU through network since the parallelism of CPU is much lower than GPU [5]. The last component is data analysis, which collects and analyses data signals and then visualizes events for end-users. The first two components are explained in our previous work [6,15]. This paper will focus on presenting the event detection in data analysis component.

2.2   Data Reduction via Signal Processing

Within the VOS for climate simulation, the analysis component can potentially receive hundreds of variables every simulation timestep (half an hour) from every single function module. To deal with the I/O challenge presented by the enormous, periodic data transfer features, signal processing is proposed. Signal processing is an enabling technology that encompasses the fundamental theory, applications, algorithms and implementations of processing or transferring information contained in many different physical, symbolic or abstract formats broadly designated as signals [6]. Because the memory and computation capability of the second resource is limited, the use of a lower sampling rate results in a implementation with less resource requirement. Nonetheless, downsampling alone causes signal components to be misinterpreted by subsequent users of the data. Therefore, for different science research requirements, different signal filter methods are needed to smooth the signal to an acceptable level. If researchers are interested in long period events result from multi physical elements anomalies, a low-pass filter can be used to remove the short-term fluctuations, and leave the longer-term trend through, since the low-pass filter only permits low-frequency signals and weakens signals with frequencies higher than the cutoff frequency. In contrast, if researchers are interested in abrupt change in a short time period, a filter can be used to pass high-frequency signals and weaken lower than cutoff frequency signals. Our data reduction process consists of two steps: first, a digital filter is used to pass low/high-frequency signal samplings and reduce high/low-frequency variable samplings and then the filtered signal sampling rate is decimated by an integer factor α, which means only keep every α th sample. Based on Nyquist sampling theorem, the sufficient α could be doubled or larger than the original frequency. Nyquist sampling theorem establishes a sufficient condition for a sample rate that permits a discrete sequence of samples to capture all the information from a continuous-time signal of finite bandwidth [13].

3   A Case Demonstration for ACME Land Model

This section reports a detailed event detection implementation and result verification for the ACME case. The ACME is a fully-coupled, global climate model that provides state-of-the-art computer simulations of the Earth's past, present, and future climate states. Within ACME, the ACME Land Model (ALM) is the active component to simulate surface energy, river routing, carbon cycle, nitrogen fluxes and vegetation dynamics [16].

3.1   ACME Land Model for NGEE Arctic Simulation

In this case study, ALM was configured as a single-landscape grid cell simulation conducted offline over Barrow, Alaska, the Next Generation Ecosystem Experiments Arctic site. The purpose of the case study was to investigate terrestrial ecosystem responses to specific atmospheric forcing. The ALM has three hierarchical scales within a model grid cell: the land unit, the snow/soil column, and the plant functional type (PFTs). Each grid cell has a different quantity of land units with various columns, and each column has multiple PFTs. For demonstration purposes, the observation system only tracks the variable flow of a CNAllocation module which has been developed to allocate key chemical elements of a plant (such as carbon, nitrogen and phosphorus) within a terrestrial ecosystem.

3.2 Detection Framework

For the single CNAllocation module, the data flow includes three hundred variables. The NGEE simulation generates and sends out variables every half hour. The whole simulation period is 30 years, which means the data analysis component receives hundreds of multi-dimensional variables for $30 * 365 * 48 = 525600$ times. To manage the huge quantities of data generated by the simulation, each of which had a large frequency, we employed frequency domain signal processing. The framework is schematically illustrated in Fig. 2, which identifies anomalies of various durations and spatial extents in the Barrow Ecosystem Observatory (BEO) land unit datasets. In the first step, the framework filters out the interesting elements from the dimensional arrays and then apples decimation process to reduce the 30 years worth of variables. To find the average monthly pattern, only the first 6 years worth of data are initially selected. Once the monthly pattern for each variable is calculated from the training set, the framework proposes a detection algorithm based on Euclidean distance and compares the Euclidean distance the 30 years' data with the monthly pattern. If the normalized distance exceeds a threshold, the framework marks this variable in this month and this year as an anomaly alert. Finally, if the number of accumulated alerts in one year is very large, this time period is considered as an interesting event. Each detected event can consist of several patch boxes and can last for several time steps. Below is the detailed detection process.

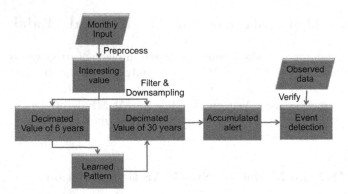

Fig. 2. Detection framework. It first decimates 30 years' variables values, then uses first 6 years' data to find averaged monthly patterns, last tracks the Euclidean distance to find anomalies.

3.3 Event Detection

Variable Preprocess. The climate change system defines, generates and calculates nutrient dynamics as the way they are in an ecosystem (build up, retain, transfer etc.). In our work, the module CNAllocation has 320 nutrient dynamics related variables, some of which are one-dimensional array, and some of which are two-dimensional array. For example, in *cnstate_vars%activeroot_prof_col* (number of active root distributed through column), the first dimension denotes the column number and the second dimension stores the active root numbers for that relevant column. The variable *carbonstate_vars%leafc_storage_patch* is a one-dimensional array with 32 elements that stand for the C storage in a leaf for every PFT level. The purpose of this step is to select out four elements from the default, since the BEO site only has four different plant types. Table 1 shows the indexes of these plant types and their meanings.

Table 1. Variable's PFT index meaning.

PFT index	Meaning
0	Not vegetated plants
9	Shrub with broadleaf and evergreen
11	Boreal shrub with broadleaf and deciduous
12	Arctic grass with c3

Data Process. To simultaneously save memory and retain as many of the data's contours as possible, the framework uses low-pass filter and down sampling data processing method. For example, the variable *carbonflux_vars%cpool_to_xsmrpool_patch* in year 1997, maintenance of respiration storage pool, the original values shown in the upper left panel of Fig. 3 include all year-round (17520 timestep) value of a single variable. The size of these data requires around 0.07 MB in disk space. The total store memory would be 672 MB if we catch and store all variables' information that is not necessary and burdensome for in-situ analysis. However, if the framework applies the data reduction method directly to the original dataset, the signal becomes aliased of original continuous signal, just as the information shown in the lower left panel of Fig. 3. The first and third quarters information are phased out. In other words, whether the decimated signal information maintains the original features massively depends on which decimator the algorithm chooses. If the decimator reflects the variable's frequency, the output signal line will be similar to the original; otherwise, the signal line will change considerably. The framework applies low-pass filter first in consideration of long run trends and anomalies. The right two panels in Fig. 3 represent the result of the low-pass method and the subsequent downsampling output, respectively, which together maintain the original features. In the experiment, the downsampling decimator $1/\alpha$ was set to $1/48$, which eventually downsized the one-year variable's memory to 1.49 KB for single timestep.

Pattern Estimation. The framework estimates the monthly averaged pattern for every variable in each month (Jan–Dec) using the simulation data of the past six years' and gets $12 * 320 = 3840$ bench month patterns in total. Every thin line

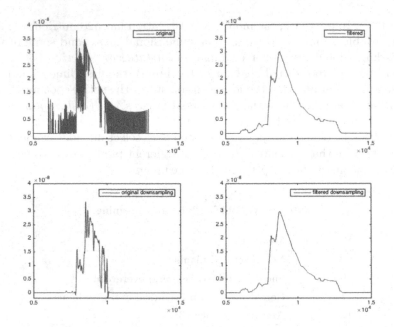

Fig. 3. Downsampling and interpolation. The left panel shows the result directly come from downsampled signals. The right panel shows result signals through filtering and downsampling, which is more accurate than left.

in Fig. 4 shows the value and pattern of July a conopyflux variable. The name of this variable is $CNCarbonFlux\%cpool\_to\_xsmrpool\_patch$, which represents the flux from total carbon pool to the maintenance respiration storage pool, and the thick blue line represents the averaged pattern of this variable in July.

Anomaly Identification. Based on the monthly averaged patterns, we can compare the Euclidean distance between the data in each individual month and the monthly averaged pattern using:

$$D_i = \sqrt{\sum_t [X_i(t) - \bar{X}(t)]^2},$$ (1)

$$\bar{X}(t) = avg[X_j(t)], j \in [i - N, i - 1]$$ (2)

The distance is normalized to get a more robust relationships to adjust values measurement from different scales to same scales and reduce the effect of data anomalies. Below is used to normalize every Euclidean distance to range in $[0, 1]$:

$$\widetilde{D}_i = \left[\frac{D_i - \min\limits_j D_j}{\max\limits_j D_j - \min\limits_j D_j} \right]^+,$$ (3)

$$j \in [i - N, i - 1]$$ (4)

Below is used to evaluate whether the variable of individual month becomes anomaly:

$$Alert = \begin{cases} 0 & \tilde{D}_i > \gamma, \\ 1 & \tilde{D}_i \leq \gamma. \end{cases} \tag{5}$$

If the normalized distance is larger than the set up threshold of value 0.8, the framework will flag the input simulation data streams as an interesting anomaly alert. Figure 4 shows the variable *cpool_to_xsmrpool_patch* of July 1992 is an extreme anomaly because the normalized distance is big.

Event Detection. The framework identifies the entire anomaly for every single variable in every month of 30 years and records the total number of alerts in each month. Figure 5 displays accumulated alert count in 30 years with 320 variables. The overall anomaly peaks can be found in the monthly comparison curve and are accumulated among the year dots. Four extreme events were detected from the horizontal comparison. These events happened in May 1991, which had more than 120 alerts, October 2000, which has 180 alerts, Jun and Jul 1997 and Sep 1998 which had more than 100 alerts. From the vertical comparison, the year of 1997, 1998 and 2000 have the most alerts caused by extreme events. Based on this analysis, we can see that extreme weather events may take place in year 1997, 1998 from Jun to Sep and year 2000 from Jun to Nov. Further verification is needed to for the detection results. Furthermore, we need to investigate what kind of event occurred and the cause of those events.

3.4   Event Verification

In the last step, we verify the event through the input data and identify the event type. The climate experience tells us that temperature and precipitation are the top two factors that affect the results. Therefore, the two variables from year 1990 to 2000 were collected and analyzed. Figure 6 show the temperature at the beginning of December in year 1995 was high and the month had large temperature fluctuation. In year 1996, the temperature trend was similar to that of year 1995, but temperature was higher than any other years. These two curves explain the year 1996 had a warm winter that was part of an arctic warming trend. This trend is most observable during winter. Although most ecosystem activity is in dormancy in cold winter, soil microbial activity can still be significant especially if lasting or significant warming occurs. This includes enhanced soil heterotrophic respiration, methane generation, and nitrogen mineralization and its cascading reactions like nitrification and denitrification. The consequent Inorganic N accumulation during winter period can also cause large denitrification in early spring due to snow melting, which cause saturated soil conditions. Therefore, in the years 1997 and 1998, there was a great deal of variation among different variables, which caused many alerts. Figure 7 compares precipitation from year 1995 to 2000, showing that the daily precipitation in Year 2000 was greater than that in the other years. Heavy precipitation or rainfall usually causes

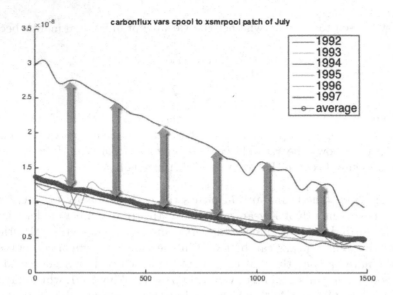

Fig. 4. July pattern comparison of variable *cpool_to_xsmrpool_patch* from year 1992 to year 1997. Among them, bold line is the July averaged pattern. (Color figure online)

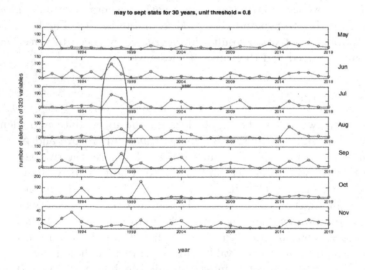

Fig. 5. Accumulated 320 variables anomaly alert count comparison from May to Nov. in 30 years. Year 1997 and year 1998 have continuous events since the alert counts keep peak among all these years.

soil saturation (i.e. anaerobic conditions), which favors methane production, and N gaseous emission from mineralization, nitrification and especially denitrification. Extreme rainfall has a huge impact on spontaneous and large fluxes of greenhouse N gas and methane from soils. Therefore, the numbers of alerts are significant from July to November in Year 2000.

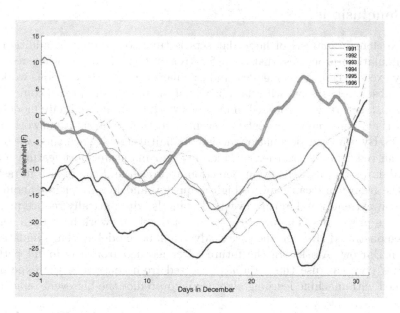

Fig. 6. December daily temperature in F from year 1991 to year 1996, which explains why year 1997 and year 1998 have more than 100 anomaly alerts. December daily temperature in the year 1996 was higher than any other years' and the warmer winter feature could also be reflected from Fig. 5's November alert count. The warming trend therefore caused a great deal of variation among different variables in year 1997 and year 1998.

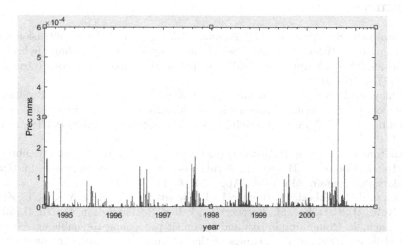

Fig. 7. Daily precipitation from years 1995 to year 2000. The precipitation in the second half of 2000 is heavier than any other years, which verify our detection result that from Jun to Nov, the total alert count is high due to the extreme rainfall's impact on spontaneous and large fluxes of greenhouse N gas and methane from soils.

4   Conclusions

Climate change analysis of large datasets is time-consuming; in addition, the post-simulation processes that transfer tremendous data to other resources rapidly exceed the latter's memory and calculation power. In previous work, the virtual observable system with data flow analysis parser and in-situ communication infrastructure was proposed in previous work to analyze climate model data in real time. This paper presents an event detection analysis framework under the VOS. By using the decimation method in digital signal processing, the framework can reduce data transfer considerably and maintain most features of the original data. Through the event detection approach and the in-situ infrastructure, the framework can capture high frequency and low frequency anomalies, long-term extremes and abrupt events. It can also dramatically reduce pressure on remote processors. The practical values of this framework have been verified and demonstrated through the case study of a land model system simulation at BEO in Barrow, Alaska. In the future, after learned from the found patterns "features", we can use the variables collected from censors in the experiment combined with machine learning algorithms to predict the big event in advance.

Acknowledgements. This research was funded by the U.S. Department of Energy (DOE), Office of Science, Biological and Environmental Research (BER) program, and Advanced Scientific Computing Research (ASCR) program, and LDRD #8389. This research used resources of the Oak Ridge Leadership Computing Facility at the Oak Ridge National Laboratory, which is supported by the Office of Science of the U.S. Department of Energy under Contract No. DE-AC05-00OR22725.

References

1. Aljawarneh, S., Aldwairi, M., Yassein, M.B.: Anomaly-based intrusion detection system through feature selection analysis and building hybrid efficient model. J. Comput. Sci. (2017). http://linkinghub.elsevier.com/retrieve/pii/S1877750316305099
2. Atchley, S., Dillow, D., Shipman, G., Geoffray, P., Squyresz, J.M., Bosilcax, G., Minnich, R.: The common communication interface (CCI). In: Proceedings - Symposium on the High Performance Interconnects, Hot Interconnects (CCI), pp. 51–60 (2011)
3. Spampinato, C., Beauxis-Aussalet, E., Palazzo, S., Beyan, C., van Ossenbruggen, J., He, J., Boom, B., Huang, X.: A rule-based event detection system for real-life underwater domain. Mach. Vis. Appl. **25**, 99–117 (2014)
4. Bennett, J.C., Abbasi, H., Bremer, P.-T., Grout, R., Gyulassy, A., Jin, T., Klasky, S., Kolla, H., Parashar, M., Pascucci, V., Pebay, P., Thompson, D., Yu, H., Zhang, F., Chen, J.: Combining in-situ and in-transit processing to enable extreme-scale scientific analysis. In: Proceedings of the International Conference on High Performance Computing, Networking, Storage and Analysis (SC 2012), 9 p. IEEE Computer Society Press, Los Alamitos (2012). Article 49
5. Du, P., Luszczek, P., Tomov, S., Dongarra, J.: Soft error resilient QR factorization for hybrid system with GPGPU. J. Comput. Sci. **4**(6), 457–464 (2013). http://linkinghub.elsevier.com/retrieve/pii/S1877750313000161

6. Moura, J.: What is signal processing? [President's Message]. IEEE Signal Process. Mag. **26**(6), Article no. 2009 (2009)
7. Nissen, K.M., Ulbrich, U.: Will climate change increase the risk of infrastructure failures in Europe due to heavy precipitation? In: EGU General Assembly Conference Abstracts, vol. 18, p. 7540 (2016)
8. Pitman, E.B., Patra, A.K., Kumar, D., Nishimura, K., Komori, J.: Two phase simulations of glacier lake outburst flows. J. Comput. Sci. **4**(1–2), 71–79 (2013). http://linkinghub.elsevier.com/retrieve/pii/S1877750312000440
9. Gao, X., Schlosser, C.A., Xie, P., Monier, E., Entekhabi, D.: An analogue approach to identify heavy precipitation events: evaluation and application to CMIP5 climate models in the United States. J. Clim. **27**, 5941–5963 (2014)
10. Santer, B.D., Mears, C., Doutriaux, C., Caldwell, P., Gleckler, P.J., Wigley, T.M.L., Solomon, S., Gillett, N.P., Ivanova, D., Karl, T.R., Lanzante, J.R., Meehl, G.A., Stott, P.A., Taylor, K.E., Thorne, P.W., Wehner, M.F., Wentz, F.J.: Separating signal and noise in atmospheric temperature changes: the importance of timescale. J. Geophys. Res.: Atmos. **116**, 1–19 (2011)
11. Santos, L.C.B., Almeida, J., Santos, J.A., Guimar, S.J.F., Ara, A.D.A., Alberton, B., Morellato, L.P.C., Torres, R.S.: Phenological event detection by visual rhythm dissimilarity analysis (2014)
12. Hegerl, G.C., Crowley, T.J., Allen, M., Hyde, W.T., Pollack, H.N., Smerdon, J., Zorita, E.: Detection of human influence on a new, validated 1500-year temperature reconstruction. J. Clim. **20**, 650–667 (2006)
13. Shannon, C.: Editorial note on "Communication in the presence of noise". Proc. IEEE **72**(12), 1713 (1984)
14. Shirvani, A., Nazemosadat, S.M.J., Kahya, E.: Analyses of the Persian Gulf sea surface temperature: prediction and detection of climate change signals. Arab. J. Geosci. **8**, 2121–2130 (2015)
15. Wang, D., Yuan, F., Ridge, O., Pei, Y., Yao, C., Hernandez, B., Steed, C.: Virtual observation system for earth system model: an application to ACME land model simulations. Int. J. Adv. Comput. Sci. Appl. **8**(2), 171–175 (2017)
16. Yao, Z., Jia, Y., Wang, D., Steed, C., Atchley, S.: In situ data infrastructure for scientific unit testing platform 1. Procedia Comput. Sci. **80**, 587–598 (2016). http://linkinghub.elsevier.com/retrieve/pii/S1877050916307591
17. Zscheischler, J., Mahecha, M.D., Harmeling, S., Reichstein, M.: Detection and attribution of large spatiotemporal extreme events in earth observation data. Ecol. Inform. **15**, 66–73 (2013). https://doi.org/10.1016/j.ecoinf.2013.03.004

Enabling Adaptive Mesh Refinement
for Single Components in ECHAM6

Yumeng Chen[✉], Konrad Simon, and Jörn Behrens

Department of Mathematics, Center for Earth System Research and Sustainability,
Universität Hamburg, 20144 Hamburg, Germany
yumeng.chen@uni-hamburg.de

Abstract. Adaptive mesh refinement (AMR) can be used to improve
climate simulations since these exhibit features on multiple scales which
would be too expensive to resolve using non-adaptive meshes. In particular, long-term climate simulations only allow for low resolution simulations using current computational resources. We apply AMR to single
components of the existing earth system model (ESM) instead of constructing a complex ESM based on AMR. In order to compatibly incorporate AMR into an existing model, we explore the applicability of a
tree-based data structure. Using a numerical scheme for tracer transport
in ECHAM6, we test the performance of AMR with our data structure utilizing an idealized test case. The numerical results show that
the augmented data structure is compatible with the data structure of
the original model and also demonstrate improvements of the efficiency
compared to non-adaptive meshes.

Keywords: AMR · Data strucuture · Climate modeling

1 Introduction

Atmospheric components of earth system models used for paleo-climate simulations currently utilize mesh resolutions of the order of hundreds of kilometers.
Since hundreds of components need to be computed on each mesh node, computational resources are limited even with such low resolution. However, relevant processes, such as desert dust or volcano ash clouds, cannot be resolved
with sufficient fidelity to capture the relevant chemical concentrations and local
extent. Improving resolution even in one single component should improve the
general simulation result due to more accurate interactions among different components [1].

AMR dynamically refines a given mesh locally based on user-defined criteria.
This approach is advantageous, when local features need higher resolution or
accuracy than the overall simulation, since the computational effort scales with
the number of mesh nodes or cells. Compared to uniform refinement fewer cells
are added for the same quality of results. Berger and Oliger [2] introduced this
approach for hyperbolic problems using a finite difference method on structured

© Springer International Publishing AG, part of Springer Nature 2018
Y. Shi et al. (Eds.): ICCS 2018, LNCS 10861, pp. 56–68, 2018.
https://doi.org/10.1007/978-3-319-93701-4_5

meshes. Since then the method has gained popularity due to its applicability in a variety of multi-scale problems in computational physics. However, implementation of numerical algorithms on adaptive meshes is more complicated than on uniform meshes. In order to ameliorate the difficulty, various established AMR software implementations are available [3–8]. These packages can generate meshes on complex geometries and provide tools to manage AMR. For example, Jablonowski et al. [9] proposed a general circulation model on the sphere using the AMR library by Oehmke and Stout [5]. McCorquodale et al. [10] built a shallow water model on a cubed-sphere using the Chombo library [8]. However, it is difficult to incorporate these so-called dynamical cores into current climate models for imminent use.

We enable adaptive mesh refinement (AMR) for selected constituents of an atmospheric model, ECHAM6 [11], with a tree-based data structure. Unlike many other AMR implementations that use specially designed mesh data structures and implement numerical schemes in their context our approach aims at a seamless integration into an existing code. Thus, the data structures presented in this paper remain transparent to the hosting program ECHAM6, while enabling locally high resolution. The most natural data structures for efficient AMR implementation are tree-based, more precisely forest of trees data structures [7]. The forest of trees data structure is a collection of trees, which allows the flexibility of adding or deleting cells on the mesh. On the other hand, as an atmospheric general circulation model that solves the equations of atmospheric dynamics and physics on non-adaptive meshes, ECHAM6 uses arrays as its predominant data structure. In order to seamlessly incorporate AMR into individual components of the hosting software ECHAM6, we use the forest of trees data structure combined with a doubly linked list such that it can take arrays as input, while retaining flexibility of the tree structure. We also combine the forest of trees data structure with an index system similar to [12] to uniquely identify individual cells on adaptive meshes and facilitate search operations.

We describe our implementation of AMR in Sect. 2, which includes the description of our indexing system, data structure and the AMR procedure. In Sect. 3, we present the transport equation as an example to demonstrate the performance of our data structure for AMR on an idealized test case. We conclude and plan our future work in Sect. 4.

2   Method

We explore the use of the forest of trees data structure to incorporate an AMR approach into ECHAM6. Our implementation is similar to the forest of trees by Burstedde et al. [7], but it is less complicated because our application is limited to 2-D structured rectangular meshes. In order to facilitate the implementation, we use the index system by [12].

2.1   Index System

ECHAM6 uses arrays for rectangular mesh management. 2-D arrays are indexed by pairs and each entry of the arrays represents a cell on the mesh. The use of an index system greatly helps the construction of numerical schemes for solving partial differential equations and the search of adjacent cells on the mesh.

If we construct the mesh by recursively refining the cells on the domain starting from one cell that covers the whole domain, the index of each cell can be computed correspondingly. After one refinement of the cell (i, j), the resulting four cells have indexes $(i, j = 0, 1, 2, \ldots)$:

$$
\begin{aligned}
(2i, 2j+1) \quad & (2i+1, 2j+1) \\
(2i, 2j) \quad & (2i+1, 2j)
\end{aligned}
\tag{1}
$$

If the mesh is coarsened, every four fine cells coalesce and the index of the resulting coarse cell is:

$$
(\lfloor \tfrac{i}{2} \rfloor, \lfloor \tfrac{j}{2} \rfloor)
\tag{2}
$$

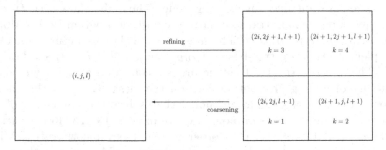

Fig. 1. Illustration of the refinement and coarsening process of a single cell and the corresponding index. k represents the index of the children in the tree

This works perfectly on uniformly refined meshes as all cell indices increase proportionally with each refinement. Thus, each pair can uniquely define a cell. However, conflicts can occur on adaptive meshes, where cells with different levels of refinement appear at the same time. Such conflicts can cause ambiguous cell identification, which in turn may result in the use of wrong values for numerical schemes leading to erroneous numerical results. We adopt the concept of an additional index for the refinement level, l, from [12]. The idea can be illustrated in 1-D cases. If the mesh is generated by recursively refining all cells on the domain from one cell covering the whole domain, we can get the number of cells $nx = 2^l$, where l is the number of refinements. We define the number of refinements as refinement level:

$$
l = \log_2 nx
\tag{3}
$$

The refinement level is defined for each cell. Once a cell is refined, the refinement level of this cell increases by one. Hence, on uniformly refined meshes, all cells have the same refinement level. Our goal is to enable adaptivity on existing meshes. Since the number of cells on the existing mesh is not necessarily an even number, we take $\lceil \log_2 nx \rceil$ as the refinement level, l, such that $nx \leq 2^l$. This concept can be extended to 2-D cases:

$$l = \lceil \log_2 \max(nx, ny) \rceil \tag{4}$$

where nx and ny are the number of cells of the input mesh in each dimension, respectively. Since cells on adaptive meshes have various refinement levels, the triple (i, j, l) forms the index of a cell such that no conflicts can occur. After refining the cell (i, j, l), the index becomes:

$$(2i + a, 2j + b, l + 1) \tag{5}$$

where $a = 0, 1$ and $b = 0, 1$. If four cells are coarsened into one, the four cells coalesce and the index of the resulting cell is:

$$(\lfloor \tfrac{i}{2} \rfloor, \lfloor \tfrac{j}{2} \rfloor, l - 1) \tag{6}$$

Such index system guarantees that each cell owns a unique index on the mesh. The system is shown in Fig. 1.

2.2   Data Structure

Without adaptivity, a cell is treated as an entry of a 2-D array on 2-D meshes. However, arrays lack the flexibility to organize cells on adaptive meshes. In order to enable adaptivity with existing meshes, it is natural to adopt the idea of a forest of trees to manage AMR [7]. A schematic illustration is shown in Fig. 2. A forest is a set of trees. In our application, a tree node represents a cell. Each entry of the input array is a root of a tree. Hence, the number of trees in the data structure depends on the number of cells on the input mesh. The input array can also be viewed as a forest, where each tree just has one root. The roots of the trees are presented as a 1-D array in our current implementation. This reduces the data structure to arrays as in ECHAM6 for non-adaptive meshes. If the input mesh has $nx \times ny$ number of cells, where nx and ny is the number of cells in each dimension, the index of each cell in the forest is $nx \times j + i$, where

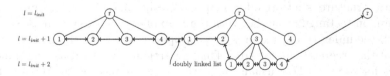

Fig. 2. Illustration of the data structure. The numbers in the tree node represent the indices of children. l is the refinement level, l_{init} is the initial refinement level and r represents the root of each tree. The two way connectors are a representation of a doubly linked list. Each tree node represents a cell and the leaves of the trees are active cells on the computational mesh. A mesh corresponding to this tree is shown in Fig. 3.

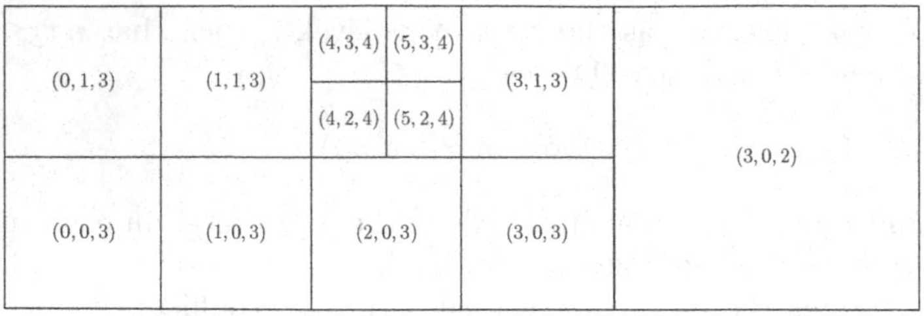

Fig. 3. The mesh organized by the forest of trees shown in Fig. 2. The index of each cell on the adaptive mesh avoids the conflicts at different refinement levels. The initial refinement level, l_{init}, is 2

(i, j), with $i = 0, \ldots, (nx - 1)$, and $j = 0, \ldots, (ny - 1)$, is the index of the cell in the input mesh. This is the same as the row-wise ordering that transforms values on 2-D meshes into 1-D vectors for numerical computation. We maintain the index of each cell from the (original) input mesh and compute the refinement level of cells in the input mesh by Eq. 4. The refinement level of cells in the roots of the trees is defined as initial refinement level, l_{init}. The refinement process divides a cell into four cells, which is equivalent to adding four children to the current tree node of the tree. The children become leaves of the tree and appear on the mesh as a cell and we refer these leaves as active tree nodes, while the parent is non-active tree node as it is not treated as a cell on the mesh. The four children of each tree node in the tree are indexed by k. It is necessary to relate, k, with the index system of cells, (i, j, l). Using a, b in Eq. 5, $k = a + 2b + 1$. An example of index k in cells after refinement is shown in Fig. 1 and the index of children in the tree is shown in Fig. 2. The index a and b can be recovered from (i, j, l):

$$a = i - 2\left\lfloor \frac{i}{2} \right\rfloor$$
$$b = j - 2\left\lfloor \frac{j}{2} \right\rfloor$$

(7)

Correspondingly, as a reverse operation of mesh refinement, the coarsening is equivalent to deleting four leaves that share the same parent. Here, the parent node is again marked as active tree node, which appears as a cell on the mesh. The data structure is intuitive for adaptive meshes and enables a simple search algorithm on rectangular meshes with the help of our index system. Searching a cell with the index (i, j, l) requires $l - l_{init}$ operations, which is the same as the depth of the tree node in the tree. This is particularly useful as the numerical schemes for solving PDEs usually need values at adjacent cells. While a forest of trees is a suitable data structure for adaptive refinement and coarsening, the numerical computation of PDEs usually requires (many) traversals of all active cells of the mesh. It is inefficient to traverse each of the trees just to access the leaves. Therefore, a doubly linked list is used to connect all the leaves as shown in Fig. 2. A linked list can meet the requirement for repeated traversals of the mesh. Similar to arrays, only n operations are required for the traversal of the whole mesh, where n is the number of cells on the mesh. Also, the tree nodes on the doubly linked list can be added or removed flexibly and therefore it is well suited for AMR.

2.3 Adaptive Algorithm and Refinement Strategy

The effectiveness of the AMR also depends on the refinement procedure. Our refinement strategy is inspired by the adaptive semi-Lagrangian algorithm in [13] and is similar to most AMR procedures [14–16]. Assuming a one level time stepping method is used, the implementation involves two meshes. One mesh, M^n, keeps information of the nth time step, and another, M^{n+1}, keeps the information of the $(n + 1)^{st}$ time step. The computation of nt time steps are summarized in Algorithms 1 and 2. ECHAM6 has an independent module for tracer transport. If the AMR method is integrated into ECHAM6, ECHAM6 would parse information on the coarse meshes in the form of arrays to the AMR module. The information on coarse resolutions are supposed to be interpolated.

Data: M^n
Initialize the input mesh M^n;
Perform **mesh refinement procedure** on mesh M^n based on the initial condition of the PDE;
Recompute the initial condition on refined mesh M^n;
Generate mesh M^{n+1} for new time step, which is a copy of mesh M^n;
for $n = 1$ **to** nt **do**
    Perform **mesh refinement procedure** on mesh M^{n+1};
    Solve the PDE and store results on mesh M^{n+1};
    Regenerate mesh M^n as a copy of mesh M^{n+1} for next time step;
end

Algorithm 1. The process of solving the PDEs with AMR. nt is the total number of time steps, and the input data is from an array. The mesh refinement procedure mentioned above is iterative in itself. The details of the step **mesh refinement procedure** at each time step can be found in Algorithm 2.

We limit the differences of refinement levels between adjacent cells to guarantee a relatively smooth resolution variation since abrupt resolution changes can result in artificial wave reflections [17]. This also facilitates the search for adjacent cells since the number of adjacent cells for each cell is less or equal to two.

Data: M
$numofiter = 0;$
$numofcoarsened = numofrefined = 1;$
if $M == M^{n+1}$ **then**
   | Solve PDE by a first-order scheme (predictor step);
end
while $numofcoarsened/ = 0$ **do**
   Mark cells that will be coarsened according to a coarsening criterion;
   Remove coarsening marker for those cells with neighbors differing by more than one level;
   Update mesh and obtain number of coarsened cells $numofcoarsened$;
end
while $numofiter < N$ **or** $numofrefined/ = 0$ **do**
   if $M == M^{n+1}$ **then**
      | Solve PDE by a first-order scheme (predictor step);
   end
   Mark cells that will be refined according to a refinement criterion;
   Mark those cells with neighbors differing by more than one level for refinement;
   Update mesh and refinement levels of cells and obtain number of refined cells $numofrefined$;
   $numofiter = numofiter + 1;$
end

Algorithm 2. The **mesh refinement procedure** in each time step. N is the maximum number of iterations, $numofcoarsened$ is the number of cells coarsened in the current iteration, $numberofrefined$ is the number of cells refined in the iteration, $numofiter$ records the total number of iterations.

3   Results

We test our data structure for adaptive mesh management with an idealized moving vortices test case [18]. The test case is designed to test transport schemes on the sphere. We generate the initial condition of tracer concentration and velocity as arrays and parse these into our data structure such that we can use our own implementation instead of adding the test case into ECHAM6. We use the Flux-Form Semi-Lagrangian (FFSL) [19] transport scheme in ECHAM6, which is a finite volume scheme that conserves mass and permits long time steps. The scheme uses an operator splitting technique, which computes 2-D problems by applying a 1-D solver four times. Here, we choose the cell-integrated semi-Lagrangian scheme [20] as the 1-D solver, where a piecewise parabolic function is used as reconstruction function.

3.1   Moving Vortices Test Case

In this test case, two vortices are developing at opposite sides of the sphere while rotating around the globe. The test case simulates 12 days of model time and has the benefit that an analytical solution is available. The velocity field is given by:

$$u = a\omega_r \{\sin\theta_c(t)\cos\theta - \cos\theta_c(t)\cos[\lambda - \lambda_c(t)]\sin\theta\}$$
$$+ u_0(\cos\theta\cos\alpha + \sin\theta\cos\lambda\sin\alpha), \tag{8}$$
$$v = a\omega_r\cos\theta_c(t)\sin[\lambda - \lambda_c(t)] - u_0\sin\lambda\sin\alpha,$$

where u_0 is the velocity of the background flow that rotates the vortices around the globe, (λ, θ) is the longitude and latitude, $(\lambda_c(t), \theta_c(t))$ is the center of the current vortex. In our experiment, we set $u_0 = \frac{2\pi a}{12\text{ days}}$, where a is the radius of the earth and $(\lambda_c(0), \theta_c(0)) = (\frac{3\pi}{4}, 0)$. The computation of the position of the vortex center can be found in [18]. ω_r is the angular velocity of the vortices:

$$\omega_r = \begin{cases} \frac{3\sqrt{3}u_0\ \text{sech}^2(r)\ \tanh(r)}{2ar} & r \neq 0 \\ 0 & r = 0 \end{cases} \tag{9}$$

where $r = r_0\cos\theta'$. θ' is the position of the rotated sphere where the vortex center is at the north and south poles and r is the radial distance of the vortex. We set $r_0 = 3$.

The moving vortices test case is particularly useful but hard test for AMR schemes because the tracer does not only appear in a limited area, which is common in climate simulations. It covers a large area of the globe and the concentration of the tracer is:

$$\rho = 1 - \tanh[\frac{r'}{\gamma}\sin(\lambda' - \omega_r t)] \tag{10}$$

where $r' = r_0\cos\theta_d$, and θ_d is the departure position of background rotation and λ' is the departure position on the rotated sphere where the vortices' centers are at the poles at $t = 0$.

We choose to set the flow orientation to $\alpha = \frac{\pi}{4}$ considering that this could be the most challenging test set-up for operator splitting schemes [14]. Since the vortices are moving around the globe and the mesh has different sizes around the sphere, the maximum Courant number changes with time. The maximum Courant number appears when the vortices move close to the poles. We use a maximum Courant number of 0.96. A snapshots of the numerical solution on adaptively refined meshes is shown in Fig. 4.

Similar to [14], we use a gradient based criterion. Since we use a cell-based AMR, each cell is assigned an indicator value, θ. This value is computed as the maximum of gradients in cell mean values with respect to the four adjacent cells:

$$\theta = \max(\frac{\partial\rho}{a\cos\theta\partial\lambda}, \frac{\partial\rho}{a\partial\theta}) \tag{11}$$

If $\theta > \theta_r$, the algorithm refines the cell; if $\theta < \theta_c$, the algorithm coarsens the cell. The threshold of $\theta_r = 1$ and $\theta_c = 0.95$ is chosen for this test case. This criterion is justified by the fact that flux-form semi-Lagrangian schemes show little numerical diffusion when strong variations in the tracer are highly resolved. Still, only limited areas are covered by fine resolution cells. The refinement criterion

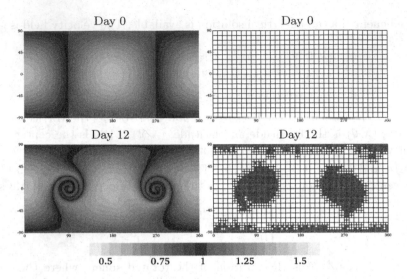

Fig. 4. Numerical solution of the moving vortices test case with base resolution of $10°$ and 2 levels of refinement which leads to fine grid resolution $2.5°$. The left column shows the numerical solution and the right column shows the corresponding mesh evolution.

successfully captures areas where vortices are located because strong distortion of the tracer distribution leads to large gradient in tracer concentrations ρ. Due to the higher resolution around the poles and the highly distorted velocity field, the mesh is refined around the poles even if the vortices do not directly cross the poles. This leads to extra high resolution cells on adaptive meshes. A better representation of the velocity field on refined meshes still helps to get more accurate results.

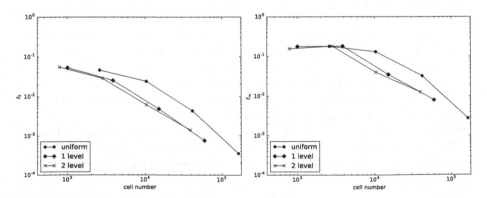

Fig. 5. Convergence rate of the numerical solution with respect to the cell number on the domain. The left one shows the ℓ_2 and the right shows the ℓ_∞-norm

The convergence rate in Fig. 5 shows that, although the results on the non-adaptive mesh can have the best accuracy, similar accuracy can be achieved with fewer cells using adaptive meshes. It is expected that the numerical result on the adaptive mesh is less accurate because the initial condition is defined on a coarser resolution. Furthermore, the ℓ_2 and ℓ_∞ norms are a measure of the global accuracy and the results on the coarse resolution have an impact on the error. Nevertheless, AMR shows improvement in the accuracy compared with the non-adaptive mesh on coarse resolutions. The results are consistent with the results from [14].

Figure 6 show that the wall clock time for tests on adaptive meshes is less than on uniform meshes with the same finest resolution. The test is run in serial. The wall clock time is measured on Debian 3.2 operating system and the machine has 4 Intel Xeon X5650 CPUs, each of which has 6 cores with a clock speed of 2.67 GHz and 12 MB L3 cache. The machine also has a RAM of 24 GB. It is worth noting that the wall clock time is affected by various factors and is not an accurate measure of the effectiveness of AMR. In particular, the implementation is not fully optimized. A more objective measure is that AMR runs use fewer cells compared to uniform meshes with the same resolution. The cell number shown in Fig. 6 represents the average number of cells over all time steps. For this test case the ratio of cell number on adaptive meshes to cell number on uniform meshes remains approximately constant even with different finest resolutions. A possible explanation is that the vortices develop only after some simulation time. Therefore, the (uniform) coarse mesh cell number dominates the average over time. The cell number and the time consumption is also quite problem dependent. In the cross-pole solid body rotation test case by [21], the cell number shows a different variation in terms of resolutions.

It could be argued that the cell number is not the only a measure of the usefulness of AMR. Compared with the non-adaptive meshes, the data structure and extra steps that allows us to enable AMR can lead to overhead, as stated in the Algorithm 2. However, with careful choice of the refinement criterion, fewer memory and less time is required relative to the implementations on non-adaptive meshes. This is because numerical schemes use less time with fewer cells and the overhead can be compensated as shown in Table 1. Additionally, it is expected that an optimized implementation has similar behavior while the specific values may differ. In [7] successful optimization and parallelization of forest of trees data structures could be demonstrated.

Compared with wall clock time, the cell number is more closely related to the memory usage. As shown in Fig. 7, the adaptive mesh runs use significantly less memory compared with non-adaptive mesh runs. Similar memory usage appears on all maximum resolutions.

The test case shows that forest of trees data structure is able to handle AMR with various initial refinement levels. Although the implementation is not fully optimized, benefits of AMR can still be observed. With the current refinement criterion, AMR achieves better accuracy with less memorie and time usage. AMR runs require less wall clock time and fewer cells than uniformly refined simulations at the same finest resolution. The results also show that the forest of trees data structure can successfully handle the information from arrays.

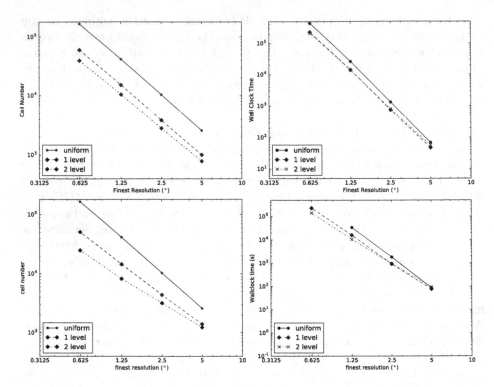

Fig. 6. Used time and cell number of the numerical scheme in the moving vortices test case using a *loglog* plot. The upper left graph shows the cell number on the mesh with the same finest resolution and the upper right graph shows the time used on different refinement levels with the same finest resolution in serial in moving vortices test cases. The lower left and lower right is the cell number and the time consumption for solid body rotation test case.

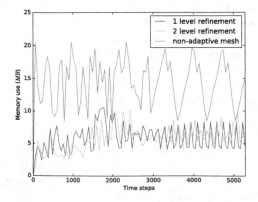

Fig. 7. Time evolution of the total heap memory usage for different refinement levels using moving vortices test case with a maximum resolution of 2.5° on the mesh

Table 1. The time used for different components of the adaptive mesh refinement. Update represents the time used for FFSL, velocity is the time used for updating the velocity for next time step and update mesh from M^n to M^{n+1}, refine is the extra time used for refinement, including the predicting time and mesh refinement.

Finest Resolution	Zero level refinement		One level refinement			Two level refinement		
	Update	Velocity	Update	Refine	Velocity	Update	Refine	Velocity
5°	8.162	60.80	3.33	30.37	17.81	2.65	36.84	21.64
2.5°	1193.81	132.56	466.45	291.14	52.89	459.91	338.74	38.55
1.25°	2216.10	23883.67	937.61	8977.73	5843.90	622.01	7150.97	6111.59

4   Summary and Future Work

We explore the use of a forest of trees data structure to enable AMR in single components of an existing atmospheric model. Our data structure is tested on a tracer transport scheme used in the atmospheric model ECHAM6 for an idealized test case.

We show that our data structure is compatible with the arrays used in ECHAM6. Compatibility between the array data structure used in ECHAM6 and the forest of trees is guaranteed as the forest of trees can simply be reduced to an array on non-adaptive meshes. We combine a forest of trees data structure with an indexing system for mesh management. The data structure is equivalent to arrays on the uniform meshes since no leaves are present on the trees. With the help of a doubly linked list the traversal of potentially adaptively refined meshes is the same as a traversal of an array and the operation for finding arbitrary cells by index is limited by the level of refinements for adaptivity. Therefore, the asymptotical computational complexity of the numerical scheme on adaptive meshes does not increase over the scheme on non-adaptive meshes.

We use a simple gradient based refinement criterion for our numerical test. Although the scheme is not fully optimized and parallelized less computation time is used for AMR while similar accuracy can be achieved using fewer cells - provided the refinement criterion is chosen with care. The results of the AMR runs show less memory and time use compared to non-adaptive meshes.

Acknowledgment. This work was supported by German Federal Ministry of Education and Research (BMBF) as Research for Sustainability initiative (FONA); www.fona.de through Palmod project (FKZ: 01LP1513A).

References

1. Aghedo, A.M., Rast, S., Schultz, M.G.: Sensitivity of tracer transport to model resolution, prescribed meteorology and tracer lifetime in the general circulation model ECHAM5. Atmos. Chem. Phys. **10**(7), 3385–3396 (2010)
2. Berger, M.J., Oliger, J.: Adaptive mesh refinement for hyperbolic partial differential equations. J. Comput. Phys. **53**(3), 484–512 (1984)

3. Berger, M.J., LeVeque, R.J.: Adaptive mesh refinement using wave-propagation algorithms for hyperbolic systems. SIAM J. Numer. Anal. **35**, 2298–2316 (1998)
4. MacNeice, P., Olson, K.M., Mobarry, C., De Fainchtein, R., Packer, C.: PARAMESH: a parallel adaptive mesh refinement community toolkit. Comput. Phys. Commun. **126**(3), 330–354 (2000)
5. Oehmke, R.H., Stout, Q.F.: Parallel adaptive blocks on a sphere. In: PPSC (2001)
6. Bohrens, J., Rakowsky, N., Hiller, W., Handorf, D., Läuter, M., Päpke, J., Dethloff, K.: amatos: parallel adaptive mesh generator for atmospheric and oceanic simulation. Ocean Model. **10**(1–2), 171–183 (2005)
7. Burstedde, C., Wilcox, L.C., Ghattas, O.: p4est: scalable algorithms for parallel adaptive mesh refinement on forests of octrees. SIAM J. Sci. Comput. **33**(3), 1103–1133 (2011)
8. Adams, M., Schwartz, P.O., Johansen, H., Colella, P., Ligocki, T.J., Martin, D., Keen, N., Graves, D., Modiano, D., Van Straalen, B., et al.: Chombo software package for AMR applications-design document. Technical report (2015)
9. Jablonowski, C., Oehmke, R.C., Stout, Q.F.: Block-structured adaptive meshes and reduced grids for atmospheric general circulation models. Philos. Trans. R. Soc. Lond. A: Math. Phys. Eng. Sci. **367**(1907), 4497–4522 (2009)
10. McCorquodale, P., Ullrich, P., Johansen, H., Colella, P.: An adaptive multiblock high-order finite-volume method for solving the shallow-water equations on the sphere. Commun. Appl. Math. Comput. Sci. **10**(2), 121–162 (2015)
11. Stevens, B., Giorgetta, M., Esch, M., Mauritsen, T., Crueger, T., Rast, S., Salzmann, M., Schmidt, H., Bader, J., Block, K., et al.: Atmospheric component of the MPI-M Earth System Model: ECHAM6. J. Adv. Model. Earth Syst. **5**(2), 146–172 (2013)
12. Ji, H., Lien, F.S., Yee, E.: A new adaptive mesh refinement data structure with an application to detonation. J. Comput. Phys. **229**(23), 8981–8993 (2010)
13. Behrens, J.: An adaptive semi-Lagrangian advection scheme and its parallelization. Monthly Weather Rev. **124**(10), 2386–2395 (1996)
14. Jablonowski, C., Herzog, M., Penner, J.E., Oehmke, R.C., Stout, Q.F., Van Leer, B., Powell, K.G.: Block-structured adaptive grids on the sphere: advection experiments. Monthly Weather Rev. **134**(12), 3691–3713 (2006)
15. Blayo, E., Debreu, L.: Adaptive mesh refinement for finite-difference ocean models: first experiments. J. Phys. Oceanogr. **29**(6), 1239–1250 (1999)
16. Behrens, J.: Atmospheric and ocean modeling with an adaptive finite element solver for the shallow-water equations. Appl. Numer. Math. **26**(1–2), 217–226 (1998)
17. Ullrich, P.A., Jablonowski, C.: An analysis of 1D finite-volume methods for geophysical problems on refined grids. J. Comput. Phys. **230**(3), 706–725 (2011)
18. Nair, R.D., Jablonowski, C.: Moving vortices on the sphere: a test case for horizontal advection problems. Monthly Weather Rev. **136**(2), 699–711 (2008)
19. Lin, S.J., Rood, R.B.: Multidimensional flux-form semi-Lagrangian transport schemes. Monthly Weather Rev. **124**, 2046–2070 (1996)
20. Nair, R.D., Machenhauer, B.: The mass-conservative cell-integrated semi-Lagrangian advection scheme on the sphere. Monthly Weather Rev. **130**(3), 649–667 (2002)
21. Williamson, D.L., Drake, J.B., Hack, J.J., Jakob, R., Swarztrauber, P.N.: A standard test set for numerical approximations to the shallow water equations in spherical geometry. J. Comput. Phys. **102**(1), 211–224 (1992)

Efficient and Accurate Evaluation
of Bézier Tensor Product Surfaces

Jing Lan[1], Hao Jiang[2](✉), and Peibing Du[3]

[1] Rongzhi College, Chongqing Technology and Business University,
Chongqing, China
[2] College of Computer, National University of Defense Technology,
Changsha, China
haojiang@nudt.edu.cn
[3] Northwest Institute of Nuclear Technology, Xi'an, China

Abstract. This article proposes a bivariate compensated Volk and Schumaker (`CompVSTP`) algorithm, which extends the compensated Volk and Schumaker (`CompVS`) algorithm, to evaluate Bèzier tensor product surfaces with floating-point coefficients and coordinates. The `CompVSTP` algorithm is obtained by applying error-free transformations to improve the traditional Volk and Schumaker tensor product (`VSTP`) algorithm. We study in detail the forward error analysis of the `VSTP`, `CompVS` and `CompVSTP` algorithms. Our numerical experiments illustrate that the `Comp-` `VSTP` algorithm is much more accurate than the `VSTP` algorithm, relegating the influence of the condition numbers up to second order in the rounding unit of the computer.

Keywords: Bézier tensor product surfaces
Volk and Schumaker algorithm · Compensated algorithm
Error-free transformation · Round-off error

1 Introduction

Tensor product surfaces are bivariate polynomials in tensor product form. In monomial basis, tensor product polynomials are expressed in the following form,

$$p(x, y) = \sum_{i=0}^{n} \sum_{j=0}^{m} c_{i,j} x^i y^j.$$

In Computer Aided Geometric Design (CAGD), tensor product surfaces are usually represented in Bézier form [1]

$$p(x, y) = \sum_{i=0}^{n} \sum_{j=0}^{m} c_{i,j} B_i^n(x) B_i^m(y), \quad (x, y) \in [0, 1] \times [0, 1],$$

Partially supported by National Natural Science Foundation of China (No. 61402495, No. 61602166), National Natural Science Foundation of Hunan Province in China (2018JJ3616) and Chongqing education science planning project 2015-GX-036, which research on the construction for Chongqing smart education.

where $B_i^k(t)$ is the Bernstein polynomial of degree k as

$$B_i^k(t) = \binom{k}{i}(1-t)^{k-i}t^i, \quad t \in [0,1], \quad i = 0, 1, \ldots, k.$$

The de Casteljau algorithm [2,3] is the usual polynomial evaluation algorithm in CAGD. Nevertheless, evaluating a polynomial of degree n, the de Casteljau algorithm needs $\mathcal{O}(n^2)$ operations, in contrast to the $\mathcal{O}(n)$ operations of the Volk and Schumaker (VS) algorithm [4]. The VS basis $z_n := (z_0^n(t), z_1^n(t), \ldots, z_n^n(t))(t \in [0,1])$ is given by $z_i^n(t) = t^i(1-t)^{n-i}$. Otherwise, the VS algorithm consist of Horner algorithm. For evaluating tensor product surfaces, de Casteljau and VS algorithms are more stable and accurate than Horner algorithm [1]. And these three algorithms satisfy the relative accuracy bound

$$\frac{|p(x,y) - \widehat{p}(x,y)|}{|p(x,y)|} \leq \mathcal{O}(u) \times cond(p,x,y),$$

where $\widehat{p}(x,y)$ is the computed result, u is the unit roundoff and $cond(p,x,y)$ is the condition number of $p(x,y)$.

From 2005 to 2009, Graillat et al. proposed compensated Horner scheme for univariate polynomials in [5–7]. From 2010 to 2013, Jiang et al. presented compensated de Casteljau algorithms to evaluate univariate polynomials and its first order derivative in Bernstein basis in [8], to evaluate bivariate polynomials in Bernstein-Bézier form in [9], and to evaluate Bézier tensor product surfaces in [10]. From 2014 to 2017, Du et al. improved Clenshaw-Smith algorithm [11] for Legendre polynomial series with real number coefficients, bivariate compensated Horner algorithm [12] for tensor product polynomials and the quotient-difference algorithm [13] which is a double nested algorithm. All these algorithms can yield a full precision accuracy in double precision as applying double-double library [14].

This paper presents new compensated VS algorithms, which have less computational cost than compensated de Casteljau algorithm, to evaluate tensor product polynomial surfaces by applying error-free transformations which is exhaustively studied in [15–17]. The relative accuracy bound of our proposed compensated algorithms is satisfied

$$\frac{|p(x,y) - \widehat{p}(x,y)|}{|p(x,y)|} \leq u + \mathcal{O}(u^2) \times cond(p,x,y),$$

where $\widehat{p}(x,y)$ is computed by the compensated algorithms.

The rest of the paper is organized as follows. Section 2 introduces basic notation in error analysis, error-free transformations and condition numbers are also given. Section 3 presents the new compensated VS tensor product algorithm and its error analysis. Finally all the error bounds are compared in numerical experiments in Sect. 4.

2   Preliminary

2.1   Basic Notations

We assume to work with a floating-point arithmetic adhering to IEEE-754 floating-point standard rounding to nearest. In our analysis we assume that there is no computational overflow or underflow. Let $op \in \{\oplus, \ominus, \otimes, \oslash\}$ represents a floating-point computation, and the evaluation of an expression in floating-point arithmetic is denoted $fl(\cdot)$, then its computation obeys the model

$$a \ op \ b = (a \circ b)(1 + \varepsilon_1) = (a \circ b)/(1 + \varepsilon_2), \tag{1}$$

where $a, b \in \mathbb{F}$ (the set of floating-point numbers), $\circ \in \{+, -, \times, \div\}$ and $|\varepsilon_1|, |\varepsilon_2| \leq u$ (u is the round-off unit of the computer). We also assume that if $a \circ b = x$ for $x \in \mathbb{R}$, then the computed result in floating-point arithmetic is denoted by $\hat{x} = a \ op \ b$, and its perturbation is ϵx, i.e.

$$\hat{x} = x + \epsilon x. \tag{2}$$

The following definition and properties will be used in the forward error analysis (see more details in [18]).

Definition 1. *We define*

$$1 + \theta_n = \prod_{i=1}^{n}(1 + \delta_i)^{\rho_i}, \tag{3}$$

where $|\delta_i| \leq u, \rho_i = \pm 1$ *for* $i = 1, 2, \ldots, n$, $|\theta_n| \leq \gamma_n := \dfrac{nu}{1 - nu} = nu + \mathcal{O}(u^2)$ *and* $nu < 1$.

Some basic properties in Definition 1 are given by:

- $u + \gamma_k \leq \gamma_{k+1}$,
- $i\gamma_k < \gamma_{ik}$,
- $\gamma_k + \gamma_j + \gamma_k\gamma_j \leq \gamma_{k+j}$,
- $\gamma_i\gamma_j \leq \gamma_{i+k}\gamma_{j-k}$, if $0 < k < j - i$.

2.2   Error-Free Transformations

The development of some families of more stable algorithms, which are called *compensated algorithms*, is based on the paper [15] on error-free transformations (EFT). For a pair of floating-point numbers $a, b \in \mathbb{F}$, when no underflow occurs, there exists a floating-point number y satisfying $a \circ b = x + y$, where $x = \text{fl}(a \circ b)$ and $\circ \in \{+, -, \times\}$. Then the transformation $(a, b) \longrightarrow (x, y)$ is regarded as an EFT. For division, the corresponding EFT is constructed using the remainder, so its definition is slightly different (see below). The EFT algorithms of the sum, product and division of two floating-point numbers are the TwoSum algorithm [19], the TwoProd algorithm [20] and the DivRem algorithm [21,22], respectively.

2.3   Condition Numbers

The condition number of polynomials is with respect to the difficulty of the evaluation algorithm. We assume to evaluate a bivariate polynomial $p(x, y)$ in basis $u \in \mathcal{U}$ at the point (x, y), then for any $(x, y) \in I$, we have

$$
\begin{aligned}
|p(x, y) - \hat{p}(x, y)| &= |\sum_{i=0}^{n} \sum_{j=0}^{m} c_{i,j} u_i^n(x) u_i^m(y)| \\
&\leq \sum_{i=0}^{n} \sum_{j=0}^{m} |c_{i,j}| |u_i^n(x)| |u_i^m(y)|.
\end{aligned}
\tag{4}
$$

We assume that

$$
\bar{p}(x, y) := \sum_{i=0}^{n} \sum_{j=0}^{m} |c_{i,j}| |u_i^n(x)| |u_i^m(y)|,
\tag{5}
$$

then the relative condition number is

$$
cond(p, x, y) = \frac{\bar{p}(x, y)}{|p(x, y)|}.
\tag{6}
$$

In [23], it is known that the condition number in VS basis is as same as in Bernstein basis.

3   The Compensated VS Algorithm for Bézior Tensor Product Surfaces

In this section, we show the VS algorithms, including univariate and bivariate ones. We provide a compensated VSTP algorithm for evaluating Bézior tensor product polynomials. Its forward error bound is also given in the end.

3.1   VS Algorithm

The VS algorithm is a nested-type algorithm for the evaluation of bivariate polynomials of total degree n by Schumaker and Volk [4]. Basically, the VS tensor product algorithm could be represented by the univariate VS algorithm.

Theorem 1 states the forward error bound of VS algorithm.

Theorem 1 [24]. *Let $p(t) = \sum_{i=0}^{n} c_i z_i^n(t)$ with floating point coefficients c_i and a floating point value t. Consider the computed result $\hat{p}(t)$ with the VS algorithm and its corresponding theoretical result $p(t)$, if $4nu < 1$ where u is the unit roundoff, then*

$$
|p(t) - \hat{p}(t)| \leq \gamma_{4n} \sum_{i=0}^{n} |c_i z_i^n(t)|.
\tag{7}
$$

Similar as Theorem 4 in [10], the forward error bound of the VSTP algorithm is easily performed in Theorem 2.

Algorithm 1. Volk-Schumaker algorithm [4] ($x \in [0,1]$)

---

function $res = \text{VS}(p, x)$
if $x \geq 1/2$
    $q = (1 \ominus x) \oslash x$
    $f = \text{Horner}((p_1, p_2, \ldots, p_n), q)$
    $res = f \otimes x^n$
else
    $q = x \oslash (1 \ominus x)$
    $f = \text{Horner}((p_{n-1}, p_{n-2}, \ldots, p_0), q)$
    $res = f \otimes (1 \ominus x)^n$
end

Algorithm 2. VS tensor product algorithm

---

function $VSTP(p, x, y)$
for $i = n : -1 : 0$
    $\widehat{b}_{i,0} = VS(c_{i,:}, y)$
end
$\widehat{a}_0 = VS(\widehat{b}_{:,0}, x)$
$VSTP(p, x, y) \equiv \widehat{a}_0$

Theorem 2. *Let* $p(x, y) = \sum_{i=0}^{n} \sum_{j=0}^{m} c_{i,j} z_i^n(x) z_i^m(y)$ *with floating point coefficients* $c_{i,j}$ *and floating point values* x, y. *Consider the computed result* $\widehat{p}(x, y)$ *of the VSTP algorithm and its corresponding theoretical result* $p(x, y)$, *if* $(4n + 4m + 1)u < 1$ *where* u *is the unit roundoff, then*

$$|p(x, y) - \widehat{p}(x, y)| \leq \gamma_{4(n+m)+1} \bar{p}(x, y), \tag{8}$$

where $\bar{p}(x, y)$ *is defined in (5) in VS basis.*

3.2 The CompVSTP Algorithm

The CompVS algorithm [23] is proposed by Delgado and Peña, which is as accurate as computing in twice the working precision by VS algorithm. In this section, in order to easily provide the forward error bound of CompVS algorithm, we show a compensated Horner algorithm with double-double precision input in Algorithm 3. A compensated power evaluation algorithm in Algorithm 4 is also given.

In Algorithm 3, assuming input x is real number, and we split x into three parts, i.e. $x = x^{(h)} + x^{(l)} + x^{(m)}$, where $x^{(h)}, x^{(l)} \in \mathbb{F}$, $x, x^{(m)} \in \mathbb{R}$ and $|x^{(l)}| \leq u|x^{(h)}|, |x^{(m)}| \leq u|x^{(l)}|$. Since the perturbation of input $x^{(m)}$ in Algorithm 3 is $\mathcal{O}(u^2)$, we just need to consider x in double-double precision. According to Theorem 3.1 in [25], the proof of forward error bound of Algorithm 3 in the following theorem is similar as Theorem 12 in [11].

Theorem 3. *If* $p(x) = \sum_{i=0}^{n} a_i x^i$ ($n \geq 2$) *with floating point coefficients* a_i *and a double-double precision number* x. *And* $\widehat{eb}_0$ *is the computed result err of the CompHorner2 algorithm,* eb_0 *is corresponding theoretical result of* $\widehat{eb}_0$. *Then*

$$|\epsilon b_0 - \widehat{\epsilon b_0}| \le \gamma_{3n-1}\gamma_{3n} \sum_{i=0}^{n} |a_i||x^i|. \tag{9}$$

Graillat proposes a compensated power evaluation algorithm [26] as follows.

Algorithm 3. Compensated Horner scheme with double-double precision inputs

function $[res, err] = \texttt{CompHorner2}(p, x^{(h)}, x^{(l)})$
$\widehat{b}_{n+1} = \widehat{\epsilon b}_{n+1} = 0$
for $i = n : -1 : 0$
  $[s_i, \pi_i] = \texttt{TwoProd}(\widehat{b}_{i+1}, x^{(h)})$
  $[\widehat{b}_i, \sigma_i] = \texttt{TwoSum}(s_i, a_i)$
  $\widehat{\epsilon b}_i = \widehat{\epsilon b}_{i+1} \otimes x^{(h)} \oplus \widehat{b}_{i+1} \otimes x^{(l)} \oplus \pi_i \oplus \sigma_i$
end
$[res, err] = [\widehat{b}_0, \widehat{\epsilon b}_0]$
$\texttt{CompHorner2}(p, x) \equiv \widehat{b}_0 \oplus \widehat{\epsilon b}_0$

Algorithm 4. Compensated power evaluation [26]

function $[res, err] = \texttt{CompLinPower}(x, n)$
$p_0 = x$
$e_0 = 0$
for $i = 1 : n - 1$
  $[p_i, \pi_i] = \texttt{TwoProd}(p_{i-1}, x)$
end
$[res, err] = [p_n, \texttt{Horner}((\pi_1, \pi_2, \ldots, \pi_{n-1}), x)]$
$\texttt{CompLinpower}(x, n) \equiv res \oplus err$

Theorem 4 [26]. *If $p(x) = x^n$ ($n \ge 2$) with a floating-point number x. And $\widehat{e}$ is the computed result err of the CompLinpower algorithm, e is corresponding theoretical result of $\widehat{e}$. Then*

$$|e - \widehat{e}| \le \gamma_n \gamma_{2n}|x^n|. \tag{10}$$

In [23], Delgado and Peña present the running error analysis of CompVS algorithm, but they do not propose its forward error analysis. Here, combining Algorithms 3 and 4, we show the CompVS algorithm in the following algorithm which is expressed a little different in [23].

In Algorithm 5, we can easily obtain that $[q^{(h)}, q^{(l)}]$ is the double-double form of $q = (1 - x)/x$ if $x \ge 1/2$ or $q = x/(1 - x)$ if $x > 1/2$. Then, according to Theorems 1, 3 and 4, the forward error bound of CompVS algorithm is proposed in Theorem 5.

Algorithm 5. Compensated Volk-Schumaker algorithm ($x \in [0,1]$)

---

function $[res, err] = \texttt{CompVS}(\mathbf{p}, \mathbf{x})$
$[r, \rho] = \texttt{TwoSum}(1, -x)$
if $x \geq 1/2$
    $[q^{(h)}, \beta] = \texttt{DivRem}(r, x)$
    $q^{(l)} = (\rho \oplus \beta) \oslash x$
    $[f, e_1] = \texttt{CompHorner2}((p_1, p_2, \ldots, p_n), q^{(h)}, q^{(l)})$
    $[s, e_2] = \texttt{CompLinPower}(x, n)$
    $[res, err] = [f \otimes s, e_1 \otimes s \oplus e_2 \otimes f]$
else
    $[q^{(h)}, \beta] = \texttt{DivRem}(x, r)$
    $q^{(l)} = (\beta \ominus \rho \otimes q^{(h)}) \oslash r$
    $[f, e_1] = \texttt{CompHorner2}((p_{n-1}, p_{n-2}, \ldots, p_0), q^{(h)}, q^{(l)})$
    $[s, e_2] = \texttt{CompLinPower}(r, n)$
    $[res, err] = [f \otimes s, e_1 \otimes s \oplus e_2 \otimes f]$
end
$\texttt{CompVS}(x, n) \equiv res \oplus err$

Theorem 5. *If $p(t) = \sum_{i=0}^{n} c_i z_i^n(t)$ with floating point coefficients c_i and a floating point value t. And $\widehat{\epsilon b_0}$ is the computed result err of the CompVS algorithm, ϵb_0 is corresponding theoretical result of $\widehat{\epsilon b_0}$. Then*

$$|\epsilon b_0 - \widehat{\epsilon b_0}| \leq \gamma_{3n+1}\gamma_{3n+2} \sum_{i=0}^{n} |c_i z_i^n(t)|. \tag{11}$$

Proof. In Algorithm 5, we assume that $\widehat{f} + e_1 = \sum_{i=1}^{n} p_i q^i$ and $\widehat{s} + e_2 = x^n$. Then, we can obtain that $p(t) = (\widehat{f} + e1)(\widehat{s} + e2)$ and assume that $e = e_1\widehat{s} + e_2\widehat{f} + e_1 e_2$. Since $\widehat{e} = \widehat{e}_1 \otimes \widehat{s} \oplus \widehat{e}_2 \otimes \widehat{f}$, we have

$$|e - \widehat{e}|$$
$$\leq |(1+u)^2[(e_1 - \widehat{e}_1)\widehat{s} + (e_2 - \widehat{e}_2)\widehat{f} + e_1 e_2] - (2u + u^2)e| \tag{12}$$
$$\leq (2u + u^2)|e| + (1+u)^2(|e_1 - \widehat{e}_1||\widehat{s}| + |e_2 - \widehat{e}_2||\widehat{f}|).$$

From Theorem 1, let $\bar{p}(t) = |c_i z_i^n(t)|$, we obtain that

$$|e| \leq \gamma_{4n}\bar{p}(t). \tag{13}$$

Thus

$$(2u + u^2)|e| \leq \gamma_2\gamma_{4n+1}\bar{p}(t). \tag{14}$$

According to Theorem 3, we have

$$(1+u)^2|e_1 - \widehat{e}_1||\widehat{s}| \leq \gamma_{3n}\gamma_{3n+1}\bar{p}(x) + \mathcal{O}(u^2). \tag{15}$$

According to Theorem 4, we have

$$(1+u)^2|e_2 - \widehat{e}_2||\widehat{f}| \leq \gamma_{n+1}\gamma_{2n+1}\bar{p}(x) + \mathcal{O}(u^2). \tag{16}$$

From (14), (15) and (16), we can deduce (11).

In fact, $p(x) = \widehat{p}(x) + \epsilon b_0$, where ϵb_0 is corresponding theoretical error of the computed result $\widehat{p}(x)$. In order to correct the result by Algorithms 1 and 5 find an approximate value $\widehat{\epsilon b_0}$ of ϵb_0. Motivated by this principle, we propose to use the CompVS algorithm instead of VS algorithm in Algorithm 2 to improve the accuracy of VSTP algorithm. According to Algorithm 2, we assume that

$$b_{i,0} = \widehat{b}_{i,0} + err_{i,0}^{(1)}, \quad 0 \le i \le n, \tag{17}$$

where $err_{i,0}^{(1)}$ is the theoretical error of $\widehat{b}_{i,0} = VS(c_{i,:}, y)$ and

$$b_{i,0} = \sum_{j=0}^{m} c_{i,j} z_i^m(y), \tag{18}$$

is the exact result for each i. Similarly, we have

$$\tilde{a}_0 = \widehat{a}_0 + err^{(2)}, \tag{19}$$

where $err^{(2)}$ is the theoretical error of $\widehat{a}_0 = VS(\widehat{b}_{:,0}, x)$ and

$$\tilde{a}_0 = \sum_{i=0}^{n} \widehat{b}_{i,0} z_i^n(x), \tag{20}$$

is the exact result. According to (17)–(20), we can deduce

$$\sum_{i=0}^{n} \sum_{j=0}^{m} c_{i,j} z_i^n(x) z_i^m(y) = \widehat{a}_0 + \sum_{i=0}^{n} err_{i,0}^{(1)} z_i^n(x) + err^{(2)}, \tag{21}$$

i.e.

$$p(x,y) = \widehat{p}(x,y) + \sum_{i=0}^{n} err_{i,0}^{(1)} z_i^n(x) + err^{(2)}. \tag{22}$$

Using CompVS algorithm, we can easily get the approximation values of $err_{i,0}^{(1)}$ and $err^{(2)}$, i.e. $\widehat{err}_{i,0}^{(1)}$ and $\widehat{err}^{(2)}$. Thus, we propose the CompVSTP algorithm for evaluating Bézier tensor product polynomials in Algorithm 6.

From (21) and (22), we assume that $e_1 = \sum_{i=0}^{n} err_{i,0}^{(1)} z_i^n(x)$ and $e_2 = err^{(2)}$ so that the real error of the computed result is $e = e_1 + e_2$, i.e. $p(x,y) = \widehat{p}(x,y) + e$. Firstly, we present the bound of $|e_1 - \widehat{e}_1|$ in Lemma 1.

Lemma 1. *From Algorithm 6, we assume that $e_1 = \sum_{i=0}^{n} err_{i,0}^{(1)} z_i^n(x)$. Then we have*

$$|e_1 - \widehat{e}_1| \le (\gamma_{3n+1}\gamma_{3n+2}(1 + \gamma_{4m}) + \gamma_{4n}\gamma_{4m}\bar{p}(x,y), \tag{23}$$

where $\bar{p}(x,y)$ is defined in (5) in VS basis.

Algorithm 6. Compensated VSTP algorithm ($x \in [0,1]$)

function $[res, err] = \mathtt{CompVSTP}(p, x, y)$
$f_{i,j}^{(0)} = b_{i,j}$
for $i = 1 : m$
    $[\widehat{f}_{i,0}^{(1)}, \widehat{e}_{i,0}] = \mathtt{CompVS}(f_{i,:}^{(0)}, y)$
end
$[\widehat{f}_{0,0}^{(2)}, \widehat{e2}] = \mathtt{CompVS}(\widehat{f}_{:,0}^{(1)}, x)$
$[res, err] = [\widehat{f}_{0,0}^{(2)}, \widehat{e2} \oplus \mathtt{VS}(\widehat{e1}_{:,0}, x)]$
$\mathtt{CompVSTP}(p, x, y) \equiv res \oplus err$

Proof. We denote that

$$\bar{e}_1 = \sum_{i=0}^{n} \widehat{err}_{i,0}^{(1)} z_i^n(x). \tag{24}$$

Hence, we have

$$|e_1 - \widehat{e}_1| \leq |e_1 - \bar{e}_1| + |\bar{e}_1 - \widehat{e}_1|. \tag{25}$$

According to Theorem 5, we have

$$|err_{i,0}^{(1)} - \widehat{err}_{i,0}^{(1)}| \leq \gamma_{3n+1}\gamma_{3n+2} \sum_{j=0}^{m} |c_{i,j} z_i^m(y)|, \tag{26}$$

thus

$$|e_1 - \bar{e}_1| = \sum_{i=0}^{n} |err_{i,0}^{(1)} - \widehat{err}_{i,0}^{(1)}| z_i^n(x)$$

$$\leq \gamma_{3n+1}\gamma_{3n+2} \sum_{i=0}^{n} \sum_{j=0}^{m} |c_{i,j} z_i^n(x) z_i^m(y)|. \tag{27}$$

According to Theorem 1, we obtain

$$|\bar{e}_1 - \widehat{e}_1| \leq \gamma_{4m} \sum_{i=0}^{n} |\widehat{err}_{i,0}^{(1)} z_i^n(x)|. \tag{28}$$

Then we have that

$$|\widehat{err}_{i,0}^{(1)}| \leq |err_{i,0}^{(1)}| + |err_{i,0}^{(1)} - \widehat{err}_{i,0}^{(1)}|. \tag{29}$$

By Theorem 1, we have

$$|err_{i,0}^{(1)}| \leq \gamma_{4n} \sum_{j=0}^{m} |c_{i,j} z_i^m(y)|. \tag{30}$$

From (26), (29) and (30), we deduce that

$$|\widehat{err}_{i,0}^{(1)}| \leq (\gamma_{3n+1}\gamma_{3n+2} + \gamma_{4n}) \sum_{j=0}^{m} |c_{i,j} z_i^m(y)|, \tag{31}$$

and then from (28) we obtain

$$|\bar{e}_1 - \widehat{e}_1| \leq \gamma_{4m}(\gamma_{3n+1}\gamma_{3n+2} + \gamma_{4n})\bar{p}(x,y). \tag{32}$$

Hence, from (25), (27) and (32), we can obtain (23).

Then, we present the bound of $|e_2 - \widehat{e}_2|$ in Lemma 2.

Lemma 2. *From Algorithm 6, we assume that $e_2 = err^{(2)}$. Then we have*

$$|e_2 - \widehat{e}_2| \leq \gamma_{3m+1}\gamma_{3m+2}(1 + \gamma_{4m})\bar{p}(x,y), \tag{33}$$

where $\bar{p}(x,y)$ is defined in (5) in VS basis.

Proof. According to Theorem 5, we have

$$|e_2 - \widehat{e}_2| \leq \gamma_{3m+1}\gamma_{3m+2}\sum_{i=0}^{n}|\widehat{b}_{i,0}z_i^n(x)|. \tag{34}$$

From Theorem 1, we obtain

$$|\widehat{b}_{i,0}| \leq \sum_{j=0}^{m}(1 + \gamma_{4m})|c_{i,j}z_i^m(y)|. \tag{35}$$

Hence, from (34) and (35), we can deduce (33).

Above all, the forward error bound of CompVSTP algorithm is performed in the following theorem.

Theorem 6. *Let $p(x,y) = \sum_{i=0}^{n}\sum_{j=0}^{m}c_{i,j}z_i^n(x)z_i^m(y)$ with floating point coefficients $c_{i,j}$ and floating point values x,y. The forward error bound of Algorithm 6 is*

$$|CompVSTP(p,x,y) - p(x,y)| \leq u|p(x,y)| + 3(\gamma_{4n+2}^2 + \gamma_{4m+2}^2)\bar{p}(x,y), \tag{36}$$

where $\bar{p}(x,y)$ is defined in (5) in VS basis.

Proof. We assume that $e_1 = \sum_{i=0}^{n} err_{i,0}^{(1)}x^i$ and $e_2 = err^{(2)}$ so that $e = e_1 + e_2$. From (22), we have

$$p(x,y) = \widehat{p}(x,y) + e, \tag{37}$$

and from Algorithm 6, we have

$$\mathtt{CompVSTP}(p,x,y) = \widehat{p}(x,y) \oplus \widehat{e}. \tag{38}$$

Hence

$$\begin{aligned}|\mathtt{CompVSTP}(p,x,y) - p(x,y)| &\leq |(1+u)(p(x,y) - e + \widehat{e}) - p(x,y)| \\ &\leq u|p(x,y)| + (1+u)|e - \widehat{e}|.\end{aligned} \tag{39}$$

Since $\widehat{e} = \widehat{e}_1 \oplus \widehat{e}_2$, we have

$$|e - \widehat{e}| \leq |(1 + u)(e_1 - \widehat{e}_1 + e_2 - \widehat{e}_2) - ue| \qquad (40)$$
$$\leq u|e| + (1 + u)(|e_1 - \widehat{e}_1| + |e_2 - \widehat{e}_2|).$$

From Theorem 2, we obtain that

$$|e| \leq \gamma_{4(n+m)+1} \bar{p}(x, y). \qquad (41)$$

Thus

$$u(1+u)|e| \leq \gamma_1 \gamma_{4(n+m+1)} \bar{p}(x, y) \leq \gamma_{4n+2} \gamma_{4m+2} \bar{p}(x, y) \leq \frac{1}{2}(\gamma_{4n+2}^2 + \gamma_{4m+2}^2)\bar{p}(x, y). \qquad (42)$$

According to Lemma 1, we have

$$(1 + u)^2 |e_1 - \widehat{e}_1| \leq (2\gamma_{4n+1}^2 + \gamma_{4n+1}\gamma_{4m+1})\bar{p}(x, y)$$
$$\leq (\frac{5}{2}\gamma_{4n+1}^2 + \frac{1}{2}\gamma_{4m+1}^2)\bar{p}(x, y). \qquad (43)$$

According to Lemma 2, we have

$$(1 + u)^2 |e_2 - \widehat{e}_2| \leq 2\gamma_{4m+1}^2 \bar{p}(x, y). \qquad (44)$$

From (42), (43) and (44), we can deduce (36).

According to the relative condition number defined in (6), we can deduce Corollary 1.

Corollary 1. *Let* $p(x, y) = \sum_{i=0}^{n} \sum_{j=0}^{m} c_{i,j} z_i^n(x) z_i^m(y)$ *with floating point coefficients* $c_{i,j}$ *and floating point values* x, y. *The forward relative error bound of Algorithm 6 is*

$$\frac{|CompVSTP(p, x, y) - p(x, y)|}{|p(x, y)|} \leq u + 3(\gamma_{4n+2}^2 + \gamma_{4m+2}^2)cond(p, x, y). \qquad (45)$$

4 Numerical Experiments

In this section, we compare CompVSTP algorithm against an implementation of VSTP algorithm that applies the double-double format [14,27] which we denote as DDVSTP algorithm. In fact, since the working precision is double precision, the double-double arithmetic is the most efficient way to yield a full precision accuracy of evaluating polynomials. Moreover, we also compare CompVSTP algorithm against compensated de Casteljau (CompDCTP) algorithm [10].

All our experiments are performed using IEEE-754 double precision as working precision. All the programs about accuracy measurements have been written in Matlab R2014a on a 1.4-GHz Intel Core i5 Macbook Air. We focus on the

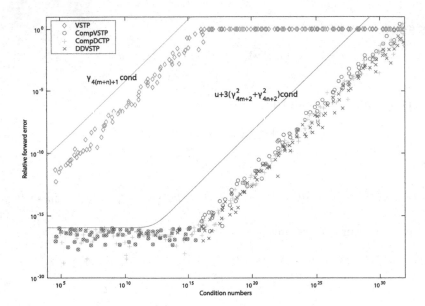

Fig. 1. Accuracy of evaluation of ill-conditioned Bézier tensor product polynomials with respect to the condition number

relative forward error bounds for ill-conditioned Bézier tensor product polynomials. We use a similar GenPoly algorithm [10,21] to generate tested polynomials $p(x, y)$. The generated polynomials are 6×7 degree with condition numbers varying from 10^4 to 10^{36}, x and y are random numbers in $[0, 1]$ and the inspired computed results of all the tested polynomials are 1. We evaluate the polynomials by the VSTP, CompVSTP, CompDCTP, DDVSTP algorithms and the Symbolic Toolbox, respectively, so that the relative forward errors can be obtained by $(|p_{res}(x, y) - p_{sym}(x, y)|)/|p_{sym}(x, y)|$ and the relative error bounds are described from Corollary 1. Note that the condition number of Bézier tensor product polynomials in Bernstein basis evaluated by CompDCTP algorithm is as same as in VS basis evaluated by CompVSTP algorithm. Then we present the relative forward errors of evaluation of the tested polynomials in Fig. 1. As we can see, the relative errors of CompVSTP, CompDCTP and DDVSTP algorithms are both smaller than u ($u \approx 1.16 \times 10^{-16}$) when the condition number is less than 10^{16}. And the accuracy of them is decreasing linearly for the condition number larger than 10^{16}. However, the VSTP algorithm can not yield the working precision; the accuracy of which decreases linearly since the condition number is less than 10^{16}.

At last, we give the computational cost of VSTP, CompVSTP, CompDCTP and DDVSTP algorithms.

- **VSTP:** $(3n + 2)(m + 1) + 3m + 2$ flops,
- **CompVSTP:** $(50n + 26)(m + 1) + 50m + 26 + 1$ flops,
- **CompDCTP:** $(24n^2 + 24n + 7)(m + 1) + 24m^2 + 24m + 7 + 1$ flops,
- **DDVSTP:** $(68n + 120)(m + 1) + 68m + 120$ flops.

CompVSTP and DDVSTP algorithms require almost 17 and 23 times flop than VSTP algorithm, respectively. Meanwhile, CompDCTP algorithm requires $\mathcal{O}(n^2 m)$ flop which is much more than $\mathcal{O}(nm)$. Hence, CompVSTP algorithm only needs about 73.5% of flops counting on average of DDVSTP algorithm and needs much less computational cost than CompDCTP algorithm. Meanwhile, CompVSTP algorithm is as accurate as CompDCTP and DDVSTP algorithms.

5 Conclusions and Further Work

In this paper, we present CompVSTP algorithm to evaluate Bézier tensor product polynomials, which are compensated algorithms that obtaining an approximate error to correct the computed results by original algorithm. The proposed algorithm is as accurate as computing in double-double arithmetic which is the most efficient way to yield a full precision accuracy. Moreover, it needs fewer flops than counting on average with double-double arithmetic.

A similar approach can be applied to other problems to obtain compensated algorithms. For example we can consider the evaluation of ill-conditioned tensor product polynomials in orthogonal basis like Chebyshev and Legendre basis. Instead of tensor product surfaces, we can consider triangle surfaces like Bernstein-Bézier form. We can also study compensated algorithms for multivariate polynomials.

References

1. Farin, G.: Curves and Surfaces for Computer Aided Geometric Design, 4th edn. Academic Press Inc., SanDiego (1997)
2. Mainar, E., Peña, J.: Error analysis of corner cutting algorithms. Numer. Algorithms **22**(1), 41–52 (1999)
3. Barrio, R.: A unified rounding error bound for polynomial evaluation. Adv. Comput. Math. **19**(4), 385–399 (2003)
4. Schumaker, L., Volk, W.: Efficient evaluation of multivariate polynomials. Comput. Aided Geom. Des. **3**, 149–154 (1986)
5. Graillat, S., Langlois, P., Louvet, N.: Compensated Horner scheme. Technical report, University of Perpignan, France (2005)
6. Graillat, S., Langlois, P., Louvet, N.: Algorithms for accurate, validated and fast polynomial evaluation. Jpn. J. Ind. Appl. Math. **26**, 191–214 (2009)
7. Langlois, P., Louvet, N.: How to ensure a faithful polynomial evaluation with the compensated Horner algorithm. In: Proceedings 18th IEEE Symposium on Computer Arithmetic, pp. 141–149. IEEE Computer Society (2007)
8. Jiang, H., Li, S.G., Cheng, L.Z., Su, F.: Accurate evaluation of a polynomial and its derivative in Bernstein form. Comput. Math. Appl. **60**(3), 744–755 (2010)
9. Jiang, H., Barrio, R., Liao, X.K., Cheng, L.Z.: Accurate evalution algorithm for bivariate polynomial in Bernstein-Bźier form. Appl. Numer. Math. **61**, 1147–1160 (2011)
10. Jiang, H., Li, H.S., Cheng, L.Z., Barrio, R., Hu, C.B., Liao, X.K.: Accurate, validated and fast evaluation of Bézier tensor product surfaces. Reliable Comput. **18**, 55–72 (2013)

11. Du, P.B., Jiang, H., Cheng, L.Z.: Accurate evaluation of polynomials in Legendre basis. J. Appl. Math. **2014**, Article ID 742538 (2014)
12. Du, P.B., Jiang, H., Li, H.S., Cheng, L.Z., Yang, C.Q.: Accurate evaluation of bivariate polynomials. In: 2016 17th International Conference on Parallel and Distributed Computing, Applications and Technologies, pp. 51–55 (2016)
13. Du, P.B., Barrio, R., Jiang, H., Cheng, L.Z.: Accurate Quotient-Difference algorithm: error analysis, improvements and applications. Appl. Math. Comput. **309**, 245–271 (2017)
14. Li, X.S., Demmel, J.W., Bailey, D.H., Henry, G., Hida, Y., Iskandar, J., Kahan, W., Kapur, A., Martin, M.C., Tung, T., Yoo, D.J.: Design, implementation and testing of extended and mixed precision BLAS. ACM Trans. Math. Softw. **28**(2), 152–205 (2002)
15. Ogita, T., Rump, S., Oishi, S.: Accurate sum and dot product. SIAM J. Sci. Comput. **26**, 1955–1988 (2005)
16. Rump, S., Ogita, T., Oishi, S.: Accurate floating-point summation part I: faithful rounding. SIAM J. Sci. Comput. **31**, 189–224 (2008)
17. Rump, S., Ogita, T., Oishi, S.: Accurate floating-point summation part II: Sign, k-fold faithful and rounding to nearest. SIAM J. Sci. Comput. **31**, 1269–1302 (2008)
18. Higham, N.J.: Accuracy and Stability of Numerical Algorithm, 2nd edn. SIAM, Philadelphia (2002)
19. Knuth, D.E.: The Art of Computer Programming: Seminumerical Algorithms, 3rd edn. Addison-Wesley, Boston (1998)
20. Dekker, T.J.: A floating-point technique for extending the available precision. Numer. Math. **18**, 224–242 (1971)
21. Louvet, N.: Compensated algorithms in floating-point arithmetic: accuracy, validation, performances, Ph.D. thesis, Université de Perpignan Via Domitia (2007)
22. Pichat, M., Vignes, J.: Ingénierie du contrôle de la préision des calculs sur ordinateur. Technical report, Editions Technip (1993)
23. Delgado, J., Peña, J.: Algorithm 960: POLYNOMIAL: an object-oriented Matlab library of fast and efficient algorithms for polynomials. ACM Trans. Math. Softw. **42**(3), 1–19 (2016). Article ID 23
24. Delgado, J., Peña, J.: Running relative error for the evaluation of polynomials. SIAM J. Sci. Comput. **31**, 3905–3921 (2009)
25. Peña, J., Sauer, T.: On the multivariate Horner scheme. SIAM J. Numer. Anal. **37**(4), 1186–1197 (2000)
26. Graillat, S.: Accurate floating point product and exponentiation. IEEE Trans. Comput. **58**(7), 994–1000 (2009)
27. Hida, Y., Li, X.Y., Bailey, D.H.: Algorithms for quad-double precision floating point arithmetic. In: 15th IEEE Symposium on Computer Arithmetic, pp. 155–162. IEEE Computer Society (2001)

Track of Agent-Based Simulations, Adaptive Algorithms and Solvers

Agent-Based Simulations, Adaptive Algorithms and Solvers: Preface

Maciej Paszyński

AGH University of Science and Technology, Al. Mickiewicza 30, 30-059
Kraków, Poland
paszynsk@agh.edu.pl

Abstract. The aim of this workshop is to integrate results of different domains of computer science, computational science, and mathematics. We invite papers oriented toward simulations, either hard simulations by means of finite element or finite difference methods, or soft simulations by means of evolutionary computations, particle swarm optimization, and other. The workshop is most interested in simulations performed by using agent-oriented systems or by utilizing adaptive algorithms, but simulations performed by other kind of systems are also welcome. Agent-oriented system seems to be the attractive tool useful for numerous domains of applications. Adaptive algorithms allow significant decrease of the computational cost by utilizing computational resources on most important aspect of the problem.[1]

Keywords: Agent-based simulations · Adaptive-algorithms · Solvers

Introduction

This is the fourteen workshop on "Agent-Based Simulations, Adaptive Algorithms and Solvers" (ABS-AAS) organized in the frame of the International Conference on Computational Science (ICCS). The workshop at Wuxi follows meetings hold in Krakow 2004, Atlanta 2005, Reading 2006, Beijing 2007, Krakow 2008, Baton Rouge 2009, Amsterdam 2010, Singapore 2011, Omaha 2012, Barcelona 2013, Cairns 2014, Reykjavik 2015, San Diego 2016 and Zurich 2017 in frame on ICCS series of conferences. The history of previous ABS-AAS workshops is illustrated in Fig. 1.

The co-chairmen of the workshop currently involve prof. Robert Schaefer from AGH University, Kraków, Poland, prof. David Pardo from the University of the Basque Country UPV/EHU, Bilbao, Spain, and prof. Victor Manuel Calo from Curtin Univeristy, Perth, Western Australia.

We have a scientific committee with researchers from several countries, including Poland, Spain, Australia, United States, Brasil, Saudi Arabia, Ireland, Chile. These locations are illustrated in Fig. 2.

---

[1] home.agh.edu.pl/iacs.

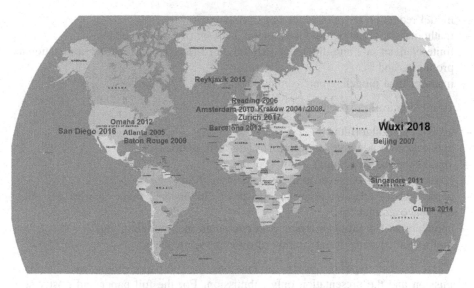

Fig. 1 Past locations of the workshop.

Fig. 2 Scientiffic committee from different countries.

The papers submitted to the workshop falls into either theoretical brand, like:

- multi-agent systems in high-performance computing,
- efficient adaptive algorithms for big problems,
- low computational cost adaptive solvers,
- fast solvers for isogeometric finite element method,
- agent-oriented approach to adaptive algorithms,

- model reduction techniques for large problems,
- mathematical modeling and asymptotic analysis of large problems,
- finite element or finite difference methods for three dimensional or non-stationary problems, and
- mathematical modeling and asymptotic analysis.

or the application sphere, like:

- agents based algorithms,
- application of adaptive algorithms in large simulations,
- simulation and large multi-agent systems,
- applications of isogeometric finite element method,
- application of adaptive algorithms in three dimensional finite element and finite difference simulations,
- application of multi-agent systems in computational modeling, and
- multi-agent systems in integration of different approaches.

There are three types of possible submissions, the full paper submission, the poster submission and the presentation only submission. For the full paper and poster submission, the whole paper is reviewed by the scientific committee. This year we had 11 full paper submissions, and we rejected 5 submissions to keep the high level of the workshop. On top of that, there are abstract only submissions which do not require a full paper review. Usually, authors of these submissions prefer to submit the full paper to some high impact factor journal after the conference. Thus, these submissions are usually of high quality, and this year we had 5 presentation-only submissions, and all of them have been accepted. Summing up, this year we had 14 submissions, with 6 full papers accepted [6, 7, 9–11], 5 presentation only [1–5], and 5 rejected.

The topics of the papers fall into two categories. The first one includes theoretical analysis and implementation aspects of the finite element method simulations, from adaptive finite element method in 1.5 dimensions to space-time formulations [1, 3], through isogeometric finite element method simulations [2, 4] finishing with different aspects of large-scale parallel simulations [5, 6]. The second one include agent-based simulations of swarm computations [7], pedestrian modeling [8], behavioral modeling [9], through image coding [10] finishing with sociological simulations [11].

References

1. Shahriari, M., Rojas, S., Pardo, D., Rodriguez-Rozas, A., Bakr, S.A., Calo, V.M., Muga, I., Munoz-Matute, J.: A Fast 1.5D Multi-scale Finite Element Method for Borehole Resistivity Measurements
2. Garcia-Lozano, D., Pardo, D., Calo, V.M., Munoz-Matute, J.: Refined Isogeometric Analysis (rIGA): A multi-field application on a fluid flow scenario
3. Munoz-Matute, J., Pardo, D., Calo, V.M., Alberdi Celaya, E.: Space-Time Goal-Oriented Adaptivity and Error Estimation for Parabolic Problems employing Explicit Runge-Kutta Methods

4. Jopek, K., Woźniak, M., Paszyński, M.: Algorithm for estimation of FLOPS per mesh node and its application to reduce the cost of isogeometric analysis
5. Woźniak, M., Łoś, M., Paszyński, M.: Hybrid memory parallel alternating directions solver library with linear cost for IGA-FEM
6. Podsiadło, K., Łoś, M., Siwik, L., Woźniak, M.: An algorithm for tensor product approximation of three-dimensional material data for implicit dynamics simulations. In: Shi, Y. et al. (eds.) ICCS 2018. LNCS, vol. 10861, pp. 156–168 (2018)
7. Płaczkiewicz, L., Sendera, M., Szlachta, A., Paciorek, M., Byrski, A., Kisiel-Dorohinicki, M., Godzik, M.: Hybrid swarm and agent-based evolutionary optimization. In: Shi, Y. et al. (eds.) ICCS 2018. LNCS, vol. 10861, pp. 89–102 (2018)
8. Kuang Tan, S., Hu, N., Cai, W.: Data-driven agent-based simulation for pedestrian capacity analysis. In: Shi, Y. et al. (eds.) ICCS 2018. LNCS, vol. 10861, pp. 103–116 (2018)
9. Kudinov, S., Smirnov, E., Malyshev, G., Khodnenko, I.: Planning optimal path networks using dynamic behavioral modeling. In: Shi, Y. et al. (eds.) ICCS 2018. LNCS, vol. 10861, pp. 129–141 (2018)
10. Dhou, K.: A novel approach for Image coding and compression based on a modified wolf sheep predation model. LNCS (2018)
11. Derevitskii, I., Severiukhina, O., Bochenina, K., Voloshin, D., Lantseva, A., Boukhanovsky, A.: Multiagent contextdependent model of opinion dynamics in a virtual society. LNCS (2018)

Hybrid Swarm and Agent-Based Evolutionary Optimization

Leszek Placzkiewicz, Marcin Sendera, Adam Szlachta, Mateusz Paciorek, Aleksander Byrski$^{(\boxtimes)}$, Marek Kisiel-Dorohinicki, and Mateusz Godzik

Department of Computer Science, Faculty of Computer Science, Electronics and Telecommunications, AGH University of Science and Technology, Al. Mickiewicza 30, 30-059 Krakow, Poland
leszekplaczkiewicz@gmail.com, marcin.sendera@gmail.com, adam.szlachta@gmail.com, godzik.mateusz@gmail.com, {mpaciorek,olekb,doroh}@agh.edu.pl

Abstract. In this paper a novel hybridization of agent-based evolutionary system (EMAS, a metaheuristic putting together agency and evolutionary paradigms) is presented. This method assumes utilization of particle swarm optimization (PSO) for upgrading certain agents used in the EMAS population, based on agent-related condition. This may be perceived as a method similar to local-search already used in EMAS (and many memetic algorithms). The obtained and presented in the end of the paper results show the applicability of this hybrid based on a selection of a number of 500 dimensional benchmark functions, when compared to non-hybrid, classic EMAS version.

1 Introduction

Solving difficult search problems requires turning to unconventional methods. Metaheuristics are often called "methods of last resort" and are successfully applied to solving different problems that cannot be solved with deterministic means in a reasonable time. Moreover, metaheuristics do not assume any knowledge about the intrinsic features of the search space, that helps a lot in solving complex problems such as combinatorial ones. It has also been proven that there is always need for searching for novel metaheuristics, as there is no Holy Grail of metaheuristics computing, and there is no one method that could solve all the possible problems with the same accuracy (cf. Wolpert and MacReady [21]). One has however to retain common sense and not produce the metaheuristics only for the sake of using another inspiration (cf. Sorensen [18]).

In 1996, Krzysztof Cetnarowicz proposed the concept of an Evolutionary Multi-Agent System (EMAS) [7]. The basis of this agent-based metaheuristic are agents—entities that bear appearances of intelligence and are able to make decisions autonomously. Following the idea of population decomposition and evolution decentralization, the main problem is decomposed into sub-tasks, each of which is entrusted to an agent. One of the most-important features of EMAS is

Y. Shi et al. (Eds.): ICCS 2018, LNCS 10861, pp. 89–102, 2018.
https://doi.org/10.1007/978-3-319-93701-4_7

the lack of global control—agents co-evolve independently of any superior management. Another remarkable advantage of EMAS over classic population-based algorithms is the parallel ontogenesis—agents may die, reproduce, or act at the same time. EMAS was successfully applied to solving many discrete and continuous problems, and was thoroughly theoretically analyzed, along with preparing of formal model proving its potential applicability to any possible problem (capability of being an universal optimizer, based on Markov-chain analysis and ergodicity feature) [3].

Particle swarm optimization [11] is an iterative algorithm commonly used for mathematical optimization of certain problems. Particle swarm optimization was originally proposed for simulating social behavior, and was used for simulating the group movement of fish schools, bird flocks, and so on. But the algorithm was also found to be useful for performing mathematical optimization after some simplification. The algorithm considers a number of particles moving in the search space, utilizing the available knowledge (generated by a certain particle and its neighbors) regarding the current optimal solutions, providing the user with an attractive technique retaining both exploitation and exploration features.

Memetic algorithms originate from Richard Dawkins' theory of memes. Meme is understood as a "unit of culture" that carries ideas, behaviors, and styles. This unit spreads among people by being passed from person to person within a culture by speech, writing, and other means of direct and indirect communication. The actual implementation of memetic algorithms proposed by Pablo Moscato is based on coupling local-search technique with evolutionary process, either on the reproduction level (e.g. during mutation: lamarckian memetization) or on the evaluation level (baldwinian memetization).

The hybrid method presented in this paper is based on coupling two metaheuristics, namely EMAS and PSO, using the memetic approach, i.e. allowing the agents in EMAS to run PSO-based "local-search". It should be noted, that PSO is a global optimization technique, and thus its synergy with EMAS seems to be even more attractive than e.g. introducing of a certain steepest-descent method that we have already done in the past [13].

The paper is organized as follows. After this introduction a number of hybrid PSO and evolutionary methods are referenced, leading the reader to the short recalling of EMAS basics and later presenting the PSO and its hybridization with EMAS. Next the experimental results comparing the base model of EMAS with the PSO-memetic one are shown, and finally the paper is concluded with some remarks.

2   Hybrid Particle Swarm Optimization

There exist many methods which can be used to hybridize Genetic Algorithms (GA) with Particle Swarm Optimization (PSO). One of them, called GA-PSO, has been presented by Kao and Zahara [10]. Their algorithm starts with generating a population of individuals of a fixed size $4N$ where N is a dimension of the solution space. The fitness function is calculated for each individual, the population is sorted by the fitness value and divided into two $2N$ subpopulations. The top $2N$ individuals are further processed using standard real-coded GA operators: crossover and mutation. Crossover is defined as a random linear combination of two vectors and happens with 100% probability. The probability of mutation is fixed at 20%. The obtained subpopulation of $2N$ individuals is used to adjust the remaining $2N$ individuals in PSO method. This operation involves the selection of the global best particle, the neighborhood and the velocity updates. The result is sorted in order to perform the next iteration. The algorithm stops when the convergence criterion is met, that is when a standard deviation of the objective function for $N + 1$ best individuals is below a predefined threshold (authors suggest 10^{-4}). The article shows the performance of the hybrid GA-PSO algorithm using a suit of 17 standard test functions and compares it to the results obtained with different methods (tabu search, simulated annealing, pure GA, and some modifications). In some cases GA-PSO performs clearly better, but in general behaves very competitive.

Similar method has been used by Li et al. [19]. Their algorithm, called PGHA (PSO GA Hybrid Algorithm), divides the initial population into two parts which then perform GA and PSO operators respectively. The subpopulations are recombined into new population which is again divided into two parts for the next population. Authors successfully used this technique for creation optimal antenna design.

Another method of hybridization of PSO and GA has been presented by Gupta and Yadav in [9] as PSO-GA hybrid. In their algorithm there are two populations, PSO and GA based, running independently and simultaneously. Occasionally, after a predefined number of iterations $N1$, certain number $P1$ of individuals from each system are designated for an exchange. The results authors obtained showed clear superiority of their PSA-GA hybrid technique over plain PSO and GA algorithms. The article compares GA, PSO and PSO-GA hybrid in the application of optimization 2nd and 3rd Order Digital Differential Operators.

There also exist GA/PSO hybrids for combinatorial problems. Borna and Khezri developed a new method to solve Traveling Salesman Problem (TSP) called MPSO [2]. Their idea is to perform the PSO procedure, but without using velocity variable. Instead, the crossover operator between *pbest* (particle's best position) and *gbest* (global best position) is used to calculate new positions. Both *pbest* and *gbest* values are updated as in normal PSO algorithm. Authors show that their MPSO technique gives better accuracy than other methods.

A combination of GA and PSO for combinatorial vehicle routing optimization problem (VRP) has been presented by Xu et al. [22]. Their algorithm starts with parameters and population initialization. Then the step of particle encoding is performed in order to calculate fitness function of each particle for VRP problem in the following step. Then *pbest* and *gbest* values are updated as in standard PSO. After that particles positions and velocities are recalculated using special crossover formulas which use a random value from a defined range to describe crossover probability. If the fitness of offspring is lower than the fitness of parents it is discarded, otherwise it replaces the parents. The algorithm is performed in loop until the stop conditions are met. The test results show that the proposed algorithm can find the same solutions as the best-known, but has overall better performance than other algorithms.

AUC-GAPSO is a hybrid algorithm proposed by Ykhlef and Alqifari in order to solve winner determination problem in multiunit double internet auction [23]. In each iteration the chromosomes are updated using specialized for this problem crossover and mutation operators. After that a PSO step is performed and new *gbest* and *pbest* together with new positions and velocities are calculated. If *gbest* is not being changed for more than one fourth of the maximum number of generations, the algorithm stops as no further improvement is assumed. Authors showed that their method performs superior to plain AUC-GA giving higher performance and reduced time to obtain satisfactory optimization results.

Different variation of PSO-GA hybrid has been presented by Singh et al. [17]. Their technique, called HGPSTA, is similar to ordinary GA. PSO is used to enhance individuals before performing crossover and mutation operators. Once the fitness values of all individuals are calculated, the most successful first half is selected for further processing using crossover. Parents are selected by roulette wheel method. Mutation is then performed on entire population. HGPSTA (Hybrid Genetic Particle Swarm Technique Algorithm) has been used to identify the paths of software that are error prone in order to generate software test cases. Authors demonstrated that the method needs less iterations to deliver 100% test coverage than plain GA and PSO.

The performance of GA is also improved by incorporating PSO in the work of Nazir et al. [16]. Individuals are enhanced by PSO step after crossover and mutation operations are performed. There are some innovations to the basic algorithm. The first one is that the probability of taking PSO enhancement into account varies according to a special formula. The second one is that if *gbest* value remains a number of times unchanged it is updated to prevent from getting trapped in local extremum. The method has been used to select the most significant features in gender classification using facial and clothing information.

Another hybrid method has been presented by Abd-El-Wahed, Mousa and El-Shorbagy [1], who apply it to solve constrained nonlinear optimization problems. The entire procedure is based on interleaving steps of PSO and GA mechanisms. Moreover the algorithm incorporates a calculation and usage of modified dynamic constriction factor to maintain the feasibility of a particle. In GA part selection, crossover and mutation are used, as well as elitist strategy. The last step of an iteration is to repair infeasible individuals to make them feasible again. Authors show an excellent performance of the algorithm for a presented set of test problems.

Algorithm presented by Mousavi et al. in [15] is a mixture of PSO and GA steps. The PSO part is performed first (updating particles' positions and velocities), then standard selection, crossover and mutation steps follow. Before and after the GA part the boundary check is done for each particle. If a particle is out of predefined boundary then a new random particle is generated until it fits into the boundary. Authors successfully applied their GA-PSO method in multi-objective AGV (automated guided vehicles) scheduling in a FMS (flexible manufacturing system) problem. The study shows that GA-PSO outperforms single PSO and GA algorithms in this application.

Kuo and Han in [14] describe and evaluate three hybrid GA and PSO algorithms, HGAPSO-1, HGAPSO-2, HGAPSO-3. The first two are taken from other studies, whereas the last one is invented by the authors. This method follows the general PSO procedure, but if *gbest* is unchanged in given iteration, then each particle is additionally updated using mutation operator. The idea is to prevent premature convergence to a local optimum. Moreover the elitist policy is applied in the last step. Positions of particles are checked to fit into a defined range, also a velocity value is constrained by a predefined upper limit. Authors show that their version is superior to the other two described. They apply the method to solving bi-level linear programming problem.

Another overview of PSO hybridizations is presented in [20] by Thangaraj, Pant, Abraham and Bouvry. The research also include some other algorithms used in conjunction with PSO like differential evolution, evolutionary programming, ant colony optimization, sequential quadratic programming, tabu search, gradient descend, simulated annealing, k-means, simplex and others. A small subset of them is chosen for further performance comparison using a set of standard numerical problems like Rosenbrock function, DeJong function etc.

Summing up the presented state-of-the-art, one can clearly see that many approaches using Genetic Algorithm with PSO for improvement of the solutions were realized, however none of them considered hybridization in fully autonomous environment. Thus we would like to present an agent-based metaheuristic that utilizes PSO selectively, by certain agent, and its decision is fully autonomous.

3   Evolutionary Multi Agent-Systems

Evolutionary Multi Agent-System [7] can be treated as an interesting and quite efficient metaheuristic, moreover with a proper formal background proving its correctness [3]. Therefore this system has been chosen as a tool for solving the problem described in this paper.

Evolutionary processes are by nature decentralized and therefore they may be easily introduced in a multi-agent system at a population level. It means that agents are able to *reproduce* (generate new agents), which is a kind of cooperative interaction, and may *die* (be eliminated from the system), which is the result of competition (selection). A similar idea with limited autonomy of agents located in fixed positions on some lattice (like in a cellular model of parallel evolutionary algorithms) was developed by Zhong et al. [24]. The key idea of the decentralized model of evolution in EMAS [12] was to ensure full autonomy of agents.

Such a system consists of a relatively large number of rather simple (reactive), homogeneous agents, which have or work out solutions to the same problem (a common goal). Due to computational simplicity and the ability to form independent subsystems (sub-populations), these systems may be efficiently realized in distributed, large-scale environments (see, e.g. [4]).

Agents in EMAS represent solutions to a given optimization problem. They are located on islands representing distributed structure of computation. The islands constitute local environments, where direct interactions among agents may take place. In addition, agents are able to change their location, which makes it possible to exchange information and resources all over the system [12].

In EMAS, phenomena of inheritance and selection—the main components of evolutionary processes—are modeled via agent actions of *death and reproduction* (see Fig. 1). As in the case of classical evolutionary algorithms, inheritance is accomplished by an appropriate definition of reproduction. Core properties of the agent are encoded in its genotype and inherited from its parent(s) with the use of variation operators (mutation and recombination). Moreover, an agent may possess some knowledge acquired during its life, which is not inherited. Both inherited and acquired information (phenotype) determines the behavior of an agent. It is noteworthy that it is easy to add mechanisms of diversity enhancement, such as allotropic speciation (cf. [6]) to EMAS. It consists in introducing population decomposition and a new action of the agent based on moving from one evolutionary island to another (migration) (see Fig. 1).

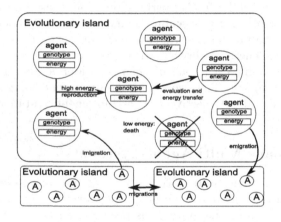

Fig. 1. Evolutionary multi-agent system (EMAS)

Assuming that no global knowledge is available, and the agents being autonomous, selection mechanism based on acquiring and exchanging non-renewable resources [7] is introduced. It means that a decisive factor of the agent's fitness is still the quality of solution it represents, but expressed by the amount of non-renewable resource it possesses. In general, the agent gains resources as a reward for "good" behavior, and looses resources as a consequence of "bad" behavior (behavior here may be understood as, e.g. acquiring sufficiently good solution). Selection is then realized in such a way that agents with a lot of resources are more likely to reproduce, while a low level of resources increases the possibility of death. So according to classical Franklin's and Graesser's taxonomy—agents of EMAS can be classified as Artificial Life Agents (a kind of Computational Agents) [8].

Many optimization tasks, which have already been solved with EMAS and its modifications, have yielded better results than certain classical approaches. They include, among others, optimization of neural network architecture, multi-objective optimization, multimodal optimization and financial optimization. EMAS has thus been proved to be a versatile optimization mechanism in practical situations. A summary of EMAS-related review has is given in [5].

EMAS may be held up as an example of a cultural algorithm, where evolution is performed at the level of relations among agents, and cultural knowledge is acquired from the energy-related information. This knowledge makes it possible to state which agent is better and which is worse, justifying the decision about reproduction. Therefore, the energy-related knowledge serves as situational knowledge. Memetic variants of EMAS may be easily introduced by modifying evaluation or variation operators (by adding an appropriate local-search method).

4   From Classic to Hybrid PSO

In the basic particle swarm optimization [11] implementation, the potential solutions are located in a subspace of D-dimensional Euclidean space R^D limited in each dimension (usually a D-dimensional hypercube). The search space is a domain of the optimized quality function $f : R^D \rightarrow R$.

A particle is a candidate solution described by three D-dimensional vectors: position $X = x_d, d \in [1 \dots D]$; velocity $V = v_d, d \in [1 \dots D]$; best known position $P = p_d, d \in [1 \dots D]$. A swarm is a set of m particles. The swarm is associated with a D-dimensional vector $G = g_d, d \in [1 \dots D]$ which is swarm's best known position (the solution with the currently highest quality).

The execution of the algorithm begins by initializing the start values. Each particle I belonging to the swarm S is initialized with the following values:

1. position X of the particle I is initialized with a random vector belonging to the search space A
2. best known position is initialized with current particle's position: $P \leftarrow X$
3. velocity V of the particle I is initialized with a random vector belonging to the search space A
4. swarm's best position is updated by the following rule: $if\ f(P) < f(G)\ then\ G \leftarrow P$

Once all the particles are initialized and uniformly distributed in the search space, the main part of the algorithm starts executing. During each iteration of the algorithm, the following steps are executed. These steps of the algorithm are executed until a termination criteria are met. The most common termination criteria for the particle swarm optimization are:

Algorithm 1

```
for each particle I in swarm S do
    update particle's velocity:
```
$$V \leftarrow r_g(G - X) + r_p(P - X) + \omega V; r_g, r_p \in [0,1]$$
```
    update particle's position:
```
$$X \leftarrow X + V$$
```
    where ω is the inertia factor
    update particle's best position:
```
$$if \ f(X) < f(P) \ then \ P \leftarrow X$$
```
    update global best position:
```
$$if \ f(P) < f(G) \ then \ G \leftarrow P$$
```
end for
```

---

1. number of executed iterations reaches a specified value,
2. swarm's best position exceeds a specified value,
3. the algorithm found global optimum,
4. swarm's best positions in two subsequent iterations are the same.

The idea of hybridization of EMAS with PSO follows the cultural and memetic inspirations, by utilizing the PSO-defined movements of the solutions (agents' genotypes) as a kind of additional "local-search" algorithm for making the "worse" agents better by updating their solutions (see Fig. 2). This is not entirely a local-search algorithm, as PSO of course is a well-known global optimization technique, however the planned synergy seems to be attractive and thus not prone to early-convergence problems.

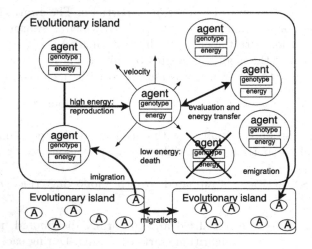

Fig. 2. Evolutionary multi-agent system with PSO modification (PSO-EMAS)

In the proposed hybrid algorithm, the agent may be treated either as regular EMAS agent—when its energy is higher than certain, fixed level, and as

PSO particle—when its energy is lower (a dedicated energy threshold, so called "move" energy is considered a parameter of the algorithm). Thus better agents are evolved using well-known evolutionary methods, while worse agents update their solutions based on PSO rules.

5 Experimental Results

The experiments were performed taking advantage of AgE 3 platform[1], which is distributed, agent-based computational platform developed by Intelligent Information Systems Group. The platform was further developed in order to combine PSO with EMAS. The tests were executed on Samsung NP550P5C with Intel CORE i5-3210M @ 2.5 GHz; 8 GB RAM; Ubuntu 14.04.5 LTS.

5.1 Experimental Setting

In the PSO aspect of the hybrid algorithm, an agent can move in the search space only when its energy value is lower than 40. The max/min velocity parameters determine the size of the move performed by an agent. Other parameters presented below relate to the formula below, which is used for updating agent's velocity.

$$v_{i,d}^{t+1} \leftarrow \omega \cdot v_{i,d}^t + r_p(p_{i,d} - x_{i,d}) + r_g(g_d - x_{i,d})$$

where:

- $v_{i,d}^t$ describes i-th agent's (particle) d-th component of its velocity in t-th step of algorithm;
- r_p and r_g are random numbers within (0, 1) range;
- $p_{i,d}$ is i-th agent's local best position d-th component value;
- $x_{i,d}$ is i-th agent's current position d-th component value;
- g_d is globally best position d-th component value;
- ω is a weight considering current velocity of particle.

The most important parameters set for the compared systems were as follows:

- EMAS parameters: Population size: 50; Initial energy: 100; Reproduction predicate: energy above 45; Death predicate: energy equal to 0; Crossover operator: discrete crossover; Mutation operator: uniform mutation; Mutation probability: 0.05; Reproduction energy transfer: proportional, 0.25; Fight energy transfer: 5.0;
- PSO parameters: Move energy threshold: 40; Maximum velocity: 0.05; ω 0.5.

For each dimensionality and algorithm variant (EMAS or PSO-EMAS hybrid) optimization tests were performed 30 times and the stopping condition was time-related, namely each experiment could last only for 200 s.

---

[1] http://www.age.agh.edu.pl.

5.2   Discussion of the Results

The main objective of the tests was to compare optimization results achieved for
PSO-EMAS hybrid with those obtained for EMAS approach. The experiments
were realized in the following sequence.

In the beginning, selected benchmark problems (Rastrigin in Fig. 3a, Rosenbrock in Fig. 3b, Schwefel in Fig. 3c and Whitley in Fig. 3d) were optimized in
500 dimensions, in order to realize preliminary checking of the compared algorithms. As shown in Fig. 3 in all the considered cases the hybrid of PSO and
EMAS did significantly better, however it is to note, that in all the cases the
actual global optima were not approached closely, probably because of arbitrarily chosen algorithm parameters. Thus, in order to do further examination, any
of these problems could have been selected, therefore we have selected Rastrigin
problem, as this is a very popular benchmark and we have already used it many
times in our previous research.

Next, the parameters of the constructed hybrid (namely move energy, maximum velocity, weights of personal and global optima and weight of the previous
vector in PSO update) were tested on 500 dimensional Rastrigin problem. The
results of these tests are presented in Fig. 4.

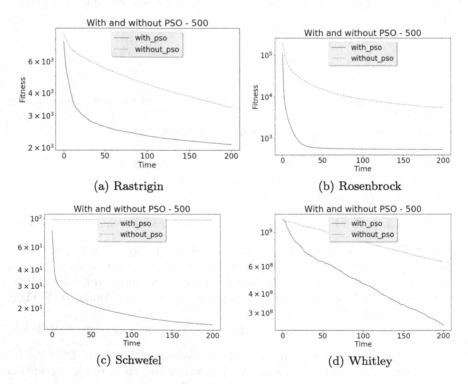

Fig. 3. Comparison of EMAS and PSO-EMAS fitness for selected 500 dimensional
benchmark functions optimization

Testing the move energy (see Fig. 4a) it is easy to see that the best results were obtained for its value 40 (out of tested values between 5 and 60). It is to note, that the reproduction energy is 45, so the difference is quite small: the agents apparently participate in PSO hybrid until their energy becomes close to the reproduction threshold. Then the PSO action is suspended and the agents participate in EMAS part of the hybrid, acting towards reproduction.

Testing the maximum velocity (see Fig. 4b) can be summarized with a quite natural and predictable solution: from the values between 0.03 and 1.0 the value of 0.05 turned out to be the best in the tested case, suggesting that too high values of the velocity cap will bring the examined hybrid to a random stochastic search type algorithm, hampering the intelligent search usually realized by meta-heuristic algorithms.

The graph showing the dependency of the weight of the previous vector ω (see Fig. 4c) yielded 0.5 as the optimal value of this parameter for the tested case. Again, similar to the observation of the move energy, not too big value (considering the tested range) turned out to be the best. It is quite predictable, as almost "copying" the previous vector would stop the exploration process, while complete forgetting about this vector would lose the "metaheuristic" information turning the whole algorithm to a purely random walk technique.

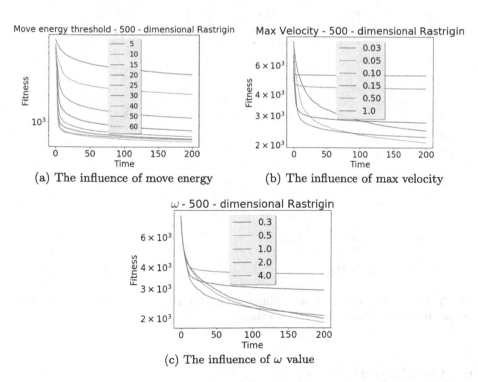

(a) The influence of move energy   (b) The influence of max velocity

(c) The influence of ω value

Fig. 4. Optimization of 500-dimensional Rastrigin problem using various values of PSO parameters

Finally, the Rastrigin problem was tested in different dimensions (10, 50, 100, 200, 300, 500), using the best values of the hybrid parameters found in the previous step. For Rastrigin problem in less than 200-dimensional domains standard EMAS achieved better results than hybrid variant, as shown on Fig. 5 and in Table 1. However in higher dimensional problems PSO-EMAS hybrid significantly outperforms standard algorithm yielding both better fitness values and lower standard deviations. The latter highlights good reproducibility of conducted experiments, as opposed to results of EMAS in 500-dimensional Rastrigin experiments.

Table 1. Final results found by EMAS and PSO-EMAS with standard deviation for optimization of Rastrigin function in different dimensions

Dimensions	EMAS average	EMAS std. dev.	PSO-EMAS average	PSO-EMAS std. dev.
10	0.00	0.00	0.00	0.00
50	0.00	0.00	12.15	8.78
100	1.40	0.40	52.26	6.62
200	108.81	9.60	143.45	13.14
300	464.16	35.80	251.19	27.51
500	3343.55	216.58	546.88	28.50

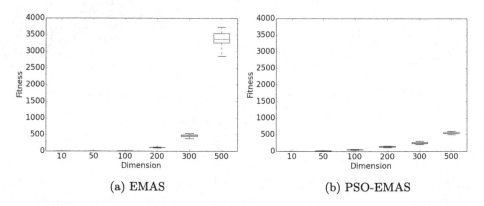

(a) EMAS   (b) PSO-EMAS

Fig. 5. Comparison of final fitness values for EMAS and PSO-EMAS using the best parameters found during the experimentation.

6   Conclusion

In the paper a PSO and EMAS hybrid was presented and tested against several selected, popular benchmark functions. The research consisted in preliminary testing different benchmark functions using arbitrarily chosen parameters, then a detailed study on the best values for the PSO parameters based on Rastrigin function in 500 dimensions was realized, and finally the efficacy of EMAS and PSO-EMAS was tested for the Rastrigin function in different dimensions, using the above-mentioned parameter values.

The results show that the hybrid version is significantly better than the original one in some of the considered cases. Moreover, not only final fitness values were similar or better (obtained in the assumed time of 200 s) but also in most of the tested cases better fitness was significantly earlier obtained by the hybrid version of the algorithm. In the future we plan to propose new PSO and EMAS hybrid algorithms, as well as do broader experimentation with the presented PSO-EMAS metaheuristic.

Acknowlegment. The research presented in this paper was partially supported by the Grant of the Dean of Faculty of Computer Science, Electronics and Telecommunications, AGH University of Science and Technology, for Ph.D. Students.

References

1. Abd-El-Wahed, W.F., Mousa, A.A., El-Shorbagy, M.A.: Integrating particle swarm optimization with genetic algorithms for solving nonlinear optimization problems. J. Comput. Appl. Math. **235**(5), 1446–1453 (2011)
2. Borna, K., Khezri, R.: A combination of genetic algorithm and particle swarm optimization method for solving traveling salesman problem. Cogent Math. **2**(1) (2015)
3. Byrski, A., Schaefer, R., Smołka, M., Cotta, C.: Asymptotic guarantee of success for multi-agent memetic systems. Bull. Pol. Acad. Sci.-Tech. Sci. **61**(1), 257–278 (2013)
4. Byrski, A., Debski, R., Kisiel-Dorohinicki, M.: Agent-based computing in an augmented cloud environment. Comput. Syst. Sci. Eng. **27**(1), 7–18 (2012)
5. Byrski, A., Dreżewski, R., Siwik, L., Kisiel-Dorohinicki, M.: Evolutionary multi-agent systems. Knowl. Eng. Rev. **30**(2), 171–186 (2015)
6. Cantú-Paz, E.: A summary of research on parallel genetic algorithms. IlliGAL Report No. 95007. University of Illinois (1995)
7. Cetnarowicz, K., Kisiel-Dorohinicki, M., Nawarecki, E.: The application of evolution process in multi-agent world (MAW) to the prediction system. In: Tokoro, M. (ed.) Proceedings of the 2nd International Conference on Multi-Agent Systems (ICMAS 1996), pp. 26–32. AAAI Press (1996)
8. Franklin, S., Graesser, A.: Is it an agent, or just a program?: a taxonomy for autonomous agents. In: Müller, J.P., Wooldridge, M.J., Jennings, N.R. (eds.) ATAL 1996. LNCS, vol. 1193, pp. 21–35. Springer, Heidelberg (1997). https://doi.org/10.1007/BFb0013570
9. Gupta, M., Yadav, R.: New improved fractional order differentiator models based on optimized digital differentiators. Sci. World J. **2014**, Article ID 741395 (2014)
10. Kao, Y.-T., Zahara, E.: A hybrid genetic algorithm and particle swarm optimization for multimodal functions. Appl. Soft Comput. **8**(2), 849–857 (2008)
11. Kennedy, J., Eberhart, R.: Particle swarm optimization. In: Proceedings of International Conference on Neural Networks, vol. 4, pp. 1942–1948, November 1995

12. Kisiel-Dorohinicki, M.: Agent-oriented model of simulated evolution. In: Grosky, W.I., Plášil, F. (eds.) SOFSEM 2002. LNCS, vol. 2540, pp. 253–261. Springer, Heidelberg (2002). https://doi.org/10.1007/3-540-36137-5_19

13. Korczynski, W., Byrski, A., Kisiel-Dorohinicki, M.: Buffered local search for efficient memetic agent-based continuous optimization. J. Comput. Sci. **20**(Suppl. C), 112–117 (2017)

14. Kuo, R.J., Han, Y.S.: A hybrid of genetic algorithm and particle swarm optimization for solving bi-level linear programming problem - a case study on supply chain model. Appl. Math. Model. **35**(8), 3905–3917 (2011)

15. Mousavi, M., Yap, H.J., Musa, S.N., Tahriri, F., Md Dawal, S.Z.: Multi-objective AGV scheduling in an FMS using a hybrid of genetic algorithm and particle swarm optimization. PLOS ONE **12**(3), 1–24 (2017)

16. Nazir, M., Majid-Mirza, A., Ali-Khan, S.: PSO-GA based optimized feature selection using facial and clothing information for gender classification. J. Appl. Res. Technol. **12**(1), 145–152 (2014)

17. Singh, A., Garg, N., Saini, T.: A hybrid approach of genetic algorithm and particle swarm technique to software test case generation. Int. J. Innov. Eng. Technol. **3**, 208–214 (2014)

18. Sörensen, K.: Metaheuristics—the metaphor exposed. Int. Trans. Oper. Res. **22**(1), 3–18 (2015)

19. Li, W.T., Xu, L., Shi, X.W.: A hybrid of genetic algorithm and particle swarm optimization for antenna design. In: Progress in Electromagnetics Research Symposium, vol. 2 (2008)

20. Thangaraj, R., Pant, M., Abraham, A., Bouvry, P.: Particle swarm optimization: hybridization perspectives and experimental illustrations. Appl. Math. Comput. **217**(12), 5208–5226 (2011)

21. Wolpert, D.H., Macready, W.G.: No free lunch theorems for optimization. IEEE Trans. Evol. Comput. **67**(1), 67–82 (1997)

22. Xu, S.-H., Liu, J.-P., Zhang, F.-H., Wang, L., Sun, L.-J.: A combination of genetic algorithm and particle swarm optimization for vehicle routing problem with time windows. Sensors **15**(9), 21033–21053 (2015)

23. Ykhlef, M., Alqifari, R.: A new hybrid algorithm to solve winner determination problem in multiunit double internet auction. **2015**, 1–10 (2015)

24. Zhong, W., Liu, J., Xue, M., Jiao, L.: A multiagent genetic algorithm for global numerical optimization. IEEE Trans. Syst. Man Cybern. Part B: Cybern. **34**(2), 1128–1141 (2004)

Data-Driven Agent-Based Simulation
for Pedestrian Capacity Analysis

Sing Kuang Tan[1([⊠])], Nan Hu[2], and Wentong Cai[1]

[1] School of Computer Science and Engineering, Nanyang Technological University,
Singapore, Singapore
{singkuang,aswtcai}@ntu.edu.sg
[2] Institution of High Performance Computing,
Agency for Science Technology and Research, Singapore, Singapore
hun@ihpc.a-star.edu.sg

Abstract. In this paper, an agent-based data-driven model that focuses on path planning layer of origin/destination popularities and route choice is developed. This model improves on the existing mathematical modeling and pattern recognition approaches. The paths and origins/destinations are extracted from a video. The parameters are calibrated from density map generated from the video. We carried out validation on the path probabilities and densities, and showed that our model generates better results than the previous approaches. To demonstrate the usefulness of the approach, we also carried out a case study on capacity analysis of a building layout based on video data.

1 Introduction

Capacity analysis is to measure of the amount of pedestrian traffic a building layout can handle. To apply crowd simulation models in real applications, we can vary the inflow of people into a building layout to determine the capacity of the amount of pedestrian traffic the layout can handle by measuring the pedestrians' speeds and densities. It can be used to detect congested regions, and underutilized regions in a building layout. And these can be further used to evaluate different policies for crowd management and optimization (e.g., it can be used for event planning when a large crowd is expected). In summary, capacity analysis is useful to measure the effectiveness of a layout and plans for upgrading layout or managing the crowd.

Existing works on capacity analysis using agent-based simulation specify the pedestrians' movement rules in a layout manually [16,17]. Then the density distribution of the pedestrians is analyzed to determine the bottlenecks in the layout. Molyneaux et al. [8] proposed pedestrian management strategies such as the use of access gate and flow separation. Fundamental diagram [13] can be used to assess the capacity of a building layout and crowd management policy. Metrics [10] such as speed, travel time and level-of-service are used. Current works *use manually defined routes to do simulation for capacity analysis.* They

© Springer International Publishing AG, part of Springer Nature 2018
Y. Shi et al. (Eds.): ICCS 2018, LNCS 10861, pp. 103–116, 2018.
https://doi.org/10.1007/978-3-319-93701-4_8

only analyze speeds and densities in fundamental diagram, *ignoring the origin/destination (OD) popularities*. We developed more sophisticated metric to *analyze the histogram of density distributions* (see Sect. 4.3) instead of instantaneous density [5] or average density [16,17] in previous works. By deriving interpersonal distances from densities, we can understand the safety and comfort of the pedestrians better.

Using agent-based modeling and simulation for capacity planning has many advantages over previous methods of mathematical analysis using statistical route choices [9,12]. It can model the effect of changes in the environment, e.g., adding a new obstacle that lies in the walking paths of the pedestrians; and the detailed crowd behaviors such as group behaviors and inter-personal collision avoidance which the mathematical modeling approach cannot handle. As collision avoidance behavior is generally well studied [4,7] and data-driven path planning presents a more challenging research issue to form realistic crowd dynamics, we focus our study here on learning the route choice preference and the preference of selecting the origins (O) and destinations (D) in the layout. We formulate the OD popularities, and route choice model between a given OD pair in this work. Parameters of our model are calibrated through differential evolution genetic algorithm (GA) using a crowd density map extracted from KLT tracks [11]. Then from the learned parameters, capacity analysis is carried out on the layout.

The following components are generally required in agent-based simulation for capacity planning: identification of OD and routes, route choice model, and determination of OD popularities. With these components, pedestrian simulation can then be performed to get the pedestrian tracks. Capacity analysis metrics are then applied to the tracks to measure the amount of pedestrian traffic a building layout can handle.

The paper is organized as follows: Sect. 2 describes the related works. Section 3 describes our data-driven framework (OD and route identification, route choice model, pedestrian simulation and lastly parameters calibration). Section 4 presents a case study. Section 5 concludes this paper.

2   Related Works

Many crowd models have been proposed and developed over the years. For the high level behaviors of pedestrians, the choice of origin and destination using OD matrix [1] and the preference of different routes due to their differences in lengths and differential turns using statistical route choice [9] can be used. There is also a vector field model that maps each pedestrian position to the velocity vector based on the position of the pedestrian in the building layout [21]. A model of the adaption of each pedestrian speed and direction according to the distances and angles to nearby obstacle and destination [20] is created through genetic programming. For the low level behaviors of pedestrians, there are social force model [7] and RVO2 model [4]. Existing work learns route choice from density maps using mathematical modeling and optimization [12], which cannot *model the dynamic behavior* of the pedestrians such as the obstacle collision avoidance behavior when an obstacle is added to the simulation. Unlike the existing mathematical route choice models that model the average statistical behavior of pedestrians over time, our model can simulate the instantaneous behaviors of agents with more precise positions than a discrete position layout used in mathematical modeling.

Recently there is a trend towards data-driven based approach to model crowd and calibrate model parameters. For calibrating interpersonal collision avoidance model parameters from videos, there is an anomaly detection approach [2]. An approach that extracts example behaviors from videos and use these examples to avoid collisions in agent-based pedestrian simulation is introduced in [19]. Interpersonal collision avoidance parameters can also be calibrated through laboratory experiments using deterministic approach [18] or non-deterministic approach [6]. Entry and exit regions transition probabilities can be learned either from the density maps [14] or from the KLT tracks [15]. Current works on data-driven modeling mostly focus on low-level pedestrian behavior models or do pattern recognitions on video or trajectories data. Instead of extracting patterns from data, we learn navigation behaviors of pedestrians that can be applied in an agent-based pedestrian simulation. This simulation can later be used to study different scenarios.

Crowd model parameters calibrations are often non-convex and require heuristic-based optimization algorithm such as genetic algorithm to search for good parameter values. Differential evolution genetic algorithm has shown to outperform many other variants of genetic algorithm on a wide set of problems [3]. In this paper, we followed similar approach as described in [22] to use differential evolution genetic algorithm and density-based calibration.

3   Data-Driven Framework

In this section, we will discuss about the framework of our data-driven agent-based pedestrian simulation model.

3.1   Overview of the Framework

The overview of our framework is shown in Fig. 1. A crowd simulation model is built based on empirical data extracted from videos, in particular, to capture the high-level motion of path planning through OD popularities and route choice modeling. The model is used to create agent-based simulation which is in turn used for capacity analysis of a given layout. It is conducted based on the calibrated simulation model. We will describe these in detail in the subsequent sub-sections.

To model the path planning behaviors of crowds, OD popularities and a route choice model for a given OD need to be determined. In this work, we focus on distilling OD popularities and calibrate route choice model parameters using video data.

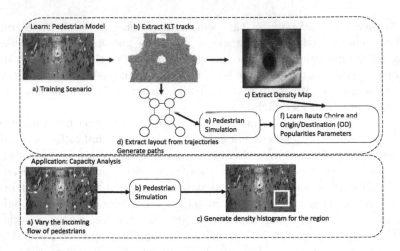

Fig. 1. The workflow of our framework from learning model to capacity analysis

3.2 OD and Path Identification

To get a full picture of the pedestrians in a building layout, the camera is preferably looking downward between 135 to 180° angle to the plane normal of the ground to minimize perspective distortion. The video can be in monochrome with a resolution high enough to get a few corner points on each pedestrian for tracking.

For a given video dataset, first image transformation is applied to remove perspective distortion of the camera. It is done by manually labeling some points in the ground plane in the video frame with the actual positions in the actual layout. The perspective transformation matrix is determined from the actual positions and pixel coordinates of the frame. Then an inverse perspective transform is applied on the video frame. The image transformation is also applied to the list of KLT tracks ρ_{KLT} (each track consists of a sequence of points (q_x, q_y), each of which is represented by (track_id, q_x, q_y, time)). Finally, we accumulate all the points in the KLT trajectories on a density map (grid size W by H) of the whole layout covered by the video. The density value at grid location (i, j) or distribution $\Pr(\text{M}(i, j))$ is determined by:

$$\Pr(\text{M}(i,j)) = \frac{1}{T} r^{\text{mask}}(i,j) \sum_{u=-h_{\text{size}}}^{h_{\text{size}}} \sum_{v=-h_{\text{size}}}^{h_{\text{size}}} \sum_{n} r_n(i+u, j+v) h(u,v) \tag{1}$$

$$T = \sum_{i,j} r^{\text{mask}}(i,j) \sum_{u=-h_{\text{size}}}^{h_{\text{size}}} \sum_{v=-h_{\text{size}}}^{h_{\text{size}}} \sum_{n} r_n(i+u, j+v) h(u,v) \tag{2}$$

$$r^{\text{mask}}(i,j) = \mathbb{1}_{\sum_n r_n(i,j) > 0} \tag{3}$$

$$i = \{1, 2, \ldots, W\} \text{ and } j = \{1, 2, \ldots, H\} \tag{4}$$

where $r_n(i, j) = 1$ if track n passes through grid position (i, j). 1 is an indicator function which is 1 when the condition is true, else it is 0. $h(u, v)$ represents the smoothing filter of size h_{size}. Note that each track contributes one density count to a grid point in the density map and the points on each track are interpolated so that it is continuous. The density value is then normalized by the total density values so that it becomes a probability distribution. The grid points of the density map that are zeros form the mask map (r^{mask}) and these grid points are not used for calibrating the model parameters. These mask regions represent the walls and other barriers in the layout that the pedestrians cannot move into. The smoothing function $h(u, v)$ can be a Gaussian or uniform function.

The high density regions of the transformed ρ_{KLT} of a building layout are extracted by clustering all the (q_x, q_y) positions from the tracks using a Gaussian Mixture Modeling (GMM) algorithm as waypoints. The entrances of the layout (OD) can also be extracted by clustering. The number of clusters is selected using the elbow method by increasing the number of clusters until there is no significant increase in the maximum likelihood value of the clustering result. The W by H grid points of the layout is broken down into voronoi regions where each grid point is labeled to the nearest waypoint center and each mask region remains unlabeled without assigning to any waypoint. Two waypoint voronoi regions are adjacent if the pedestrian can walk from the first waypoint to the second waypoint without transversing other waypoints. We link the adjacent waypoints (voronoi) to form a topology map of the layout. For all pairs of OD, all possible paths (paths without repeating nodes) are generated between the OD.

3.3 Path Selection Model

Distance and turn distance are the commonly used path descriptors as the choice of path by the pedestrian is highly dependent on these two descriptors. These two descriptors are revised from [12]. The path descriptors of each path (p), namely the distance and turn distance, are computed using the formulas as follows:

$$\text{desc}_{\text{dist}}(p) = \frac{\sum_{i=1}^{N-1} \sqrt{(q_x^{(i+1)} - q_x^{(i)})^2 + (q_y^{(i+1)} - q_y^{(i)})^2}}{\sqrt{(q_x^{(N)} - q_x^{(1)})^2 + (q_y^{(N)} - q_y^{(1)})^2}} - 1 \tag{5}$$

$$\text{desc}_{\text{turn\_dist}}(p) = \frac{1}{\Pi} \sum_{i=1}^{N-2} \min(|\text{angle}_{i+2} - \text{angle}_{i+1}|, 2\pi - |\text{angle}_{i+2} - \text{angle}_{i+1}|) \tag{6}$$

$$\text{angle}_i = tan^{-1}(\frac{q_y^{(i)} - q_y^{(i-1)}}{q_x^{(i)} - q_x^{(i-1)}}) \tag{7}$$

where N is the number of waypoints for path p, $(q_x^{(i)}, q_y^{(i)})$ is the centroid position of the i-th waypoint of p and angle_i is the direction (in radians) between the waypoints $i - 1$ and i. O and D centroids will be $(q_x^{(1)}, q_y^{(1)})$ and $(q_x^{(N)}, q_y^{(N)})$

respectively. The path descriptors distance and turn distance are normalized by the straight line distance between the OD and π respectively so that the descriptors are invariant to the scale size of the layout. We added these normalization techniques to the path descriptors introduced in [12] to improve learning performance.

The probability of taking p given o and d is then formulated as $\Pr(p|o,d)$ function as below,

$$\Pr(p|o,d) = \frac{\mathrm{Pref}(p)}{\sum_{p' \text{ between } o \text{ and } d} \mathrm{Pref}(p')} \tag{8}$$

$$\mathrm{Pref}(p) = e^{\alpha \times \mathrm{desc}_{\mathrm{dist}}(p) + \beta \times \mathrm{desc}_{\mathrm{turn\_dist}}(p)}. \tag{9}$$

$\Pr(o,d)$ is the probability of selecting a pair of OD. $\mathrm{Pref}(p)$ is preference of taking a particular path and it has a value between zero to positive infinity. In the expression $\Pr(p|o,d)$, the preference is normalized to a probability value between zero and one. The parameters α and β are to be learned empirically through the GA described later. The frequency of selecting p (number of times p is selected per second), $f(p)$ is therefore

$$f(p) = \sum_{o \in O, d \in D} \Pr(p|o,d) f(o,d) \tag{10}$$

where $f(o,d)$ is the frequency of selecting a pair of OD, which will be also learned through GA.

3.4   Parametrized Pedestrian Simulation

For each origin o, the simulation algorithm will generate a number of agents to be added to o using a Poisson distribution

$$n \sim \frac{e^{-k} k^n}{n!} \tag{11}$$

where $k = f(o) = \sum_{d \in D} f(o,d)$ and $f(o,d)$ (i.e., OD popularity) is a value in the simulation parameters. The destination of the agent a_i will be set according to

$$\Pr(d|O(a_i)) = \frac{f(O(a_i), d)}{\sum_{d' \in D} f(O(a_i), d')} \tag{12}$$

where $O(a_i)$ is the origin of agent a_i. These parameters are evolved by the GA to find a good set of values. The parameters will be described in more detail in the next section. For a layout of m entrances, there are $\frac{m(m-1)}{2}$ pairs (the permutation of arbitrary two out of m entrances) of OD. We assume that the o and d for each agent cannot be the same, and for a given (o,d) pair, agents have the same probability moving from o to d and from d to o. This assumption is made so as to keep the set of the OD popularities parameters smaller and manageable. It also leads to better learning by preventing the creation of an overparameterized model.

For each origin o, new agents are added to the simulation at a fixed (i.e., every 5 s) interval according to Eq. (11). The destination (d) and path (p) of each agent is selected according to Eq. (12) and Eq. (8) respectively. They are assigned with the list of waypoints of $p \in P$ from o to d. The particular position (a waypoint is represented as a 2D Gaussian distribution learned from GMM) is selected randomly within the Gaussian distribution range of the waypoint,

$$(q_x, q_y) \sim \sqrt{\det(2\pi\Sigma_j)}e^{-\frac{1}{2}(\mathbf{q}-\mu_j)^T\Sigma_j^{-1}(\mathbf{q}-\mu_j)} \tag{13}$$

where μ_j and Σ_j are derived from GMM clustering, and $\mathbf{q}$ is the vector form of (q_x, q_y). Each agent is then following $p \in P$ from o through a list of waypoints to d. Agents avoid each other using a collision avoidance mechanism while moving between two consecutive waypoints. In this study, we apply the Reciprocal Velocity Obstacle (RVO2) method [4] for collision avoidance. RVO2 collision avoidance algorithm basically finds the best velocity vector for each agent to avoid collision. Once an agent reaches d, it will be removed from the simulation. Agents' trajectories through simulation are then aggregated. The density map is then created from the agents' trajectories in the same way as from the ρ_{KLT}. The detail description of our agent-based simulation procedure is shown in Fig. 2.

3.5   Path Selection Parameter and OD Popularity Determination

Our goal is to develop an agent-based model that behaves similarly to the video by having the same density distribution. In this model, we focus on the path planning layer of behaviors, which needs to set the route choice and OD popularities. The route choice and OD popularities will be the parameters to be calibrated by our GA. (Differential evolution) GA is very suitable for this problem as the cost function is non-convex. GA will reduce the number of simulation runs needed to do global optimization and it is important as each simulation run is a time-consuming process. As the parameters space is bounded by a set of minimum and maximum ranges instead of discrete values, this also makes GA very suitable.

First a population of random parameters are generated. The parameters are ordered in this particular order, $<\{f(o, d)|o \in O, d \in D\}, \alpha, \beta>$ where (α, β) are the route choice parameters. Then the fitness value of every individual of the population is calculated by running simulations using the parameter values of the individual, and compare the simulated density map with the ground truth density map using the formula below:

$$\text{fitness}, \lambda = \sqrt{\sum_{i=1}^{W}\sum_{j=1}^{H}(\Pr(\text{M}(i,j)|\rho_{simulate}) - \Pr(\text{M}(i,j)|\rho_{KLT}))^2} \tag{14}$$

Our Pedestrian Simulation

Input:
$f(o)$: Frequency of selecting a particular o
$Pr(d|o)$: The probability of selecting a d given o
$Pr(p|o, d)$: The probability of selecting a path p of a pair of OD
Return: the list of tracks $\rho_{simulate}$
Agent Generation Procedure:
   for Every small time interval (i.e. 5 seconds interval) **do**
      for Every origin o in layout **do**
         Generate n number of agents using a Poisson distribution, Eq.(11)
         Set the origin of each generated agent to o
         Set the position of each generated agents to o position
         Put these generated agents into the simulation
      end for
   end for
Agent Navigation Procedure:
   for Each active agent a_i with id $= \mathrm{id}(a_i)$ and $o = \mathrm{O}(a_i)$ **do**
      Select the destination $\mathrm{D}(a_i)$ for agent a_i using $Pr(d|\mathrm{O}(a_i))$, Eq.(12)
      Select a path for agent a_i using $Pr(p|\mathrm{O}(a_i), \mathrm{D}(a_i))$
      for For every waypoints w_j on the path **do**
         Generate a position (q_x, q_y) on the waypoint using Eq.(13)
         Move agent a_i to position (q_x, q_y)
         Record the track of agent, $(\mathrm{id}(a_i), q_x, q_y, time)$ into $\rho_{simulate}$
         if Agent a_i reached the destination $\mathrm{D}(a_i)$ **then**
            Remove the agent a_i
         end if
      end for
   end for

Fig. 2. Procedure of our pedestrian simulation

where $Pr(\mathrm{M}(i, j))$ is the probability of finding an agent/a pedestrian on a grid point (i, j) of the density map, W and H are the width and height of the density map. Note that $Pr(\mathrm{M})$ sums to one and greater than zero and the mask regions of the density map are not used for parameter calibration. We use a probability distribution for the density map because we do not have the density values from the KLT tracks, but the relative densities between the grid points. As usual the population parameter values are evolved using differential evolution mutation and crossover methods to generate new offsprings. The fitness of these offsprings are evaluated using simulations and the fitness formula above. The offsprings will replace their parents if their fitness values are smaller than their parents. After several generations, the population will converge to a good set of parameter values.

4   Case Study

In this section, we will describe our scenario, evaluate our framework and lastly carry out capacity analysis using our framework.

4.1   Scenario Description

An agent-based crowd simulation, performing the path planning of crowds through the proposed route choice and OD popularities model, is developed in Java for the Grand Station dataset [23]. This dataset consists of a 33 minutes and 20 s video containing 50010 frames with a framerate of 25 fps at the resolution 720 × 480. A set of about 40000 KLT tracks, ρ_{KLT}, is also provided with the dataset. The GA is implemented in Matlab and for each set of parameter values, a multiple instances of the crowd simulation are executed. The average result over 4 runs is used for fitness evaluation. In this case, there are 8 entrances and therefore we have 28 pairs of OD. And another two route choice parameters, so we have in total 30 parameters. We choose a population size of 30 for the GA (we have also experimented with a population size of 100 and it leads to similar fitness value). We set the size of the density map to be 100 by 100 grid points to make it more manageable.

4.2   Evaluation of the Proposed Framework

In this section, we will compare our model (Model) against three baseline models: uniform OD popularity and shortest path (UniMod), existing vector-field model (VecMod) [21], and existing pedestrian-obstacle-destination model (Pod-Mod) [20]. The ground truth (GT) will be derived from the ρ_{KLT}.

Figure 3 shows the density maps generated from our model and other existing approaches. We applied a small 5 by 5 window average filter to the density map (i.e., $h(u,v) = 1$ and $h_{size} = 2$, see Eq. (4)) to filter out the randomness. Our approach matches the ground truth density map better than other approaches by more than 10% (by comparing the fitness values in the figure). As VecMod learns the path of the pedestrian from the directions of the ρ_{KLT} instead of from the density map of the ρ_{KLT}, it cannot model the variations of movements across the open space as well as our route choice approach. PodMod learns a deterministic function of movement for each OD pair, it only allows the pedestrian to move along one path instead of probabilistically select one of the paths in our route choice approach.

OD popularities parameters are calibrated by GA and simulation. The popularities can be estimated from the density map because the density between a high popularity OD will be higher and likewise the density between a low popularity OD will be lower. As for the OD popularities, Fig. 4(a) shows the relative popularity of each pair OD and Fig. 4(b) shows the density map obtained from the training video without applying any smoothing function (i.e., $h(u,v) = 0$ and $h_{size} = 0$, see Eq. (4)). The high popularities between the bottom and right entrances further confirm what is shown in the video.

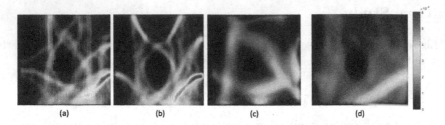

Fig. 3. Density maps generated by (a) VecMod [21], (b) PodMod [20], (c) our model and (d) GT. (Fitness, $\lambda = $ (a) 6.159×10^{-3} (b) 6.329×10^{-3} (c) $\mathbf{4.216 \times 10^{-3}}$)

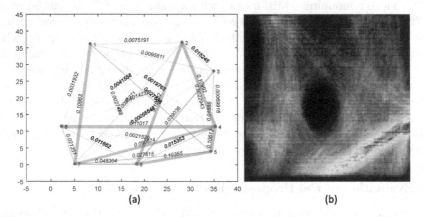

Fig. 4. (a) Relative popularities of learned OD popularities, (b) GT density map without applying any smoothing filter (see text for more details)

We compared the learned path probabilities with the path probabilities of the ρ_{KLT}. As the ρ_{KLT} are broken without OD information, we cannot directly map each track to a specific path. So we match each track to all paths with which the track matches partially, and evenly distribute the probabilities of the tracks to the matching list of paths. To specify it formally,

$$\Pr(p = \text{path}_i | \text{GT}) = \frac{1}{\alpha_i} \text{ if } \alpha_i > 0, \text{else } 0 \tag{15}$$

where $\alpha_i = \#$ of tracks in ρ_{KLT} match sub-path of path_i and a KLT track matches sub-path of path_i if the track contains a 'substring' of the path_i's waypoints. The following distance functions are used for comparison:

$$\text{Total Variation Distance} = \sum_i |\Pr(p = \text{path}_i | \text{Model}) - \Pr(p = \text{path}_i | \text{GT})|$$

$$\text{Histogram Intersection} = \sum_i min(\Pr(p = \text{path}_i | \text{Model}), \Pr(p = \text{path}_i | \text{GT})).$$

$$\tag{16}$$

These two distance functions are commonly used for comparing between two probability distributions (it is the lower the better for variation distance; whereas it the higher the better for histogram intersection). UniMod is used as a baseline model as it is commonly assumed if we have no information of how often one pedestrian will choose a pair of OD over another pair.

Our model is better in terms of the two distance functions than the baseline UniMod. The distances (GT versus our model/GT versus UniMod) for total variation and histogram intersection are **1.9624**/1.9965 and **0.0188**/0.0017 respectively. The popularities across different pairs of OD are non-uniform as we observed that there are much more people walking from some of the entrances.

4.3 Capacity Analysis

Following the work described in [10], we choose three metrics for capacity analysis,

$$\text{Density Distribution}, \eta(d) = \sum_t \mathbf{1}_{\text{density}(t) >= d}$$

$$\text{Average Travel Speed}, \theta = \frac{1}{M} \sum_{i=1}^{M} \text{Speed}(a_i)$$

$$\text{Travel Speed Index}, \vartheta = \frac{\theta}{\theta_{\text{free\_flow}}} \tag{17}$$

where density(t) is the density of the region at time t, Speed(a_i) is the speed of agent i, M is the number of agents in the region and $\theta_{\text{free\_flow}}$ is the average speed of the agents when the density is 0. $\eta(d)$ is the number of time steps where the density is greater than or equal to a specified amount d. $\eta(d)$ is selected because it has been used to determine the safety and comfort of the pedestrians [5]. θ is selected as it can tell us the time taken for a pedestrian to move through the region and give us the level of congestion. ϑ gives us the percentage of additional time that is needed to move through the crowded region compared to when the region has no crowd.

We varied the OD popularities by multiplying them using a fixed constant between 1 to 11. Figure 5(a) shows $\eta(d)$ (time step $= 0.25$ s). Figure 5(b) shows θ and ϑ. Figure 5(c) shows the region where the density and speeds are inspected for the different OD popularity values. This region is selected as it lies along the highest density path when the popularities are at normal values.

As the popularities get higher, the total number of people increases linearly, but the density increases non-linearly. The changes in the density (Fig. 5(a)) is non-linear and there is a tipping point of significant increase when the popularities increase from 7 to 8 times. The increase in density starts to slow down after 8 times. For instance, for $\eta(0.5)$, when the popularities are increased from 7 to 8 times, the frequency increases by more than 4 times. This makes intuitive sense as the density increases, the speeds of pedestrians decrease due to more collision avoidance and this in turn leads to larger increase in density. As the

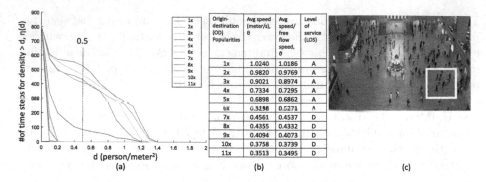

Fig. 5. (a) Density and (b) speed changes due to increase in OD popularities. (c) Region under analysis

Origin-destination (OD) Popularities	Avg speed (meter/s), θ	Avg speed/ free flow speed, θ	Level of service (LOS)
1x	1.0240	1.0186	A
2x	0.9820	0.9769	A
3x	0.9021	0.8974	A
4x	0.7334	0.7295	A
5x	0.6898	0.6862	A
6x	0.5298	0.5271	A
7x	0.4561	0.4537	D
8x	0.4355	0.4332	D
9x	0.4094	0.4073	D
10x	0.3758	0.3739	D
11x	0.3513	0.3495	D

density further increases, jams occur at some parts of the layout and this reduces the rate of increment of the density at the region under study. The capacities at different regions are also affected by layout structure which determines where and how density is accumulated. This kind of dynamic behavior is difficult to model mathematically and the results are different for different layouts.

We can also see that as the popularities get higher, θ decreases, where the rate of decreases is higher between 3 to 7 times of normal popularities. This is due to the same observation as the density. However the decrease in speed is not as obvious as the increase in density. For the level of service (LOS) [5], it is 'A' (free circulation) when the increase of popularity is below 7 times, but it changes drastically to 'D' (restricted and reduced speed for most pedestrians) when the increase of popularity is above or equal 7 times. For ϑ, a value of 1 indicates that the average travel speed is at its optimal speed and is not affected by the density (due to small randomness in the simulation, ϑ can be slightly larger than 1 as in the 1st row of the table).

5   Conclusion

We have developed a data-driven agent-based framework that focuses on the path planning layer. And this framework can be used for capacity analysis. We have carried out experiments and analysis on the learned parameters and density map of our model, performed capacity analysis on hypothetical situation where the OD popularities were varied by a constant multiplier.

The model created can be used for analyzing different crowd management policies, sudden increase in crowd densities, and other novel scenarios. In the future, we will automate crowd management strategies through optimization of speeds of the pedestrians at different locations or re-routing the pedestrians, enforced by marshallers on the ground.

The assumption we make here is that as density increases uniformly, people's path planning is not affected much by the density increment, but still by space syntax (layout). There is one imperfection in our model is that it does not model change in a pedestrian route due to very high density congestion. Congestion model is important as we continuously increase the number of agents in the simulation for capacity analysis, it will definitely lead to very serious congestion at some point. As our future work, we will add congestion model into the current route choice model to model the change of pedestrian behaviors during congestion to tackle this problem. We are also planning to use virtual reality experiments to collect data under controlled environment.

Acknowledgement. Singkuang Tan, Nan Hu, and Wentong Cai would like to acknowledge the support from the grant: IHPC-NTU Joint R&D Project on "Symbiotic Simulation and Video Analysis of Crowds".

References

1. Asakura, Y., Hato, E., Kashiwadani, M.: Origin-destination matrices estimation model using automatic vehicle identification data and its application to the Han-Shin expressway network. Transportation **27**(4), 419–438 (2000)
2. Charalambous, P., Karamouzas, I., Guy, S.J., Chrysanthou, Y.: A data-driven framework for visual crowd analysis. In: CGF, vol. 33, pp. 41–50. Wiley Online Library (2014)
3. Das, S., Suganthan, P.N.: Differential evolution: a survey of the state-of-the-art. TEVC **15**(1), 4–31 (2011)
4. Fiorini, P., Shiller, Z.: Motion planning in dynamic environments using velocity obstacles. IJRR **17**(7), 760–772 (1998)
5. Fruin, J.J.: Pedestrian planning and design. Technical report (1971)
6. Guy, S.J., Van Den Berg, J., Liu, W., Lau, R., Lin, M.C., Manocha, D.: A statistical similarity measure for aggregate crowd dynamics. TOG **31**(6), 190 (2012)
7. Helbing, D., Molnár, P.: Social force model for pedestrian dynamics. Phys. Rev. E **51**, 4282–4286 (1995)
8. Molyneaux, N., Scarinci, R., Bierlaire, M.: Pedestrian management strategies for improving flow dynamics in transportation hubs. In: STRC (2017)
9. Prato, C.G.: Route choice modeling: past, present and future research directions. J. Choice Model. **2**(1), 65–100 (2009). https://doi.org/10.1016/S1755-5345(13)70005-8. http://www.sciencedirect.com/science/article/pii/S1755534513700058
10. Rao, A.M., Rao, K.R.: Measuring urban traffic congestion-a review. IJTTE **2**(4) (2012)
11. Shi, J., Tomasi, C.: Good features to track. In: CVPR, pp. 593–600 (1994). https://doi.org/10.1109/CVPR.1994.323794
12. Tan, S.K.: Visual detection and crowd density modeling of pedestrians. Ph.D. thesis, SCSE, NTU (2017). http://hdl.handle.net/10356/72746
13. Vanumu, L.D., Rao, K.R., Tiwari, G.: Fundamental diagrams of pedestrian flow characteristics: a review. ETRR **9**(4), 49 (2017)
14. Wang, H., Ondřej, J., O'Sullivan, C.: Trending paths: a new semantic-level metric for comparing simulated and real crowd data. TVCG **23**(5), 1454–1464 (2017)
15. Wang, H., O'Sullivan, C.: Globally continuous and non-Markovian crowd activity analysis from videos. In: Leibe, B., Matas, J., Sebe, N., Welling, M. (eds.) ECCV 2016. LNCS, vol. 9909, pp. 527–544. Springer, Cham (2016). https://doi.org/10.1007/978-3-319-46454-1_32

16. Wang, H., Yu, L., Qin, S.: Simulation and optimization of passenger flow line in Lanzhou West Railway Station. In: Sierpiński, G. (ed.) TSTP 2017. Advances in Intelligent Systems and Computing, vol. 631, pp. 61–73. Springer, Cham (2017). https://doi.org/10.1007/978-3-319-62316-0_5

17. Wang, R., Zhang, Y., Yue, H.: Developing a new design method avoiding latent congestion danger in urban rail transit station. Transp. Res. Procedia **25**, 4083–4099 (2017)

18. Wolinski, D., J Guy, S., Olivier, A.H., Lin, M., Manocha, D., Pettré, J.: Parameter estimation and comparative evaluation of crowd simulations. In: CGF, vol. 33, pp. 303–312. Wiley Online Library (2014)

19. Zhao, M., Turner, S.J., Cai, W.: A data-driven crowd simulation model based on clustering and classification. In: DS-RT, pp. 125–134. IEEE (2013)

20. Zhong, J., Cai, W., Lees, M., Luo, L.: Automatic model construction for the behavior of human crowds. Appl. Soft Comput. **56**, 368–378 (2017). https://doi.org/10.1016/j.asoc.2017.03.020

21. Zhong, J., Cai, W., Luo, L., Yin, H.: Learning behavior patterns from video: a data-driven framework for agent-based crowd modeling. In: AAMAS, pp. 801–809 (2015). http://dl.acm.org/citation.cfm?id=2773256

22. Zhong, J., Hu, N., Cai, W., Lees, M., Luo, L.: Density-based evolutionary framework for crowd model calibration. J. Comput. Sci. **6**, 11–22 (2015)

23. Zhou, B., Wang, X., Tang, X.: Understanding collective crowd behaviors: learning a mixture model of dynamic pedestrian-agents. In: CVPR, pp. 2871–2878. IEEE (2012)

A Novel Agent-Based Modeling Approach for Image Coding and Lossless Compression Based on the Wolf-Sheep Predation Model

Khaldoon Dhou[(✉)]

University of Missouri – St. Louis, St. Louis, USA
dhouk@umsl.edu

Abstract. In this article, the researcher develops an image coding technique which is based on the wolf-sheep predation model. In the design, images are converted to virtual worlds of sheep, routes and wolves. Wolves in this model wander around searching for sheep while the algorithm tracks their movement. A wolf has seven movements which capture all the directions of the wolf. In addition, the researcher introduces one extra move of the wolf the purpose of which is to provide a shorter string of movements and to enhance the compression ratio. The first coordinates and the movements of the wolf are tracked and recorded. Then, arithmetic coding is applied on the string of movements to further compress it. The algorithm was applied on a set of images and the results were compared with other algorithms in the research community. The experimental results reveal that the size of the compressed string of wolf movements offer a higher reduction in space and the compression ratio is higher than those of many existing compression algorithms including G3, G4, JBIG1, JBIG2 and the recent agent-based model of ant colonies.

Keywords: Agent-based modeling · Wolf-sheep predation model
Binary image coding · Compression · Arithmetic coding

1 Introduction

A binary or a bi-level image is a computerized image which holds two values for each pixel. These values are normally black and white. Binary images can be used in a variety of applications such as analyzing textual documents and representing gnomic strings [24,35]. One advantage of binary images is their small size compared to grayscale and color images. A concern that remains to impact the image processing domain is the growing of extremely large amounts of data everyday. This issue makes it crucial to explore new image compression techniques. A tremendous amount of work has been done in the field of image compression and researchers tackled the problem from different perspectives. JBIG1 is an international standard designed to compress binary images such as

© Springer International Publishing AG, part of Springer Nature 2018
Y. Shi et al. (Eds.): ICCS 2018, LNCS 10861, pp. 117–128, 2018.
https://doi.org/10.1007/978-3-319-93701-4_9

fax documents [13]. JBIG2 is a newer standard in binary image compression. In JBIG2, an image is typically decomposed into distinct parts and each part is encoded via a separate method [23]. In addition to JBIG1 and JBIG2 standards, researchers employed different techniques for binary image coding and compression such as the Freeman [6,7], arithmetic [26] and Huffman coding [11].

The extensive literature review reveals that agent-based modeling is a new direction in image compression and coding. Recent work by Mouring et al. [20] indicates that agent-based modeling is an effective and a promising approach to capture the characteristics of a binary image which allows coding and compression. In fact, utilizing the rules of biological ants (i.e. pheromone), the ant colonies algorithm offered by Mouring et al. [20] could outperform well-known algorithms such as JBIG1 and JBIG2. The present research aims at challenging the ant colonies model via utilizing the movements of wolves in a wolf-sheep predation model. Interestingly, it has less details and easier to implement while generating better compression results than the ant-colonies model [20]. In the wolf-sheep predation model, wolves wander around to find sheep to prey on in order to avoid dying. To this end, a binary image is converted to a contour image which is then converted to a virtual world of sheep and routes where a wolf can have certain moves according to specified rules. The purpose of the wolf movements is to identify sheep and thus, such movements can serve as a new image representation. These movements are also designed to take advantage of the arithmetic coding which is used to compress the final string of the wolf movements. Additionally, since it is an agent-based model, the researcher can control the number of agents that work simultaneously in the virtual world, which in turn, generates different results depending on the specifications of each particular image. Agent-based modeling also offers the capability to add certain behavior depending on the type of the agent. The researcher can explore with different settings and identify the best parameters to choose. These features make this algorithm different than many other image processing techniques. The main contributions of this article are the following:

- The present model takes advantage of the wolf-sheep predation model to produce a higher compression ratio than many other existing methods in the field of binary image compression including JBIG1 and JBIG2 standards. The extensive literature review did not reveal any previous work which utilized the wolf-sheep predation model in binary image compression.
- Agent-based modeling is a new direction in image compression and coding. The utilization of agent-based modeling allows the exploration of different behaviors which makes the agent-based modeling approach different than many other classical coding approaches in the literature [16,17,37].
- The current study introduces a new wolf movement, which is captured via a total of eight possible directions. This is less than the number of chains in the researcher's previous work in chain coding [37] where there were 10 possible chains.

– The algorithm is simple to implement compared to JBIG1 [13], JBIG2 [22, 23] and the ant colonies model [20]. Interestingly, it could outperform all of them in all the testing images.

The paper is organized as follows: related work in agent-based modeling and binary image coding and compression is presented in Sect. 2. The proposed model is described in Sect. 3. The results and discussion regarding the application of this algorithm on a dataset and the comparison with other algorithms in the research community are discussed in Sect. 4. Finally, Sect. 5 provides conclusions.

2   Related Work

This section explores existing work in agent-based modeling domain related to the movements and shows how this influences this research in image compression. Furthermore, it explores related work in image coding and compression and demonstrates an agent movement as a new approach utilized in image coding and representation.

2.1   Agent-Based Modeling

Agent-based modeling has been an attractive domain to researchers from different backgrounds and it is aimed at solving many real-life problems. It is a way to simulate systems consisting of interacting agents. Research reveals that agent-based modeling plays a crucial role in solving many computer science problems. A highly remarkable achievement in the field of agent-based modeling is the development of Netlogo [31], which is a programming environment designed to help different audiences including domain experts with no prior programming background. Netlogo has a library which is preloaded with a considerable amount of models utilized by researchers from different fields such as biology, computing, earth science, games, psychology, arts, physics and mathematics. These models can help investigators understand many life problems with complex phenomena.

One of the most well-known Netlogo models is the wolf-sheep predation model [30, 33], which investigates the balance of ecosystems consisting of predators and preys. One alteration of the model is to include wolves and sheep where wolves are looking for sheep to restore their energy and thus, avoid dying. Additionally, this variation allows sheep and wolves to reproduce at a certain rate, which enables them to persist. In another more complex alteration, it models sheep, wolves and grass where sheep must eat grass to preserve their energy. This model has been subjected to further research and development and it has been examined from various views such as offering instruction in life sciences [8] and agent-based modeling research [5]. Whilst many research studies have been carried out on the wolf sheep predation model, none of them utilized it in image processing domain. The wolf-sheep predation model inspired the present study and it was mainly used in image coding and compression.

Similarly, Wilensky [32] has introduced the ethnocentrism model which proposes that there are many circumstances which contribute to developing an ethnocentric behavior. In this model, agents use different cooperation strategies such as collaborating with everyone and collaborating within the same group. Numerous scholars have investigated the ethnocentrism model and its applications. Bausch [2] has demonstrated more collaboration when certain groups are eliminated. In 2015, the paths model was developed and it is concerned with how pathways come out along usually traveled ways where people are more inclined to follow popular routes taken by other people before them [9]. These paths can be influential in developing agent-based models which contain paths agents can walk through depending on many circumstances. Furthermore, analyzing the behavior of human agents has been examined in literature. Kvassay et al. [14] have developed a new approach which depends on casual partitioning to examine the human behavior via an agent-based model. In another study, Carbo et al. [3] have introduced an agent-based simulation to assess an ambient intelligence scheme which measures satisfaction and time savings depending on agents. They use Netlogo to simulate an airport with travelers passing through different stops such as shopping and boarding gates.

Ant colonies have been a subject of research in agent-based modeling. The ants model simulates a virtual environment of ants searching for food according to a set of rules [29]. When an ant discovers a food item, it carries it back to the nest while releasing a pheromone which can be sniffed by the surrounding ants. Pheromone attracts ants to that food source. The extensive literature review reveals one study utilizing agent-based modeling in binary image compression by Mouring et al. [20]. They have built a model for image compression which simulates an ant colony. In their study, an image is converted to a virtual environment with ants moving over the routes and searching for food items. The search process in the algorithm is influenced by the pheromones released and the other ants in the neighborhood. The results of the ant colonies algorithm were promising and they could significantly produce better compression ratios than JBIG1 and JBIG2. The difference between this research and the ant colonies algorithm by Mouring et al. [20] is that this algorithm has a new set of rules which were not utilized in the ant colonies research. In turn, the compression ratios of the wolf-sheep predation model are higher than those obtained by the ant colonies model offered by Mouring et al. [20] in all the testing images.

2.2   Binary Image Compression

With the introduction of Internet and social media, there is a continual increase in the amounts of data generated everyday. This makes it imperative to explore new mechanisms to process and compress the data in order to transmit it efficiently over the media channels. The topic of compression has attracted much attention in the research community and it has been extensively studied from different perspectives. One of the most remarkable achievements that has drawn the attention of many image compression researchers is arithmetic encoding [26,34]. This technique is widely used by investigators from different domains and was subject to further improvement and development over the years. Anandan and Sabeenian [1] have described a method to compress medical images using Fast

Discrete Curvelet Transform and coded the coefficients using arithmetic coding. In a different study, Masmoudi and Masmoudi [18] have investigated a new mechanism for lossless compression which utilizes arithmetic coding and codes an image block by block. Recently, Shahriyar et al. [27] have proposed a lossless depth coding mechanism based on a binary tree which produces a compression ratio between 20 to 80. Furthermore, Zhou [39] has proposed an algorithm which exploits the redundancy in 2D images and improved the arithmetic coding to provide a better compression of the data.

Literature shows that researchers incorporate arithmetic encoding with other image processing techniques. A widely used approach in the field of data compression is the chain coding which has been developed further after Freeman Code [7]. It keeps track of the image contour information and records each traversed direction. The subject of chain coding has been extensively explored and analyzed over the years. Minami and Shinohara [19] have introduced a new concept called the multiple grid chain code which utilizes square grids in encoding lines. Furthermore, Zhao et al. [38] have introduced a new approach to identify the related parts in a bi-level image. Another advancement is the representation of voxel-based objects via chain code strings by Martínez et al. [17]. In a different vein, Liu and Žalik [16] have presented a new chain code where the elements were encoded based on the relative angle difference between the current and the previous direction. Then, they have compressed the resulting string using Huffman coding. Likewise, Zahir and Dhou [37] have introduced a chain coding technique for lossy and lossless compression which takes advantage of the sequence of the consecutive directions and encodes them using a particular set of rules. In a different vein, Yeh et al. [36] have presented the Ideal-segmented Chain Coding (IsCC) method which employs 4-connected chains that can move in certain directions.

Along with improvements, the subject of chain code has been utilized in many applications. For example, Decker et al. [4] have introduced a new tracking mechanism to be used in endoscopy which overcomes the obstacles in soft surgery. Additionally, Ngan et al. [21] have employed the 3D chain codes in representing the paths of human movement. Coding was also used by researchers for different purposes in image processing. For example, Priyadarshini and Sahoo [25] have proposed a new method for lossless image compression of Freeman coding. Their method has achieved an average space saving of 18% and 50% for Freeman 8-directional and 4-directional chain codes, respectively. In another study, Liaghati et al. [15] have proposed a compression method for ROI maps which relies onto partitioning the image into blocks of the same size, applying a conversion on each block and then running code for compression.

Although all the previous methods handle the problem of image coding and compression from different perspectives, the extensive literature review has revealed that there is only one study utilizing the agent-based model of ant colonies in binary image coding and compression [20]. In this research a different model is utilized for image coding and compression which takes advantage of the wolf-sheep predation model and as shown, the results could outperform many

existing methods in the research community including the recent ants model
and JBIG family [10,12,13,20,23,28,39]. Despite the fact that image coding
and compression has research grounds in image processing [6,7,16,25,37,38], an
agent-based modeling approach has a number of attractive advantages over the
classical approaches of chain coding the considerable literature review revealed:

- The researcher can add an agent behavior to be included in the model. For
  example, in the agent-based model utilizing ant colonies for image coding and
  compression, Mouring et al. [20] have utilized the concept of pheromone to
  attract ants to move to certain locations of the image. Similarly, the researcher
  can add more behavior to the wolf-sheep predation model such as the concepts
  of the grass and reproduction. This does not exist in chain coding.
- Agents can work on different parts of the image at the same time. For instance,
  the ant colonies algorithm has the proximity awareness feature, which allows
  the virtual ants to move to certain parts of the image with less density of
  ants. The number of agents working on the image is a parameter which can
  be controlled by the programmer. Likewise, in the wolf-sheep predation model,
  the researcher can control the number and the directions of wolves depending
  on the virtual world.
- Agent-based modeling approaches can have less number of movements as
  opposed to the chain coding directions in some chain coding approaches. For
  example, the lossless chain coding technique offered by Zahir and Dhou [37]
  provides a total of ten directions while the ant colonies algorithm has four or
  five movement possibilities depending on whether the movement is related or
  normal. Likewise, in the current wolf-sheep predation model, the movement
  of the wolf can only have one of eight possibilities.

3   The Proposed Agent-Based Modeling Algorithm

In this paper, the researcher proposes an algorithm for bi-level image coding
based on the wolf-sheep predation model [30] which can also be used in binary
image compression. The idea of the model is based on the movements of wolves
to find sheep in a predatory-prey system. The researcher believes that this work
paves the way for a new direction on image analysis using agent-based modeling.
In the present model, a moving agent is represented by a wolf and the movement
is for the purpose of searching for sheep. At the beginning, a binary image is
converted to a contour representation which is then transformed to a virtual
world consisting of a wolf, sheep and routes where the wolf can walk to search
for the sheep. Each zero pixel in the binary image is replaced by a route and
each 1 pixel is replaced by a sheep as shown in the example in Fig. 1.

The wolf starts from the upper-left position and starts searching for sheep
and once he finds a sheep, he moves to that location and so on. Each time a wolf
moves to a new location, the movement is recorded based on the previous one.
There are seven pertinent moves in the system which capture all the directions
of the wolf in the virtual environment. These movements depend on the location
of the wolf, the direction of attack and the location of the sheep as in Fig. 2.

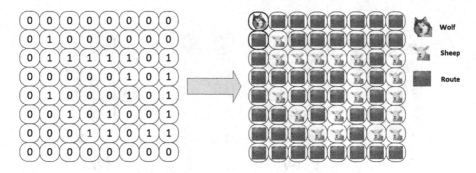

Fig. 1. An example of a binary image converted to a virtual world of sheep, routes and a wolf searching for sheep

For example, if the wolf moves in the same direction as its previous move, the movement is recorded as Straight Move (SM). If the wolf moves sharp in the right direction, the movement is recorded as Right Move (RM). There is one exception to the straight movement of the wolf: If the wolf has the ability to move 8 consecutive steps in the same direction (i.e. Straight Move). In such a case, the movement is recorded as Big Straight Move (BSM).

Other than the movement exception listed, the movement is encoded according to Fig. 2(a) through (g). The reason why the researcher designed the movement to include an exception is because he experimented with a large number of images and found that the percentage of occurrence of the Straight Move (SM) was about 50% of the time. Thus, by having the movement exception, the algorithm can achieve a high reduction on the agent movement, which in turn, provides a better compression ratio. In other words, using BSM movements offers further reduction to the series of movements and allows the arithmetic coding to provide a higher compression ratio when applied on the string representing the wolf movements. Some other movements of the wolf occur very rarely in images and thus, it would be of no value to have exceptions concerning them. After obtaining the chain of wolf movements, the researcher compressed them using arithmetic encoding, the purpose of which was to reduce the number of bits in the string. Figure 3 provides an example of coding an image using the current algorithm.

4   Results and Discussion

The proposed wolf sheep predation model was tested on a set of 8 binary images from [39]. The same set of images was used in the study of ant colonies by Mouring et al. [20]. For more information about the images, please refer to [39]. The experimental results showed that the number of bits resulting from compressing the wolf movements in the present model via arithmetic coding could outperform the results of many existing algorithms. Table 1 shows the results of

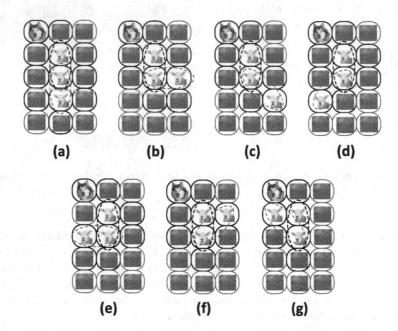

Fig. 2. (a) Straight Move (b) Left Move; (c) Cross Left Move; (d) Cross Right Move; (e) Right Move; (f) Reverse Left Move; (g) Reverse Right Move

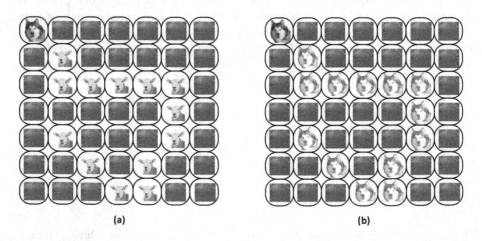

Fig. 3. An example of a wolf movement for the purpose of coding. The wolf starts searching from the upper-left portion of an image and then moves to the first location where he finds a sheep. Then, the wolf finds a sheep in a neighborhood location, thus moves to that location and so on. The relative movement of the wolf can be represented as: LM, SM, SM, SM, RM, SM, CRM, CLM, RM, CRM and SM

Table 1. Number of bits generated after compressing the chain of wolf movements using arithmetic coding in a wolf-sheep predation model as opposed to the number of bits generated by other existing algorithms [10, 12, 13, 20, 23, 28, 39]

Image	Original	G3	G4	JBIG1	JBIG2	Ant colonies model	Wolf-sheep predation model
Image 1	65280	26048	19488	15176	15064	8556	6982
Image 2	202320	29856	12208	8648	8616	4892	4433
Image 3	187880	26000	11184	8088	8072	4342	4009
Image 4	81524	14176	6256	5080	5064	2591	2221
Image 5	40000	11712	5552	5424	5208	2314	1902
Image 6	96472	21872	9104	7336	7328	3935	3527
Image 7	414720	102208	81424	62208	58728	43966	37323
Image 8	83600	20064	8192	7200	6984	3319	3101
Total	1171796	251936	153408	119160	115064	73915	63498

the current wolf-sheep predation model as compared to other algorithms in the research community.

Using the data in Table 1, the space savings metric was calculated using the equation below:

$$Space\ savings = 1 - \frac{Compressed\ Size}{Uncompressed\ Size} \qquad (1)$$

The space savings metric was calculated for the wolf-sheep predation model as compared to other existing techniques. The space savings metric was 78.500%, 86.908%, 89.831%, 90.181% and 93.692% for G3, G4, JBIG1, JBIG2 and Ant Colonies Model, respectively while it was 94.511% for the current wolf sheep predation model. In addition, the current model uses one of eight codes to represent each movement (SM, LM, RM, CLM, CRM, RLM, RRM and BSM) as opposed to the previous work by Zahir and Dhou [37] which involved one of 10 codes to represent each direction.

5   Conclusion

The aim of the present study is to investigate the role of a modified wolf-sheep predation model in image coding and compression. In particular, a set of movements of wolves is designed the purpose of which is to encode and compress binary images. Specifically, eight wolf movements are introduced including a big movement which help further reduction of the string employed in image representation. The experimental results show that in terms of bit reduction offered by the compressed string of movements, the present agent-based model is superior to many other methods in binary compression including JBIG2 [22, 23] and the ant colonies algorithm [20]. Furthermore, the present method is easier to program than JBIG methods and the ant colonies algorithm.

The evidence from the findings of this study is that agent-based modeling can be utilized as a new approach in the field of image coding and analysis. The empirical findings of this study provide a new understanding to an agent-based modeling and its application in binary image coding compression. Furthermore, this research serves as a base for future studies that investigate the movements of agents in image analysis and representation.

A limitation of this study is that it does not address utilizing agent-based modeling in compressing grayscale and color images. Additionally, it is only limited to image coding and compression. Future work includes testing the algorithm on a larger set of images and applying the chains of agent movement in further image analysis. Furthermore, this project can be a starting point to more research in image analysis and compression of grayscale and color images using agent-based modeling approaches.

References

1. Anandan, P., Sabeenian, R., et al.: Medical image compression using wrapping based fast discrete curvelet transform and arithmetic coding. Circ. Syst. **7**(08), 2059 (2016)
2. Bausch, A.W.: The geography of ethnocentrism. J. Conflict Resolut. **59**(3), 510–527 (2015)
3. Carbo, J., Sanchez-Pi, N., Molina, J.: Agent-based simulation with NetLogo to evaluate ambient intelligence scenarios. J. Simul. **12**(1), 42–52 (2018)
4. Decker, R.S., Shademan, A., Opfermann, J.D., Leonard, S., Kim, P.C., Krieger, A.: Biocompatible near-infrared three-dimensional tracking system. IEEE Trans. Biomed. Eng. **64**(3), 549–556 (2017)
5. Fachada, N., Lopes, V.V., Martins, R.C., Rosa, A.C.: Towards a standard model for research in agent-based modeling and simulation. PeerJ Comput. Sci. **1**, e36 (2015)
6. Freeman, H.: On the encoding of arbitrary geometric configurations. IRE Trans. Electron. Comput. **2**, 260–268 (1961)
7. Freeman, H.: Computer processing of line-drawing images. ACM Comput. Surv. (CSUR) **6**(1), 57–97 (1974)
8. Ginovart, M.: Discovering the power of individual-based modelling in teaching and learning: the study of a predator-prey system. J. Sci. Educ. Technol. **23**(4), 496–513 (2014)
9. Grider, R., Wilensky, U.: NetLogo paths model. Center for Connected Learning and Computer-Based Modeling, Northwestern University, Evanston, IL (2015). http://ccl.northwestern.edu/netlogo/models/Paths
10. Hampel, H., Arps, R.B., Chamzas, C., Dellert, D., Duttweiler, D.L., Endoh, T., Equitz, W., Ono, F., Pasco, R., Sebestyen, I., et al.: Technical features of the JBIG standard for progressive bi-level image compression. Sig. Process. Image Commun. **4**(2), 103–111 (1992)
11. Huffman, D.A.: A method for the construction of minimum-redundancy codes. Proc. IRE **40**(9), 1098–1101 (1952)
12. JBIG1: Progressive bilevel image compression. International Standard 11544 (1993)

13. Kuhn, M.: JBIG-KIT. University of Cambridge (2017). http://www.cl.cam.ac.uk/~mgk25/jbigkit/
14. Kvassay, M., Krammer, P., Hluchỳ, L., Schneider, B.: Causal analysis of an agent-based model of human behaviour. Complexity **2017**, 1–18 (2017)
15. Liaghati, A.L., Shen, H., Pan, W.D.: An efficient method for lossless compression of bi-level ROI maps of hyperspectral images. In: Aerospace Conference, 2016 IEEE, pp. 1–6. IEEE (2016)
16. Liu, Y.K., Žalik, B.: An efficient chain code with huffman coding. Pattern Recogn. **38**(4), 553–557 (2005)
17. Martínez, L.A., Bribiesca, E., Guzmán, A.: Chain coding representation of voxel-based objects with enclosing, edging and intersecting trees. Pattern Anal. Appl. **20**(3), 825–844 (2017)
18. Masmoudi, A., Masmoudi, A.: A new arithmetic coding model for a block-based lossless image compression based on exploiting inter-block correlation. SIViP **9**(5), 1021–1027 (2015)
19. Minami, T., Shinohara, K.: Encoding of line drawings with a multiple grid chain code. IEEE Trans. Pattern Anal. Mach. Intell. **2**, 269–276 (1986)
20. Mouring, M., Dhou, K., Hadzikadic, M.: A novel algorithm for bi-level image coding and lossless compression based on virtual ant colonies. In: 3rd International Conference on Complexity, Future Information Systems and Risk, pp. 72–78. Setúbal - Portugal (2018)
21. Ngan, P.T.H., Hochin, T., Nomiya, H.: Similarity measure of human body movement through 3D chaincode. In: 2017 18th IEEE/ACIS International Conference on Software Engineering, Artificial Intelligence, Networking and Parallel/Distributed Computing (SNPD), pp. 607–614. IEEE (2017)
22. Ono, F., Rucklidge, W., Arps, R., Constantinescu, C.: JBIG2 - the ultimate bi-level image coding standard. In: ICIP, pp. 140–143 (2000). http://dblp.uni-trier.de/db/conf/icip/icip2000.html#OnoRAC00
23. Ono, F., Rucklidge, W., Arps, R., Constantinescu, C.: JBIG2-the ultimate bi-level image coding standard. In: 2000 International Conference on Image Processing, Proceedings, vol. 1, pp. 140–143. IEEE (2000)
24. Pan, J., Hu, Z., Su, Z., Yang, M.H.: l_0-regularized intensity and gradient prior for deblurring text images and beyond. IEEE Trans. Pattern Anal. Mach. Intell. **39**(2), 342–355 (2017)
25. Priyadarshini, S., Sahoo, G.: A new lossless chain code compression scheme based on substitution. Int. J. Signal Imaging Syst. Eng. **4**(1), 50–56 (2011)
26. Sayood, K.: Introduction to Data Compression. Newnes, Boston (2012)
27. Shahriyar, S., Murshed, M., Ali, M., Paul, M.: Lossless depth map coding using binary tree based decomposition and context-based arithmetic coding. In: 2016 IEEE International Conference on Multimedia and Expo (ICME), pp. 1–6. IEEE (2016)
28. Tompkins, D.A., Kossentini, F.: A fast segmentation algorithm for bi-level image compression using JBIG2. In: 1999 International Conference on Image Processing, ICIP 1999, Proceedings, vol. 1, pp. 224–228. IEEE (1999)
29. Wilensky, U.: Ants model. Center for Connected Learning and Computer-Based Modeling, Northwestern University, Evanston, IL (1997). http://ccl.northwestern.edu/netlogo/models/Ants
30. Wilensky, U.: NetLogo wolf sheep predation model. Center for connected learning and computer-based modeling, Northwestern University, Evanston (1997). http://ccl.northwestern.edu/netlogo/models/WolfSheepPredation

31. Wilensky, U.: NetLogo. Center for Connected Learning and Computer-Based Modeling, Northwestern University, Evanston, IL (1999). http://ccl.northwestern.edu/netlogo/
32. Wilensky, U.: NetLogo ethnocentrism model. Northwestern University, Evanston, Center for Connected Learning and Computer-based Modeling (2003)
33. Wilensky, U., Reisman, K.: Thinking like a wolf, a sheep, or a firefly: learning biology through constructing and testing computational theories—an embodied modeling approach. Cogn. Instr. **24**(2), 171–209 (2006)
34. Witten, I.H., Neal, R.M., Cleary, J.G.: Arithmetic coding for data compression. Commun. ACM **30**(6), 520–540 (1987)
35. Xie, X., Zhou, S., Guan, J.: CoGI: towards compressing genomes as an image. IEEE/ACM Trans. Comput. Biol. Bioinf. **12**(6), 1275–1285 (2015)
36. Yeh, M.C., Huang, Y.L., Wang, J.S.: Scalable ideal-segmented chain coding. In: 2002 International Conference on Image Processing, Proceedings, vol. 1, pp. I–197. IEEE (2002)
37. Zahir, S., Dhou, K.: A new chain coding based method for binary image compression and reconstruction. In: Picture Coding Symposium, pp. 1321–1324 (2007)
38. Zhao, X., Zheng, J., Liu, Y.: A new algorithm of shape boundaries based on chain coding. In: ITM Web of Conferences, vol. 12, p. 03005. EDP Sciences (2017)
39. Zhou, L.: A new highly efficient algorithm for lossless binary image compression. ProQuest (2007)

Planning Optimal Path Networks
Using Dynamic Behavioral Modeling

Sergei Kudinov[1(✉)], Egor Smirnov[1], Gavriil Malyshev[1], and Ivan Khodnenko[2]

[1] Institute for Design and Urban Studies, ITMO University, Birzhevaya Liniya 14,
199034 Saint Petersburg, Russia
{sergei.kudinov,g.malyshev}@corp.ifmo.ru,
smirnov.egor.v@gmail.com
[2] High-Performance Computing Department, ITMO University, Birzhevaya Liniya 4,
199034 Saint Petersburg, Russia
ivan.khodnenko@corp.ifmo.ru

Abstract. Mistakes in pedestrian infrastructure design in modern cities decrease transfer comfort for people, impact greenery due to appearance of desire paths, and thus increase the amount of dust in the air because of open ground. These mistakes can be avoided if optimal path networks are created considering behavioral aspects of pedestrian traffic, which is a challenge. In this article, we introduce Ant Road Planner, a new method of computer simulation for estimation and creation of optimal path networks which not only considers pedestrians' behavior but also helps minimize the total length of the paths so that the area is used more efficiently. The method, which includes a modeling algorithm and its software implementation with a user-friendly web interface, makes it possible to predict pedestrian networks for new territories with high precision and detect problematic areas in existing networks. The algorithm was successfully tested on real territories and proved its potential as a decision making support system for urban planners.

Keywords: Path formation · Agent-based modeling · Human trail system
Group behavior · Pedestrian flows simulation · Stigmergy

1 Introduction

Pedestrian infrastructure is a crucial part of urban environment, forming the basis of city territory accessibility because the last part of a trip is normally walked [1]. Thus, planning and organizing a comfortable pedestrian infrastructure is vitally important for urban development. Path network optimality is among key factors determining the comfort value of the way [2], as pedestrians tend to consider the optimal route to be the most comfortable [3].

From the pedestrian's point of view, the decisive factor when choosing the route is the highest connectivity that enables the pedestrian to get from the departure point to the destination point with minimum effort and in the minimum time possible, i.e. using the shortest way [4]. However, in terms of city planning, economics and environmental protection, minimizing the costs of path network creation is equally important, as well

© Springer International Publishing AG, part of Springer Nature 2018
Y. Shi et al. (Eds.): ICCS 2018, LNCS 10861, pp. 129–141, 2018.
https://doi.org/10.1007/978-3-319-93701-4_10

as minimizing the paved area in order to increase the green area and for other purposes. A compromise is possible which would provide a comfortable pedestrian infrastructure without linking all possible attraction points to each other using paved paths, although finding this kind of solution might be challenging.

In this article, a computer simulation method is discussed which makes it possible to design optimal path networks. The method considers both pedestrians' behavioral demands and the need to minimize the total length of the paths. The method was tested on real urban territories, showed high accuracy in predicting problematic areas of existing pedestrian networks, and demonstrated a good calculation speed.

2   Related Work

Usage of behavioral modeling methods for designing pedestrian infrastructure is currently underrepresented in research literature. Today, many simulation methods and software tools allow for modeling pedestrian flow motion in a predefined route network, which makes it possible to predict interaction between agents and prevent jams during public events and in emergency situations [5]. These are based on the social force model [6] and the cellular automata model [7], and their main application area is capacity estimation, but using these methods for calculating optimal path networks seems to be impossible.

Nevertheless, simulation methods aimed at building an optimal path network do exist, although they are not widespread due to their restricted application or their unsuitability for practical implementation.

2.1   Active Walkers

The Active Walkers method based on a greedy pathfinding algorithm was developed by Dirk Helbing and was aimed at modeling the forming of animal and human paths [8]. It makes it possible to model the forming of desire paths across lawns on territories with non-optimal path networks. The territory for the algorithm is defined by a grid with outlined borders and preset attraction points between which the agents simulating the pedestrians are distributed. The agent motion equation considers, among other things, the direction to the destination point and presence of existing paths nearby. This way the forming of desire paths is modeled as the agents move across the grid cells. At the end of the simulation, the modeled path network is formed by the grid cells through which the highest number of agents moved.

The drawback of this method is that the greedy pathfinding algorithm is not predictive, so an agent within the simulation makes its way to the destination based only on the comfort of each next step and the direction to the destination. The agent has no information on the complexity of the landscape or the location of obstacles, so it cannot start bypassing an obstacle until coming close to it [9]. This limits the applicability of Active Walkers to particular cases where territories have no complex shaped obstacles or dead ends, which makes the algorithm inefficient for creating an optimal path network on real urban territories with a complex configuration.

2.2 The Method by the Central Research and Project Institute for Urban Planning

This method was developed by the USSR Institute for Urban Planning that worked on planning developing urban territories and public accommodation. The method is stated in a set of instructions for mathematical and geometrical calculation of an optimal pedestrian network [10]. These design guidelines are based on a method of designing optimal networks for pedestrian communications [11]. Location of all destination points and obstacles, as well as a set of significant links between the given points needs to be considered as input data. The optimality criteria for the network created is the observance of the network feasibility condition which means that the angle between the pedestrian's motion direction and the direction to the destination point does not exceed 30°. This condition is of geometric nature and is closely related to the psychological mechanism regulating pedestrians' behavior as they move towards the destination. A subconscious visual on-site estimation of the angle between the motion direction in each point of the route and the direction to the destination plays the main role in this mechanism.

The algorithm allows for mathematical calculation and design of optimal path networks on urban territories, as it considers pedestrians' behavioral demands as well as economic and environmental factors, which makes it possible to create comfortable path networks with a minimum total length. The main drawback of the algorithm is lack of software implementation, which makes its wide use impossible. Moreover, the algorithm can only be used for pedestrian infrastructure planning for new territories and cannot be applied to optimize existing pedestrian networks where it is unreasonable to reconstruct the territory completely.

3 Proposed Methodology

The optimal path network creation method proposed in this article is called Ant Road Planner and is based on agent modeling performed by A* algorithm, a modification of Dijkstra's pathfinding algorithm. An important feature of this algorithm is its ability to consider changes to the area map introduced by agents as optimal paths are formed by them.

This method is somewhat similar to algorithms of the so called ant colony optimization family. In these algorithms, ant-like agents choose their ways randomly based on "pheromone" traces left by other ants [12]. Trampledness of the lawn in the task in question can be compared to the pheromone traces in ant colony optimization algorithms. However, there are differences as well. The suggested method uses determined pathfinding based on full information on the navigation graph, unlike ant colony optimization algorithms in which the next step is chosen randomly. This helps to avoid problems typical of all greedy and randomized algorithms which find non-optimal paths in case there are complex-shaped obstacles.

The method is implemented in a software solution written in Java with a web interface, which makes it possible to use it as a practical support tool for decision making in pedestrian infrastructure design [13]. This enables testing the algorithm on a large number of real territories with the help of urban planning experts.

3.1 Input Data

As input data, the algorithm requires detailed information on the configuration of the territory for which an optimal path network is being created. This information includes the location of obstacles, attraction points (shops, building entrances, playgrounds etc.), existing elements of pedestrian infrastructure, and different types of landscape surface. For this purpose, the algorithm uses a vector map of the territory. The web interface supports GeoJSON maps imported from GIS systems as well as DXF files from CAD systems.

The attraction points within the algorithm are divided into several types:

- Generators which agents go out from but which cannot be their destinations
- Attractors which can be agents' destinations but cannot generate agents
- Universal points performing both functions.

A combination of different types of attraction points can handle situations when pedestrians do not move between certain attraction points. For example, pedestrians do not normally walk between different entrances to the same house, so these entrances can be marked as generators.

Locations of agent generators are shown on the map, as well as walkability of the territory parts ranging from zero for obstacles to maximum for official paths (Fig. 1). In order to obtain high-quality results, it is important to set relative popularity of agent attraction points correctly. The attraction points within the model are divided into two types: "popular" and "less popular", which correspond to the relative number of people choosing them.

Fig. 1. Preparing territory map in Ant Road Planner web interface.

3.2 Building the Navigation Graph

At the initialization step, the input data is processed by the algorithm for future simulation. A navigation graph $G(V, E)$ is built based on the map. In order to do this, a hexagonal grid is applied over the map, the centers of the hexangular blocks forming the vertex set of the graph V. If there is no impassable obstacle between the centers of the two adjacent blocks, i.e. an agent can walk between them, these nodes are linked with edges constituting set E. In Fig. 2, the points represent the vertex set, the vertices corresponding to the hexangular cells of the grid, and the thin lines between the points represent the edge set. Hexagonal grid was chosen instead of more common orthogonal one in order to increase the precision of route forming [14].

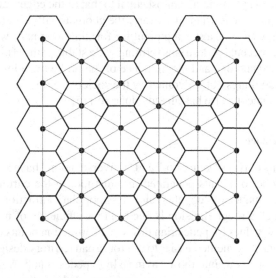

Fig. 2. Hexagonal grid and the navigation graph.

The weight W of each edge e is represented by the difference of two components: constant $W_{const}(e)$ determined by the type of surface, and variable $W_{var}(e)$ representing the trampledness:

$$W(e) = W_{const}(e) - W_{var}(e) \tag{1}$$

Initial trampledness equals 0. $W_{const}(e)$ equals 1 for official paths with hard pavement; these have no variable component. For lawns, $W_{const}(e)$ is suggested to be 2.7. This value was calculated empirically in a series of algorithm tests on reference territory maps. In order to do this, such values were selected for the variables that the pedestrian network resulting from the simulation for each territory was as close as possible to the official and desire path network existing on the real territory.

3.3 Agents' Behavioral Model

Agents $p(i)$ that model pedestrians within the algorithm are divided into two groups – "decent" and "indecent" – to simulate the behavior of different types of pedestrians. For agents of the first type, the key factor when choosing the direction is the condition of the surface (lawn). "Decent" agents will not leave the path and start crossing the lawn if it is not significantly trampled. Moreover, they will stick to this type of behavior even if the way along official paths is longer than along desire paths that are not trampled enough. "Indecent" agents tend to always take the shortest way regardless of the existence and trampledness of the path across the lawn. That is, $W_{var}(e)$ for them is always taken to equal the maximum acceptable value W_{max}. Thus, the weight of the edges representing the lawn is always minimal, almost equal to that of the edges representing paved paths. As a result, these pedestrians use nearly the geometrically shortest ways directly across the lawns and serve as a starting point for forming long narrow paths which are then used by other, "decent" pedestrians forming wide stable paths. This behavior represents pedestrians' psychology and the influence of the broken windows theory: People are more prone to do things not welcomed by the society (in this case – walking across lawns) if they see someone else has already done so [15].

3.4 Simulation Process

The attraction points of types "generator" and "universal point" have a capacity C which represents the number of agents generated in unit time. In the current version of the algorithm, the performance of "popular" and "less popular" attraction points differs by a factor of two. Such a rough division is due to labor efficiency of measurements and prediction of precise values for pedestrian flows in all attraction points of real territories. Thus, in order to make the method easier to use for urban territory designers, we suggest dividing the attraction points into those having a high pedestrian flow (e.g. public transport stops) and those having a lower flow (e.g. one of the entrances to a residential building).

Agents of different types are distributed equally within each attraction point but "indecent" agents constitute 5–10% of the total number of simulated agents. This proportion in the algorithm is chosen empirically.

Attraction points of types "attractor" and "universal point" have an operating radius R. It determines the maximum straight line distance between attraction points creating agents for this destination point. Agents' destinations are chosen randomly from a list of attractors and universal points with suitable operating radius.

The following happens at each step of the simulation:

1. Agents $p(i)$ walk a certain distance S proportional to the specified speed v. At the end of the simulation step, agent's position on the current edge is saved to parameter S_L:

$$S_L = (S \bmod L)/L, \text{ where } L \text{ is the length of the graph edge.} \tag{2}$$

2. Trampledness of the graph edge $W_{var}(e)$ increases by a constant value of the trampledness increment ΔW_{ped} after each agent who walked the whole length of the edge till the end on this step of the simulation:

$$W'_{var}(e) = W_{var}(e) + \Delta W_{ped} \tag{3}$$

Trampledness of surrounding edges increases as well. The purpose and mechanism of this process are described in detail below.

3. Agents reaching their destinations disappear. New agents appear in attraction point of types "generator" and "universal point". Each point generates a new agent after a set number of simulation steps, while popular points generate pedestrians two times more often. Agent creation frequency can be set manually (if statistics or an estimation of the number of pedestrians are available) or equals 2 pedestrians a minute by default. This value was chosen empirically and is explained below.
4. Trampledness of each graph edge $W_{var}(e)$ decreases by a constant value ΔW_{dis} reflecting the path "dissolution" process, for example as a result of greenery regrowth.

$$W''_{var}(e) = W'_{var}(e) - \Delta W_{dis} \tag{4}$$

Increasing the trampledness of the edges surrounding the edge walked enables the algorithm to model realistic width of desire paths and implement a path adhesion mechanism. This mechanism is necessary to replace multiple parallel paths with a single one which is equally preferable for pedestrians using the neighboring paths.

Let $W_{var}(ej)$ be the trampledness of edge j that neighbors edge i which the agent walks. After the agent walks the edge i, trampledness $W_{var}(ej)$ of the surrounding edges increases by the induced trampledness ΔW_{ind}:

$$W'_{var}(ej) = W_{var}(ej) + \Delta W_{ind}, \tag{5}$$

Induced trampledness is calculated as the product of the trampledness increment of the edge walked ΔW_{ped} and a variable remoteness factor $D(x)$ representing the distance between the node located at the far end of the calculated edge j and the node located at the far end of the walked edge i, where remoteness x is the distance between the nodes:

$$\Delta W_{ind} = \sum_i \Delta W_{ped\,i} * D(x)_i, \{D \in \mathbb{R}: 0 \leq D \leq 1\} \tag{6}$$

Range r of induced trampledness depends on the stage of the simulation on which the calculation takes place. As part of path adhesion mechanism development, experimental estimation of maximum range and possible curves illustrating the dependence of the factor D on the distance x was carried out. The task was to find such a curve that adding induced trampledness caused by neighboring edges used by agents would change the trampledness of the unused edge located between them by a value comparable to

ΔW_{ped}. It was found out that a suitable dependence is described by an equation of a cubic parabola:

$$D(x) = -4\left|\left(\frac{x}{r}\right)^3\right| + 6\left|\left(\frac{x}{r}\right)^2\right| - 3\left|\left(\frac{x}{r}\right)\right| + 1 \tag{7}$$

Figure 3 shows how induced trampledness emerges when simulating path adhesion.

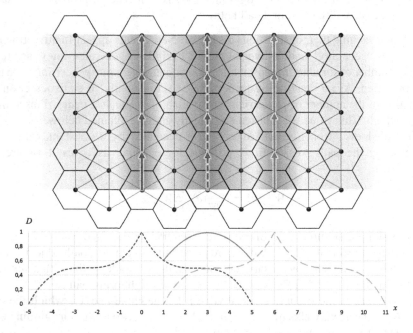

<table>
<tr><td>↑ ↑</td><td>The edge e(i) along which the agent moves.</td></tr>
<tr><td>┇ ┇</td><td>$W_{var}(ei)$ increases by ΔW_{ped}</td></tr>
<tr><td>↑</td><td>The edge e(j) exposed to induced trampledness of two edges used by agents.</td></tr>
<tr><td></td><td>$W_{var}(ej)$ increases by ΔW_{ind}</td></tr>
</table>

Fig. 3. Path adhesion process at the first stage of the simulation.

Range r is chosen to equal 5 m for the first half of all the simulation steps. This range of induced trampledness is enough to start the adhesion process for paths located close to each other, which was determined by experiments. However, wide areas of high trampledness appear as a result of this process. For the path resulting from adhesion to have a realistic width, at the second stage of the simulation the trampledness of the surrounding edges is spread over a distance of $r \approx 1.5$ m from the edge walked.

The weight $W(e)$ of the same edge e for different agents p within the model can differ. The weight determines the attractiveness of the territory part for the given agent, which is inversely related to the weight. Agents walking the territory choose the direction for the next step based on the edge weight. As the agents walk along the edge, its weight may decrease as the trampledness $W_{var}(e)$ increases, which reflects the increase of attractiveness as the path becomes more trampled. $W_{var}(e)$ is limited from below by zero for intact lawn (which has not been walked by agents yet) and from above by W_{max} which equals 1.6. This value is chosen in such a way that the weight of the edge across the lawn area always exceeds that of the edge following a paved path. As a result, even a lawn area with maximum trampledness will have a slightly lower attractiveness (up to 10%) than a similar official path, all other factors held equal.

The following formula is used for the weight $W(e)$ of the edge e for the agent:

$$W(e) = (W_{const}(e) - W_{var}(e)) * L \tag{8}$$

Based on the parameter limits described above, untouched lawn is 2.7 times less comfortable than a paved path for a "decent" agent, and a well-trampled lawn is only 1.1 times less comfortable. An "indecent" agent pays no attention to the trampledness of the lawn, so for it the weight of the edge across the lawn always equals 1.1.

Trampledness $W_{var}(e)$ for the edge e after simulation step i can be expressed as follows:

$$W_{var}(e) = \Delta W_{ped} * P_{count}(e, i) + \Delta W_{ind} - \Delta W_{dis\neg}, \text{ where}$$
$$P_{count}(e, i) \text{ is the number of agents who walked the edge } e \text{ at step } i. \tag{9}$$

In the model, agents plot their routes according to the A* algorithm. The simulation continues until the preset number of steps is reached. Intermediate results can be estimated at each step.

After the simulation finishes, Ant Road Planner software environment forms a graphical layout representing the distribution of trampledness over the territory and showing the areas with the most intensive flow, where agents typically leave official paths and form desire paths.

4 Experiments and Results

The main parameters of the algorithm, such as the proportion of "indecent" agents or $W_{const}(e)$ for different types of surface, were chosen empirically based on experiment results. Three examples of existing urban territories were used: a small 50×50 m backyard, a large 150×150 m yard and a 500×300 m park section. A comprehensive examination of possible parameter values and their combinations was carried out with a simulation run for each set of values. Then the prediction suggested by the algorithm was visually compared to on-site data on the path layout. A parameter set was selected that produced a simulation result as close to the real path layout as possible.

After that, several simulations of new territories (not used for parameter selection) were carried out in order to test the quality of the model obtained.

As an example, we analyzed a pedestrian network on a territory of a housing estate in St. Petersburg, Russia. This territory has a complex configuration with numerous obstacles and attraction points and has an existing path network but many of its parts are non-optimal and do not correspond to pedestrians' demands. As a result, there are a lot of desire paths on the territory.

For the purpose of the experiment, the attraction points of the territory were analyzed. The territory map and the data gathered was uploaded to the simulation using the Ant Road Planner web interface, after which a simulation was performed using the suggested algorithm. The calculations were performed with Intel Core i5-760 CPU (8 MB Cache, 2.80 GHz) and 16 GB DDR3 667 MHz RAM. The following parameters were set for the simulation: territory area – 192,500 m^2, grid density – 0.451 m^2 per 1 hexagonal block, simulation step duration – 5 s, simulation duration – 5,760 steps. The calculation time for the chosen territory was 3 h 56 min. The simulation result is a sketch map of the territory with highlighted areas recommended for inclusion into the official path network. Here is the resulting map together with a satellite shot of the territory for side-by-side comparison. Satellite shots from Yandex.Maps (Fig. 4) are used in this article.

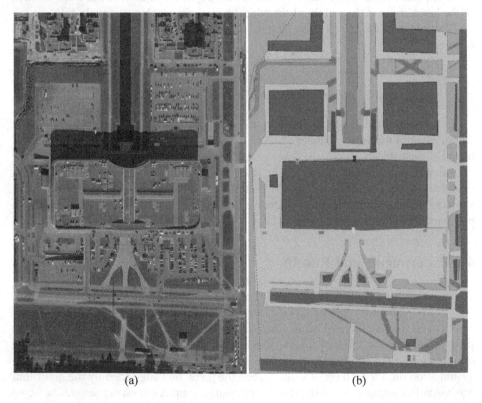

(a)   (b)

Fig. 4. Simulation result visualization for pedestrian motion across the territory. (a) Satellite shot of the territory, (b) A sketch map by Ant Road Planner. (Color figure online)

Areas suggested by the algorithm to be included in the official path network are marked in red. Colored rectangles denote the locations of agent attraction points.

In order to estimate the precision of predictive simulation, the sections of path layout suggested by the algorithm were compared to the gathered on-site data on the location of desire paths on the territory. Typical examples of non-optimal network areas for which the algorithm suggested creating additional official paths are listed below.

Figure 5a shows a satellite shot and the simulation result for the area between a tram stop and a housing estate (location coordinates: 59.847732, 30.144792). Existing sideways only go along the carriageway and bypass the lawn, which encourages pedestrians to make desire paths. The paths suggested by the algorithm mainly coincide with the existing desire paths. Figure 5b shows a photo of the area between a sideway and a car parking which are separated by a lawn (location coordinates: 59.850742, 30.143564). The algorithm predicted the necessity of creating a path in this place, which is confirmed by on-site research. Figure 5c shows the area near the crossroads (location coordinates: 59.848019, 30.146786). Pedestrians walking from the crossroads towards the housing estate and back also take a shortcut across the lawn because official paths suggest a longer way. In this case the algorithm also correctly predicted the need to improve the connectivity of the attraction points. Finally, Fig. 5d shows an interesting example of a paved path that was not included in the initial design but was created by residents on their own (location coordinates: 59.851035, 30.143597). However, a typical mistake was made by locating the two paths perpendicularly, which resulted in trampling the surrounding area. For this case, the algorithm also predicted the necessity of paving a diagonal path.

(a) The green area between the tram stop and the   (b) The lawn between the sideway and the
     housing estate   parking

  (c) The area near the crossroads   (d) Sideways intersecting at a right angle

Fig. 5. Comparison of areas suggested by the algorithm for improvement of the territory with desire paths existing in the territory (Color figure online)

Thus, using Ant Road Planner when this territory was designed would have helped to avoid lawn trampling in many places when creating an optimal path network, as well as ensure a comfortable pedestrian infrastructure.

In addition, Ant Road Planner was used in experiments in estimating the optimality of pedestrian networks, not only in residential areas but also in parks. The algorithm also demonstrated high prediction accuracy and was adopted for experimental operation by the city administration in order to estimate the optimality of pedestrian networks planned within green area creation and renovation projects.

5   Conclusions and Future Work

Computer modeling of path networks helps avoid design errors and ensure a comfortable pedestrian infrastructure. Ant Road Planner demonstrated good results and high modeling accuracy when tested on numerous real territories. Pedestrian networks designed on the basis of its results have the highest connectivity of attraction points while maintaining the lowest possible total length of the paths and taking into account pedestrians' behavior as they move across the territory. Ant Road Planner open-source web-interface can be used by urban planners even now to design pedestrian infrastructure while considering pedestrians' demands, eliminating labor-efficient manual calculations and minimizing time costs for on-site research. Current drawbacks of the algorithm, such as presence of empirically fitted coefficients and disregarding certain environment factors, will be eliminated as part of the follow-up study by conducting on-site experiments and more detailed analysis of factors affecting pedestrians' behavior as they move across urban territories. For example, the decision making mechanism when a pedestrian chooses a desire path instead of an official one, the dependency between pedestrians' behavior and the weather, the type of surface, the time of day, and illumination need to be refined, as well as study of lawn trampledness and greenery regrowth at the sites of desire paths.

The updated method which makes it possible to suggest optimal path networks for real urban territories with numerous obstacles featuring ultimate accuracy and a user-friendly interface can be widely adopted in design and engineering activities and used to develop plans for improvement and creation of urban territories that will be comfortable for the people.

References

1. Kumar, A.: A systems approach to assess and improve the last-mile access to mass transits, p. 89. Department of Industrial and Systems Engineering, National University of Singapore (2015)
2. Mudron, I., Pachta, M.: Pedestrian network design and optimisation based on pedestrian shortcuts and needs. In: GIS Ostrava 2013 – Geoinformatics for City Transformation Proceedings, pp. 175–184, Ostrava (2013)
3. Vahidi, H., Yan, W.: How is an informal transport infrastructure system formed? Towards a spatially explicit conceptual model. Open Geosp. Data Softw. Stand. 1, 8 (2016)

4. Al-Widyan, F., Al-Ani, A., Kirchner, N., Zeibots, M.: An effort-based evaluation of pedestrian route choice. Sci. Res. Essays **12**(4), 42–50 (2017)
5. Okazaki, S., Matsushita, S.: A study of simulation model for pedestrian movement with evacuation and queuing. In: Proceedings of the International Conference on Engineering for Crowd Safety, pp. 271–280 (1993)
6. Helbing, D., Molnár, P.: Social force model for pedestrian dynamics. Phys. Rev. E **51**(5), 4282–4286 (1995)
7. Weifeng, F., Lizhong, Y., Weicheng, F.: Simulation of bi-direction pedestrian movement using a cellular automata model. Phys. A: Stat. Mech. Appl. **321**(3), 633–640 (2003)
8. Helbing, D., Keltsch, J., Molnar, P.: Modelling the evolution of human trail systems. Nature **388**(6637), 47–50 (1997)
9. Girdhar, A., Antonaglia, J.: Investigation of trail formation with the active walker model. Atomic-Scale Simulations (2013)
10. The Central Research and Project Institute for Urban Planning: Guidelines for Pedestrian Network Design, Moscow (1989)
11. Romm, A.P.: Pedestrian networks. Academia Archit. Constr. **2**, 45–49 (2006)
12. Dorigo, M., Stützle, T.: Ant colony optimization: overview and recent advances. In: Gendreau, M., Potvin, J.Y. (eds.) Handbook of Metaheuristics. ISOR, vol. 146, pp. 227–263. Springer, Boston (2010). https://doi.org/10.1007/978-1-4419-1665-5_8
13. Smirnov, E., Gurevich, M.: Ant Road Planner – Pedestrian simulator webpage. http://antroadplanner.ru/editor/editor. Accessed 09 Apr 2018
14. Nitzsche, C.: Cellular automata modeling for pedestrian dynamics. Bachelor thesis (2013)
15. Keizer, K., Lindenberg, S., Steg, L.: The spreading of disorder. Science **322**(5908), 1681–1685 (2008)

Multiagent Context-Dependent Model of Opinion Dynamics in a Virtual Society

Ivan Derevitskii[✉], Oksana Severiukhina, Klavdiya Bochenina,
Daniil Voloshin, Anastasia Lantseva, and Alexander Boukhanovsky

ITMO University, Saint Petersburg, Russia
iderevitskiy@gmail.com, oseveryukhina@gmail.com,
k.bochenina@gmail.com, achoched@gmail.com,
a.a.lantseva@gmail.com, Boukhanovsky@mail.ifmo.ru

Abstract. To describe the diversity of opinions and dynamics of their changes in a society, there exist different approaches—from macroscopic laws of political processes to individual-based cognition and perception models. In this paper, we propose mesoscopic individual-based model of opinion dynamics which tackles the role of context by considering influence of different sources of information during life cycle of agents. The model combines several sub-models such as model of generation and broadcasting of messages by mass media, model of daily activity, contact model based on multiplex network and model of information processing. To show the applicability of the approach, we present two scenarios illustrating the effect of the conflicting strategies of informational influence on a population and polarization of opinions about topical subject.

Keywords: Context-dependent modeling · Multiagent modeling
Opinion dynamics · Virtual society

1 Introduction

Modeling of evolving human opinions can be used for a deep understanding and influence on the processes of dissemination of information about publicly significant events and topics. Models of the opinions dynamics imitate the dissemination of information about political companies [1] and entertaining content [2], the interaction of agents in social networks [3] and training online communities [4].

Wide variety of models that are used to study opinion dynamics can be divided into three different levels: (i) macromodels, reflecting the longitudinal dynamics of public sentiment at the level of the entire population and its strata, (ii) mesomodels, capturing interactions between individuals via network-based or multiagent approach, and (iii) micromodels, describing decision-making process of an individual. However, at the moment there is a lack of models, linking the different levels (i.e. society, communities and individuals) in frames of a holistic system. In this study, we address the problem of modeling the opinion dynamics from a perspective of emergence, dissemination and influence of information processes in a virtual society. Here and further by virtual society we mean a simplified digital image of a society aimed to represent its main entities and interactions between them.

© Springer International Publishing AG, part of Springer Nature 2018
Y. Shi et al. (Eds.): ICCS 2018, LNCS 10861, pp. 142–155, 2018.
https://doi.org/10.1007/978-3-319-93701-4_11

We consider aggregated opinion dynamics at the population level as the result of informational influence at the micro-level. Linking of micro- and macro-levels takes place in a mesoscopic context-dependent model (Edmonds in his recent study [5] underlines that accounting context in social sciences is a way to integrate qualitative and quantitative models, and to understand emergent social processes while combining formal and data-driven approaches). In frames of this study, a time-aware context binds together agents, information channels and information messages, thereby determining conditions of information spread. Another important implication of using contexts is an opportunity to account for different types of behavior and reactions in different situations. Examples of contexts in a virtual society are social network (or even particular page in it) and household.

Proposed mesoscopic model presents several mechanisms of tackling the contexts: (i) individual model of context switching sets daily schedule of online and offline contexts, (ii) link between two agents (an edge of a complex network) may be activated only if they are in the same context, (iii) agents have context-dependent memory and patterns of behavior including rules of choice of information channels within the context. Simulation of peer-to-peer interaction together with influence of one-to-many information channels (e.g. mass media or opinion leaders) allows to explore the aggregated dynamics of a virtual society for predefined types and preferences of agents and scenarios of population-level informational influence.

The rest of the paper is organized as follows. Section 2 presents a brief overview of related works. Section 3 describes main entities of the proposed model, their evolution laws and the relationships between them. Section 4 provides the results and interpretation of two simulated illustrative scenarios ("Information war" and "Opinion on the hot topic"). Finally, Sect. 5 discusses the borders of applicability of proposed model and further research directions.

2 Related Works

Agent-based approaches for modeling of opinion dynamics can be classified according to several distinctive features: way of presenting opinion and modeling process (discrete, continuous), rules for changing opinions (homogeneous or heterogeneous parameters of agents, the influence of agents' views on each other, various constraints on interactions, etc.), way of representing a network and interaction of agents, type of information to be disseminated.

Discrete opinion models allow to investigate areas where one of the possible solutions must be taken, for instance, a binary view (yes or no) or a range of values, like in [6, 7]. However, such models do not allow investigating processes related to negotiation problems or fuzzy attitudes. This drawback can be eliminated using continuous models. Lorenz [8] points out that domain of continuous opinion dynamics models covers decision of multiple types of task consensus, information spread, influence etc. In addition, the variables giving the opinion can be changed continuously (see, e.g. [9]). In this paper, Martins investigates continuous opinion models based on the interaction of simplified agents. Author compares the results of the application of

Bayesian updating rules to estimating certainty about the value of a continuous variable (representing their opinion for a given topic) to confidence interval-based approaches.

One of the prime questions that is being answered in the field of opinion dynamic is how actors (or agents, which is a common term for modeling research) change their opinion through interactions. Classical opinion models operate with static rules which are universal for all the agents. To take into consideration different types of behavior, there have been carried out attempts of introducing heterogeneous rules of opinion change. For instance, the work of Salzarulo [10] seeks to improve the model known as social judgement, previously introduced by Jager and Amblard [11], which assigns constant rejection/agreement rates for interaction of agents. Salzarulo's model of meta-contrast incorporates the self-categorization theory to provide the formalization of the embeddedness of the opinion update rules in the context of interaction. In addition, there are studies devoted to the fact that agents can interact with each other if they have close opinion about problem under consideration (for example, in work of Lorenz [8]). In the paper [12], authors suggest an approach to the formation of communities where the agents are grouped together with a similar opinion and can sever ties with agents if their opinion is very different.

Characteristics of the network that binds agents together socially (when the network describes the structure of sustained relations between agents) or communicatively (through recurring or single-time acts of information exchange) are extensively studied in the works dedicated to opinion modeling. For instance, in [13] authors suggest that there is a randomness threshold that leads to convergence to central opinion which is in line with Salzarulo [10] who additionally assumes that non-random small-world networks can produce extreme opinions. Further, Grabowski and Kosiński [14] highlight the role of critical phenomena in opinion dynamics. Two major factors contributing to these are the influence of mass media and the global context of interaction. Other studies connect the evolution of the opinions with the evolution of the networks representing relations between agents. For instance, in [15] authors conclude that at different scales, given the dynamic nature of social relationships, the strategies for active opinion propagation undertaken by a group shall be diverse as to gain support yet maintain integrity.

What distinguishes our work from the majority of research articles on opinion dynamics is that though it operates with networks and mechanisms of their construction, it as well looks into the diversity of the types of users and the features of how information can be obtained by users using the context change.

3 Model Description

3.1 Model Entities

Proposed model of information spreading in a society describes the change in the attitude of agents to entities (other agents, opinion leaders), information channels (media), and information sources. We assume that each agent is characterized with a set of constant social values which determines the attitude to other entities. In other words, each agent has a position (represented as vector) in a space of social values, and the distance is this space between two entities influences their opinion about each other. An agent shares the position with members of his or her social group. A position on an agent is assumed to be fixed, but an agent can change his vision of social values of other entities according to a received information messages (IMs). This results in changing the distance between entities.

Formally, an agent as a member of a social group is represented by a tuple $A = (V, Y, M, G, C(G))$ where V is a vector encoding the position in the space of social values (each element of V ranges from -1 to 1), Y is a set of vectors with current positions of other entities, M is the set of IMs stored in memory, G is the social group to which the agent belongs, $C(G)$ is a schedule of context switching that depends on the agent's social group.

Agents receive information messages during peer-to-peer interaction or passive perception in 'one-to-all' (e.g. media broadcasting) cases. The information messages (IM) are transmitted using information channels and are represented by the tuple $IM = (s, r, q, x, y, b, c)$ where s is a source, r is a receiver, q is a topic (it denotes a unique event to be discussed and serves as a unique id for a group of messages), x denotes who expresses the relation (the message generator), y - to whom the relation is expressed (the subject), $b \in [-1, 1]$ - evaluation of the subject, $c \in [0, 1]$ - credibility of IM. A subject and a topic also have their positions in a space of social values. Received information messages change agents' opinion. Evolution of opinion for an agent on the subject is then simulated by a long-term model of information processing. This model calculates the result of informational influence taking into consideration memory of an agent (e.g. history of interaction with an information source, current positions of other entities in a place of social values).

The model of society imitates the process of information exchange in a population on a range of topics. The model is based on a simplification that the person (the agent in the model) receives information messages from two sources: the media (mass media) and other people. We also assume that there is special type of agents called opinion leaders whose aim is to disseminate their opinion within a population. The opinion leaders may use broadcasting facilities of mass media and may prefer different contexts and schedules of working with audience. Agents constituting the audience of mass media also have own preferences of information sources and context switching. Thus, a model of society includes two sub-models: (i) the model of interaction of opinion leaders with media (and thus with the audience of media), and (ii) the model of context switching which regulates interaction of agents with media and peer-to-peer interactions of agents. Here a context binds together sources and receivers of information messages in a timely manner.

3.2 The "Opinion Leader-Media" Model

The "Opinion leader (OL)-Media" model determines conditions of generation and transfer of information messages from the OL to agents through the media. Each OL in the model has a schedule that characterizes the frequency and the type of messages transmitted to each media in model. The media is an entity that receives, transforms, stores and transmits information messages to an agent. At each iteration, OL can broadcast a message to one of the media. Then the message is filtered and stored in the media memory (interaction is based on [17]). After that, the agent in a suitable context ("Media context" and "Online media context", depending on the type of media) receives all IM stored in the media memory. The memory of each media is updated every few days.

An example of the interaction scheme of an agent with OL is shown in Fig. 1. The scheme uses the following notation: *IM* - information message; *L(IM)* - leader's information message; *F_np* - newspaper filter; *F_tv* - TV filter; *F_on* - online media filter.

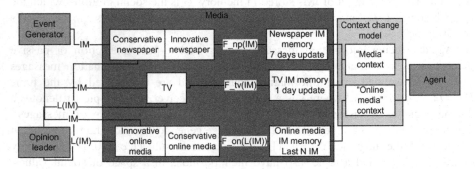

Fig. 1. Media-agent interaction scheme

After getting into the media, the information message is transformed in accordance with the filtering model (if a source of information is considered as unreliable, a media may replace the attitude with its own position), which based on [9]:

$$F(IM(T)) = d\frac{IM(T) + P(T)}{2} + (1 - d)P(T), \qquad (1)$$

where *F(IM (T))* is an opinion after filtering, *IM(T)* is an opinion encoded in initial information message, *P* is an opinion of the media about topic *T*, *d* is the degree of confidence in the source. In the tuple, only one parameter changes after filtering - an opinion on the topic. If the value of the expression is greater than 1 (modulus), it is considered equal to ±1.

3.3   The "Agent-Agent" Model

Circulation of information messages between agents is regulated by: (i) the model of context switching (a context determines occupation of an agent at a given time, for example, sleep or work), and (ii) the contact network of agents, which determines the interaction of agents within the same context (for example, agents can send messages to each other if there is a working contact between them, and they are simultaneously in the context of "communication with colleagues").

As mentioned above, each agent has a G - social group, and C(G) denotes a schedule of contexts that depend on a social group. A context is an element from the set of all contexts available for a modeling scenario, meaning the current occupation of an agent. Within the scenarios presented in the work, contexts that include "communication" are significant (agents in them can exchange messages within the "Agent-Agent" model), as well as the "media" context (receiving messages in the "Opinion Leader-Media model"). The schedule of context switching $C(G)$ is a set of triples (time of beginning, time of end, type of context). The schedule must cover the entire simulation time.

For an exchange of messages between two agents, three conditions must be met. First, the agent should be in a context suitable for exchanging messages with other agents. Secondly, the agent must be connected by a special type of edge in the contact network graph with another agent in the same context. And third, there should be messages for exchange in the memory of agent.

A contact network is created at the beginning of the simulation, and is an undirected graph without self-loops. The edges of the graph are divided into 3 categories: friends, family, colleagues/classmates (thus, in fact this network is a multiplex).

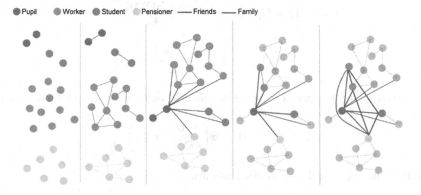

Fig. 2. Stages of generation of the contact network

The procedure of generating a contact network consists of four steps. The first stage is the assignment of the age category and social group to each agent. Then, edges are randomly generated within the members of social groups, as well as the types of these edges. The third stage of network generation is the creation of "family" edges. For each of the members of a fixed social group, edges are created with members of the other social groups. The types of edges are assigned randomly. Then, "family ties" can occur between the "family" edges agents associated with the agents of different social groups. The last stage is the creation of friendly relations between the representatives of other social groups. Figure 2 shows all the steps described.

When the agent is in a fitting context (one of the communication contexts, for example, "communication with family"), and there are agents suitable for sending messages, a pair of agents for communication are randomly chosen. After this, we randomly select the agent-sender, which transmits to the other agent a random message from a fixed number of the last.

The agent's opinion about other entities of the model (agents, and opinion leaders) is formed based on distance in the space of social values (SV). Values are the moral foundations that people rely on to form an attitude towards other entities. The mechanism for changing attitudes to other entities is described in detail in the section "The long-term behavior model". The vector of social values is a vector of the dimension of the number of social values, with values from the interval $[-1; 1]$. Each value corresponds to the ratio of the agent to the SV from -1 (sharply negative) to 1 (sharply positive).

3.4   The Long-Term Behavior Model

This model runs to recalculate the values of fields of long-term memory of agent after each context change. Using a set of IMs obtained within the context, the long-term behavior model updates the values of the relation to other entities ($\varphi_k(t)$ - the relation to the k-th entity), opinion about the relation of other entities to social values ($\gamma_k(t)$ - the relation of k-th entity to one of possible social values).

The updated opinion on the newsbreaks is calculated by the following formulas:

$$O_\chi(t+1) = O_\chi(t) + \alpha \frac{\sum_{k=1}^{K_\chi} b_{\chi k} c_{\chi k} v_k (\varphi/2 + 1)}{K_\chi} \tag{2}$$

$$|O_\chi(t+1)| \leq \frac{\sum_k |v_k|}{M} \tag{3}$$

Then the values for representing social values of other entities must be recalculated:

$$\gamma_k(t+1) = \gamma_k(t) + \alpha \left(\frac{\sum b}{K} - \gamma_k(t) \right) \frac{\sum c}{K} \tag{4}$$

as well as the agent's relation to other entities:

$$\varphi_k = 1 - \frac{d(v, \gamma_k)}{\sqrt{M}}, \tag{5}$$

where K is the number of messages, b and c are the values of the evaluation and credibility in the messages, M is the number of social values, α is the rigidity coefficient, and $d(v, \gamma_k)$ is the Euclidean distance between the vectors.

3.5   Simulation Cycle

Figure 3 shows the scheme of simulation cycle. At the beginning of the simulation, basic parameters and components are initialized, such as the contact network, the context change model, the agents' relation to entities and social values. In addition, the identity of each agent is initialized to one of the social groups. Belonging to the social group is used in the initialization of the degree of radicalism of the agent. Then, a simulation run is started, consisting in the sequential execution of an iterative procedure, which includes the following steps: generating messages and storing them in the media memory; updating the current context of each agent; receiving messages from media memory by agents in suitable contexts; sharing of messages between agents; recalculation of the attitude of agents to the entities of the model; collection of statistics of the model.

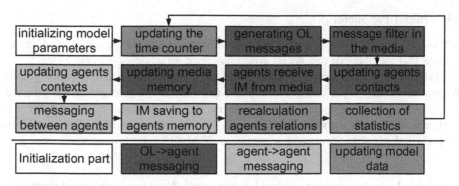

Fig. 3. Scheme of simulation cycle

4 Experimental Study

Proposed model is complex in a sense that it describes different types of entities (each one with built-in sub-models of external activity and opinion dynamics) and relationships between them (via contexts and networks). To use this framework, one needs to specify the input parameters of models, and the rules of evolution of parameters for a given input. The experimental study presented further was aimed to validate the proposed way of combining the models by considering simple scenarios of informational influence. These scenarios were constructed in a way allowing interpretable and predictable results of a given strategy of influence on the population. Thus, it becomes possible to compare the results from our model with predicted output. By doing so, we show that proposed mesoscopic model may reproduce the results on a macro level by aggregating the results of a micro-level. The program was implemented using Python programming language. The computation time for the scenario "Information war" (for three months, 1000 agents) is 170 s.

Table 1. Basic schedule of context switching for different social groups (an example).

	Pupils	Students	Workers	Pensioners
8:00–9:00	Internet Media			Communication with family
9:00–12:00	Study		Work	Rest
12:00–13:00	Communication with one-grader/classmates/colleagues			Communication with friends
13:00–14:00	Study			Rest
14:00–15:00	Way home			Personal business
15:00–16:00	Communication with friends			Communication with friends
16:00–18:00	Hobby			
18:00–19:00	Communication with family			
19:00–21:00	Media			
21:00–8:00	Sleep			

4.1   Initial Parameters

We use the assumption that the agent has an identical schedule every day. Also, we assume that members of one social group have one schedule.

Table 1 shows the schedules of contexts for members of different social groups. Within the scenarios presented in the work, there are four social groups: pupils, students, workers and pensioners. Table 2 presents data on the statistics of the number of connections between agents of different age (and social groups) based on data from [18]. Casual edges are generated according to Table 2.

Table 2. Average number of edges between agents, depending on the social group.

	Share of total agents	Pupil	Student	Worker	Pensioner
Pupil (15–18)	10%	6.39	2.02	3.62	0.49
Student (19–24)	10%	1.67	4.40	5.2	0.57
Worker (25–59)	50%	0.7	0.97	6.72	1.88
Pensioner (60+)	30%	0.37	0.61	3.47	3.09

Table 3. Edges type for social groups.

	Friend edge	Colleagues and etc. edge	Family edge
Pupil–pupil	0.2	0.8	0
Student–student	0.2	0.8	0
Worker–worker	0.2	0.7	0.1
Pensioner–pensioner	1	0	0
Other types	0.2	0.7	0.1

The types of edges are assigned in accordance with Table 3, that indicates the probabilities of assigning a specific type of edge to the rib, depending on the social groups of agents. The number of recent messages from which the message is selected for transmission in these scenarios is five.

Social Values Initialization

Social values (within the framework of the scenarios presented in the work) are: justice, freedom, conformism, progress, traditional values. We use values based on work [19].

The vector of social values of the agent is initialized at the beginning of modeling and does not change in its process. The initialization algorithm consists of three steps. The first step is to randomly assign to the agent the direction of the views: "innovator" or "conservator". Then, depending on the direction of the views, the agent is given a degree of radicalism (according to Fig. 4a and b). The vector of social values is calculated in accordance with Fig. 4 (bottom), depending on the degree of radicalism.

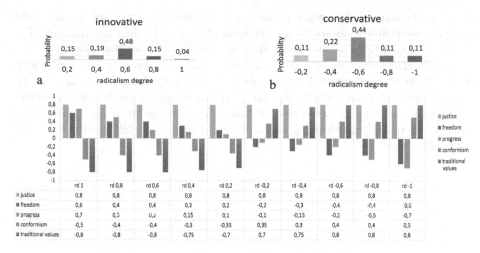

Fig. 4. Data for the initialization of social values

4.2 Scenario "Information War"

We developed the scenario "Information war" with the aim to investigate the dynamics of opinions about opinion leaders with different social values (in this case, conservative and innovative). We simulate the translation of leaders' attitudes toward social values (stage one), the conservative leader's broadcast of disinformation about the innovative leader (stage two), and the "exposure" of the conservative leader (stage three). In the scenario, we simulate the broadcasting by the two opinion leaders ("Conservator" and "Innovator") of their attitude to social values and change of opinions about these leaders in society.

The model simulates the work of five media: "Innovative Newspaper", "Conservative Newspaper", "Innovative Internet Media", "Conservative Internet Media", "TV". To identify the intensity of the appearance of opinion leaders in these media, we collected the data on the speeches of Russian politicians in five Russian media.[1]

The scenario consists of 3 stages (each with 30 model days). At the first stage, each of the opinion leaders broadcasts through the media their attitude to random SV. At the second stage, with an intensity of once every 1.5 h, the casual media receives reports of the leader-innovator's negative attitude to the values "freedom" and "progress."

In the third stage, with an intensity of once every 1.5 h, messages are sent to the random media that refute the reports of the second stage. With the same intensity, reports are received about the negative attitude of the leader-conservative to the SC "justice". The script was launched for 1000 agents and 90 days of modeling time. In this scenario, a simplification is used, which is that the trust of all agents to both opinion leaders is equal to 1.

Figure 5 shows the graphs of the change in attitude towards the conservative (Fig. 5a) and innovative (Fig. 5b) opinion leaders. As can be seen from Fig. 5a, at the

---

[1] kremlin.ru; www.spb.kp.ru; navalny.com; tvrain.ru; www.1tv.ru.

first stage the attitude of innovator agents to the Leader-Innovator improves, and to the Leader-Conservative worsens, as reports about their social values are received. The attitude of conservative agents during the first stage varies in the opposite way.

At the second stage, the attitude towards the Leader-Conservative does not change (in the absence of messages). The relationship to the Leader-Innovator changes in the opposite (in comparison with the first stage) because the messages themselves contain the opposite meaning. In the third stage, the ratio of all agents to the Conservative Agent is significantly deteriorating, due to the good opinion of each agent to the social value of "justice."

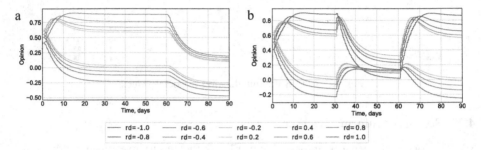

Fig. 5. Opinion about two OL depending on the degree of radicality: (a) - conservative, (b) - innovative; "rd" in legend - radicalism degree

4.3   Scenario "Opinion on the Hot Topic"

This experiment was aimed to study change of opinions about the topics and the people involved in spreading the information. The purpose of this scenario is to show the process of opinion's polarization in society regarding to hot topics.

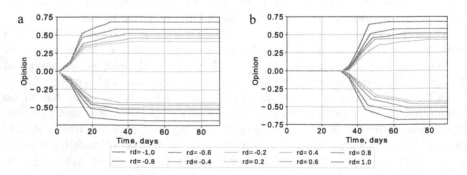

Fig. 6. Opinion about two topics depending on the degree of radicality: (a) - conservative, (b) - innovative; "rd" in legend - radicalism degree (Color figure online)

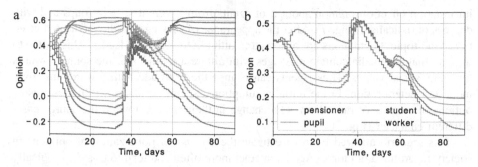

Fig. 7. Opinion about the source of information, depending on: (a) the degree of radicalism, (b) - the social group (Color figure online)

This scenario has all the same assumptions about entities and social values as in the previous scenario. Model describes the behavior of 1000 agents and the source of information (e.g. government) that creates the messages related to social values about two topics: conservative and innovative. For conservative topic IMs contain negative attitude towards freedom/progress and positive towards traditional values/conformism. In contrast, for innovative topic IMs contain positive attitude towards freedom/progress and negative towards traditional values/conformism. Messages are broadcasted through the media. We assume that conservatives are more likely to trust conservative media and agents with similar SVs (same for innovators). Therefore, innovators read innovative media, conservatives are conservative (newspaper and Internet-media).

The scenario was simulated within 90 days. The first 30 days of the entity broadcast through the media conservative topics, the following days - innovative. Thus, after 30 days, the messages regarding to first topics are gradually replaced by messages dedicated to the second one (Fig. 8).

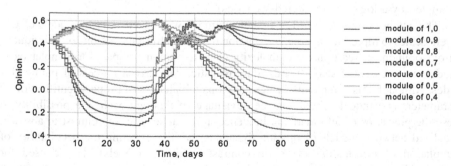

Fig. 8. Influence of the radicality of the assessment in information messages (Color figure online)

Figure 6 shows the peculiarity of the influence on the formation time of opinions in different groups. On all the charts of color denotes radicalism degree from innovative (red color) to the conservative (blue color). The messages generated by the source of information effect on opinion about it of agents from different social groups and with degrees of radicalism (Fig. 7). After the appearance of messages in the media dedicated to second topic, fluctuations are observed in attitude towards the leader. This is due to the fact that the media contain messages with different attitudes of the source towards the same social values. Thus, agents can change their attitude both towards improvement and deterioration. In the initial assumptions, social groups have different distributions of degrees of radicalism, so a change in their attitude toward the source has a different character (Fig. 7b).

This scenario allowed us to investigate the process of polarization of opinions in society regarding a hot topic. Agents interact more often and tend to trust ideologically "close" media (conservatives read conservative media, innovators read innovative), so there is a polarization effect and a change in the attitude to the leader when he discusses different topics.

5 Conclusion and Future Works

In this paper, we propose a multiagent context-dependent model of the dynamics of opinions based on distance in the space of social values. The model includes message exchange between agents based on varying contexts and a multiplex contact network, as well as a model for transmitting the information via the media. In addition, a long-term information processing model is proposed that regulates the effect of the received message on the agent's opinion. Experimental study demonstrates expressive abilities of a model in two scenarios: "Information war" and "Opinion on the hot topics" illustrating the effect of the conflicting strategies of informational influence on a population and polarization of opinions about topical subject. For these synthetic scenarios, parameters of a model were identified partially based on the evidence from a published literature, partially from the observed data. The results of experiments show that the model reproduces the expected dynamics of opinions (which is implicitly prompted by a logic of considered scenarios).

This study is mostly aimed at demonstrating a way of combining models of different scales to reproduce aggregated opinion dynamics from the actions of individuals. In our opinion, increase in the complexity of this solution compared to simpler basic models is an essential step towards more realistic, data-driven models of public attitudes. Although this complexity brings additional challenges of proper identification of parameters and model calibration, the advantage of this approach is a possibility to describe processes of informational influence in a real society (in contrast to abstract, idealized network models of opinion dynamics) while respecting the peculiarities of circulation of information flows (in contrast to macro models). To be used for real-world scenarios, the model has to be supplemented with a calibration tool which allows to choose the optimal implementation of sub-models (e.g. model of opinion update) and to tune sub-models according to an observable data (from social networks and traditional mass-media to the sociological surveys).

Acknowledgments. This research was supported by The Russian Scientific Foundation, Agreement #14-21-00137-II (02.05.2017).

References

1. Gatti, M., Cavalin, P., Neto, S.B., Pinhanez, C., dos Santos, C., Gribel, D., Appel, A.P.: Large-scale multi-agent-based modeling and simulation of microblogging-based online social network. In: Alam, S.J., Parunak, H. (eds.) MABS 2013. LNCS, vol. 8235, pp. 17–33. Springer, Heidelberg (2014). https://doi.org/10.1007/978-3-642-54783-6_2
2. Ryczko, K., Domurad, A., Buhagiar, N., Tamblyn, I.: Hashkat: large-scale simulations of online social networks. Soc. Netw. Anal. Min. **7**, 4 (2017)
3. Peng, W., Shuang, Y., Jingjing, Z., Qingning, G.: Agent-based modeling and simulation of evolution of netizen crowd behavior in unexpected events public opinion. Data Anal. Knowl. Discov. **31**, 65–72 (2015)
4. Zhang, Y., Tanniru, M.: An agent-based approach to study virtual learning communities. In: Proceedings of the 38th Annual Hawaii International Conference on System Sciences, HICSS 2005, p. 11c (2005)
5. Edmonds, B.: The room around the elephant: tackling context-dependency in the social sciences. In: Johnson, J., Nowak, A., Ormerod, P., Rosewell, B., Zhang, Y.-C. (eds.) Non-Equilibrium Social Science and Policy. UCS, pp. 195–208. Springer, Cham (2017). https://doi.org/10.1007/978-3-319-42424-8_13
6. Hu, H.-B., Wang, X.-F.: Discrete opinion dynamics on networks based on social influence. J. Phys. A Math. Theoret. **42**, 225005 (2009). https://doi.org/10.1088/1751-8113/42/22/225005
7. Yildiz, E., Acemoglu, D., Ozdaglar, A., Saberi, A., Scaglione, A.: Discrete Opinion Dynamics with Stubborn Agents*
8. Lorenz, J.: Continuous opinion dynamics under bounded confidence: a survey. Int. J. Mod. Phys. C **18**, 1819–1838 (2007)
9. Martins, A.C.R.: Bayesian updating rules in continuous opinion dynamics models. J. Stat. Mech.: Theory Exp. **2009**, P02017 (2009)
10. Salzarulo, L.: A continuous opinion dynamics model based on the principle of meta-contrast. J. Artif. Soc. Soc. Simul. **9** (2006)
11. Jager, W., Amblard, F.: Uniformity, bipolarization and pluriformity captured as generic stylized behavior with an agent-based simulation model of attitude change. Comput. Math. Organ. Theory **10**, 295–303 (2005)
12. Yu, Y., Xiao, G., Li, G., Tay, W.P., Teoh, H.F.: Opinion diversity and community formation in adaptive networks. Chaos Interdisc. J. Nonlinear Sci. **27**, 103115 (2017)
13. Amblard, F., Deffuant, G.: The role of network topology on extremism propagation with the relative agreement opinion dynamics. Phys. A Stat. Mech. Appl. **343**, 725–738 (2004)
14. Grabowski, A., Kosiński, R.A.: Ising-based model of opinion formation in a complex network of interpersonal interactions. Phys. A Stat. Mech. Appl. **361**, 651–664 (2006)
15. Benczik, I.J., Benczik, S.Z., Schmittmann, B., Zia, R.K.P.: Opinion dynamics on an adaptive random network. Phys. Rev. E **79**, 46104 (2009)
16. Leifeld, P.: Polarization of coalitions in an agent-based model of political discourse. Comput. Soc. Netw. **1**, 7 (2014)
17. Sobkowicz, P.: Opinion dynamics model based on cognitive biases. arXiv Preprint arXiv1703.01501 (2017)
18. Mossong, J., Hens, N., Jit, M., Beutels, P., Auranen, K., Mikolajczyk, R., Massari, M., Salmaso, S., Tomba, G.S., Wallinga, J., et al.: Social contacts and mixing patterns relevant to the spread of infectious diseases. PLoS Med. **5**, e74 (2008)
19. Graham, J., Haidt, J., Nosek, B.A.: Liberals and conservatives rely on different sets of moral foundations. J. Pers. Soc. Psychol. **96**, 1029 (2009)

An Algorithm for Tensor Product Approximation of Three-Dimensional Material Data for Implicit Dynamics Simulations

Krzysztof Podsiadło, Marcin Łoś, Leszek Siwik[✉], and Maciej Woźniak

AGH University of Science and Technology, Krakow, Poland
{podsiadlo,los,siwik,wozniak}@agh.edu.pl

Abstract. In the paper, a heuristic algorithm for tensor product approximation with B-spline basis functions of three-dimensional material data is presented. The algorithm has an application as a preconditioner for implicit dynamics simulations of a non-linear flow in heterogeneous media using alternating directions method. As the simulation use-case, a non-stationary problem of liquid fossil fuels exploration with hydraulic fracturing is considered. Presented algorithm allows to approximate the permeability coefficient function as a tensor product what in turn allows for implicit simulations of the Laplacian term in the partial differential equation. In the consequence the number of time steps of the non-stationary problem can be reduced, while the numerical accuracy is preserved.

1 Introduction

The alternating direction solver [1,2] has been recently applied for numerical simulations of non-linear flow in heterogeneous media using the explicit dynamics [3,4].

The problem of extraction of liquid fossil fuels with hydraulic fracturing technique has been considered there. During the simulation two (contradictory) goals i.e., the maximization of the fuel extraction and the minimization of the ground water contamination have been considered [4,14]. The numerical simulations considered there are performed using the explicit dynamics with B-spline basis functions from isogeometric analysis [5] for approximation of the solution [6,7]. The resulting computational cost of a single time step is linear, however the number of time steps is large due to the Courant-Fredrichs-Lewy (CFL) condition [8]. In other words, the number of time steps grows along with the mesh dimensions.

Our ultimate goal is to extend our simulator for implicit dynamics case, following the idea of the implicit dynamics isogeometric solver proposed in [9]. The problem is that the extension is possible only if the permeability coefficients of the elliptic operator are expressed as the tensor product structure. Thus, we

© Springer International Publishing AG, part of Springer Nature 2018
Y. Shi et al. (Eds.): ICCS 2018, LNCS 10861, pp. 156–168, 2018.
https://doi.org/10.1007/978-3-319-93701-4_12

focus on the algorithm approximating the permeability coefficients with tensor products iteratively.

The algorithm is designed to be a preconditioner for the implicit dynamics solver. With such the preconditioner the number of time steps of the non-stationary problem can be reduced, while the numerical accuracy preserved.

Our method presented in this paper is an alternative for other methods available for approximating coefficients of the model, e.g., adaptive cross approximation [15].

2   Explicit and Implicit Dynamics Simulations

Following the model of the non-linear flow in heterogeneous media presented in [1] we start with our explicit dynamics formulation of the problem of non-linear flow in heterogeneous media where we seek for the pressure scalar field u:

$$\left(\frac{\partial u(x,y,z)}{\partial t}, v(x,y,z)\right) = \left(\left(K(x,y,z)e^{\mu u(x,y,z)}\right)\nabla u(x,y,z), \nabla v(x,y,z)\right)$$
$$+ \left(f(x,y,z), v(x,y,z)\right) \quad \forall v \in V \tag{1}$$

Here μ stands for the dynamic permeability constant, $K(x,y,z)$ is a given permeability map, and $f(x,y,z)$ represents sinks and sources of the pressure, modeling pumps and sinks during the exploration process.

The model of non-linear flow in heterogeneous media is called exponential model [12] and is taken from [10,11].

In the model, the permeability consists of two parts, i.e., the static one depending on the terrain properties, and the dynamic one reflecting the influence of the actual pressure.

The broad range of the variable known as the saturated hydraulic conductivity along with the functional forms presented above, confirm the nonlinear behavior of the process.

The number of time steps of the resulting explicit dynamics simulations are bounded by the CFL condition [8], requesting to reduce the time step size when increasing the mesh size. This is important limitation of the method, and can be overcome by deriving the implicit dynamics solver.

Following the idea of the implicit dynamics solvers presented in [9], we move the operator to the left-hand side:

$$\left(\frac{\partial u}{\partial t}, v\right) - \left(\left(K(x,y,z)e^{\mu u(x,y,z)}\right)\nabla u, \nabla v\right) = (f,v) \quad \forall v \in V, \tag{2}$$

where we skip all arguments but the permeability operator.

In order to proceed with the alternating directions solver, the operator on the left-hand-side needs to be expressed as a tensor product:

$$\left(\frac{\partial u}{\partial t}, v\right) - \left(\left(K(x)e^{\mu \overline{u}(x)}K(y)e^{\mu \overline{u}(y)}K(z)e^{\mu \overline{u}(z)}\right)\nabla u, \nabla v\right) =$$
$$(f,v) + \left(K(x)K(y)K(z)e^{\mu \overline{u}(x)}e^{\mu \overline{u}(y)}e^{\mu \overline{u}(z)} - K(x,y,z)e^{\mu u(x,y,z)}\nabla u, \nabla v\right) \quad \forall v \in V \tag{3}$$

It is possible if we express the static permeability in a tensor product form:

$$K(x, y, z) = K(x)K(y)K(z) \tag{4}$$

using our tensor product approximation algorithm described in Sect. 3.

Additionally, we need to replace the dynamic permeability with an arbitrary selected tensor product representation:

$$u(x, y, z) = \overline{u}(x)\overline{u}(y)\overline{u}(z) \tag{5}$$

It can be done by adding and subtracting from the left and the right hand sides the selected tensor product representation.

One simple way to do that is to compute the average values of u along particular cross-sections, namely using:

$$u(x, y, z) = \sum_{i=1}^{N_x} \left(\sum_{j=1}^{N_y} \left(\sum_{k=1}^{N_z} \left(d_{ijk} B_{i,p}(x) B_{j,p}(y) B_{k,p}(z) \right) \right) \right) \tag{6}$$

so we define:

$$\overline{u}(x) = \sum_{i=1}^{N_x} \overline{u}_i B_{i,p}(x) \tag{7}$$

$$\overline{u}(y) = \sum_{j=1}^{N_y} \overline{u}_j B_{j,p}(y) \tag{8}$$

$$\overline{u}(z) = \sum_{k=1}^{N_z} \overline{u}_k B_{k,p}(z) \tag{9}$$

and

$$\overline{u}_i = \frac{\sum_{j=1}^{N_y} \left(\sum_{k=1}^{N_z} (d_{ijk}) \right)}{N_y N_z}; \quad \overline{u}_j = \frac{\sum_{i=1}^{N_x} \left(\sum_{k=1}^{N_z} (d_{ijk}) \right)}{N_x N_z}; \quad \overline{u}_k = \frac{\sum_{i=1}^{N_x} \left(\sum_{j=1}^{N_y} (d_{ijk}) \right)}{N_x N_y} \tag{10}$$

In other words, we approximate the static permeability and we replace the dynamic permeability.

Finally we introduce the time steps, so we deal with the dynamic permeability explicitly, and with the static permeability implicitly:

$$\left(u_{t+1}, v \right) - \left(\left(K(x)e^{\mu \overline{u}_t(x)} K(y)e^{\mu \overline{u}_t(y)} K(z)e^{\mu \overline{u}_t(z)} \right) \nabla u_{t+1}, \nabla v \right) =$$
$$(f, v) + \left(K(x)K(y)K(z)e^{\mu \overline{u}(x)} e^{\mu \overline{u}(y)} e^{\mu \overline{u}(z)} - K(x, y, z)e^{\mu u_t(xyz)} \nabla u_t, \nabla v \right) \quad \forall v \in V \tag{11}$$

In the following part of the paper the algorithm for expression of an arbitrary material data function as the tensor product of one dimensional functions that can be utilized in the implicit dynamics simulator is presented.

3   Kronecker Product Approximation

As an input of our algorithm we take a scalar function defined over the cube shape three-dimensional domain. We call this function a bitmap, since often the material data is given in a form of a discrete 3D bitmap.

First, we approximate this bitmap with B-spline basis functions using fast, linear computational cost isogeometric L2 projections algorithm.

$$Bitmap(x,y,z) \approx \sum_{i=1}^{N_x} \Big(\sum_{j=1}^{N_y} \Big(\sum_{k=1}^{N_z} \Big(d_{ijk} B_{i,p}(x) B_{j,p}(y) B_{k,p}(z) \Big) \Big) \Big) \qquad (12)$$

Now, our computational problem can be stated as follows:

Problem 1. We seek coefficients $a_1^x, \ldots, a_{N_x}^x, b_1^y, \ldots, b_{N_y}^y, c_1^z, \ldots, c_{N_z}^z$ to get the minimum of

$$F(a_1^x, \ldots, a_{N_x}^x, b_1^y, \ldots, b_{N_y}^y, c_1^z, \ldots, c_{N_z}^z)$$

$$= \int_{\Omega} \Big[\Big(\sum_{i=1}^{N_x} a_i B_{i,p}^x \Big) \Big(\sum_{j=1}^{N_y} b_j B_{j,p}^y \Big) \Big(\sum_{k=1}^{N_z} c_k B_{k,p}^z - \sum_{i=1}^{N_x} \Big(\sum_{j=1}^{N_y} \Big(\sum_{k=1}^{N_z} \big(d_{ijk} B_{i,p}(x) B_{j,p}(y) B_{k,p}(z) \big) \Big) \Big) \Big) \Big]^2$$

$$= \int_{\Omega} \Big[\sum_{i=1}^{N_x} \Big(\sum_{j=1}^{N_y} \Big(\sum_{k=1}^{N_z} \big(a_i b_j c_k - d_{ijk} B_{i,p}(x) B_{j,p}(y) B_{k,p}(z) \big) \Big) \Big) \Big]^2 \qquad (13)$$

The minimum is realized when the partial derivatives are equal to zero:

$$\frac{\partial F}{\partial a_l^x}(a_1^x, \ldots, a_{N_x}^x, b_1^y, \ldots, b_{N_y}^y, c_1^z, \ldots, c_{N_z}^z) = 0 \qquad (14)$$

$$\frac{\partial F}{\partial b_l^y}(a_1^x, \ldots, a_{N_x}^x, b_1^y, \ldots, b_{N_y}^y, c_1^z, \ldots, c_{N_z}^z) = 0 \qquad (15)$$

$$\frac{\partial F}{\partial c_l^z}(a_1^x, \ldots, a_{N_x}^x, b_1^y, \ldots, b_{N_y}^y, c_1^z, \ldots, c_{N_z}^z) = 0 \qquad (16)$$

We compute these partial derivatives:

$$\frac{\partial F}{\partial a_l^x}(a_1^x, \ldots, a_{N_x}^x, b_1^y, \ldots, b_{N_y}^y, c_1^z, \ldots, c_{N_z}^z) = 0$$

$$= \int_{\Omega} \Big[\sum_{j=1}^{N_y} \Big(\sum_{k=1}^{N_z} \big(2(a_l b_j c_k - d_{ljk}) \Big(\frac{\partial (a_i b_j c_k)}{\partial a_l^x} - \frac{\partial (d_{ijk})}{\partial a_l^x} \Big) B_{l,p}^x B_{j,p}^y B_{k,p}^z \big) \Big) \Big] = 0, \qquad (17)$$

where the internal term:

$$\frac{\partial (a_i b_j c_k)}{\partial a_l^x} = \frac{\partial (a_i) b_j c_k}{\partial a_l^x} + a_i \frac{\partial (b_j c_k)}{\partial a_l^x} = b_j c_k \delta_{il} + 0, \qquad (18)$$

thus

$$= \int_\Omega [\sum_{j=1}^{N_y} (\sum_{k=1}^{N_z} (2(a_l b_j c_k - d_{ljk}) b_j c_k B_{l,p}^x B_{j,p}^y B_{k,p}^z)] = 0, \quad l = 1, \dots, N_x \quad (19)$$

Similarly we proceed with the rest of partial derivatives to obtain:

$$= \int_\Omega [\sum_{i=1}^{N_x} (\sum_{k=1}^{N_z} (2(a_i b_l c_k - d_{ilk}) a_i c_k B_{i,p}^x B_{l,p}^y B_{k,p}^z)] = 0, \quad l = 1, \dots, N_y \quad (20)$$

$$= \int_\Omega [\sum_{i=1}^{N_x} (\sum_{j=1}^{N_y} (2(a_i b_j c_l - d_{ijl}) a_i b_j B_{i,p}^x B_{j,p}^y B_{l,p}^z)] = 0, \quad l = 1, \dots, N_z \quad (21)$$

This is equivalent to the following system of equations:

$$\sum_{j=1}^{N_y} (\sum_{k=1}^{N_z} 2(a_l b_j c_k - d_{ljk}) b_j c_k) = 0 \quad (22)$$

$$\sum_{i=1}^{N_x} (\sum_{k=1}^{N_z} 2(a_i b_l c_k - d_{ilk}) a_i c_k) = 0 \quad (23)$$

$$\sum_{i=1}^{N_x} (\sum_{j=1}^{N_y} 2(a_i b_j c_c - d_{ijl}) a_i b_j) = 0 \quad (24)$$

We have just got a non-linear system of $N_x + N_y + N_z$ equations with $N_x + N_y + N_z$ unknowns:

$$a_l (\sum_{j=1}^{N_y} (\sum_{k=1}^{N_z} (b_j c_k) b_j c_k)) = \sum_{j=1}^{N_y} (\sum_{k=1}^{N_z} (d_{ljk} b_j c_k)) \quad (25)$$

$$b_l (\sum_{i=1}^{N_x} (\sum_{k=1}^{N_z} (a_i c_k) a_i c_k)) = \sum_{i=1}^{N_x} (\sum_{k=1}^{N_z} (d_{ilk} a_i c_k)) \quad (26)$$

$$c_l (\sum_{i=1}^{N_x} (\sum_{j=1}^{N_y} (a_i b_j) a_i b_j)) = \sum_{i=1}^{N_x} (\sum_{j=1}^{N_y} (d_{ijl} a_i b_j)), \quad (27)$$

what implies:

$$a_l = \frac{\sum_{j=1}^{N_y} (\sum_{k=1}^{N_z} d_{ljk} b_j c_k)}{\sum_{j=1}^{N_y} (\sum_{k=1}^{N_z} (b_j c_k)^2)} \quad (28)$$

$$b_l = \frac{\sum_{i=1}^{N_x} (\sum_{k=1}^{N_z} d_{ilk} a_i c_k)}{\sum_{i=1}^{N_x} (\sum_{k=1}^{N_z} (a_i c_k)^2)} \quad (29)$$

We insert these coefficients into the third equation:

$$c_l \sum_{i=1}^{N_x} \left(\sum_{j=1}^{N_y} \left(\frac{\sum_{m=1}^{N_y} \left(\sum_{n=1}^{N_z} d_{imn} b_m c_n \right)}{\sum_{m=1}^{N_y} \left(\sum_{n=1}^{N_z} (b_m c_n)^2 \right)} \right)^2 \left(\frac{\sum_{m=1}^{N_x} \left(\sum_{n=1}^{N_z} d_{mjn} a_m c_n \right)}{\sum_{m=1}^{N_x} \left(\sum_{n=1}^{N_z} (a_m c_n)^2 \right)} \right)^2 \right)$$

$$= \sum_{i=1}^{N_x} \left(\sum_{j=1}^{N_y} d_{ijl} \frac{\sum_{m=1}^{N_y} \left(\sum_{n=1}^{N_z} d_{imn} b_m c_n \right)}{\sum_{m=1}^{N_y} \left(\sum_{n=1}^{N_z} (b_m c_n)^2 \right)} \frac{\sum_{m=1}^{N_x} \left(\sum_{n=1}^{N_z} d_{mjn} a_m c_n \right)}{\sum_{m=1}^{N_x} \left(\sum_{n=1}^{N_z} (a_m c_n)^2 \right)} \right)$$

(30)

$$c_l \sum_{i=1}^{N_x} \left(\sum_{j=1}^{N_y} \left(\sum_{m=1}^{N_y} \left(\sum_{n=1}^{N_z} d_{imn} b_m c_n \right) \right) \left(\sum_{m=1}^{N_x} \left(\sum_{n=1}^{N_z} d_{mjn} a_m c_n \right) \right) \right)$$

$$= \sum_{i=1}^{N_x} \left(\sum_{j=1}^{N_y} d_{ijl} \right) \left(\sum_{n=1}^{N_z} \left(\sum_{m=1}^{N_y} (b_m c_n)^2 \right) \right) \left(\sum_{n=1}^{N_z} \left(\sum_{m=1}^{N_x} (a_m c_n)^2 \right) \right)$$

(31)

$$c_l \sum_{i=1}^{N_x} \left(\sum_{j=1}^{N_y} \left(\sum_{n=1}^{N_z} \left(\sum_{m=1}^{N_y} d_{imn} b_m c_n \right) \right) \left(\sum_{n=1}^{N_z} \left(\sum_{m=1}^{N_x} d_{mjn} a_m c_n \right) \right) \right)$$

$$= \sum_{i=1}^{N_x} \left(\sum_{j=1}^{N_y} d_{ijl} \right) \left(\sum_{n=1}^{N_z} \left(\sum_{m=1}^{N_y} (b_m c_n)^2 \right) \right) \left(\sum_{n=1}^{N_z} \left(\sum_{m=1}^{N_x} (a_m c_n)^2 \right) \right)$$

(32)

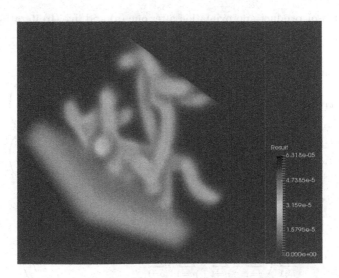

Fig. 1. The original configuration of static permeability

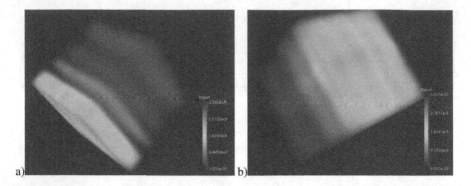

Fig. 2. The result obtained from the heuristic algorithm (a) and from the heuristic plus genetic algorithms (b).

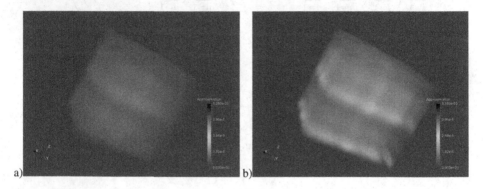

Fig. 3. The tensor product approximation after one (a) and five (b) iterations of Algorithm 1.

$$
c_l \sum_{i=1}^{N_x} \left(\sum_{j=1}^{N_y} \left(\sum_{n=1}^{N_z} \left(\sum_{m=1}^{N_y} d_{imn} b_m c_n \right) \right) \left(\sum_{m=1}^{N_x} d_{mjn} a_m c_n \right) \right)
$$
$$
= \sum_{i=1}^{N_x} \left(\sum_{j=1}^{N_y} d_{ijl} \right) \left(\sum_{m=1}^{N_y} (b_m c_n)^2 \right) \left(\sum_{n=1}^{N_z} \left(\sum_{m=1}^{N_x} (a_m c_n)^2 \right) \right)
\tag{33}
$$

$$
\sum_{i=1}^{N_x} \left(\sum_{j=1}^{N_y} \left(\sum_{n=1}^{N_z} \left(\sum_{m=1}^{N_y} \left(\sum_{o=1}^{N_x} d_{ojn} a_o c_n d_{imn} b_m c_n c_l \right) \right) \right) \right)
$$
$$
= \sum_{i=1}^{N_x} \left(\sum_{j=1}^{N_y} \left(\sum_{n=1}^{N_z} \left(\sum_{m=1}^{N_y} \left(\sum_{o=1}^{N_x} (a_o c_n b_m c_n)^2 d_{ijl} \right) \right) \right) \right)
\tag{34}
$$

The above is true when

$$
d_{imn} b_m c_n c_l d_{ojn} a_o c_n = (a_o c_n b_m c_n)^2 d_{ijl},
\tag{35}
$$

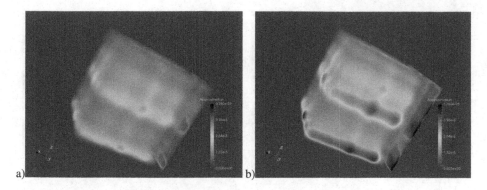

Fig. 4. The tensor product approximation after ten (a) and fifty (b) iterations of Algorithm 1.

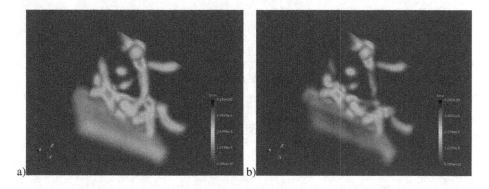

Fig. 5. The error of the tensor product approximation after one (a), and five (b) iterations of Algorithm 1.

so:

$$d_{imn}c_l d_{ojn} = a_o c_n b_m c_n d_{ijl} \tag{36}$$

thus:

$$\frac{d_{ojn}d_{imn}}{d_{ijl}} = \frac{a_o c_n b_m c_n}{c_l} \tag{37}$$

We can setup now a_1, b_1, and c_1 arbitrary and compute c_l using the derived proportions.

In a similar way we compute a_l, namely we insert:

$$b_l = \frac{\sum_{i=1}^{N_x} \left(\sum_{k=1}^{N_z} d_{ilk}a_i c_k \right)}{\sum_{i=1}^{N_x} \left(\sum_{k=1}^{N_z} \left(a_i c_k \right)^2 \right)} \tag{38}$$

$$c_l = \frac{\sum_{i=1}^{N_x} \left(\sum_{j=1}^{N_y} d_{ijl}a_i b_j \right)}{\sum_{i=1}^{N_x} \left(\sum_{j=1}^{N_y} \left(a_i b_j \right)^2 \right)} \tag{39}$$

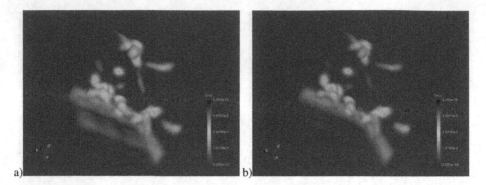

a)   b)

Fig. 6. The error of the tensor product approximation after ten (a), and fifty (b) iterations of Algorithm 1.

into

$$
a_l\Big(\sum_{j=1}^{N_y}\Big(\sum_{k=1}^{N_z}\Big(\sum_{m=1}^{N_x}\Big(\sum_{n=1}^{N_z}(d_{mjn}a_m c_n)\Big)\Big)\Big(\sum_{m=1}^{N_x}\Big(\sum_{n=1}^{N_y}(d_{mnk}a_m b_n)\Big)\Big)\Big)\Big)\Big)
$$
$$
=\Big(\sum_{j=1}^{N_y}\Big(\sum_{k=1}^{N_z}d_{ljk}\Big)\Big(\sum_{m=1}^{N_x}\Big(\sum_{n=1}^{N_z}(a_m c_n)^2\Big)\Big)\Big(\sum_{m=1}^{N_x}\Big(\sum_{n=1}^{N_y}(a_m b_n)^2\Big)\Big)\Big),
$$

(40)

then:

$$
a_l\Big(\sum_{j=1}^{N_y}\Big(\sum_{k=1}^{N_z}\Big(\Big(\sum_{m=1}^{N_x}\Big(\sum_{n=1}^{N_z}d_{mjn}a_m c_n\Big)\Big(\sum_{o=1}^{N_y}d_{mok}a_m b_o\Big)\Big)\Big)\Big)\Big)
$$
$$
=\sum_{j=1}^{N_y}\Big(\sum_{k=1}^{N_z}d_{ljk}\Big)\Big(\sum_{m=1}^{N_x}\Big(\sum_{n=1}^{N_z}(a_m c_n)^2\Big)\Big)\Big(\sum_{m=1}^{N_x}\Big(\sum_{o=1}^{N_y}(a_m b_o)^2\Big)\Big),
$$

(41)

and finally:

$$
\sum_{j=1}^{N_y}\Big(\sum_{k=1}^{N_z}\Big(\Big(\sum_{m=1}^{N_x}\Big(\sum_{n=1}^{N_z}\Big(\sum_{o=1}^{N_y}a_l d_{mok}a_m b_o d_{mjn}a_m c_n\Big)\Big)\Big)\Big)\Big)
$$
$$
=\sum_{j=1}^{N_y}\Big(\sum_{k=1}^{N_z}\Big(\sum_{m=1}^{N_x}\Big(\sum_{n=1}^{N_z}\Big(\sum_{m=1}^{N_x}\Big(\sum_{n=1}^{N_z}(a_m b_o a_m c_n)^2 d_{ljk}\Big)\Big)\Big)\Big)\Big),
$$

(42)

what results in:

$$
a_l d_{mok}a_m b_o d_{mjn}a_m c_n = (a_m b_o a_m c_n)^2 d_{ljk},
$$

(43)

so:

$$
a_l d_{mok}d_{mjn} = a_m b_o a_m c_n d_{ljk},
$$

(44)

thus:

$$\frac{d_{mok}d_{mjn}}{d_{ljk}} = \frac{a_m b_o a_m c_n}{a_l} \tag{45}$$

We compute b_l from (we already have a_i and c_k):

$$b_l = \frac{\sum_{i=1}^{N_x}\left(\sum_{k=1}^{N_z} d_{ilk}a_i c_k\right)}{\sum_{i=1}^{N_x}\left(\sum_{k=1}^{N_z}\left(a_i c_k\right)^2\right)} \tag{46}$$

The just analyzed Problem 1 has multiple solutions, and the algorithm presented above finds one exemplary solution, for the assumed values of a_1, b_1, and c_1.

This however may not be the optimal solution, in the sense of equation (13), and thus we may improve the quality of the solution executing simple genetic algorithm, with the individuals representing the parameters $a_1^x, \ldots, a_{N_x}^x, b_1^y, \ldots, b_{N_y}^y, c_1^z, \ldots, c_{N_z}^z$, and with the fitness function defined as (13).

4 Iterative Algorithm with Evolutionary Computations

The heuristic algorithm mixed with the genetic algorithm, as presented in Sect. 3, is not able to find the solution with 0 error, for non-tensor product structures, since we approximate $N * N$ data with $2 * N$ unknowns. Thus, the iterative algorithm presented in 1 is proposed, with the assumed accuracy ϵ.

Algorithm 1. Iterative algorithm with evolutionary computations

---

1: m=1
2: Bitmap[m](x,y,z)=K(x,y,z)
3: **repeat**
4: Find d_{ijk} for Bitmap[m](x,y,z) $\approx \sum_{i=1}^{N_x}\left(\sum_{j=1}^{N_y}\left(\sum_{k=1}^{N_z}\left(d_{ijk}B_{i,p}(x)B_{j,p}(y)B_{k,p}(z)\right)\right)\right)$
    using the linear computational cost isogeometric L2 projection algorithm
5: Find $a_1^x, \ldots, a_{N_x}^x, b_1^y, \ldots, b_{N_y}^y, c_1^z, \ldots, c_{N_z}^z$ to minimize
    $F[m]\left(a_1^x, \ldots, a_{N_x}^x, b_1^y, \ldots, b_{N_y}^y, c_1^z, \ldots, c_{N_z}^z\right)$ given by (13) using the heuristic algorithm
    to generate initial population and the genetic algorithm to improve the tensor product
    approximations
6: $m = m + 1$
7: Bitmap[m](x,y,z)=Bitmap[m-1](x,y,z)-$\left(\sum_{i=1}^{N_x} a_i B_{i,p}^x\right)\left(\sum_{j=1}^{N_y} b_j B_{j,p}^y\right)\left(\sum_{k=1}^{N_z} c_k B_{k,p}^z\right)$
8: **until** $F[m]\left(a_1^x, \ldots, a_{N_x}^x, b_1^y, \ldots, b_{N_y}^y, c_1^z, \ldots, c_{N_z}^z\right) \geq \epsilon$

In the aforementioned algorithm we approximate the static permeability as a sequence of tensor product approximations:

$$K(x,y,z) = \sum_{m=1}^{M} K_m^x(x)K_m^y(y)K_m^z(z) \tag{47}$$

Practically, it is realized according to the following equations:

$$\left(u_{t+m}, v\right) - \left(K_m^x(x)e^{\mu\overline{u}_{t+m-1}(x)}\right)\left(K_m^y(x)e^{\mu\overline{u}_{t+m-1}(y)}\right)\left(K_m^z(x)e^{\mu\overline{u}_{t+m-1}(z)}\right)\nabla u_{t+m}, \nabla v\right)$$

$$= - \sum_{n=1, m\neq n} \left(K_n^x(x)e^{\mu\overline{u}_{t+n}(x)}K_n^y(y)e^{\mu\overline{u}_{t+n}(y)}K_n^z(z)e^{\mu\overline{u}_{t+n}(z)}\nabla u_{t+n}, \nabla v\right)$$

$$+ (f, v) \mid K_m^x(x)K_m^y(y)K_m^z(z)$$

$$\left[\left(e^{\mu\overline{u}_{t+m}(x)}e^{\mu\overline{u}_{t+m-1}(y)}e^{\mu\overline{u}_{t+m-1}(z)}\right) - e^{\mu\overline{u}_{t+m-1}(x,y,z)}\right]\nabla u, \nabla v\right) \quad \forall v \in V$$

$$\tag{48}$$

5 Numerical Results

We conclude the paper with the numerical results concerning the approximation of the static permeability map. The original static permeability map is presented in Fig. 1. The first approximation has been obtained from the heuristic algorithm described in Sect. 3. We used the formulas (25)–(27) with the suitable substitutions. In the first approach we first compute the values of a, next, the values of b and finally the values of c. As the initial values we picked $\sqrt[3]{d_{111}}$.

Deriving this method further we decided to compute particular points in the order of a_2, b_2, c_2, a_3, b_3 and so on. This gave us the final result presented in Fig. 2a.

We have improved the approximation by post-processing with the generational genetic algorithm as implemented in jMetal package [13] with variables from [0,1] intervals. The fitness function was defined as:

$$f(a_1, \ldots, a_{N_x}, b_1, \ldots, b_{N_y}, c_1, \ldots, c_{N_z}) = \sum_{i=1}^{N_x}\sum_{l=1}^{N_y}\sum_{k=1}^{N_z}\left(d_{ilk} - a_i b_l c_k\right)^2 \tag{49}$$

The results are summarized in Fig. 2b.

To improve the numerical results we have employed the Algorithm 1. In Figs. 3 and 4 results obtained after 1, 5, 10 and 50 iterations of Algorithm 1 are presented.

In order to analyze the accuracy of the tensor product approximation, we also present in Figs. 5 and 6 the error after 1, 5, 10, 50 iterations. We can read from these Figures, how the error decreases when adding particular components.

6 Conclusions and the Future Work

In the paper the heuristic algorithm for tensor product approximation of material data for implicit dynamics simulations of non-linear flow in heterogeneous media is presented.

The algorithm can be used as a generator of initial configurations for a genetic algorithm, improving the quality of the approximation. The future work will involve the implementation of the implicit scheme and utilizing the proposed algorithms as a preconditioner for obtaining tensor product structure of the material data.

We have analyzed the convergence of our tensor product approximation method but assessing how the convergence influences the reduction of the iteration number of the explicit method will be the matter of our future experiments.

Our intuition is that 100 iterations (100 components of the tensor product approximation) should give a well approximation, and thus we can use the implicit method not bounded by the CFL condition, which will require 100 substeps in every time step.

Acknowledgments. This work was supported by National Science Centre, Poland, grant no. 2014/15/N/ST6/04662. The authors would like to acknowledge prof. Maciej Paszyński for his help in this research topic and preparation of this paper.

References

1. Łoś, M., Woźniak, M., Paszyński, M., Dalcin, L., Calo, V.M.: Dynamics with matrices possessing kronecker product structure. Proc. Comput. Sci. **51**, 286–295 (2015). https://doi.org/10.1016/j.procs.2015.05.243
2. Łoś, M., Woźniak, M., Paszyński, M., Lenharth, A., Amber-Hassan, M., Pingali, K.: IGA-ADS: isogeometric analysis FEM using ADS solver. Comput. Phys. Commun. **217**, 99–116 (2017). https://doi.org/10.1016/j.cpc.2017.02.023
3. Woźniak, M., Łoś, M., Paszyński, M., Dalcin, L., Calo, V.M.: Parallel fast isogeometric solvers for explicit dynamics. Comput. Inf. **36**(2), 423–448 (2017). https://doi.org/10.4149/cai.2017.2.423
4. Siwik, L., Łoś, M., Kisiel-Dorohinicki, M., Byrski, A.: Hybridization of isogeometric finite element method and evolutionary mulit-agent system as a tool-set for multi-objective optimization of liquid fossil fuel exploitation with minimizing groundwater contamination. Proc. Comput. Sci. **80**, 792–803 (2016). https://doi.org/10.1016/j.procs.2016.05.369
5. Łoś, M.: Fast isogeometric L2 projection solver for non-linear flow in non-homogenous media, Master Thesis, AGH University, Krakow, Poland (2015)
6. Hughes, T.J.R., Cottrell, J.A., Bazilevs, Y.: Isogeometric analysis: CAD, finite elements, NURBS, exact geometry and mesh refinement. Comput. Methods Appl. Mech. Eng. **194**(39), 4135–4195 (2005). https://doi.org/10.1016/j.cma.2004.10.008
7. Cottrell, J.A., Hughes, T.J.R., Bazilevs, Y.: Isogeometric Analysis: Toward Unfication of CAD and FEA. Wiley, New York (2009). The Attrium, Southern Gate, Chichester, West Sussex
8. Courant, R., Friedrichs, K., Lewy, H.: On the partial difference equations of mathematical physics. In: AEC Research and Development Report, NYO-7689. AEC Computing and Applied Mathematics Centre-Courant Institute of Mathematical Sciences, New York (1956)
9. Paszyński M, Łoś, M., Calo, V.M.: Fast isogeometric solvers for implicit dynamics. Comput. Math. Appl. (2017, submitted to)
10. Alotaibi, M., Calo, V.M., Efendiev, Y., Galvis, J., Ghommem, M.: Global-local nonlinear model reduction for flows in heterogeneous porous media. Comput. Methods Appl. Mech. Eng. **292**, 122–137 (2015). https://doi.org/10.1016/j.cma.2014.10.034

11. Efendiev, Y., Ginting, V., Hou, T.: Multiscale finite element methods for nonlinear problems and their applications. Commun. Math. Sci. **2**(4), 553–589 (2004). https://doi.org/10.4310/CMS.2004.v2.n4.a2
12. Warrick, A.W.: Time-dependent linearized in filtration: III. Strip and disc sources. Soil Sci. Soc. Am. J. **40**, 639–643 (1976)
13. Nebro, A.J., Durillo, J.J., Vergne, M.: Redesigning the jMetal Multi-objective optimization framework. In: Proceedings of the Companion Publication of the 2015 Annual Conference on Genetic and Evolutionary Computation, GECCO Companion 2015 (2015)
14. Siwik, L., Los, M., Kisiel-Dorohinicki, M., Byrski, A.: Evolutionary multiobjective optimization of liquid fossil fuel reserves exploitation with minimizing natural environment contamination. In: Rutkowski, L., Korytkowski, M., Scherer, R., Tadeusiewicz, R., Zadeh, L.A., Zurada, J.M. (eds.) ICAISC 2016. LNCS (LNAI), vol. 9693, pp. 384–394. Springer, Cham (2016). https://doi.org/10.1007/978-3-319-39384-1_33
15. Goreinov, S.A., Tyrtyshnikov, E.E., Zamarashkin, N.L.: A theory of pseudoskeleton approximations. Linear Algebra Appl. **261**(1–3), 1–21 (1997). https://doi.org/10.1016/S0024-3795(96)00301-1

Track of Applications of Matrix Methods in Artificial Intelligence and Machine Learning

Applications of Matrix Methods in Artificial Intelligence and Machine Learning

Kourosh Modarresi

Adobe Inc., San Jose, CA, USA
kouroshm@alumni.stanford.edu

Objectives and Description of the Workshop. With availability of large amount of data, the main challenge of our time is to get insightful information from the data. Therefore, artificial intelligence and machine learning are two main paths in getting the insights from the data we are dealing with. The data we currently have is a new and unprecedented form of data, "Modern Data". "Modern Data" has unique characteristics such as, extreme sparsity, high correlation, high dimensionality and massive size. Modern data is very prevalent in all different areas of science such as Medicine, Environment, Finance, Marketing, Vision, Imaging, Text, Web, etc. A major difficulty is that many of the old methods that have been developed for analyzing data during the last decades cannot be applied on modern data. One distinct solution, to overcome this difficulty, is the application of matrix computation and factorization methods such as SVD (singular value decomposition), PCA (principal component analysis), and NMF (non- negative matrix factorization), without which the analysis of modern data is not possible. This workshop covers the application of matrix computational science techniques in dealing with Modern Data.

Keywords: Artificial intelligence · Machine learning
Matrix factorization

On Two Kinds of Dataset Decomposition

Pavel Emelyanov[1,2]([⊠]) [iD]

[1] A.P. Ershov Institute of Informatics Systems,
Lavrentiev av. 6, 630090 Novosibirsk, Russia
[2] Novosibirsk State University, Pirogov st. 1, 630090 Novosibirsk, Russia
emelyanov@mmf.nsu.ru

Abstract. We consider a Cartesian decomposition of datasets, i.e. finding datasets such that their unordered Cartesian product yields the source set, and some natural generalization of this decomposition. In terms of relational databases, this means reversing the SQL `CROSS JOIN` and `INNER JOIN` operators (the last is equipped with a test verifying the equality of a tables attribute to another tables attribute). First we outline a polytime algorithm for computing the Cartesian decomposition. Then we describe a polytime algorithm for computing a generalized decomposition based on the Cartesian decomposition. Some applications and relating problems are discussed.

Keywords: Data analysis · Databases · Decision tables
Decomposition · Knowledge discovery · Functional dependency
Compactification · Optimization of boolean functions

1 Introduction

The analysis of datasets of different origins is a most topical problem. Decomposition methods are powerful analysis tools in data and knowledge mining as well in many others domains. Detecting the Cartesian property of a dataset, i.e. determining whether it can be given as an unordered Cartesian product of two (or several) datasets, as well as its generalizations, appears to be important in at least four out of the six classes of data analysis problems, as defined by the classics in the domain [9], namely in anomaly detection, dependency modeling, discovering hidden structures in datasets and constructing a more compact data representation. Algorithmic treatment this property has interesting applications, for example, for relational databases, decision tables, and some other table–based modeled domains, such as Boolean functions.

Let us consider the Cartesian product $\times$ of two relations given in the form of tables in Fig. 1. It corresponds to the SQL–operator `T1 CROSS JOIN T2`. In the first representation of the product result, where the "natural" order of rows and

This work is supported by the Ministry of Science and Education of the Russian Federation under the 5–100 Excellence Programme and the grant of Russian Foundation for Basic Research No. 17–51–45125.

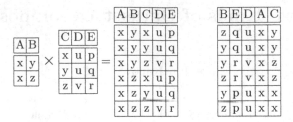

Fig. 1. Cartesian product of tables.

columns is preserved, a careful reader can easily recognize the Cartesian structure of the table. However, this is not so easy to do for the second representation, where the rows and columns are randomly shuffled, even though the table is small. In the sequel, we will only consider the relations having no key of any kind and assume that the tuples found in the relations are all different.

Only in the first twenty–five years after Codd had developed his relational data model, more than 100 types of dependencies were described in the literature [14]. Cartesian decomposition underlies the definitions of the major dependency types encompassed by the theory of relational databases. This is because the numerous concepts of dependency are based on the *join* operation, which is inverse to Cartesian decomposition. Recall that the *join dependency* is the most common kind of dependencies considered in the framework of the fifth normal form. A relation R satisfies the join dependency $\bowtie (A_1, \ldots, A_n)$ for a family of subsets of its attributes $\{A_1, \ldots, A_n\}$ if R is the union of the projections on the subsets A_i, $1 \leqslant i \leqslant n$. Thus, if A_i are disjoint, we have the Cartesian decomposition of the relation R into the corresponding components–projections.

For the case $n = 2$ the join dependency is known in the context of the fourth normal form under the name *multivalued dependency*. A relation R for a family of subsets of its attributes $\{A_0, A_1, A_2\}$ satisfies the multivalued dependency $A_0 \mapsto A_1$ iff R satisfies the join dependency $\bowtie (A_0 \cup A_1, \ A_0 \cup A_2)$. Thus for each A_0-tuple of values, the projection of R onto $A_1 \cup A_2$ has a Cartesian decomposition. Historically, multivalued dependencies were introduced earlier than join dependencies [8] and attracted wide attention as a natural variant thereof.

An important task is the development of efficient algorithms for solving the computationally challenging problem of finding dependencies in data. A lot of research has been devoted to mining functional dependencies (see surveys [10,12]), while the detection of more general dependencies, like the multivalued ones, has been studied less. In [16], the authors propose a method based on directed enumeration of assumptions/conclusions of multivalued dependencies (exploring the properties of these dependencies to narrow the search space) with checking satisfaction of the generated dependencies on the relation of interest. In [13], the authors employ an enumeration procedure based on the refinement of assumptions/conclusions of the dependencies considered as hypotheses. Notice that when searching for functional dependencies $A \mapsto B$ on a relation R, once an assumption A is guessed, the conclusion B can be efficiently found. For multivalued dependencies, this property is not trivial and leads to the issue of efficient recognition of Cartesian decomposition (of the projection of R on the attributes not contained in A). Thus, the algorithmic results presented in this paper can be viewed as a foundation for the development of new methods for detecting the general kind dependencies, in particular, multivalued and join dependencies.

In [7] we considered the problem of Cartesian decomposition for the relational data model. A conceptual implementation of the decomposition algorithm in Transact SQL was provided. Its time complexity is polynomial. This algorithm is based on an algorithm for the disjoint (no common variables between components) AND–decomposition of Boolean functions given in ANF, which, in fact is an algorithm of the factorization of polylinear polynomials over the finite field of the order 2 (Boolean polynomials), described by the authors in [5,6]. Notice that another algorithm invented by Bioch [1] also applied to this problem is more complex because it essentially depends on a number of different values of attributes.

The relationship between the problems of the Cartesian decomposition and factorization of Boolean polynomials can be easily established. Each tuple of the relation is a monomial of a polynomial, where the attribute values play the role of variables. Importantly, the attributes of the same type are considered different. Thus, if in a tuple different attributes of the same type have equal values, the corresponding variables are different. NULL is also typed and appears as a different variable. For example, for the relation above the corresponding polynomial is

$$z_B \cdot q \cdot u \cdot x_A \cdot y_C + y_B \cdot q \cdot u \cdot x_A \cdot y_C +$$
$$y_B \cdot r \cdot v \cdot x_A \cdot z_C + z_B \cdot r \cdot v \cdot x_A \cdot z_C +$$
$$y_B \cdot p \cdot u \cdot x_A \cdot x_C + z_B \cdot p \cdot u \cdot x_A \cdot x_C =$$
$$x_A \cdot (y_B + z_B) \cdot (q \cdot u \cdot y_C + r \cdot v \cdot z_C + p \cdot u \cdot x_C)$$

Subsequently, we use this correspondence between relational tables and polynomials. This polynomial will also be referred as the table's polynomial.

Apparently, however, datasets with pure Cartesian product structure are rare. Cartesian decomposition has natural generalizations allowing us to solve more complex problems. For example, it is shown [4] that more polynomials can be decomposed if we admit that decomposition components can share variables from some prescribed set. We could use the same idea for the decomposition of datasets. Hopefully, the developed decomposition algorithm for datasets, in contrast to [4], does not depend on number of shared variables and therefore remains practical for large tables.

Fig. 2 is an adapted example from [17] extended by one table. This example comes from the decision support domain which is closely related to database management [15] and has numerous applications. From the mathematical point of view, a decision table is a map defined, sometimes partially, by explicit listing arguments and results (a set of rules or a set of implications "conditions–conclusions"). The well–known example is truth tables, which are widely used to represent Boolean functions. The decomposition of a decision table is finding the representation of the map $F(X)$ in the form $G(X_1, H(X_2))$, $X = X_1 \cup X_2$, which may not be unique. The map H can be treated as a new, previously unknown concept. This explication leads to a new knowledge about the data of interest and its more compact presentation.

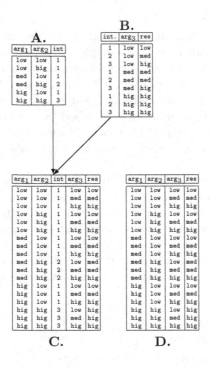

A.

arg$_1$	arg$_2$	int
low	low	1
low	hig	1
med	low	1
med	hig	2
hig	low	1
hig	hig	3

B.

int.	arg$_3$	res
1	low	low
2	low	med
3	low	hig
1	med	med
2	med	med
3	med	hig
1	hig	hig
2	hig	hig
3	hig	hig

C.

arg$_1$	arg$_2$	int	arg$_3$	res
low	low	1	low	low
low	low	1	med	med
low	low	1	hig	hig
low	hig	1	low	low
low	hig	1	med	med
low	hig	1	hig	hig
med	low	1	low	low
med	low	1	med	med
med	low	1	hig	hig
med	hig	2	low	med
med	hig	2	med	med
med	hig	2	hig	hig
hig	low	1	low	low
hig	low	1	med	med
hig	low	1	hig	hig
hig	hig	3	low	hig
hig	hig	3	med	hig
hig	hig	3	hig	hig

D.

arg$_1$	arg$_2$	arg$_3$	res
low	low	low	low
low	low	med	med
low	low	hig	hig
low	hig	low	low
low	hig	med	med
low	hig	hig	hig
med	low	low	low
med	low	med	med
med	low	hig	hig
med	hig	low	med
med	hig	med	med
med	hig	hig	hig
hig	low	low	low
hig	low	med	med
hig	low	hig	hig
hig	hig	low	hig
hig	hig	med	hig
hig	hig	hig	hig

Fig. 2. Examples of decision tables.

Fig. 2 gives two examples of the interrelation between bigger and smaller decision tables. The rules of **Table C** explicitly repeat the "conclusion" for subrules. Thereby, we can detect the three dependencies

$$\text{arg}_1, \text{arg}_2 \mapsto \text{int}, \quad \text{int}, \text{arg}_3 \mapsto \text{res}, \quad \text{and} \quad \text{arg}_1, \text{arg}_2, \text{arg}_3 \mapsto \text{res}$$

The rules of **Table D** are more lapidary; they have no intermediate "conclusions" (the column int), and therefore this table has only the third dependency.

In the other words, **Table B** is a compacted version of **Table C** (and **D** as well) where compactification is based on a new concept described by **Table A**. In the map terms, informally

$$\mathbf{C}(\text{arg}_1, \text{arg}_2, \text{int}, \text{arg}_3) = \mathbf{D}(\text{arg}_1, \text{arg}_2, \text{arg}_3) = \mathbf{B}(\mathbf{A}(\text{arg}_1, \text{arg}_2), \text{arg}_3).$$

Table C may appear as a result of the routine design of decision tables (a set of business rules) by analysts. Yet another natural source of these tables is SQL queries. In SQL terms, the decompositions mentioned above are the reversing operators of the following kind:

```
SELECT T1.*, T2.* EXCEPT(Attr2)
  FROM T1 INNER JOIN T2
    ON T1.Attr1 = T2.Attr2
```

for **Table C** and

```
SELECT T1.* EXCEPT(Attr1), T2.* EXCEPT(Attr2)
  FROM T1 INNER JOIN T2
    ON T1.Attr1 = T2.Attr2
```

for **Table D**. Here, EXCEPT(list) is an informal extension of SQL used to exclude list from the resulting attributes. We will denote this operator as $\times_{A1=A2}$ also.

Among numerous approaches to the decomposition of decision tables via finding functional dependencies we would mention the approaches [2,11,17] having the same origins as our investigations: decomposition methods for logic circuits optimizations. These approaches perform the case exemplified by **Table D** which evidently occurs more frequently in the K&DM domain. They construct some auxiliary graphs and use the graph–coloring techniques to derive new concepts. Additional consideration are taken into account because the new concept derivation may be non–unique.

In this paper, we give a polynomial–time algorithm to solve **Table C** decomposition problem. It is based on Cartesian decomposition; therefore, we will briefly describe it. Also it explores the idea of taking into account shared variables. Namely, as it is easy to see, the values of an attribute assumed to be connector–attribute compose such a set of shared variables. They will be presented in both derived components of decomposition, appearing as conclusions and conditions, respectively.

Among possible applications of this algorithm we consider decomposition problems of Boolean tables. In particular, we demonstrate how it can be used to provide the disjunctive Shannon's decomposition of some special form and how it can be used in some generalized approach to designing decompositions for Boolean functions given in the form of truth tables with *don't care* values. In addition, some relating problems are discussed.

2 Cartesian Decomposition

First, we give a description for the AND–decomposition of Boolean polynomials which serves as a basis for the Cartesian decomposition of datasets. Then we outline its SQL–implementation for relational databases.

2.1 Algorithm for Factorization of Boolean Polynomials

Let us briefly mention the factorization algorithm given in [5,6]. It is assumed that the input polynomial F has no trivial divisors and contains at least two variables.

1. Take an arbitrary variable x from F.
2. Let $\Sigma_{same} := \{x\}, \Sigma_{other} := \varnothing$, and $F_{same} := 0, F_{other} := 0$.
3. Compute $G := F_{x=0} \cdot F'_x$.
4. For each variable $y \in Var(F) \setminus \{x\}$:
   if $G'_y = 0$ then $\Sigma_{other} := \Sigma_{other} \cup \{y\}$
   else $\Sigma_{same} := \Sigma_{same} \cup \{y\}$
5. If $\Sigma_{other} = \varnothing$, then output $F_{same} := F, F_{other} := 1$ and stop.
6. Restrict each monomial of F onto Σ_{same} and add every obtained monomial to F_{same}; the monomial is added once to F_{same}.
7. Restrict each monomial of F onto Σ_{other} and add every obtained monomial to F_{other}; the monomial is added once to F_{other}.

Remark 1. The decomposition components F_{same} and F_{other} possess the following property. The polynomial F_{same} is not further decomposable, while the polynomial F_{other} may be decomposed. Hence, we should apply the algorithm to F_{other} to derive a finer decomposition.

The worst–time complexity of the algorithm is $O(L^3)$, where L is the length of the polynomial F, i.e., for the polynomial over n variables having M monomials of lengths $m_1, \ldots, m_M$, $L = \sum_{i=1}^{M} m_i = O(nM)$. In [5] we also show that the algorithm can be implemented without computing the product $F_{x=0} \cdot F'_x$ explicitly.

2.2   SQL–Implementation of Decomposition Algorithm

A decomposition algorithm for relational tables implements the steps of the factorization algorithm described above. An implementation of this algorithm in Transact SQL is given in [3].

In terms of polynomials, it is easy to formulate and prove the following property: if two variables always appear in different monomials (i.e., there is no monomial in which they appear simultaneously) then these variables appear in different monomials of the same decomposition component if a decomposition exists. A direct consequence of this observation is that for each relation attribute it is enough to consider just one value of this attribute because the others must belong to the same decomposition component (if it exists).

Trivial Attribute Elimination. If some attribute of a relation has only one value, we have a case of trivial decomposition. In terms of polynomials, this condition can be written as $F = x \cdot F'_x$. This attribute can be extracted into a separate table. In what follows, we assume that there are no such trivial attributes.

Preliminary Manipulations. This creates auxiliary strings which are needed to form SQL queries. At the first step, we need to select a "variable" x, with respect to which decomposition will be constructed. We need to find two sets of attributes forming the tables as decomposition components. As mentioned above,

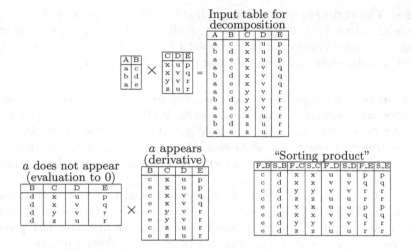

Fig. 3. Example of Cartesian Decomposition

we can take an arbitrary value of an arbitrary attribute of the table. Next, we create the string representing table attributes and their aliases corresponding to the product $F_{x=0} \cdot F'_x$ (in terms of polynomials). The prefixes F_ and S_ correspond to $F_{x=0}$ and F'_x.

Creation of Duplicates Filter. After that, we create a string of a logical expression allowing us to reduce the size of the table–product through the exclusion of duplicate rows; they appear exactly twice. In terms of polynomials, these are the monomials of the polynomial-product with the coefficient 2, which can be obviously omitted in the field of the order 2. In an experimental evaluation we observed that the share of such duplicates reached 80%. Since this table is used for bulk queries, its size significantly impacts the performance.

Retrieval of "Sorting Product". The table-product allowing for sorting attributes with respect to the component selected is created in the form VIEW. It is worth noting that it can be constructed in different ways. A "material- ized" VIEW can significantly accelerate the next massively executed query to this table–product. It is easy to see that the table corresponding to the full product is bigger than the original table. In the example given above it would contain 32 rows. However, its size can be reduced substantially by applying the duplicates filter. The view SortingProduct contains only 8 rows.

Partition of Attributes. The membership of a variable y in a component con- taining the variable x selected at the first step is decided by checking whether the partial derivative of the polynomial $\frac{\partial}{\partial y}(F_{x=0} \cdot F'_x)$ is not equal to zero (in the finite field of order 2). They are from different components iff this derivative vanishes. This corresponds to checking whether a variable appears in the monomials in the second degree (or is absent at all). In SQL terms, an attribute A belongs to another component (with respect to the attribute of x) if each row of the sorting table contains equal values at F_A and S_A columns.

Retrieval of Decomposition. At the previous steps, we find a partition of attributes and constructs strings representing it. If the cycle is completed and the string for the second component is empty, then the table is not decomposable. Otherwise, the resulting tables–components are produced by restricting the source table onto the corresponding component attributes and selecting unique tuples.

To verify the new concepts discovery algorithms, Jupan and Bohanec described an artificial dataset establishing characteristics of cars (see, for example, [17]). As it is pure Cartesian product of several attribute domains representing characteristics, the decomposition algorithm given above produces a set of linear factors.

At the same time, disjointly decomposable Boolean polynomials are rare:

Proposition 1. *If a random polynomial F has M monomials defined over $n > 2$ variables without trivial divisors, then*

$$\mathbb{P}[F \text{ is } \varnothing\text{--}undecomposable] > 1 - \left(1 - \frac{\phi(M)}{M}\right)^n > 1 - \left(1 - \frac{1}{e^\gamma \ln \ln M + \frac{3}{\ln \ln M}}\right)^n,$$

where ϕ and γ are Euler's totient function and constant, respectively.

Remark 2. For database tables M is the relation's cardinality (number of the table's rows) and n is the number of different values in the table which can be estimated as $O(dM)$ where d is the relation's degree (number of the table's attributes). Notice that polynomials corresponding to database tables have a particular structure and, therefore, the bound can be improved.

3   One Generalization of Cartesian Decomposition

As "pure" Cartesian decomposition is rare, it is naturally to detect other tractable cases and to develop new kinds of decompositions for them. One way is to abandon the strict requirement on decomposition components to be disjoint on values. It is shown [4] that more Boolean polynomials can be decomposed if we admit that decomposition components can share variables from some prescribed set. We would use the same idea for decomposition of datasets. Arbitrariness of choice of variables results in an exponential growth of the algorithm complexity with respect to the number of variables. Hopefully, table–based datasets have a particular structure that can be taken into account. Namely, we can take as shared variables only those which corresponds to the same attribute. This attribute connects original datasets (items of them) on base of the equality of theirs values. In this case, the decomposition algorithm does not depend on the number of shared variables in contrast to the Boolean polynomials case and therefore appears practical for large tables.

3.1   Decomposition with Explicit Attribute–Connector

For the decomposition of tables with an explicit connector–attribute, the Cartesian decomposition is a crucial step. In general, this decomposition consists of the following steps:

A	B	C	D	E
a	p	u	x	1
b	q	u	x	1
a	p	u	y	2
a	q	v	y	2
b	p	u	x	3
b	p	v	y	3

$$P = [\{\{A,B\},\{C\},\{D\}\}, \\ \{\{A\},\{B,C\},\{D\}\}, \\ \{\{A\},\{B\},\{C,D\}\}]$$

Fig. 4. An undecomposable table with decomposable sub–tables for the connector–attribute E.

1. Subdivide the original table into k sub–tables such that all sub–table rows contain the same value at the connector–attribute (this attribute should be excluded for further manipulations).
2. For each sub–table perform the full Cartesian decomposition (i.e. all components are undecomposable), skipping the last step (projection on partition of attributes). Notice that all trivial components appear in the partition of attributes as singleton sets. Then we have a set of partitions $P = [p_1, \ldots, p_k]$ of table attributes $\mathcal{A}$, where one partition corresponds to the Cartesian decomposition of one sub–table.
3. We cannot use a simple projection on partition of attributes because it is possible that all sub–tables are decomposable while the entire table is not (an example at Fig. 4). The table of interest is decomposable if there exists a minimal closure of the parts of attribute partitions across all sub–tables (if parts of different partitions have a common attribute, then both parts are joined with the resulting closure) such that this closure does not coincide with the entire set of the table attributes. This simple procedure can be done in $O(|P| \cdot |\mathcal{A}|^2)$ steps.
   1. Select any attribute set π of any partition from P.
   2. Initialize the result set R by π.
       //when the algorithm stops then R contains component attributes
   3. Initialize the active set A by π.
       //it contains attributes that will be treated at the next closure steps
   4. While $A \neq \varnothing$ do:
   5.   Take any attribute a from A; remove it from A.
   6.   For each $p \in P$ do:
   7.   Select from p the attribute set π containing a.
   8. $A := A \cup (\pi \setminus R)$.

9. $R := R \cup \pi$.

10. If $R = \mathcal{A}$ then the table is not decomposable; otherwise, it is.

11. If decomposable then R and $\mathcal{A} \backslash R$ are the attribute sets of the components of decomposition.

12. For each sub–table perform projections on these attribute sets.

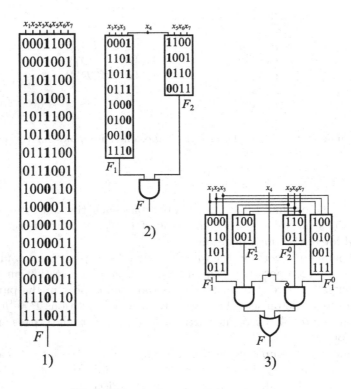

Fig. 5. Circuit decomposition example.

3.2   Applications to Boolean Tables

The interplay of K&DM and logic circuit optimization is quite important and fruitful. An interesting application of this decomposition algorithm is logic circuit optimization. Indeed, every Boolean table (with different rows) is the true/false part of the truth table of some Boolean function (the set of satisfying/unsatisfying vectors). This algorithm allows us to find tables corresponding to Boolean functions of the following Shannon's OR–decomposition, where $F_{x=0}$ and $F_{x=1}$ components have finer disjoint Cartesian decomposition

$$F(U, V, x) = \overline{x} F(U, V, 0) \vee x F(U, V, 1) = \overline{x} F_1^0(U) F_2^0(V) \vee x F_1^1(U) F_2^1(V).$$

A number of function that are decomposable in this way can be easily counted. For simplicity's sake they are $n^2 2^{n-2} - O(n2^n)$.

An example is shown at Fig. 5. The original circuit **(1)** is given in the form of the satisfying vectors table (on missing inputs the output is false). The connector–attribute corresponding to the input x_4 is given in **bold**. The composition **(2)** is the simplest result of decomposition as

$$F(x_1, \ldots, x_7) = F_1(x_1, x_2, x_3, x_4) \wedge F_2(x_4, x_5, x_6, x_7).$$

But evidently, the connector–attribute can be replaced by a simpler controlling wire. F_k^v is a part of the function F_k, $k = 0, 1$, with the value $v = 0, 1$, at x_4. The result is the composition **(3)**. Notice that the derived Boolean functions given by the tables have a specific structure and can be specifically optimized.

Table 1. (a) Decomposition example. (b) Function–combinator.

x_1	x_2	x_3	x_4	F
1	0	0	0	0
0	0	1	0	1
0	0	0	1	1
0	1	1	0	1
0	1	0	1	1
1	1	1	0	1
1	1	0	1	1
1	0	1	1	0

$=$

x_1	x_2	F_1
0	0	1
1	0	0
0	1	1
1	1	1

$\times_{F_1 = F_2}$

x_3	x_4	F_2
0	0	0
1	0	1
0	1	1
1	1	0

x	y	H
0	0	0
1	1	1
DC	DC	

a) Decomposition example.   b) Function–combinator.

Yet another application of this decomposition emerges when we consider the decomposition of a truth table with *don't care* (*DC*) inputs and outputs with respect to the resulting column. The following example at Table 1 plainly explains this idea. The decomposition components defines the *not–DC* part of the truth table.

The complete form of the original Boolean function can be defined by the function–combinator H

$$F(x_1, x_2, x_3, x_4) = H(F(x_1, x_2), F(x_3, x_4)).$$

Note that by extending definition on *DC*s we can deduce different kinds of decompositions (eliminating DC). For example, if we extend H to the definition of the disjunction (OR) then we establish the disjoint OR–decomposition of Boolean functions given in the form of truth tables with *DC*.

4   Further Work

To achieve deeper optimization we asked [5,6] how to find a representation of a Boolean function in the ANF–form $F(X, Y) = G(X)H(Y) + D(X, Y)$, i.e.

the relatively small "defect" $D(X,Y)$ extends or shrinks the pure "Cartesian product".

In the scope of decomposition of Boolean functions given in the form of truth tables with DC finding small extensions (redefinition of several DCs) may cause more compact representations.

Clearly, finding representation of the table's polynomial in the form

$$F(X,Y) = \sum_k G_k(X)H_k(Y), \quad X \cap Y = \varnothing,$$

i.e. complete decomposition without any "defect", solves **Table D** decomposition problem. Here, valuation of k corresponds to a new concept (an implicit connector–attribute), which will serve as a result of the compacting table and an argument of the compacted table. Although, apparently, such decompositions (for example, this one, is trivial, where each monomial is treated separately) always exist, not all of them are meaningful from the K&DM point of view. Formulating additional constraints targeting decomposition algorithms is an interesting problem.

Finding a "defect" $D(X,Y)$ can be considered as completing the original "dataset" $F(X,Y)$ to derive some "conceptual" decompositions. In other words, $D(X,Y)$ represents incompleteness or noise/artifacts of the original dataset if we need to add or to remove data, respectively. It is relative because divers completions are possible. It can be Cartesian or involve explicit/implicit connectors. For example, there always exists a trivial completion ensuring Cartesian decomposition into linear factors

$$F(X) + D(X) = \prod_{i=1}^{n} \sum_{x_i^j \in A_i} x_i^j$$

where x_i^j are variables representing different values of a A_i domain (the ith–column of the table) as for the mentioned above CARS–example of Bohanec and Jupan.

A simple observation is inspired by considering non–linear factors that can appear under some completions. For example, if A and B domains belong to the same non–decomposable factor then all the factor's monomials $a_i b_j$ form values of a new concept that is a subconcept of $A \times B$. It can serve for the reduction of dataset dimension (degree of a relation) and space requirements to represent domain values.

References

1. Bioch, J.C.: The complexity of modular decomposition of boolean functions. Discrete Appl. Math. **149**(1–3), 1–13 (2005)
2. Bohanec, M., Zupan, B.: A function-decomposition method for development of hierarchical multi-attribute decision models. Decis. Support Syst. **36**(3), 215–233 (2004)

3. Emelyanov, P.: Cartesian decomposition of tables. Transact SQL. http://algo.nsu. ru/CartesianDecomposition.sql
4. Emelyanov, P.: AND–decomposition of boolean polynomials with prescribed shared variables. In: Govindarajan, S., Maheshwari, A. (eds.) CALDAM 2016. LNCS, vol. 9602, pp. 164–175. Springer, Cham (2016). https://doi.org/10.1007/ 978-3-319-29221-2_14
5. Emelyanov, P., Ponomaryov, D.: Algorithmic issues of conjunctive decomposition of boolean formulas. Program. Comput. Softw. **41**(3), 162–169 (2015)
6. Emelyanov, P., Ponomaryov, D.: On tractability of disjoint AND-decomposition of boolean formulas. In: Voronkov, A., Virbitskaite, I. (eds.) PSI 2014. LNCS, vol. 8974, pp. 92–101. Springer, Heidelberg (2015). https://doi.org/10.1007/978-3-662-46823-4_8
7. Emelyanov, P., Ponomaryov, D.: Cartesian decomposition in data analysis. In: Proceedings of the Siberian Symposium on Data Science and Engineering (SSDSE 2017), pp. 55–60 (2017)
8. Fagin, R., Vardi, M.: The theory of data dependencies: a survey. In: Mathematics of Information Processing: Proceedings of Symposia in Applied Mathematics, vol. 34, pp. 19–71. AMS, Providence (1986)
9. Fayyad, U., Piatetsky-Shapiro, G., Smyth, P.: From data mining to knowledge discovery in databases. AI Mag. **17**(3), 37–54 (1996)
10. Liu, J., Li, J., Liu, C., Chen, Y.: Discover dependencies from data - a review. IEEE Trans. Knowl. Data Eng. **24**(2), 251–264 (2012)
11. Mankowski, M., Łuba, T., Jankowski, C.: Evaluation of decision table decomposition using dynamic programming classifiers. In: Suraj, Z., Czaja, L. (eds.) Proceedings of the 24th International Workshop on Concurrency, Specification and Programming (CS&P 2015), pp. 34–43 (2015)
12. Papenbrock, T., Ehrlich, J., Marten, J., Neubert, T., Rudolph, J., Schoenberg, M., Zwiener, J., Naumann, F.: Functional dependency discovery: an experimental evaluation of seven algorithms. Proc. VLDB Endowment **8**(10), 1082–1093 (2015)
13. Savnik, I., Flach, P.: Discovery of multivalued dependencies from relations. Intell. Data Anal. **4**(3–4), 195–211 (2000)
14. Thalheim, B.: An overview on semantical constraints for database models. In: Proceedings of the 6th International Conference on Intellectual Systems and Computer Science, pp. 81–102 (1996)
15. Vanthienen, J.: Rules as data: decision tables and relational databases. Bus. Rules J. **11**(1) (2010). http://www.brcommunity.com/a2010/b516.html
16. Yan, M., Fu, A.W.: Algorithm for discovering multivalued dependencies. In: Proceedings of the 10th International Conference on Information and Knowledge Management (CIKM 2001), pp. 556–558. ACM, New York (2001)
17. Zupan, B., Bohanec, M.: Experimental evaluation of three partition selection criteria for decision table decomposition. Informatica **22**, 207–217 (1998)

A Graph-Based Algorithm for Supervised Image Classification

Ke Du[1], Jinlong Liu[2(✉)], Xingrui Zhang[2], Jianying Feng[2], Yudong Guan[2], and Stéphane Domas[1]

[1] FEMTO-ST Institute, UMR 6174 CNRS,
University of Bourgogne Franche-Comté, 90000 Belfort, France
[2] School of Electronics and Information Engineering,
Harbin Institute of Technology, Harbin 150000, China
yq20@hit.edu.cn

Abstract. Manifold learning is a main stream research track used for dimensionality reduction as a method to select features. Many variants have been proposed with good performance. A novel graph-based algorithm for supervised image classification is introduced in this paper. It makes the use of graph embedding to increase the recognition accuracy. The proposed algorithm is tested on four benchmark datasets of different types including scene, face and object. The experimental results show the validity of our solution by comparing it with several other tested algorithms.

Keywords: Graph-based · Supervised learning · Image classification

1 Introduction

In the last years, machine learning has been playing an important role in many domains, especially in image recognition and classification. It has shown the great power for effective learning. In supervised learning, a physical phenomenon is described by a mapping between predict or labeled data. In this domain, graph-based algorithms have drawn great attention [1–5]. A lot of efforts have been done by using graph-based learning methods to various topics, such as regression [6] and dimensionality reduction [7].

Techniques that address the latter problem were proposed to reduce the multi-dimensional data dimensionality. It aims to find relevant subsets for feature description. It yields a smaller set of representative features while preserving the optimal salient characteristics. Hence, not only the processing time can be decreased, but also a better generalization of the learning models can be achieved. The algorithms mentioned above rely on both the manifold structure and learning mechanism [8–10]. Therefore, in many cases, it is possible to achieve better performance than other conventional methods. However, all of these methods firstly define the characterized manifold structure and then perform a regression [5]. As a result, the constructed graphs have great effects on

© Springer International Publishing AG, part of Springer Nature 2018
Y. Shi et al. (Eds.): ICCS 2018, LNCS 10861, pp. 184–193, 2018.
https://doi.org/10.1007/978-3-319-93701-4_14

the performance. Indeed, the graph spectral is fixed in the following regression steps.

Taking into consideration the above remarks, we introduce in this paper a graph-based algorithm for efficient supervised image classification. It applies the models of graph-based dimensionality reduction and sparse regression simultaneously. Besides, an iterative locally linear graph weight algorithm is applied to acquire graph weights and improve the recognition accuracy. Finally, we inspect the optimization problem of the proposed approach and we demonstrate the situations to solve it.

The rest of the paper is structured as follows. In Sect. 2, the graph embedding model is introduced. Section 3 details the proposed graph-based supervised classification algorithm. Section 4 presents the experiments carried out on benchmark datasets to verify the effectiveness of the proposed algorithm by comparing with other art-of-state algorithms. The analysis of the experimental results are also given. Finally, in Sect. 5, we draw conclusions and discuss the works for the future research.

2   Related Works

2.1   Notations and Preliminaries

In order to make the paper self-contained, the notations used in the paper are introduced. $\mathbf{X} = [\mathbf{x}_1, \mathbf{x}_2, \cdots, \mathbf{x}_l, \mathbf{x}_{l+1}, \cdots, \mathbf{x}_{l+u}] \in \mathbb{R}^{d \times (l+u)}$ is defined as the sample data matrix, where $\mathbf{x}_i \big|_{i=1}^{l}$ and $\mathbf{x}_j \big|_{j=l+1}^{l+u}$ are the labeled and unlabeled samples, respectively. l and u are the total numbers of labeled and unlabeled samples, respectively, and d is the sample dimension. Let N be the total number of samples. The label of each sample $\mathbf{x}_i$ is denoted by $y_i \in 1, 2, ..., C$, where C relates to the total number of classes. Let $\mathbf{S} \in \mathbb{R}^{(l+u) \times (l+u)}$ be the graph similarity matrix, where $\mathbf{S}_{ij}$ represents the similarity between $\mathbf{x}_i$ and $\mathbf{x}_j$ as given by the Cosine or the Gaussian Kernel ($\mathbf{S}$ is symmetric). To make it clear, Table 1 shows all the nations and descriptions in this paper.

2.2   Graph Embedding

In graph embedding, each node of a constructed graph $\mathbf{G} = \{\mathbf{X}, \mathbf{S}\}$ relates to a data point $\mathbf{x}_i \in \mathbf{X}$ [11]. The graph embedding is aimed at finding an optimal matrix $\mathbf{Y}$ with a lower dimension that can make the best description of the similarity between the data well. The optimal $\mathbf{Y}$ is given by

$$\arg \min_{\mathbf{Y}} (\mathbf{Y}^T \mathbf{X} \mathbf{L} \mathbf{X}^T \mathbf{Y})$$

$$s.t. \ \mathbf{Y}^T \mathbf{X} \mathbf{D} \mathbf{Y}^T \mathbf{A} = \mathbf{I} \tag{1}$$

Where $\mathbf{L} = \mathbf{D} - \mathbf{S}$ gives the Laplacian matrix, $\mathbf{D}$ is a diagonal matrix and $\mathbf{I}$ is an identity matrix.

Table 1. Notations and descriptions.

Notation	Description
d	Dimensionality of original data
N	Number of data samples
l	Number of labeled samples
u	Number of unlabeled samples
C	Number of classes
$\mathbf{x}_i$	The i-th original data sample
y_i	The label of $\mathbf{x}_i$
$\mathbf{S}$	Graph similarity matrix
$\mathbf{W}$	Linear transformation matrix
$\mathbf{D}$	Diagonal matrix
$\mathbf{I}$	Identity matrix
$\mathbf{L}$	Laplacian matrix
$\mathbf{X}_l$	Labeled train samples matrix
$\mathbf{X}_u$	Unlabeled test samples matrix
$\mathbf{X}$	Original data matrix
$\mathbf{Y}$	Low dimensional matrix

In fact, different algorithms for dimensionality reduction result in various intrinsic graphs $\mathbf{G} = \{\mathbf{X}, \mathbf{S}\}$. The most used algorithms to reduce the dimensionality include Principal Components Analysis (PCA), Linear Discriminant Analysis (LAD), Locally Linear Embedding (LLE) [12], Locality Preserving Projections (LPP) [2], ISOMAP [13], etc.

3   Proposed Algorithm

3.1   Similarity Matrix S

Firstly, a nearest neighbors method is used to determine k neighbors $(k \leq N)$ for each node. Asuming that i and j are two nodes linked by an edge, if i is among the k nearest neighbors of j, or if j is among the k nearest neighbors of i. It is obvious that this relation is symmetric.

Secondly, the similarity matrix $\mathbf{S}$ is computed. It is introduced in [14,15]. In order to acquire better performance for recognition and classification, the matrix $\mathbf{S}$ is computed in a high-dimensional data space. The regularizer $L_{1/2}$ is used as an unbiased estimator in this paper. It is used to improve the sparsity of matrix $\mathbf{S}$ for the minimization problem. Additionally, for graph embedding, the condition $\mathbf{S} \geq 0$ is added. The process of minimization can be presented as:

$$\min_{\mathbf{S}\geq 0} \sum_i \left\| \mathbf{x}_i - \sum_j \mathbf{S}_{i,j}\mathbf{x}_j \right\|^2 + \alpha\|\mathbf{S}\|_{\frac{1}{2}} + \beta\|\mathbf{S}\|^2$$

$$= \min_{\mathbf{S}\geq 0} \|\mathbf{X} - \mathbf{XS}\|^2 + \alpha\|\mathbf{S}\|_{\frac{1}{2}} + \beta\|\mathbf{S}\|^2$$

$$\Rightarrow \min_{\mathbf{S}\geq 0} Tr\left(\tilde{\kappa} - 2\tilde{\kappa}\mathbf{S} + \mathbf{S}^T\tilde{\kappa}\mathbf{S}\right) + \alpha\|\mathbf{S}\|_{\frac{1}{2}} + \beta Tr\left(\mathbf{S}^T\mathbf{S}\right) \tag{2}$$

Where α and β are the free parameters, $\tilde{\kappa}$ the kernel of $\mathbf{X}$ and $\|\mathbf{S}\|_{\frac{1}{2}} = \sum_i \sum_j \mathbf{S}_{i,j}^{1/2}$.

Thus, Eq. (2) could be rewritten as:

$$\min_{\mathbf{S}\geq 0} Tr\left[\left(\tilde{\kappa} - 2\tilde{\kappa}\mathbf{S} + \mathbf{S}^T\tilde{\kappa}\mathbf{S}\right) + \beta\mathbf{S}^T\mathbf{S}\right] + \alpha\|\mathbf{S}\|_{\frac{1}{2}} \tag{3}$$

Furthermore, Eq. (3) is equivalent to

$$\min_{\mathbf{S}\geq 0} Tr\left[\mathbf{S}^T\left(\beta\mathbf{I} + \tilde{\kappa}\right)\mathbf{S} - 2\tilde{\kappa}\mathbf{S} + \tilde{\kappa}\right] + \alpha\|\mathbf{S}\|_{\frac{1}{2}} \tag{4}$$

It should be noticed that minimizing Eq.(4) is subjected to $\mathbf{S} \geq 0$. Let $\varsigma \geq 0$ be the corresponding Lagrange multipliers. The Lagrange function $F(\mathbf{S})$ can be presented as:

$$F(\mathbf{S}) = Tr\left[\mathbf{S}^T\left(\beta\mathbf{I} + \tilde{\kappa}\right)\mathbf{S} - 2\tilde{\kappa}\mathbf{S} + \tilde{\kappa}\right] + \alpha\|\mathbf{S}\|_{\frac{1}{2}} + Tr\left(\varsigma\mathbf{S}^T\right) \tag{5}$$

Then, partial derivative of both sides leads to

$$\frac{\partial F(\mathbf{S})}{\partial \mathbf{S}_{ij}} = \left(-2\tilde{\kappa} + 2\tilde{\kappa}\mathbf{S} + 2\beta\mathbf{S} + \frac{1}{2}\alpha\mathbf{S}^{-\frac{1}{2}} + \varsigma\right)_{ij} \tag{6}$$

Where $\mathbf{S}^{-\frac{1}{2}}$ is equivalent to the inverse matrix of principal square-rooting matrix $\mathbf{S}^{\frac{1}{2}}$.

Then, the Karush-Kuhn-Tucker(KKT) condition $\varsigma\mathbf{S} = 0$ for $\mathbf{S}$ is

$$\left(-2\mathbf{X} + 2\mathbf{XS} + 2\beta\mathbf{S} + \frac{1}{2}\alpha\mathbf{S}^{-\frac{1}{2}} + \varsigma\right)_{ij}\mathbf{S}_{ij} = 0 \tag{7}$$

Eq. (7) can be reformulated as:

$$(-\tilde{\kappa}_{ij} + (\tilde{\kappa}\mathbf{S} + \beta\mathbf{S} + \frac{1}{2}\alpha\mathbf{S}^{-\frac{1}{2}})_{ij})\mathbf{S}_{ij} = 0 \tag{8}$$

An iterative process to retrieve $\mathbf{S}$ is expressed by

$$\mathbf{S}_{ij} \leftarrow \frac{\mathbf{X}}{(\mathbf{XS} + \beta\mathbf{S} + \frac{1}{4}\alpha\mathbf{S}^{-\frac{1}{2}})_{ij}}\mathbf{S}_{ij} \tag{9}$$

In fact, Eq. (9) only shows the computation for one iteration and it repeats many times until the result is convergence. Finally, we acquire the similarity matrix $\mathbf{S}$ for graph projection.

3.2   Graph Embedding Learning

The work described in [16] proposed a novel graph-based embedding framework for feature selection with unsupervised learning, named Joint Embedding Learning and Sparse Regression (JELSR). This unsupervised method aims at ranking the original features by performing non-linear embedding learning and sparse regression concurrently. JELSR inspired us to develop a method with graph embedding algorithm for supervised learning in the domain of image classification.

Based on graph embedding and sparse regression optimization function, we can optimize it by making the following operation:

$$\ell(\mathbf{W}, \mathbf{Y}) = \underset{\mathbf{W}, \mathbf{Y} \, s.t. \mathbf{Y}^T \mathbf{Y} = \mathbf{I}}{\arg\min} \left(trace(\mathbf{Y}^T \mathbf{L} \mathbf{Y}) + \mu(\left\| \mathbf{W}^\mathbf{T} \mathbf{X} - \mathbf{Y} \right\|_2^2 + \gamma \|\mathbf{W}\|_{2,1}) \right) \quad (10)$$

Where γ and μ are two regularization parameters. $\mathbf{W}$ represents the linear transform matrix, m is the graph embedding dimensionality, and $\mathbf{Y}$ denotes the data matrix of embedding non-linear projection of $\mathbf{X}$. The $\ell_{2,1}$ norm of $\mathbf{W}$ is given by $\|\mathbf{W}\|_{2,1} = \sum_{i=1}^{d} \|\hat{\mathbf{w}}_i\|_2$. $\hat{\mathbf{w}}_i$ is the i-th row of $\mathbf{W}$.

Respecting to the matrix $\mathbf{W}$, we can get the derivative of $\ell(\mathbf{W}, \mathbf{Y})$ as follows,

$$\frac{\partial \ell(\mathbf{W}, \mathbf{Y})}{\partial \mathbf{W}} = 2\mathbf{X}\mathbf{X}^T \mathbf{W} - 2\mathbf{X}\mathbf{Y}^T + 2\gamma \mathbf{U}\mathbf{W} = 0 \quad (11)$$

Where $\mathbf{U} \in \mathbb{R}^{d \times d}$ is a diagonal matrix. The i-th diagonal element is $\mathbf{U}_{ii} = \frac{1}{2\|\hat{\mathbf{w}}_i\|_2}$.

Thus, we have the equation as follows:

$$\mathbf{W} = (\mathbf{X}\mathbf{X}^T + \gamma \mathbf{U})^{-1} \mathbf{X}\mathbf{Y}^T \quad (12)$$

Equation (10) can be reformulated as:

$$\begin{aligned}
\ell(\mathbf{W}, \mathbf{Y}) &= \underset{\mathbf{W}, \mathbf{Y} \, s.t. \mathbf{Y}^T \mathbf{Y} = \mathbf{I}}{\arg\min} \left(trace(\mathbf{Y}^T \mathbf{L}\mathbf{Y}) + \mu(\left\| \mathbf{W}^\mathbf{T} \mathbf{X} - \mathbf{Y} \right\|_2^2 + \gamma \|\mathbf{W}\|_{2,1}) \right) \\
&= tr(\mathbf{Y}\mathbf{L}\mathbf{Y}^T) + \mu(tr(\mathbf{W}^T \mathbf{X}\mathbf{X}^T \mathbf{W}) - 2tr(\mathbf{W}^T \mathbf{X}\mathbf{Y}^T) \\
&\quad + tr(\mathbf{Y}\mathbf{Y}^T) + \gamma tr(\mathbf{W}^T \mathbf{U}\mathbf{W})) \\
&= tr(\mathbf{Y}\mathbf{L}\mathbf{Y}^T) + \mu(-tr(\mathbf{W}^T(\mathbf{X}\mathbf{X}^T + \gamma \mathbf{U})\mathbf{W}) + tr(\mathbf{Y}\mathbf{Y}^T)) \\
&= tr(\mathbf{Y}(\mathbf{L} + \mu \mathbf{I} - \mu \mathbf{X}^T \mathbf{A}^{-1} \mathbf{X})\mathbf{Y}^T) \quad (13)
\end{aligned}$$

Where $\mathbf{A} = \mathbf{X}\mathbf{X}^T + \gamma \mathbf{U}$.

Taking the objective function and the constraint $\mathbf{Y}\mathbf{Y}^T = \mathbf{I}$ into account, the optimization problem turns to

$$\arg\min_{\mathbf{Y}} tr(\mathbf{Y}(\mathbf{L} + \mu \mathbf{I} - \mu \mathbf{X}^T \mathbf{A}^{-1} \mathbf{X})\mathbf{Y}^T) \ \ s.t. \ \mathbf{Y}\mathbf{Y}^T = \mathbf{I} \quad (14)$$

If $\mathbf{A}$ and $\mathbf{L}$ are fixed, The Eigen decomposition of matrix $(\mathbf{L} + \mu \mathbf{I} - \mu \mathbf{X}^T \mathbf{A}^{-1} \mathbf{X})$ can be used as the solution to the optimization problem in Eq. (14). We select m eigenvectors corresponding to the m smallest eigenvalues in order. These eigenvectors are suitable to build a graph-based embedding which is used for image classification.

4 Experiments

We have tested our method on four different datasets. They contains scenes (8 Sports Event Categories Dataset and Scene 15 Dataset), faces (ORL Face Dataset) and objects (COIL-20 Object Dataset). These images have been used in different groups to train and test. The details of the experiments and results are described in the following.

4.1 Dataset Configurations

The details of how the images in the four datasets are configurated are listed as follows.

8 Sports Event Categories Dataset includes 8 sports event categories (provided by Li and Fei-Fei) [17]. We have used 130 images in every category, thus a total of 1040.

Scene 15 Dataset includes 4485 gray level images of 15 different scenes including indoor and outdoor scenes [18]. We use 130 images in every category, thus a total of 1950.

ORL Face Dataset consists of 10 different images of each 40 distinct subjects [19].

COIL-20 Objects Dataset contains 1440 images of 20 objects (provided by Columbia Object Image Library) [20]. We select 70 images out of 72 for each object as a subset.

We have tested different distributions between training and testing images. For the first three datasets, we have used 50% and 70% of images for training twice, leaving 50% and 30% for testing, respectively. For the last dataset, we have used 10% and 20% of images for training, remaining 90% and 80% for testing, respectively.

4.2 Graph Performance Comparison

In this experiment, the graph calculated from the similarity matrix S is firstly tested with by comparing with that of other classical similarity measure algorithms, such as KNN graph and ℓ_1 graph. Table 2 displays the performance of graphs based on different similarity measure algorithms. In order to make the comparison, Laplacian Eigenmaps (LE) is chosen as the projection algorithm and the classification algorithm is 1NN classifier. From the results, it can be concluded that the kernelized sparse non-negative graph matrix S is able to produce a graph weight matrix much better than the KNN graph and ℓ_1 graph methods.

4.3 Effect of Proposed Algorithm

The block-based Local Binary Patterns (LBP) is used as the image descriptor, where the number of blocks is set to 10×10. The LBP descriptor is the

Table 2. The best average recognition rates (%) on 10 random splits of different graph algorithms.

Datasets	8 Sports		Scene 15		ORL Face	
Training images	50%	70%	50%	70%	50%	70%
KNN graph	52.31	54.31	42.36	45.33	89.80	92.08
ℓ_1 graph	53.81	57.31	46.72	49.23	89.95	93.67
Proposed algorithm	**54.83**	**57.44**	**50.49**	**52.67**	**92.10**	**94.50**

uniform one having 59 features. For ORL Face and COIL-20 Objects datasets, we use image raw brightnesses. The proposed algorithm is tested by comparing with the following five algorithms including LLE, Supervised Laplacian Eigenmaps (SLE) [21], Manifold Regularized Deep Learning Architecture (MRDL) [14], Semi-Supervised Discriminant Embedding (SDE)[22] and S-ISOMAP [23]. For MRDL method, we used two layers. Image classification is carried out in the obtained subspace using the Nearest Neighbor Classifier (NN). The experimental results are listed in Tables 3, 4, 5, and represented as graphs in Figs. 1 and 2.

Table 3. The best average recognition rates (%) of 8 Sports Event Categories Dataset on 10 random splits.

8 Sports scene	P = 50%	P = 70%
LLE	44.92	49.10
SLE	51.40	50.90
MRDL	51.77	52.85
S-ISOMAP	51.88	54.68
SDE	51.98	55.96
Proposed algorithm	**55.92**	**57.60**

Table 4. The best average recognition rates (%) of Scene 15 Dataset on 10 random splits.

Scene 15 dataset	P = 50%	P = 70%
LLE	44.26	47.42
SLE	50.48	50.65
MRDL	46.59	47.91
S-ISOMAP	42.74	45.28
SDE	46.10	48.07
Proposed algorithm	**51.83**	**58.59**

Table 5. The best average recognition rates (%) of COIL-20 Object Dataset on 10 random splits.

COIL-20 object	P = 10%	P = 20%
LLE	91.81	94.71
SLE	82.03	88.56
MRDL	88.00	88.86
Proposed algorithm	**93.80**	**96.88**

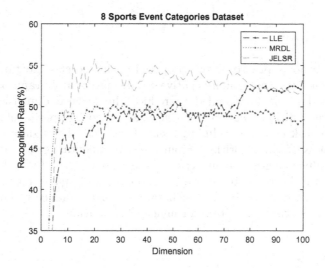

Fig. 1. Recognition accuracy vs. feature dimension for 8 Sports Event Categories Dataset.

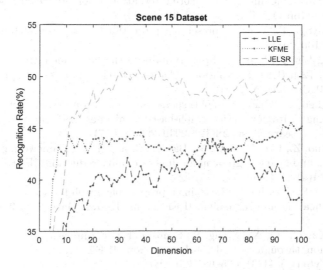

Fig. 2. Recognition accuracy vs. feature dimension for Scene 15 Dataset.

As presented by the results, we can draw the following conclusions. Generally, the proposed non-linear graph embedding method has enhanced performances compared with the other algorithms tested on different datasets in Tables 3, 4 and 5. Especially, compared with the MRDL algorithm, the best recognition rate of COIL-20 Object Dataset is increased by 15.80%. As the curves shown in Figs. 1 and 2, the recognition rates do not increase along with the dimension of features. Therefore, the proposed method can perform well without using large quantity of features. It can reduce the time and space complexity of training and classification.

5   Conclusions

By emplying a novel procedure, we proposed an image classification algorithm related to kernelized sparse non-negative graph matrix and graph-based sparse regression method. It is intended to reduce the feature dimensionality and improve the recognition accuracy in image classification. Experiments are carried out on benchmark datasets including scene, faces and object datasets to check the effectiveness of our algorithm. From the experimental results, it is obvious that the introduced algorithm outperforms the others tested. In the future, some optimization will be made to ensure the robustness of sparse regression. Some modifications are also needed to ameliorate the performance of our proposed graph-based supervised algorithm for image classification.

References

1. Zhu, X., Ghahramani, Z., Lafferty, J.D.: Semi-supervised learning using gaussian fields and harmonic functions. In: 20th International Conference on Machine Learning, Washington DC, USA, pp. 912–919 (2003)
2. He, X., Niyogi, P.: Locality preserving projections. Adv. Neural Inf. Proc. Syst. **2**(5), 153–160 (2004)
3. Cheng, H., Liu, Z., Yang, J.: Sparsity induced similarity measure for label propagation. In: 12th IEEE International Conference on Computer Vision (ICCV), pp. 317–324. IEEE, Kyoto (2009)
4. Pei, X., Chen, C., Guan, Y.: Joint sparse representation and embedding propagation learning: a framework for graph-based semisupervised learning. IEEE Trans. Neural Netw. Learn. Syst. **28**(12), 2949–2960 (2017)
5. Shi, X., Guo, Z., Lai, Z., Yang, Y., Bao, Z., Zhang, D.: A framework of joint graph embedding and sparse regression for dimensionality reduction. IEEE Trans. Image Process. **24**(4), 1341–1355 (2015)
6. Ni, B., Yan, S., Kassim, A.: Learning a propagable graph for semisupervised learning: classification and regression. IEEE Trans. Knowl. Data Eng. **24**(1), 114–126 (2012)
7. Nie, F., Xu, D., Li, X., Xiang, S.: Semisupervised dimensionality reduction and classification through virtual label regression. IEEE Trans. Syst. Man Cybern. Part B (Cybern.) **41**(3), 675–685 (2011)

8. He, X., Cai, D., Han, J.: Semi-supervised discriminant analysis. In: 11th IEEE International Conference on Computer Vision (ICCV), pp. 1–7. IEEE, Rio de Janeiro (2007)

9. Yan, S., Xu, D., Yang, Q., Zhang, L., Tang, X., Zhang, H.J.: Discriminant analysis with tensor representation. In: IEEE Computer Society Conference on Computer Vision and Pattern Recognition, pp. 526–532. IEEE, San Diego (2005)

10. Yan, S., Xu, D., Zhang, B., Zhang, H.J., Yang, Q., Lin, S.: Graph embedding and extensions: a general framework for dimensionality reduction. IEEE Trans. Pattern Anal. Mach. Intell. **29**(1), 40–51 (2007)

11. Brand, M.: Continuous nonlinear dimensionality reduction by kernel eigenmaps. In: International Joint Conference on Artificial Intelligence (IJCAI), pp. 547–554. ACM, Acapulco (2010)

12. Roweis, S.T., Saul, L.K.: Nonlinear dimensionality reduction by locally linear embedding. Science **290**(5500), 2323–2326 (2000)

13. Tenenbaum, J.B., De, S.V., Langford, J.C.: A global geometric framework for non-linear dimensionality reduction. Science **290**(5500), 2319–2323 (2000)

14. Yuan, Y., Mou, L., Lu, X.: Scene recognition by manifold regularized deep learning architecture. IEEE Trans. Neural Netw. Learn. Syst. **26**(10), 2222–2233 (2015)

15. Kong, D., Ding, C.H.Q., Huang, H., Nie, F.: An iterative locally linear embedding algorithm. In: 29th International Conference on Machine Learning (ICML), Edinburgh, Scotland, UK (2010)

16. Hou, C., Nie, F., Li, X., Yi, D., Wu, Y.: Joint embedding learning and sparse regression: a framework for unsupervised feature selection. IEEE Trans. Cybern. **44**(6), 793–804 (2014)

17. Li, L.J., Li, F.F.: What, where and who? Classifying events by scene and object recognition. In: 11th IEEE International Conference on Computer Vision (ICCV), pp. 1–8. IEEE, Rio de Janeiro (2007)

18. Lazebnik, S., Schmid, C., Ponce, J.: Beyond bags of features: spatial pyramid matching for recognizing natural scene categories. In: IEEE Computer Society Conference on Computer Vision and Pattern Recognition, vol. 2, pp. 2169–2178. IEEE, New York (2006)

19. Samaria, F.S., Harter, A.C.: Parameterisation of a stochastic model for human face identification. In: 2ed IEEE Workshop on Applications of Computer Vision, pp. 138–142. IEEE, Sarasota (2010)

20. Nene, S.A., Nayar, S.K., Murase, H.: Columbia object image library (coil-20). Technical report CUCS-005-96, Location (1996)

21. Raducanu, B., Dornaika, F.: A supervised non-linear dimensionality reduction approach for manifold learning. Pattern Recogn. **45**(6), 2432–2444 (2012)

22. Yu, G., Zhang, G., Domeniconi, C., Yu, Z., You, J.: Semi-supervised classification based on random subspace dimensionality reduction. Pattern Recogn. **45**(3), 1119–1135 (2012)

23. Geng, X., Zhan, D.C., Zhou, Z.H.: Supervised nonlinear dimensionality reduction for visualization and classification. IEEE Trans. Syst. Man Cybern. Part B (Cybern.) **35**(6), 1098–1107 (2005)

An Adversarial Training Framework
for Relation Classification

Wenpeng Liu[1,2], Yanan Cao[1(✉)], Cong Cao[1], Yanbing Liu[1], Yue Hu[1], and Li Guo[1]

[1] Institute of Information Engineering, Chinese Academy of Sciences, Beijing, China
{liuwenpeng,caoyanan,caocong,liuyanbing,huyue,guoli}@iie.ac.cn
[2] School of Cyber Security, University of Chinese Academy of Sciences, Beijing, China

Abstract. Relation classification is one of the most important topics in Natural Language Processing (NLP) which could help mining structured facts from text and constructing knowledge graph. Although deep neural network models have achieved improved performance in this task, the state-of-the-art methods still suffer from the scarce training data and the overfitting problem. In order to solve this problem, we adopt the adversarial training framework to improve the robustness and generalization of the relation classifier. In this paper, we construct a bidirectional recurrent neural network as the relation classifier, and append word-level attention to the input sentence. Our model is an end-to-end framework without the use of any features derived from pre-trained NLP tools. In experiments, our model achieved higher F1-score and better robustness than comparative methods.

Keywords: Relation classification · Deep learning · Adversarial training
Attention mechanism

1 Introduction

Relation Classification is the process of recognizing the semantic relations between pairs of *nominals*. It is a crucial component in natural language processing and could be defined as follows: given a sentence S with the annotated pairs of nominals e_1 and e_2, we aim to identify the relations between e_1 and e_2. For example: "The [singer]$_{e1}$, who performed three of the nominated songs, also caused a [commotion]$_{e2}$ on the red carpet." Our goal is to find out the relation of marked entities *singer* and *commotion*, which is obviously recognized as *Cause-Effect* (e_1, e_2) relation in this demonstration.

Traditional relation classifiers generally focused on features representation or kernel-based approaches which rely on full-fledged NLP tools, such as POS tagging, dependency parsing and semantic analysis [13, 14]. Although these approaches are able to exploit the symbolic structures in sentences, they still suffer from the weakness of using handcrafted features. In recently years, deep learning models which extract features automatically, have achieved big improvements on this task. Commonly used models include convolutional neural network (CNN), recurrent neural network (RNN) and other complex hybrid networks [7, 8]. In the most recent past, some researchers combined features representation with neural network models to utilize more characteristics, such as the shortest dependency path [2].

© Springer International Publishing AG, part of Springer Nature 2018
Y. Shi et al. (Eds.): ICCS 2018, LNCS 10861, pp. 194–205, 2018.
https://doi.org/10.1007/978-3-319-93701-4_15

Although deep neural network architectures have achieved state-of-the-art perform-ance, to train an optimized model relies on a large amount of labeled data, otherwise it will lead to overfitting. Due to the high cost of manually tagging samples, in many specific tasks, labeled data is scarce and may not fully sustain the training of a deep supervised learning model. For example, in relation classification task, the standard dataset just contains 10,717 annotated sentences. To prevent overfitting, strategies such as dropout [16] and adding random noise [17, 18] have been proposed, but the effec-tiveness is limited.

In order to address this problem, we innovatively adopt the *adversarial training* framework for classifying the inter-relations between nominals. We generate *adversa-rial examples* [11, 12] for labeled data by making small perturbations on word embed-dings of the input, which significantly increase the loss incurred by our model. Then, we regularize our classifier using adversarial training technique, i.e. training the model to correctly classify both unmodified examples and perturbed ones. This strategy not only improves the robustness to adversarial examples, but also promotes generalization performance for original examples. In this work, we construct a bidirectional LSTM model as a relation classifier. Beyond the basic model, we use a word-level attention mechanism [6] on the input sentence to capture its most important semantic information. This framework is an end-to-end one without using extra knowledge and NLP systems.

In experiments, we run our model and ten typical comparative methods on the SemEval-2010 Task 8 dataset [13]. Our model achieved an F1-score of 88.7% and outperformed other methods in the literature, which demonstrates the effectiveness of adversarial training.

2   Related Work

Traditional methods for relation classification are mainly based on features representa-tion or kernel-based approaches which rely on a mature NLP tools, such as POS tagging, dependency parsing and semantic analysis. [21] propose a shortest path dependency kernel for relation classification, the main idea of which is that the relation strongly relies on the dependency path between two given entities. Besides considering the structural information, [20] introduce semantic information into kernel methods. In these approaches, the use of features extracted by NLP tools results in cascaded error. On the other hand, handcrafted features of data have bad reusability for other tasks.

In order to extract features automatically, recent researches focus on utilizing deep learning models for this task and have achieved big improvements. [9] proposed convo-lutional neural networks (CNNs), which uses word embedding and position as input. [5, 7] observed that recurrent neural networks (RNNs) with long-short term memory (LSTMs) could improve addressing this problem. Recently, [6] proposed CNNs with two levels of attention for this task in order to better discern patterns in heterogeneous contexts, which achieved the best effect. What is more, some researchers combined features representation with neural network in order to utilize more linguistic informa-tion. The typical operations are neural architecture which leverages the shortest depend-ency path-based CNNs [2], and the SDP-LSTM model [5]. Existing studies revealed that, deep and rich neural network architectures are more capable of information integration and abstraction, while the annotated data maybe not sufficient for the further promotion of performance.

Adversarial Training was originally introduced by image classification [12]. Then it is adapted to text classification and extended to some semi-supervised tasks by [10]. Predecessors' work demonstrated that the learned input with adversarial training have improved in quality, which solved overfitting problem to some extent. Having a similar intuition, [18] added random noise to the input and hidden layer during training, however the effectiveness of randomly adding mechanism is limited. As another strategy for prevent overfitting, dropout [16] is a regularization method widely used for many tasks. We especially conducted an experiment to make a comparison among adversarial training and these methods.

3   Our Model

Given a sentence s with a pair of entities e_1 and e_2 annotated, the task of relation classification is to identify the semantic relation between and e_1 and e_2 in accordance with a set of predefined relation types (all types will be displayed in Sect. 4). Figure 1 shows the overall architectures of our adversarial neural relation classification (ANRC).

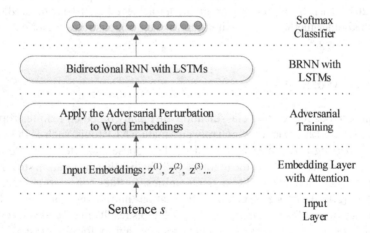

Fig. 1. Overall architecture for adversarial neural relation classification

The input of architecture is encoded using vector representations including word embedding, context and positional embedding. What's more, word-level attention could be used to capture the relevance of words with respect to the target entities. In order to enhance the robustness of model, adversarial examples are leveraged in input embeddings. After that, bidirectional recurrent neural network is used to capture information in different levels of abstraction, and the last layer is a softmax classifier to optimize classification results.

3.1 Input Representation with Word-Level Attention

Given a sentence s, each word w_i is converted into a real-valued vector r^{w_i}. The position embedding of w_i is mapped to a vector of dimension d^{wpe}, tagged as WPE (word position embeddings) proposed by [9]. Consequently, the word embedding and the word position embedding of each word w_l are concatenated to form the input, $emb_x = \{[r^{w_1}, wpe^{w_1}], [r^{w_2}, wpe^{w_2}], \ldots, [r^{w_N}, wpe^{w_N}]\}$. Afterwards, the convolutional operation is applied to each window of size k of successive windows in $emb_x = \{r^{w_1}, r^{w_2}, \ldots, r^{w_N},\}$, ultimately, we define vector z_n as the concatenation of a sequence of k word embedding, centralized in the n-th word:

$$Z_n = (r^{w_{n-(k-1)/2}}, \cdots, r^{w_{n+(k-1)/2}})^T \tag{1}$$

Word-Level Attention. Attention mechanism makes the neural network look back to the key parts of the source text when it is trying to predict the next token of a sequence. Attentive neural networks have been applied successfully in sequence-to-sequence learning tasks. In order to fully capture the relationships and interest of specific words with the target nominals, we design a model to automatically learn this relevance for relation classification like [6].

Contextual Relevance Matrices. Take notice of the example in Fig. 2, we can easily observe that the non-entity word "cause" is of great significance to determine the relation of entity pair. For the sake of characterizing the contextual correlations and connections between entity mention e_j and non-entity word w_i, we leverage two diagonal attention matrix A^j with value $A^j_{i,i} = f(e_j, w_i)$, which is computed as the inner product between embeddings of the entity e_j and word w_i respectively. Based on the diagonal attention matrixes, the relativeness of the i-th word with respect to j-th entity ($j \in \{1, 2\}$) could be calculated as Eq. (1):

S: The [singer], who performed three of the nominated songs, also caused a [commotion] on the red carpet.

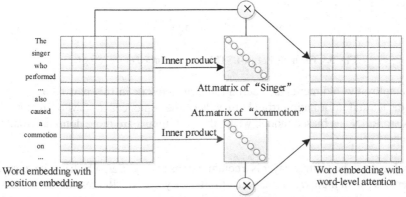

Fig. 2. Word-level attention on input

$$\alpha_i^j = \frac{\exp\left(A_{i,i}^j\right)}{\sum_{i'=1}^n \exp\left(A_{i',i'}^j\right)} \tag{2}$$

Input Attention Composition. Next, we combine the two relevance factors α_i^1 and α_i^2 with compositional word embedding z_n above in for recognizing the relation via a simple average algorithm as:

$$r_i = z_i \cdot \frac{\alpha_i^1 + \alpha_i^2}{2} \tag{3}$$

Finally, we've got the final output of word-level attention mechanism, a matrix $R = [r_1, r_2, ..., r_n]$ where n is the sentence length, regarded as input vectors feed into neural network we construct.

3.2 Bi-LSTM Network for Classification

Bi-LSTM Network. As a text classification model, we use a LSTM-based neural network model which is used in the state-of-the-art works [1, 7] and the experimental results show its effectiveness for this problem. Beyond the basic model, we adopt in our method a variant introduced by [15]. The LSTM-based recurrent neural network consists of four components: an input gate, a forget gate, an output gate, and a memory cell .

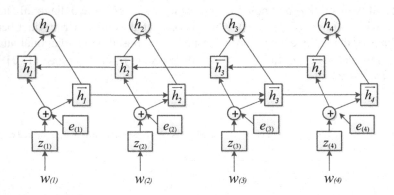

Fig. 3. The model of Bi-LSTMs and perturbed embeddings

We employ the bidirectional recurrent neural network in this part so as to better capture the textual information from both ends of the sentences in view of the fact that the standard RNN is a biased model, where the later inputs are more dominant than the earlier inputs.

Softmax Layer. The softmax layer is a commonly used classifier, which can be regarded as a generalization of multivariate classifier from binary Logistic Regression (LR) one. For this part, we use it to predict the label y from a discrete set of classes Y for a sentence. We denote s as the input sentence and θ as the parameters of a classifier. The output of Bi-LSTM

h is the input of the classifier (Eq. (4)). Simply taking the summation over the log probabilities of all those labels yields the final loss function as Eq. (5).

$$p(y|s; \theta) = \text{softmax}(W_y * h + b_y) \tag{4}$$

$$L(s; \theta) = - \sum_{i=1}^{|Y|} \log P\big(y_i|s; \theta\big) \tag{5}$$

3.3 Adversarial Training

Adversarial examples are generated by making small perturbations to the input, which is designed to significantly increase the loss incurred by a machine learning model. And *adversarial training* is a way of regularizing supervised learning algorithms to improves robustness to small, approximately word case perturbations. It's a process of training a model to correctly classify unmodified examples and adversarial examples.

As shown in Fig. 3, we apply the adversarial perturbation to word embeddings, rather than directly to the input, which is similar to [10]. We denote the concatenation of a sequence of word embedding vectors $[z^{(1)}, z^{(2)}, ..., z^{(T)}]$ as s'. Then we define the adversarial perturbation e_{adv} on s' as Eq. (6). Here e is a perturbation on the input and $\hat{\theta}$ denotes a fixed copy of the current value of θ.

$$e_{adv} = arg \min_{\|e\| \le \epsilon} -L\big(s' + e; \hat{\theta}\big) \tag{6}$$

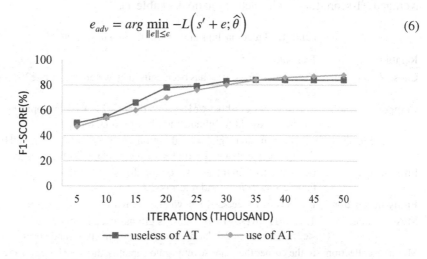

Fig. 4. Training progress of ANRC and ANRC minus AT across iterations

When applied to a classifier, adversarial training adds e_{adv} to the cost as Eq. (7) instead of Eq. (5), where N in Eq. (7) denotes the number of labeled examples. The adversarial training is carried out to minimize the negative log-likelihood plus L_{adv} with stochastic gradient descent.

$$L_{adv}(s';\theta) = -\frac{1}{N}\sum_{n=1}^{N}\log p(y_n|s'_n + e_{adv,n};\theta) \tag{7}$$

At each step of training, we identify the worst perturbations e_{adv} against the current model $p(y|s';\hat{\theta})$, and train the model to be robust to such perturbations through minimizing Eq. (7) with respect to θ. However, Eq. (6) is computationally intractable for neural nets. Inspired by [11], we approximate this value by linearizing $L(s';\theta)$ around s as Eq. (8).

$$e_{adv} = \frac{\epsilon g}{\|g\|}, \text{ where } g = \nabla_s L(s';\hat{\theta}) \tag{8}$$

4   Experiments and Results

4.1   Datasets

Our experiments are conducted on SemEval-2010 Task 8 dataset, which is widely used for relation classification [13]. The dataset contains 10,717 annotated examples, including 8,000 sentences for training and 2,717 for testing. The relationships between nominals in the corpus are classified into 10 categories, which are list as below. We adopt the official evaluation metric to evaluate our systems, which is based on macro-averaged F1-score for the nine actual relations (Table 1).

Table 1. 9 relationships and examples in our dataset

Relation	Example
Cause-effect	"The <e1>burst</e1> has been caused by water hammer<e2>pressure</e2>"
Component-whole	The ride-on <e1>boat</e1> <e2>tiller</e2> was developed by engineers Arnold S. Juliano and Dr. Eulito U. Bautista
Content-container	This cut blue and white striped cotton <e1>dress</e1> with red bands on the bodice was in a <e2>trunk</e2> of vintage Barbie clothing
Entity-origin	One basic trick involves a spectator choosing a <e1>card</e1> from the<e2>deck</e2> and returning it
Entity-destination	Both his <e1>feet</e1> have been moving into the <e2>ball</e2>
Message-topic	This <e1>love</e1> of nature's gift has been reflected in <e2>artworks</e2> dating back more than a thousand years
Member-collection	In the corner there are several gate captains and a <e1>legion</e1> of Wu <e2>crossbowmen</e2>
Instrument-agency	A <e1>thief</e1> who tried to steal the truck broke the igenition with <e2>screwdriver</e2>
Product-producer	A <e1>factory</e1> for <e2>cars</e2> and spareparts was built in Russia
Other	The following information appeared in the <e1>notes</e1> to consolidated financial <e2>statements</e2> of some corporate annual reports

4.2 Comparative Methods

To evaluate the effectiveness of our model, we compare its performance with notable traditional machine learning approaches and deep learning models including CNN, RNN and other neural network architectures. The comparative methods are introduced in the following.

- **Traditional machine learning algorithms:** As a traditional handcrafted-feature based classification, [19] fed extracted features from many external corpora to an SVM classifier and achieved 82.2% F1 score.
- **RNN based models:** MV-RNN is a recursive neural network build on the constituency tree and achieved a comparable performance with SVM [22]. SDP-LSTM is a type of gated recurrent neural network, and it is the first attempt to use LSTM in this task and it raised the F1-score to 83.7% [5].
- **CNN based models:** [9] construct a CNN on the word sequence and integrated word position embedding, make a breakthrough on the task. CR-CNN extended the basic CNN by replacing the common softmax cost function with a ranking-based cost function [3], and achieved an F1-score of 84.1%. Using a simple negative sampling method, depLCNN + NS introduced additional samples from other corpora like the NYT dataset. And this strategy effectively improved the performance to 85.6% F1-score [4]. Att-Pooling-CNN appended multi-level attention to the basic CNN model, and have achieved the state-of-the-art F1-score in relation classification task [6].
- **RNN combined with CNN:** DepNN is a convolutional neural network with a recursive neural network designed to model the subtrees, and achieve an F1-score of 83.6% [2].

4.3 Experimental Setup

We utilize the word embeddings with 200 dimensions released by Stanford[1]. For model parameters, we set the dimension of the entity position feature vector as 20. We use Adam optimizer with batch size 64, an initial learning rate of 0.001 and a 0.99 learning rate exponential decay factor at each training step. The word window size on the convolutional layer is fixed to 3. We also leverage dropout method to training the neural network with 0.5 dropout ratio. For adversarial training, we empirically choose "ϵ" = 0.02. We trained for 50,000 steps for each method in contrast experiments.

We run all experiments using TensorFlow on two Tesla V100 GPUs. Our model took about 8 min per epoch on average.

4.4 Results Analysis

Comparation with Other Models. Table 2 presents the best effect achieved by our adversarial-training based model (ANRC) and comparative methods. We observe that our model achieves an F1-score of 88.7%, outperforming the state-of-the-art models.

---

[1] https://nlp.stanford.edu/projects/glove/.

Table 2. Results of our model and comparative methods

Model	F1 (%)
Methods of traditional classifier	
SVM [19]	82.2
Neural networks with dependency features	
MVRNN [22]	82.4
Hybrid FCM [24]	83.4
SDP-LSTM [5]	83.7
DRNNs [1]	85.8
SPTree [23]	84.5
Neural works (End-to-end)	
CNN+Softmax [9]	82.7
CR-CNN [3]	84.1
DepNN [2]	83.6
depLCNN+NS [4]	85.6
Att-Pooling-CNN [6]	88.0
Our architecture	
ANRC	88.7

From the results in Table 2, we can also find that, in the end-to-end frameworks the CNN architectures have achieved better performance than RNN ones. Besides, the employment of negative sampling in depLCNN+NS promote the F1-score to more than 85%. And the attention mechanism introduced in the Att-Pooling-CNN model significantly improved the effectiveness of relation classification. Although we use a Bi-LSTM as the basic classification model, there is still some improvement in the performance, which proved the effectiveness of adversarial training framework.

Robustness of Adversarial Training. In order to test the robustness of our model, we delete half of the training data, and evaluate the models' precision on training data and test data respectively. All using the Bi-LSTM model with attention as the relation classifier, we adopt three different strategies to prevent overfitting: adversarial training plus dropout, adding random noise plus dropout, and just using dropout. Comparative results are shown in Table 3. Although the Adversarial Training+Dropout method has a little precision loss on training data, it achieves an acceptable precision on test data which prominently outperforms other strategies. It demonstrates that training with adversarial perturbations well alleviated the overfitting in the case of scarce training data. Meanwhile, our model has stronger robustness to small, approximately word case perturbations.

Table 3. F1-score in the case of halving training data

Strategy for reducing overfitting	Precision (training data)	Precision (test data)
Dropout	83.1%	59.6%
Random noise+dropout	82.3%	66.4%
Adversarial training+dropout	81.0%	75.5%

Convergence of Adversarial Training. We compare the convergence behavior of our method using adversarial training to that of the baseline Bi-LSTM model with attention. We plot the performance of each iteration of these two models in Fig. 4. From this figure, we find that training with adversarial examples converges more slowly while the final F1 score is higher. It enlightens us that, we could pre-trained the model without adversarial training to faster the process.

5   Conclusion and the Future Work

In this paper, we proposed an adversarial training framework for relation classification, named ANRC, to improve the performance and robustness of relation classification. Experimental results demonstrate that, training with adversarial perturbations outperformed the method with random perturbations and dropout in term of reducing overfitting. And, our model using a Bi-LSTM relation classifier with word-level attention outperforms previous models. In the future work, we will construct various relation classifier models and apply the adversarial training framework on other tasks.

Acknowledgement. This work was supported by the National Key Research and Development program of China (No. 2016YFB0801300), the National Natural Science Foundation of China grants (No. 61602466).

References

1. Xu, Y., Jia, R., Mou, L., Li, G., Chen, Y., Lu, Y., Jin, Z.: Improved relation classification by deep recurrent neural networks with data augmentation. In: Proceedings of COLING 2016, the 26th International Conference on Computational Linguistics: Technical Papers, pp. 1461–1470 (2016)
2. Liu, Y., Wei, F., Li, S., Ji, H., Zhou, M., Wang, H.: A dependency-based neural network for relation classification. In: Proceedings of the 53rd Annual Meeting of the Association for Computational Linguistics (2015)
3. dos Santos, C., Xiang, B., Zhou, B.: Classifying relations by ranking with convolutional neural networks. In: Proceedings of the 53rd Annual Meeting of the Association for Computational Linguistics (2015)
4. Xu, K., Feng, Y., Huang, S., Zhao, D.: Semantic relation classification via convolutional neural networks with simple negative sampling. In: Proceedings of the 2015 Conference on Empirical Methods in Natural Language Processing, pp. 536–540 (2015)
5. Xu, Y., Mou, L., Li, G., Chen, Y., Peng, H., Jin, Z.: Classifying relations via long short term memory networks along shortest dependency paths. In: Proceedings of the 2015 Conference on Empirical Methods in Natural Language Processing, pp. 1785–1794 (2015)
6. Wang, L., Cao, Z., de Melo, G., Liu, Z.: Relation classification via multi-level attention CNNs. In: Proceedings of the 54th Annual Meeting of the Association for Computational Linguistics, Volume 1: Long Papers, vol. 1, pp. 1298–1307 (2016)
7. Cai, R., Zhang, X., Wang, H.: Bidirectional recurrent convolutional neural network for relation classification. In: Proceedings of the 54th Annual Meeting of the Association for Computational Linguistics, Volume 1: Long Papers, vol. 1, pp. 756–765 (2016)

8. Zeng, D., Liu, K., Chen, Y., Zhao, J.: Distant supervision for relation extraction via piecewise convolutional neural networks. In: Proceedings of the 2015 Conference on Empirical Methods in Natural Language Processing, pp. 1753–1762 (2015)

9. Zeng, D., Liu, K., Lai, S., Zhou, G., Zhao, J.: Relation classification via convolutional deep neural network. In: Proceedings of COLING 2014, the 25th International Conference on Computational Linguistics: Technical Papers, pp. 2335–2344 (2014)

10. Miyato, T., Dai, A.M., Goodfellow, I.: Adversarial training methods for semi-supervised text classification. arXiv preprint arXiv:1605.07725 (2016)

11. Goodfellow, I.J., Shlens, J., Szegedy, C., Goodfellow, I.J., Shlens, J., Szegedy, C.: Explaining and harnessing adversarial examples. In: ICML, pp. 1–10 (2015)

12. Szegedy, C., Zaremba, W., Sutskever, I., Bruna, J., Erhan, D., Goodfellow, I., Fergus, R.: Intriguing properties of neural networks. arXiv preprint arXiv:1312.6199 (2013)

13. Hendrickx, I., Kim, S.N., Kozareva, Z., Nakov, P., Ó Séaghdha, D., Padó, S., Pennacchiotti, M., Romano, L., Szpakowicz, S.: Semeval-2010 task 8: multi-way classification of semantic relations between pairs of nominals. In: Proceedings of the Workshop on Semantic Evaluations: Recent Achievements and Future Directions, pp. 94–99. Association for Computational Linguistics (2009)

14. Kambhatla, N.: Combining lexical, syntactic, and semantic features with maximum entropy models for extracting relations. In: Proceedings of the ACL 2004 on Interactive poster and demonstration sessions, p. 22. Association for Computational Linguistics (2004)

15. Zaremba, W., Sutskever, I.: Learning to execute. arXiv preprint arXiv:1410.4615 (2014)

16. Srivastava, N., Hinton, G., Krizhevsky, A., Sutskever, I., Salakhutdinov, R.: Dropout: a simple way to prevent neural networks from overfitting. J. Mach. Learn. Res. 15(1), 1929–1958 (2014)

17. Poole, B., Sohl-Dickstein, J., Ganguli, S.: Analyzing noise in autoencoders and deep networks. arXiv preprint arXiv:1406.1831 (2014)

18. Xie, Z., Wang, S.I., Li, J., Lévy, D., Nie, A., Jurafsky, D., Ng, A.Y.: Data noising as smoothing in neural network language models. arXiv preprint arXiv:1703.02573 (2017)

19. Rink, B., Harabagiu, S.: UTD: classifying semantic relations by combining lexical and semantic resources. In: Proceedings of the 5th International Workshop on Semantic Evaluation, pp. 256–259. Association for Computational Linguistics (2010)

20. Plank, B., Moschitti, A.: Embedding semantic similarity in tree kernels for domain adaptation of relation extraction. In: Proceedings of the 51st Annual Meeting of the Association for Computational Linguistics, Volume 1: Long Papers, vol. 1, pp. 1498–1507 (2013)

21. Bunescu, R.C., Mooney, R.J.: A shortest path dependency kernel for relation extraction. In: Proceedings of the Conference on Human Language Technology and Empirical Methods in Natural Language Processing, pp. 724–731. Association for Computational Linguistics (2005)

22. Socher, R., Huval, B., Manning, C.D., Ng, A.Y.: Semantic compositionality through recursive matrix-vector spaces. In: Proceedings of the 2012 Joint Conference on Empirical Methods in Natural Language Processing and Computational Natural Language Learning, pp. 1201–1211. Association for Computational Linguistics (2012)

23. Miwa, M., Bansal, M.: End-to-end relation extraction using LSTMs on sequences and tree structures. arXiv preprint arXiv:1601.00770 (2016)
24. Yu, M., Gormley, M., Dredze, M.: Factor-based compositional embedding models. In: NIPS Workshop on Learning Semantics, pp. 95–101 (2014)

Topic-Based Microblog Polarity Classification Based on Cascaded Model

Quanchao Liu[1,2(✉)], Yue Hu[1,2], Yangfan Lei[2], Xiangpeng Wei[2], Guangyong Liu[4], and Wei Bi[3]

[1] Institute of Information Engineering, Chinese Academy of Science, Beijing, China
liuquanchao@iie.ac.cn
[2] University of Chinese Academy of Science, Beijing, China
[3] SeeleTech Corporation, San Francisco, USA
[4] Beijing, China

Abstract. Given a microblog post and a topic, it is an important task to judge the sentiment towards that topic: positive or negative, and has important theoretical and application value in the public opinion analysis, personalized recommendation, product comparison analysis, prevention of terrorist attacks, etc. Because of the short and irregular messages as well as containing multifarious features such as emoticons, and sentiment of a microblog post is closely related to its topic, most existing approaches cannot perfectly achieve cooperating analysis of topic and sentiment of messages, and even cannot know what factors actually determined the sentiment towards that topic. To address the issues, MB-LDA model and attention network are applied to Bi-RNN for topic-based microblog polarity classification. Our cascaded model has three distinctive characteristics: (i) a strong relationship between topic and its sentiment is considered; (ii) the factors that affect the topic's sentiment are identified, and the degree of influence of each factor can be calculated; (iii) the synchronized detection of the topic and its sentiment in microblog is achieved. Extensive experiments show that our cascaded model outperforms state-of-the-art unsupervised approach JST and supervised approach SSA-ST significantly in terms of sentiment classification accuracy and F1-Measure.

Keywords: Cascaded model · Attention model · LDA model
Bi-RNN · Sentiment analysis · Microblog topic

1 Introduction

With the fast development of social network, more and more Chinese, especially young people, are enjoying the convenience brought by the social network. Take microblog for example, people have published various topics, such as entertainment news, political events, sports reports, etc. They express their various sentiment and opinions towards the topic with multiple forms of media. However, the unique features appear in microblog, such as the sparsity of topics, contact relation, retweet, the short message, the homophonic words, abbreviations, the network language (the popular words), emoticons, etc. These make it very difficult to analyze microblog's topic and its sentiment.

© Springer International Publishing AG, part of Springer Nature 2018
Y. Shi et al. (Eds.): ICCS 2018, LNCS 10861, pp. 206–220, 2018.
https://doi.org/10.1007/978-3-319-93701-4_16

To address the issues, a new cascade model, which excavates the topic of microblog and takes into account the relationship between the topic and its sentiment, is proposed. Our cascaded model aims to identify microblog topic and its sentiment more automatically and efficiently. It mainly has three distinctive advantages: (i) a novel MB-LDA model, which takes both contact relation and document relation into consideration based on LDA, is introduced to mining microblog topic, and the strong relationship between topic and its sentiment is considered in a model; (ii) attention network is introduced to identifying the factors that affect the topic's sentiment and calculating the degree of influence of each factor; (iii) because both MB-LDA model and attention network are considered when using Bi-RNN to judge the sentiment towards the topic, the synchronized detection of the topic and its sentiment in microblog is achieved.

The rest of our paper will be organized as follows. In Sect. 2, we briefly summarize related works. Section 3 gives an overview of data construction, including the dictionaries of sentiment words, internet slang and emoticons. Section 4 gives an overview for cascaded model, including principles, graph models, related resources needed. The experimental results are reported in Sect. 5. Lastly, we conclude in Sect. 6.

2 Related Works

2.1 Topic Model

The present text topic recognition technologies mainly are: traditional topic mining algorithm, topic mining algorithm based on linear algebra, topic mining algorithm based on probability model. The traditional topic model can be traced back to the algorithm of text clustering, and it maps the unstructured data in the text into the points in the vector space by VSM (vector space model), and then uses traditional clustering algorithm to achieve text clustering. Usually text clustering has division-based algorithm, hierarchical-based algorithm, density-based algorithm and so on. However, these clustering algorithms generally depend on the distance calculation between the text and the distance calculation in the mass text is difficult to define; in addition, the clustering result is to distinguish the categories and doesn't give the semantic information, it is not conducive to people's understanding. LSA (latent semantic analysis) is a new method for mining text topics based on linear algebra, proposed by [1]. LSA uses the dimensionality reduction method of SVD to excavate the latent structure (semantic structure) of documents, and then we query and analyze correlation in low dimensional semantic space. By means of SVD and other mathematical methods, the implicit correlation can be well mined. However, the limitation of LSA is that it does not solve the "polysemous" problem of the text, because a word only has one coordinate in semantic space (that is the average of the word more than one meaning), instead of using multiple coordinate to express more than one meaning, and what's more, SVD involves matrix operations, the computational cost is large, and the calculation results in many dimensions is negative, which makes the understanding of the topic is not intuitive.

The third topic model is generative probability model. It assumes that the topic can generate words according to certain rules. When text words are known, the topic distribution of text set can be calculated by probability. The most representative topic model are PLSA (probabilistic latent semantic analysis) and LDA (latent dirichlet allocation). Based on the study of LSA, PLSA is proposed by [2], which combines the maximum likelihood method and the generation model. It follows the dimension reduction of LSA: the text is a kind of high dimensional data when it is represented with TF·IDF, the number of topics is limited and the topic corresponds to the low dimensional semantic space, the topic mining is to project the document from the high dimensional space to the semantic space by reducing the dimension. LDA is a breakthrough extension of the PLSA by adding a priori distribution of Dirichlet on the basis of PLSA. The founder of LDA [3] point out that PLSA does not use a unified probability model in the probability calculation of the document corresponding to the topic, too many parameters will lead to overfitting, and it is difficult to assign a probability to a document outside the training set. Based on these defects, LDA introduces the super parameters and form a Bayesian model with 3 layers "document-topic-word", and then the model is derived by using the probability method to find the semantic structure of the text and to mine the topic of the text.

In recent years, the research on topic model has been deepened, and a variety of models have been derived, such as Dynamic topic model [4], Syntactic topic model [5] and so on. There are also models that consider the relationships between texts, such as Link-PLSA-LDA and HTM (Hypertext Topic Model). Link-PLSA-LDA is a topic model proposed by [6] for citation analysis. In this model, the quoted text is generated by PLSA, and the citation text is generated by LDA, and the model assumes that the two has the same topic. HTM is a topic model proposed by [7] for hypertext analysis. In the process of generating text, HTM adds the influence factors of hyperlinks to mine the topic and classify the text for the hypertext.

2.2 Microblog Sentiment Analysis

Sentiment analysis is one of the fastest growing research areas in computer science, making it challenging to keep track of all the activities in the area. In the research domain of sentiment analysis, polarity classification for twitter has been concerned for some time, such as Tweetfeel, Twendz, Twitter Sentiment. In previous related work, [8] use distant learning to acquire sentiment data. They use tweets ending in positive emoticons like ":)" as positive and negative emoticons like ":(" as negative. They build models using Naives Bayes (NB), MaxEnt (ME) and Support Vector Machines (SVM), and they report SVM outperforms other classifiers. In terms of feature space, they try a Unigram, Bigram model in conjunction with parts-of-speech (POS) features. They note that the unigram model outperforms all other models. However, the unigram model isn't suitable for Chinese microblog, and we make full use of new emoticons which appear frequently in Chinese microblog.

Another significant effort for sentiment classification on Twitter data is by [9]. They use polarity predictions from three websites as noisy labels to train a model. They propose the use of syntax features of tweets like retweet, hashtags, link, punctuation and exclamation marks in conjunction with features like prior polarity of words and

POS of words. In order to improve target-dependent twitter sentiment classification, [10] incorporate target-dependent features and take the relations between twitters into consideration, such as retweet, reply and the twitters published by the same person. We extend their approach by adding a variety of Chinese dictionaries of sentiment, internet slang, emoticons, contact relation and document relation (forwarding), and then by using attention network and Bi-RNN to achieve the sentiment towards the topic.

The problem we address in this paper is to identify microblog topic and its sentiment automatically and synchronously. So the input of our task is a collection of microblogs and the output is topic labels and sentiment polarity assigned to each of the microblogs.

3 Data Description

Microblog allows users to post real time messages and are commonly displayed on the Web as shown in Fig. 1. "# #" identifies the microblog topic, "//" labels user's forwarding relation (document relation), "@" specified the user who we speak to (contact relation).

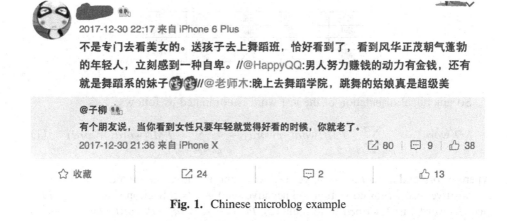

Fig. 1. Chinese microblog example

People usually use sentiment words, internet slang and emoticons to express their opinions and sentiment in microblog. According to [11], the sentiment word is one of the best sentiment features representations of text, and the rich sentiment words can be conductive to improving sentiment analysis. Internet slang that more and more people use in social network is also important factor for polarity classification. The constructions of them are not only a significant foundation, but also a time-consuming, labor-intensive work. In order to obtain sentiment polarity on microblog topic, we use the same method to construct some dictionaries based on [12].

3.1   The Dictionary of Sentiment Words

In order to obtain more abundant sentiment words, we regard these sentiment words provided by HowNet[1] and National Taiwan University Sentiment Dictionary (NTUSD)[2] as the foundation, and then use lexical fusion strategy to enrich the dictionary of sentiment words.

[13] uses lexical fusion strategy to compute the degree of correlation between test word and seed words that have more obvious sentiment polarity, and then obtain sentiment polarity of test word. We respectively take 20 words as seed words in this paper, as shown in Tables 1 and 2.

Table 1. Seed words with positive polarity

辉煌	美妙	漂亮	俱佳	动听
体面	淳美	良好	出色	完美
美丽	精英	优秀	高手	先进
快乐	最佳	优质	幸福	积极

Table 2. Seed words with negative polarity

罪恶	诅咒	责备	丑陋	丑恶
藐小	累赘	错误	失败	麻烦
不良	恶意	色情	暴力	讨厌
魔鬼	野蛮	腐败	流氓	残酷

So emotional orientation of the test word is computed as follows:

$$SO(word) = \sum_{pword \in Pset} PMI(word, pword) - \sum_{nword \in Nset} PMI(word, nword) \quad (1)$$

where *pword* and *nword* are positive seed word and negative seed word, *Pset* and *Nset* are positive seed words collection and negative seed words collection respectively. *PMI (word$_1$, word$_2$)* is described in formula (2), *P(word$_1$&word$_2$)*, *P(word$_1$)* and *P(word$_2$)* are probabilities of *word$_1$* and *word$_2$* co-occurring, *word$_1$* appearing, and *word$_2$* appearing in a microblog respectively. When *SO(word)* is greater than zero, sentiment polarity of word is positive. Otherwise it is negative.

$$PMI(word_1, word_2) = \log(\frac{P(word_1 \& word_2)}{P(word_1) P(word_2)}) \quad (2)$$

---

[1] http://www.keenage.com/html/c_index.html.

[2] http://nlg18.csie.ntu.edu.tw:8080/opinion/index.html.

3.2   The Dictionary of Internet Slang

People usually use homophonic words, abbreviated words and network slang to express their opinions in social network, and [14] has analysed the sentiment of twitter data. Sometimes new words, produced by important events or news reports, are used to express their opinions. So we use the dictionary of internet slang appeared in [12] to support microblog topic polarity classification, containing homophonic words, abbreviated words, network slang and many new words. Table 3 shows part of the dictionary.

Table 3. Part of the dictionary of internet slang

Internet slang	Meaning	Polarity
达人	高人	Positive
狂顶	强烈支持	Positive
萝莉	16岁以下的可爱小女孩	Positive
灰常桑心	非常伤心	Negative
菜鸟	网上低手	Negative

3.3   The Dictionary of Emoticons

We construct the dictionary of emoticons by combining emotional symbol library in microblog with other statistical methods. The former is used to select obvious emotion symbols in microblog, such as Sina, Tencent microblog et al. The latter chooses emoticons used in other social network, containing user-generated emoticons.

Firstly, two laboratory personnel obtain emotional symbol library, and keep the emoticons with the same sentiment polarity after their analysis, and then get rid of emotional symbols with ambiguous polarity, the result is described in Table 4.

Table 4. Part of the dictionary of emoticons

Emoticons	Meaning	Polarity
	Good	Positive
	给力	Positive
	鄙视	Negative
	怒骂	Negative

Secondly, in order to enrich the dictionary of emoticons, especially user-generated emoticons in social network, two laboratory personnel collect and analyse sentiment polarity, and finally obtain the result shown in Table 5.

Table 5. Part of the dictionary of user-generated emoticons

Emoticons	Meaning	Polarity
:o)	大笑	Positive
:)	微笑	Positive
T_T	哭泣	Negative
:(	伤心	Negative

In order to deal with the content conveniently, we pre-process all the microblogs and replace all the emoticons with their "Meaning" by looking up the dictionary of emoticons.

4   The Cascaded Model

4.1   MB-LDA Model for Microblog Topic Mining

MB-LDA is based on the research of LDA, and makes unified modeling for microblog's contact relation and text relation. It is suitable for microblog topic mining. The parameters of the model are shown in Table 6.

Table 6. Parameter definition description

Id	Parameter	Definition
1	α, α_c	Hyperparameters for θ_d and θ_c
2	β	Hyperparameter for φ
3	c	Contactor in conversation message (@)
4	θ_c	Topic distribution associated with contactor c
5	θ_d	Topic distribution over microblog d
6	$\theta_{d_{RT}}$	Topic distribution over retweet microblog d
7	λ	Weight parameters for retweet microblog
8	φ	Word distribution over topics
9	r	Retweet relation in conversation message (//)
10	φ	Word distribution over topics
11	w	Word in microblogs
12	z_i	Topic of word i
13	π_c	Bool parameters to decide specific microblogs

Bayesian network diagram of MB-LDA is shown in Fig. 2, c and r are used to represent the relation of the contact and the retweet respectively. At first, MB-LDA extracts the relation φ between the words and the topic which follows the Dirichlet distribution of the parameter β. Usually conversation message in microblog begins with

"@", it is difficult to judge whether it is conversation message when "@" appears in other positions. In this paper we only consider contact relation in microblog beginning with "@". When MB-LDA generates a microblog, we regard the microblog beginning with "@" as conversation message and set $\pi_c = 1$, and then extract the relation θ_c between each topic and the contact c which follows the Dirichlet distribution of the parameter α_c, and assign α_c to the relation θ_d between the microblog d and each topic; Otherwise set $\pi_c = 0$, directly extract the relation θ_d between each topic and the microblog d which follows the Dirichlet distribution of the parameter α.

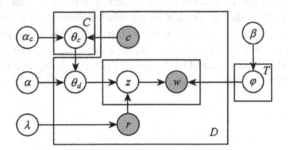

Fig. 2. Bayesian network of MB-LDA

Throughout the microblog sets, the topic probability distribution θ is defined as follows:

$$P(\theta|\alpha, \alpha_c, c) = P(\theta_c|\alpha_c)^{\pi_c} P(\theta_d|\alpha)^{1-\pi_c} \tag{3}$$

Secondly, how to identify retweet relation? If microblog contains "//", we regard the relation between retweet microblog d_{RT} and each topic as $\theta_{d_{RT}}$, and extract r from the Bernoulli distribution with parameter λ, as well as extract the topic probability z_{dn} of the current word from the polynomial distribution with parameters $\theta_{d_{RT}}$ or θ_d. However, we set $r = 0$ when "//" doesn't exist in microblog, and extract the topic probability z_{dn} of the current word from the polynomial distribution with parameter θ_d. Finally, the specific words are extracted from the polynomial distribution with the parameter $\varphi_{z_{dn}}$. More the details about MB-LDA model, see [15].

In microblog, the joint probability distribution of all the words and their topics is shown as follows:

$$P(w, z|\lambda, \theta, \beta) = P(r|\lambda)P(z|\theta)P(w|z, \beta) = P(r|\lambda)P(z|\theta_d)^{1-r}P(z|\theta_{d_{RT}})^{r}P(w|z, \beta) \tag{4}$$

4.2 Hierarchical Attention Network

Traditional approaches of text polarity classification represent documents with sparse lexical features, such as n-grams, and then use a linear model or kernel methods on this representation. More recent approaches used deep learning, such as convolutional neural networks and recurrent neural networks based on long short-term memory (LSTM) to learn text representations. However, a better sentiment representation can be obtained in this paper by incorporating knowledge of microblog structure in the attention network. We know that not all parts of a microblog are equally relevant for judging the microblog polarity and that determining the relevant sections involves modeling the interactions of the words, not just their presence in isolation.

Words form sentences, sentences form a document. In the application of micro-blog's polarity classification, we introduce hierarchical attention network created by Zichao Yang into our cascaded model. Our intention is to let the network to pay more or less attention to individual emotional factor when constructing microblog's polarity classifier. The overall architecture is shown in Fig. 3. It consists of five parts: a word sequence encoder, a word-level attention layer, a sentence encoder, a sentence-level attention layer and softmax layer. The details of different parts have been described in [16], we don't introduce them anymore.

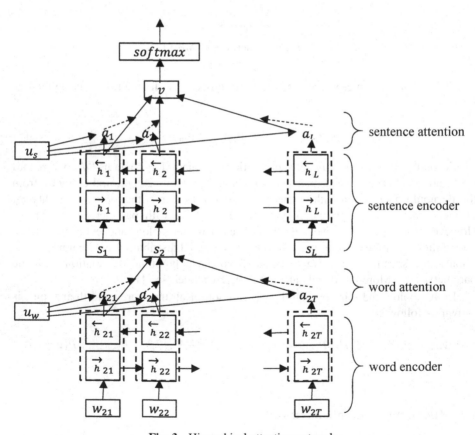

Fig. 3. Hierarchical attention network

4.3   The Cascaded Model Architecture for Topic Polarity Classification

Although attention-network-based approaches to polarity classification have been quite effective, it is difficult to identify the topic and give the polarity towards that topic synchronously. We combine the MB-LDA model and attention network to generate the cascaded model. The overall architecture of the cascaded model is shown in Fig. 4. T_{w_i} expresses the probability of the word w_i belongs to the topic T, where $i \in [1, T]$. The advantages of this architecture are as follows: (i) polarity classification is carried out on the basis of the results of topic recognition; (ii) the information input into the neural network takes into account the probability T_{w_i}.

The processing steps are as follows:

(i)   The MB-LDA model is used to obtain the topics of microblog data sets and the top 50 sentiment words in each topic. These sentiment words are selected from the topic according to the dictionary of sentiment words.

(ii)   Both the microblogs and the topic probabilities of each sentiment words from the same topic are used as the input of hierarchical attention network.

(iii)   The polarity classification of each microblog of each topic is achieved in the softmax layer.

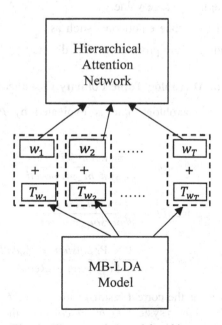

Fig. 4. The cascaded model architecture

5 Experiments and Results

In order to quantitatively analyze the performance of the cascade model, we use 4 different real microblog topic datasets to do experiments, and analyze the accuracy of polarity classification, the influence of topic number on accuracy, and the influence of emoticons on accuracy.

5.1 Data Sets

The labeled data sets in NLP&CC 2012[3] & 2013[4], a total of 405 microblogs, are provided by *Tencent Weibo*, including four topics: *hui_rong_an*, *ipad*, *kang_ri_shen_ju_sample* and *ke_bi_sample*. We reserve the microblog labeled with "*opinionated* = *Y*" and "*forward*" on behalf of "*//*" (retweet) in a microblog. When the number of "polarity = 'POS'" in microblog is more than or equal to the number of "polarity = 'NEG'", we think that microblog is positive. Otherwise, it is negative, and according to the polarity tagging, we randomly add the corresponding emoticons to microblog to enrich the emotional characteristics of the data sets.

In order to avoid over-fitting or under-fitting, we adopt 10-fold cross-validation in the experiments. Namely data sets would be randomly divided into 10 parts, 9 parts of them are used as training sets and the others are used to test. We repeat the process for 10 times and finally take the average value.

In addition, in order to encode emoticons, such as " 👍 ", "T_T", and so on, we carry out the corresponding string processing "Good" and "哭泣".

5.2 The Evaluation of Microblog Topic Polarity Classification

Polarity classification on microblog topic is evaluated by *Precision*, *Recall* and *F-measure*.

$$\Pr ecision = \frac{\#system\_correct}{\#system\_proposed} \tag{5}$$

$$\mathrm{Re}call = \frac{\#system\_correct}{\#person\_correct} \tag{6}$$

$$F - measure = \frac{2 \times \Pr ecision \times \mathrm{Re}call}{\Pr ecision + \mathrm{Re}call} \tag{7}$$

Where *#system_correct* is the correct result from system, *#system_proposed* is the whole number of microblogs from system, *#person_correct* is the number of microblogs that has been annotated correctly by people, *#weibo_topic* is the number of microblogs containing topic words, *#weibo_total* is the whole number of microblogs in the collection.

---

[3] http://tcci.ccf.org.cn/conference/2012/pages/page04_eva.html.
[4] http://tcci.ccf.org.cn/conference/2013/pages/page04_eva.html.

5.3 Results

In order to evaluate microblog topic polarity recognition ability, considering the semi-supervised learning of the cascaded model, we compare it with the most representative unsupervised learning model JST [17], semi-supervised learning model SSA-ST [18] and supervised learning model SVM in four data sets for microblog topic polarity classification. The results of the experiment are shown in Table 7. The value in the table shows the average value of the correct rate of each group of data.

Table 7. The comparison of polarity classification in 4 data sets

Model name	Precision	Recall	F-measure
JST	71.09	62.3	66.41
SSA-ST	78.9	74.32	76.54
SVM	89.1	85.19	87.1
Cascaded model	**86.74**	**81.35**	**83.96**

From the above table, we can see that the precision of polarity classification in cascaded model is higher than that of unsupervised model JST and semi-supervised model SSA-ST, while our result is similar to that of supervised model SVM. The reason is that our cascaded model has strong ability to identify emotional characteristics, and we find that the attention network has higher weight in features' calculation. This helps us quickly identify key elements that affect microblog's topic polarity. Although the experimental results of the cascaded model are lower than SVM, the cascaded model can discover topics and achieve higher polarity classification with fewer training sets.

Because the cascaded model can synchronously detect the topic and its polarity in microblog data sets, it is necessary to explore the interaction between polarity classification and topic detection. We carry out an experimental analysis that how does the number of topics affect the precision of polarity classification. The results of the experiment are shown in Fig. 5.

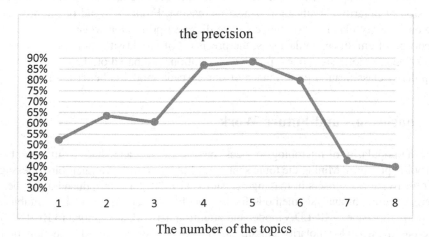

Fig. 5. The influence of the number of topics on the precision of polarity classification

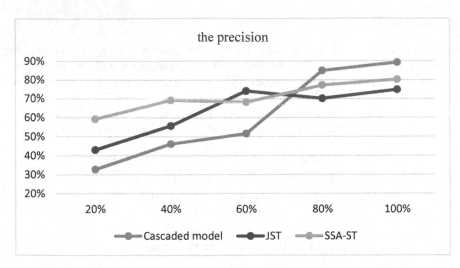

Fig. 6. The influence of the proportion of emoticons on the precision of polarity classification

As shown in Fig. 5, the influence of different numbers of topics generated by the cascaded model is different on the same data sets. The inappropriate number of topics will reduce the precision of microblog's polarity classification. Too little number of topics can reduce the correlation between the topic and its polarity. Too much number of topics can make the complete topic fragmented, which improves the noises of polarity classification and reduces the precision.

At the same time, we know that usually emoticons can effectively improve the effect of polarity classification, so what is the quantitative correlation between the two? We are gradually raising the number of microblogs containing emoticons in four data sets, that is to increase the proportion of microblogs with emoticons. The results of the experiment are shown in Fig. 6.

Figure 6 shows that with the increase of the number of emoticons in microblog, the precision of polarity classification is also increasing. From the trend of the precision, different polarity classification models have different promotion when we increase the proportion of emoticons in data sets, the precision of all classification models and the proportion of emoticons is linear positive correlation, and based on the topic identified, the polarity classification performance of our cascade model is better obviously.

6 Conclusions and Future Work

With the popularity of microblog services, people can see and share reality events on microblog platform. Mining the topic sentiment hidden in massive microblog messages can effectively assist users in making decisions. [19, 20] have introduced a number of different sentiment analysis methods for twitter, but our approach is also suitable for twitter. In this paper, MB-LDA model and attention network are applied to Bi-RNN for topic-based microblog polarity classification, and the synchronized detection of the topic and its sentiment in microblog is achieved.

Acknowledgments. This paper is financially supported by The National Key Research and Development Program of China (No. 2017YFB0803003) and National Science Foundation for Young Scientists of China (No. 6170060558). We would like to thank the anonymous reviewers for many valuable comments and helpful suggestions. Our future work will be carried out in the following aspects: firstly, the file attribute information of microblog users is incorporated into microblog message emotional polarity and thematic reasoning in order to improve the accuracy of polarity classification; Secondly, more explicit emotional features are excavated into the attention network to improve the accuracy of the polarity classification.

References

1. Deerwester, S., Dumais, S.T., Furnas, G.W., et al.: Indexing by latent semantic analysis. J. Assoc. Inf. Sci. Technol. **41**(6), 391–407 (1990)
2. Hofmann, T.: Probabilistic latent semantic indexing. In: International ACM SIGIR Conference on Research and Development in Information Retrieval, pp. 50–57. ACM (1999)
3. Blei, D.M., Ng, A.Y., Jordan, M.I.: Latent dirichlet allocation. J. Mach. Learn. Res. Arch. **3**, 993–1022 (2003)
4. Blei, D.M., Lafferty, J.D.: Dynamic topic models. In: International Conference, DBLP, pp. 113–120 (2006)
5. Boydgraber, J., Blei, D.M.: Syntactic topic models. In: Advances in Neural Information Processing Systems, pp. 185–192 (2008)
6. Nallapati, R., Cohen, W.: Link-PLSA-LDA: a new unsupervised model for topics and influence of blogs. In: ICWSM (2008)
7. Sun, C., Gao, B., Cao, Z., et al.: HTM: a topic model for hypertexts. In: Conference on Empirical Methods in Natural Language Processing, pp. 514–522. Association for Computational Linguistics (2008)
8. Go, A., Bhayani, R., Huang, L.: Twitter sentiment classification using distant supervision. CS224N Project report, Stanford (2009)
9. Barbosa, L., Feng, J.: Robust sentiment detection on Twitter from biased and noisy data. In: Proceedings of COLING 2010 Beijing, China, pp. 36–44 (2010)
10. Long, J., Yu, M., Zhou, M., et al.: Target-dependent Twitter sentiment classification. In: Proceedings of the 49th Annual Meeting of the Association for Computational Linguistics, Portland, Oregon, pp. 151–160 (2011)
11. Du, W., Tan, S., Yun, X., et al.: A new method to compute semantic orientation. J. Comput. Res. Dev. **46**(10), 1713–1720 (2009)
12. Liu, Q., Feng, C., Huang, H.: Emotional tendency identification for micro-blog topics based on multiple characteristics. In: 26th Pacific Asia Conference on Language, Information and Computation (PACLIC 26), pp. 280–288 (2012)
13. Wang, S., Li, D., Wei, Y.: A method of text sentiment classification based on weighted rough membership. J. Comput. Res. Dev. **48**(5), 855–861 (2011)
14. Agarwal, A., Xie, B., Vovsha, I., et al.: Sentiment analysis of Twitter data. In: Proceedings of the Workshop on Language in Social Media (LSM 2011), Portland, Oregon, pp. 30–38 (2011)
15. Zhang, C., Sun, J., Ding, Y.: Topic mining for microblog based on MB-LDA model. J. Comput. Res. Dev. **48**(10), 1795–1802 (2011)

16. Yang, Z., Yang, D., Dyer, C., et al.: Hierarchical attention networks for document classification. In: Conference of the North American Chapter of the Association for Computational Linguistics: Human Language Technologies, pp. 1480–1489 (2017)
17. Lin, C., He, Y., Everson, R., et al.: Weakly supervised joint sentiment-topic detection from text. IEEE Trans. Knowl. Data Eng. **24**(6), 1134–1145 (2012)
18. Hu, X., Tang, L., Tang, J., et al.: Exploiting social relation for sentiment analysis in microblogging. In: Proceedings of the 6th International Conference on Web Search and Data Mining. Rome, Italy, pp. 537–546 (2013)
19. Nakov, P.: Semantic sentiment analysis of Twitter data. arXiv preprint arXiv:1710.01492 (2017)
20. Wang, B., Liakata, M., Tsakalidis, A., et al.: TOTEMSS: topic-based, temporal sentiment summarisation for Twitter. In: Proceedings of the IJCNLP 2017, System Demonstrations, pp. 21–24 (2017)

An Efficient Deep Learning Model
for Recommender Systems

Kourosh Modarresi[✉] and Jamie Diner

Adobe Inc., San Jose, CA, USA
kouroshm@alumni.stanford.edu, diner@adobe.com

Abstract. Recommending the best and optimal content to user is the essential part of digital space activities and online user interactions. For example, we like to know what items should be sent to a user, what promotion is the best one for a user, what web design would fit a specific user, what ad a user would be more susceptible to or what creative cloud package is more suitable to a specific user.

In this work, we use deep learning (autoencoders) to create a new model for this purpose. The previous art includes using Autoencoders for numerical features only and we extend the application of autoencoders to non-numerical features.

Our approach in coming up with recommendation is using "matrix completion" approach which is the most efficient and direct way of finding and evaluating content recommendation.

Keywords: Recommender systems · Artificial intelligence · Deep learning

1 Introduction

1.1 An Overview of Matrix Completion Approach

With the advancements in data collection and the increased availability of data, the problem of missing values will only intensify. Traditional approaches to treating this problem just remove rows and/or column that have missing values but, especially in online applications, this will mean removing most of the rows and columns as most data collected is sparse. Naïve approaches impute missing values with the mean or median of the column, which changes the distribution of the variables and increases the bias in the model. More complex approaches create one model for each column based on the other variables; our test show that this work well for small matrices but the computational time increases exponentially as more columns are added. For only numerical datasets, matrix factorization using SVD-based models proved to work on the Netflix Prize but has the drawback of inferring a linear combination between variables and not working well with mixed datasets (continuous and categorical). For sequential data, researches have been done using Recurrent Neural Networks (RNN). However, the purpose of this paper is to create a general matrix completion algorithm that does not depend on the data being sequential and works with both continuous and categorical variables that would be the founding block of a Recommendation System. A novel model is proposed using an autoencoder to reconstruct each row and impute

© Springer International Publishing AG, part of Springer Nature 2018
Y. Shi et al. (Eds.): ICCS 2018, LNCS 10861, pp. 221–233, 2018.
https://doi.org/10.1007/978-3-319-93701-4_17

the unknown values based on the known values, with a cost function that optimizes separately the continuous and categorical variables. Tests show that this method outperforms the performance of more complex models with a fraction of the execution time.

Matrix Completion is a problem that's been around for decades but took prominence in 2006 with the Netflix Price, where the first model to beat Netflix's baseline recommender system by more than 10% would win 1 million dollars. In such a dataset, each row represented a different user and each column a different movie. When a user i rated movie j, the position ij of the matrix would reflect the rating, otherwise it would be a missing value. This is a very particular type of dataset, as every column represented a movie from which a limited number of ratings was possible (1–5). It is fair to say that the difference between the values in the columns reflect the taste of the user but, in a general sense, each column represents the same concept i.e., a movie. Most of the research in matrix completion and recommendation systems have been done on datasets of this type, predicting the rating that a user will give on a movie, song, book, or any other content. However, most of the datasets, created in the real world, are not of this type as each column may represent a different type of data. Thus, the data could be demographical (age, income, etc.), geographical (city, state, etc.), medical (temperature, blood pressure, etc.), just to name a few. Any dataset may have missing values, and the purpose of this work is to create a general model that imputes these missing values and recommends contents in the face of having all possible type of data.

1.2   The State of the Art

Naïve Approaches
The most basic approach is to fill the missing values with the mean or median (for continuous variables) or the mode (for categorical variables). This method presents two clear problems: the first is that it is changing the distribution of the variable by giving more prominence and over-representation to the imputed variable than it really has in the data, and the second is that bias is introduced to the model, as the output is the same for all the missing values in a specific column. This is specially a problem for highly sparse datasets. It is important to notice that a variation of this method exists where the mean or median of the *row* (instead of the column) is imputed, but only works for continuous variables. The mode could be used for both continuous and categorical but will still present the problems described earlier. Some more models can be found in [1, 6, 48, 66–68].

Collaborative Filtering and Content-Based Filtering
Collaborative filtering is one of the main methods for completing *Netflix*-style datasets. In collaborative filtering, a similarity between rows (or columns) is calculated and used to compute a weighted average of the known values to impute the missing values. This method only works for numerical datasets, and is not scalable as similarity must be computed for all pairs (which is very computationally expensive).

Content-Based filtering uses attributes of the columns to find the similarity between them and then calculate the weighted average to impute. This method only works for numerical datasets.

SVD Based

The Singular Value Decomposition works by finding the latent factors of the matrix by factorizing it into 3 matrices:

$$X = U\Sigma V^T$$

Where U is an m x m unitary matrix, Σ is a diagonal matrix of dimensions m x n and V is an n x n unitary matrix. The matrix Σ represent the singular values of matrix X, and the columns of U and V are orthonormal. It reconstructs the matrix X by finding its low-rank approximation. A preprocessing step for this method is pre-imputing the missing values, usually with the mean of the column, as missing values are not permitted. This method is one of the most popular one as it was the winning solution of the Netflix Prize, but has the drawback of only working on numerical datasets, inferring a linear combination of the columns, and usually are fit for *Netflix*-style datasets.

More Complex Approaches

More complex approaches create one model for each variable with missing values, using the rows with known values in a column as the training set. A model is trained using all the variables, except the one column, as the input, and that column as the output. After a model is trained, the missing values are estimated by predicting the output of the other rows. The principal drawback of these methods is that the number of models that have to be trained increase with the number of columns of the dataset, therefore it is very computationally expensive for large datasets. This framework can work for mixed datasets or for numerical only datasets, depending on the model used. Pre-imputing missing values is needed for this framework as missing values are not permitted, usually with the mean of the column.

Some implementations of these models use Random Forest (missForest, works for mixed datasets), chained equations (mice, works for numerical only), EMB (Amelia, works for mixed datasets in theory but in this paper only the numerical part worked), FAMD (missMDA, works for mixed datasets).

2 Our Deep Learning Model

2.1 The General Framework

When designing the model, three main objectives were considered:

- Minimize reconstruction error for continuous variables
- Minimize reconstruction error for categorical variables
- Eliminate the effect of missing values in the model

Our proposed method uses autoencoders to reconstruct the dataset and impute the missing values. The concept originates from idea of SVD method through using deep learning model. Autoencoders are an unsupervised method that tries to reconstruct the input in the output using a neural network that is trained using backpropagation.

A general overview of the model is shown in Fig. 1.

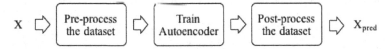

Fig. 1. The general overview of the model.

2.2 The Step of Pre-process the Dataset

The dataset can be of three types: all continuous, all categorical, or mixed (some columns are continuous and some categorical). Therefore, the first step of pre-processing the data is finding out which columns are numerical and which are categorical. The procedure followed in this work, to achieve this, is shown in Fig. 2, below.

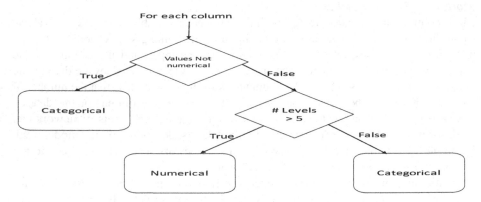

Fig. 2. The column type definition.

Once the column type is known, each of the continuous columns (if they exist) are normalized using Min Max Scaling. This way, every numerical column is scaled between 0 and 1. This step of normalization of data is a necessary step in the application of Neural Networks. The minimum and maximum values for each column are saved to be able to rescale the reconstructed matrix to the original scale.

After normalizing the continuous columns, the next step is encoding the categorical columns. For simplicity purposes, and because the order of the columns is not relevant in the model, all the continuous columns are moved to the beginning of the matrix and the categorical columns to the end. Then, each categorical column is encoded using One-Hot encoding, where one new column is created for each level of each categorical variable. The column with the label has a value of 1 and the rest a value of 0.

At this step, the matrix is all numerical and every column is between 0 and 1. For the reasons that will be explained in Sect. 2.3, three masks will be extracted from the encoded dataset:

- Missing Value Mask: same shape as the encoded matrix, where the missing values are encoded as 0 and the non-missing values as 1.
- Numerical Mask: a vector of the same length as the number of columns, where the continuous columns (if exist) are encoded as 1 and the categorical columns (if exist) are encoded as 0.
- Categorical Mask: the complement of the numerical mask, where the continuous columns are encoded as 0 and the categorical as 1.

The last step in encoding the matrix is converting all missing values to 0. This serves two purposes: the first is that neural networks can't handle missing values, and the other is to remove the effect of these missing nodes in the neural network. Once the encoded matrix and the three masks are created, the training step can begin.

2.3 Training the Autoencoder

To train the autoencoder, each row of the encoded matrix is treated as the input and output at the same time. Therefore, the number of nodes in the input (n_input) and output layer are equal to the number of columns in the encoded matrix.

The architecture that was defined consists of 3 hidden layers. The design is symmetrical with the number of nodes of each of the hidden layers as follows:

- Hidden Layer 1: *n_input/2*
- Hidden Layer 2: *n_input/4*
- Hidden Layer 3: *n_input/2*

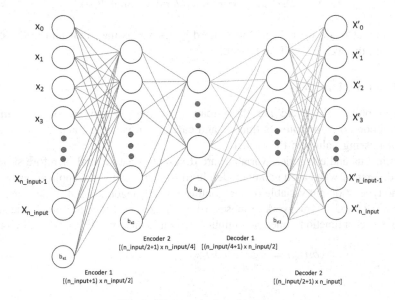

Fig. 3. The network architecture.

There are two encoding layers and two decoding layers. The reason why the number of nodes for the hidden layers is smaller than the input layer is due to the idea of projecting the data onto a lower dimension and find the latent factors to reconstruct the data set from there.

Figure 3 shows the autoencoder neural network architecture, with the dimensions of each encoding/decoding layer. The "+1" in the first dimension of each encoder/decoder is the bias term that was added.

The activation function that was used for each of the nodes is the sigmoid given as,

$$\sigma(x) = \frac{1}{1 + e^{-x}}$$

The output of each encoder and decoder are computed as follows:

$$Encoder\,1 = \sigma(X * W_{E1} + B_{E1})$$

Where $*$ denotes matrix multiplication, W_{E1} are the weights for encoder 1 learned from the network (initialized randomly) and B_{E1} is the bias of the encoder 1 learned from the network (initialized randomly). This result is fed to the second encoder,

$$Encoder\,2 = \sigma(Encoder\,1 * W_{E2} + B_{E2})$$

Similarly, for the Decoders:

$$Decoder\,1 = \sigma(Encoder\,2 * W_{D1} + B_{D1})$$

$$X' = Decoder\,2 = \sigma(Decoder\,1 * W_{D2} + B_{D2})$$

The output of decoder 2 has the same dimensions as the input and is the output from which the weights will be trained.

2.4 The Cost Functions

As stated previously, there are three main objectives in this work; to minimize reconstruction error for both continuous and categorical variables, and to eliminate the effect of missing values in the model.

Continuous and categorical variables are different in nature, and therefore should be treated differently when used in any model. In most neural networks applications, there is only one type of output variable (either continuous or categorical) but in this case, there may be mixed nodes. This work proposes using a mixed cost function that is the sum of two separate cost functions, one for continuous variables and one for categorical variables.

$$cost_{total} = \underset{W,B}{\mathrm{argmin}}(cost_{continuous} + cost_{categorical})$$

To be able to distinguish between continuous and categorical variables, the numerical and categorical masks, that are created earlier, will be used.

For the purpose of the third objective, the missing values mask will be used to only consider the error of values that are *not* missing. By using this approach, there is no need to pre-impute missing values as they will have no effect on the overall cost function.

Mathematically, the continuous cost function is as follows:

$$cost_{continuous} = \sum\nolimits_{i,j} \left(\left(X'_{ij} - X_{ij} \right) \delta_{num_j} \delta_{miss_{ij}} \right)^2$$

Where X'_{ij} is the output of Decoder 2 for position ij, X_{ij} is the same value in the original encoded matrix, δ_{num_j} is the value in the numerical mask for column j, and $\delta_{miss_{ij}}$ is the value in the missing value mask for position ij. It is clear that this cost will only consider values that are in columns that are numerical ($\delta_{num_j} = 1$) and that are not missing in the original matrix ($\delta_{miss_{ij}} = 1$).

The categorical cost function is given by the cross entropy:

$$cost_{categorical} = - \sum_{i,j} \left(X_{ij} \ln\left(X'_{ij} \right) + \left(1 - X_{ij} \right) \ln\left(1 - X'_{ij} \right) \right) \delta_{cat_j} \delta_{miss_{ij}}$$

Similarly, X'_{ij} is the output of Decoder 2 for position ij, X_{ij} is the same value in the original encoded matrix, δ_{cat_j} is the value in the categorical mask for column j, and $\delta_{miss_{ij}}$ is the value in the missing value mask for position ij. It is clear that this cost will only consider values that are in columns that are categorical ($\delta_{cat_j} = 1$) and that are not missing in the original matrix ($\delta_{miss_{ij}} = 1$). The total cost function is minimized using Gradient Descent. The learning rate for these tests was set at a default of 0.01.

2.5   The Post-processing of the Dataset

The output of the Autoencoder is a matrix where all the numerical columns are at the beginning, and all the categorical columns are split among different columns, with a value between 0 and 1, at the end. The goal is to reconstruct the original matrix, with the columns in the same order and each categorical variable as one column with different levels.

The first step is computing the "prediction" for the categorical variables, that is, the level of the categorical variables that obtained the highest score after the decoder 2. Once the category is found, the name of the column is assigned as the category or level for that variable. This is repeated for all categorical variables.

Once each categorical column is decoded to its original form and levels, the columns are reordered using the order of the original dataset. Then, the numerical variables are scaled back using the minimum and maximum values saved during the pre-processing step for each column.

At this point, the matrix is in the same shape and scale as the original matrix; with all the missing values imputed.

The model in this work is based on a deep learning model using autoencoder for content recommendation based on the solution of the matrix completion problem. The main idea that this work proposes is extending the state of the art to impute missing values of any type of dataset, and not just numerical. One of the principal idea of this work is the application of a new cost function, a mixed cost function, that has not been done before. This function detects which columns are continuous and which are categorical, and computes the proper error depending on the type of the data. This improves considerably the performance of the model and can be extended to any neural network application that requires output nodes of mixed types.

3   The Results and Conclusion

3.1   The Data Set and the Results

For this analysis, 15 publicly available datasets [12–26] were used. The dataset was selected such that the data set would be diverse with respect to sparsity level, domain or application, amount of numerical vs categorical data, and the number of rows and columns.

To create a more varied selection of data, 100 bootstrap samples were created from each of the datasets by selecting a random number of rows, a random number of columns, and a random number of missing values.

To measure the performance of continuous variables, the Normalized Root Mean Squared Error (NRMSE) measure is used. The reason this metric is used is that we could compare the performance of difference datasets regardless of the range or variance it has. The lower the NRMSE score, the better.

$$NRMSE = \sqrt{\frac{mean\left(\left(x_{true} - x_{pred}\right)^2\right)}{var\left(x_{true}\right)}}$$

To measure the performance of categorical variables, the Accuracy is used. The higher the accuracy score, the better.

$$Accuracy = mean\left(x_{true} = x_{pred}\right)$$

The execution time is measured in seconds. The lower the execution time, the better.

To compare the performance of our model vs other state of the art models, seven packages in R were used as baselines models: *Amelia* [51], *impute* [49], *mice* [72], *missForest* [70], *missMDA* [59], *rrecsys* [11], and *softImpute* [48]. The models in these packages are state of the art solutions for the matrix completion problem and cover all the models described in the introduction.

The number of missing values ranged from 0 to 100%, but limitations on other packages only allowed only up to 80% on most models, and 20% on Amelia package model.

Figure 4 shows the performance of the models with 1500 bootstrap samples (100 per dataset) measured by the NRMSE. It can be seen that the model proposed in this paper outperforms all of the models, with less variation in the results. The closest model, Amelia, was only tested with up to 20% sparsity but our autoencoder still improves the median NRMSE by 11% (0.09293 vs 0.10395).

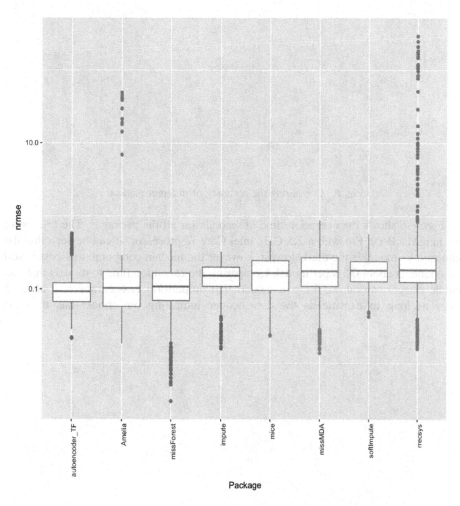

Fig. 4. Comparing the performance using NRMSE.

Figure 5 shows the accuracy of categorical variables for all packages that are able to handle them. Out of the seven packages that were tested to compare, only four are able to impute categorical variables. The model proposed in this paper sits right in the middle in terms of median performance with large variation in the results.

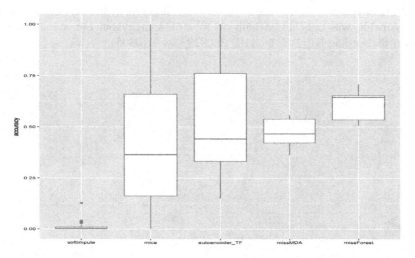

Fig. 5. Comparing the accuracy of different models.

Figure 6 shows the execution time in seconds for all the packages. The tests were run in a MacBook Pro with a 2.5 GHz Intel Core i7 processor. It can be seen that the autoencoder model is the third slowest, however the median computational cost is still reasonable at about 0.5 s per model. Comparing the execution time to models that can handle categorical values, the two models that outperform in accuracy take about 5 times as long to execute as the autoencoder indicating our model has the best

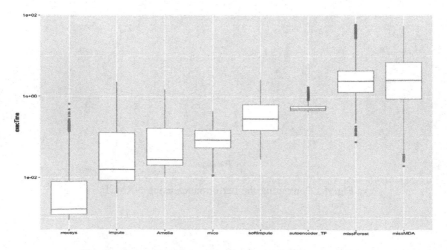

Fig. 6. Comparing the execution time of different models.

performance for NRMSE for all models tested. Thus, for the models that can handle mixed datasets, our model has the best tradeoff between accuracy and execution time.

The results indicate our model outperforms existing models. It has the best NRMSE of all models, and has the best trade-off accuracy and computational complexity as the two models.

References

1. Becker, S., Bobin, J., Candès, E.J.: NESTA, a fast and accurate first-order method for sparse recovery. SIAM J. Imaging Sci. **4**(1), 1–39 (2009)
2. Bjorck, A.: Numerical Methods for Least Squares Problems. SIAM, Philadelphia (1996)
3. Boyd, S., Vandenberghe, L.: Convex Optimization. Cambridge University Press, Cambridge (2004)
4. Breese, J.S., Heckerman, D., Kadie, C.: Empirical analysis of predictive algorithms for collaborative filtering. In: Proceedings of Fourteenth Conference on Uncertainty in Artificial Intelligence. Morgan Kaufmann (1998)
5. Cai, J.-F., Candès, E.J., Shen, Z.: A singular value thresholding algorithm for matrix completion. SIAM J. Optim. **20**(4), 1956–1982 (2008)
6. Candès, E.J., Recht, B.: Exact matrix completion via convex optimization. Found. Comput. Math. **9**, 717–772 (2008)
7. Candès, E.J.: Compressive sampling. In: Proceedings of the International Congress of Mathematicians, Madrid, Spain (2006)
8. Chen, P.-Y., Wu, S.-Y., Yoon, J.: The impact of online recommendations and consumer feedback on sales. In: Proceedings of the 25th International Conference on Information Systems, pp. 711–724 (2004)
9. Cho, Y.H., Kim, J.K., Kim, S.H.: A personalized recommender system based on web usage mining and decision tree induction. Expert Syst. Appl. **23**, 329–342 (2002)
10. Claypool, M., Gokhale, A., Miranda, T., Murnikov, P., Netes, D., Sartin M.: Combining content-based and collaborative filters in an online newspaper. In: Proceedings of the ACM SIGIR 1999 Workshop on Recommender Systems (1999)
11. Çoba, L., Zanker, M.: rrecsys: an R-package for prototyping recommendation algorithms. In: RecSys 2016 Poster Proceedings (2016)
12. Data, Abalone. https://archive.ics.uci.edu/ml/datasets/abalone
13. Data, Air Quality. https://archive.ics.uci.edu/ml/datasets/Air+Quality
14. Data, Batting. http://www.tgfantasybaseball.com/baseball/stats.cfm
15. Data, Bike. https://archive.ics.uci.edu/ml/datasets/bike+sharing+dataset
16. Data, Boston. https://archive.ics.uci.edu/ml/datasets/housing
17. Data, CASP. https://archive.ics.uci.edu/ml/datasets/Physicochemical+Properties+of+Protein+Tertiary+Structure
18. Data, Census: Click on the "Compare Large Cities and Towns for Population, Housing, Area, and Density" link on Census 2000. https://factfinder.census.gov/faces/nav/jsf/pages/community_facts.xhtml
19. Data, Concrete. https://archive.ics.uci.edu/ml/datasets/Concrete+Compressive+Strength
20. Data, Data_akb. https://archive.ics.uci.edu/ml/dtasets/ISTANBUL+STOCK+EXCHANGE#
21. Data, Parkinsons. https://archive.ics.uci.edu/ml/datasets/parkinsons
22. Data, S&P. http://www.cboe.com/products/stock-index-options-spx-rut-msci-ftse/s-p-500-index-options/s-p-500-index/spx-historical-data
23. Data, Seeds. http://archive.ics.uci.edu/ml/datasets/seeds

24. Data, Waveform. https://archive.ics.uci.edu/ml/datasets/Waveform+Database+Generator+ (Version+2)
25. Data, Wdbc. https://archive.ics.uci.edu/ml/datasets/Breast+Cancer+Wisconsin+%28Prognos tic%29
26. Data, Yacht. http://archive.ics.uci.edu/ml/datasets/yacht+hydrodynamics
27. d'Aspremont, A., El Ghaoui, L., Jordan, M.I., Lanckriet, G.R.G.: A direct formulation for sparse PCA using semidefinite programming. SIAM Rev. **49**(3), 434–448 (2007)
28. Davies, A.R., Hassan, M.F.: Optimality in the regularization of ill-posed inverse problems. In: Sabatier, P.C. (ed.) Inverse Problems: An Interdisciplinary Study. Academic Press, London (1987)
29. DeMoor, B., Golub, G.H.: The restricted singular value decomposition: properties and applications. SIAM J. Matrix Anal. Appl. **12**(3), 401–425 (1991)
30. Donoho, D.L., Tanner, J.: Sparse nonnegative solutions of underdetermined linear equations by linear programming. Proc. Natl. Acad. Sci. **102**(27), 9446–9451 (2005)
31. Efron, B., Hastie, T., Johnstone, I., Tibshirani, R.: Least angle regression. Ann. Stat. **32**, 407–499 (2004)
32. Elden, L.: Algorithms for the regularization of ill-conditioned least squares problems. BIT **17**, 134–145 (1977)
33. Elden, L.: A note on the computation of the generalized cross-validation function for ill-conditioned least squares problems. BIT **24**, 467–472 (1984)
34. Engl, H.W., Hanke, M., Neubauer, A.: Regularization methods for the stable solution of inverse problems. Surv. Math. Ind. **3**, 71–143 (1993)
35. Engl, H.W., Hanke, M., Neubauer, A.: Regularization of Inverse Problems. Kluwer, Dordrecht (1996)
36. Engl, H.W., Kunisch, K., Neubauer, A.: Convergence rates for Tikhonov regularisation of non-linear ill-posed problems. Inverse Prob. **5**, 523–540 (1998)
37. Engl, H.W., Groetsch, C.W. (eds.): Inverse and Ill-Posed Problems. Academic Press, London (1987)
38. Gander, W.: On the linear least squares problem with a quadratic Constraint. Technical report STAN-CS-78-697, Stanford University (1978)
39. Golub, G.H., Van Loan, C.F.: Matrix Computations. Computer Assisted Mechanics and Engineering Sciences, 4th edn. Johns Hopkins University Press, US, (2013)
40. Golub, G.H., Van Loan, C.F.: An analysis of the total least squares problem. SIAM J. Numer. Anal. **17**, 883–893 (1980)
41. Golub, G.H., Kahan, W.: Calculating the singular values and pseudo-inverse of a matrix. SIAM J. Numer. Anal. Ser. B **2**, 205–224 (1965)
42. Golub, G.H., Heath, M., Wahba, G.: Generalized cross-validation as a method for choosing a good ridge parameter. Technometrics **21**, 215–223 (1979)
43. Guo, S., Wang, M., Leskovec, J.: The role of social networks in online shopping: information passing, price of trust, and consumer choice. In: ACM Conference on Electronic Commerce (EC) (2011)
44. Häubl, G., Trifts, V.: Consumer decision making in online shopping environments: the effects of interactive decision aids **19**, 4–21 (2000)
45. Hastie, T., Tibshirani, R., Friedman, J.: The Elements of Statistical Learning; Data mining, Inference and Prediction. Springer, New York (2001). https://doi.org/10.1007/978-0-387-84858-7
46. Hastie, T.J., Tibshirani, R.: Handwritten Digit Recognition via Deformable Prototypes. AT&T Bell Laboratories Technical report (1994)
47. Hastie, T., Tibshirani, R., Eisen, M., Brown, P., Ross, D., Scherf, U., Weinstein, J., Alizadeh, A., Staudt, L., Botstein, D.: 'Gene Shaving' as a method for identifying distinct sets of genes with similar expression patterns. Genome Biol. **1**, 1–21 (2000)

48. Hastie, T., Mazumder, R.: Matrix Completion via Iterative Soft-Thresholded SVD (2015)
49. Hastie, T., Tibshirani, R., Narasimhan, B., Chu, G.: Package 'impute'. CRAN (2017)
50. Hofmann, B.: Regularization for Applied Inverse and Ill-Posed problems. Teubner, Stuttgart, Germany (1986)
51. Honaker, J., King, G., Blackwell, M.: Amelia II: A program for Missing Data (2012)
52. Anger, G., Gorenflo, R., Jochum, H., Moritz, H., Webers, W. (eds.): Inverse Problems: principles and Applications in Geophysics, Technology, and Medicine. Akademic Verlag, Berlin (1993)
53. Hua, T.A., Gunst, R.F.: Generalized ridge regression: a note on negative ridge parameters. Commun. Stat. Theory Methods **12**, 37–45 (1983)
54. Iyengar, V.S., Zhang, T.: Empirical study of recommender systems using linear classifiers. In: Cheung, D., Williams, G.J., Li, Q. (eds.) PAKDD 2001. LNCS (LNAI), vol. 2035, pp. 16–27. Springer, Heidelberg (2001). https://doi.org/10.1007/3-540-45357-1_5
55. Jeffers, J.: Two case studies in the application of principal component. Appl. Stat. **16**, 225–236 (1967)
56. Jolliffe, I.: Principal Component Analysis. Springer, New York (1986). https://doi.org/10.1007/978-1-4757-1904-8
57. Jolliffe, I.T.: Rotation of principal components: choice of normalization constraints. J. Appl. Stat. **22**, 29–35 (1995)
58. Jolliffe, I.T., Trendafilov, N.T., Uddin, M.: A modified principal component technique based on the LASSO. J. Comput. Graph. Stat. **12**(3), 531–547 (2003)
59. Josse, J., Husson, F.: missMDA: a package for handling missing values in multivariate data analysis. J. Stat. Softw. **70**(1) (2016)
60. Linden, G., Smith, B., York, J.: Amazon.com recommendations: item-to-item collaborative filtering. Internet Comput. **7**(1), 76–80 (2003)
61. Mazumder, R., Hastie, T., Tibshirani, R.: Spectral regularization algorithms for learning large incomplete matrices. JMLR **2010**(11), 2287–2322 (2010)
62. McCabe, G.: Principal variables. Technometrics **26**, 137–144 (1984)
63. Modarresi, K., Golub, G.H.: An adaptive solution of linear inverse problems. In: Proceedings of Inverse Problems Design and Optimization Symposium (IPDO2007), 16–18 April 2007, Miami Beach, Florida, pp. 333–340 (2007)
64. Modarresi, K.: A Local Regularization Method Using Multiple Regularization Levels, Stanford, April 2007
65. Modarresi, K., Golub, G.H.: An efficient algorithm for the determination of multiple regularization parameters. In: Proceedings of Inverse Problems Design and Optimization Symposium (IPDO), 16–18 April 2007, Miami Beach, Florida, pp. 395–402 (2007)
66. Modarresi, K.: Recommendation system based on complete personalization. Procedia Comput. Sci. **80C** (2016)
67. Modarresi, K.: Computation of recommender system using localized regularization. Procedia Comput. Sci. **51C** (2015)
68. Modarresi, K.: Algorithmic Approach for Learning a Comprehensive View of Online Users. Procedia Comput. Sci. **80C** (2016)
69. Sedhain, S., Menon, A.K., Sanner, S., Xie, L.: AutoRec: autoencoders meet collaborative. In: WWW 2015 (2015)
70. Stekhoven, D.: Using the missForest Package. CRAN (2012)
71. Strub, F., Mary, J., Gaudel, R.: Hybrid Collaborative Filtering with Autoencoders (2016)
72. Van Buuren, S., Groothuis-Oudshoorn, K.: MICE: multivariate imputation by chained equations in R. J. Stat. Softw. **45**(3), 1–67 (2011)

Standardization of Featureless Variables for Machine Learning Models Using Natural Language Processing

Kourosh Modarresi$^{(\boxtimes)}$ and Abdurrahman Munir

Adobe Inc., San Jose, CA, USA
kouroshm@alumni.stanford.edu, munir@adobe.com

Abstract. AI and machine learning are mathematical modeling methods for learning from data and producing intelligent models based on this learning. The data these models need to deal with, is normally a mixed of data type where both numerical (continuous) variables and categorical (non-numerical) data types. Most models in AI and machine learning accept only numerical data as their input and thus, standardization of mixed data into numerical data is a critical step when applying machine learning models. Having data in the standard shape and format that models require often a time consuming, nevertheless very significant step of the process.

Keywords: Machine learning · Natural Language Processing
Mixed type variables

1 Introduction

1.1 Motivation

As an example, when we have a data set (below) combined of many variables where all are numerical ones except two variables of categorical type (gender and marital status) as following [50]:

Table 1. Original mixed variables

User	Age	Income	Gender	Marital status
1	31	90,000	M	Single
2	45	45,000	M	Married
3	63	34,000	M	Divorced
4	33	65,000	F	Divorced
5	47	87,000	F	Single
6	38	39,000	M	Married
7	26	120,000	M	Married
8	25	32,000	F	Married
9	29	55,000	F	Single
10	44	33,000	F	Single

© Springer International Publishing AG, part of Springer Nature 2018
Y. Shi et al. (Eds.): ICCS 2018, LNCS 10861, pp. 234–246, 2018.
https://doi.org/10.1007/978-3-319-93701-4_18

When applying many machine learning models, the models need the data to be numerical data type. Thus, the categorical data should be converted into numerical type. The most efficient way of converting the categorical variable is the introduction of dummy variables (one hot encoding) for which a new (dummy) variable is created for each category (except the last category – since it'd be dependent on the rest of dummy variables, i.e., its value could be determined when all other dummy variables are known) of the categorical variable. These dummy variables are binary variables and could assume only two values, 1 and 0. The value 1 means the sample has the value of that variable and 0 means the opposite.

Here, for this example, we have two categorical variables:

1. Gender: there are only two categories, so we need to create one dummy variable.
2. Marital Status: there are three categories so we need to create two new dummy variables.

The result after the creation of dummy variables is shown in Table 2.

Table 2. The original variables after the introduction of dummy variables.

User	Age	Income	Dummy variable-1 (female)	Dummy variable-2 (married)	Dummy variable-3 (single)
1	31	90000	0	0	1
2	45	45000	0	1	0
3	63	34000	0	0	0
4	33	65000	1	0	0
5	47	87000	1	0	1
6	38	39000	0	1	0
7	26	120000	0	1	0
8	25	32000	1	1	0
9	29	55000	1	0	1
10	44	33000	1	0	1

After this transitional step, we could use any machine learning model for this data set as all its variables are numerical one.

In general, for any categorical variable of "m" categories (classes), we need to create "m − 1" dummy variables. The problem arises when any specific categorical variable has large (based on our work, that means larger than 8) number of categories. The reason is that, in these cases, the number of dummy variables need to be created becomes too large causing the data to become of high dimension. The high dimensionality of data leads to "curse of dimensionality" problem and thus all related issues related to "curse of dimensionality" such as the need of "exponential increase in the number of data rows" and "difficulties of distance computation" would appear. Obviously, one needs to avoid the situation since, in addition to these problems, curse of dimensionality also leads to misleading results from any machine learning models such as finding false patterns discovered based on noise or random chance. Besides all of that, higher dimension leads to higher "computational cost" and "slow model response and lower robustness", all of which should be avoided. Therefore, in the process of transformation of categorical data into numerical data types, we must reduce the number of newly created numerical variables to reduce the dimension of data [50].

Two examples of the case of categorical variables of large categories or classes are "country of residence" and "URL related data such as the last site visited by the user". For the first variable, there are more than 150 categories and for the second, there is potentially as many categories as the number of users which is a very large (in the order of millions) number. To address these types of problem, this work establishes a new approach of reducing the number of categories (when the number of categories in a categorical variable in larger than 10) to K categories for $K \leq 10$. This way, we will create a limited number of dummy variables to replace the categorical variable in the data set.

For some types of categorical variables such as "country of residence", we may find some attributes online and thus, using these attributes and applying clustering models and web scraping, we can create only a handful of dummy variable to replace the categorical variables of large categories [50].

But, there are other type of categorical variables, such as "URL" variable, where it is not possible to scrap features online and thus the above method [50] cannot be applied. This paper focuses on a method of dealing with this type of categorical data.

2   The Approach Used in This Work

2.1   The Difficulties in Dealing with Modern Data

Quite often, the models in machine learning are models that use only numeric data. Though, practically all data that are used in machine learning are mixed type, numerical and categorical data. When used for machine learning models that could use only numerical data, mixed data types are handled using three different approaches: first approach is trying to, instead, using models that could handle mixed data type, second approach is to ignore (drop) categorical variables. The last approach is converting categorical variables to numerical type by introducing dummy variables. The first approach introduces many limitations as there are only a limited number of models that could handle mixed data and those models are often not the best model fitting the data set. The second approach leads to ignoring much of the information in data set, i.e., the categorical data. The practical approach is the third one, i.e., conversion of categorical data into numerical data. As we explained above, this can be done correctly only when all categorical variables have only limited number of categories (10 or less). Else, it leads to high dimensional data that causes, among other problems, machine learning models to produce meaningless (biased) results. In other words, when the variable has many classes, this approach becomes infeasible because the number of variables will be too much for the numeric models to handle.

This work detects a much smaller number of "latent classes" that are the underpinning classes or categories for the original categories of each categorical variable. This way, the high dimensionality is avoided and thus, we can use these latent classes to perform the dummy variable generation described above to use any machine learning. The small number of latent categories are detected using k-means clustering.

The basic idea is that categorical variables that have many values (or unique values for each sample) provide little information for other samples. To maintain the useful information from these variables, the best method is to keep that useful (latent) information. This invention does it by finding the latent categories by clustering all categories into similar groups. Using k-means clustering of the categories of any categorical variable, we may two distinct cases. First, is when each category has given features or attributes. This is rarely seen in the data sets. The second case is when there are no such attributes about each of the categories and we need to create them.

In the cases, we have features for all categories or classes of any variable, we could use k-means clustering directly. Though, quite often, there is no attributes information about these classes in the data sets. This work uses NLP [2, 13, 18–20, 53, 57] models (Natural Language Processing) to address the case of categorical variables without any attributes or features. The objective is to find a small number of dummy variables replacing the categorical variable, that we want to convert to a numerical one.

We show our approach for the very important example of URL variable.

2.2 Application of Our Model by Using the Example of URL Data

Categorical variables having URL are important example of these types of categorical variables. They are frequently present in click data and often have very large possible values, sometime as much as the number of users.

To extract the latent categories from these URL variables, we try to cluster them into similar URL's i.e. URLs with similar paths. We choose to extract a word and character using n-gram vector representations from the URL's, then cluster these vector representations using K-means clustering.

URL clustering is a great example because of the difficulty of the task. The difficulty is not only as a result of the number of URLs but also because of the lack of information (attributes) about them that can be used for clustering. When there is no information available about the variables, we need to use NLP. It important that we use NLP to perform the clustering because we have no knowledge of the format of the URLs, i.e., we have no attributions for each URL and clustering cannot be done without attributes. In this case, we use NLP to build the needed attributes for the URLs. When URLs have the same domain, like www.google.com, then the clusters would all be under www.google.com. However, the URLs could also be under multiple domains in which case the clusters would be under multiple domains. A predetermined algorithm would not be able to dynamically handle this variability. This is another reason that, in the case of URLs as an example, we use NLP to cluster them based off syntactic similarity, specifically word bigrams i.e. groups of three words. Our categorical variable has 500 categories, all under the domain of www.adobe.com. A few of these categories are;

http://www.adobe.com/creativecloud.html?promoid=NGWGRLB2&mv=other

http://www.adobe.com/creativecloud/photography.html?promoid=NQCJRBTZ&mv=other

http://www.adobe.com/creativecloud/buy/students.html?promoid=P79NQTWV&mv=other

http://www.adobe.com/creativecloud/business/teams.html?promoid=NYTLR3CX&mv=other

http://www.adobe.com/creativecloud/business/enterprise.html?promoid=NV3KR73Y&mv=other

http://www.adobe.com/creativecloud/buy/education.html?promoid=NLMHRGL1&mv=other

http://www.adobe.com/products/photoshop.html?promoid=PC1PQQ5T&mv=other

http://www.adobe.com/products/illustrator.html?promoid=PGRQQLFS&mv=other

http://www.adobe.com/products/indesign.html?promoid=PLHRQGPR&mv=other

http://www.adobe.com/products/premiere.html?promoid=PQ7SQBYQ&mv=other

http://www.adobe.com/products/experience-design.html?promoid=PYPVQ3HN&mv=other

Fig. 1. The example of URL variable list with 500 different categories.

For the algorithm to work best, we first strip the URL's of any characters that provide little information for clustering (since these words may introduce no new information). These words include punctuation and common words such as "http" and "www". We, thus, perform pre-processing on this list which includes removing punctuation, queries (anything after the character "?"), and stop-words (http, com, www, html, etc.). After this step, we are left with the URLs as space separated words representing the path of URL (Fig. 2);

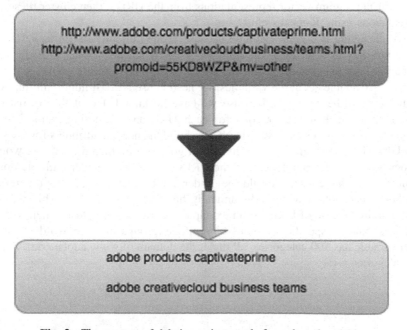

Fig. 2. The process of deleting noisy words from the url variable.

A sample of the result looks like (Fig. 3):

```
adobe creativecloud business teams
adobe creativecloud desktop-app
adobe creativecloud business enterprise
adobe creativecloud business teams
adobe creativecloud business enterprise
adobe creativecloud business teams plans
adobe creativecloud

adobe creativecloud buy students
adobe creativecloud buy education
adobe creativecloud buy students
adobe creativecloud buy students
adobe creativecloud buy education
adobe creativecloud buy government
adobe creativecloud buy government
```

Fig. 3. The url data after the removal of words that may be irrelevant for clustering.

One of the most popular tools in NLP is the ones involving representation of words with a numerical vector representation in an n dimensional space. Using the context of a word, it can be mapped into an n-dimensional vector space. Learned representations such as word embedding is increasingly popular for modeling semantics in NLP. This is done by reducing semantic composition to simple vector operations. We've modified and extended traditional representation learning techniques [13, 18, 50] to support multiple word senses and uncertain representations.

In this work, we used a modification so that, instead of projecting individual words, we project whole URLs containing multiple words. We use these words and their contexts as features for the projection of the whole URL (Fig. 4).

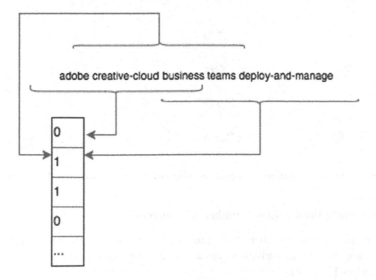

Fig. 4. Vector representation of the url data.

Using the cleaned list, we extract vector representations of the URL's using the tool "Sally". Sally is a tool that maps a set of strings to a set of vectors. The features that we use for this mapping are bi-gram words and tri-gram characters. Thus, using word bigrams of the URLs as features, we project the URLs into vector space using "Sally". Sally represents the URLs using a sparse matrix representation. This means that the URLs are projected into very long vectors with each dimension representing a word trigram that has been seen in the dataset. If a trigram has been observed in the URL its value in the vector is 1. Otherwise the value is 0. This results in a long vector with most values equal to 0 and a few values equal to 1. All the vectors together make a matrix that is a sparse matrix because of its many 0 values. Finally, we used K-means clustering on the embedding. Given that the URLs have been transformed into points in n-dimensional vector space, K-means clustering can find groups of points and partitions them as a cluster in the dataset. Given a number K which is the number of clusters for the algorithm to discover, K-means finds the best partitioning of the dataset such that the points in the clusters are mutually as similar as possible. In the context of URLs this means finding the groups of URLs that share the most word trigrams. Figure 5 shows that the best K values is 10.

Clusters	Word tri-grams	Char tri-grams
3	.149	.224
4	.176	.215
5	.167	.203
6	.172	.199
7	.215	.211
8	.208	.251
9	.210	.244
10	.233	.221

Fig. 5. The computation of optimal number of clustering using word tri-grams.

2.3 Computing the Optimal Number of Clusters

To compute the optimal number of clusters, we use Silhouette method which is based on minimizing the dissimilarities inside a cluster and maximizing the dissimilarities among clusters [31, 50]:

The Silhouette model computes s(i) for each data point in the data set for each K:

$$s(i) = \frac{b(i) - a(i)}{\max\{a(i), b(i)\}}$$

Where $a(i)$ is the mean distance of point i to all the other points in its cluster. Also, $b(i)$ is the mean distance to all the points in its closest cluster, i.e., $b(i)$ is the minimum mean distance of point i to all clusters that i is not a member of.

The optimal K is the K that maximizes the total score s(i) for all data set. The score values lie in the range of [−1, 1] with −1 to be the worst possible score and +1 to be the optimal score. Thus, the closest (average score of all points) score to +1 is the optimal one and the corresponding K is the optimal K. Our experiments show that the value of K has upper bound of 10. Here, we use not only the score but the maximum separation and compactness of the clusters, as measured by distance between clusters and uniformity of the width of clusters, to test and validate our model simultaneously when computing optimal K. Figure 6 depicts Silhouette model for different K [50].

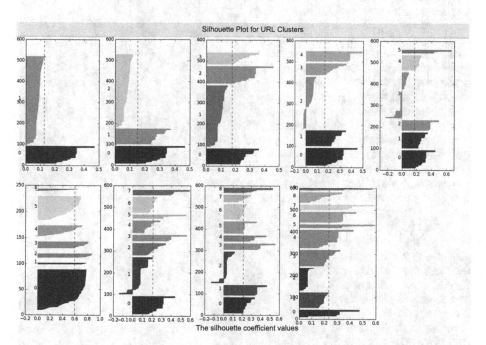

Fig. 6. Using silhouette model to compute the optimal number of clusters, to be 10.

Using the results from silhouette model, we use k-means clustering to cluster the URL data. Some of the clusters are shown in Fig. 7.

```
adobe data-analytics-cloud
 adobe data-analytics-cloud analytics
 adobe data-analytics-cloud
 adobe data-analytics-cloud analytics
 adobe data-analytics-cloud
 adobe data-analytics-cloud
 adobe data-analytics-cloud analytics
 adobe data-analytics-cloud
 adobe data-analytics-cloud analytics
 adobe data-analytics-cloud analytics
 adobe data-analytics-cloud analytics
 adobe data-analytics-cloud analytics select
 adobe data-analytics-cloud analytics prime
 adobe data-analytics-cloud analytics ultimate
 adobe data-analytics-cloud analytics video
 adobe data-analytics-cloud analytics predictive-intelligence
 adobe data-analytics-cloud analytics live-stream
 adobe data-analytics-cloud analytics data-workbench
 adobe data-analytics-cloud analytics mobile-app-analytics
 adobe data-analytics-cloud analytics capabilities
 adobe data-analytics-cloud analytics new-capabilities
 adobe data-analytics-cloud analytics resources
 adobe data-analytics-cloud analytics learn-support
 adobe data-analytics-cloud analytics select
 adobe data-analytics-cloud analytics prime
 adobe data-analytics-cloud analytics ultimate
 adobe data-analytics-cloud analytics video
 adobe data-analytics-cloud analytics predictive-intelligence
 adobe data-analytics-cloud analytics live-stream
 adobe data-analytics-cloud analytics data-workbench
 adobe data-analytics-cloud analytics mobile-app-analytics
 adobe data-analytics-cloud analytics marketing-attribution
 adobe data-analytics-cloud analytics analysis-workspace

 adobe products photoshop
 adobe products illustrator
 adobe products indesign
 adobe products premiere
 adobe products experience-design
 adobe products elements-family
 adobe products special-offers
 adobe products photoshop
 adobe products photoshop-lightroom
 adobe products illustrator
 adobe products premiere
 adobe products indesign
 adobe products experience-design
 adobe products captur
```

Fig. 7. Some of the clusters for the url data.

As the figure above shows, our method has grouped together URLs with similar paths and separated URLs with dissimilar paths.

3   The Results and Conclusion

This project provides a method of converting categorical variables to numerical variables so machine learning models could use data. For this conversion to be plausible for categorical variables with many classes, we propose that clustering can be used to decrease the number of classes in the variable to a small number for dummy variable generation. Though, some variables may have accessible features which makes it possible to cluster them, but many variables lack the information or features that would be needed for clustering models. This work deal effectively with these types of categorical variables and assumes no extra features and information may be available, neither explicitly nor implicitly – by web scraping, for such variables. For the model to work, we used NLP to create a vector representation of the variables. Then, we use the vector representation to cluster the variables, i.e., clustering the categories of the variables.

This work provides a new and only practical method of dealing with the standardization of categorical variables when the variables have large number of categories or classes and have no explicitly or implicitly available features. Our model avoids the deletion of the categorical variables and thus loss of information that causes machine learning models to produce meaningless results. This work also leads to the avoidance of creating high dimensional data where "curse of dimensionality" leads to high computational cost, need of exponentially larger data sets, distorted values for distance metrics and biased models.

References

1. Ahn, D., Jijkoun, V., Mishne, G., Müller, K., de Rijke, M., Schlobach, S.: Using Wikipedia at the TREC QA track. In: Proceedings of TREC (2004)
2. Auer, S., Bizer, C., Kobilarov, G., Lehmann, J., Cyganiak, R., Ives, Z.: DBpedia: a nucleus for a web of open data. In: Aberer, K., et al. (eds.) ASWC/ISWC -2007. LNCS, vol. 4825, pp. 722–735. Springer, Heidelberg (2007). https://doi.org/10.1007/978-3-540-76298-0_52
3. Backstrom, L., Leskovec, J.: Supervised random walks: predicting and recommending links in social networks. In: ACM International Conference on Web Search and Data Mining, WSDM (2011)
4. Bahdanau, D., Cho, K., Bengio, Y.: Neural machine translation by jointly learning to align and translate. In: International Conference on Learning Representations, ICLR (2015)
5. Baudiš, P.: YodaQA: a modular question answering system pipeline. In: POSTER 2015-19th International Student Conference on Electrical Engineering, pp. 1156–1165 (2015)
6. Baudiš, P., Šedivý, J.: Modeling of the question answering task in the YodaQA system. In: Mothe, J., Savoy, J., Kamps, J., Pinel-Sauvagnat, K., Jones, G.J.F., SanJuan, E., Cappellato, L., Ferro, N. (eds.) CLEF 2015. LNCS, vol. 9283, pp. 222–228. Springer, Cham (2015). https://doi.org/10.1007/978-3-319-24027-5_20

7. Becker, S., Bobin, J., Candès, E.J.: NESTA: a fast and accurate first-order method for sparse recovery. SIAM J. Imag. Sci. **4**(1), 1–39 (2009)
8. Bjorck, A.: Numerical Methods for Least Squares Problems. SIAM, Philadelphia (1996)
9. Blei, D.M., Ng, A.Y., Jordan, M.I.: Latent Dirichlet allocation. J. Mach. Learn. Res. **3**, 993–1022 (2003)
10. Bollacker, K., Evans, C., Paritosh, P., Sturge, T., Taylor, J.: Freebase: a collaboratively created graph database for structuring human knowledge. In: Proceedings of the 2008 ACM SIGMOD International Conference on Management of Data, pp. 1247–1250. ACM (2008)
11. Brill, E., Dumais, S., Banko, M.: An analysis of the AskMSR question-answering system. In: Empirical Methods in Natural Language Processing, EMNLP, pp. 257–264 (2002)
12. Boyd, S., Vandenberghe, L.: Convex Optimization. Cambridge University Press, Cambridge (2004)
13. Buscaldi, D., Rosso, P.: Mining knowledge from Wikipedia for the question answering task. In: International Conference on Language Resources and Evaluation, LREC, pp. 727–730 (2006)
14. Candès, E.J., Recht, B.: Exact matrix completion via convex optimization. Found. Comput. Math. **9**, 717–772 (2008)
15. Candès, E.J.: Compressive sampling. In: Proceedings of the International Congress of Mathematicians, Madrid, Spain (2006)
16. Candès, E.J., Tao, T.: Near-optimal signal recovery from random projections: universal encoding strategies. IEEE Trans. Inf. Theory **52**, 5406–5425 (2004)
17. Caruana, R.: Multitask learning. In: Thrun, S., Pratt, L. (eds.) Learning to Learn, pp. 95–133. Springer, Boston (1998). https://doi.org/10.1007/978-1-4615-5529-2_5
18. Chen, D., Bolton, J., Manning, C.D.: A thorough examination of the CNN/Daily Mail reading comprehension task. In: Association for Computational Linguistics, ACL (2016)
19. Chen, D., Fisch, A., Weston, J., Bordes, A.: Reading Wikipedia to answer open-domain questions. arXiv:1704.00051 (2017)
20. Collobert, R., Weston, J.: A unified architecture for natural language processing: deep neural networks with multitask learning. In: International Conference on Machine Learning, ICML (2008)
21. d'Aspremont, A., El Ghaoui, L., Jordan, M.I., Lanckriet, G.R.G.: A direct formulation for sparse PCA using semidefinite programming. SIAM Rev. **49**(3), 434–448 (2007)
22. Efron, B., Hastie, T., Johnstone, I., Tibshirani, R.: Least angle regression. Ann. Stat. **32**, 407–499 (2004)
23. Eldén, L.: Algorithms for the regularization of ill-conditioned least squares problems. BIT **17**, 134–145 (1977)
24. Eldén, L.: A note on the computation of the generalized cross-validation function for ill-conditioned least squares problems. BIT **24**, 467–472 (1984)
25. Engl, H.W., Groetsch, C.W. (eds.): Inverse and Ill-Posed Problems. Academic Press, London (1987)
26. Fader, A., Zettlemoyer, L., Etzioni, O.: Open question answering over curated and extracted knowledge bases. In: ACM SIGKDD International Conference on Knowledge Discovery and Data Mining, pp. 1156–1165 (2014)
27. Fazel, M., Hindi, H., Boyd, S.: A rank minimization heuristic with application to minimum order system approximation. In: Proceedings American Control Conference, vol. 6, pp. 4734–4739 (2001)
28. Golub, G.H., Van Loan, C.F.: Matrix Computations, 4th edn. Computer Assisted Mechanics and Engineering Sciences, Johns Hopkins University Press, Baltimore (2013)

29. Golub, G.H., Van Loan, C.F.: An analysis of the total least squares problem. SIAM J. Numer. Anal. **17**, 883–893 (1980)
30. Golub, G.H., Heath, M., Wahba, G.: Generalized cross-validation as a method for choosing a good ridge parameter. Technometrics **21**, 215–223 (1979)
31. Hastie, T., Tibshirani, R., Friedman, J.: The Elements of Statistical Learning; Data Mining, Inference and Prediction. Springer, New York (2001). https://doi.org/10.1007/978-0-387-21606-5
32. Hastie, T.J., Tibshirani, R.: Handwritten digit recognition via deformable prototypes. Technical report. AT&T Bell Laboratories (1994)
33. Hein, T., Hofmann, B.: On the nature of ill-posedness of an inverse problem in option pricing. Inverse Probl. **19**, 1319–1338 (2003)
34. Hewlett, D., Lacoste, A., Jones, L., Polosukhin, I., Fandrianto, A., Han, J., Kelcey, M., Berthelot, D.: WikiReading: a novel large-scale language understanding task over wikipedia. In: Association for Computational Linguistics, ACL, pp. 1535–1545 (2016)
35. Hill, F., Bordes, A., Chopra, S., Weston, J.: The Goldilocks principle: reading children's books with explicit memory representations. In: International Conference on Learning Representations, ICLR (2016)
36. Hua, T.A., Gunst, R.F.: Generalized ridge regression: a note on negative ridge parameters. Commun. Stat. Theory Methods **12**, 37–45 (1983)
37. Jolliffe, I.T., Trendafilov, N.T., Uddin, M.: A modified principal component technique based on the LASSO. J. Comput. Graph. Stat. **12**, 531–547 (2003)
38. Kirsch, A.: An Introduction to the Mathematical theory of Inverse Problems. Springer, New York (1996). https://doi.org/10.1007/978-1-4419-8474-6
39. Mardia, K., Kent, J., Bibby, J.: Multivariate Analysis. Academic Press, New York (1979)
40. Manning, C.D., Surdeanu, M., Bauer, J., Finkel, J., Bethard, S.J., McClosky, D.: The stanford CoreNLP natural language processing toolkit. In: Association for Computational Linguistics, ACL, pp. 55–60 (2014)
41. Marquardt, D.W.: Generalized inverses, ridge regression, biased linear estimation, and nonlinear estimation. Technometrics **12**, 591–612 (1970)
42. Mazumder, R., Hastie, T., Tibshirani, R.: Spectral regularization algorithms for learning large incomplete matrices. JMLR **2010**(11), 2287–2322 (2010)
43. McCabe, G.: Principal variables. Technometrics **26**, 137–144 (1984)
44. Miller, A.H., Fisch, A., Dodge, J., Karimi, A.-H., Bordes, A., Weston, J.: Key-value memory networks for directly reading documents. In: Empirical Methods in Natural Language Processing, EMNLP, pp. 1400–1409 (2016)
45. Mintz, M., Bills, S., Snow, R., Jurafsky, D.: Distant supervision for relation extraction without labeled data. In: Association for Computational Linguistics and International Joint Conference on Natural Language Processing, ACL/IJCNLP, pp. 1003–1011 (2009)
46. Modarresi, K., Golub, G.H.: An adaptive solution of linear inverse problems. In: Proceedings of Inverse Problems Design and Optimization Symposium, IPDO 2007, Miami Beach, Florida, 16–18 April, pp. 333–340 (2007)
47. Modarresi, K.: A local regularization method using multiple regularization levels, Stanford, CA, April 2007
48. Modarresi, K.: Algorithmic approach for learning a comprehensive view of online users. Proc. Comput. Sci. **80**(C), 2181–2189 (2016)
49. Modarresi, K.: Computation of recommender system using localized regularization. Proc. Comput. Sci. **51**(C), 2407–2416 (2015)
50. Modarresi, K., Munir, A.: Generalized variable conversion using K-means clustering and web scraping. In: ICCS 2018 (2018, Accepted)

51. Rajpurkar, P., Zhang, J., Lopyrev, K., Liang, P.: SQuAD: 100,000 + questions for machine comprehension of text. In: Empirical Methods in Natural Language Processing, EMNLP (2016)
52. Ryu, P.-M., Jang, M.-G., Kim, H.-K.: Open domain question answering using Wikipedia-based knowledge model. Inf. Process. Manag. **50**(5), 683–692 (2014)
53. Seo, M., Kembhavi, A., Farhadi, A., Hajishirzi, H.: Bidirectional attention flow for machine comprehension. arXiv preprint arXiv:1611.01603 (2016)
54. Tarantola, A.: Inverse Problem Theory. Elsevir, Amsterdam (1987)
55. Tibshirani, R.: Regression shrinkage and selection via the LASSO. J. Roy. Stat. Soc. Ser. B **58**(1), 267–288 (1996)
56. Tikhonov, A.N., Goncharsky, A.V. (eds.): Ill-Posed Problems in the Natural Sciences. MIR, Moscow (1987)
57. Wang, Z., Mi, H., Hamza, W., Florian, R.: Multi-perspective context matching for machine comprehension. arXiv preprint arXiv:1612.04211 (2016)
58. Witten, R., Candès, E.J.: Randomized algorithms for low-rank matrix factorizations: sharp performance bounds. Algorithmica **72**, 264–281 (2013)
59. Zhou, Z., Wright, J., Li, X., Candès, E.J., Ma, Y.: Stable principal component pursuit. In: Proceedings of International Symposium on Information Theory, June 2010
60. Zou, H., Hastie, T., Tibshirani, R.: Sparse principal component analysis. J. Comput. Graph. Stat. **15**(2), 265–286 (2006)

Generalized Variable Conversion Using K-means Clustering and Web Scraping

Kourosh Modarresi[(✉)] and Abdurrahman Munir

Adobe Inc., San Jose, CA, USA
kouroshm@alumni.stanford.edu, munir@adobe.com

Abstract. The world of AI and Machine Learning is the world of data and learning from data so the insights could be used for analysis and prediction. Almost all data sets are of mixed variable types as they may be quantitative (numerical) or qualitative (categorical). The problem arises from the fact that a long list of methods in Machine Learning such as "multiple regression", "logistic regression", "k-means clustering", and "support vector machine", all to be as examples of such models, designed to deal with numerical data type only. Though the data, that need to be analyzed and learned from, is almost always, a mixed data type and thus, standardization step must be undertaken for all these data sets. The standardization process involves the conversion of qualitative (categorical) data into numerical data type.

Keywords: Mixed variable types · NLP · K-means clustering

1 Introduction

1.1 Why this Work is Needed

AI and machine learning are mathematical modeling methods for learning from data and producing intelligent models based on this learning. The data these models need to deal with, is normally a mixed data type of both numerical (continuous) variables and categorical (non-numerical) data types. Most models in AI and machine learning accept only numerical data as their input and thus, standardization of mixed data into numerical data is a critical step when applying machine learning models. Having data in the standard shape and format that models require is often a time consuming, nevertheless very significant step of the process.

As an example, when we have a data set (below) combined of many variables where all variables are numerical ones except two variables of categorical type (gender and marital status) as following (Table 1):

© Springer International Publishing AG, part of Springer Nature 2018
Y. Shi et al. (Eds.): ICCS 2018, LNCS 10861, pp. 247–258, 2018.
https://doi.org/10.1007/978-3-319-93701-4_19

Table 1. Original mixed variables

User	Age	Income	Gender	Marital status
1	31	90,000	M	Single
2	45	45,000	M	Married
3	63	34,000	M	Divorced
4	33	65,000	F	Divorced
5	47	87,000	F	Single
6	38	39,000	M	Married
7	26	120,000	M	Married
8	25	32,000	F	Married
9	29	55,000	F	Single
10	44	33,000	F	Single

When applying many machine learning models, the models need the data to be numerical data type. Thus, the categorical data should be converted into numerical type. The most efficient way of converting the categorical variable is the introduction of dummy variables (one hot encoding) for which a new (dummy) variable is created for each category (except the last category – since it'd be dependent on the rest of dummy variables, i.e., its value could be determined when all other dummy variables are known) of the categorical variable. These dummy variables are binary variables Queryand could assume only two values, 1 and 0. The value 1 means the sample has the value of that variable and 0 means the opposite.

Here, for this example, we have two categorical variables:

1. Gender: there are only two categories, so we need to create one dummy variable.
2. Marital Status: there are three categories so we need to create two new dummy variables.

The result after the creation of dummy variables is shown in Table 2.

Table 2. The original variables after the introduction of dummy variables.

User	Age	Income	Dummy variable-1 (Female)	Dummy variable-2 (Married)	Dummy variable-3 (Single)
1	31	90000	0	0	1
2	45	45000	0	1	0
3	63	34000	0	0	0
4	33	65000	1	0	0
5	47	87000	1	0	1
6	38	39000	0	1	0
7	26	120000	0	1	0
8	25	32000	1	1	0
9	29	55000	1	0	1
10	44	33000	1	0	1

Now, we could use any machine learning model for this data set as all its variables are of the numerical type.

In general, for any categorical variable of "m" categories (classes), we need to create "m − 1" dummy variables. The problem arises when any specific categorical variable has large (based on our work, that means larger than 8) number of categories. The reason is that, in these cases, the number of dummy variables need to be created becomes too large causing the data to become of high dimension. The high dimensionality of data leads to "curse of dimensionality" problem and thus all related issues related to "curse of dimensionality" such as the need of "exponential increase in the number of data rows" and "difficulties of distance computation" would appear. Obviously, one needs to avoid the situation since, in addition to these problems, curse of dimensionality also leads to misleading results from any machine learning models such as finding false patterns discovered based on noise or random chance. Besides all of that, higher dimension leads to higher "computational cost" and "slow model response and lower robustness", all of which should be avoided. Therefore, in the process of transformation of categorical data into numerical data types, we must reduce the number of newly created numerical variables to reduce the dimension of data.

2 The Model

2.1 The Problem of Mixed Variables

The Vast majorities of the models in machine learning are models that use only numeric data. Though, practically all data that are used in machine learning are mixed type, numerical and categorical data. When used for machine learning models that could use only numerical data, mixed data types are handled using three different approaches: first approach is trying to, instead, using models that could handle mixed data type, second approach is to ignore (drop) categorical variables. The last approach is converting categorical variables to numerical type by introducing dummy variables or one hot encoding. The first approach introduces many limitations as there are only a limited number of models that could handle mixed data and those models may not the best model fitting the data sets. The second approach leads to ignoring much of the information in the data sets, i.e., the categorical data.

The practical approach is the third one, i.e., conversion of categorical data into numerical data. As we explained above, this can be done correctly only when all categorical variables have only limited number of categories. Else, it leads to high dimensional data that causes, among other problems, machine learning models to produce meaningless (biased) results. In other words, when the variable has many classes, this approach becomes infeasible because the number of variables will be too high for the numeric models to handle.

We can classify categorical variables into three types of variables. The first type is the ones without any clear and explicit features (like url, concatenated data, acronyms and so on). The second type of categorical variable occur when we have features (attributes) readily available as a part of data sets (or metadata). This is rarely seen in the data sets of the real world. In these cases that we have features for all categories or classes of any variable, we could use k-means clustering directly and follow it with the rest of the steps in this work. The third categorical data type is the case of categorical data without those readily available features. This paper addresses this last type of data where, quite often, there is no attributes information about these classes in the data sets and thus this we use NLP, Natural Language Processing [2, 13, 18–20, 40, 44, 45, 52, 56], models to establish these attributes. For our invention, we use web scraping to detect all features or attributes for our data sets. Then using these features, we use k-means clustering to compute a limited number of clusters that would represent the number of newly created features for the categorical data.

In this work, we also determine the upper bound for the number of new numerical variable created for conversion and representation of categorical variable. Besides, we define our way of testing the correctness and validation of our approach.

Therefore, to address these types of problem, this work establishes a new approach of reducing the number of categories (when the number of categories in a categorical variable in larger than 10) to K categories for $K \leq 10$. We do it by clustering the categories of each of such categorical variable into k clusters, using k-means clustering. We compute the number of clusters, k, using silhouette method. We also use Silhouette method also to verify correctness of our models simultaneously. Then, the number of dummy variable needs to be created for any categorical variable of such will be reduced to K dummy variables, one for each cluster. Thereafter, the standardization is done by introducing K dummy variables.

Using the method explained above, this work detects a much smaller number of "latent classes", that in general could be some of the original attributes or some linear or non-linear combination of the original attributes, that are the underpinning classes or categories for the original categories of each categorical variable. This way, the high dimensionality is avoided and thus, we can use these latent classes to perform the dummy variable generation procedure that is described above to be used for any machine learning model. The small number of latent categories are detected using k-means clustering.

The basic idea is that categorical variables that have many values (or unique values for each sample) provide little information for other samples. To maintain the useful information from these variables, the best method may be to keep that useful (latent) information. This paper does it by finding the latent categories by clustering all categories into similar groups.

2.2   Computing the Number of Cluster K and Testing the Model

In this work, including for the three examples, to compute the optimal number of clusters, the upper bound for the number of clusters, and for testing and validation of our model, we use Silhouette method which is based on minimizing the dissimilarities inside a cluster and maximizing the dissimilarities among clusters:

The Silhouette model computes s(i) for each data point in the data set for each K:

$$s(i) = \frac{b(i) - a(i)}{\max\{a(i), b(i)\}}$$

Where $a(i)$ is the mean distance of point i to all the other points in its cluster. Also, $b(i)$ is the mean distance to all the points in its closest cluster, i.e., $b(i)$ is the minimum mean distance of point i to all clusters that i is not a member of.

The optimal K is the K that maximizes the total score s(i) for all data set. The score values lie in the range of $[-1, 1]$ with -1 to be the worst possible score and $+1$ to be the optimal score. Thus, the closest (average score of all points) score to $+1$ is the optimal one and the corresponding K is the optimal K. Our experiments show that the value of K has upper bound of 10. Here, we use not only the score but the maximum separation and compactness of the clusters, as measured by distance between clusters and uniformity of the width of clusters, to test and validate our model simultaneously when computing optimal K.

In this work, we display the application of our model using three examples of categorical variables of large categories or classes. The first example is "country of residence" where there are over 175 categories or classes (countries). Secondly, we consider "city of residence (in the US)" as the second example where we use 183 most populated cities in the US. The third example of categorical variable with large categories that we use as an application of our model is "vegetables". For the vegetables, we have found records of 52 different classes (types of vegetables). In these examples, we show, that using our approach, we can find a small number of grouping within these variables and that these groupings can then be appended to the original data as dummy numeric variables to be used alongside the numeric variables.

2.3   The First Example of Categorical Variable, "Country of Residence"

Again, the issue is that there are so many categories for this categorical variable (country of residence), i.e., 175 categories. So, we need to create 174 dummy variables that would lead to a very high dimensional data and hence to "curse of dimensionality", as explained above. Here, we used clustering to group a list of 175 countries. For this

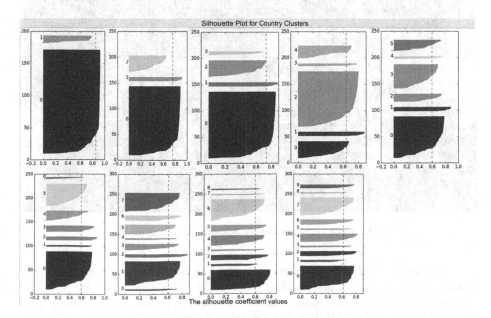

Fig. 1. The Silhouette plots displaying the optimal K to be 8.

case, syntactic similarity is useless since the name of a country has no relation to its attributes. Thus, we extracted the features from "www.worldbank.com". The seven features that we extracted, for each country, were: population, birth rate, mortality rate, life expectancy, death rate, surface area and forest area. These features were first normalized then K-means clustering was performed on the samples, again with a range of K from 2 to 10. Based off the silhouette plots in the following figure, Fig. 1, we can see that the algorithm performed well with K equal to 8:

country clustering output after k-means clustering is:

Antigua and Barbuda Burundi Belgium Bangladesh Bahrain Barbados China Comoros Cabo Verde Cyprus Czech Republic Germany Denmark Dominican Republic Micronesia Fed. Sts. United Kingdom Gambia Guam Haiti Indonesia Israel Italy Jamaica Japan Kiribati Korea Rep. Kuwait Lebanon St. Lucia Liechtenstein Sri Lanka Luxembourg St. Martin (French part) Maldives Malta Mauritius Malawi Nigeria Netherlands Nepal Pakistan Philippines Puerto Rico Korea Dem. People?s Rep. West Bank and Gaza Qatar Rwanda South Asia Singapore El Salvador Sao Tome and Principe Seychelles Togo Thailand Tonga Trinidad and Tobago Uganda St. Vincent and the Grenadines Virgin Islands (U.S.) Vietnam

Australia Botswana Canada Guyana Iceland Libya Mauritania Suriname

Angola Bahamas Brazil Bhutan Chile Estonia Kyrgyz Republic Lao PDR Peru Sudan Solomon Islands Somalia Sweden Uruguay Vanuatu Zambia

Central African Republic Gabon Kazakhstan Russian Federation

Afghanistan Belarus Cameroon Congo Dem. Rep. Colombia Djibouti Fiji Faroe Islands Georgia Guinea Guinea-Bissau Equatorial Guinea Iran Islamic Rep. Latin America & Caribbean (excluding high income) Liberia Lithuania Madagascar Montenegro Mozambique Nicaragua Panama United States Yemen Rep. South Africa

Argentina Congo Rep. Algeria Finland Mali New Caledonia Niger Norway New Zealand Oman Papua New Guinea Paraguay Saudi Arabia

Albania United Arab Emirates Austria Azerbaijan Benin Burkina Faso Bulgaria Bosnia and Herzegovina Cote d'Ivoire Costa Rica Ecuador Egypt Arab Rep. Spain Ethiopia Greece Honduras Croatia Hungary Ireland Iraq Jordan Kenya Cambodia Lesotho Morocco Moldova Mexico Macedonia Myanmar Malaysia Poland Portugal French Polynesia Romania Senegal Sierra Leone Serbia Slovak Republic Slovenia Tajikistan Timor-Leste Tunisia Turkey Tanzania Ukraine Uzbekistan

For n_clusters = 8 The average silhouette_score is : 0.608186424138

Fig. 2. The K-means clustering output for the first example.

In this example, the features extracted were not from only one domain, such as economic features only or just physical features. The advantage, of having a diverse domain features, is that the clusters that are formed will be more meaningful as they represent higher variation of data. For example, if our only feature was country size then the clustering algorithm would cluster algorithms with similar size. Additionally, if our only feature was country population then the algorithm would cluster countries with similar sizes. However, by using the different types of features, the algorithm could find clusters of countries that have both similar sizes and similar populations. For example, big countries with small populations could be in the same cluster as well as small countries that have large populations - - based their overall similarities computed using many various features.

2.4   The Second Example of Categorical Variable, "City of Residence" Using Web Scraping

To extract features for our categorical data (cities), we web scraped Wikipedia pages because of their abundant and concise data. The extraction came from the infobox on Wikipedia pages which contain quick facts about the article. We used five features which mainly pertained to the various attributes of the cities: land area, water area, elevation, population, and population density. For the most part, this was the only information available for direct extraction via Wikipedia pages. We extracted features for 183 U.S. cities then performed the same K-means clustering as in the previous examples to group the set into similar cities in each cluster. The most important aspect of this example is the web scraping. Whereas in the previous example, the features

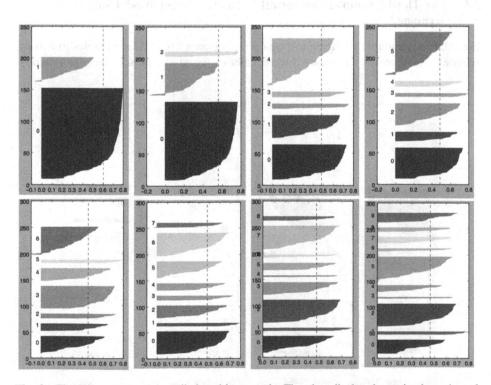

Fig. 3. The Silhouette model applied to this example. The plots display the optimal number of cluster to be K = 8.

San Francisco-California Boston-Massachusetts Long Beach-California Oakland-California Anaheim-California Riverside
-California Stockton-California Cincinnati-Ohio Saint Paul-Minnesota Lincoln-Nebraska Chula Vista-California St. Pe
tersburg-Florida Norfolk-Virginia Chandler-Arizona Madison-Wisconsin Glendale-Arizona Irvine-California Irving-Texa
s Fremont-California Gilbert-Arizona San Bernardino-California Richmond-Virginia Spokane-Washington Tacoma-Washingt
on Akron-Ohio Grand Prairie-Texas Newport News-Virginia Santa Clarita-California Vancouver-Washington Sioux Falls-S
outh Dakota Rockford-Illinois Joliet-Illinois Dayton-Ohio Hampton-Virginia McAllen-Texas Thousand Oaks-California G
ainesville-Florida Lafayette-Louisiana Denton-Texas Evansville-Indiana Springfield-Illinois Peoria-Illinois Palm Ba
y-Florida West Palm Beach-Florida

Colorado Springs-Colorado Aurora-Colorado Boise-Idaho Salt Lake City-Utah Lancaster-California Palmdale California
Surprise-Arizona Victorville-California Midland-Texas

For n_clusters = 8 The average silhouette_score is : 0.483367645642

Fig. 4. The city clustering output after K-means clustering.

were taken from prebuilt online datasets, in this example we automatically built our own dataset by web scraping Wikipedia pages and constructing the features from this dataset. This shows that despite having a variable with many classes and no available information about the classes, we can extract the information necessary to perform the clustering. The following figure shows the silhouette model outcome:

As indicated, the silhouette plot for city clusters shows the number of newly variables, replacing 183 cities (categories), should be 8. Some of these clusters are shown here:

2.5 The Third Example: Categorical Variable, "Vegetables" Using Web Scraping

For the final example, we again use web scraping on a list of 52 vegetables to extract features. The features we extracted were: calories, protein, carbohydrates, and dietary

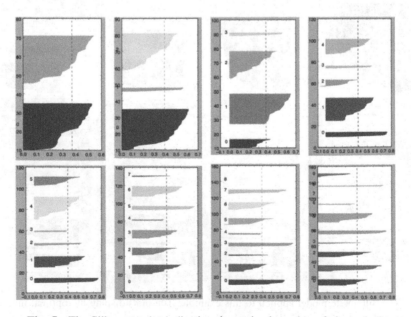

Fig. 5. The Silhouette plot indicating the optimal number of cluster is 7.

fiber. Like the previous example, we used Wikipedia articles to extract the features. Once again, this example shows the practicality of using web scraping as a means of automatically collecting features to build features for a dataset and then perform clustering on the dataset. The clustering of vegetables demonstrates the wide variety of variable types that our method can be applied to. The Silhouette plots is shown below with the optimal k to be 7:

Some of the clusters are shown below:

```
Broccoli Cabbage Celery Celtuce Broccoli Cauliflower Green bean Okra Cardoon Celery Daikon

Beetroot Garlic Leek Onion Shallot Beetroot Carrot Jerusalem artichoke Potato Rutabaga Sweet potato Taro

Watercress Nori

Chicory Endive Artichoke Kohlrabi Turnip

Bok choy Collard greens Komatsuna Lettuce Rapini Spinach Asparagus Chives Bamboo shoot

Amaranth Pea Radicchio Black-eyed pea Chickpea Lentil Mung bean Pea Snap pea Wakame

For n_clusters = 7 The average silhouette_score is : 0.42576581221
```

Fig. 6. Some of the clusters for the example three.

As shown by the images above, our algorithm is able to cluster the list of vegetables into groups based on similar nutritional benefit.

3 Conclusion

This work deals with the problem of converting categorical variables (to numerical ones) when the variables have high number of classes. We have shown the application of our model using three examples: countries, cities and vegetables. We use NLP plus clustering to show that even when there is no available information about the attributes, we could still perform clustering for the purpose of standardization of data. In the second example, we extracted external information about the values and then applied clustering using the information (features). In the second and third examples, we automatically extracted features from online resources. This information is needed for clustering. These three examples show that as long as there exists information about a variable, somewhere online, this information can be extracted and used for clustering. The final objective is to use the clustering method to drastically reduce the number of dummy variables that must be created in place of the categorical data type. Our model is practical and easy to use. It is an essential step in pre-processing data for many machine learning models.

References

1. Ahn, D., Jijkoun, V., Mishne, G., Müller, K., de Rijke, M., Schlobach, S.: Using Wikipedia at the TREC QA track. In: Proceedings of TREC (2004)
2. Auer, S., Bizer, C., Kobilarov, G., Lehmann, J., Cyganiak, R., Ives, Z.: DBpedia: a nucleus for a web of open data. In: Aberer, K., Choi, K.-S., Noy, N., Allemang, D., Lee, K.-I., Nixon, L., Golbeck, J., Mika, P., Maynard, D., Mizoguchi, R., Schreiber, G., Cudré-Mauroux, P. (eds.) ASWC/ISWC -2007. LNCS, vol. 4825, pp. 722–735. Springer, Heidelberg (2007). https://doi.org/10.1007/978-3-540-76298-0_52
3. Backstrom, L., Leskovec, J.: Supervised random walks: predicting and recommending links in social networks. In: ACM International Conference on Web Search and Data Mining (WSDM) (2011)
4. Bahdanau, D., Cho, K., Bengio, Y.: Neural machine translation by jointly learning to align and translate. In: International Conference on Learning Representations (ICLR) (2015)
5. Baudiš, P.:YodaQA: a modular question answering system pipeline. In: POSTER 2015-19th International Student Conference on Electrical Engineering, pp. 1156–1165 (2015)
6. Baudiš, P., Šedivý, J.: Modeling of the question answering task in the YodaQA system. In: Mothe, J., Savoy, J., Kamps, J., Pinel-Sauvagnat, K., Jones, Gareth J.F., SanJuan, E., Cappellato, L., Ferro, N. (eds.) CLEF 2015. LNCS, vol. 9283, pp. 222–228. Springer, Cham (2015). https://doi.org/10.1007/978-3-319-24027-5_20
7. Becker, S., Bobin, J., Candès, E.J.: NESTA: a fast and accurate first-order method for sparse recovery. SIAM J. Imaging Sci. **4**(1), 1–39 (2009)
8. Bjorck, A.: Numerical Methods for Least Squares Problems. SIAM, Philadelphia (1996)
9. Blei, D.M., Ng, A.Y., Jordan, M.I.: Latent Dirichlet allocation. J. Mach. Learn. Res. **3**, 993–1022 (2003)
10. Bollacker, K., Evans, C., Paritosh, P., Sturge, T., Taylor, J.: Freebase: a collaboratively created graph database for structuring human knowledge. In: Proceedings of the 2008 ACM SIGMOD International Conference on Management of Data, pp. 1247–1250. ACM (2008)
11. Brill, E., Dumais, S., Banko, M.: An analysis of the AskMSR question-answering system. In: Empirical Methods in Natural Language Processing (EMNLP), pp. 257–264 (2002)
12. Boyd, S., Vandenberghe, L.: Convex Optimization. Cambridge University Press, Cambridge (2004)
13. Buscaldi, D., Rosso, P.: Mining knowledge from Wikipedia for the question answering task. In: International Conference on Language Resources and Evaluation (LREC), pp. 727–730 (2006)
14. Candès, E.J., Recht, B.: Exact matrix completion via convex optimization. Found. Comput. Math. **9**, 717–772 (2008)
15. Candès, E.J.: Compressive sampling. In: Proceedings of the International Congress of Mathematicians, Madrid, Spain (2006)
16. Candès, E.J., Tao, T.: Near-optimal signal recovery from random projections: universal encoding strategies. IEEE Trans. Inform. Theor. **52**, 5406–5425 (2004)
17. Caruana, R.: Multitask learning. In: Thrun, S., Pratt, L. (eds.) Learning to Learn, pp. 95–133. Springer, Boston (1998). https://doi.org/10.1007/978-1-4615-5529-2_5
18. Chen, D., Bolton, J., Manning, C.D.: A thorough examination of the CNN/daily mail reading comprehension task. In: Association for Computational Linguistics (ACL) (1998). 2016
19. Chen, D., Fisch, A., Weston, J., Bordes, A.: Reading Wikipedia to Answer Open-Domain Questions, arXiv:1704.00051 (2017)

20. Collobert, R., Weston, J.: A unified architecture for natural language processing: deep neural networks with multitask learning. In: International Conference on Machine Learning (ICML) (2008)
21. d'Aspremont, A., El Ghaoui, L., Jordan, M.I., Lanckriet, G.R.G.: A direct formulation for sparse PCA using semidefinite programming. SIAM Rev. **49**(3), 434–448 (2007)
22. Efron, B., Hastie, T., Johnstone, I., Tibshirani, R.: Least angle regression. Ann. Stat. **32**, 407–499 (2004)
23. Elden, L.: Algorithms for the regularization of Ill-conditioned least squares problems. BIT **17**, 134–145 (1977)
24. Elden, L.: A note on the computation of the generalized cross-validation function for Ill-conditioned least squares problems. BIT **24**, 467–472 (1984)
25. Engl, H.W., Groetsch, C.W. (eds.): Inverse and Ill-Posed Problems. Academic Press, London (1987)
26. Fader, A., Zettlemoyer, L., Etzioni, O.: Open question answering over curated and extracted knowledge bases. In: ACM SIGKDD International Conference on Knowledge Discovery and Data Mining, pp. 1156–1165 (2014)
27. Fazel, M., Hindi, H., Boyd, S.: A rank minimization heuristic with application to minimum order system approximation. In: Proceedings American Control Conference, vol. 6, pp. 4734–4739 (2001)
28. Golub, G.H., Van Loan, C.F.: Matrix Computations, 4th edn. Computer Assisted Mechanics and Engineering Sciences, Johns Hopkins University Press, US (2013)
29. Golub, G.H., Van Loan, C.F.: An analysis of the total least squares problem. SIAM J. Numer. Anal. **17**, 883–893 (1980)
30. Golub, G.H., Heath, M., Wahba, G.: Generalized cross-validation as a method for choosing a good ridge parameter. Technometrics **21**, 215–223 (1979)
31. Hastie, T., Tibshirani, R., Friedman, J.: The Elements of Statistical Learning. SSS. Springer, New York (2009). https://doi.org/10.1007/978-0-387-84858-7
32. Hastie, T.J., Tibshirani, R.: Handwritten digit recognition via deformable prototypes. Technical report, AT&T Bell Laboratories (1994)
33. Hein, T., Hofmann, B.: On the nature of ill-posedness of an inverse problem in option pricing. Inverse Prob. **19**, 1319–1338 (2003)
34. Hewlett, D., Lacoste, A., Jones, L., Polosukhin, I., Fandrianto, A., Han, J., Kelcey, M., Berthelot, D.: Wikireading: a novel large-scale language understanding task over Wikipedia. In: Association for Computational Linguistics (ACL), pp. 1535–1545 (2016)
35. Hill, F., Bordes, A., Chopra, S., Weston, J.: The goldilocks principle: reading children's books with explicit memory representations. In: International Conference on Learning Representations (ICLR) (2016)
36. Hua, T.A., Gunst, R.F.: Generalized ridge regression: a note on negative ridge parameters. Comm. Stat. Theor. Methods **12**, 37–45 (1983)
37. Jolliffe, I.T., Trendafilov, N.T., Uddin, M.: A modified principal component technique based on the LASSO. J. Comput. Graph. Stat. **12**, 531–547 (2003)
38. Kirsch, A.: An Introduction to the Mathematical Theory of Inverse Problems. Springer, New York (1996). https://doi.org/10.1007/978-1-4419-8474-6
39. Mardia, K., Kent, J., Bibby, J.: Multivariate Analysis. Academic Press, New York (1979)
40. Manning, C.D., Surdeanu, M., Bauer, J., Finkel, J., Bethard, S.J., McClosky, D.: The stanford corenlp natural language processing toolkit. In: Association for Computational Linguistics (ACL), pp. 55–60 (2014)
41. Marquardt, D.W.: Generalized inverses, ridge regression, biased linear estimation and nonlinear estimation. Technometrics **12**, 591–612 (1970)

42. Mazumder, R., Hastie, T., Tibshirani, R.: Spectral regularization algorithms for learning large incomplete matrices. JMLR **11**, 2287–2322 (2010)
43. McCabe, G.: Principal variables. Technometrics **26**, 137–144 (1984)
44. Miller, A.H., Fisch, A., Dodge, J., Karimi, A.-H., Bordes, A., Weston, J.: Key-value memory networks for directly reading documents. In: Empirical Methods in Natural Language Processing (EMNLP), pp. 1400–1409 (2016)
45. Mintz, M., Bills, S., Snow, R., Jurafsky, D.: Distant supervision for relation extraction without labeled data. In: Association for Computational Linguistics and International Joint Conference on Natural Language Processing (ACL/IJCNLP), pp. 1003–1011 (2009)
46. Modarresi, K., Golub, G.H.: An adaptive solution of linear inverse problems. In: Proceedings of Inverse Problems Design and Optimization Symposium (IPDO2007), 16–18 April, Miami Beach, Florida, pp. 333–340 (2007)
47. Modarresi, K.: A local regularization method using multiple regularization levels, Stanford, CA, April 2007
48. Modarresi, K.: Algorithmic approach for learning a comprehensive view of online users. Procedia Comput. Sci. **80C**, 2181–2189 (2016)
49. Modarresi, K.: Computation of recommender system using localized regularization. Procedia Comput. Sci. **51**, 2407–2416 (2015)
50. Rajpurkar, P., Zhang, J., Lopyrev, K., Liang, P.: SQuAD: 100,000+ questions for machine comprehension of text. In: Empirical Methods in Natural Language Processing (EMNLP) (2016)
51. Ryu, P.-M., Jang, M.-G., Kim, H.-K.: Open domain question answering using Wikipedia-based knowledge model. Inf. Process. Manag. **50**(5), 683–692 (2014)
52. Seo, M., Kembhavi, A., Farhadi, A., Hajishirzi, H.: Bidirectional attention flow for machine comprehension. arXiv preprint arXiv:1611.01603 (2016)
53. Tarantola, A.: Inverse Problem Theory. Elsevier, Amsterdam (1987)
54. Tibshirani, R.: Regression shrinkage and selection via the LASSO. J. Roy. Stat. Soc. Ser. B **58**(1), 267–288 (1996)
55. Tikhonov, A.N., Goncharsky, A.V. (eds.): Ill-Posed Problems in the Natural Sciences. MIR, Moscow (1987)
56. Wang, Z., Mi, H., Hamza, W., Florian, R.: Multi-perspective context matching for machine comprehension. arXiv preprint arXiv:1612.04211 (2016)
57. Witten, R., Candès, E.J.: Randomized algorithms for low-rank matrix factorizations: sharp performance bounds. To appear in Algorithmica (2013)
58. Zhou, Z., Wright, J., Li, X., Candès, E.J., Ma, Y.: Stable principal component pursuit. In: Proceedings of International Symposium on Information Theory, June 2010
59. Zou, H., Hastie, T., Tibshirani, R.: Sparse principal component analysis. J. Comput. Graph. Stat. **15**(2), 265–286 (2006)

Parallel Latent Dirichlet Allocation on GPUs

Gordon E. Moon$^{(\boxtimes)}$, Israt Nisa, Aravind Sukumaran-Rajam$^{(\boxtimes)}$,
Bortik Bandyopadhyay, Srinivasan Parthasarathy, and P. Sadayappan$^{(\boxtimes)}$

The Ohio State University, Columbus, OH 43210, USA
{moon.310,nisa.1,sukumaranrajam.1,bandyopadhyay.14,parthasarathy.2,
sadayappan.1}@osu.edu

Abstract. Latent Dirichlet Allocation (LDA) is a statistical technique for topic modeling. Since it is very computationally demanding, its parallelization has garnered considerable interest. In this paper, we systematically analyze the data access patterns for LDA and devise suitable algorithmic adaptations and parallelization strategies for GPUs. Experiments on large-scale datasets show the effectiveness of the new parallel implementation on GPUs.

Keywords: Parallel topic modeling
Parallel Latent Dirichlet Allocation · Parallel machine learning

1 Introduction

Latent Dirichlet Allocation (LDA) is a powerful technique for topic modeling originally developed by Blei et al. [2]. Given a collection of documents, each represented as a collection of words from an active vocabulary, LDA seeks to characterize each document in the corpus as a mixture of latent topics, where each topic is in turn modeled as a mixture of words in the vocabulary.

The sequential LDA algorithm of Griffiths and Steyvers [3] uses collapsed Gibbs sampling (CGS) and was extremely compute-intensive. Therefore, a number of parallel algorithms have been devised for LDA, for a variety of targets, including shared-memory multiprocessors [13], distributed-memory systems [7,12], and GPUs (Graphical Processing Units) [6,11,14,15,17]. In developing a parallel approach to LDA, algorithmic degrees of freedom can be judiciously matched with inherent architectural characteristics of the target platform. In this paper, we conduct an exercise in architecture-conscious algorithm design and implementation for LDA on GPUs.

In contrast to multi-core CPUs, GPUs offer much higher data-transfer bandwidths from/to DRAM memory but require much higher degrees of exploitable parallelism. Further, the amount of available fast on-chip cache memory is orders of magnitude smaller in GPUs than CPUs. Instead of the fully sequential collapsed Gibbs sampling approach proposed by Griffiths et al. [3], different forms of *uncollapsed* sampling have been proposed by several previous efforts [10,11]

© Springer International Publishing AG, part of Springer Nature 2018
Y. Shi et al. (Eds.): ICCS 2018, LNCS 10861, pp. 259–272, 2018.
https://doi.org/10.1007/978-3-319-93701-4_20

in order to utilize parallelism in LDA. We perform a systematic exploration of the space of partially collapsed Gibbs sampling strategies by

(a) performing an empirical characterization of the impact on convergence and perplexity, of different sampling variants and
(b) conducting an analysis of the implications of different sampling variants on the computational overheads for inter-thread synchronization, fast storage requirements, and implications on the expensive data movement to/from GPU global memory.

The paper is organized as follows. Section 2 provides the background on LDA. Section 3 presents the high-level overview of our new LDA algorithm (AGA-LDA) for GPUs, and Sect. 4 details our algorithm. In Sect. 5, we compare our approach with existing state-of-the-art GPU implementations. Section 6 summarizes the related works.

2 LDA Overview

Latent Dirichlet Allocation (LDA) is an effective approach to topic modeling. It is used for identifying latent topics distributions for collections of text documents [2]. Given D documents represented as a collection of words, LDA determines a latent topic distribution for each document. Each document j of D

Algorithm 1. Sequential CGS based LDA

Input: $DATA$: D documents and $\mathbf{x}$ word tokens in each document, V: vocabulary size, K: number of topics, α, β: hyper-parameters
Output: DT: document-topic count matrix, WT: word-topic count matrix, NT: topic-count vector, Z: topic assignment matrix

```
1: repeat
2:     for document = 0 to D − 1 do
3:         L ← document_length
4:         for word = 0 to L − 1 do
5:             current_word ← DATA[document][word]
6:             old_topic ← Z[document][word]
7:             decrement WT[current_word][old_topic]
8:             decrement NT[old_topic]
9:             decrement DT[document][old_topic]
10:            sum ← 0
11:            for k = 0 to K − 1 do
```
$$12: \quad \text{sum} \leftarrow \text{sum} + \frac{WT[current\_word][k]+\beta}{NT[k]+V\beta}\ (DT[document][k] + \alpha)$$
```
13:            p[k] ← sum
14:            end for
15:            U ← random_uniform() × sum
16:            for new_topic = 0 to K − 1 do
17:                if U < p[new_topic] then
18:                    break
19:                end if
20:            end for
21:            increment WT[current_word][new_topic]
22:            increment NT[new_topic]
23:            increment DT[document][new_topic]
24:            Z[document][word] ← new_topic
25:        end for
26:    end for
27: until convergence
```

---

documents is modeled as a random mixture over K latent topics, denoted by θ_j. Each topic k is associated with a multinomial distribution over a vocabulary of V unique words denoted by ϕ_k. It is assumed that θ and ϕ are drawn from Dirichlet priors α and β. LDA iteratively improves θ_j and ϕ_k until convergence. For the ith word token in document j, a topic-assignment variable z_{ij} is sampled according to the topic distribution of the document $\theta_{j|k}$, and the word x_{ij} is drawn from the topic-specific distribution of the word $\phi_{w|z_{ij}}$. Asuncion et al. [1] succinctly describe various inference techniques, and their similarities and differences for state-of-the-art LDA algorithms. A more recent survey [4] discusses in greater detail the vast amount of work done on LDA. In context of our work, we first discuss two main variants, viz., *Collapsed Gibbs Sampling (CGS)* and *Uncollapsed Gibbs Sampling (UCGS)*.

Collapsed Gibbs Sampling. To infer the posterior distribution over latent variable z, a number of studies primarily used Collapsed Gibbs Sampling (CGS) since it reduces the variance considerably through marginalizing out all prior distributions of $\theta_{j|k}$ and $\phi_{w|k}$ during the sampling procedure [7,15,16]. Three key data structures are updated as each word is processed: a 2D array DT maintaining the document-to-topic distribution, a 2D array WT representing word-to-topic distribution, and a 1D array NT holding the topic-count distribution. Given the three data structures and all words except for the topic-assignment variable z_{ij}, the conditional distribution of z_{ij} can be calculated as:

$$P(z_{ij} = k | \mathbf{z}^{\neg ij}, \mathbf{x}, \alpha, \beta) \propto \frac{WT_{x_{ij}|k}^{\neg ij} + \beta}{NT_k^{\neg ij} + V\beta}(DT_{j|k}^{\neg ij} + \alpha) \tag{1}$$

where $DT_{j|k} = \sum_w S_{w|j|k}$ denotes the number of word tokens in document j assigned to topic k; $WT_{w|k} = \sum_j S_{w|j|k}$ denotes the number of occurrences of word w assigned to topic k; $NT_k = \sum_w N_{w|k}$ is the topic-count vector. The superscript $\neg ij$ means that the previously assigned topic of the corresponding word token x_{ij} is excluded from the counts. The hyper-parameters, α and β control the sparsity of DT and WT matrices, respectively. Algorithm 1 shows the sequential CGS based LDA algorithm.

Uncollapsed Gibbs Sampling. The use of Uncollapsed Gibbs Sampling (UCGS) as an alternate inference algorithm for LDA is also common [10,11]. Unlike CGS, UCGS requires the use of two additional parameters θ and ϕ to draw latent variable z as follows:

$$P(z_{ij} = k | \mathbf{x}) \propto \phi_{x_{ij}|k}\theta_{j|k} \tag{2}$$

Rather than immediately using DT, WT and NT to compute the conditional distribution, at the end of each iteration, newly updated local copies of DT, WT and NT are used to sample new values on θ and ϕ that will be levered in the next iteration. Compared to CGS, this approach leads to slower convergence since the dependencies between the parameters (corresponding word tokens) is not fully being utilized [7,11]. However, the use of UCGS facilitates a more straightforward parallelization of LDA.

3   Overview of Parallelization Approach for GPUs

As seen in Algorithm 1, the standard CGS algorithm requires updates to the DT, WT and NT arrays after each sampling step to assign a new topic to a word in a document. This is inherently sequential. In order to achieve high performance on GPUs, a very high degree of parallelism (typically thousands or tens/hundreds of thousands of independent operations) is essential. We therefore divide the corpus of documents into mini-batches which are processed sequentially, with the words in the mini-batch being processed in parallel. Different strategies can be employed for updating the three key data arrays DT, WT and NT. At one extreme, the updates to all three arrays can be delayed until the end of processing of a mini-batch, while at the opposite end, immediate concurrent updates can be performed by threads after each sampling step. Intermediate choices between these two extremes for processing updates also exist, where some of the data arrays are immediately updated, while others are updated at the end of a mini-batch. There are several factors to consider in devising a parallel LDA scheme on GPUs:

- Immediate updates to all three data arrays DT, WT and NT would likely result in faster convergence since this corresponds most closely to fully CGS. At the other extreme, delayed updates for all three arrays may be expected to result in the slowest convergence, with immediate updates to a subset of arrays resulting in an intermediate rate of convergence.
- Immediate updating of the arrays requires the use of atomic operations, which are very expensive on GPUs, taking orders of magnitude more time than arithmetic operations. Further, the cost of atomics depends on the storage used for the operands, with atomics on global memory operands being much more expensive than atomics on data in shared memory.
- While delayed updates mean that we can avoid expensive atomics, additional temporary storage will be required to hold information about the updates to be performed at the end of a mini-batch, since storage is scarce on GPUs, especially registers and shared-memory.
- The basic formulation of CGS requires an expensive division operation (Eq. 1) in the innermost loop of the computation for performing sampling. If we choose to perform delayed updates to DT, an efficient strategy can be devised whereby the old DT entries corresponding to a minibatch can be scaled by the division operation by means of the denominator term in Eq. 1 once before processing of a mini-batch commences. This will enable the innermost loop for sampling to no longer requires an expensive division operation.

In order to understand the impact on convergence rates for different update choices for DT, WT and NT, we conducted an experiment using four datasets and all possible combinations of immediate versus delayed updates for the three key data arrays. As shown in Fig. 1, standard CGS (blue line) has a better convergence rate per-iteration than fully delayed updates (red line). However, standard CGS is sequential and is not suitable for GPU parallelization. On the other hand, delayed update scheme is fully parallel but suffers from a lower convergence rate per-iteration. In our scheme, we divide the documents into mini-batches. Each document within a mini-batch is processed using delayed updates. At the end of each mini-batch, DT, WT and NT are updated and the next mini-batch uses the updated DT, WT and NT values. Note that the mini-batches are processed sequentially.

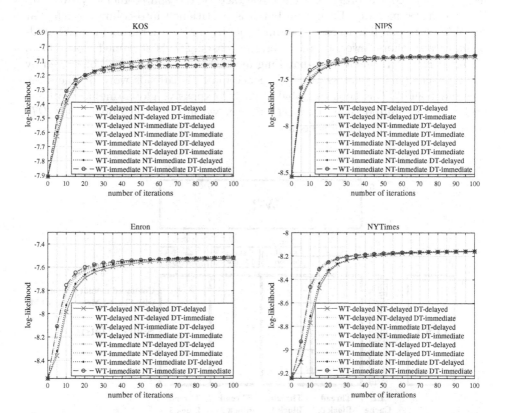

Fig. 1. Convergence over number of iterations on KOS, NIPS, Enron and NYTimes datasets. The mini-batch sizes are set to 330, 140, 3750 and 28125 for KOS, NIPS, Enron and NYTimes, respectively. X-axis: number of iterations; Y-axis: per-word log-likelihood on test set. (Color figure online)

Each data structure can be updated using either delayed updates or atomic operations. In delayed updates, the update operations are performed at the end of each mini-batch and is faster than using atomic operations. The use of atomic operations to update DT, WT and NT makes the updates closer to standard sequential CGS, as each update is immediately visible to all the threads. Figure 1 shows the convergence rate of using delayed updates and atomic updates for each DT, WT and NT. Using atomic-operations enables a better convergence rate per-iteration. However, global memory atomic operations are expensive compared to shared memory atomic operations. Therefore, in order to reduce the overhead of atomic operations, we map WT to shared memory. In addition to reducing the overhead of atomics, this also helps to achieve good data reuse for WT from shared memory.

In order to achieve the required parallelism on GPUs, we parallelize across documents and words in a mini-batch. GPUs have a limited amount of shared-memory per SM. In order to take advantage of the shared-memory, we map WT to shared-memory. Each mini-batch is partitioned into columns such that the WT corresponding to each column panel fits in the shared-memory. Shared-memory also offers lower atomic operation costs. DT is streamed from global memory. However, due to mini-batching most of these accesses will be served by the L2 cache (shared across all SMs). Since multiple threads work on the same document and DT is kept in global memory, expensive global memory atomic updates are required to update DT. Hence, we use delayed updates for DT. Figure 2 depicts the overall scheme.

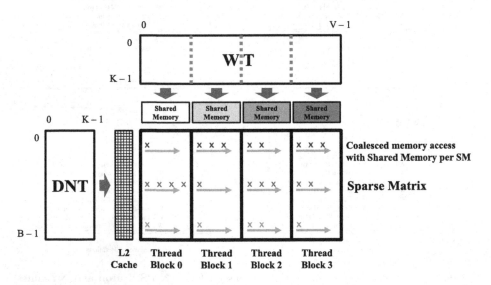

Fig. 2. Overview of our approach. V: vocabulary size, B: number of documents in the current mini-batch, K: number of topics

4   Details of Parallel GPU Algorithm

As mentioned in the overview section, we divide the documents into mini-batches. All the documents/words within a mini-batch are processed in parallel,

Algorithm 2. GPU implementation of sampling kernel

Input: $DOC\_IDX, WORD\_IDX, Z\_IDX$: document index, word index and topic index for each nnz in CSB format corresponding to the current mini-batch, $lastIdx$: a vector which stores the start index of each tile, V: vocabulary size, K: number of topics, β: hyper-parameter

```
 1: tile_id = block_id
 2: tile_start = lastIdx[tile_id]
 3: tile_end = lastIdx[tile_id + 1]
 4: shared_WT[column_panel_width][K]
 5: warp_id = thread_id / WARP_SIZE
 6: lane_id = thread_id % WARP_SIZE
 7: n_warp_k = thread_block_size / WARP_SIZE
    // Coalesced data load from global memory to shared memory
 8: for i=warp_id to column_panel step n_warp_k do
 9:    for w = 0 to K step WARP_SIZE do
10:       shared_WT[i][w+lane_id] = WT[(tile_id×col_panel_width+i)][w+lane_id]
11:    end for
12: end for
13: __syncthreads()
14: for nnz = thread_id+tile_start to tile_end step thread_block_size do
15:    curr_doc_id = DOC_IDX[nnz]
16:    curr_word_id = WORD_IDX[nnz]
17:    curr_word_shared_id = curr_word_id − tile_id × column_panel_width
18:    old_topic = Z_IDX[nnz]
19:    atomicSub (shared_WT[curr_word_shared_id][old_topic], 1)
20:    atomicSub (NT[old_topic], 1)
21:    sum = 0
22:    for k = 0 to K − 1 do
23:       sum += (shared_WT[curr_word_shared_id][k]+β)×DNT[curr_doc_id][k]
24:    end for
25:    U = curand_uniform() × sum
26:    sum = 0
27:    for new_topic = 0 to K − 1 do
28:       sum += (shared_WT[curr_word_shared_id][k]+β)×DNT[curr_doc_id][k]
29:       if U < sum then
30:          break
31:       end if
32:    end for
33:    atomicAdd (shared_WT[curr_word_shared_id][new_topic], 1)
34:    atomicAdd (NT[new_topic], 1)
35:    Z_IDX[nnz] = new_topic
36: end for
    // Update WT in global memory
37: for i=warp_id to column_panel step n_warp_k do
38:    for w = 0 to K step WARP_SIZE do
39:       WT[(tile_id×col_panel+i)][w+lane_id] = shared_WT[i][w+lane_id]
40:    end for
41: end for
42: __syncthreads()
```

and the processing across mini-batches is sequential. All the words within a mini-batch are partitioned to form column panels. Each column panel is mapped to a thread block.

Shared Memory: Judicious use of shared-memory is critical for good performance on GPUs. Hence, we keep WT in shared-memory which helps to achieve higher memory access efficiency and lower cost for atomic operations. Within a mini-batch, WT gets full reuse from shared-memory.

Reducing Global Memory Traffic for the Cumulative Topic Count: In the original sequential algorithm (Algorithm 1) the cumulative topic is computed by multiplying WT with DT and then dividing the resulting value with NT. The cumulative count with respect to each topic is saved in an array p as shown in Line 13 in Algorithm 1. Then a random number is computed and is scaled by the topic-count-sum across all topics. Based on the scaled random number the cumulative topic count array is scanned again to compute the new topic. Keeping the cumulative count array in global memory will increase the global memory traffic especially as these accesses are uncoalesced. As data movement is much more expensive than computations, we do redundant computations to reduce data movement. In order to compute the topic-count-sum across all topics, we perform a dot product of DT and WT in Line 23 in Algorithm 2. Then a random number which is scaled by the topic sum is computed. The product of DT and WT is recomputed, and based on the value of scaled random number, the new topic is selected. This strategy helps to save global memory transactions corresponding to $2 \times number\,of\,words \times number\,of\,topics$ (read and write) words.

Reducing Expensive Division Operations: In Line 12 in Algorithm 1, division operations are used during sampling. Division operations are expensive in GPUs. The total number of division operations during sampling is equal to *total number of words across all documents* $\times$ *number of features*. We can precompute $DNT = DT/NT$ (Algorithm 4) and then use this variable to compute the cumulative topic count as shown in Line 23 in Algorithm 2. Thus a division is performed per document as opposed to per word which helps to reduce the total number of division operations to *total number of documents* $\times$ *number of features*.

Reducing Global Memory Traffic for DT (DNT): In our algorithm, DT is streamed from global memory. The total amount of DRAM (device memory) transactions can be reduced if we can substitute DRAM access with L2 cache accesses. Choosing an appropriate size for a mini-batch can help to increase L2 hit rates. For example, choosing a low mini-batch size will increase the probability of L2 hit rates. However, if the mini-batch size is very low, there will not be enough work in each mini-batch. In addition, the elements of the sparse matrices are kept in segmented Compressed Sparse Blocks (CSB) format. Thus, the threads with a column panel process all the words in a document before moving on to the next document. This ensures that within a column panel the temporal reuse of DT (DNT) is maximized.

Algorithm 2 shows our GPU algorithm. Based on the column panel, all the threads in a thread block collectively bring in the corresponding WT elements from global memory to shared memory. WT is kept in column major order. All the threads in a warp bring one column of WT and different wraps bring different columns of WT (Line 10). Based on the old topic, the copy of WT in shared memory and NT is decremented using atomic operations (Lines 19 and 20).

The non-zero elements within a column panel are cyclically distributed across threads. Corresponding to the non-zero, each thread computes the topic-count-sum by computing the dot product of WT and DNT (Line 23). A random number is then computed and scaled by this sum (Line 25). The product of WT and DNT is then recomputed to find the new topic with the help of the scaled random number (Line 28). Then the copy of WT in shared memory and NT is incremented using atomic operations (Lines 33 and 34).

At the end of each column panel, each thread block collectively updates the global WT using the copy of WT kept in shared memory (Line 39).

Algorithm 3. GPU implementation of updating the DT

Input: DOC_IDX, Z_IDX: document index and topic index for each nnz in CSB format corresponding to the current mini-batch

1: curr_doc_id = DOC_IDX[thread_id]
2: new_topic = Z_IDX[thread_id]
3: **atomicAdd** (DT[curr_doc_id][new_topic], 1)

Algorithm 4. GPU implementation of updating the DNT

Input: V: vocabulary size, α, β: hyper-parameters

1: curr_doc_id = blockIdx.x
2: DNT[curr_doc_id][thread_id] = $\frac{DT[curr\_doc\_id][thread\_id]+\alpha}{NT[thread\_id]+V\beta}$

At the end of each mini-batch, we need to update DT and pre-compute DNT for the next mini-batch. Algorithm 3 shows our algorithm to compute DT. All the DT elements are initially set to zero using cudaMemset. We iterate over all the words across all the documents. Corresponding to the topic of each word, we increment the document topic count using atomic operations (Line 3). The pre-computation of DNT is shown in Algorithm 4. In this algorithm, each document is processed by a thread block and the threads within a thread block are distributed across different topics. Based on the document and thread id, each thread computes the DNT as shown in Line 2.

5   Experimental Evaluation

Two publicly available GPU-LDA implementations, **Lu-LDA** by Lu et al. [6] and **BIDMach-LDA** by Zhao et al. [17], are used in the experiments to compare the performance and accuracy of the approach developed in this paper. We label our new implementation as Approximate GPU-Adapted LDA (**AGA-LDA**). We also use GibbsLDA++ [8] (**Sequential CGS**), a standard C++ implementation of sequential LDA with CGS, as a baseline. We use four datasets: the KOS, NIPS, Enron and NYTimes from the UCI Machine Learning Repository [5]. While Table 2 shows the characteristics of the datasets, Table 1 shows the configuration of the machines used for experiments.

Table 1. Machine configuration

Machine	Details
GPU	GTX TITAN (14 SMs, 192 cores/MP, 6 GB Global Memory, 876 MHz, 1.5 MB L2 cache)
CPU	Intel(R) Xeon(R) CPU E5-2680(28 core)

Table 2. Dataset characteristics. D is the number of documents, W is the total number of word tokens and V is the size of the active vocabulary.

Dataset	D	W	V
KOS	3,430	467,714	6,906
NIPS	1,500	1,932,365	12,375
Enron	39,861	6,412,172	28,099
NYTimes	299,752	99,542,125	101,636

In BIDMach-LDA, the train/test split is dependent on the size of the mini-batch. To ensure a fair comparison, we use the same train/test split across different LDA algorithms. The train set consists of 90% of documents and the remaining 10% is used as the test set. BIDMach-LDA allows changing the hyperparameters such as α. We tuned the mini-batch size for both BIDMach-LDA and AGA-LDA and we report the best performance. In AGA-LDA, the hyperparameters, α and β are set to 0.1. The number of topics (K) in all experiments is set to 128.

5.1   Evaluation Metric

To evaluate the accuracy of LDA models, we use the per-word log-likelihood on the test set. The higher the log-likelihood, the better the generalization of the model on unseen data.

$$log(p(\mathbf{x}^{test})) = \prod_{ij} log \sum_{k} \frac{WT_{w|k} + \beta}{\sum_{w} WT_{w|k} + V\beta} \frac{DT_{j|k} + \alpha}{\sum_{k} DT_{j|k} + K\alpha} \qquad (3)$$

$$\text{per-word log-likelihood} = \frac{1}{W^{test}} log(p(\mathbf{x}^{test})) \qquad (4)$$

where W^{test} is the total number of word tokens in the test set. For each LDA model, training and testing algorithms are paired up.

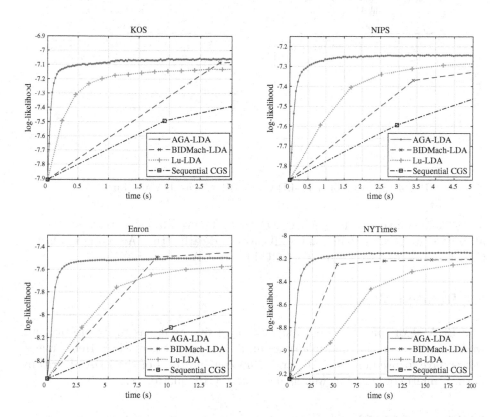

Fig. 3. Convergence over time on KOS, NIPS, Enron and NYTimes datasets. The mini-batch sizes are set to 330, 140, 3750 and 28125 for KOS, NIPS, Enron and NYTimes, respectively.

5.2 Speedup

Figure 3 shows the log-likelihood versus elapsed time of the different models. Compared to BIDMach-LDA, AGA-LDA achieved 2.5×, 15.8×, 2.8× and 4.4× on the KOS, NIPS, Enron and NYTimes datasets, respectively. AGA-LDA consistently performs better than other GPU-based LDA algorithms on all datasets. Figure 4 shows the speedup of our approach over BIDMach-LDA and Lu-LDA. The y-axis in Fig. 4 is the ratio of time for BIDMach-LDA and Lu-LDA to achieve

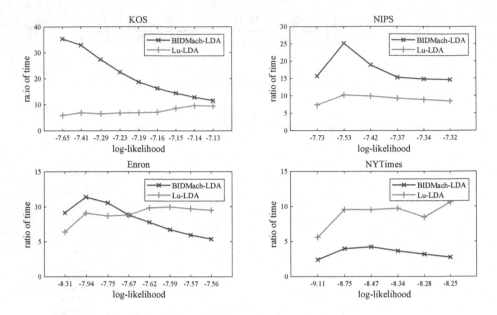

Fig. 4. Speedup of AGA-LDA over BIDMach-LDA and Lu-LDA.

a log-likelihood to how long AGA-LDA took. The result shows that y-values of all points are greater than one for all cases, indicating that AGA-LDA is faster than the existing state-of-the-art GPU-based LDA algorithms.

6   Related Work

The LDA algorithm is computationally expensive as it has to iterate over all words in all documents multiple times until convergence is reached. Hence many works have focused on efficient parallel implementations of the LDA algorithm both in multi-core CPU as well as many-core GPU platforms.

Multi-core CPU Platform. Newman et al. [7] justifies the importance of distributed algorithms for LDA for large scale datasets and proposed an *Approximate Distributed LDA (AD-LDA)* algorithm. In AD-LDA, documents are partitioned into several smaller chunks and each chunk is distributed to one of the many processors in the system, which performs the LDA algorithm on this pre-assigned chunk. However, global data structures like word-topic count matrix and topic-count matrix have to be replicated to the memory of each processor, which are updated locally. At the end of each iteration, a reduction operation is used to update all the local counts thereby synchronizing the state of the different matrices across all processors. While the quality and performance of the LDA algorithm is very competitive, this method incurs a lot memory overhead and has performance bottleneck due to the synchronization step at the end of each iteration. Wang et al. [12] tries to address the storage and communication overhead by an efficient MPI and MapReduce based implementation. The efficiency of CGS for LDA is further improved by Porteous et al. [9] which leveraging the sparsity structure of the respective probability vectors, without any approximation scheme. This allows for accurate yet highly scalable algorithm. On the other hand, Asuncion et al. [1] proposes approximation schemes for CGS based LDA in the distributed computing paradigm for efficient sampling with competitive accuracy. Xiao and Stibor [13] proposes a dynamic adaptive sampling technique for CGS with strong theoretical guarantees and efficient parallel implementation. Most of these works either suffer from memory overhead and synchronization bottleneck due to multiple local copies of global data-structures which are later used for synchronization across processors, or have to update key data structures using expensive atomic operations to ensure algorithmic accuracy.

Many-Core GPU Platform. One of the first GPU based implementations using CGS is developed by Yan et al. [15]. They partition both the documents and the words to create a set of disjoint chunks, such that it optimizes memory requirement, avoids memory conflict while simultaneously tackling a load imbalance problem during computation. However, their implementation requires maintaining local copies of global topic-count data structure. Lu et al. [6] tries to avoid too much data replication by generating document-topic counts on the fly and also use succinct sparse matrix representation to reduce memory cost. However, their implementation requires atomic operations during the global update phase which increases processing overhead. Tristan et al. [11] introduces a variant of UCGS technique which is embarrassingly parallel with competitive performance. Zhao et al. [17] proposes a state-of-the-art GPU implementation which combines the SAME (State Augmentation for Marginal Estimation) technique with mini-batch processing.

7 Conclusion

In this paper, we describe a high-performance LDA algorithm for GPUs based on approximated Collapsed Gibbs Sampling. The AGA-LDA is designed to achieve high performance by matching characteristics of GPU architecture. The algorithm is focused on reducing the required data movement and overheads due to atomic operations. In the experimental section, we show that our approach achieves significant speedup when compared to the existing state-of-the-art GPU LDA implementations.

References

1. Asuncion, A., Welling, M., Smyth, P., Teh, Y.W.: On smoothing and inference for topic models. In: Proceedings of the Twenty-Fifth Conference on Uncertainty in Artificial Intelligence, pp. 27–34. AUAI Press (2009)

2. Blei, D.M., Ng, A.Y., Jordan, M.I.: Latent Dirichlet allocation. JMLR **3**, 993–1022 (2003)
3. Griffiths, T.L., Steyvers, M.: Finding scientific topics. Proc. Natl. Acad. Sci. **101**(Suppl 1), 5228–5235 (2004)
4. Jelodar, H., Wang, Y., Yuan, C., Feng, X.: Latent Dirichlet allocation (LDA) and topic modeling: models, applications, a survey. arXiv:1711.04305 (2017)
5. Lichman, M.: UCI machine learning repository (2013). http://archive.ics.uci.edu/ml
6. Lu, M., Bai, G., Luo, Q., Tang, J., Zhao, J.: Accelerating topic model training on a single machine. In: Ishikawa, Y., Li, J., Wang, W., Zhang, R., Zhang, W. (eds.) APWeb 2013. LNCS, vol. 7808, pp. 184–195. Springer, Heidelberg (2013). https://doi.org/10.1007/978-3-642-37401-2_20
7. Newman, D., Asuncion, A., Smyth, P., Welling, M.: Distributed algorithms for topic models. JMLR **10**, 1801–1828 (2009)
8. Phan, X.H., Nguyen, C.T.: GibbsLDA++: AC/C++ implementation of latent dirichlet allocation (LDA) (2007)
9. Porteous, I., Newman, D., Ihler, A., Asuncion, A., Smyth, P., Welling, M.: Fast collapsed Gibbs sampling for latent Dirichlet allocation. In: SIGKDD. ACM (2008)
10. Tristan, J.B., Huang, D., Tassarotti, J., Pocock, A.C., Green, S., Steele, G.L.: Augur: data-parallel probabilistic modeling. In: NIPS (2014)
11. Tristan, J.B., Tassarotti, J., Steele, G.: Efficient training of LDA on a GPU by mean-for-mode estimation. In: ICML (2015)
12. Wang, Y., Bai, H., Stanton, M., Chen, W.-Y., Chang, E.Y.: PLDA: parallel latent Dirichlet allocation for large-scale applications. In: Goldberg, A.V., Zhou, Y. (eds.) AAIM 2009. LNCS, vol. 5564, pp. 301–314. Springer, Heidelberg (2009). https://doi.org/10.1007/978-3-642-02158-9_26
13. Xiao, H., Stibor, T.: Efficient collapsed Gibbs sampling for latent Dirichlet allocation. In: ACML (2010)
14. Xue, P., Li, T., Zhao, K., Dong, Q., Ma, W.: GLDA: parallel Gibbs sampling for latent Dirichlet allocation on GPU. In: Wu, J., Li, L. (eds.) ACA 2016. CCIS, vol. 626, pp. 97–107. Springer, Singapore (2016). https://doi.org/10.1007/978-981-10-2209-8_9
15. Yan, F., Xu, N., Qi, Y.: Parallel inference for latent Dirichlet allocation on graphics processing units. In: NIPS (2009)
16. Zhang, B., Peng, B., Qiu, J.: High performance LDA through collective model communication optimization. Proc. Comput. Sci. **80**, 86–97 (2016)
17. Zhao, H., Jiang, B., Canny, J.F., Jaros, B.: Same but different: fast and high quality Gibbs parameter estimation. In: SIGKDD. ACM (2015)

Improving Search Through A3C Reinforcement Learning Based Conversational Agent

Milan Aggarwal[1]([✉]), Aarushi Arora[2], Shagun Sodhani[1],
and Balaji Krishnamurthy[1]

[1] Adobe Systems Inc., Noida, India
milan.ag1994@gmail.com, kbalaji@adobe.com
[2] IIT Delhi, Hauz Khas, Delhi, India

Abstract. We develop a reinforcement learning based search assistant which can assist users through a sequence of actions to enable them realize their intent. Our approach caters to subjective search where user is seeking digital assets such as images which is fundamentally different from the tasks which have objective and limited search modalities. Labeled conversational data is generally not available in such search tasks, to counter this problem we propose a stochastic virtual user which impersonates a real user for training and obtaining bootstrapped agent. We develop A3C algorithm based context preserving architecture to train agent and evaluate performance on average rewards obtained by the agent while interacting with virtual user. We evaluated our system with actual humans who believed that it helped in driving their search forward with appropriate actions without being repetitive while being more engaging and easy to use compared to conventional search interface.

Keywords: Subjective search · Reinforcement learning
Virtual user model · Context aggregation

1 Introduction

Within the domain of "search", the recent advances have focused on personalizing the search results through recommendations [17,28]. While the quality of recommendations have improved, the conventional search interface has not innovated much to incorporate useful contextual cues which are often missed. Conventional search interface enables the end user to perform a keyword based faceted search where the end user types in her search query, applies some filters and then modifies the query based on the results. This iterative interaction naturally paves way for incorporating conversations in the process. Instead of the search engine just retrieving the "best" result set, it can interact with the user to collect more contextual cues. For example, if a user searches for "birthday gift", the search engine could follow-up by asking "who are you buying the

© Springer International Publishing AG, part of Springer Nature 2018
Y. Shi et al. (Eds.): ICCS 2018, LNCS 10861, pp. 273–286, 2018.
https://doi.org/10.1007/978-3-319-93701-4_21

gift for". Such information and interaction can provide more human-like and engaging search experience along with assisting user in discovering their search intent. In this work we address this problem by developing a Reinforcement Learning (RL) [18] based conversational search agent which interacts with the users to help them in narrowing down to relevant search results by providing them contextual assistance.

RL based dialogue agents have been designed for tasks like restaurant, bus and hotel reservation [16] which have limited and well-defined objective search modalities without much scope for subjective discussion. For instance, when searching for a restaurant, the user can specify her preferences (budget, distance, cuisines etc.) due to which the problem can be modeled as a slot filling exercise. In contrast, suppose a designer is searching for digital assets (over a repository of images, videos etc.) to be used in a movie poster. She would start with a broad idea and her idea would get refined as the search progresses. The modified search intent involves an implicit cognitive feedback which can be used to improve the search results. We train our agent for this type of search task where it is modeled as a sequence of alternate interactions between the user and the RL agent. The extent to which the RL agent could help the user depends on the sequence and the type of actions it takes according to user behavior. Under the RL framework, intermediate rewards is given to the agent at each step based on its actions and state of conversational search. It learns the applicability of different actions through these rewards. In addition to extrinsic rewards, we define auxiliary tasks and provide additional rewards based on agent's performance on these tasks. Corresponding to the action taken by the agent at each turn, a natural language response is selected and provided to the user. Since true conversational data is not easily available in search domain, we propose to use query and session log data to develop a stochastic virtual user environment to simulate training episodes and bootstrap the learning of the agent.

Our contributions are three-fold: (1) formulating conversational interactive search as a reinforcement learning problem and proposing a generic and easily extendable set of states, actions and rewards; (2) developing a stochastic user model which can be used to efficiently sample user actions while simulating an episode; (3) we develop A3C (Asynchronous Advantage Actor-Critic) [13] algorithm based architecture to predict policy and state value functions of RL agent.

2   Related Work

There have been various attempts at modeling conversational agents, as dialogue systems [4,10,20,26] and text-based chat bots [5,11,12,21,24]. Some of these have focused on modeling goal driven RL agent such as indoor way finding system [5] to assist humans to navigate to their destination and visual input agents which learn to navigate and search object in 3-D environment space [27].

RL based dialogue systems have been explored in the past. For example, [20] uses User Satisfaction (US) as the sole criteria to reward the learning agent and completely disregards Task Success (TS). But US is a subjective metric and is much harder to measure or annotate real data with. In our formulation, we provide a reward for task success at the end of search along with extrinsic and auxiliary rewards at intermediate steps (discussed in Sect. 3.4). Other RL based information seeking agents extract information from the environment by sequentially asserting questions but these have not been designed on search tasks involving human interaction and behavior [2].

RL has also been used for improving document retrieval through query reformulation where the agent sequentially reformulates a given complex query provided by the user [14,15]. But their work focuses on single turn episodes where the model augments the given query by adding new keywords. In contrast, our agent engages the user directly into the search which comprises of sequence of alternate turns between user and agent with more degrees of freedom (in terms of different actions the agent can take).

To minimize human intervention while providing input for training such agents in spoken dialogue systems, simulated speech outputs have been used to bypass spoken language unit [4]. This approach enables to reduce the system's dependence on hand engineered features. User models for simulating user responses have been obtained by using LSTM which learns inter-turn dependency between the user actions. They take as input multiple user dialogue contexts and outputs dialogue acts taking into account history of previous dialogue acts and dependence on the domain [1].

Often task oriented dialogue systems are difficult to train due to absence of real conversations and subjectivity involved in measuring shortcomings and success of a dialogue [7]. Evaluation becomes much more complex for subjective search systems due to absence of any label which tells whether the intended task had been completed or not. We evaluate our system through rewards obtained while interacting with the user model and also on various real world metrics (discussed in experiments section) through human evaluation.

3   System Model

3.1   Reinforcement Learning

Reinforcement Learning is the paradigm to train an agent to interact with the environment in a series of independent episodes where each episode comprises of a sequence of turns. At each turn, the agent observes state s of the environment ($s \in \mathbf{S}$ - set of possible states) and performs an action from $\mathbf{A}$ - set of possible actions which changes the state of the environment and the agent gets the corresponding reward [18]. An optimal policy maximizes cumulative reward that the agent gets based on the actions taken from start till the final terminal state.

3.2   Agent Action Space

Action space $\mathbf{A}$ is designed to enable the search agent to interact with the user and help her in searching the desired assets conveniently. The agent actions

Table 1. Probe intent actions

Action	Description
Probe use case	Ask about where assets will be used
Probe to refine	Ask the user to further refine query if less relevant search results are retrieved
Cluster categories	Ask the user to select from categorical options related to her query

Table 2. General actions

Action	Description
Show results	Display results corresponding to most recent user query
Add to cart	Suggest user to bookmark assets for later reference
Ask to download	Suggest user to download some results if they suit her requirement
Ask to purchase	Advise the user to buy some paid assets
Provide discount	Offer special discounts to the user based on search history
Sign up	Ask the user to create an account to receive updates regarding her search
Ask for feedback	Take feedback about the search so far
Provide help	List possible ways in which the agent can assist the user
Salutation	Greet the user at the beginning; say goodbye when user concludes the search

can be divided into two sets - the set of probe intent actions - **P** and general actions - **G** as described in Tables 1 and 2 respectively. The agent uses the probe intent actions **P** to explicitly query the user to learn more about her context. For instance, the user may make a very open-ended query resulting in a diverse set of results even though none of them is a good match. In such scenarios, the agent may prompt the user to refine her query or add some other details like where the search results would be used. Alternatively, the agent may cluster the search results and prompt the user to choose from the clustered categories. These actions serve two purposes - they carry the conversation further and provide various cues about the search context which is not evident from input query.

The set **G** consists of generic actions like displaying assets retrieved corresponding to the user query, providing help to the user etc. The set **G** comprises of actions for carrying out the functionality which the conventional search interface provides like "presenting search results". We also include actions which promote the business use cases (such as prompting the user to signup with her email, purchase assets etc.). The agent is rewarded appropriately for such prompts depending on the subsequent user actions.

3.3   State Space

We model the state representation in order to encapsulate facets of both search and conversation. The state s at every turn in the conversation is modeled using the history of user actions - *history_user*,[1] history of agent actions - *history_agent*, relevance scores of search results - *score_results* and *length_conv* which represents number of user responses in the conversation till that point.

The variables *history_user* and *history_agent* comprises of user and agent actions in last k turns of the conversational search respectively. This enables us to capture the context of the conversation (in terms of sequence of actions taken). Each user-action is represented as one-hot vector of length 9 (number of unique user actions). Similarly, each agent-action has been represented as a one-hot vector of length 12. The history of the last 10 user and agent actions is represented as concatenation of these one-hot vectors. We use zero padded vectors wherever current history comprises of less than 10 turns.

The variable *score_results* quantifies the degree of similarity between most recent query and the top 10 most relevant search assets retrieved. They have been used to incorporate the dependency between the relevance of probe intent actions and quality of search results retrieved. *length_conv* has been included since appropriateness of other agent actions like *sign up* may depend on the duration for which the user has been searching.

3.4 Rewards

Reinforcement Learning is concerned with training an agent in order to maximize some notion of cumulative reward. In general, the action taken at time t involves a long term versus short term reward trade-off. This problem manifests itself even more severely in the context of conversational search. For instance, let us say that the user searches for "nature". Since the user explicitly searched for something, it would seem logical to provide the search results to the user. Alternatively, instead of going for immediate reward, the agent could further ask the user if she is looking for "posters" or "portraits" which would help in narrowing down the search in the long run.

Since we aim to optimize dialogue strategy and do not generate dialogue utterances, we assign the rewards corresponding to the appropriateness of the action considering the state and history of the search. We have used some rewards such as task success (based on implicit and explicit feedback from the user during the search) which is also used in PARADISE framework [22]. We model the total reward which the agent gets in one complete dialogue as:

$$R_{total} = r_{Task\ Completion}(search) + \sum_{t \in turns} (r_{extrinsic}(t) + r_{auxiliary}(t))$$

Task Completion and Extrinsic Rewards. First kind of reward (r_{TC}) is based on the completion of the task (Task Completion TC) which is download and purchase in the case of our search problem. This reward is provided once at the end of the episode depending on whether the task is completed or not.

---

[1] *History_user* includes most recent user action to which agent response is pending in addition to remaining history of user actions.

As second kind of rewards, we provide instantaneous extrinsic rewards [6] - ($r_{extrinsic}$) based on the response that the user gives subsequent to an agent action. We categorize the user action into three feedback categories, namely good, average or bad. For example, if the agent prompts the user to refine the query and the user does follow the prompt, the agent gets a high reward while if the user refuses, a low reward is given to the agent. A moderate reward will be given if the user herself refines the query without the agent's prompt.

Auxiliary Rewards. Apart from the extrinsic rewards, we define a set of auxiliary tasks T_A specific to the search problem which can be used to provide additional reward signals, $r_{auxiliary}$, using the environment. We define $T_A = \{\#$ click result, # add to cart, # cluster category click, if sign up option exercised$\}$. $r_{auxiliary}$ is determined and provided at every turn in the search based on the values of different auxiliary tasks metrics defined in T_A till that turn in the search. Such rewards promotes a policy which improves the performance on these tasks.

3.5 Stochastic User Model Details

The RL agent is trained to learn the optimal action policy requiring actual conversational search data which is not available as conversational agents have not been used for search task we defined. To bypass this issue and bootstrap training, we propose a user model that simulates user behavior to interact with the agent during training and validation. Our methodology can be used to model a virtual user using any query and log sessions data.

We developed a stochastic environment where the modeled virtual human user responds to agent's actions. The virtual human user has been modeled using query sessions data from a major stock photography and digital asset marketplace which contain information on queries made by real users, the corresponding clicks and other interactions with the assets. This information has been used to generate a user which simulates human behavior while searching and converses with the agent during search episode. We map every record in the query log to one of the user actions as depicted in Table 3. Figure 1 shows an example mapping from session data to user action. To model our virtual user, we used the query and session log data of approximately 20 days.

The virtual user is modeled as a finite state machine by extracting conditional probabilities - $P(User\ Action\ u|\ History\ h\ of\ User\ Actions)$. These probabilities are employed for sampling next user action given the fixed length history of her actions in an episode. The agent performs an action in response to the sampled user action and the process continues.

The query and session log data has been taken from an asset search platform where the marketer can define certain offers/promotions which kick in when the user takes certain actions, for instance the user can be prompted to add some images to cart (via a pop-up box). User's response to such prompts on the search interface is used as proxy to model the effect of RL agent on virtual user's

Session Data	Mapped User Action
shopping ; content_type : all ; NO_OFFSET ; search	*new query*
shopping ; content_type : all ; 100 ; search	*request more*
child while shopping ; content_type:all ; NO_OFFSET ; search	*refine query*
child while shopping ; content_type:all ; NO_OFFSET ; click	*click result*
child while shopping ; content_type: landscape ; NO_OFFSET ; search	*cluster category click*

Fig. 1. Example of mapping session data to user actions. The session data comprises of sequence of logs, each log comprises of search query, filters applied (content type), offset field and interaction performed by the user (such as search, click etc.)

Table 3. Mapping between query logs and user actions

User action	Mapping used
New query	First query or most recent query with no intersection with previous ones
Refine query	Query searched by user has some intersection with previous queries
Request more	Clicking on next set of results for same query
Click result	User clicking on search results being shown
Add to cart	When user adds some of searched assets to her cart for later reference
Cluster category click	When user clicks on filter options like orientation or size
Search similar	Search assets with similar series, model etc.

sampled action subsequent to different probe actions by the agent. This ensures that our conditional probability distribution covers the entire probability space of user behavior.

3.6 Q-Learning

The agent can be trained through *Q-learning* [23] which consists of a real valued function $Q : S \times A \to \mathbb{R}$. This Q-function maps every state-action pair (s, a) to a Q-value which is a numerical measure of the expected cumulative reward the agent gets by performing a in state s. In order to prevent the agent from always exploiting the best action in a given state, we employ an $\epsilon-$ greedy exploration policy [25], $0 < \epsilon < 1$. The size of our state space is of the order of $\approx 10^7$. For Q-learning, we use the table storage method where the Q-values for each state is stored in a lookup table which is updated at every step in a training episode.

3.7 A3C Algorithm

In this algorithm, we maintain a value function V_π and a stochastic policy π as a function of the state. The policy $\pi : A \times S \to \mathbb{R}$ defines a probability distribution

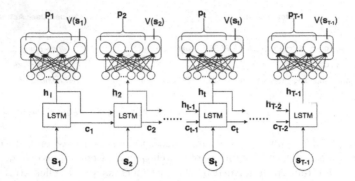

Fig. 2. A3C architecture for predicting policy $\mathbf{p_t}$ and value $V(\mathbf{s_t})$.

$\pi(a|s)$ over the set of actions which the agent may take in state s and is used to sample agent action given the state. The value function $V_\pi : S \to \mathbb{R}$ represents the expected cumulative reward from current time step in an episode if policy π is followed after observing state s i.e. $V_\pi(s) = \mathbb{E}_{a \sim \pi(.|s)}[Q_\pi(s,a)]$.

Search Context Preserving A3C Architecture. We propose a neural architecture (Fig. 2) which preserves the context of the conversational search for approximating the policy and value functions. The architecture comprises of a LSTM [8] which processes the state at a time step t (input $\mathbf{i_t} = \mathbf{s_t}$) and generates an embedding $\mathbf{h_t}$ which is processed through a fully connected layer to predict the probability distribution over different actions using softmax function [3] and value of the input state separately. In A3C algorithm, the agent is allowed to interact with the environment to roll-out an episode. The network parameters are updated after completion of every n-steps in the roll-out. An n-step roll-out when the current state is s_t can be expressed as $(s_t, a_t, r_t, s_{t+1}, v_{s_t}) \to (s_{t+1}, a_{t+1}, r_{t+1}, s_{t+1}, v_{s_{t+1}}) \to \cdots \to (s_{t+n-1}, a_{t+n-1}, r_{t+n-1}, s_{t+n}, v_{s_{t+n-1}})$. The parameters are tuned by optimizing the loss function $loss_{total}$ which can be decomposed into - $loss_{policy}$, $loss_{value}$, $loss_{entropy}$. $loss_{value}$ is defined as:

$$loss_{value}(\theta) = (V_{target}(s_i) - V(s_i; \theta))^2, \quad i = t, t+1, \ldots, t+n-1$$
$$where, V_{target}(s_i) = \sum_{k=0}^{t+n-i-1} \gamma^k r_{k+i} + \gamma^{n+t-i} V(s_{t+n}; \theta) \tag{1}$$

Thus an n-step roll-out allows us to estimate the target value of a given state using the actual rewards realized and value of the last state observed at the end of the roll-out. Value of a terminal state s_T is defined as 0. In a similar way, the network is trained on $loss_{policy}$ which is defined as:

$$loss_{policy}(\theta) = -\log(p(a_i|s_i; \theta)) * A(a_i, s_i; \theta), \quad i = t, t+1, \ldots, t+n-1, where$$
$$A(a_i, s_i; \theta) = \sum_{k=0}^{t+n-i-1} \gamma^k r_{k+i} + \gamma^{n+t-i} V(s_{t+n}; \theta) - V(s_i; \theta) \tag{2}$$

The above loss function tunes the parameter in order to shift the policy in favor of actions which provides better advantage $A(a_t, s_t, \theta)$ given the state s_t.

This advantage can be interpreted as additional reward the agent gets by taking action a_t in state s_t over the average value of the state $V(s_t; \theta)$ as the reference. However, this may bias the agent towards a particular or few actions due to which the agent may not explore other actions in a given state. To prevent this, we add entropy loss to the total loss function which aims at maximizing the entropy of probability distribution over actions in a state.

$$loss_{entropy}(\theta) = -\sum_{a \in \mathbf{A}} -p(a|s_i; \theta)\log(p(a|s_i; \theta)), \quad i = t, t+1, \ldots, t+n-1 \quad (3)$$

4   Experiments

In this section, we evaluate the trained agent with the virtual user model and discuss the results obtained with the two reinforcement learning techniques, A3C and Q-learning, and compare them. For each algorithm, we simulate validation episodes after each training episode and plot the average rewards and mean value of the states obtained during the validation episodes. We also developed a chat-search interface where real users can interact with the trained agent during their search.[2]

4.1   A3C Using User Model

The global model is obtained using 10 local agents which are trained in parallel threads (each trained over 350 episodes). We compare the validation results using this global model for different state representations for conversational search and hyper-parameter settings such as discount factor (γ) (which affects exploration vs exploitation trade-off) and the LSTM size which controls the context preserving capacity of our architecture.

Varying Discount Factor. We experiment with 3 values of discount factor and fix the LSTM size to 250. Figure 3 shows the validation trend in average rewards for different discount factors. Greater discount factor (lower value of γ) lowers weights for the future rewards due to which the agent tries to maximize the immediate rewards by taking the greedy actions. We validate this by computing the variance in the results for each case. The variance values for the 3 cases ($\gamma = 0.90, 0.70, 0.60$) are 1.5267, 1.627, and 1.725 respectively. Since the agent takes more greedy actions with higher discount factors, the variance in the reward values also increases since the greedy approach yields good rewards in some episodes and bad rewards in others.

---

[2] Supplementary material containing snapshots and demo video of the chat-search interface can be accessed at https://drive.google.com/open?id=0BzPI8zwXMOi WNk5hRElRNG4tNjQ.

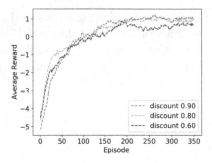

Fig. 3. Plot of average validation reward against number of training episodes for A3C agent. The size of LSTM is 250 for each plot with varying discount factor. Higher value of discount results in better average rewards.

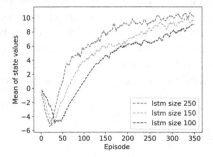

Fig. 4. Plot of mean of state values observed in an episode for A3C agent. Different curves correspond to different LSTM size. The discount value is $\gamma = 0.90$ for each curve. Better states (higher average state values) are observed with larger LSTM size since it enables the agent to remember more context while performing actions.

Varying Memory Capacity. We vary the size of the LSTM as 100, 150 and 250 to determine the effect of size of the context preserved. Figure 4 depicts the trend in mean value of states observed in an episode. We observe that larger size of the LSTM results in better states since average state value is higher. This demonstrates that a bigger LSTM size providing better capacity to remember the context results in agent performing actions which yield improved states.

4.2   Q-Learning Using User Model

We experimented with values of different hyper-parameters for Q-learning such as discount (γ) and exploration control parameter (ϵ) determined their optimal values to be 0.70 and 0.90 respectively based on trends in average reward value at convergence. We compare the A3C agent (with LSTM size 250 and $\gamma = 0.90$ with the Q-learning agent (Fig. 5). It can be observed that the A3C agent is able to obtain better averaged awards (≈ 1.0) in validation episodes upon convergence as compared to the Q-agent which obtains ≈ 0.20. Since A3C algorithm performs and generalize better than Q-learning approach, we evaluated it through professional designers.

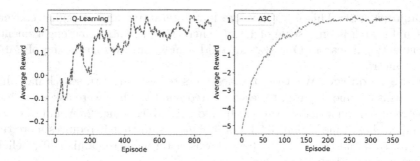

Fig. 5. Plot of average reward observed in validation episodes with Q-agent (left) with $\gamma = 0.70$ and $\epsilon = 0.90$) and A3C agent (right) with $\gamma = 0.90$ and LSTM size $= 250$. The average reward value at convergence is larger for A3C agent than Q-agent.

4.3   Human Evaluation of Agent Trained Through A3C

To evaluate the effectiveness of our system when interacting with real humans, we asked professional designers to search images which they will use while designing a poster on natural scenery using both our conversational search agent and conventional search interface provided by stock photography marketplace and collected feedback from 12 designers. We asked them to rate our conversational search system on following metrics. Table 4 shows average rating value of each of these metrics.

1. **Information flow** to measure the extent to which the agent provide new information and suggestions which helped in driving the search forward (on a scale of 1 to 5 where 5 represents high information flow).
2. **Appropriateness** of actions to measure the suitability of actions taken by the agent during the search in terms of coherence (on a scale of 1 to 5 where 5 denotes that it took right actions at right time during the search).
3. **Repetitiveness** to measure how repetitive was the agent's actions in providing assistance during their search (on a scale of 1–5 where 1 represents not repetitive at all).

Table 4. Human evaluation ratings for agent trained through A3C

Metric	Average rating
Information flow	2.58
Appropriateness	2.67
Repetitiveness	2.50

We also asked the designers to compare our system to conventional search interface in terms of following metrics:

1. **Engagement:** This is to measure how interactive and engaging conversational search is on a scale of 1 to 5 where 1 represents same engagement as conventional search. Our system could achieve an average rating of 2.67 in this metric.
2. **Time Required:** We asked the designers to compare two search modalities in terms of time required to reach desired results. They were asked to choose between conversational search required - 1. More time, 2. About the same time, 3. Less time. About 33.3% of designers said that it requires more time, 16.7% said that conversational search was faster while remaining 50% believed that it required about the same time.
3. **Ease of Use:** We asked them to choose one of three options - conversational search is, 1. Difficult to use and adds additional burden, 2. About the same to use, 3. Much easier to use, compared to conventional search. 33.3% of the designers believed that conversational search is easier, 41.7% said that it is the same while 25% believed that it is difficult to use it for search.

The above evaluation shows that although we trained the bootstrapped agent through user model, it performs decently well with actual users by driving their search forward with appropriate actions without being much repetitive. The comparison with conventional search shows that out system is much more engaging, requires about the same time while being easier to use than conventional search. Following is an example interaction between assistant and real human:

> **User:** show some images of mountains
> **Agent:** We also have many images in these categories, should I show you some?
> **User:** nature mountains
> **Agent:** Where will you use these images?
> **User:** i am organizing adventure sports
> **Agent:** Check out the images
> **User:** can you show some more
> **Agent:** Images can be added to cart for building a separate collection of stuff that you like. You can simply click on add to cart button
> **User:** <User adds few assets to cart>
> **Agent:** Want me to get you anything else?
> **User:** i want people riding bike on mountains
> **Agent:** We also have many images in these categories, should I show you some? - high mountains, hiking sports mountains, mountaineering mountains
> **User:** hiking sports mountains
> **Agent:** Signing up takes a moment, just give me your email id
> **User:** ABC@XYZ.com

5   Conclusion

In this paper, we develop a Reinforcement Learning based search assistant to interact with customers to help them search digital assets suited to their usecase. We model the rewards, state space, action space and develop an A3C based architecture which leverages the context of search to predict the policy. The trained agent is able to obtain higher average rewards in the validation episodes with virtual user and observes states with better values indicative of providing better search experience. As the next step, we would deploy our system to collect true conversational data which can be used to fine tune the current model as well as to train a new model which can generate the natural language responses in addition to deciding the action. In different search domains, designing the state and action space can take significant time which makes every situation an absolutely new task to be solved. To approach this issue as a future work, another system can be designed which helps in the automation of state space characterization with the help of system query logs.

References

1. El Asri, L., He, J., Suleman, K.: A sequence-to-sequence model for user simulation in spoken dialogue systems. arXiv preprint arXiv:1607.00070 (2016)
2. Bachman, P., Sordoni, A., Trischler, A.: Towards information-seeking agents. arXiv preprint arXiv:1612.02605 (2016)
3. Bridle, J.S.: Probabilistic interpretation of feedforward classification network outputs, with relationships to statistical pattern recognition. In: Soulié, F.F., Hérault, J. (eds.) Neurocomputing. NATO ASI Series, vol. 68, pp. 227–236. Springer, Heidelberg (1990). https://doi.org/10.1007/978-3-642-76153-9_28
4. Cuayáhuitl, H.: *SimpleDS*: a simple deep reinforcement learning dialogue system. In: Jokinen, K., Wilcock, G. (eds.) Dialogues with Social Robots. LNEE, vol. 999, pp. 109–118. Springer, Singapore (2017). https://doi.org/10.1007/978-981-10-2585-3_8
5. Cuayhuitl, H., Dethlefs, N.: Spatially-aware dialogue control using hierarchical reinforcement learning. ACM Trans. Speech Lang. Process. (TSLP) **7**(3), 5 (2011)
6. Deci, E.L., Koestner, R., Ryan, R.M.: A meta-analytic review of experiments examining the effects of extrinsic rewards on intrinsic motivation. Psychol. Bull. **125**, 627 (1999)
7. Dodge, J., Gane, A., Zhang, X., Bordes, A., Chopra, S., Miller, A., Szlam, A., Weston, J.: Evaluating prerequisite qualities for learning end-to-end dialog systems. arXiv preprint arXiv:1511.06931 (2015)
8. Hochreiter, S., Schmidhuber, J.: Long short-term memory. Neural Comput. **9**(8), 1735–1780 (1997)
9. Kingma, D., Ba, J.: Adam: a method for stochastic optimization. arXiv preprint arXiv:1412.6980 (2014)
10. Levin, E., Pieraccini, R., Eckert, W.: Learning dialogue strategies within the Markov decision process framework. In: Proceedings of the 1997 IEEE Workshop on Automatic Speech Recognition and Understanding, pp. 72–79. IEEE (1997)
11. Li, J., Galley, M., Brockett, C., Spithourakis, G.P., Gao, J., Dolan, B.: A persona-based neural conversation model. arXiv preprint arXiv:1603.06155 (2016)
12. Li, J., Monroe, W., Ritter, A., Galley, M., Gao, J., Jurafsky, D.: Deep reinforcement learning for dialogue generation. arXiv preprint arXiv:1606.01541 (2016)
13. Mnih, V., Badia, A.P., Mirza, M., Graves, A., Lillicrap, T., Harley, T., Silver, D., Kavukcuoglu, K.: Asynchronous methods for deep reinforcement learning. In: International Conference on Machine Learning, pp. 1928–1937 (2016)

14. Narasimhan, K., Yala, A., Barzilay, R.: Improving information extraction by acquiring external evidence with reinforcement learning. arXiv preprint arXiv:1603.07954 (2016)
15. Nogueira, R., Cho, K.: Task-oriented query reformulation with reinforcement learning. arXiv preprint arXiv:1704.04572 (2017)
16. Peng, B., Li, X., Li, L., Cao, J., Celikyilmaz, A., Lee, S., Wong, K.-F.: Composite task-completion dialogue policy learning via hierarchical deep reinforcement learning. In: Proceedings of the 2017 Conference on Empirical Methods in Natural Language Processing, pp. 2221–2230 (2017)
17. Shani, G., Heckerman, D., Brafman, R.I.: An MDP-based recommender system. J. Mach. Learn. Res. **6**(Sep), 1265–1295 (2005)
18. Sutton, R.S., Barto, A.G.: Reinforcement Learning: An Introduction, vol. 1. MIT Press, Cambridge (1998)
19. Sutton, R.S., McAllester, D.A., Singh, S.P., Mansour, Y.: Policy gradient methods for reinforcement learning with function approximation. In: Advances in Neural Information Processing Systems, pp. 1057–1063 (2000)
20. Ultes, S., Budzianowski, P., Casanueva, I., Mrkic, N., Barahona, L.R., Pei-Hao, S., Wen, T.-H., Gaic, M., Young, S.: Domain-independent user satisfaction reward estimation for dialogue policy learning. In: Proceedings of Interspeech 2017, pp. 1721–1725 (2017)
21. Vinyals, O., Le, Q.: A neural conversational model. arXiv preprint arXiv:1506.05869 (2015)
22. Walker, M.A., Litman, D.J., Kamm, C.A., Abella, A.: PARADISE: a framework for evaluating spoken dialogue agents. In: Proceedings of the Eighth Conference on European Chapter of the Association for Computational Linguistics, pp. 271–280. Association for Computational Linguistics (1997)
23. Watkins, C.J.C.H.: Learning from delayed rewards. Ph.D. dissertation. Kings College, Cambridge (1989)
24. Weston, J., Chopra, S., Bordes, A.: Memory networks. arXiv preprint arXiv:1410.3916 (2014)
25. Wunder, M., Littman, M.L., Babes, M.: Classes of multiagent Q-learning dynamics with epsilon-greedy exploration. In: Proceedings of the 27th International Conference on Machine Learning, ICML 2010, pp. 1167–1174 (2010)
26. Zhao, T., Eskenazi, M.: Towards end-to-end learning for dialog state tracking and management using deep reinforcement learning. arXiv preprint arXiv:1606.02560 (2016)
27. Zhu, Y., Mottaghi, R., Kolve, E., Lim, J.J., Gupta, A., Fei-Fei, L., Farhadi, A.: Target-driven visual navigation in indoor scenes using deep reinforcement learning. In: 2017 IEEE International Conference on Robotics and Automation, ICRA, pp. 3357–3364. IEEE (2017)
28. Wei, J., He, J., Chen, K., Zhou, Y., Tang, Z.: Collaborative filtering and deep learning based recommendation system for cold start items. Expert Syst. Appl. **69**, 29–39 (2017)

Track of Architecture, Languages, Compilation and Hardware Support for Emerging ManYcore Systems

Architecture Emulation and Simulation of Future Many-Core Epiphany RISC Array Processors

David A. Richie[1] and James A. Ross[2(✉)]

[1] Brown Deer Technology, Forest Hill, MD, USA
drichie@browndeertechnology.com
[2] U.S. Army Research Laboratory, Aberdeen Proving Ground, MD 21005, USA
james.a.ross176.civ@mail.mil

Abstract. The Adapteva Epiphany many-core architecture comprises a scalable 2D mesh Network-on-Chip (NoC) of low-power RISC cores with minimal uncore functionality. The Epiphany architecture has demonstrated significantly higher power-efficiency compared with other more conventional general-purpose floating-point processors. The original 32-bit architecture has been updated to create a 1,024-core 64-bit processor recently fabricated using a 16 nm process. We present here our recent work in developing an emulation and simulation capability for future many-core processors based on the Epiphany architecture. We have developed an Epiphany SoC device emulator that can be installed as a virtual device on an ordinary x86 platform and utilized with the existing software stack used to support physical devices, thus creating a seamless software development environment capable of targeting new processor designs just as they would be interfaced on a real platform. These virtual Epiphany devices can be used for research in the area of many-core RISC array processors in general.

Keywords: RISC · Network-on-Chip · Emulation · Simulation
Epiphany

1 Introduction

Recent developments in high-performance computing (HPC) provide evidence and motivation for increasing research and development efforts in low-power scalable many-core RISC array processor architectures. Many-core processors based on two-dimensional (2D) RISC arrays have been used to establish the first and fourth positions on the most recent list of top 500 supercomputers in the world [1]. Further, this was accomplished without the use of commodity processors and with instruction set architectures (ISAs) evolved from a limited ecosystem, driven primarily by research laboratories. At the same time, the status quo in HPC of relying upon conventional commodity processors to achieve the next level of supercomputing capability has encountered major setbacks. Increasing research into new and innovative architectures has emerged as a significant recommendation as we transition into a post-Moore era [2] where old trends and conventional wisdom will no longer hold.

Y. Shi et al. (Eds.): ICCS 2018, LNCS 10861, pp. 289–300, 2018.
https://doi.org/10.1007/978-3-319-93701-4_22

At the same time, there is increasing momentum for a shift to open hardware models to facilitate greater innovation and resolve problems with the ecosystems that presently provide the majority of computing platforms. Open hardware architectures, especially those based on principles of simplicity, are amenable to analysis for reliability, security, and correctness errata. This stands in stark contrast to the lack of transparency we find with existing closed architectures where security and privacy defects are now routinely found years after product deployment [3]. Open hardware architectures are also likely to spark more rapid and significant innovation, as was seen with the analogous shift to open-source software models. Recognition of the benefits of an open hardware architecture can be seen in the DARPA-funded RISC-V ISA development, which has recently lead to the availability of a commercial product and is based on a BSD open source licensed instruction set architecture.

Whereas the last decade was focused mainly on using architectures provided by just a few large commercial vendors, we may be entering an era in which architectures research will become increasingly important to define, optimize, and specialize architectures for specific classes of applications. A reduction in barriers to chip fabrication and open source hardware will further advance an open architecture model where increasing performance and capability must be extracted with innovative design rather than a reliance on Moore's Law to bring automatic improvements.

More rapid and open advances in hardware architectures will require unique capabilities in software development to resolve the traditional time lag between hardware availability and the software necessary to support it. This problem is long standing and one that is more pragmatic than theoretical. Significant software development for new hardware architectures will typically only begin once the hardware itself is available. Although some speculative work can be done, the effectiveness is limited. Very often the hardware initially available will be in the form of a development kit that brings unique challenges, and will not entirely replicate the target production systems. Based on our experience with Epiphany and other novel architectures, the pattern generally follows this scenario. Efforts to develop hardware/software co-design methodologies can benefit development in both areas. However in this work we are proposing an approach that goes further.

Modern HPC platforms are almost universally used for both development and production. With increasing specialization to achieve extreme power and performance metrics for a given class of problems, high-performance architectures may become well designed for a specific task, but not well suited to supporting software development and porting. An architecture emulation and simulation environment, which replicates the interfacing to real hardware, could be utilized to prepare software for production use beyond the early hardware/software co-design phase. As an example, rather than incorporate architectural features into a production processor to make it more capable at running compiler and development tools, the production processor should be purpose-built, with silicon and power devoted to its specific production requirements. A more general-purpose support platform can then be used to develop and test both software and hardware designs at modest scale in advance of deployment on production systems.

The focus of this research has been on the Epiphany architecture, which shares many characteristics with other RISC array processors, and is notable at the present time as the most power-efficient general-purpose floating-point processor demonstrated in silicon. To the best of our knowledge, Epiphany is the only processor architecture that has achieved the power-efficiency projected to be necessary for exascale. The Adapteva Epiphany RISC array architecture [4] is a scalable 2D array of low-power RISC cores with minimal un-core functionality supported by an on-chip 2D mesh network for fast inter-core communication. The Epiphany-III architecture is scalable to 4,096 cores and represents an example of an architecture designed for power-efficiency at extreme on-chip core counts. Processors based on this architecture exhibit good performance/power metrics [5] and scalability via a 2D mesh network [6, 7], but require a suitable programming model to fully exploit the architecture. A 16-core Epiphany-III processor [8] has been integrated into the Parallella mini-computer platform [9] where the RISC array is supported by a dual-core ARM CPU and asymmetric shared-memory access to off-chip global memory. Most recently, a 1024-core, 64-bit Epiphany-V was fabricated by DARPA and is anticipated to have much higher performance and energy efficiency [10].

The overall motivation for this work stems from ongoing efforts to investigate future many-core processors based on the Epiphany architecture. At present we are investigating the design of a hybrid processor based on a 2D array of Epiphany-V compute cores with several RISC-V supervisor cores acting as an on-die CPU host. In support of such efforts, we need to develop a large-scale emulation and simulation capability to enable rapid design and specialization by allowing testing and software development using simulated virtual architectures. In this work, a special emphasis is placed on achieving a seamless transition between emulated architectures and physical systems. The overall design and implementation of the proposed emulation and simulation environment will be generally applicable to supporting more general research and development of other many-core RISC array processors.

The main contributions presented here are as follows: we present a description of the design and implementation of an Epiphany architecture emulator that can be used to construct virtual Epiphany devices on an ordinary x86 workstation for software development and testing. Early results from testing and validation of the Epiphany ISA emulator are presented.

2   Background

The Adapteva Epiphany MIMD architecture is a scalable 2D array of RISC cores with minimal uncore functionality connected with a fast 2D mesh Network-on-Chip (NoC). The Epiphany-III (16-core) and Epiphany-IV (64-core) processors have a RISC CPU core that support a 32-bit RISC ISA with 32 KB of shared local memory per core (used for both program instructions and data), a mesh network interface, and a dual-channel DMA engine. Each RISC CPU core contains a 64-word register file, sequencer, interrupt handler, arithmetic logic unit, and a floating point unit. The fully memory-mapped architecture allows shared memory access to global off-chip memory and shared non-uniform memory access to the local memory of each core. The Epiphany-V processor, shown in Fig. 1, was extended to support 64-bit addressing and floating-point operations. The 1,024-core Epiphany-V processor was fabricated by DARPA at 16 nm.

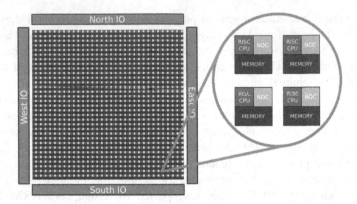

Fig. 1. The Epiphany-V RISC array architecture. A tiled array of 64-bit RISC cores are connected through a 2D mesh NoC for signaling and data transfer. Communication latency between cores is low, and the amount of addressable data contained on a mesh node is low (64 KB). Three on-chip 136-bit mesh networks enable on-chip read transactions, on-chip write transactions, and off-chip memory transactions.

The present work leverages significant research and development efforts related to the Epiphany architecture, and which produced the software stack to support many-core processors like Epiphany. Previous work included investigating a parallel programming models for the Epiphany architecture, including threaded MPI [11], OpenSHMEM [12, 13], and OpenCL [14] support for the Epiphany architecture. In all cases the parallel programming model involved explicit data movement between the local memory of each core in the RISC array, or to/from the off-chip global DRAM. The absence of a hardware cache necessitated this movement to be controlled in software explicitly. Also relevant to the present work, progress was made in the development of a more transparent compilation and run-time environment whereby program binaries could be compiled and executed directly on the Epiphany co-processor of the Parallella platform without the use of an explicit host/coprocessor offload model [15].

3   Simulation Framework for Future Many-Core Architectures

There are several technical objectives addressed in the design and implementation of a simulation framework for Epiphany-based many-core architectures. First and foremost, the ISA emulator(s) must enable fast emulation of real compiled binaries since they are to be used for executing real application code, and not merely for targeted testing of sub-sections of code. This will require a design that emphasizes efficiency and potential optimization. An important application will be the use of virtual devices operating at a level of performance that, albeit slower than real hardware, is amenable to executing large applications.

Cycle-accurate correctness of the overall system is not an objective of the design, since the goal is not to verify the digital logic of a given hardware design; sufficient tools already exist for this purpose as part of the VLSI design process. The goal instead is to ensure that the emulation and simulation environment is able to execute real applications with correct results and with the overall performance modeled sufficiently well so as to reproduce meaningful metrics. Thus, performance modeling is done by way of directly executing compiled binary code rather than employing theoretical models of the architecture. The advantage of this approach is that it will simultaneously provide a natural software development environment for proposed architectures and architecture changes without the need for physical devices. The software development and execution environment should not appear qualitatively different between simulation and execution on real hardware.

3.1   Epiphany Architecture Emulator

The design and implementation of an emulator for the Epiphany architecture is initially focused on the 32-bit architecture since physical devices are readily available for testing. The more recent extension of the ISA to support 64-bit instructions will be addressed in future work. The emulator for the 32-bit Epiphany architecture is implemented as a modular C++ class, in order to support the rapid composition and variation of specific devices for testing and software development. Implementing the emulator directly in C++, and without the use of additional tools or languages, avoids unnecessary complexity and facilitates modifications and experimentation. In addition, the direct implementation of the emulator in C++ will allow for the highest levels of performance to be achieved through low-level optimization. The emulator class is primarily comprised of an instruction dispatch method, implementations of the instructions forming the ISA, and additional features external to the RISC core but critical for the architecture functionality, such as the DMA engines.

The present design uses an instruction decoder based on an indirect threaded dispatch model. The Epiphany instruction decode table was analyzed to determine how to efficiently dispatch the 16-bit and 32-bit instructions of the ISA. Examining the lowest 4 bits of any instruction can be used to differentiate 16-bit and 32-bit instruction. For 16-bit instructions, it was determined that the lower 10 bits could efficiently dispatch the instruction by way of a pre-initialized call table for all 16-bit instructions. For 32-bit instructions, it was determined that a compressed bit-field of {b19...b16|b9...b0} could efficiently dispatch instructions by way of a larger pre-initialized call table that extends the table used for 16-bit instructions. The instruction call table is sparse, representing a balance of trade-offs between table size and dispatch efficiency.

The instruction dispatch design will allow for any instruction to stall in order to support more realistic behaviors. Memory and network interfaces are implemented as separate abstractions to allow for different memory and network models. Initially, a simple memory mapped model is used, and the incorporation of more complex and accurate memory models will be introduced in future work. The emulator supports the Epiphany architecture special registers, dual DMA engines, and interrupt handler. The DMA engines and interrupt support are based on a direct implementation of the behaviors described in the Epiphany architecture reference, and are controlled by the relevant special registers.

As will be described in more detail below, the emulator was validated using applications developed in previous work and has been demonstrated to correctly execute complex code that included interrupts, asynchronous DMA transfers, and host-coprocessor synchronization for host callback capabilities and direct Epiphany program execution without supporting host code.

3.2 Virtual Epiphany Devices

Rather than incorporate the emulator into a stand-alone tool, the chosen design allows the use of the emulator to create virtual Epiphany devices that present an interface identical to that of a physical coprocessor and is indistinguishable from a user application. This is accomplished by creating a nearly identical interface to that which is found on the Parallella boards. On this platform, the dual-core ARM host and the Epiphany-III device share 32 MB of mapped DRAM, and the Epiphany SRAM and registers are further mapped into the Linux host address space. The result is that with one exception of an ioctl() call intended to force a hard reset of the device, all inter-actions occur via reads and writes to specific memory locations. Further, the COPRTHR-2 API uses these mappings to create a unified virtual address space (UVA) between the ARM host and Epiphany coprocessor so that no address translation is required when transferring control from host to coprocessor.

Low-level access to the Epiphany coprocessor is provided by the device special file mounted on the Linux host file system at /dev/epiphany/mesh0. The setup of the UVA described above is carried out entirely through mmap() calls of this special file from within the COPRTHR software stack. Proper interaction with the Epiphany device requires nothing more than knowing the required mappings and the various protocols to be executed via ordinary reads and writes to memory. In order to create a virtual Epiphany device, a shared memory region is mounted at /dev/shm/e32.0.0 that repli-cates the memory segments of a physical Epiphany device, as shown in Fig. 2.

The emulator described in Sect. 3 is then used to compose a device of the correct number of cores and topology, and then run "on top" of this shared memory region. By this, it is meant that the emulator core will have mapped its interfacing of registers, local SRAM, and external DRAM to specific segments of the shared memory region. By simply redirecting the COPRTHR API to map/dev/shm/e32.0.0 rather than/dev/epiphany/mesh0, user applications executing on the host see no difference in func-tionality between a physical and virtual Epiphany device.

The only real distinction is the replacement of the ioctl() call mentioned above with a direct back-channel mechanism for forcing the equivalent of a hard reset of the virtual device. In addition, whereas the device special file is mapped as though it represented the full and highly sparse 1 GB address space of the Epiphany architecture, the shared memory region is stored more compactly to optimize the storage required for repre-senting a virtual Epiphany device. This is achieved by removing unused segments of the Epiphany address space for a given device, and storing only the core-local memory, register files, and global memory segments within the shared memory region. As an example, for a 256-core device with 32 MB of global memory, the compressed address

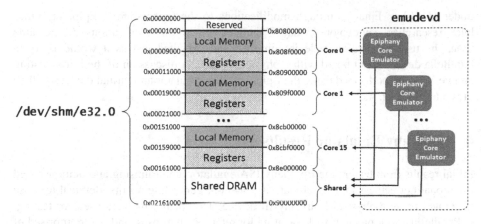

Fig. 2. The shared memory region replicates the physical memory segments of an Epiphany processor. Each emulated core has virtual local and global addresses which match the physical addressing.

space of the device will only occupy 42 MB rather than a sparse the sparse 1 GB address space.

The Linux daemon process emudevd creates this shared memory region and then operates in either active or passive mode. In active mode, an emulator is started up and begins executing on the shared memory region. If subsequently the user executes a host application that utilizes the Epiphany coprocessor, it will find the virtual device to be active and running, just as it would find a physical device.

The result of fully decoupling the emulator and user applications has an interesting benefit. Having a coprocessor in an uncertain state is closer to reality, and there is initially a low-level software requirement to develop reliable initialization procedures to guarantee that an active coprocessor can be placed in a known state regardless of the state in which it is found. This was the case during early software development for the Epiphany-III processor and the Parallella board. Issues of device lockup and unrecoverable states were common until a reliable procedure was developed. If a user application were executed through a "safe" emulator tool placing the emulated device in a known startup state, this would be overly optimistic and avoid common problems encountered with real devices. The decoupling of the emulator and user application replicates realistic conditions and provides visibility into state initialization that was previously only indirectly known or guessed at during early software development.

It is worth emphasizing the transparency and utility of these virtual Epiphany devices. The Epiphany GCC and COPRTHR tool chains are easily installed on an x86 platform, and with which Epiphany/Parallella application code can be cross-compiled. By simply installing and running the emudevd daemon on the same x86 platform, it is possible to then execute the cross-compiled code directly on the x86 platform. The result is a software development and testing environment equivalent to that of a Parallella development board. Furthermore, the virtual device is configurable in terms of the number of cores and other architectural parameters. It is also possible to install multiple virtual devices appearing as separate shared memory device special files under /dev/shm. Finally, through modifications to the (open-source) Epiphany emulator, researchers can explore "what-if" architecture design modifications. At the same time, the user application code is compiled and executed just as it would be on a Parallella development board with a physical device. A discussion of the initial testing and verification performed using the Epiphany ISA emulator and virtual devices will be presented in Sect. 4.

4 Epiphany Emulator Results

Initial results from testing the Epiphany ISA emulator are promising and demonstrated functional correctness in a benchmark application, generating results identical to those generated using a physical Epiphany-III device. Two platforms were used for testing. A Parallella development board was used for reference purposes, and was comprised of a Zynq 7020 dual-core ARM CPU and a 16-core Epiphany-III coprocessor, and with a software stack consisting of Ubuntu Linux 15.04, GCC 4.9.2 for compiling host applications, GCC 5.2.0 for cross-compiling Epiphany binaries, and the COPRTHR-2 SDK for providing software support for the Epiphany coprocessor. Emulation was tested on an ordinary x86 workstation with an eight-core AMD FX-8150 CPU, and with a software stack consisting of Linux Mint 17.3, GCC 5.3.0 for compiling host applications, GCC 5.4.0 for cross-compiling Epiphany binaries, and the COPRTHR-2 SDK for providing software support for the Epiphany coprocessor.

Two test cases were used for initial debugging and then validation of the Epiphany architecture emulator. The first test application involved a simple "Hello, World!" type program that used the COPRTHR host-coprocessor interoperability. This represents a non-trivial interaction between the host application and the code executed on the Epiphany coprocessor. The test code was compiled on the x86 workstation using the COPRTHR coprcc compiler option '-fhost' to generate a single host executable that will automatically run the cross-compiled Epiphany binary embedded within it. We note that the test code was copied over from a Parallella development board and left unmodified. When executing the host program just as it would be executed on the Parallella development platform, the application ran successfully on the x86 workstation using the Epiphany emulator. From the perspective of the host-side COPRTHR API, the virtual Epiphany device appears to be a physical Epiphany coprocessor that was simply mounted at a different location within the Linux file system.

A variation of this "Hello, World!" type program was also tested using an explicit host program to load and execute a function on one or more cores of the Epiphany coprocessor. For this test, the Epiphany binary was first compiled using the GCC cross-compiler on the x86 workstation, with results being very similar to the first successful test case. A cross-compiled Epiphany binary was then copied over from the Parallella platform and used directly on the x86 workstation with emulation. Using the binary compiled on the different platform, no differences in behavior were observed. This demonstrated that Epiphany binaries could be copied from the Parallella platform and executed without modification using emulation on the x86 workstation. Using the COPRTHR shell command coprsh we were able to execute the test program using various numbers of cores up to 16, with success in all cases. From a user perspective, the "look and feel" of the entire exercise did not differ from that experienced with software development on a Parallella development board.

The overall results from the above testing demonstrated that the test codes previously developed on the Parallella platform using the COPRTHR API could be compiled and executed via emulation on an ordinary workstation, seamlessly, and using an identical workflow. For a more demanding test of the emulator, a benchmark application was used that exercises many more features of the Epiphany coprocessor.

The Cannon matrix-matrix multiplication benchmark was implemented in previous work for Epiphany using the COPRTHR API with threaded MPI for inter-core data transfers [11]. This application code was highly optimized and used previously for extensive benchmarking of the Epiphany architecture and provides a non-trivial test case for the emulator for several reasons. The Cannon algorithm requires significant data movement between cores as sub-matrices are shifted in alternating directions. These inter-core data transfers are implemented using a threaded MPI interface, and specifically the MPI_Sendrecv_replace() call which requires precise inter-core synchronization. Finally, the data transfers from shared DRAM to core-local memory are performed using DMA engines. As a result, this test case places significant demands on the architecture emulator and is built up from complex layers of support with the COPRTHR device-side software stack. For a complete and detailed discussion of this Epiphany benchmark application see reference [11].

Figure 3 shows the actual workflow and output from the command-line used to build and execute the benchmark on the x86 workstation with the emulated virtual Epiphany device. This workflow is identical to that which is used on a Parallella platform, and the benchmark executes successfully without error. It was mentioned above that the application code leverages the COPRTHR software stack; it is important to emphasize again that no changes have been made to the COPRTHR software stack to support emulation. The virtual Epiphany devices create a seamless software development and testing capability, and appear to the supporting middleware to be real devices.

The idea behind using emulated devices is that they allow for testing and software development targeting future architecture changes. The previously developed matrix-matrix multiplication benchmark allowed command line options to control the size of the matrices and the number of threads used on the Epiphany device. With a physical Epiphany-III, the range of valid parameters was limited to 16 threads, with submatrices required to fit in the core-local memory of the coprocessor core executing each thread. Using emulated Epiphany devices, it was possible to execute this benchmark on 64 and 256 cores, and with larger matrices.

The results from this testing are shown in Table 1 where for each combination of device, matrix size, and thread count, the total execution time for the benchmark is reported in terms of 1,000 s of device clocks and wall-clock time in milliseconds. For each reported result, the numerical accuracy of the calculated matrix satisfied the default error test requiring that the relative error of each matrix element be less than 1% as compared with the analytical result. This criterion was used consistently in identifying coding errors during benchmark development, and is used here in validating the successful executing of the benchmark through emulation.

```
] gcc -I$COPRTHR_INC_PATH -c cannon_host.c

] gcc -rdynamic -o cannon.x cannon_host.o \
  -L$COPRTHR_LIB_PATH -lcoprthr -lcoprthrcc -lm -ldl

] coprcc -o cannon_tfunc.e32 cannon_tfunc.c \
  -L$COPRTHR_LIB_PATH -lcoprthr_mpi

] ./cannon.x -d 4 -n 32

COPRTHR-2-BETA (Anthem) build 20180118.0014
main: Using -n=32, -s=1, -s2=1, -d=4
main: dd=0
main: 0x2248420 0x223f3f0
main: mpiexec time 0.117030 sec
main: # errors: 0
```

Fig. 3. Workflow and output from the command-line used to build and execute the Cannon matrix-matrix multiplication benchmark on the x86 workstation using the emulated virtual Epiphany device. The workflow and execution is unchanged from that used on the Epiphany Parallella platform where the benchmark was first developed. This seamless interface to the Epiphany ISA emulator enables a testing and software development environment for new designs that is identical to production hardware.

Data for certain combinations of device, matrix size, and thread count are not shown due to several factors. First, results for larger thread counts require devices with at least as many cores. Additionally, the size of the matrices is limited by core count since the distributed submatrices must fit in core-local memory, which for the purposes of testing was kept at 32 KB. Finally, smaller matrices have a lower limit in terms of the number of threads that can be used, and this limit is impacted by a four-way loop unrolling in the optimized matrix-matrix multiplication algorithm.

The overall trend shows that the emulator executes the benchmark in fewer clocks when compared to a physical device. This result is expected, since the instruction execution at present is optimistic and does not account for pipeline stalls. Having such an optimistic mode of emulation is not necessarily without utility, since it allows for faster functional testing of software. The emulator also, as expected, takes longer to execute the benchmark than a physical device. Future work will attempt to address the issue of enabling more realistic clock cycle estimates while also optimizing the emulator for faster execution in terms of wall clock time. Finally, it should be noted that the scaling of wall clock time with the number of emulated cores is expected since the emulator is presently not parallelized in any way.

Of importance is the fact that as a result of this work, the software stack for devices that do not yet exist in silicon may be developed. A case in point can be seen in the results for the 256-core device which does not correspond to any fabricated Epiphany device. The ability to prepare software in advance of hardware will shorten significantly the traditional lag that accompanies hardware and then software development.

Table 1. Performance results for the execution of the Cannon matrix-matrix multiplication benchmark using physical and emulated devices for different matrix sizes and thread counts. Results are shown in terms of 1,000 s of device clocks (wall clock time in milliseconds)

Matrix	Threads	Epiphany-III	Emulated Device		
		16-core	16-core	64-core	256-core
16^2	1	104 (2.7)	46 (59)	60 (340)	79 (2667)
	4	90 (2.8)	11 (53)	12 (310)	16 (2485)
	16	109 (2.7)	14 (57)	14 (325)	18 (2288)
32^2	1	201 (3.1)	112 (138)	127 (682)	145 (4032)
	4	155 (3.1)	37 (86)	38 (448)	41 (2712)
	16	145 (3.1)	22 (70)	23 (325)	26 (2311)
	64	–	–	47 (569)	51 (2868)
64^2	4	479 (4.5)	201 (298)	202 (1421)	205 (7679)
	16	311 (4.0)	73 (141)	73 (672)	77 (3773)
	64	–	–	64 (663)	67 (3358)
	256	–	–	–	258 (8773)
128^2	16	1062 (9.4)	400 (561)	400 (2395)	404 (13522)
	64	–	–	165 (1230)	168 (6033)
	256	–	–	–	291 (9831)
256^2	64	–	–	816 (4849)	820 (23651)
	256	–	–	–	490 (15731)

5   Conclusion and Future Work

An Epiphany 32-bit ISA emulator was implemented that may be configured as a virtual many-core device for testing and software development on an ordinary x86 platform. The design enables a seamless interface allowing the same tool chain and software stack to be used to target and interface to the virtual device in a manner identical to that of real physical devices. This has been done in the context of research into the design of future many-core processors based on the Epiphany architecture. The emulator has been validated for correctness using benchmarks previously developed for the Epiphany Parallella development platform, which work without modification using emulated devices.

Efforts to develop the software support for simulating and evaluating future many-core processor designs based on the Epiphany architecture reflects ongoing work. In the near term, the emulator will be improved with better memory models and instruction pipeline timing to allow for the prediction of execution time for software applications. The emulator will be extended to support the more recent 64-bit ISA which is backward compatible with the 32-bit Epiphany architecture. With direct measurements taken from the Epiphany-V SoC the emulator will be refined to produce predictive metrics such as clock cycle costs for software execution. With this calibration, general specializations to the architecture can then be explored with real software applications.

Acknowledgements. This work was supported by the U.S. Army Research Laboratory. The authors thank David Austin Richie for contributions to this work.

References

1. https://www.top500.org/lists/2017/11/. Accessed 04 Feb 2018
2. https://www.nitrd.gov/nitrdgroups/images/b/b4/NSA_DOE_HPC_TechMeetingReport.pdf. Accessed 04 Feb 2018
3. https://spectreattack.com/spectre.pdf, https://meltdownattack.com/meltdown.pdf. Accessed 04 Feb 2018
4. Adapteva introduction. http://www.adapteva.com/introduction/. Accessed 08 Jan 2015
5. Olofsson, A., Nordström, T., Ul-Abdin, Z.: Kickstarting high-performance energy-efficient manycore architectures with Epiphany. ArXiv Preprint arXiv:14125538 (2014)
6. Wentzlaff, D., Griffin, P., Hoffmann, H., Bao, L., Edwards, B., Ramey, C., Mattina, M., Miao, C.-C., Brown III, J.F., Agarwal, A.: On-chip interconnection architecture of the tile processor. IEEE Micro **27**(5), 15–31 (2007)
7. Taylor, M.B., Kim, J., Miller, J., Wentzlaff, D., Ghodrat, F., Greenwald, B., Hoffman, H., Johnson, P., Lee, W., Saraf, A., Shnidman, N., Strumpen, V., Amarasinghe, S., Agarwal, A.: A 16-issue multiple-program-counter microprocessor with point-to-point scalar operand network. In: 2003 IEEE International Solid-State Circuits Conference (ISSCC), pp. 170–171 (2003)
8. E16G301 Epiphany 16-core microprocessor. Adapteva Inc., Lexington, MA, Datasheet Rev. 14 March 2011
9. Parallella-1.x reference manual. Adapteva, Boston Design Solutions, Ant Micro, Rev. 14 September 2009
10. Epiphany-V: A 1024-core processor 64-bit System-On-Chip. http://www.parallella.org/docs/e5_1024core_soc.pdf. Accessed 10 Feb 2017
11. Richie, D., Ross, J., Park, S., Shires, D.: Threaded MPI programming model for the epiphany RISC array processor. J. Comput. Sci. **9**, 94–100 (2015)
12. Ross, J., Richie, D.: Implementing OpenSHMEM for the adapteva epiphany RISC array processor. In: International Conference on Computational Science, ICCS 2016, San Diego, California, USA, 6–8 June 2016
13. Ross, J., Richie, D.: An OpenSHMEM implementation for the adapteva epiphany coprocessor. In: Gorentla Venkata, M., Imam, N., Pophale, S., Mintz, T.M. (eds.) OpenSHMEM 2016. LNCS, vol. 10007, pp. 146–159. Springer, Cham (2016). https://doi.org/10.1007/978-3-319-50995-2_10
14. Richie, D.A., Ross, J.A.: OpenCL + OpenSHMEM hybrid programming model for the adapteva epiphany architecture. In: Gorentla Venkata, M., Imam, N., Pophale, S., Mintz, T.M. (eds.) OpenSHMEM 2016. LNCS, vol. 10007, pp. 181–192. Springer, Cham (2016). https://doi.org/10.1007/978-3-319-50995-2_12
15. Richie, D., Ross, J.: Advances in run-time performance and interoperability for the adapteva epiphany coprocessor. Proc. Comput. Sci. **80** (2016). https://doi.org/10.1016/j.procs.2016.05.47

Automatic Mapping for OpenCL-Programs on CPU/GPU Heterogeneous Platforms

Konrad Moren[1](✉) and Diana Göhringer[2](✉)

[1] Fraunhofer Institute of Optronics, System Technologies and Image Exploitation IOSB, 76275 Ettlingen, Germany
konrad.moren@iosb.fraunhofer.de
[2] Adaptive Dynamic Systems, TU Dresden, 01062 Dresden, Germany
diana.goehringer@tu-dresden.de

Abstract. Heterogeneous computing systems with multiple CPUs and GPUs are increasingly popular. Today, heterogeneous platforms are deployed in many setups, ranging from low-power mobile systems to high performance computing systems. Such platforms are usually programmed using OpenCL which allows to execute the same program on different types of device. Nevertheless, programming such platforms is a challenging job for most non-expert programmers. To enable an efficient application runtime on heterogeneous platforms, programmers require an efficient workload distribution to the available compute devices. The decision how the application should be mapped is non-trivial. In this paper, we present a new approach to build accurate predictive-models for OpenCL programs. We use a machine learning-based predictive model to estimate which device allows best application speed-up. With the LLVM compiler framework we develop a tool for dynamic code-feature extraction. We demonstrate the effectiveness of our novel approach by applying it to different prediction schemes. Using our dynamic feature extraction techniques, we are able to build accurate predictive models, with accuracies varying between 77% and 90%, depending on the prediction mechanism and the scenario. We evaluated our method on an extensive set of parallel applications. One of our findings is that dynamically extracted code features improve the accuracy of the predictive-models by 6.1% on average (maximum 9.5%) as compared to the state of the art.

Keywords: OpenCL · Heterogeneous computing
Workload scheduling · Machine learning · Compilers · Code analysis

1 Introduction

One of the grand challenges in efficient multi-device programming is the workload distribution among the available devices in order to maximize application performance. Such systems are usually programmed using OpenCL that allows executing the same program on different types of device. Task distribution-mapping

© Springer International Publishing AG, part of Springer Nature 2018
Y. Shi et al. (Eds.): ICCS 2018, LNCS 10861, pp. 301–314, 2018.
https://doi.org/10.1007/978-3-319-93701-4_23

defines how the total workload (all OpenCL-program kernels) is distributed among the available computational resources. Typically application developers solve this problem experimentally, where they profile the execution time of kernel function for each available device and then decide how to map the application. This approach error prone and furthermore, it is very time consuming to analyze the application scaling for various inputs and execution setups. The best mapping is likely to change with different: input/output sizes, execution-setups and target hardware configurations [1,2]. To solve this problem, researchers focus on three major performance-modeling techniques on which mapping-heuristic can be based: simulations, analytical and statistical modeling. Models created with analytical and simulation techniques are most accurate and robust [3], but they are also difficult to design and maintain in a portable way. Developers often have to spend huge amount of time to create a tuned-model even for a single target architecture. Since modern hardware architectures are rapidly changing those methods are likely to be out of the date. The last group, statistical modeling techniques overcome those drawbacks, where the model is created by extracting program parameters, running programs and observing how the parameters variation affects their execution times. This process is independent of the target platform and easily adaptable. Recent research studies [4–9] have already proved that predictive models are very useful in wide range of applications. However, one major concern for accurate and robust model design is the selection of program features.

Efficient and portable workload mapping requires a model of corresponding platform. Previous work on predictive modeling [10–13] restricted their attention to models based on features extracted statically, avoiding dynamic application analysis. However, performance related information, like the number of memory transactions between the caches and main memory, is known only during the runtime.

In this paper, we present a novel method to dynamically extract code features from the OpenCL programs which we use to build our predictive models. With the created model, we predict which device allows the best relative application speed-up. Furthermore, we developed code transformation and analysis passes to extract the dynamic code features. We measure and quantify the importance of extracted code-features. Finally, we analyze and show that dynamic code features increase the model accuracy as compared to the state of the art methods. Our goal is to explore and present an efficient method for code feature extraction to improve the predictive model performance. In summary:

- We present a method to extract OpenCL code features that leads to more accurate predictive models.
- Our method is portable to any OpenCL environment with an arbitrary number of devices. The experimental results demonstrate the capabilities of our approach on three different heterogeneous multi-device platforms.
- We show the impact of our newly introduced dynamic features in the context of predictive modeling.

This paper is structured as follows. Section 2 gives an overview of the related work. Section 3 presents our approach. In Sect. 4 we describe the experiments. In Sect. 5 we present results and discuss the limitations of our method. In the last section, we draw our conclusion and show directions for the future work.

2 Background and Existing Approaches

Several related studies have tackled the problem of feature extraction from OpenCL programs, followed by the predictive model building.

Grewe and O'Boyle [10] proposed a predictive model based on static OpenCL code features to estimate the optimal split kernel-size. Authors present that the estimated split-factor can be used to efficiently distribute the workload between the CPU and the GPU in a heterogeneous system.

Magni et al. [11] presented the use of predictive modeling to train and build a model based on Artificial Neural Network algorithms. They predict the correct coarsening factor to drive their own compiler tool-chain. Similarly to Grewe they target almost identical code features to build the model.

Kofler et al. [12] build the predictive-model based on Artificial Neural Networks that incorporates static program features as well as dynamic, input sensitive features. With the created model, they automatically optimize task partitioning for different problem sizes and different heterogeneous architectures.

Wen et al. [13] described the use of machine learning to predict the proper target device in context of a multi-application workload distribution system. They build the model based on the static OpenCL code features with few run-time features. They included environment related features, which provide only information about the computing-platform capabilities. This approach is most related to our work. They also study building of the predictive model to distribute the workloads in a context of the heterogeneous platform.

One observation is that all these methods extract code features statically during the JIT compilation phase. We believe, that our novel dynamic code analysis, can provide more meaningful and valuable code features. We justify our statement by profiling the Listing 1.1.

```
 1 kernel
 2 void floydWarshall( global uint * pathDist,global uint * path,
 3           const uint numNodes, const uint pass)
 4 {
 5   const int xValue = get_global_id(0);
 6   const int yValue = get_global_id(1);
 7   const int oldWeight = pathDist[yValue * numNodes + xValue];
 8   const int tempWeight = (pathDist[yValue * numNodes + pass] +
 9   pathDist[pass * numNodes + xValue]);
10   if (tempWeight < oldWeight){
11     pathDist[yValue * numNodes + xValue] = tempWeight;
12     path[yValue * numNodes + xValue] = pass;
13   }}
```

Listing 1.1. AMD-SDK FloydWarshall kernel

The results are shown in Fig. 1. These experiments demonstrate the execution times of the Listing 1.1 executed with varying input values (*numNodes*, *pass*)

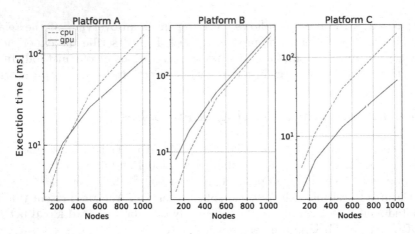

Fig. 1. Profiling results for an AMD-SDK FloydWarshall kernel function on test platforms. The target architectures are detailed in the Sect. 4.1. The Y-Axis presents the execution time in milliseconds, the X-Axis shows the varying number of nodes.

and execution-configurations on our experimental platforms. We can observe that even for a single kernel function, the optimal mapping considerably depends on the input/output sizes and the capabilities of the platform. In Listing 1.1 the arguments *numNodes* and *pass* control effectively the number of requested cache lines. According to our observations, many of the OpenCL programs rely on kernel input arguments, known only at the enqueuing time. In general, input values of OpenCL-function arguments are unknown at the compilation time. Many performance related information, like the memory access pattern, number of executed statements, could possibly be dependent on these parameters. This is a crucial shortcoming in previous approaches. The code-statements dependent on values known during the program execution are undefined and could not provide quantitative information. Since current state of the art methods analyze and extract code features only statically, new methods are needed. In the next section, we present our framework that addresses this problem.

3   Proposed Approach

This section describes the design and the implementation of our dynamic feature extraction method. We present all the parts of our extraction approach: transformation and feature building. We describe which code parameters we extract and how we build the code features from them. Finally, we present our methodology to train and build the statistical performance model based on the extracted features.

3.1   Architecture Overview

Figure 2 shows the architecture of our approach. We modify and extend the default OpenCL-driver to integrate our method. First, we use the binary LLVM-

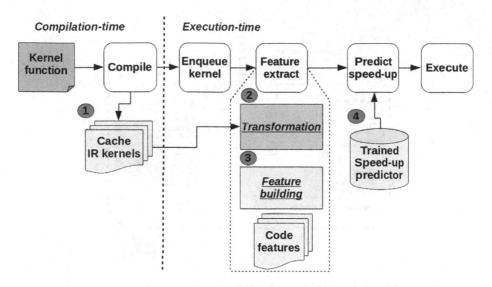

Fig. 2. Architecture of the proposed approach.

IR representation of the kernel function and cache it in the driver memory ❶. We reuse IR functions during enqueuing to the compute-device. During the enqueuing phase, cached IR functions with known parameters are used as inputs to the transformation engine. At the time of enqueuing, the values of input arguments, the kernel code and the NDRange sizes are known and remain constant. A semantically correct OpenCL program always needs this information to properly execute [14]. Based on this observation, our transform module ❷ rewrites the input OpenCL-C kernel code to a simplified version. This kernel-IR version is analyzed to build the code features ❸. Finally we deploy our trained predictive model and embed it as a last stage in our modified OpenCL driver ❹. Following sections describe steps ❶–❹ in more details.

3.2 Dynamic Code Feature Analysis and Extraction

The modified driver extends the default OpenCL driver by three additional modules. First, we extend and modify the *clBuildProgram* function in OpenCL API. Our implementation adds a caching system ❶ to reduce the overhead of invoking transformation and feature-building modules. We store internal LLVM-IR representations in the driver memory to efficiently reuse it in the transformation module ❷. Building the LLVM-IR module is done only once, usually at the application beginning. The transformation module ❷ is implemented within the *clEnqueueNdRangeKernel* OpenCL API function. This module rewrites the input OpenCL-C kernel code to a simplified version. The Fig. 3 shows the transformation architecture. The module includes two cache objects, which store original and pre-transformed IR kernel functions. We apply transformations in two phases $T1$ and $T2$. First phase $T1$, we load for a specific kernel name the

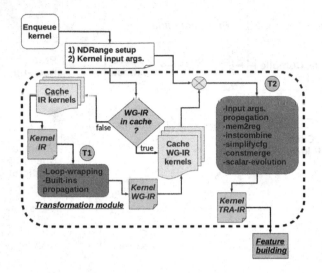

Fig. 3. Detailed view on our feature extraction module.

IR-code created during ❶ and then wrap the code region with work-item loops. The wrapping technique is a known method described by Lee [15] and already applied in other studies [16,17]. The work-group IR-function generation is performed at kernel enqueue time, when the group size is known. The known work-group size makes it possible to set constant values to the work-item loops. In a second phase $T2$, we load the transformed work-group IR and propagate constant input values. After this step, the IR includes all specific values not only the symbolic expressions. The remaining passes of $T2$ further simplifies the code. The Listing 1.2 presents the intermediate code after the transformation $T1$ and input argument values propagation. Due to the space limitation, we do not present the original LLVM-IR code but a readable-intermediate representation.

```
1  kernel
2  void floydWarshall( global uint * pathDist ,global uint * path)
3  {
4    for(int yValue=0; yValue<1024; yValue++){
5      for(int xValue=0; xValue<1024; xValue++){
6        const int oldWeight = pathDist[yValue * 1024 + xValue];
7        const int tempWeight = (pathDist[yValue * 1024 + 16] +
8        pathDist[16 * 1024 + xValue]);
9        if (tempWeight < oldWeight){
10         pathDist[yValue * 1024 + xValue] = tempWeight;
11         path[yValue * 1024 + xValue] = 16;
12       }
13     }
14   }
15 }
```

Listing 1.2. The readable-intermediate representation of Listing 1.1 after input and built-in constants propagation. The execution parameters are: numNodes = 1024, pass = 16, work-group sizes = (1,1), global sizes = (1024,1024)

We can observe that the constant propagation pass, enables to determine how the memory accesses are distributed. Now the system can extract not only how many load and stores are requested, but also how are they distributed. With pure static code analysis, this information is not available. Additionally, compared to the pure static methods we analyze more accurately the instructions. Our method simplifies the control flow graph and analyzes only the executable instructions. In contrast, the static code analysis scans all basic blocks also these that are not used. Furthermore, we extract for each load and store instructions the Scalar Evolution (SCEV) expressions. The extracted SCEV expressions represent the evolution of loop variables in a closed form [18,19]. A SCEV consist of a starting value, an operator and an increment value. They have the format $\{<base>, +, <step>\}$. The base of an SCEV defines its value at loop iteration zero and the step of an SCEV defines the values added on every subsequent loop iteration [20]. For example, the SCEV expression for the load instruction in Listing 1.2 on line 6 has the form $\{\{\%pathDist, +, 4096\}, +, 4\}$. We can see that this compact representation describes the memory access of the kernel input argument $\%pathDist$. With this information, we analyze the SCEVs for existing loads and stores to infer the memory access. We group the extracted memory accesses in four groups. First invariant accesses with the stride zero. Stride zero accesses (i.e., invariant) means that the memory access index is the same for all loop iterations in a work-group. The second group, consecutive accesses with stride one. Stride one means that the memory access index increases by one for consecutive loop iterations. The third group, non-consecutive accesses with the stride N, where N means that the memory access index is neither invariant nor stride one. Finally, the last group, the unknown accesses with the stride X. In general, SCEV expression can have an unknown value due to a dependence on the results calculated during the code execution. Table 1 presents all extracted information about the kernel function.

The selected features are not specific for any micro-architecture or device type. We extract the existing OpenCL-C arithmetic, control and memory instructions. Additionally in contrast to other approaches, we extract the memory access pattern. The selection of the features is a design specific decision. We analyze in more detail the importance of selected features in Sect. 4.2. In the next section, we use our extracted features to create the training data and describe how we train our predictive model.

3.3   Building the Prediction Model

Building machine-learning based models involves the collection of data that is used in the model training and evaluation. To retrieve the data we execute, extract features and measure the execution time for various test applications. We use different applications implemented in: the NVIDIA OpenCL SDK [21], the AMD APP SDK [14], and the Polybench OpenCL v2.5 [22]. We execute the applications with different input data sizes. The purpose of this is twofold. First, the variable sizes of input data let us collect more training data and second, the data is more diverse due to the implicit change in work-group sizes. Many of these

Table 1. Features extracted with our dynamic analysis method. These features are used to build the predictive model.

	Features	Description
F1	$(arithmetic\_inst)/(all\_inst)$	Computational intensity ratio
F2	$(memory\_inst)/(all\_inst)$	Memory intensity ratio
F3	$(control\_inst)/(all\_inst)$	Control intensity ratio
F4	$datasize$	Global memory allocated
F5	$globalWorkSize$	Number of global threads
F6	$localWorkSize$	Number of local threads
F7	$workGroups$	Number of work-groups
F8	$Stride0$	Invariant memory accesses
F9	$Stride1$	Consecutive memory accesses
F10	$StrideN$	Scatter/gather memory accesses
F11	$StrideX$	Unknown memory accesses

applications adapt the number of work-groups with the change of input/output data sizes. By varying the input variables of applications, we create the data set with 5887 samples. The list of application is shown in Table 2.

In our approach, we execute presented OpenCL programs on the CPU and the GPU to measure the speedup of the GPU execution for each individual kernel over the CPU. Furthermore, to consider various costs of data transfers on architectures with discrete and integrated GPUs, we measure the transfer times between the CPU and GPU. We define it as DT. To model the real cost of the execution on the GPUs, we add the DT to the GPU execution time. Finally, in a last step we combine the CPU/GPU execution times and label the kernel-code to one of five speed-up classes. The Eq. 1 defines the speed-up categories for our predictive model.

$$
Speedup\_class = \begin{cases}
Class1 & \frac{CPU}{GPU+DT} \leq 1x\,(no\ speedup) \\
Class2 & 1x < \frac{CPU}{GPU+DT} \leq 3x \\
Class3 & 3x < \frac{CPU}{GPU+DT} \leq 5x \\
Class4 & 5x < \frac{CPU}{GPU+DT} \leq 7x \\
Class5 & \frac{CPU}{GPU+DT} \geq 7x
\end{cases}
\tag{1}
$$

In our experiments, we use the Random Forest (RF) classifier. The reason for this is twofold. First, the RF classifier enables to build the relative feature importance ranking. In Sect. 5 we use this metric to explore the relative feature importance on the classification accuracy. The second one is that, the classifiers based on decision trees are usually fast. We also investigated other machine learning algorithms but due to the space limitations, we will not show a detailed comparison of these classifiers. Finally, once the model is trained we use the trained model during the runtime ❹ to determine the kernel scheduling.

Table 2. The applications used to train and evaluate our predictive model.

Suite	Application	Input sizes	Application	Input sizes
AMD SDK	Binary search	80K–1M	Bitonic sort	8K–64K
	Binomial option	1K–64K	Black Scholes	34M
	DCT	130K–20M	Fast Walsh transform	2K–32K
	Floyd Warshall	1K–64K	LU decomposition	8M
	Monte Carlo Asian	4M–8M	Matrix multiplication	130K–52M
	Matrix transpose	130K–50M	Quasi random sequence	4K
	Reduction	8K	RadixSort	8K–64K
	Simple convolution	130K–1M	Scan large arrays	4K–64K
Nvidia SDK	DXT compression	2M–6M	Median filter	3M
	Dot product	9K–294K	FDTD3d	8M–260M
	HMM	2M–4M	Tridiagonal	320K–20M
Polybench	Atax	66K–2M	Bicg	66K–2M
	Gramschmidt	15K–1M	Gesummv	130K–5M
	Correlation	130K–5M	Covariance	130K–52M
	Syrk	190K–5M	Syr2k	190K–5M

4   Experimental Evaluation

4.1   Hardware and Software Platforms

We evaluate on three CPU+GPU platforms. The details are shown in Table 3. All platforms have Intel CPUs, two platforms include discrete GPUs. The third platform is an Intel SoC (System on Chip) with integrated CPU/GPU. We use LLVM 3.8 with Ubuntu-Linux 16.04 LTS to drive our feature extraction tool. The host-side compiler is GCC 5.4.0 with -O3 option. On the device-side Intel OpenCL SDK 2.0, NVIDIA Cuda SDK 8.0 and AMD OpenCL SDK 2.0 provide compilers.

4.2   Evaluation of the Model

We train and evaluate two speed-up models with different features to compare our approach with the state of the art. The first model, is based on our dynamic feature extraction method. Table 1 shows the features applied to build the model. To train and build the second model, we extract statically only the code features $F1$–$F7$ from the kernel function (i.e. during the JIT-compilation). The memory access features $F8$-$F11$ known only during the runtime are not included.

Table 3. Hardware platforms

Platform A	CPU I7-4930K	GPU Radeon R9-290
Architecture	Ivy Bridge	Hawaii
Core count	6 (12 w/HT)	2560
Core clock	3.9 GHz	0.9 GHz
Memory bandwidth	59.7 GB/s	320 GB/s
Platform B	CPU I7-6600U	GPU HD-520
Architecture	Skylake	Skylake
Core count	2 (4 w/HT)	192
Core clock	3.4 GHz	1.0 GHz
Memory bandwidth	34.1 GB/s	25.6 GB/s
Platform C	CPU Xeon E5-2667	GPU Geforce GTX 780 Ti
Architecture	Sandy Bridge	Kepler
Core count	6 (12 w/HT)	2880
Core clock	3.5 GHz	0.9 GHz
Memory bandwidth	51.2 GB/s	288.4 GB/s

For both models, we apply the following train and evaluation method. We split 10 times our dataset into train and test sets. Each time we randomly select 33% of dataset samples for the evaluation process. The remaining 67% are used to train the model. Figure 4 presents the confusion matrix for the evaluation scenario.

We observe that the prediction accuracy for the model created with dynamic features is higher than for the model based on static features. On the Platform A the model based on dynamic features have a 90.1% mean accuracy. The accuracy values is an average over testing scenarios. We calculate the accuracy as the ratio between sum of values on the diagonal in Fig. 4 to all values. We observe similar results for two other Platforms B and C. The mean accuracies for the remaining platforms are 77% and 84% for Platforms B and C respectively. Overall, we can report increase of the prediction accuracy with dynamically extracted features by 9.5%, 4.9% and 4.1% for the tested Platforms. We observe also that, the model based on dynamic features leads to lower slowdowns. We can observe from Fig. 4 that the model with static features predicts less accurate, the error rate is 19.4%, for the dynamic model only 9.9%. More importantly, we can see that the distribution of errors is different. Overall, we can observe that the number of miss-predictions, values below and above the diagonal, is higher for the model created with static features. In the worst case, the model based on statically extracted features predicts only 36 times correctly the $7x$ speed-up on the GPU. This point corresponds to the lowest row in the confusion matrix presented in Fig. 4.

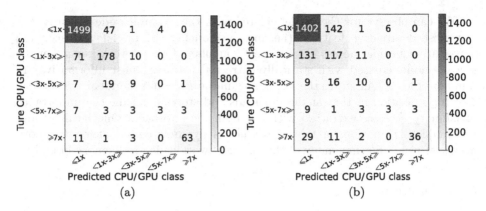

Fig. 4. The confusion matrix for platform A, (a) results for the model with dynamic features (b) results without dynamic features.

5   Discussion

We find out in our experiments that the predictive models designed with the dynamic code features are more accurate and lead to lower performance degradation in context of workload distribution. To further explore the impact of dynamic features on the classification, we analyze the relative feature importance. The selected RF classifier enables to build the relative feature importance ranking. The relative feature importance metric is based on two statistical methods Gini-impurity and the Information gain. More details about the RF classifier and the feature importance metric are included in the [23]. Figure 5 presents the relative feature importance for the both models presented in the previous section.

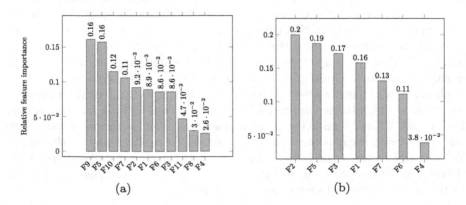

Fig. 5. Relative feature importance for the classifier (a) trained with dynamic features and (b) with statically extracted features. The values on X-Axis are features presented in Table 1, the Y-Axis represents the ranking of relative feature importance.

We can observe for the model created with the dynamic code features that the most informative features (i.e. mostly reducing the model variance), are consecutive memory access $F9$ and the $F5$ number of global work-items. For the second model created with statically extracted features, most informative are number of loads and stores the $F2$ and again the $F5$ count of global work-items. The high position in the ranking for loads and stores confirms the importance of memory accesses extracted with our dynamic approach. One intuitive and reasonable explanation for the importance of dynamic code features (memory accesses) would be that many of the analyzed workloads are memory-bound.

5.1 Limitations

Our dynamic approach described in previous sections increases a classification accuracy. However, the proposed and described method in this paper has also several limitations. Our memory access analysis is limited to a sub-set of all possible code variants. The Scalar Evolution pass computes only the symbolic expressions for combinations of constants, loop variables and static variables. It supports only a common integer arithmetic like addition, subtraction, multiplication or unsigned division [20]. Other possible code variants and resulting statements lead to unknown values. Another aspect is the feature extraction time. Compared to the pure static methods our dynamic method generates an overhead during the runtime. We can observe the variable overhead between 0.3 and 4 ms, dependent on the platform capabilities and the code complexity.

6   Conclusion and Outlook

Deploying data parallel applications using the right hardware is essential for improving application performance on heterogeneous platforms. A wrong device selection and as a result not efficient workload distribution may lead to a significant performance loss. In this paper, we propose a novel systematic approach to build the predictive model that estimates the compute device with an optimal application speed-up. Our approach uses dynamic features available only during the runtime. This improves the prediction accuracy independently of the applications and hardware setups. Therefore, we believe that our work provides an effective and adaptive approach for users who are looking for high performance and efficiency on heterogeneous platforms. The performed experiments and results encourage us to extend and improve our methodology in the future. We will extract and experiment with other code features and classifiers. Additionally, we will improve our feature extraction method to further increase the model accuracy and reduce the overall runtime.

References

1. Calotoiu, A., Hoefler, T., Poke, M., Wolf, F.: Using automated performance modeling to find scalability bugs in complex codes. In: Gropp, W., Matsuoka, S., (eds.) International Conference for High Performance Computing, Networking, Storage and Analysis, Denver, CO, USA, SC 2013, 17–21 November 2013, pp. 45:1–45:12. ACM, New York (2013)
2. Hoefler, T., Gropp, W., Kramer, W., Snir, M.: Performance modeling for systematic performance tuning. In: State of the Practice Reports, SC 2011, pp. 6:1–6:12. ACM,New York (2011)
3. Lopez-Novoa, U., Mendiburu, A., Miguel-Alonso, J.: A survey of performance modeling and simulation techniques for accelerator-based computing. IEEE Trans. Parallel Distrib. Syst. **26**(1), 272–281 (2015)
4. Bailey, D.H., Snavely, A.: Performance modeling: understanding the past and predicting the future. In: Cunha, J.C., Medeiros, P.D. (eds.) Euro-Par 2005. LNCS, vol. 3648, pp. 185–195. Springer, Heidelberg (2005). https://doi.org/10.1007/11549468_23
5. Nagasaka, H., Maruyama, N., Nukada, A., Endo, T., Matsuoka, S.: Statistical power modeling of GPU kernels using performance counters. In: Green Computing Conference, pp. 115–122. IEEE Computer Society (2010)
6. Kerr, A., Diamos, G.F., Yalamanchili, S.: Modeling GPU-CPU workloads and systems. In: Kaeli, D.R., Leeser, M., (eds.) Proceedings of 3rd Workshop on General Purpose Processing on Graphics Processing Units, GPGPU 2010, Pittsburgh, Pennsylvania, USA, 14 March 2010. ACM International Conference Proceeding Series, vol. 425, pp. 31–42. ACM (2010)
7. Dao, T.T., Kim, J., Seo, S., Egger, B., Lee, J.: A performance model for GPUs with caches. IEEE Trans. Parallel Distrib. Syst. **26**(7), 1800–1813 (2015)
8. Baldini, I., Fink, S.J., Altman, E.R.: Predicting GPU performance from CPU runs using machine learning. In: SBAC-PAD, Washington, DC, USA, pp. 254–261. IEEE Computer Society (2014)
9. Tripathy, B., Dash, S., Padhy, S.K.: Multiprocessor scheduling and neural network training methods using shuffled frog-leaping algorithm. Comput. Ind. Eng. **80**, 154–158 (2015)
10. Grewe, D., O'Boyle, M.F.P.: A static task partitioning approach for heterogeneous systems using OpenCL. In: Knoop, J. (ed.) CC 2011. LNCS, vol. 6601, pp. 286–305. Springer, Heidelberg (2011). https://doi.org/10.1007/978-3-642-19861-8_16
11. Magni, A., Dubach, C., O'Boyle, M.F.P.: Automatic optimization of thread-coarsening for graphics processors. In: Amaral, J.N., Torrellas, J., (eds.) PACT, pp. 455–466. ACM (2014)
12. Kofler, K., Grasso, I., Cosenza, B., Fahringer, T.: An automatic input-sensitive approach for heterogeneous task partitioning. In: Malony, A.D., Nemirovsky, M., Midkiff, S.P., (eds.) ICS, pp. 149–160. ACM (2013)
13. Wen, Y., Wang, Z., O'Boyle, M.F.P.: Smart multi-task scheduling for OpenCL programs on CPU/GPU heterogeneous platforms. In: 21st International Conference on High Performance Computing, HiPC 2014, Goa, India, 17–20 December 2014, pp. 1–10 (2014)
14. AMD: AMD APP SDK v2.9 (2014)

15. Lee, J., Kim, J., Seo, S., Kim, S., Park, J., Kim, H., Dao, T.T., Cho, Y., Seo, S.J., Lee, S.H., Cho, S.M., Song, H.J., Suh, S., Choi, J.: An OpenCL framework for heterogeneous multicores with local memory. In: Salapura, V., Gschwind, M., Knoop, J. (eds.) 19th International Conference on Parallel Architecture and Compilation Techniques (PACT 2010), Vienna, Austria, 11–15 September 2010, pp. 193–204. ACM (2010)

16. Kim, H.S., Hajj, I.E., Stratton, J.A., Lumetta, S.S., Hwu, W.M.: Locality-centric thread scheduling for bulk-synchronous programming models on CPU architectures. In: Olukotun, K., Smith, A., Hundt, R., Mars, J. (eds.) Proceedings of the 13th Annual IEEE/ACM International Symposium on Code Generation and Optimization, CGO 2015, San Francisco, CA, USA, 07–11 February 2015, pp. 257–268. IEEE Computer Society (2015)

17. Jo, G., Jeon, W.J., Jung, W., Taft, G., Lee, J.: OpenCL framework for arm processors with neon support. In: Proceedings of the 2014 Workshop on Programming Models for SIMD/Vector Processing. WPMVP 2014, pp. 33–40. ACM, New York (2014)

18. Zima, E.V.: On computational properties of chains of recurrences. In: Proceedings of the 2001 International Symposium on Symbolic and Algebraic Computation. ISSAC 2001, p. 345. ACM, New York (2001)

19. Engelen, R.A.: Efficient symbolic analysis for optimizing compilers. In: Wilhelm, R. (ed.) CC 2001. LNCS, vol. 2027, pp. 118–132. Springer, Heidelberg (2001). https://doi.org/10.1007/3-540-45306-7_9

20. Grosser, T., Größlinger, A., Lengauer, C.: Polly - performing polyhedral optimizations on a low-level intermediate representation. Parallel Process. Lett. **22**(4) (2012)

21. Nvidia: NVIDIA OpenCL SDK code samples (2014)

22. Grauer-Gray, S., Xu, L., Searles, R., Ayalasomayajula, S., Cavazos, J.: Auto-tuning a high-level language targeted to GPU codes. In: Innovative Parallel Computing (InPar), pp. 1–10, May 2012

23. Breiman, L.: Random forests. Mach. Learn. **45**(1), 5–32 (2001)

Track of Biomedical and Bioinformatics Challenges for Computer Science

11th Workshop on Biomedical and Bioinformatics Challenges for Computer Science: New Computational Models, Algorithms and Computer Architectures

Mario Cannataro[1], Riccardo Dondi[1], Giuseppe Agapito[1],
Mauro Castelli[3], Italo Zoppis[4],
and Rodrigo Weber dos Santos[5]

[1] Data Analytics Research Center,
University Magna Græcia of Catanzaro, Italy
[2] University of Bergamo, Italy
[3] NOVA Information Management School (NOVA IMS),
Universidade Nova de Lisboa, Campus de Campolide,
1070-312 Lisboa, Portugal
[4] University of Milano-Bicocca, Italy
[5] Graduate Program in Computational Modeling,
Federal University of Juiz de Fora, Brazil
rodrigo.weber@ufjf.edu.br

Abstract. Emerging technologies in biomedicine and bioinformatics are generating an increasing amount of complex data. To tackle the growing complexity associated with life science challenges, bioinformatics and computational biology researchers need to explore, develop and apply novel computational concepts, methods, and tools. The 11th Workshop on Biomedical and Bioinformatics Challenges for Computer Science (BBC) aimed to present the development and use of new computational models, algorithms, and computer hardware applied to different problems of life sciences and biomedical engineering. This short paper summarizes the accepted works presented at the workshop.

Keywords: Bioinformatics · Biomedicine
Computational modeling · High performance computing

Supported by CAPES, CNPq, UFJF, FAPEMIG, and Data Analytics Research Center.

Preface

Bioinformatics and biomedical engineering are interdisciplinary in nature. In addition to biomedicine and biology, many other disciplines are integrated, such as mathematics and systems theory, computational modeling and high-performance computing, just to name a few.

Emerging life sciences applications need to use bioinformatics tools, biological data banks, patient's molecular and clinical data as well as epidemiology data in a coordinated way. Therefore, new challenges to computer science arise from huge amounts of data to be integrated and the computing power necessary to analyze those big data sets or to simulate complex biological and biomedical systems. The aim of this Special Section is to discuss challenges and future directions of bioinformatics and biomedical algorithms, computational models, computer hardware and applications; and relate these to the accepted papers of the 11th Workshop on Biomedical and Bioinformatics Challenges for Computer Science, held in Wuxi, China, 11–13 June, 2018. The first edition of this workshop took place in Krakow, Poland, in 2008 [1], and since then a couple of special issues with extended papers presented at the workshops were published [2–4].

Crossing Multiple Scales of Biomedicine

The papers presented in this Special Section deals with different scales of biology and biomedicine.

Wienbrandt *et al.* in their paper *1,000x Faster than PLINK: Genome-Wide Epistasis Detection with Logistic Regression Using Combined FPGA and GPU Accelerators* deal with challenges at the level of the genes.

Vizza *et al.* in their paper *On blood viscosity and its correlation with biological parameters* study how cells, such as Hematocrits and Erythrocytes influence human blood viscosity.

Katsushima *et al.* in their paper *Development of Octree-Based High-Quality Mesh Generation Method for Biomedical Simulation* present a simulation of the biomechanics of the tibia bone.

Reis *et al.* in their paper *Combining Data Mining Techniques to Enhance Cardiac Arrhythmia Detection* present how to use ECG signals, Electrocardiograms, taken non-invasively from patient to infer the electrical behavior of the heart.

Chillarón *et al.* in their paper *CT medical imaging reconstruction using direct algebraic methods with few projections* study how to reconstruct images of the human body from x-rays.

Finally, Varella *et al.* in their paper *A Stochastic Model to Simulate the Spread of Leprosy in Juiz de Fora* present a new model to describe the spread and dynamics of the Hansen's disease within a particular population of a Brazilian city.

Therefore, the selected papers presented in this Special Section deal with diverse spatial and time scales of life, from genes to population dynamics, passing through cells, organs and the human body.

Computational Models

Although the papers presented in this Special Section use computational modeling to address different challenges, the reader can find a great variety of types of models.

Empirical models are used in the works of Vizza *et al.* and Reis *et al.* in order to capture the relation between blood cells and viscosity, and the relation between ECG signals and cardiac pathologies, respectively.

On the other hand, mechanistic models are used by Katsushima *et al.*, Chillarón *et al.*, and Varella *et al.*. Katsushima *et al.* present simulations of the structural biomechanics of the tibia bone using partial differential equations. These simulations can be used to help the planning of High Tibial Osteotomy (HTO), a surgical procedure that aims to disperse excessive load on the bone due to bow leg deformation. Chillarón *et al.* also use deterministic models, in the form of algebraic equations, in order to reconstruct CT-images from X-rays.

Finally, mechanistic but stochastic models are proposed by Varella *et al.* to describe the evolution of the Hansen's disease within a particular city. Stochastic models were needed to capture the limited number of infected persons, as described by the public health database of the aforementioned city.

Therefore, the selected papers presented in this Special Section use different types of models, from empirical to mechanistic, from deterministic to stochastic ones.

New Algorithms

All the papers presented in this Special Section propose new algorithms or new implementations to address different challenges of biomedicine and bioinformatics.

Wienbrandt *et al.* developed a new parallel algorithm to compute a logistic regression. The algorithm is based on a modified version of the classical Newton's method specially tailored to FPGAs and GPUs.

Katsushima *et al.* developed an octree-based high-quality mesh generator to support biomedical simulations, such as those based on the Finite Element Method.

Reis *et al.* combine different data mining techniques, such as clustering, feature selection, oversampling strategies and automatic classification algorithms to create efficient classification models to identify cardiac diseases based on ECG signals.

Chillarón *et al.* present two new direct algebraic algorithms for CT-imaging reconstruction, one based on Sparse QR (SPQR), and another based on singular values decomposition (SVD).

Finally, Varella *et al.* implement the Gillespie algorithm to solve the new proposed stochastic and compartmental model of epidemiology.

High Performance Computing

Modern challenges of life sciences involve a large amount of data and complex models, posing considerable requirements for computing power and storage resources. Not surprisingly, high performance computing is often used to deal with these complexities.

The numerical methods developed and presented by Chillarón *et al.* for CT-imaging reconstruction were run on a cluster composed of 128 cores.

The simulations of the structural biomechanics of the tibia bone performed by Chillarón *et al.* were executed on a shared-memory system composed of a total of 512 cores.

Finally, the new parallel algorithms to assess gene-gene interactions developed by Wienbrandt *et al.* were executed on a modern and heterogeneous high-performance platform that combines CPUs, FPGAs, and GPUs. The combinations of FPGAs and GPUs resulted in a speedup of more than one thousand when compared to a classical parallel algorithm that was executed on 32 cores. These new computer architectures enabled the reduction of execution times from months to a couple of hours.

Conclusion

Modern biology and medicine are on a regular basis challenging computer science in many aspects: (i) by demanding new concepts and models or the integration of them; (ii) by promoting the development of new algorithms, methods and techniques to solve problems that arise from life sciences or biomedical engineering; (iii) and even by requesting novel computer architectures that can cope with the ever-increasing tasks of processing large amount of data and simulation of complex computational models. The selection of papers of the 11th Workshop on Biomedical and Bioinformatics Challenges for Computer Science discusses all these issues and suggest novel directions and approaches to tackle them.

References

1. Cannataro, M., Romberg, M., Sundnes, J., Weber dos Santos, R.: Bioinformatics challenges to computer science. In: Bubak, M., van Albada, G.D., Dongarra, J., Sloot, P.M.A. (eds.) ICCS 2008. LNCS, vol. 5103. Springer, Heidelberg (2008)
2. Cannataro, M., Romberg, M., Sundnes, J., Weber dos Santos, R.: Special section: Biomedical and bioinformatics challenges to computer science. Future Gener. Comput. Syst. **26**(3), 421–423 (2010). https://doi.org/10.1016/j.future.2009.https://doi.org/10.00
3. Cannataro, M., Weber dos Santos, R., Sundnes, J., Veltri, P.: Advanced computing solutions for health care and medicine. J. Comput. Sci. **3**(5), 250–253 (2012). https://doi.org/10.1016/j.jocs.2012.07.002
4. Agapito, G., Cannataro, M., Castelli, M., Dondi, R., Zoppis, I.: Editorial of the special issue of the 10th workshop on biomedical and bioinformatics challenges for computer science BBC 2017. Computers **7**(1), (2018). https://doi.org/10.3390/computers7010017

Combining Data Mining Techniques to Enhance Cardiac Arrhythmia Detection

Christian Gomes[1(✉)], Alan Cardoso[1], Thiago Silveira[2], Diego Dias[1],
Elisa Tuler[1], Renato Ferreira[3], and Leonardo Rocha[1]

[1] Universidade Federal de São João del-Rei, São João del-Rei, Brazil
{christian,alanc,diegodias,etuler,lcrocha}@ufsj.edu.br
[2] Tsinghua University, Beijing, China
zhuangzq16@mails.tsinghua.edu.cn
[3] Universidade Federal de Minas Gerais, Belo Horizonte, Brazil
renato@dcc.ufmg.br

Abstract. Detection of Cardiac Arrhythmia (CA) is performed using the clinical analysis of the electrocardiogram (ECG) of a patient to prevent cardiovascular diseases. Machine Learning Algorithms have been presented as promising tools in aid of CA diagnoses, with emphasis on those related to automatic classification. However, these algorithms suffer from two traditional problems related to classification: (1) excessive number of numerical attributes generated from the decomposition of an ECG; and (2) the number of patients diagnosed with CAs is much lower than those classified as "normal" leading to very unbalanced datasets. In this paper, we combine in a coordinate way several data mining techniques, such as clustering, feature selection, oversampling strategies and automatic classification algorithms to create more efficient classification models to identify the disease. In our evaluations, using a traditional dataset provided by the UCI, we were able to improve significantly the effectiveness of Random Forest classification algorithm achieving an accuracy of over 88%, a value higher than the best already reported in the literature.

Keywords: Cardiac Arrhythmia Detection · Automatic classification
Machine learning

1 Introduction

Cardiovascular diseases are still one of the leading causes of death in the world. One of the major abnormalities associated with these diseases is Cardiac Arrhythmia (CA), which can be detected by the specialist through a clinical analysis of the patient's electrocardiogram (ECG). Early detection of CA can aid in treatment, significantly reducing the risk of patient's life. However,

---

This work was partially supported by CNPq, CAPES, Fapemig, INWEB and MAsWeb.

Y. Shi et al. (Eds.): ICCS 2018, LNCS 10861, pp. 321–333, 2018.
https://doi.org/10.1007/978-3-319-93701-4_24

their discovery in the onset of the first clues is a difficult task since they involve evaluating the several variables present in an ECG.

In order to assist specialists in the diagnosis of cardiovascular diseases, a recent and promising line of research has been adopted, that corresponds the use of methods based on Machine Learning in the detection of Arrhythmia [18]. From a previous set of ECG examinations duly and manually classified by medi cal specialists, a learning technique is applied resulting in a classification model. So, this model can be used by the physician in the evaluation/classification of new patient's ECG. However, the process of creating effective classification models is challenged by two main issues: (1) each ECG consists of a very large set of attributes; and (2) datasets related to ECG assessments are very unbalanced, since the number of patients diagnosed with CA is much smaller than those classified as "normal". While the first question is related to computational cost [24], the second one limits the learning process of the smaller classes [7], which are precisely the targets of the models in this scenario.

The questions mentioned above can be solved employing some data preprocessing strategies, on which the most common ones are Feature Selection techniques (FS) [2,17,24] and oversampling approaches [4,7,8]. FS consists of techniques that can measure the importance of each attribute in the construction of the classification model for a given base, returning those attributes more relevant, aiming to solve the first question previously presented. Oversampling consists of replicate/combine samples related to smaller classes, generating new samples to compose the dataset with a smaller unbalance, increasing the amount of information associated with the smaller classes, thus relating to the second question. Regarding the techniques of oversampling, although we find significant results in the literature related to efficacy in collections of data whose unbalance is even more pronounced, as in the CA detection scenario, the excessive generation of artificial samples can generate distortions which compromise the effectiveness of the classification model generated. From this finding, recently in [26], the authors present a technique called Classification using lOcal clustering with OverSampling (COG-OS), which consists, briefly, in the application of some clustering technique in classes splitting them into other smaller classes and then applying oversampling techniques considering the new distribution of generated classes. The authors' premise is that fewer artificial samples need to be generated, thereby reducing distortions in the generation of the classification model.

Therefore, in this paper, we proposed the combination, in a coordinated way, of several data mining and data preprocessing techniques aiming at the generation of more efficient (lower computational cost) and efficient classification models for the CA detection problem. More specifically, different classification algorithms were evaluated, combined with FS, clustering and oversampling techniques. To evaluate our proposal, we consider one of the collections of data related to the CA more referenced in the literature [16]. In our experimental analysis, we demonstrate that these strategies are complementary and, when appropriately combined, can result in a more efficient classification model. For example, while a classification model constructed based on the algorithm Random Forest using the collection of data without any preprocessing results in an accuracy of 63%, the model generated after the application of an FS technique achieve an accuracy of 72%. Moreover, the model generated after the application of clustering and oversampling strategies results in an accuracy of approximately 82%. Finally, the model that combines all these strategies achieves an accuracy of over 88%, a value higher than the best already reported in the literature.

Roadmap. The remaining of paper is organized as follows. Section 2 presents some related works. The work methodology is presented in Sect. 3. In Sect. 4 the results of the experimental evaluation are discussed and the conclusions and future work are presented in Sect. 5.

2   Related Work

In recent years, several investigations related to the classification of CA have been performed, with the primary objective being the detection of arrhythmia using classification models. Felipe et al. [19] developed some CA classification models using eight different sets of variables related to the onset of CA in people. These variables were collected in real time from patients hospitalized at the Hospital Center of Porto, such as vital signs, laboratory results, among others. These are well-controlled data (not public) and related only to hospitalized patients, resulting in a relatively balanced collection, different from the collection considered in our study. Using the SVM classification algorithm, the authors achieved a 95% of accuracy.

Samad et al. [22] compared three classifiers based on their accuracy for the detection of the cardiac arrhythmia in the UCI dataset [16], the same one used in our paper. The classification algorithms k-NN, Naive Bayes and Decision Tree were used. The most relevant result was obtained by k-NN, reaching an accuracy of 66.96%. Moreover, this paper provides a detailed explanation of the conversion of an ECG into numerical values for using in machine learning tasks. Shivajirao et al. [14] created an intelligent system based on artificial neural networks to determine the classification of the presence or absence of CA, also using the UCI dataset. The authors used the Multilayer Perceptron model with the Backpropagation technique, reaching an accuracy of 86.67%, the best-reported result in the literature for this collection. As we will show in Sect. 4, combining Feature Selection (FS), clustering and oversampling techniques, we achieve superior results (i.e., 88.8% accuracy).

An FS technique is used to designate a score for each attribute to assess its importance in the learning task. In [28], the authors compare the performance of some metrics, such as Information Gain (IG), χ^2, Odds Ratio (OR) and Correlation Coefficient (CC). In our paper, we consider *CfsSubsetEval* [12]. Concerning clustering techniques, there are several proposals in the literature [5]. These are from straightforward and usable techniques in several scenarios, such as K-Means [10], to some more elaborate and accurate for certain contexts, such as subspace clustering [1] and partitioning clustering [5]. In our paper, we consider only the K-Means, but other strategies can be evaluated in the future, as detailed in Sect. 5.

Finally, regarding oversampling techniques, Wu et al. [26] have developed an approach to address the problem of class unbalance that overcomes the other ones to predict rare classes. The method, titled Classification using lOcal clustering (COG), applies a clustering technique to divide the major classes into smaller subclasses. A significant improvement in the efficacy of supervised classification algorithms was observed in the results. A variation of the COG was also shown by applying the local clustering method together with an oversampling technique. This change was called Classification using lOcal clustering with OverSampling (COG-OS), being one of the techniques adopted in our approach.

3   Methodology

In this section, we present the methodology adopted to combine different data mining techniques, such as feature selection, oversampling and automatic supervised classification algorithms to improve the process of automatically identifying Cardiac Arrhythmia. First, we present the techniques considered by each step of our methodology. Next, we present the different strategies followed by the methodology to combine the techniques, which corresponds to evaluating the classification algorithms applying different data preprocessing approaches (i.e., feature selection, clustering and oversampling). Finally, we present the metrics adopted to evaluate each one of the combinations.

3.1   Data Mining Techniques

In this section, we present the algorithms considered in our paper. For all of them, we adopt the implementations provided by Weka [25], an educational software package, which has several data mining algorithms implemented, including classification, feature selection, oversampling and clustering. Next, we detail these algorithms.

Feature Selection. For this paper we considered the *CfsSubsetEval* [12], which calculates, for each subset of attributes, the correlation of each of them with the dataset classes. In this case, it is desirable the subset that has a high correlation with a class in which each attribute of the subset has a low correlation with each other. Thus, it adds/removes attributes until it reaches a subset that has only the most relevant attributes to predict the desired class.

Clustering. The clustering algorithm chosen was the K-Means [9], which consists of partitioning the objects into K groups where each object belongs to a group. The algorithm creates K centers in the object space and continues to change the location of its centers until the number of objects in each center from one iteration to another does not modify. The WCSS value is determined by Eq. 1, where S_k is the set of observations in the kth cluster and $\bar{x}_{kj}$ is the jth variable of the cluster center for the kth cluster.

To determine the number K, the *Within-Cluster Sum of Squares* (WCSS) value must be analyzed, which is the sum done within each cluster between its objects and its center squared. It is necessary to observe the WCSS metric ranging the value of K (i.e., from 1 to 10).

$$\text{WCSS} = \sum_{k=1}^{K} \sum_{i \in S_k} \sum_{j=1}^{p} (x_{ij} - \bar{x}_{kj})^2 \tag{1}$$

Oversampling. The oversampling algorithm chosen was SMOTE [7], which consists of creating synthetic instances of rare classes. For each class that we want to create objects to make the dataset balanced, SMOTE uses k neighbor objects to combine and generate a synthetic instance that is close to those k objects.

Classification Algorithms. In our analysis, supervised classification algorithms considered state-of-the-art have been chosen, which address the problem through different approaches. They are:

- **Naive Bayes:** probabilistic algorithm that calculates the probability of a given new instance belonging to each of the available classes in a collection. It is one of the most widely used learning machine methods that combine efficiency and simplicity [23,24].
- **Random Forest:** it is an algorithm based on the bagging approach, in which a set of m decision trees are trained considering different training set samples. Then, each of these trees is considered in the algorithm final decision to classify a new instance [6,20].
  Support Vector Machine (SVM): this algorithm maps the training set as points in a vector space, trying to define the boundaries of the space that separates each one of the classes. New instances are mapped into this vector space and assigned to the class according to their location. It is considered the most effective algorithm in the literature [15].
- **k-Nearest Neighbor (k-NN):** this is a lazy nonlinear classification algorithm in which the classification consists of assigning a new instance for the majority class related to k closest instances in a vector space [21,27].

For all algorithms, weka default parameters were used.

3.2 Combination Approaches

In Fig. 1 we illustrate the combination approaches proposed to be evaluated in this work. Below we detail each of them. For all them, it is important to provide a missing values treatment in the dataset, which consists of removing/replacing all missing values from the dataset attributes.

1. **Classification Without Preprocessing:** in this step, classification using the selected classification algorithms is done without any preprocessing;
2. **FS Classification:** in this step the goal is to apply the FS technique to remove attributes that do not add value to the classification, using only a subset of relevant attributes. After that, it is generated new classification models that are evaluated the quality achieved in comparison to the results without applying any preprocessing techniques;
3. **Classification with the COG-OS Technique:** for this step of the methodology, considering all the attributes, the COG-OS method mentioned in Sect. 2 is applied to the dataset. This method consists in applying the clustering algorithm in the majority class ("normal" ECG), redistributing its instances into k smaller classes. Then, the oversampling technique is applied in the minority classes (arrhythmia ECG) to achieve a class balance in the dataset. Finally, the classification algorithms are applied again for a new round of results evaluation;
4. **Classification with FS and COG-OS Combined:** in this step the two techniques (FS and COG-OS) are applied together. The FS technique is applied to select the most relevant subset of attributes, and the COG-OS is applied to the resulting dataset. With the fully-treated dataset, all classification algorithms are executed, and the results are compared once again.

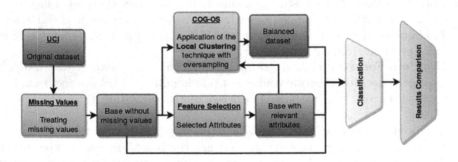

Fig. 1. Data Mining combination approaches for identifying Cardiac Arrhythmia.

3.3 Evaluation Metrics

In our evaluations, we consider two metrics: Accuracy and Macro F-Measure (Macro-F1). Accuracy measures the global effectiveness regarding all decisions made by the classifier (that is, the inverse of error rate). Macro-F1 on the other hand, measures the classification effectiveness regarding each class independently. It corresponds the mean of the F-Measure values obtained for each possible class in the dataset.

To define the F-Measure metric, we need to understand two main concepts:

- Precision: number of items classified as positive is positive;
- Recall: number of relevant items selected.

The F-Measure (**F1**) is the harmonic mean between precision and recall:

$$F1 = 2 * \frac{\text{precision} * \text{recal}}{\text{precision} + \text{recall}} \qquad (2)$$

We propose to use the K-fold Cross Validation Strategy [3] with K = 10, which consists of splitting the total dataset into ten mutually exclusive subsets of the same size, and from that, a subset is used for testing, and the remaining nine subsets are used for the model training. This process is repeated ten times, alternating the test subset. In the end, the reported results in the next section refer to the average of the Accuracies and Macro-F1 obtained in the ten repetitions.

4   Experimental Evaluation

In this section, we present the experimental results regarding each combination approach described in the previous section, considering a real dataset related to CA detection.

4.1   Experimental Setup

Dataset. The dataset used was created by Guvenir et al. [11] and made available by UCI[1], being characterized by a transformation of ECGs into numerical attributes for the application of data mining algorithms. This base has missing values and ambiguous samples that need to be addressed for a more efficient use of classification algorithms. The original dataset has 280 attributes. The base has 16 classes; class 01 refers to normal ECGs; class 13 refers to ECGs that do not have a classification, and the others refer to ECGs with the presence of some arrhythmia. Three of these classes were disregarded because they did not have any associated instances. Figure 2 depicts the distribution of occurrences between classes. As we can see, this is a highly unbalanced dataset, so some classes of arrhythmia have two instances, while the normal ECG class has 245 instances.

Treatment of Missing Values. In a previous dataset analysis, we identified that one of the attributes (V14) had 390 missing values instances, which was removed from our analyses. For the remainder of the attributes, the missing values treatment was performed using the packet *mice* provided in conjunction with the R language. This packet has a function for replacing incomplete values by synthetic plausible ones according to all columns, losing no data consistency. At all stages of our experimental evaluation, we used the data collection resulting from this treatment.

---

[1] https://archive.ics.uci.edu/ml/datasets/Arrhythmia.

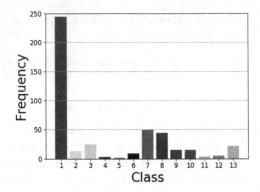

Fig. 2. Distributing instances between classes in the UCI dataset.

4.2 Analysis of Results

The first result was reached through the evaluation of classification algorithms without the use of preprocessing techniques. Table 1 presents the accuracy and Macro-F1 values achieved by each evaluated by the classification algorithm. As we can see, the algorithm Random Forest was the one that obtained the best value for Macro-F1 and accuracy in the unbalanced dataset, where Naive Bayes achieved an approximate value. The value achieved can be considerate low since in the unbalanced dataset most of the classes of arrhythmia are not classified correctly. That happens because the created models were trained on an unbalanced dataset, bias to normal class, which is the most frequent.

Table 1. Results achieved in the unbalanced original dataset classification.

Algorithm	Accuracy	Macro-F1
Naive Bayes	62.0%	61.0%
Random Forest	69.9%	62.3%
k-NN	58.1%	45.6%
SVM Linear	54.2%	38.1%

The second result set refers to the combination of the classification algorithms and the FS technique, and the results are presented in Table 2. The FS algorithm was able to decrease the number of attributes from the 280 ones presenting in the original dataset, selecting only the 23 most relevant attributes. We can observe that almost all classifiers, except SVM, get improvements in the classification quality considering only the 23 most relevant attributes. It is important to note that, in addition to the improving classification models, using FS techniques can also improve efficiency in the process to create classification models.

The third step consists in the use of the COG technique as a preprocessing step for classification. In the arrhythmia dataset, only the "normal" class has

Table 2. Results achieved in classification after applying the FS technique.

Algorithm	Accuracy	Macro-F1
Naive Bayes	68.4%	66.2%
Random Forest	75.7%	72.7%
k-NN	63.9%	55.2%
SVM Linear	54.2%	38.1%

numerous objects, so the clustering is applied to divide it into smaller subclasses. The best value for WCSS was achieved for four clusters ($K = 4$). The last step is the application of the oversampling technique to obtain a more relevant balancing between the classes. The new class distribution achieved using this strategy is presented in Fig. 3.

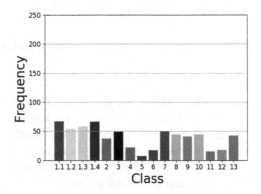

Fig. 3. Resulting dataset after applying the COG-OS approach.

Based on the resulting dataset from the application of the COG-OS, the classification was performed to compare with the previous results. Table 3 shows the classification results considering all the 280 original attributes of the dataset. We can observe that almost all classifiers, except SVM, get expressive improvements in the classification quality considering the COG-OS technique, demonstrating that efforts to mitigate unbalance between classes are able to improve considerably the quality of classification models for detecting Cardiac Arrhythmia.

Table 3. Results achieved in the classification after applying the COG-OS approach.

Algorithm	Accuracy	Macro-F1
Naive Bayes	70.1%	70.0%
Random Forest	82.6%	81.9%
k-NN	65.6%	62.5%
SVM Linear	30.4%	32.2%

The fourth and final step consisted in combining the local clustering, oversampling and FS techniques as a preprocessing step, that is, COG-OS was applied to the dataset with only 23 attributes. The new class distribution achieved using this strategy is presented in Fig. 4.

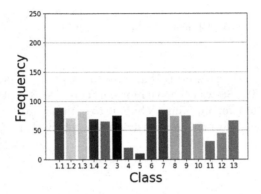

Fig. 4. Resulting dataset after applying the COG-OS approach considering the 23 most relevant attributes.

Table 4 presents the results achieved by the classification algorithms considering the dataset distribution shown in Fig. 4. As we can see, the combination of techniques was very effective, further increasing the quality of the classifications. While the accuracy achieved by Naive Bayes in original dataset was 61%, for the preprocessed dataset the accuracy was 71.3%. A more expressive result is achieved by Random Forest algorithm, 62.3% of accuracy in original dataset and 88.8% in preprocessed dataset.

Table 4. Results obtained in the classification after applying the COG-OS approach considering the 23 most relevant attributes.

Algorithm	Accuracy	Macro-F1
Naive Bayes	71.9%	71.3%
Random Forest	88.9%	88.8%
k-NN	71.9%	70.6%
SVM Linear	29.4%	32.2%

4.3   Discussion

The FS techniques and the COG-OS method showed an excellent strategy in improving the effectiveness of the chosen classifiers, except the SVM. The algorithm that obtained the best results was the Random Forest, reaching a Macro-F1 of nearly 90%, making it the best result already reported in the literature for the CA detection. Table 5 shows how it was possible to gradually increase the value of accuracy and, mainly, of the Macro-F1 value of the Random Forest algorithm. That is an important scientific breakthrough showing that the combination of different data mining strategies can significantly aid in the construction of classification models that assist medical specialists in the detection of CA.

Table 5. Random Forest result achieved at each step of our methodology.

Preprocessing techniques	Macro-F1
None	62.3%
FS	72.7%
COG-OS	81.9%
FS + COG-OS	**88.8%**

5   Conclusion and Future Works

In this paper, it has been demonstrated that the unbalance between classes of a dataset related to CA detection negatively influences the process of creating supervised classification models using traditional classifiers algorithms. The large majority of arrhythmia diagnoses are classified as normal, and cases of disease incidence are rare. In this way, several preprocessing strategies combined with automatic classification techniques were evaluated to create a more efficient classification models to assist specialists in the detection of the disease. More specifically, the results of this paper demonstrated that classification models constructed from a more relevant attributes subset, selected through an FS technique, tend to improve the quality of the models generated significantly. In an analogous and complementary way, it has been demonstrated that an oversampling strategy, combined with a clustering approach (COG-OS), also results in effective models. Besides, combining both strategies was achieved an even better classification model, surpassing the best result reported in the literature. More specifically, using the classification Random Forest algorithm, considering only the 23 most relevant attributes and applying the COG-OS oversampling strategy, a Macro-F1 of 88.8% was obtained, surpassing the 86% achieved in [14] for the same UCI dataset.

As a future work, the goal is to improve the prediction of arrhythmia further using other classification algorithms, clustering and oversampling [13] in the steps proposed in this work. Also, a detailed analysis of the 23 selected attributes can facilitate the arrhythmia detection in an ECG, finding out the relationships of these attributes in their respective ECG.

References

1. Agrawal, R., Gehrke, J., Gunopulos, D., Raghavan, P.: Automatic subspace clustering of high dimensional data for data mining applications. In: Proceedings of SIGMOD 1998, pp. 94–105. ACM, New York (1998)
2. Alelyani, S., Tang, J., Liu, H.: Feature selection for clustering: a review. Data Clust.: Algorithms Appl. **29**, 110–121 (2013)
3. Arlot, S., Celisse, A., et al.: A survey of cross-validation procedures for model selection. Stat. Surv. **4**, 40–79 (2010)
4. Barua, S., Islam, M.M., Yao, X., Murase, K.: Mwmote-majority weighted minority oversampling technique for imbalanced data set learning. IEEE Trans. Knowl. Data Eng. **26**(2), 405–425 (2014)
5. Berkhin, P.: A survey of clustering data mining techniques. In: Kogan, J., Nicholas, C., Teboulle, M. (eds.) Grouping Multidimensional Data, pp. 25–71. Springer, Heidelberg (2006). https://doi.org/10.1007/3-540-28349-8_2
6. Breiman, L.: Random forests. Mach. Learn. **45**(1), 5–32 (2001)
7. Chawla, N.V., Bowyer, K.W., Hall, L.O., Kegelmeyer, W.P.: Smote: synthetic minority over-sampling technique. J. Artif. Int. Res. **16**(1), 321–357 (2002). http://dl.acm.org/citation.cfm?id=1622407.1622416
8. Douzas, G., Bacao, F.: Self-organizing map oversampling (SOMO) for imbalanced data set learning. Expert Syst. Appl. **82**, 40–52 (2017)
9. Faber, V.: Clustering and the continuous K-Means algorithm. Los Alamos Sci. **22**, 138–144 (1994)
10. Farivar, R., Rebolledo, D., Chan, E., Campbell, R.H.: A parallel implementation of K-Means clustering on GPUs. In: Proceedings of PDPTA 2008, USA, pp. 340–345, July 2008
11. Guvenir, H.A., Acar, B., Demiroz, G., Cekin, A.: A supervised machine learning algorithm for arrhythmia analysis. In: Computers in Cardiology, pp. 433–436. IEEE (1997)
12. Hall, M.A.: Correlation-based feature subset selection for machine learning. Ph.D. thesis, University of Waikato, Hamilton, New Zealand (1998)
13. Han, H., Wang, W.-Y., Mao, B.-H.: Borderline-SMOTE: a new over-sampling method in imbalanced data sets learning. In: Huang, D.-S., Zhang, X.-P., Huang, G.-B. (eds.) ICIC 2005. LNCS, vol. 3644, pp. 878–887. Springer, Heidelberg (2005). https://doi.org/10.1007/11538059_91
14. Jadhav, S.M., Nalbalwar, S., Ghatol, A.: Artificial neural network based cardiac arrhythmia classification using ECG signal data. In: 2010 International Conference on Electronics and Information Engineering (ICEIE), vol. 1, p. V1-228. IEEE (2010)
15. Joachims, T.: Making large-scale support vector machine learning practical. In: Advances in Kernel Methods, pp. 169–184. MIT Press, Cambridge (1999). http://dl.acm.org/citation.cfm?id=299094.299104
16. Lichman, M.: UCI machine learning repository (2013). https://archive.ics.uci.edu/ml/datasets/Arrhythmia
17. Liu, H., Motoda, H.: Feature Selection for Knowledge Discovery and Data Mining, vol. 454. Springer, Heidelberg (2012). https://doi.org/10.1007/978-1-4615-5689-3
18. Özçift, A.: Random forests ensemble classifier trained with data resampling strategy to improve cardiac arrhythmia diagnosis. Comput. Biol. Med. **41**(5), 265–271 (2011)

19. Portela, F., Santos, M.F., Silva, Á., Rua, F., Abelha, A., Machado, J.: Preventing patient cardiac arrhythmias by using data mining techniques. In: 2014 IEEE Conference on Biomedical Engineering and Sciences (IECBES), pp. 165–170. IEEE (2014)

20. Salles, T., Gonçalves, M., Rodrigues, V., Rocha, L.: Broof: exploiting out-of-bag errors, boosting and random forests for effective automated classification. In: Proceedings of the 38th International ACM SIGIR Conference on Research and Development in Information Retrieval, SIGIR 2015, pp. 353–362. ACM, New York (2015). http://doi.acm.org/10.1145/2766462.2767747

21. Salles, T., Rocha, L., Mourão, F., Gonçalves, M., Viegas, F., Meira, W.: A two-stage machine learning approach for temporally-robust text classification. Inf. Syst. **69**(Suppl. C), 40–58 (2017). https://doi.org/10.1016/j.is.2017.04.004, http://www.sciencedirect.com/science/article/pii/S0306437917301801

22. Samad, S., Khan, S.A., Haq, A., Riaz, A.: Classification of arrhythmia. Int. J. Electr. Energy **2**(1), 57–61 (2014)

23. Viegas, F., Gonçalves, M.A., Martins, W., Rocha, L.: Parallel lazy semi-naive Bayes strategies for effective and efficient document classification. In: Proceedings of the 24th ACM International on Conference on Information and Knowledge Management, CIKM 2015, pp. 1071–1080. ACM, New York (2015). http://doi.acm.org/10.1145/2806416.2806565

24. Viegas, F., Rocha, L., Gonçalves, M., Mourão, F., Sá, G., Salles, T., Andrade, G., Sandin, I.: A genetic programming approach for feature selection in highly dimensional skewed data. Neurocomputing (2017). https://doi.org/10.1016/j.neucom.2017.08.050, http://www.sciencedirect.com/science/article/pii/S0925231217314716

25. Weka: Weka - interface classifier (2016). http://weka.sourceforge.net/doc.dev/weka/classifiers/Classifier.html. Accessed 02 Dec 2017

26. Wu, J., Xiong, H., Wu, P., Chen, J.: Local decomposition for rare class analysis. In: Proceedings of the 13th ACM SIGKDD International Conference on Knowledge Discovery and Data Mining, pp. 814–823. ACM (2007)

27. Zhang, M.L., Zhou, Z.H.: A k-nearest neighbor based algorithm for multi-label classification. In: 2005 IEEE International Conference on Granular Computing, pp. 718–721. IEEE (2005)

28. Zheng, Z., Wu, X., Srihari, R.: Feature selection for text categorization on imbalanced data. ACM SIGKDD Explor. Newsl. **6**, 80–89 (2004)

CT Medical Imaging Reconstruction Using Direct Algebraic Methods with Few Projections

Mónica Chillarón[1]([⊠]) [iD], Vicente Vidal[1] [iD], Gumersindo Verdú[2] [iD],
and Josep Arnal[3] [iD]

[1] Departamento de Sistemas Informáticos y Computación (DSIC),
Universitat Politècnica de València, Valencia, Spain
mnichipr@inf.upv.es, vvidal@dsic.upv.es
[2] Instituto de Seguridad Industrial, Radiofísica y Medioambiental (ISIRYM),
Universitat Politècnica de València, Valencia, Spain
gverdu@iqn.upv.es
[3] Departamento de Ciencia de la Computación e Inteligencia Artificial (DCCIA),
Universidad de Alicante, Alicante, Spain
arnal@ua.es

Abstract. In the field of CT medical image reconstruction, there are two approaches you can take to reconstruct the images: the analytical methods, or the algebraic methods, which can be divided into iterative or direct.

Although analytical methods are the most used for their low computational cost and good reconstruction quality, they do not allow reducing the number of views and thus the radiation absorbed by the patient.

In this paper, we present two direct algebraic approaches for CT reconstruction: performing the Sparse QR (SPQR) factorization of the system matrix or carrying out a singular values decomposition (SVD). We compare the results obtained in terms of image quality and computational time cost and analyze the memory requirements for each case.

Keywords: CT · Medical imaging · Reconstruction
Matrix factorization · QR · SVD · Few projections

1 Introduction and Background

In medical imaging, CT (computerized tomography) [18,24] is one of the most significant tests to perform a diagnosis. Thus, it is imperative to develop reconstruction algorithms that provide high-quality images as well as high computational time efficiency. Having fast algorithms is essential to have short-term results of a CT scan available to medical professionals.

The reconstruction methods can be divided into two types, depending on their nature. On the one hand, we find the analytical algorithms. They are based on the application of the Fourier transform on the data obtained from the

© Springer International Publishing AG, part of Springer Nature 2018
Y. Shi et al. (Eds.): ICCS 2018, LNCS 10861, pp. 334–346, 2018.
https://doi.org/10.1007/978-3-319-93701-4_25

projection of x-rays on an object, called sinogram. On the other hand, we have the algebraic methods, whether direct or iterative, which make a mathematical approach to the reconstruction problem.

In clinical practice, the most widespread methods are the analytical ones. This is due to the reduced computational time cost involved, which can be vital in emergency diagnoses. However, algebraic methods allow reducing the number of projections, and therefore the radiation to which we expose the patient.

Since hardware elements evolve at high speed and also their cost decreases constantly, using algebraic approaches to solve these problems has become possible. Although they involve a high computational cost, nowadays it is less significant thanks to parallel computing (multiple CPUs, GPU computing, clusters, etc.) [12]. If we add the enhancement of main memory in new equipments, it is now feasible to implement these methods for large size problems as is our case.

The aim of this work is to achieve the resolution of the CT image reconstruction problem by means of two direct algebraic factorization methods. The first one, called multifrontal sparse QR (SPQR), and implemented in the library 'SuiteSparseQR, a multifrontal multithreaded sparse QR factorization package' [7], allows solving the equation of reconstruction problem more directly than the iterative methods we studied previously (such as ART [1], SART [2] or LSQR [22]). This is achieved by calculating the QR factorization of the sparse system matrix A to simulate its pseudo-inverse.

The second method is the singular values decomposition (SVD) of the system matrix A, which is carried out through the parallel implementation of the method included in the SLEPc [14] to simulate, as in the previous case, the pseudo-inverse of the matrix.

Since these methods are not widespread in clinical practice, the validity of both approaches will be tested. We will check the quality of the reconstructed image by working with a smaller number of projections in order to reduce the radiation induced to the patient, and analyze the computation resources necessary to perform the decomposition of the matrix A. This point will be vital for the use of these algebraic methods, since the matrices are large and can suppose a high demand for RAM.

2 Materials and Methods

2.1 CT Image Reconstruction Problem

In a CT reconstruction problem, using an algebraic approach we need to solve the equations system defined by the Eq. (1), where A (2) represents the system matrix, a sparse matrix that measures the weight of the influence that each ray has on the reconstructed image [5, 16]. The size of the matrix A is M × N, where M is the number of traced rays, and N is the size in pixels of the image to be reconstructed. The vector g (3) represents the sinogram or projections vector and u (4) the solution image. Both the system matrix and the sinogram vector have been calculated with Joseph's Forward Projection method [17].

$$A * u = g \tag{1}$$

$$A = a_{i,j} \in \mathbb{R}^{MxN} \tag{2}$$

$$g = [g_1, g_2, \ldots, g_M]^T \in \mathbb{R}^M \tag{3}$$

$$u = [u_1, u_2, \ldots, u_N]^T \in \mathbb{R}^N \tag{4}$$

The projections have been generated for a phantom corresponding to the mathematical representation of the human head developed by the Forbild Phantom Group [10], using the medical image program CONRAD [20] to generate the phantom reference images. This is defined by simple geometric objects that represent head elements with different densities such as bone, tissue, gray matter, etc.

When reconstructing a CT image for a given physical configuration of the scanner, the associated matrix A is always the same. What changes is the sinogram (g), that represents the studied object. If it were possible to calculate a pseudo-inverse A^+ of the matrix A [13,19], the image could be obtained more directly without solving a large equations system. This means the computational cost would be reduced to a matrix-vector product. But this idea not viable since the explicit calculation of the matrix A^+ is prohibitive for a high resolution and many views in the reconstruction. The reason why is that A^+ can be dense and contaminated due to rounding errors.

Another possibility is to calculate implicitly an approximation of the range and use it to simulate the pseudo-inverse. The two methods that we have considered to solve this approach are explained in the following subsections

2.2 Projections Reduction

In the acquisition of the data, the important factors that influence the reconstruction of the image are two, the number of samples per projection (detectors) and the number of projections. A reduced number of any of these two variables will cause the formation of artifacts in the reconstructed image when using analytical methods: rings by the Gibbs phenomenon, streaks and lines and Moiré pattern, amongst others [3].

To prevent such problems, we should take into account the Nyquist theorem [21], which says the sampling rate must be greater than twice the bandwidth of the sampled signal. If we undersample we get the aforementioned artifacts. The classical analytical procedure of image reconstruction (filtered back projection FBP) is a fast process but it needs a complete set of projections to obtain high-quality images. The exact number depends on the physical characteristics of the scanner, but typically the minimum number of projections to take is 360.

If the aim is to reduce the dose absorbed by the patient, we should take the fewer number of projections possible, so we should use different methods that can work with less projections, such as iterative or direct methods. In our previous works [6,8,9,23] it has been shown that it is possible to use few views, between 30 and 90, while using iterative methods to reconstruct high-quality images. However, the computational cost is high for these algorithms.

In order to take an approach that is not iterative, we propose the SPQR and SVD methods. In this way, the computational cost of the reconstruction could be reduced, so we could reconstruct images faster in real time. We will check if its application to the CT image reconstruction allows reducing the number of views in equal measure than the methods that we used previously.

2.3 Sparse Pivoting QR Factorization

The first new direct method used to solve the equations system is the Multi-frontal Sparse QR (SPQR) [7]. It is a method that performs a QR [13] factorization of a large sparse matrix in a sequence of dense frontal matrices. In this way, we can form the pseudo-inverse of the system matrix.

The software used to perform this factorization is implemented in the SuiteSparseQR library, which uses BLAS and LAPACK, and Intel Threading Building Block to exploit parallelism. This allows processing heavy matrices, which is key in the reconstruction of CT images since A is large for high resolutions.

The QR factorization of the matrix A comprises its decomposition as a product of two matrices (5), where Q is orthogonal and R is upper triangular.

$$A = QR \tag{5}$$

$$AP = QR \tag{6}$$

However, when A is considerably large and sparse, this decomposition can be prohibitive since Q could not be sparse. Here, the decomposition with pivoting (6) must be used. The resolution would be:

- If $m \geq n$ we have to solve (7). That means a matrix-vector product of Q^T by the vector g, the resolution of an upper triangular system with the matrix R and a rearrangement with permutation matrix P.
- If $m < n$ we have to solve (8), that is reordering the vector g, then solve a triangular system and finally make the product of the resulting vector by the matrix Q.

$$u = P * (R^{-1}(Q^T * g)) \tag{7}$$

$$u = Q * (R^{-T}(P^T * g)) \tag{8}$$

2.4 Q-Less Sparse QR Factorization

If we want to spare memory, we can compute the QR decomposition without saving the Q explicitly. In this way we would have to transform the equations to obtain the solution vector u, which would be as follows:

- If $m \geq n$ we have to solve the system $Q * R * g = u$. By multiplying both sides of equation by A^T, we obtain: $(Q * R)^T * Q * R * g = A^T * u$. Since Q is orthogonal, performing the matrix operations to solve for u, we reach the solution Eq. (9).

$$u = R^{-1} * R^{-T}(A^T * g) \tag{9}$$

– If $m < n$ we would work with the QR decomposition of A^T. By a similar reasoning to the previous case, the solution of the system would correspond to calculate (10), which requires the same operations but in a different order.

$$u = A^T * R^{-1} * (R^{-T} * g) \tag{10}$$

Note that the Q matrix is not used for the calculation of u and therefore this process requires fewer memory resources.

2.5   Singular Values Decomposition

The singular values decomposition performs the k-order factorization (11) [4,11,19]. In this factorization, $U \in \mathbb{R}^{Mxk}$ and $V \in \mathbb{R}^{kxN}$ are matrices whose columns are orthogonal and are called left-hand and right-hand singular vectors, where k is the number of singular values computed. $\Sigma \in \mathbb{R}^{kxk}$ is a diagonal matrix that has the singular values in decreasing order. The software we use to apply this algorithm is the SVD solver included in the eigenvalues calculation parallel library SLEPc. Applying this factorization, we can transform the equations system into the product (13), taking the pseudo-inverse as (12)

$$A = U\Sigma V^T \tag{11}$$

$$A^+ = V\Sigma^{-1}U^T \tag{12}$$

$$u = A^+ g \tag{13}$$

Note that the storage cost of this decomposition is of order (M * k) + (k * N) elements. When k grows, the memory resources necessary to carry out the decomposition increase. Once the decomposition of the system matrix has been calculated, resolving the problem consists on the product of two dense matrices by a vector,thus the computational cost is of order ((M + N) * k) flops.

Since we can do this decomposition 'offline', it can be calculated and stored and it can be ready when a CT image has to be reconstructed. Therefore, we can replace an iterative method with a much simpler and less computationally expensive matrix multiplication problem. In our application, we are interested in the case where $k = N$, in which case we have enough information to reconstruct the image with great precision.

3   Results and Discussion

In order to check the validity of both methods, we used a cluster belonging to the Universitat Politécnica de Valéncia to perform the factorizations. The cluster consists of 4 RX500S7 servers with four Intel Xeon E5-4620 8 core processors (32 cores per node) and 256 GB DDR3 RAM (8 GB/core ratio) per node.

3.1   Memory Requirements

For the SPQR factorization, we have used the code developed for Matlab. We reserve a single node in the cluster. In this node which we can consume a maximum of 250 GB of main memory. With these resources, it has been possible to compute the QR decomposition corresponding to the system matrix for an image resolution from 32×32 up to 256×256 with 30 views. Besides, using the Q-less QR factorization we have been able to use up to 90 views with the 256×256 resolution, which is important as we will explain in Sect. 3.3. For the analogous case of resolution 512×512, considering 30 views, the matrix has not been factorized due to lack of RAM.

Regarding the SVD decomposition, all cases of 30 views have been computed, except for the 512×512 resolution case. For this process, we have reserved up to 32 processors with 15 GB of RAM per processor, which means up to 240 GB. Despite making use of distributed memory, we can not reserve over one server node at a time, similar to the sequential case. In addition, the SVD process requires more memory than the SPQR, so with the same characteristics, it has not been possible to reach the case of 90 views for the 256×256 resolution.

3.2   Computational Time Efficiency

Although the factorization time is not critical in this scenario, it is convenient to have an approximation of the computation time required for each matrix size. In addition, we want to make a comparison between the two proposed methods. Table 1 shows the results in seconds of computational time cost to carry out the decompositions.

Table 1. Factorization time

Resolution	Factorization method	
	SPQR	SVD
	Time (secs.)	
32×32 30 views	1.2	9
64×64 30 views	5.6	50
128×128 30 views	151	1900
256×256 30 views	3270	12000
256×256 60 views	12336	-
256×256 90 views	16400	-

As we can observe, the factorization time in both cases is satisfactory. Although it may seem that with the SVD decomposition it is too high, we must bear in mind that this calculation will be performed only once and 'offline', which makes it a non-critical calculation. As shown in the table, the computational time efficiency of the SPQR method is greater, which can be justified because this calculation is performed in a single node, and therefore does not require distributed memory as does the SVD. Since SVD implements the communication through MPI messages, it generates an extra time associated with interprocess communications, which makes the temporary efficiency much worse.

3.3 Image Quality

Regarding the quality of the images obtained by performing a reconstruction with both methods, the results are reflected in Table 2. To measure the quality, we used the PSNR metric [15], which shows the noise level of a image compared to a reference image, and also the SSIM metric [15], which indicates the structural similarity between both images, based on the shape of the elements it contains.

Table 2. Reconstructed images quality

Resolution	SPQR		SVD	
	PSNR	SSIM	PSNR	SSIM
32 × 32 30 views	228	1	238	1
64 × 64 30 views	213	1	224	1
128 × 128 30 views	255	1	221	1
256 × 256 30 views	38	0.03	30	0.29
256 × 256 60 views	32.5	0.03	-	-
256 × 256 90 views	150	1	-	-

In both cases we can see that up to the resolution 128 × 128, the results of the reconstruction are very good, getting a PSNR greater than 200 in all cases (considering that a PSNR close to 100 can be considered a perfect reconstruction to the perception of the eye human). In addition, all cases obtain an SSIM equal to 1, which means that structurally the image is accurate. The result of the reconstruction by SVD with resolution 128 × 128 can be seen in Fig. 1b. If we compare it with the reference image for the same resolution (Fig. 1a), we observe that they are almost identical and the reconstruction does not have artifacts or noise. However, for the 256 × 256 resolution and 30 views, the result is of very poor quality for both methods, being the PSNR of both around 30. The reconstructed images, that we can see in Fig. 2 are very noisy and although we get to perceive elements of the phantom, it is not seen clearly enough.

The poor quality of this reconstruction is due to the fact that for this particular case (256 × 256 and 30 views), the sub-matrix extracted from the system matrix is rank deficient, as shown in Table 3. Therefore, the equations system is ill-conditioned, which leads to missing information necessary for the reconstruction. We observe that in the rest of the cases with smaller resolutions the sub-matrix retains the full rank, so we have no problem when reconstructing using these algebraic methods.

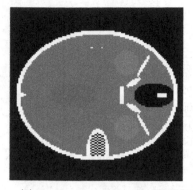
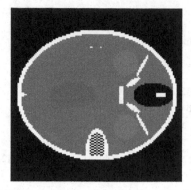

(a) Reference image 128x128   (b) SVD reconstruction 128x128 30 views

Fig. 1. Reference and reconstructed 128×128 images

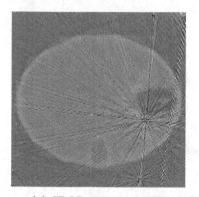
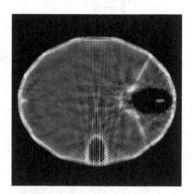

(a) SPQR reconstruction   (b) SVD reconstruction

Fig. 2. Reconstructions 256×256 30 views

If we analyze the rank of the sub-matrices when we work with the largest resolutions, we can observe that we need to use more views in order to reach full rank. For 256×256 pixels reconstructions, we should use at least 90 views, which means we still reduce the number of views with respect to traditional methods. For 512×512 resolution, we need over 180 views, approximately 260, to keep the full rank on the sub-matrix. That means that even if we could still reduce a few views compared with other methods, the resulting reconstruction problem would have larger dimensions than we can compute.

We have verified that the rank of the matrix used has direct effect on the reconstructed image. In Fig. 3 we present the singular vector of a full-rank sub-matrix. As we can see, we have a few dominant values, approximately 1000, and then they start to decrease. When we reach the 8000th value, it looks like they stabilize and are close to 0. If we look to the detail window on the plot, we can observe that the last 1600 values, even if they are close to 0, vary between 0.03 and 0.01, which is still a significant number in this case. Therefore, this means we can not disregard any singular value.

Table 3. Rank study

Resolution	Number of views				
	180	120	90	60	30
	N° of columns/rank				
32 × 32	1024/1024	1024/1024	1024/1024	1024/1024	1024/1024
64 × 64	4096/4096	4096/4096	4096/4096	4096/4096	4096/4096
128 × 128	16384/16384	16384/16384	16384/16384	16384/16384	16384/16384
256 × 256	65536/65536	65536/65536	65536/65536	65536/49380	65536/30093
512 × 512	262144/149551	262144/100842	262144/76000	262144/50963	262144/25608

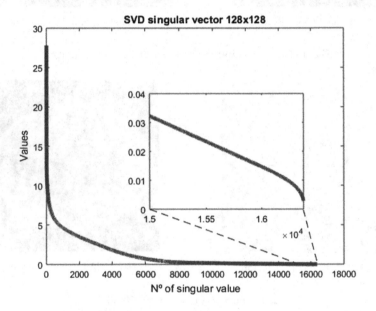

Fig. 3. Singular vector 128 × 128

In Fig. 4 we can observe how varying the number of singular values, we get very different reconstructions. As explained before, we do not reach optimal quality until we use the full rank. We observe the same effect with SPQR if we vary the number of views.

In Fig. 5 we see the difference between taking 30, 60, and 90 for the 256 × 256 resolution matrix. With 60 projections we increase the rank, so the image is slightly better than with 30, as can be observed in the edges of the phantom. But it is not until we reach 90 views that the image is of good quality.

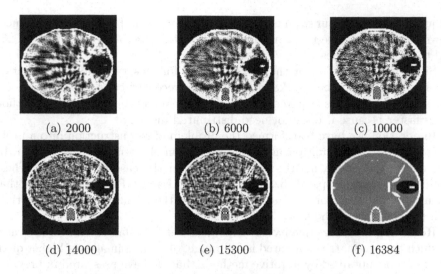

(a) 2000   (b) 6000   (c) 10000

(d) 14000   (e) 15300   (f) 16384

Fig. 4. Reconstruction varying singular values 128×128

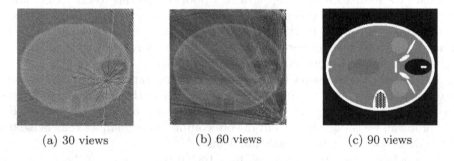

(a) 30 views   (b) 60 views   (c) 90 views

Fig. 5. SPQR 256×256 reconstructions

4   Conclusion

In the present work, we have proposed two sparse matrix factorization methods that can be used for CT image reconstruction. In this way, we simulate the use of the pseudoinverse of the system matrix to transform the initial problem solution into a simpler one. The main challenge of these methods is the high consumption of memory to perform the computation, so we had to make use of a high performance computing cluster.

In this cluster it has been possible to calculate the SPQR factorization up to a resolution of 256×256 pixels and 90 views. In addition, the SVD up to 256×256 and 30 views. Although with the SVD method we have not obtained satisfactory results for higher resolutions, through SPQR we have managed to perform a reconstruction of very high quality with 90 views and full rank. This translates into a very significant difference in the doses of x-rays to which patients should be exposed. Taking into account that the direct methods are based on the

Nyquist theorem, for our scanner configuration, they would use significantly more views. However, we are reducing them to 90 in the case of resolution 256×256 and to 30 in lower ones.

Since the calculation of the factorizations for this type of reconstruction problem can be done before the moment of the reconstruction itself and stored, the computation times required for all cases are acceptable, the SPQR method being faster because it does not need distributed memory.

In addition, we have transformed the problem of reconstruction into a problem of matrix-vector multiplication and resolution of a triangular system in the case of the QR and a matrix-vector product in the case of the SVD. These resolutions are highly parallelizable in both CPU and GPU, which means that having the matrices stored we could accomplish the reconstructions faster than with the previous methods.

Regarding the image quality obtained, it is very satisfactory for all the cases in which the sub-matrix generated is full range, obtaining images of higher quality than those obtained by iterative methods that we have presented in previous works, such as LSQR [4]. However, the moment the sub-matrix becomes rank deficient, the reconstructed image is of very poor quality due to the lack of information. In future works, it is proposed to introduce regularization algorithms to increase the range of sub-matrices, or a filter in the image that, as with the LSQR method, are combined in a certain way that allows a more quality approximation to be made despite having an ill-conditioned problem.

In addition, it is necessary to analyze the implementation of the factorizations in order to improve the use of RAM memory, and in this way to factorize the corresponding matrix for 512×512 pixels, which is the objective resolution. For this problem, we set out to use out-of-core computing techniques that make use of the disk to avoid main memory problems.

In conclusion, we can say that we have tested the viability of the SPQR and SVD direct algebraic methods applied to CT image reconstruction. In spite of not having reconstructed images of very high quality, we have verified that with these methods it is possible to reduce the dose of radiation to a great extent if the matrix can be computed.

At this point of our work we have two resolution options: For rapid reconstructions with low dose and medium resolutions, factoring methods. For high-resolution reconstructions and slightly worse quality, the LSQR + FISTA + STF iterative method, which is slower but guarantees good results.

Acknowledgements. This research has been supported by "Universitat Politècnica de València" and the Spanish Ministry of Economy and Competitiveness under Grant TIN2015-66972-C5-4-R co-financed by FEDER funds, as well as "Generalitat Valenciana" under PROMETEOII/2014/008 project and ACIF/2017/075 predoctoral grant.

References

1. Andersen, A.H.: Algebraic reconstruction in CT from limited views. IEEE Trans. Med. Imag. **8**(1), 50–55 (1989)
2. Andersen, A.H., Kak, A.C.: Simultaneous algebraic reconstruction technique (SART): a superior implementation of the ART algorithm. Ultrason. Imag. **6**(1), 81–94 (1984)
3. Barrett, J.F., Keat, N.: Artifacts in CT: recognition and avoidance. RadioGraphics **24**(6), 1679–1691 (2004). https://doi.org/10.1148/rg.246045065. PMID: 15537976
4. Berry, M.W., Pulatova, S.A., Stewart, G.: Algorithm 844: computing sparse reduced-rank approximations to sparse matrices. ACM Trans. Math. Softw. (TOMS) **31**(2), 252–269 (2005)
5. Brooks, R., Chiro, G.D.: Principles of computer assisted tomography (CAT) in radiographic and radioisotopic imaging. Phys. Med. Biol. **21**(5), 689–732 (1976)
6. Chillarón, M., Vidal, V., Segrelles, D., Blanquer, I., Verdú, G.: Combining grid computing and Docker containers for the study and parametrization of CT image reconstruction methods. Proc. Comput. Sci. **108**, 1195–1204 (2017). https://doi.org/10.1016/j.procs.2017.05.065. International Conference on Computational Science, ICCS 2017, Zurich, Switzerland, 12–14 June 2017. http://www.sciencedirect.com/science/article/pii/S1877050917306038
7. Davis, T.A.: Algorithm 915, SuitesparseQR: multifrontal multithreaded rank-revealing sparse QR factorization. ACM Trans. Math. Softw. **38**(1), 8:1–8:22 (2011). https://doi.org/10.1145/2049662.2049670
8. Flores, L., Vidal, V., Verdú, G.: Iterative reconstruction from few-view projections. Proc. Comput. Sci. **51**, 703–712 (2015)
9. Flores, L.A., Vidal, V., Mayo, P., Rodenas, F., Verdú, G.: Parallel CT image reconstruction based on GPUs. Radiat. Phys. Chem. **95**, 247–250 (2014)
10. FORBILD Phantom Group. http://www.imp.uni-erlangen.de/forbild/english/results/index.htm. Accessed Sept 2016
11. Golub, G., Kahan, W.: Calculating the singular values and pseudo-inverse of a matrix. J. Soc. Ind. Appl. Math. Ser. B Numer. Anal. **2**, 205–224 (1965). https://doi.org/10.1137/0702016
12. Golub, G.H., Ortega, J.M.: Scientific Computing: An Introduction with Parallel Computing. Academic Press, Cambridge (1993). http://www.amazon.com/Scientific-Computing-An-Introduction-Parallel/dp/0122892534
13. Golub, G.H., Van Loan, C.F.: Matrix Computations. Johns Hopkins University Press, Baltimore (2013)
14. Hernandez, V., Roman, J.E., Vidal, V.: SLEPc: a scalable and flexible toolkit for the solution of eigenvalue problems. ACM Trans. Math. Softw. (TOMS) **31**(3), 351–362 (2005)
15. Hore, A., Ziou, D.: Image quality metrics: PSNR vs. SSIM. In: 2010 20th International Conference on Pattern Recognition, pp. 2366–2369. IEEE, August 2010. https://doi.org/10.1109/ICPR.2010.579, http://ieeexplore.ieee.org/document/5596999/
16. Hounsfield, G.: Computerized transverse axial scanning (tomography): part I. Description of system. Br. J. Radiol. **46**, 1016–1022 (1973)
17. Joseph, P.: An improved algorithm for reprojecting rays through pixel images. IEEE Trans. Med. Imag. **1**(3), 192–196 (1982)
18. Kak, A.C., Slaney, M.: Principles of computerized tomographic imaging. Soc. Ind. Appl. Math. (2001). https://doi.org/10.1137/1.9780898719277

19. Katsikis, V.N., Pappas, D., Petralias, A.: An improved method for the computation of the Moore-Penrose inverse matrix. Appl. Math. Comput. **217**(23), 9828–9834 (2011)
20. Maier, A., Hofmann, H.G., Berger, M., Fischer, P., Schwemmer, C., Wu, H., Müller, K., Hornegger, J., Choi, J.H., Riess, C., et al.: CONRAD—A software framework for cone-beam imaging in radiology. Med. Phys. **40**(11) (2013)
21. Nyquist, H.: Certain topics in telegraph transmission theory. Trans. Am. Inst. Electr. Eng. **47**(2), 617–644 (1928)
22. Paige, C.C., Saunders, M.A.: LSQR: an algorithm for sparse linear equations and sparse least squares. ACM Trans. Math. Softw. **8**(1), 43–71 (1982)
23. Parcero, E., Flores, L., Sánchez, M., Vidal, V., Verdú, G.: Impact of view reduction in CT on radiation dose for patients. Radiat. Phys. Chem. **137**, 173–175 (2016)
24. Radon, J.: On the determination of functions from their integral values along certain manifolds. IEEE Trans. Med. Imag. **5**(4), 170–176 (1986)

On Blood Viscosity and Its Correlation
with Biological Parameters

Patrizia Vizza[1], Giuseppe Tradigo[2], Marianna Parrilla[1], Pietro Hiram Guzzi[1],
Agostino Gnasso[1], and Pierangelo Veltri[1(✉)]

[1] Magna Graecia University, 88100 Catanzaro, Italy
{vizzap,hguzzi,gnasso,veltri}@unicz.it, marianna.parrilla@gmail.com
[2] University of Calabria, 87036 Rende, Italy
g.tradigo@dimes.unical.it

Abstract. In recent years interest in blood viscosity has increased significantly in different biomedical areas. Blood viscosity, a measure of the
resistance of blood flow, related to its thickness and stickiness, is one
of the main biophysical properties of blood. Many factors affect blood
viscosity, both in physiological and in pathological conditions.
  The aim of this study is to estimate blood viscosity by using the
regression equation of viscosity which is based on hematocrit and total
plasma proteins. It can be used to perform several observations regards
the main factors which can influence blood viscosity. The main contribution regards the correlation between viscosity values and other important
biological parameters such as cholesterol. This correlation has been supported by performing statistical tests and it suggest that the viscosity
could be the main risk factor in cardiovascular diseases. Moreover, it is
the only biological measure being correlated with the other cardiovascular risk factors. Results obtained are compliant with values obtained by
using the standard viscosity measurement through a viscometer.

Keywords: Blood viscosity · Regression equation
Cardiovascular disease

1 Introduction

Blood is a fluid in a viscous, red and opaque state, which is distributed in the
body through the circulatory system. It is a non-Newtonian fluid composed by
many cells with different features and tasks [1]. Blood consists of two parts: (i)
a liquid part, called plasma, and (ii) a corpuscular part, formed by cells or fragments of cells. The former represents the 54% of the circulating blood mass and it
is composed by 90% of water and 10% of inorganic substances, including critical
proteins which are fundamental for sustaining health and life. The latter contains the so-called figurative elements including red blood cells (or erythrocytes),
white blood cells (or leukocytes) and platelets (thrombocytes), as well as some
liquid particles. The platelets are cellular fragments essential for coagulation and

© Springer International Publishing AG, part of Springer Nature 2018
Y. Shi et al. (Eds.): ICCS 2018, LNCS 10861, pp. 347–353, 2018.
https://doi.org/10.1007/978-3-319-93701-4_26

in case of vessel lesion. The white blood cells defense the organism in the case of pathogens aggression. The red blood cells represent the 40–50% of total volume so that this high concentration influences the behavior of the blood more than the other blood cells. Moreover, they are particularly important in the study of rheology and blood flow dynamics, but also in hemorrhage which is specifically aimed at the study of blood and viscosity. The volumetric concentration of erythrocytes in the blood is commonly known as hematocrit which is responsible for blood viscosity. In fact, it indicates the relationship between the liquid and the corpuscular parts of the blood expressed as a percentage or a fraction. Blood viscosity represents the inherent resistance of blood to flow and it is obtained by summing the viscosity of hematocrit with the viscosity of plasma [2]. In the International System, the unit of measure used for viscosity is "Pascal-Second" ($Pa \cdot s$). In general, the viscosity coefficient of a fluid indicates the ratio between the force applied per unit area and the relative velocity gradient, called shear rate and expressed in s^{-1}. The force per unit area that produces the shear rate is called shear stress and is expressed in $dyne/cm^2$. The relationship between shear stress and shear rate corresponds to viscosity. The main factor that influences blood viscosity is hematocrit. Red blood cells, in contrast to white blood cells and platelets, strongly influence viscosity by: (i) volumetric fraction: its increase leads to an increase in viscosity; (ii) rouleaux development: the aggregation of red blood cells increases viscosity; (iii) cells warping: a decrease in the deformability of red blood cells leads to an increase in viscosity [3].

The relationship between volumetric fraction and dynamic viscosity is a nonlinear relationship. Viscosity grows rapidly for hematocrit values above 45%.

1.1 Related Work

Recently, the interest in studying blood viscosity has significantly increased because it has been shown that alterations in its normal values can be related to diseases [4–7]. Viscosity can be determined by (i) a reduction in plasma, (ii) a change in the volume or number of red blood cells, (iii) an increase in blood coagulation capacity [8–10]. These events cause greater resistance in blood flow, forcing the heart to increase its contraction force. Conventional methods for measuring blood viscosity include the use of different types of viscometers [11]. They cannot perform a direct measure but they estimate an experimental parameter related to viscosity in a known manner. Moreover, they present disadvantages in terms of avoiding to deal with heavy and expensive equipment, large sample consumption, and long measurement time. To overcome these limitations, new measurement techniques have been proposed in literature [12]. A quick method to measure blood viscosity, which allows to verify the accuracy of predictions and to biologically determine the variability of the blood viscosity and its components, is based on a regression equation [13–16]. These study are based on this regression equation and they are been conducted on demographic and laboratory variables in normal subjects to identify deviations related to cardiovascular diseases.

2 Methods

The dataset used for the experiment contains features from 4320 subjects who enrolled at the Laboratory of Clinical Biochemistry in University of Magna Graecia. The subjects attended the laboratory from January to December 2016 for routine blood tests. Every subject, between 12 and 100 years old, gave written informed consent to this research conforming to the ethical guidelines of the Declaration of Helsinki, as reflected in a priori approval by the Ethical Committee of Mater Domini Hospital in Catanzaro, Italy. Moreover, features of the dataset have been acquired by taking into consideration all clinical variabilities (e.g. temperature, use of anticoagulants). For each subject, the number of clinical record has been linked to an identifier associated with personal data (e.g. date of birth, sex) and the examination date. In this study, the regression equation has been applied to the dependent variable (blood viscosity) and has been correlated to the independent variables (e.g. proteins, hematocrit). The goal is to estimate a functional relationship between the dependent variable and the independent variables. Blood viscosity have been calculated for different shear rates:

- Shear rate 208 s^{-1} with (x, y, z) = (0.12, 0.17, 2.07);
- Shear rate 104 s^{-1} with (x, y, z) = (0.12, 0.19, 2.13);
- Shear rate 52 s^{-1} with (x, y, z) = (0.14, 0.22, 2.6);
- Shear rate 5.2 s^{-1} with (x, y, z) = (0.46, 0.62, 14.25).

The Eq. 1 used for the Whole Blood Viscosity (WBV) is [17]:

$$WBV = x \cdot HCT + y \cdot TP - z \tag{1}$$

WBV is the dependent variable and HCT (hematocrit, expressed in percentage) and TP (plasma protein concentration, expressed in g/dL) are the independent clinical variables. Blood viscosity is dependent because it depends on the value of proteins and hematocrit and also on the variables x, y, z, (related to the thickness of vessels) defined according to the shear rate. Moreover, viscosity also depends on the cutting speed because blood is a non-Newtonian fluid, due to the presence of cells, so the viscosity is closely linked to the speed gradient.

All the variables have been measured in the laboratories of Clinical Biochemistry and Clinical Pathology of the Mater Domini Polyclinic. Possible correlations between blood viscosity and hematocrit, proteins and shear rate have been evaluated for two groups of subjects divided by sex and age. The viscosity correlation with other important variables has been analyzed to validate the correct functioning of the organism. In particular, the serum calcium has been examined and the analysis has been performed based on five different serum calcium values:

- Group 1: serum calcium ≤ 9 mg/dl;
- Group 2: serum calcium > 9 mg/dl and ≤ 9.3 mg/dl;
- Group 3: serum calcium > 9.3 mg/dl and ≤ 9.6 mg/dl;
- Group 4: serum calcium > 9.6 mg/dl and ≤ 9.8 mg/dl;
- Group 5: serum calcium > 9.8 mg/dl.

Statistical analysis has been performed by using T-test with a significance level of 0.05. The association between viscosity and calcium has been studied by using a Pearson correlation. Multiple regression analysis has been used to evaluate the correlation adjusted for age between viscosity and hematocrit, proteins and share rate. The analysis of variance ANOVA has been performed to compare the multivariate means among the 5 calcium groups.

3 Results

The overall population consists of 4320 subjects (1922 women and 2398 men) in an age range between 12 and 100 years. In order to manage the data, apply the regression equation and perform the analysis, IBM Watson (www.ibm.com/watson-analytics) has been used. Watson Analytics is a cloud-based software for data analysis and visualization containing modules able to find useful information through statistical and machine learning models. Table 1 reports mean and standard deviation values for age, hematocrit, proteins and serum calcium variables. Women are younger than men and show significantly lower hematocrit. Proteins and serum calcium are similar for women and men.

Table 1. Values of clinical and biochemical parameters.

Variable	Total	Women	Men
Number	4320	1922	2398
Age (years)	56.25 ± 18.27	53.61 ± 19.08	58.36 ± 17.31
Hematocrit (%)	40.77 ± 5.17	39.03 ± 4.36	42.16 ± 5.36
Proteins (g/dL)	7.03 ± 0.66	7.06 ± 0.64	7.01 ± 0.68
Serum calcium (mg/dL)	9.37 ± 0.49	9.39 ± 0.47	9.35 ± 0.51

The higher values of hematocrit in men is due to the higher testosterone levels. In fact, erythrocytes are produced in the bone marrow thanks to the stimulating action of erythropoietin (EPO), an action that depends on several factors, including the concentration of testosterone. Table 2 reports the viscosity calculated by using the regression equation and related to the different values of shear-rate. Viscosity increases significantly and progressively as the shear-rate decreases, both for men and women. Since blood is a non-Newtonian fluid, viscosity increases as the cutting speed decreases.

Pearson correlation and T-test have been performed to evaluate correlations between viscosity and age, hematocrit, proteins and calcium. These results are reported in Table 3. A weak correlation between age and viscosity can be observed and the T-test produces a result statistically significant with a p-value < 0.001, confirming the weak relation. A significant and direct association between hematocrit and viscosity can be highlighted. This is a direct relationship, hence viscosity increases with the increase of the hematocrit. By considering the gender, higher values are reported in male, which can be explained

Table 2. Blood viscosity values divided according to shear-rate values.

Variable	Shear rate 208	Shear rate 104	Shear rate 52	Shear rate 5.2
Total viscosity	5.74 ± 0.66	5.82 ± 0.67	6.68 ± 0.78	14.28 ± 2.54
Viscosity for women	5.53 ± 0.57	5.62 ± 0.58	6.45 ± 0.67	13.50 ± 2.17
Viscosity for men	5.90 ± 0.69	5.99 ± 0.71	6.87 ± 0.83	14.90 ± 2.68

Table 3. Pearson coefficient for viscosity and age, hematocrit and proteins and related p-values.

Correlation	Women	Men	Total	p-value
Age-viscosity	-0.10	-0.27	-0.15	<0.001
Hematocrit-viscosity	0.98	0.99	0.99	<0.001
Proteins-viscosity	0.46	0.50	0.49	<0.001
Calcium-viscosity	0.42	0.45	0.44	<0.001

by viscosity being closely related to hematocrit. This strong correlation is statistically confirmed by a p-value < 0.001. Moreover, Pearson correlation confirms a moderate correlation between proteins and viscosity and between calcium and viscosity, both with a p-value < 0.001. Blood viscosity increases with the increase of proteins but the presence of proteins is not highly influential, therefore it does not influence the viscosity trend excessively. The correlation between the serum calcium and blood viscosity has been calculated to evaluate the presence of a major cardiovascular risk. The dataset has been subdivided into five groups with respect to the different calcium values (as reported in the previous section). Table 4 reports the dimension of each group in term of number of subjects, mean and standard deviation (SD) value for blood viscosity.

Table 4. Blood viscosity for each group representative of specific calcium level.

	Group 1	Group 2	Group 3	Group 4	Group 5	Total
Dimension	888	783	969	534	692	3870
Mean	5.26	5.66	5.82	5.95	6	5.71
SD	0.73	0.61	0.56	0.53	0.6	0.67

We note a mean blood viscosity that increases with the increase of the calcium values in each group. ANOVA statistical test has been applied between the mean values and the result indicates a significant difference between the means of the groups. Then, the Turkey-Kramer Post-Hoc test has been applied because the groups present a different dimension and also in this case a significant difference between means is reported, especially between the first and the last group (Groups 1 and 5). Hematocrit values have been evaluated related to the five groups for their strong correlation with blood viscosity. Results are reported in Table 5.

Table 5. Hematocrit for each group representative of specific calcium level.

	Group 1	Group 2	Group 3	Group 4	Group 5	Total
Dimension	888	783	969	534	692	3870
Mean	37.63	40.29	41.36	42.2	42.41	40.59
SD	5.73	4.69	4.54	4.29	4.78	5.24

4 Discussion

The main result of this study is that blood viscosity can be calculated by applying the regression equation proposed in this paper. The obtained results have been compared to the ones obtained through a viscometer instrument and they show a statistical similarity (test results and details not reported), thus confirming the validity of the method. The second result is the evaluation and the identification of the main factors influencing blood viscosity. Hematocrit, plasma viscosity and erythrocyte deformability are factors independently associated with viscosity at high and low shear rates. Viscosity increases significantly as shear rate decreases and hematocrit increases. Viscosity at high shear rates is strongly influenced by erythrocyte deformability, while at low shear rates it is influenced by the aggregation of red blood cells. These characteristics also depend on the properties of erythrocytes and plasma. Another result is the evidence of a significant correlation between serum calcium and viscosity. Results also show that blood viscosity is one of the risk factors for cardiovascular diseases and it is a biological measure correlated with all the other major cardiovascular risk factors, such as an excessive calcium increase. In particular, a higher blood viscosity is due to an increase in calcium level. By acting on the amount of calcium, this reflects on cholesterol and, consequently, on viscosity.

5 Conclusion

We presented a cross-sectional study to evaluate the application of the regression equation on blood viscosity measurements. The increase in blood viscosity as a pathogenetic factor for the development of cardiovascular complications and diseases has been evaluated with respect to specific clinical and biological parameters. A significant correlation between serum calcium and viscosity, both in men and women, is reported. This suggests that the calcium supplement in the population should be done with caution. The result of this study is in line with results obtained by using the standard blood viscosity measurement, validating the proposed method and verifying the effect of calcium on cardiovascular risks.

Acknowledgments. This contribution has been funded by grant POR FESR/FSE Regione Calabria for SISTABENE and PIHGIS projects.

References

1. Rogers, K.: Blood: Physiology and Circulation (The Human Body). The Rosen Publishing Group, New York (2010)
2. Goslinga, H.: Blood Viscosity and Shock: The Role of Hemodilution, Hemoconcentration and Defibrination. Springer, Heidelberg (1984). https://doi.org/10.1007/978-3-642-69260-4
3. Chien, S.: Determinants of blood viscosity and red cell deformability. Scand. J. Clin. Lab. Invest. **41**(1981), 712 (2009)
4. Chen, G., Zhao, L., Liu, Y., Liao, F., Han, D., Zhou, H.: Regulation of blood viscosity in disease prevention and treatment. Chin. Sci. Bull. **57**(16), 1946–1952 (2012)
5. Mazza, A., Fruci, B., Guzzi, P., D'Orrico, B., Malaguarnera, R., Veltri, P., Fava, A., Belfiore, A.: In PCOS patients the addition of low-dose spironolactone induces a more marked reduction of clinical and biochemical hyperandrogenism than metformin alone. Nutr. Metab. Cardiovasc. Dis. **24**(2), 132–139 (2014)
6. Palopoli, L., Rombo, S.E., Terracina, G., Tradigo, G., Veltri, P.: Improving protein secondary structure predictions by prediction fusion. Inf. Fus. **10**(3), 217–232 (2009)
7. Vizza, P., Curcio, A., Tradigo, G., Indolfi, C., Veltri, P.: A framework for the atrial fibrillation prediction in electrophysiological studies. Comput. Methods Program. Biomed. **120**(2), 65–76 (2015)
8. Sloop, G.D.: Blood Viscosity: Its Role in Cardiovascular Pathophysiology and Hematology. Nova Science Publishers, Inc., Hauppauge (2017)
9. De Napoli, I.E., Zanetti, E.M., Fragomeni, G., Audenino, A.L., Catapano, G.: Transport modeling of convection-enhanced hollow fiber membrane bioreactors for therapeutic applications. J. Membr. Sci. **471**, 347–361 (2014)
10. Caruso, M.V., Gramigna, V., Renzulli, A., Fragomeni, G.: Computational analysis of aortic hemodynamics during total and partial extra-corporeal membrane oxygenation and intra-aortic balloon pump support. Acta Bioeng. Biomech. **18**(3), 3–9 (2016)
11. Schramm, G.A.: A Practical Approach to Rheology and Rheometry, 2nd edn. Thermo Haake Rheology, Karlsruhe (1994)
12. Kim, B.J., Lee, S.Y., Jee, S., Atajanov, A., Yang, S.: Micro-viscometer for measuring shear-varying blood viscosity over a wide-ranging shear rate. Sensors (Basel.) **17**(6), E1442 (2017)
13. Stoeff, S., Jovtchev, S., Trifonova, N.: Whole blood viscosity assessment in arterial hypertension: a mathematical approach. Measurements **6**(9), 10 (2012)
14. Sahin, B., Yigitarslan, S.: The equation for prediction of blood viscosity from biochemical laboratory data. In: AIP Conference Proceedings, vol. 1653, no. 1 (2015)
15. Ruef, P., Gehm, J., Gehm, L., Felbinger, C., Pöschl, J., Kuss, N.: Determination of whole blood and plasma viscosity by means of flow curve analysis. Gen. Physiol. Biophys. **33**(3), 285–293 (2014)
16. Çinar, Y., Şenyol, A.M., Duman, K.: Blood viscosity and blood pressure: role of temperature and hyperglycemia. Am. J. Hypertens. **14**(5), 433–438 (2001)
17. Pop, G.A., Chang, Z.Y., Slager, C.J., Kooij, B.J., van Deel, E.D., Moraru, L., Quak, J., Meijer, G.C., Duncker, D.J.: Catheter-based impedance measurements in the right atrium for continuously monitoring hematocrit and estimating blood viscosity changes; an in vivo feasibility study in swine. Biosens. Bioelectron. **19**(12), 1685–1693 (2004)

Development of Octree-Based High-Quality Mesh Generation Method for Biomedical Simulation

Keisuke Katsushima[1]([⊠]), Kohei Fujita[1,2], Tsuyoshi Ichimura[1,2], Muneo Hori[1,2], and Lalith Maddegedara[1,2]

[1] Department of Civil Engineering, Earthquake Research Institute, The University of Tokyo, Bunkyo, Tokyo, Japan
{keisuke-k,fujita,ichimura,hori,lalith}@eri.u-tokyo.ac.jp
[2] RIKEN Center for Computational Science, Kobe, Japan

Abstract. This paper proposes a robust high-quality finite element mesh generation method which is capable of modeling problems with complex geometries and multiple materials and suitable for the use in biomedical simulation. The previous octree-based method can generate a high-quality mesh with complex geometries and multiple materials robustly allowing geometric approximation. In this study, a robust mesh optimization method is developed combining smoothing and topology optimization in order to correct geometries guaranteeing element quality. Through performance measurement using sphere mesh and application to HTO tibia mesh, the validity of the developed mesh optimization method is checked.

Keywords: Mesh generation · Multiple materials
Mesh optimization · Biomedical simulation

1 Introduction

Numerical simulations of biomedical bodies are expected to bring new knowledge to medicine and bioengineering field through discovering pathology developing mechanisms and optimizing surgical procedures. In particular, biomedical simulations based on finite element (FE) analysis which can analyze arbitrarily shaped field have been an active research topic recently. Thanks to the emergence of medical image diagnostic apparatus such as CT scans and MRI scans, it has become relatively easy to acquire detailed geometric information of biomedical bodies including inner structures without dissection. For the realization of reliable biomedical FE simulations, the mesh generation of biomedical bodies, which have complex geometries and multiple materials generally came to be a large current bottleneck and development of robust mesh generation method which is capable of complex geometries and multiple materials is required.

Though some meshing methods tailored for specific problems such as modeling of soils [1], realized robust mesh generation, they are not capable of complex

© Springer International Publishing AG, part of Springer Nature 2018
Y. Shi et al. (Eds.): ICCS 2018, LNCS 10861, pp. 354–367, 2018.
https://doi.org/10.1007/978-3-319-93701-4_27

geometries and multiple materials. As a prototype of a robust generation method of mesh consisting of complex geometries and multiple materials, octree-based fast mesh generation method which can generate global mesh by tetrahedralizing cubes locally using look up table [2, 3] has been developed. This method has high affinity with a mesh generation of biomedical bodies thanks to the ability to use brightness values of two dimensional images as an input. However, mesh generated by this method contains small geometrical approximation, which leads to the bad convergence and local concentration of feature amount, such as stress and strain in analysis results. In order to use this method in biomedical simulations which requires high accuracy, modification of geometrical approximation remains to be settled.

Geometrical modification needs to be performed guaranteeing that invalid elements (i.e., inside out elements and greatly distorted elements) will not be generated which are unacceptable in numerical analysis. Therefore, simple geometrical modification which smooths only boundary nodes is not satisfactory due to the generation of invalid elements especially near boundary surfaces. Frequently boundary nodes get locked because of the restriction of the element quality guarantee and then geometrical modification does not progress any more. To escape from this situation topology optimization (i.e., changing node-element connectivity) is useful and it has been reported that combination of smoothing and topology optimization leads to generation of high quality mesh.

In this study, with the objective of the use in biomedical FE simulations, a robust mesh optimization method to modify geometric approximation guaranteeing mesh quality is developed. Consequently, combining with the previous method, a robust generation method of high-quality mesh whose geometries follow input geometries with multiple materials is established. Mesh optimization method is developed combining smoothing and topology optimization as previous studies. While modifying surface geometries of mesh by smoothing, situation that boundary nodes get locked because of generated bad elements is avoided by topology optimization.

The rest of this paper is organized as follows. Previous mesh generation method and mesh optimization method developed in this study are explained in Sect. 2. Performance measurement of developed method is performed in Sect. 3. Developed method is applied to tibia model after HTO surgery in Sect. 4. Section 5 summarizes this paper.

2   Methodology

Mesh generation method developed in this study follows the procedures shown in Fig. 1. In the first half, initial mesh is generated using octree-based mesh generation method. By allowing small geometric approximation, boundary surfaces of multiple materials are explicitly resolved with robustness, mesh conformity is ensured and mesh quality is guaranteed. However, geometric approximation, which leads to bad convergence and local concentration of feature amount in analysis results is undesirable. In the second half, mesh optimization reduces the magnitude of geometric approximation. This mesh optimization method repeats smoothing and topology optimization and thus the geometric approximation is reduced according to the number of iterations. In the following subsections, we explain the overview of octree-based mesh generation method and mesh optimization method.

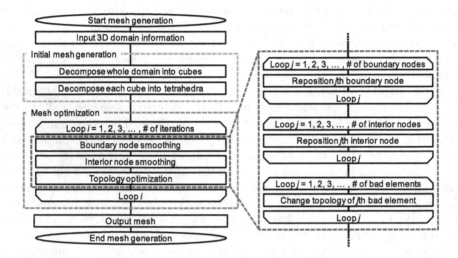

Fig. 1. Flowchart of developed mesh generation method

2.1   Overview of Octree-Based Mesh Generation Method

Using closed triangular patches discretizing surface information of each material region as an input, this method generates conforming mesh with linear tetrahedral elements robustly. The target domain is decomposed into multi-scale cubes using an orthogonal octree structure and then each cube is decomposed into tetrahedral elements. The former process is referred to as "cube generation" and the latter process as "cube decomposition" in this paper.

Cube Generation. Using closed triangular patches defining each material region as an input, the target domain (Fig. 2a) is recursively decomposed into multi-scale cubes by orthogonal octree structure (Fig. 2b). While fine cubes are allocated near material boundaries in order to resolve detailed geometries of boundary surfaces, coarse cubes are allocated inside material regions to generate mesh with minimum degree of freedoms. The size of boundary cubes, which have input material boundaries inside and are allocated near material boundaries is the smallest and referred to as "resolution" in this paper. Since large gap in size between neighboring cubes will directly lead to generation of bad quality tetrahedral elements and deterioration in analysis accuracy, size difference between neighboring cubes is restricted to be within one level. At the same

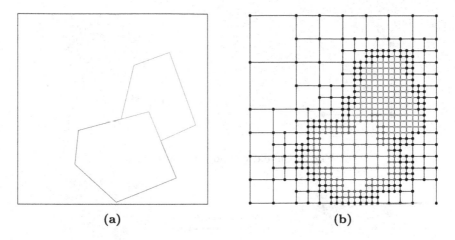

(a)   (b)

Fig. 2. Cube generation procedure in 2D

time, sizes of cubes inside material regions are restricted to be smaller than the size prescribed for each material to generate fine enough mesh required for numerical analysis. Each node is allocated material information which identifies the material region the node belongs to.

Cube Decomposition. Each cube is decomposed into tetrahedral elements referring to look up table using material information of nodes as an input (Fig. 3a–b). Mesh generation resolving multiple material boundaries is enabled by constructing boundary cube decomposition look up table using multiple material marching cubes method [4] which can define boundary surfaces of multiple materials inside structured grid. Moreover, by storing cube decomposition patterns in look up table which guarantee mesh conformity between neighboring cubes, tetrahedralization of each cube is realized.

Following procedures explained above, a conforming linear tetrahedral mesh with complex geometries and multiple materials is generated robustly. Uniqueness of all procedures involved in cube generation and decomposition assures the robustness in mesh generation. Though originally the input is material region definition in 3D, it is possible to allocate material information of each node from brightness values of image information in 2D. Therefore, it is not difficult to modify current source code to use 2D image as an input and this method has high affinity with mesh generation of biomedical bodies. However, mesh generated by this method contains geometric approximation whose size is half of the resolution at maximum. This is due to the location restriction of new boundary nodes to lattice points in 3D when decomposing boundary cubes with input material boundaries inside and defining new material boundaries (Fig. 4). Though guaranteeing mesh conformity and quality, this geometric approximation is undesirable since bad convergence and local concentration of feature amount will be brought

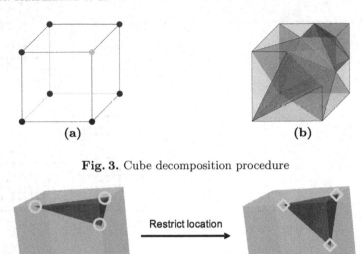

Fig. 3. Cube decomposition procedure

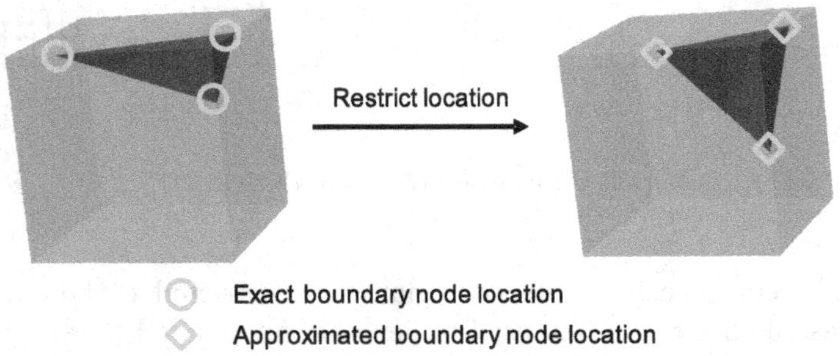

Restrict location

○ Exact boundary node location
◇ Approximated boundary node location

Fig. 4. Geometric approximation

together in FE analysis. In next subsection, mesh optimization method to reduce geometric approximation is developed.

2.2   Mesh Optimization

Overview of Mesh Optimization. Mesh optimization can be classified into to two groups, smoothing and topology optimization according to the modification content of mesh information. The former smoothing changes positions of nodes while preserving mesh topology, or node-element connectivity. The latter topology optimization changes mesh topology while preserving node positions. Smoothing, which repositions node is available for geometric modification, but in many cases nodes get locked because of the generation of bad quality elements during the iteration of smoothing. Quality of elements with boundary nodes tends to be bad and in particular, it often becomes impossible to improve quality of elements with four boundary nodes by smoothing [5]. In such cases, topology optimization is effective to improve element quality and reportedly combination of smoothing and topology optimization leads to mesh with better quality [6,7].

On the other hand, mesh optimization can be classified into global optimization and local optimization according to the size of domain to optimize in one process. While topology optimization is always performed locally since global topology optimization means global mesh generation, smoothing can be performed either locally or globally. Global smoothing, which repositions all nodes in whole mesh which are free to move at the same time is reduced to solve constrained non-linear programming problem in order to move nodes guaranteeing element quality firmly. However, in addition to the difficulty of the formulation of the objective function, obtaining global solution requires large computation and often fails since there is no guarantee of convergence in general cases. In local smoothing, which moves all nodes inside each small domain which are free to move at the same time, the optimization of the whole mesh is achieved by solving local optimization problems in each small domain. While having advantages such as the easy convergence of each local optimization which requires small computation and the suitability for parallelization, local optimization has disadvantages such as the increase of the overall computation because of the iteration of local optimization in each small domain [8] and convergence to local solution depending on the objective function [8].

In this study, mesh optimization method combining smoothing and topology optimization is developed following previous studies. Since topology on boundary surfaces is maintained while nodes are repositioned and element topology inside material regions is changed, mesh fineness on surface is preserved. Developed method is designed to modify geometry by iterating unit process consisting of smoothing and topology optimization. Smoothing improves surface geometries of mesh while topology optimization avoids such a situation that nodes get locked because of bad quality elements. Both smoothing and topology optimization in unit process are preformed locally and iteratively in many small domains. By adopting local processes which have small computation for smoothing and topology optimization, steady geometric improvement guaranteeing that no element violates the predetermined value of element quality metric. Moreover, room is left for acceleration envisaging the application to a large-scale mesh by adopting local processes which can be naturally parallelized.

In the following subsections, preparation required for mesh optimization is explained first, and then boundary node smoothing, interior node smoothing, and topology optimization of low quality elements which consists of unit process of mesh optimization are explained.

Preparation. First, as a preparation for mesh optimization, construction of boundary cube decomposition look up table with two materials which does not contain any element consisting of four boundary nodes and assignment of projection destinations to boundary nodes. In smoothing, tetrahedral elements consisting of four boundary nodes are undesirable. Since boundary nodes are moved toward projection destinations, quality of tetrahedral elements sharing boundary nodes tend to deteriorate and especially tetrahedral elements consisting of four boundary nodes should not exist. Therefore, in this study, decomposition look up table of boundary cube with two materials, which is frequently refereed to when generating initial mesh is improved to have no tetrahedral element consisting of four boundary nodes. Additionally it is required to choose projection destinations for each boundary node from input triangle patches defining material surfaces in advance of mesh optimization processes. This projection destination information will be used to move boundary nodes toward desirable position to improve mesh geometry. As for the assignment of projection destination of edge-centered boundary node, one triangle patch which has intersection with the edge on which the edge-centered node exists is chosen from input triangle patches. Projection destinations of face-centered boundary node is set to be the union of the projection destinations of the edge-centered boundary nodes which are on the same face. Therefore, face-centered boundary node can have four projection destinations at maximum. Based on the same idea, projection destinations of cube-centered boundary node is set to be the union of the projection destinations of the edge-centered boundary nodes which are on the same cube. Cube-centered boundary node can have twelve projection destinations at maximum.

Boundary Node Smoothing. Each boundary node has its own projection destination information. In this process, after Laplacian smoothing, boundary nodes are moved toward their projection destinations. Since the void domain of the target problem is also considered as one material, boundary nodes which are shared with air part and another material are also moved.

- Boundary node Laplacian smoothing

Position of boundary nodes is improved to mitigate the distortion of elements brought by boundary node repositioning. This process is essential to avoid such a situation that boundary nodes get locked because of the approach of boundary nodes in the iteration of mesh optimization. Laplacian smoothing is adopted as a determining method of new position on the ground of the easiness of implementation and small computation. However, simple movement to the arithmetic mean of all neighbouring nodes of the boundary node may result in further position from the projection destinations because of the neighbouring interior nodes. This phenomena will be remarkable with boundary nodes sharing air part (Fig. 5a–b). Therefore, in this study, boundary nodes are moved to the arithmetic mean of all neighbouring boundary nodes (Fig. 5a–c). Whether inside out element or low quality element is generated by this node repositioning is checked at every step to deal with the disadvantage of Laplacian smoothing. In case these invalid elements are generated, boundary nodes are moved by half of the movement vector. Thus, the boundary node Laplacian smoothing procedure is summarized as:

1. Calculate the arithmetic mean of neighbouring boundary nodes and movement vector from the current position.
2. Calculate new position by adding movement vector to the current position.
3. When moved to new position, if inside out element or low quality element whose element quality metric value violates predetermined value is generated, half the movement vector and go to 2.
4. Move to new position.

Note that this boundary node Laplacian smoothing is performed only in the first half of the mesh optimization iterations since it does not always move each boundary node toward its own projection destination.

- Movement of boundary node toward boundary surface

Boundary nodes are moved to boundary surfaces designated by projection destination information. New position is set to be the foot of a perpendicular line projected from the current position to the boundary surface (Fig. 5c–d). In case these invalid elements such as inside out elements or low quality elements are generated, boundary nodes are moved by half of the movement vector. Since there were some cases that a element get stuck in other element, the movement vector is also halved in these cases. Movement vector of boundary node which has two or more projection destinations is set to be the arithmetic mean of all movement vectors toward each boundary surfaces. Thus, movement procedure of boundary node toward boundary surface is summarized as:

1. Calculate movement vector from the current position to the foot of a perpendicular line on the boundary surface (Fig. 6). If boundary node has two or more projection destinations, calculate the arithmetic mean of all movement vectors toward each boundary surfaces.
2. Calculate new position by adding movement vector to the current position.
3. When moved to new position, if inside out element or low quality element whose element quality metric value violates predetermined value is generated or a element get stuck in other element, half the movement vector and go to 2.
4. Move to new position.

However, sometimes the above procedure cannot move boundary nodes sufficiently. One possibility of this phenomena is because of the activation of element quality restriction since there are other boundary nodes which share the boundary surface with the boundary node to move on the way to the new position. This problem stems from the fact that movement vector is simply set to be in the direction of the foot of a perpendicular line on the boundary surface. Therefore, when the above procedure failed to work, some perturbation is added to the movement vector and movement in the direction of boundary surface avoiding other boundary nodes is enabled. Perturbation vector is set by random number and its magnitude is set to be half of the magnitude of the movement vector. Since the magnitude ratio of movement vector and perturbation vector is constantly 1:2, new position is assured to be closer to the boundary surface than the current position. Thus, movement procedure of boundary node toward boundary surface with perturbation is summarized as:

1. Calculate movement vector from the current position to the foot of a perpendicular line on the boundary surface. If boundary node has two or more projection destinations, calculate the arithmetic mean of all movement vectors toward each boundary surfaces.
2. Set perturbation vector whose magnitude is half of the magnitude of movement vector using random number.
3. Calculate new position by adding movement vector and perturbation vector to the current position.

4. When moved to new position, if inside out element or low quality elements whose element quality metric value violates predetermined value is generated or a element get stuck in other element, half the movement vector and go to 3.
5. Move to new position.

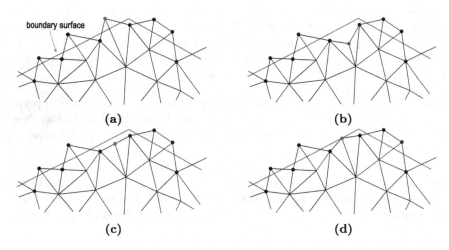

Fig. 5. Example of mesh near air part. Small dots represent boundary nodes. The boundary node represented by the red dot in (a) is going to be repositioned. While simple Laplacian smoothing results in (b) pulled by interior nodes, developed method results in (c) near the boundary surface. Next, projection to boundary surface results in (d). (Color figure online)

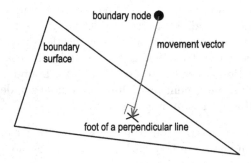

Fig. 6. Movement vector toward boundary surface

Interior Node Smoothing. This process improves position of interior nodes. The objective of this process is to relieve the distortion of elements near boundary surfaces which is brought by moving boundary nodes to boundary surfaces in entire mesh. By repositioning interior nodes and mitigating the distortion near boundary surfaces, further movement of boundary nodes to boundary surfaces is intended. New position of interior nodes is determined by Laplacian smoothing and in case of the generation of invalid elements, interior nodes are moved by half of the movement vector. Thus, smoothing procedure of interior node is summarized as:

1. Calculate the arithmetic mean of neighbouring nodes and movement vector from the current position.
2. Calculate new position by adding movement vector to the current position.
3. When moved to new position, if inside out element or low quality element whose element quality metric value violates predetermined value is generated, half the movement vector and go to 2.
4. Move to new position.

Topology Optimization. Topology of elements whose quality became almost no better than the predetermined value in the iteration of mesh optimization is changed. Topology optimization involving more elements tends to bring about better results since the number of patterns to change topology increases. Therefore, in this study, the algorithm of topology optimization is designed to change topology of several elements at the same time. First, an interior node composing low quality element is chosen. The reason why boundary node is not chosen is to maintain the topology of material boundary surfaces. Next, the surface triangles of the polygon consisting of tetrahedral elements which share the interior node is extracted. This process deletes the interior node and all tetrahedral elements sharing this interior node. Finally, using constrained Delaunay tetrahedralization, the polygon is decomposed into tetrahedral elements preserving the surface triangles. New nodes generated in this process are restricted inside the polygon. However, if a tetrahedral element consisting of four boundary nodes or a low quality tetrahedral element is generated, topology optimization is not performed. Advantages of these processes are the topology preservation on boundary surfaces and the tendency to improve the element quality by changing the topology of several elements at the same time. Thus, topology optimization procedure is summarized as:

1. Choose an interior node composing a low quality element.
2. Extract all tetrahedral elements sharing the interior node and construct polygon
3. Extract surface triangles from the polygon.
4. Perform constrained Dealunay tetrahedralization preserving surface triangles.
5. If and only if no tetrahedra consisting of four boundary nodes or no low quality tetrahedra whose element quality metric value violates predetermined value is generated, change topology.

3   Performance Measurement

Performance of mesh optimization method developed in previous section is measured. Considering that geometric approximation can become large on curved surfaces, sphere with a diameter of 8 is used. Figure 8a shows initial sphere mesh with resolution 0.1 before mesh optimization. The mesh consists of 452,280 linear tetrahedral elements, 90,813 nodes, 272,439 degrees of freedom, and 30,070 boundary nodes. Geometric approximation is clearly visible. On the other hand, sphere mesh after mesh optimization is shown in Fig. 8b, which has smoother surface. In this mesh optimization, the total number of iterations consisting of smoothing and topology optimization set 50, while Laplacian smoothing of boundary nodes is performed only in the first 25 iterations. Allowable maximum aspect ratio is set 30. Aspect ratio, a, represents an indicator of element quality and an element with a smaller a value is considered to exhibit better quality (a becomes 1 for a regular tetrahedron). Figure 9a shows maximum distance and average distance between each node and boundary surface on which the node should be in terms of iterations. Before mesh optimization shown as 0th iteration, maximum distance is 4.96E$-$2 which almost match the half size of resolution 0.1 and average distance is 1.67E$-$2. While distance increases in some part of iterations until 25th iteration, after 26th iteration distance monotonically decreases since Laplacian smoothing of boundary nodes is not performed and after finishing 50th iteration both maximum and average distance are small enough. Moreover, after 38th iteration, maximum and average distance almost converged to 4.25E$-$15 and 1.9E$-$16 respectively. Figure 9b shows cumulative relative frequency distribution of element aspect ratio inside overall mesh. Max aspect ratio changed from 4.87 to 30 through mesh optimization. It can be understood that nodes moved to the limit of allowable maximum aspect ratio. Even after mesh optimization, 95% of all elements have aspect ratio smaller than 10 and overall mesh quality is still maintained (Fig. 9).

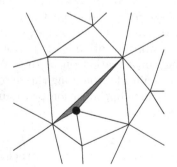
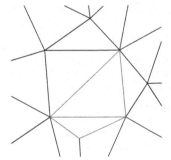

(a) Before topology optimization   (b) After topology optimization

Fig. 7. Topology optimization of low quality element. Change topology of elements sharing the interior node represented with the black dot.

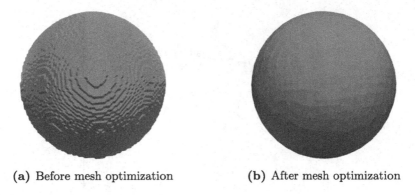

(a) Before mesh optimization   (b) After mesh optimization

Fig. 8. Mesh optimization of sphere mesh (Res. 0.1)

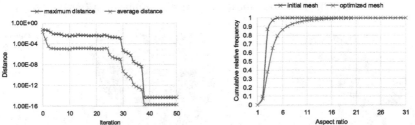

(a) Maximum and average distance be- (b) Transition of aspect ratio through
tween boundary nodes and boundary   mesh optimization
surfaces in terms of iterations

Fig. 9. Performance measurement results

4 Application Example

High tibial osteotomy (HTO) is a surgical procedure to disperse excessive load on
the inner side of the thigh due to bow leg deformation toward the outer side of the
thigh. For the realization of less invasive HTO surgery, quantitative evaluation of
stress distribution applied to the bone, such as presence of stress concentration,
is considered to be effective. This time, using two tibia meshes after HTO with
and without mesh optimization respectively, linear elastic analysis under static
load was performed and the validity of the developed mesh generation method
was verified by comparing stress distributions between them.

The tibia of the right leg of an adult male was used [9, 10]. Setting the resolution to 0.05 cm, tibia mesh consisting of 5,459,851 linear tetrahedral elements,
1,073,949 nodes and 3,221,847 degrees of freedom was generated (Fig. 10). Initial
mesh generation took 157 s using 64 cores and mesh optimization took 7,947 s
using 1 core of SGI UV 300. SGI UV300 is a 512 core, 24.5-TB cache-coherent
shared memory system consisting of 32 sockets of 16-core Intel Xeon E7-8867
v3 CPUs and 768 slots of 32 GB DDR4 DRAM connected with SGI NUMAlink
ASIC technology. Smooth surface of the generated mesh can be seen.

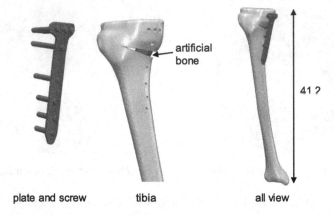

plate and screw   tibia   all view

Fig. 10. HTO tibia mesh after mesh optimization (cm)

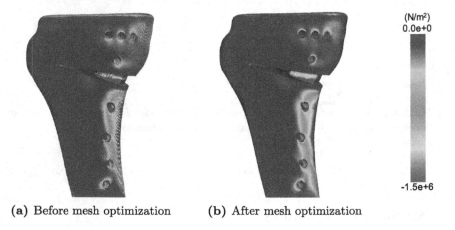

(a) Before mesh optimization   **(b)** After mesh optimization

Fig. 11. Comparison of maximum principal stress distribution

Next, linear elastic structural analysis was performed using generated tibia mesh. As a boundary condition, static load was applied on the top face of tibia in downward direction and lower half part was fixed. Comparison of minimum principal stress distributions between two meshes is shown in Fig. 11. While contour line on the mesh before mesh optimisation is rough, contour line on the mesh after mesh optimisation is smooth. It is suggested that mesh optimization method developed in this study reduces local concentration of stress and enables quality assurance of numerical analysis by mesh refinement. Though the inner material of tibia used in this analysis was assumed to be uniform for simplicity, making use of the ability to resolve multiple material boundaries of developed mesh generation method, analysis considering heterogeneous material distribution inside bone would be easily realizable.

5   Closing Remarks

In this study, by developing mesh optimization method which modifies geometric approximation of previous mesh generation method, robust generation method of high-quality mesh with complex geometries and multiple materials is established. Steady geometry modification guaranteeing element quality is realized by iterating local smoothing and topology optimization. Performance measurement using sphere mesh confirmed that geometry is finely improved. Comparing stress distributions of tibia meshes, it is suggested that mesh optimization method realizes numerical simulations whose quality can be assured by mesh refinement. One of the future works would be the acceleration of mesh optimization method. Current mesh optimization takes some days to complete optimization of mesh with $O(10^7)$ elements. Considering that initial mesh with $O(10^9)$ elements can be generated in several hours, by accelerating mesh optimization method whose room for parallelization possibility is left, mesh generation for large-scale biomedical simulations would be easily possible.

References

1. Ichimura, T., Hori, M., Bielak, J.: A hybrid multiresolution meshing technique for finite element three-dimensional earthquake ground motion modelling in basins including topography. Geophys. J. Int. **177**(3), 1221–1232 (2009)
2. Fujita, K., Katsushima, K., Ichimura, T., Hori, M., Lalith, M.: Octree-based multiple-material parallel unstructured mesh generation method for seismic response analysis of soil-structure systems. Procedia Comput. Sci. **80**, 1624–1634 (2016)
3. Fujita, K., Katsushima, K., Ichimura, T., Horikoshi, M., Nakajima, K., Hori, M., Maddegedara, L.: Wave propagation simulation of complex multi-material problems with fast low-order unstructured finite-element meshing and analysis. In: Proceedings of International Conference on High Performance Computing in Asia-Pacific Region (2017)
4. Wu, Z., Sullivan, J.M.: Multiple material marching cubes algorithm. Int. J. Numer. Methods Eng. **58**(2), 189–207 (2003)
5. Xu, K., Cheng, Z.Q., Wang, Y., Xiong, Y., Zhang, H.: Quality encoding for tetrahedral mesh optimization. Comput. Graph. **33**(3), 250–261 (2009)
6. Freitag, L.A., Ollivier-Gooch, C.: Tetrahedral mesh improvement using swapping and smoothing. Int. J. Numer. Methods Eng. **40**(21), 3979–4002 (1997)
7. Klingner, B.M., Shewchuk, J.B.: Aggressive tetrahedral mesh improvement. In: Brewer, M.L., Marcum, D. (eds.) Proceedings of the 16th International Meshing Roundtable, pp. 3–23. Springer, Heidelberg (2007). https://doi.org/10.1007/978-3-540-75103-8_1
8. Freitag, L.A., Knupp, P.M., Munson, T., Shontz, S.: A comparison of inexact Newton and coordinate descent mesh optimization techniques. In: Proceedings of the 13th International Meshing Roundtable. Sandia National Laboratories, pp. 243–254, September 2004
9. GrabCAD: Tibia TOMOFIX Plate for HTO. https://grabcad.com/
10. GrabCAD: Design of osseointegrated Implant for tibial bone. https://grabcad.com/

1,000x Faster Than PLINK: Genome-Wide Epistasis Detection with Logistic Regression Using Combined FPGA and GPU Accelerators

Lars Wienbrandt[✉], Jan Christian Kässens, Matthias Hübenthal,
and David Ellinghaus

Institute of Clinical Molecular Biology, University Medical Center Schleswig-Holstein,
Campus Kiel, Kiel University, Kiel, Germany
{l.wienbrandt,j.kaessens,m.huebenthal,d.ellinghaus}@ikmb.uni-kiel.de

Abstract. Logistic regression as implemented in PLINK is a powerful and commonly used framework for assessing gene-gene (GxG) interactions. However, fitting regression models for each pair of markers in a genome-wide dataset is a computationally intensive task. Performing billions of tests with PLINK takes days if not weeks, for which reason pre-filtering techniques and fast epistasis screenings are applied to reduce the computational burden.

Here, we demonstrate that employing a combination of a Xilinx Ultra-Scale KU115 FPGA with an Nvidia Tesla P100 GPU leads to runtimes of only minutes for logistic regression GxG tests on a genome-wide scale. In particular, a dataset of 53,000 samples genotyped at 130,000 SNPs was analyzed in 8 min, resulting in a speedup of more than 1,000 when compared to PLINK v1.9 using 32 threads on a server-grade computing platform. Furthermore, on-the-fly calculation of test statistics, p-values and LD-scores in double-precision make commonly used pre-filtering strategies obsolete.

Keywords: Genome-wide association study (GWAS)
Genome-wide interaction study (GWIS)
Gene-gene (GxG) interaction · Linkage disequilibrium (LD) · BOOST
Hardware accelerator · Hybrid computing · Heterogeneous architecture

1 Introduction

Gene-gene (GxG) interactions (epistasis) are believed to be a significant source of unexplained genetic variation causing complex chronic diseases. Several studies provided evidence for statistical GxG interaction between the top disease-associated single nucleotide polymorphisms (SNPs) of complex chronic diseases, including ankylosing spondylitis [21], Behçet's disease [15], type 2 diabetes [14], and psoriasis [6]. Particularly, in psoriasis a significant interaction

© Springer International Publishing AG, part of Springer Nature 2018
Y. Shi et al. (Eds.): ICCS 2018, LNCS 10861, pp. 368–381, 2018.
https://doi.org/10.1007/978-3-319-93701-4_28

($p = 6.95 \times 10^{-6}$) as measured by logistic regression has been detected between the genes *ERAP1* (*rs27524*) and *HLA-C* (*rs10484554*). The biological consequence of this interaction is that the *ERAP1* SNP only has an effect in individuals carrying at least one copy of the risk allele at the *HLA-C* SNP.

In general, detection of GxG interactions poses a great challenge for genome-wide association studies (GWAS) due to the computational burden of testing billions of pairs of SNPs (as a result of the number of tests being quadratic in the number of SNPs). Traditional logistic regression analysis is still the gold-standard to detect statistical GxG interactions in case/control studies, but too slow in practice to screen for GxG interactions on a genome-wide scale. Thus, many approximate methods for epistasis screening have been proposed applying a variety of heuristic and filtering techniques to conduct genome-wide interaction studies (GWIS) in a reasonable amount of time. Well-established methods include the Kirkwood Superposition Approximation (KSA) of the Kullback-Leibler divergence implemented in BOOST [23] as well as the joint effects test introduced by Ueki et al. [22]. Another exhaustive interaction method, called GWIS [7], employs a permutation-based approach to calibrate test statistics. Similarly, MBMDR [3] uses permutations to adjust the p-value of the significance test. However, it is able to reduce the dimensionality of any problem into one dimension categorizing into high-risk, low-risk and no evidence groups before calculating a chi-squared test statistic. Other tools defining different test statistics include BiForce [8], iLOCi [18] and EDCF [27]. The latter uses a clustering approach in order to reduce the computational burden. Recently, entropy-based measures for GxG interaction detection gained increasing attention. A well-written overview can be found in [5].

However, no convincing GxG loci have been identified exclusively from GWIS using these approaches. Many of the methods derive an upper bound on the test statistic in order to prune the search space and conduct follow-up model-fitting analysis using logistic regression on a pre-filtered subset of pairs [24]. Furthermore, the computational load for preliminary epistasis screenings is not negligible. Accordingly, several tools emerged to speedup this process employing hardware accelerators, such as GPUs in GBOOST [28] or SHEsisEpi [9]. Another way to reduce the computational burden is to reduce the number of SNPs in advance by pre-filtering for linkage disequilibrium (LD), although it can be shown that SNPs supposed to be in LD may also reveal an interaction effect [2,10].

An attempt to reduce the computational load for logistic regression tests is made in [17] by using GLIDE [11]. To our knowledge, GLIDE is the fastest currently available GPU implementation of the logistic regression GxG interaction test. More recently, CARAT-GxG [16] emerged. It also offers linear regression including covariate analysis on GPUs, but provides a poor performance when compared to GLIDE (12 days for a dataset containing 500,000 SNPs and not more than 1,000 samples using 32 Nvidia Tesla M2070 GPUs).

In this paper, we show that we are able to perform an exhaustive genome-wide logistic regression analysis for SNP-SNP interactions on datasets consisting of hundreds of thousands of SNPs and tens of thousands of samples in minutes, thus eliminating the needs for epistasis screening or LD-filtering as a preprocessing step. If required, LD-filtering can directly be applied as a postprocessing step, thanks to on-the-fly calculation of r^2. Furthermore, we perform our calculations in double-precision floating point format in order to overcome precision problems that may occur during floating point accumulations.

We run our benchmark against PLINK v1.9 using 32 threads on a computing system with two Intel Xeon E5-2667v4 eight-core CPUs. We already gain a 10–11 times speedup by sacrificing the support for sample covariates (re-enabling it in our method is still under development) and adapting the logistic regression test to be used with contingency tables. This reduces the computational complexity from $\mathcal{O}(NT)$ to $\mathcal{O}(N + T)$ (with N indicating the number of samples and T the number of iterations required for a single test). By harnessing a combination of only two hardware accelerators, namely a Xilinx Kintex UltraScale KU115 FPGA and an Nvidia Tesla P100 GPU, we gain another 100 times speedup resulting in a total of >1,000 times speedup compared to multi-threaded PLINK on a server-grade platform. Exemplary, for analyzing a dataset consisting of 130k SNPs and 53k samples our method requires only 8 min while PLINK running with 32 threads almost requires 6 days. Finally, it turns out that our method is even more than 300 times faster than GLIDE, which harnesses 12 Nvidia GTX 580 GPUs.

2 Pairwise Epistasis Testing

2.1 Logistic Regression Test

In this article we address the efficient implementation of a genotype-based statistical test for binary traits. Let Y be a random variable correlated with the trait. Correspondingly, for the trait being a disease, we define the two possible outcomes of Y as $Y = 1$ if the sample is a *case* affected by the disease, and $Y = 0$ if the samples is a *control* unaffected by the disease. Furthermore, for a pairwise test, we define X_A and X_B as random variables correlated with the observation of genotypes at SNPs A and B, respectively. The possible outcomes of $X_{A/B}$ are $g_{A/B} \in \{0, 1, 2\}$ representing the observed genotype (0 = homozygous reference, 1 = heterozygous, 2 = homozygous variant). PLINK [4,20] uses the following multiplicative logistic regression affection model with β_3 indicating the interaction effect of SNPs A and B.

$$\ln \frac{P(Y = 1 | X_A = g_A, X_B = g_B)}{P(Y = 0 | X_A = g_A, X_B = g_B)} = \beta_0 + \beta_1 g_A + \beta_2 g_B + \beta_3 g_A g_B \tag{1}$$

PLINK employs Newton's method to iteratively obtain ML estimates of the model parameters. It firstly generates a covariate matrix $\mathbf{C}$ with entries C_{ij} whereby i indicates a sample of the input dataset and $j \in 0, 1, 2, 3$ indicates a column for each β_j. The matrix is defined as follows:

$$C_{i0} = 1, \quad C_{i1} = g_{iA}, \quad C_{i2} = g_{iB} \quad \text{and} \quad C_{i3} = g_{iA} g_{iB} \tag{2}$$

In detail, for a variable number of iterations $t = 0, \ldots, T - 1$, fitting the vector $\boldsymbol{\beta}$ is performed in a stepwise manner. $\boldsymbol{\beta}^{(0)}$ is initialized with $\beta_j^{(0)} = 0 \; \forall j$ for the first iteration $t = 0$.

1. For each sample i, compute intermediate variables

$$p_i^{(t)} = \bar{p}_i^{(t)} - y_i \quad \text{and} \quad v_i^{(t)} = \bar{p}_i^{(t)} \left(1 - \bar{p}_i^{(t)} \right) \tag{3}$$

where

$$\bar{p}_i^{(t)} = \left(1 + \exp\left(-\sum_j \beta_j^{(t)} C_{ij} \right) \right)^{-1}. \tag{4}$$

2. Compute gradient

$$\boldsymbol{\nabla}^{(t)} = \left\{ \nabla_j^{(t)} \right\}_{j=0}^{3} = \sum_i C_{ij} p_i^{(t)}. \tag{5}$$

3. Compute Hessian matrix

$$\boldsymbol{H}^{(t)} = \left\{ h_{jk}^{(t)} \right\}_{j,k=0}^{3} = \begin{cases} 0 & \text{if } k > j \\ \sum_i C_{ij} C_{ik} v_i^{(t)} & \text{if } k \le j \end{cases}. \tag{6}$$

4. Compute $\boldsymbol{\Delta\beta}^{(t)} = \left\{ \Delta\beta_j^{(t)} \right\}_{j=0}^{3}$ by efficiently solving the linear system

$$\boldsymbol{H}^{(t)} \boldsymbol{\Delta\beta}^{(t)} = \boldsymbol{\nabla}^{(t)} \tag{7}$$

using the Cholesky decomposition of $\boldsymbol{H}^{(t)}$.
5. Update model parameters

$$\boldsymbol{\beta}^{(t+1)} \leftarrow \boldsymbol{\beta}^{(t)} - \boldsymbol{\Delta\beta}^{(t)}. \tag{8}$$

If $\sum_j \Delta\beta_j^{(t)}$ approaches zero, i.e. there is no more significant change, the process stops with $\boldsymbol{\beta}^{(t+1)}$ as the current result. Otherwise, the next iteration is started with step 1. However, if the change does not converge to zero, the process stops after a fixed number of iterations. PLINK uses at maximum 16 iterations and a close-to-zero threshold of 0.0001. Additional tests for convergence failure are implemented but omitted here for the sake of brevity.

The result of the logistic regression test in PLINK is composed of three components, namely the test statistic, its approximate p-value and the odds-ratio. The test statistic χ^2 is calculated as

$$\chi^2 = \frac{\beta_3}{\varepsilon^2}. \tag{9}$$

ε is the standard error for the $g_A g_B$-term in (1). It can directly be determined by solving the linear system $\boldsymbol{H}^{(t)} e = (0, 0, 0, 1)$ and defining $\varepsilon^2 = e_3$.

According to PLINK, the test statistic is assumed to follow a chi-squared distribution χ_1^2 with one degree of freedom, which implies that the approximate p-value can directly be determined from its cumulative distribution function. Finally, the odds-ratio is defined as e^{β_3}.

Obviously, steps 1 to 3 in each iteration have linear complexity in N, i.e. $\mathcal{O}(N)$ whereby N is the number of samples. Let T be the number of iterations, then $\mathcal{O}(NT)$ is the total complexity for a single test. In the next Sects. 2.2 and 2.3, we show how to do a linear precomputing step to generate a contingency table and how to apply the contingency table in the logistic regression test, which results in a constant computation complexity for each iteration.

2.2   Contingency Tables

For any SNP pair (A, B) a contingency table represents the number of samples in a dataset that carry a specific genotype information. In particular, an entry n_{ij} represents the number of samples that carry the information $g_A = i$ at SNP A and $g_B = j$ at SNP B. Thus, a contingency table for pairwise genotypic tests contains 3×3 entries. Since we are focusing on binary traits, we require a contingency table for each state, w.l.o.g. one for the $case$ and $control$ group, respectively, and denote their entries by n_{ij}^{case} and n_{ij}^{ctrl} (see Fig. 1).

cases $(Y = 1)$	SNP A 0	1	2		controls $(Y = 0)$	SNP A 0	1	2
SNP B 0	n_{00}^{case}	n_{01}^{case}	n_{02}^{case}		SNP B 0	n_{00}^{ctrl}	n_{01}^{ctrl}	n_{02}^{ctrl}
1	n_{10}^{case}	n_{11}^{case}	n_{12}^{case}		1	n_{10}^{ctrl}	n_{11}^{ctrl}	n_{12}^{ctrl}
2	n_{20}^{case}	n_{21}^{case}	n_{22}^{case}		2	n_{20}^{ctrl}	n_{21}^{ctrl}	n_{22}^{ctrl}

Fig. 1. Contingency tables for cases and controls. n_{ij} reflect the number of occurrences for the corresponding genotype combination in a given pair of SNPs.

For a given SNP pair generating the contingency tables is clearly linear in the number of samples. In the next section (Sect. 2.3) we show how to incorporate contingency tables into logistic regression.

2.3   Logistic Regression with Contingency Tables

The information in the contingency tables for case and control group can be used to simplify steps 1 to 3 in Sect. 2.1. Steps 4 and 5 as well as the calculation of the test statistic, the odds-ratio and the p-value remain the same.

1. From a given contingency table we compute the following intermediate variables.

$$p_{ij}^{(t)} = \left(1 + \exp\left(-\left(\beta_0^{(t)} + i\beta_1^{(t)} + j\beta_2^{(t)} + ij\beta_3^{(t)}\right)\right)\right)^{-1} \qquad (10)$$

$$p_{ij}^{(t),\text{ctrl}} = p_{ij}^{(t)}, \quad p_{ij}^{(t),\text{case}} = p_{ij}^{(t)} - 1, \quad v_{ij}^{(t)} = p_{ij}^{(t)}\left(1 - p_{ij}^{(t)}\right)\left(n_{ij}^{\text{case}} + n_{ij}^{\text{ctrl}}\right)$$
(11)

2. The gradient $\boldsymbol{\nabla}^{(t)}$ from (5) can now be computed as

$$\boldsymbol{\nabla}^{(t)} = \left(\sum_{ij} N_{ij}^{(t)}, \sum_{ij} i N_{ij}^{(t)}, \sum_{ij} j N_{ij}^{(t)}, \sum_{ij} ij N_{ij}^{(t)}\right)$$
(12)

where

$$N_{ij}^{(t)} = \left(n_{ij}^{\text{case}} p_{ij}^{(t),\text{case}} + n_{ij}^{\text{ctrl}} p_{ij}^{(t),\text{ctrl}}\right)$$
(13)

3. The Hessian matrix $\boldsymbol{H}^{(t)}$ from (6) evaluates to

$$\boldsymbol{H}^{(t)} = \left\{h_{pq}^{(t)}\right\}_{p,q=0}^{3} = \begin{pmatrix} \sum v_{ij}^{(t)} & 0 & 0 & 0 \\ \sum i v_{ij}^{(t)} & \sum i^2 v_{ij}^{(t)} & 0 & 0 \\ \sum j v_{ij}^{(t)} & \sum ij v_{ij}^{(t)} & \sum j^2 v_{ij}^{(t)} & 0 \\ \sum ij v_{ij}^{(t)} & \sum i^2 j v_{ij}^{(t)} & \sum ij^2 v_{ij}^{(t)} & \sum i^2 j^2 v_{ij}^{(t)} \end{pmatrix}$$
(14)

where each sum is evaluated over all indexes i and j.

Obviously, the complexity of each iteration step is now constant, i.e. $\mathcal{O}(1)$. As in Sect. 2.1, let N be the total number of samples and T the number of iterations. We recall the complexity of the method used by PLINK with $\mathcal{O}(NT)$. Our proposed method improves this complexity to $\mathcal{O}(N+T)$ which can directly be observed in a significant increase in computation speed (see Sect. 4).

2.4 Linkage Disequilibrium

Our ultimate aim is the exhaustive testing of all SNP pairs on a genome-wide scale without pre-filtering with regard to linkage disequilibrium (LD). However, to be able to apply posthoc LD filtering we compute the r^2-score on-the-fly. r^2 is a measure of similarity between two SNPs. It is defined as

$$r^2 = \frac{D^2}{p_A(1 - p_A)p_B(1 - p_B)} \quad \text{with} \quad D = p_{AB} - p_A p_B.$$
(15)

D is the distance between the observed allele frequency p_{AB} at loci A and B and the expected allele frequency $p_A p_B$ assuming statistical independence. Thus, r^2 is a normalized measure for D which can be used for comparison of different SNP pairs. The allele frequencies p_A and p_B can directly be determined as

$$p_A = \frac{2n_{00} + 2n_{10} + 2n_{20} + n_{01} + n_{11} + n_{21}}{2N}$$
(16)

$$p_B = \frac{2n_{00} + 2n_{01} + 2n_{02} + n_{10} + n_{11} + n_{12}}{2N}$$
(17)

whereby $n_{ij} = n_{ij}^{\text{case}} + n_{ij}^{\text{ctrl}}$ for all i, j. Unfortunately, the determination of the allele frequency p_{AB} from genotypic data is not straightforward. This is due to the unknown phase when two heterozygous genotypes face each other in a SNP pair. Basically, it can be defined as

$$p_{AB} = \frac{2n_{00} + n_{01} + n_{10} + x}{2N} \tag{18}$$

with x meeting $x \leq n_{11}$. x has to satisfy the following equation whose solution is omitted here for simplicity:

$$(f_{00} + x)(f_{11} + x)(n_{11} - x) = (f_{01} + n_{11} - x)(f_{10} + n_{11} - x)x \tag{19}$$

where f_{ij} is the number of allele combinations ij we know for sure, e.g. $f_{00} = 2n_{00} + n_{01} + n_{10}$ and $f_{11} = 2n_{22} + n_{21} + n_{12}$.

PLINK does not compute the r^2-score jointly with the logistic regression test. However, one can create a table of r^2 scores explicitly for all pairs of a given range (`--r2` switch), or compute the r^2-score for a single pair (`--ld` switch). This process is in linear complexity for each pair of SNPs to determine the respective allele frequencies. In comparison, we are using the information of the precomputed contingency table which allows us to calculate the r^2-score in constant time.

3   Implementation

3.1   Heterogeneous FPGA-GPU Computing Architecture

Our implementation targets a heterogeneous FPGA-GPU computing architecture. We improved our architecture proposed in [26] by adding high-end off-the-shelf components, namely a server-grade mainboard hosting two Intel Xeon E5-2667v4 8-core CPUs @ 3.2 GHz and 256 GB of RAM, an NVIDIA Tesla P100 GPU, and an Alpha Data ADM-PCIE-8K5 FPGA accelerator card.

The GPU accelerator is equipped with 16 GB of graphics memory and is connected via PCI Express Gen3 x16. The FPGA accelerator hosts a recent Xilinx Kintex UltraScale KU115 FPGA with two attached 8 GB SODIMM memory modules. It is connected via PCI Express Gen3 x8 allowing high-speed communication with the host and the GPU. The system runs a Ubuntu 17.10 Linux OS (Kernel version 4.13).

Due to driver restrictions, it is currently not possible to perform direct peer transfers, i.e. moving data from an FPGA accelerator to a GPU or vice-versa. Therefore, both devices are placed in slots that are served by the same CPU to reduce transmission overhead as described in [13].

According to the PCIe specifications, the net transmission rate between FPGA and GPU is about 7.3 GB/s. This absolutely fits our application demands, such that the transmission interface does not become a bottleneck.

3.2   Task Distribution

Similar to our method for testing third-order SNP interactions based on information gain [26], we split the application into three subtasks. Firstly, the creation of pairwise contingency tables (see Sect. 2.2) is done by the FPGA module. Secondly, all computations required for the logistic regression test based on the contingency tables are performed by the GPU. And thirdly, the host collects and filters the results created by the GPU.

As before, data transmission between the modules is performed by DMA transfers via PCI Express, and since there is no direct connection between the FPGA and the GPU module, the transmission of the contingency tables is redirected via the host memory.

The input dataset is assumed to be in binary PLINK format, i.e. three files in .bed, .bim, .fam format. The output is in plain text format containing for each result the information on the respective SNP pair (name and ID), χ^2 test statistic, odds-ratio, approximate p-value and r^2-score.

Contingency Table Creation on the FPGA. The FPGA pipeline for contingency table generation is based on our previous work for pairwise [12,25] and third-order interactions [26]. Thus, we omit details here and only remark the differences.

Shortly summarized, the pipeline consists of a chain of 480 process elements (PEs) divided into two subchains of 240 PEs each. After a short initialization phase, the chain produces 480 contingency tables in parallel while the genotype data of one SNP is streamed through the pipeline at a speed of 266 MHz and 8 genotypes/cycle. This sums up to a peak performance of about 40.8 million contingency tables per second for a dataset containing about 50,000 samples, as used in our performance evaluation in Sect. 4.

In previous publications, we used a sparse contingency table representation lacking support for unknown genotypes. The disadvantage of such a design is, that datasets containing unknown genotypes could not be supported because the assumption that the sum of all entries stays the same over all tables is disproved in the presence of unknowns. In order to remove this limitation, we now transfer complete tables from the FPGA to the GPU. Unfortunately, this increases the transmission rate significantly. Therefore, we encode each table entry into two bytes, i.e. 18 B per table. For each pair of corresponding case and control tables 4 B for the pair ID is added, which accumulates to 40 B per table pair. Hence, the peak transmission rate for the example above is about 816 MB/s, compared to 245 MB/s required for the sparse representation. However, the peak transmission rate of the architecture is 7.3 GB/s according to PCIe Gen3 specifications which theoretically allows us to process datasets down to 5,200 samples without the transmission link becoming the bottleneck.

Processing Contingency Tables on the GPU. The GPU stores the buffers from the FPGA containing contingency tables in graphics memory. We used a transmission buffer size of 256 MB which may hold up to 6.7 million table pairs. The computation process follows a simple parallelization scheme over GPU threads. By setting the block size to the maximum supported block size and the grid size to evenly distribute the contingency tables over the blocks, each thread processes exactly one contingency table pair, and only one kernel call per buffer is required.

Logistic regression and LD computation have been implemented as described in Sects. 2.3 and 2.4. However, in contrast to PLINK, we use the double precision floating point format in all our computations. The output is written into a result buffer. We provide one result buffer for each table transmission buffer, which is transferred to the host as soon as processing a table buffer has finished.

By evenly distributing the contingency tables over the blocks, we most likely introduce an unequal load resulting from a varying number of Newton iterations per thread. However, the average number of iterations per block remains virtually constant.

Transmission Buffer Management and Result Collection on the Host. We used a similar transmission buffer management as presented in [26], but introduced some improvements. In order to reduce transmission overhead, we used different adapted buffer sizes for contingency table transmission between FPGA and GPU, and result transmission from GPU to host. We used a transmission buffer size of 256 MB for contingency tables leading to 230.4 MB for results (reserving space for one result per contingency table pair). As before, the buffers are page-locked to ensure a fast transmission without delay, and the number of buffers allocated for each connection is equal (eight per default).

Multiple threads on the host system perform the collection of results by filtering by a given significance threshold and finally providing them sorted with regard to the test statistic. For this purpose, the min-max fine heap data structure [1,13] is employed. Each thread keeps its own instance of a min-max heap to avoid lock conditions and inserts a result only if the test statistic exceeds the threshold. Then, the output file is composed by iteratively extracting the single best result over all heaps until the heaps are drained or the number of requested results is reached, whichever occurs first.

The complete workflow on our heterogeneous FPGA-GPU-based architecture is illustrated in Fig. 2.

4   Performance Evaluation

For performance evaluation we prepared six datasets based on in-house cohorts. Dataset "A" and "B" contain 14,513 and 19,085 cases of autoimmune diseases, respectively, and share a common collection of 34,213 healthy controls. Modified instances of sets "A" and "B" were generated by applying an LD filter with r^2-threshold of 0.2, resulting in sets "A LD" and "B LD", respectively. Furthermore, we reduced the latter two datasets to only comprise SNPs located on

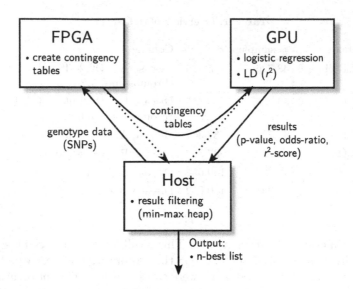

Fig. 2. Workflow on our heterogeneous system. 1. Genotypic data is sent to the FPGA. 2. For each pair of SNPs the FPGA creates contingency tables. 3. The contingency tables are sent to the GPU employing a memory buffer on the host. 4. The GPU calculates the logistic regression and LD. 5. Results (p-value, odds-ratio and LD-score) are transferred back to host. 6. Result are filtered using a min-max heap on host.

chromosomes 5 and 6. The resulting sets have been denoted by "A LD chr5,6" and "B LD chr5,6". An overview of these datasets can be found in Table 1.

Our target system was the architecture described in Sect. 3.1. We compiled our implementation with GCC 5.4.1 and CUDA 9.0. The FPGA code was written in VHDL and compiled with Xilinx Vivado 2017.3. For comparison, we used the to date most recent 64-bit PLINK v1.9 built published on Jan 9th, 2018. We ran PLINK on all six datasets in two ways. Firstly, we computed the standard logistic regression tests with flags `--epistasis --epi1 5e-8` which filters the results by a genome-wide significance threshold of $5 \cdot 10^{-8}$ according to the approximate p-value. Secondly, we applied a faster epistasis screening test with the BOOST [23] method (included in PLINK) with the same threshold flag, but replacing `--epistasis` with `--fast-epistasis boost`. Both runs used all available 32 threads (`--threads`) on our 2x Intel Xeon E5-2667v4 system.

We ran our implementation from a hybrid built, i.e. using both accelerators (Xilinx Kintex UltraScale KU115 FPGA and Nvidia Tesla P100 GPU) and a CPU-only built using all 32 threads. In contrast to PLINK, our implementations perform all calculations in double-precision floating point format, while PLINK only uses single-precision. Furthermore, we calculated the r^2-score in order to test for linkage disequilibrium on all SNP pairs, which PLINK does not.

We verified the correctness of our implementation by comparing our results with the PLINK results. At first, we encountered a lot of differences in the score and also in the order. Thus, we modified the source code of PLINK to let it do the

Table 1. Overview of datasets.

Dataset	# samples	# SNPs	Comment
A LD chr5, 6	48,726	5,725	Disease A, LD0.2-filtered, only chromosomes 5, 6
B LD chr5, 6	53,298	5,725	Disease B, LD0.2-filtered, only chromosomes 5, 6
A LD	48,726	37,358	Disease A, LD0.2-filtered
B LD	53,298	37,358	Disease B, LD0.2-filtered
A	48,726	130,052	Disease A, complete
B	53,298	130,052	Disease B, complete

calculations in double-precision as well. This modification increased the runtime of PLINK by a factor of about 5.7, but the results were almost exactly equal now, showing that the inconsistencies were caused by the different precisions. We believe the remaining small inconsistencies were due to numerical problems in PLINK when accumulating small floating-point values over all samples in steps 2 and 3 of computing the logistic regression test (see (5) and (6) in Sect. 2.1).

The wall-clock runtimes were measured with the GNU time command and without additional system load. The results are listed in Table 2. The measures demonstrate that by applying our method that reduces runtime complexity by using contingency tables, we can gain a 10–11 times speedup. With an additional application of the combination of two hardware accelerators, namely FPGA and GPU, we gain an additional speedup of about 100, resulting in a total computation speed that it is more than 1,000 times faster than that of PLINK on a server-grade high-end platform. The performance is underlined by the additional burden on our implementation, which is a higher calculation precision and the additional on-the-fly r^2-score computation, which is not performed by the PLINK software. Furthermore, our full logistic regression test is still almost 7 times faster than the quick but imprecise pre-scanning method BOOST [23].

However, Table 2 also shows, that small datasets, that have a very short runtime on our hybrid system, do not gain a high speedup. The reason is a large overhead for file reading, buffer preparation, device initialization and file output. In particular, these processes take about 10 seconds for the two smallest datasets in our ensemble, which implies a total pipeline run of less than two seconds for the real task. Since this processes cannot be simplified for a single task, we implemented a scheduling system that allows exclusive access to the accelerator pipeline for parallel tasks, but pre- and post-processing can be run concurrently.

We exemplary compared our computational speed to GLIDE [11]. For this purpose, we extrapolated GLIDE's presented interaction speed to the number of samples used in our evaluation datasets. Combined with the number of interaction tests required for our data, we calculated the runtime of GLIDE for dataset

"A" as 44.7 h and for dataset "B" as 48.9 h. This leads to a speedup of 361 and 364 respectively.

Table 2. Wall-clock runtimes and speedup of the hybrid FPGA-GPU logistic regression test compared to PLINK [19] logistic regression (`--epistasis`) and PLINK BOOST (`--fast-epistasis boost`) and our CPU-only implementation, all using 32 threads on two Intel Xeon E5-2667v4 processors. Our CPU-only and hybrid implementations additionally calculate the r^2-score (LD) and do all computations in double-precision format (vs. single-precision without r^2 in PLINK).

Dataset	PLINK		Hybrid		Speedup	
	log.reg.	BOOST	CPU-only	FPGA-GPU	CPU only	Hybrid
A LD chr5,6	15 m 48 s	7 s	1 m 32 s	11 s	10.30	86.18
B LD chr5,6	16 m 48 s	8 s	1 m 39 s	12 s	10.18	84.00
A LD	11 h 09 m 38 s	4 m 05 s	57 m 51 s	50 s	11.58	803.56
B LD	11 h 49 m 32 s	4 m 34 s	1 h 02 m 45 s	53 s	11.31	803.25
A	5 d 14 h 06 m	49 m 34 s	11 h 40 m 12 s	7 m 25 s	11.49	**1,084.85**
B	5 d 18 h 18 m	54 m 34 s	12 h 39 m 05 s	8 m 03 s	10.93	**1,030.81**

5 Conclusions and Future Work

In this paper, we presented two ways of improving performance of PLINK's logistic regression epistasis test [4,20]. Firstly, we reduced the computational complexity from $\mathcal{O}(NT)$ to $\mathcal{O}(N+T)$ for a single test by introducing contingency tables (see Sect. 2). This already led to a speedup of a factor of more than 10 for all our example datasets, although we were even calculating in double-precision format.

The second improvement was made by applying a two-step hardware acceleration pipeline (see Sect. 3). By generating contingency tables on a Kintex Ultra-Scale KU115 FPGA and computing the logistic regression based on the tables on an Nvidia Tesla P100 GPU, we gained a total speedup of more than 1,000 when compared to the original PLINK v1.9 software run with 32 threads on a server-grade two processor (Intel Xeon E5-2667v4) system.

Furthermore, we demonstrated that by employing contingency tables, the LD-score r^2 can be computed on-the-fly. In combination, this provides a powerful tool for epistasis analysis on large datasets, making LD-filtering deprecated as a pre-processing step.

Consequently, we are able to calculate a full logistic regression test in double-precision format on all pairs of hundreds of thousands of SNPs with tens of thousands of samples in a few minutes and allow to filter the results by score and/or by LD in the post-processing stage.

Currently, our method does not support the use of a covariate matrix as additional user input. However, we are currently working on a solution based on weighted contingency tables in order to be able to incorporate covariate information.

In order to make the system available for the scientific community, we are currently working on a much more powerful successor by enhancing it with three additional Xilinx UltraScale FPGAs and Nvidia Tesla P100 GPUs. Furthermore, we aim to develop a web interface to allow scientists to perform genome-wide epistasis tests on our system.

References

1. Atkinson, M.D., Sack, J.R., Santori, N., et al.: Min-max heaps and generalized priority queues. Commun. ACM **29**(10), 996–1000 (1986)
2. Bulik-Sullivan, B.K., Loh, P.R., Finucane, H.K., et al.: LD score regression distinguishes confounding from polygenicity in genome-wide association studies. Nat. Genet. **47**, 291–295 (2015). https://doi.org/10.1038/ng.3211
3. Cattaert, T., Calle, M.L., Dudek, S.M., et al.: Model-based multifactor dimensionality reduction for detecting epistasis in case-control data in the presence of noise. Ann. Hum. Genet. **75**(1), 78–89 (2011)
4. Chang, C.C., Chow, C.C., Tellier, L.C., Vattikuti, S., Purcell, S.M., Lee, J.J.: Second-generation PLINK: rising to the challenge of larger and richer datasets. Gigascience **4**, 1–16 (2015). https://doi.org/10.1186/s13742-015-0047-8
5. Ferrario, P.G., König, I.R.: Transferring entropy to the realm of GxG interactions. Briefings in Bioinform., 1–12 (2016). https://doi.org/10.1093/bib/bbw086
6. Genetic Analysis of Psoriasis Consortium, et al.: A genome-wide association study identifies new psoriasis susceptibility loci and an interaction between HLA-C and ERAP1. Nat. Genet. **42**, 985–990 (2010). https://doi.org/10.1038/ng.694
7. Goudey, B., Rawlinson, D., Wang, Q., et al.: GWIS: model-free, fast and exhaustive search for epistatic interactions in case-control GWAS. Lorne Genome 2013 (2013)
8. Gyenesei, A., Moody, J., Semple, C.A., et al.: High-throughput analysis of epistasis in genome-wide association studies with BiForce. Bioinformatics **28**(15), 1957–1964 (2012). https://doi.org/10.1093/bioinformatics/bts304
9. Hu, X., Liu, Q., Zhang, Z., et al.: SHEsisEpi, a GPU-enhanced genome-wide SNP-SNP interaction scanning algorithm, efficiently reveals the risk genetic epistasis in bipolar disorder. Cell Res. **20**, 854–857 (2010)
10. Ibrahim, Z.M., Newhouse, S., Dobson, R.: Detecting epistasis in the presence of linkage disequilibrium: a focused comparison. In: 2013 IEEE Symposium on CIBCB, pp. 96–103 (2013). https://doi.org/10.1109/CIBCB.2013.6595394
11. Kam-Thong, T., Azencott, C.A., Cayton, L., et al.: GLIDE: GPU-based linear regression for detection of epistasis. Hum. Hered. **73**, 220–236 (2012). https://doi.org/10.1159/000341885
12. Kässens, J.C., Wienbrandt, L., et al.: Combining GPU and FPGA technology for efficient exhaustive interaction analysis in GWAS. In: 2016 IEEE 27th International Conference on ASAP, pp. 170–175 (2016). https://doi.org/10.1109/ASAP.2016.7760788
13. Kässens, J.C.: A hybrid-parallel architecture for applications in bioinformatics. No. 2017/4 in Kiel Computer Science Series, Department of Computer Science, CAU Kiel (2017). Dissertation, Faculty of Engineering, Kiel University. https://doi.org/10.21941/kcss/2017/4

14. Keaton, J.M., Hellwege, J.N., Ng, M.C.Y., et al.: Genome-wide interaction with selected type 2 diabetes loci reveals novel loci for type 2 diabetes in African Americans. Pac. Symp. Biocomput. **22**, 242–253 (2016). https://doi.org/10.1142/9789813207813_0024

15. Kirino, Y., Bertsias, G., Ishigatsubo, Y., et al.: Genome-wide association analysis identifies new susceptibility loci for Behçet's disease and epistasis between HLA-B*51 and ERAP1. Nat. Genet. **45**, 202–207 (2013). https://doi.org/10.1038/ng.2520

16. Lee, S., Kwon, M.S., Park, T.: CARAT-GxG: CUDA-accelerated regression analysis toolkit for large-scale gene-gene interaction with GPU computing system. Cancer Inform. **13s7**, CIN.S16349 (2014). https://doi.org/10.4137/CIN.S16349

17. van Leeuwen, E.M., Smouter, F.A.S., Kam-Thong, T., et al.: The challenges of genome-wide interaction studies: lessons to learn from the analysis of HDL blood levels. PLoS ONE **9**, e109290 (2014). https://doi.org/10.1371/journal.pone.0109290

18. Piriyapongsa, J., Ngamphiw, C., Intarapanich, A., et al.: iLOCi: a SNP interaction prioritization technique for detecting epistasis in genome-wide association studies. BMC Genom. **13**(Suppl 7), S2 (2012). https://doi.org/10.1186/1471-2164-13-s7-s2

19. Purcell, S., Chang, C.: PLINK v1.90p 64-bit, 9 January 2018. www.cog-genomics.org/plink/1.9/

20. Purcell, S., Neale, B., Todd-Brown, K., et al.: PLINK: a tool set for whole-genome association and population-based linkage analyses. Am. J. Hum. Genet. **81**, 559–575 (2007). https://doi.org/10.1086/519795

21. The Australo-Anglo-American Spondyloarthritis Consortium (TASC), et al.: Interaction between ERAP1 and HLA-B27 in ankylosing spondylitis implicates peptide handling in the mechanism for HLA-B27 in disease susceptibility. Nat. Genet. **43**, 761–767 (2011). https://doi.org/10.1038/ng.873

22. Ueki, M., Cordell, H.J.: Improved statistics for genome-wide interaction analysis. PLoS Genet. **8**(4), e1002625 (2012). https://doi.org/10.1371/journal.pgen.1002625

23. Wan, X., Yang, C., Yang, Q., et al.: BOOST: a fast approach to detecting gene-gene interactions in genome-wide case-control studies. Am. J. Hum. Genet. **87**(3), 325–340 (2010)

24. Wang, Y., Liu, G., Feng, M., Wong, L.: An empirical comparison of several recent epistatic interaction detection methods. Bioinformatics **27**(21), 2936–2943 (2011)

25. Wienbrandt, L., Kässens, J.C., González-Domínguez, J., et al.: FPGA-based acceleration of detecting statistical epistasis in GWAS. Proc. Comput. Sci. **29**, 220–230 (2014). https://doi.org/10.1016/j.procs.2014.05.020

26. Wienbrandt, L., Kässens, J.C., et al.: Fast genome-wide third-order SNP interaction tests with information gain on a low-cost heterogeneous parallel FPGA-GPU computing architecture. Proc. Comput. Sci. **108**, 596–605 (2017). https://doi.org/10.1016/j.procs.2017.05.210

27. Xie, M., Li, J., Jiang, T.: Detecting genome-wide epistases based on the clustering of relatively frequent items. Bioinformatics **28**(1), 5–12 (2012)

28. Yung, L.S., Yang, C., Wan, X., et al.: GBOOST: a GPU-based tool for detecting gene-gene interactions in genome-wide case control studies. Bioinformatics **27**(9), 1309–1310 (2011)

Track of Computational Finance and Business Intelligence

Deep Learning and Wavelets for High-Frequency Price Forecasting

Andrés Arévalo[1(✉)], Jaime Nino[1], Diego León[2], German Hernandez[1], and Javier Sandoval[1]

[1] Universidad Nacional de Colombia, Bogotá, Colombia
{ararevalom,jhninop,gjhernandezp}@unal.edu.co,
javier.sandoval@uexternado.edu.co
[2] Universidad Externado de Colombia, Bogotá, Colombia
diego.leon@uexternado.edu.co

Abstract. This paper presents improvements in financial time series prediction using a Deep Neural Network (DNN) in conjunction with a Discrete Wavelet Transform (DWT). When comparing our model to other three alternatives, including ARIMA and other deep learning topologies, ours has a better performance. All of the experiments were conducted on High-Frequency Data (HFD). Given the fact that DWT decomposes signals in terms of frequency and time, we expect this transformation will make a better representation of the sequential behavior of high-frequency data. The input data for every experiment consists of 27 variables: The last 3 one-minute pseudo-log-returns and last 3 one-minute compressed tick-by-tick wavelet vectors, each vector is a product of compressing the tick-by-tick transactions inside a particular minute using a DWT with length 8. Furthermore, the DNN predicts the next one-minute pseudo-log-return that can be transformed into the next predicted one-minute average price. For testing purposes, we use tick-by-tick data of 19 companies in the Dow Jones Industrial Average Index (DJIA), from January 2015 to July 2017. The proposed DNN's Directional Accuracy (DA) presents a remarkable forecasting performance ranging from 64% to 72%.

Keywords: Short-term forecasting · High-frequency forecasting
Computational finance · Deep Neural Networks
Discrete Wavelet Transform

1 Introduction

Modeling and forecasting financial time series continue to be a very difficult task [6,16–18,21]. Techniques to address this problem can be split into two categories: analytical models and Machine Learning. On one hand, analytical techniques include statistical and stochastic models, such as Linear Regression (LR), Multiple Linear Regression (MLR), Autoregressive Integrated Moving Average (ARIMA), Generalized Autoregressive Conditional Heteroskedasticity

© Springer International Publishing AG, part of Springer Nature 2018
Y. Shi et al. (Eds.): ICCS 2018, LNCS 10861, pp. 385–399, 2018.
https://doi.org/10.1007/978-3-319-93701-4_29

(GARCH/N-GARCH), Brownian Motion (BM), Diffusion, Poisson and Levy Processes. On the other hand, Machine Learning Techniques (MLT) include Decisions Trees, Artificial Neural Networks (ANN), Fuzzy Systems, Kernel Methods, Support Vector Machines (SVM) and recently, Deep Neural Networks (DNN), an extension of Artificial Neural Networks [6,16,20].

We selected Deep Learning because MLT are good while dealing with non-linearities and complexities, such as those present in financial data, in addition to its capabilities to handle large amounts of data, such as those present on HFD. Moreover, we decided to use wavelets as a feature generator because the sequential behavior of HFD, there are many transactions at the same price and changes (price jumps), under normal market conditions should occur with not high variance. Moreover, Deep Learning has been successfully applied in many different fields including price forecasting, as a result, we think that this kind of representation can improve previous results achieved in [1].

The paper is organized as follows: Sect. 2 presents a theoretical overview of Time Series, ARIMA, Artificial Neural Networks, and Wavelets. Section 3 presents the proposed model to forecast one-minute pseudo-log-returns. Section 4 presents some baseline models which are used to compare performance against the proposed method. Section 5 presents final results and their analysis. Finally, Sect. 6 presents conclusions and recommendations for future research.

2 Theory Overview

2.1 Financial Time Series

A time series is a sequence of successive data points with a time order. A Financial Time Series (FTS) is a sequence of financial data points, like price, volume (quantity of financial asset), or any transformation of the previous ones. A FST is a non-stationary process. Formally, a FST X is denoted: $X = X_t : t \in T$.

Where T is an index set, where each element is labeled by a date time stamp, and it is associated only with one data point for a specific financial asset.

Forecasting models seek to predict aptly the next value of the series X without the knowledge of future. F, the predicted time series, is the sequence of predicted values. In order to assess model's performance of F, it is necessary to determine the similarity between X and F. Popular similarity measures for time series include [14]:

− Mean Squared Error (MSE): A scale dependent measure.

$$MSE = \frac{1}{n} \sum_{t=1}^{n} (X_t - F_t)^2 \tag{1}$$

− Directional Accuracy (DA): A scale independent measure. Percent of predicted directions that matches the original time series. DA is widely used in finance [22].

$$DA = \frac{100\%}{n-1} \sum_{t=2}^{n} 1_{sign(X_t - X_{t-1}) = sign(F_t - F_{t-1})} \tag{2}$$

Where 1 is an indicator function: $1_A = f(x) = \begin{cases} 1, & A = \text{True} \\ 0, & A = \text{False} \end{cases}$

A common transformation to make a FST stationary consists of getting the Log-return or pseudo-log-return series.

Log-Return. Let p_t be the current closing price and p_{t-1} the previous closing price.

$$R = \ln \frac{p_t}{p_{t-1}} \cdot 100\% = (\ln p_t - \ln p_{t-1}) \cdot 100\% \tag{3}$$

From a log-return R, the price p_t can be reconstructed as follows: $p_t = p_{t-1} \cdot e^{\frac{R}{100\%}}$

Pseudo-Log-Return. It is a logarithmic difference (log of quotient) between average prices on consecutive minutes. Let $\overline{p_t}$ be the current one-minute average price and $\overline{p_{t-1}}$ the previous one-minute average price.

$$\hat{R} = \ln \frac{\overline{p_t}}{\overline{p_{t-1}}} \cdot 100\% = (\ln \overline{p_t} - \ln \overline{p_{t-1}}) \cdot 100\% \tag{4}$$

Pseudo-returns can be reconstructed just as log-returns: $\overline{p_t} = \overline{p_{t-1}} \cdot e^{\frac{\hat{R}}{100\%}}$

2.2   ARIMA

Traditionally, econometric models dominate the forecasting arena, where statistical linear methods such as ARIMA. ARIMA(p, d, q) and (Auto-Regressive Integrated Moving Average with orders p, d, q), are the most frequently used. In general, these models are a set of discrete time linear equations with noise, of the form:

$$\left(1 - \sum_{k=1}^{p} \alpha_k L^k\right)(1-L)^d X_t = \left(1 - \sum_{k=1}^{q} \beta_k L^k\right)\epsilon_t. \tag{5}$$

Particularly, ARIMA forecasting equation is a linear regression-type equation, in which the predictors consist of lags of a dependent variable and lags of predicted errors, where p is the number of autoregressive terms, d is the number of nonseasonal differences needed for stationarity, and q is the number of lagged forecast errors in the prediction equation.

Despite the relative success of these models, they have low capacity to capture market movements, given complexities and non-linear relationships [6] exhibit in financial markets. For these reasons machine learning methods have emerged as an important alternative to handle this kind of problem, since they are able to recognize complex patterns, and they have the ability to process large amounts of data.

2.3   Artificial Neural Networks

The first class of ANN was the Feed-forward Neural Network (FNN), which has multiple neurons connected to each other, but there are no cycles or loops in the network. Therefore, the information always moves forward from input to output nodes. A Multilayer Perceptron (MLP), which is a FNN subtype, has an input, multiple hidden layers, and one output layer. Each layer has a finite number of neurons that are fully connected to all neurons in the next layer [11].

Since the late 1980s, techniques using ANNs have been widely used to forecast financial time series, due to its ability to extract essential features and to learn complex information patterns in high dimensional spaces [8,16,21,23].

Deep learning (DL) models have demonstrated a greater effectiveness in both classification and prediction tasks, in different domains such as video analysis, audio recognition, text analysis and image processing. Models based on DL attracts the interest of general public because they are able to learn useful representations from raw data, avoiding the local minimum issue of ANNs, by learning in a layered way using a combination of supervised and unsupervised learning to adjust weights W. Nevertheless its advantages, DL applications in computational finance are limited [3,4,7,24,25,28].

Within DL there is a wide variety of architectures, the most simple one uses MLP. However, for the purpose of this paper, we will be using more complex ones such as Recurrent Neural Networks (RNN), Gate Recurrent Units (GRU) and Long Short Term Memory (LSTM). A RNN is an ANN that has connections from output units to input ones, such that a directed cycle is formed. Under this architecture, the network is feedback by the output data; this allows modeling temporal behavior dynamics when storing previous inputs or outputs in an internal memory [11,13,19]. The first known application of a RNN in finance "Stock price pattern recognition-a recurrent neural network approach" was published in [15].

Historically, RNN are better at learning time series, because they are designed to identify patterns through time. But they include a greater complexity than the MLP, and therefore they are more difficult to train. In 1997, the Long Short-Term Memory (LSTM), a kind of RNN, was proposed in [13]. It solved some issues of recurrent networks related to learning too much time dependencies; LSTMs are capable of learning in a balanced way both long and short-term dependencies [10]. Recently, [5] proposed Gated Recurrent Unit (GRU), a variation of LSTM. It combines several internal components of the LSTM; making it simpler than LSTM because it has fewer parameters to be fitted during the training phase.

2.4   Wavelets

A wavelet is a wave function with an average value of zero. One key difference is duration; wavelets, unlike sinusoids, have a finite duration, that is, they have a beginning and an end [9]. Wavelets are a useful way to extract key features from signals in order to reproduce them without having to save or keep the complete signal. Moreover, wavelets possess additional advantages that help to overcome non-stationarity associated with financial time series. In order to get a theoretical background on wavelets, it is important to start with Multi-resolution Analysis (MRA).

Definition 1: A MRA on R is a sequence of subspaces V_j, $j \in Z$ on functions L^2 on R that satisfies the following properties [12,26]:

- $\forall j \in Z, V_j \subset V_{j+1}$
- if f(x) is C_c^0 on R, then f(x) $\in \overline{span}$ $V_j, j \in Z$. Given $\epsilon > 0, \exists$ $j \in Z$ and a function g(x) $\in V_j$, such that $\|f - g\|_2 < \epsilon$
- $\bigcap_{j \in Z} V_j = 0$
- A function $f(x) \in V_0$ if and only if $f(2x) \in V_{j+1} \forall j \in Z$
- $\exists$ a function $\varphi(x), L^2$ on R, called the scaling function, such that $\{\tau_n \varphi(x)\}$ is an orthonormal system of translates and $V_0 = \overline{span}\{\tau_n \varphi(x)\}$

MRA allows an exact calculation of the wavelet coefficients for an L^2 function. Let $\{V_j\}$ an MRA with scaling function $\varphi(x)$, therefore [26]:

- $\varphi(x) = \sum_n h(n)\varphi_{1,n}(x)$, is the scaling function.
- $\psi(x) = \sum_n g(n)\varphi_{1,n}(x)$, is the corresponding wavelet.

Where $g(n) = (-1)^n \overline{h(1-n)}$, is the wavelet filter.

Wavelets transforms could be either continuous or discrete. Since financial time series are discrete, Discrete Wavelet Transform (DWT) is more suitable to filter the data. DWT is defined as follows [26]:

Having a signal $c_o(n)$, its DWT is a sequence collection: $\{d_j(k) : 1 \leq j \leq J; k \in Z\} \cup \{c_j(k) : k \in Z\}$, where

$$c_{j+1}(n) = (Hc_j)(n)$$
$$d_{j+1}(n) = (Gc_j)(n)$$
$$c_j(n) = (H^*c_{j+1})(n) + (G^*d_{j+1})(n)$$

$$(Hc)(k) = \sum_n c(n)\overline{h(n-2k)}$$

$$(Gc)(k) = \sum_n c(n)\overline{g(n-2k)}$$

$$(6)$$

Wavelet analysis offers the following advantages [12]:

- It does not require a strong assumption about the data generation process.
- It provides information in both time and frequency domains.
- It has the ability to locate discontinuities in the data.

However, it has some disadvantages [12]: It requires that the length of the data be 2^j. It is not shift invariant. Finally, it may shift data peaks, causing wrong approximations when compared to the original data.

Table 1. Dataset description

Company	Exchange	Symbol	# Ticks	File size
Apple	NASDAQ	AAPL	146.98 M	7.1 GB
American Express	NYSE	AXP	4.15 M	197 MB
Boeing	NYSE	BA	3.55 M	168 MB
Caterpillar	NYSE	CAT	4.59 M	218 MB
Cisco Systems	NASDAQ	CSCO	58.11 M	2.8 GB
Chevron	NYSE	CVX	7.1 M	340 MB
DuPont Corporation	NYSE	DD	3.66 M	170 MB
Walt Disney	NYSE	DIS	6.34 M	304 MB
General Electric	NYSE	GE	4.76 M	224 MB
Goldman Sachs	NYSE	GS	3.2 M	151 MB
The Home Depot	NYSE	HD	4.35 M	206 MB
IBM	NYSE	IBM	3.59 M	173 MB
Intel	NASDAQ	INTC	70.47 M	3.4 GB
Johnson & Johnson	NYSE	JNJ	5.77 M	278 MB
JPMorgan Chase	NYSE	JPM	7.9 M	375 MB
Coca-Cola	NYSE	KO	3.72 M	174 MB
McDonald's	NYSE	MCD	0.57 M	28 MB
3M	NYSE	MMM	2.63 M	127 MB
ExxonMobil	NYSE	XOM	8.13 M	386 MB
Total			349.56 M	17 GB

Because in a previous work [1], a simple DNN achieved good predictability on high frequency data for two different NYSE equities, we will use DWT as a feature selector, to test the DNN's ability to improve forecasting capabilities when using as inputs features extracted from wavelet analysis of price sequences.

3   Proposed Method

3.1   Dataset Description

Data from the Dow Jones Industrial Average (Dow30) is used. Dow30 is the second-oldest U.S. market index and consists of 30 major US companies. Tick-by-tick data from 19 randomly chosen companies are used. Data were downloaded from January 1st, 2015 to July 31th, 2017. Table 1 shows some dataset descriptors.

3.2   Preprocessing

HFD means high transaction frequency (microseconds to seconds), our approach includes representing a typical one minute for this kind of data. We know that

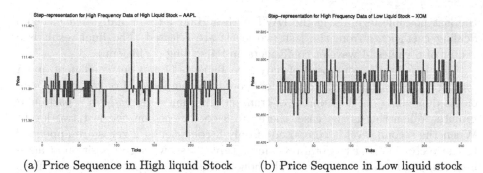

(a) Price Sequence in High liquid Stock   (b) Price Sequence in Low liquid stock

Fig. 1. Stock sequences

prices can vary dramatically in financial markets, however, given the liquidity of $DOW\,30's$ instruments, under normal market conditions, they should exhibit the following characteristics:

- There are many transactions, occurring within short intervals (usually milliseconds/microseconds).
- Prices should not have much volatility between ticks.
- There should not be many different prices.
- Price jumps should not be very wide.

This means that for a typical one minute period, any instrument should exhibit similar behavior. The average number of price jumps (measured in cents) is lower as the price jump is larger, and usually, the less liquid stocks exhibit bigger jumps between ticks. There is a strong correlation between an average number of ticks per minute and the number of streaks or sequences occurring at the same price. That is $P_t = P_{t-1}$. Moreover, we can see that nearly 50% of the ticks have the same price in most of the stocks, except for the more liquids (AAPL, CSCO, INTC), where this measure is near 72% on average. We infer that price discovery is more efficiently performed. As a result, there is a larger proportion of ticks at the same price. In contrast, less liquid stocks exhibit a lower percentage of ticks at the same price, and wider price jumps between ticks. Graphically, this behavior is seen in Fig. 1a and b; The charts have a step style that makes them very similar. This kind of behavior is suitable for wavelet decomposition since the signal exhibits stepped changes between points. This is the reason to use DWT, in order to choose Wavelets coefficients as inputs, because on HFD traded prices can be interpreted as price intervals. Next, we will illustrate in detail the steps to select inputs for the DNN.

All data were summarized at a one-minute level. For each minute, the one-minute pseudo-log-return is calculated. Average prices are calculated from all of the ticks for the particular minute. Moreover, the tick-by-tick series is compressed to 8 values using the DWT.

A log transformation is applied to all tick-by-tick prices on a minute, then iterated differences are performed. The resulting time series is decomposed until the last possible level using the DWT with a Haar filter. Finally, Wavelet and Scaling coefficients from the last two levels are selected. The final result is a vector of 8 values: 4 wavelet coefficients and 4 scaling coefficients.

The last level is composed of only 2 coefficients (1 wavelet coefficient and 1 scaling coefficient). But the one before could be composed of only 4 or 6 coefficients depending on the number of transactions that were made in a particular minute. When this is the case, there are 8 coefficients on the last two levels. When the second level is composed of only 8 coefficients, 2 zeros are appended to the vector in order to obtain 8 values. Table 2a shows decomposition of numbers ranging from 1 to 12. Table 2b shows number decomposition ranging from 1 to 8.

Table 2. Compressed tick-by-tick series using DWT: case I

Level	Wavelet Coefficients						Scaling Coefficients					
3	5.65						24.04					
2	2		2		2		5		13		21	
1	0.70	0.70	0.70	0.70	0.70	0.70	2.12	4.94	7.77	10.60	13.43	16.26
Time series:	1	2	3	4	5	6	7	8	9	10	11	12
Final vector:	5.65	2	2	2	24.04	5	13	21				

(a) Case I

Level	Wavelet Coefficients				Scaling Coefficients			
3	5.65				24.04			
2	2		2		5		13	
1	0.70	0.70	0.70	0.70	2.12	4.94	7.77	10.60
Time series:	1	2	3	4	5	6	7	8
Final vector:	5.65	2	2	0	12.72	5	13	0

(b) Case II

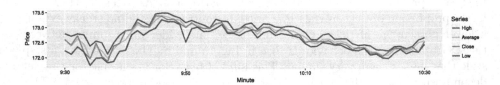

Fig. 2. Example of 60 one-minute prices.

3.3   Modeling

Figure 2 shows the average price, a good descriptor of market behavior. The highest or lowest prices are usually found within a confidence range of average price, therefore the next highest and lowest prices can be estimated from a predicted average price. The closing price is the last price within a minute, it can be the highest/lowest price inclusive. Unlike the average price, the highest, lowest and close are exposed largely to market dynamics.

Since this work's objective is to build the best possible forecaster, average prices could be more suitable for this purpose than closing prices. With a good average price forecast, it is known that traded prices will match at some point in time the predicted average during the next minute.

Selected inputs consist of 27 values: The last 3 one-minute pseudo-log-returns and the last 3 compressed tick-by-tick time series (8×3). The selected output is the next predicted one-minute pseudo-log-returns.

The network architecture consists of one input layer, 5 hidden layers, and one output layer. For each hidden layer, the number of neurons decreases with a constant factor $\frac{1}{5}$, (27, 22, 17, 11 and 6 neurons respectively). The output layer has one neuron. All neurons in hidden layers use a ***Tanh*** activation function, whereas the output neuron uses a ***Linear*** activation function. Figure 3 shows the architecture overview.

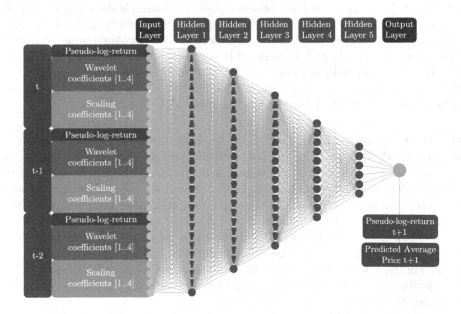

Fig. 3. DNN's architecture

4 Experiments

The proposed method will be compared against the following methods or models, in order to verify its performance (Table 3).

Table 3. Experiment summary

Method	Architecture	Inputs	Reason to use
ARIMA	Analytical formula	Logarithmic rescale	Traditional econometric forecasting model
DNN	5 layers	4 categories, described in [1,2]	Baseline work
GRU	2 layers	Same as proposed method	More suitable DL topologies for time series
LSTM	2 layers	Same as proposed method	More suitable DL topologies for time series

ARIMA: Although it has good performance over in-sample datasets, it has bad performance over out-sample datasets. The time series were rescaled to a logarithmic scale to help to stabilize strong growth trends. And then, many ARIMA models were fitted with the Augmented Dickey-Fuller Test, the Auto and Cross-Covariance and Correlation Function Estimation (ACF) and the Partial Auto and Cross-Covariance and Correlation Function Estimation (PACF). Finally, for each dataset, the ARIMA model with the lowest AIC was selected.

DNN: [1,2] proposed a DNN which also forecasts the next one-minute pseudo-log-return. DNN's inputs are composed of four groups: the current time (hour and minute), the last n one-minute pseudo-log-returns, the last n one-minute standard deviations of prices and the last n one-minute trend indicators, where n is the window size. The trend indicator is a statistical measure computed as the linear model's slope ($price = at + b$) fitted on transaction prices for a particular minute. LSTM and GRU architectures only have two layers, whereas our base work exhibits a five layers network. The main reason to change the number of layers was training times. Given the memory effect of GRU and LSTM, complexity of these topologies is greater, therefore reducing the number of layers decreases training times.

5 Results and Analysis

The dataset was split up into two parts: an in-sample dataset (first 85%) and an out-sample dataset (last 15%). For each symbol and machine learning model, ten artificial networks were trained and then the average error was calculated and reported. Overall, all networks had homogeneous and stable results.

Figure 4 shows the Model Performances during the training and testing phases. Figure 5a shows the Model Performances per Symbol during the training and testing phases, whereas Fig. 5b shows the DA performance on a wider scale.

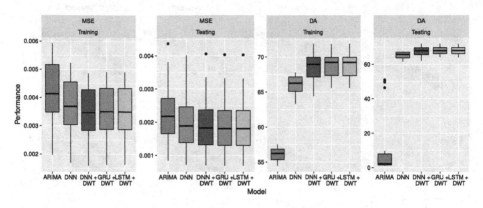

Fig. 4. Model's performance during the training and testing phases

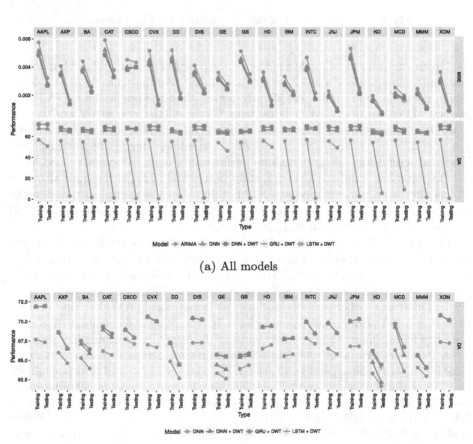

(a) All models

(b) All models except ARIMA

Fig. 5. Model's performance per symbol during the training and testing phases

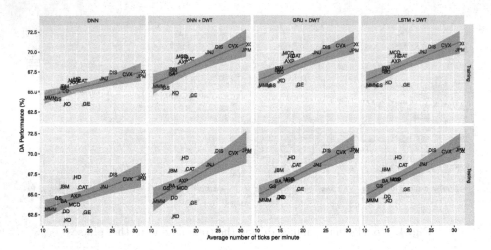

Fig. 6. Average number of ticks per minute vs. DA performance

Given the analysis of models performance over out-sample datasets, machine learning techniques had a much better performance compared to ARIMA. Meanwhile, networks using DWT are slightly better than the one without DWT; On average, DNN without DWT, DNN with DWT, GRU with DWT and LSTM with DWT achieved a MSE of 0.002026, 0.001963, 0.001941 and 0.001939, and a DA of 65.27%, 67.38%, 67.74% and 67.72% respectively during the testing phase. The best model was GRU, though its performance is almost equal to LSTM.

On the other hand, GRU is definitely better than LSTM, because although it has the same performance as LSTM, GRU has less complexity and fewer parameters than LSTM, therefore, the training time is reduced and this method is more suitable for use in a real environment.

Overall, DNNs can learn market dynamics with reasonable precision and accuracy over out-sample datasets. But DA performance may be correlated to liquidity. For instance, symbols AAPL, CSCO and INTC, which exhibit the most liquidity, got much better DA performance, close to 72%, 68%, and 68% respectively. Otherwise, other symbols that are less liquid, like MMM (10 ticks/minute) had a lower DA performance, close to 64%. It is important to mention that more liquidity means more data, the raw material for Machine Learning Techniques.

A Pearson Correlation Test and a Spearman Correlation Test were performed in order to verify the dependency between the average number of ticks per minute and DA performance archived by each machine learning model on all out-sample datasets. The Pearson correlation archived by DNN without DWT, DNN with DWT, GRU with DWT and LSTM with DWT on all symbols were 0.4407459, 0.4524886, 0.4695877 and 0.4648353 respectively. Whereas, the Spearman correlation achieved by DNN without DWT, DNN with DWT, GRU with DWT and LSTM with DWT over all symbols were 0.7684211, 0.7368421, 0.7649123 and 0.7701754 respectively.

The Spearman correlation suggests that there is a non-linear correlation between liquidity and DA Performance. Hence, as liquidity is higher, the proposed model has greater effectiveness. It is important to clarify that the model effectiveness will be stuck at some unknown point, in other words, the proposed models would never reach 100% precision despite the liquidity of a particular instrument.

Figure 6 shows the relationship between the average number of ticks per minute and DA Performance for each machine learning model. Stocks with higher liquidity, (AAPL, CSCO, and INTC), were excluded for better visualization. As we can see, the most traded the stock the best model predicts. Also, it draws a fitted Generalized Additive Model (GAM).

6 Conclusions

Traders collectively repeat the behavior of the traders that preceded them [27]. Those patterns can be learned by a DNN. The proposed strategy replicates the concept of predicting prices for short-time periods.

Feature selection is a very important step while building a machine learning model. Moreover, frequency domain with temporal resolution, produced by the DWT, allows the network to identify more complex patterns in the time series.

In liquid stocks there are many ticks in a minute, therefore the mean is more stable than another less liquid stocks. As a result, the final average price time series has less noise, therefore, a machine learning technique can perform better for these kinds of stocks.

Within the deep learning arena, there are more models than the ones depicted here. As a result, a possible research opportunity could be to evaluate model's performance against other DL models such as Deep Belief Networks, Convolutional Networks, Deep Coding Networks, among others. Overall, Deep Learning techniques can learn market dynamics with a reasonable precision and accuracy, for instance, using recurrent networks increased model's performance.

Another opportunity would be to explore higher resolution levels, other wavelet filters families such as Daubechies, Coiflets, Symlets, Discrete Meyer, Biorthogonal, among others, as well as other discrete transformations.

References

1. Arévalo, A., Niño, J., Hernández, G., Sandoval, J.: High-frequency trading strategy based on deep neural networks. In: Huang, D.-S., Han, K., Hussain, A. (eds.) ICIC 2016. LNCS (LNAI), vol. 9773, pp. 424–436. Springer, Cham (2016). https://doi.org/10.1007/978-3-319-42297-8_40
2. Arévalo Murillo, A.R.: Short-term forecasting of financial time series with deep neural networks. bdigital.unal.edu.co (2016). http://www.bdigital.unal.edu.co/54538/
3. Arnold, L., Rebecchi, S., Chevallier, S., Paugam-Moisy, H.: An introduction to deep learning. In: ESANN (2011). https://www.elen.ucl.ac.be/Proceedings/esann/esannpdf/es2011-4.pdf

4. Chao, J., Shen, F., Zhao, J.: Forecasting exchange rate with deep belief networks. In: 2011 International Joint Conference on Neural Networks, pp. 1259–1266. IEEE, July 2011. https://doi.org/10.1109/IJCNN.2011.6033368

5. Cho, K., van Merrienboer, B., Gulcehre, C., Bahdanau, D., Bougares, F., Schwenk, H., Bengio, Y.: Learning phrase representations using RNN encoder-decoder for statistical machine translation. In: Proceedings of the 2014 Conference on Empirical Methods in Natural Language Processing (EMNLP), pp. 1724–1734, June 2014. http://arxiv.org/abs/1406.1078

6. De Gooijer, J.G., Hyndman, R.J.: 25 years of time series forecasting. Int. J. Forecast. 22(3), 443–473 (2006). https://doi.org/10.1016/j.ijforecast.2006.01.001

7. Ding, X., Zhang, Y., Liu, T., Duan, J.: Deep learning for event-driven stock prediction. In: Proceedings of the Twenty-Fourth International Joint Conference on Artificial Intelligence (ICJAI) (2015). http://ijcai.org/papers15/Papers/IJCAI15-329.pdf

8. Gallo, C., Letizia, C., Stasio, G.: Artificial neural networks in financial modelling (2006). http://citeseerx.ist.psu.edu/viewdoc/download?doi=10.1.1.114.2740&rep=rep1&type=pdf

9. Gençay, R., Selçuk, F., Whitcher, B.: An Introduction to Wavelets and Other Filtering Methods in Finance and Economics. Academic Press, Cambridge (2002)

10. Goodfellow, I., Bengio, Y., Courville, A.: Deep Learning. MIT press, Cambridge (2016). http://www.deeplearningbook.org

11. Haykin, S.: Neural Networks and Learning Machines. Prentice Hall, Upper Saddle River (2009)

12. He, T.X., Nguyen, T.: Wavelet analysis and applications in economics and finance. Res. Rev. J. Stat. Math. Sci. 1(1), 22–37 (2015)

13. Hochreiter, S., Schmidhuber, J.: Long short-term memory. Neural Comput. 9(8), 1735–1780 (1997). https://doi.org/10.1162/neco.1997.9.8.1735

14. Hyndman, R.J., Koehler, A.B.: Another look at measures of forecast accuracy. Int. J. Forecast. 22(November), 679–688 (2005). http://www.sciencedirect.com/science/article/pii/S0169207006000239%5Cncore.ac.uk/download/pdf/6340761.pdf

15. Kamijo, K., Tanigawa, T.: Stock price pattern recognition-a recurrent neural network approach. In: International Joint Conference on Neural Networks, pp. 215–221 (1990). http://ieeexplore.ieee.org/lpdocs/epic03/wrapper.htm?arnumber=5726532

16. Krollner, B., Vanstone, B., Finnie, G.: Financial time series forecasting with machine learning techniques: a survey (2010). http://works.bepress.com/bruce_vanstone/17/

17. Li, X., Huang, X., Deng, X., Zhu, S.: Enhancing quantitative intra-day stock return prediction by integrating both market news and stock prices information. Neurocomputing 142, 228–238 (2014). https://doi.org/10.1016/j.neucom.2014.04.043

18. Marszałek, A., Burczyński, T.: Modeling and forecasting financial time series with ordered fuzzy candlesticks. Inf. Sci. 273, 144–155 (2014). https://doi.org/10.1016/j.ins.2014.03.026

19. Medsker, L., Jain, L.C.: Recurrent Neural Networks: Design and Applications. International Series on Computational Intelligence. CRC Press, Boca Raton (1999)

20. Mills, T.C., Markellos, R.N.: The Econometric Modelling of Financial Time Series. Cambridge University Press, Cambridge (2008). https://doi.org/10.1017/CBO9780511817380

21. Preethi, G., Santhi, B.: Stock market forecasting techniques: a survey. J. Theor. Appl. Inf. Technol. 46(1), 24–30 (2012)

22. Schnader, M.H., Stekler, H.O.: Evaluating predictions of change. J. Bus. **63**(1), 99–107 (1990)
23. Sureshkumar, K., Elango, N.: Performance analysis of stock price prediction using artificial neural network. Global journal of computer science and Technology **12**, 19–26 (2012). http://computerresearch.org/index.php/computer/article/view/426
24. Takeuchi, L., Lee, Y.: Applying deep learning to enhance momentum trading strategies in stocks (2013)
25. Tsay, R.S.: Analysis of Financial Time Series, vol. 543. Wiley, Hoboken (2005)
26. Walnut, D.F.: An Introduction to Wavelet Analysis. Birkhäuser, Boston (2002)
27. Wilder, J.W.: New Concepts in Technical Trading Systems. Trend Research (1978)
28. Yeh, S., Wang, C., Tsai, M.: Corporate Default Prediction via Deep Learning (2014). http://teacher.utaipei.edu.tw/~cjwang/slides/ISF2014.pdf

Kernel Extreme Learning Machine
for Learning from Label Proportions

Hao Yuan[1,4,5], Bo Wang[3], and Lingteng Niu[2,4,5(✉)]

[1] School of Mathematical Sciences, University of Chinese Academy of Sciences,
Beijing 100049, China
yuanhao15@mails.ucas.ac.cn
[2] School of Economics and Management, University of Chinese Academy of Sciences,
Beijing 100190, China
niulf@ucas.ac.cn
[3] School of Information Technology and Management,
University of International Business and Economics, Beijing 100029, China
wangbo@uibe.edu.cn
[4] Research Center on Fictitious Economy & Data Science,
Chinese Academy of Sciences, Beijing 100190, China
[5] Key Laboratory of Big Data Mining and Knowledge Management,
Chinese Academy of Sciences, Beijing 100190, China

Abstract. As far as we know, Inverse Extreme Learning Machine (IELM) is the first work extending ELM to LLP problem. Due to basing on extreme learning machine (ELM), it obtains the fast speed and achieves competitive classification accuracy compared with the existing LLP methods. Kernel extreme learning machine (KELM) generalizes basic ELM to the kernel-based framework. It not only solves the problem that the node number of the hidden layer in basic ELM depends on manual setting, but also presents better generalization ability and stability than basic ELM. However, there is no research based on KELM for LLP. In this paper, we apply KELM and design the novel method LLP-KELM for LLP. The classification accuracy is greatly improved compared with IELM. Lots of numerical experiments manifest the advantages of our novel method.

Keywords: Learning from label proportions
Extreme learning machine · Kernel · Classifier calibration

1 Introduction

In the age of big data, there are a huge number of varied data, but manually labeling these data is very difficult and expensive [10, 19, 34, 35]. In order to solve the situation, many machine learning techniques called weak-label learning are proposed. They don't require the complete labeling information and can achieve good generalization performance. There are many specific techniques of weak-label learning, such as semi-supervised learning (SSL) [3, 17, 33], learning from

© Springer International Publishing AG, part of Springer Nature 2018
Y. Shi et al. (Eds.): ICCS 2018, LNCS 10861, pp. 400–409, 2018.
https://doi.org/10.1007/978-3-319-93701-4_30

partial labels [5, 16, 31], multi-instance learning (MIL) [1, 2, 7, 21, 32] and learning from label proportions (LLP) [4, 6, 8, 18, 22, 23, 25–30]. In this paper, the problems of LLP are concerned on and investigated.

In LLP, the training instances are divided into bags and there are no labels for every instance. The only known information about labels is the label proportion for every bag. The goal of LLP is to get a instance-level classifier to give the predictions of the class labels for the new instances. An intuitive instruction of LLP problem is shown in Fig. 1.

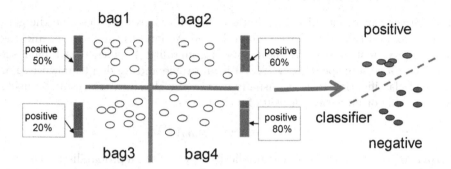

Fig. 1. Illustration of LLP. Consider the binary classification problem, each instance has the positive or negative label. Now there are 4 bags for training: bag1, bag2, bag3, bag4. The proportions of positive instances in each bag are 50%, 60%, 20%, 80%, respectively. By using the 4 bags with the proportions, we get a instance classifier.

LLP attracts a lot of attention and has many applications, such as privacy protection, spam filter, computer vision and medical research. Let's take medical research as a detailed example. Of course, it is also an application of LLP for privacy protection [27]. In medical research, we want to study the outbreak pattern of a new type of flu. Whether each patient is infected with this new type of flu virus is a private information between the patient and the doctor. However, the statistics can be obtained on the proportion of patients diagnosed with this new flu who went to hospital for treatment. Some information about the basic physical condition of patients is also available. Based on these, LLP methods can be used to predict whether each patient is infected with the new flu virus. According to the prediction of LLP methods, the medical researchers can explore the specific relationship between this new type of flu and individual physical condition. After establishing the corresponding relationship, they can develop corresponding measures to better treat this disease and prevent large-scale infections.

For the sake of addressing the problems of LLP, many algorithms have been proposed [4, 6, 8, 18, 22, 23, 25–30]. Recently, Cui et al. [6] presented an approach based on extreme learning machine (ELM) [12–15] called inverse extreme learning machine (IELM). Compared with the existing methods, it speeds up the training process and achieves competitive classification results. However, the

LLP methods based on ELM have not been well studied. In this paper, we design a new LLP method LLP-KELM, which links inverse classifier calibration [6,24,27] to kernel extreme learning machine (KELM) [13]. It overcomes the disadvantage that the node number of hidden layer need to be manually set. Moreover, the performance has been significantly improved than IELM.

2   Related Work

2.1   Classifier Calibration Methods

On a dataset, an probability distribution $P(X, Y)$ is given to describe the generation process of data instances. where Y and X denotes the label set and the sample space, respectively. Without loss of generality, Y is set to a binary set $\{+1, -1\}$. Generally speaking, $P(X, Y)$ is an oracle and we don't known it. For a general classification task, we usually obtain the classification result by using the sign value of numerical decision function, i.e.,

$$class(x) = sign(f_{Num}(x)).$$

In order to produce a probabilistic prediction, we can use a probabilistic classifier f_{Prob}. It estimates the class probability conditioned on the given sample x, i.e.

$$f_{Prob}(x) \approx P(Y = 1|x).$$

When we want to get the probability output and expect to improve the performance of numerical classifier, calibrating the numerical classifier is a standard approach. Therefore, we need to find a good appropriate function to scale the numerical decision values into the probability values:

$$\sigma(f_{Num}(x)) \approx P(Y = 1|x).$$

Platt calibration [24] is one of probabilistic calibration techniques. It has been validated that this method is quite efficient for many numerical decision functions. It can transform decision outputs to posterior probabilities by the equation:

$$\sigma_{Platt}(f(x)) = \frac{1}{\exp(B - Af(x)) + 1}.$$

In above equation, the parameters B and A can be solved by maximum likelihood estimation.

2.2   Extreme Learning Machine

The work [14] proposed a single-hidden-layer feed-forward networks (SLFNs) learning system called ELM. ELM unifies the classification and regression in the same framework. ELM runs extremely fast and can be easily implemented.

We briefly describe the special form of ELM models, which only have one output node as follows: Given N training instances $(\boldsymbol{x}_i, y_i)_{i=1}^N$, where $\boldsymbol{x}_i \in \mathbb{R}^n$

denotes the feature vector, $y_i \in \mathbb{R}$ denotes the corresponding target value. Suppose that the SLFNs with M hidden nodes have activation function $z(\boldsymbol{x})$, then the model of SLFNs can be represented as

$$\sum_{j=1}^{M} \beta_j z(\boldsymbol{w}_j.\boldsymbol{x}_i + b_j) = o_i, \quad i = 1, 2, .., N. \tag{1}$$

Here, $\boldsymbol{w}_j \in \mathbb{R}^n$ and $\beta_j \in \mathbb{R}$ denote the input and output weight, respectively.

In order to make the output o_i be as close as possible to the target y_i, the loss function of SLFNs is build as

$$\min_{\{\beta_j, \boldsymbol{w}_j, b_j\}_{j=1}^{M}} \sum_{i=1}^{N} |o_i - y_i|^2. \tag{2}$$

(2) can be transformed compactly as:

$$\min_{\boldsymbol{\beta}, \{\boldsymbol{w}_j, b_j\}_{j=1}^{M}} \|\mathbf{Q}\boldsymbol{\beta} - Y\|_2^2. \tag{3}$$

Here, $\boldsymbol{\beta} = [\beta_1, \beta_2, ..., \beta_M]^T$, $Y = [y_1, y_2, ..., y_N]^T$, Q ($q(\boldsymbol{x})$ can be regard as the feature mapping) can be expressed as:

$$
\begin{aligned}
\mathbf{Q} &= \begin{bmatrix} \boldsymbol{q}(\boldsymbol{x}_1) \\ \vdots \\ \boldsymbol{q}(\boldsymbol{x}_N) \end{bmatrix} = \begin{bmatrix} q_1(\boldsymbol{x}_1) & \cdots & q_M(\boldsymbol{x}_1) \\ \vdots & \vdots & \vdots \\ q_1(\boldsymbol{x}_N) & \cdots & q_M(\boldsymbol{x}_N) \end{bmatrix} \\
&= \begin{bmatrix} z(\boldsymbol{w}_1 \boldsymbol{x}_1 + b_1) & \cdots & z(\boldsymbol{w}_M \boldsymbol{x}_1 + b_M) \\ \vdots & \vdots & \vdots \\ z(\boldsymbol{w}_1 \boldsymbol{x}_N + b_1) & \cdots & z(\boldsymbol{w}_M \boldsymbol{x}_N + b_M) \end{bmatrix}_{N \times M}
\end{aligned} \tag{4}
$$

In the training phase of ELM, $\{\boldsymbol{w}_j, b_j\}_{j=1}^{L}$ are randomly produced and don't need to be learned. So, the tuned parameters $\boldsymbol{\beta}$ of the learning system ELM can be solved by means of the least squares methods. The solution $\boldsymbol{\beta}^\star$ is

$$\mathbf{Q}^\dagger Y, \tag{5}$$

where the notation $\dagger$ operates the Moore-Penrose generalized inverse of a matrix. Finally, ELM is represented as

$$f(\boldsymbol{x}) = \boldsymbol{q}(\boldsymbol{x})\boldsymbol{\beta}^\star. \tag{6}$$

According to the theory of matrix computation [9], when $\mathbf{Q}$ is full row-rank,

$$\boldsymbol{\beta}^\star = \mathbf{Q}^T(\mathbf{Q}\mathbf{Q}^T)^{-1}Y, \tag{7}$$

when $\mathbf{Q}$ is full column-rank,

$$\boldsymbol{\beta}^\star = (\mathbf{Q}^T\mathbf{Q})^{-1}\mathbf{Q}^T Y. \tag{8}$$

3   KELM for LLP

In LLP, InvCal [27] is the first method to adopt the process of inverting calibration for a classifier, IELM method [6] also used the inverse process. In this paper, the idea also will be used.

A binary classification situation is considered as follows. The training instances $\{x_i, y_i^*\}_{i=1}^N$ are expressed as the form of K bags: $\{B_k, P_k\}_{k=1}^K$, where B_k represents the k-th bag including N_k instances $\{x_i, y_i^*\}_{i=1}^{N_k}$.

We denote $y_i^* \in \{+1, -1\}$ the unknown ground truth label of each instance x_i. Then, for the k-th bag B_k, the proportions of positive instances (i.e. the conditional probability)can be calculated by

$$P_k = \frac{|\{i|x_i \in B_k, y_i^* = +1\}|}{|B_k|}, k = 1, 2 \ldots K. \tag{9}$$

If the instance labels are modeled as $\{y_i\}_{i=1}^N$, for the k-th bag, the modeled label proportion can be expressed as

$$p_k = \frac{|\{i|x_i \in B_k, y_i = +1\}|}{|B_k|}, k = 1, 2 \ldots K. \tag{10}$$

Here, we can treat p_k as the estimate value of P_k.

Now, LLP problem formulation has been completed and we know the bags $\{B_k\}_{k=1}^K$ and the corresponding proportions $\{p_k\}_{k=1}^K$. Next, We will inverse the process of classifier calibration [6,27]. Firstly, each bag B_k is regarded as an instance X_k, which is called the "super-instance". The super-instance X_k is presented as the mean value of all instances in B_k, i.e., $X_k = (\sum_{x_i \in B_k} x_i)/|B_k|$. Secondly, a soft label $\sigma^{-1}(p_k)$ are generated. The generation process is described as follows: (1) We fix the scaling function in classifier calibration methods. Here, we use the scaling function σ_{Platt} in the Platt calibration and let the parameter $A = 1, B = 0$. (2) We calculate the inverse of the scaling function $\sigma_{Platt}^{-1}(p) = -log(1/p - 1)$ and get the soft label $y_k^s = \sigma_{Platt}^{-1}(p_k)$ of each super-instance X_k.

After obtaining the super-instance X_k and the soft label y_k^s, the LLP problem is converted to a supervised learning problem, i.e., a regression problem. We expect the regression model f can fits y_k^s well over each super-instance X_k. In this paper, KELM is adopted to better solve the regression problem. In KELM, Mercer's conditions are applied and the ELM kernel function is defined as: $\kappa(x_i, x_j) = \langle q(x_i), q(x_j) \rangle = K_{i,j}$, where $\langle, \rangle$ represents the inner product operation, q is the feature mapping function in formula (4). Here, lots of kernel function can be used, such as polynomial kernel, RBF kernel and so on. In Eq. (7), a positive number C can be added to all the diagonal elements of $\mathbf{QQ}^T$ motivated by the ridge regression theory [11], and $\mathbf{QQ}^T$ can be replaced by the kernel matrix $\mathbf{K}$. When a new instance x comes, we compute the kernel matrix k_x between x and $\{X_k\}_{k=1}^K$ and then get the corresponding response y_x by formula (11), the label y of x can be obtained by the sign of y_x. The novel model LLP-KELM can be formalized as:

$$f(x) = q(x)\mathbf{Q}^T(\frac{\mathbf{I}}{C} + \mathbf{Q}\mathbf{Q}^T)^{-1}Y$$

$$= \mathbf{k}_x(\frac{\mathbf{I}}{C} + \mathbf{Q}\mathbf{Q}^T)^{-1}Y \tag{11}$$

$$= \begin{bmatrix} \kappa(x, X_1) \\ \vdots \\ k(x, X_N) \end{bmatrix}^T (\frac{\mathbf{I}}{C} + \mathbf{K})^{-1}Y,$$

Here, $\mathbf{K}$ represents the kernel matrix of the super-instances $\{X_k\}_{k=1}^K$, Y is the vector of the soft labels $\{y_k^s\}_{k=1}^K$. We summarize the process of LLP-KELM as Algorithm 1.

Algorithm 1. LLP-KELM

Require: A training set in bags $\{(B_k, p_k)\}_{k=1}^K$, the kernel function κ, the parameter
$\quad\quad$ C and a test instance x
Ensure: The predicted label y of the instance x
1: Compute the bag-level super-instances $\{X_k\}_{k=1}^K$
2: compute the kernel matrix $\mathbf{K}$ of $\{X_k\}_{k=1}^K$ by the kernel function κ
3: compute $Y = [y_1^s, ..., y_K^s]^T$ by the inverse function of σ: $\sigma^{-1}(p_k), k = 1, 2, .., K$.
4: compute the inverse of $\frac{\mathbf{I}}{C} + \mathbf{K}$
5: compute $\beta^\star = (\frac{\mathbf{I}}{C} + \mathbf{K})^{-1}Y$
6: compute the kernel matrix $\mathbf{k}_x$ between x and the super-instances $\{X_k\}_{k=1}^K$
7: compute the responding $y_x = \mathbf{k}_x\beta^\star$
8: get the predicted label $y = sign(y_x)$
9: **return** the predicted label y

---

4   Numerical Experiment

We conduct the experiment to verify the performances of our novel method LLP-KELM in this section. From the paper [6], we know that IELM can produce the comparable classification accuracy and has very fast training speed compared with other advanced methods in many public datasets. Therefore, it is appropriate that we choose IELM as the only baseline. We run the experiment code on a server with Windows Server OS. Its configurations are Intel(R) Xeon(R) CPU E5-2640 at 2.6 GHz and 128 GB main memory. MATLAB R2013a 64-bit version is used as the programming IDE.

4.1   Benchmark Datasets

Different algorithms are compared in real-world classification datasets obtained from the UCI repository [20] and LibSVM collection[1]. We only consider the binary classification datasets. For each dataset, the features are scaled. The statistics for these used datasets are shown in Table 1.

---

[1] https://www.csie.ntu.edu.tw/~cjlin/libsvmtools/datasets/.

Table 1. Statistics of the used data. According to the sample number, data are list one by one.

Datasets	# of samples	# of features
Spect	267	22
Heart	270	13
Liver-disorders	345	5
Vote	435	16
Credit-a	690	15
Diabetes	768	8
Fourclass	862	2
Splice	1000	60
German.numer	1000	24
A1a	1605	119

4.2 Experimental Settings

In order to generate the data form of LLP problems, we randomly split various datasets in Table 1 into lots of bags with fixed bag size. In this paper, the bag sizes which are used are 2, 4, 8, 16, 32, 64. We utilize grid search and 5-fold cross validation to find the best parameters and evaluate the performance. The performance are evaluated based on test accuracy on the instance level.

For the baseline IELM, we follow the paper [6] and adopt the same parameter setting rule. The node number of hidden layer ranges from the set $\{5, 10, 15, 20, 25, \ldots, 200\}$. For our proposed method, the RBF kernel $\kappa(u, v) = \exp(-\gamma \|u - v\|_2^2)$ is considered. The logarithm of parameters, $\log_{10} C$ and $\log_{10} \gamma$, are adjusted from the set $\{-3, -2, -1, 0, 1, 2, 3\}$.

4.3 Results and Analysis

The experiment results on the various datasets are reported in Table 2. We use the bold figures to state the best accuracy of our experiments. Table 2 displays the mean test accuracies of 5-fold cross validation with standard deviation. As shown in Table 2, our novel method LLP-KELM overwhelmingly outperforms the baseline IELM on the test accuracy in most situations. We take some examples to illustrate the results. The datasets "splice", we observe that the accuracy of LLP-KELM and IELM are respectively 82.80%, 75.10% in the bag size 2. In the setting of bag size 4, the accuracy value are respectively 79.30%, 70.10%. It is obvious that LLP-KELM is much better than IELM on the test accuracy. In other bag size setting, this is also true. We can also notice that the accuracies of the two methods LLP-KELM and IELM decrease with the bag size increasing in some ways. This indicates that the larger the bag size, the harder it is to correctly classify the instances in the bags. This is a great challenge in LLP.

Table 2. Mean test accuracies (mean ± std%) of 5-fold cross validation with different bag sizes: 2, 4, 8, 16, 32, 64.

Datasets	Method	Bag Size					
		2	4	8	16	32	64
Spect	LLP-KELM	80.91 ± 3.55	80.13 ± 4.00	81.30 ± 3.56	81.66 ± 6.69	80.13 ± 4.41	79.39 ± 4.47
	IELM	80.17 ± 3.46	77.13 ± 5.15	73.81 ± 8.31	72.61 ± 8.34	78.25 ± 7.57	81.66 ± 2.29
Heart	LLP-KELM	82.96 ± 4.01	85.93 ± 3.84	81.85 ± 2.41	77.04 ± 5.65	74.44 ± 5.77	73.33 ± 9.85
	IELM	82.22 ± 4.46	80.37 ± 2.81	76.30 ± 7.90	70.74 ± 12.92	67.04 ± 6.60	75.56 ± 6.06
Liver-disorders	LLP-KELM	69.28 ± 7.20	63.48 ± 5.27	62.32 ± 5.42	57.97 ± 4.81	58.84 ± 5.29	58.26 ± 5.16
	IELM	68.41 ± 4.40	62.03 ± 7.20	60.00 ± 6.28	60.00 ± 6.28	53.91 ± 8.84	52.46 ± 11.10
Vote	LLP-KELM	96.32 ± 1.89	95.40 ± 1.41	94.48 ± 0.96	93.56 ± 2.38	91.95 ± 1.82	87.82 ± 5.05
	IELM	95.63 ± 0.51	92.87 ± 3.08	89.43 ± 4.48	91.03 ± 4.48	91.95 ± 4.53	87.36 ± 7.22
Credit-a	LLP-KELM	86.38 ± 3.05	85.36 ± 3.05	85.22 ± 4.43	85.22 ± 3.22	83.48 ± 5.48	79.71 ± 7.19
	IELM	85.94 ± 1.80	81.16 ± 5.45	81.30 ± 2.48	79.86 ± 2.73	74.64 ± 5.66	77.54 ± 4.23
Diabetes	LLP-KELM	77.73 ± 1.30	75.78 ± 1.92	74.87 ± 0.96	74.48 ± 2.24	70.32 ± 2.18	69.27 ± 3.92
	IELM	76.43 ± 0.58	74.35 ± 1.28	72.39 ± 3.37	69.66 ± 4.99	69.80 ± 4.48	60.78 ± 13.32
Fourclass	LLP-KELM	81.22 ± 6.12	79.01 ± 3.61	77.03 ± 4.11	76.22 ± 7.66	75.18 ± 3.95	74.02 ± 5.76
	IELM	78.54 ± 4.11	75.88 ± 4.03	67.52 ± 4.91	62.41 ± 12.23	59.98 ± 8.58	55.21 ± 9.45
Splice	LLP-KELM	82.80 ± 1.96	79.30 ± 2.14	74.00 ± 5.42	71.00 ± 5.33	61.50 ± 3.18	60.50 ± 7.95
	IELM	75.10 ± 3.21	70.10 ± 4.60	66.10 ± 4.16	63.40 ± 2.13	61.30 ± 2.46	60.20 ± 6.39
German.numer	LLP-KELM	75.00 ± 2.62	74.60 ± 2.04	73.30 ± 3.93	70.90 ± 1.85	70.10 ± 1.64	71.00 ± 3.54
	IELM	73.70 ± 2.36	71.60 ± 3.07	66.60 ± 4.38	67.00 ± 2.85	64.50 ± 4.43	63.40 ± 2.58
A1a	LLP-KELM	83.12 ± 1.68	82.18 ± 1.48	80.12 ± 2.98	78.69 ± 2.60	78.38 ± 2.61	76.88 ± 2.30
	IELM	79.31 ± 3.17	75.26 ± 2.58	72.40 ± 3.97	68.72 ± 5.56	71.21 ± 7.83	74.58 ± 4.90

5 Conclusion

We design a novel LLP method called LLP-KELM, which significantly improves the method IELM. In LLP-KELM, the kernel version of ELM and the inverse process of classifier calibration are fully utilized. In most situation of our experiments, it can gain the better performances than IELM. In conclusion, our novel method LLP-KELM is feasible for LLP and can be applied in many practical applications.

Acknowledgments. This research was supported by the National Natural Science Foundation of China (Grant No. 11331012, No. 11671379) and UCAS Grant (No. Y55202LY00).

References

1. Amores, J.: Multiple instance classification: review, taxonomy and comparative study. Artif. Intell. **201**(4), 81–105 (2013)
2. Andrews, S., Tsochantaridis, I., Hofmann, T.: Support vector machines for multiple-instance learning. Adv. Neural Inf. Process. Syst. **15**(2), 561–568 (2002)
3. Chapelle, O., Scholkopf, B., Zien, A.: Semi-supervised learning. IEEE Trans. Neural Netw. **20**(3), 542 (2009). Chapelle, O., et al. (eds.) (2006)
4. Chen, B.C., Chen, L., Ramakrishnan, R., Musicant, D.R.: Learning from aggregate views. In: 22nd International Conference on Data Engineering, ICDE 2006, p. 3. IEEE (2006)

5. Cour, T., Sapp, B., Taskar, B.: Learning from partial labels. J. Mach. Learn. Res. **12**(May), 1501–1536 (2011)
6. Cui, L., Zhang, J., Chen, Z., Shi, Y., Yu., P.S.: Inverse extreme learning machine for learning with label proportions. In: Proceedings of IEEE International Conference on Big Data (2017)
7. Dietterich, T.G., Lathrop, R.H., Lozano-Pérez, T.: Solving the Multiple Instance Problem with Axis-Parallel Rectangles. Elsevier Science Publishers Ltd., Amsterdam (1997)
8. Fan, K., Zhang, H., Yan, S., Wang, L., Zhang, W., Feng, J.: Learning a generative classifier from label proportions. Neurocomputing **139**, 47–55 (2014)
9. Golub, G.H., Van Loan, C.F.: Matrix Computations, 3rd edn. Johns Hopkins University Press, Baltimore (1996)
10. Hady, M.F.A., Schwenker, F.: Semi-supervised learning. In: Bianchini, M., Maggini, M., Jain, L. (eds.) Handbook on Neural Information Processing. ISRL, vol. 49, pp. 215–239. Springer, Heidelberg (2013). https://doi.org/10.1007/978-3-642-36657-4_7
11. Hoerl, A.E., Kennard, R.W.: Ridge regression: biased estimation for nonorthogonal problems. Technometrics **12**(1), 55–67 (2000)
12. Huang, G.B., Wang, D.H., Lan, Y.: Extreme learning machines: a survey. Int. J. Mach. Learn. Cybern. **2**(2), 107–122 (2011)
13. Huang, G.B., Zhou, H., Ding, X., Zhang, R.: Extreme learning machine for regression and multiclass classification. IEEE Trans. Syst. Man Cybern. Part B (Cybern.) **42**(2), 513–529 (2012)
14. Huang, G.B., Zhu, Q.Y., Siew, C.K.: Extreme learning machine: a new learning scheme of feedforward neural networks. In: Proceedings of the 2004 IEEE International Joint Conference on Neural Networks, vol. 2, pp. 985–990. IEEE (2004)
15. Huang, G.B., Zhu, Q.Y., Siew, C.K.: Extreme learning machine: theory and applications. Neurocomputing **70**(1), 489–501 (2006)
16. Jin, R., Ghahramani, Z.: Learning with multiple labels. In: Advances in Neural Information Processing Systems, pp. 921–928 (2003)
17. Joachims, T.: Transductive inference for text classification using support vector machines. In: Sixteenth International Conference on Machine Learning, pp. 200–209 (1999)
18. Kück, H., de Freitas, N.: Learning about individuals from group statistics. In: Proceedings of the Twenty-First Conference on Uncertainty in Artificial Intelligence, UAI 2005, pp. 332–339. AUAI Press, Arlington (2005). http://dl.acm.org/citation.cfm?id=3020336.3020378
19. Li, Y.F., Tsang, I.W., Kwok, J.T., Zhou, Z.H.: Convex and scalable weakly labeled SVMs. J. Mach. Learn. Res. **14**(1), 2151–2188 (2013)
20. Lichman, M.: UCI machine learning repository (2013). http://archive.ics.uci.edu/ml
21. Maron, O., Lozano-Pérez, T.: A framework for multiple-instance learning. In: Advances in Neural Information Processing Systems, pp. 570–576 (1997)
22. Musicant, D.R., Christensen, J.M., Olson, J.F.: Supervised learning by training on aggregate outputs. In: Seventh IEEE International Conference on Data Mining, pp. 252–261 (2007)
23. Patrini, G., Nock, R., Caetano, T., Rivera, P.: (Almost) no label no cry. In: Advances in Neural Information Processing Systems, pp. 190–198 (2014)
24. Platt, J.C.: Probabilistic outputs for support vector machines and comparisons to regularized likelihood methods. Adv. Large Margin Classif. **10**(4), 61–74 (1999)

25. Qi, Z., Wang, B., Meng, F., Niu, L.: Learning with label proportions via NPSVM. IEEE Trans. Cybern. **PP**(99), 1–13 (2017)
26. Quadrianto, N., Smola, A.J., Caetano, T.S., Le, Q.V.: Estimating labels from label proportions. J. Mach. Learn. Res. **10**(3), 2349–2374 (2009)
27. Rueping, S.: SVM classifier estimation from group probabilities. In: Proceedings of the 27th International Conference on Machine Learning, ICML 2010, pp. 911–918 (2010)
28. Stolpc, M., Morik, K.: Learning from label proportions by optimizing cluster model selection. In: Gunopulos, D., Hofmann, T., Malerba, D., Vazirgiannis, M. (eds.) ECML PKDD 2011. LNCS, vol. 6913, pp. 349–364. Springer, Heidelberg (2011). https://doi.org/10.1007/978-3-642-23808-6_23
29. Yu, F.X., Choromanski, K., Kumar, S., Jebara, T., Chang, S.F.: On learning from label proportions. arXiv preprint arXiv:1402.5902 (2014)
30. Yu, F., Liu, D., Kumar, S., Jebara, T., Chang, S.: ∝SVM for learning with label proportions. In: Proceedings of the 30th International Conference on Machine learning (2013)
31. Zhang, M.L., Yu, F., Tang, C.Z.: Disambiguation-free partial label learning. IEEE Trans. Knowl. Data Eng. **29**(10), 2155–2167 (2017)
32. Zhang, Q., Goldman, S.A.: EM-DD: an improved multiple-instance learning technique. In: International Conference on Neural Information Processing Systems: Natural and Synthetic, pp. 1073–1080 (2001)
33. Zhou, D., Bousquet, O., Lal, T.N., Weston, J., Schölkopf, B.: Semi-supervised learning by maximizing smoothness. J. Mach. Learn. Res. (2004)
34. Zhou, Z.H.: A brief introduction to weakly supervised learning. Natl. Sci. Rev. **5**, 44–53 (2017)
35. Zhu, X.: Semi-supervised learning literature survey. Comput. Sci. **37**(1), 63–77 (2005)

Extreme Market Prediction for Trading Signal with Deep Recurrent Neural Network

Zhichen Lu[1,2,3], Wen Long[1,2,3(✉)], and Ying Guo[1,2,3]

[1] School of Economics and Management, University of Chinese Academy of Sciences, Beijing 100190, People's Republic of China
longwen@ucas.ac.cn
[2] Research Center on Fictitious Economy and Data Science, Chinese Academy of Sciences, Beijing 100190, People's Republic of China
[3] Key Laboratory of Big Data Mining and Knowledge Management, Chinese Academy of Sciences, Beijing 100190, People's Republic of China

Abstract. Recurrent neural network are a type of deep learning units that are well studied to extract features from sequential samples. They have been extensively applied in forecasting univariate financial time series, however their application to high frequency multivariate sequences has been merely considered. This paper solves a classification problem in which recurrent units are extended to deep architecture to extract features from multi-variance market data in 1-minutes frequency and extreme market are subsequently predicted for trading signals. Our results demonstrate the abilities of deep recurrent architecture to capture the relationship between the historical behavior and future movement of high frequency samples. The deep RNN is compared with other models, including SVM, random forest, logistic regression, using CSI300 1-minutes data over the test period. The result demonstrates that the capability of deep RNN generating trading signal based on extreme movement prediction support more efficient market decision making and enhance the profitability.

Keywords: Recurrent neural networks · Deep learning
High frequency trading · Financial time series

1 Introduction

Financial time series forecasting, especially stock price forecasting has been one of the most difficult problems for researchers and speculators. The difficulties are mainly caused by the uncertainty and noise of samples, the generation of samples are not just consequence of historical behavior information contained in samples, but also influenced by information beyond historical samples such as macro economy, investor sentiment etc. Traditional statistics methods were well prefered to fit financial time series consider the their robustness to noise

© Springer International Publishing AG, part of Springer Nature 2018
Y. Shi et al. (Eds.): ICCS 2018, LNCS 10861, pp. 410–418, 2018.
https://doi.org/10.1007/978-3-319-93701-4_31

and good explaination. But consider it's pool fitting capability, their implement on sending signal for trading were mostly undesirable. Machine learning method were exploited to this problem and get considerable progress but bottleneck are lead by their sensitivity to parameters and tendency to overfitting.

In recent years, deep learning method have shown remarkable progress in many tasks such as computer visions [9,15], nature language process [7], speech recognition [5] etc. The deep architecture have shown powerful capabilities of feature extraction and fitting,and the auxiliary tricks such as dropout [14],batch normalization [6] etc. and optimizer such as Rmsprop, Adam [8], Nadam etc. were designed to improve the efficiency of training and figure problems of over-fitting, gradient vanish, gradient explosion that substantially led by the deep architecture and non-linear mapping during training. In application on financial time series prediction,numerous studies have shown that neural network is a very effective tool in financial time series forecasting [2,13,16]. Weigend et al. [12,17,18] compared the performance of neural network with that of traditional statistics methods in predicting financial time series and neural network showed superior forecasting ability than tradition ways. NN models were firstly applied to solve problem in financial domain in White research [19], five different exchange rates were predicted by feedforward and recurrent networks and it was shown in their finding that performance of predictions can be improved by applying NN. Some works show that neural networks are efficient and profitable in forecasting financial time series [4]. Some combinations of multiple neural networks or NN with other method are also proposed for financial time series forecasting. For example, a hybrid artificial method based on neural network and genetic algorithm was used to model daily exchange rates [11].

In this paper, we extended recurrent neural network into deep architecture as a classifier to predict the movement trend of stock price. The performance of models were evaluated on CSI 300 stock index and the results of classification were considered as trading signal to evaluate the profitability.

2   Recurrent Neural Networks with Deep Architecture

2.1   RNN

RNNs [20] are sequence learners which have achieved much success in applications such as natural language understanding, language generation, video processing, and many other tasks [1,3,10]. A simple RNN is formed by a repeated application of a function F_h to the input sequence $\mathcal{X}_t = (X_1, \ldots, X_T)$.For each time step $t = 1, \ldots, T$,the function generates a hidden state h_t:

$$h_t = F_h(X_t, h_{t-1}) = \sigma(W_h X_t + U_h h_{t-1} + b_h) \tag{1}$$

for some non-linear activation function $\sigma(x)$, where X_t denotes the input at time t, W_h denotes the weight of connection between input and hidden state, U_h denotes the weight of connection between the hidden states h_t and h_{t-1}, and b_h denotes the bias of activation.

2.2 Batch Normalization

With the depth of a net work growing, problems such as gradient explosion and gradient vanish may be incurred, and some approach were proposed to alleviate these problems, one of them was batch normalization [6]. The main idea of batch normalization is to perform normalization on the output of each layers for each mini batch [BN], and to reduce internal covariate shift of each layer's activation, the mean and variance of the distribution are parameterized and learned while training. A batch normalization layer can be formulated as:

$$\hat{x}^k = \frac{x^k - E[x^k]}{\sqrt{Var[x^k]}} \qquad (2)$$

$$y^k = \gamma^k \hat{x}^k + \beta^k \qquad (3)$$

where x^k is the activation of kth layer, y^k is the output after batch normalization, γ and β are parameters of batch normalization to be learned.

2.3 Deep Recurrent Architecture

To address the problem of stock price prediction, we extend recurrent neural networks into deep architecture. The input of model are multi-variance time series of high frequency market data. At each frame, the hidden outputs h_t from recurrent layer are fully connected to the next recurrent layer so that the recurrent units are stacked into deeper architecture. Between each stacked recurrent layers, batch normalization are performed on each time axis so that the output of each recurrent units can be normalized to avoid the problems that may led by scale of activation while training on mini-batch. At the last recurrent layer, the last normalized frame was connected to a fully connected perception and output with a softmax layers. The details of our deep architecture are presented in Fig. 1.

3 Data and Preprocessing Methodology

3.1 Sampling

To exploit trading signal from historical market behavior (open, close, high, low, amount, volumns), market data of CSI 300 from the period Jan. 2016 to Dec. 2016 with frequency of 1-minute were sampled into short sequence by constant windows with length of 120, normalization are performed on each univariate time series of each segmented sequence.

3.2 Labeling Methodology

The profitability not only depend on the correctness of prediction on the movement direction of price, but also the margin of price movement that captured

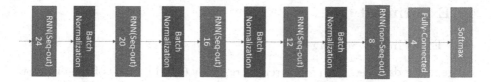

Fig. 1. RNN architecture for financial time series prediction.

by trading signal. So we label samples by assign those whose future prices rise or fall sharply into two single classes and the others as another class, which is defined as:

$$
L_t = \begin{cases} 1 & r_t > r_\theta \\ 0 & \text{Others} \\ -1 & r_t < r_{1-\theta} \end{cases}
$$

where L_t denotes the label of sample X_t, $r_t = ln\dfrac{close_{t+t_{forward}}}{close_t}$ denotes the logarithm return of the stock index $t_{forward}$ minutes after t, and θ denotes the threshold of labeling with $p(r_t > r_\theta) = \theta$ and $p(r_t < r_{1-\theta}) = \theta$. Another reason of the labeling methodology is that samples contain higher noise when the price fluctuates in a narrow range, dependency between history behavior and future trend are tend to be weaker than other two situations. Detail statistics of training and test sets are shown in Table 1.

Table 1. Statistic of data sets

(a) Number of samples in each class with different θ.

θ	Training sets			Testing sets		
	Rise	Fluctuation	Fall	Rise	Fluctuation	Fall
0.1	12239	12277	12194	2454	2412	2370
0.15	18355	18397	18315	4511	4386	4261
0.2	24470	24504	24433	6880	6761	6642
0.25	30588	30622	30551	9667	9521	9375
0.3	36699	36738	36665	12982	12652	12322

(b) tuples $(r_\theta, r_{1-\theta})$ in different θ and $t_{forward}$

θ	$t_{forward} = 5$	$t_{forward} = 10$	$t_{forward} = 15$	$t_{forward} = 20$	$t_{forward} = 25$	$t_{forward} = 30$
0.1	(0.0026,-0.0025)	(0.0036,-0.0035)	(0.0044,-0.0042)	(0.0051,-0.0049)	(0.0057,-0.0054)	(0.0063,-0.0059)
0.15	(0.0019,-0.0018)	(0.0027,-0.0026)	(0.0033,-0.0031)	(0.0039,-0.0036)	(0.0044,-0.0039)	(0.0048,-0.0043)
0.2	(0.0014,-0.0013)	(0.0022,-0.002)	(0.0026,-0.0024)	(0.003,-0.0027)	(0.0034,-0.003)	(0.0038,-0.0033)
0.25	(0.0011,-0.001)	(0.0017,-0.0015)	(0.0021,-0.0019)	(0.0024,-0.0021)	(0.0027,-0.0023)	(0.003,-0.0025)
0.3	(0.0008,-0.0007)	(0.0013,-0.0011)	(0.0016,-0.0014)	(0.0019,-0.0016)	(0.0021,-0.0017)	(0.0023,-0.0019)

4 Experiment

4.1 Experiment Setting

We generate data sets with 5 different thresholds θ and 6 kinds of time window $t_{forward}$ of prediction to train 30 RNNs. While training models and learning the parameters, back propagation and stochastic gradient descent(SGD) are used for updating the weights of neurons, dropout rates are 0.25 among recurrent layers and 0.5 in fully connected layers, and the batch size is 320. The learning rate of optimizer are 0.5 at the start of training, and decayed by 0.5 if the accuracy on validation sets haven't improve for 20 epochs. A early stop condition is set, which is that accuracy on validation sets haven't improve for 150 epochs.

4.2 Results Discussion

The performance of each model on test set are shown in Fig. 2. We find that the prediction accuracy increases as the threshold decreases, which is likely because the samples corresponded to larger margin of rise or fall show stronger dependency between features and labels. However, the change of time windows of prediction do not show obvious effect on model performance. Specifically, the model with $\theta = 0.1, t_{forward} = 10$ reaches the best performance with the accuracy of 48.31%, which is remarkable for 3-classes financial time series prediction, and can give powerful support for market practice.

We further test our 30 data sets on SVM, Random Forest, Logistic Regression and traditional statistic model linear regression to compare results with RNN, the best five results of each model on 30 data sets are shown in Table 2. We can find that the performance of RNN is far better than any of the three traditional machine learning models or linear regression, and the accuracy of SVM, the best of the other four models, is outperformed by that of RNN about 4%.

4.3 Market Simulation

We simulate real stock trading based on the prediction of RNN to evaluate the market performance. We follow a strategy proposed by Lavrenko et al. are followed: if the model predicts the new sample as positive class, our system will purchase 100,000 CYN worth of stock at next minutes with open price. We assume 1,000,000 CYN are available at the start moment and trading signal will not be executed when cash balance is less than 100,000 CYN. After a purchase, the system will hold the stock for $t_{forward}$ minutes corresponding to the prediction window of model. If during that period we can sell the stock to make profit of r_θ (threshold profit rate of labeling) or more, we sell immediately, otherwise, at the end of $t_{forward}$ minute period, our system sells the stock with the close price. If the model predicts the new sample as negative class, our system will have a short position of 100,000 CNY worth of stock. Similarly, system will hold the stock for $t_{forward}$ minutes. If during the period the system can buy the stock at $r_{1-\theta}$ lower than shorted, the system close the position of short by buying the

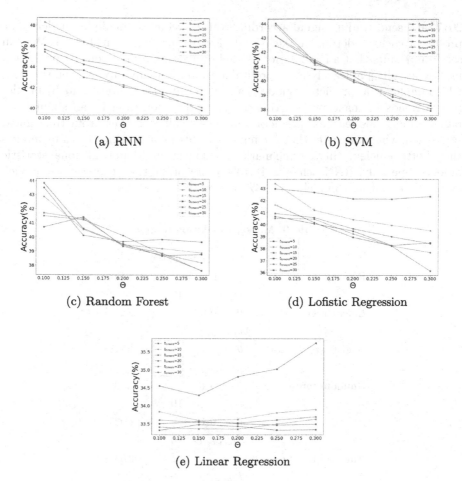

(a) RNN

(b) SVM

(c) Random Forest

(d) Lofistic Regression

(e) Linear Regression

Fig. 2. Performance of each model on 30 datasets.

Table 2. Best 5 results of each model on 30 data sets

	RNN	SVM	Logistic regression	Random forest	Linear regression
1	$t_{forward} = 10\, \theta = 0.1$ 48.31%	$t_{forward} = 20\, \theta = 0.1$ 44.03%	$t_{forward} = 10\, \theta = 0.1$ 43.41%	$t_{forward} = 20\, \theta = 0.1$ 43.83%	$t_{forward} = 5\, \theta = 0.3$ 35.75%
2	$t_{forward} = 5\ \ \theta = 0.1$ 47.40%	$t_{forward} = 10\, \theta = 0.1$ 43.89%	$t_{forward} = 5\ \ \theta = 0.1$ 42.97%	$t_{forward} = 5\ \ \theta = 0.1$ 43.52%	$t_{forward} = 5\, \theta = 0.25$ 35.03%
3	$t_{forward} = 10\, \theta = 0.15$ 46.45%	$t_{forward} = 25\, \theta = 0.1$ 43.13%	$t_{forward} = 5\ \ \theta = 0.15$ 42.67%	$t_{forward} = 10\, \theta = 0.1$ 42.88%	$t_{forward} = 5\, \theta = 0.2$ 34.81%
4	$t_{forward} = 5\ \ \theta = 0.15$ 46.40%	$t_{forward} = 30\, \theta = 0.1$ 43.12%	$t_{forward} = 5\ \ \theta = 0.3$ 42.33%	$t_{forward} = 25\, \theta = 0.1$ 41.71%	$t_{forward} = 5\, \theta = 0.1$ 34.55%
5	$t_{forward} = 15\, \theta = 0.1$ 45.67%	$t_{forward} = 15\, \theta = 0.1$ 42.44%	$t_{forward} = 5\ \ \theta = 0.2$ 42.13%	$t_{forward} = 15\, \theta = 0.1$ 41.50%	$t_{forward} = 5\, \theta = 0.15$ 34.29%

stock to cover. Or else, at the end of the period, system will close the position in the same way at the close price of the end of period.

To simulate this strategy we use models trained on training sets to predict the future trend of stock in each minute from April 18th 2016 to January 30th

2017, and send trading signal according to the prediction made by models. The profits of each model on market simulation are presented in Table 3. We can see from results that all simulations based on trading signals sent by prediction models are all significantly more profitable than randomly buy and sell strategy, which implies that prediction models can catch suitable trading points by predict future trends to make profit. Among these prediction models, all simulations based on machine learning prediction models result in higher profit than linear regression, which indicates that the non-linear fitting of machine learning models show better efficiency in extreme market signal learning than traditional statistic models. Specially, RNN achieves 18.13% more profit than the statistic model, even the second best model is 11.13% less profit than RNN.

Table 3. Market simulation results

	Hyper-parameter	Profit
RNN	$\theta = 0.1$	**24.50%**
	$t_{forward} = 10$	
Linear regression	$\theta = 0.3$	6.37%
	$t_{forward} = 5$	
Logistic regression	$\theta = 0.1$	13.37%
	$t_{forward} = 10$	
Random forest	$\theta = 0.1$	9.65%
	$t_{forward} = 10$	
SVM	$\theta = 0.1$	12.93%
	$t_{forward} = 10$	
Random buy and sell	—	1.03%
	$t_{forward} = 10$	

5   Conclusion

In this paper we extend RNN into deep structure to learning the extreme market from the sequential samples of historical behavior. High frequency market data of CSI 300 are used to train the deep RNN and the deep structure do improve the accuracy of prediction compared with the traditional machine learning method and statistical method. In the sight of practice, this paper presents the applicability of deep non-linear mapping on financial time series, and 48.31% accuracy for 3-classes classification is meaningful for practice in market. And we further prove the better profitability of deep RNN in market simulation than that of any traditional machine learning models or statistic models.

Acknowledgement. This research was partly supported by the grants from National Natural Science Foundation of China (No. 71771204, 71331005, 91546201).

References

1. Bhattacharya, A., Parlos, A.G., Atiya, A.F.: Prediction of MPEG-coded video source traffic using recurrent neural networks. IEEE Trans. Signal Process. **51**(8), 2177–2190 (2002)
2. Cheng, W., Wagner, L., Lin, C.H.: Forecasting the 30-year us treasury bond with a system of neural networks. Neuroizest J. **4**, 10–16 (1996)
3. Dauphin, Y., Yao, K., Bengio, Y., Deng, L., Hakkani-Tur, D., He, X., Heck, L., Tur, G., Yu, D., Zweig, G.: Using recurrent neural networks for slot filling in spoken language understanding. IEEE/ACM Trans. Audio Speech Lang. Process. **23**(3), 530–539 (2015)
4. Emam, A.: Optimal artificial neural network topology for foreign exchange forecasting. In: Proceedings of the 46th Annual Southeast Regional Conference on XX, pp. 63–68. ACM (2008)
5. Graves, A., Mohamed, A., Hinton, G.: Speech recognition with deep recurrent neural networks. In: 2013 IEEE International Conference on Acoustics, Speech and Signal Processing (ICASSP), pp. 6645–6649. IEEE (2013)
6. Ioffe, S., Szegedy, C.: Batch normalization: accelerating deep network training by reducing internal covariate shift. In: International Conference on Machine Learning, pp. 448–456 (2015)
7. Kim, Y.: Convolutional neural networks for sentence classification. arXiv preprint arXiv:1408.5882 (2014)
8. Kingma, D., Ba, J.: Adam: a method for stochastic optimization. arXiv preprint arXiv:1412.6980 (2014)
9. Krizhevsky, A., Sutskever, I., Hinton, G.E.: Imagenet classification with deep convolutional neural networks. In: Advances in Neural Information Processing Systems, pp. 1097–1105 (2012)
10. Mikolov, T., Karafit, M., Burget, L., Cernock, J., Khudanpur, S.: Recurrent neural network based language model. In: INTERSPEECH 2010, Conference of the International Speech Communication Association, Makuhari, Chiba, Japan, September, pp. 1045–1048 (2010)
11. Nag, A.K., Mitra, A.: Forecasting daily foreign exchange rates using genetically optimized neural networks. J. Forecast. **21**(7), 501–511 (2002)
12. Panda, C., Narasimhan, V.: Forecasting exchange rate better with artificial neural network. J. Policy Model. **29**(2), 227–236 (2007)
13. Sharda, R., Patil, R.B.: Connectionist approach to time series prediction: an empirical test. J. Intell. Manuf. **3**(5), 317–323 (1992)
14. Srivastava, N., Hinton, G.E., Krizhevsky, A., Sutskever, I., Salakhutdinov, R.: Dropout: a simple way to prevent neural networks from overfitting. J. Mach. Learn. Res. **15**(1), 1929–1958 (2014)
15. Szegedy, C., Liu, W., Jia, Y., Sermanet, P., Reed, S., Anguelov, D., Erhan, D., Vanhoucke, V., Rabinovich, A.: Going deeper with convolutions. In: Proceedings of the IEEE Conference on Computer Vision and Pattern Recognition, pp. 1–9 (2015)
16. Van Eyden, R.J.: The Application of Neural Networks in the Forecasting of Share Prices (1996)
17. Weigend, A.S.: Predicting sunspots and exchange rates with connectionist networks. In: Nonlinear Modeling and Forecasting, pp. 395–432 (1992)

18. Weigend, A.S., Rumelhart, D.E., Huberman, B.A.: Generalization by weight-elimination with application to forecasting. In: Advances in Neural Information Processing Systems, pp. 875–882 (1991)
19. White, H.: Economic prediction using neural networks: the case of IDM daily stock returns. In: IEEE International Conference on Neural Networks, vol. 2, pp. 451–458 (1988)
20. Williams, R.J., Zipser, D.: A Learning Algorithm for Continually Running Fully Recurrent Neural Networks. MIT Press, Cambridge (1989)

Multi-view Multi-task Support Vector Machine

Jiashuai Zhang[1(✉)], Yiwei He[2], and Jingjing Tang[1]

[1] School of Mathematical Sciences, University of Chinese Academy of Science,
Beijing 100049, China
zhangjiashuai16@mails.ucas.ac.cn
[2] School of Computer and Control Engineering,
University of Chinese Academy of Science, Beijing 101408, China

Abstract. Multi-view Multi-task (MVMT) Learning, a novel learning paradigm, can be used in extensive applications such as pattern recognition and natural language processing. Therefore, researchers come up with several methods from different perspectives including graph model, regularization techniques and feature learning. SVMs have been acknowledged as powerful tools in machine learning. However, there is no SVM-based method for MVMT learning. In order to build up an excellent MVMT learner, we extend PSVM-2V model, an excellent SVM-based learner for MVL, to the multi-task framework. Through experiments we demonstrate the effectiveness of the proposed method.

Keywords: SVM-based · MVMT learning · PSVM-2V
Regularization method

1 Introduction

With the promotion of diversified information acquisition technology, many samples are characterized in many ways, and thus there are a variety of multi-view learning theories and algorithms. Those works have already been extensively used in the practical applications such as pattern recognition [1] and natural language processing [2]. However, multi-view learning merely solves a single learning task.

In many real-world applications, problems exhibit dual-heterogeneity. To state it clearly, a single task has features due to multiple views (i.e., feature heterogeneity); different tasks are related with one another through several shared views (i.e., task heterogeneity) [3]. Confronted with this problem, neither multi-task learning nor multi-view learning is suitable to model. Aiming at settling this complex problem, a novel learning paradigm (i.e. multi-view multi-task learning, or MVMT Learning) has been proposed, which deals with multiple tasks with multi-view data.

He and Lawrence [3] firstly proposed a graph-based framework ($GraM^2$) to figure out MVMT problems. Correspondingly, an effective algorithm ($IteM^2$) was designed to solve the problem. Zhang and Huan [4] developed a regularized

© Springer International Publishing AG, part of Springer Nature 2018
Y. Shi et al. (Eds.): ICCS 2018, LNCS 10861, pp. 419–428, 2018.
https://doi.org/10.1007/978-3-319-93701-4_32

method to settle MVMT learning based on co-regularization. Algorithm based on share structure to deal with multi-task multi-view learning [5]was also proposed afterwards. Besides classification problem, Zhang et al. [6] introduced a novel problem named Multi-task Multi-view Cluster Learning. In order to deal with this special cluster problem, the author presented an algorithm based on graph model to handle nonnegative data at first [6]. Then an improved algorithm [7] was introduced to solve the negative data set.

For decades, SVMs have been acknowledged as powerful tools in machine learning [8,9]. Therefore, many SVM-based algorithms have been proposed for MVL and MTL separately. Although there are several methods dealing with the MVMT learning, models based on SVM have not yet to be established. In order to make use of the excellent performance of SVM, we incorporate multi-task learning into the existing SVM-based multi-view model.

From the perspective of MVL, both consensus principle and complementarity principle are essential for MVL. While the consensus principle emphasizes the agreement among multiple distinct views, the complementary principle suggests that different views share complementary information. Most MVL algorithms achieve either consensus principle or complementary principle. However, a novel MVL model PSVM-2V under the framework of Privileged SVM satisfies both consensus and complementary through combining the LUPI and MVL [10].

In this paper, we construct a new model PSVM-2VMT by extending the PSVM-2V model to the multi-task learning framework. In a single task, we take advantage of PSVM-2V to learn from multiple distinct views; among different tasks, we add regularized terms to ensure the parameters of the same view are similar to each other. Hence, we establish a SVM-based model to solve the MVMT learning. According to the conventional solution of SVM problem, we derive the dual problem of the primal problem and then adopt the classical quadratic programming (QP) solver. We conduct experiments to demonstrate the effectiveness of our model.

To sum up, there are two main contributions of this paper. Firstly, we extend the PSVM-2V model to the multi-task learning framework. Secondly, we conduct experiments on multi-view multi-task data sets, and the results validate the effectiveness of our method.

The rest of this paper is organized as follows. In Sect. 2, we survey related work. Concrete model and corresponding optimization method are presented in Sects. 3 and 4. In Sect. 4, we carry on experiments to demonstrate the effectiveness of our model. At last, we conclude our work in Sect. 5.

2   Related Work

2.1   Multi-task Learning

Multi-task learning (MTL) is a learning paradigm with the help of other tasks to improve the generalization performance of original task [11]. Specifically, characterizing the relationships among tasks is the core of MTL.

In the early study of MTL, we assume that different tasks are closely related. Multi-Task feature learning is a classical method based on this assumption.

According to the relationship between the original feature space and learned feature space, there are two distinctive methods, i.e. feature transformation methods and feature selection methods. Multi-Task feature learning (MTFL) [12] transformed original feature space into low-dimension common feature space. Multi-Task feature selection (MTFS) [13] was the first method to select feature from the original feature space in multi-task learning by adding $l_{2,1}$ norm of the weight matrix to the objective function. There were other developments in feature selection by substituting different norms such as $l_{\infty,1}$ [14], capped-$l_{p,1}$ [15].

Besides MTFL, there were others methods brought up based on the positive relation correlation. The regularized multi-task support vector machine [16] extended SVM into the multi-task learning framework by confining parameters for all tasks as similar as possible. Parameswaran and Weinberger [17] extended large margin nearest neighbor (lmnn) algorithm to the MTL paradigm.

However, the assumption of positive tasks correlation is too strong to conform the practical situation. Therefore, researchers come up with distinct models to figure out the outlier tasks and negative task correlation. Thrun and O'Sullivan [18] firstly came up with the task clustering method by introducing a weighted nearest neighbor classifier for each task. Bakker and Heskes [19] developed a multi-task Bayesian neural network model. The work by Jacob et al. [20] explored task clusters under the regularization framework using three orthogonal terms.

Learning the task relationships automatically from data is an advanced learning method. In [21], the covariance matrix of tasks relationships was learned by assuming the data samples conforming to Gauss distribution. Multi-task relationship learning (MTRL) [22] also learned the covariance matrix of tasks relationship but through a more direct way, assuming parameter matrix conforming to the matrix normal distribution. [23] was similar to MTRL, but the model construct the covariance matrix of tasks relationship as well we feature.

2.2   Multi-view Learning

Multi-view learning (MVL) makes use of the data coming from multiple sources to explore the latent knowledge. For MVL models both consensus principle and complementary principle are crucial principles to obey [10]. According to different application, existing multi-view learning is mainly divided into tree categories: co-training, multiple kernel learning and subspace learning [24].

Co-training utilizes the complementary information among multiple views to learn alternatively, minimizing the disagreement and thus improving the model generalization. Multiple kernel learning explores the connection among multiple views by integrating distinctive kernel functions corresponding to distinctive feature spaces. Subspace learning assumes multiple views share common latent space. Although these three learning methods are seemingly diverse, they all follow consensus principle and complementary principle.

With the extensive study of MVL, there are a variety of SVM-based MVL models. Brefeld and Scheffer [25] developed the Co-EM SVM to exploit the unlabeled data. SVM-2K [26] was proposed to take advantage of two views by combining SVM and the distance minimization version of KCCA. In [27],

Li et al. linked co-training to random sampling building up a new model MTSVM. The work by Xu et al. [28] introduced the theory of the information bottleneck to multi-view learning. Rakotomamonjy et al. suggested a multi-view intact space learning algorithm [29] by incorporating the encoded complementary information to MVL.

2.3 Multi-view Multi-task Learning

Many real-world problems are so complicated that they usually require to learn several tasks at the same time with diverse data sources. Because this kind of problems own task heterogeneity as well as feature heterogeneity, multi-task learning or multi-view learning cannot provide solution for these kind of problems. Existing multi-task learning merely takes advantage of the relatedness among different tasks ignoring the consistency within distinct views; however, existing multi-view learning have not yet to take the information from other tasks into consideration. Therefore, multi-view multi-task learning (MVMTL) comes into being recently.

A graph-based framework $(GraM^2)$ to deal with multi-task multi-view problem was proposed in [3]. He and Lawrence assumed that in a single task each of the view keep consistency with other views, and the shared views among different tasks own the similar predictions. Under this situation, shared views became the bridge to connect distinct tasks. Correspondingly, an effective algorithm $(IteM^2)$ was designed to solve the problem. However, the $GraM^2$ framework only aimed at nonnegative data set. In order to expand the range of data set to the negative data, a regularized framework was proposed. Based on the co-regularization in a single task, Zhang and Huan [4] added regularized multi-task learning method into the co-regularization model. Algorithm based on share structure to deal with multi-view multi-task learning [5] was also proposed afterwards. Save for aiming at classification problem, in [6] Zhang et al. introduced a novel problem named Multi-view Multi-task Cluster Learning. In order to deal with this special cluster problem, they presented an algorithm based on graph model to handle nonnegative data at first [6]. Then an improved algorithm [7] was introduced to solve more general data set including negative data.

3   PSVM-2VMT Model

There are several multi-view multi-task learning methods based on different perspective such as graph models and co-regularized methods. However, models based on SVM have not yet to been studied. SVMs, as traditional powerful machine learning models, outperformance most other learning methods. Hence, we propose a SVM-based model to deal with the MVMT learning. We firstly apply an advanced multi-view learning method PSVM-2V within each task and then learn multiple related tasks simultaneously using regularization techniques. Through extending PSVM-2V model to multi-task learning framework, we establish a powerful model based on SVM to solve MVMT problem.

3.1 Notation and Problem Overview

Consider a multi-view multi-task learning problem with T tasks. In each task, there is a supervised multi-view learning problem with data set (X_t, Y_t), where X_t comes from multiple sources. In order to make use of all tasks simultaneously with all views, an unified model is needed to learn the decision function $f(x)$ for every view in every task. In this paper, our proposed model is based on PSVM-2V. As a result, there are only two views have been taking into considerations. The scripts of A and B represent the certain two views. Suppose we use lowercase letter t to present the serial number of tasks, then there are l_t samples for task t and the ith training point in task t is presented as $(x_{i_t}^A, x_{i_t}^B, y_{j_t})$. In proposed model, w_A^t, w_B^t denote weight vectors for views A and B in task t. C, C^A, C^B, γ, θ are hyperparameters remain to be chosen.

3.2 PSVM-2V

PSVM-2V model is a novel MVL method which incorporates Learning Using Privileged Information (LUPI) into MVL [10]. This model takes views A and B into consideration, regarding each view as the other view's privileged information. The concrete formulation of PSVM-2V is presented as follow:

$$\min_{w_A, w_B} \frac{1}{2}(\|w_A\|^2 + \gamma\|w_B\|^2) + C^A\sum_{i=1}^{l}\xi_i^{A^*} + C^B\sum_{i=1}^{l}\xi_i^{B^*} + C\sum_{i=1}^{l}\eta_i$$

$$\begin{aligned}
\text{s. t.} \quad & |(w_A \cdot \phi_A(x_i^A)) - (w_B \cdot \phi_B(x_i^B))| \leqslant \varepsilon + \eta_i, \\
& y_i(w_A \cdot \phi_A(x_i^A)) \geqslant 1 - \xi_i^{A^*}, \\
& y_i(w_B \cdot \phi_B(x_i^B)) \geqslant 1 - \xi_i^{B^*}, \\
& \xi_i^{A^*} \geqslant y_i(w_B \cdot \phi_B(x_i^B)), \ \xi_i^{A^*} \geqslant 0, \\
& \xi_i^{B^*} \geqslant y_i(w_A \cdot \phi_A(x_i^A)), \ \xi_i^{B^*} \geqslant 0, \\
& \eta_i \geqslant 0, \ i = 1, \cdots, l.
\end{aligned} \quad (1)$$

3.3 PSVM-2VMT

Existing PSVM-2V only aims at single task with two views. When we are confronted with multiple tasks, one direct way to extend the PSVM-2V is to learn each of the multiple task individually, the optimization goal is presented below:

$$\min_{w_A^t, w_B^t} \sum_{t=1}^{T}\left[\frac{1}{2}(\|w_A^t\|^2 + \gamma\|w_B^t\|^2) + C^A\sum_{i_t=1}^{l_t}\xi_{i_t}^{A^*} + C^B\sum_{i_t=1}^{l_t}\xi_{i_t}^{B^*} + C\sum_{i_t=1}^{l_t}\eta_{i_t}\right] \quad (2)$$

Apparently Eq. (2) has not utilize the relationship among different tasks. To use the relationship among multiple tasks, we add a regularized term in the objective function. We chose the least square loss as the formulation of the regularized term, on one hand this regularization term limits the change of weight among tasks, on the other hand it is easy to optimize by calculating the gradient. At last, we gain the following model:

$$
\min_{w_A^t, w_B^t} \sum_{t=1}^{T} \left[\frac{1}{2}(\|w_A^t\|^2 + \gamma\|w_B^t\|^2) + C^A \sum_{i_t=1}^{l_t} \xi_{i_t}^{A^*} + C^B \sum_{i_t=1}^{l_t} \xi_{i_t}^{B^*} + C \sum_{i_t=1}^{l_t} \eta_{i_t} \right]
$$
$$
+ \frac{\theta}{2} \sum_{t \neq t'} (\|w_A^t - w_A^{t'}\|^2 + \|w_B^t - w_B^{t'}\|^2)
$$

s. t. $|(w_A^t \cdot \phi_A(x_{i_t}^A)) - (w_B^t \cdot \phi_B(x_{i_t}^B))| \leqslant \varepsilon + \eta_{i_t}$,

$$y_{i_t}(w_A^t \cdot \phi_A(x_{i_t}^A)) \geqslant 1 - \xi_{i_t}^{A^*},$$

$$y_{i_t}(w_B \cdot \phi_B(x_{i_t}^B)) \geqslant 1 - \xi_{i_t}^{B^*},$$

$$\xi_{i_t}^{A^*} \geqslant y_{i_t}(w_B^t \cdot \phi_B(x_{i_t}^B)),\ \xi_{i_t}^{A^*} \geqslant 0,$$

$$\xi_{i_t}^{B^*} \geqslant y_{i_t}(w_A^t \cdot \phi_A(x_{i_t}^A)),\ \xi_{i_t}^{B^*} \geqslant 0,$$

$$\eta_{i_t} \geqslant 0,\ i_t = 1, \cdots, l_t. \tag{3}$$

According to the traditional method to settle the SVM problem, deriving the corresponding dual problem is an effective way to simplify the primal problem. Hence, we take Eq. (3) as primal problem and derive the dual problem. On the basis of the dual theory, we calculate the derivative of the Lagrangian function, gain the KKT conditions and obtain the dual problem as shown in Eq. (4).

$$
\min \sum_{t=1}^{T} [(\theta + \frac{1}{2} - \theta T) \sum_{i_t,j_t=1}^{l_t} (\alpha_{i_t}^A y_{i_t} - \beta_{i_t}^+ + \beta_{i_t}^- - \lambda_{i_t}^B y_{i_t})(\alpha_{j_t}^A y_{j_t} - \beta_{j_t}^+ + \beta_{j_t}^- - \lambda_{j_t}^B y_{j_t}) \kappa_A(x_{i_t}^A, x_{j_t}^A)
$$
$$
+ (\theta + \frac{1}{2\gamma} - \theta T) \sum_{i_t,j_t=1}^{l_t} (\alpha_{i_t}^B y_{i_t} + \beta_{i_t}^+ - \beta_{i_t}^- - \lambda_{i_t}^A y_{i_t})(\alpha_{j_t}^B y_{j_t} + \beta_{j_t}^+ - \beta_{j_t}^- - \lambda_{j_t}^A y_{j_t}) \kappa_B(x_{i_t}^B, x_{j_t}^B)]
$$
$$
+ \theta \sum_{t \neq t'} [\sum_{i_t=1}^{l_t} \sum_{j_{t'}=1}^{l_{t'}} (\alpha_{i_t}^A y_{i_t} - \beta_{i_t}^+ + \beta_{i_t}^- - \lambda_{i_t}^B y_{i_t})(\alpha_{j_{t'}}^A y_{j_{t'}} - \beta_{j_{t'}}^+ + \beta_{j_{t'}}^- - \lambda_{j_{t'}}^B y_{j_{t'}}) \kappa_A(x_{i_t}^A, x_{j_{t'}}^A)
$$
$$
+ \sum_{i_t=1}^{l_t} \sum_{j_{t'}=1}^{l_{t'}} (\alpha_{i_t}^B y_{i_t} + \beta_{i_t}^+ - \beta_{i_t}^- - \lambda_{i_t}^A y_{i_t})(\alpha_{j_{t'}}^B y_{j_{t'}} + \beta_{j_{t'}}^+ - \beta_{j_{t'}}^- - \lambda_{j_{t'}}^A y_{j_{t'}}) \kappa_B(x_{i_t}^B, x_{j_{t'}}^B)]
$$
$$
+ \sum_{t=1}^{T} [\varepsilon \sum_{i_t=1}^{l_t} (\beta_{i_t}^+ + \beta_{i_t}^-) - \sum_{i_t=1}^{l_t} (\alpha_{i_t}^A + \alpha_{i_t}^B)]
$$

s. t. $\alpha_{i_t}^A + \lambda_{i_t}^A \leqslant C^A,\ \alpha_{i_t}^B + \lambda_{i_t}^B \leqslant C^B,\ \beta_{i_t}^+ + \beta_{i_t}^- \leqslant C$,

$$\alpha_{i_t}^A, \alpha_{i_t}^B, \beta_{i_t}^+, \beta_{i_t}^-, \lambda_{i_t}^A, \lambda_{i_t}^B \geqslant 0. \tag{4}$$

Because the formulation of dual problem in Eq. (4) is a classical convex QPP, we can solve the problem using QP solver. Moreover, using the KKT conditions we have the following conclusions without proof, which is similar to the conclusions in [30]. Suppose that $\alpha_A^1\top, \alpha_B^1\top, \beta_+^1\top, \beta_-^1\top, \lambda_A^1\top$, $\lambda_B^1\top, \ldots, \alpha_A^T\top, \alpha_B^T\top, \beta_+^T\top, \beta_-^T\top, \lambda_A^T\top, \lambda_B^T\top$ is a solution of Eq. (4), then the solutions w_A^t and w_B^t of Eq. (3) can be formulated as follows.

$$
w_A^t = \sum_{i_t=1}^{l_t} (\alpha_{i_t}^A y_{i_t} - \beta_{i_t}^+ + \beta_{i_t}^- - \lambda_{i_t}^B y_{i_t}) \phi_A(x_{i_t}^A), \tag{5}
$$

$$w_B^t = \frac{1}{\gamma} \sum_{i_t=1}^{l_t} (\alpha_{i_t}^B y_{i_t} + \beta_{i_t}^+ - \beta_{i_t}^- - \lambda_{i_t}^A y_{i_t}) \phi_B(x_{i_t}^B). \tag{6}$$

Since in PSVM-2V there is a assumption that each view has sufficient information to learn a classifier, we assume that in PSVT-2VMT two discriminative classifiers learning from different feature views are equally important. Hence, we have the following prediction function to predict the label of a new sample (x_t^A, x_t^B) for task t:

$$f_t = sign(f_t(x_t^A, x_t^B)) = sign(0.5(w_A^{t}{}^{*\top} \phi_A(x_t^A) + w_B^{t}{}^{*\top} \phi_B(x_t^B))). \tag{7}$$

where w_A^t* and w_B^t* are the optima of Eq. (3)

In summary, we can predict using Eq. (7) when both the two views of a new sample are available.

4   Numerical Experiment

In this section, we demonstrate the effectiveness of proposed model for binary classification based on 10 data sets obtained from *Animals with Attributes (AwA)*. We carry out experiments on a Windows workstation with Inter Core CPU(i7-6700K@4.00 GHz) and 32-GB RAM. In order to measure the performance of different models, we take the accuracy as a criterion. Through using fivefold cross validation, we gain the best parameter for each model. The details of experiments are as follow.

4.1   Experimental Setup

Data Sets. *Animals with Attributes:* The *Animals with Attributes (AwA)*[1] contains 30475 images of 50 animals classes with six pre-extracted feature representations for each image. In our experiments, we take the 252-dimensional HOG features and the 2000-dimensional L_1 normalized SURF descriptors as views A and B. Moreover, we take out ten classes as train and test data sets and construct nine binary classifications regarding as nine tasks. There are 200 samples selected randomly for each task to train. Table 1 shows the details of these nine tasks.

Parameters. In PSVM-2VMT, there are several hyperparameters which influence the performance of model. In order to obtain the best parameters for all models, we implement fivefold cross validation. Empirically, the smaller the parameter ϵ in SVM is, the performance of SVM is better. Hence, we set ϵ to be 0.001. For convenience, we set $C = C^A = C^B$. Under this situation, there are still four hyperparameters including kernel parameter σ, penalty parameter C, θ and nonnegative parameter γ need to be chosen. We adopt grid search as a means of choosing hyperparameters. Since a grid search usually picks values approximately on a logarithmic scale, we select those four hyperparameter from $\{10^{-3}, 10^{-2}, 10^{-1}, 1, 10^1, 10^2, 10^3\}$.

---

[1] Available at http://attributes.kyb.tuebingen.mpg.de.

Table 1. Details of multiple tasks

Task number	Classification problem
Task 1	Chimpanzee vs Giant panda
Task 2	Chimpanzee vs Leopard
Task 3	Chimpanzee vs Persian cat
Task 4	Chimpanzee vs Pig
Task 5	Chimpanzee vs Hippopotamus
Task 6	Chimpanzee vs Humpback whale
Task 7	Chimpanzee vs Raccoon
Task 8	Chimpanzee vs Rat
Task 9	Chimpanzee vs Seal

4.2   Experimental Results

We use PSVM-2VMT to settle MVMT learning aiming at the aforementioned
tasks. Due to the limitation of QP solver for large-scale data set, we choose two
tasks as the input of PSVM-2VMT. Hence, we obtain 80 results for each task
pair combination, as shown in Table 2. Select the optimal accuracy for each task,
we draw the histogram as shown in Fig. 1.

Table 2. Performance on PSVM-2VMT based on 2 tasks

Training task	1:75.28	1:76.3	1:75.44	1:76.42	1:76.56	1:76.46	1:75.78	1:75.27
	2:84.34	3:82.4	4:75.15	5:79.82	6:95.52	7:76.45	8:68.31	9:83.72
Training task	1:75.28	1:76.3	1:75.44	1:76.42	1:76.56	1:76.46	1:75.78	1:75.27
	2:84.34	3:82.4	4:75.15	5:79.82	6:95.52	7:76.45	8:68.31	9:83.72
Training task	2:83.82	2:83.99	2:80.38	2:**86.86**	2:83.5	2:82.95	2:83.87	2:84.54
	1:76.64	3:82.22	4:71.4	5:78.41	6:96.1	7:77.8	8:68.89	9:83.37
Training task	3:80.95	3:80.95	3:80.95	3:82.13	3:81.8	3:**82.57**	3:81.89	3:81.41
	1:**77.69**	2:83.19	4:72.68	5:80.4	6:**97.13**	7:78.66	8:68.91	9:83.34
Training task	4:72.33	4:73.15	4:72.57	4:71.99	4:72.12	4:72.66	4:72.12	4:71.58
	1:76.81	2:84.04	3:81.3	5:**81.59**	6:96.7	7:76.28	8:65.86	9:84.45
Training task	5:79.22	5:78.86	5:80.04	5:79.19	5:78.6	5:78.6	5:78.6	5:79.75
	1:75.74	2:85.14	3:81.49	4:71.81	6:95.77	7:76.07	8:72.11	9:84.3
Training task	6:96.3	6:96.3	6:96.3	6:96.3	6:96.3	6:96.3	6:95.59	6:96.71
	1:77.06	2:82.38	3:81.7	4:72.18	5:78.92	7:77.48	8:71.04	9:83.72
Training task	7:75.84	7:76.23	7:**78.89**	7:76.55	7:77.13	7:77.11	7:76.13	7:76.13
	1:76.11	2:86.3	3:81.84	4:**75.81**	5:79.64	6:96.21	8:65.76	9:83.66
Training task	8:65.6	8:65.6	8:65.6	8:65.6	8:65.6	8:69.91	8:65.44	8:68.91
	1:76.94	2:84.46	3:81.79	4:72.63	5:79.46	6:95.72	7:77.09	9:84.48
Training task	9:83.64	9:84.46	9:84.11	9:84.39	9:84.7	9:84.78	9:84.78	9:**84.78**
	1:75.98	2:86.08	3:81.03	4:71.78	5:79.13	6:96.35	7:76.27	8:**75.11**

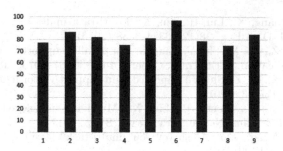

Fig. 1. Best accuracy of 9 tasks

5   Conclusion

In this paper, we proposed a novel model based on SVM to settle the MVMT learning. The existing model PSVM-2V is an effective model for MVL achieving both consensus and complementary principle. Based on PSVM-2V, we construct PSVM-2VMT to settle the MVMT learning. We have derived the corresponding dual problem and adopted the classical QP to solve it. Experimental results demonstrated the effectiveness of our models. In the future, we will design correspond speedup algorithm to solve our problems. Furthermore, because we assume all tasks are related in PSVM-2VMT, we will explore more complicated task relationship in the future study.

Acknowledgments. This work has been partially supported by grants from National Natural Science Foundation of China (Nos. 61472390, 71731009, 71331005, and 91546201), and the Beijing Natural Science Foundation (No. 1162005).

References

1. Su, H., Maji, S., Kalogerakis, E., Learned-Miller, E.: Multi-view convolutional neural networks for 3D shape recognition. In: Proceedings of the IEEE International Conference on Computer Vision, pp. 945–953 (2015)
2. Dhillon, P., Foster, D.P., Ungar, L.H.: Multi-view learning of word embeddings via CCA. In: Advances in Neural Information Processing Systems, pp. 199–207 (2011)
3. He, J., Lawrence, R.: A graph-based framework for multi-task multi-view learning. In: ICML, pp. 25–32 (2011)
4. Zhang, J., Huan, J.: Inductive multi-task learning with multiple view data. In: Proceedings of the 18th ACM SIGKDD International Conference on Knowledge Discovery and Data Mining, pp. 543–551. ACM (2012)
5. Jin, X., Zhuang, F., Wang, S., He, Q., Shi, Z.: Shared structure learning for multiple tasks with multiple views. In: Blockeel, H., Kersting, K., Nijssen, S., Železný, F. (eds.) ECML PKDD 2013. LNCS (LNAI), vol. 8189, pp. 353–368. Springer, Heidelberg (2013). https://doi.org/10.1007/978-3-642-40991-2_23
6. Zhang, X., Zhang, X., Liu, H.: Multi-task multi-view clustering for non-negative data. In: IJCAI, pp. 4055–4061 (2015)

7. Zhang, X., Zhang, X., Liu, H., Liu, X.: Multi-task multi-view clustering. IEEE Trans. Knowl. Data Eng. **28**(12), 3324–3338 (2016)
8. Tian, Y., Qi, Z., Ju, X., Shi, Y., Liu, X.: Nonparallel support vector machines for pattern classification. IEEE Trans. Cybern. **44**(7), 1067–1079 (2014)
9. Tian, Y., Ju, X., Qi, Z., Shi, Y.: Improved twin support vector machine. Sci. China Math. **57**(2), 417–432 (2014)
10. Tang, J., Tian, Y., Zhang, P., Liu, X.: Multiview privileged support vector machines. IEEE Trans. Neural Netw. Learn. Syst. (2017)
11. Zhang, Y., Yang, Q.: A survey on multi-task learning. arXiv preprint arXiv:1707.08114 (2017)
12. Argyriou, A., Evgeniou, T., Pontil, M.: Multi-task feature learning. In: Advances in Neural Information Processing Systems, pp. 41–48 (2007)
13. Obozinski, G., Taskar, B., Jordan, M.: Multi-task feature selection. Statistics Department, UC Berkeley, Technival report 2 (2006)
14. Liu, H., Palatucci, M., Zhang, J.: Blockwise coordinate descent procedures for the multi-task lasso, with applications to neural semantic basis discovery. In: Proceedings of the 26th Annual International Conference on Machine Learning, pp. 649–656. ACM (2009)
15. Gong, P., Ye, J., Zhang, C.: Multi-stage multi-task feature learning. In: Advances in Neural Information Processing Systems, pp. 1988–1996 (2012)
16. Evgeniou, T., Pontil, M.: Regularized multi-task learning. In: Proceedings of the Tenth ACM SIGKDD International Conference on Knowledge Discovery and Data Mining, pp. 109–117. ACM (2004)
17. Parameswaran, S., Weinberger, K.Q.: Large margin multi-task metric learning. In: Advances in Neural Information Processing Systems, pp. 1867–1875 (2010)
18. Thrun, S., O'Sullivan, J.: Discovering structure in multiple learning tasks: the TC algorithm. In: ICML, vol. 96, pp. 489–497 (1996)
19. Bakker, B., Heskes, T.: Task clustering and gating for Bayesian multitask learning. J. Mach. Learn. Res. **4**(May), 83–99 (2003)
20. Jacob, L., Vert, J.P., Bach, F.R.: Clustered multi-task learning: a convex formulation. In: Advances in Neural Information Processing Systems, pp. 745–752 (2009)
21. Bonilla, E.V., Chai, K.M., Williams, C.: Multi-task Gaussian process prediction. In: Advances in Neural Information Processing Systems, pp. 153–160 (2008)
22. Zhang, Y., Yeung, D.Y.: A convex formulation for learning task relationships in multi-task learning. arXiv preprint arXiv:1203.3536 (2012)
23. Zhang, Y., Schneider, J.G.: Learning multiple tasks with a sparse matrix-normal penalty. In: Advances in Neural Information Processing Systems, pp. 2550–2558 (2010)
24. Xu, C., Tao, D., Xu, C.: A survey on multi-view learning. arXiv preprint arXiv:1304.5634 (2013)
25. Brefeld, U., Scheffer, T.: Co-EM support vector learning. In: Proceedings of the Twenty-first International Conference on Machine learning, p. 16. ACM (2004)
26. Sonnenburg, S., Rätsch, G., Schäfer, C., Schölkopf, B.: Large scale multiple kernel learning. J. Mach. Learn. Res. **7**(Jul), 1531–1565 (2006)
27. Muslea, I., Minton, S., Knoblock, C.A.: Active + semi-supervised learning = robust multi-view learning. In: ICML, vol. 2, pp. 435–442 (2002)
28. Xu, C., Tao, D., Xu, C.: Large-margin multi-viewinformation bottleneck. IEEE Trans. Pattern Anal. Mach. Intell. **36**(8), 1559–1572 (2014)
29. Suzuki, T., Tomioka, R.: SpicyMKL. arXiv preprint arXiv:0909.5026 (2009)
30. Deng, N., Tian, Y., Zhang, C.: Support Vector Machines: Optimization Based Theory, Algorithms, and Extensions. CRC Press, Boca Raton (2012)

Research on Stock Price Forecast Based on News Sentiment Analysis—A Case Study of Alibaba

Lingling Zhang[(✉)], Saiji Fu, and Bochen Li

University of Chinese Academy of Sciences, Beijing 100190, China
zll933@163.com

Abstract. Based on the media news of Alibaba and improvement of L&M dictionary, this study transforms unstructured text into structured news sentiment through dictionary matching. By employing data of Alibaba's opening price, closing price, maximum price, minimum price and volume in Thomson Reuters database, we build a fifth-order VAR model with lags. The AR test indicates the stability of VAR model. In a further step, the results of Granger causality tests, impulse response function and variance decomposition show that VAR model is successful to forecast variables *dopen*, *dmax* and *dmin*. What's more, news sentiment contributes to the prediction of all these three variables. At last, MAPE reveals *dopen*, *dmax* and *dmin* can be used in the out-sample forecast. We take *dopen* sequence for example, document how to predict the movement and rise of opening price by using the value and slope of *dopen*.

Keywords: News sentiment · Dictionary matching · Stock price forecast

1 Introduction

As one of the most common sources of daily life information, it is unavoidable for media news to be decision-making basis for individuals, institutions and markets. Nevertheless, even in the recognition of the vital position of news, it can be difficult for investors to screen out effective information and make investment plan to max-imize profits. Recently, more and more investors' and financial analysts' attentions have been paid on news sentiment. In May 2017, in the Global Artificial Intelligence Technology Conference (GAITC), held in the National Convention Center, it is pro-posed that AI will play an increasingly crucial role in the financial field in future. And text mining is going to has a promising application prospects. However, manually extracting news sentiment from news text turns out to be difficult and time-consuming.

At present, the sentiment analysis in financial mainly includes two aspects, investor sentiment and text sentiment. Nevertheless, most of Chinese scholars' researches are focused on text sentiment. With the rapid development of Internet and AI, structural data analysis is far from enough to meet the need of people's daily life. Hence, the sentiment analysis of news text in this study is of great implication.

The effective source of information is the guarantee of text sentiment analysis. Kearney and Liu summarize various information sources, including public corporate

© Springer International Publishing AG, part of Springer Nature 2018
Y. Shi et al. (Eds.): ICCS 2018, LNCS 10861, pp. 429–442, 2018.
https://doi.org/10.1007/978-3-319-93701-4_33

disclosures, media news and Internet postings [1]. Dictionary matching and machine learning are the common methods of text sentiment analysis, with its own pros and cons. Dictionary matching [2–6] is relatively simple, but the subjectivity of the artificial dictionary is larger and the accuracy is limited. On the contrary, machine learning [7–10] is able to avoid subjective problems and improve accuracy, but it comes with a higher cost and much more work. In domestic study, public sentiment analysis is getting more and more popular. However, Chinese dictionaries, especially in specific areas, have not been established. Most of scholars rely on Cnki Dictionary, which is not suitable for financial analysis. Additionally, unstructured data as such Micro-blog and comments [11] are often utilized in domestic public sentiment analysis, which is too subjective consciousness compared with media news. Thus, immense volume of data is required to match the professional and literal dictionary. As a result, foreign dictionary turns out to be more mature and suitable, together with a wide use of English language, dictionary matching has gained its popularity. Words in dictionary matching are divided into three categories: positive, negative and neutral. It is worth of noting that constructing or selecting a sentiment dictionary that is applicable to financial study. What's more, designing an appropriate weighting scheme has been a breakthrough in text sentiment analysis.

The stock market is closely concerned by investors. The study of the stock price forecast has also become a heated and difficult problem in recent years. At present, econometric analysis [12–16] in stock price prediction model has been very mature, such as linear regression model, vector autoregressive model, Markov chain model, BP neural network model, GARCH model [15–20]. In spite of this, unstructured data is not fully utilized, resulting the inability for pure mathematical model to achieve accurate forecast of stock market. Therefore, it provides a new method of combing quantitative news sentiment with traditional mathematical model.

The rest of paper is organized as follows. In Sect. 2, we construct a VAR model based on news sentiment analysis. In Sect. 3, we conduct a series of empirical tests, including data processing, unit root test, Granger causality test, impulse response function analysis and variance decomposition. In Sect. 4, we test the forecast effect of in-static and out-static sample. Finally, in Sect. 5, we conclude and give future work of our research.

2 Construction of VAR Model

2.1 News Sentiment Analysis

This article mainly uses the news released by the media as the source of information. In order to ensure more comprehensive information contained in the news, this article takes Alibaba as an example, using Gooseeker software to capture press release date, news content and news links of 4569 news from 12 news reports including Sina Finance, China Daily, PR Newswire, The Dow Jones Network, Economic Times, Seeking Alpha, etc. The frequency of the data is based on the day, from September 19, 2014 (the day that Alibaba listed). As a representative of unstructured data, news needs to be processed through the process of Fig. 1 [4].

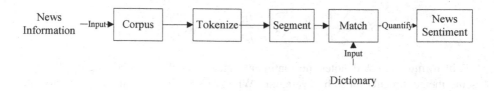

Fig. 1. Main process of news sentiment.

Among the process, (1) corpus, namely the collection of news, needs to be further processed in order to become useful information; (2) tokenize, that is the secondary processing of the corpus. This article combines the regular expression module in Python with Excel to remove the collection of non-essential characters in corpus; (3) segment is transforming a string into single words according to a certain characteristic; (4) match is the key means to complete the word and dictionary matching, which can be considered as the transition from unstructured data to structured data. This paper chooses the L & M dictionary as matching dictionary. This dictionary contains a number of positive and negative words, and is more suitable for the field of finance and economics. For example, "tax" is considered as a negative vocabulary in other dictionaries while a neutral vocabulary in L & M dictionary [1]. This dictionary consists of words with the same root but different meanings and different roots but the same meaning. For instance, the word "care" and "careless" have the same stem, but the meaning is exactly the opposite. The word "gram" and "grammar" also have the same root, with irrelevant meaning as well. Currently, some scholars adopt the method of stem and root matching, which will cause the problem of low accuracy. In view of the root matching will bring statistical error to some extent, this paper sacrifices matching efficiency in exchange for a higher match accuracy by treating words with the same root as different words and making the L&M dictionary a regular one dimensional array. Through matching, this article statistics the frequency of positive words and negative words appearing in each piece of news respectively, and imports the matching result into Mysql database; (5) Quantification is the destination of unstructured data into structured data. This paper defines the result of quantification as sentiment. The choice of the quantification formula is directly related to the forecast effect of the stock price in the later period. Therefore, it is very important to select a reasonable formula.

Due to the impact of the event itself, there will be the same source of different news reports and different sources of the same report. For the former, it may be necessary to sum the word frequency to quantify the text; for the latter, averaging the word frequency may be more appropriate. In order to avoid the tedious work-load of above two methods, this paper adopts the sampling method for approximate treatment. That is to say, if the sampling results show that most of the news comes from different events, then all news of the same day is regarded as different events, otherwise, it is regarded as the same event. Based on the above factors, this article selects formula (1) and use of SQL statements to quantify the news sentiment. The advantage of this formula is that regardless of whether the news of the same day is eventually treated as the same event or different event, the result is the same. At present, the formula is also quite popular with scholars [21].

$$S' = \frac{\sum PF/n - \sum NF/n}{\sum PF/n + \sum NF/n} = S = \frac{\sum PF - \sum NF}{\sum PF + \sum NF} \tag{1}$$

In formula (1), S denotes the sentiment values calculated by adding up, S' represents the sentiment values by averaging. When $S(S') > 0$, the sentiment demonstrates positive, investors may be optimistic about the situation on the day, on the contrary, the sentiment takes on negative, investors may be pessimistic. PF indicates the frequency of positive words appearing on a particular day's news, and NF indicates the frequency of negative words appearing on a particular day's news.

2.2   Construction of Stock Price Forecasting Model

The stock market, as an active zone for investors, is often regarded as a barometer of economic activity and plays a decisive role in the development of the national economy. Choosing and building a reasonable stock price forecasting model is of great significance to all countries, enterprises and individuals. Based on the literature of stock price forecast, this paper summarizes the variables commonly used in predecessors' stock price forecasting, including the three categories of technical indicators, macroeconomic variables and stock price raw data [11, 22–24]. Among them, the adoption of technical indicators combined with the original data is popular, and the forecast results are often satisfactory. However, the effective market hypothesis put forward by Eugene Fama in 1970 holds that all valuable information has been timely, accurately and fully reflected in the stock price movements. Even though the theory is still controversial, it can be thought that the past transaction information affects the investor sentiment on the one hand. On the other hand, the investor sentiment also indicates the volatility of the future stock market. That is, the original stock price data not only contains the information needed by investors, but also by the external sentiment. Based on this, this article assumes that the combination of raw data and sentiment value of stock price can predict the trend of future stock price. In summary, this article initially identifies the variables in the model as follows: closing price (*close*), opening price(*open*), minimum(*min*), maximum(*max*), trading volume(*volume*) and news sentiment(*sentiment*).

Considering the significant time series features and the lasting effects of each variable, this paper determines to construct a time series model. However, for the commonly used time series models such as AR (p), MA (p), and ARMA (p), the model for solving the univariate problem is served in spite of the lag effect. Taking all factors into consideration, this article focuses on the VAR (p) model. VAR model is often used to predict interconnected time-series systems and to analyze the dynamic impact of stochastic disturbances on the variable system, thus explaining the impact of various economic shocks on the formation of economic variables. At present, VAR model is widely sought after by many economists. Its general form can be expressed as formula (2).

$$Y_t = \alpha_0 + \alpha_1 Y_{t-1} + \alpha_2 Y_{t-2} + \ldots + \alpha_p Y_{t-p} + \varepsilon_t \quad t = 1, 2, \ldots, T \tag{2}$$

Where Y_t is an n-dimensional endogenous variable, $t \in T$, α_i ($i \in N$, $0 \le i \le p$) is the parameter matrix to be estimated, εt is an n-dimensional random vector, $E(\varepsilon_t) = 0$, p denotes the lag order. Equation (2) can be called VAR (p) model. Ignoring the constant term, Eq. (2) can be abbreviated as Eq. (3).

$$A(L)Y_t = \varepsilon_t \tag{3}$$

Among them, $A(L) = I_n - \alpha_1 L - \alpha_2 L_2 - \ldots - \alpha_p L_p$, $A(L) \in R^{n \times n}$, L is a lag operator. The formula (3) is generally called the unrestricted vector autoregressive model [25].

In summary, the preliminary non-restrictive VAR(2) model to be established in this paper is shown in Eq. (4).

$$
\begin{pmatrix} close_t \\ open_t \\ min_t \\ max_t \\ volume_t \\ sentiment_t \end{pmatrix} = \alpha_0 + \alpha_1 \begin{pmatrix} close_{t-1} \\ open_{t-1} \\ min_{t-1} \\ max_{t-1} \\ volume_{t-1} \\ sentiment_{t-1} \end{pmatrix} + \alpha_2 \begin{pmatrix} close_{t-2} \\ open_{t-2} \\ min_{t-2} \\ max_{t-2} \\ volume_{t-2} \\ sentiment_{t-2} \end{pmatrix} + \ldots \alpha_p \begin{pmatrix} close_{t-p} \\ open_{t-p} \\ min_{t-p} \\ max_{t-p} \\ volume_{t-p} \\ sentiment_{t-p} \end{pmatrix} + \begin{pmatrix} \varepsilon_{1t} \\ \varepsilon_{2t} \\ \varepsilon_{3t} \\ \varepsilon_{4t} \\ \varepsilon_{5t} \\ \varepsilon_{6t} \end{pmatrix}
\tag{4}
$$

3 Empirical Test of VAR Model

3.1 Data Source and Processing of Stock Price

The stock data in this article is sourced from the Thomson Reuters database. We extract opening price, closing price, the maximum price, the minimum price and trading volume from the database for a total of 633 trading days from September 19, 2014 (listed) to March 24, 2017. The data frequency is the day. In the meantime, in order to test the final out-of-sample prediction effect of the model, this paper specifically selects a total of 575 transaction days from September 19, 2014 to December 30, 2016 as sample data to input into the models, and the remaining data in total of 57 from January 3, 2017 to March 24, 2017 are reserved for the test data to test the model. Eviews9.0 is selected as the measurement software of this article.

In data processing, the six variables of the model are standardized to eliminate the dimensional difference between the variables. Generally believed that the absolute value of more than 3 can be considered as abnormal values after the standardization of the data. The results show that the trading volume data on the day of Sept. 19, 2014 is close to 17 and much higher than 3 after standardization, which is attributable to the noticeably higher number of news media coverage on the listing day that leads to the overwhelming reaction of the public and the abnormal trading volume. In order to avoid the large error brought to the model by the extreme trading volume on the listing day, this paper excludes the data on the date of listing before the model is constructed, and keeps the stock price data and sentiment values of the remaining 574 trading days.

3.2   Unit Root Test of VAR Model

The application of VAR model requires that the sequence be stable, otherwise, it is easy to produce false regression [12]. For example, wrong conclusion may be made within are two variables with no economic relationship. However, the sequences encountered in real life are often non-stationary, which need to be differenced to obtain the smooth sequence. In order to eliminate the phenomenon of pseudo-regression, we use the ADF test to test the sequence of model variables. The results are shown in Table 1.

Table 1. T ADF test results.

Variables	Test statistics	1% threshold	5% threshold	10% threshold	P value	Stable or not
volume	−12.54943	−3.974123	−3.417668	−3.131264	0.0000	Yes
sentiment	−19.04287	−3.974123	−3.417668	−3.131264	0.0000	Yes
dclose	−22.44971	−3.974152	−3.417681	−3.131272	0.0000	Yes
dopen	−26.25389	−3.974152	−3.417681	−3.131272	0.0000	Yes
dmax	−22.09662	−3.974152	−3.417681	−3.131272	0.0000	Yes
dmin	−22.26319	−3.974152	−3.417681	−3.131272	0.0000	Yes

The results show that volume and sentiment are I (0) processes, close, open, max and min are I (1) processes, denoted as *dclose, dopen, dmax* and *dmin* respectively. There is a clear mapping between close and *dclose*. When *dclose* > 0, it can be inferred that today's closing price is higher than the closing price yesterday, on the contrary, the closing price today is lower than yesterday's closing price, the remaining variables are the same to be obtained. Finally, the six stationary sequences of *dclose, dopen, dmax, dmin, volume* and *sentiment* are added to the VAR model. Taking lag 2 as an example, the transition from formula (4) to formula (5) is made.

$$
\begin{pmatrix} dclose_t \\ dopen_t \\ dmin_t \\ dmax_t \\ volume_t \\ sentiment_t \end{pmatrix} = \alpha_0 + \alpha_1 \begin{pmatrix} dclose_{t-1} \\ dopen_{t-1} \\ dmin_{t-1} \\ dmax_{t-1} \\ volume_{t-1} \\ sentiment_{t-1} \end{pmatrix} + \alpha_2 \begin{pmatrix} dclose_{t-2} \\ dopen_{t-2} \\ dmin_{t-2} \\ dmax_{t-2} \\ volume_{t-2} \\ sentiment_{t-2} \end{pmatrix} + \begin{pmatrix} \varepsilon_{1t} \\ \varepsilon_{2t} \\ \varepsilon_{3t} \\ \varepsilon_{4t} \\ \varepsilon_{5t} \\ \varepsilon_{6t} \end{pmatrix} \quad (5)
$$

3.3   Determination of Lag Period in VAR Model

The determination of lag order is directly related to the quality of the model. On the one hand, the larger the lag order, the more realistic and comprehensive the information reflected. On the other hand, an excessively large lag order will lead to a decrease of the freedom degree of the model and an increase of the estimated parameters, thereby increasing the error and decreasing the prediction accuracy. Based on this, the proper lagging order plays a decisive role. In this paper, the 8-order lag test is carried in VAR (2) model by Eviews9.0, the results shown in Table 2.

Table 2. Lag period test results.

Lag	LogL	LR	FPE	AIC	SC	HQ
0	522.8801	NA	6.49e−09	−1.826431	−1.780439	−1.808481
1	1098.340	1136.687	9.64e−10	−3.732651	−3.410706	−3.606999
2	1227.335	252.0639	6.94e−10	−4.061255	−3.463357*	−3.827900
3	1321.375	181.7657	5.65e−10	−4.266342	−3.392491	−3.925286*
4	1382.570	116.9841	5.17e−10	−4.355370	−3.205566	−3.906612
5	1426.921	83.84496	5.02e−10*	−4.384881*	−2.959124	−3.828421
6	1461.213	64.09933	5.06e−10	−4.378843	−2.677133	−3.714681
7	1489.105	51.54672	5.21e−10	−4.350195	−2.372532	−3.578331
8	1526.057	67.50489*	5.19e−10	−4.353557	−2.099941	−3.473991

According to the principle of asterisk at most, it is determined that the model is optimal for 5 lags, so the VAR(5) model is established as Eq. (6).

$$Y_t = \alpha_0 + \alpha_1 Y_{t-1} + \alpha_2 Y_{t-2} + \alpha_3 Y_{t-3} + \alpha_4 Y_{t-4} + \alpha_5 Y_{t-5} + \varepsilon_t \tag{6}$$

Among them, $Y = \begin{pmatrix} dclose \\ dopen \\ dmin \\ dmax \\ volume \\ sentiment \end{pmatrix}$, $\alpha_0 = \begin{pmatrix} c_1 \\ c_2 \\ c_3 \\ c_4 \\ c_5 \\ c_6 \end{pmatrix}$, $\varepsilon_t = \begin{pmatrix} \varepsilon_{1t} \\ \varepsilon_{2t} \\ \varepsilon_{3t} \\ \varepsilon_{4t} \\ \varepsilon_{5t} \\ \varepsilon_{6t} \end{pmatrix}$

The results of the VAR model can be estimated by OLS.

The AR test is used to determine the stability of the VAR(5) model, as shown in Fig. 2, all the characteristic roots of the model fall within the unit circle, indicating that the model is stable.

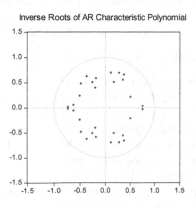

Inverse Roots of AR Characteristic Polynomial

Fig. 2. Discrimination of model stability.

3.4   Empirical Analysis of VAR(5) Model

Even the stability of the VAR model is indicated in the above analysis, it still is unlikely to explain the whether and to what extent does the news sentiment contribute to the model. Therefore, we use the Granger causality tests, impulse response function and variance decomposition analysis to analyze the model in a further step.

(1) Granger Causality Tests

The causality test for the time series data of 6 variables in this study is conducted using "Granger Causality Test", respectively. Table 3 summarizes the test results where the P value is less than 0.05. The P value for variable *dopen* is 0.0000, pointing out that variable *dopen* has significant impact on the lagged items *dclose, dmax, dmin*, volume and sentiment. That is to say, variables *dclose, dmax, dmin* and *volume* can be capitalized to forecast *dopen*. Also, *dmax* and *dmin* have significant impact on the lagged items of the rest of variables.

Table 3. Granger causality test results.

Variables	H0	Chi 2	Prob > Chi 2	Accept the H0 or not
dopen	*dclose, dmax, dmin, volume* and *sentiment* do not casue *dopen*	957.2198	0.0000	No
dmax	*dclose, dopen, dmin, volume* and *sentiment* do not casue *dmax*	224.9506	0.0000	No
dmin	*dclose, dopen, dmax, volume* and *sentiment* do not casue *dmin*	242.9907	0.0000	No

(2) Impulse Response Function

Based on the stability of model, the impulse response function explains the response of an endogenous variable to one of the innovations. It traces the effects on present and future values of the endogenous variable of one standard deviation shock to one of the innovations. According to Granger Causality test, we examine the response of variables *dopen, dmax* and *dmin* to residual disturbance.

(1) The Response of Variable *dopen*

It can be seen from the Fig. 3 that variable, the shock of one standard deviation at the current period has a strong impact on variable *dopen*, which begins to fluctuate around 0 since period 3, nearly vanishing at period 9. Likewise, given an unexpected shock in *dclose, dopen* will initially increase and starts to fall afterwards, fluctuating around 0. This response has acted in line with the shock of itself, converging to 0 at period 9. The relationship between sequences *dopen* and *dmin, dmax* and *volume* is not significant. With the existence of lags, the effect on the sequence is also small, exhibiting a fluctuating trend till period 9. In line with that, the lag also exists in the response of *dopen* to *sentiment* at current period. The link between *sentiment* and *dope*n can be quite complex as it can either be positive or negative, which gradually disappears at period 8.

Hence, we can draw the conclusion that except *dopen* itself, only variables *dclose* and *sentiment* have a significant influence on *dopen*.

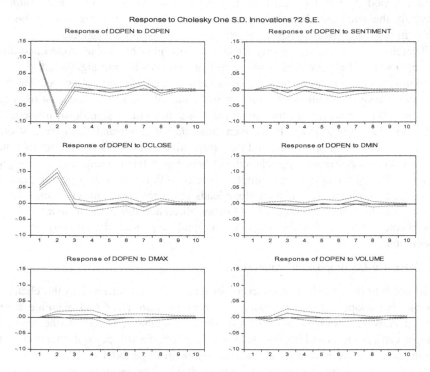

Fig. 3. Response of variable *dopen* to system variables.

(2) The Response of Variable *dmax*

Due to limited space, the figure of the response of variable *dmax* is not shown here. However, the result depicts that the link between *dmax* and *dmax* presents up-and-down trends till period 3. Like the response of *dopen* to *dopen*, the trend gets close to 0 then. At current period, the variable *dclose* has an even stronger shock to *dmax* than *dmax* itself. The impact gets weaker since period 2, almost decreasing to 0 since period 3. In the event of a one standard deviation shock in *dopen*, *dmax* will decrease up until period 2, after which it will increase. The *dmax* will decrease again up until period 4. It takes about 9 periods for *dmax* to fully become stable. Finally, the result obtained from the IRF suggests a 1 period lag time facing a one standard deviation shock of *sentiment*, then rising and falling, gradually showing no response till period 9.

Accordingly, except *dmax* itself, only variables *dclose*, *dopen* and *sentiment* have a significant influence on *dmax*. The degrees of impact are in their stated order.

(3) The Response of Variable *dmin*

Due to limited space, the figure of the response of variable *dmin* is not shown here. However, the result describes that variable *min* will be positively affected by *dclose*, *dopen* and *dmin* at current period. These influences then start to decline and get close to 0 since period 3. The lags exist in the response to *dmax*, *volume* and *sentiment*, especially the *sentiment*. It takes about 7 periods these 3 variables to fully become stable. In particular, *volume* has a general positive effect on the sequences.

Therefore, variable *dmin* is only affected significantly by *dclose*, *dopen* and *dmin*. The relationships between *dmin* and the rest of variables are not significant.

In this paper, we focus on how the news sentiment effects stock price. As what have been stated above, variable *sentiment* can make contribution to the forecast of *dopen*, *dmax* and *dmin*. In particular, the *dopen* and *dmax* have more significant influence on sentiment, compared to *dmin*. In the meantime, *dopen*, *dmax* and *dmin* are first order difference sequence of *open*, *max* and *min*, respectively. It is easy to find out that there turns out to be a corresponding relationship between difference sequence and original sequence. Taking the *dopen* for example, if *dopen* > 0, it means the opening price has the tendency to climb. And a larger slope leads to higher price, and vice versa. In line with *dopen*, the value and slope of first order difference sequence of *dmax* and *dmin* also enable us to predict the trend of original sequence, determining investor's expectation.

(3) Variance Decomposition Analysis

In order to discover how does every structural shock contribute to the change of variable, we adopt *Relative Variance Contribution Rate (RVC)* to examine a relationship between variable j and the response of variable i. Based on the results of Granger causality tests and impulse response function, we will pay our attention on the decomposition analysis of *dopen*, *dmax* and *dmin* from period 1 to 10.

Firstly, we run the analysis with variable *dopen*. The result shows that variables *dclose* and *dopen* contribute most to *dopen*, next are *sentiment* and *dmax*, whereas *dmin* and *volume* barely have no impact on the forecast of *dopen*, in accordance with the result of impulse response function.

Secondly, Variance decomposition of variable *dmax* presents that our finding further confirms the earlier impulse response function: one standard deviation shock of *dmax* makes the greatest contribution the *dmax*, then are the *dclose*, *dopen* and *sentiment*. Particularly, the effect of *sentiment* is small at first, and becomes larger as the time goes by.

Finally, the result of variance decomposition of *dmin* shows that the effects of six variables on *dmin* last for 10 periods. The variables making the largest contribution is *dmin* and *dclose*. Also there are similar but non-trivial responses of *dmin* to the rest of variables. The influence of *sentiment* on *dmin* is small in the initial stage, after which it will increase.

Due to limited space, the result of variance decomposition tables is not shown here. It can be concluded that the results of variance decomposition of *dopen*, *dmax* and *dmin* are essentially in agreement with the results of previous impulse response function. News sentiment variable *sentiment* has significant effect on all three variables.

The impacts of *sentiment* on *dmax* and *dmin* are small in the initial stage, after which it will become greater. Our conclusion is consistent with Larkin and Ryan, which documents that news is successfully able to predict stock price movement, although the predictive movement only accounts for 1.1% of whole movement [25].

4 Discussion on Forecast Effect of VAR(5) Model

4.1 Forecast Effect of in-Static Sample

Even though news sentiment can be used to forecast stock price, the forecasting effect remains unknown. We adopt 575 samples of variable *dopen* to achieve in-sample forecast. Sample 250–400 from 22/04/2016–17/09/2015 is randomly chosen to present a clearer observation. Figure 4 reveals the comparison between the actual value sequence (in solid line) and forecast value sequence (in dashed line).

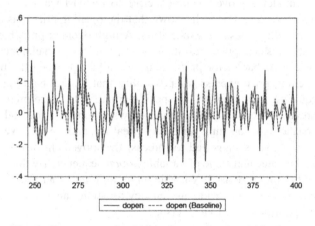

Fig. 4. Forecast result of in-static sample of variable *dopen*.

In a further step, *mean absolute percentile error* (*MAPE*) is used to evaluate the in-sample forecasting accuracy. The *MAPE* of *dopen, dmax* and *dmin* are all less than 10 (2.12, 2.48 and 5.33, respectively), enabling extrapolation forecasts of these three variables.

4.2 Forecast Effect of Out-Static Sample

Figure 5 depicts comparison between actual value sequence (in solid line) and forecast value sequence (in dashed line), using the samples from 576 to 632, which date from 03/01/2017 to 24/03/2017. The out-sample prediction is generally satisfactory, where the forecast sequence is nearly line with original sequence. Even the specific abnormal data indicates the correct movement.

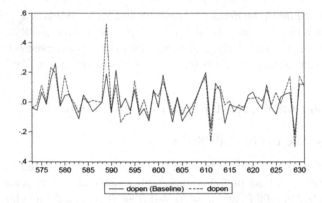

Fig. 5. Forecast result of out-static sample of variable *dopen*.

The VAR(5) model is proved to be effective to forecast variable *dopen* by using either in or out sample data. It is well-known that the opening price acts as a signal for stock market, indicating investor's expectation. A high opening price means investors are optimistic about stock price, resulting in a promising development of market. Nevertheless, it can be harder for profit taking or arbitrage when the price goes too high; A low opening price express the possibility that market is going to be bad or whipsawed, requiring combing with the specific situation to make prediction; A price closed to the previous session's closing price shows no obvious rise and fall. Hence, a thorough understanding of opening price is of great importance for investors. Impulse response function above is suggested to forecast the movement of opening price, by giving a look at the value and slope of variable *dopen* sequence. By this way investor's expectation can be further revised. Variable *dmax* and *dmin* can also be predicted by conducting the same method. A wide discrepancy illustrates an active stock market and a greater profit opportunity, and vice versa.

5   Conclusion and Future Work

In this study, we have proposed a forecast model to predict news sentiment around stock price. Base on dictionary matching, unstructured news text is transformed into structured news sentiment. We build a fifth-order VAR model with lags using the data of original stock price, including opening price, closing price, maximum price, minimum price and volume of transaction. Granger causality tests, impulse response function and variance decomposition analysis are employed to analyze the data of Alibaba news and its stock transaction. The result identifies the ability of VAR model to forecast variable *dopen, dmax* and *dmin*. In other words, news sentiment makes contribution to predict all these three variables. What's more, variable *dopen* is used to examine the predict effect of VAR model. The forecast sequence is accordance with original sequence, successfully to reflect the sequence general movement. However, due to the complexity of stock market, limited ability of author, more explanatory variables need to be concerned in the model, enhancing investor's decision in a further step.

References

1. Kearney, C., Liu, S.: Textual sentiment analysis in finance: a survey of methods and models. Finan. Anal. **33**(3), 171–185 (2013)
2. Tetlock, P.: Giving content to investor sentiment: the role of media in the stock market. J. Finan. **62**(3), 1139–1168 (2007)
3. Tetlock, P., Saar-Tsechansky, M., Macskassy, S.: More than words: quantifying language to measure firms' fundamentals. J. Finan. **63**(3), 1437–1467 (2008)
4. Chowdhury, S.G., Routh, S., Chakrabarti, S.: News analytics and sentiment analysis to predict stock price trends. Int. J. Comput. Sci. Inf. Technol. **5**(3), 3595–3604 (2014)
5. Loughran, T., Mcdonald, B.: When is a liability not a liability? Textual analysis, dictionaries, and 10-Ks. J. Finan. **66**(1), 35–65 (2011)
6. Ferguson, N.J., Philip, D., Lam, H.Y.T., Guo, J.: Media content and stock returns: the predictive power of press. Multinatl. Finan. J. **19**(1/1), 1–31 (2015)
7. Schumaker, R.P., Zhang, Y., Huang, C.N., Chen, H.: Evaluating sentiment in financial news articles. Decis. Support Syst. **53**(3), 458–464 (2012)
8. Schumaker, R.P., Chen, H.: A quantitative stock prediction system based on financial news. Inf. Process. Manag. **45**(5), 571–583 (2009)
9. Feng, L.I.: The Information content of forward-looking statements in corporate filings—a Naïve [1] Bayesian machine learning approach. J. Account. Res. **48**(5), 1049–1102 (2010)
10. Sehgal, V., Song, C.: SOPS: stock prediction using web sentiment. In: ICDM Workshops. IEEE (2007)
11. Zhu, M.J., Jiang, H.X., Xu, W.: Stock price prediction based on the emotion and communication effect of financial micro-blog. J. Shandong Univ. (Nat. Sci.) **51**(11), 13–25 (2016)
12. Cao, Y.B.: Study on the influence of open market operation on stock price – an empirical analysis based on VAR model. Econ. Forum **7**, 88–94 (2014)
13. Liu, L.: A Research on the Relationship between Stock Price and Macroeconomic Variables Based on Vector Autoregression Model. Hunan University (2006)
14. Yu, Z.J., Yang, S.L.: A model for stock price forecasting based on error correction. Chin. J. Manag. Sci. 1–5 (2013)
15. Xu, F.: GARCH model of stock price prediction. Stat. Decis. **18**, 107–109 (2006)
16. Chen, Z.X., He, X.W., Geng, Y.X.: Macroeconomic variables predict stock market volatility. In: International Institute of Applied Statistics Studies, pp. 1–4 (2008)
17. Xu, W., Li, Y.J.: Quantitative analysis of the impact of industry and stock news on stock price. Money China **20**, 31–32 (2015)
18. Sun, Q., Zhao, X.F.: Prediction and analysis of stock price based on multi-objective weighted markov chain. J. Nanjing Univ. Technol. (Nat. Sci. Ed.) **30**(3), 89–92 (2008)
19. Xu, X.J., Yan, G.F.: Analysis of stock price trend based on BP neural network. Zhejiang Finan. **11**, 57–59 (2011)
20. Peng, Z.X., Xia, L.T.: Markov chain and its application on analysis of stock market. Mathematica Applicata **S2**, 159–163 (2004)
21. Gao, T.M.: Method and Modeling of Econometric Analysis: Application and Example of EViews. Tsinghua University Press, Beijing (2009)
22. Chen, X.H., Peng, Y.L., Tian, M.Y.: Stock price and volume forecast based on investor sentiment. J. Syst. Sci. Math. Sci. **36**(12), 2294–2306 (2016)
23. Zhang, S.J., Cheng, G.S., Cai, J.H., Yang, J.W.: Stock price prediction based on network public opinion and support vector machine. Math. Pract. Theory **43**(24), 33–40 (2013)

24. Xie, G.Q.: Stock price prediction based on support vector regression machine. Comput. Simul. **4**, 379–382 (2012)
25. Larkin, F., Ryan, C.: Good news: using news feeds with genetic programming to predict stock prices. In: O'Neill, M., Vanneschi, L., Gustafson, S., Esparcia Alcázar, A.I., De Falco, I., Della Cioppa, A., Tarantino, E. (eds.) EuroGP 2008. LNCS, vol. 4971, pp. 49–60. Springer, Heidelberg (2008). https://doi.org/10.1007/978-3-540-78671-9_5

Parallel Harris Corner Detection on Heterogeneous Architecture

Yiwei He[1], Yue Ma[2], Dalian Liu[3(✉)], and Xiaohua Chen[4]

[1] School of Computer and Control Engineering,
University of Chinese Academy of Sciences, Beijing, China
heyiwei16@mails.ucas.ac.cn

[2] School of Mathematical Sciences, University of Chinese Academy of Sciences,
Beijing, China
mayue115@mails.ucas.ac.cn

[3] Department of Basic Course Teaching, Beijing Union University, Beijing, China
ldlluck@sina.com

[4] Dean's office, Beijing Union University, Beijing, China
lytxiaohua@buu.edu.cn

Abstract. Corner detection is a fundamental step for many image processing applications including image enhancement, object detection and pattern recognition. Recent years, the quality and the number of images are higher than before, and applications mainly perform processing on videos or image flow. With the popularity of embedded devices, the real-time processing on the limited computing resources is an essential problem in high-performance computing. In this paper, we study the parallel method of Harris corner detection and implement it on a heterogeneous architecture using OpenCL. We also adopt some optimization strategy on the many-core processor. Experimental results show that our parallel and optimization methods highly improve the performance of Harris algorithm on the limited computing resources.

Keywords: Harris corner detection · Heterogeneous architecture
Parallel computing · OpenCL

1 Introduction

Corner detection is an important problem in many image processing applications including edge detection, object detection and pattern recognition [1]. It is a fundamental step in image processing. Recent years, with the development of embedded devices or high-performance computing, the real-time computing plays a crucial role in many applications, such as video game, communication app and media player. Especially in the area of computer vision, applications always require that the system can be request clients in a few seconds. As an indispensable corner detection algorithm, Harris corner detector has been successfully used in the image processing [25], such as feature selection or edge

© Springer International Publishing AG, part of Springer Nature 2018
Y. Shi et al. (Eds.): ICCS 2018, LNCS 10861, pp. 443–452, 2018.
https://doi.org/10.1007/978-3-319-93701-4_34

detection. It is also accelerated based on different strategy or various compute devices. However, much of them ignore the limitations of computing resources like embedded device, and they do not fully take advantage of the heterogeneous architecture.

Over past decades, the performance of computing device has achieved a significant development. Many large-scale computing tasks are benefited from modern processors like GPU, CPU or FPGA. Especially growing in many-core processors, massive algorithms have been parallelled and implemented on the many-core processor which could improve the efficiency of computing [11]. The general purpose computing on GPU pushed the revolution of many applications like machine learning, and more and more algorithms are transplanted to the many-core compute platforms. GPU also push the improvement of machine learning research. Many methods would be benefited from the high-performance of GPU [7, 10, 15, 19–22, 24].

However, large-scale computing task is suitable for the host or server devices. For the embedded devices, the limited computing resources cannot satisfy the complexity of massive data processing or the real-time reaction. For example, some image applications on the Android or IOS which should be reacted in a few seconds. Thus, how to fully utilize the limited computation resource is a key problem which is needed to solve urgently. Two types of strategy are used to speed up. One is reducing the complexity of an algorithm, and the other is optimizing based on the architecture of computing device. In real applications, the implementation is always combined this two idea to optimize the software.

In this paper, we parallel the Harris corner detection algorithm and implement it in an environment of heterogeneous architecture which is composed of many-core and multi-core processors. We also adopt some optimization for methods basing on this unique design. We implement the algorithm by OpenCL, which is an open source parallel library working for heterogeneous architecture and it is commonly used in cross computation platforms. Experimental results prove that our implementation is accuracy and efficiency. The rest paper is organized as follow: Sect. 2 introduces the background and Harris corner detection, Sect. 3 makes an instruction of heterogeneous architecture under the cross-platform software library OpenCL and the related work of parallel Harris corner algorithm implementation. Section 4 introduces details of our implementation and optimization. Section 5 lists the accuracy of detection and computing efficiency. At last, we give the conclusion and explanation.

2   Background of Harris Corner Detection

Harris corner detector is developed basing on Moravec corner detection to mark the location of corner points precisely [5]. It is a corner detection operator which is widely used in computer vision algorithms to extract corners and infer features of an image [23]. It also contributes to the area of computer vision [8]. At the rest of this section, we give an overview of the formulation of the Harris corner detection and its algorithm.

A corner is defined as the intersection of two edges. The main idea of Harris algorithm is that the corner would emerge when the value of an ROI (region of interest) variant dynamically with the shift to nearby regions [2]. The algorithm set a window scan the ROI in all directions; if it has a high gradient, we can infer that there may be corners in this region. We define $I(x, y)$ as a pixel in the input image, (u, v) is the offset of shifted region from the ROI. $w(x, y)$ is represented a convolution function which is Gaussian filter here. The function of the variable is defined as follow:

$$E(u, v) = \sum_{x,y} w \otimes (x, y) \left[I(x + u, y + v) - I(x, y) \right] \tag{1}$$

where $\otimes$ is represented as a convolution operator. And then we make an approximation with shifted ROI value based on Taylor series expansion equation.

$$I(x + u, y + v) \approx I(x, y) + I_x(x, y) u + I_y(x, y) v \tag{2}$$

By substituting (2) into (1) and approximate the result can be converted to matrix form:

$$E(u, v) \approx [u \ v] \sum_{x,y} w(x, y) \otimes \begin{bmatrix} I_x^2(x, y) & I_x(x, y) I_y(x, y) \\ I_x(x, y) I_y(x, y) & I_y^2(x, y) \end{bmatrix} \begin{bmatrix} u \\ v \end{bmatrix} \tag{3}$$

$$= (u \ v) \, w(x, y) \otimes M \begin{pmatrix} u \\ v \end{pmatrix} \tag{4}$$

The matrix H which named Harris matrix is defined as:

$$H = \sum_{x,y} w(x, y) \otimes \begin{bmatrix} I_x^2(x, y) & I_x(x, y) I_y(x, y) \\ I_x(x, y) I_y(x, y) & I_y^2(x, y) \end{bmatrix} \tag{5}$$

To determine whether the pixel is a corner point or not, we need to compute pixel criterion score $c(x, y)$ for each pixel. The function is given by

$$c(x, y) = det(H) - k(trace(H))^2 \tag{6}$$

$$= \lambda_1 \lambda_2 - k(\lambda_1 + \lambda_2)^2 \tag{7}$$

where λ_1, λ_2 are the eigenvalues of the Harris matrix H. At the last step, we calculate the criterion score $c(x, y)$ for each pixel, if the score higher than the threshold and it is the maximum value in the scan area, we mark this pixel as a corner point. The description of Harris corner detection algorithm is list in Algorithm 1.

3   Heterogeneous Architecture and Related Work

3.1   Heterogeneous Architecture

Since the improving requirement of complexity for large-scale computing, the performance of processors become more efficiently. Many-core and multi-core

---

Algorithm 1. Harris Corner Detection

Require: Input image I parameter k,
Ensure: optimal α and M
  1: Compute image gradient I_x and I_y for every pixel;
  2: Compute the element in the Harris Matrix H
  3: **repeat** Each pixel
  4:     Define ROI of pixel by Gaussian filter
  5:     Update Harris matrix H
  6:     Compute eigenvalues of Harris matrix H
  7:     Compute corner score of the pixel
  8: **until**
  9: Threshold corner score
10: Mark pixel as corner point for maximum corner score

---

processors make a significant contribution to many fields [9]. CPU specialize in logic operation, and contrast, GPU does well in float or integer computing. These two kinds processors cooperate each other to enhance the computing speed. This structure of CPU-GPU is a typical kind of heterogeneous architecture. Figure 1 shows an example of heterogeneous architecture.

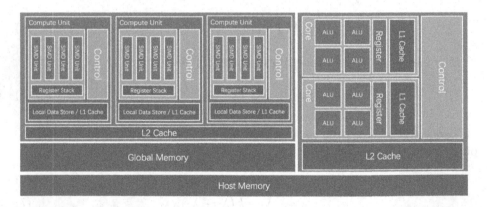

Fig. 1. Multi-core and many-core heterogeneous architecture. There are several compute units in the GPU and each of them contains SIMD (single instruction multi data) unit, register stack and local data store. Most square of CPU is used to be memory, like cache and register.

However, some factors limit the development of processors, including memory access and power wall, particularly the finite square of the chip for the requirement of embedded devices. With the popularity of embedded devices, the square wall of a chip is a limitation. Thus, how to fully utilize resource on-chip, like register, local memory and compute units, is a critical problem in future.

In this paper, we consider the heterogeneous architecture, which is composed of a GPU and a CPU. For implementation, we adopt a parallel open source library named OpenCL that can be performed on various devices. It is a popular framework for programming in the heterogeneous environment. It abstracts compute devices into the same structure and constructs a communication function among compute units or devices. The most advantage of OpenCL is cross-platform. Figure 2 shows the abstract structure in OpenCL.

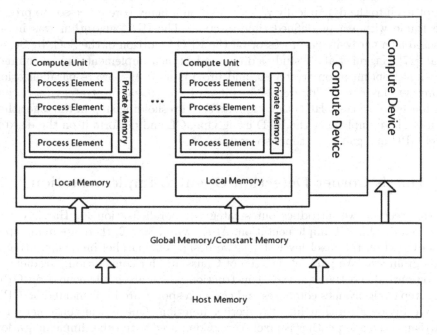

Fig. 2. OpenCL open source library abstracts computing devices in a unified framework [18]. The compute units are organized in clusters, compute devices are highest level contain several compute units which are composed by dozens of process element. Memory resources are organized in a multi-level style. The nearest from process elements are register, then in the order of local memory, global memory and host memory.

3.2 Related Works

Corner detection techniques are being widely used in many computer vision applications for example in object recognition and motion detection to find suitable candidate points for feature registration and matching. High-speed feature detection is a requirement for many real-time multimedia and computer vision applications. Harris corner detector (HCD) as one of many corner detection algorithm has become a viable solution for meeting real-time requirements of the applications. There are many works to improve the efficiency of the algorithm, and some parallel implementations has been developed on different platforms. In previous work, several implementation have been proposed which target a specific device or some particular aspects of the algorithm. Saidani et al. [16] used the Harris algorithm for the detection of interest points in an image as a benchmark to compare the performance of several parallel schemes on a Cell processor. To attain further speedup, Phull et al. [13] proposed the implementation of this low complexity corner detector algorithm on a parallel computing architecture, a GPU software library namely Compute Unified Device Architecture (CUDA). Paul and his co-author [12] present a new resource-aware Harris corner-detection algorithm for many-core processors. The novel algorithm can adapt itself to the dynamically varying load on a many-core processor to process the frame within a predefined time interval. The HDC algorithm was implemented as a hardware co-processor on the FPGA portion of the SoC, by Schulz et al. [17]. Haggui et al. [3] study a direct and explicit implementation of common and novel optimization strategies, and provide a NUMA-aware parallelization. Moreover, Jasani et al. [6] proposed a bit-width optimization strategy for designing hardware-efficient HCD that exploits the thresholding step in the algorithm. Han et al. [4] implement the HCD using OpenCL and perform it on the desktop level GPU and gain a 77 times speedup.

4   Harris Corner Detection OpenCL Implementation

In this section, we introduce our strategy of parallelization for Harris corner detection in OpenCL implementation. As shown in Sect. 2, there are many operators based on the pixel level. Thus, we design our parallel implementation in pixel grain size. We parallel the step of Gaussian blur convolution, Gradient X, Y computing and Harris matrix construction which are implemented on GPU. The step of eigenvalues computes and corner response are implemented on CPU.

We divide algorithm into two kernel function. One is the construction of Harris matrix, and another is pixel score. Compared with other implementation, we decrease the number of the kernels. We integrate the function into one kernel as far as possible for the reason that it can reduce the time of communication between host and kernel device, like host memory and graphics memory. It also increases the ratio of data reuse and speeds up the program. In our design, we assume that the computing resource is limited, such as register, shared memory or computing unit, and our primary target is speeding up our program in the limited resource.

4.1   Kernel of Convolution and Matrix Construction

The compute of Gaussian blur convolution, image gradient and Harris matrix are merged into one kernel. For this kernel, we construct a computing space which is the same dimension as an input image. Every thread deals a pixel task and output one Harris matrix. All outputs in threads compose a complete Harris matrix. For a thread In this kernel, we first compute the gradient X $I_x(x, y)$and gradient Y $I_y(x, y)$ of this pixel and then compute its own $I_x^2(x, y)$, $I_y^2(x, y)$ and $I_x(x, y) I_y(x, y)$. Finally, we use the operation of Gaussian blur convolution to filter the pixel with its neighbourhood. The procedure description of this kernel is shown in Fig. 3.

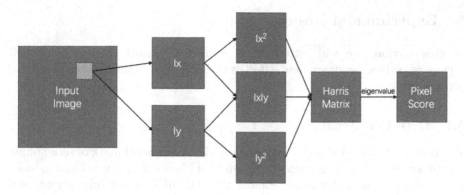

Fig. 3. The figure indicates the process for the algorithm of Harris corner detection.

Optimization strategy: The pixel level computing is beneficial for many-core architecture since its high parallelism and numerical value compute. We utilize this advantage of convolution that every thread compute a mask filter. However, in the process of convolution or gradient compute, it exists many memory access. It is low efficiency when read data from global memory to compute unit frequently. To solve this problem, we move pixels nearby target to shared memory on-chip first. This method could improve the local data repetition rate and make computing units access data which are stored in the consecutive address, namely combination access. In our implementation, we set the local pixel to the size of local computing space.

4.2 Kernel of Corner Response

After the first kernel computing, we get the corner score for every pixel in the ROI which we defined. These corner scores can report the probability of a corner point existing in the corresponding ROI. If a corner score is a negative value, it means there may be an edge in this region, and a small value indicates this area may be a flat region. Thus, we need to get the score values which are larger than the threshold, which indicate that there exists a corner in the ROI of this pixel. At last, we adopt the non-maximum suppression (NMS) stage which is aim to get the local maximum value. We set the pixel which have local maximum value as a corner point.

In our implementation, we fix a $3 * 3$ window to search the neighborhood nearby the pixel. Every thread in the computing space is assigned a $3 * 3$ region, and if the corner score is larger than the threshold and it is the maximum value of this region, we set this pixel as a corner point. Similar to kernel convolution, we store consecutive data together from global memory to the local data memory on-chip. For limited store resource like register, we prefer the search window as little as possible.

5   Experimental Results

In this section, we will introduce experimental results for our implementation regarding accuracy and effectiveness on our heterogeneous hardware architecture.

5.1   Detection Accuracy

We use the function *HarrisCorner* in *OpenCV* as our benchmark of serial implementation. OpenCV is an open source software library, and it is utilized in image processing and computer vision. Similar with OpenCL, it can take advantage of the cross-platform and hardware acceleration based on heterogeneous compute device [14]. Figure 4 shows the results of corner detection.

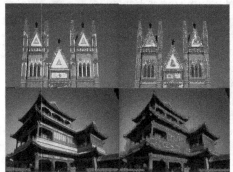

Fig. 4. The experimental results are shown in this figure. The corners detected by algorithms are in the red circles. The left image for each of sub-images is the detection result of baseline method, which is the function in OpenCV. The right image for each of sub-images is the results of our paralleled method. Contrast, our method is more stable and more precisely. (Color figure online)

5.2   Performance Results

To evaluate our implementation, we perform our experiments on MacOS with OpenCL 1.2. The hardware configure is a CPU of 2.6 GHz Intel Core i5 and a many-core processor namely Intel Iris. Iris is a lightweight GPU with limited compute units and memory, which provides 40 stream processors. It is a typically many-core processor with limited computing resource.

Comparing with OpenCV function *HarrisCorner*, our implementation (image size: 640 × 480) on the CPU-GPU architecture could get speedup of 11.7. With the ROI increasing, the speedup is improved. It proves that our design is efficiency. The experimental results are lists in Table 1.

Table 1. We change the size of ROI to test the compute time. This table list the compute time on CPU and heterogeneous device. When the size of ROI augment, the speedup is increasing.

Size of ROI	CPU time (ms)	Heterogeneous time (ms)	Speedup
3 × 3	120.34	11.05	10.89
5 × 5	144.10	10.94	13.17
7 × 7	147.43	11.09	13.29
Average	137.29	11.03	12.45

6 Conclusion

In this paper, we have paralleled the Harris corner detection algorithm and implemented it on the heterogeneous architecture using OpenCL. Our implementation has achieved an acceleration compared with open library function in OpenCV. Our design considers the utilization of memory resource. It increases memory reuse ratio as possible. We implement Harris corner detection on a limited resource device and gain a speedup.

Acknowledgments. This work has been partially supported by grants from the National Natural Science Foundation of China (Nos. 61472390, 71731009, 71331005 and 91546201), the Beijing Natural Science Foundation (No. 1162005), Premium Funding Project for Academic Human Resources Development in Beijing Union University.

References

1. Ben-Musa, A.S., Singh, S.K., Agrawal, P.: Object detection and recognition in cluttered scene using Harris corner detection. In: 2014 International Conference on Control, Instrumentation, Communication and Computational Technologies, pp. 181–184, July 2014
2. Dey, N., Nandi, P., Barman, N., Das, D., Chakraborty, S.: A comparative study between Moravec and Harris corner detection of noisy images using adaptive wavelet thresholding technique. Comput. Sci. (2012)
3. Haggui, O., Tadonki, C., Lacassagne, L., Sayadi, F., Ouni, B.: Harris corner detection on a NUMA manycore. Future Gener. Comput. Syst. (2018)
4. Han, X., Ge, M., Qinglei, Z.: Harris corner detection algorithm on OpenCL architecture. Comput. sci. **41**(7), 306–309, 321 (2014)
5. Harris, C.: A combined corner and edge detector. In: 1988 Proceedings of the 4th Alvey Vision Conference, no. 3, pp. 147–151 (1988)
6. Jasani, B.A., Lam, S., Meher, P.K., Wu, M.: Threshold-guided design and optimization for Harris corner detector architecture. IEEE Trans. Circ. Syst. Video Technol. **PP**(99), 1 (2017)
7. Li, D., Tian, Y.: Global and local metric learning via eigenvectors. Knowl.-Based Syst. **116**, 152–162 (2017)
8. Lowe, D.G.: Object recognition from local scale-invariant features. In: Proceedings of the 7th IEEE International Conference on Computer Vision, p. 1150 (2002)

9. Mittal, S., Vetter, J.S.: A survey of CPU-GPU heterogeneous computing techniques. ACM Comput. Surv. **47**(4), 1–35 (2015)
10. Niu, L., Zhou, R., Tian, Y., Qi, Z., Zhang, P.: Nonsmooth penalized clustering via ell_p regularized sparse regression. IEEE Trans. Cybern. **47**(6), 1423–1433 (2017)
11. Owens, J.D., Houston, M., Luebke, D., Green, S., Stone, J.E., Phillips, J.C.: GPU computing. Proc. IEEE **06**(5), 879–899 (2008)
12. Paul, J., et al.: Resource-aware Harris corner detection based on adaptive pruning. In: Maehle, E., Römer, K., Karl, W., Tovar, E. (eds.) ARCS 2014. LNCS, vol. 8350, pp. 1–12. Springer, Cham (2014). https://doi.org/10.1007/978-3-319-04891-8_1
13. Phull, R., Mainali, P., Yang, Q., Alface, P.R., Sips, H.: Low complexity corner detector using CUDA for multimedia application. In: International Conferences on Advances in Multimedia, MMEDIA (2011)
14. Pulli, K., Baksheev, A., Kornyakov, K., Eruhimov, V.: Real-time computer vision with OpenCV. Commun. ACM **55**(6), 61–69 (2012)
15. Qi, Z., Meng, F., Tian, Y., Niu, L., Shi, Y., Zhang, P.: Adaboost-LLP: a boosting method for learning with label proportions. IEEE Trans. Neural Netw. Learn. Syst. **PP**(99), 1–12 (2018)
16. Saidani, T., Lacassagne, L., Falcou, J., Tadonki, C., Bouaziz, S.: Parallelization schemes for memory optimization on the cell processor: a case study on the Harris corner detector. In: Stenström, P. (ed.) Transactions on High-Performance Embedded Architectures and Compilers III. LNCS, vol. 6590, pp. 177–200. Springer, Heidelberg (2011). https://doi.org/10.1007/978-3-642-19448-1_10
17. Schulz, V.H., Bombardelli, F.G., Todt, E.: A Harris corner detector implementation in SoC-FPGA for visual SLAM. In: Santos Osório, F., Sales Gonçalves, R. (eds.) LARS/SBR -2016. CCIS, vol. 619, pp. 57–71. Springer, Cham (2016). https://doi.org/10.1007/978-3-319-47247-8_4
18. Stone, J.E., Gohara, D., Shi, G.: OpenCL: a parallel programming standard for heterogeneous computing systems. Comput. Sci. Eng. **12**(3), 66–73 (2010)
19. Tang, J., Tian, Y.: A multi-kernel framework with nonparallel support vector machine. Neurocomputing **266**, 226–238 (2017)
20. Tang, J., Tian, Y., Zhang, P., Liu, X.: Multiview privileged support vector machines. IEEE Trans. Neural Netw. Learn. Syst. **PP**(99), 1–15 (2017)
21. Tian, Y., Ju, X., Qi, Z., Shi, Y.: Improved twin support vector machine. Sci. China Math. **57**(2), 417–432 (2014)
22. Tian, Y., Qi, Z., Ju, X., Shi, Y., Liu, X.: Nonparallel support vector machines for pattern classification. IEEE Trans. Cybern. **44**(7), 1067–1079 (2014)
23. Weijer, V.D., Gevers, T., Geusebroek, J.M.: Edge and corner detection by photometric quasi-invariants. IEEE Trans. Pattern Anal. Mach. Intell. **27**(4), 625–630 (2005)
24. Xu, D., Wu, J., Li, D., Tian, Y., Zhu, X., Wu, X.: SALE: self-adaptive lsh encoding for multi-instance learning. Pattern Recogn. **71**, 460–482 (2017)
25. Zhu, J., Yang, K.: Fast Harris corner detection algorithm based on image compression and block. In: IEEE 2011 10th International Conference on Electronic Measurement Instruments, vol. 3, pp. 143–146, August 2011

A New Method for Structured Learning with Privileged Information

Shiding Sun[1], Chunhua Zhang[1(✉)], and Yingjie Tian[2]

[1] School of Information, Renmin University of China, Beijing 100872, China
zhangchunhua@ruc.edu.cn
[2] Research Center on Fictitious Economy and Data Science,
Chinese Academy of Science, Beijing 100190, China

Abstract. In this paper, we present a new method JKSE+ for structured learning. Compared with some classical methods such as SSVM and CRFs, the optimization problem in JKSE+ is a convex quadratical problem and can be easily solved because it is based on JKSE. By incorporating the privileged information into JKSE, the performance of JKSE+ is improved. We apply JKSE+ to the problem of object detection, which is a typical one in structured learning. Some experimental results show that JKSE+ performs better than JKSE.

Keywords: SVM · One-class SVM · Structured learning
Object detection · Privileged information

1 Introduction

This paper deals with the structured learning problems which learn function: $f : \mathcal{X} \to \mathcal{Y}$, where the elements of $\mathcal{X}$ and $\mathcal{Y}$ are structured objects such as sequences, trees, bounding boxes, strings. Structured learning arises in lots of real world applications including multi-label classification, natural language parsing, object detection, and so on. Conditional random fields [5,6], maximum margin markov networks [9] and structured output support vector machines (SSVM) [10] have been developed as powerful tools to predict the structured data. The common approach of these methods is to define a linear scoring function based on a joint feature map over inputs and outputs. There are some drawbacks in these methods. On the one hand, to apply them one requires clearly labeled training sets. Experiments show that some incorrect or incomplete labels can reduce their performance. On the other hand, training these models is computationally cost. So it is difficult or infeasible to solve large scale problems except for some special output structures.

C. Zhang—This work has been partially supported by grants from National Natural Science Foundation of China (Nos. 61472390, 71731009, 71331005, 91546201 and 11771038), and the Beijing Natural Science Foundation (No. 1162005).

© Springer International Publishing AG, part of Springer Nature 2018
Y. Shi et al. (Eds.): ICCS 2018, LNCS 10861, pp. 453–461, 2018.
https://doi.org/10.1007/978-3-319-93701-4_35

To overcome these drawbacks, a method called Joint Kernel Support Estimation (JKSE) has been proposed in [7]. JKSE is a generative method as it relies on learning the support of the joint-probability density of inputs and outputs. This makes it robust in handling mislabeled data. At the same time, The optimization problem is convex and can be efficiently solved because the one-class SVM is used in it. However, JKSE is not as powerful as SSVM [2]. So we focus on the following problem: How to improve the performance of JKSE? To answer this question, we introduce the privileged information into JKSE.

Privileged information [11] provides useful high-level knowledge that is used only at training time. For example, in the problem of object detection, these information includes the object's parts, attributes and segmentations. More reliable models [3,4,8,11] can be learned by incorporating these high-level information into SVM, SSVM, one-class SVM.

In this paper, we propose a new method called JKSE+ based on JKSE with privileged information and apply it to the problem of object detection. Some experiments show that our new method JKSE+ performs better than JKSE.

The rest of this paper is organized as follows. We first review the method JKSE in Sect. 2, then introduce our new method JKSE+ in Sect. 3, and the experimental results are presented in Sect. 4.

2   Related Work

This section considers the following structured learning problem: given the training set: $\{(x_1, y_1), ..., (x_l, y_l)\}$, where $x_i \in \mathcal{X}$, $y_i \in \mathcal{Y}$. $\mathcal{X}$ and $\mathcal{Y}$ are the space of inputs and outputs with some structures respectively. Assume that the input-output pairs (x, y) follow a joint probability distribution $p(x, y)$. Our goal is to learn a mapping: $g : \mathcal{X} \rightarrow \mathcal{Y}$ such that for a new input $x \in \mathcal{X}$, the corresponding label $y \in \mathcal{Y}$ can be determined by maximizes the posterior probability $p(y|x)$.

As we all know, The discriminative method directly models the conditional distribution $p(y|x)$, and the generative method directly models the joint distribution $p(x, y)$. These two methods are equivalent, i.e. $\arg\max\limits_{y \in \mathcal{Y}} p(y|x) = \arg\max\limits_{y \in \mathcal{Y}} p(x, y)$ for any $x \in \mathcal{X}$. JKSE is a generative method. Suppose that $p(x, y) = \frac{1}{Z} \exp(\langle w, \Phi(x, y)\rangle)$. Here, $Z \equiv \sum_{x,y} \exp(\langle w, \Phi(x, y)\rangle)$, and Z is a normalization constant. We can ignore Z during training and testing. The JKSE method translates the task of learning a joint probability distribution $p(x, y)$ into a one-class SVM problem to estimate the joint probability distribution $p(x, y)$.

In training phase, JKSE solves the following problem:

$$\min_{w,\xi,\rho} \frac{1}{2} \| w \|^2 + \frac{1}{vl} \sum_{i=1}^{l} \xi_i - \rho$$
$$s.t. \quad \langle w, \Phi(x_i, y_i)\rangle \geq \rho - \xi_i, \quad i = 1, 2, ..., l, \tag{1}$$
$$\xi_i \geq 0, \quad i = 1, 2, ..., l.$$

To get its solution, JKSE solve its dual problem:

$$\min_{\alpha} \sum_{i=1}^{l} \sum_{j=1}^{l} \alpha_i \alpha_j K\left((x_i, y_i), (x_j, y_j)\right)$$
$$s.t. \quad 0 \leq \alpha_i \leq \tfrac{1}{vl}, \quad i = 1, ..., l, \tag{2}$$
$$\sum_{i=1}^{l} \alpha_i = 1.$$

where $K\left((x, y), (x', y')\right) \equiv \langle \Phi(x, y), \Phi(x', y') \rangle$ is a joint feature kernel function. If α^* is the solution to the above problem (2), then the solution to the primal problem (1) for w is given as follows:

$$w^* = \sum_{i=1}^{l} \alpha_i^* \Phi(x_i, y_i). \tag{3}$$

Furthermore, in the inference step, for a new input $x \in \mathcal{X}$, the corresponding label y is given by:

$$y = \arg\max_{y \in \mathcal{Y}} \sum_{i=1}^{l} \alpha_i K\left((x_i, y_i), (x, y)\right). \tag{4}$$

3   JKSE+

Assume that we have some privileged information, $(x_1^*, x_2^*, ..., x_l^*) \in \mathcal{X}^*$ that is available only at the training phase but not available on the test phase. Now we consider the following privileged structured learning problem:

Given a training set $T = \{(x_1, x_1^*, y_1), ..., (x_l, x_l^*, y_l)\}$ where $x_i \in \mathcal{X}$, $x_i^* \in \mathcal{X}^*$, $y \in \mathcal{Y}$, $i = 1, ..., l$, our goal is to find a mapping: $g : x \to y$, such that the label of y for any x can be predicted by $y = g(x)$.

Now we discuss how the privileged information can be incorporated into the framework of JKSE. Suppose that there exists the best but unknown function: $\arg\max_{y \in \mathcal{Y}} \langle w_0, \Phi(x, y) \rangle$. The function $\xi(x)$ of the input x is defined as follows:

$$\xi^0 = \xi(x) = [\rho - \langle w_0, \Phi(x, y) \rangle]_+$$

where $[\eta]_+ = \begin{cases} \eta, & if \quad \eta \geq 0, \\ 0, & otherwise. \end{cases}$ If we know the value of the function $\xi(x)$ on each input $x_i (i = 1, ..., l)$ such as we know the triplets $\left(x_i, \xi_i^0, y_i\right)$ with $\xi_i^0 = \xi(x_i), i = 1, ..., l$, we can get improved prediction. However, in reality, this is impossible. Instead we use a correcting function to approximate the function $\xi(x)$. Similar to one-class SVM with privileged information in [3], we replace ξ_i by a mixture of values of the correcting function $\psi(x_i^*) = \langle w^*, \Phi(x_i^*, y_i) \rangle + b^*$ and some values ζ_i, and get the primal problem of JKSE+:

$$\min_{w,w^*,b^*,\rho,\varsigma} \frac{vl}{2} \| w\|^2 + \frac{\gamma}{2} \| w^*\|^2 - vl\rho + \sum_{i=1}^{l} [\langle w^*, \Phi^* (x_i, y_i)\rangle + b^* + \varsigma_i]$$
$$\text{s.t.} \quad \langle w, \Phi (x_i, y_i)\rangle \geq \rho - (\langle w^*, \Phi^* (x_i^*, y_i)\rangle + b^*), \quad i = 1, ..., l, \tag{5}$$
$$\langle w^*, \Phi^* (x_i^*, y_i)\rangle + b^* + \varsigma_i \geq 0, \varsigma_i \geq 0, \quad i = 1, ..., l.$$

The Lagrange function for this problem is:

$$L (w, w^*, b^*, \rho, \varsigma, \mu, \alpha, \beta) = \frac{vl}{2} \| w\|^2 + \frac{\gamma}{2} \| w^*\|^2 - vl\rho$$

$$+ \sum_{i=1}^{l} [\langle w^*, \Phi^* (x_i, y_i)\rangle + b^* + \varsigma_i]$$

$$- \sum_{i=1}^{l} \mu_i \varsigma_i - \sum_{i=1}^{l} \alpha_i [\langle w, \Phi (x_i, y_i)\rangle - \rho + \langle w^*, \Phi^* (x_i^*, y_i)\rangle + b^*]$$

$$- \sum_{i=1}^{l} \beta_i [\langle w^*, \Phi^* (x_i^*, y_i)\rangle + b^* + \varsigma_i] \tag{6}$$

The KKT conditions are as follows:

$$\nabla_w L = vlw - \sum_{i=1}^{l} \alpha_i \Phi (x_i, y_i) = 0, \tag{7}$$

$$\nabla_{w^*} L = \gamma w^* + \sum_{i=1}^{l} \Phi^* (x_i^*, y_i) - \sum_{i=1}^{l} \alpha_i \Phi^* (x_i^*, y_i) - \sum_{i=1}^{l} \beta_i \Phi^* (x_i^*, y_i), \tag{8}$$

$$\frac{\partial L}{\partial b^*} = l - \sum_{i=1}^{l} \alpha_i - \sum_{i=1}^{l} \beta_i = 0, \tag{9}$$

$$\frac{\partial L}{\partial \rho} = -vl + \sum_{i=1}^{l} \alpha_i = 0, \tag{10}$$

$$\frac{\partial L}{\partial \varsigma_i} = 1 - \beta_i - \mu_i = 0, i = 1, ..., l, \tag{11}$$

$$\rho - (\langle w^*, \Phi^* (x_i^*, y_i)\rangle + b^*) - \langle w, \Phi (x_i, y_i)\rangle \leq 0, i = 1, ..., l, \tag{12}$$

$$- (\langle w^*, \Phi^* (x_i^*, y_i)\rangle + b^* + \varsigma_i) \leq 0, i = 1, ..., l, \tag{13}$$

$$-\varsigma_i \leq 0, i = 1, ..., l, \tag{14}$$

$$\alpha_i [\rho - (\langle w^*, \Phi^* (x_i^*, y_i)\rangle + b^*) - \langle w, \Phi (x_i, y_i)\rangle] = 0, i = 1, ..., l, \tag{15}$$

$$\beta_i [\langle w^*, \Phi^* (x_i^*, y_i)\rangle + b^* + \varsigma_i] = 0, i = 1, ..., l, \tag{16}$$

$$\mu_i \varsigma_i = 0, i = 1, ..., l, \tag{17}$$

$$\alpha_i \geq 0, \beta_i \geq 0, \mu_i \geq 0, i = 1, ..., l. \tag{18}$$

From the above KKT conditions and setting $\delta_i = 1 - \beta_i$, we can get that

$$w = \frac{1}{vl} \sum_{i=1}^{l} \alpha_i \Phi(x_i, y_i), \tag{19}$$

$$w^* = \frac{1}{\gamma} \sum_{i=1}^{l} (\alpha_i - \delta_i) \Phi^*(x_i^*, y_i), \tag{20}$$

$$\sum_{i=1}^{l} \delta_i = \sum_{i=1}^{l} \alpha_i = vl, \tag{21}$$

$$0 \le \delta_i \le 1, i = 1, ..., l. \tag{22}$$

So, we can get the dual problem is as follows:

$$\begin{aligned}
\max_{\alpha, \delta} \; & -\frac{1}{2vl} \sum_{i=1}^{l} \sum_{j=1}^{l} \alpha_i \alpha_j K\left((x_i, y_i), (x_j, y_j)\right) \\
& - \sum_{i=1}^{l} \sum_{j=1}^{l} \frac{1}{2\gamma} (\alpha_i - \delta_i) K^*\left((x_i^*, y_i), (x_j^*, y_j)\right)(\alpha_j - \delta_j) \\
s.t. \quad & \sum_{i=1}^{l} \alpha_i = vl, \quad \alpha_i \ge 0, \\
& \sum_{i=1}^{l} \delta_i = vl, \quad 0 \le \delta_i \le 1.
\end{aligned} \tag{23}$$

We use $K\left((x_i, y_i), (x_j, y_j)\right)$ and $K^*\left((x_i^*, y_i), (x_j^*, y_j)\right)$ to replace the inner product $\langle \Phi(x_i, y_i), \Phi(x_j, y_j) \rangle$ and $\langle \Phi^*(x_i^*, y_i), \Phi^*(x_j^*, y_j) \rangle$. Therefore, the model's decision function is $f(x, y) = \sum_{i=1}^{l} \alpha_i K\left((x_i, y_i), (x, y)\right)$.

We can learn this mapping in JKSE framework as

$$y = g(x) = \arg\max_{y \in \mathcal{Y}} f(x, y) = \arg\max_{y \in \mathcal{Y}} \sum_{i=1}^{l} \alpha_i K\left((x_i, y_i), (x, y)\right). \tag{24}$$

Here, the function $f(x, y)$ is equivalent to a matching function. For example in object detection, when the overlap of an object and a bounding box is higher, the value of the function is greater. Therefore, we output y that maximizes the value of $f(x, y)$.

Our new algorithm JKSE+ is given as follows:

Algorithm 1

(1) Given a training set $T = \{(x_1, x_1^*, y_1), ..., (x_l, x_l^*, y_l)\}$ where $x_i \in \mathcal{X}$, $x_i^* \in \mathcal{X}^*$, $y \in \mathcal{Y}$, $i = 1, .., l$;
(2) Choose the appropriate kernel function $K(u, v)$, $K^*(u', v')$ and penalty parameters $v > 0, \gamma > 0$;

(3) Construct and solve convex quadratic programming problem:

$$\max_{\alpha,\delta} -\frac{1}{2vl} \sum_{i=1}^{l} \sum_{j=1}^{l} \alpha_i \alpha_j K\left((x_i, y_i), (x_j, y_j)\right)$$

$$-\sum_{i=1}^{l} \sum_{j=1}^{l} \frac{1}{2\gamma} \left(\alpha_i - \delta_i\right) K^*\left((x_i^*, y_i), (x_j^*, y_j)\right) \left(\alpha_j - \delta_j\right)$$

$$s.t. \quad \sum_{i=1}^{l} \alpha_i = vl, \quad \alpha_i \geq 0,$$

$$\sum_{i=1}^{l} \delta_i = vl, \quad 0 \leq \delta_i \leq 1.$$

get the solution $(\alpha^*, \delta^*) = (\alpha_1^*, ...\alpha_l^*, \delta_1^*, ..., \delta_l^*)$.
(4) Construct decision function:

$$y = g(x) = \arg\max_{y \in \mathcal{Y}} f(x, y) = \arg\max_{y \in \mathcal{Y}} \sum_{i=1}^{l} \alpha_i^* K\left((x_i, y_i), (x, y)\right).$$

4 Experiments

In this section, we apply our new method to the problem of object detection. In object detection, given a set of pictures, we hope to learn a mapping $g : \mathcal{X} \to \mathcal{Y}$, when inputing a picture, we can get the object's position in the picture by mapping g. Obviously, it is a typical one of structured learning and can be solved by our new method. Some experiments are made in this section.

4.1 Dataset

We use dataset Caltech-UCSD Birds 2011 (CUB-2011) [12] to evaluate our algorithm. This dataset contains two hundred species of birds, each of which has sixty pictures. Each picture contains only one bird, the bird's position in the picture is indicated by a bounding box. In addition, this dataset provides privilege information, including the bird's attribute information for each image described as a 312-dimensional vector and segmentation masks.

4.2 Features and Privileged Information

Our feature descriptor adopts the bag-of-visual-words model based on SURF descriptor [1]. We use attribute informations and segmentation masks as privileged information. For the feature extraction of segmentation mask, we use the same strategy as the original image for feature extraction, that is SURF based bag-of-visual-words feature descriptor. It is clear that the feature space of privileged information provides more information relative to the feature space of the original image so that the object's location in the image can be better detected.

We select 50 pictures as the training set and 10 pictures as the test set. The dimensionality of original visual feature descriptors is 200. In addition, attribute information is described as a 312-dimensional vector, each dimension is a binary variable. We extract the 500-dimensional feature descriptors based on the same bag-of-visual-words model from segmentation masks as in the original picture. So the privilege information has a dimension of 812-dimensional vectors.

In Fig. 1, we can see that more feature descriptors can be extracted in the segmentation masks, which is beneficial to improve the overlap of object detection.

 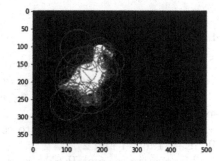

Fig. 1. The picture on the left is the feature descriptor of the original picture. The picture on the right is the feature descriptor of the segmentation mask, which is used as privilege information when training.

Table 1. Dataset

Data_ID	Name
001	Black_footed_Albatross
002	Laysan_Albatross
003	Sooty_Albatross
004	Groove_billed_Ani
005	Crested_Auklet
006	Least_Auklet
007	Parakeet_Auklet
008	Rhinoceros_Auklet
009	Brewer_Blackbird
010	Red_winged_Blackbird

4.3   Kernal Function

We use the following version of the chi-square kernel function $\left(\chi^2 - \text{kernel}\right)$:

$$K\left(u,v\right) = K^*\left(u,v\right) = e^{-\theta \sum_{i=1}^{n} \frac{(u_i - v_i)^2}{u_i + v_i}}, u \in R^n, v \in R^n.$$

This kernel is most commonly applied to histograms generated by bag-of-visual-words model in computer vision [13].

Table 2. Overlap ratio of Object Detection

Model	Data_ID									
	001	002	003	004	005	006	007	008	009	010
JKSE	40.974	34.281	**55.808**	28.948	38.719	47.705	51.414	31.695	**54.044**	34.285
JKSE+	**46.241**	**42.933**	46.347	**30.323**	**44.660**	**51.455**	**53.692**	**40.342**	49.919	**37.866**
DIFF	+5.267	+8.652	−9.461	+1.375	+5.941	+3.750	+2.278	+8.647	−4.125	+3.581

4.4 Experimental Results

To evaluate our JKSE+, we compare it with JKSE. During the training, we adjust the parameters v, γ, θ on a $8 \times 8 \times 8$ space spanning values $[10^{-4}, 10^{-3}, ..., 10^3]$. For JKSE, we also adjust the parameter v, θ on a 8×8 space spanning values $[10^{-4}, 10^{-3}, ..., 10^3]$.

We chose ten different birds to compare the detection results of JKSE and JKSE+ (Tables 1 and 2).

The overlap ratio of JKSE+ is higher than that of JKSE in eight datasets.

5 Conclusion

We propose a new method for structured learning with privilege information based on JKSE. Firstly, compared with some traditional methods SSVM, CRFs for structured learning, the resulting optimization problem in our new model JKSE+ is convex and can be easily solved. Secondly, compared with JKSE, the prediction performance of JKSE is improved by using the privileged information. Lastly, we apply JKSE+ to the problem of object detection. Some experimental results show that JKSE+ performs better than JKSE in most cases.

For future work, we will consider some extensions of the JKSE+ method. For example, at the training stage privileged information are provided only for a fraction of inputs or privileged information are described in many different spaces, and so on.

References

1. Bay, H., Ess, A., Tuytelaars, T., Van Gool, L.: Speeded-up robust features (SURF). Comput. Vis. Image Underst. **110**(3), 346–359 (2008)
2. Blaschko, M.B., Lampert, C.H.: Learning to localize objects with structured output regression. In: Forsyth, D., Torr, P., Zisserman, A. (eds.) ECCV 2008. LNCS, vol. 5302, pp. 2–15. Springer, Heidelberg (2008). https://doi.org/10.1007/978-3-540-88682-2_2
3. Burnaev, E., Smolyakov, D.: One-class SVM with privileged information and its application to malware detection. In: 2016 IEEE 16th International Conference on Data Mining Workshops (ICDMW), pp. 273–280. IEEE (2016)

4. Feyereisl, J., Kwak, S., Son, J., Han, B.: Object localization based on structural SVM using privileged information. In: Advances in Neural Information Processing Systems, pp. 208–216 (2014)
5. Lafferty, J., McCallum, A., Pereira, F.C.: Conditional random fields: probabilistic models for segmenting and labeling sequence data (2001)
6. Lafferty, J., Zhu, X., Liu, Y.: Kernel conditional random fields: representation and clique selection. In: Proceedings of the Twenty-First International Conference on Machine Learning, p. 64. ACM (2004)
7. Lampert, C.H., Blaschko, M.B.: Structured prediction by joint kernel support estimation. Mach. Learn. **77**(2–3), 249 (2009)
8. Tang, J., Tian, Y., Zhang, P., Liu, X.: Multiview privileged support vector machines. IEEE Trans. Neural Netw. Learn. Syst. 1–15 (2017)
9. Taskar, B., Guestrin, C., Koller, D.: Max-margin Markov networks. In: Advances in Neural Information Processing Systems, pp. 25–32 (2004)
10. Tsochantaridis, I., Joachims, T., Hofmann, T., Altun, Y.: Large margin methods for structured and interdependent output variables. J. Mach. Learn. Res. **6**(Sep), 1453–1484 (2005)
11. Vapnik, V., Vashist, A.: A new learning paradigm: learning using privileged information. Neural Netw. **22**(5–6), 544–557 (2009)
12. Wah, C., Branson, S., Welinder, P., Perona, P., Belongie, S.: The caltech-ucsd birds-200-2011 dataset (2011)
13. Zhang, J., Marszałek, M., Lazebnik, S., Schmid, C.: Local features and kernels for classification of texture and object categories: a comprehensive study. Int. J. Comput. Vis. **73**(2), 213–238 (2007)

An Effective Model Between Mobile Phone Usage and P2P Default Behavior

Huan Liu[1], Lin Ma[2,3]($\boxtimes$), Xi Zhao[2,4], and Jianhua Zou[1]

[1] School of Electrical and Information Engineering,
Xi'an Jiaotong University, Xi'an 710049, China
liuhuanli@stu.xjtu.edu.cn, jhzou@sei.xjtu.edu.cn
[2] School of Management, Xi'an Jiaotong University, Xi'an 710049, China
malinxjtu@163.com
[3] State Key Laboratory for Manufacturing Systems Engineering,
Xi'an 710049, China
[4] Shaanxi Engineering Research Center of Medical and Health Big Data, Xi'an
710049, China
zhaoxi1@mail.xjtu.edu.com

Abstract. P2P online lending platforms have become increasingly developed. However, these platforms may suffer a serious loss caused by default behaviors of borrowers. In this paper, we present an effective default behavior prediction model to reduce default risk in P2P lending. The proposed model uses mobile phone usage data, which are generated from widely used mobile phones. We extract features from five aspects, including consumption, social network, mobility, socioeconomic, and individual attribute. Based on these features, we propose a joint decision model, which makes a default risk judgment through combining Random Forests with Light Gradient Boosting Machine. Validated by a real-world dataset collected by a mobile carrier and a P2P lending company in China, the proposed model not only demonstrates satisfactory performance on the evaluation metrics but also outperforms the existing methods in this area. Based on these results, the proposed model implies the high feasibility and potential to be adopted in real-world P2P online lending platforms.

Keywords: P2P default behavior Prediction · Mobile phone usage
Joint decision model

1 Introduction

The P2P (peer-to-peer) online lending platforms provide micro-credit services by playing a mediating role between individual lenders and borrowers. Compared with traditional lending institutions, these platforms show lower costs, convenient conditions, and quick loan process. For above advantages, more and more individuals and investors are attracted by P2P platforms, especially in developing countries. In China, the online lending industry shows transaction size had

© Springer International Publishing AG, part of Springer Nature 2018
Y. Shi et al. (Eds.): ICCS 2018, LNCS 10861, pp. 462–475, 2018.
https://doi.org/10.1007/978-3-319-93701-4_36

reached 28 thousand billion RMB, increasing 137% over than 2015 [11].The number of P2P platforms had grown to 2307 in 2016, which increase year-on-year by 2.81%.

However, the investment of lenders on P2P platforms may suffer a serious loss caused by default behaviors of borrowers, which may cause a critical customer churn problem to the platforms. In order to reduce risk in P2P lending, the platforms generally adopt risk control mechanism to filter some high default risk borrowers. Actually, the risk control mechanism may face serious challenges from several perspectives. First, to ensure profitability of platform, the cost on risk control must be as low as possible, which causes a high limit in restricting the facticity inspect of individuals information. Second, without other monitoring mechanism required by traditional banks, a pre-approval credit checking process is crucial to decrease the loss of default. Third, since the target customs are the mass individuals, the credit control mechanism must have the capability to handle users without or limited credit records in the credit behavior. All these challenges put forward for an automated risk control mechanism, which provides pre-approval credit estimate with high accuracy and reliable data source.

The growing need has motivated several studies in reducing the risk for P2P lending. Based on credit related records, such as FICO, credit history, etc., some researchers reduce the risk by rejecting loans with high potential default risk [5], by transferring the problem to a portfolio optimizing investment decision problem [8], or by replacing default loss as profit scoring to increase the overall income [22]. Other researchers try to find the connection between default behavior and soft information [3,7,26,29]. All these aforementioned studies are effective to reduce the risk of P2P lending. However, there still exist several questions when applying on developing countries. Due to the immature credit system, not all borrowers have credit records. And the mass applicants make it difficult for platforms to verify off-line self-reported applications. These restrictions narrow the generality of the methods.

In this paper, we present a general and reliable joint decision model to predict default behaviors on P2P lending platform from mobile phone usage data. Mobile phone usage data contains a series of records from the call, message, data volume, and App usage. The great value of mobile phone usage data has already been discovered in analysing user behaviors, personality traits, socioeconomic status, consumption patterns, and economic characteristics [13,15–17,20,23,28], which are correlated with credit default behavior [3,6,7,12,26,29]. Moreover, the ubiquity of mobile phones guarantees the extensive application of the proposed model, and the portability and versatility of smartphones ensure the data volume and multi-descriptions of each individual, and the automatic generating characteristic ensures the facticity of data. Supported by above conclusions, the proposed model using mobile phone usage data has great potential and advantages in predicting P2P default behavior.

The main contributions of this paper are threefold. (1) We present a risk control mechanism for P2P online lending platforms, which can realize automated and agile loan approval. (2) We propose a quantitative model to predict the default behavior of individuals, which can be implemented in the risk control mechanism of P2P online lending platforms. (3) We verify our proposed model on a real-world dataset, and gain satisfactory performance not only on the evaluation metrics but also on the comparison with existing models in this area.

2   Related Work

P2P online lending served as a marketplace for individuals to directly borrow money from others through Internet [1]. Benefit from the services with lower charge and without any confining of space [8,30], P2P lending and platforms are growing rapidly. However, limited by information asymmetry and guarantee fund, platforms cannot perform precision default assessment for each loan applicant, which may lead to a high default rate. This situation attracts researchers to study increasing the profit of lenders and reducing the default rate of borrowers. In this work, we focus on the particular problem of building a quantitative model to predict individual default behavior on P2P loan repayment, which acts as a pre-approval credit checking in decreasing the risk for P2P lending.

Some researchers focus on recognizing default behavior of loan applicants by using financial and credit data. Emekter et al. [5] measured loan performances by credit records and historical data from LendingClub. Using the same data source, Polena and Regner [19] defined different ranks of loan risk. Different technologies also were used to predict defaults probability on borrowers, such as random forest classification [14], Bayesian network [27], logistic regression [21], decision tree [29], fuzzy SVM algorithm [25]. When data about individuals' credit is available, these methods achieved high precision on evaluating credit. However, limited by collecting credible individual data, the performance of the methods may decrease when applying on developing countries.

Other researchers try to understand the correlation between individual default behavior and soft information that can be correlated with the default probability. Gathergood [6] inferred personality traits and socioeconomic status correlated with credit behavior. Lin et al. [12] found that the significant and verifiable relational network associated with a high possible on low default risk. Chen et al. [3] studied relationships between social capital and repayment performance, discovering that borrowers structural social capital may have a negative effect on his/her repayment performance. Zhang et al. [29] used social media information to constitute a credit scoring model. Wang et al. [26] studied the connection between borrowers self-report loan application documents and the risk of loans by text analysis. Gonzalez and Loureiro [7] focused on the characteristics of both lender and borrower on the P2P lending decision. These studies illustrate the existing relationship between soft information and credit scoring, especially prove that individuals' behaviors on other perspectives can affect default behavior.

Mobile phone usage data have been studied for modeling users and community dynamics in a wide range of applications. In [15,16,23], mobile phone usage data were used for modeling users, such as inferring personality traits and socioeconomic status. In [9,10], phone usage data have already been used for analyzing behavior and psychology. Chiara Renso et al. [20] proposed methods on movement pattern discovery and human behavior inference. Parent et al. [17] summarized the approaches on mining behavior patterns from semantic trajectories. Mobile phone usage data can also reflect one's purchase habits and natural attributes [28]. Liu et al. [13] proposed a model to extract factors from trajectories and construct the connection between these factors and rationality decisions. All these studies proved the close relationship between phone usage data and human reactions to socio-economic activities, which can affect default behavior as previously discussed. To the best of our knowledge, in the default behavior prediction on P2P online lending, we are the first to build a machine learning model to predict P2P default behavior using mobile phone usage data.

3   Mechanism Overview and Data Description

3.1   Mechanism Overview

The main purpose of risk control mechanism is to reduce the default rate of borrowers. According to the adoptive common mechanism on P2P lending platforms [30], we design the mechanism as demonstrated in Fig. 1. When a borrower applies for loans on a P2P platform, the risk control mechanism is triggered. Firstly, the loan approval process encrypts borrower's ID and sends it to risk control service provider via API. Secondly, risk control service performs the default prediction and sends the result back. Thirdly, depending on the assessment result, loan approval process decides whether or not post the borrower's loan application. Finally, if the loan application is posted online, lenders access the application and conclude the transaction. In order to preserve the privacy of borrowers, phone usage data are kept within risk control service providers. In this mechanism, the risk control service provider refers to a mobile carrier. As soon as risk control service received the loan request, it decrypts the encrypted ID and retrieves the applicant's phone usage data. Then, the default prediction model analyses the borrower's daily behavior and predicts the default probability of borrower and returns assessment consequence to the P2P platform. The detail of the prediction model is introduced in Sect. 4.

3.2   Data Description

Mobile Phone Usage Dataset. Mobile phone usage data consists individuals demographic information and telecommunication services records, which contain detailed call, message, and data volume. These records are generated during the communication between a mobile phone and base transceiver stations (BTSs) of its carrier. Generally, a specific BTS, automatically selected according to the distance and signal strength, provides the requested services while logs detailed phone usage behaviors. Our mobile phone usage dataset is from one

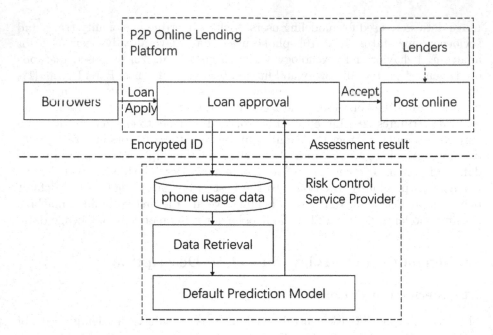

Fig. 1. A figure caption is always placed below the illustration. Please note that short captions are centered, while long ones are justified by the macro package automatically.

of the mobile carriers in China. Specifically, for message service, the recorded information includes the time stamp and the contact ID. For phone call service, the location and call duration is added to the aforementioned items. Both these records can describe when and where individual contact others by phone or message. For data volume service, the detail information contains the time stamp, the location, and the data volume. In addition, we obtain the statistical data for each App on the frequency and data volume spend in every month. Besides these direct information from the records, users' movement behaviors can be implied by locations of the selected BTSs. Despite losing a large volume of content in data such as message texts, voices during calls, and App data, these meta-level records reach a good balance between user privacy and behavioral representation power.

Actual Default Behavior Dataset. Our actual default behavior dataset of borrowers is from a P2P lending company in China, which contains 3027 subjects. Before advancing this study, the ethical problem of collecting and analyzing subjects' behavior data requires careful consideration. The ethical and legal approval is granted by the contract we signed. The data has been anonymized on subjects' name, ID, and phone numbers. Encryption techniques are applied by mobile carriers. It's impossible for us to decrypt and identify the participants.

4   Methodology

In this section, we will discuss the default behavior prediction sub-process, as the decisive role of the risk control process. Based on the realization procedure, we separate the sub-process into two parts. First, we extract features from mobile phone usage data on five aspects. Second, we build a joint decision model for the default behavior prediction combining two popular machine learning algorithms.

4.1   Feature Extraction

According to the existing feature pools on mobile data [9,10,18] and characteristics of our data, we extract a set of features conveying user behavioral information from 5 aspects, including consumption, social network, mobility, socioeconomic, and individual attribute. These features describe the phone usage behavior from different fields, as depicted in Table 1.

Table 1. Extracted Features from five different aspects.

Feature set	Features clusters	Records type	Number
Consumption features	Communication consumption	Calls & messages	22
	MONET consumption	Data volume	6
	Telecommunication consumption	Basic information	10
	Consumption entropy	Calls & messages	4
Social network features	Connections quantity	Calls & messages	2
	Connections entropy	Calls & messages	2
Mobility features	Mobility sphere	Calls & data volume	2
	Mobility quantity	Calls & data volume	8
	Mobility entropy	Calls & data volume	3
Socioeconomic features	Age & gender	Basic information	2
Individual attribute features	App frequency	App usage data	8
	App data volume	App usage data	6
	Specific app usage behavior	App usage data	17

Consumption Features. Consumption features reflect the amount of usage on the communications network, and we provide a high-level view of the statistical criteria for calls, SMS, and internet usage.

Communication Consumption. Statistics of usage time on call, SMS and Internet services, including the average, the maximum, the minimum number, the variance of usage frequency in one day, and the number of days that have records, The number and the proportion of communications during the night(19pm to 7am of next day). The rate of communications occurred at home or at the workplace. The interval refers to the time interval between two interactions, including the average, the maximum, the minimum, the variance number.

MONET Consumption. Statistical features focus on the Data Volume records occurred when the individuals using mobile internet, including the average, the maximum, the minimum number, the variance of usage frequency in one day, and the number of days that have records, The number and the proportion of internet usage during the night(19pm to 7am of next day).

Telecommunication Consumption. Individuals telecommunication service records, which consist of shutdown times in last year, total data volume used in last year, total expenditure on the mobile phone in last year, the number and cost of international and internal roams days in last year, time of network, star level.

Consumption Entropy. We compute the number of call and SMS for different temporal partitions: by day, and by the time of the day (eight periods of time, 0 am to 3 am, 3 am to 6 am). We use Shannons entropy to compute communications day entropy and communications time entropy. The former can reflect the usage time regularity in every day of one mouth, and the latter reflects the usage time regularity in eight periods of one mouth.

Social Network Features. Social network features are related to the characteristics of the graph of connections between different individuals, which can transmit information about social-related traits such as empathy of personality.

Connections Quantity. The number of unique contacts from both calls and SMS, which can be used to measure the degrees in the Social network.

Connections Entropy. We count the number of Connections time between the individuals and the unique contacts, and compute Shannons entropy to measure the contacts regularity.

Mobility Features. Mobility features focus on mobility patterns of the individuals in daily life, which can be inferred from the position of BTSs connected by the individuals.

Mobility Sphere. The minimum radius which encompasses all the locations (BTS), and the distance between home and workplace of the individuals.

Mobility Quantity. The record of Locations (BTSs) from both call and Data Volume services, including the average, the maximum, the minimum number, the variance of Locations in one day, and the number of days that have Locations, The number and the proportion of Locations during the night(19 pm to 7 am of next day). The number of locations where 80% of communications occurred.

Mobility Entropy. We count the frequency for each location the individual stay on, and compute Shannons entropy to measure the locations regularity. Moreover, we compute the number of call and SMS for different locations (BTS), and use Shannons entropy to compute connections space entropy, which reflects the space regularity of connections.

Socioeconomic Features. Socioeconomic features are related to demographic information (age, gender), which required in specific P2P products. We get those features from the basic information of individuals.

Individual Attribute Features. Individual attribute features refer to individuals' operation behaviors through an electronic device. In our data, the extracted features reflect individuals operation behaviors on mobile phones, which are mainly the App usage behaviors. These behaviors which have been proved can reflect differences on psychological level [10]. Specifically, payment, financial, and P2P online lending Apps usage features are extracted to compare the different operation preference on economic status related Apps of individuals.

App Frequency. The number of installed Apps and the categories of Apps, statistics of usage frequency of Apps, including the total, the average, the variance, the maximum, the minimum usage frequency; the regularity on usage frequency.

App Data Volume. Statistics of data volume spend on Apps, including the total, the average, the variance, the maximum, the minimum data volume spent; the regularity of data volume spent.

Specific App Usage Behavior. The usage features on different categories of Apps, which consist of financial Apps, payment Apps, and the combination of financial and payment Apps. The feature set includes the number of installed Apps, the proportion of Apps, the number of Apps that belongs to the top5 frequently used Apps in different categories, and the number of Apps that belongs to the top5 frequently used Apps. Especially, for P2P online lending Apps, the total usage time on Apps, the total data volume spending on Apps, the regularity of usage frequency and the data volume are extracted.

4.2   Model Building

We select supervised learning to build our default behavior prediction model of P2P Online Lending. To this end, we represent individuals in the presented feature space, which we extract from the mobile phone usage data. Every presented feature for an individual contains total 92 features. We select actual default behavior of 3027 subjects. After data pre-processing on aggregating to structural data, data cleaning i.e., 2999 subjects are included in the experiments and 28 subjects have been filtered due to missing data. To train and test the effect of our model, we randomly split the dataset into two parts, where 80% are used for training (2399 subjects) and 20% (600 subjects) are used for testing.

We try two different classification methods to compare their performance in this specific problem setting: Random Forests (RF) [2] and Light Gradient Boosting Machine (LightGBM) [24]. Random Forests algorithm is a combination of tree predictors such that each tree depends on the values of a random vector sampled independently and with the same distribution for all trees in the forest, which is widely used in classification problems. LightGBM is a highly efficient Gradient Boosted Decision Trees method proposed by Microsoft, which has faster training efficiency, low memory usage, higher accuracy, and support parallelization learning for processing large scale data.

Considering different methods have different advantages, we construct a joint decision model, which makes a default risk judgment through combining Random Forests with LightGBM. To build the proposed model, we train two independent submodels by using Random Forests algorithm and LightGBM algorithm separately. The final prediction result of the proposed model is determined by the average value of the two default possibilities, which are given by the two submodels. To give an example, if the default possibilities from the two submodels are 0.7 and 0.8, the ultimate default possibility judged by the proposed model is 0.75, which is the average value of 0.7 and 0.8. In order to tune the hyper-parameters automatically, we use grid-search strategy and fivefold cross validation over the entire training set for both of the two submodels. Finally, we get the optimal parameters of the Random Forests submodel and LightGBM submodel respectively, which make up the optimal parameters of the proposed model. According to the contrast result on the same testing phase, the proposed model has a better performance in the default behavior prediction for P2P Online Lending.

5   Experimental Results

In this section, we report the experimental results on real-world dataset as described in Sect. 3. Considering the unbalanced nature of the ground truth, we used the following four metrics to evaluate the prediction performance of default behavior, i.e., Precision, Recall, F1 score, AUCROC [4]. We use the AUCROC to measure the discriminatory ability. And the Precision, Recall, and F1 score are used to evaluate the correctness of the categorical predictions.

5.1 Feature Performance

In order to compare the performance of the features from mobile phone usage data as described in Sect. 4, we use three different features sets to build our models, i.e., CSMS features set only, IA features set only, CSMS+IA features set. CSMS features set contains Consumption features, Social network features, Mobility features, and Socioeconomic features, which we extract from the daily CDR records data and basic information registered by the mobile carriers. IA features set contains Individual attribute features, which we extract from the special data of App usage. Using Random Forest and LightGBM methods, we build models on these three features sets respectively, and use AUCROC to measure the Classification performance. The compared results are depicted in Table 2. Obviously, the combination of CSMS+IA features has better performance in AUCROC on the two methods. Based on this conclusion, and we select CSMS+IA features set to build the default behavior prediction model.

Table 2. Classification performance (AUCROC) of different feature categories on different two methods.

Categories	Random forests	LightGBM
CSMS features set	0.72	0.72
IA features set	0.69	0.69
CSMS+IA features set	**0.76**	**0.77**

5.2 Comparison of the Methods

To accomplishing default behavior prediction, we adopt a joint decision model, which makes a default risk judgment through combining Random Forests with LightGBM as described in Sect. 4. We also use Random Forest method and LightGBM method individually to compare their performance with the proposed model in this specific problem setting. Three different models have been performed, and Fig. 2 shows the performance of these models on four evaluation metrics. We found the proposed model achieving the best performance on Recall (0.885), F1 score (0.819), and AUCROC (0.774), which also has the better Precision (0.782), just 0.02 lower than LightGBM (0.784). According to the contrast result above, the proposed model has quantitative performance on the P2P default behavior Prediction.

5.3 Comparison Against Existing Methods

The performance of the proposed method has also been compared with existing methods. In the state-of-art studies [14], random forest model has been trained on Lending Club dataset to assess the individual default risk. As depicted in Table 3, the proposed method has higher AUCROC (0.774), Recall (0.885) and

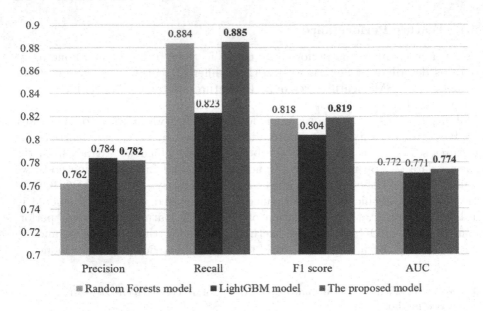

Fig. 2. A figure caption is always placed below the illustration. Please note that short captions are centered, while long ones are justified by the macro package automatically.

Table 3. The performance comparison between our method and the existing methods

Methods	AUCROC	Precision	Recall
[14]	0.71	0.56	0.87
[21]	-	0.646	-
[18]	0.725	0.29	-
Our method	**0.774**	**0.782**	**0.885**

Precision (0.782) than [14] with AUCROC of 0.71, Recall of 0.87 and Precision of 0.56, which depict the proposed method has better prediction performance. We also compare the performance with [21] following the same protocol on the division of test samples. They developed a logistic regression model to predict default also on data from Lending Club. As depicted in Table 3, our performance on Precision (0.782) are better than [21], which has Precision of 0.646. This shows that the proposed method is a more conservative model tending to reject more applicants to protect the P2P platforms from possible financial loss. These results demonstrate the feasibility of adopting the proposed method for P2P lending platforms. Moreover, we compare the performance with [18], where they build a Gradient Boosted Trees (GBT) classifier model to assess the users financial risk on credit card data, collected by a financial institution operating in the considered Latin American country. As depicted in Table 3, our proposed method has higher AUCROC (0.774) and Precision(0.782) than [18] with AUCROC of 0.725 and Precision of 0.29, These results demonstrate that the proposed method may have a better performance not only on P2P lending platforms but also on other financial risk platforms.

6   Conclusion

In this paper, we propose a risk control mechanism for P2P online lending platforms, which has a potential to be employed in countries lack of reliable personal credit evaluation system. We further propose a default behavior prediction model, which provides pre-approval credit estimate using mobile phone usage data in this mechanism. We extract features from five aspects, including consumption, social network, mobility, socioeconomic, and individual attribute. Specifically, we adopt a joint decision model, which makes a default behavior judgment through combining Random Forests with Light Gradient Boosting Machine. Lastly, we validate the proposed model using real-world dataset.

The experimental results demonstrate that the features combining all five aspects are most predictive for the future default behaviors of borrowers. Compared with other classifiers, the proposed model has achieved the best performance in terms of evaluation metrics. Moreover, the proposed model shows better performance when comparing to the existing methods in this problem setting.

In the future, we plan to measure the distinguishing power of the different features of our model in detail. Furthermore, we are interested in assessing how our risk control mechanism changes as a function of the P2P online lending products analyzed.

References

1. Boase, J., Ling, R.: Measuring mobile phone use: self-report versus log data. J. Comput.-Mediated Commun. **18**(4), 508–519 (2013)
2. Breiman, L.: Random forests. Mach. Learn. **45**(1), 5–32 (2001)
3. Chen, X., Zhou, L., Wan, D.: Group social capital and lending outcomes in the financial credit market : an empirical study of online peer-to-peer lending. Electron. Commer. Res. Appl. **15**(C), 1–13 (2016)
4. Davis, J., Goadrich, M.: The relationship between precision-recall and roc curves. In: Proceedings of the International Conference on Machine Learning, ICML 2006, New York, NY, USA, pp. 233–240 (2006)
5. Emekter, R., Tu, Y., Jirasakuldech, B., Lu, M.: Evaluating credit risk and loan performance in online Peer-to-Peer (P2P) lending. Appl. Econ. **47**(1), 54–70 (2015)
6. Gathergood, J.: Self-control, financial literacy and consumer over-indebtedness. Soc. Sci. Electron. Publishing **33**(3), 590–602 (2012)
7. Gonzalez, L., Loureiro, Y.K.: When can a photo increase credit? The impact of lender and borrower profiles on online peer-to-peer loans. J. Behav. Exp. Financ. **2**, 44–58 (2014)
8. Guo, Y., Zhou, W., Luo, C., Liu, C., Xiong, H.: Instance-based credit risk assessment for investment decisions in P2P lending. Eur. J. Oper. Res. **249**(2), 417–426 (2015)

9. Harari, G.M., Lane, N.D., Wang, R., Crosier, B.S., Campbell, A.T., Gosling, S.D.: Using smartphones to collect behavioral data in psychological science: opportunities, practical considerations, and challenges. Perspect. Psychol. Sci. **11**(6), 838–854 (2016)

10. Harari, G.M., Müller, S.R., Aung, M.S., Rentfrow, P.J.: Smartphone sensing methods for studying behavior in everyday life. Curr. Opin. Behav. Sci. **18**, 83–90 (2017)

11. JiaZhuo, W., Hongwei, X.: China's Online Lending Industry in 2015. Tsinghua University Press, Beijing (2015)

12. Lin, M., Prabhala, N.R., Viswanathan, S.: Judging borrowers by the company they keep: social networks and adverse selection in online peer-to-peer lending. SSRN eLibrary (2009)

13. Liu, S., Qu, Q., Wang, S.: Rationality analytics from trajectories. ACM Trans. Knowl. Discov. Data (TKDD) **10**(1), 10 (2015)

14. Malekipirbazari, M., Aksakalli, V.: Risk assessment in social lending via random forests. Expert Syst. Appl. **42**(10), 4621–4631 (2015)

15. de Montjoye, Y.-A., Quoidbach, J., Robic, F., Pentland, A.S.: Predicting personality using novel mobile phone-based metrics. In: Greenberg, A.M., Kennedy, W.G., Bos, N.D. (eds.) SBP 2013. LNCS, vol. 7812, pp. 48–55. Springer, Heidelberg (2013). https://doi.org/10.1007/978-3-642-37210-0_6

16. Oliveira, R.D., Karatzoglou, A., Cerezo, P.C., Oliver, N.: Towards a psychographic user model from mobile phone usage. In: CHI 11 Extended Abstracts on Human Factors in Computing Systems, pp. 2191–2196 (2011)

17. Parent, C., Spaccapietra, S., Renso, C., Andrienko, G., Andrienko, N., Bogorny, V., Damiani, M.L., Gkoulalas-Divanis, A., Macedo, J., Pelekis, N., et al.: Semantic trajectories modeling and analysis. ACM Comput. Surv. (CSUR) **45**(4), 42 (2013)

18. Pedro, J.S., Proserpio, D., Oliver, N.: MobiScore: towards universal credit scoring from mobile phone data. In: Ricci, F., Bontcheva, K., Conlan, O., Lawless, S. (eds.) UMAP 2015. LNCS, vol. 9146, pp. 195–207. Springer, Cham (2015). https://doi.org/10.1007/978-3-319-20267-9_16

19. Polena, M., Regner, T., et al.: Determinants of borrowers default in P2P lending under consideration of the loan risk class. Jena Econ. Res. Pap. **2016**, 023 (2016)

20. Renso, C., Baglioni, M., de Macedo, J.A.F., Trasarti, R., Wachowicz, M.: How you move reveals who you are: understanding human behavior by analyzing trajectory data. Knowl. Inf. Syst. **37**, 1–32 (2013)

21. Serrano-Cinca, C., Gutierrez-Nieto, B., López-Palacios, L.: Determinants of default in P2P lending. PLoS ONE **10**(10), e0139427 (2015)

22. Serrano-Cinca, C., Gutierrez-Nieto, B.: The use of profit scoring as an alternative to credit scoring systems in peer-to-peer (P2P) lending. Decis. Support Syst. **89**(C), 113–122 (2016)

23. Soto, V., Frias-Martinez, V., Virseda, J., Frias-Martinez, E.: Prediction of socioeconomic levels using cell phone records. In: Konstan, J.A., Conejo, R., Marzo, J.L., Oliver, N. (eds.) UMAP 2011. LNCS, vol. 6787, pp. 377–388. Springer, Heidelberg (2011). https://doi.org/10.1007/978-3-642-22362-4_35

24. Wang, D., Zhang, Y., Zhao, Y.: LightGBM: an effective miRNA classification method in breast cancer patients. In: International Conference, pp. 7–11 (2017)

25. Wang, M., Zheng, X., Zhu, M., Hu, Z.: P2P lending platforms bankruptcy prediction using fuzzy SVM with region information. In: 2016 IEEE 13th International Conference on e-Business Engineering (ICEBE), pp. 115–122. IEEE (2016)

26. Wang, S., Qi, Y., Fu, B., Liu, H.: Credit risk evaluation based on text analysis. Int. J. Cogn. Inform. Nat. Intell. **10**(1), 1–11 (2016)

27. Wang, X., Zhang, D., Zeng, X., Wu, X.: A Bayesian investment model for online P2P lending. In: Su, J., Zhao, B., Sun, Z., Wang, X., Wang, F., Xu, K. (eds.) Frontiers in Internet Technologies. CCIS, vol. 401, pp. 21–30. Springer, Heidelberg (2013). https://doi.org/10.1007/978-3-642-53959-6_3
28. Wu, S., Kang, N., Yang, L.: Fraudulent behavior forecast in telecom industry based on data mining technology. Commun. IIMA **7**(4), 1 (2014)
29. Zhang, Y., Jia, H., Diao, Y., Hai, M., Li, H.: Research on credit scoring by fusing social media information in online peer-to-peer lending. Procedia Comput. Sci. **91**, 168–174 (2016)
30. Zhao, H., Ge, Y., Liu, Q., Wang, G., Chen, E., Zhang, H.: P2P lending survey: platforms, recent advances and prospects. ACM Trans. Intell. Syst. Technol. (TIST) **8**(6), 72 (2017)

A Novel Data Mining Approach Towards Human Resource Performance Appraisal

Pei Quan[1,2], Ying Liu[1,2], Tianlin Zhang[1,2], Yueran Wen[3],
Kaichao Wu[4], Hongbo He[4], and Yong Shi[2,5,6,7]

[1] School of Computer and Control, University of Chinese Academy of Sciences,
Beijing 100190, China
quanpei17@mails.ucas.ac.cn, yingliu@ucas.ac.cn
[2] Key Lab of Big Data Mining and Knowledge Management,
Chinese Academy of Sciences, Beijing 100190, China
[3] School of Labor and Human Resources, Renmin University of China,
Beijing 100872, China
[4] Computer Network Information Center, Chinese Academy of Sciences,
Beijing 100190, China
[5] School of Economics and Management,
University of Chinese Academy of Sciences, Beijing 100190, China
yshi@ucas.ac.cn
[6] Research Center on Fictitious Economy and Data Science,
Chinese Academy of Sciences, Beijing 100190, China
[7] College of Information Science and Technology,
University of Nebraska at Omaha, Omaha, NE 68182, USA

Abstract. Performance appraisal has always been an important research topic in human resource management. A reasonable performance appraisal plan lays a solid foundation for the development of an enterprise. Traditional performance appraisal programs are labor-based, lacking of fairness. Furthermore, as globalization and technology advance, in order to meet the fast changing strategic goals and increasing cross-functional tasks, enterprises face new challenges in performance appraisal. This paper proposes a data mining-based performance appraisal framework, to conduct an *automatic* and *comprehensive* assessment of the employees on their working ability and job competency. This framework has been successfully applied in a domestic company, providing a reliable basis for its human resources management.

Keywords: Performance appraisal · Data mining · Enterprise strategy
Job competency

1 Introduction

The six modules of human resources: recruitment, configuration, training, development, performance management, compensation and benefit management, are interconnected. Among them, performance management is the core in practical businesses. With performance management, companies can reward and punish good or bad performance, and implement performance-based wages. Businesses can also identify

© Springer International Publishing AG, part of Springer Nature 2018
Y. Shi et al. (Eds.): ICCS 2018, LNCS 10861, pp. 476–488, 2018.
https://doi.org/10.1007/978-3-319-93701-4_37

weaknesses and deliver targeted training with proper performance management. Based on specific circumstances of internal and external recruitment, they can also achieve better matchings of positions and employees. Thus, a performance appraisal system which meets the requirement of enterprise strategic goals and current market conditions can fully release the potential of employees, and greatly mobilize their enthusiasm for the overall business development.

In practice, most employee performance appraisal approaches follow the traditional *manual* method for evaluation and supervision. It is very labor intensive, incomprehensive and unfair in domains where work is difficult to quantify, as well as large companies with thousands of employees and many departments. Therefore, the results of performance appraisal are not accurate, and cannot achieve the expectations. In addition, the market and policies of enterprises are changing rapidly, and their strategic objectives are also being constantly adjusted. Dynamically evaluating the relationship between actual work and strategic goals, and establishing real-time performance appraisal system are urgent problems in human resources management. In addition, with the development of society, the complexity of work is getting higher and higher, and job competition is becoming more intense. Thus, it is difficult to solve problems completely through employees' inherent knowledge. Therefore, it is necessary to *automatically* evaluate workability of staffs, based on the actual requirements of positions and the development of the employees. It is very useful to supervise the continuous growth of employees, as a basis for training and staffing.

In this paper, we use data mining algorithms to solve the above problems. The main contributions of our work include two aspects: **work performance** and **job competency**. We propose an automatic, comprehensive and fair performance appraisal framework which meets the strategic objectives of the enterprise and the needs of the market. Firstly, through text analysis of plans and summaries in the employee's work report, and the strategic objectives of the enterprise, the **work performance** of the employees can be evaluated from three aspects: job value, executive ability and content of the report. In the evaluation of **job competency**, the competency model of positions is extracted from the competency requirements of the job, and match with external knowledge sources such as books, images and other information in the internal knowledge base. Our model will automatically generate questions from the above core concepts. By investigating employee's answers, we can evaluate their job competency.

Currently, this performance appraisal framework has been highly recognized by human resources experts and has been widely used by thousands of employees at Company H and Company J. In addition, Company H is one of the largest high-tech companies in China. In practical application, this framework plays a role in encouraging staff to work actively and speeding up the realization of corporate strategic objectives, and contributes to the employee assessment and personnel adjustment.

The paper is organized as follows: Sect. 2 provides related work and backgrounds of human resource performance evaluation and data mining algorithms. Section 3 presents our methodology. Section 4 discusses implementation details and experiment results. Section 5 summaries this paper.

2 Related Work

In the field of **performance appraisal**, it is generally difficult to have a comprehensive assessment of staff performance. Various performance appraisal methods have their own advantages and disadvantages. Therefore, the study of personnel performance appraisal theory still needs to be further improved, especially in fitting performance appraisal methods to be in line with actual needs. At present, the main research methods are as followed.

Key Performance Indicators (KPIs) are one of the most commonly used methods [1, 2]. They are the key factors that determine the effectiveness of a business strategy. They turn a business strategy into internal processes and activities, and continuously strengthen the key competitiveness of enterprises and achieve high returns. The KPI method is based on annual target, combined with analysis of employee performance differences, and then periodically agreed on the key quantitative indicators of enterprises, ministries and individuals to build performance appraisal system.

360° assessment method is a more comprehensive performance evaluation method, also known as comprehensive evaluation method, with a wide range of sources of assessment results, and multi-level features [3]. 360°, as the name implies, refers to an all-round evaluation of employee performance. In terms of examiners, they include internal and external customers, as well as superior leaders, colleagues, subordinates, and employee themselves. The specific implementation process can be summarized as following: Firstly, the employees listen and fill out the questionnaire. Then, the managers evaluate the performance of different aspects of performance. When analyzing and discussing the assessment results, the two sides have conducted a full study and discussion to formulate the performance targets for the next year. The advantage of this method is to break the traditional way of superior evaluation of subordinates. It can avoid the phenomenon of "halo effect", "center trend", "personal prejudice and check blind spot" which is very common for the examiner in the traditional evaluations.

Date mining methodologies have been developed for exploration and analysis, by automatic or semi-automatic means, of large quantities of data to discover meaningful patterns and rules [4]. Indeed, such data including employees' seldom used data and work summary can provide a rich resource for knowledge discovery and decision support. Therefore, data mining is discovery-driven, not assumption-driven. Data mining involves various techniques including statistics, neural networks, decision tree, genetic algorithm.

Data mining has been applied in many fields such as marketing [5], finance [6], traffic [7], health care [8], customer relationship management [9], and educational data mining [10]. However, data mining has not been used well in human resource management. In particular, Chien and Chen [11] used data mining in the high-technology industry to analyze the ability of employees to improve personnel selection and enhance the quality of employees.

With the gradual development of data mining and text analysis, more and more fields apply data mining algorithms on domain specific data analysis, and gain positive results. For example, Tang et al. employ a multiview privileged SVM model to exploit complementary information among multiple feature sets, which can be an interesting future direction for our work, as we process data from multiple sources [22]. However, there are few cases which combine performance evaluation and data mining at present. Therefore, this paper proposes a novel comprehensive performance appraisal framework based on data mining and text analysis, which combines a employees' work performance, corporate strategic objectives and position competence. It provides a promising way for human resource management.

3 Methodology

This paper constructs an automatic framework for human resource data mining to evaluate the employees' work from their work summary and self-improvement. As the main contribution and novelty of our work, we extensively apply NLP and data mining technologies to areas of work performance, job competency and self-growth material recommendation. Under our methodology, working ability and job competencies could be quantified and the decision makers can have an easier and better understanding on employees' comprehensive ability. The evaluation results can be used to effectively adjust enterprise position structure reasonably and improve matching of staff and posts. The performance appraisal framework is shown in Fig. 1.

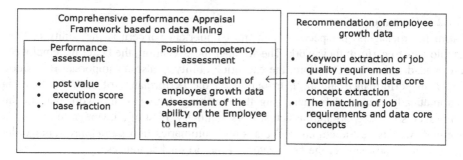

Fig. 1. The performance appraisal framework

3.1 Assessment of Work Performance of Employee Based on Text Analysis

Each employee submits a job report periodically, including the company's strategic objectives, the employee's expected plan, and a summary of the employee's actual work during that period. Since each report submitted is reviewed by the manager of the employee, the reliability of the report's content can be guaranteed. Therefore, our framework applies text analysis on the employee's work reports, and conducts analysis on the position value, the execution score and the basic score, and thus obtains the employee's work performance result. The specific assessment is as follows:

3.1.1 Position Score

The most intuitive manifestation of the value of an employee is the impact of his/her work on the strategic goals of the organization. Therefore, we correlate the work plan in the employee's work report with the strategic objectives of the enterprise. The two sources of paragraph text are firstly divided into words by CRF segmentation method. Since sentences often contain "stop words" that appears frequently but not semantically relevant (e.g. is, this, etc.), in this work we remove such words. In addition, Chinese expression is abundant, and synonyms are often used to describe the same thing. We use a Chinese synonym dictionary, and transform semantically similar words into the same form. Finally, we identify similar documents based on a set of common keywords. We employ cosine similarity [12, 13] commonly used in text analysis, to characterize the correlation between two segments of text. The formula for calculating post value based on cosine similarity is as follows.

$$Position\_Score = sim(v_1, v_2) = \frac{v_1 \cdot v_2}{|v_1||v_2|} \tag{1}$$

Where $v_1 \cdot v_2 = \sum_{i=1}^{t} v_{1i}v_{2i}$, $|v_1| = \sqrt{v_1 \cdot v_1}$, v is a word vector used to describe the content of a passage by word segmentation and removal of stop words. The higher the value of Position_Score, the higher the correlation between the two paragraphs.

3.1.2 Execution Score

From the managers' perspective, their most important concern is the ability of their employees to perform their work. The stronger the execution, the better the employees are considered to be. Therefore, the execution ability is also an important evaluation index in performance appraisal. In our work, the performance of each employee is automatically measured by analyzing the matching degree of the work plan in the employee's work report and his actual work summary. First of all, similar to the above method, we divide the employees' plans and summaries into participles, remove the stop words, and then get the key vectors of the original sentences.

$$Execution\_Score = \frac{\sum_{i=1}^{t} F(i)}{m} \tag{2}$$

Here $F(i)$ is the completion of each plan. Based on the different degree adverbs identified in the summary, each program is assigned a discount ratio for varying degrees, which is provided by the domain experts. The detailed scores are shown in Table 1, where m is the total number of plans listed by the employees.

Table 1. Discount ratio of different adverbs of degree comparison table

Adverbs of degree	Discount ratio
{基本完成, 初步完成, 大体上, 几乎完成} (almost done)	0.8
{未完成, 尚未, 没有完成, 有待完成} (not yet)	0.6

3.1.3 Basis Score

In addition to the two aspects of the above assessment, the quality of the employee's report should also be evaluated. Through analysis of the employees' plan and summary after the participle, the sentence that lacks predicate is regarded as the residual sentence, and we use the total number of the residual sentences in the report to evaluate the employee. Employees who have few words or who copy the same content from the plan are assigned lower scores.

3.1.4 Total Score of Work Performance

The score of the above parts are summed up the following formula (3):

$$Work\_Score = \alpha \cdot Position\_Score + \beta \cdot Execution\_Score + (1 - \alpha - \beta) \cdot Basis\_Score \quad (3)$$

The values of α and β denote the weights of the position value and the execution scores respectively. The values of α and β are set according to the actual situation of different companies, which are company-specific. For example, Company J wants to assess the ability of employees, but also encourages employees to better complete tasks in line with the strategic objectives of the enterprise, so the value of α and β will both be set to high values of 0.4.

3.2 Assessment of Employee Job Competency

As globalization and technology advance, the working procedures in companies are becoming diversified and complicated, and cross-functional tasks are also increased while new jobs are still constantly created. For employees, the ability of self-improvement is especially important. Therefore, based on position characteristics and requirements of employees, our work selects the most suitable data from the internal databases and external data sources for employees to meet their job requirements. Through analysis of the learning behavior of employees, we evaluate the employees' job competency.

3.2.1 Automatic Multi-source-data Core Concept Extraction

In order to improve the ability to work, and face the complex tasks, employees have to continuously learn knowledge from internal databases and external data sources. It is very important to obtain the core content of each material and generate a reasonable summary for each source quickly and efficiently, for the growth and progress of employees. Here, we employ a combination of TF-IDF algorithm and TextRank algorithm (based on graph model) to automatically extract data [14]. The algorithm can be described as a three-step process including sentence representation, ranking, and selection. The following paragraphs will describe each of the steps [15, 16].

Sentence representation

In the TextRank algorithm, it is impossible to process plain text information directly. Therefore, each sentence must be transformed into the weight vector of the word, and then TextRank could be carried out by the similarity between each sentence vector. When converting to sentence weight vector, one possible approach would be to only count the number of occurrences of the term in the sentence, but that will give usual term preference over unusual terms, even if unusual terms often defines a text better than the usual terms that most text contains. To account for this, the frequency of a term is weighted with the inverse document frequency (IDF). The purpose of IDF is to boost the value of rare terms [17]. This is done by taking the logarithm of the number of documents N in the given corpus divided by the number of documents that contains a given term nt.

$$\log \frac{N}{n_t} \tag{4}$$

The IDF-score will be high for a term if it is only present in a small number of documents in the corpus. The IDF-score is combined with the term frequency (TF) to give the so-called TF-IDF score. The TF-IDF for a given term t, document d and corpus D, is defined as:

$$tf - idf(t, d, D) = tf(t, d) \cdot idf(t, D) \tag{5}$$

Through the calculation of TF-IDF, we attach an initial weight to each term in the sentence. So the input text is represented as a graph, where each sentence is converted to a node where an edge between two nodes denotes the similarity between the two sentences.

Sentence ranking

After the sentence weight initialization, we proceed to calculate the importance of each sentence in the whole text through an iterative way [18, 19]. The specific iterative process is shown as follows in (6):

$$WS(V_i) = \frac{1-d}{n} + d * \sum_{V_j \in In(V_i)} \frac{w_{ij}}{\sum_{V_k \in Out(V_j)} w_{jk}} WS(V_j) \tag{6}$$

Here, $WS(V_i)$ denotes the weight of sentence i, $\sum_{V_k \in Out(V_j)} w_{jk}$ denotes the contribution of each adjacent sentence. w_{ij} denotes the similarity between sentence i and sentence j, while $WS(V_j)$ denotes the weight of sentence j in the last iteration. The initial weight of array WS is 1/n, where n is the total number of sentences in the passage. d is a damping coefficient in a range of 0 to 1, denoting a probability of pointing to other arbitrary points from a particular point in the graph, and the general value is set at 0.85.

Sentence selection

The last step is to select which sentences to be extracted as the summary. In this case, we select N sentences with the highest scores. The specific value of N is selected in Sect. 4 through specific experimental results.

Also, as books are more structured than plain text, the title of each chapter is often closer to the subject of the paragraph than other sentence. Therefore, we enhance the weight of different sentences based on the title of the book when initializing the weight of each sentence, so as to achieve the purpose of highlighting the topic. The specific lifting effect will be shown in the Sect. 4.

In addition, external data sources and internal databases contain a large number of images, video and other information. We extract metadata to obtain the text description, and then use the same way to process the multi-source-data core concept extraction.

3.2.2 Intelligent Matching of Job Requirements and Learning Materials

After extracting core concepts of multi-source-data, we next consider how to recommend the most suitable learning materials for employees in different positions. First of all, through the analysis of position requirements of our competency model, a set of widely recognized job function requirements in the field of human resources is described, and the key words of quality requirements of different positions are obtained. Here we use the BM25 information retrieval model [20], with the formula (7).

$$RSV_d = \sum_{t \in q} \log \left[\frac{N}{df_t} \right] \cdot \frac{(k_1 + 1)\text{tf}_{td}}{k_1[(1 - b) + b \times (L_d/L_{ave})] + \text{tf}_{td}} \tag{7}$$

RSV_d denotes the weight of term t in the document d, L_d and L_{ave} denotes the length of document d and the average length of the entire document. k_1 and b are two free variables, usually $k_1 \in [1.2, 2.0]$, $b = 0.75$.

The keywords of quality requirements are used as query morphemes, and the core concept set of extracted data is used as a set of retrieved documents. The retrieval results of core qualities are arranged according to the order of matching score varying from large to small. This is the order in which learning materials are recommended for the employee.

3.2.3 Employee Competency Evaluation

Using the above methods, we choose the most suitable learning materials for different positions of employees, and then evaluate the learning effect of each employee to get the job competency of employees for that position. Based on the above process, we have developed a program to record the behavior information of employees in the process of material learning. By calculating Pearson correlation coefficient, sensitive data including employee name, personnel code and irrelevant attributes are deleted.

Since it is a classification problem, we use the decision tree model. The final test result is used as the prediction target, and other attributes are used as input. We construct a learning effect evaluation model based on employee learning behavior, and the results of the model are used to evaluate the job competency of employees in this position. The results of the model and the analysis are described in detail in Sect. 4.

3.3 Employee Comprehensive Performance Appraisal

Through the above two modules, we automatically evaluate employees' work performance and job competency respectively, and the final assessment scores are as shown in (8):

$$PAScore = \alpha_1 \cdot Work\_Score + \alpha_2 \cdot Competency\_Score \qquad (8)$$

Work_Score denotes the work performance of employees, and *Competency_Score* denotes the job competency. These two parts reflect the employees' current competence and the future growth potential. These two parts are very important indicators for the development of an enterprise. Different companies have different levels of concern for these two indicators. Therefore, enterprises can adjust the weights of the two parts according to their actual situations, and get the comprehensive performance appraisal results that meet their own business needs. For example, Company H, which is one of the largest high-tech companies in China, has intensively employed our model to evaluate their employees. Positive feedbacks are obtained from Company H.

4 Experiment

4.1 Textual Core Concept Extraction Based on Graph Model

In our textual core concept extraction experiment, we employ the famous "principle of salary management" in the field of human compensation. The book contains about 4.65 million Chinese characters. It is the latest textbook of original salary management in China. It is very suitable for the employees' self-learning scene in the assessment of competency. We compare the key sentence proposed by the author with the core concepts extracted by the TextRank graph model algorithm, to verify whether the core concept extraction method based on TF-IDF and TextRank is suitable for this scenario. Then, according to the results, we choose the most appropriate number of core concept sentences. Here, we introduce the precision and NDCG [21] as the evaluation indexes. These two evaluation criteria are shown in (9) and (10):

$$P = \frac{x_i \cap y_i}{n} \qquad (9)$$

$$NDCG = Z \sum_{p=1}^{n} \frac{2^{r_p} - 1}{\log(1 + p)} \qquad (10)$$

In the formula of precision, x_i denotes the set of extracted sentences, y_i denotes the set of author's intention, n denotes the number of extracted sentences. In the formula of NDCG, Z is a regularization term, r_p denotes the score of the sentence p. Accuracy is used to evaluate the degree of matching between the extraction result and the author's intention. The higher the accuracy is, the more representative the author's intention is.

The NDCG value is used to evaluate the difference between the weight ranking of the core concepts and the key sentence ranking of the author's intention. The higher the value is, the more accurate the sentence ranking is. Because of the structure of the article, we can enhance the weight of the key information based on its title information. The results of the experiment in the "*concept of compensation*" is presented in Table 2:

Table 2. Result of core concept extraction experiment

Number of test groups	Number of sentences extracted	Whether or not to optimize based on title	Precision	NDCG
1	10	No	1.0	0.6776
	10	Yes	1.0	0.739
2	20	No	0.9	0.6426
	20	Yes	1.0	0.7445
3	30	No	0.8333	0.6702
	30	Yes	1.0	0.7408

Through our experiments, it is evident that the improvement based on the title has a significant effect on the extraction of the core concept, and the effect is best when the number of sentences is 20.

Therefore, in actual use, we select 20 sentences with the title enhancement, we can automatically get very accurate core concepts. It provides a reliable basis for personalized recommendation based on the characteristics of employee quality.

4.2   Employee Competency Evaluation Based on Decision Tree

In this part of the experiment, we use the learning behavior data from 1735 employees of Company H to build a decision tree model. These data are valid data obtained through the background when employees use the learning program. 1132 pieces of data are used as training sets and 603 are used is test sets. Three decision tree models, C & RT, CHAID and C5.0, are used to construct the model. Here, we define the precision in (11):

$$P = \frac{n_t}{n} \tag{11}$$

n_t denotes the number of correctly classified samples, and n denotes the number of total samples.

The outcome shown in Table 3:

Table 3. Outcome of different decision tree models

Decision tree model types	Number of correctly classified samples	Number of wrongly classified samples	Precision
C&RT	599	4	99.34%
CHAID	599	4	99.34%
C5.0	601	2	99.67%

The classification accuracy obtained by C5.0 model is the highest. The decision tree model using C5.0 is shown in Fig. 2:

With the above decision tree model, we get job competency evaluation model based on employee learning behavior. The indexes that can best reflect the learning

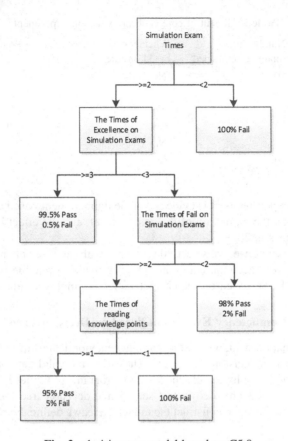

Fig. 2. decision tree model based on C5.0

ability of the employee include: the number of times to participate in the simulated examinations, the excellent times of the test results, the number of times of unqualified examination results and the number of times of reading the key knowledge points. Our model results can also be used to guide the employee learning and skill-set building. For example, one implication is that learning should be accompanied by taking simulation tests and reading core knowledge points.

5   Conclusion

Human resource performance appraisal index system has great application values in enterprise management. It is of great significance to tap the potential of employees, motivate the enthusiasm of employees, and to ensure the overall performance of enterprises. In this paper, we developed a comprehensive employee performance appraisal framework based on data mining and text analysis. Our framework has been successfully applied in Company H and Company J. It effectively improves the fairness in the performance appraisal procedures and fits the latest strategies of the enterprises.

It also evaluates the adaptability of employees and obtains a more complete performance appraisal method. Our work can help enterprises to rationally allocate and adjust their positions. Based on the requirements, they can formulate corresponding growth plans for their employees, motivate their work enthusiasm, and enhance their working ability and efficiency.

Acknowledgement. This project was partially supported by Grants from Natural Science Foundation of China #71671178/#91546201/#61202321, and the open project of the Key Lab of Big Data Mining and Knowledge Management. It was also supported by Hainan Provincial Department of Science and Technology under Grant No. ZDKJ2016021, and by Guangdong Provincial Science and Technology Project 2016B010127004.

References

1. Ding, X.R., Deng, X.M., Luo, J.: The development of key performance evaluation system of nurse staff. Chin. Nurs. Manag. (2009)
2. AlRababah, A.A.: A new model of information systems efficiency based on key performance indicator (KPI). Int. J. Adv. Comput. Sci. Appl. **8**(3), 80–83 (2017)
3. Hardison, C.M., et al.: 360-degree assessments (2015)
4. Han, J., Kamber, M.: Data Mining: Concepts and Techniques. Data Mining Concepts Models Methods & Algorithms, 2 edn., vol. 5, no. 4, pp. 1–18 (2011)
5. Shmueli, G., Bruce, P.C., Patel, N.R.: Data Mining for Business Analytics: Concepts, Techniques, and Applications in XLMiner, 3rd edn. Wiley, Hoboken (2016)
6. Olson, D.L., Wu, D.D.: Data mining models and enterprise risk management. Enterprise Risk Management Models. STBE, pp. 119–132. Springer, Heidelberg (2017). https://doi.org/10.1007/978-3-662-53785-5_9
7. Li, L., Shrestha, S., Hu, G.: Analysis of road traffic fatal accidents using data mining techniques. In: IEEE International Conference on Software Engineering Research, Management and Applications, pp. 363–370. IEEE (2017)
8. Chaurasia, V.: Early prediction of heart diseases using data mining techniques. Carib. J. Sci. Technol. **1**, 208–217 (2013)
9. Rygielski, C., Wang, J.C., Yen, D.C.: Data mining techniques for customer relationship management. Technol. Soc. **24**(4), 483–502 (2002)
10. Stefan, S., Joksimovic, S., Kovanovic, V., Baker, R.S., Gasevic, D.: Tools for educational data mining: a review. J. Educ. Behav. Stat. **42**(1), 85–106 (2017)
11. Chien, C.F., Chen, L.F.: Data mining to improve personnel selection and enhance human capital: a case study in high-technology industry. Expert Syst. Appl. **34**(1), 280–290 (2008)
12. Li, B., Han, L.: Distance weighted cosine similarity measure for text classification. In: Yin, H., Tang, K., Gao, Y., Klawonn, F., Lee, M., Weise, T., Li, B., Yao, X. (eds.) IDEAL 2013. LNCS, vol. 8206, pp. 611–618. Springer, Heidelberg (2013). https://doi.org/10.1007/978-3-642-41278-3_74
13. Shen, Y.-C., et al.: A cross-database comparison to discover potential product opportunities using text mining and cosine similarity (2017)
14. Shouzhong, T., Minlie, H.: Mining microblog user interests based on TextRank with TF-IDF factor. J. China Univ. Posts Telecommun. **23**(5), 40–46 (2016)
15. Audich, D.A., Dara, R., Nonnecke, B.: Extracting keyword and keyphrase from online privacy policies. In: Eleventh International Conference on Digital Information Management, pp. 127–132. IEEE (2017)

16. Karlsson, S.: Using semantic folding with TextRank for automatic summarization (2017)
17. Ibrahim, M., Murshed, M.: From TF-IDF to learning-to-rank: an overview (2016)
18. Barrios, F., et al.: Variations of the similarity function of textrank for automated summarization (2016)
19. Page, L.: The PageRank citation ranking: bringing order to the web. Stanford Digital Libraries Working Paper, vol. 9, no. 1, pp. 1–14 (1998)
20. Niu, J., et al.: OnSeS: a novel online short text summarization based on BM25 and neural network. In: IEEE Global Communications Conference, pp. 1–6 (2017)
21. Wang, Y., et al.: A theoretical analysis of NDCG ranking measures. In: Proceedings of the 26th Annual Conference on Learning Theory (COLT 2013) (2013)

Word Similarity Fails in Multiple Sense Word Embedding

Yong Shi[1,3,4,5], Yuanchun Zheng[2,3,4], Kun Guo[3,4,5(✉)], Wei Li[3,4,5], and Luyao Zhu[3,4,5]

[1] College of Information Science and Technology, University of Nebraska at Omaha, Omaha, NE 68182, USA
[2] School of Computer and Control Engineering, University of Chinese Academy of Sciences, Beijing 101408, China
[3] Key Laboratory of Big Data Mining and Knowledge Management, Chinese Academy of Sciences, Beijing 100190, China
[4] Research Center on Fictitious Economy & Data Science, Chinese Academy of Sciences, Beijing 100190, China
[5] School of Economics and Management, University of Chinese Academy of Sciences, Beijing 100190, China
guokun@ucas.ac.cn

Abstract. Word representation is one foundational research in natural language processing which full of challenges compared to other fields such as image and speech processing. It embeds words to a dense low-dimensional vector space and is able to learn syntax and semantics at the same time. But this representation only get one single vector for a word no matter it is polysemy or not. In order to solve this problem, sense information are added in the multiple sense language models to learn alternative vectors for each single word. However, as the most popular measuring method in single sense language models, word similarity did not get the same performance in multiple situation, because word similarity based on cosine distance doesn't match annotated similarity scores. In this paper, we analyzed similarity algorithms and found there is obvious gap between cosine distance and benchmark datasets, because the negative internal in cosine space does not correspond to manual scores space and cosine similarity did not cover semantic relatedness contained in datasets. Based on this, we proposed a new similarity methods based on mean square error and the experiments showed that our new evaluation algorithm provided a better method for word vector similarity evaluation.

1 Introduction

Word embedding is an effective distributed method for word representation in natural language precessing (NLP) which can obtain syntax and semantic information from amount of unlabeled corpus. Comparing with local representation like one-hot encoding, distributed representation maps word or sentence to a

© Springer International Publishing AG, part of Springer Nature 2018
Y. Shi et al. (Eds.): ICCS 2018, LNCS 10861, pp. 489–498, 2018.
https://doi.org/10.1007/978-3-319-93701-4_38

dense low dimensional vector space. And properties like word syntax and semantic information distributed on all dimensions. However, these models assumed that each word only have one single vector and ignored polysemy situation in languages which called word disambiguation. For instance, '*apple*' is not only a technology company but also a kind of fruits. In a sentence, once the context environment determined, the meaning of the word is also determined. According to this, multiple sense word embedding is proposed, each word has various number of word vectors and corresponding sense vectors. And the biggest difference between single sense and multiple sense language model is the sense information. Therefore, we can choose proper word vector based on sense information and get more accurate representation in sentences.

Another problem after get embedding is the evaluation process. Different language models has different patterns and structures, some of them focus on word similarity and others focus on word syntax and semantic. To summarize, researchers proposed two different evaluations called intrinsic and extrinsic evaluation, which evaluated word vectors with different priorities. Intrinsic evaluation includes word similarity, word analogy and synonym question, extrinsic evaluation includes experiments which using embedding as the initialization of neural networks like text classification, semantic analysis and named entity recognition. But there are none one evaluation algorithm covered all these evaluations, intrinsic evaluation methods may fail in extrinsic measuring, so evaluation methods become more and more important in language models and NLP tasks.

In intrinsic evaluation, word similarity algorithm is the most-used method to measure semantic similarity. But the vector scores computed by cosine are different with manual annotated similarity scores, because cosine value only measure similarity while annotated value contained similarity and relatedness at the same time, which caused mismatch in similarity evaluation. In this paper, we analyzed multiple sense language models and word similarity evaluations, and studied the reason which caused mismatch between cosine scores and manual scores. Based on this, we proposed a new method based on mean square error to evaluate the performance of different language models. We also proposed a new word similarity benchmark datasets with our new annotation method.

This paper is organized as follows: Sect. 2 reviewed multiple sense word embedding models, and word similarity evaluation methods are analyzed and our new evaluation method is proposed in Sect. 3, Sect. 4 listed some experiments results between different word similarity evaluations, and we gave our conclusion in the final section.

2   Related Work

Raw words or sentences need to be represented by vectors before input into algorithms, therefore representation learning had became foundational field in NLP. In 1954, Harris [1] proposed distributed hypothesis which point that syntax would be similar if words had the same contexts, and this hypothesis was a footstone in language modeling. Researcher designed lots of models according to the distributed hypothesis. Assume $S = (w_1, w_2, \ldots, w_n)$ is a sentence with n words. We use $P(S)$ in 1 to represent the joint probability of this sentence, and probability would be decrease if replacing any word in S. The gold of language model is to maximum joint probability of a sentence, but the difficult of conditional probability would be growth exponential in the tail of S because we need to consider more history words. Therefore, a context window cover $2k$ words would be chosen to replace the whole sentence, $C(w_i) = w_{i-k}, \ldots, w_{i-1}, w_{i+1}, \ldots, w_{i+k}$ means all context words in this window.

$$P(S) = \prod_{i=1}^{n} p(w_i|w_1, w_2, \ldots, w_{i-1}) \approx \prod_{i=1}^{n} p(w_i|C(w_i)) \tag{1}$$

$$P(S) = \prod_{i=1}^{n} \prod_{j=1}^{a_i} p(w_i^j|C(w_i^j)) \approx \prod_{i=1}^{n} \prod_{j=1}^{a_i} p(w_i^j|C(w_i)) \tag{2}$$

In single sense models, each word has only one vector w_i, the goal of language model is to maximum the probability of S. When extend to multiple sense language model, each word has a_i word vectors $(w_i^1, w_i^2, \ldots, w_i^{a_i})$ and corresponding sense vectors $(c_i^1, c_i^2, \ldots, c_i^{a_i})$, models must decide which sense is the best one in current context from candidate senses. Once determine sense index, word vector would be updated by the same algorithm with single sense models. Therefore, we can modified sentence probability with 2. In this equation, sense information and corresponding vectors are added as extra data in the inner multiplication.

Bengio [2] first exploited a feed-forward neural network for modeling language, they used a three layer neural network to modeling sentence and got a word embedding at the same time. But it is very time consuming because the output layer is a softmax layer and the number of neural units are the same with dimension of dictionary. Mnih [3] proposed a Log-Bilinear language model (LBL), in their model, a bilinear structure replace the three layers and accelerate the algorithms effectively. After that, Mikolov [4] tried to used recurrent neural network to model language because sentences are sequence data essentially. They [5] also proposed two popular language models named continuous bag-of-words (CBOW) model and skip-gram model, and two efficient accelerate algorithms named hierarchical softmax and negative sampling. Figure 1(a) indicated two model structures in word2vec, the CBOW model predict target word w_i by its neighbor context words $C(w_i) = \{w_{i-k}, \ldots, w_{i-1}, w_{i+1}, w_{i+k}\}$, and Skip-gram had a symmetrically structure that predict context word by target word.

Collobert [6] designed a more complex network with a score function to replace the softmax layer. They used a union probability $p(w_1, w_2, \ldots, w_n)$ in 3 rather than a approximate conditional probability, and $f_\theta(x)$ is a neural network based score function. Original sentence S is a positive sample, and $S^{(w)}$ which central word was replaced by a random chosen word is a negative sample. Then made the score of positive sample at least one point more than negative samples.

$$P(S) = \sum_{w \in \mathcal{D}} \max\{0, 1 - f_\theta(S) + f_\theta(S^{(w)})\} \tag{3}$$

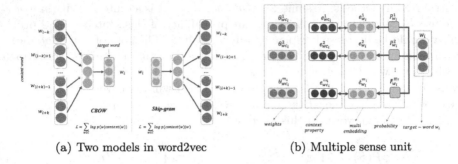

(a) Two models in word2vec   (b) Multiple sense unit

Fig. 1. Single sense and multiple sense language models

All the previous models only considered local context and ignore the global information, and Pennington [7] proposed Glove model which has the same thought as previous models but considered more situation of the concurrence of words. This mode adapted advantages both from latent semantic analysis [8] and CBOW model. The results showed that Glove perform well in small corpus and more flexible in big corpus than word2vec. Except unsupervised learning models, Joulin [9] proposed a supervised method based on text classification to train word vectors and reduce the learning time from days to several hours, Bojanowski [10] put sub-words into models as extra information and enriched samples for training, they also released fastText[1] toolkits to train embeddings or to finish text classification task. No matter predicate-based or score function-based models, they all take advantage of the great power of the neural network. More and more complex and useful networks began adapted in language models. As a special design of recurrent neural network, long-short memory network (LSTM) is a better way to model sequence data with different gates.

Models mentioned in previous part are all single sense language models which assumed that one word have only one vector no matter how many different context environment may occur in corpus. Several efforts have been made in multiple sense language modeling. Huang [11] proposed a two-stage learning methods based on cluster algorithms, they first clustered words to many groups and labeled word using theirs cluster center, then trained word vector by these replaced centers. But clustering process would be the biggest block in this algorithm because it spend lots of time. Effort have been made to solve this problem. Neelakantan [12] proposed a non-parametric estimation methods based on skip-gram model to learn multiple prototype vectors, they used a latent variable to represent the sense vector and get better performance in word similarity benchmark. Zheng [13] designed a universal multiple sense unit and embed into CBOW model to learning multiple word embedding and got different representations for each word. Tian [14] proposed a new method based on EM algorithm, Li [15] proposed a new model to learn sense information and used Chinese Restaurant

---

[1] https://github.com/facebookresearch/fastText.

Process to recognize the number of senses for different word. Figure 1(b) is a basic cell structure in multiple sense language model, it is more complex than an ordinary neural unit.

Some researchers began to explore the internal explanation of similarity evaluation. Gladkova [16] discussed methods of intrinsic evaluation of word embeddings and hoped to draw attention of both computational and theoretical linguists to get a better evaluation method. Chiu [17] found word embeddings can't get the same performance in intrinsic or extrinsic evaluations. Li [15] explored if multiple sense word embedding can improve natural language understanding and found that single sense word embedding can beat multiple sense word embedding with a bigger dimension size. All of this lead to the suspicion of multiple sense models.

3 Methodology

Another important part in natural language processing is the evaluation because we don't know if vectors contains similarity or analogy properties or not. Language models based on distributed hypothesis consider words have same meaning if they have same context, therefore, similarity evaluation is the most intuitive test for the quality of language models and word vectors. As one of the most used intrinsic evaluation, cosine distance indicated in 4 measured semantic distance between word pairs, and this test has been the most popular evaluations.

$$cos(w_1, w_2) = \frac{w_1 w_2}{\|w_1\|\|w_2\|} \tag{4}$$

In multiples sense models, each word may contains many vectors, Huang proposed another four different similarity distances with multiple vectors. In 5, $AvgSim$ means average of all the possible match of word vectors, and $AvgSimC$ adds the probability of every sense occur in corpus. And the $LocalSim$ only use the best match one to represent all the situations, this may be the most close to multiple sense vectors at all. And another special distance is global similarity which is the cosine distance between two global vectors.

$$AvgSim(w_1, w_2) = \frac{1}{K^2} \sum_{i=1}^{K} \sum_{j=1}^{K} d(v_i(w_1), v_j(w_2)) \tag{5}$$

$$AvgSimC(w_1, w_2) = \frac{1}{K^2} \sum_{i=1}^{K} \sum_{j=1}^{K} p(c_1, w_1, i) p(c_2, w_2, j) d(v_i(w_1), v_j(w_2)) \tag{6}$$

$$LocalSim(w_1, w_2) = d(v_s(w_1, k_1), v_s(w_2, k_2)) \tag{7}$$

$$GlobalSim(w_1, w_2) = d(v_g(w_1), v_g(w_2)) \tag{8}$$

Embedding trained by neural networks whose object function is 1 or 2 would catch semantic information like word similarity and word relatedness. But these vectors represent words' context situations other than word property itself. For example, 'good' and 'bad' would be have a high cosine score because they always appear in the same context environment. Similarity score computed by word vector pairs is in the range $[-1, 1]$ while manual annotated scores in the range $[0, 10]$. The negative part would be difficult to map in the same scope.

WS353 is a common used dataset with 353 word pairs and their manual annotated similarity scores. For example, '*tiger cat 7.35*' is one record in WS353, two words '*tiger*' and '*cat*' are word pairs used in similarity algorithms, value in the third column means annotated similarity score of word pairs which range from 0 to 10, higher score represent two word are more similar. After get similarity score of each word vector pairs, correlation coefficient in 9 is one index that can measure the degree of correlation between estimated scores and human language. And X is a cosine similarity vector based on cosine distance, Y is a same size vector of annotated similarity scores. A higher value means that word embedding catch more semantic information and grammar structures.

$$\rho(X, Y) = \frac{\sum_{i=1}^{n}(x_i - \bar{X})(y_i - \bar{Y})}{\sqrt{\sum_{i=1}^{n}(x_i - \bar{X})\sum_{i=1}^{n}(y_i - \bar{Y})}} \tag{9}$$

In order to analysis the effectiveness of word embeddings, two new evaluation algorithms were proposed in this paper. The first one is fake similarity, we used manual annotated scores to find the best match word vectors and recomputed cosine distance and pearson correlation coefficient. The fake similarity was designed as 10, $v_f(x)$ means vector x are the most similar to manual scores from word's multiple embeddings. This fake similarity measures the best conditions that embedding can achieve compared to human language. 'Fake' means that annotated scores were already used in advance.

$$FakeSim(w_1, w_2) = \frac{1}{K^2}d(v_f(w_1), v_f(w_2)) \tag{10}$$

The second evaluation method is mean square error (MSE) in 11, it is the difference between manual scores and what is estimated.

$$MSE(X, Y) = \frac{1}{n}\sum_{i=1}^{n}(X^i - Y^i)^2 \tag{11}$$

There are many similarity benchmark datasets in intrinsic evaluation, Table 1 listed some similarity benchmark datasets that always used in intrinsic evaluation. WS353 is the most used dataset included 353 word pairs and their annotated similarity scores. Another two datasets created from WS353 are WS353Sim and WS353Rel, and WS353Sim include 203 records that each word pair have similarity while WS353Rel contains 252 records that each word pair are more related to each other. As for multiple sense word embedding, SCWS dataset provide 2003 word pairs with their context environment and annotated scores. Each record has two words and two whole sentences including two words. Datasets like this can be used both in single sense word embedding and multiple sense embedding.

Table 1. Datasets used in word similarity evaluation

Dataset	Word Paris	Evaluation	Source
WS353	353	Single sense	Finkelstein [18]
WS353Sim	203	Single sense	Agirre [19]
WS353Rel	252	Single sense	Agirre [19]
SCWS	2003	Multiple sense	Huang [11]
MEN	3000	Single sense	Bruni [20]

Cosine distance is range from -1 to 1 while manual annotated scores did not cover the negative scope. Therefore, there must be a mismatch between two scores. To solve this problem, we can shift all the values to positive part, but zero is a special point in this situation. And there's another method, we can mirror all negative scores to positive range.

4   Experiments

Multiple sense word embedding is the best method for word disambiguation in unsupervised learning filed. Many researchers proposed their own well-designed models for learning word vectors and share their own datasets for word similarity evaluation. Multiple sense skip gram is one of the best multiple sense language model, we download their trained word vectors and got computed four correlation coefficient using similarity algorithms mentioned in 5 and 10. In the experiment, we choose pre-trained multiple sense word vectors with 50 dimension size choose sense window is 5 (with 5 words in both left and right of current word). In MSSG word vectors, each word has a global vector and corresponding sense vectors, global vector updated every time while sense vector updated when match its context vector in the training process. In fact, global vector is the same as single sense word embedding.

As for benchmark dataset, we removed all the records that didn't not appear in MSSG dictionary. After getting the cosine scores and annotated scores, we reorder the annotated scores from small to large and just showed by the green point line in Fig. 2, and the red point means the paired cosine scores.

In Fig. 2, the distance between red point and green point reflect the offset between manual scores and cosine scores. We can find in Fig. 2(a), (b), (c) and (d) that computed cosine scores are a little bit close to the positive range. We can get more accurate numerical comparison in Table 2. In this table, subscript number 1 means we used 1947 pairs of valid words from SCWS datasets, and subscript number 2 means the left 1723 word pairs after removing 241 word pairs with duplicate word. $]rho$ is the correlation coefficient and e means MSE while e' is the result after normalization. From the result we can find that local similarity did not get best performance while global vector get the highest value

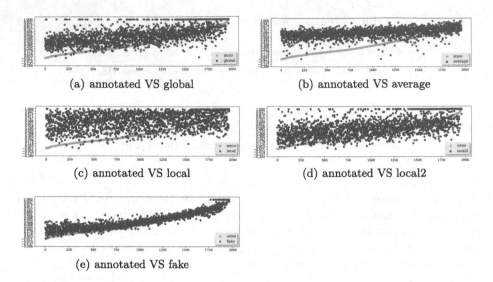

(a) annotated VS global   (b) annotated VS average

(c) annotated VS local   (d) annotated VS local2

(e) annotated VS fake

Fig. 2. Similarity of scores scatter with different cosine algorithms (Color figure online)

Table 2. Correlation coefficient and MSE on MSSG word vectors

-	GlobalSim	AvgSim	LocalSim	LocalSim2	FakeSim
ρ_1	0.634	0.481	0.256	0.543	0.946
ρ_2	0.543	0.388	0.248	0.456	0.943
e_1	16.767	16.493	15.981	16.935	-
e_2	12.077	11.333	10.882	11.998	-
e_1'	15.807	15.585	15.633	16.294	-
e_2'	10.968	10.540	10.585	11.303	-

in correlation measuring. And we add global vector into sense vectors to enrich the source of *LocalSim2*, but it also fails to overtaken the *GlocalSim*. There are many reasons that can influence the results include context windows and similarity algorithms.

We also analyzed the influence of different context window size indicated in Fig. 3. Because MSSG word vectors are trained with context window 5, so we choose the context window size in range [1, 10]. The results showed that sense vector didn't play ideal role, but the global vector perform better. We guess that global vector catch more semantic information and sense vectors didn't get fully trained and even get incorrect updated. Therefore, single sense word embedding or global vector would be enough in most NLP tasks.

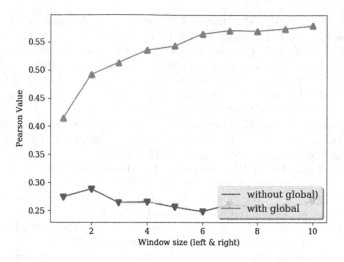

Fig. 3. Window size analysis

5 Conclusion

Multiple sense word embedding is a better way for word disambiguation, it considers specific meaning of a word in context environment. But models may not get better performance if it can not determine sense information. Sometimes, single sense or global word vector can achieve same results with multiple sense vectors and more flexible during serialization process. As most used intrinsic evaluation, word similarity is an efficient measuring for word vectors. But the gap between estimated annotated scores and cosine similarity-based scores influence the performance of similarity evaluation. In this paper, we designed a new similarity distance $fakeSim$ and used mean square error to evaluate the performance of word similarity and found that word similarity fails in multiple sense word embedding evaluation, there are still a long way to reach the desired goal.

Acknowledgements. This work is supported by the National Natural Science Foundation of China No. 91546201, No. 71331005 and No. 71501175, Shandong Independent Innovation and Achievement Transformation Special Fund of China (2014ZZCX03302), and the Open Project of Key Laboratory of Big Data Mining and Knowledge Management, Chinese Academy of Sciences.

References

1. Harris, Z.S.: Distributional structure. Word **10**(2–3), 146–162 (1954)
2. Bengio, Y., Ducharme, R., Vincent, P., Jauvin, C.: A neural probabilistic language model. J. Mach. Learn. Res. **3**(Feb), 1137–1155 (2003)
3. Mnih, A., Hinton, G.: Three new graphical models for statistical language modelling. In: Proceedings of the 24th International Conference on Machine Learning, pp. 641–648. ACM (2007)

4. Mikolov, T., Karafiát, M., Burget, L., Cernockỳ, J., Khudanpur, S.: Recurrent neural network based language model. In: Interspeech, vol. 2, p. 3 (2010)
5. Mikolov, T., Chen, K., Corrado, G., Dean, J.: Efficient estimation of word representations in vector space. arXiv preprint arXiv:1301.3781 (2013)
6. Collobert, R., Weston, J.: A unified architecture for natural language processing: deep neural networks with multitask learning. In: Proceedings of the 25th International Conference on Machine Learning, pp. 160–167. ACM (2008)
7. Pennington, J., Socher, R., Manning, C.: GloVe: global vectors for word representation. In: Proceedings of the 2014 Conference on Empirical Methods in Natural Language Processing, EMNLP, pp. 1532–1543 (2014)
8. Landauer, T.K., Foltz, P.W., Laham, D.: An introduction to latent semantic analysis. Discourse Process. **25**(2–3), 259–284 (1998)
9. Joulin, A., Grave, E., Bojanowski, P., Mikolov, T.: Bag of tricks for efficient text classification. arXiv preprint arXiv:1607.01759 (2016)
10. Bojanowski, P., Grave, E., Joulin, A., Mikolov, T.: Enriching word vectors with subword information. arXiv preprint arXiv:1607.04606 (2016)
11. Huang, E.H., Socher, R., Manning, C.D., Ng, A.Y.: Improving word representations via global context and multiple word prototypes. In: Proceedings of the 50th Annual Meeting of the Association for Computational Linguistics: Long Papers, vol. 1, pp. 873–882. Association for Computational Linguistics (2012)
12. Neelakantan, A., Shankar, J., Passos, A., McCallum, A.: Efficient non-parametric estimation of multiple embeddings per word in vector space. arXiv preprint arXiv:1504.06654 (2015)
13. Zheng, Y., Shi, Y., Guo, K., Li, W., Zhu, L.: Enhanced word embedding with multiple prototypes. In: 2017 4th International Conference on Industrial Economics System and Industrial Security Engineering, IEIS 2017, pp. 1–5. IEEE (2017)
14. Tian, F., Dai, H., Bian, J., Gao, B., Zhang, R., Chen, E., Liu, T.Y.: A probabilistic model for learning multi-prototype word embeddings. In: COLING, pp. 151–160 (2014)
15. Li, J., Jurafsky, D.: Do multi-sense embeddings improve natural language understanding? CoRR (2015)
16. Gladkova, A., Drozd, A.: Intrinsic evaluations of word embeddings: what can we do better? In: Proceedings of the 1st Workshop on Evaluating Vector-Space Representations for NLP, Stroudsburg, PA, USA, pp. 36–42. Association for Computational Linguistics (2016)
17. Chiu, B., Korhonen, A., Pyysalo, S.: Intrinsic evaluation of word vectors fails to predict extrinsic performance. In: Proceedings of the 1st Workshop on Evaluating Vector Space Representations for NLP, pp. 1–6 (2016)
18. Finkelstein, L., Gabrilovich, E., Matias, Y., Rivlin, E., Solan, Z., Wolfman, G., Ruppin, E.: Placing search in context: the concept revisited. In: Proceedings of the 10th International Conference on World Wide Web, pp. 406–414. ACM (2001)
19. Agirre, E., Alfonseca, E., Hall, K., Kravalova, J., Paşca, M., Soroa, A.: A study on similarity and relatedness using distributional and WordNet-based approaches. In: Proceedings of Human Language Technologies: The 2009 Annual Conference of the North American Chapter of the Association for Computational Linguistics, pp. 19–27. Association for Computational Linguistics (2009)
20. Bruni, E., Boleda, G., Baroni, M., Tran, N.K.: Distributional semantics in technicolor. In: Proceedings of the 50th Annual Meeting of the Association for Computational Linguistics: Long Papers, vol. 1, pp. 136–145. Association for Computational Linguistics (2012)

Track of Computational Optimization, Modelling and Simulation

A Hybrid Optimization Algorithm for Electric Motor Design

Mokhtar Essaid[1]([⊠]), Lhassane Idoumghar[1], Julien Lepagnot[1],
Mathieu Brévilliers[1], and Daniel Fodorean[2]

[1] IRIMAS, University of Haute-Alsace, 68093 Mulhouse, France
{mokhtar.essaid, lhassane.idoumghar, Julien.lepagnot,
Mathieu.brevilliers}@uha.fr
[2] Department of Electrical Machines and Drives,
Technical University of Cluj-Napoca, 400114 Cluj-Napoca, Romania
daniel.fodorean@emd.utcluj.ro

Abstract. This paper presents a hybrid algorithm employed to reduce the weight of an electric motor, designed for electric vehicle (EV) propulsion. The approach uses a hybridization between Cuckoo Search and CMAES to generate an initial population. Then, the population is transferred to a new procedure which adaptively switches between two search strategies, i.e. one for exploration and one for exploitation. Besides the electric motor optimization, the proposed algorithm performance is also evaluated using the 15 functions of the CEC 2015 competition benchmark. The results reveal that the proposed approach can show a very competitive performance when compared with different state-of-the-art algorithms.

Keywords: Electric motors · Hybridization · Cuckoo search · CMAES

1 Introduction

Metaheuristics are widely used to solve complex optimization problems within a reasonable time. According to [3], most of metaheuristics have the common following characteristics: they are nature-inspired, and based on stochastic components (randomness). Besides, a balance should be preserved between the diversification and exploitation phases [5]. Otherwise, metaheuristics would suffer from falling in local optima (weak diversification) or from slow convergence (weak exploitation). To overcome these limitations, hybridization between different algorithmic components appears to be an appropriate choice. Hybrid metaheuristics have attracted a lot of attention from researchers to solve optimization problems. It has been proven that choosing an appropriate combination of algorithmic concepts can lead to a successful solving of many hard optimization problems [2].

In this paper, we propose a hybrid algorithm to optimize the weight of electric motors within electric vehicles. The hybridization is based on a CMAES-enhanced Cuckoo Search (CS) which provides a well distributed initial population. Then, the population is transferred to a surrogate model-based LSHADE to optimize the solutions obtained so far.

© Springer International Publishing AG, part of Springer Nature 2018
Y. Shi et al. (Eds.): ICCS 2018, LNCS 10861, pp. 501–517, 2018.
https://doi.org/10.1007/978-3-319-93701-4_39

LSHADE is a recent version of differential evolution algorithm (DE) that incorporates success-history based parameter adaptation [17] with Linear Population Size Reduction (LPSR) [18]. The main motivation for using LSHADE as the main optimizer is its high adaptability when solving many optimization problems [1]. In addition to that, LSHADE ranked first at the CEC 2014 competition. However, our approach relies on a modification of this algorithm, where we aim to improve its exploration capability by integrating the K-means clustering algorithm to generate the central individuals of a given population. Then, we apply a Lévy Flight movement on them to generate new individuals. The proposed approach is evaluated using the 15 test functions of the CEC 2015 benchmark and it is compared with LSHADE, DE and Cuckoo Search (CS). This experimentation shows that our proposition obtains very competitive results on the electric motor problem at hand and on the CEC 2015 benchmark.

The rest of this paper is organized as follows. In Sect. 2, the electric motor problem is discussed. In Sect. 3, the algorithmic components of our proposition are presented. In Sect. 4, our approach is explained in details. Then, the results are discussed in Sect. 5. Finally, Sect. 6 concludes the paper.

2 Electric Motor Design

Here the application under study is introduced. The hybrid optimization approach will be applied to optimize the design of an electric motor used to propel an electric vehicle (EV). Concerning the EV application one can observe that from the first hybrid vehicle in series production, the Toyota Prius Hybrid, have past about 20 years. At that time, the permanent magnet synchronous machine (PMSM) used to propel the hybrid vehicle was designed at 6 000 r/min. The PMSM structure from today's Prius Hybrid has a double speed, 12 000 r/min. Moreover, for all other manufacturers, the electric motors used for the traction present a speed level in the same range: BMW-i3 is running at a top speed of 11 400 r/min, Renault-Zoe at 11 300 r/min, etc. The idea of increasing the speed of the electric propulsion is due to the improved power density (i.e., power/weight ratio) of the high speed traction motor: the higher the speed of the motor, the better the power density. Since the power density is improved, meaning that for the desired out power, the weight of the machine is reduced, the operation range (the main drawback of electric vehicles today), meaning the autonomy of the electric car, can be increased [6, 7]. Also, by reducing the weight and consequently the volume of the electric motor, one could consider to increase the capacity of the supplying battery, again, with a clear advantage on terms of vehicle's autonomy.

For the above reasons our interest was to find the best suited motor topology, capable to run at higher speeds. We have established the desired output power, which is 20 kW, while the motor is supplied from a battery of 380 Vdc. In Fig. 1(a) is presented the 3D view of the high speed PMSM which was designed to run at 22 000 r/min and where one can identify the main components of the active parts of the machine, meaning: the stator and rotor parts, the inset permanent magnets (PMs) with the appropriate polarity. All the calculation of the obtained performances are made on the length of the machine (Lm in Fig. 1(a)). The analysis with respect to the obtained performances of the designed highs-speed PMSM is carried out with a numerical finite element method (FEM). Based on this one will get the electromagnetic and mechanical performances. This analysis stands for validation of the analytical design of the machine and will also be used to verify the optimized results proposed by our optimization approach. In Fig. 1(b) is presented, in several slices on the length of the machine, the flux density repartition while the machine is running at high speed. Based on this analysis we can see which machine's iron regions present a risk of saturation. Since we are using very good steel, we can conclude that the machine is not oversaturated.

The structure is designed to have only 2 magnetic poles. Since the frequency of the supply is proportional to the machine's magnetic poles and since the iron losses of the machine are proportional to the square of the frequency, it means that the machine efficiency is drastically affected by the frequency/poles values. Thus, having the lowest possible number of poles will offer the possibility to reduce at maximum the frequency of the machine, and finally to have the most appropriate magnetic configuration. And from this point on, we can consider to optimize the structure itself in order to obtain the best power density (power/weight ratio).

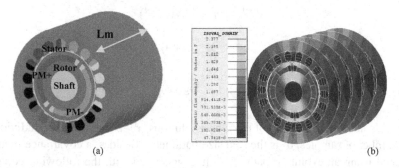

Fig. 1. (a) 3D view of the considered high-speed PMSM; (b) Numerical FEM analysis for flux density distribution on the high-speed PMSM

3 Approach Components

We provide in this section a brief presentation of the algorithmic components used in our proposition.

3.1 CMA-ES

The Covariance Matrix Adaptation Evolution Strategy (CMA-ES) is a class of evolutionary algorithms where the new population is generated by sampling from a probability distribution constructed during the optimization process. CMA-ES is briefly explained in Algorithm 1.

Algorithm 1: Pseudocode of CMA-ES algorithm
1. $\lambda \leftarrow$ number of samples per iteration
2. $\mu \leftarrow$ number of recombination points
3. Initialize state variables $m, \sigma, C = I, p_\sigma = 0, p_c = 0$
4. Repeat
5.   For $i = 1$ to λ do
6. $x_i^{(t+1)} \leftarrow$ sample i^{th} solution according to (1)
7. $f_i \leftarrow$ evaluate i^{th} solution
8.   End for
9.   Sort the new solutions and find the first μ solutions
10. $m^{(t+1)} \leftarrow$ update the mean value according to (2)
11. $p_c^{(t+1)} \leftarrow$ update anisotropic evolution path according to (4)
12. $C^{(t+1)} \leftarrow$ update the covariance matrix according to (5)
13. $p_\sigma^{(t+1)} \leftarrow$ update isotropic evolution path according to (6)
14. $\sigma^{(t+1)} \leftarrow$ update the step size using isotropic path length according to (7)
15. Until (stopping condition = true)

In this algorithm, solutions are generated using a multivariate normal distribution N with mean m and a covariance C. According to [11], a new solution x^{t+1} is generated as follows:

$$x^{t+1} = m^t + \sigma^t N(0, C^t) \tag{1}$$

$$m^t = \sum_{i=1}^{\mu} w_i x_{i:\lambda}^t \tag{2}$$

$$w_i = \log\left(\mu + \frac{1}{2}\right) - \log(i), \sum_{i=1}^{\mu} w_i = 1 \tag{3}$$

where m^t is the weighted mean of the μ best solutions, $x_{i:\lambda}^t$ is the tth ranked individual, λ is the number of samples, σ^t is the step size parameter. Besides, a covariance matrix C^t is adapted using an evolution path p_c^{t+1}. It is generated with the following equation:

$$p_c^{t+1} = (1 - c_c)p_c^t + \sqrt{c_c(2 - c_c)} \frac{\sqrt{\mu}}{\sigma^t} (m^{t+1} - m^t) \tag{4}$$

$$C^{t+1} = (1 - c_{cov})C^t + c_{cov}p_c^{t+1}(p_c^{t+1})^T \tag{5}$$

where c_c and $c_{cov} \in [0, 1]$ are learning rates for p_c^{t+1} and C^{t+1} respectively.

Moreover, the step size parameter is updated through the evolution path p_σ^{t+1} as below:

$$p_\sigma^{t+1} = (1 - c_\sigma)p_\sigma^t + \sqrt{c_\sigma(2 - c_\sigma)} \sqrt{\mu} B^t m^{t+1} \tag{6}$$

where c_σ is a learning rate controller, and B^t is the normalized eigenvectors of C^t. Then, σ^{t+1} is updated as follows:

$$\sigma^{t+1} = \sigma^t \exp\left(\frac{||p_\sigma^{t+1}|| - T_n}{d_\sigma T_n}\right) \tag{7}$$

$$T_n = \sqrt{n}\left(1 - \frac{1}{4n} + \frac{1}{21n^2}\right) \tag{8}$$

where n represents the problem dimension and $d_\sigma > 1$ is a damping parameter.

3.2 Cuckoo Search

Cuckoo search (CS) is an optimization algorithm that simulates brood parasitism of cuckoo birds [19]. These birds lay their eggs in other bird's nests. When host birds find the foreign eggs, they will either throw them, or abandon the nest. Following this model, each egg represents a solution, and each new solution is represented by a cuckoo egg. Cuckoo bird replaces bad eggs in the host nest with better feasible eggs. Moreover, CS algorithm simulates the food foraging process of many animals and insects [8]. Commonly, the foraging path of animals is a random walk where the next move depends on the actual location and the transition probability to the next location. However, Lévy flight random walk is proved to be more efficient for searching [8]. In CS, a balanced combination of local random walk and a global random walk is obtained through a switching parameter P_a. The local random walk is written as:

$$x_i^{t+1} = x_i^t + s \otimes H(P_a - \epsilon) \otimes \left(x_j^t - x_k^t\right) \tag{9}$$

where $\otimes$ represents entry-wise multiplications x_j^t, x_k^t are solutions randomly selected and H is heaviside function. ϵ and s are random numbers generated from a uniform distribution. The global random walk is handled using Lévy flights:

$$x_i^{t+1} = x_i^t + a \otimes \text{Lévy}(\beta) \tag{10}$$

where

$$a = a_0 \otimes \left(\left(x_j^t - x_i^t\right)\right) \tag{11}$$

$$\text{Lévy}(\beta) = \frac{u}{|v|^{1/\beta}} \tag{12}$$

a_0 is a step size scaling factor and β is Lévy Flights exponent. Finally, u and v are two numbers with zero means and associated variance. Indeed, using Lévy Flights and combining local and global search capabilities makes CS a very efficient algorithm. *CS* pseudo-code is presented in Algorithm 2.

Algorithm 2: Pseudocode of CS algorithm
1. Initialize a population of n host nests x_i (i=1,2.... n)
2. While stop criterion is not reached
3. Get a cuckoo (say i) randomly and generate a new solution according to (10)
4. Evaluate its fitness F_i
5. Choose randomly a nest among n (say j)
6. If ($F_i < F_j$)
7. Replace j by the new solution
8. End
9. Abandon a fraction (p_a) of worse nests
10. Build new nests according to (9)
11. Keep the best solutions among the current nests and the new generated ones
12. Rank the solutions and find the current best
13. End while

3.3   K-means

K-means is a widely used clustering algorithm. The parameter K is a given integer representing the number of centers. The algorithm assigns each point from a given set of points to the nearest center among the K centers [14]. Algorithm 3 presents the pseudo-code of K-means.

Algorithm 3: Pseudocode of K-means algorithm
1. Input: A data set D
2. Output: K clusters
3. Choose k centers $C_1, C_2, ... C_k$ randomly from n points $(X_1, X_2, .. X_n)$
4. Assign point X_i, i=1,2, ..., n to the nearest center C_j, $j\in\{1, 2, ...,k\}$
5. Compute new cluster centers as follows:
6. $C_i^* = \frac{1}{|C_i|}\Sigma_{X_j\in C_i} X_j$, $i = 1, 2, ..., k$
7. Stop if termination criterion is satisfied. Otherwise, continue from step 3

3.4   LSHADE

LSHADE is an adaptive version of differential evolution algorithm (*DE*). It incorporates success-history-based parameter adaptation [17] with Linear Population Size Reduction (LPSR) [18]. The convergence performance of LSHADE is improved by using the mutation strategy current to-pBest/1/bin [20] to generate mutant vectors. It is proved that this strategy is very efficient for the generation of high quality individuals [20].

Current to-pBest/1/bin is expressed as follows:

$$v_{i,g} = x_{i,g} + F\left(x_{best,g} - x_{i,g}\right) + F\left(x_{r1,g} - x_{r2,g}\right) \tag{13}$$

where $x_{best,g}$ is a randomly selected parent from the top best individuals of the current individuals. To maintain the diversity of the population, an archive A is proposed. The parent solutions that are not selected are added to this archive. Moreover, success-history-based parameter adaptation is a mechanism used to store successful CR, F values that performed well in the past generations. After the generation of a new trial vector u_i, it is compared with its parent. If u_i is better, then the CR and F parameters are stored in the sets S_{CR}, S_F respectively. Finally, the memories M_{CR} and M_F are updated using these successful parameters according to the following equations:

$$M_{CR} = \begin{cases} meanw_A(S_{CR}) & if\ S_{CR} \neq \emptyset \\ M_{CR} & otherwise \end{cases} \tag{14}$$

$$M_F = \begin{cases} meanw_L(S_F) & if\ S_F \neq \emptyset \\ M_F & otherwise \end{cases} \tag{15}$$

where $meanw_A$ is the weighted mean and $meanw_L$ is the Lehmar mean.

For further details about LSHADE, we refer the reader to [18].

3.5   Radial Basis Function (RBF)

Surrogate models can be used as approximation models for the cost functions of optimization problems [10]. There are several surrogate models in the literature such as polynomial Response Surface Model RSM, Kriging and Radial Basis Function (RBF). In our proposition, RBF has been chosen thanks to its acceptable accuracy and to its relative simplicity compared to other surrogate models. A brief description of the RBF surrogate model is presented. Assuming that we have n given points $x_1, x_2, ..., x_n$ whose true function values $f(x_i)$ are known. In this method, an interpolant is used as follows:

$$s(x) = \sum_{i=1}^{k} w_i \emptyset(|x - x_i|) + b^T x + a, \quad x \in R^D \tag{16}$$

where $w = (w_1, w_2, ... w_n)^T \in R^n$, $b \in R^D$, $a \in R$, and $\emptyset$ is a cubic basis function. Moreover, the parameters w, b, a are obtained by solving the following system of linear equations:

$$\begin{pmatrix} \Phi & P \\ P^T & 0 \end{pmatrix} \begin{pmatrix} w \\ c \end{pmatrix} = \begin{pmatrix} F \\ 0 \end{pmatrix} \tag{17}$$

where Φ is the $n \times n$ matrix with $\Phi_{i,j} = \emptyset\left(\|x_i - x_j\|_2\right), c = (b^T, a)^T,$

$$F = (f(x1), f(x2), ..., f(xn))^T$$

and

$$P^T = \begin{pmatrix} x_1 & x_2 & \cdots & x_n \\ 1 & 1 & \cdots & 1 \end{pmatrix} \tag{18}$$

For more details about RBF surrogate model, the reader can refer to [10].

4 The Proposed Approach

An initialization strategy can play an important role on the algorithm performance. Several works have investigated the effect of initialization techniques in finding the global optima such as [12]. In our approach, a CMA-ES-enhanced CS initialization technique is proposed to provide well-distributed points over the search space. Our goal is to investigate the high capability of CS in exploring the search space as well as the CMA-ES, which is able to provide high quality solutions with a limited number of evaluations. First, CMA-ES algorithm is run for a certain number of evaluations. Then, the produced solution is provided along with a randomly generated population to CS procedure. The goal is to speed up the convergence rate of CS and lead the search towards well-distributed individuals. Afterwards, the population *pop* of *pop_size* individuals obtained from the last iteration of CS is used to train the RBF model. Thereafter, it will be provided to the main procedure of our proposition.

Since it is important for a metaheuristic to show a good balance between exploration and exploitation, we propose a technique to handle this issue. For each generation of the main procedure, it is decided with a probability *PLV* whether the algorithm performs the global search procedure, or whether one iteration of the modified LSHADE is performed instead as a local search procedure. The global search procedure consists of a clustering algorithm and a Lévy Flight perturbation. The clustering is used for its high capability of avoiding redundant search points during the search process [15] as well as its efficiency in performing global search [8, 9]. The clustering is considered as a search operator that exploits the whole information of the population to generate a certain number of centers (new individuals). In our approach, the K-means algorithm is chosen because it has experimentally shown a superior performance than other algorithms as the fuzzy c-means (FCM) which is demonstrated in the results. K-means is exploited in order to generate K central individuals of the current population. Then, the central individuals are relocated to potentially more promising areas of the search space using Lévy Flight perturbation. The Lévy Flight movement is applied according to:

$$step\_size_i = 0.001 * step_i * (z_i - best) \ i = 1, 2, \ldots K \tag{19}$$

where $step_i$ is generated according to (11), *best* is the best solution so far and z is the set of the central individuals. Then, the new trial individuals are generated as follows:

$$z_i = z_i + step\_size_i \tag{20}$$

As a replacement strategy, the best *pop_size* individuals of $pop \cup z$ are selected for the next iteration. Then, *PLV* parameter is decreased to progressively shift the search process from exploration to exploitation. This parameter is updated according to the following equation:

$$PLV = \max\left\{0, PLV - \frac{current\_fes}{\max\_fes}\right\} \tag{21}$$

Algorithm 4: One generation of our SLSHADE algorithm
1. Given a population of *pop_size* individuals
2. Given S_{CR}, S_F
3. Compute M_{CR}, and M_F according to (14), (15)
4. Generate a mutant population pop_a according to (13)
5. Generate a mutant population pop_b according to (22)
6. Evaluate approximately pop_a and pop_b using RBF surrogate model
7. Choose the population containing the best solution
8. For each x_i in the population
9.   Use binomial crossover to generate the trial vector u_i
10.   Evaluate u_i using the actual objective function
11.   If f(u_i) < f(x_i)
12. $x_{i+1} \leftarrow u_i$, $A \leftarrow x_i$, $S_{CR} \leftarrow CR_i$, $S_F \leftarrow F_i$
13.   Else
14. $x_{i+1} = x_i$
15.   End If
16. End for
17. Reduce the population by using LPSR

The decreasing procedure makes the approach more exploitative during the search process by enhancing the possibility of performing the exploitation procedure.

As a local search technique, a proposed surrogate model-based LSHADE (SLSHADE) algorithm is used, which is depicted in Algorithm 4. LSHADE is an adaptive version of DE that proved its high capability in solving a wide range of complex optimization problems. Its parameter adaptation strategy allows achieving an efficient exploitation [4]. In SLSHADE, we modify the mutation strategy by using an additional mutation equation and a simple switching technique to choose the best mutation operator for the next generation. The proposed mutation equation is as follows:

$$v_{i,g} = \left(x_{i,best} - x_{i,g}\right) + step\_size_i \tag{22}$$

where $step\_size_i$ is computed according to (11), and $x_{i,best}$ is the i_{th} best solution in the current population. To save the limited budget of evaluations, we use the RBF for an approximated evaluation. After applying the two search operators (Eqs. (13) and (22)), RBF is used to approximate the fitness of the two mutant populations. Afterwards, the population that contains the best solution is chosen to perform the binomial crossover of LSHADE. To provide a fair approximation, the RBF model is updated using the current population after each quarter of the available budget. The pseudo-code of the full proposition is depicted in Algorithm 5.

Algorithm 5: Pseudocode of the proposed approach

1. Archive $A \leftarrow \emptyset$
2. $S_{CR} \leftarrow \emptyset$, $S_F \leftarrow \emptyset$ // sets of successful CR and F in the previous generation
3. Set all values in M_{CR}, M_F to 0.5
4. Generate a solution S_{cmaes} using CMA-ES for a number of evaluation α
5. Perform CS to generate pop of pop_size individuals for a number of evaluation ρ
6. Train the RBF surrogate model using each individual in pop and its fitness
7. While $current\_fes < Budget$
8.   If $(current\_fes < max\_fes)$ and $(rand < PLV)$
9.   For $i=1:T$
10.   Generate K central individuals of pop using K-means
11.   Generate a step size for each center using Lévy flights
12.   Generate new individuals according to (20)
13.   Evaluate individuals and replace the bad individuals of the population
14. $current\_fes \leftarrow current\_fes + K$
15.   End for
16.   Decrease PLV according to equation (21)
17.   Else
18.   Perform SLSHADE (pop, S_{CR}, S_F)
19.   End if
20.   Update the RBF model using the current population after each quarter of the budget
21. End while

5   Experimental Results

This section presents an evaluation of our proposition on the problem at hand. We compare it with LSHADE as well as CS [19] and DE [16]. Moreover, we evaluated our algorithm on the 15 functions of the CEC 2015 test suite [13] in order to provide difficult test cases. The parameter setting of the compared algorithms are given in Table 1.

Table 1. Parameter setting of the compared algorithms

Algorithm	Parameters	Electric motor design problem	CEC 2015
Our proposition	α	$D * 1000$	$D * 1000$
	ρ	$D * 1000$	$D * 1000$
	pop_size	200	200
	k	$pop\_size/4$	$pop\_size/4$
	PLV	0.8	0.8
	$Budget$	10^6	$D * 10000$
	max_fes	$2/3 * Budget$	$1/3 * Budget$
	T	100	1
CS	P_a	0.25	0.25
	b	1.5	1.5
DE	CR	0.5	0.5
	F	0.5	0.5
LSHADE	r^{init}	18	18
	r^{arc}	2.6	2.6
	p	0.11	0.11
	Size of archive A	6	6

5.1   Comparison on CEC 2015 Benchmark

The comparison has been carried out using the CEC 2015 test suite. The benchmark contains 15 functions to be minimized with a limited budget of 10000 * D evaluations, where D is the dimension of the search space. Table 2 presents in detail the characteristics of CEC 2015 benchmark. The performance is evaluated using $D = 30$ and we performed 30 runs for each function.

Table 2. Problem definitions for the CEC 2015 competition on learning-based real-parameter single objective optimization

No	Function	Range	F_i
1	Rotated high conditioned elliptic function	$[-100, 100]^D$	100
2	Rotated cigar function	$[-100, 100]^D$	200
3	Shifted and rotated Ackley's function	$[-100, 100]^D$	300
4	Shifted and rotated Rastrigin's function	$[-100, 100]^D$	400
5	Shifted and rotated Schwefel's function	$[-100, 100]^D$	500
6	Hybrid function 1	$[-100, 100]^D$	600
7	Hybrid function 2	$[-100, 100]^D$	700
8	Hybrid function 3	$[-100, 100]^D$	800
9	Composition function 1	$[-100, 100]^D$	900
10	Composition function 2	$[-100, 100]^D$	1000
11	Composition function 3	$[-100, 100]^D$	1100
12	Composition function 4	$[-100, 100]^D$	1200
13	Composition function 5	$[-100, 100]^D$	1300
14	Composition function 6	$[-100, 100]^D$	1400
15	Composition function 7	$[-100, 100]^D$	1500

To demonstrate the importance of each component, an experimentation has been conducted to compare the proposed algorithm with other variants. In the first variant, the initialization method is removed and it is called "*variant-1*". In the second variant, the switching technique to the global search procedure is disabled. The algorithm becomes a hybridization between the proposed initialization method and SLSHADE. Moreover, to demonstrate the clustering impact in producing new individuals, K-means algorithm has been replaced by the FCM clustering algorithm "*variant-3*".

Each column from Table 3 shows best, mean and standard deviation of each algorithm for each function. The best fitness found for each function is in bold. Mean results that are significantly better than the ones of the other algorithms, according to the Kruskal-Wallis statistical test at 95% confidence level followed by a Tukey-Kramer post hoc test are also in bold. The results presented in Table 4 show a superior performance of our proposition over the other algorithms. It can significantly outperform LSHADE in 6 functions, DE and CS in 15 functions. The comparison with the three variants reveals that our proposition could achieve better performance as well. It can outperform variant-1 in 8 functions which shows the importance of the proposed initialization method. Similarly, disabling the global search has a major effect on the algorithm. *Variant-2* performs significantly worse than the proposition in 8 functions.

Table 3. Comparison of CS, DE, LSHADE and our proposition on CEC 2015 test suite

		CS	DE	LSHADE	Variant-1	Variant-2	Variant-3	Our proposition
F1	Best	4.06E+06	1.84E+07	**100**	100.00	100.00	100.00	**100**
	Mean	5.88E+06	3.25E+07	100.00	100.00	100.00	100.00	**100**
	Std	1.09E+06	6.62E+06	6.34+E 05	0.02	8.6e−04	4.2e−03	0
F2	Best	1.00E+11	1.39E+04	**200**	200.00	200.00	200.00	**200**
	Mean	1.00E+11	7.50E+06	**200**	200.00	200.00	200.00	**200**
	Std	0	4.78E+04	0	3.07e−14	2.63e−14	7.46e−15	0
F3	Best	320.80	320.60	320	320.03	320.05	320.04	**319.99**
	Mean	320.90	320.68	320.05	320.07	320.09	320.09	**319.99**
	Std	0.03	0.03	0.01	0.01	0.01	0.01	0
F4	Best	525.86	532.89	404.98	405.98	408.97	406.97	**403.99**
	Mean	575.17	547.86	**410.04**	**410.25**	415.76	415.18	**410.19**
	Std	19.99	8.26	2.04	2.58	7.01	4.08	2.19
F5	Best	3 499.36	5 368.68	**1 315.40**	1490.93	1992.54	1899.11	1 618.87
	Mean	4 053.09	5 940.68	**1 768.50**	**1865.59**	2370.67	2348.35	2 147.12
	Std	193.60	234.93	200.44	181.26	195.42	199.84	229.57
F6	Best	5.64E+04	8.84E+05	673.18	676.37	**654.09**	663.72	712.41
	Mean	1.08E+05	2.20E+06	1 021.14	1014.76	861.93	**796.49**	928.25
	Std	2.89E+04	8.09E+05	215.63	230.03	129.32	88.51	151.84
F7	Best	711.84	712.73	705.85	705.56	704.928	705.07	**703.15**
	Mean	713.41	713.71	**706.84**	**706.84**	706.24	706.15	706.40
	Std	0.91	0.36	0.56	0.63	0.68	0.55	0.94
F8	Best	5 384.50	1.34E+05	810.82	811.42	806.97	**801.21**	811.71
	Mean	9 497.06	4.12E+05	906.48	909.34	852.84	**838.76**	859.89
	Std	1 941.79	1.39E+05	68.79	80.78	43.78	39.22	62.67
F9	Best	1 004.23	1 003.27	**1 002.37**	1002.59	1002.39	1002.42	1 002.43
	Mean	1 004.79	1 003.50	**1 002.81**	1002.85	1002.72	1002.75	1 002.80
	Std	0.24	0.15	0.18	0.14	1.3e−01	0.14	0.15
F10	Best	1.22E+04	1.01E+05	1 413.77	1265.26	1170.70	1152.72	**1 100**
	Mean	2.38E+04	5.13E+05	**1 691.50**	1609.82	5330.32	1474.494	1563.60
	Std	4864.28	1.81E+05	171.69	223.07	17629.47	200.49	178.13
F11	Best	1 428.42	1 694.51	1 500	1500	1400.75	1400.72	**1 400.7**
	Mean	1 443.50	1 874.25	1 515.42	1519.98	**1410.13**	**1406.101**	1 401.10
	Std	9.86	125.368	23.28	27.34	9.26	8.03	0.56
F12	Best	1 305.67	1 306.58	1 303.42	1303.53	1303.24	1303.24	**1 303.2**
	Mean	1 306.46	1 307.71	**1 304.02**	1303.95	1303.83	1303.78	1 304
	Std	0.36	0.55	0.26	0.23	0.27	0.23	0.38
F13	Best	1 300.02	1 300.02	1 300.02	1300.02	1300.02	1300.02	**1 300**
	Mean	1 300.02	1 300.02	1 300.02	1300.02	1300.02	1300.02	**1 300**
	Std	0	0	0	2.1e−04	2.75e−04	2.57e−04	0
F14	Best	3.33E+04	3.49E+04	3.25E+04	34167.93	32486.61	32499.62	**1 500**
	Mean	3.39E+04	3.51E+04	3.44E+04	34832.79	34085.43	34132.58	**1 500**
	Std	402.35	117.80	735.88	208.95	667.58	625.16	0
F15	Best	1 606.34	1 600.00	**1 600**	1600.00	1600.00	1600.00	**1600**
	Mean	1 607.50	1 600.00	**1 600**	1600.00	1600.00	1600.00	**1600**
	Std	0.59	0	0	0	4.22e−14	0	0

Variant-3 shows slightly better performance when compared to *variant-1* and *variant-2*. However, the proposition can significantly outperform it in 7 functions. These results demonstrates the impact of clustering. It is observed that both clustering methods can significantly improve the performance of the proposed algorithm.

Table 4. Comparison using Kruskal-Wallis test on CEC 2015 test suite

vs	Our proposition	D = 30
LSHADE	+(better)	1
	−(worse)	6
	=(no sig)	8
CS	+(better)	0
	−(worse)	15
	=(no sig)	0
DE	+(better)	0
	−(worse)	15
	=(no sig)	0
Variant-1	+(better)	1
	−(worse)	8
	=(no sig)	6
Variant-2	+(better)	0
	−(worse)	8
	=(no sig)	7
Variant-3	+(better)	1
	−(worse)	7
	=(no sig)	7

5.2 Comparison on HS-PMSM

The paper's objective is to reduce HS-PMSM weight and by that, increase EV's autonomy. The problem at hand is a multi-objective problem, where the objective functions are as follows:

1. The first objective function concerns the mass of the electric motor m_{atot}:

$$m_{atot} = m_{cooper} + m_{stat} + m_{rot} + m_{pm} \qquad (23)$$

where m_{cooper} is the cooper mass, m_{stat} is the stator iron mass, m_{rot} is the rotor iron mass, and m_{pm} is the magnets mass.

2. The second objective function is to maximize the output power density. It is written as follows:

$$P_{out} = P_{in} + \sum losses \qquad (24)$$

where P_{out} is the output power density, P_{in} is the input density, and the sum of losses mainly contains the mechanical, iron and copper loss component.

Table 5. The problem constraints

Parameter	Symbol	Unity	Variation limits
Output power	P_{out}	W	[19995; 20005]
Current consumption	I_s	A	[20; 56]
Motor torque	T_m	Nm	[8.5; 8.6]
Motor's efficiency	η	-	[0.9; 0.99]
Motor's power factor	PF	-	[0.81; 0.99]
Rotor inner diameter	Dir	mm	[22; 70]
Slot filling factor	τ	-	[0.1; 0.5]

The two objective functions are aggregated to obtain the following new objective function which will be optimized using the proposed algorithm:

$$\min j(x) = -\frac{P_{out}}{m_{atot}} + penality \qquad (25)$$

where

$$penality = 10^4 \sum_{i=1}^{7} C_i \qquad (26)$$

$C_i = 0$ if the constraint i is satisfied, 1 otherwise.

The set of constraints are presented in Table 5. There are 8 variables for the optimization problem at hand, i.e. 8 geometrical parameters controlling the electric motor structure. The parameters are presented in Table 6.

Table 6. The geometrical parameters for the weight optimization

Symbol	Description	Variation limits
Dis	Inner stator diameter	[50; 80] mm
hjr	Rotor yoke height	[7; 15] mm
histm	Tooth isthmus	[0.5; 2] mm
hjs	Stator yoke height	[8; 15] mm
wt	Tooth width	[3.5; 8] mm
gap0	Air-gap length	[0.5; 1.5] mm
hmp	PM height	[4; 8] mm
Lm	Machine's length	[100; 160] mm

To conduct a fair comparison, the proposed algorithm has been run 30 times. We collected the best, the mean, the median, the worst, and the standard deviation of each algorithm. It is observed from Table 7 that our proposition obtains the best solution compared to the other algorithms.

Table 7. Results on the real problem after 30 runs

	CS	DE	L-SHADE	*Variant-1*	*Variant-2*	*Variant-3*	Our proposition
Best	−3.308e+03	−3.156e+03	−3.197e+03	**−3.397e+03**	−3.318e+03	−3.380e+03	**−3.397e+03**
Mean	−3.131e+03	−2.910e+03	−3.044e+03	−3.114e+03	−3.202e+03	−3.188e+03	**−3.397e+03**
Median	−3.179e+03	−3.024e+03	−2.816e+03	−2.937e+03	−3.283e+03	−3.210e+03	**−3.397e+03**
Worst	−3.034e+03	−2.848e+03	−2.797e+03	−2.935e+03	−3.130e+03	−3.085e+03	**−3.397e+03**
Std	88.52	91.23	107	112.10	49.03	58.36	**0**

Besides, a stable performance is achieved, since the proposition could obtain the best solution in each run. The comparison between the 3 variants reveals that variant-2 could obtain the best results. It demonstrates clearly the importance of the proposed initialization method. *Variant-3* shows an inferior performance when compared to the proposition. Thus, it can be concluded that each component of our proposition tends to be effective and the combination as a whole leads to a successful algorithm. Further details about the optimal solution found by our proposition are depicted in Table 8. Regarding the optimized obtained results, the proposed algorithm could achieve an important gain of 28% in the mass. Moreover, it could achieve a gain of 17% and 29% decreasing the mechanical loss and the iron loss stator respectively.

Table 8. The best geometrical parameters with the optimized factors

Symbol	Original motor	Optimized motor	Gain %
m_{atot}	8.2513 kg	5.8885 kg	**+28.63**
P_{out}	20000 W	20005 W	**+0.25e−3**
P_{out}/m_{tot}	2.42 kW/kg	3.39 kW/kg	**+28.653**
Iron loss stator	225.73 W	158.9 W	**+29.60**
Mechanical loss	352.69 W	292.15 W	**+17.16**
Efficiency	0.9596	0.9607	**+1.01**
Power factor	0.8187	0.8100	**−1.06**
Dis	63 mm	66.7 mm	
hjr	10.5 mm	9.3 mm	
histm	1.5 mm	1 mm	
hjs	11.8 mm	9.8 mm	
wt	5 mm	4 mm	
gap	1 mm	0.9 mm	
hmp	6 mm	4 mm	
Lm	135 mm	100 mm	

6 Conclusion

The paper has presented a successful hybridization to solve numerical optimization problems. The proposition consists in combining 2 state-of-art algorithms as an initialization method. Then, the produced population is transferred to the main procedure. The latter switches between the global and the local search procedures giving progressively the priority to the local search procedure to adaptively enhance exploitation in the algorithm. The proposition has been tested on CEC 2015 test suite and on the optimization of an electric motor. The obtained results have shown a stable and competitive performance compared to other state-of-art algorithms. Besides, a superior performance of K means over FCM clustering algorithm has been noticed in the global search procedure. Thus, as a future work, we aim to justify this superiority by conducting an experimentation integrating visualization tools, in order to analyze the behavior of each clustering method. We also aim to integrate recent landscape analysis strategies to switch between the search operators (local and global search) in order to investigate their influence on the algorithm performance.

References

1. Awad, N.H., Ali, M.Z., Suganthan, P.N., Reynolds, R.G.: An ensemble sinusoidal parameter adaptation incorporated with L-SHADE for solving CEC2014 benchmark prolems. In: 2016 IEEE Congress on Evolutionary Computation (CEC), pp. 2958–2965 (2016)
2. Blum, C., Puchinger, J., Raidl, G.R., Roli, A.: Hybrid metaheuristics in combinatorial optimization: a survey. Appl. Soft Comput. **11**(6), 4135–4151 (2011)
3. Boussaid, I., Lepagnot, J., Siarry, P.: A survey on optimization metaheuristics. Inf. Sci. **237**, 82–117 (2013)
4. Brest, J., Maucec, M.S., Boskovic, B.: iL-SHADE: improved L-SHADE algorithm for single objective real-parameter optimization. In: 2016 IEEE Congress on Evolutionary Computation (CEC), pp. 1188–1195 (2016)
5. Crepinsek, M., Liu, S.H., Mernik, M.: Exploration and exploitation in evolutionary algorithms. ACM Comput. Surv. **45**(3), 1–33 (2013)
6. Fodorean, D., Idoumghar, L., N'diaye, A., Bouquain, D., Miraoui, A.: Simulated annealing algorithm for the optimisation of an electrical machine. IET Electr. Power Appl. **6**(9), 735–742 (2012)
7. Fodorean, D., Idoumghar, L., Szabo, L.: Motorization for an electric scooter by using permanent-magnet machines optimized based on a hybrid metaheuristic algorithm. IEEE Trans. Veh. Technol. **62**(1), 39–49 (2013)
8. Gao, W., Yen, G.G., Liu, S.: A cluster-based differential evolution with self-adaptive strategy for multimodal optimization. IEEE Trans. Cybern. **44**(8), 1314–1327 (2014)
9. Halder, U., Das, S., Maity, D.: A cluster-based differential evolution algorithm with external archive for optimization in dynamic environments. IEEE Trans. Cybern. **43**(3), 881–897 (2013)
10. Han, Z.H., Zhang, K.S.: Surrogate-based optimization. In: Real-World Applications of Genetic Algorithms. InTech (2012)
11. Hansen, N., Muller, S.D., Koumoutsakos, P.: Reducing the time complexity of the derandomized evolution strategy with covariance matrix adaptation (CMA-ES). Evol. Comput. **11**(1), 1–18 (2003)
12. Kazimipour, B., Li, X., Qin, A.K.: A review of population initialization techniques for evolutionary algorithms. In: 2014 IEEE Congress on Evolutionary Computation (CEC), pp. 2585–2592 (2014)
13. Liang, J., Qu, B., Suganthan, P., Chen, Q.: Problem definitions and evaluation criteria for the CEC 2015 competition on learning-based real-parameter single objective optimization. Technical report, Computational Intelligence Laboratory, Zhengzhou University, Zhengzhou China, Nanyang Technological University, Singapore (2014)

14. MacQueen, J.: Some methods for classification and analysis of multivariate observations. In: Proceedings of the Fifth Berkeley Symposium on Mathematical Statistics and Probability, pp. 281–297. University of California Press, Berkeley, California (1967)
15. Pence, I., Cesmeli, M.S., Senel, F.A., Cetisli, B.: A new unconstrained global optimization method based on clustering and parabolic approximation. Expert Syst. Appl. **55**, 493–507 (2016)
16. Storn, R., Price, K.: Differential evolution - a simple and efficient heuristic for global optimization over continuous spaces. J. Global Optim. **11**(4), 341–359 (1997)
17. Tanabe, R., Fukunaga, A.: Evaluating the performance of shade on CEC 2013 benchmark problems. In: 2013 IEEE Congress on Evolutionary Computation, pp. 1952–1959 (2013)
18. Tanabe, R., Fukunaga, A.S.: Improving the search performance of SHADE using linear population size reduction. In: 2014 IEEE Congress on Evolutionary Computation (CEC), pp. 1658–1665 (2014)
19. Yang, X.S., Deb, S.: Cuckoo search via Lévy flights. In: 2009 World Congress on Nature and Biologically Inspired Computing (NaBIC). IEEE (2009)
20. Zhang, J., Sanderson, A.: JADE: adaptive differential evolution with optional external archive. IEEE Trans. Evol. Comput. **13**(5), 945–958 (2009)

Dynamic Current Distribution
in the Electrodes of Submerged Arc Furnace
Using Scalar and Vector Potentials

Yonatan Afework Tesfahunegn[1(✉)], Thordur Magnusson[2],
Merete Tangstad[3], and Gudrun Saevarsdottir[4]

[1] Engineering Optimization and Modeling Center,
School of Science and Engineering, Reykjavik University,
Mentavegur 1, 101 Reykjavik, Iceland
yonatant@ru.is
[2] United Silicon, Stakksbraut 9, 230 Reykjanesbæ, Iceland
tm@silicon.is
[3] Department of Materials Science and Engineering, NTNU,
7491 Trondheim, Norway
merete.tangstad@ntnu.no
[4] School of Science and Engineering, Reykjavik University,
Menntavegur 1, 101 Reykjavik, Iceland
gudrunsa@ru.is

Abstract. This work presents computations of electric current distributions inside an industrial submerged arc furnace. A 3D model has been developed in ANSYS Fluent that solves Maxwell's equations based on scalar and vector potentials approach that are treated as transport equations. In this paper, the approach is described in detail and numerical simulations are performed on an industrial three-phase submerged arc furnace. The current distributions within electrodes due to skin and proximity effects are presented. The results show that the proposed method adequately models these phenomena.

Keywords: Current distribution · Skin effect · Proximity effect
Submerged arc furnace

1 Introduction

Current distribution is critical for proper operation of Submerged Arc Furnaces for silicon production. Control systems do not offer this information as it is not directly measurable, but metallurgists operate furnaces based on experienced interpretation of available data. A number of recent dig-outs of industrial furnaces have expanded available information on location-dependent charge properties, thus enabling numerical models with reasonably realistic domain configurations. This has the potential to enhance understanding of critical process parameters allowing more accurate furnace control.

A masters thesis by Krokstad [1] published in 2014 describes measurements of the electrical conductivity of silicon carbide and Vangskåsen [2] in 2012 looked in detail at

© Springer International Publishing AG, part of Springer Nature 2018
Y. Shi et al. (Eds.): ICCS 2018, LNCS 10861, pp. 518–527, 2018.
https://doi.org/10.1007/978-3-319-93701-4_40

the metal producing mechanisms. Molnas [3] and Nell [4] have also published data on digout samples and material analysis that are relevant. These are some of the basic components necessary to set up a reasonably realistic modeling domain with correct physical properties to model the current distribution within a furnace, and therefore there is now a unique opportunity to create a model which enables understanding of the current distribution in the furnace. These results can be used in the development of furnace control strategies that can allow improved silicon recovery and current efficiency.

A number of researchers have published results on current distribution of Submerged Arc Furnaces using Finite Volume Method (FVM) and Finite Element Method (FEM). Palsson and Jonsson [5] used FEM to analyze the skin and proximity effects in Soderberg electrodes for FeSi furnace. In the paper, a cross-section of the furnace is modeled in 2D and solved to obtain a time-harmonic solution of AC currents in the electrodes. Toh *et al.* [6] used FVM to model steelmaking process. In their approach, they follow scalar and vector potentials to implement Maxwell's equations. Diahnaut [7] presented computations of the electric field in SAF using CFD. The author showed the effect of contact resistance by studying the contact between two coke particles before dealing with a full-scale furnace. The furnace was partitioned into layers to consider different materials, and no assumptions were made regarding the current path. Bezuidenhout *et al.* [8] applied CFD on a three-phase electric smelting furnace to investigate the electrical aspects, thermal and flow behavior. They showed relationships between electrode positions, current distribution and slag electrical resistivity. Darmana *et al.* [9] developed a modeling concept applicable for SAFs using CFD that considers various physical phenomena such as thermodynamics, electricity, hydrodynamics, heat radiation and chemical reactions. Wang *et al.* [10] investigated the thermal behavior inside three different electric furnaces for MgO production.

This paper presents computations of electric current distributions inside an industrial submerged arc furnace. A 3D model has been developed in ANSYS Fluent [11] that solves Maxwell's equations based on scalar and vector potentials approach that are treated as transport equations. They are implemented using User Define Scalar (UDS). In the next sections, the process of producing silicon, and the proposed approach are described in detail. The proposed methodology is applied to an industrial three-phase submerged arc furnace. At this stage, not all the furnace components are included in the analysis. Only the three electrodes and the outer boundary of the furnace are considered. Hence, the current distributions within the electrodes due to skin-effect (current flowing near the electrode surface) and proximity-effect are presented.

2   The Process

In the silicon production process, quartz and carbon materials are fed into a Submerged Arc Furnace. The raw material mix fills up the furnace and forms a charge. Three electrodes sticking into the charge from above. The energy for the reactions in the furnace is provided by electric heating from the current passed to the furnace through the electrodes, but each carries one of three phases of 50 Hz AC current, canceling out at a star-point in the furnace.

The overall reaction for producing Silicon metal is:

$$SiO_2 + 2C = Si + 2CO(g) \tag{1}$$

This reaction, however, happens through a series of sub-reactions, changing the properties of the charge along the way as intermediary reaction products are formed. The current passes from the electrodes through the raw-material charge and an electric arc burning at the tip of the electrode. The arc, which consists of thermal plasma in the range of 10000–30000 K provides heat for energy consuming silicon producing reaction (4) while the SiC forming reaction and SiO(g) condensation, reactions (2) and (3), happen at a lower temperature further up in the furnace [12]:

$$SiO(g) + 2C = SiC + CO(g) \tag{2}$$

$$2SiO(g) = Si + SiO_2 \tag{3}$$

$$SiO_2 + SiC = SiO(g) + CO(g) + Si(1) \tag{4}$$

It is extremely important for the silicon recovery in this process that there is a balance between the high temperature reactions (4) and the low temperature reactions (2) and (3). Therefore, it is necessary that sufficient heat is released in the arc, while a certain part should be released in the raw-material charge.

The current distribution is not well known for silicon furnaces, and cannot be directly measured. Saevarsdottir et al. [13] calculated that the arc could be maximum 10–15 cm, based on the electrical parameters. Although there have been publications on this subject, (for example [14]), no results from an accurate model where the current distribution can be calculated have been published to date.

The geometry of the zones in a silicon furnace depends on the operation history, and hence a number of different geometries, sizes and compositions are possible in various parts of the furnace. A report from recent excavations of industrial furnaces published by Tranell et al. [15] describe various zones in a FeSi furnace. Myrhaug [16] reported similar features from a pilot scale excavation operating around 150 kW. Tangstad et al. [17] published results from excavation of industrial furnaces, where the interior of the furnace is divided into zones depending on the materials and their degree of conversion. Mapping the material distribution gives a basis for quantifying the location-dependent physical properties of the charge materials such as the electrical conductivity.

3 Computational Model

In this section, we describe the mathematical modeling, the furnace geometry, material properties, mesh generation and boundary conditions.

3.1   Mathematical Modeling

In this paper, we will focus only on the electrical aspects of SAF. The 3D electrical model is developed in ANSYS Fluent [11] based on scalar and vector potentials approach to solve the Maxwell's equations. This will capture the time-dependent effects, the induction of magnetic field and the resulting magnetic forces in the system, but for the considerations in this paper, we will not deal with the magnetic forces. In the Maxwell's equations we have taken the following assumptions:

a. The current displacement is zero $\left(\frac{\partial D}{\partial t} = 0\right)$. This is valid as the frequency of the AC-period is low (50 Hz).
b. Charge density is ignored which is the result of (a).

Hence the modified Maxwell's equations are the following [18]

$$\nabla \cdot B = 0 \tag{5}$$

$$\nabla \times E = -\frac{\partial B}{\partial t} \tag{6}$$

$$\nabla \times B = \mu J \tag{7}$$

$$\nabla \cdot J = 0 \tag{8}$$

From Ohm's law [18]:

$$J = \sigma E \tag{9}$$

where B, E, D, J, μ and σ represent magnetic flux density, electric field, electric flux density, electric current density, magnetic permeability and electrical conductivity, respectively.

Introducing scalar and vector potentials, ϕ and A the unknowns in Maxwell's equations will be reduced from six (three components of E and B) to four (ϕ and three components of A). In the study of electromagnetism [18], especially when potentials are introduced two identities are important, i.e., the curl of the gradient of any scalar field is zero ($\nabla \times \nabla \phi = 0$), and the divergence of the curl of any vector field is zero ($\nabla \cdot \nabla \times A = 0$). Hence after some manipulations and substitution, we get the following relationships:

$$E = -\nabla \phi - \frac{\partial A}{\partial t} \tag{10}$$

$$B = \nabla \times A \tag{11}$$

$$\nabla(\nabla \cdot A) - \nabla^2 A = \mu J \tag{12}$$

Taking the divergence of Eq. (10) and assuming Coulomb condition ($\nabla \cdot A = 0$) [18], we get the following equations:

$$\nabla^2 \phi = 0 \tag{13}$$

$$\sigma \frac{\partial A}{\partial t} - \nabla \cdot \left(\frac{1}{\mu} \nabla A \right) = -\sigma \nabla \phi \tag{14}$$

In Eq. (14) the gradient of the scalar potential is a source. Even though Eq. (13) is already implemented in ANSYS Fluent MHD module, it is not supported to impose time-varying voltage or current. Hence we need to develop four UDS transport equations to solve Eqs. (13) and (14). By using the distribution of scalar potential ϕ and of vector potential A obtained by solving Eqs. (13) and (14) with suitable boundary conditions, the following relation can calculate the distribution of electric current density.

$$J = -\sigma \nabla \phi - \sigma \frac{\partial A}{\partial t} \tag{15}$$

The distribution of magnetic flux density can be obtained by Eq. (11).

3.2 Furnace Geometry and Material Properties

To verify the proposed approach, it is suitable to use benchmark problems. However, there are no available benchmark problems that have either analytical or experimental solutions related to submerged arc furnaces. Palsson and Jonsson [5] have used a two-dimensional FEM model that has three electrodes. In their model, the variation along the axis of the electrodes is neglected. Hence, they considered a cross-sectional area of a furnace. In the FEM model, it is convenient to apply current at a node of the electrodes. In the FVM model it is not possible to impose current on a node. It should be applied normal to a surface area. This means that in this paper, a 3D FVM model should be created. To replicate the 2D model, the length of electrodes should be sufficiently long to make the effect of the boundary will be negligible. All simulation results of the simulation will be reported in the middle cross-section. The 3D domain is shown in Fig. 1. The dimensions of the the modeling domain are taken from [5].

The electrode electrical conductivity is assumed to be $\sigma = 3 \times 10^4$ and the relative permeability is $\mu_r = 1$. The conductivity and relative permeability in the furnace is 0 and 1 respectively.

3.3 Mesh Generation and Boundary Conditions

Mesh generation is a crucial part of any computational method. It has a significant influence on the runtime and memory use of simulation, as well as the accuracy and stability of the solution. The material volumes (electrodes and the furnace part) were meshed using ICEM-CFD [19]. The mesh is generated using unstructured grid. After performing preliminary grid convergence study, the minimum and maximum element sizes are set 5 and 30 cm, respectively. To reduce the cell count, the unstructured mesh is converted to a polyhedral mesh in ANSYS Fluent reducing the cell count by almost two thirds, thus enabling faster convergence and saving computational expense.

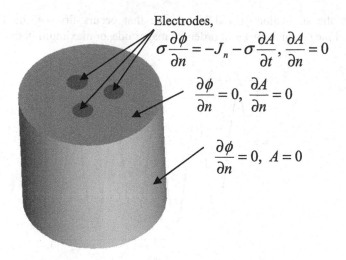

Fig. 1. Computational domain with boundary conditions

The boundary conditions are indicated as shown in Fig. 1. Note that the same boundary conditions are applied on the top and bottom surfaces of the furnace. It is assumed that there is no magnetic flux through the furnace wall. Applying such condition imposes that the vector potential $\mathbf{A}$ is constant, which involves the simple case $\mathbf{A} = 0$ at the outer boundary. The boundary condition $\partial\phi/\partial n = 0$, where n is the normal vector on the outer side of the furnace combined with $\mathbf{A} = 0$ imposes that there is no current flow out of the furnace.

The top and bottom surfaces of the electrodes defined as conductive walls by applying the respective phase currents as current density. Here, a total current density of 118 kA RMS [5] divided by the electrode cross-section area is applied on the top and the bottom surfaces of the electrodes but with a phase shift of 120° between them. Thus the current density on electrode k; $k = 0, 1, 2$ is

$$J_k = \frac{118}{A_e\sqrt{2}}\sin\left(2\pi ft + \frac{2\pi k}{3}\right) \tag{16}$$

where A_e, f and t are the cross-sectional area of electrode, frequency and time.

4 Results

In this section, we study the skin and proximity effects on the electrodes using the proposed method as described in Sect. 3. In this work, the frequency is taken as 50 Hz which is the standard frequency in furnace operation. The solver setup is a second order upwind scheme based on an implicit formulation. The iterative convergence of each solution is examined by monitoring the overall residual, which is the sum (over all the cells in the computational domain) of the L^2 norm (also known as least squares) of all the governing equations solved in each cell. The solution convergence criterion throughout the simulation period is the one that occurs first of the following: a reduction of the residuals by eight orders of magnitude, or maximum iterations of 1000.

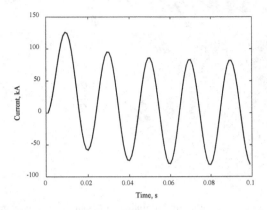

Fig. 2. Comparison between input and simulated current

To achieve reasonable and stable result, several simulations have been performed for over four periods. As it can be seen in Fig. 2, for the first three periods the current was unstable.

A grid convergence study has been conducted to discern the effect of grid refinement based on a total current. For the study, three different levels of grid refinements with time-step (Δt) of 0.001 have been considered. The three grids are coarse, medium and fine grids with total cells of 154829, 293476 and 486656, respectively. The results are shown in Fig. 3. The maximum difference between fine and coarse models is about 4.5 kA and between fine and medium is approximately 0.6 kA. Consequently, utilization of the medium grid will be sufficient for further analysis.

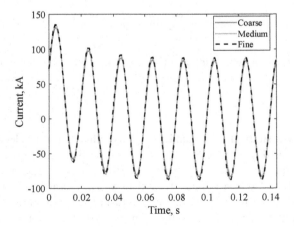

Fig. 3. Grid convergence study

Tesla

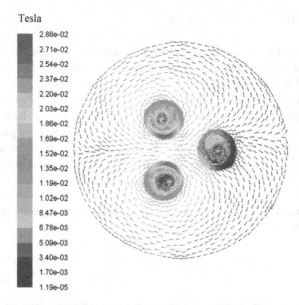

Fig. 4. Magnetic flux density in the middle section

Figure 4 shows the magnetic field in the cross-section of the furnace at one-time point. At this particular time, the two electrodes in the left have higher current but in opposite directions and less current is flowing through the third electrode. Figure 5 indicates the resulting non-uniform current distributions on the electrodes. The non-uniformity is the result of skin-effect and proximity-effect.

A/m^2

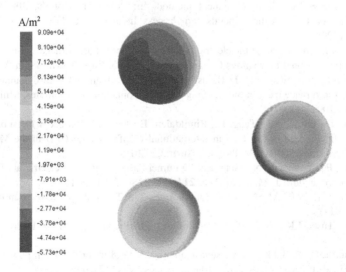

Fig. 5. Current densities within the three electrodes

5 Conclusions

This work proposed scalar and vector potentials approach to solve the time-dependent Maxwell's equations for determining electric current distributions inside submerged arc furnaces. A 3D finite volume model has been developed in ANSYS Fluent and implemented using User Define Scalar (UDS). We have considered a simplified furnace that consists of three electrodes and check the validity of the simulation results based on the skin-effect and the proximity effect. The results show that the proposed method can handle these effects. As a future work the proposed method will be applied to a real industrial submerged arc furnace that contains several components such as electrodes, arcs, crater and crater wall.

Acknowledgments. The Icelandic Technology development fund is greatly acknowledged for their funding of this work.

References

1. Krokstad, M.: Electrical resistivity of industrial SiC crusts. MSc-thesis, NTNU (2014)
2. Vangskåsen, J.: Metal-producing mechanisms in the carbothermic silicon process. MSc. thesis, NTNU (2012)
3. Mølnås, H.: Investigation of SiO condensate formation in the silicon process. Project report in TMT 4500. NTNU, Norway (2010)
4. Nell, J., Joubert, C.: Phase Chemistry of digout samples from a ferrosilicon furnace. In: The 13th International Ferroalloys Congress, pp. 265–271. Almaty, Kazakhstan (2013)
5. Palsson, H., Jonsson, M.: Finite element analysis of proximity effects in Soderberg electrodes. https://www.hi.is/∼magnusj/ritverk/proximit.pdf. Accessed 07 Jan 2018
6. Toh, T., Yamasaki, N., Seki, T., Tanaka, J.: Magnetohydrodynamic simulation in steel making process by 3D finite element method. In: Proceedings of the 4th International Conference on CFD in the Minerals and Process Industries SINTEF/NTNU. Trondheim, Norway (2005)
7. Dhainaut, M.: Simulation of the electric field in a submerged arc furnace. In: Proceedings of the 10th International Ferroalloys Congress, pp. 605–613. Cape Town, South Africa (2004)
8. Bezuidenhout, J.J., Eksteen, J.J., Bardshaw, S.M.: Computational fluid dynamic modelling of an electric furnace used in the smelting of PGM containing concentrates. Miner. Eng. **22** (11), 995–1006 (2009)
9. Darmana, D., Olsen, J.E., Tang, K., Ringldalen, E.: Modelling concept for submerged arc furnaces. In: Proceedings of the 9th International Conference on CFD in the Minerals and Process Industries CSIRO. Melbourne, Australia (2012)
10. Wang, Z., Fu, Y., Wang, N., Feng, L.: 3D numerical simulation of electric arc furnaces for the MgO production. J. Mat. Pro. Tec. **214**(11), 2284–2291 (2014)
11. FLUENT, ver. 17.0, ANSYS Inc., Southpointe, 275 Technology Drive, Canonsburg, PA 15317 (2017)
12. Schei, A., Tuset, J.K., Tveit, H.: Production of high silicon alloys. Tapir Forlag, Trondheim (1998)
13. Sævarsdottir, G.A., Bakken, J.A., Sevastyanenko, V.G., Liping, G.: High power AC arcs in metallurgical furnaces. High Temp. Mater. Process. **5**(1) (2001)

14. Saevarsdottir, G.A., Bakken, J.A.: Current distribution in submerged arc furnaces for silicon metal/ferrosilicon production. In: Proceedings of the 12th International Ferroalloys Congress, pp. 717–728. Helsinki, Finland (2010)
15. Tranell, G., Andersson, M., Ringdalen, E., Ostrovski, O., Stenmo, J.J.: Reaction zones in a FeSi75 furnace – results from an industrial excavation. In: Proceedings of the 12th International Ferroalloys Congress, pp. 709–715. Helsinki, Finland (2010)
16. Myrhaug, E.H.: Non-fossil reduction materials in the silicon process -properties and behavior. Ph.D. thesis, NTNU (2003)
17. Tangstad, M., Ksiazek, M., Andersen, J.E.: Zones and materials in the Si furnace. In: Silicon for the Chemical and Solar Industry XII. Trondheim, Norway (2014)
18. Griffiths, D.J., College, R.: Introduction to Electrodynamics, 3rd edn. Prentice-Hall Inc., USA (1999)
19. ICEM-CFD, ver . 17.0, ANSYS Inc., Southpointe, 275 Technology Drive, Canonsburg, PA 15317 (2017)

Optimising Deep Learning by Hyper-heuristic Approach for Classifying Good Quality Images

Muneeb ul Hassan[1], Nasser R. Sabar[2]([✉]) [iD], and Andy Song[1]([✉])

[1] RMIT University, Melbourne, VIC 3000, Australia
muneeb_hassan@outlook.com, andy.song@rmit.edu.au
[2] La Trobe University, Melbourne, VIC 3083, Australia
n.sabar@latrobe.edu.au

Abstract. Deep Convolutional Neural Network (CNN), which is one of the prominent deep learning methods, has shown a remarkable success in a variety of computer vision tasks, especially image classification. However, tuning CNN hyper-parameters requires expert knowledge and a large amount of manual effort of trial and error. In this work, we present the use of CNN on classifying good quality images versus bad quality images without understanding the image content. The well known data-sets were used for performance evaluation. More importantly we propose a hyper-heuristic approach for tuning CNN hyper-parameters. The proposed hyper-heuristic encompasses of a high level strategy and various low level heuristics. The high level strategy utilises search performance to determine how to apply low level heuristics to automatically find an appropriate set of CNN hyper-parameters. Our experiments show the effectiveness of this hyper-heuristic approach which can achieve high accuracy even when the training size is significantly reduced and conventional CNNs can no longer perform well. In short the proposed hyper-heuristic approach does enhance CNN deep learning.

Keywords: Hyper-heuristics · Deep learning · CNN · Optimisation

1 Introduction

Deep learning is a fast growing area in Artificial Intelligence as it has achieved remarkable success in many fields apart from the well publicised Go player - AlphaGo [1]. These fields include real time object detection [2], image classification [3] and video classification [4]. It also performed well in speech recognition [5] and natural language processing [6]. Major deep learning methods are Convolutional Neural Network, Deep Belief Network and Recurrent Neural Network. One of the problems of these deep learning methods is the configuration of the learning process because these learning algorithms are sensitive to parameters and a good performance is often the result of a good parameter combination. However finding a good combination is not a trivial task. For example the parameters in

Y. Shi et al. (Eds.): ICCS 2018, LNCS 10861, pp. 528–539, 2018.
https://doi.org/10.1007/978-3-319-93701-4_41

Convolutional Neural Network typically involve batch size, drop out rate, learning rate and training duration. They all can significantly impact the learning performance of deep learning on a particular task. In this study we will address this issue by introducing a hyper-heuristic approach to automatically tune these parameters. The particular problem in this study is image classification. We would like to train a deep network classifier to differentiate good quality images versus bad ones regardless the image content. The problem itself is novel.

Image Classification has been studied of many decades and is one of the key areas in computer vision. The task of image classification is to differentiate between images according to their categories. Image classification usually has a set of targets for example handwritten digits in images [7], human faces appeared on photos [8], various human behaviours captured in video image frames [3] and target objects like cars and books. However, in many real world scenarios, image quality, which is independent of image content, is also of significant importance. It is highly desirable that good photos can be separated from bad photos automatically. Bad images then could be improved or rejected from an image collection so less resources would be consumed. An extension on this is to even automatically select aesthetic images. The aim of this study is the first step, utilising deep learning to differentiate good images from images of obvious poor quality such as blurred images and noisy images. In particular the research goal of this study is to answer the following questions:

1. How to formulate deep learning to differentiate between images of good quality and images of bad quality without understanding the image content?
2. To what extend the training samples can be reduced while still maintaining good accuracy in classifying good vs bad images?
3. How to automatically tune the deep learning parameters to achieve good classification results?

Hence our investigation is also organised in three components. The first part is try to determine a suitable convolutional network structure as a classifier for good and bad images. Secondly, we study the impact of the training size on the classification performance. Thirdly, a hyper-heuristic approach is introduced to evolve the appropriate parameter combinations.

In Sect. 2 the image datasets are introduced. Section 3 describes the deep learning methodology while Sect. 4 describes the hyper-heuristic methodology. Section 5 shows the experiments with results. The conclusion is presented in Sect. 6.

2 Image Data Sets

In this study the well know image classification benchmark, the MNIST dataset is used to represent the good images [7]. MNIST is a standardized image collection which consists of handwritten digits from 0 to 9. Each digit is a 28×28 pixel gray scale image. MNIST comes with a training set which consists of 60000 such images of digits and a test set which contains 10000 similar images.

A variation of MNIST dataset which is called noisy MNIST or n-MNIST, is used to represent the bad images [9]. There are three subsets of n-MNIST:

1. MNIST with motion blur
2. MNIST with additive white gaussian noise (awgn)
3. MNIST with AWGN and reduced contrast.

These datasets are the exact replicas of original MNIST but with additional noise. Each image in n-MNIST is also 28×28 gray scale. There are 60000 training examples and 10000 test examples. The labels in training and test data-sets are hard encoded, e.g. each label is a 1×10 vector (Figs. 1, 2, 3 and 4).

Fig. 1. Example of images from MNIST dataset [10]

Fig. 2. Example of images from motion blur dataset.

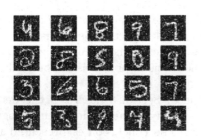

Fig. 3. Example of images from AWGN dataset

Fig. 4. Example of images from additive white AWGN dataset.

The MNIST with motion blur filter is created by imitating a motion of came by 5 pixels with an angle of $15°$ which makes the filter a vector for horizontal and vertical motions. The MNIST with AWGN is created by introducing additive white Gaussian noise with signal to noise ratio of 9.5. The MNIST with reduced contrast and AWGN is created by introducing contrast range with AWGN with signal to noise ratio of 12 [9].

3   Deep Learning Methodology

In this study, we use the well-know convolutional neural network (CNN) through Keras and Tensorflow. Keras is a high-level neural network API which is built on top of Tensorflow. With keras, we can define models with different standalone configurable modules which then can be combined to form a neural network model. Tensorflow is a deep learning library developed by Google [11]. Tensorflow is a directed graph which consists of nodes and it also maintain and update the state of the node. Every node has zero or more input and zero or more outputs. Value flow among the node to node and values are arbitrary long arrays called tensors. An example of a tensor graph is shown in Fig. 5. That is a simple equation of cost computed as a function of rectified Linear Unit (ReLu) in which the matrix of weights W and input x are multiplied then adding a bias b.

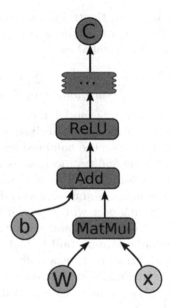

Fig. 5. A Tensorflow computation graph [11]

For our image classification tasks, we use two 2D convolution layers (convolution2D), with a 2D max pooling layer (MaxPooling) placed after the second convolution layer. The output of MaxPooling is flattened to a one dimensional vector which will be passed through a fully connected dense layer. The dense layer and a drop out layer are introduced after the MaxPooling2D layer to produce better generalization. For all the layers the Rectified Linear Unit (ReLu) activation is used. The output of dense layer uses the softmax activation for probabilistic classification.

The hyper-parameters of the CNN learning are listed below. The optimization target in this study is to find a good combination of these hyper-parameters and ultimately lead to a better accuracy:

1. The batch size - the number of training examples used in one iteration.
2. The number of epochs - representing the number of iteration over the entire data set.
3. The number of neurons in the fully connected layer.
4. Drop out probability.
5. The learning rate.
6. The Rho factor.
7. The epsilon factor.

During the learning, we split the training data into a training set and a validation set. Validation data consist of 20% of the original training set and the training set uses the rest. During training, the validation loss is monitored. When it stops decreasing or starts increasing then the training will terminate to avoid over-fitting.

Once the learning is terminated, the trained network will be applied on the test image set to obtain test accuracy. The accuracy in this study is simply classification accuracy which is calculated as

$$Accuracy = \frac{\sum True\ Positive + \sum True\ Negative}{Total\ number\ of\ Images} \tag{1}$$

There are other ways to evaluate the model, for example ROC, F-measure and MSE. Only classification accuracy measure described above is used for simplicity reason. Also our image datasets are quite balanced and true and false cases are equally important. Hence training and test accuracies are sufficient to guide the learning and to indicate the performance of learned models.

Our second aim is to see how training size would impact the learning. It is obvious that the computational cost will be less if the training set is small. However a data set, which is too small, would not be representative enough to enable good learning. Therefore it is important to find the right balance between good performance vs computational cost, especially in real world applications. In this study we try to find minimum size for training which can still lead to reasonable test performance. Logarithmic scale is used here, in the order of 2^n, 2^{n-1}, 2^{n-2}, until 2^3 and 2^2.

Note the size reduction only applies on the training data. The test set, which contains 10000 MNIST images (good) and 10000 n-MNIST images (bad), is consistently used in all experiments. Only test accuracy is used to report the learning performance unless specified otherwise.

4   Hyper-heuristic Parameter Optimisation

Hyper-heuristics have been proposed for selecting and generating heuristics to solve a particular problem [12]. It has been successful in many different fields [12–18]. The aim of hyper-heuristic is to find and assemble good optimisation heuristics. Different operations or techniques can be introduced as heuristics so the overall optimisation could be more effective and more efficient.

Hyper-heuristic often begins from randomly generated initial solution and then iteratively improve the solution. A traditional selection hyper-heuristic approach has two key components: low level heuristics and high level strategy. The low level heuristics operate on the solution space. The quality of solution is being evaluated by the objective function from the domain. Whereas high level strategy operate on the heuristic space. It will form heuristics to improve the result and secondly it will also determine whether to accept or reject the generated solution by the acceptance criterion. The components of this framework are briefly described below:

4.1   High Level Strategy

The high level strategy uses the past search performance of low level heuristics to decide which heuristic should be applied at each decision point. It selects one from a pool of heuristics in the low level. This work uses the Multi-Armed Bandit (MAB) as an on-line heuristic selector [19,20]. MAB is based on the record of past performance, e.g. the performance in previous iterations. The record stores an empirical reward and confidence level. The former is the average rewards achieved by that heuristic. The confidence level is the number of times that the heuristic has been selected. The higher values of these two scores indicate better quality of the heuristic [21]. MAB goes through all heuristics one by one and selects the one which returns the maximum value when applied Eq. (2).

$$\arg\max_{i=LLH_1...LLH_n} \left(q_{i(t)} + c\sqrt{\frac{2log \sum_{i=LLH_1}^{LLH_n} n_{i(t)}}{n_{i(t)}}} \right) \tag{2}$$

where LLH_n is the total number of heuristics in the low level, $n_{i(t)}$ is number of times that i^{th} heuristic has been applied up to time t and $q_{i(t)}$ is the empirical reward of the ith heuristics up to time t which is calculated as follows: $q_{i(t)} = q_{i(t)} + \Delta$, where Δ is the difference between the quality of the old and new solutions.

4.2   Acceptance Criterion

Acceptance criterion is in the high level and is independent of the domain. Monte Carlo acceptance criterion is used in this study [15]. A solution that improve the objective function will be accepted if the following condition is met [21].

$$R < exp(\Delta f) = exp(f_t - f_{t-1}) \tag{3}$$

where R is the random number between $[0, 1]$ and Δf is the difference between performance at $(t-1)$th and (t)th iterations.

4.3   Low Level Heuristics

In this work, 18 heuristics are included in the low level. Every heuristic has different characteristics hence may lead to different search behaviours. We use the following six heuristics to form the set of low level heuristics. Each heuristic is used in several ways to change one, two, three, real values parameters only, integer parameters only or all parameters.

Parametrised Gaussian Mutation

$$X_i = X_i + N(0, \sigma^2) \tag{4}$$

where σ^2 is 0.5 times the standard deviation [21].

There another three operators which are the same as above but with different σ values ranged from 0.2, 0.3 and 0.4 of the standard deviation.

Differential Mutation

$$X_i = X_i + F \times (X_{1i} - X_{2i}) \forall i = 1...n \tag{5}$$

where X_i is the decision variable for a given solution and $X_1 i$ is the best solution and F is the scaling factor [21].

Arithmetic Crossover

$$X_i = \lambda \times X_i + (1 - \lambda) \times X_{1i}, \forall i = 1...N \tag{6}$$

where λ is random number with range 0 to 1. X_i is the current solution and $X_1 i$ is the current best solution [21].

4.4 Initial Solution

This in our study is a set of CNN parameters that need to be tuned. These parameters are represented as an array. Each parameter initially is randomly generated. The random function is as follows:

$$x_p = l_p + Rand_p(0, 1) \times (u_p - l_p), p = 1...p \tag{7}$$

where p is the total number of parameters to be tuned. $Rand_p$ returns a random number within 0 and 1. l_p and u_p are lower bound and upper bound respectively for that parameter [21].

5 Experiments and Results

The first set of experiments are for image classifications. There are two most commonly used optimisers that were studied, namely Adam and Adadelta. In [22], it was mentioned that Adam and Adadelta provide the best convergence during the learning process. Table 1 show the classification performance on noisy

MNIST sets with these two optimisers. The learning rate was set as 0.2 for all experiments. This preliminary experiments show that Adadelta can achieve better accuracy in comparison with Adam.

Table 1. Experiment with training on MNIST and testing on n-MNIST

Datasets	Optimiser	Learning rate	Train accuracies	Test accuracies	Epochs
mnist-m-b	Adam	0.2	0.9828	0.9631	4
mnist-m-b	Adadelta	0.2	0.9732	0.9660	4
mnist-awgn	Adam	0.2	0.9810	0.7023	4
mnist-awgn	Adadelta	0.2	0.9737	0.7897	4
mnist-rc-awgn	Adam	0.2	0.9814	0.5287	4
mnist-rc-awgn	Adadelta	0.2	0.9740	0.6676	4

After a range of preliminary experiments, we settled on the settings include the optimisation algorithm, learning rate, drop out rate and number of neurons in the dense layer to start our experiment on classifying the noisy-MNIST and MNIST images. The images for training data are more than 60,000. We decrease the data size by half starting from $2^{16} = 65540$ images to see the impact on test accuracy. For each size we repeat the experiment 30 times. The results are shown in Table 2 including the average training accuracies and test accuracies of the 30 runs. The epochs are all set as 10 to be consistent.

As we can see from Table 2, the classification performance between training on 65540 images and 512 images are not much different, meaning 512 is sufficient for training image classifiers to recognise good quality images. The drop in performance between 512 and 64 images is not major as well. The set of 32 images starts showing significant performance loss indicating more training images are required. When the training size is as small as 4, the test accuracy becomes 50% which is pretty much random guessing for this binary classification task.

The above experiments confirm that the size of training dataset does impact on training. In the next set of experiments the hyper-heuristic approach presented in Sect. 4 is added in the learning process to tune the network parameters. The results are shown in Table 3 which listed the average test accuracies of 30 runs on training set of size 512 to that of size 4. Sizes above 512 are not included as the results from these sets would be all similar and close to 100%. For comparison purposes, the test results of training without the hyper-heuristic approach from Table 2 are repeated in the middle column of Table 3.

From test accuracies listed in Table 3 we can see the big improvement introduced by the hyper-heuristics approach on sizes 32 and 16. For larger size there are still performance increases but there are not much room for improvement. For smaller size like size 4, the sample is too few to be learnable hence the parameter tuning could not be much of help. This result indicates that with the hyper-heuristic tuning approach, it is possible to reduce the required training

Table 2. Experiment with different training sizes

Training size	Training accuracies	Test accuracies	Epochs
65540	0.9999	1.0	10
32770	1.0	1.0	10
16384	0.9999	1.0	10
8192	0.9998	1.0	10
4096	0.9979	0.9998	10
2048	0.9866	0.9917	10
1024	0.9639	0.9922	10
512	0.9043	0.9910	10
256	0.7500	0.9891	10
128	0.6078	0.9898	10
64	0.7031	0.9824	10
32	0.7600	0.7905	10
16	0.5625	0.6959	10
8	0.5205	0.6469	10
4	0.5000	0.5022	10

Table 3. Experiment with different training size using hyper-heuristic approach

Size of training data	Test accuracies (No HH)	Ttest accuracies (with HH)
512	0.9910	0.9990
256	0.9891	0.9990
128	0.9898	0.9988
64	0.9824	0.9911
32	0.7905	0.9165
16	0.6959	0.9068
8	0.6469	0.6872
4	0.5022	0.5211

size. For applications of which training examples are few or expensive to obtain, our parameter optimisation could be very helpful.

To investigate the computational cost of the parameter optimisation, we also measured the running time of the above experiments which were all conducted on a machine with Intel core i3 with processor 1.90 GHz, 4.00 GB RAM and 64-bit Windows 10. The results are presented in Fig. 6 which shows the average time in seconds of 30 runs of learning on sizes 4, 8 up to 128, with and without the hyper-heuristic parameter optimisation. As can be seen on the figure, the optimisation process does take extra time. However the time increase is acceptable, maximum of a double time in the case of 128 training images. In comparison, exact methods for combinatorial optimisation are too expensive to be practical.

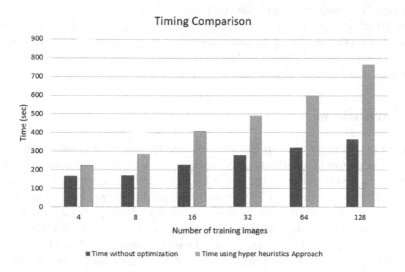

Fig. 6. Comparison on running time with and without hyper-heuristic optimization

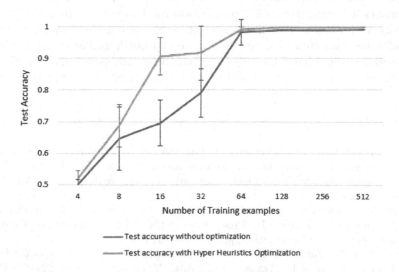

Fig. 7. Test accuracies with and without hyper-heuristic parameter optimisation

From the above experiments we can see the hyper-heuristic approach can greatly improve learning without requiring too much extra computational resources. To further illustrate the differences realised by our hyper-heuristic approach, the test performance on different sizes are plotted as in Fig. 7. The lines represent the average of 30 runs, while the bars on size 4 to size 64 are the standard deviation of these 30 runs of using and without using hyper-heuristic optimisation. As can be seen in this figure, the gap at size 16 and at size 32 are significant. To verify the significance, T-tests are conducted on test accuracies on size 16 which resulted a p-value of 0.000002, and on size 32 which resulted a p-value of 0.000025. These p-values are way below the null hypothesis threshold 0.05, showing the differences that hyper-heuristic optimisation made on test performance are indeed significant.

6   Conclusions

In this work, we utilised deep learning to classify images of good quality versus images of poor quality without understanding or examining the image content. Based on our investigation using MNIST and n-MNIST benchmark, we can conclude that deep learning with convolutional neural networks can handle this type of image classification tasks and can achieve high performance with sufficient amount of training images. Our study also confirms that the learning performance is affected by training size. Learning image quality classifiers does not need large amount of samples. However the learning would still suffer if the training set is too small.

Another important part of this study is introducing hyper-heuristic approach based parameter optimisation to automatic configure the learning. Through our experiments it is clear that this optimisation method can improve the learning especially when the training size is not sufficient but not too few. Furthermore, the additional computational cost introduced by our hyper-heuristic method is not too expensive. That makes this method attractive especially in real world applications where training samples might be expensive or difficult to obtain.

References

1. Silver, D., Huang, A., Maddison, C.J., Guez, A., Sifre, L., Van Den Driessche, G., Schrittwieser, J., Antonoglou, I., Panneershelvam, V., Lanctot, M., et al.: Mastering the game of go with deep neural networks and tree search. Nature 529(7587), 484–489 (2016)
2. Redmon, J., Divvala, S., Girshick, R., Farhadi, A.: You only look once: unified, real-time object detection. In: Proceedings of the IEEE Conference on Computer Vision and Pattern Recognition, pp. 779–788 (2016)
3. Ji, S., Wei, X., Yang, M., Kai, Y.: 3D convolutional neural networks for human action recognition. IEEE Trans. Pattern Anal. Mach. Intell. 35(1), 221–231 (2013)
4. Karpathy, A., Toderici, G., Shetty, S., Leung, T., Sukthankar, R., Fei-Fei, L.: Large-scale video classification with convolutional neural networks. In: Proceedings of the IEEE Conference on Computer Vision and Pattern Recognition, pp. 1725–1732 (2014)
5. Graves, A., Mohamed, A., Hinton, G.: Speech recognition with deep recurrent neural networks. In: 2013 IEEE International Conference on Acoustics, Speech and Signal Processing (icassp), pp. 6645–6649. IEEE (2013)

6. Hermann, K.M., Kocisky, T., Grefenstette, E., Espeholt, L., Kay, W., Suleyman, M., Blunsom, P.: Teaching machines to read and comprehend. In: Advances in Neural Information Processing Systems, pp. 1693–1701 (2015)
7. LeCun, Y., Bottou, L., Bengio, Y., Haffner, P.: Gradient-based learning applied to document recognition. Proc. IEEE **86**(11), 2278–2324 (1998)
8. Taigman, Y., Yang, M., Ranzato, M.A., Wolf, L.: Deepface: closing the gap to human-level performance in face verification. In: Proceedings of the IEEE Conference on Computer Vision and Pattern Recognition, pp. 1701–1708 (2014)
9. Basu, S., Karki, M., Ganguly, S., DiBiano, R., Mukhopadhyay, S., Gayaka, S., Kannan, R., Nemani, R.: Learning sparse feature representations using probabilistic quadtrees and deep belief nets. Neural Process. Lett. **45**, 1–13 (2015)
10. Liu, C.-L., Nakashima, K., Sako, H., Fujisawa, H.: Handwritten digit recognition: benchmarking of state-of-the-art techniques. Pattern Recogn. **36**(10), 2271–2285 (2003)
11. Abadi, M., Agarwal, A., Barham, P., Brevdo, E., Chen, Z., Citro, C., Corrado, G.S., Davis, A., Dean, J., Devin, M., et al.: Tensorflow: large-scale machine learning on heterogeneous distributed systems. arXiv preprint arXiv:1603.04467 (2016)
12. Burke, E.K., Hyde, M., Kendall, G., Ochoa, G., Özcan, E., Woodward, J.R.: A classification of hyper-heuristic approaches. In: Gendreau, M., Potvin, J.Y. (eds.) Handbook of Metaheuristics, pp. 449–468. Springer, Boston (2010). https://doi.org/10.1007/978-1-4419-1665-5_15
13. Sabar, N.R., Kendall, G.: Population based Monte Carlo tree search hyper-heuristic for combinatorial optimization problems. Inf. Sci. **314**, 225–239 (2015)
14. Sabar, N.R., Zhang, X.J., Song, A.: A math-hyper-heuristic approach for large-scale vehicle routing problems with time windows. In: 2015 IEEE Congress on Evolutionary Computation (CEC), pp. 830–837. IEEE (2015)
15. Sabar, N.R., Ayob, M.: Examination timetabling using scatter search hyper-heuristic. In: 2nd Conference on Data Mining and Optimization 2009, DMO 2009, pp. 127–131. IEEE (2009)
16. Sabar, N.R., Ayob, M., Kendall, G., Qu, R.: Grammatical evolution hyper-heuristic for combinatorial optimization problems. Strategies **3**, 4 (2012)
17. Sabar, N.R., Ayob, M., Kendall, G., Qu, R.: Automatic design of a hyper-heuristic framework with gene expression programming for combinatorial optimization problems. IEEE Trans. Evol. Comput. **19**(3), 309–325 (2015)
18. Abdullah, S., Sabar, N.R., Nazri, M.Z.A., Turabieh, H., McCollum, B.: A constructive hyper-heuristics for rough set attribute reduction. In: 2010 10th International Conference on Intelligent Systems Design and Applications (ISDA), pp. 1032–1035. IEEE (2010)
19. Sabar, N.R., Ayob, M., Kendall, G., Qu, R.: A dynamic multiarmed bandit-gene expression programming hyper-heuristic for combinatorial optimization problems. IEEE Trans. Cybern. **45**(2), 217–228 (2015)
20. Sabar, N.R., Abawajy, J., Yearwood, J.: Heterogeneous cooperative co-evolution memetic differential evolution algorithm for big data optimization problems. IEEE Trans. Evol. Comput. **21**(2), 315–327 (2017)
21. Sabar, N.R., Turky, A.M., Song, A.: Optimising deep belief networks by hyper-heuristic approach. In: CEC 2017-IEEE Congress on Evolutionary Computation (2017)
22. Ruder, S.: An overview of gradient descent optimization algorithms. arXiv preprint arXiv:1609.04747 (2016)

An Agent-Based Distributed Approach for Bike Sharing Systems

Ningkui Wang$^{(\boxtimes)}$, Hayfa Zgaya, Philippe Mathieu, and Slim Hammadi

Univ. Lille, CNRS, Centrale Lille, UMR 9189 - CRIStAL Centre de Recherche en Informatique Signal et Automatique de Lille, 59000 Lille, France
ningkui.wang@centralelille.fr

Abstract. Shared bikes are wildly welcomed and becoming increasing popular in the world, as a result, quite a few bike sharing systems have been conducted to provide services for bike users. However, current bike sharing systems are not flexible and considerate enough for public bike users because of the fixed stations and not well emphasized about user's satisfactions. In this paper, an agent-based distributed approach for bike sharing systems is proposed, this approach aims at helping users obtain a needed shared bike successfully and efficiently. We pay more attention on user's preferences to improve the satisfaction to the target shared bike, meanwhile, trust and probability are considered to improve the efficiency and success rate. To the end, results from simulation studies demonstrate the effectiveness of our proposed method.

Keywords: Computer science · Agent · Trust · Optimization
Resource assignment · Bike sharing system · Preference

1 Introduction

The first bike sharing system was launched in Amsterdam in 1965 [20,24]. Since then, many cities have developed the bike sharing system for the purpose of providing an economical, convenient and environmentally way for the travelers. Until December 2017, more than 18880500 self-service public use bikes and pedelecs (electric assisted bicycles) have been put into use in 1525 cities. In addition, 417 cities are planning or under construction of utilizing shared bikes [5,9]. The shared bikes play an increasing important role in our lives [14,22].

Bike sharing can be simply defined as many shared bikes distributed in the city for multiple users. A bike user is able to get access to shared bikes when logs in the bike sharing system. So far, models include public bike share (PBS) can be classified into about eight categories according to their operating mechanisms (Resource: Models of bike share) [1]. We divide bike sharing models into two types, either station based using docks or non station based free-floating

Supported by CRIStAL (Research center in Computer Science, Signal and Automatic Control of Lille) (UMR 9189) and China Scholarship Council (CSC).

© Springer International Publishing AG, part of Springer Nature 2018
Y. Shi et al. (Eds.): ICCS 2018, LNCS 10861, pp. 540–552, 2018.
https://doi.org/10.1007/978-3-319-93701-4_42

dock-less. Self-service public bike sharing on street docking, smart bikes and geo-fencing are typical models that users have to rent and return shared bikes to fixed stations or within virtual geo-fencing. Free-floating systems allow the smart bikes to be dropped anywhere safety around the city [1]. In this paper, we focus on smart bike sharing system without restrictions of fixed locations. We consider a system to be more flexible and convenient for shared bike users. Accordingly, we propose an agent based distributed approach which makes contributions to general resource distribution systems. The remained of the paper is organized as follows, related works and proposed method are given in Sects. 2 and 3, respectively. In Sect. 4, a practical example is analyzed to show the working process and effectiveness of our proposed approach. Some conclusions and future works end the paper in the last section.

2   Related Works

In the past decades, significant attention has been devoted to task assignment in distributed systems. In [11], Jiang summarized the works on task allocations and load balances according to the characteristic differences between distributed systems, mainly about typical control, typical resource optimization, the methods of reaching reliability and so on [11]. In bike sharing systems, users need shared bikes to satisfy their requests, it can also be regarded as a task assignment problem.

Quite a few researchers have devoted themselves into public bikes. The existing literatures about this topic are numerous, most of their works focus on the following research points. Firstly, the related works mainly focus on the development history and advantages of shared bikes [7,22]. Then, they pay much attention to concerning the policies and the satisfaction analysis for the cyclists [7,15,23]. Fishman et al. [8] analyzed some factors that influence potential users for choosing shared bikes. In literature [2], a methodology is proposed to quantify user's perception and satisfaction about bike sharing, results show that safety and information are the two influential aspects that influence most.

Finally, relevant works are conducted considering the system designers and controllers. They mainly concentrate on the number and locations of the fixed bike stations, the number of shared bikes to put into service and the imbalance in bike distribution [4,10,12]. A good understanding of the operating mechanism is helpful for the system optimization exploitation. In a bike sharing system, the fixed station location is essential and it has been studied from the operational research point of view [4,10,12,25]. Hu and Liu [10] proposed a mathematical location model of finding the optimal location to minimize the total fixed system cost for bike renting and the redistribution. In [25], a network flow model to estimate the flow of bikes within the network and the number of trips supported is proposed. In [4], a mathematical model to formulate public bike station distribution is conducted to minimize the total travel time and investment budget. To stress the unbalance distribution problem, the redistribution strategy is adopted [9,16,19,26]. In literature [16], vehicles are used to redistribute the bikes. Preisler et al. [19] built an incentive scheme that encourages users to pass nearby stations for selecting and returning bikes, thereby redistributing them in a self-organized fashion. In [26], Wong and Cheng established an actual path distance optimization method for the shared bike redistribution.

These approaches are helpful for the proper functioning of bike sharing systems. However, operating bike sharing systems and redistributing strategies cost plenty money [13], so we would like to consider a system without fixed stations and the redistribute strategy will no longer be needed.

3 Proposed Method

The agent concept is quite important in both artificial intelligent and mainstream computer science, it can be defined to denote a hardware or commonly the software-based computer system that holds the properties of autonomy, social ability, reactivity and pro-activeness [17,27]. In this part, we present an agent-based distributed approach for bike sharing system. In the system, all agents work together to rent or return shared bikes efficiently and freely.

When a user needs to travel by shared bikes, she attempts to send requests to all the bike agents in the system. After she receives the responses from bike agents, evaluations of the shared bikes are conducted according to her preferences and the responses. Simultaneously, the reliability of the responses is calculated by its own experiences and the other agents' information. Meanwhile, the probability of getting the shared bike can be obtained. These three factors work together to improve the satisfaction for users. The proposed agent based distributed approach is detailed discussed as follows, some explanations about the common variables are listed in Table 1, their specific meanings are also discussed in the text.

Table 1. Some commonly used variables and explanations

m : Numbers of users	i : the ith user
n : Numbers of shared bikes	j : the jth shared bike
p : Numbers of influential aspects	k : the kth influential aspect
q : Numbers of sub-factors of kth aspect	l : the lth sub-factor of kth aspect
$e_{i,j,k}$: $User_i$'s requests on j on kth aspect	$r_{j,i,k}$: Bike j' responses to i about k
pf_{ij} : Preference evaluations of i to j	M_{ij} : Trust evaluation of i to j
p_{ij} : Probability for i to get j	E_{ij} : The final assessment of i to j

3.1 User's Preferences—Shared-Bike Evaluations

Choosing a shared bike according to the user's preferences should completely depend on the user's own judgements. In fact, considering the user's preferences is essential, for example, a shared bike user prefers to have a bike with basket if she has brought a heavy goods. For the economic saving users, they would like to choose cheaper bikes, similarly, the deposit-payed shared bikes are always their only choices.

Evaluating the shared bikes according to a user's preferences is a multi-attribute decision making problem. In the bike sharing system, we assume that

- 1: There are m users which can be represented as $Users = \{User_1, User_2 ... User_i ... Userm\}$.
- 2: n shared bikes exist in the system, denoted as $Bikes = \{Bike_1, Bike_2 ... Bike_j ... Bike_n\}$.
- 3: p mainly influential aspects of evaluating the bikes denoted as $Aspects = \{Aspect_1, Aspect_2 ... Aspect_k ... Aspect_p\}$.
- 4: For each influential aspect, q sub-factors are considered, for aspect k, we have $Subfactors = \{Subf_{k1}, Subf_{k2} ... Subf_{kl} ... Subf_{kq}\}$.

When a bike user needs a shared bike at time t, she firstly needs to give her own requirements about the sub-factors of some influential aspects, they can be represented as

$$e_{i,j,k} = (e_{i,j,k,1}, e_{i,j,k,2} ... e_{i,j,k,l} ... e_{i,j,k,q}), \tag{1}$$

where $e_{i,j,k,l}$ represents the evaluation result given by $User_i$ to $Bike_j$ about the main influential $Aspect_k$, l shows the influential sub-factor. For example, when $User_i$ demands a shared bike, she believes that bike type is one of the influential aspects, three sub-factors, $V'LILLE$, $Mobike$ and "OfO" are considered. For $User_i$, $V'Lille$ and $Mobike$ can be chosen while she prefers $V'Lille$ much, as a result, she gives her requirements as $e_{i,j,1} = (0.8, 0.2, 0)$. Similarly, all the other factors can be judged in the same way.

Then the user advocates her requests to the shared bike agents and bikes immediately reply with boolean values $True$ or $False$. Their responses can be represented by

$$r_{j,i,k} = (Boolean(k1), ... Boolean(kl), ... Boolean(kq)). \tag{2}$$

For example, when considering the shared bike types, $Bike_j$ belongs to "OfO", so its response can be $r_{j,i,1} = (0, 0, 1)$ when evaluating bike types.

Obviously, not all the influential aspects are of equal importance, so we need to know their actual weights. Many methods can be used for the calculation of weights, such as principal component analysis, analytic hierarchy process (AHP), entropy method and coefficient of variation method [29]. Coefficient of variation method is a simple but efficient method which bases on the resolution information contained in the evaluation index. The coefficient of variation is defined as the ratio of the standard deviation σ to the mean $\bar{\mu}$. The bigger the coefficient of variation is, the greater the weight is assigned.

We suppose that q sub-factors effect on influential $Aspect_k$, let $\overline{\mu_k}$ be the average value of all the index of sub-factors, σ_k be the standard deviation of the index $Sub_{i,j,k}$, then the coefficient of variation of this index is $Coff(i,j,k) =$

$\frac{\sigma_k}{\mu_k}$. After that we normalize all the coefficients of variation and the weights of $Aspect_k$ can be obtained by

$$W_{i,j,k} = \frac{Coff(i,j,k)}{\sum_{k=1}^{P}(Coff(i,j,k))}. \tag{3}$$

When all the sub-factors are discussed, then final preference evaluations of $User_i$ to $Bike_j$ can be concluded as

$$preference(i,j) = pf_{ij} = \sum_{k=1}^{p}\{W_{i,j,k}(e_{i,j,k} \cdot r_{j,i,k})\}. \tag{4}$$

In the bike sharing system, at time t, all m users and n free bikes have been evaluated according to user's own preferences. The evaluation results of available bikes at time t can be denoted as

$$Preference(User(i),Bike(j))(t) = \begin{bmatrix} & Bike(1) \dots Bike(j) \dots Bike(n) \\ User(1) & pf_{11}(t) \dots pf_{1j}(t) \dots pf_{1n}(t) \\ \dots & \dots \quad \dots\dots \\ User(i) & pf_{i1}(t) \dots pf_{ij}(t) \dots pf_{in}(t) \\ \dots & \dots \quad \dots \quad \dots \\ User(m) & pf_{m1}(t) \dots pf_{mj}(t) \dots pf_{mn}(t) \end{bmatrix}. \tag{5}$$

At different time, whenever there is a new request message, a new preference matrix is generated. Users would like to choose a bike with higher evaluation values. However, agents might response with unreliable information, meanwhile, the well-evaluated bikes might be pursued by other users. Therefore, trust and probability to get the target bike are formulated.

3.2   Trust Evaluation

Trust can be regarded as the expectation given by all members of a society, they believe that the existing natural or moral social orders persist, just as we believe that the sun rises from the east and fall to the west [18,28,30]. Yu et al. summarized that the proposed methods to evaluate the agents' trust can be divided into four main categories [28], they are direct trust evaluation models, indirect/reputation-based trust evaluation models, socio-cognitive trust evaluation models and organization trust evaluation models. The mostly frequently used are direct trust evaluation models which depend on the direct interaction experience. The indirect/reputations-based trust evaluation models rely on the recommendation results from a third comity in the same system. These two trust evaluation models are easy to be accessed and efficient in distributed systems. As a result, these main trust evaluation models have been considered simultaneously. Dempster-Shafer theory of evidence is used for the representation of semantic assessment and weighted Dempster's combination rule is adopted for the combination of different information.

3.2.1 Dempster-Shafer Theory of Evidence

Dempster-Shafer theory of evidence also known as evidence theory which was proposed by Dempster and Shafer [6,21]. This theory is efficient in uncertainty representation, Dempster's combination rule has the ability to combine different basic probability assignments (BPA). In this paper, evidence theory is adopted to represent the trust and reputation, then Dempster's combination rule is used for the fusion of these two aspects. Some details about evidence theory are introduced as follows.

Definition 1 (The frame of discernment). *The frame of discernment* U, *consisted of* N *mutually exclusive and collectively exhaustive elements, can be defined as* $U = (e_1, ...e_h...e_N)$, *satisfying* $\cap e_h = \emptyset$.

Definition 2 (Basic probability assignment). *The power set of* U *represented by* 2^U, *any elements belong to* 2^U *is said to be propositions, the basic probability assignment is defined as a mapping from the power set to* $[0,1]$ *which represented by* $m : 2^U \rightarrow [0,1]$, *the following conditions are satisfied,*

$$m(\emptyset) = 0 \quad and \quad \sum_{A \subseteq 2^U} m(A) = 1; \tag{6}$$

where $\emptyset$ is an empty set and A is a subset of 2^U, the function $m(A)$ represents how strongly the evidence supports A. Any propositions of which $m(A)$ is non-zero is called a focal element and the set of all the focal elements is core.

Definition 3 (Dempster's rule of combination). *For any two BPAs* m_1 *and* m_2, *the Dempster's rule of combination which can be represented by* $m = m_1 \oplus m_2$ *is defined as*

$$m(A) = \begin{cases} \frac{1}{1-K} \sum_{B \cap C = A} m_1(B) m_2(C), & A \neq \emptyset; \\ 0, & A = \emptyset; \end{cases} \tag{7}$$

with $K = \sum_{B \cap C = \emptyset} m_1(B) m_2(C)$, *where* A, B *and* C *are the elements of* 2^U, K *is a normalization constant which means the conflict coefficient of two BPAs.*

Definition 4 (Weighted Dempster's combination rule). *In this paper, not all the BPAs are of the equal importance, so the weighted Dempster's combination rule is adopted. The modification of the Dempster's combination is conducted on the BPAs, the weights of the BPAs operate on the core of the power set, then the incomplete part is assigned to the frame of discernment. For the BPA which is defined in the frame work* $\{A, B\}$, *where* $m_1(A) = a$; $m_1(B) = b$; $m_1(A, B) = 1 - (a + b)$. *Its weight is denoted as* w_1, *where* $w_1 \in [0,1]$, *Then the BPA is modified by weight as*

$$m_1(A) = aw_1; \quad m_1(B) = bw_1; \quad m_1(A, B) = 1 - (a + b)w_1; \tag{8}$$

Finally, we can use Dempster's combination rule for the BPAs combination.

3.2.2 Agent's Trust

As explained, agent's trust is calculated from two aspects, the direct interaction experiences and indirect reputations. The direct trust evaluation is authenticity assessments consist of p aspects because the agents give their responses from p aspects. The users give their objective judgements by comparing the responses to the actual state of affairs, these judgement values $TrustE_{i,j,k}$ is between $[0, 1]$ where 1 means that the agent has provided an actual real response and 0 means that the agent was totally lying. We can use the Dempster-Shafer theory of evidence for the representation of the results, here the frame of discernment is defined as $U = \{Trust, NotTrust\} = \{T, nT\}$.

When translating the evaluating results into Dempster-Shafer theory of evidence, they can be denoted as

$$\begin{cases} m(T) = min\{TrustE_{i,j,1}, TrustE_{i,j,2}, ...TrustE_{i,j,p}\} \\ m(nT) = max\{1 - TrustE_{i,j,1}, 1 - TrustE_{i,j,2}, ...1 - TrustE_{i,j,p}, \} \\ m(T, nT) = 1 - [m(T) + m(nT)]. \end{cases} \quad (9)$$

For the trust evaluation, the current data is more reliable than the past ones because the characteristics of agents are always changeable. So we define a decay function that decays with time. Supposing the historical interaction happens at time T, we define decay function as

$$f_D(t) = \rho^{t-T}, \quad 0 < \rho < 1 \ and \ Limit \leq T \leq t. \quad (10)$$

we are now at time t and $Limit$ shows the interaction before this time is no longer reliable.

Similarly, the indirect reputations is also evaluated with the same approach of generating BPAs for direct trust. The final evaluation results can be represented as

$$\begin{cases} M_{DirectTrust} = M_{DT} = (m_D\{T\}, m_D\{nT\}, m_D\{T, nT\}); \\ M_{IndirectReputation} = M_{IR} = (m_I\{T\}, m_I\{nT\}, m_I\{T, nT\}). \end{cases} \quad (11)$$

Then the weighted Dempster's combination rule is used to combine both direct trust and indirect reputation,

$$M_{ij} = M_{DT}^{W_D} \oplus M_{IR}^{W_R}. \quad (12)$$

where $M_{DT}^{W_D}$ and $M_{IR}^{W_R}$ are the final evaluations about direct trust and indirect reputation, their weights represented by $W_D = f_D(t)w_{DT}$ and $W_R = f'_D(t)w_{IR}$ where w_{DT} and w_{IR} are the weights of direct trust and indirect reputation respectively, the values belong to $[0, 1]$. Of the final overall evaluation results, we would take more attention on the reliability value, i.e., $M_{ij}(T)$.

3.3   Probability of Getting the Selected Shared Bike

In dynamic bike sharing systems, all users can also rent the target bike before a user's arrival. In this situation, users prefer selecting a bike with high probability. Many research works consider bike appearance probability by population density [3]. In this part, we consider probability according to bicycle numbers in one domain within the user's reach.

Supposing $User_i$ needs to find a bike in time period $[0, t]$, her walking speed is V_{User_i}. Therefore, all the bikes in the circle whose radius is $V_{User_i} * t$ with user's position regarded as the center are available. As shown in Fig. 1, all the small blue circles in big dark circle are target shared bikes for the user represented by red five-pointed stars.

Firstly, we set a threshold $\sigma = t$. This threshold is also the time limitation for $User_i$ to find a bike. Then the travel salesman problem (TSP) algorithm is operated starts from any node with this threshold as the maximum traveling time. Traditional TSP is a shortest distance problem about traveling among x cities once and only once, starting and returning from the same place. Here we adopt TSP algorithm to classify all possible target bikes into sets which satisfies the traveling time in each set is smaller than the time limitation. If the time is still not exceed to the threshold when reaching at one node, the target bike is added to the set, otherwise, we start another TSP algorithm. Our goal is to obtain the minimum number of sets.

To the end, all reachable bikes have been divided into N sets, we can obtain the probabilities for $User_i$ to receive $Bike_j$ at time t by

$$p_{ij}(t) = \frac{Total\ numbers\ in\ set\ N}{Total\ numbers\ in\ the\ circle} = \frac{\sum(n_{set(i)})}{\sum(N_{Total})}. \tag{13}$$

Where $\sum(n_{set(i)})$ shows the total number in set i and $\sum(N_{Total})$ shows the total numbers available for $User_i$.

3.4   The Agent-Based Distributed Approach

As explained above, in the bike sharing system contains n users and m shared bikes. At time t, $User_i$ needs to find a shared bike before time T, according to her requests and bike agents' responses, evaluations of the three main factors are all obtained. $pf_{ij}(t)$ represents her preferences, $M_{ij}(T)$ describes the credibility level and $p_{ij}(t)$ shows the probability of getting the bike. So a user needs to give overall evaluations to rank and decide to select which shared bike. The overall ranking results can be obtained by multiplication of the factors as follows

$$E_{ij} = pf_{ij}(t) \times M_{ij}(T) \times p_{ij}(t). \tag{14}$$

Then a user sets off for the best evaluated shared bike rapidly. If the ideal bike is still there when she reaches at the target location, she rents it. Otherwise, she immediately spreads her new requests for shared bikes. The distributed approach is summarized as choosing best bikes from i free sharing bikes for j requesters denoted as Algorithm $BBU(i, j)$, it is shown in Algorithm 1 as follows.

4   Practical Example Simulations

In this part, a practical example is given to show how the proposed approach works and its effectiveness for users to find needed shared bikes.

Algorithm 1. BBU(i,j): Best Bikes for Users

    Location Initializations: m Agents(Shared Bike Requesters) & n Agents(Free Shared Bikes);

    if New requests for shared bikes appear at time t (Eq. 1) **then**

        Shared bikes responses (Eq. 2); Evaluate and rank all free shared bikes (Eqs. 3-15); Set off for the best one;

        if Target shared bike is still reachable; **then**

            Select the target shared bike;

        else

            BBU(i,j)

        end if

    end if

4.1 A Practical Example

We suppose that three shared bike companies run a total 1000 shared bikes in a system, the shared bikes can be placed freely in anywhere safety in the city. At time t, 30 users are looking for shared bikes among 300 free bikes. Locations for bikes and users distribution are shown in Fig. 1, the small blue circles represent the free-parking shared bikes, users are denoted by small red five-pointed stars. The dark circles whose centers are red five-pointed stars denote that all shared bikes inside are available.

Fig. 1. Distribution of the shared bikes and users (Color figure online)

We suppose $User_i$ is interested in four aspects when explaining her preferences, they are bike types ($Aspect_1$), whether there is a basket ($Aspect_2$), old and new degree ($Aspect_3$) and size ($Aspect_4$). All the influential aspects have influential sub-factors, the details are shown as below,

$$\begin{cases} Subf_{11} : V'Lille, Subf_{12} : Mobike, Subf_{13} : OfO; \; Subf_{31} : New, Subf_{32} : Old; \\ Subf_{21} : With\ a\ basket; \; Subf_{22} : Without\ a\ basket; \; Subf_{41} : Big, Subf_{42} : Small; \end{cases} \tag{15}$$

$User_i$ needs to send her requests to available bike agents. This process completes in her phone according to the API connected to the system. For example, $User_i$ can give her requires as $e_{i,j,1} = (0.8, 0.2, 0)$, $e_{i,j,2} = (1, 0)$, $e_{i,j,3} = (0.4, 0.6)$ and $e_{i,j,4} = (0.5, 0.5)$. As is shown, we find that user i chooses $V'Lille$ or $Mobike$, and she prefers $V'Lille$. she needs the bike with basket so the bikes without basket are no longer considered. she prefers old shared bikes. From the forth aspect, bike size makes no sense.

By analyzing the original data entered by user i, weights of the corresponding aspects are obtained based on the coefficient of variation method shown in Eq. 3. The corresponding average value $\overline{\mu_k}$, standard deviation σ_k and weights are shown in Table 2.

Table 2. Weights of the four main influential aspects

Aspects	$Aspect_1$	$Aspect_2$	$Aspect_3$	$Aspect_4$
$user_i$	(0.8,0.2,0)	(1.0, 0)	(0.4, 0.6)	(0.5, 0.5)
$\overline{\mu_k}$	$\frac{1}{3}$	0.5	0.5	0.5
σ_k	$\frac{\sqrt{26}}{15}$	0.5	0.1	0
$W_{(i,j,k)}$	0.36	0.53	0.11	0

All shared bikes respond if $User_i$'s requests is received. Here we suppose three bikes give their responses as shown in Table 3.

Table 3. Three bikes' responses to user i

Aspects	$Aspect_1$	$Aspect_2$	$Aspect_3$	$Aspect_4$
$r_{1,i}$	(1,0,0)	(0, 1)	(0, 1)	(1, 0)
$r_{2,i}$	(1,0,0)	(1, 0)	(1, 0)	(1, 0)
$r_{3,i}$	(0,1,0)	(1, 0)	(0, 1)	(0, 1)

Preference evaluations can be obtained by Eq. 4. For $User_i$, the evaluations of the three bikes are $pf_{i,1} = 0.354$, $pf_{i,2} = 0.862$ and $pf_{i,3} = 0.668$. Then the responses' reliability are calculated according to the historical experience. $User_i$ has used shared bike 1 twice which happened three and five days ago respectively. she has used shared bike 2 five hours ago and never uses shared bike 3, so from her own point of view, she has to evaluate bikes from four aspects whether the bike has replied with exact results and she gives bike 1 two evaluations as $TrustE(i,1)(t_1) = (1,1,1,0.8)$ and $TrustE(i,1)(t_2) = (1,1,0.9,0.8)$. Then the information can be denoted by Dempster-Shafer theory of evidence as $m_{i,1}^1(T) = 0.8$, $m_{i,1}^1(nT) = 0.2$, $m_{i,1}^1(T,nT) = 0$ and $m_{i,1}^2(T) = 0.8$, $m_{i,1}^2(nT) = 0.2$, $m_{i,1}^2(T,nT) = 0$.

The weighted Dempster' combination rule is adopted for the combination. We define $\rho = 0.95$ in delay function. The two times are separately three and five days ago, so the decay values are $0.95^3 = 0.8574$ and $0.95^5 = 0.7738$, they are regarded as the weights for combination of direct trust. The modified evaluations according to Eq. 8 are denoted as follows,

$$\begin{cases} m_{i,1}^1(T) = 0.6859 \\ m_{i,1}^1(nT) = 0.1715 \\ m_{i,1}^1(T,nT) = 0.1426 \end{cases} and \begin{cases} m_{i,1}^2(T) = 0.6190 \\ m_{i,1}^2(nT) = 0.1548 \\ m_{i,1}^2(T,nT) = 0.2262 \end{cases} \tag{16}$$

Then the combined results are $M_{i,1}^1(T) = 0.8480$; $M_{i,1}^1(nT) = 0.1110$; $M_{i,1}^1(T,nT) = 0.0410$. Similarly, another user K provides him the indirect reputation evaluation and the results are $M_{K,1}^2(T) = 0.5$, $M_{K,1}^2(nT) = 0.3$, $M_{K,1}^2(T,nT) = 0.2$.

For direct trust and indirect reputation, she trusts herself more and the weights are $W_D = 1$ and $W_R = 0.7$. Finally, the overall trust evaluations are calculated from both direct experience and indirect reputation by Eq. 12, the combined results for $Bike_1$ are $M_{i,1}(T) = 0.8738$, $M_{i,1}(nT) = 0.1032$ and $M_{i,1}(T,nT) = 0.0230$.

Similarly, the trust evaluations about bike 2 and 3 are conducted. Here we suppose the trust values respectively are 0.832 and 0.65 to bike 2 and 3. Simultaneously, the probabilities are conducted while we suppose they are 0.7, 0.553 and 0.75 respectively.

To the end, we would like to choose not only an ideal and reliable bike, but also a bike with high probability to be received. For the three bikes,

$$\begin{cases} E_{i1} = pf_{i,1} \times M_{i,1}(T) \times p_{i,1} = 0.354 \times 0.8738 \times 0.7 = 0.2165 \\ E_{i2} = pf_{i,2} \times M_{i,2}(T) \times p_{i,2} = 0.862 \times 0.832 \times 0.553 = 0.3966 \\ E_{i3} = pf_{i,3} \times M_{i,3}(T) \times p_{i,3} = 0.668 \times 0.65 \times 0.75 = 0.3257 \end{cases} \tag{17}$$

The final results are compared and $User_i$ chooses bike 2. With the same process, all users rank reachable shared bikes and set off for the best one.

4.2   Results Comparison and Analysis

As discussed in the last subsection, three aspects, namely bike evaluations, agent trust and probability are evaluated for 30 users to select best bikes from 300 free bikes. Looking for bikes randomly is used for the comparison with the proposed method in this paper. Moving randomly is the method that frequently be used nowadays. When a user and a bike gets close, the user evaluates whether this bike is acceptable. If she is satisfied about the bike, then the bike is selected and both the shared bike and user are removed to satisfied set. Otherwise, the user sets off randomly again to search for a needed bike.

The proposed method in this paper is regarded as another approach. A user evaluates all the possible bikes firstly and then sets off for the appropriate bike. Obviously, this method is more efficient and a user can receive the satisfied bike much more faster than the randomly approach.

5   Conclusions

In the bike sharing system, fixed bike stations are always the main restriction for the users to rent and return the shared bikes freely, the redistribute strategy are widely considered for the imbalances of supply and demand in the fixed stations in order to satisfy all the users. In this paper, we discussed a more freely environment for bike sharing system where the fixed stations are no longer existed. Users rent and return bikes anywhere in the city. We also considered for the users to choose satisfied shared bikes according to her own demands or preferences. There are many other future works, the proposed method needs to be compared to other approaches, more methods about uncertainty and data fusion will be adopted for trust evaluations.

Acknowledgment. This work is supported by CRIStAL (Research center in Computer Science, Signal and Automatic Control of Lille) (UMR 9189) and China Scholarship Council (CSC).

References

1. Carplus, bikeplus (2017). https://www.carplusbikeplus.org.uk/
2. Bordagaray, M., Ibeas, A., dellOlio, L.: Modeling user perception of public bicycle services. Procedia-Soc. Behav. Sci. **54**, 1308–1316 (2012)
3. Buck, D., Buehler, R.: Bike lanes and other determinants of capital bikeshare trips. In: 91st Transportation Research Board Annual Meeting (2012)
4. Chen, Q., Sun, T.: A model for the layout of bike stations in public bike-sharing systems. J. Adv. Transp. **49**(8), 884–900 (2015)
5. DeMaio, P., Meddin, R.: The bike-sharing world map (2017). http://www.bikesharingmap.com/
6. Dempster, A.P.: Upper and lower probabilities induced by a multivalued mapping. Ann. Math. Stat. **38**(2), 325–339 (1967)
7. Fishman, E.: Bikeshare: a review of recent literature. Transp. Rev. **36**(1), 92–113 (2016)
8. Fishman, E., Washington, S., Haworth, N.: Bike share: a synthesis of the literature. Transp. Rev. **33**(2), 148–165 (2013)
9. Ghosh, S., Varakantham, P., Adulyasak, Y., Jaillet, P.: Dynamic repositioning to reduce lost demand in bike sharing systems. J. Artif. Intell. Res. **58**, 387–430 (2017)
10. Hu, S.R., Liu, C.T.: An optimal location model for a bicycle sharing program with truck dispatching consideration. In: 2014 IEEE 17th International Conference on Intelligent Transportation Systems (ITSC), pp. 1775–1780. IEEE (2014)

11. Jiang, Y.: A survey of task allocation and load balancing in distributed systems. IEEE Trans. Parallel Distrib. Syst. **27**(2), 585–599 (2016)
12. Lin, J.R., Yang, T.H.: Strategic design of public bicycle sharing systems with service level constraints. Transp. Res. Part E: Logistics Transp. Rev. **47**(2), 284–294 (2011)
13. Lin, J.H., Chou, T.C.: A geo-aware and VRP-based public bicycle redistribution system. Int. J. Veh. Technol. **2012**, 1–14 (2012)
14. Midgley, P.: The role of smart bike-sharing systems in urban mobility. Journeys **2**(1), 23–31 (2009)
15. Murphy, H.: Dublin bikes: an investigation in the context of multimodal transport. Dublin, Ireland, M.Sc. Sustainable Development, Dublin Institute of Technology (2010)
16. Obrien, O., Cheshire, J., Batty, M.: Mining bicycle sharing data for generating insights into sustainable transport systems. J. Trans. Geogr. **34**, 262–273 (2014)
17. Pham, V.A., Karmouch, A.: Mobile software agents: an overview. IEEE Commun. Mag. **36**(7), 26–37 (1998)
18. Pinyol, I., Sabater-Mir, J.: Computational trust and reputation models for open multi-agent systems: a review. Artif. Intell. Rev. **40**(1), 1–25 (2013)
19. Preisler, T., Dethlefs, T., Renz, W.: Self-organizing redistribution of bicycles in a bike-sharing system based on decentralized control. In: 2016 Federated Conference on Computer Science and Information Systems (FedCSIS), pp. 1471–1480. IEEE (2016)
20. Samet, B., Couffin, F., Zolghadri, M., Barkallah, M., Haddar, M.: Performance analysis and improvement of the bike sharing system using closed queuing networks with blocking mechanism (2017)
21. Shafer, G.: A Mathematical Theory of Evidence, vol. 20, no. 1, p. 242 (1976)
22. Shaheen, S., Guzman, S., Zhang, H.: Bikesharing in Europe, the Americas, and Asia: past, present, and future. Transp. Res. Rec.: J. Transp. Res. Board **2143**, 159–167 (2010)
23. Shaheen, S.A.: Public bikesharing in North America: early operator and user understanding, MTI report 11–19 (2012)
24. Shaheen, S.A.: Introduction shared-use vehicle services for sustainable transportation: carsharing, bikesharing, and personal vehicle sharing across the globe. Int. J. Sustain. Transp. **7**(1), 1–4 (2013)
25. Shu, J., Chou, M.C., Liu, Q., Teo, C.P., Wang, I.L.: Models for effective deployment and redistribution of bicycles within public bicycle-sharing systems. Oper. Res. **61**(6), 1346–1359 (2013)
26. Wong, J.T., Cheng, C.Y.: Exploring activity patterns of the taipei public bikesharing system. J. East. Asia Soc. Transp. Stud. **11**, 1012–1028 (2015)
27. Wooldridge, M., Jennings, N.R.: Intelligent agents: theory and practice. Knowl. Eng. Rev. **10**(2), 115–152 (1995)
28. Yu, H., Shen, Z., Leung, C., Miao, C., Lesser, V.R.: A survey of multi-agent trust management systems. IEEE Access **1**, 35–50 (2013)
29. Zhulin, F., Yu, Q., Quan, Y., Xiaolin, C.: The real-time assessment of freeway traffic state based on variation coefficient method. In: 2016 Eighth International Conference on Measuring Technology and Mechatronics Automation (ICMTMA), pp. 811–816. IEEE (2016)
30. Zupancic, E., Trcek, D.: Qade: a novel trust and reputation model for handling false trust values in e-commerce environments with subjectivity consideration. Technol. Econ. Dev. Econ. **23**(1), 81–110 (2017)

A Fast Vertex-Swap Operator for the Prize-Collecting Steiner Tree Problem

Yi-Fei Ming, Si-Bo Chen, Yong-Quan Chen, and Zhang-Hua Fu[(✉)]

Robotics Laboratory for Logistics Service,
Institute of Robotics and Intelligent Manufacturing,
The Chinese University of Hong Kong, Shenzhen, Shenzhen 518172, China
{115010203,115010121}@link.cuhk.edu.cn, yqchen@cuhk.edu.cn,
Fzh.cuhksz@gmail.com

Abstract. The prize-collecting Steiner tree problem (PCSTP) is one of the important topics in computational science and operations research. The vertex-swap operation, which involves removal and addition of a pair of vertices based on a given minimum spanning tree (MST), has been proven very effective for some particular PCSTP instances with uniform edge costs. This paper extends the vertex-swap operator to make it applicable for solving more general PCSTP instances with varied edge costs. Furthermore, we adopt multiple dynamic data structures, which guarantee that the total time complexity for evaluating all the $O(n^2)$ possible vertex-swap moves is bounded by $O(n) \cdot O(m \cdot \log n)$, where n and m denote the number of vertices and edges respectively (if we run Kruskal's algorithm with a Fibonacci heap from scratch after swapping any pair of vertices, the total time complexity would reach $O(n^2) \cdot O(m + n \cdot \log n)$). We also prove that after applying the vertex-swap operation, the resulting solutions are necessarily MSTs (unless infeasible).

Keywords: Computational complexity · Network design
Prize-collecting Steiner tree · Vertex-swap operator
Dynamic data structures

1 Introduction

The prize-collecting Steiner tree problem (PCSTP) has a wide range of applications, e.g., design of utility network, telecommunication network, signal processing. As a variant of the classic Steiner tree problem in graphs, the PCSTP is *NP-hard*, thus being important in the field of computational science.

Given an undirected graph $G = (V, E)$ with a set V ($|V| = n$) of vertices and a set E ($|E| = m$) of edges, where each edge $e \in E$ is associated with a non-negative edge cost c_e, and each vertex $v \in V$ is associated with a non-negative prize p_v (vertex v is a customer vertex if $p_v > 0$ and a non-customer vertex otherwise), the goal of the PCSTP is to find a subtree $T = (V_T, E_T)$ of G in

© Springer International Publishing AG, part of Springer Nature 2018
Y. Shi et al. (Eds.): ICCS 2018, LNCS 10861, pp. 553–560, 2018.
https://doi.org/10.1007/978-3-319-93701-4_43

which the total cost of edges in the tree plus the total prize of vertices not in the tree is minimized, i.e., [1]:

$$Minimize \ f(T) = \sum_{e \in E_T} c_e + \sum_{v \notin V_T} p_v. \tag{1}$$

Many algorithms have been proposed to solve the PCSTP, including several heuristics, such as multi-start local-search algorithm combined with perturbation [2], trans-genetic hybrid algorithm [3], divide-and-conquer meta-heuristic method [4], knowledge-guided tabu search [5], etc. Among various heuristics for solving the PCSTP, local search enjoys popularity in the literature, which commonly relies on two basic move operators, i.e., vertex addition and vertex deletion. Typically, the vertex addition (deletion) operator tries to add (delete) a vertex $v \notin V_T(v' \in V_T)$ to (from) an original minimum spanning tree (MST) and then tries to reconstruct a new MST, leading to a neighboring solution. Though these two basic move operators are generally effective, improvements could be achieved by introducing a new vertex-swap operator, which substitutes one vertex in the original MST with another one out of the original MST, and then reconstructs a new MST as the neighboring solution.

Unfortunately, although the basic idea of the vertex-swap operator is natural, it has not been widely employed in the existing PCSTP heuristics, possibly due to its unaffordable complexity: if we choose to reconstruct an MST using Kruskal's algorithm (with the aid of a Fibonacci heap) from scratch after swapping any pair of vertices, the overall time complexity for evaluating all the $O(n^2)$ possible vertex-swap moves would reach $O(n^2) \cdot O(m + n \cdot \log n)$, being unaffordable for large-sized (even mid-sized) instances.

During the 11th DIMACS Implementation Challenge, Zhang-Hua Fu (corresponding author of this paper) and Jin-Kao Hao implemented a dynamic vertex-swap operator [6], based on which they proposed a local-search heuristic [5], which won three out of the eight PCSTP competing sub-categories of the DIMACS challenge. Actually, the vertex-swap operator contributed significantly to the outstanding performance of the proposed algorithm. However, its application was limited to a number of particular PCSTP instances with uniform edge costs. In this paper, we extend the previous work in order to develop an efficient vertex-swap operator which is suitable for more general PCSTP instances, not only limited to the ones with uniform edge costs. With the aid of dynamic data structures, the time complexity for evaluating all the $O(n^2)$ possible vertex-swap moves could be reduced from $O(n^2) \cdot O(m + n \cdot \log n)$ to $O(n) \cdot O(m \cdot \log n)$. The details as well as proof of complexity and correctness are given below.

2   Method and Complexity

Given a solution $T = (V_T, E_T)$ of the PCSTP, two basic move operators (vertex-addition and vertex-deletion) are commonly used, which adds a vertex $v' \notin V_T$ to (respectively, removes a vertex $v \in V_T$ from) V_T, and then tries to reconstruct an

MST denoted by MST($V_T \cup \{v'\}$) (respectively, MST($V_T \backslash \{v\}$)). Corresponding to these two move operators, two sub-neighborhoods are defined as follows:

$$N_1(T) = MST(V_T \cup \{v'\}), \forall v' \notin V_T,$$
$$N_2(T) = MST(V_T \backslash \{v\}), \forall v \in V_T. \tag{2}$$

Based on the above two basic operators, the vertex-swap operator consists of the following two phases (outlined in Algorithm 1). The solutions are represented as dynamic data structures such as ST-trees [7,8], which takes $O(\log n)$ time to perform basic operations, i.e., searching, removing and inserting an edge.

Algorithm 1. Procedure of evaluating all the $O(n^2)$ possible vertex-swap moves.

Input: An MST $T = (V_T, E_T)$
Output: Cost difference $\Delta(v, v')$ after swapping any vertices $v \in V_T$ and $v' \notin V_T$
$T^* \leftarrow T$ //T^* always denotes the incumbent solution
for each vertex $v \in V_T$ (processed in post order) **do**
    $T^* \leftarrow Deletion(T^*, v)$ //apply the deletion phase to T^* relative to v
    $T^{Del} \leftarrow T^*$
    for each vertex $v' \notin V_T$ **do**
        $T^* \leftarrow Addition(T^*, v')$ //apply the addition phase to T^* relative to v'
        if T^* is a tree **then**
            $\Delta(v, v') \leftarrow f(T^*) - f(T)$
        else
            $\Delta(v, v') \leftarrow Null$
        end if
        $T^* \leftarrow T^{Del}$ //restore the solution before addition (only restore the changes)
    end for
    $T^* \leftarrow T$ //restore the original solution (only restore the changes)
end for

Vertex Deletion Phase: Given an original MST $T = (V_T, E_T)$, for a chosen vertex $v \in V_T$, we first remove it from T, together with the edges incident to v. This operation leads to an minimum spanning forest (MSF) consisting of a number of sub-trees (consider an MST as a special case of MSF with only one sub-tree, so as follows), where each sub-tree is an MST. After that, we try to reconnect the remaining sub-trees as far as possible. To do this, it suffices to compact each sub-tree into a super-vertex, and then run Kruskal's algorithm on the subgraph consisting of all the super-vertices along with edges between different super-vertices (if there are multiple edges between two super-vertices, just retain the one with the lowest cost). After this process, we get an MSF consisting of k ($k \geq 1$) sub-trees: $T_1, T_2, \cdots, T_k$, where each sub-tree is an MST and there is no edge between any two different sub-trees.

Complexity: As illustrated in Algorithm 1, given an original MST $T = (V_T, E_T)$, each vertex $v \in V_T$ should be deleted only once. Using the dynamic data structures slightly adapted from the vertex-elimination operator detailed in [9], which process the vertices of V_T in post order and classify the edges of E_T into horizontal edges (stored in lists) and vertical edges (stored in logarithmic-time heaps and updated dynamically), the total time complexity of this phase is bounded by $O(m \cdot \log n)$ (proven in [9]).

Vertex Addition Phase: For a chosen vertex $v' \notin V_T$, add it to each sub-tree T_i $(1 \leq i \leq k)$ of the above MSF, to form a new MST. To do this, Spira and Pan [10] showed that for one sub-tree $T_i = (V_{T_i}, E_{T_i})$, it is enough to determine the MST on sub-graph $G' = (V_{T_i} \cup \{v'\}, E_{T_i} \cup E_N(T_i, v'))$, where $E_N(T_i, v')$ denotes the collection of edges connecting v' to T_i. For each edge e incident to v', if $e \in E_N(T_i, v')$, insert e into T_i at first and then check if a cycle is formed. If so, remove the edge with the highest cost on the cycle [9]. After repeating this process for every edge e, a new MST is reconstructed (unless infeasible).

Complexity: After performing the vertex deletion phase for each vertex $v \in V_T$, we try to add every vertex out of V_T (added one by one) into the resulting MSF and then eliminate cycles. During this process, at most m edges would be inserted or removed in total. With the help of ST tree, it takes $O(\log n)$ to insert/remove one edge to/from a sub-tree [7,8]. Therefore, after deleting each vertex $v \in V_T$, the complexity of adding all the vertices is $O(m) \cdot O(\log n)$. Since at most $O(|V_T|) \leq O(n)$ vertices should be deleted, the total complexity of the vertex addition phase is bounded by $O(n) \cdot O(m \cdot \log n)$.

   In addition to above two phases, we further analyze the complexity of storage and restoration. As illustrated in Algorithm 1, we only store and restore the changed vertices and edges whenever needed, instead of the whole tree. During the whole procedure, every edge belonging to E_T is deleted twice by the **vertex deletion phase**, and at most $2|E_T|$ edges are added to connect the sub-trees. Furthermore, during the **vertex addition phase**, each edge (in total m edges) is added at most n times (at most once after deleting each vertex of V_T), and at most $m \cdot n$ edges are deleted (totally no more than added edges) to eliminate cycles. It means at most $O(m \cdot n)$ changes in total should be stored and restored. Since the complexity for storing or restoring a change is $O(1)$ and $O(\log n)$ respectively, the total complexity of these steps is $O(n) \cdot O(m \cdot \log n)$.

Summary: Given an original MST $T = (V_T, E_T)$, the total complexity for evaluating all the $O(n^2)$ vertex-swap based neighboring solutions (Algorithm 1) is bounded by $O(n) \cdot O(m \cdot \log n)$.

   Figure 1 gives an example, where sub-figure (a) is the original graph consisting of 4 customer vertices (drawn in boxes, each with a prize of 1) and 2 non-customer vertices (drawn in circles). Sub-figure (b) is an initial solution (MST) with an objective value of 6. Now we show how to swap vertex 2 with vertices 4 and 6 (similar for others). At first, we remove vertex 2 and its incident edges, leading to a MSF shown in sub-figure (c). Then we run Kruskal's algorithm to reconnect these sub-trees (regarding each sub-tree as a super-vertex), leading to the MSF shown in sub-figure (d), where vertex 1 is reconnected to vertex 5. Furthermore, to add vertex 4, we add the edge between vertex 1 and vertex 4 first, and add the edge between vertex 4 and vertex 5, which leads to a cycle. To eliminate the cycle, we remove the edge between vertex 1 and vertex 5, leading to the solution shown in sub-figure (e), which is infeasible. Similarly, for vertex 6, we at first restore the solution before addition of vertex 4, and insert in sequence three edges (between vertex 6 and vertices 1, 3, 5 respectively), then we remove the edge between vertex 1 and vertex 5 to eliminate cycle, resulting a MST with an objective value of 5 ($\Delta(2,6) = -1$), as shown in sub-figure (f).

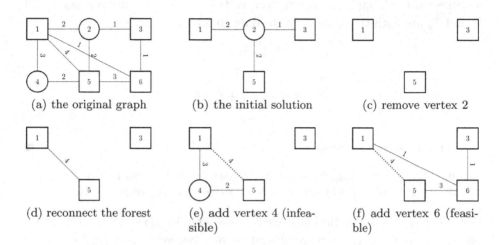

(a) the original graph   (b) the initial solution   (c) remove vertex 2

(d) reconnect the forest   (e) add vertex 4 (infeasible)   (f) add vertex 6 (feasible)

Fig. 1. Example showing how to apply the swap-vertex move operator

3 Proof of Correctness

Now we prove that using above dynamic techniques, the final solution after swapping any pair of vertices is necessarily an MST (unless being a forest).

Lemma 1. Given an MST $T = (V_T, E_T)$, performing the vertex deletion phase with respect to vertex $v \in V_T$ would lead to an minimal spanning forest (MSF), consisting of $k \geq 1$ sub-trees (denoted by $T_1, T_2, \cdots T_k$ respectively, and each is an MST).

Proof: Proven in [11].   ■

Lemma 2. For any vertex $v' \notin V_T$, if v' can be connected to sub-tree T_i ($1 \leq i \leq k$), after performing the vertex addition phase, T_i would become a new MST denoted by T_i' ($V_{T_i'} = V_{T_i} \cup \{v'\}$).

Proof. Proven in [9].   ■

For Lemmas 3 to 5, we consider two trees (unnecessarily MSTs) $T_i' = (V_{T_i'}, E_{T_i'})$ and $T_j' = (V_{T_j'}, E_{T_j'})$, which satisfy the following two conditions:

(1) v' is the only common vertex between $V_{T_i'}$ and $V_{T_j'}$, i.e., $V_{T_i'} \cap V_{T_j'} = \{v'\}$.
(2) There is no direct edge between $V_{T_i'} \backslash \{v'\}$ and $V_{T_j'} \backslash \{v'\}$.

Lemma 3. By merging T_i' and T_j', the resulting graph $G' = (V_{G'}, E_{G'}) = (V_{T_i'} \cup V_{T_j'}, E_{T_i'} \cup E_{T_j'})$ is a tree.

Proof: (1) T_i' and T_j' are both trees, thus any vertex $h \in V_{T_i'} \backslash \{v'\}$ ($g \in V_{T_j'} \backslash \{v'\}$) is connected to v', implying that any two vertices of $V_{T_i'} \cup V_{T_j'}$ are connected. (2) T_i' and T_j' are both trees, and v' is the only common vertex, so:

$$|V_{G'}| = |V_{T_i'}| + |V_{T_j'}| - 1,$$
$$|E_{G'}| = |E_{T_i'}| + |E_{T_j'}|$$
$$= |V_{T_i'}| - 1 + |V_{T_j'}| - 1$$
$$= |V_{G'}| - 1$$

Above information indicates that G' is a tree. ∎

Lemma 4. Any tree T_{any} based on vertex set $V_{T_i'} \cup V_{T_j'}$ can be exactly partitioned into two sub-trees based on vertex set $V_{T_i'}$ and $V_{T_j'}$ respectively.

Proof: (1) T_{any} is a tree, thus no cycle exists among $V_{T_i'} \cup V_{T_j'}$, so no cycle exists among $V_{T_i'}$ and $V_{T_j'}$. (2) Now we prove that any two vertices $h, g \in V_{T_i'}$ can be connected only via vertices of $V_{T_i'}$. Since T_{any} is a tree, there must be one and only one path connecting h and g. Assume another vertex $l \in V_{T_j'} \backslash \{v'\}$ appears on this path, since there is no edge between $V_{T_i'} \backslash \{v'\}$ and $V_{T_j'} \backslash \{v'\}$, v' must appear on the path from h to l, so does on the path from l to g, leading to a cycle (v' appears twice), contradicting to the statement that T_{any} is a tree, indicating $V_{T_i'}$ is internally connected. Similarly, $V_{T_j'}$ is internally connected. ∎

Lemma 5. If T_i' and T_j' are both MSTs with cost $C_{T_i'} = \sum_{e \in E_{T_i'}} c_e = C_{T_i'}^{min}$ and $C_{T_j'} = \sum_{e \in E_{T_j'}} c_e = C_{T_j'}^{min}$ respectively, the graph G' formed by merging T_i' and T_j' is also an MST with cost $C_{G'} = \sum_{e \in E_{G'}} c_e = C_{T_i'}^{min} + C_{T_j'}^{min}$.

Proof: (1) According to Lemma 3, G' is a tree with cost $C_{G'} = C_{T_i'}^{min} + C_{T_j'}^{min}$. (2) According to Lemma 4, any solution T_{any} based on vertex set $V_{T_i'} \cup V_{T_j'}$ can be exactly partitioned into two sub-trees based on vertex set $V_{T_i'}$ and $V_{T_j'}$, so its cost $C_{any} \geq C_{T_i'}^{min} + C_{T_j'}^{min} = C_{G'}$, implying that the cost of G' is minimized. ∎

Theorem 1. Given an initial MST $T = (V_T, E_T)$, after performing the procedure illustrated in Algorithm 1, the final solution after swapping a pair of vertices $v \in V_T$ and $v' \notin V_T$ is necessarily an MST (unless infeasible).

Proof: (1) According to Lemma 1, applying the vertex deletion phase respect to vertex $v \in V_T$ leads to a MSF consisting of $k \geq 1$ sub-trees $T_1, T_2, \cdots, T_k$ (each is an MST). (2) Assume $v' \notin V_T$ can be connected to every sub-tree obtained above (otherwise, the solution after swapping v with v' is a forest, being infeasible), according to Lemma 2, after applying the vertex addition phase with respect to vertex v', each sub-tree $T_i(1 \leq i \leq k)$ becomes a new MST T_i'. (3) Note that any two sub-trees T_i' and T_j' ($1 \leq i \neq j \leq k$) satisfy the two conditions mentioned before Lemma 3. According to Lemma 5, the graph formed by combining T_i' and T_j' is an MST. By induction, the whole graph formed by combining $T_1', T_2', \cdots, T_k'$ is an MST (unless infeasible). ∎

4 Conclusion

This paper develops an efficient vertex-swap operator for the prize-collecting Steiner tree problem (PCSTP), which is applicable to general PCSTP instances with varied edge costs, not only limited to instances with uniform edge costs. A series of dynamic data structures are integrated to guarantee that the total time complexity for evaluating all the $O(n^2)$ possible vertex-swap moves is bounded by $O(n) \cdot (m \cdot \log n)$, instead of the complexity $O(n^2) \cdot O(m + n \cdot \log n)$ by running Kruskal's algorithm from scratch after swapping any pair of vertices (with the aid of a Fibonacci heap). We also prove that using the developed techniques, the resulting solutions are necessarily minimum spanning trees (unless infeasible).

Acknowledgements. This paper is partially supported by the National Natural Science Foundation of China (grant No: U1613216), the State Joint Engineering Lab on Robotics and Intelligent Manufacturing, and Shenzhen Engineering Lab on Robotics and Intelligent Manufacturing, from Shenzhen Gov, China.

References

1. Johnson, D.S., Minkoff, M., Phillips, S.: The prize collecting Steiner tree problem: theory and practice. In: Proceeding of the Eleventh Annual ACM-SIAM Symposium on Discrete Algorithms, Philadelphia, USA, pp. 760–769 (2000)
2. Canuto, S.A., Resende, M.G.C., Ribeiro, C.C.: Local search with perturbations for the prize collecting Steiner tree problem in graphs. Networks **38**, 50–58 (2001)
3. Goldbarg, E.F.G., Goldbarg, M.C., Schmidt, C.C.: A hybrid transgenetic algorithm for the prize collecting Steiner tree problem. J. Univers. Comput. Sci. **14**, 2491–2511 (2008)
4. Akhmedov, M., Kwee, I., Montemanni, R.: A divide and conquer matheuristic algorithm for the prize-collecting Steiner tree problem. Comput. Oper. Res. **70**, 18–25 (2016)
5. Fu, Z.H., Hao, J.K.: Knowledge-guided local search for the prize-collecting Steiner tree problem in graphs. Knowl.-Based Syst. **128**, 78–92 (2017)
6. Fu, Z.H., Hao, J.K.: Swap-vertex based neighborhood for Steiner tree problems. Math. Progr. Comput. **9**, 297–320 (2017)
7. Sleator, D.D., Tarjan, R.E.: A data structure for dynamic trees. J. Comput. Syst. Sci. **26**, 362–391 (1983)

8. Sleator, D.D., Tarjan, R.E.: Self-adjusting binary search trees. J. ACM **32**, 652–686 (1985)
9. Uchoa, E., Werneck, R.F., Fast local search for Steiner trees in graphs. In: 2010 Proceedings of the Twelfth Workshop on Algorithm Engineering and Experiments, ALENEX. pp. 1–10. Society for Industrial and Applied Mathematics (2010)
10. Spira, P.M., Pan, A.: On finding and updating spanning trees and shortest paths. SIAM J. Comput. **4**, 375–380 (1975)
11. Das, B., Michael, C.L.: Reconstructing a minimum spanning tree after deletion of any node. Algorithmica **31**, 530–547 (2001)

Solving CSS-Sprite Packing Problem Using a Transformation to the Probabilistic Non-oriented Bin Packing Problem

Soumaya Sassi Mahfoudh$^{(\boxtimes)}$ (iD), Monia Bellalouna (iD), and Leila Horchani (iD)

Laboratory CRISTAL-GRIFT, National School of Computer Science,
University of Manouba, Manouba, Tunisia
soumaya.lsm@gmail.com, monia.bellalouna@gmail.com,
leila.horchani@gmail.com

Abstract. CSS-Sprite is a technique of regrouping small images of a web page, called tiles, into images called sprites in order to reduce network transfer time. CSS-sprite packing problem is considered as an optimization problem. We approach it as a probabilistic non-oriented two-dimensional bin packing problem $(2PBPP|R)$. Our main contribution is to allow tiles rotation while packing them in sprites. An experimental study evaluated our solution, which outperforms current solutions.

Keywords: Bin packing · Non-oriented · CSS-sprite
Image compression

1 Introduction

It was reported in [16] that 61.3% of all HTTP requests to servers are images. In fact, for each image we need a HTTP request. This action includes interaction between the web server and the user. Web server is characterized by a long delay due to the messages transporting the request through the network stack, the request treatment at the server and the location of the resources in the server cache. So to reduce web interactions, web designers resort to CSS-sprite technique, whose main idea is to regroup small images, called tiles, in pictures called, sprites.

Figure 1(a) shows a sprite and Fig. 1(b) shows a part of Cascading Style Sheet (CSS) [27] file. The size of each of the three tiles in Fig. 1(a) is 17 Kilobytes (KB). If tiles are used separately, we need to load each tile apart, which means that we are going to load 51 KB. However, if we use the sprite Fig. 1(a), we need only to load 21 KB. And this is not all, for in order to load each tile, we need a HTTP request instead of loading the sprite only once and saving it on the cache. We can imagine the amount of reduction in the case of thousands of tiles.

To our knowledge, CSS was introduced by [1] then popularized by [23]. CSS-sprite generators pack all tiles in one or multiple sprites. Yet, they are still forcing the packing of tiles without rotation.

© Springer International Publishing AG, part of Springer Nature 2018
Y. Shi et al. (Eds.): ICCS 2018, LNCS 10861, pp. 561–573, 2018.
https://doi.org/10.1007/978-3-319-93701-4_44

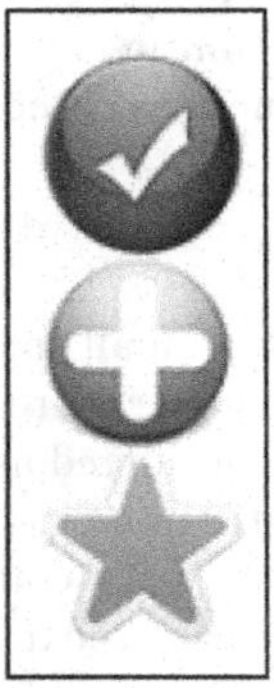

```
<style>
.image1
{background: url("sprites.png")
0  0 no-repeat;
width:204px; height:204px
}
.image2
{background: url("sprites.png")
0 -204px  no-repeat;
width:204px; height:204px
}
.image3
{background: url("sprites.png")
0 -408px 0 no-repeat;
width:204px; height:204px
}
</style>
```

(a)   Sprite.png   (b) Part of CSS file
image

Fig. 1. Example of use of CSS-sprite

Css-sprite problem is a practical problem with multiple facets involving combinatorial optimization problems, image compression and network performance. These facets will be presented in further sections. In the next section, we will present our approach which allows tiles rotation while constructing sprites. In Sect. 3, we will present in details geometric packing as well as chosen heuristics. In Sect. 4, we will describe briefly image processing. Section 5 is dedicated to outline communication performance. The last section is devoted to the evaluation of our solution.

2   Problem Formulation

Formally, CSS-sprite packing problem is defined as follows: given a set of tiles $\Gamma_n = \{t_1, \ldots, t_n\}$ in standard formats (such as JPEG, PNG and GIF). We intend to combine them into a sprite or a set of sprites S to minimize network transfer time. CSS-sprite packing is a NP-Hard problem [20]. The major problem is the large number of tiles and the presence of distorted tiles. Css-sprite packing is considered as an optimization problem of the class 2D packing problems because tiles and sprites are rectangles. Contemporary CSS-sprite generators pack tiles in one or many sprites but do not consider two important aspects:

1. Tiles rotation.
2. The presence of distorted tiles.

In fact, though it is technically possible to rotate images using CSS, tiles rotation has not been used in CSS-sprite packing so far [20], which may cause wasted space illustrated in Fig. 2. Wasted space drains memory and excessive memory usage affects browser performance. One possible approach to overcame wasted space in sprites is to model CSS-sprite problem as a two-dimensional probabilistic non-oriented bin packing problem. Following the notation [18], this problem is denoted by 2PBPP|R. 2PBPP|R is a branch of Probabilistic Combinatorial Optimization Problems (PCOP).

The idea of PCOPs comes from Jaillet [14,15]. Among several motivations PCOPs were introduced to formulate and analyze models which are more appropriate for real world problems. PBPP was first studied in [5].

2PBPP|R is essentially a 2BPP|R where one is asked to pack a varying number of rectangular items: where we assume that a list L_n of n rectangular items is given, and that some items disappear from L_n. The subset of present items is packed without overlapping and with the possibility of rotation by 90° into the minimum number of identical bins. Table 1 represents the similarities between 2PBPP|R and CSS-sprite problem.

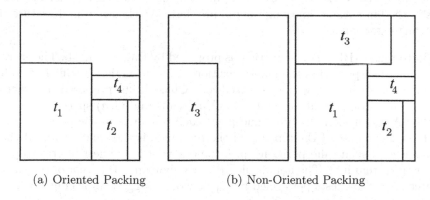

(a) Oriented Packing   (b) Non-Oriented Packing

Fig. 2. Example of wasted space

Solving CSS-sprite problem, is a tantamount to solving an instance of 2PPBP|R. The possible optimization methods to solve bin-packing problems are exact methods, heuristics, meta-heuristics. Even though, it is guaranteed that exact methods can find an optimal solution, the difficulty of obtaining an optimal solution increases drastically if the problem size increases, due to the fact that is an NP-hard problem.

Table 1. Analogy between 2PPBP|R and CSS-sprite technique

$2PBPP|R$	CSS-sprite
L_n: set of rectangular items	Γ_n: set of tiles
Bins with same capacity	Sprites with same size
Rectangular items	Tiloε
Items rotation $90°$	Tiles rotation $90°$
Absent items	Distorted, unused tiles
Minimize the average number of bins	Better fulfil sprites

3   Geometric Packing

Css-sprite packing was firstly solved manually [23] then multiple solutions were proposed. Moreover, a great number of sprite generators have been proposed. A recent survey of existing solutions were proposed by [20]. But we are only interested in those which exploit 2D packing heuristics. Table 2 groups this category of solutions identified by short name and web address. In fact, in CSS-sprite packing problem, decisions of choosing the position of tiles need to be made without full knowledge of the rest of the input. We have an incrementally appearing input, where the input needs to be processed in the order in which it comes. The input is only completely known at the end of the problem.

So, to solve this situation we consider some fast online algorithms. Such algorithms receive the tiles one at a time and need to decide where to place tiles in the bin without knowing the full problem. We choose from literature the following algorithms:

1. Bottom Left (BL): The heuristic was proposed by Baker et al. [4]. The current item is then packed in the lowest position of open bin, left justified; if no bin can allocate it, a new one is initialized. Chazelle [6] proposed an efficient implementation of this algorithm in $\mathcal{O}(n^2)$ time and $\mathcal{O}(n)$ space.
2. Best Area Fit (BAF): Orient and place each rectangle to the position where the y-coordinate of the top side of the rectangle is the smallest and if there are several such valid positions, pick the one that is smallest in area to place the next item into. The item is placed in the bottom left corner of the chosen area. Based on tests performed by [2], it would suggest an average of $\mathcal{O}(n^3)$ time and $\mathcal{O}(n)$ space.
3. Item Maxim Area (IMA): This heuristic was proposed by [9] as an extension of the Best-Fit heuristic for 2D packing problems. At each step of item packing, a choice of the couple (item to be packed, receiving area) is made.
   This choice is based on the criteria which takes into account the characteristics of the item and those of the candidate area. Given an item $a_i(w_i, h_i)$ in a given orientation and an area ma that can contain it, let dx_i and dy_i (respectively w_{ma} and h_{ma}) be the projections of the edges of a_i (respectively ma) on the x- and y-axis. Given four real numbers: q_1, q_2, q_3 and q_4 such that $0 \le q_k \le 1; k = 1, \ldots, 4$ and $\sum_{k=1,\ldots,4} q_k = 1$, the criteria can be written as follows:

Table 2. Sprite generators using 2D packing algorithms

	Short name	Output format	2D packing heuristic	Web address
A	Glue	PNG PNG8	Binary-tree [11]	http://glue.readthedocs.io/en/latest/
	Zerosprites	PNG PNG8	Korf's algorithm [13] B*-tree [8]	http://zerosprites.com/
	Pypack	PNG	Extension of binary-tree [11]	http://jwezorek.com/2013/01/sprite-packing-in-python/
	JSGsf	PNG	Binary-tree [11]	https://github.com/jakesgordon/sprite-factory/
	Isaccc	PNG	Rectangle packing [10]	https://www.codeproject.com/Articles/140251/Image-Sprites-and-CSS-Classes-Creator
	Simpreal	PNG JPEG GIF BMP	Colum or row mode	http://simpreal.org.ua/csssprites/#!source
B	Codepen	PNG	Tiles sorting by area width or height	https://codepen.io/JFarrow/full/scxKd
	Csgencom	PNG JPEG GIF	Not specified	http://css.spritegen.com/
	Cdplxsg	PNG	Tree [7,21]	http://spritegenerator.codeplex.com/
	Txturepk	Many formats	MaxRects [3] Bottom-left [4]	https://www.codeandweb.com/texturepacker/documentation
	Stitches	PNG	Not specified	http://draeton.github.io/stitches/
	Sstool	PNG	Not specified	https://www.leshylabs.com/apps/sstool/
	Canvas	PNG	Korf's algorithm [17]	https://timdream.org/canvas-css-sprites/en/
	Shoebox	PNG	Not specified	https://renderhjs.net/shoebox/
	Retina	PNG JPEG GIF	Colum row diagonal mode	http://www.retinaspritegenerator.com/
	Csspg	PNG JPEG GIF	Binary-tree top-down left-right	https://www.toptal.com/developers/css/sprite-generator
	Spritepack	PNG8 PNG32 PNG24 JPEG GIF	FFDH [19] BFDH [19] Bottom-left [4]	http://www.cs.put.poznan.pl/mdrozdowski/spritepack/

$$O(a_i, ma) = q_1 \frac{w_i h_i}{w_{ma} h_{ma}} + q_2 \frac{dx_i}{w_{ma}} + q_3 \frac{dy_i}{h_{ma}} + q_4 \frac{w_i^2 + h_i^2}{w_{ma}^2 + h_{ma}^2}$$

The couple (item to be packed, maximal area that will accommodate it) is the one that maximizes the criteria cited above. The choice of IMA was based on the elaborated experiments [9], which conclude that IMA dominates several heuristics from literature however theoretically the complexity of this heuristic is $\mathcal{O}(n^5)$.

4   Image Processing

Processing images is a primordial step in CSS-sprite packing whose purpose is to reduce tiles sizes, and so implicitly decrease transfer time and sprites size. It involves tiles transformation and tiles compression.

1. Tiles Transformation: Tiles are images in standard image formats as JPEG, PNG and GIF. All GIFs tiles were converted to PNG, which reduces image size [24]. JPEG tiles were transformed to PNG if PNG format is smaller than JPEG image.
2. Tiles compression: Presenting image compression techniques and standards is beyond the scope of this paper. But we recommend readers to take a look at several survey papers [22,25] to understand the concept of image compression techniques and standards. In fact, no method can be considered good for all images, nor are all methods equally good for a particular type of image. Compression methods perform in different manner in accordance with different kinds of images.
   Recently, Google Incorporation proposed a compression tool named Zopfli [3]. Zopfli algorithm is based on Huffman coding. It was proved that Zopfli yields the best compression ratio [12].
   As we mentioned before, images often represent the majority of bytes uploaded to a web page. Therefore, image optimization is essential for saving bytes and the most important performance improvement. For better results, sprites were post-compressed for the minimum size. This means that sprites obtained after packing tiles are further compressed for the minimum size.

5   Communication Performance

Obviously, we consider that measuring the quality of sprites is equivalent to determining the network transfer time. However, certain factors make it hardly possible. In fact, transfer time is unpredictable and non-deterministic. So, it remains impossible to use detailed methods of packet level simulation to calculate sprites transfer time since those methods are quite time consumers [20]. Thus, [26] proposed to use flow models to evaluate the quality of sprites.

We exploited the flow model proposed by [20] which was validated in real settings. Table 3 presents the parameters of our model:

Table 3. Model parameters

Parameter	Definition
S	Set of sprites
m	Number of sprites
f_i	Size of sprite S_i in bytes
F	Size of set S
c	Number of communication channels
$B(c)$	Accumulated bandwidth of c
L	Communication latency (startup time)
$T(S,c)$	Transfer time as a function of S and c

The transfer time of a set of sprites over c concurrent channels is modeled by the following formula [20]:

$$T(S,c) = max\left\{\frac{1}{c}\sum_{i=1}^{m}(L + \frac{f_i}{B(c)/c}), \max_{\{i=1..m\}}\{L + \frac{f_i}{B(c)/c})\}\right\} \qquad (1)$$

Since the web site performance is not only affected by the server but also by the user side such as browser and computer performance, so performance parameters should be measured on their real populations.

6 Computational Results

In this section, we compare our approach to solve CSS-sprite packing problem, named SpriteRotate, with alternative sprite generators. The main contribution of our approach is to rotate tiles by 90° while constructing sprites.

SpriteRotate has been implemented in Java using Eclipse Jee Neon IDE. All tests were performed on typical PC with i5-5200U CPU (2.2 GHz), 12 GB of RAM and Windows 8.

Based on experiments through real visitors [20], transfer time model parameters have been set to $L = 352$ ms, $c = 3$ and $B(c) = 631$ Kilobit (Kb)/s. For image compression, Zoplfli compression level has been set to the strongest level 9.

Generated sprites by SpriteRotate include the position of tile in the sprite, which sprite contains a considered tile and whether the output is one sprite or multiple sprites. Besides, we specify if the tile in the sprite is rotated or not to facilitate the extraction of tiles from CSS file. SpriteRotate offers two output formats: PNG and JPEG.

Thereafter, we applied the following procedure. In the first experiments, we considered only a set of sprite generators which construct one sprite. Since SpriteRotate builds a number of sprites, we modified SpriteRotate code to generate a single sprite. In fact, group A of solutions in Table 2 were excluded from the evaluation because of: failure to work properly or dead applications. Only solutions from group B were chosen for comparison.

In the second series of tests, SpriteRotate has been compared to Spritepack [20], which is a recent solution which generates multiple sprites. The comparison focused on the sizes of the sprites and the objective function: transfer time.

In order to evaluate SpriteRotate, we considered 10 tiles sets from test sets collected in [20]. The tiles are skins and other reusable GUI elements of popular open source web applications. But unfortunately most of them are too simple, consisting of few tiles with identical shape and tiles format. Nevertheless, this tiles test sets allow evaluating our approach in realistic settings. The instances in Table 4 are chosen to represent a spectrum of possible situations: from Joomla Busines14a tile set of size smaller than 20 KB (29 tiles) to Vbulletin Darkness with 1010 tiles and over 11.2 Megabytes (MB) total size.

The results of the first evaluations are collected in Tables 5 and 6, which show the sprite size f_i and resulted transfer time $T(S, c)$ of SpriteRotate compared to alternative generators. Each column represents results for each generator. Column labeled "Min" and "Max" represents respectively the minimum and the maximum gain rate obtained by SpriteRotate relatively to alternative generators. Row "Average" is the average size of the sprite through all test instances. An empty cell means that generators has not been able to generate a sprite. It is clear that SpriteRotate outperformed the alternative generators in sprite size and transfer time. Codepen generator considered as the second generator, multiplied on average sprite size by a factor 4 compared to SpriteRotate's (17 in worst case). Similarly, transfer time was multiplied on average by a factor of 5 compared to the SpriteRotate's objective function (and 28 in the worst case). In absolute terms, SpriteRotate decreases sprite size from 16 KB to 279 KB. As consequence, a very considerable gain was obtained. SpriteRotate succeed to reduce transfer time from 370 ms up to 71 s.

In the case of Vbulletin Darkness instance (1010 tiles), TexturePacker and SpriteRotate were only able to give result. In fact, SpriteRotate lowers sprite size by 800 KB and transfer time by 30 s.

Through computational results, SpriteRotate was able to generate sprites to all tiles instances with up to 1010 tiles. SpriteRotate produced a transfer time of seconds compared to few tens for considered generators. This is a very substantial improvement for the objective function (1). Overall, although our solution was not designed to generate one sprite with the smallest file size, it still outperforms competitors.

In the second round of comparison, SpriteRotate has been evaluated to Spritepack. The comparison also focused on sprites size and transfer time. Due to lack of results related to Spritepack, the comparison was only performed on 5 tiles sets. The results are collected in Table 7.

For small tiles instances with up to 32 tiles, SpriteRotate was able to reduce sprites size by a factor of 1.2 to 4. In absolute terms, the reduction was from 1.5 KB to 18 KB. As a consequence, transfer time $T(S, c)$ was reduced from 60 ms to 720 ms.

For moderate instance Oscommerce Pets (162 tiles), the improvement of transfer time, by 1.82 s, was driven by reduce in sprites size by 47 KB.

To conclude this experimental comparison, the proposed approach, SpriteRotate, focused on solving CSS-sprite packing using a transformation to a probabilistic non oriented bin-packing problem. The main contribution was allowing tiles rotation. SpriteRotate was compared to 9 alternative generators on tiles instances, of popular open source web applications, with up to 1010 tiles. Our experimental study has demonstrated that SpriteRotate outperformed the alternative generators.

Though SpriteRotate is not necessarily constructing optimum sprites because we are dealing with NP-Hard problem. Thus, we can conclude that tiles rotation

Table 4. Test instances

Instance name	Number of tiles	Tiles classification			URL
		PNG	GIF	JPEG	
Magneto Hardwood	9	3	5	1	http://www.themesbase.com/Magento-Skins/download/?dl=7396
Sprite Creator	26	26	0	0	http://www.codeproject.com/KB/HTML/SpritesAndCSSCreator/SpriteCreator_v2.0.zip
Joomla Busines14a	29	28	0	1	http://www.joomla24.com/Joomla_2.5_%10_1.7_Templates/Joomla_2.5_%10_1.7_Templates/Business_14.html
Mojoportal Thehobbit	32	28	3	1	https://www.mojoportal.com
Squirrel Mail_outlook	73	16	57	0	https://sourceforge.net/projects/squirreloutlook/
Myadmin Cleanstrap	198	196	2	0	https://github.com/phpmyadmin/themes/tree/master/cleanstrap/img
Prestashop Matrice	212	52	139	21	http://dgcraft.free.fr/blog/index.php/category/themes-prestashop/
Smf Classic	317	62	254	1	http://www.themesbase.com/SMF-Themes/7339_Classic.html
Vbulletin Darkness	1010	646	351	13	https://www.bluepearl-skins.com/forums/topic/5544-darkness-free-vbulletin-skins/

Table 5. Comparison of SpriteRotate to alternative generators on size of sprite f_i(Kb)

	Codepen	Csgencom	Cdplxsg	Stitches	Sstool	Retina	Shoebox	Txturepk	Sprite Rotate	Min	Max
Magneto Hardwood	296	738	568	23	782	831	506	746	16	5	815
Sprite Creator	113	43	437	394	473	427	453	434	15	28	457
Joomla Busines14a	33	24	15	15	23	24	15	21	5	10	28
Mojoportal Thehobbit	59	149	159	197	192	205	146	160	7	52	190
Squirrelmail Outlook	66	102	89	121	105	114	62	98	50	16	71
Oscommerce Pets	273	1601	1612	1680	1711	1903	1627	608	35	238	1868
Myadmin Cleanstrap	47	63	55	86	70	82	56	45	23	22	41
Prestashop Matrice	62	138	136	165	144	-	123	133	51	112	515
Smf Classic	107	-	220	265	239	-	133	205	25	82	240
Vbulletin Darkness	-	-	-	-	-	-	-	839	39	800	800
Average	132	357.2	365	326	415	480	346	348.35	26.96	136	502

Table 6. Comparison of SpriteRotate to alternative generators on objective function $T(S, c)(s)$

	Codepen	Csgencom	Cdplxsg	Stitches	Sstool	Retina	Shoebox	TSxturepk	Sprite Rotate	Min	Max
Magneto Hardwood	11.47	28.09	21.70	12.16	30.06	31.93	19.58	28.81	0.98	10.49	38.05
Sprite Creator	4.59	1.96	16.77	15.16	18.32	16.57	17.56	16.84	0.93	1.03	17.39
Joomla Busines14a	15.92	1.25	9.15	1.11	1.22	1.27	0.92	1.17	0.55	0.37	15.37
Mojoportal Thehobbit	4.69	5.99	6.32	7.75	7.56	8.14	5.9	6.43	0.61	4.08	7.53
Squirrel Mail	2.83	4.18	3.69	4.95	4.34	4.68	2.71	4.08	2.25	0.46	2.7
Oscommerce Pets	10.6	60.53	60.94	64.12	65.37	72.66	62.17	23.45	0.73	9.87	71.93
Myadmin Cleanstrap	2.11	2.72	2.41	3.62	3.01	3.47	2.49	2.06	1.25	0.81	2.22
Prestashop Matrice	2.68	5.53	5.11	6.62	5.82	-	5.02	5.4	2.29	0.57	7.98
Smf Classic	4.37	-	8.62	10.31	9.33	-	5.40	8.14	1.3	3.07	9.16
Vbulletin Darkness	-	-	-	-	-	-	-	32.23	1.8	30.43	30.43

Table 7. Comparison of SpriteRotate to Spritepack on size of sprites $(F(Kb))$ and objective function $(T(S,c)(s))$

	Spritepack			SpriteRotate		
	m	F	$T(S,c)$	m	F	$T(S,c)$
Magneto Hardwood	3	36	1.7	1	16.7	0.98
Squirrelmail Outlook	1	8.71	0.68	1	7.31	0.62
Joomla Busines14a	1	23.76	1.25	1	5.44	0.55
Mojoportal Thehobbit	7	19.31	1.08	4	7.38	0.63
Oscommerce Pets	6	84	3.54	6	36.05	1.72

have a great influence on reducing sprites size and the objective function: transfer time.

This section will conclude with some general remarks about SpriteRotate. The solution was able to provide sprites for all test sets in practically acceptable time. SpriteRotate processing time is split between image processing, geometric packing and postprocessing. The three stages consumed in average 70%, 20%, 10% of total processing time, respectively. Thus, image compression is the most time-consuming step.

Concerning image compression, we detected that for tiles with sizes lower than 1 Kb, there was not a modification in tiles sizes. As matter of fact, image compression was efficient for tiles with sizes larger than 3 Kb.

SpriteRotate is considered as a research tool and not an industrial one. In fact, image compression techniques and packing algorithms are evolving so other heuristics and image compression standards can be tried as well as integrating further input formats.

7   Conclusion

In this paper, we have approached the CSS-sprite packing problem into two-dimensional non-oriented probabilistic bin packing problem (2PBPP|R). We followed the relation between CSS-sprite packing and 2PBPP|R and proposed our approach which allowed for the first time to rotate tiles while generating sprites. Furthermore, in order to manage efficiently the big number of tiles, it was necessary to exploit 2PBPP heuristics. Our experiments on real-world sets validated our approach, which performs better than alternative approaches.

Acknowledgments. The first author extends her sincere thanks to Seifeddine Kaoeuch for his help.

References

1. Fast rollovers without preload. http://wellstyled.com/css-nopreload-rollovers. html. Accessed 29 September 2017
2. A thousand ways to pack the bin - a practical approach to two-dimensional rectangle bin packing. http://clb.demon.fi/files/RectangleBinPack.pdf Accessed 10 July 2017
3. Alakuijala, J., Vandevenne, L.: Data compression using Zopfli.Google inc. (2013). https://github.com/google/zopfli. Accessed 08 January 2017
4. Baker, B., Coffman, E., Rivest, R.: Orthogonal packing in two dimensions. SIAM J. Comput. **9**(4), 846–855 (1980)
5. Bellalouna, M.: Problèmes d'optimisation combinatoires probabilistes. Ph.D. thesis, Ecole Nationale des Ponts et Chaussees (1993)
6. Chazelle, B.: The bottom-left bin-packing heuristic: an efficient implementation. IEEE Trans. Comput. **32**(8), 697–707 (1983)
7. Chen, P.H., Chen, Y., Goel, M., Mang, F.: Approximation of two-dimensional rectangle packing. Technical report (1999)
8. Chen, T.C., Chang, Y.W.: Modern floorplanning based on b*-tree and fast simulated annealing. Trans. Comp.-Aided Des. Integr. Circ. Sys. **25**, 637–650 (2006)
9. El Hayek, J., Moukrim, A., Nègre, S.: New resolution algorithm and pretreatments for the two-dimensional bin-packing problem. Comput. Oper. Res, **35**(10), 3184–3201 (2008)
10. Framework, N.: Rectangle packing. http://nuclexframework.codeplex.com/. Accessed 25 January 2018
11. Gordon, J.: Binary tree bin packing algorithm. https://codeincomplete.com/posts/bin-packing/. Accessed 08 September 2017
12. Habib, A., Rahman, M.S.: Balancing decoding speed and memory usage for Huffman codes using quaternary tree. Appl. Inform. **4**(1), 39–55 (2017)
13. Huang, E., Korf, R.: Optimal rectangle packing: an absolute placement approach. J. Artif. Intell. Res. **46**, 47–87 (2013)
14. Jaillet, P.: A priori solution of a traveling salesman problem in which a random subset of the customers are visited. Oper. Res. **36**(6), 929–936 (1988)
15. Jaillet, P.: Analysis of probabilistic combinatorial optimization problems in euclidean spaces. Math. Oper. Res. **18**(1), 51–70 (1993)
16. Jeon, M., Kim, Y., Hwang, J., Lee, J., Seo, E.: Workload characterization and performance implications of large-scale blog servers. ACM Trans. Web (TWEB) **6**, 16 (2012)
17. Korf, R.: Optimal rectangle packing: new results. In. Proceedings of the Thirteenth International Conference on Automated Planning and Scheduling, ICAPS 2004, pp. 142–149 (2004)
18. Lodi, A.: Algorithms for two-dimensional bin packing and assignment problems. Ph.D. thesis, Université de bologne (1999)
19. Lodi, A., Martello, S., Vigo, D.: Recent advances on two-dimensional bin packing problems. Discret. Appl. Math. **123**(1–3), 379–396 (2002)
20. Marszalkowski, J., Mizgajski, J., Mokwa, D., Drozdowski, M.: Analysis and solution of CSS-sprite packing problem. ACM Trans. Web (TWEB) **10**(1), 283–294 (2015)
21. Murata, H., Fujiyoshi, K., Nakatake, S., Kajitani, Y.: Rectangle-packing-based module placement. In: Kuehlmann, A. (ed.) The Best of ICCAD, pp. 535–548. Springer, Boston (2003). https://doi.org/10.1007/978-1-4615-0292-0_42

22. Rehman, M., Sharif, M., Raza, M.: Image compression: a survey. Res. J. Appl. Sci. Eng. Technol. **7**(4), 656–672 (2014)
23. Shea, D.: CSS sprites: image slicings kiss of death. A List Apart (2013)
24. Stefanov, S.: Image optimization, part 3 : four steps to file size reduction. http://yuiblog.com/blog/2008/11/14/imageopt-3/. Accessed 29 Jan 2017
25. Taubman, D., Marcellin, M.: JPEG2000 Image Compression Fundamentals, Standards and Practice: Image Compression Fundamentals, Standards and Practice, vol. 642. Springer Science & Business Media, Boston (2012). https://doi.org/10.1007/978-1-4615-0799-4
26. Velho, P., Schnorr, M., Casanova, H., Legrand, A.: On the validity of flow-level TCP network models for grid and cloud simulations. ACM Trans. Model. Comput. Simul. (TOMACS) **23**, 23 (2013)
27. Wium Lie, H., Bos, B.: Cascading style sheets. World Wide Web J. **2**, 75–123 (1997)

Optimization of Resources Selection for Jobs Scheduling in Heterogeneous Distributed Computing Environments

Victor Toporkov$^{(\boxtimes)}$ and Dmitry Yemelyanov

National Research University "Moscow Power Engineering Institute",
ul. Krasnokazarmennaya, 14, Moscow 111250, Russia
{ToporkovVV,YemelyanovDM}@mpei.ru

Abstract. In this work, we introduce slot selection and co-allocation algorithms for parallel jobs in distributed computing with non-dedicated and heterogeneous resources (clusters, CPU nodes equipped with multicore processors, networks etc.). A single slot is a time span that can be assigned to a task, which is a part of a parallel job. The job launch requires a co-allocation of a specified number of slots starting and finishing synchronously. The challenge is that slots associated with different heterogeneous resources of distributed computing environments may have arbitrary start and finish points, different pricing policies. Some existing algorithms assign a job to the first set of slots matching the resource request without any optimization (the first fit type), while other algorithms are based on an exhaustive search. In this paper, algorithms for effective slot selection are studied and compared with known approaches. The novelty of the proposed approach is in a general algorithm selecting a set of slots efficient according to the specified criterion.

Keywords: Distributed computing · Economic scheduling
Resource management · Slot · Job · Allocation · Optimization

1 Introduction

Modern high-performance distributed computing systems (HPCS), including Grid, cloud and hybrid infrastructures provide access to large amounts of resources [1,2]. These resources are typically required to execute parallel jobs submitted by HPCS users and include computing nodes, data storages, network channels, software, etc. The actual requirements for resources amount and types needed to execute a job are defined in resource requests and specifications provided by users.

This work was partially supported by the Council on Grants of the President of the Russian Federation for State Support of Young Scientists (YPhD-2297.2017.9), RFBR (grants 18-07-00456 and 18-07-00534) and by the Ministry on Education and Science of the Russian Federation (project no. 2.9606.2017/8.9).

© Springer International Publishing AG, part of Springer Nature 2018
Y. Shi et al. (Eds.): ICCS 2018, LNCS 10861, pp. 574–583, 2018.
https://doi.org/10.1007/978-3-319-93701-4_45

HPCS organization and support bring certain economical expenses: purchase and installation of machinery equipment, power supplies, user support, etc. As a rule, HPCS users and service providers interact in economic terms and the resources are provided for a certain payment. Thus, as total user job execution budget is usually limited, we elaborate an actual task to optimize suitable resources selection in accordance with a job specification and a restriction to a total resources cost.

Economic mechanisms are used to solve problems like resource management and scheduling of jobs in a transparent and efficient way in distributed environments such as cloud computing and utility Grid. In [3], we elaborate a hierarchical model of resource management system which is functioning within a VO. Resource management is implemented using a structure consisting of a metascheduler and subordinate job schedulers that interact with batch job processing systems. The significant and important feature for approach proposed in [3] as well as for well-known scheduling solutions for distributed environments such as Grids [1,2,4–6], is the fact that the scheduling strategy is formed on a basis of efficiency criteria. The metascheduler [3,6] implements the economic policy of a VO based on local resource schedules. The schedules are defined as sets of slots coming from resource managers or schedulers in the resource domains, i.e. time intervals when individual nodes are available to perform a part of a parallel job. In order to implement such scheduling schemes and policies, first of all, one needs an algorithm for finding sets of simultaneously available slots required for each job execution. Further we shall call such set of simultaneously available slots with the same start and finish times as execution *window*.

In this paper we study algorithms for optimal or near-optimal resources selection by a given criterion with the restriction to a total cost. Additionally we consider solutions to overcome complications with different resources types, their heterogeneity, pre-known reservations and maintenance works.

2   Related Works

The scheduling problem in Grid is NP-hard due to its combinatorial nature and many heuristic-based solutions have been proposed. In [5] heuristic algorithms for slot selection, based on user-defined utility functions, are introduced. NWIRE system [5] performs a slot window allocation based on the user defined efficiency criterion under the maximum total execution cost constraint. However, the optimization occurs only on the stage of the best found offer selection. First fit slot selection algorithms (backtrack [7] and NorduGrid [8] approaches) assign any job to the first set of slots matching the resource request conditions, while other algorithms use an exhaustive search [2,9,10] and some of them are based on a linear integer programming (IP) [2,9] or mixed-integer programming (MIP) model [10]. Moab scheduler [11] implements the backfilling algorithm and during a slot window search does not take into account any additive constraints such as the minimum required storage volume or the maximum allowed total allocation cost. Moreover, it does not support environments with non-dedicated resources.

Modern distributed and cloud computing simulators GridSim and CloudSim [12,13] provide tools for jobs execution and co-allocation of simultaneously available computing resources. Base simulator distributions perform First Fit allocation algorithms without any specific optimization. CloudAuction extension [13] of CloudSim implements a double auction to distribute datacenters' resources between a job flow with a fair allocation policy. All these algorithms consider price constraints on individual nodes and not on a total window allocation cost. However, as we showed in [14], algorithms with a total cost constraint are able to perform the search among a wider set of resources and increase the overall scheduling efficiency.

GrAS [15] is a Grid job-flow management system built over Maui scheduler [11]. In order to co-allocate already partially utilized and reserved resources GrAS operates on a set of slots preliminary sorted by their start time. Resources co-allocation algorithm retrieves a set of simultaneously available slots (a window) with the same start and finish times even in heterogeneous environments. However the algorithm stops after finding the first suitable window and, thus, doesn't perform any optimization except for window start time minimization.

Algorithm [16] performs job's response and finish time minimization and doesn't take into account constraint on a total allocation budget. [17] performs window search on a list of slots sorted by their start time, implements algorithms for window shifting and finish time minimization, doesn't support other optimization criteria and the overall job execution cost constraint.

AEP algorithm [18] performs window search with constraint on a total resources allocation cost, implements optimization according to a number of criteria, but doesn't support a general case optimization. Besides AEP doesn't guarantee same finish time for the window slots in heterogeneous environments and, thus, has limited practical applicability.

In this paper, we propose algorithms for effective slot selection based on user defined criteria that feature linear complexity on the number of the available slots during the job batch scheduling cycle. The novelty of the proposed approach consists in allocating a set of simultaneously available slots. The paper is organized as follows. Section 3 introduces a general scheme for searching slot sets efficient by the specified criterion. Then several implementations are proposed and considered. Section 4 contains simulation results for comparison of proposed and known algorithms. Section 5 summarizes the paper and describes further research topics.

3   Resource Selection Algorithm

3.1   Problem Statement

We consider a set R of heterogeneous computing nodes with different performance p_i and price c_i characteristics. Each node has a local utilization schedule known in advance for a considered scheduling horizon time L. A node may be turned off or on by the provider, transfered to a maintenance state, reserved to perform computational jobs. Thus, it's convenient to represent all available resources as a set of slots. Each slot corresponds to one computing node on which it's allocated and may be characterized by its performance and price.

In order to execute a parallel job one needs to allocate the specified number of simultaneously idle nodes ensuring user requirements from the resource request. The resource request specifies number n of nodes required simultaneously, their minimum applicable performance p, job's computational volume V and a maximum available resources allocation budget C. The required window length is defined based on a slot with the minimum performance. For example, if a window consists of slots with performances $p \in \{p_i, p_j\}$ and $p_i < p_j$, then we need to allocate all the slots for a time $T = \frac{V}{p_i}$. In this way V really defines a computational volume for each single node subtask. Common start and finish times ensure the possibility of inter-node communications during the whole job execution. The total cost of a window allocation is then calculated as $C_W = \sum_{i=1}^{n} T * c_i$.

These parameters constitute a formal generalization for resource requests common among distributed computing systems and simulators.

Additionally we introduce criterion f as a user preference for the particular job execution during the scheduling horizon L. f can take a form of any additive function and vary from a simple window start time or cost minimization to a general independent parameter maximization with the restriction to a total resources allocation cost C. As an example, one may want to allocate suitable resources with the maximum possible total data storage available before the specified deadline.

3.2   General Window Search Procedure

For a general window search procedure for the problem statement presented in Sect. 3.1, we combined core ideas and solutions from algorithm AEP [18] and systems [15,17]. Both related algorithms perform window search procedure based on a list of slots retrieved from a heterogeneous computing environment.

Following is the general square window search algorithm. It allocates a set of n simultaneously available slots with performance $p_i > p$, for a time, required to compute V instructions on each node, with a restriction C on a total allocation cost and performs optimization according to criterion f. It takes a list of available slots ordered by their non-decreasing start time as input.

1. Initializing variables for the best criterion value and corresponding best window: $f_{max} = 0$, $W_{max} = \{\}$.
2. From the slots available we select different groups by node performance p_i. For example, group P_k contains resources allocated on nodes with performance $p_i \geq P_k$. Thus, one slot may be included in several groups.
3. Next is a cycle for all retrieved groups P_i starting from the max performance P_{max}. All the sub-items represent a cycle body.
   (a) The resources reservation time required to compute V instructions on a node with performance P_i is $T_i = \frac{V}{P_i}$.
   (b) Initializing variable for a window candidates list $S_W = \{\}$.

(c) Next is a cycle for all slots s_i in group P_i starting from the slot with the minimum start time. The slots of group P_i should be ordered by their non-decreasing start time. All the sub-items represent a cycle body.

    i. If slot s_i doesn't satisfy user requirements (hardware, software, etc.) then continue to the next slot (3c).

    ii. If slot length $l(s_i) < T_i$ then continue to the next slot (3c).

    iii. Set the new window start time $W_i.start = s_i.start$.

    iv. Add slot s_i to the current window slot list S_W.

    v. Next a cycle to check all slots s_j inside S_W.

        A. If there are no slots in S_W with performance $P(s_j) == P_i$ then continue to the next slot (3c), as current slots combination in S_W was already considered for previous group P_{i-1}.

        B. If $W_i.start + T_i > s_j.end$ then remove slot s_j from S_W as it can't consist in a window with the new start time $W_i.start$.

    vi. If S_W size is greater or equal to n, then allocate from S_W a window W_i (a subset of n slots with start time $W_i.start$ and length T_i) with a maximum criterion value f_i and a total cost $C_i < C$. If $f_i > f_{max}$ then reassign $f_{max} = f_i$ and $W_{max} = W_i$.

4. End of algorithm. At the output variable W_{max} contains the resulting window with the maximum criterion value f_{max}.

In this algorithm a list of slots-candidates S_W *moves* through the ordered list of all slots from each performance group P_i. During each iteration, when a new slot is added to the list (step 3(c)vi), any combination of n slots from S_W can form a suitable window if satisfy a restriction on the maximum allocation cost. In (3(c)vi) an optimal subset of n slots is allocated from S_W according to the criterion f with a restriction on the total cost. If this intermediate window W_i provides better criterion value compared to the currently best value ($f_i > f_{max}$) then we reassign variables W_{max} and f_{max} with new values. In this a way the presented algorithm is similar to the maximum value search in an array of f_i values.

3.3 Optimal Slot Subset Allocation

Let us discuss in more details the procedure which allocates an optimal (according to a criterion f) subset of n slots out of S_W list (algorithm step 3(c)vi).

For some particular criterion functions f a straightforward subset allocation solution may be offered. For example for a window finish time minimization it is reasonable to return at step 3(c)vi the first n *cheapest* slots of S_W provided that they satisfy the restriction on the total cost. These n slots (as any other n slots from S_W at the current step) will provide $W_i.finish = W_i.start + T_i$, so we need to set $f_i = -(W_i.start + T_i)$ to minimize the finish time. And at the end of the algorithm variable W_{max} will represent a window with the minimum possible finish time $W_{max}.finish = -f_{max}$.

The same logic applies for a number of other important criteria, including window start time, finish time and a total cost minimization.

However in a general case we should consider a subset allocation problem with some additive criterion: $Z = \sum_{i=1}^{n} c_z(s_i)$, where $c_z(s_i) = z_i$ is a target optimization characteristic value provided by a single slot s_i of W_i.

In this way we can state the following problem of an optimal n - size window subset allocation out of m slots stored in S_W:

$$Z = x_1 z_1 + x_2 z_2 + \cdots + x_m z_m, \tag{1}$$

with the following restrictions:

$$x_1 c_1 + x_2 c_2 + \cdots + x_m c_m \leq C$$

$$x_1 + x_2 + \cdots + x_m = n$$

$$x_i \in \{0, 1\}, i = 1, \ldots, m,$$

where z_i is a target characteristic value provided by slot s_i, c_i is total cost required to allocate slot s_i for a time T_i, x_i - is a decision variable determining whether to allocate slot s_i ($x_i = 1$) or not ($x_i = 0$) for a window W_i.

This problem relates to the class of integer linear programming problems, which imposes obvious limitations on the practical methods to solve it. However we used 0–1 knapsack problem as a base for our implementation. Indeed, the classical 0–1 knapsack problem with a total weight C and items-slots with weights c_i and values z_i have the same formal model (1) except for extra restriction on the number of items required: $x_1 + x_2 + \cdots + x_m = n$. To take this into account we implemented the following dynamic programming recurrent scheme:

$$f_i(C_j, n_k) = \max\{f_{i-1}(C_j, n_k), f_{i-1}(C_j - c_i, n_k - 1) + z_i\}, \tag{2}$$

$$n_k = 1, \ldots, n, i = 1, \ldots, m, C_j = 1, \ldots, C,$$

where $f_i(C_j, n_k)$ defines the maximum Z criterion value for n_k - size window allocated out of first i slots from S_W for a budget C_j. For the actual implementation we initialized $f_i(C_j, 0) = 0$, meaning $Z = 0$ when we have no items in the knapsack. Then we perform forward propagation and calculate $f_i(C_j, n_k)$ values for $n_k = 1, \ldots, n$. For example $f_i(C_j, 1)$ stands for $Z \to max$ problem when we can have only one item in the knapsack. Based on $f_i(C_j, 1)$ we can calculate $f_i(C_j, 2)$ using (2) and so on. So after the forward induction procedure (2) is finished the maximum value $Z_{max} = f_m(C, n)$. x_i values are then obtained by a backward induction procedure.

An estimated computational complexity of the presented recurrent scheme is $O(m * n * C)$, which is n times harder compared to the original knapsack problem ($O(m * C)$). However in practical job resources allocation cases this overhead doesn't look very large as we may assume that $n \ll m$ and $n \ll C$. On the other hand, this subset allocation procedure (2) may be called multiple times during the general square window search algorithm (step 3(c)vi).

4   Simulation Study

4.1   Simulation Environment Setup

An experiment was prepared as follows using a custom distributed environment simulator [3,18]. For our purpose, it implements a heterogeneous resource domain model: nodes have different usage costs and performance levels. A space-shared resources allocation policy simulates a local queuing system (like in GridSim or CloudSim [12]) and, thus, each node can process only one task at any given simulation time.

During the experiment series we performed a window search operation for a job requesting $n = 7$ nodes with performance level $p_i >= 1$, computational volume $V = 800$ and a maximum budget allowed is $C = 644$. The computing environment includes 100 heterogeneous computational nodes. Each node performance level is given as a uniformly distributed random value in the interval [2, 10]. So the required window length may vary from 400 to 80 time units. The scheduling interval length is 1200 time quanta which is enough to run the job on nodes with the minimum performance. The additional resources load (advanced reservations, maintenance windows) is distributed hyper-geometrically resulting in up to 30% utilization for each node.

Additionally an independent value $q_i \in [0; 10]$ is randomly generated for each computing node i to compare algorithms against $Q = \sum_{i=1}^{n} q_i$ window allocation criterion.

4.2   Algorithms Comparison

We implemented the following window search algorithms based on the general window search procedure introduced in Sect. 3.2.

1. *FirstFit* performs a square window allocation in accordance with a general scheme described in Sect. 3.2. Returns first suitable and affordable window found [15,17].
2. *MinFinish*, *MinRuntime* and *MinCost* implements general scheme and returns windows with a minimum finish time, runtime (the difference between finish and start times) and execution cost correspondingly.
3. *MaxQ* implements a general square window search procedure with an optimal slots subset allocation (2) to return a window with maximum total Q value.
4. *MultipleBest* algorithm searches for multiple non-intersecting alternative windows using FirstFit algorithm. When all possible window allocations are retrieved the algorithm searches among them for alternatives with the minimum start time, finish time, runtime, cost and the maximum Q. In this way *MultipleBest* is similar to [5] approach.

Figure 1 presents average window start time, runtime and finish time obtained by these algorithms based on 3000 independent simulation experiments. As expected, *FirstFit*, *MinFinish* and *MultipleBest* have the same minimum window finish time. Furthermore, they were able to start window at the beginning of the scheduling interval during each experiment($t_{start} = 0$). This is quite a probable event, since we are allocating 7 nodes out of 100 available, however partially utilized, nodes.

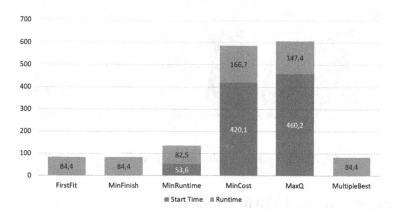

Fig. 1. Simulation results: average start time, runtime and finish time in computing environment with 100 nodes

Under such conditions *FirstFit* and *MinFinish* become practically the same algorithm: general window allocation scheme starts search among nodes with maximum performance. Thereby *FirstFit* combines minimum start time criterion with the maximum performance nodes. *MinRuntime* was able to slightly decrease runtime compared to *FirstFit* by using nodes with even higher performance, but starting a little later.

Windows allocated by *MinCost* and *MaxQ* are usually started closer to the middle of the scheduling interval. Late start time allowed these algorithms to perform a window search optimization among a wider variety of available nodes combinations. For example, average window allocation cost with the minimum value $C_W = 477$ is provided by *MinCost* (remember that we set $C = 644$ as a window allocation cost limit). *MinCost* advantage over *MultipleBest* approach is almost 17%. The advantage over other considered algorithms, not performing any cost optimization, reaches 24%.

Finally Fig. 2 shows average $Q = \sum_{i=1}^{n} q_i$ value obtained during the simulation. Parameter q_i was generated randomly for each node i and is independent from node's cost, performance and slots start times. Thereby we use it to evaluate the general scheme (2) efficiency against optimization problem where no simple and accurate solution could possibly exist. Note that as q_i was generated randomly on a $[0; 10]$ interval and a single window should consist of 7 slots, we had the following practical limits specific for our experiment: $Q \in [0; 70]$.

As can be seen from Fig. 2, *MaxQ* is indeed provided the maximum average value $Q = 61.8$, which is quite close to the practical maximum, especially compared to other algorithms. *MaxQ* advantage over *MultipleBest* is 18%. Other algorithms provided *average* Q value exactly in the middle of $[0; 70]$ interval and *MaxQ* advantage over them is almost 44%.

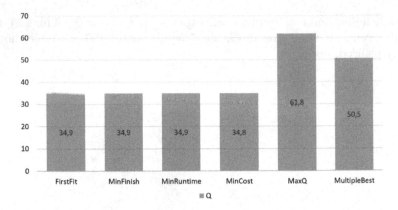

Fig. 2. Simulation results: average window Q value

5   Conclusion and Future Work

In this work, we address the problem of slot selection and co-allocation for parallel jobs in distributed computing with non-dedicated resources. For this purpose a general *square* window allocation algorithm was proposed and considered. A special slots subset allocation procedure is implemented to support a general case optimization problem.

Simulation study proved algorithms' optimization efficiency according to their target criteria. A general case implementation showed 44% advantage over First Fit algorithms and 18% over a simplified *MultipleBest* optimization heuristic. As a drawback, the general case algorithm has a high computational complexity compared to *FirstFit*.

In our further work, we will refine resource co-allocation algorithms in order to decrease their computational complexity. Another research direction will be focused on a practical resources allocation tasks implementation based on the proposed general case approach.

References

1. Lee, Y.C., Wang, C., Zomaya, A.Y., Zhou, B.B.: Profit-driven scheduling for cloud services with data access awareness. J. of Parallel Distrib. Comput. **72**(4), 591–602 (2012)
2. Garg, S.K., Konugurthi, P., Buyya, R.: A linear programming-driven genetic algorithm for meta-scheduling on utility grids. Int. J. Parallel Emergent Distrib. Syst. **26**, 493–517 (2011)
3. Toporkov, V., Tselishchev, A., Yemelyanov, D., Bobchenkov, A.: Composite scheduling strategies in distributed computing with non-dedicated resources. Procedia Comput. Sci. **9**, 176–185 (2012)
4. Buyya, R., Abramson, D., Giddy, J.: Economic models for resource management and scheduling in grid computing. J. Concurrency Comput.: Pract. Exp. **5**(14), 1507–1542 (2002)

5. Ernemann, C., Hamscher, V., Yahyapour, R.: Economic scheduling in grid computing. In: Feitelson, D.G., Rudolph, L., Schwiegelshohn, U. (eds.) JSSPP 2002. LNCS, vol. 2537, pp. 128–152. Springer, Heidelberg (2002). https://doi.org/10.1007/3-540-36180-4_8
6. Kurowski, K., Nabrzyski, J., Oleksiak, A., Weglarz, J.: Multicriteria aspects of grid re-source management. In: Nabrzyski, J., Schopf, J.M., Weglarz, J. (eds.) Grid Resource Management. State of the Art and Future Trends, pp. 271–293. Kluwer Academic Publishers (2003)
7. Aida, K., Casanova, H.: Scheduling mixed-parallel applications with advance reservations. 17th IEEE International Symposium on HPDC, pp. 65–74. IEEE CS Press, New York (2008)
8. Elmroth, E., Tordsson, J.: A standards-based grid resource brokering service supporting advance reservations, coallocation and cross-grid interoperability. J. Concurrency Comput.: Pract. Exp. 25(18), 2298–2335 (2009)
9. Takefusa, A., Nakada, H., Kudoh, T., Tanaka, Y.: An advance reservation-based co-allocation algorithm for distributed computers and network bandwidth on QoS-guaranteed grids. In: Frachtenberg, E., Schwiegelshohn, U. (eds.) JSSPP 2010. LNCS, vol. 6253, pp. 16–34. Springer, Heidelberg (2010). https://doi.org/10.1007/978-3-642-16505-4_2
10. Blanco, H., Guirado, F., Lérida, J.L., Albornoz, V.M.: MIP model scheduling for multi-clusters. In: Caragiannis, I., Alexander, M., Badia, R.M., Cannataro, M., Costan, A., Danelutto, M., Desprez, F., Krammer, B., Sahuquillo, J., Scott, S.L., Weidendorfer, J. (eds.) Euro-Par 2012. LNCS, vol. 7640, pp. 196–206. Springer, Heidelberg (2013). https://doi.org/10.1007/978-3-642-36949-0_22
11. Moab Adaptive Computing Suite. http://www.adaptivecomputing.com/
12. Calheiros, R.N., Ranjan, R., Beloglazov, A., De Rose, C.A.F., Buyya, R.: CloudSim: a toolkit for modeling and simulation of cloud computing environments and evaluation of resource provisioning algorithms. J. Softw.: Pract. Exp. 41(1), 23–50 (2011)
13. Samimi, P., Teimouri, Y., Mukhtar, M.: A combinatorial double auction resource allocation model in cloud computing. J. Inf. Sci. 357(C), 201–216 (2016)
14. Toporkov, V., Toporkova, A., Bobchenkov, A., Yemelyanov, D.: Resource selection algorithms for economic scheduling in distributed systems. In: Proceedings of International Conference on Computational Science, ICCS 2011, 1–3 June 2011, Singapore, Procedia Computer Science, vol. 4, pp. 2267–2276. Elsevier (2011)
15. Kovalenko, V.N., Kovalenko, E.I., Koryagin, D.A., et al.: Parallel job management in the grid with non-dedicated resources, Preprint of Keldysh Institute of Applied Mathematics of Russian Academy of Sciences, Moscow, no. 63 (2007)
16. Makhlouf, S., Yagoubi, B.: Resources Co-allocation Strategies in Grid Computing. In: CEUR Workshop Proceedings, CIIA, vol. 825 (2011)
17. Netto, M.A.S., Buyya, R.: A Flexible resource co-allocation model based on advance reservations with rescheduling support. Technical report, GRIDS-TR-2007-17, Grid Computing and Distributed Systems Laboratory, The University of Melbourne, Australia, 9 October 2007
18. Toporkov, V., Toporkova, A., Tselishchev, A., Yemelyanov, D.: Slot selection algorithms in distributed computing. J. Supercomput. 69(1), 53–60 (2014)

Explicit Size-Reduction-Oriented Design of a Compact Microstrip Rat-Race Coupler Using Surrogate-Based Optimization Methods

Slawomir Koziel[1]([✉]) [iD], Adrian Bekasiewicz[2] [iD], Leifur Leifsson[3] [iD], Xiaosong Du[3], and Yonatan Tesfahunegn[1] [iD]

[1] Engineering Optimization and Modeling Center,
School of Science and Engineering, Reykjavík University,
Menntavegur 1, 101, Reykjavík, Iceland
{koziel,yonatant}@ru.is
[2] Faculty of Electronics Telecommunications and Informatics,
Gdansk University of Technology, Narutowicza 11/12, 80-233 Gdansk, Poland
bekasiewicz@ru.is
[3] Department of Aerospace Engineering, Iowa State University,
Ames, IA 50011, USA
{leifur,xiaosong}@iastate.edu

Abstract. In this paper, an explicit size reduction of a compact rat-race coupler implemented in a microstrip technology is considered. The coupler circuit features a simple topology with a densely arranged layout that exploits a combination of high- and low-impedance transmission line sections. All relevant dimensions of the structure are simultaneously optimized in order to explicitly reduce the coupler size while maintaining equal power split at the operating frequency of 1 GHz and sufficient bandwidth for return loss and isolation characteristics. Acceptable levels of electrical performance are ensured by using a penalty function approach. Two designs with footprints of 350 mm^2 and 360 mm^2 have been designed and experimentally validated. The latter structure is characterized by 27% bandwidth. For the sake of computational efficiency, surrogate-based optimization principles are utilized. In particular, we employ an iterative construction and re-optimization of the surrogate model involving a suitably corrected low-fidelity representation of the coupler structure. This permits rapid optimization at the cost corresponding to a handful of evaluations of the high-fidelity coupler model.

Keywords: Microwave couplers · Rat-race couplers · Coupler optimization
Surrogate-based optimization · Computer-aided design · Compact coupler
Compact microstrip resonant cells

1 Introduction

Design of compact microwave structures is an important yet challenging task because size reduction stays in conflict with other objectives concerning electrical performance of the circuit [1–4]. In case of many classes of structures such as couplers, several

© Springer International Publishing AG, part of Springer Nature 2018
Y. Shi et al. (Eds.): ICCS 2018, LNCS 10861, pp. 584–592, 2018.
https://doi.org/10.1007/978-3-319-93701-4_46

criteria have to be handled at the same time (e.g., power split error, achieving a specific operating frequency, minimization of return loss, etc.) [3–5]. Another problem is that due to considerable electromagnetic (EM) cross-couplings present in highly compressed layouts of miniaturized structures [6–10], equivalent network models (typically used as design tools) are highly inaccurate [3, 9]. Reliable evaluation of the circuit performance can only be realized by means of full-wave EM analysis, which is computationally expensive [4, 5]. Consequently, design through numerical optimization—although highly desirable—is very difficult. On one hand, manual design approaches (e.g., parameter sweeps) do not allow for simultaneous control of the structure size and electrical responses [2]. On the other hand, conventional optimization algorithms exhibit high computational cost due to a large number of EM simulations necessary for convergence [11].

In this paper, an explicit size reduction of a compact microstrip coupler is considered. Small size of the circuit is partially obtained through tightly arranged layout based on a combination of high- and low-impedance transmission lines which allows efficient utilization of the available space. Furthermore, geometrical dimensions of the circuit are obtained through numerical optimization oriented towards explicit size reduction. Surrogate-based methods [12–16] are used to speed up the design process. More specifically, we utilize variable-fidelity models and space mapping technology [12, 16] to construct the surrogate model, further utilized as a prediction tool that iteratively guides the optimization process towards the optimum design. Simultaneous control of the coupler size and its electrical performance parameters is achieved by means of a penalty function approach. The optimized coupler structure exhibits small size of 350 mm^2 and acceptable performance in terms of power split as well as bandwidth. Only slight loosening of the size constraint (to 360 mm^2) leads to considerable bandwidth improvement to 270 MHz. Both designs have been fabricated and experimentally validated.

2 Design Optimization Procedure

In this section, an optimization procedure utilized to obtain a minimum-size coupler design is discussed. Specifically, we formulate design optimization problem and describe utilized design optimization algorithm. The numerical results and comparison of the structure with the state-of-the-art couplers are given in Sect. 4, whereas its experimental validation is given in Sect. 5.

2.1 Problem Formulation

The primary objective is to minimize the coupler size $A(x)$. On the other hand, the design process is also supposed to ensure sufficient electrical performance of the structure. We consider the following requirements [4]:

- $d_S = |S_{21,f}(x) - S_{31,f}(x)| \leq \varepsilon$ at the operating frequency (here, we set $\varepsilon = 0.2$ dB);
- $S_{\max} = \max(\min\{S_{11,f}(x), S_{41,f}(x)\}) \leq S_m$ (we assume $S_m = -25$ dB);
- $f_{S11,f}(x)$ and $f_{S41,f}(x)$, i.e., the frequencies realizing minimum of $S_{11,f}(x)$ and $S_{41,f}(x)$, respectively, are as close to the operating frequency f_0 as possible.

The design optimization problem is formulated as [11]

$$x^* = \arg\min_x U\left(\mathbf{R}_f(x)\right) \tag{1}$$

where $\mathbf{R}_f$ is a high-fidelity EM simulation model of the structure as described above, whereas x^* is the optimum design to be found. In order to take into account all of these goals the objective function is defined as follows

$$\begin{aligned} U(x) &= A(x) + \beta_1(\max\{(d_S - \varepsilon)/\varepsilon, 0\})^2 \\ &\quad + \beta_2(\max\{(S_{\max} - S_m)/|S_m|, 0\})^2 \\ &\quad + \beta_{f1}|(f_{S_{11f}}(x) - f_0)/f_0|^2 + \beta_{f2}|(f_{S_{41f}}(x) - f_0)/f_0|^2 \end{aligned} \tag{2}$$

This formulation is supposed to ensure (with certain tolerance) equal power split (controlled by d_S) as well as sufficient return loss and isolation (controlled by $S_{\max}$) at the operating frequency. The coefficients β_1, β_2, β_{f1}, and β_{f2} are chosen so that the corresponding penalty functions take noticeable values (when compared to $A(x)$) for relative violations larger than a few percent.

2.2 Surrogate-Based Coupler Optimization

For the sake of computational efficiency the design process is executed using surrogate-based optimization methods with variable-fidelity EM models [11]. More specifically, direct solving of (1) is replaced by an iterative procedure

$$x^{(i+1)} = \arg\min_x U\left(\mathbf{R}_s^{(i)}(x)\right) \tag{3}$$

that yields a series $x^{(i)}$, $i = 0, 1, \ldots$, of approximations to x^*, with $\mathbf{R}_s^{(i)}$ being a surrogate model at iteration i. Here, the surrogate is constructed by suitable correction of the low-fidelity model $\mathbf{R}_c$ as mentioned in the previous section. The model correction is realized using space mapping [11]. In this work, we utilized frequency scaling and additive response correction. Frequency scaling is realized by evaluating the low-fidelity model at a set of frequencies that are transformed with respect to the original frequency sweep $F = [f_1 \ldots f_m]$ (at this the high-fidelity model is simulated) as follows $F' = [\alpha_0 + \alpha_1 f_1 \ldots \alpha_0 + \alpha_1 f_m]$. Here, α_0 and α_1 are coefficients found (using nonlinear regression) so as to minimize the misalignment between the scaled low- and high-fidelity models, i.e., $\|\mathbf{R}_c'(x^{(i)}) - \mathbf{R}_f(x^{(i)})\|$. The additive response correction is applied on the top of frequency scaling so that we have $R_s^{(i)}(x) = R_c'(x) + [R_f(x^{(i)}) - R_c'$ $(x^{(i)})]$. The correction term $[R_f(x^{(i)}) - R_c'(x^{(i)})]$ ensured zero-order consistency between the surrogate and the high-fidelity model at the current iteration point $x^{(i)}$.

3 Numerical Results and Comparisons

Consider a rectangular-shaped, equal-split rat-race coupler (RRC) is shown in Fig. 1. It consists of two horizontal and four vertical compact microstrip resonant cells (CMRSs) [9]. The cells contain folded high-impedance lines interconnected with low-impedance stubs, which allows obtaining complementary geometry that ensures tight filling of the structure interior and thus good utilization of available space. This is critical for achieving considerable miniaturization rate. On the other hand, the circuit contains a relatively small number of geometry parameters which facilitates its further design optimization process.

The coupler is implemented on a Taconic RF-35 substrate ($\varepsilon_r = 3.5$, $\tan\delta = 0.0018$, $h = 0.762$ mm). The geometry parameters are $x = [w_1\ w_2\ w_3\ d_1\ d_2\ l_1]^T$, whereas $w_0 = 1.7$ is fixed (all dimensions in mm). The design procedure involves fine and coarsely discretized EM models of the RRC, both evaluated in CST Microwave Studio [17]. The high-fidelity model R_f contains $\sim 700{,}000$ mesh cells and its simulation time on a dual Intel E5540 machine is 52 min. The low-fidelity model R_c has $\sim 150{,}000$ cells (simulation time 4 min).

The considered structure has been designed using the above outlined methodology. The final design (here, denoted as design A) is $x_A^* = [4.979\ 0.179\ 1.933\ 0.197\ 0.164$ $2.568]^T$. The footprint of the optimized circuit is only 350 mm^2. Obtained frequency characteristics of the structure are shown in Fig. 2. In the next step, for the sake of improved coupler performance, the area constraint has been increased to 360 mm^2 and the circuit has been re-optimized. The parameter vector of an alternative design (denoted as coupler B) is $x_B^* = [4.395\ 0.244\ 2.263\ 0.199\ 0.233\ 2.499]^T$. The frequency responses of the structure are shown in Fig. 3.

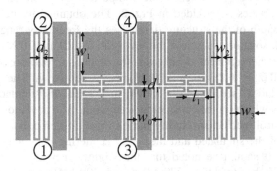

Fig. 1. Geometry of the considered compact microstrip rat-race coupler.

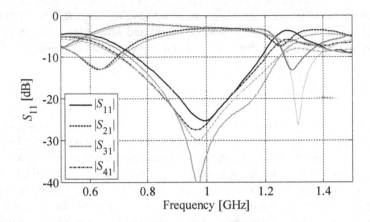

Fig. 2. Simulated (black) and measured (gray) characteristics of the design A; layout area 350 mm^2.

Utilization of variable-fidelity simulation models in combination with space mapping technology permits low cost of the optimization process, equivalent to less than twenty evaluations of the high-fidelity coupler model for both designs (A and B).

Both coupler designs have been compared with other state-of-the-art structures [9, 19–22] in terms of the bandwidth and miniaturization rate (expressed in terms of the guided wavelength λ_g defined for the operating frequency and the given substrate parameters). The results collected in Table 1 indicate that both coupler realizations provide competitive miniaturization while ensuring broader bandwidth than other structures with similar sizes.

4   Experimental Validation

Both coupler designs have been fabricated and measured. Photograph of manufactured coupler A is shown in Fig. 4, whereas the comparison of its simulated and measured frequency characteristics is provided in Fig. 2. The obtained results indicate that the operational bandwidth of the structure defined as the frequency range for which both the reflection and isolation are below the level of −20 dB is 170 MHz for simulation and 220 MHz for measurement. Moreover, the simulated and measured power split error at $f_0 = 1$ GHz is 0.25 dB and 0.59 dB, respectively. The phase difference between ports 2 and 3 (see Fig. 1) is shown in Fig. 5a. Its simulated and measured value is about 8.7° which can be considered acceptable. The deviation from 0° is due to lack of phase control mechanism during the optimization process.

Comparison of the simulated and measured scattering parameters of coupler B is shown in Fig. 3. It should be noted that the slightly increased size has resulted in increase of −20 dB bandwidth to 270 MHz and 290 MHz for simulation and measurement, respectively.

The simulated power split error and phase difference (cf. Fig. 5b) at f_0 are 0.2 dB and 4.7°, whereas measured values are 0.7 dB and 5.6°, respectively. One should

Table 1. A comparison of competitive compact coupler designs

Coupler	Bandwidth %	Dimensions mm × mm	Effective λ_g	Miniaturization %[*]
Design [19]	39.0	32.4 × 51.9	0.20 × 0.32	53.6
Design [20]	17.2	38.5 × 38.5	0.19 × 0.19	73.8
Design [21]	16.8	22.4 × 22.4	0.14 × 0.14	85.8
Design [9]	20.2	22.8 × 17.0	0.13 × 0.09	91.5
Design [22]	15.1	6.67 × 52.5	0.04 × 0.28	92.2
Design A	17.0	12.1 × 29.0	0.07 × 0.16	92.2
Design B	27.0	11.2 × 32.2	0.06 × 0.18	92.1

[*] w.r.t. conventional RRC (effective λ_g: 0.26 × 0.53, size: 4536 mm^2) [9].

emphasize that the considered RRC structure is sensitive for fabrication inaccuracies which is the reason of noticeable discrepancies between the simulated and the measured responses [9]. The key electrical properties of both coupler designs have been gathered in Table 2.

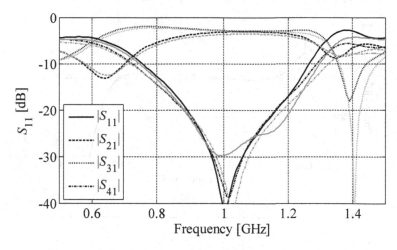

Fig. 3. Simulated (black) and measured (gray) responses of the design B; layout area constraint $A(x) \leq 360$ mm^2.

Table 2. Key features of couplers A and B: simulation vs measurements

$f_0 = 1$ GHz	Coupler A		Coupler B	
	Simulated	Measured	Simulated	Measured
$|S_{11}|$	−25.3 dB	−33.4 dB	−41.7 dB	−29.9 dB
$|S_{21}|$	−3.17 dB	−3.73 dB	−3.05 dB	−3.70 dB
$|S_{31}|$	−2.92 dB	−3.14 dB	−2.85 dB	−3.02 dB
$|S_{41}|$	−26.2 dB	−28.3 dB	−36.8 dB	−34.7 dB
Bandwidth	170 MHz	220 MHz	270 MHz	290 MHz
$\angle S_{21} - \angle S_{31}$	8.48°	8.92°	4.73°	5.57°

Fig. 4. Photograph of the fabricated coupler prototype (design A).

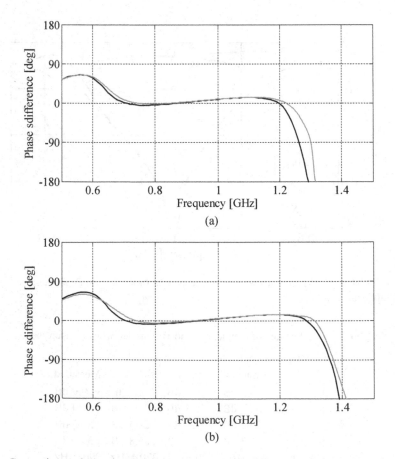

(a)

(b)

Fig. 5. Comparison of simulated and measured phase difference of the proposed compact couplers: (a) design A; and (b) design B.

5 Conclusions

In this work, an explicit size reduction of a compact coupler structure implemented in microstrip technology has been considered. Due to highly-packed geometry of the considered structure, as well as appropriate handling of all design requirements, a very small size of 350 mm^2 can be achieved (with 17% bandwidth). At the same time, optimization for electrical performance (with the maximum size constrained to 360 mm^2) leads to bandwidth increase to 27% with respect to the operating frequency of 1 GHz. Utilization of variable-fidelity electromagnetic simulations as well as space mapping technology allowed us to maintain low cost of the optimization process. Here it is equivalent to less than twenty evaluations of the high-fidelity model of the coupler under design. The structure has been favorably compared with benchmark compact couplers. Simulation results are supported with measurement data. Future work will focus on utilization of the method for design of compact multi-band coupler structures.

References

1. Koziel, S., Bekasiewicz, A., Kurgan, P.: Size reduction of microwave couplers by EM-driven optimization. In: International Microwave Symposium (2015)
2. Zheng, S.Y., Yeung, S.H., Chan, W.S., Man, K.F., Leung, S.H.: Size-reduced rectangular patch hybrid coupler using patterned ground plane. IEEE Trans. Microwave Theory Techn. **57**(1), 180–188
3. Bekasiewicz, A., Koziel, S., Zieniutycz, W.: A structure and design optimization of novel compact microscrip dual-band rat-race coupler with enhanced bandwidth. Microwave Opt. Technol. Lett. **58**(10), 2287–2291 (2016)
4. Koziel, S., Bekasiewicz, A., Kurgan, P., Bandler, J.W.: Rapid multi-objective design optimization of compact microwave couplers by means of physics-based surrogates. IET Microwaves, Antennas Propag. **10**(5), 479–486 (2015)
5. Koziel, S., Kurgan, P., Pankiewicz, B.: Cost-efficient design methodology for compact rat-race couplers. Int. J. RF Microwave Comput. Aided Eng. **25**(3), 236–242 (2015)
6. Tseng, C.-H., Chen, H.-J.: Compact rat-race coupler using shunt-stub-based artificial transmission lines. IEEE Microwaves Wirel. Compon. Lett. **18**(11), 734–736 (2008)
7. Liao, S.-S., Sun, P.-T., Chin, N.-C., Peng, J.-T.: A novel compact-size branch-line coupler. IEEE Microwaves Wirel. Compon. Lett. **15**(9), 588–590 (2005)
8. Tseng, C.-H., Chang, C.-L.: A rigorous design methodology for compact planar branch-line and rat-race couplers with asymmetrical T-structures. IEEE Trans. Microwave Theory Tech. **60**(7), 2085–2092 (2012)
9. Bekasiewicz, A., Kurgan, P.: A compact microstrip rat-race coupler constituted by nonuniform transmission lines. Microwave Opt. Technol. Lett. **56**(4), 970–974 (2014)
10. Tsai, K.-Y., Yang, H.-S., Chen, J.-H., Chen, Y.-J.: A miniaturized 3 dB branch-line hybrid coupler with harmonics suppression. IEEE Microwaves Wirel. Compon. Lett. **21**(10), 537–539 (2011)
11. Koziel, S., Yang, X.S., Zhang, Q.J. (eds.): Simulation-Driven Design Optimization and Modeling for Microwave Engineering. Imperial College Press, London (2013)
12. Koziel, S., Leifsson, L. (eds.): Surrogate-Based Modeling and Optimization. Springer, New York (2013). https://doi.org/10.1007/978-1-4614-7551-4

13. Koziel, S., Bekasiewicz, A.: Rapid microwave design optimization using adaptive response scaling. IEEE Trans. Microwave Theory Techn. **64**(9), 2749–2757 (2016)
14. Bekasiewicz, A., Koziel, S.: Response features and circuit decomposition for accelerated EM-driven design of compact impedance matching transformers. Microwave Opt. Techn. Lett. **58**(9), 2130–2133 (2016)
15. Queipo, N.V., Haftka, R.T., Shyy, W., Goel, T., Vaidynathan, R., Tucker, P.K.: Surrogate-based analysis and optimization. Prog. Aerosp. Sci. **41**(1), 1–28 (2005)
16. Koziel, S., Bandler, J.W., Cheng, Q.S.: Reduced-cost microwave component modeling using space-mapping-enhanced EM-based kriging surrogates. Int. J. Numer. Model. Electron. Netw. Devices Fields **26**(3), 275–286 (2013)
17. CST Microwave Studio, ver. 2013. CST AG, Darmstadt (2013)
18. Koziel, S., Bekasiewicz, A.: Expedited geometry scaling of compact microwave passives by means of inverse surrogate modeling. IEEE Trans. Microwave Theory Techn. **63**(12), 4019–4026 (2015)
19. Zhang, C.F.: Planar rat-race coupler with microstrip electromagnetic bandgap element. Microwave Opt. Techn. Lett. **53**(11), 2619–2622 (2011)
20. Shao, W., He, J., Wang, B.-Z.: Compact rat-race ring coupler with capacitor loading. Microwave Opt. Techn. Lett. **52**(1), 7–9 (2010)
21. Wang, J., Wang, B.-Z., Guo, Y.X., Ong, L.C., Xiao, S.: Compact slow-wave microstrip rat-race ring coupler. Electron. Lett. **43**(2), 111–113 (2007)
22. Koziel, S., Bekasiewicz, A., Kurgan, P.: Rapid multi-objective simulation-driven design of compact microwave circuits. Microwave Opt. Techn. Lett. **25**(5), 277–279 (2015)

Stochastic-Expansions-Based Model-Assisted Probability of Detection Analysis of the Spherically-Void-Defect Benchmark Problem

Xiaosong Du[1], Praveen Gurrala[2], Leifur Leifsson[1($\boxtimes$)], Jiming Song[2],
William Meeker[3], Ronald Roberts[4], Slawomir Koziel[5],
and Yonatan Tesfahunegn[5]

[1] Computational Design Laboratory, Iowa State University, Ames, IA, USA
{xiaosong, leifur}@iastate.edu
[2] Department of Electrical and Computer Engineering, Iowa State University,
Ames, IA, USA
{praveeng, jisong}@iastate.edu
[3] Department of Statistics, Iowa State University, Ames, IA, USA
wqmeeker@iastate.edu
[4] Center for Nondestructive Evaluation, Iowa State University, Ames, IA, USA
rroberts@iastate.edu
[5] Engineering Optimization and Modeling Center,
School of Science and Engineering, Reykjavik University,
Menntavegur 1, 101 Reykjavik, Iceland
{koziel, yonatant}@ru.is

Abstract. Probability of detection (POD) is used for reliability analysis in nondestructive testing (NDT) area. Traditionally, it is determined by experimental tests, while it can be enhanced by physics-based simulation models, which is called model-assisted probability of detection (MAPOD). However, accurate physics-based models are usually expensive in time. In this paper, we implement a type of stochastic polynomial chaos expansions (PCE), as alternative of actual physics-based model for the MAPOD calculation. State-of-the-art least-angle regression method and hyperbolic sparse technique are integrated within PCE construction. The proposed method is tested on a spherically-void-defect benchmark problem, developed by the World Federal Nondestructive Evaluation Center. The benchmark problem is added with two uncertainty parameters, where the PCE model usually requires about 100 sample points for the convergence on statistical moments, while direct Monte Carlo method needs more than 10000 samples, and Kriging based Monte Carlo method is oscillating. With about 100 sample points, PCE model can reduce root mean square error to be within 1% standard deviation of test points, while Kriging model cannot reach that level of accuracy even with 200 sample points.

Keywords: Spherically-void-defect · Nondestructive evaluation
Model-assisted probability of detection · Monte Carlo sampling
Surrogate modeling

© Springer International Publishing AG, part of Springer Nature 2018
Y. Shi et al. (Eds.): ICCS 2018, LNCS 10861, pp. 593–603, 2018.
https://doi.org/10.1007/978-3-319-93701-4_47

1 Introduction

The concept of probability of detection (POD) (Sarkar *et al.* 1998) was initially developed to quantitatively describe the detection capabilities of nondestructive testing (NDT) systems (Blitz and Simpson 1996). A commonly used term is "90% POD" and "90% POD with 95% confidence interval", which are written as a_{90} and $a_{90/95}$, respectively. POD curves were initially only based on experiments. The POD can be enhanced by utilizing physics-based computational models, such as the full wave ultrasonic testing simulation model (Gurrala *et al.* 2017), and the model-assisted probability of detection (MAPOD) methodology (Thompson *et al.* 2009; Aldrin *et al.* 2009, 2010, 2011). MAPOD can be performed using the hit/miss method (MIL-HDBK-1823), linear regression method (MIL-HDBK-1823 2009), or the Bayesian inference method (Aldrin *et al.* 2013; Jenson *et al.* 2013). Typically, the true physics-based simulation models are directly employed in the analysis.

Unfortunately, evaluating the simulation models can be time-consuming. Moreover, the MAPOD analysis process requires multiple evaluations. Consequently, the use of MAPOD with computationally expensive physics-based simulation models can be challenging to complete in a timely fashion. This has motivated the use of surrogate models (Aldrin *et al.* 2009, 2010, 2011; Miorelli *et al.* 2016; Siegler *et al.* 2016; Ribay *et at.* 2016) to alieve the computational burden. Deterministic surrogate models, such as Kriging interpolation (Aldrin *et al.* 2009, 2010, 2011; Du *et al.* 2016) and support vector regression (SVR) (Miorelli *et al.* 2016), have been successfully applied in this area. Stochastic surrogate models, such as polynomial chaos expansions (PCE) (Knopp *et al.* 2011; Sabbagh *et al.* 2013), are another option and have recently been utilized for MAPOD analysis (Du *et al.* 2017).

In this work, we integrate PCE models with least-angle regression (LAR) and hyperbolic sparse truncation schemes (Blatman *et al.* 2009, 2010, 2011), which can solve efficiently for the coefficients of PCE models. The proposed method is demonstrated on a spherically-void-defect NDT case, which is a benchmark case developed by the World Federal Nondestructive Evaluation Center (WFNDEC). For the purpose of this work, we use the Thompson-Gray analytical model (Gray 2012) for the ultrasonic testing simulation. The results of the MAPOD analysis using the PCE-based surrogate models are compared with direct Monte Carlo sampling (MCS) and the true model, and with MCS and deterministic Kriging surrogate models.

The paper is organized as follows. Next section gives a description of the analytical ultrasonic testing simulation model. The MAPOD analysis process is given in Sect. 3. Section 4 describes the deterministic and stochastic surrogate models. The numerical results are presented in Sect. 5. Finally, the paper ends with conclusion.

2 Ultrasonic Testing Simulation Model

The spherically-void-defect benchmark problem (shown in Fig. 1) was proposed by the WFDEC in 2004. The spherically void defect, whose radius is 0.34 mm, is included in a fused quartz block, which is surrounded by water. A spherically focused transducer, the radius of which is 6.23 mm, is used to detect this defect. The frequency range is set to be [0, 10 MHz].

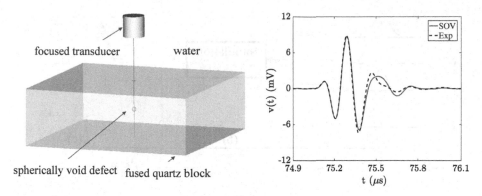

Fig. 1. Setup of the spherically-void-defect benchmark case (left) and results of comparison between experimental data (Exp) and the analytical solution (SOV).

The analytical model, used in this work, is known as the Thompson-Gray model (Gray 2012). This model is based on paraxial approximation of the incident and scattered ultrasonic waves, computing the spectrum of voltage at the receiving transducer in terms of the velocity diffraction coefficients of the transmitting/receiving transducers, scattering amplitude of the defect and a frequency-dependent coefficient known as the system-efficiency function (Schmerr *et al.* 2007). In this work, velocity diffraction coefficients were calculated using the multi-Gaussian beam model and scattering amplitude of the spherical-void was calculated using the method of separation of variables (Schmerr 2013). The system efficiency function, which is a function of the properties and settings of the transducers and the pulser, was taken from the WFNDEC archives. The time-domain pulse-echo waveforms are computed by performing FFT on the voltage spectrum. The foregoing system model was shown to be very accurate in predicting pulse-echo from the spherical void if the paraxial approximation is satisfied and radius of the void is small. To guarantee the effectiveness of this analytical model on the benchmark problem mentioned above, it is validated on this case with experimental data, given in Fig. 1, through which shows that the results match well.

3 Framework for Model-Assisted Probability of Detection

POD is essentially the quantification of inspection capability starting from the distributions of variability, and describes its accuracy with confidence bounds, also known as uncertain bounds (Spall 1997). In many cases, the final product of a POD curve is the flaw size, a, for which there is a 90% probability of detection. This flaw size is denoted a_{90}. The 95% upper confidence bound on a_{90} is denoted as $a_{90/95}$. The POD is typically determined through experiments which are both time-consuming and costly. This motivated the MAPOD methods with the aim for reducing the number of experimental sample points by introducing insights physics-based simulations (Thompson *et al.* 2009).

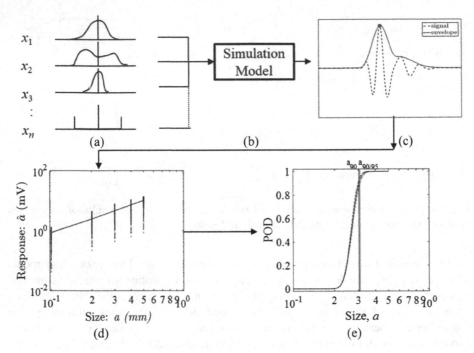

Fig. 2. General process of model-assisted probability of detection: (a) probabilistic inputs; (b) simulation model; (c) response (amplitude in this work); (d) "$\hat{a}$ vs. a" plot, (e) POD curves.

The main elements for generating POD curves using simulations is shown in Fig. 2. The process starts by defining the random inputs with specific statistical distributions (Fig. 2a). Next, the inputs are propagated through the simulation model (Fig. 2b). In this work, the simulation model is calculated using an analytical model (described in Sect. 2), to obtain the quantity of interest, which is the maximum signal amplitude obtained from the signal envelope (Fig. 2c). When doing detection tests for the same defect size, the results vary due to uncertainty/noise existing within the system. Usually, arbitrary number of sample runs are taken for each defect size, then a linear regression is made based on the results to obtain the so-called "$\hat{a}$ vs. a" plot (Fig. 2d). With this information, the POD at each defect size can be obtained, thereby, the POD curves are generated (Fig. 2e).

4   Surrogate Modeling

This section describes the surrogate models used in this work. In particular, we use the deterministic Kriging interpolation surrogate model (Du *et al.* 2016), and the stochastic PCE surrogate models. More specifically, we use the least-angle regression (LAR) method (Blatman *et al.* 2010, 2011) with the hyperbolic truncation technique (Blatman *et al.* 2009).

4.1 Deterministic Surrogate Models via Kriging

Kriging (Ryu *et al.* 2002) model, also known as Gaussian process regression, is a type of interpolation method, taking all observed data as sample points and minimizing the mean square error (MSE) to reach the most appropriate model coefficients. It has the generalized formula as sum of the trend function, $\mathbf{f}^T(\mathbf{x})\boldsymbol{\beta}$, and a Gaussian random function $Z(\mathbf{x})$:

$$y(x) = \mathbf{f}^T(\mathbf{x})\boldsymbol{\beta} + Z(\mathbf{x}), \mathbf{x} \in \mathbb{R}^m, \tag{1}$$

where $\mathbf{f}(\mathbf{x}) = [f_0(\mathbf{x}), \dots, f_{p-1}(\mathbf{x})]^T \in \mathbb{R}^p$ is defined with a set of the regression basis functions, $\boldsymbol{\beta} = [\beta_0(\mathbf{x}), \dots, \beta_{p-1}(\mathbf{x})]^T \in \mathbb{R}^p$ denotes the vector of the corresponding coefficients, and $Z(\mathbf{x})$ denotes a stationary random process with zero mean, variance and nonzero covariance. In this work, Gaussian exponential correlation function is adopted, thus the nonzero covariance is of the form

$$Cov[Z(\mathbf{x}), Z(\mathbf{x}')] = \sigma^2 \exp\left[-\sum_{k=1}^m \theta_k |x_k - x_k'|^{p_k} \right], \ 1 < p_k \le 2 \tag{2}$$

where $\boldsymbol{\theta} = [\theta_1, \theta_2, \dots, \theta_m]^T$, $\mathbf{p} = [p_1, p_2, \dots, p_m]^T$, denote the vectors of unknown hyper model parameters to be tuned.

After further derivation (Sacks 1989), the Kriging predictor $\hat{y}(\mathbf{x})$ for any untried $\mathbf{x}$ can be written as

$$\hat{y}(\mathbf{x}) = \beta_0 + \mathbf{r}^T(\mathbf{x})\mathbf{R}^{-1}(\mathbf{y}_S - \beta_0 \mathbf{1}), \tag{3}$$

where β_0 comes from generalized least squares estimation.

A unique feature of Kriging model is that it provides an uncertainty estimation (or MSE) for the prediction, which is very useful for sample-points refinement. Further details are beyond the scope of this paper, readers who have interests are suggested to go through Forrester *et al.* (2008).

4.2 Stochastic Surrogate Models via Polynomial Chaos Expansions

In this work, the stochastic expansions are generated using non-intrusive PCE (Xiong *et al.* 2010, 2011). PCE theory enables the fast construction of surrogate models, as well as an efficient statistical analysis of the model responses. More specifically, to the calculate coefficients more efficiently and accurately, we use the LAR algorithms (Blatman *et al.* 2010, 2011) and the hyperbolic truncation scheme (Blatman *et al.* 2009).

4.2.1 Generalized Polynomial Chaos Expansions

PCE is a type of stochastic surrogate model, having the generalized formulation of (Wiener 1938)

$$Y = M(\mathbf{X}) = \sum_{i=1}^{\infty} \alpha_i \Psi_i(\mathbf{X}), \tag{4}$$

where, $\mathbf{X} \in \mathbb{R}^M$ is a vector with random independent components, described by a probability density function $f_{\mathbf{X}}$, $Y = M(\mathbf{X})$ is a map of $\mathbf{X}$, i is the index of ith polynomial term, Ψ is multivariate polynomial basis, and α is corresponding coefficient of basis function. In practice, the total number of sample points needed does not have to be infinite, instead, a truncated form of the PCE is used

$$M(\mathbf{X}) \approx M^{PC}(\mathbf{X}) = \sum_{i=1}^{P} \alpha_i \Psi_i(\mathbf{X}), \tag{5}$$

where, $M^{PC}(\mathbf{X})$ is the approximate truncated PCE model, P is the total number of required sample points and can be calculated as

$$P = \frac{(p+n)!}{p!n!}, \tag{6}$$

where, p is the required order of PCE, and n is the total number of random variables.

4.2.2   Least-Angle Regression

When solving for coefficients of the PCE, this works selects state-of-the-art LAR method, which treats the observed data of actual model as a summation of PCE predictions at the same design points and corresponding residual (Efron et al. 2004)

$$M(\mathbf{X}) = M^{PC}(\mathbf{X}) + \varepsilon_P = \sum_{i=1}^{P} \alpha_i \Psi_i(\mathbf{X}) + \varepsilon_P \equiv \boldsymbol{\alpha}^T \Psi(\mathbf{X}) + \varepsilon_P, \tag{7}$$

where ε_p is the residual between $M(\mathbf{X})$ and $M^{PC}(\mathbf{X})$, which is to be minimized in least-squares methods.

Then the initial problem can be converted to a least-squares minimization problem

$$\hat{\boldsymbol{\alpha}} = \arg \min E[\boldsymbol{\alpha}^T \Psi(\mathbf{X}) - M(\mathbf{X})]. \tag{8}$$

Adding one more regularization term to favor low-rank solution (Udell et al. 2016)

$$\hat{\boldsymbol{\alpha}} = \arg \min E[\boldsymbol{\alpha}^T \psi(\mathbf{x}) - M(\mathbf{x})] + \lambda ||\boldsymbol{\alpha}||_1, \tag{9}$$

where λ is a penalty factor, $||\boldsymbol{\alpha}||_1$ is L1 norm of the coefficients of PCE. The LAR algorithm, solving for the least-squares minimization problem (Eq. (9) in this work), is very efficient in calculation, and can accept an arbitrary number of sample points.

4.2.3   Hyperbolic Truncation Technique

Commonly used basic truncation scheme has been applied to PCE as shown in Eqs. (5) and (6) to make it in a summation of finite number of terms. In order to reduce the number of sample points needed for coefficient regression, the hyperbolic truncation technique, also known as q-norm method (Blatman *et al.* 2009), is applied here. The main idea is to reduce the interaction terms, since they do not have much effect on the PCE prediction due to the sparsity-of-effect principle (Blatman *et al.* 2009).

The hyperbolic truncation technique follows the formula (Blatman *et al.* 2009)

$$A^{M,p,q} = \left\{ \alpha \in A^{M,p} : \left(\sum_{i=1}^{M} \alpha_i^q \right)^{1/q} \leq p \right\}. \tag{10}$$

Here, when $q = 1$, it is the same as basic truncation scheme, while $q < 1$, it can reduce the interactive terms further based on basic truncation schemes.

4.2.4   Calculation of Statistical Moments

After solving for the coefficients, statistical moments can be obtained from those coefficients directly, due to the orthonormal characteristics of PCE basis.

The mean value of PCE is (Blatman *et al.* 2009)

$$\mu^{PC} = E[M^{PC}(\mathbf{X})] = \alpha_1, \tag{11}$$

where α_1 is the coefficient of the constant basis term $\Psi_1 = 1$. The standard deviation of PCE is

$$\sigma^{PC} = E[(M^{PC}(\mathbf{X}) - \mu^{PC})^2] = \sum_{i=2}^{P} \alpha_i^2, \tag{12}$$

where it is the summation on coefficients of non-constant basis terms only.

5   Results

The proposed approach is illustrated on the spherically-void-defect benchmark problem with two uncertain parameters (see Fig. 1). In this work, the probe angle, θ, and the probe F-number, F, are considered as uncertain, with normal $N(0°, 1°)$ and uniform U (13, 15) distributions, respectively. The distributions are shown in Fig. 3.

Figure 4 gives the results of the surrogate modeling construction. In particular, Fig. 4 shows the root mean square error (RMSE) as a function of the number of samples. From Fig. 4a, the LAR sparse (LARS) PCE model can reduce the RMSE value to less than 1% (also smaller than 1% σ of testing points) using 190 Latin hypercube sampling (LHS) random sample points. The Kriging interpolation model reaches the lowest RMSE value of around 10%. Figure 4b shows how the RMSE of the surrogate model varies with the defect size.

Statistical moments are always representative of a population of samples. Figure 5 compares the convergence on the statistical moments from the PCE model, Monte Carlo sampling (MCS) with the true model, and MCS based on the Kriging model. From the figure, it can be seen that LARS PCE method has a faster convergence rate

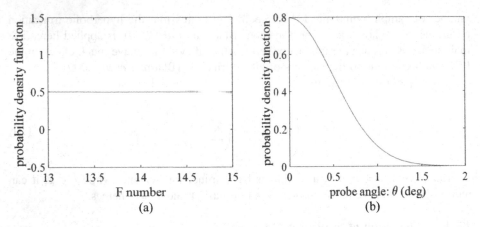

Fig. 3. Statistical distributions of uncertainty parameters: (a) F-number; (b) probe angle: θ.

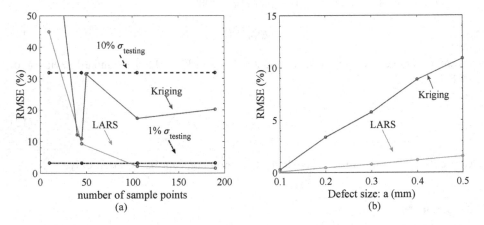

Fig. 4. RMSE for Kriging and LARS PCE: (a) RMSE for 0.5 mm defect; (b) RMSE for various defect sizes.

than MCS with the true model and MCS with the Kriging model with a difference in the number of sample points of around 2 orders of magnitude.

The LARS PCE models are used to generate the "$\hat{a}$ vs. a" plot and the POD curves, as shown in Fig. 6a and b, respectively. Through the POD curves, we obtain the a_{50}, a_{90}, and $a_{90/95}$ information to compare the results based on the LARS PCE models with those from using MCS with the Kriging model and true model (see Table 1). We can see that the important POD metrics from the LARS PCE model match well with those from true model. More specifically, the relative differences between the LARS PCE model and the true model on a_{50}, a_{90}, and $a_{90/95}$ are 0.05%, 0.35%, and 0.39%, respectively. However, the relative differences between MCS with the Kriging model and MCS with the true model are −2.22%, −25.7%, −29.65%, respectively.

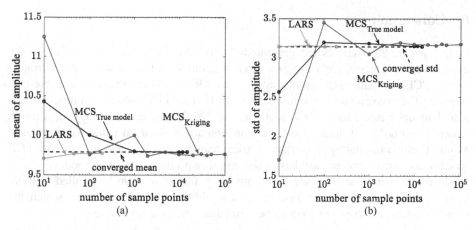

Fig. 5. Convergence on the statistical moments: (a) convergence on the mean; (b) convergence on the standard deviation. Here, MCS_{True} model is MCS on true model, while $MCS_{Kriging}$ is MCS on Kriging model.

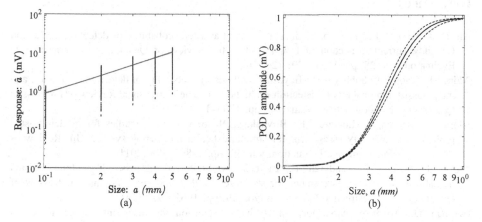

Fig. 6. POD generation using the LARS PCE model: (a) "$\hat{a}$ vs. a" plots; (b) POD curves.

Table 1. Comparison on the POD metrics obtained using MCS with the true model, MCS with the Kriging model, and the LARS PCE model. Here Δ is the relative difference with true model.

	a_{50}/Δ	a_{90}/Δ	$a_{90/95}/\Delta$
MCS-true	0.3747/N/A	0.5951/N/A	0.6395/N/A
MCS-Kriging	0.3831/− 2.22%	0.7484/− 25.76%	0.8291/− 29.65%
LARS PCE	0.3745/0.05%	0.593/0.35%	0.637/0.39%

6 Conclusion

In this paper, POD curves are generated through MAPOD framework. Due to the expensive time costs of physics-based simulation model, a type of stochastic surrogate model, PCE surrogate model, is integrated with LAR method and hyperbolic sparse-grid scheme. The convergence on statistical moments from PCE model is compared with actual model based Monte Carlo method, and Kriging based Monte Carlo, through which a two orders of magnitude faster convergence is obtained while Kriging based Monte Carlo is oscillating. Important metrics, namely, a_{50}, a_{90}, and $a_{90/95}$, from PCE models, are also compared, and have good match with those from true model.

In future work, the surrogate-based modeling framework can be applied to more complex and time-consuming models, such as full wave model, through which the problem under test does not have to be limited as spherically void defect.

Acknowledgements. This work was funded by the Center for Nondestructive Evaluation Industry/University Cooperative Research Program at Iowa State University, Ames, USA.

References

Aldrin, J., Knopp, J., Lindgren, E., Jata, K.: Model-assisted probability of detection evaluation for eddy current inspection of fastener sites. In: Review of Quantitative Nondestructive Evaluation, vol. 28, pp. 1784–1791 (2009)

Aldrin, J., Knopp, J., Sabbagh, H.: Bayesian methods in probability of detection estimation and model-assisted probability of detection evaluation. In: The 39th Annual Review of Progress in Quantitative Nondestructive Evaluation, pp. 1733–1740 (2013)

Aldrin, J., Medina, E., Lindgren, E., Buynak, C., Knopp, J.: Case studies for model-assisted probabilistic reliability assessment for structural health monitoring systems. In: Review of Progress in Nondestructive Evaluation, vol. 30, pp. 1589–1596 (2011)

Aldrin, J., Medina, E., Lindgren, E., Buynak, C., Steffes, G., Derriso, M.: Model-assisted probabilistic reliability assessment for structure health monitoring systems. In: Review of Quantitative Nondestructive Evaluation, vol. 29, pp. 1965–1972 (2010)

Blatman, G.: Adaptive sparse polynomial chaos expansion for uncertainty propagation and sensitivity analysis. Ph.D. thesis, Blaise Pascal University - Clermont II. 3, 8, 9 (2009)

Blatman, G., Sudret, B.: An adaptive algorithm to build up sparse polynomial chaos expansions for stochastic finite element analysis. Probab. Eng. Mech. **25**(2), 183–197 (2010)

Blatman, G., Sudret, B.: Adaptive sparse polynomial chaos expansion based on least angle regression. J. Comput. Phys. **230**, 2345–2367 (2011)

Blitz, J., Simpson, G.: Ultrasonic Methods of Non-destructive Testing. Chapman & Hall, London (1996)

Nondestructive Evaluation System Reliability Assessment: MIL-HDBK-1823, Department of Defense Handbook, April 2009

Du, X., Grandin, R., Leifsson, L.: Surrogate modeling of ultrasonic simulations using data-driven methods. In: 43rd Annual Review of Progress in Quantitative Nondestructive Evaluation, vol. 36, pp. 150002-1–150002-9 (2016)

Du, X., Leifsson, L., Grandin, R., Meeker, W., Roberts, R., Song, J.: Model-assisted probability of detection of flaws in aluminum blocks using polynomial chaos expansions. In: 43rd Annual Review of Progress in Quantitative Nondestructive Evaluation (2017)

Efron, B., Hastie, T., Johnstone, I., Tibshirani, R.: Least angle regression. Ann. Stat. **32**(2), 407–499 (2004)

Forrester, A., Sobester, A., Keane, A.: Engineering Design via Surrogate Modelling: A Practical Guid. Wiley, Hoboken (2008)

Gray, T.A.: Ultrasonic measurement models – a tribute to R. Bruce Thompson. In: Review of Progress in Quantitative Nondestructive Evaluation, vol. 31, no. 1, pp. 38–53 (2012)

Gurrala, P., Chen, K., Song, J., Roberts, R.: Full wave modeling of ultrasonic NDE benchmark problems using Nystrom method. In: 43rd Annual Review of Progress in Quantitative Nondestructive Evaluation, vol. 36, pp. 150003-1–150003-8 (2017)

Jenson, F., Dominguez, N., Willaume, P., Yalamas, T.: A Bayesian approach for the determination of POD curves from empirical data merged with simulation results. In: The 39th Annual Review of Progress in Quantitative Nondestructive Evaluation, pp. 1741–1748 (2013)

Knopp, J., Blodgett, M., Aldrin, J.: Efficient propagation of uncertainty simulations via the probabilistic collocation method. In: Studies in Applied Electromagnetic and Mechanics; Electromagnetic Nondestructive Evaluation Proceedings, vol. 35 (2011)

Miorelli, R., Artusi, X., Abdessalem, A., Reboud, C.: Database generation and exploitation for efficient and intensive simulation studies. In: 42nd Annual Review of Progress in Quantitative Nondestructive Evaluation, pp. 180002-1–180002-8 (2016)

Ribay, G., Artusi, X., Jenson, F., Reece C., Lhuillier, P.: Model-assisted POD study of manual ultrasound inspection and sensitivity analysis using metamodel. In: 42nd Annual Review of Progress in Quantitative Nondestructive Evaluation, pp. 200006-1–200006-7 (2016)

Ryu, J., Kim, K., Lee, T., Choi, D.: Kriging interpolation methods in geostatistics and DACE model. Korean Soc. Mech. Eng. Int. J. **16**(5), 619–632 (2002)

Sabbagh, E., Murphy, R., Sabbagh, H., Aldrin, J., Knopp, J., Blodgett, M.: Stochastic-integral models for propagation-of-uncertainty problems in nondestructive evaluation. In: The 39th Annual Review of Progress in Quantitative Nondestructive Evaluation, pp. 1765–1772 (2013)

Sacks, J., Welch, W.J., Michell, T.J., Wynn, H.P.: Design and analysis of computer experiments. Stat. Sci. **4**, 409–423 (1989)

Sarkar, P., Meeker, W., Thompson, R., Gray, T., Junker, W.: Probability of detection modeling for ultrasonic testing. In: Thompson, D.O., Chimenti, D.E. (eds.) Review of Progress in Quantitative Nondestructive Evaluation, vol. 17, pp. 2045–2052. Springer, Boston (1998). https://doi.org/10.1007/978-1-4615-5339-7_265

Schmerr, L.: Fundamentals of Ultrasonic Nondestructive Evaluation: A Modeling Approach. Springer, Heidelberg (2013). https://doi.org/10.1007/978-3-319-30463-2

Schmerr, L., Song, J.M.: Ultrasonic Nondestructive Evaluation Systems. Springer, Heidelberg (2007). https://doi.org/10.1007/978-0-387-49063-2

Siegler, J., Leifsson, L., Grandin, R., Koziel, S., Bekasiewicz, A.: Surrogate modeling of ultrasonic nondestructive evaluation simulations. In: International Conference on Computational Science (ICCS), vol. 80, pp. 1114–1124 (2016)

Spall, J.: System understanding and statistical uncertainty bounds from limited test data. Johns Hopkins Appl. Tech. Dig. **18**(4), 473 (1997)

Thompson, R., Brasche, L., Forsyth, D., Lindgren, E., Swindell, P.: Recent advances in model-assisted probability of detection. In: 4th European-American Workshop on Reliability of NDE, Berlin, Germany, 24–26 June 2009

Udell, M., Horn, C., Zadeh, R., Boyd, S.: Generalized low rank models. Found. Trends Mach. Learn. **9**(1), 1–118 (2016)

Wiener, N.: The homogeneous chaos. Am. J. Math. **60**, 897–936 (1938)

Xiong, F., Greene, S., Chen, W., Xiong, Y., Yang, S.: A new sparse grid based method for uncertainty propagation. Struct Multidisc. Optim. **41**, 335–349 (2010)

Xiong, F., Xue, B., Yan, Z., Yang, S.: Polynomial chaos expansion based robust design optimization. In: IEEE 978-1-4577-1232-6/11 (2011)

Accelerating Optical Absorption Spectra and Exciton Energy Computation via Interpolative Separable Density Fitting

Wei Hu[1,2], Meiyue Shao[1], Andrea Cepellotti[3,4], Felipe H. da Jornada[3,4], Lin Lin[1,5], Kyle Thicke[6], Chao Yang[1(✉)], and Steven G. Louie[3,4]

[1] Computational Research Division, Lawrence Berkeley National Laboratory, Berkeley, CA 94720, USA
{whu,myshao,cyang}@lbl.gov, whuustc@ustc.edu.cn
[2] Hefei National Laboratory for Physical Sciences at Microscale, University of Science and Technology of China, Hefei 230026, Anhui, China
[3] Department of Physics, University of California, Berkeley, Berkeley, CA 94720, USA
{andrea.cepellotti,jornada,sglouie}@berkeley.edu
[4] Materials Sciences Division, Lawrence Berkeley National Laboratory, Berkeley, CA 94720, USA
[5] Department of Mathematics, University of California, Berkeley, Berkeley, CA 94720, USA
linlin@math.berkeley.edu
[6] Department of Mathematics, Duke University, Durham, NC 27708, USA
kyle.thicke@duke.edu

Abstract. We present an efficient way to solve the Bethe–Salpeter equation (BSE), a method for the computation of optical absorption spectra in molecules and solids that includes electron–hole interactions. Standard approaches to construct and diagonalize the Bethe–Salpeter Hamiltonian require at least $\mathcal{O}(N_e^5)$ operations, where N_e is the number of electrons in the system, limiting its application to smaller systems. Our approach is based on the interpolative separable density fitting (ISDF) technique to construct low rank approximations to the bare exchange and screened direct operators associated with the BSE Hamiltonian. This approach reduces the complexity of the Hamiltonian construction to $\mathcal{O}(N_e^3)$ with a much smaller pre-constant, and allows for a faster solution of the BSE. Here, we implement the ISDF method for BSE calculations within the Tamm–Dancoff approximation (TDA) in the BerkeleyGW software package. We show that this novel approach accurately reproduces exciton energies and optical absorption spectra in molecules and solids with a significantly reduced computational cost.

1 Introduction

Many-Body Perturbation Theory is a powerful tool to describe one-particle and two-particle excitations and to obtain exciton energies and absorption spectra in

© Springer International Publishing AG, part of Springer Nature 2018
Y. Shi et al. (Eds.): ICCS 2018, LNCS 10861, pp. 604–617, 2018.
https://doi.org/10.1007/978-3-319-93701-4_48

molecules and solids. In particular, Hedin's GW approximation [9] has been successfully used to compute quasi-particle (one-particle) excitation energies [11]. However, the Bethe–Salpeter equation (BSE) [23] is further needed to describe the excitations of an electron–hole pair (a two-particle excitation) in optical absorption in molecules and solids [22] and is often necessary to obtain a good agreement between theory and experiment. Solving the BSE problem requires constructing and diagonalizing a structured matrix Hamiltonian. In the context of optical absorption, the eigenvalues are the exciton energies and the corresponding eigenfunctions yield the exciton wavefunctions.

The Bethe–Salpeter Hamiltonian (BSH) consists of bare exchange and screened direct interaction kernels that depend on single-particle orbitals obtained from a quasiparticle (usually at the GW level) or mean-field calculation. The evaluation of these kernels requires at least $\mathcal{O}(N_e^5)$ operations in a conventional approach, which is very costly for large systems that contain hundreds or thousands of atoms. Recent efforts have actively explored methods to generate a reduced basis set, in order to decrease the high computational cost of BSE calculations [1,12,16,19,21].

In this paper, we present an efficient way to construct the BSH, which, when coupled to an iterative diagonalization scheme, allows for an efficient solution of the BSE. Our approach is based on the recently-developed Interpolative Separable Density Fitting (ISDF) decomposition [18]. The ISDF decomposition has been applied to accelerate a number of applications in computational chemistry and materials science, including the computation of two-electrons integrals [18], correlation energy in the random phase approximation [17], density functional perturbation theory [15], and hybrid density functional calculations [10]. In this scheme, a matrix consisting of products of single-particle orbital pairs is approximated as the product between a matrix built with a small number of auxiliary basis vectors and an expansion coefficient matrix [10]. This decomposition effectively allows us to construct low-rank approximations to the bare exchange and screened direct kernels. The construction of the ISDF-compressed BSE Hamiltonian matrix only requires $\mathcal{O}(N_e^3)$ operations when the rank of the numerical auxiliary basis is kept at $\mathcal{O}(N_e)$ and when the kernels are kept in a low-rank factored form, resulting in considerably faster computation than the $\mathcal{O}(N_e^5)$ complexity required in a conventional approach. By keeping the interaction kernel in a decomposed form, the matrix–vector multiplications required in the iterative diagonalization procedures of the Hamiltonian H_{BSE} can be performed efficiently. We can further use these efficient matrix–vector multiplications in a structure preserving Lanczos algorithm [24] to obtain an approximate absorption spectrum without an explicit diagonalization of the approximate H_{BSE}. We have implemented the ISDF-based BSH construction in the BerkeleyGW software package [4], and verified that this approach can reproduce accurate exciton energies and optical absorption spectra for molecules and solids, while significant reducing the computational cost associated with the construction of the BSE Hamiltonian.

2   Bethe–Salpeter Equation

The Bethe–Salpeter equation is an eigenvalue problem of the form

$$H_{\mathrm{BSE}}X = EX, \tag{1}$$

where X is the exciton wavefunction, E the corresponding exciton energy. The Bethe–Salpeter Hamiltonian H_{BSE} has the following block structure

$$H_{\mathrm{BSE}} = \begin{bmatrix} D + 2V_A - W_A & 2V_B - W_B \\ -2\overline{V}_B + \overline{W}_B & -D - 2\overline{V}_A + \overline{W}_A \end{bmatrix}, \tag{2}$$

where $D(i_v i_c, j_v j_c) = (\epsilon_{i_c} - \epsilon_{i_v})\delta_{i_v j_c}\delta_{i_c j_c}$ is an $(N_v N_c) \times (N_v N_c)$ diagonal matrix with $-\epsilon_{i_v}$, $i_v = 1, 2, \ldots, N_v$ the quasi-particle energies associated with valence bands and ϵ_{i_c}, $i_c = N_v + 1, N_v + 2, \ldots, N_v + N_c$ the quasi-particle energies associated with conduction bands. These quasi-particle energies are typically obtained from a GW calculation [22]. The V_A and V_B matrices represent the bare *exchange* interaction of electron–hole pairs, and the W_A and W_B matrices are referred to as the screened *direct* interaction of electron–hole pairs. These matrices are defined as follows:

$$V_A(i_v i_c, j_v j_c) = \int \bar{\psi}_{i_c}(\mathbf{r})\psi_{i_v}(\mathbf{r})V(\mathbf{r}, \mathbf{r}')\bar{\psi}_{j_v}(\mathbf{r}')\psi_{j_c}(\mathbf{r}') \,\mathrm{d}\mathbf{r}\,\mathrm{d}\mathbf{r}',$$

$$V_B(i_v i_c, j_v j_c) = \int \bar{\psi}_{i_c}(\mathbf{r})\psi_{i_v}(\mathbf{r})V(\mathbf{r}, \mathbf{r}')\bar{\psi}_{j_c}(\mathbf{r}')\psi_{j_v}(\mathbf{r}') \,\mathrm{d}\mathbf{r}\,\mathrm{d}\mathbf{r}',$$

$$W_A(i_v i_c, j_v j_c) = \int \bar{\psi}_{i_c}(\mathbf{r})\psi_{j_c}(\mathbf{r})W(\mathbf{r}, \mathbf{r}')\bar{\psi}_{j_v}(\mathbf{r}')\psi_{i_v}(\mathbf{r}') \,\mathrm{d}\mathbf{r}\,\mathrm{d}\mathbf{r}',$$

$$W_B(i_v i_c, j_v j_c) = \int \bar{\psi}_{i_c}(\mathbf{r})\psi_{j_v}(\mathbf{r})W(\mathbf{r}, \mathbf{r}')\bar{\psi}_{j_c}(\mathbf{r}')\psi_{i_v}(\mathbf{r}') \,\mathrm{d}\mathbf{r}\,\mathrm{d}\mathbf{r}', \tag{3}$$

where ψ_{i_v} and ψ_{i_c} are the valence and conduction single-particle orbitals typically obtained from a Kohn–Sham density functional theory (KSDFT) calculation respectively, and $V(\mathbf{r}, \mathbf{r}')$ and $W(\mathbf{r}, \mathbf{r}')$ are the bare and screened Coulomb interactions. Both V_A and W_A are Hermitian, whereas V_B and W_B are complex symmetric. Within the so-called Tamm–Dancoff approximation (TDA) [20], both V_B and W_B are neglected in Eq. (2). In this case, the H_{BSE} becomes Hermitian and we can focus on computing the upper left block of H_{BSE}.

Let $M_{cc}(\mathbf{r}) = \{\psi_{i_c}\bar{\psi}_{j_c}\}$, $M_{vc}(\mathbf{r}) = \{\psi_{i_c}\bar{\psi}_{i_v}\}$, and $M_{vv}(\mathbf{r}) = \{\psi_{i_v}\bar{\psi}_{j_v}\}$ be matrices built as the product between orbital pairs in real space, and $\hat{M}_{cc}(\mathbf{G})$, $\hat{M}_{vc}(\mathbf{G})$, $\hat{M}_{vv}(\mathbf{G})$ be the reciprocal space representation of these matrices. Equations (3) can then be written succinctly as

$$V_A = \hat{M}_{vc}^* \hat{V} \hat{M}_{vc}, \quad W_A = \mathrm{reshape}(\hat{M}_{cc}^* \hat{W} \hat{M}_{vv}), \tag{4}$$

where $\hat{V}$ and $\hat{W}$ are reciprocal space representations of the operators V and W respectively, and the reshape function is used to map the $(i_c j_c, i_v j_v)$th element on the right-hand side of (4) to the $(i_c i_v, j_c j_v)$th element of W_A. While in this paper we will focus, for simplicity, on the TDA model, we note that a similar set of equations can be derived for V_B and W_B.

The reason to compute the right-hand sides of (4) in the reciprocal space is that $\hat{V}$ is diagonal and an energy cutoff is often adopted to limit the number of the Fourier components of ψ_i. As a result, the leading dimension of $\hat{M}_{cc}$, $\hat{M}_{vc}$ and $\hat{M}_{cc}$, denoted by N_g, is often much smaller than that of M_{cc}, M_{vc} and M_{vv}, which we denote by N_r.

In addition to performing $\mathcal{O}(N_e^2)$ Fast Fourier transforms (FFTs) to obtain $\hat{M}_{cc}$, $\hat{M}_{vc}$ and $\hat{M}_{vv}$ from M_{cc}, M_{vc} and M_{vv}, respectively, we need to perform at least $\mathcal{O}(N_g N_c^2 N_v^2)$ floating-point operations to obtain V_A and W_A using matrix–matrix multiplications.

Note that, in order to achieve high accuracy with a large basis set, such as that of plane-waves, N_g is typically much larger than N_c or N_v. The number of occupied bands is either N_e or $N_e/2$ depending on how spin is counted. The number of conduction bands N_c included in the calculation is typically a small multiple of N_v (the precise number being a free parameter to be converged), whereas N_g is often as large as $100-10000 \times N_e$ ($N_r \sim 10 \times N_g$).

3   Interpolative Separable Density Fitting (ISDF) Decomposition

In order to reduce the computational complexity, we seek to minimize the number of integrals in Eq. (3). To this aim, we rewrite the matrix M_{ij}, where the labels i and j are indices of either valence or conducting orbitals, as the product of a matrix Θ_{ij} that contains a set of N_{ij}^t linearly independent auxiliary basis vectors with $N_{ij}^t \approx tN_e \ll \mathcal{O}(N_e^2)$ (t is a small constant referred as a rank truncation parameter) [10] and an expansion coefficient matrix C_{ij}. For large problems, the number of columns of M_{ij} (i.e. $\mathcal{O}(N_v N_c)$, or $\mathcal{O}(N_v^2)$, or $\mathcal{O}(N_c^2)$) is typically larger than the number of grid points N_r on which $\psi_n(\mathbf{r})$ is sampled, i.e., the number of rows in M_{ij}. As a result, N_{ij}^t is much smaller than the number of columns of M_{ij}. Even when a cutoff is used to limit the size of N_c or N_v so that the number of columns in M_{ij} is much less than N_g, we can still approximate M_{ij} by $\Theta_{ij} C_{ij}$ with a Θ_{ij} that has a smaller rank $N_{ij}^t \sim t\sqrt{N_i N_j}$.

To simplify our discussion, let us drop the subscript of M, Θ and C for the moment, and describe the basic idea of ISDF. The optimal low rank approximation of M can be obtained from a singular value decomposition. However, the complexity of this decomposition is at least $\mathcal{O}(N_r^2 N_e^2)$ or $\mathcal{O}(N_e^4)$. Recently, an alternative decomposition has been developed, which is close to optimal but with a more favorable complexity. This type of decomposition is called Interpolative Separable Density Fitting (ISDF) [10], which we describe below.

In ISDF, instead of computing Θ and C simultaneously, we first fix the coefficient matrix C, and determine the auxiliary basis matrix Θ by solving a linear least squares problem

$$\min \|M - \Theta C\|_F^2, \tag{5}$$

where each column of M is given by $\psi_i(\mathbf{r})\bar{\psi}_j(\mathbf{r})$ sampled on a dense real space grids $\{\mathbf{r}_i\}_{i=1}^{N_r}$, and $\Theta = [\zeta_1, \zeta_2, \ldots, \zeta_{N^t}]$ contains the auxiliary basis vectors to be determined, $\|\cdot\|_F$ denotes the Frobenius norm.

We choose C as a matrix consisting of $\psi_i(\mathbf{r})\bar{\psi}_j(\mathbf{r})$ evaluated on a subset of N^t carefully chosen real space grid points, with $N^t \ll N_r$ and $N^t \ll N_e^2$, such that the (i,j)th column of C is given by

$$[\psi_i(\hat{\mathbf{r}}_1)\bar{\psi}_j(\hat{\mathbf{r}}_1), \cdots, \psi_i(\hat{\mathbf{r}}_k)\bar{\psi}_j(\hat{\mathbf{r}}_k), \cdots, \psi_i(\hat{\mathbf{r}}_{N^t})\bar{\psi}_j(\hat{\mathbf{r}}_{N^t})]^\mathsf{T}. \tag{6}$$

The least squares minimizer is given by

$$\Theta = MC^*(CC^*)^{-1}. \tag{7}$$

Because both multiplications in (7) can be carried out in $\mathcal{O}(N_e^3)$ due to the separable structure of M and C [10], the computational complexity for computing the interpolation vectors is $\mathcal{O}(N_e^3)$.

The interpolating points required in (6) can be selected by a permutation produced from a QR factorization of M^T with Column Pivoting (QRCP) [3]. In QRCP, we choose a permutation Π such that the factorization

$$M^\mathsf{T}\Pi = QR \tag{8}$$

yields a unitary matrix Q and an upper triangular matrix R with decreasing matrix elements along the diagonal of R. The magnitude of each diagonal element R indicates how important the corresponding column of the permuted M^T is, and whether the corresponding grid point should be chosen as an interpolation point. The QRCP decomposition can be terminated when the $(N^t + 1)$-st diagonal element of R becomes less than a predetermined threshold, obtaining N^t leading columns of the permuted M^T that are, within numerical accuracy, maximally linearly independent. The corresponding grid points are chosen as the interpolation points. The indices for the chosen interpolation points $\hat{\mathbf{r}}_{N^t}$ can be obtained from indices of the nonzero entries of the first N^t columns of the permutation matrix Π. Notice that the standard QRCP procedure has a high computational cost of $\mathcal{O}(N_e^2 N_r^2) \sim \mathcal{O}(N_e^4)$, however, this cost can be reduced to $\mathcal{O}(N_r N_e^2) \sim \mathcal{O}(N_e^3)$ when QRCP is combined with the randomized sampling method [18].

4   Low Rank Representations of Bare and Screened Operators via ISDF

The ISDF decomposition applied to M_{cc}, M_{vc} and M_{vv} yields

$$M_{cc} \approx \Theta_{cc}C_{cc}, \quad M_{vc} \approx \Theta_{vc}C_{vc}, \quad M_{vv} \approx \Theta_{vv}C_{vv}. \tag{9}$$

It follows from Eqs. (3), (4) and (9) that the exchange and direct terms of the BSE Hamiltonian can be written as

$$V_A = C_{vc}^* \tilde{V}_A C_{vc}, \quad W_A = \text{reshape}(C_{cc}^* \widetilde{W}_A C_{vv}), \tag{10}$$

where $\widetilde{V}_A = \hat{\Theta}_{vc}^* \hat{V} \hat{\Theta}_{vc}$ and $\widetilde{W}_A = \hat{\Theta}_{cc}^* \hat{W} \hat{\Theta}_{vv}$ are the *projected* exchange and direct terms under the auxiliary basis $\hat{\Theta}_{vc}$, $\hat{\Theta}_{cc}$ and $\hat{\Theta}_{vv}$. Here, $\hat{\Theta}_{vc}$, $\hat{\Theta}_{cc}$ and $\hat{\Theta}_{vv}$ are reciprocal space representations of Θ_{vc}, Θ_{cc} and Θ_{vv}, respectively, that can be obtained via FFTs. Note that the dimension of the matrix $C_{cc}^* \widetilde{W}_A C_{cc}$ on the right-hand side of Eq. (10) is $N_c^2 \times N_v^2$. Therefore, it needs to be reshaped into a matrix of dimension $N_v N_c \times N_v N_c$ according to the mapping $W_A(i_c j_c, i_v j_v) \rightarrow W_A(i_v i_c, j_v j_c)$ before it can be used in the BSH together with the V_A matrix.

Once the ISDF approximations for M_{vc}, M_{cc} and M_{vv} are available, the cost for constructing a low-rank approximation to the exchange and direct terms reduces to that of computing the projected exchange and direct kernels $\hat{\Theta}_{vc}^* \hat{V} \hat{\Theta}_{vc}$ and $\hat{\Theta}_{cc}^* \hat{W} \hat{\Theta}_{vv}$, respectively. If the ranks of Θ_{vc}, Θ_{cc} and Θ_{vv} are N_{vc}^t, N_{cc}^t and N_{vv}^t, respectively, then the computational complexity for computing the compressed exchange and direct kernels is $\mathcal{O}(N_{vc}^t N_{vc}^t N_g + N_{cc}^t N_{vv}^t N_g + N_{vv}^t N_g^2)$, which is significantly lower than the complexity of the conventional approach, which is $\mathcal{O}(N_g N_c^2 N_v^2)$. When $N_{vc}^t \sim t\sqrt{N_v N_c}$, $N_{cc}^t \sim t\sqrt{N_c N_c}$ and $N_{vv}^t \sim t\sqrt{N_v N_v}$ are on the order of N_e, the complexity of constructing the compressed kernels is $\mathcal{O}(N_e^3)$.

5   Iterative Diagonalization of the BSE Hamiltonian

In the conventional approach, exciton energies and wavefunctions can be computed by using the recently developed BSEPACK library [25,26] to diagonalize the BSE Hamiltonian H_{BSE}.

When ISDF is used to construct low-rank approximations to the bare exchange and screened direct operators V_A and W_A, we should keep both matrices in the factored form given by Eq. (10). We propose to use iterative methods to diagonalize the approximate BSH constructed via the ISDF decomposition.

Within the TDA, several iterative methods such as the Lanczos [14] and LOBPCG [13] algorithms can be used to compute a few desired eigenvalues of the H_{BSE}. For each iterative step, we need to multiply H_{BSE} with a vector x of size $N_v N_c$. When V_A is kept in the factored form given by (10), $V_A x$ can be evaluated as three matrix vector multiplications performed in sequence, i.e.,

$$V_A x \leftarrow C_{vc}^* \left[\widetilde{V_A}(C_{vc}x) \right]. \tag{11}$$

The complexity of these calculations is $\mathcal{O}(N_v N_c N_{vc}^t)$. If N_{vc}^t is on the order of N_e, then each $V_A x$ can be carried out in $\mathcal{O}(N_e^3)$ operations.

Because $C_{cc}^* \widetilde{W}_A C_{vv}$ cannot be multiplied with a vector x of size $N_v N_c$ before it is reshaped, a different multiplication scheme must be used. It follows from the separable nature of C_{vv} and C_{cc} that this multiplication can be succinctly written as

$$W_A x = \text{reshape} \left[\Psi_c^* \left(\widetilde{W} \odot (\Psi_c X \Psi_v^*) \right) \Psi_v \right], \tag{12}$$

where X is a $N_c \times N_v$ matrix reshaped from the vector x, Ψ_c is a $N_{cc}^t \times N_c$ matrix containing $\psi_{i_c}(\hat{r}_k)$ as its elements, Ψ_v is a $N_{vv}^t \times N_v$ matrix containing $\psi_{i_v}(\hat{r}_k)$ as its elements, and $\odot$ denotes componentwise multiplication (Hadamard product).

The reshape function is used to turn the $N_c \times N_v$ matrix–matrix product back into a size $N_v N_c$ vector. If N_{vv}^t and N_{cc}^t are on the order of N_e, then all matrix–matrix multiplications in Eq. (12) can be carried out in $\mathcal{O}(N_e^3)$ operations. In this way, each step of the iterative method has a complexity $\mathcal{O}(N_e^3)$ and, if the number of iterative steps required to reach convergence is small, the iterative diagonalization can be solved in $\mathcal{O}(N_e^3)$ operations.

6   Estimating Optical Absorption Spectra Without Diagonalization

The optical absorption spectrum can be readily computed from the eigenpairs of H_{BSE} as

$$\varepsilon_2(\omega) = \mathrm{Im}\left[\frac{8\pi e^2}{\Omega}d_r^*((\omega - i\eta)I - H_{\mathrm{BSE}})^{-1}d_l\right], \tag{13}$$

where Ω is the volume of the primitive cell, e is the elementary charge, d_r and d_l are the right and left optical transition vectors, and η is a broadening factor used to account for the exciton lifetime.

To observe the absorption spectrum and identify its main peaks, it is possible to use a structure preserving iterative method instead of explicitly computing all eigenpairs of H_{BSE}. In Ref. [2,24], we developed a structure preserving Lanczos algorithm that has been implemented in the BSEPACK [26] library. When TDA is adopted, the structure preserving Lanczos reduces to a standard Lanczos algorithm.

7   Numerical Results

In this section, we demonstrate the accuracy and efficiency of the ISDF method when it is used to compute exciton energies and optical absorption spectrum in the BSE framework. We implemented the ISDF based BSH construction in the BerkeleyGW software package [4]. We use the *ab initio* software package Quantum ESPRESSO (QE) [6] to compute the ground-state quantities required in the GW and BSE calculations. We use Hartwigsen–Goedecker–Hutter (HGH) norm-conserving pseudopotentials [8] and the LDA [7] exchange–correlation functional in Quantum ESPRESSO. We also check these calculations in the KSSLOV software [27], which is a MATLAB toolbox for solving the Kohn-Sham equations. All the calculations were carried out on a single core at the Cori[1] systems at the National Energy Research Scientific Computing Center (NERSC).

We performed calculations for three systems at the Gamma point. In particular, we choose a silicon Si_8 system as a typical model of bulk crystals (in the $k = 0$ approximation, i.e. no sampling of the Brillouin zone) and two molecules: carbon monoxide (CO) and benzene (C_6H_6) as plotted in Fig. 1. All systems are closed shell systems, and the number of occupied bands is $N_v = N_e/2$, where

---

[1] https://www.nersc.gov/systems/cori/.

N_e is the valence electrons in the system. We compute the quasiparticle energies and the dielectric function of CO and C_6H_6 in the BerkeleyGW [4], whereas for Si_8 in the KSSLOV [27].

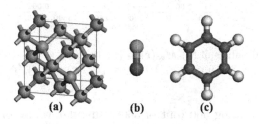

Fig. 1. Atomic structures of (a) a model silicon system Si_8, (b) carbon monoxide (CO) and (c) benzene (C_6H_6) molecules. The white, gray, red, and yellow balls denote hydrogen, carbon, oxygen, and silicon atoms, respectively. (Color figure online)

7.1   Accuracy

We first measure the accuracy of the ISDF method by comparing the eigenvalues of the BSH computed with and without the ISDF decomposition.

In our test, we set the plane wave energy cutoff required in the QE calculations to $E_{cut} = 10$ Ha, which is relatively low. However, this is sufficient for assessing the effectiveness of ISDF. Such a choice of E_{cut} results in $N_r = 35937$ and $N_g = 2301$ for the Si_8 system in a cubic supercell of size 10.22 Bohr^3, $N_r = 19683$ and $N_g = 1237$ for the CO molecule ($N_v = 5$) in a cubic cell of size 13.23 Bohr, $N_r = 91125$ and $N_g = 6235$ for the benzene molecule in a cubic cell of size 22.67 Bohr. The number of active conduction bands (N_c) and valence bands (N_v), the number of reciprocal grids and the dimensions of the corresponding BSE Hamiltonian H_{BSE} for these three systems are listed in Table 1.

Table 1. System size parameters for model silicon system Si_8, carbon monoxide (CO) and benzene (C_6H_6) molecules used for constructing corresponding BSE Hamiltonian H_{BSE}.

System	L (Bohr)	N_r	N_g	N_v	N_c	dim(H_{BSE})
Si_8	10.22	35937	2301	16	64	2048
CO	13.23	19683	1237	5	60	600
Benzene	22.67	91125	6235	15	60	1800

In Fig. 2, we plot the singular values of the matrices $M_{vc}(\mathbf{r}) = \{\psi_{i_c}(\mathbf{r})\bar{\psi}_{i_v}(\mathbf{r})\}$, $M_{cc}(\mathbf{r}) = \{\psi_{i_c}(\mathbf{r})\bar{\psi}_{j_c}(\mathbf{r})\}$ and $M_{vv}(\mathbf{r}) = \{\psi_{i_v}(\mathbf{r})\bar{\psi}_{j_v}(\mathbf{r})\}$ associated with the CO molecule. We observe that the singular values of these matrices decay rapidly.

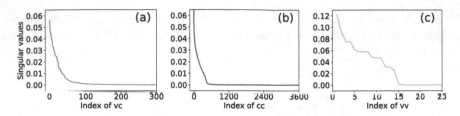

Fig. 2. The singular values of (a) $M_{vc}(\mathbf{r}) = \{\psi_{i_c}(\mathbf{r})\bar{\psi}_{i_v}(\mathbf{r})\}$ ($N_{vc} = 300$), (b) $M_{cc}(\mathbf{r}) = \{\psi_{i_c}(\mathbf{r})\bar{\psi}_{j_c}(\mathbf{r})\}$ ($N_{cc} = 3600$) and (c) $M_{vv}(\mathbf{r}) = \{\psi_{i_v}(\mathbf{r})\bar{\psi}_{j_v}(\mathbf{r})\}$ ($N_{vv} = 25$).

For example, the leading 500 (out of 3600) singular values of $M_{cc}(\mathbf{r})$ decreases rapidly towards zero. All other singular values are below 10^{-4}. Therefore, the numerical rank N^t_{cc} of M_{cc} is roughly 500 ($t = 8.3$), or roughly 15% of the number of columns in M_{cc}. Consequently, we expect that the rank of Θ_{cc} produced in ISDF decomposition can be set to 15% of N^2_c without sacrificing the accuracy of the computed eigenvalues.

This prediction is confirmed in Fig. 3, where we plot the absolute difference between the lowest exciton energy of model silicon system Si_8 computed with and without using ISDF to construct H_{BSE}. To be specific, the error in the desired eigenvalue is computed as $\Delta E = E_{ISDF} - E_{BGW}$, where E_{ISDF} is computed from the H_{BSE} constructed with ISDF approximation, and E_{BGW} is computed from a standard H_{BSE} constructed without using ISDF. We first vary one of the ratios N^t_{cc}/N_{cc}, N^t_{vc}/N_{vc} and N^t_{vv}/N_{vv} while holding the others at a constant of 1. We observe that the error in the lowest exciton energy (positive eigenvalue) is around 10^{-3} Ha, when either N^t_{cc}/N_{cc} or N^t_{vc}/N_{vc} is set to 0.1 while the other ratios are held at 1. However, reducing N^t_{vv}/N_{vv} to 0.1 introduces a significant amount of error in the lowest exciton energy, likely because $N_v = 16$ is too small. We then hold N^t_{vv}/N_{vv} at 0.5 and let both N^t_{cc}/N_{cc} and N^t_{vc}/N_{vc} vary. The variation of ΔE with respect to these ratios is also plotted as in Fig. 3. We observe that the error in the lowest exciton energy is still around 10^{-3} Ha even when both N^t_{cc}/N_{cc} and N^t_{vc}/N_{vc} are set to 0.1.

We then check the absolute error ΔE (Ha) of all the exciton energies computed with the ISDF method by comparing them with the ones obtained from a conventional BSE calculation implemented in BerkeleyGW for the CO and benzene molecules. As we can see from Fig. 4, the errors associated with these eigenvalues are all below 0.002 Ha when N^t_{cc}/N_{cc} is 0.1.

7.2   Efficiency

At the moment, our preliminary implementation of the ISDF method within the BerkeleyGW software package is sequential. Therefore, our efficiency test is limited by the size of the problem as well as the number of conducting bands (N_c) we can include in the bare and screened operators. As a result, our performance measurement does not fully reflect the computational complexity analysis presented in the previous sections. In particular, taking benzene as an example,

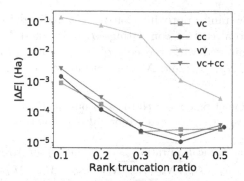

Fig. 3. The change of absolute error ΔE in the smallest eigenvalue of H_{BSE} associated with the Si_8 system with respect to different truncation levels used in ISDF approximation of M_{vc}, M_{cc} and M_{vv}. The curves labeled by 'vc', 'cc', 'vv' correspond to calculations in which only one of the ratios N_{vc}^t/N_{vc}, N_{cc}^t/N_{cc} and N_{vv}^t/N_{vv} changes while all other parameters are held constant. The curve labeled by 'vc + cc' corresponds to the calculation in which both N_{vc}^t/N_{vc} and N_{cc}^t/N_{cc} change at the same rate $(N_{vv}^t = N_{vv})$.

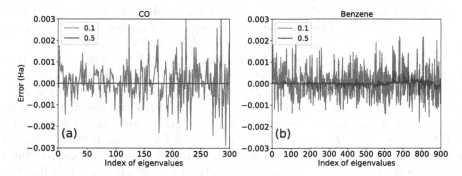

Fig. 4. Error in all eigenvalues of the BSH associated with the (a) CO and (b) benzene molecules. Two rank truncation ratios $N_{cc}^t/N_{cc} = 0.5$ $(t = 30.0)$ and $N_{cc}^t/N_{cc} = 0.1$ $(t = 6.0)$ are used in the tests.

$N_g = 6235$ is much larger than $N_v = 15$ and $N_c = 60$, therefore the computational cost of $N_g^2 N_v^2 \sim \mathcal{O}(N_e^4)$ term is much higher than the $N_g N_v^2 N_c^2 \sim \mathcal{O}(N_e^5)$ term in the conventional BSE calculations.

Nonetheless, in this section, we will demonstrate the benefit of using ISDF to reduce the cost for constructing the BSE Hamiltonian H_{BSE}. In Table 2, we focus on the benzene example and report the wall-clock time required to construct the ISDF approximations of the M_{vc}, M_{cc}, and M_{vv} matrices at different rank truncation levels. Without using ISDF, it takes $746.0\,\mathrm{s}$ to construct the reciprocal space representations of M_{vc}, M_{cc}, and M_{vv} in BerkeleyGW. Most of the time is spent in the several FFTs applied to M_{vc}, M_{cc}, and M_{vv}, in order to obtain the reciprocal space representation of these matrices. We can clearly see that by reducing N_{cc}^t/N_{cc} from 0.5 $(t = 30.0)$ to 0.1 $(t = 6.0)$, the wall-clock time used to construct the low-rank approximation to M_{cc} reduces from 578.9 to 34.3 s. Furthermore, the total cost of computing M_{vc}, M_{cc} and M_{vv} is reduced by a factor 19 when compared with the cost of a conventional approach (39.3 vs. 746.0 s) if N^t_{vc}/N_{vc}, N^t_{vv}/N_{vv} and N^t_{cc}/N_{cc} are all set to 0.1.

Table 2. The variation of time required to carry out the ISDF decomposition of M_{vc}, M_{vv} and M_{cc} with respect to rank truncation ratio for the benzene molecule.

Rank truncation ratio			Time (s) for $M_{ij}(\mathbf{r})$		
N^t_{vc}/N_{vc}	N^t_{vv}/N_{vv}	N^t_{cc}/N_{cc}	M_{vc}	M_{vv}	M_{cc}
1.0	0.5	0.5	157.0	5.8	578.9
1.0	0.5	0.1	157.0	5.8	34.3
0.1	0.1	0.1	4.3	0.7	34.3

Since the ISDF decomposition is carried out on a real-space grid, most of the time is spent in performing the QRCP in real space. Even though QRCP with random sampling has $\mathcal{O}(N^3_e)$ complexity, it has a relatively large pre-constant compared to the size of the problem. This cost can be further reduced by using the recently proposed centroidal Voronoi tessellation (CVT) method [5].

In Table 3, we report the wall-clock time required to construct the projected exchange and direct matrices $\widetilde{V}_A$ and $\widetilde{W}_A$ that appear in Eq. (10) from the ISDF approximations of M_{vc}, M_{vv}, and M_{cc}. The current implementation in BerkeleyGW requires 103,154 s (28.65 h) in a serial run for the full construction of H_{BSE}. In the present reimplementation, without ISDF, it takes $1.574 + 4.198 = 5.772$ s to construct both W_A and V_A. Note that the original implementation in BerkeleyGW is much slower as it requires a complete integration over G vectors for each pair of bands. When N^t_{cc}/N_{cc} is set to 0.1, the cost for constructing the full W_A, which has the largest complexity, is reduced by a factor 2.8. Furthermore, if N^t_{vc}/N_{vc}, N^t_{vv}/N_{vv} and N^t_{cc}/N_{cc} are all set to 0.1, we reduce the cost for constructing $\widetilde{V}_A$ and $\widetilde{W}_A$ by a factor of 63.0 and 10.1 respectively.

Table 3. The variation of time required to construct the projected bare and screened matrices $\widetilde{V}_A$ and $\widetilde{W}_A$ exhibited by the ISDF method respect to rank truncation ratio for the benzene molecule.

Rank truncation ratio			Time (s) for H_{BSE}	
N^t_{vc}/N_{vc}	N^t_{vv}/N_{vv}	N^t_{cc}/N_{cc}	$\widetilde{V}_A$	$\widetilde{W}_A$
1.0	1.0	1.0	1.574	4.198
1.0	0.5	0.1	1.574	1.474
0.1	0.1	0.1	0.025	0.414

7.3 Optical Absorption Spectra

One important application of BSE is to compute the optical absorption spectrum, which is determined by optical dielectric function in Eq. (13). Figure 5 plots the optical absorption spectra for both CO and benzene obtained from approximate H_{BSE} constructed with the ISDF method and the H_{BSE} constructed in a conventional approach implemented in BerkeleyGW. When the rank truncation ratio N_{cc}^t/N_{cc} is set to be only 0.10 ($t = 6.0$), the absorption spectrum obtained from the ISDF approximate H_{BSE} is nearly indistinguishable from that produced from the conventional approach. When N_{cc}^t/N_{cc} is set to 0.05 ($t = 3.0$), the absorption spectrum obtained from ISDF approximate H_{BSE} still preserves the main features (peaks) of the absorption spectrum obtained in a conventional approach even though some of the peaks are slightly shifted, and the height of some peaks are slightly off.

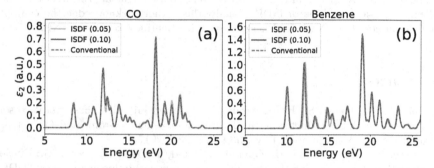

Fig. 5. Optical dielectric function (imaginary part ε_2) of (a) CO and (b) benzene molecules computed with the ISDF method (the rank ratio N_{cc}^t/N_{cc} is set to be 0.05 ($t = 3.0$) and 0.10 ($t = 6.0$)) compared to conventional BSE calculations in BerkeleyGW.

8   Conclusion and Outlook

In summary, we have demonstrated that the interpolative separable density fitting (ISDF) technique can be used to efficiently and accurately construct the Bethe–Salpeter Hamiltonian matrix. The ISDF method allows us to reduce the complexity of the Hamiltonian construction from $\mathcal{O}(N_e^5)$ to $\mathcal{O}(N_e^3)$ with a much smaller pre-constant. We show that the ISDF based BSE calculations in molecules and solids can efficiently produce accurate exciton energies and optical absorption spectrum in molecules and solids.

In the future, we plan to replace the costly QRCP procedure with the centroidal Voronoi tessellation (CVT) method [5] for selecting the interpolation points in the ISDF method. The CVT method is expected to significantly reduce the computational cost for selecting interpolating point in the ISDF procedure for the BSE calculations.

The performance results reported here are based on a sequential implementation of the ISDF method. In the near future, we will implement a parallel version suitable for large-scale distributed memory parallel computers. Such an implementation will allow us to tackle much larger problems for which the favorable scaling of the ISDF approach will be more pronounced.

Acknowledgments. This work is supported by the Center for Computational Study of Excited-State Phenomena in Energy Materials (C2SEPEM) at the Lawrence Berkeley National Laboratory, which is funded by the U.S. Department of Energy, Office of Science, Basic Energy Sciences, Materials Sciences and Engineering Division, under Contract No. DE-AC02-05CH11231, as part of the Computational Materials Sciences Program, which provided support for developing, implementing and testing ISDF for BSE in BerkeleyGW. The Center for Applied Mathematics for Energy Research Applications (CAMERA) (L. L. and C. Y.) provided support for the algorithm development and mathematical analysis of ISDF. Finally, the authors acknowledge the computational resources of the National Energy Research Scientific Computing (NERSC) center.

References

1. Benner, P., Dolgov, S., Khoromskaia, V., Khoromskij, B.N.: Fast iterative solution of the Bethe–Salpeter eigenvalue problem using low-rank and QTT tensor approximation. J. Comput. Phys. **334**, 221–239 (2017)
2. Brabec, J., Lin, L., Shao, M., Govind, N., Saad, Y., Yang, C., Ng, E.G.: Efficient algorithms for estimating the absorption spectrum within linear response TDDFT. J. Chem. Theory Comput. **11**(11), 5197–5208 (2015)
3. Chan, T.F., Hansen, P.C.: Some applications of the rank revealing QR factorization. SIAM J. Sci. Statist. Comput. **13**, 727–741 (1992)
4. Deslippe, J., Samsonidze, G., Strubbe, D.A., Jain, M., Cohen, M.L., Louie, S.G.: BerkeleyGW: a massively parallel computer package for the calculation of the quasiparticle and optical properties of materials and nanostructures. Comput. Phys. Commun. **183**(6), 1269–1289 (2012)
5. Dong, K., Hu, W., Lin, L.: Interpolative separable density fitting through centroidal Voronoi tessellation with applications to hybrid functional electronic structure calculations (2017). arXiv:1711.01531
6. Giannozzi, P., Baroni, S., Bonini, N., Calandra, M., Car, R., Cavazzoni, C., Ceresoli, D., Chiarotti, G.L., Cococcioni, M., Dabo, I., Corso, A.D., de Gironcoli, S., Fabris, S., Fratesi, G., Gebauer, R., Gerstmann, U., Gougoussis, C., Kokalj, A., Lazzeri, M., Martin-Samos, L., Marzari, N., Mauri, F., Mazzarello, R., Paolini, S., Pasquarello, A., Paulatto, L., Sbraccia, C., Scandolo, S., Sclauzero, G., Seitsonen, A.P., Smogunov, A., Umari, P., Wentzcovitch, R.M.: QUANTUM ESPRESSO: a modular and open-source software project for quantum simulations of materials. J. Phys.: Condens. Matter **21**(39), 395502 (2009)
7. Goedecker, S., Teter, M., Hutter, J.: Separable dual-space Gaussian pseudopotentials. Phys. Rev. B **54**, 1703 (1996)
8. Hartwigsen, C., Goedecker, S., Hutter, J.: Relativistic separable dual-space gaussian pseudopotentials from H to Rn. Phys. Rev. B **58**, 3641 (1998)

9. Hedin, L.: New method for calculating the one-particle Green's function with application to the electron–gas problem. Phys. Rev. **139**, A796 (1965)
10. Hu, W., Lin, L., Yang, C.: Interpolative separable density fitting decomposition for accelerating hybrid density functional calculations with applications to defects in silicon. J. Chem. Theory Comput. **13**(11), 5420–5431 (2017)
11. Hybertsen, M.S., Louie, S.G.: Electron correlation in semiconductors and insulators: band gaps and quasiparticle energies. Phys. Rev. B **34**, 5390 (1986)
12. Khoromskaia, P.B.V., Khoromskij, B.N.: A reduced basis approach for calculation of the Bethe–Salpeter excitation energies by using low-rank tensor factorisations. Mol. Phys. **114**, 1148–1161 (2016)
13. Knyazev, A.V.: Toward the optimal preconditioned eigensolver: locally optimal block preconditioned conjugate gradient method. SIAM J. Sci. Comput. **23**(2), 517–541 (2001)
14. Lanczos, C.: An iteration method for the solution of the eigenvalue problem of linear differential and integral operators. J. Res. Nat. Bur. Stand. **45**, 255–282 (1950)
15. Lin, L., Xu, Z., Ying, L.: Adaptively compressed polarizability operator for accelerating large scale *Ab initio* phonon calculations. Multiscale Model. Simul. **15**, 29–55 (2017)
16. Ljungberg, M.P., Koval, P., Ferrari, F., Foerster, D., Sánchez-Portal, D.: Cubic-scaling iterative solution of the Bethe–Salpeter equation for finite systems. Phys. Rev. B **92**, 075422 (2015)
17. Lu, J., Thicke, K.: Cubic scaling algorithms for RPA correlation using interpolative separable density fitting. J. Comput. Phys. **351**, 187–202 (2017)
18. Lu, J., Ying, L.: Compression of the electron repulsion integral tensor in tensor hypercontraction format with cubic scaling cost. J. Comput. Phys. **302**, 329–335 (2015)
19. Marsili, M., Mosconi, E., Angelis, F.D., Umari, P.: Large-scale GW-BSE calculations with N^3 scaling: excitonic effects in dye-sensitized solar cells. Phys. Rev. B **95**, 075415 (2017)
20. Onida, G., Reining, L., Rubio, A.: Electronic excitations: density-functional versus many-body Green's-function approaches. Rev. Mod. Phys. **74**, 601 (2002)
21. Rocca, D., Lu, D., Galli, G.: *Ab initio* calculations of optical absorption spectra: solution of the Bethe–Salpeter equation within density matrix perturbation theory. J. Chem. Phys. **133**, 164109 (2010)
22. Rohlfing, M., Louie, S.G.: Electron-hole excitations and optical spectra from first principles. Phys. Rev. B **62**, 4927 (2000)
23. Salpeter, E.E., Bethe, H.A.: A relativistic equation for bound-state problems. Phys. Rev. **84**, 1232 (1951)
24. Shao, M., da Jornada, F.H., Lin, L., Yang, C., Deslippe, J., Louie, S.G.: A structure preserving Lanczos algorithm for computing the optical absorption spectrum. SIAM J. Matrix. Anal. Appl. **39**(2), 683–711 (2018)
25. Shao, M., da Jornada, F.H., Yang, C., Deslippe, J., Louie, S.G.: Structure preserving parallel algorithms for solving the Bethe–Salpeter eigenvalue problem. Linear Algebra Appl. **488**, 148–167 (2016)
26. Shao, M., Yang, C.: BSEPACK user's guide (2016). https://sites.google.com/a/lbl.gov/bsepack/
27. Yang, C., Meza, J.C., Lee, B., Wang, L.-W.: KSSOLV—a MATLAB toolbox for solving the Kohn-Sham equations. ACM Trans. Math. Softw. **36**, 1–35 (2009)

Model-Assisted Probability of Detection
for Structural Health Monitoring of Flat Plates

Xiaosong Du[1], Jin Yan[2], Simon Laflamme[2], Leifur Leifsson[1(✉)],
Yonatan Tesfahunegn[3], and Slawomir Koziel[3]

[1] Computational Design Laboratory, Department of Aerospace Engineering,
Iowa State University, Ames, IA 50011, USA
{xiaosong,leifur}@iastate.edu
[2] Department of Civil, Construction, and Environmental Engineering, Iowa State University,
Ames, IA 50011, USA
{yanjin,laflamme}@iastate.edu
[3] Engineering Optimization and Modeling Center, School of Science and Engineering,
Reykjavik University, Menntavegur 1, 101 Reykjavik, Iceland
{yonatant,koziel}@ru.is

Abstract. The paper presents a computational framework for assessing quantitatively the detection capability of structural health monitoring (SHM) systems for flat plates. The detection capability is quantified using the probability of detection (POD) metric, developed within the area of nondestructive testing, which accounts for the variability of the uncertain system parameters and describes the detection accuracy using confidence bounds. SHM provides the capability of continuously monitoring the structural integrity using multiple sensors placed sensibly on the structure. It is important that the SHM can reliably and accurately detect damage when it occurs. The proposed computational framework models the structural behavior of flat plate using a spring-mass system with a lumped mass at each sensor location. The quantity of interest is the degree of damage of the plate, which is defined in this work as the difference in the strain field of a damaged plate with respect to the strain field of the healthy plate. The computational framework determines the POD based on the degree of damage of the plate for a given loading condition. The proposed approach is demonstrated on a numerical example of a flat plate with two sides fixed and a load acting normal to the surface. The POD is estimated for two uncertain parameters, the plate thickness and the modulus of elasticity of the material, and a damage located in one spot of the plate. The results show that the POD is close to zero for small loads, but increases quickly with increasing loads.

Keywords: Probability of detection · Nondestructive testing
Structural health monitoring · Model-assisted probability of detection

1 Introduction

Structural health monitoring (SHM) is used for the diagnosis and localization of damage existing in large-scale infrastructures (Laflamme et al. 2010, 2013). The increased

© Springer International Publishing AG, part of Springer Nature 2018
Y. Shi et al. (Eds.): ICCS 2018, LNCS 10861, pp. 618–628, 2018.
https://doi.org/10.1007/978-3-319-93701-4_49

utilization and insufficient maintenance of these infrastructures usually lead to high risks associated with their failures (Karbhhari 2009; Harms et al. 2010). Due to the expensive costs on repairs, timely inspection and maintenance are essential in improving health and ensuring safety of civil infrastructures (Brownjohn 2007), in turn to lengthen the sustainability.

Probability of detection (POD) (Sarkar et al. 1998) was developed to provide a quantitative assessment of the detection capability of nondestructive testing (NDT) systems (Blitz and Simpson 1996; Mix 2005). POD can be used for various purposes, for example, it can be used to demonstrate compliance with standard requirements for inspection qualification, such as "90% POD with 95% confidence". It can also be used as input to probabilistic safety assessment (Spitzer et al. 2004; Chapman and Dimitrijevic 1999) and risk-based inspection (RBI) (Zhang et al. 2017; DET NORSKE VERITAS 2009). Because of these wide applications, POD is selected as an important metric in many industrial areas to detect defects or flaws, such as cracks inside parts or structures during manufacturing or for products in service. Traditional POD determination relies on experimental information (Generazio 2008; Bozorgnia et al. 2014). However, experiments can be time-consuming and expensive.

To reduce the experimental information needed for determining the POD, model-assisted probability of detection (MAPOD) methods have been developed (Thompson et al. 2009). MAPOD has been successfully applied to various NDT systems and modalities, such as eddy current simulations (Aldrin, et al. 2009), ultrasonic testing simulations (Smith et al. 2007), and SHM models (Aldrin et al. 2010, 2011). Due to the economic benefits of MAPOD in the SHM area, several approaches have been developed, such as the uniformed approach (Thompson 2008), advanced numerical simulations (Buethe et al. 2016; Aldrin et al. 2016; Lindgren et al. 2009), and have applied those on guided wave models (Jarmer and Kessler 2015; Memmolo et al. 2016).

In this paper, a MAPOD framework for SHM of flat plates is proposed. The approach determines the POD of damage of flat plates based on the loading and the degree of damage, which depends on the change in strain field of the damaged plate relative to the healthy one. The structural behavior is modeled with a simple spring-mass system to estimate the strain field. To demonstrate the effectiveness of the proposed framework, a flat plate with fixed ends and a normal load, as well as one damaged location is investigated. The uncertain parameters used in the study are plate thickness and the material modulus of elasticity. The results show that the framework can determine the POD as a function of the load and the degree of damage.

This paper is organized as follows. Next section describes the SHM structural model. Section 3 outlines the MAPOD framework used in this work. Section 4 presents results of a numerical example on the plate model. The paper ends with conclusion and plans of future work.

2 Structural Health Monitoring Model

SHM techniques use arrays of large-area electronics measuring strain to detect local faults. In Downey et al. (2017), a fully integrated dense sensor network (DSN) for the real-time SHM of wind turbine blades was proposed and experimentally validated on a prototype skin. The sensor, called soft elastomeric capacitor (SEC), is customizable in shape and size. The SEC's unique attribute is its capability to measure additive in-plane strain. It follows that the signal needs to be decomposed into orthogonal directions in order to obtained unidirectional strain maps. The SEC based sensing skin is illustrated in Fig. 1, with the sketch Fig. 1a showing an individual SEC, and Fig. 1b showing the fully integrated DSN system.

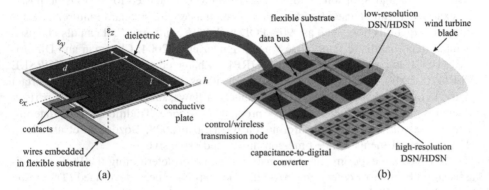

Fig. 1. Conceptual layout of a fully integrated SEC-based sensing skin for a wind turbine blade: (a) SEC with connectors and annotated axis; (b) deployment inside a wind turbine blade (Downey et al. 2017).

Inspired by the completed experimental work and SEC, a simulation model, developed as a matrix of discrete mass and stiffness elements, was constructed linking the strain to exist condition of the structures. A spring-mass system is used to represent the system being monitored, with a lumped mass at each sensor location. This model is based on the stiffness relationship between force vector F and measured displacement vector U. The additive strain is related to displacement by a transformation matrix D. Then, a static strain error function was defined to find the stiffness K by taking the difference between the predicted additive strain and field additive strain measurements.

Mindlin plate theory is used in this work to implement the plate model. In particular, the plate is divided by rectangular elements with SEC in the center for computational efficiency. On each element, the displacements in each node parallel to the undeformed middle plane, u and v, as a distance z from the centroidal axis can be expressed by

$$u = z\theta_x = z\frac{\partial w}{\partial x}, \; v = z\theta_y = z\frac{\partial w}{\partial y}, \; w = w_0,$$

where θ_x and θ_y are the rotations of the normal to the middle plane with respect to axes y and x, respectively as illustrated in Fig. 2.

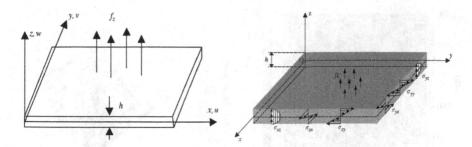

Fig. 2. Free-body diagram of a flat plate showing the stress distributions.

In this work, a fixed-ends plate is tested under a SHM system, containing 40 sensors, as shown in Fig. 3. Red regions represent the boundaries, which are fixed, so they are not considered in calculation. Cells containing blue numbers have sensors set up at centers, and strain field within the same cell is assumed to be uniform. Black numbers are computational nodes, where the calculation of strain is made.

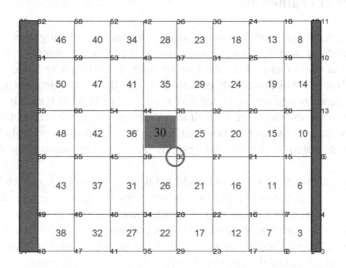

Fig. 3. SHM system setup. (Color figure online)

The red circle at node #33 shows the location where the load is applied, pointing normal to the plate. The green cell, #30, will be used to add artificial damage at its center. Contours of the deflection field contours for a healthy plate are shown in Fig. 4.

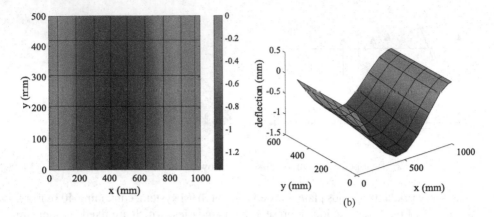

Fig. 4. Contours of deflection of the healthy plate for a force of 1 N. (Color figure online)

3   MAPOD Framework

POD is essentially the quantification of inspection capability starting from the distributions of variability, and describes its accuracy with confidence bounds, also known as uncertain bounds. In many cases, the final product of a POD curve is the flaw size, a, for which there is a 90% probability of detection. This flaw size is denoted a_{90}. The 95% upper confidence bound on a_{90} is denoted as $a_{90/95}$. The POD is typically determined through experiments which are both time-consuming and costly. This motivated the development of the MAPOD methods with the aim for reducing the number of experimental sample points by introducing insights physics-based simulations (Thompson et al. 2009).

The main elements of the proposed MAPOD framework is shown in Fig. 5. The process starts by defining the random inputs with specific statistical distributions (Fig. 5a). Next, the random inputs are propagated through the simulation model (Fig. 5b). For this step of the process, we use latin hypercube sampling (LHS) (Haddad 2013) to obtain identically independent samples from the input parameter distributions.

In this work, the simulation model is calculated using an analytical model (described in Sect. 2), to obtain the quantity of interest (Fig. 5c). In this work, the quantity of interest is the sum of the difference between current strain field and mean of healthy-plate strain field, in other words we are interested in $\Sigma(S - \mu_{S*})$ where S is the current strain field and is the mean of the healthy plate strain field.

The stiffness and strain within each cell are assumed to be the same in the structural model. Therefore, to describe the damage of the cells, we introduce a reduction parameter, α, ranging between 0 and 1. If the reduction parameter is equal to 1 there is no damage, while a value of 0 indicates total damage. We also introduce a parameter representing the degree of damage as $\gamma = 1 - \alpha$ (which ranges between 0 and 1). Values close to 1 indicate high degree of damage, and values close to 0 indicate low degree of damage.

The next step in the MAPOD process is to construct the so-called "$\hat{a}$ vs. a" plot (Fig. 5d) by drawing from the samples obtained in the last step and using linear

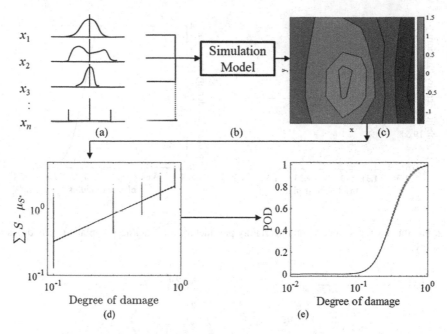

Fig. 5. Overview of model-assisted probability of detection for structural health monitoring: (a) probabilistic inputs, (b) simulation model, (c) response (strain field in this work), (d) "â vs. a" plot, (e) POD curves.

regression to plot the quantity of interest ($\Sigma(S - \mu_{S*})$) versus the degree of damage (γ). With this information, the POD at each degree of damage is determined and the POD curves are generated (Fig. 5e).

4   Results

In this study, two random input parameters are considered, the thickness of the plate and the modulus of elasticity. The thickness distribution is assumed to have an uniform distribution of $U(1.3 \text{ mm}, 1.35 \text{ mm})$ and the modulus of elasticity is assumed to have a Gaussian distribution of $N(7e4, 1e3)$. The distributions are shown in Fig. 6. The distributions are sampled one hundred times using latin hypercube sampling (LHS) (see Fig. 7). The LHS samples are propagated through the structural model with a force of $F = 1$ N without any damage. The mean strain field of those runs, μ_{S*}, is shown Fig. 8. This term is used as a reference vector, and POD curves can be generated through comparing the sum of the difference between this mean strain field and current strain field with detection threshold of system.

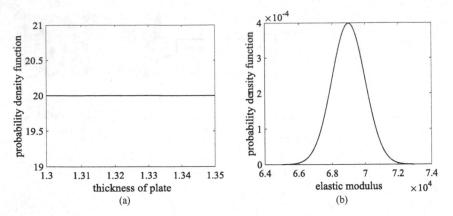

Fig. 6. Statistical distribution on uncertainty parameters: (a) thickness of plate; (b) modulus of elasticty.

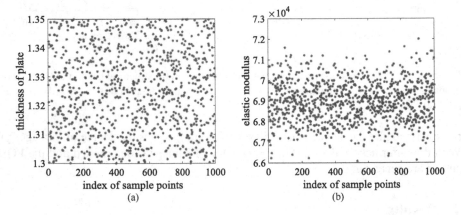

Fig. 7. Latin hyper cube (LHS) sampling: (a) thickness of plate; (b) elastic modulus.

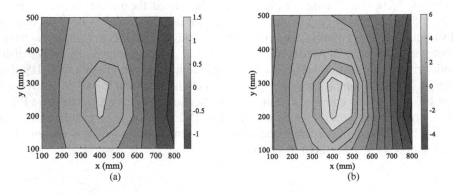

Fig. 8. Mean strain field of healthy plate: (a) $F = 1$ N; (b) $F = 4$ N.

To determine the POD of the SHM system the following computational experiments are performed using the proposed MAPOD framework (Fig. 5). An artificial damage is introduced by parametrically varying the degree of damage parameter at cell number 30 (see Fig. 3), γ_{30}, with the values of 0.1, 0.3, 0.5, 0.7, and 0.9. In each case, we take 1,000 LHS samples and propagate them through structural model to obtain the output strain fields. From those results, we take the sum of the difference between each of those strain fields and the mean strain field of the healthy plate. With the "$\hat{a}$ vs. a" plots generated, we set the detection threshold as 0.85 and determine the POD curves. The process is repeated for loads, F, ranging from low to medium to high. In this case, we use values of F of 0.1 N, 1 N, and 4 N.

The results of the MAPOD analysis giving the POD curves for the SHM system as a function of the load F and the degree of damage γ are presented in Figs. 9, 10 and 11. It can be seen that for low loads, the POD is very low, and the POD increases as the load increases. In particular, for $F = 0.1$ N, the POD is close to zero even when the damage is large. For the higher loads, the SHM system is capable of detecting the damage. More specifically, for $F = 1$ N the 50% POD, a_{50}, 90% POD, a_{90}, and 90% POD

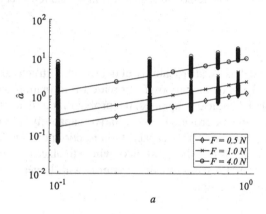

Fig. 9. Model responses at different degrees of damage, and linear regression, for various forces.

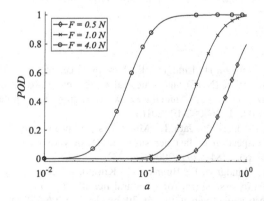

Fig. 10. POD curves versus different degrees of damage, for various forces.

with 95% confidence, $a_{90/95}$, are 0.3078, 0.5581, and 0.5776, respectively, whereas for $F = 4$ N, we have those metrics at 0.0619, 0.1157, and 0.1199, respectively. Thus, we can see that the larger load, the smaller the damage is needed to be detected, which in turn means that the detection capability is improving with increasing loads.

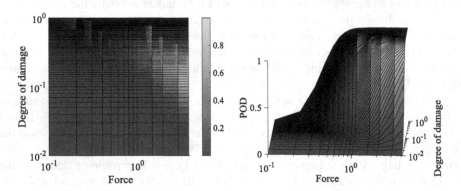

Fig. 11. POD surface with respect to degree of damage and force added, in 3D space

5   Conclusion

A framework for model-assisted probability of detection of structural health monitoring (SHM) systems of flat plates is proposed. Provided information on the uncertainties within the system and the sensor responses, the probability of detecting damage can be determined. The framework provided a quantitative capability to assess the reliability of SHM systems for flat plates. This capability is important when designing the SHM system. For example, answering the question of where to place the sensors. Future work will consider more complex cases, such as systems with larger numbers of uncertain parameters and damage locations.

Acknowledgements. This work was funded by the Center for Nondestructive Evaluation Industry/University Cooperative Research Program at Iowa State University.

References

Aldrin, J., Annis, C., Sabbagh, H., Lindgren, E.: Best practices for evaluating the capability of nondestructive evaluation (NDE) and structural health monitoring (SHM) techniques for damage characterization. In: 42th Annual Review of Progress in Quantitative Nondestructive Evaluation, pp. 200002-1–200002-10 (2016)

Aldrin, J., Knopp, J., Lindgren, E., Jata, K.: Model-assisted probability of detection evaluation for eddy current inspection of fastener sites. In: Review of Quantitative Nondestructive Evaluation, vol. 28, pp. 1784–1791 (2009)

Aldrin, J., Medina, E., Lindgren, E., Buynak, C., Knopp, J.: Case studies for model-assisted probabilistic reliability assessment for structural health monitoring systems. In: Review of Progress in Nondestructive Evaluation, vol. 30, pp. 1589–1596 (2011)

Aldrin, J., Medina, E., Lindgren, E., Buynak, C., Steffes, G., Derriso, M.: Model-assisted probabilistic reliability assessment for structure health monitoring systems. In: Review of Quantitative Nondestructive Evaluation, vol. 29, pp. 1965–1972 (2010)

Anan: Risk based inspection of offshore topsides static mechanical equipment. Det Norske Veritas, April 2009

Blitz, J., Simpson, G.: Ultrasonic Methods of Non-destructive Testing. Chapman & Hall, London (1996)

Bozorgnia, N., Schwetz, T.: What is the probability that direct detection experiments have observed dark matter. ArXiv ePrint arXiv.org/1410.6160 (2014)

Brownjohn, J.: Structural health monitoring of civil infrastructure. Philos. Trans. Roy. Soc. A Math. Phys. Eng. Sci. **365**(1851), 589–622 (2007)

Buethe, I., Dominguez, N., Jung, H., Fritzen, C.-P., Ségur, D., Reverdy, F.: Path-based MAPOD using numerical simulations. In: Wölcken, P.C., Papadopoulos, M. (eds.) Smart Intelligent Aircraft Structures (SARISTU), pp. 631–642. Springer, Cham (2016). https://doi.org/10.1007/978-3-319-22413-8_29

Chapman, J., Dimitrijevic, V.: Challenges in using a probabilistic safety assessment in a risk informed process (illustrated using risk informed inservice inspection). Reliab. Eng. Syst. Saf. **63**, 251–255 (1999)

Downey, A., Laflamme, S., Ubertini, F.: Experimental wind tunnel study of a smart sensing skin for condition evaluation of a wind turbine blade. Smart Mater. Struct. **26**, 125005 (2017)

Generazio, E.: Directed design of experiments for validating probability of detection capability of NDE systems (DOEPOD). In: Review of Quantitative Nondestructive Evaluation, vol. 27 (2008)

Haddad, R.E., Fakhereddine, R., Lécot, C., Venkiteswaran, G.: Extended latin hypercube sampling for integration and simulation. In: Dick, J., Kuo, F., Peters, G., Sloan, I. (eds.) Monte Carlo and Quasi-Monte Carlo Methods 2012. Springer Proceedings in Mathematics and Statistics, vol. 65, pp. 317–330. Springer, Heidelberg (2013). https://doi.org/10.1007/978-3-642-41095-6_13

Harms, T., Sedigh, S., Bastinaini, F.: Structural health monitoring of bridges using wireless sensor network. IEEE Instru. Meas. Mag. **13**(6), 14–18 (2010)

Jarmer, G., Kessler, S.: Probability of detection assessment of a guided wave structural health monitoring system. In: Structural Health Monitoring (2015)

Kabhari, V.M.: Design Principles for Civil Structures. Encyclopedia of Structural Health Monitoring, pp. 1467–1476. Wiley, Hoboken (2009)

Laflamme, S., Kollosche, M., Connor, J., Kofod, G.: Soft capacitive sensor for structural health monitoring of large-scale systems. J. Struct. Control **19**, 1–21 (2010)

Laflamme, S., Kollosche, M., Conor, J., Kofod, G.: Robust flexible capacitive surface sensor for structural health monitoring applications. J. Eng. Mech. **139**(7), 879–885 (2013)

Lindgren, E., Buynak, C., Aldrin, J., Medina, E., Derriso, M.: Model-assisted methods for validation of structural health monitoring systems. In: 7th International Workshop on Structural Health Monitoring, Stanford, CA (2009)

Memmolo, V., Ricci, F., Maio, L., Monaco, E.: Model-assisted probability of detection for a guided-waves based on SHM technique. In: SPIE Smart Structures and Materials and Nondestructive Evaluation and Health Monitoring, vol. 9805, pp. 980504-1–980504-12, April 2016

Mix, P.: Introduction to Nondestructive Testing. Wiley, Hoboken (2005)

Sarkar, P., Meeker, W., Thompson, R., Gray, T., Junker, W.: Probability of detection modeling for ultrasonic testing. In: Thompson, D.O., Chimenti, D.E. (eds.) Review of Progress in Quantitative Nondestructive Evaluation, vol. 17, pp. 2045–2046. Springer, Boston (1998). https://doi.org/10.1007/978-1-4615-5339-7_265

Smith, K., Thompson, B., Meeker, B., Gray, T., Brasche, L.: Model-assisted probability of detection validation for immersion ultrasonic application. In: Review of Quantitative Nondestructive Evaluation, vol. 26, pp. 1816–1822 (2007)

Spitzer, C., Schmocker, U., Dang, V.: Probability safety assessment and management. In: International Conference on Probabilistic Safety Assessment, Berlin, Germany (2004)

Thompson, R.: A unified approach to the model-assisted determination of probability of detection. In: Review of Quantitative Nondestructive Evaluation, vol. 27, pp. 1685–1692 (2008)

Thompson, R., Brasche, L., Forsyth, D., Lindgren, E., Swindell, P.: Recent advances in model-assisted probability of detection. In: 4th European-American Workshop on Reliability of NDE, Berlin, Germany, 24–26 June 2009

Zhang, M., Liang, W., Qiu, Z., Liu, Y.: Application of risk-based inspection method for gas compressor station. In: 12th International Conference on Damage Assessment of Structures, Series, vol. 842 (2017)

Track of Data, Modeling, and Computation in IoT and Smart Systems

Anomalous Trajectory Detection Between Regions of Interest Based on ANPR System

Gao Ying$^{(\boxtimes)}$, Nie Yiwen, Yang Wei, Xu Hongli, and Huang Liusheng

University of Science and Technology of China, Hefei, China
{sa516067,nyw2016}@mail.ustc.edu.cn,
{qubit,xuhongli,lshuang}@ustc.edu.cn

Abstract. With the popularization of automobiles, more and more algorithms have been proposed in the last few years for the anomalous trajectory detection. However, existing approaches, in general, deal only with the data generated by GPS devices, which need a great deal of pre-processing works. Moreover, without the consideration of region's local characteristics, those approaches always put all trajectories even though with different source and destination regions together. Therefore, in this paper, we devise a novel framework for anomalous trajectory detection between regions of interest by utilizing the data captured by Automatic Number-Plate Recognition (ANPR) system. Our framework consists of three phases: abstraction, detection, classification, which is specially engineered to exploit both spatial and temporal features. In addition, extensive experiments have been conducted on a large-scale real-world datasets and the results show that our framework can work effectively.

Keywords: Anomalous trajectory · Regions of interest
ANPR system

1 Introduction

It has been well known that "one person's noise could be another person's signal." Indeed, for some applications, the rare is more attractive than the usual. For example, when mining vehicle trajectory data, we may pay more attention to the anomalous trajectory since it is helpful to the urban transportation analysis.

Anomalous trajectory is an observation that deviates so much from other observations as to arise suspicious that it may be generated by a different mechanism. Analyzing such type of movement between regions of interest is beneficial for us to understand the road congestion, reveal the best or worst path, locate the main undertaker when traffic accidents happen and so on.

Existing trajectory-based data mining techniques mainly exploit the geo-location information provided by on-board GPS devices. [1] takes advantage of

© Springer International Publishing AG, part of Springer Nature 2018
Y. Shi et al. (Eds.): ICCS 2018, LNCS 10861, pp. 631–643, 2018.
https://doi.org/10.1007/978-3-319-93701-4_50

real-time GPS traffic data to evaluate congestion; [2] makes use of GPS positioning information to detect vehicles' speeding behaviors; [21] utilizes personal GPS walking trajectory to mine frequent route patterns. Exploiting GPS data to detect anomalous trajectories has a good performance. However, there are considerable overhead in installing GPS devices and collecting data via networks.

In this paper, we devise a novel framework for anomalous trajectory detection between regions of interest based on the data captured by ANPR system. In an ANPR system, a large number of video cameras are deployed at various locations of an area to capture and automatically recognize their license plate numbers of passing by vehicles. Each of location is often referred to as an ANPR gateway. And the trajectory of a vehicle is the concatenation of a sequence of gateways.

Compared to existing techniques that make use of GPS data, exploiting ANPR records in anomalous trajectory detection has the following advantages: high accuracy in vehicle classification, low costs of system deployment and maintenance, better coverage by monitoring vehicles and so on.

In summary, we make the following contributions in contrast to existing approaches:

1. We introduce ANPR system that not only can constantly and accurately reveal the road traffic but also almost does not need additional pre-processing works.
2. We devise a novel framework to detect anomalous trajectory between regions of interest. Specifically, we take the road distribution and road congestion into consideration.
3. Finally, using the real monitoring records, we demonstrate our devised framework can detect the anomalous trajectories correctly and effectively.

The rest of this paper is organized as follows. Section 2 presents the related works. Section 3 provides the problem statement. Section 4 gives our specific anomalous trajectory detection algorithms. Section 5 describes the results of experimental evaluation. Finally, the concluding remarks are drawn in Sect. 6.

2   Related Work

Here, we review some related and representative works. And this section can be categorized into two parts. The first part will revolve around outlier detection algorithms, whereas the second part will concentrate on the existing anonymous trajectory detection algorithms.

2.1   Outlier Detection Algorithms

A great deal of outlier detection algorithms have been developed for multi-dimensional points. These algorithms can be mainly divided into two classes: distance-based and density-based.

1. **Distance-based method:** This method is originally proposed in [7,15–17]. " An object O in a dataset T is a $DB(p,D)$-outlier if at least fraction p of the objects in T lies greater than distance D from O." This method relies deeply on the global distribution of the given dataset. So if the distribution conforms to or approximately conforms to uniform distribution, this algorithm can perform perfectly. However, it encounters difficulties when analyzing the dataset with various densities.

2. **Density-based method:** This method is proposed in [18,19]. A point is classified into an outlier if the *local outlier factor (LOF)* value is greater than a given threshold. Here, each point's LOF value depends on the local densities of its neighborhoods. Clearly, the LOF method dose not suffer from the problem above. However, the computation of LOF values require a great batch of k-nearest neighbor queries, and thus, can be computationally expensive.

2.2 Anomalous Trajectory Detection Algorithms

In recent years, more and more researchers have paid their attention to anomalous trajectory detection [3,5,6,14]:

Fontes and De Alencar [3] give a novel definition of standard trajectory in their paper, and propose that if there is at least one standard path that has enough neighborhoods nearby, then a potential anomalous trajectory that does not belong to standard group would be regarded to perform a detour, and is classified into anomalous. This rather simplistic approach even though can find out all anomalous trajectories, quantities of normal trajectories are incorrectly classified.

Lee et al. [6] propose a novel partition-and-detect framework. In their paper, they claim that even though some partitions of a trajectory show an unusual behavior, these differences may be averaged out over the whole trajectory. So, they recommend to split a trajectory into various partitions (at equal intervals), and a hybrid of distance- and density-based approaches are used to classify each partition as anomalous or not, as long as one of the partitions is classified into anomalous, the whole trajectory is considered as anomalous. However, solely using distance and density can fail to correctly classify some trajectories as anomalous.

Li [14] present an anomalous trajectory detection algorithm based on classification. In their algorithm, they first extract some common patterns named motifs from trajectories. And then they transform the set of motifs into a feature vector which will be fed into a classifier. Finally, through their trained classifier a trajectory is classified into either "normal" or "anomalous". Obviously, their algorithm depends deeply on training. However, in a real world, it is not always easy to obtain a good training set. Notice that our algorithm does not require such training.

Due to the inherent drawbacks of the GPS devices, some researchers have turned their attention to the ANPR system. Homayounfar [20] apply data clustering techniques to extract relevant traffic patterns from the ANPR data to detect and identify unusual patterns and irregular behavior of multi-vehicle convoy activities. Sun [4] propose a new anomaly detection scheme that exploits vehicle trajectory data collected from ANPR system. Their scheme is capable of detecting vehicles with the behavior of wandering round and unusual activity at specific time. However, these methods are too one-side, and there is no effective and comprehensive method to detect anomalous trajectory.

3   Problem Statement

In this section, we give several basic definitions and the formal problem statement. Before that, we make a brief synopsis of our dataset.

As mentioned before, our dataset were collected from ANPR system. By processing the ANPR data, we could get each vehicle's historical ANPR records. Each ANPR record includes the captured time, the gateway id of the capturing camera, and the license of the captured vehicle [4]. And by asking Traffic Police Bureau for help, we can obtain the latitude and longitude of every on-line gateway id.

Definition 1 (TRAJECTORY). A *trajectory* consists of a sequence of passing by points $[p_1, p_2, \ldots, p_n]$, where each point is composed of the captured time, the latitude and the longitude of the surveillance camera.

Definition 2 (CANDIDATE TRAJECTORY). Let SRC, DEST be the source region and the destination region of interest and $t = [p_1, p_2, \ldots, p_n]$ is a trajectory. t becomes a *candidate trajectory* if and only if the source region $P_1 = $ SRC and the destination region $P_n = $ DEST.

Candidate group is a set of candidate trajectories.

Definition 3 (NEIGHBORHOOD). Let t be a candidate trajectory, the neighborhoods of t can be collected by the following formula:

$$N(t, \text{maxDist}) = \{c_i \mid c_i \text{ is a candidate and dist}(t, c_i) \leq \text{maxDist} \}.$$

where $\text{dist}(t, c_i)$ can be calculated by the use of Algorithm 2, and the maxDist means maximum distance, it is a predefined threshold.

Definition 4 (STANDARD TRAJECTORY). Let t be a candidate trajectory, t is a *standard trajectory* if and only if $|N(t, maxDist)| \geq minSup$, where minSup means minimum support, it is also a predefined threshold.

Standard group is a set of standard trajectories.

Definition 5 (ANOMALOUS TRAJECTORY). A candidate trajectory will be classified into anomalous if it satisfies both of the following requirements:

1. the similarity between the candidate trajectory and the standard group is less than a given threshold S;
2. the difference between the candidate trajectory and the standard group is more than a given threshold D;

PROBLEM STATEMENT: Given a set of trajectories $T = \{t_1, t_2, \ldots, t_n\}$, a fixed S-D pair (S, D) and a candidate trajectory $t = [p_1, p_2, \ldots, p_n]$ moving from S to D. We are aimed to verify whether t is anomalous with respect to T. Furthermore, we would like to reveal the anomalous score that will be used to arrange the processing priority.

4   Anomalous Trajectory Detection Framework

In this section, we introduce our devised anomalous trajectory detection framework in details. This framework is mainly divided into three phases: abstraction, detection, classification.

4.1   Abstraction

The abstraction is aimed to abstract the candidate group and the standard group between regions of interest from a large number of unorganized ANPR records.

The first step of which is to synthetic a vehicle's trajectory. By the hand of ANPR system, we can synthetic a trajectory which is composed of the vehicle's captured records in a whole day. However, analyzing the entire trajectory of a vehicle may not be able to extract enough features. Thus, we decide to partition the whole trajectory into a set of sub trajectories based on the time interval between records. Each sub trajectory indicates an individual short-term driving trip. And in a sub trajectory, the time interval between records must be less than practical threshold *Duration*.

The second step of which is to abstract the candidate group and the standard group. By the use of the definitions presented at Definitions 2 and 4, we can abstract them quickly. However, we may run into a bad situation when we apply the method to a desert region (the desert means the region is desolate and there are so little passing by vehicles). In a desert region, there may be not enough vehicle's monitoring trajectories for us to abstract standard group. In this situation, we can find out 5 most frequently used paths to compose our standard group.

4.2   Detection

The detection is intended to calculate the similarity and difference between the candidate and the standard group. In this section, we propose *adjusting weight longest common subsequence (AWLCS)* to calculate the similarity and *adjusting weight dynamic time warping (AWDTW)* to calculate the difference.

Adjusting Longest Common Weighted Subsequence. In the beginning, we introduce the famous NP-hard problem LCS:

Problem 1. The string Longest Common Subsequence (LCS) *Problem*:
INPUT: *Two trajectories* t_1, t_2 *of length* n, m;
OUTPUT: *The length of the longest subsequence common to both strings.*

For example, for $t_1=[p_1,p_2,p_3,p_4,p_4,p_1,p_2,p_5,p_6]$ and $t_2=[p_5,p_6,p_2,p_1,p_4,p_5,$ $p_1,p_1,p_2]$, LCS(t_1,t_2) is 4, where a possible such subsequence is $[p_1,p_4,p_1,p_2]$.

Using LCS algorithm to calculate the similarity between two trajectories gives good results when the captured cameras are deployed at approximately equidistance. But if not, a problem arises. The problem is the following: some cameras are adjacent with each other, while some cameras are remote with each other, just like the situation depicted in Fig. 1. Now when we apply LCS to calculate the similarity between two trajectories, all cameras are deemed as equally important (in fact, the remote cameras play a more important role than the adjacent cameras), which neglects the road distribution definitely leading to a bad result.

Fig. 1. non-equidistant cameras

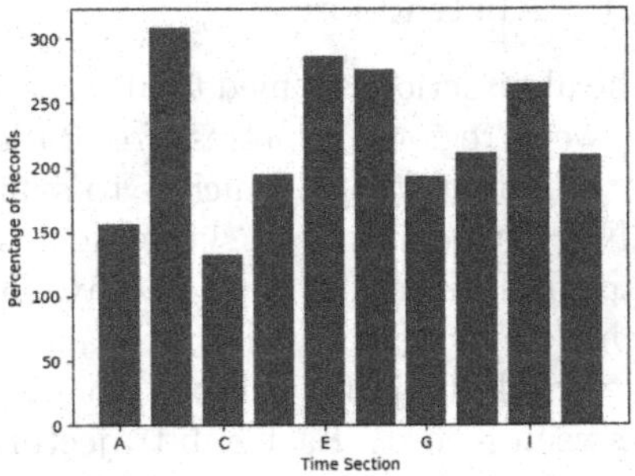

Fig. 2. Traffic volumes of captured cameras

One good way to solve this problem is to allocate different weights to different captured cameras: smaller weights to cameras that are located in dense area and bigger weights to the cameras that are located in sparse area. In there, we abstract the cameras into points. Weight of point i(w_i) can be calculated, for instance, by using the following equation:

$$w_i = \frac{c_i}{\Sigma_{k=0}^{k=n-1} c_k}, \tag{1}$$

where

$$c_i = \begin{cases} \frac{dist(p_2,p_1)}{equidistant}, & i = 0 \\ \frac{dist(p_{i+1},p_i)+dist(p_i,p_{i-1})}{2*equidistant}, & 1 < i < n - 1 \\ \frac{dist(p_n,p_{n-1})}{equidistant}, & i = n - 1 \end{cases} \tag{2}$$

The variable *equidistant* tells the distance interval on the condition that the points of a trajectory are distributed at equidistance:

$$equidistant = \frac{dist(p_n, p_1)}{n - 1} \tag{3}$$

Algorithm 1. Adjusting Weight Longest Common Subsequence

Input: A, B
Output: *the longest common weighted subsequence*
1 m := length(A);
2 n := length(B);
3 **if** $m == 0$ *or* $n == 0$ **then**
4 | return 0;

5 **else if** A[m] $==$ B[n] **then**
6 | return weight(B[n]) + AWLCS(Head(A),Head(B));

7 **else**
8 | return max(AWLCS(Head(A),B),
9 | AWLCS(A,Head(B)));

And coefficient C_i tells how far the neighbors of point p_i are located compared with a case where the points are distributed at approximately equidistant equidistance. Note that in the case of $0 < i < n - 1$, the points have two neighbors, while in the case of $i = 0$ and $i = n - 1$, the points only have one neighbor.

Now, we can present *AWLCS* in Algorithm 1.

By Algorithm 1, we can obtain the similarity measure between the candidate and one standard. As for the similarity between the candidate and the standards is the maximum between the candidate and the standard in group.

Adjusting Weight Dynamic Time Warping. We now discuss the problem of computing the difference between a candidate and the standard group using *AWDTW*.

The simplest way of calculating dynamic time warping is given by [13] using dynamic programming. This method is mainly divided into two steps. The first step is to evaluate the distance matrix of two trajectories. And the second step is to find the shortest path moving from the lower left corner DTW[0, 0] to the upper right corner DTW[n, m]. The pseudo-code is presented in Algorithm 2.

For point [i, j], it only can be arrived at insertion (previous point is [i-1, j]), or deletion (previous point is [i, j-1]), or match (previous point is [i-1, j-1]). So [i, j] must choose one of the three distance extensions to pass through point [i, j], at this time, the cumulative distance is calculated as (lines 12, 13, 14).

When we apply DTW to calculate the difference between two trajectories, we take the road congestion into consideration. It's obvious that the traffics among different roads is different, some differences even are much huge, just like the situation depicted in Fig. 2. So some experienced drivers may choose an unusual trajectory that though may deviates from the standard group, to avoid congestion.

Therefore, similar to AWLCS, the AWDTW also allocate a weight to the captured camera. However, the definition of weight in AWDTW is much different

---

Algorithm 2. Dynamic Time Warping

    Input: A, B
    Output: $DTW[n,m]$
1 m := length(A);
2 n := length(B);
3 DTW := array[0...n, 0...m];
4 **for** $i = 1; i \leq n; i + +$ **do**
5   ⌊ DTW[i, 0] := infinity;

6 **for** $j = 1; j \leq m; j + +$ **do**
7   ⌊ DTW[0, j] := infinity;

8 DTW[0,0] = 0;
9 **for** $i = 1; i \leq n; i + +$ **do**
10   **for** $j = 1; j \leq m; j + +$ **do**
11   cost:= distance(s[i], t[j]);
12   DTW[i, j] := cost + minimum(DTW[i-1, j],
13   DTW[i , j-1],
14   DTW[i-1, j-1]);

15 return DTW[n, m]

---

from that in ALCWS. Under this circumstance, we can calculate weight w_i as the ratio of average traffic volume to the traffic volume of p_i.

$$weight(p_i) = \frac{\sum_{p_k \in \phi} Vol(p_k)/|\phi|}{Vol(p_i)} \qquad (4)$$

where $Vol(p_k)$ is the traffic volume of p_k at a certain duration and ϕ is the collection of all points.

By this calculation, we will obtain a low value weight (p_i) when the point p_i's congestion is heavier than the average, and a high value weight (p_i) when the point p_i's congestion is lighter than the average. The bigger of the value weight (p_i), the higher of the chance that p_i is chosen.

When we compute the weight of a point p_k, $Vol(p_k)$ may be zero, which will bring about a serious impact on the following computation. So, we add an initial value 1 to every $Vol(p_k)$.

After defining the weight value, when we compute the distance between p_i in standard trajectory and p_j in the candidate trajectory, the distance is multiplied by the weight (p_j). After the adjustment, the distance is decreased in a congested region due to a low weight (p_j) value (<1.0), but it is increased in a uncongested region due to a high weight (p_j) value (>1.0).

Before we give the difference between the standard group and the candidate trajectory, we first introduce the inter-group distance and intra-group distance:

INTER-GRPUP DISTANCE: The inter-group distance ω is the distance between the standard group and the candidate trajectory, which is equal to the minimum between the candidate and the standard trajectory in standard group.

INTRA-GROUP DISTANCE: The intra-group distance u is the maximum distance of any two trajectories in standard group.

In order to calculate the intra-group distance u, the size of the standard group must be greater than or equal to 2. So when there is only 1 element in group, this method has lost efficacy. Under this circumstance, we randomly select 5 candidate trajectories to form our standards, at this time, u is equal to the minimum between any two standard trajectories in standard group.

After acquiring the inter-group distance and the intra-group distance, the *difference* between the candidate and the standard group can be calculated as following:

$$difference = \frac{|\omega - u|}{u} \tag{5}$$

where the ω tells us the distance between the candidate trajectory and the standard group, and the u can be regarded as the distance between a standard trajectory and the standard group, thus the $|\omega - u|$ reveals that how far away the candidate trajectory in contrast to a standard trajectory. However, we can not directly use the $|\omega - u|$ to stand for difference, because there is a great difference for different source region and the destination region. By dividing the u, it can neglect this effect.

4.3 Classfication

The classification is designed to classify the candidate trajectory into anomalous or normal according to the similarity and difference calculated in previous stage. The concrete classification method is presented in Definition 5.

Once a candidate is classified into anomalous, some actions should be taken at once. But, if a great deal of candidate trajectories are classified into anomalous at the same time, what's the processing sequences? Obviously, The bigger anonymity, the higher processing priority. Thus, we propose anomalous score to show its level of anonymity, whose computational formula is presented in the following:

$$\Delta(s, d) = \lfloor e^{\lambda(S-s)} + e^{\lambda(d-D)} \rfloor \tag{6}$$

Here, λ is a temperature parameter, s and d are the calculated similarity and difference, S and D are the aforementioned similarity threshold and difference threshold. For our experiments, we choose $\lambda = 500$. According to the computation formula, we can conclude that the bigger the similarity s, the smaller the anomalous score; the bigger the difference d, the bigger the anomalous score.

5   Experimental Evaluation

Here, we provide an empirical evaluation and analysis of our devised framework. All the experiments are run in Python 3.5 on Mac OS.

5.1   Experimental Dataset

Our dataset were collected from the ANPR system deployed at Hefei between August 15, 2017 and August 23, 2017. The total number of ANPR records is close to 100 million, which includes about 10 million trajectories. However, there is still a lack of anomalous trajectories, so we simulate the illegal drivers' escape inspection behaviors and taxi drivers' detour behaviors in real environment.

5.2   Evaluation Criteria

A classified candidate trajectory will fall into one of the following four scenarios:

1. True positive (TP): an anomalous trajectory is correctly labeled to anomalous;
2. False positive (FP): a non-anomalous trajectory is incorrectly labeled to anomalous;
3. False negative (FN): an anomalous trajectory is incorrectly labeled to non-anomalous;
4. True negative (TN): a non-anomalous trajectory is correctly labeled to non-anomalous.

According to the number of TP, FP, FN, TN, we can get the *Precision* and the *Recall*:

Precision: The *precision* concentrates on this problem: of all trajectories where we labeled to anomalous, what fraction actually be correctly labeled.

$$Precision = \frac{TP}{TP + FP}$$

Recall: The *recall* concentrates on this problem: of all trajectories that actually is anomalous, what fraction did we correctly labeled to anomalous.

$$Recall = \frac{TP}{TP + FN}$$

Obviously, the bigger of *precision and recall*, the better performance of this binary classification. However, you can't have your cake and eat it too. Thus, taking these two indicator into consideration, we choose *F1-measure* to evaluate the performance of this binary classification.

$$F1\text{-measure} = \frac{2 * Precision * Recall}{Precision + Recall}$$

5.3   Parameters Setting

As in many other data mining algorithm, the parameters setting is essential for the final experiment results. In our framework, we need to set the following five parameters: *duration threshold, maxDist, minSup, similarity threshold, difference threshold*.

Duration Threshold: In the actual drive test at Hefei, the duration that a vehicle passes through two adjacent captured point is no more than 30 min even though during rush hours. Besides, we have calculated and analysis the ANPR records, its distribution is presented at Fig. 3, the proportion of the duration that less than 30 min is up to 74.6%. Thus, we set the *duration threshold* = 30 min.

maxDist and minSup: It is obvious that with the increase of maxDist, more candidate trajectories would be included in standard group; however, with the increase of minSup, less candidate trajectories would be included in standard group. And the bigger of the size of standard group, the less of the chance of a candidate trajectory classified to anomalous. So it is important to investigate their effects on performance. In Fig. 4we plot the F1 value varies from maxDist, and In Fig. 5, we plot the F1 value varies from minSup. From these two pictures, we can conclude that the maxDist should not be set any lower than 90 and the minSup should not be set any higher than 20.

Similarity Threshold and Difference Threshold: Since similarity and difference is the threshold for determining anomalousness, it is important to investigate its effect on the performance of our devised framework. We study the effect on performance when similarity ranges from 0.0 to 1.0 and difference ranges from 1.0 to 3.0. In Fig. 6, we plot the F1 value for different values of similarity and In Fig. 7, we plot the F1 value for different values of difference. We can see that similarity should be set to 0.5 and difference should be set to 2.0 since less than or more than them the performance would significantly decrease.

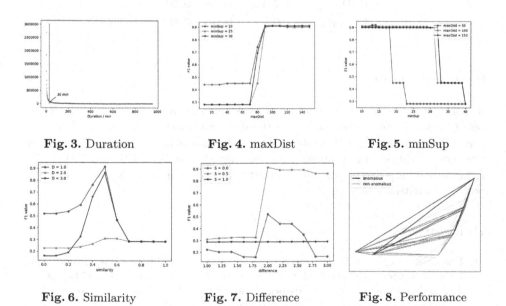

Fig. 3. Duration   Fig. 4. maxDist   Fig. 5. minSup

Fig. 6. Similarity   Fig. 7. Difference   Fig. 8. Performance

5.4 Evaluation

Figure 8 shows the result between two interest regions. We observe that many anomalous trajectories are detected. Some of the anomalous trajectories deviate so much from normal group, which are mainly caused by illegal drivers that choose an unusual path to escape polices' inspection; And some trajectories even though are similar to most of the normal trajectories, they are still be classified into anomalous, which are mainly caused by taxi drivers' and dripping drivers' detour behaviors.

Next, we evaluate the superiority of our proposed framework.

We compare its performance with two existing anomalous detection approaches: discovering trajectory outlier between regions of interest (ROF) presented in [3] and trajectory outlier detection: a partition-and-detect framework (PAD) presented in [6]. We show the experiment results in Table 1. We can see that ROF has the best recall, but worst precision, resulting great waste of the human, material and financial resources. As for PAD, it ignores temporal information in trajectory which is of great importance, so the running results are still not very good.

Table 1. Compare with ROF and PAD

Algorithms	Precision	Recall	F1 value
ROF	0.425	1.0	0.597
PAD	0.724	0.868	0.789
Our proposal	0.927	0.895	0.911

6 Conclusion

In this paper, we devise a novel framework for anomalous trajectory detection between regions of interest based on the data captured by Automatic Number-Plate Recognition (ANPR) system. Taking both spatial and temporal features into consideration, we propose two new algorithms AWLCS and AWDTW. A large number of experiments manifest that our framework significantly outperforms existing schemes.

References

1. Bacon, J., Bejan, A.I., Beresford, A.R., Evans, D., Gibbens, R.J., Moody, K.: Using real-time road traffic data to evaluate congestion. In: Jones, C.B., Lloyd, J.L. (eds.) Dependable and Historic Computing. LNCS, vol. 6875, pp. 93–117. Springer, Heidelberg (2011). https://doi.org/10.1007/978-3-642-24541-1_9
2. Mohamad, I., Ali, M.A.M., Ismail, M.: Abnormal driving detection using real time global positioning system data. In: IEEE International Conference on Space Science and Communication, pp. 1–6. IEEE (2011)

3. Fontes V, De Alencar L, Renso C, Bogorny V: Discovering trajectory outliers between regions of interest. In: Proceedings of the Brazilian Symposium on GeoInformatics, pp. 49–60. National Institute for Space Research, INPE (2013)
4. Sun, Y., Zhu, H., Liao, Y., et al.: Vehicle anomaly detection based on trajectory data of ANPR system. In: Global Communications Conference, pp. 1–6. IEEE (2016)
5. Chen, C., Zhang, D., Castro, P.S., et al.: iBOAT: isolation-based online anomalous trajectory detection. IEEE Trans. Intell. Transp. Syst. 14(2), 806–818 (2013)
6. Lee, J.G., Han, J., Li, X.: Trajectory outlier detection: a partition-and-detect framework, pp. 140–149 (2008)
7. Papadimitriou, S., Kitagawa, H., Gibbons, P.B., et al.: LOCI: fast outlier detection using the local correlation integral. In: 2003 Proceedings of the International Conference on Data Engineering, pp. 315–326. IEEE (2003)
8. Ramaswamy, S., Rastogi, R., Shim, K.: Efficient algorithms for mining outliers from large data sets. ACM SIGMOD International Conference on Management of Data, pp. 427–438. ACM (2000)
9. Bunke, H.: On a relation between graph edit distance and maximum common subgraph. Pattern Recogn. Lett. 18(9), 689–694 (1997)
10. Vlachos, M., Kollios, G., Gunopulos, D.: Discovering similar multidimensional trajectories. In: Proceedings of the International Conference on Data Engineering, p. 673. IEEE (2002)
11. Berndt, D.J.: Using dynamic time warping to find patterns in time series. KDD Workshop, pp. 359–370 (1994)
12. Salvador, S., Chan, P.: Toward accurate dynamic time warping in linear time and space. Intell. Data Anal. 11(5), 561–580 (2007)
13. Yi, B.K., Jagadish, H.V., Faloutsos, C.: Efficient retrieval of similar time sequences under time warping. In: Proceedings of the International Conference on Data Engineering, pp. 201–208. IEEE (2002)
14. Li, X., Han, J., Kim, S., et al.: ROAM: rule- and motif-based anomaly detection in massive moving object data sets. In: SIAM International Conference on Data Mining, 26–28 April 2007, Minneapolis, Minnesota, USA. DBLP (2007)
15. Knorr, E.M., Ng, R.T.: Algorithms for mining distance-based outliers in large datasets. In: International Conference on Very Large Data Bases, pp. 392–403. Morgan Kaufmann Publishers Inc. (1998)
16. Knorr, E.M., Ng, R.T., Tucakov, V.: Distance-based outliers: algorithms and applications. VLDB J. 8(3–4), 237–253 (2000)
17. Knorr, E.M., Ng, R.T.: Finding Intensional Knowledge of Distance-Based Outliers. In: VLDB, pp. 211–222 (1999)
18. Breunig, M.M., Kriegel, H.P., Ng, R.T.: LOF: identifying density-based local outliers. ACM SIGMOD International Conference on Management of Data, pp. 93–104. ACM (2000)
19. Jin, W., Tung, A.K.H., Han, J.: Mining top-n local outliers in large databases, pp. 293–298 (2001)
20. Homayounfar, A., Ho, A.T.S., Zhu, N., et al.: Multi-vehicle convoy analysis based on ANPR data. In: International Conference on Imaging for Crime Detection and Prevention, pp. 1–5. IET (2012)
21. Fu, Z., Tian, Z., Xu, Y., et al.: Mining frequent route patterns based on personal trajectory abstraction. IEEE Access PP(99), 1 (2017)

Dynamic Real-Time Infrastructure Planning and Deployment for Disaster Early Warning Systems

Huan Zhou[1], Arie Taal[1], Spiros Koulouzis[1], Junchao Wang[1], Yang Hu[1], George Suciu Jr.[2], Vlad Poenaru[2], Cees de Laat[1], and Zhiming Zhao[1(✉)] (iD)

[1] University of Amsterdam, 1098 XH Amsterdam, The Netherlands
{h.zhou,a.taal,j.wang2,y.hu,delaat,z.zhao}@uva.nl
[2] BEIA Consultant, Bucharest, Romania
{george.suciu,vlad.poenaru}@beia.ro

Abstract. An effective nature disaster early warning system often relies on widely deployed sensors, simulation based predicting components, and a decision making system. In many cases, the simulation components require advanced infrastructures such as Cloud for performing the computing tasks. However, effectively customizing the virtualized infrastructure from Cloud based time critical constraints and locations of the sensors, and scaling it based on dynamic loads of the computation at runtime is still difficult. The suitability of a Dynamic Real-time Infrastructure Planner (DRIP) that handles the provisioning within cloud environments of the virtual infrastructure for time-critical applications is demonstrated with respect to disaster early warning systems. The DRIP system is part of the SWITCH project (Software Workbench for Interactive, Time Critical and Highly self-adaptive Cloud applications).

Keywords: Cloud · Disaster early warning · Time critical systems

1 Introduction

An elastic early warning system enables people and authorities to save lives and property in case of disasters. In case of floods, a warning issued with enough time before the event will allow for reservoir operators to gradually reduce water levels, people to reinforce their homes, hospitals be prepared to receive more patients, authorities to prepare and provide help [3–5]. An early warning system often collects data from sensors, processes the information using tools such as predictive simulation, and provides warning services or interactive facilities for the public to obtain more information [1].

Depending on factors like the spatial and temporal scale of a specific environmental degradation, early warning systems are often highly distributed [8–10]. An ideal disaster early warning system needs to minimize prevention costs and increase prevention efficiency in case of flood and other possible disaster events. But there is a trade-off between timeliness, warning reliability, the cost of a false alert, and damage avoided as a function of lead time, which must be modelled to determine the cost efficiency of the outcome [6, 7].

© Springer International Publishing AG, part of Springer Nature 2018
Y. Shi et al. (Eds.): ICCS 2018, LNCS 10861, pp. 644–654, 2018.
https://doi.org/10.1007/978-3-319-93701-4_51

In this paper we focus on supporting disaster early warning systems using Cloud, and specifically highlight the challenges of customizing, provisioning, and runtime managing virtual infrastructure based on the time critical constraints from early warning systems. The research is performed in the context of EU H2020 SWITCH project. An automated infrastructure planning and provisioning tool called Dynamic Real-time infrastructure planner (DRIP) will be presented. In the rest of the paper, we will first discuss the requirement challenges of the an early warning system, and then present the basic architecture of DRIP. After that a use case is used to demonstrate the current implementation.

2 Early Warning Systems and Challenges

2.1 A Use Case of Early Warning System

The essential structure of any early warning systems depends on the objectives of the system to provide important, timely information on specific phenomena to end-users and decision-makers, thereby enabling effective response [6].

Figure 1 presents a typical use case scenario. Sensors in the field transmit information to the IP Gateway. This gateway transmits the data collected to the database server. The notification server (Interactive Voice Response + Contact Center) periodically checks the data from the database, and, if they exceed certain values set, then on different communications channels, notifications are sent to an available operator that is scheduled to process the event. The operator checks statistics data received from sensors and transmits the decision whether or not to alert Unique National System for Emergency Calls (112).

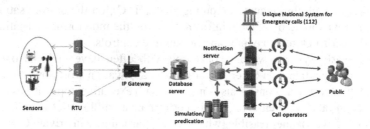

Fig. 1. Functional diagram for elastic early warning system

2.2 Requirements and Problems

The implementation of this kind of system faces several challenges, as the system must:

1. collect and process the sensor data in nearly real time;
2. detect and respond to urgent events very rapidly (i.e. this is a time-critical scenario);
3. predict the potential increase of load on the warning system when public users (customers) increase;
4. operate reliably and robustly throughout its life time;
5. be scalable when the deployment of sensors increases.

The development of such applications is usually difficult and costly, because of the high requirements for the runtime environment, and in particular the sophisticated optimisation mechanisms needed for developing and integrating the system components. In the meantime, a Cloud environment provides virtualised, elastic, controllable and quality on demand services for supporting systems like time critical applications. However, the engineering method and software tools for developing, deploying and executing classical time critical applications have not yet included the programmability and controllability provided by the Clouds; and the time critical applications cannot yet get the full potential benefits which Cloud technologies could provide.

It is still an open question whether disaster early warning systems, like the one outlined above, are suited to run in one or more private or public cloud environments. To deploy and control such time-critical systems asks for a workbench of dedicated tools each having its well defined task.

2.3   Time Critical Challenges

Laplante and Ovaska [11] define a real-time system as "a computer system that must satisfy bounded response-time constraints or risk severe consequences". The actual nature of individual response-time constraints varies. For example, often time constraints imposed on the acquisition, processing and publishing of real-time observations, not least in scenarios such as weather prediction or disaster early warning [12]. The ability to handle such scenarios is predicated on the time needed for customisation of the runtime environment and the scheduling of workflows [13, 23], while the steering of applications during complex experiments is also temporally bounded [14]. Time constraints are imposed on the scheduling and execution of tasks that require high performance or high throughput computing (HPC/HTC), on the customisation, reservation and provisioning of suitable infrastructure, on the monitoring of runtime application and infrastructure behaviour, and on runtime controls.

Disaster early systems we are concerned with often have multiple overlapping response-time constraints on different parts of the application workflow. Note that our concern of "time critical" constraints is not only with executing applications as quickly as possible, but also with ensuring stable performance within strict boundaries in the most cost-effective manner feasible (where 'cost', particularly in private Clouds, might be measured in terms of metrics other than money, such as energy consumption).

3   Dynamic Real-Time Infrastructure Planner

The Dynamic Real-time Infrastructure Planner (DRIP) is a system developed in the SWITCH project for the planning, validation and provisioning of the virtual infrastructure enlisted to support an application with time critical constraints. It is part of the SWITCH workbench, which includes two other subsystems (i) GUI for composing, executing and managing applications, namely The SWITCH Interactive Development Environment (SIDE), and (ii) a runtime monitoring and adaptation sub system, namely The Autonomous System Adaptation Platform (ASAP) [22].

3.1 Architecture and Components

The key features are modelled as a number of micro services, which are coupled via message brokers of DRIP manager. It provide a unified interface for clients such as SIDE or ASAP, as shown in Fig. 2.

1. The **infrastructure planner** uses an adapted partial critical path algorithm to produce efficient infrastructure topologies based on application workflows and constraints by selecting cost-effective virtual machines, customising the network topology among VMs, and placing network controllers for the networked VMs.
2. The **performance modeller** allows for testing of different cloud resources against different kinds of application component in order to provide performance data for use by the infrastructure planner and other components inside and outside of DRIP.
3. The **infrastructure provisioner** can automate the provisioning of infrastructure plans produced by the *planner* onto underlying infrastructure services. The provisioner can decompose the infrastructure description and provision it across multiple data centres (possibly from different providers) with transparent network configuration.
4. The **deployment agent** installs application components onto provisioned infrastructure. The deployment agent is able to schedule based on network bottlenecks, and maximize the satisfaction of deployment deadlines.
5. The **infrastructure control agents** are a set of APIs that DRIP provides to applications to control the scaling containers or VMs and for adapting network flows. They provide access to the underlying programmability provided by the virtual infrastructures, e.g., horizontal and vertical scaling of virtual machines, by providing interfaces by which the infrastructure hosting an application can be dynamically manipulated at runtime.
6. The **DRIP manager** is implemented as a web service that allows DRIP functions to be invoked by outside clients as services. Each request is directed to the appropriate component by the manager, which is responsible for coordinating the individual components and scaling them if necessary. The manager also maintains a database containing user accounts.
7. The communication between the manager and the individual components is facilitated by a **message broker**. Message brokering is an architectural pattern for message validation, transformation and routing, helping compose asynchronous, loosely coupled applications by providing transparent communication to independent components.
8. Resource information, credentials, and application workflows are all internally managed via a **knowledge base**. It maintains the descriptions of the cloud providers, resource types, performance characteristics, and other relevant information. The knowledge base also provides an interface for these agents to look up providers, resources and runtime status data during the execution of an application.

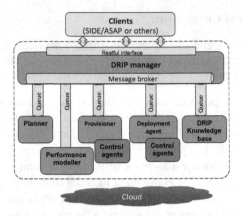

Fig. 2. DRIP implementation architecture.

Figure 3 depicts how those micro services interact.

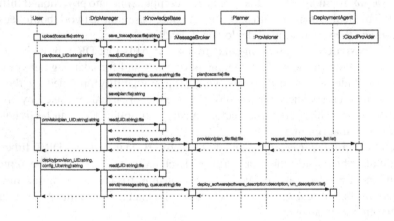

Fig. 3. Sequence diagram describing how DRIP plans and provisions virtual infrastructure and how it deploys software.

3.2 Current Prototype

The prototype of DRIP is based on industrial and community standards. The *infrastructure planner* is currently specified in YAML (formerly 'Yet Another Markup Language' but now 'YAML Ain't a Markup Language') in compliance with the Topology and Orchestration Specification for Cloud Applications (TOSCA)[1]. The *infrastructure provisioner* uses the Open Cloud Computing Interface (OCCI)[2] as its default provisioning interface, and

---

[1] https://www.oasis-open.org/committees/tosca/.
[2] http://occi-wg.org/.

currently supports the Amazon EC2[3], European Grid Initiative (EGI) FedCloud[4] and ExoGeni[5] Clouds. The *deployment agent* can deploy overlay Docker clusters using Docker Swarm or Kubernetes[6]. It may also deploy any type of customised distributed application based on Ansible playbooks[7]. The *infrastructure control agents* are set of API that DRIP provides to applications to control the infrastructure for scaling containers or VMs and adapting network flows. The *manager* provides a RESTful interface. DRIP uses the Advanced Message Queuing Protocol (AMQP) and RabbitMQ as its message broker where each process of each component is represented by a separate queue; this scalable architecture allows DRIP to be extended with additional components (e.g. planners) in order to handle larger workflows (e.g. in the case of a single DRIP service being provided to a large organisation for several applications).

The DRIP components are made available as open source under the Apache License Version 2.0; the software has been containerised and can be provisioned and deployed on federated virtual infrastructures within minimal configuration. They can be obtained either via the SWITCH release repository at https://github.com/switch-project or directly via the DRIP development repository at https://github.com/QCAPI-DRIP.

4   Experiments and Performance Characteristics

We will demonstrate how DRIP enhances the disaster early warning use case discussed in Sect. 2.

As the first step, the application logic should be modelled as a Direct Acyclic Graph (DAG) with annotation of deadlines. Figure 4 depicts the DAG of the scenario in Fig. 1. It will then be used as input for DRIP to automate the planning, provisioning, deployment of the application. In the early warning system workflow, 3 different deadlines can be defined as shown in Fig. 4. As the early warning system workflow is a service, the individual deadlines can be interpreted as deadlines in case data of a disaster is transmitted by the sensors in the field.

---

[3] https://aws.amazon.com/cn/ec2.

[4] https://www.egi.eu/federation/egi-federated-cloud/.

[5] http://www.exogeni.net/.

[6] https://kubernetes.io/.

[7] https://www.ansible.com/.

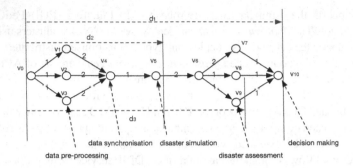

Fig. 4. Example of an abstract early warning system workflow with multiple deadlines. Global deadline d_1, and two intermediate deadlines d_2 and d_3 imposed on simulation and disaster assessment respectively.

The planner in the DRIP system *uses a 'compress-relax' Multi dEadline workflow Planning Algorithm (MEPA)* method to assign each task in the workflow to the best performing VM possible such that multiple deadlines are met, as shown in Fig. 5. To find the best combination of assignments to nodes that fulfil all deadlines a Genetic Algorithm based Planning Algorithm is applied. The effectiveness of this approach is compared to a modification of the IC_PCP algorithm, Abrishami et al. [15] that allows IC-PCP to deal with multiple deadlines. Wang et al. [17] demonstrated the performance of both approaches for task graphs generated by the GGen package [16] applying the 'fan-in/fan-out' methods, showing that the MEPA method can successfully cope with these kind of problems and allows for an easy adaptation in case more constraints play a role.

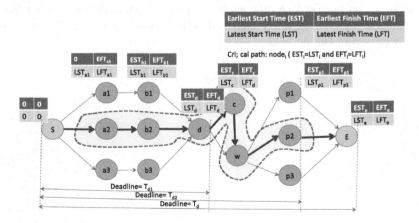

Fig. 5. Example of deadline-aware planning by DRIP. The blue nodes represent the workflow, with the critical path outlined. For each parallel group of nodes, the earliest/latest start/finish times can be extracted. (Color figure online)

Planning heavily depends on the **Performance modeler** of the DRIP subsystem to collect performance information of cloud resources. It schedules on a regular basis one or more benchmark scenarios for different cloud providers. Information on CPU, memory, disk and network I/O are collected for different VMs offered by a cloud provider. The systematic collection and sharing of such information will allow the DRIP planner to select the most suitable resources for mission-critical applications. Elzinga et al. [19] showed the functionality of this collector using the ExoGENI infrastructure platform.

Once the planner is finished, **the provision agent** provides a *flexible inter-locale Cloud infrastructure provisioning* mechanism to satisfy time-critical requirements. It is able to provision a networked infrastructure, recover from sudden failures quickly, and scale across data centers or Clouds automatically [20, 24]. This Cloud engine is able to set up a networked virtual Cloud across even public Clouds which do not explicitly support network topology, like EC2 or EGI FedCloud. For fast failure recovery the interplay of two agents, the provisioning agent and the monitoring agent. When some data center is down or inaccessible, a probe previously installed on the node can detect this. The monitoring agent can then invoke the provisioning agent to perform recovery. This is of importance in case sensors are geographically separated and data collections occurs in different cloud locations. The provisioning engine just needs to provision the specific part of the application hosted on the failed infrastructure. As the infrastructure description is already partitioned, it is easy for the agent to provision the same topology in another data center. Primary tests have been performed using the ExoGENI infrastructure platform; an example scenario is shown in Fig. 6.

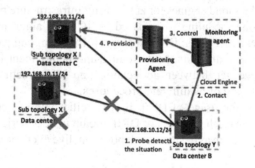

Fig. 6. Fast failure recovery.

Finally, **the deployment agent** provide a *deadline aware deployment scheduling* for time-critical applications in clouds comes into action, which accounts for deadlines on the actual deployment time of application components [21]. This is of special importance after fast failure recovery.

After the those steps, the application can be in operation for early warning, as shown in Fig. 7.

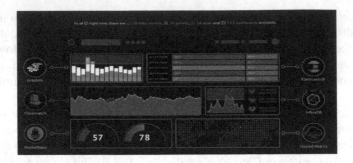

Fig. 7. The GUI of the use case prototyped using Grafana (GRAFANA: The open platform for beautiful analytics and monitoring: https://grafana.com/).

5 Summary

In this paper, we discussed the infrastructure challenges for meeting the time critical constraints for disaster early warning systems, and present a software suite called Dynamic Real-time Infrastructure Planner to automate the procedure for planning, provisioning and deploying early warning systems based on their time constraints. In the paper, the time critical constraints are not only referring to the as fast as possible but also to the deadlines that application has to meet.

There exist similar cloud engines for automating infrastructure provisioning such as Chef[8], also cloud job scheduling work based on IC_PCP algorithms [15]. However, compared to those existing work, DRIP shows the following unique features: (1) integrate infrastructure customization, provisioning and deployment into one service, to seamlessly bridge the gap between application and infrastructure, (2) time critical constraints are taken care of by different procedures.

We demonstrated the usage of DRIP in a specific type of application like early warning system; however, the purpose of DRIP meant to be generic. It has been used in several other use cases such as business collaboration, live event broadcast, and big data infrastructure.

One of the important future work will be further improve the optimization algorithm across the three steps of planning, provisioning and deployment.

Acknowledgement. This research has received funding from the European Union's Horizon 2020 research and innovation program under grant agreements 643963 (SWITCH project), 654182 (ENVRIPLUS project) and 676247 (VRE4EIC project).

---

[8] https://www.chef.io/chef/.

References

1. Suciu, G., Suciu, V., Butca, C., Dobre, C., Pop, F.: Elastic disaster early warning system using a cloud-based communication center. In: Proceedings of the 13th IEEE International Conference on Intelligent Computer Communication and Processing (2017)
2. Zhao, Z., Martin, P., Wang, J., Taal, A., Jones, A., Taylor, I., Stankovski, V., Vega, I.G., Suciu, G., Ulisses, A., Laat, C.: Developing and operating time critical applications in clouds: the state of the art and the SWITCH approach. In: The Proceedings of HOLACONF - Cloud Forward: From Distributed to Complete Computing, Procedia Computer Science, vol. 68, pp. 17–28. Elsevier (2015)
3. Zschau, J., Küppers, A.N. (eds.): Early Warning Systems for Natural Disaster Reduction. Springer, Heidelberg (2013). https://doi.org/10.1007/978-3-642-55903-7
4. Glade, T., Nadim, F.: Early warning systems for natural hazards and risks. Nat. Hazards 70(3), 1669 (2014)
5. de Groot, William J., Flannigan, Michael D.: Climate change and early warning systems for wildland fire. In: Zommers, Z., Singh, A. (eds.) Reducing Disaster: Early Warning Systems For Climate Change, pp. 127–151. Springer, Dordrecht (2014). https://doi.org/10.1007/978-94-017-8598-3_7
6. Horita, F.E., de Albuquerque, J.P., Marchezini, V., Mendiondo, E.M.: A qualitative analysis of the early warning process in disaster management. In: Proceedings of the ISCRAM 2016 Conference–Rio de Janeiro, Brazil (2016)
7. Cools, J., Innocenti, D., O'Brien, S.: Lessons from flood early warning systems. Environ. Sci. Policy 58, 117–122 (2016)
8. Alhmoudi, A., Aziz, Z.U.H.: Integrated framework for early warning system in UAE. Int. J. Disaster Resilience Built Environ. 7, 361–373 (2016)
9. Arcorace, M., Silvestro, F., Rudari, R., Boni, G., Dell'Oro, L., Bjorgo, E.: Forecast-based integrated flood detection system for emergency response and disaster risk reduction (Flood-FINDER). In: EGU General Assembly Conference Abstracts, vol. 18, p. 8770 (2016)
10. Udo, J., Jungermann, N.: Early warning system Ghana: how to successfully implement a disaster early warning system in a data scarce region. In: EGU General Assembly Conference Abstracts, vol. 18, p. 12819 (2016)
11. Laplante, P.A., Ovaska, S.J.: Real-Time Systems Design and Analysis: Tools for the Practitioner. Wiley, Hoboken (2011)
12. Poslad, S., Middleton, S.E., Chaves, F., Tao, R., Necmioglu, O., Bügel, U.: A semantic IoT early warning system for natural environment crisis management. IEEE Trans. Emerg. Top. Comput. 3(2), 246–257 (2015)
13. Zhao, Z., Grosso, P., van der Ham, J., Koning, R., de Laat, C.: An agent based network resource planner for workflow applications. Multiagent Grid Syst. 7(6), 187–202 (2011)
14. Evans, K., Jones, A., Preece, A., Quevedo, F., Rogers, D., Spasić, I., Taylor, I., Stankovski, V., Taherizadeh, S., Trnkoczy, J., Suciu, G., Suciu, V., Martin, P., Wang, J., Zhao, Z.: Dynamically reconfigurable workflows for time-critical applictions. In: Proceedings of the 10th Workshop on Workflows in Support of Large-Scale Science, p. 7. ACM (2015)
15. Abrishami, S., Naghibzadeh, M., Epema, D.: Deadline-constrained work-flow scheduling algorithms for infrastructure as a service clouds. Future Gener. Comput. Syst. 29(1), 158–169 (2013)
16. Cordeiro, D., Mounié, G., Perarnau, S., Trystram, D., Vincent, J.M., Wagner, F.: Random graph generation for scheduling simulations. In: Proceedings of the 3rd International ICST Conference on Simulation Tools and Techniques, p. 60. ICST Institute for Computer Sciences, Social-Informatics and Telecommunications Engineering (2010)

17. Wang, J., Taal, A., Martin, P., Hu, Y., Zhou, H., Pang, J., de Laat, C., Zhao, Z.: Planning virtual infrastructures for time critical applications with multiple deadline constraints. Future Gener. Comput. Syst. **75**, 365–375 (2017)
18. Wang, J., de Laat, C., Zhao, Z.: QoS-aware virtual SDN network planning. In: Proceedings of IFIP/IEEE International Symposium on Integrated Network Management. IEEE (2017)
19. Elzinga, O., Koulouzis, S., Taal, A., Wang, J., Hu, Y., Zhou, H., Martin, P., de Laat, C., Zhao, Z.: Automatic collector for dynamic cloud performance information. In: Proceedings of 12th International Conference on Networking, Architecture, and Storage (2017)
20. Zhou, H., Wang, J., Hu, Y., Su, J., Martin, P., De Laat, C., Zhao, Z.: Fast resource co-provisioning for time critical application based on networked infrastructure. In: IEEE International Conference on CLOUD, San Francisco, US (2016)
21. Hu, Y., Wang, J., Zhou, H., Martin, P., Taal, A., de Laat, C., Zhao, Z.: Deadline-aware deployment for time critical applications in clouds. In: Rivera, F.F., Pena, T.F., Cabaleiro, J.C. (eds.) Euro-Par 2017. LNCS, vol. 10417, pp. 345–357. Springer, Cham (2017). https://doi.org/10.1007/978-3-319-64203-1_25
22. Zhao, Z., Taal, A., Jones, A., Taylor, I., Stankovski, V., Vega, I.G., Hidalgo, F.J., Suciu, G., Ulisses, A., Ferreira, P, de Laat, C.: A software workbench for interactive, time critical and highly self-adaptive cloud applications (SWITCH). In: The Proceedings of IEEE CCGrid (2015)
23. Zhao, Z., van Albada, D., Sloot, P.: Agent-based flow control for HLA components. Int. J. Simul. Trans. **81**(7), 487–501 (2005)
24. Zhou, H., Hu, Y., Wang, J., Martin, P., De Laat, C., Zhao, Z.: Fast and dynamic resource provisioning for quality critical cloud applications. In: IEEE International Symposium On Real-time Computing (ISORC), York, UK (2016)

Calibration and Monitoring of IoT Devices by Means of Embedded Scientific Visualization Tools

Konstantin Ryabinin[1]([⊠])[ID], Svetlana Chuprina[1][ID], and Mariia Kolesnik[2][ID]

[1] Perm State University, Bukireva Str. 15, 614990 Perm, Russia
kostya.ryabinin@gmail.com, chuprinas@inbox.ru
[2] Perm Regional Museum/Branch Museum of Permian Antiquities,
Monastyrskaya Str. 11, 614000 Perm, Russia
kolesnik.ma@outlook.com

Abstract. In the paper we propose ontology based scientific visualization tools to calibrate and monitor various IoT devices in a uniform way. We suggest using ontologies to describe associated controllers, chips, sensors and related data filters, visual objects and graphical scenes to provide self-service solutions for IoT developers and device makers. High-level interface of these solutions enables composing data flow diagrams defining both the behavior of the IoT devices and rendering features. According to the data flow diagrams and the set of ontologies the firmware for IoT devices is automatically generated incorporating both the data visualization and device behavior code. After the firmware loading, it's possible to connect to these devices using desktop computer or smartphone/tablet, get the visualization client code over HTTP, monitor the data and calibrate the devices taking into account monitoring results. To monitor the distributed IoT networks a new visualization model based on circle graph is presented. We demonstrate the implementation of suggested approach within ontology based scientific visualization system SciVi. It was tested in a real world project of an interactive Permian Antiquities Museum exhibition creating.

Keywords: IoT devices · Scientific visualization tools
Ontology engineering · Data flow diagrams
Firmware source code generation

1 Introduction

According to the elaborate overview made by Internet Society [20], the key issues of Internet of Things (IoT) are security, privacy, interoperability, legislative framework, emerging economy and development. In the same time, the level of development automation tools for IoT is not high enough. As Texas Instruments Inc., one of the biggest manufacturers of IoT-related microelectronics, pointed, "IoT needs to be made easy for inexperienced developers" [27]. Moreover, nowadays the IoT developers community grows exponentially. Survey made

© Springer International Publishing AG, part of Springer Nature 2018
Y. Shi et al. (Eds.): ICCS 2018, LNCS 10861, pp. 655–668, 2018.
https://doi.org/10.1007/978-3-319-93701-4_52

by Tractica [28] shows that many enthusiasts become IoT developers. They create Smart Systems for homes, scientific or artistic exhibitions, and just for fun.

Due to the lack of widely supported standards [20], development of IoT devices often requires special software for designing, debugging and steering. Consequently, high-level software tools for building and managing IoT applications in a uniform way are demanded.

Growing IoT networks embrace more and more different fields of life and thereby produce huge quantity of heterogeneous data gathered by connected things. IoT systems have to be intelligent enough to make these data observable for humans, avoiding information overflow and ensuring comfortable cohabitation of humans and smart objects. The overflow problem can be solved by advanced semantic filtering of data performed inside the IoT network.

High complexity and granularity of IoT networks require powerful and ergonomic analytics tools. Especially it relates to the role of Big Data visual analytics in IoT. Modern visual tools for IoT should enable the user not only to monitor device data, but also control the behavior of smart objects and configure/reconfigure their network.

When it comes to IoT devices with different kinds of sensors, calibration and monitoring tasks become complicated. Calibration has many forms and consists in adjusting the parameters. These parameters rule the device to provide an accurate measurement according to known model, ground-truth data from laboratory instruments or already calibrated devices. Normally device manufacturer performs the basic calibration, but in some specific cases user steering is also required. For example, user may need to adjust the sensitivity of light detector to adapt it to concrete ambient lighting conditions. This kind of "user-side" calibration is often empirical and thereby requires the tools to adequately data monitoring, analyzing and predicting the adjustment results.

We propose to tackle the above mentioned IoT challenges using a single software platform based on the scientific visualization methods, corresponding rendering techniques and semantic filtering. Reusing of scientific visualization tools enables graphical representation and visual analysis of data generated by IoT devices and light-weight consumer robotic systems [23]. In this paper we focus on the monitoring and user-side calibration issues.

During the previous research work we developed a concept of a knowledge-driven multiplatform adaptive scientific visualization system (SVS), which can be integrated with third-party data sources by means of high-level tuning without source code modifications. We have implemented this concept in the system called SciVi [22]. The behavior of this system is driven by the ontologies [9] included in its knowledge base that describes the features of data sources, supported data filters, visual objects and graphical scenes. Thereby SciVi can be easily extended to cover new visualization techniques and set up for communication with arbitrary data sources including software solvers and hardware devices.

The aim of the paper is to present the extension of SciVi by self-service tools for automated embedding in IoT devices. This extension enables IoT device calibration and monitoring supported by high-quality interactive visualization. We demonstrate the results by an example of automated creation of interactive IoT-based exhibits in the Museum of Permian Antiquities (Perm, Russia).

2 Key Contributions

In this paper we describe the new capabilities of multiplatform SVS SciVi (version 3.0). The conducted research and corresponding development led to the following key results:

1. Proposed the ontology-driven approach for high-level adaptable monitoring and calibration of the heterogeneous IoT devices by means of scientific visualization and semantic filtering.
2. Proposed the circle graph-based model to graphical depiction of IoT network.
3. Implemented new SciVi high-level tools based on suggested approach to automate the process of SVS embedding into IoT device firmware to enable built-in visualization and steering.
4. Suggested the concept of interactive IoT-based museum exhibition, which uses implemented tools. Demonstrated this concept by 3D-reconstruction of Permian synapsid *Dimetrodon grandis* that exhibits the latest paleontological research results.

3 Related Work

3.1 IoT Development Tools

Since IoT is an exponentially evolving field of computer science and engineering [28], there are literary hundreds of related development tools [17]. They include software and hardware development platforms, middleware, operating systems, integration software, stacks of technologies and protocols. But most of these tools require very deep skills either in programming or in electronics, and the modern trend is to create high-level solutions available for beginners, not only for experts [27]. Such kind of solutions reduces IoT development time and increases productivity, which enables to involve more people into IoT community.

The most popular high-level state-of-the-art software solutions are Processing [18], Blynk [7], XOD [2] and NEXCOM IoT Studio [14]. The first system provides the high-level programming language and the set of libraries to simplify the development of light-weight electronic devices in terms of handling, transforming and monitoring data gathered. Being a powerful programming toolset, it still requires some additional developer's skills and provides no visual programming capabilities. Blynk is a visual programming tool enabling high-level control over the firmware logic of electronic device. It is very ergonomic, but lacks complex visualization capabilities, which are sometimes needed for data monitoring. XOD and NEXCOM IoT Studio use data flow [13] visual programming paradigm enabling user to compose firmware logic as a data transformation diagram. Data flow based programming is very intuitive and its effectiveness has been proven in many different application domains. However as well as Blynk, XOD and NEXCOM IoT Studio focus on the device logic providing just a basic dashboard-based data visualization.

While the mentioned solutions perfectly suite for solving typical IoT tasks, they cannot be easily extended for special cases like, for example, creating IoT-powered interactive museum exhibitions (see Sect. 6).

3.2 Ontology Engineeing Applied to IoT

Knowledge-driven approach based on ontology engineering methods is agile and handy for creating of complex systems [6]. Semantic Web technologies were proven to be suitable for IoT many times. One of the first research works in this field was made by Gyrard et al. [10]. As a result of this work best practices of ontology engineering usage in a context of IoT are defined.

The state-of-the-art ontology-based solutions are described in [3,25,26]. These works leverages ontology-based methods to different aspects of IoT, including network representation, security and interoperability issues. The work [11] describes ontology-based approach to create middleware for IoT. The work [8] describes powerful state-of-the-art ontology-based library code generator OLGA, which is suited for IoT firmware programmers. Finally, W3C Consortium published reusable ontology IoT-Lite of resources, entities and services related to IoT [29].

Despite many successful results, the ontology-driven IoT monitoring and calibration issues are still open. According to our knowledge there are no popular state-of-the-art solutions leveraging ontology engineering for visual analytics of IoT-generated data (see Sect. 5).

3.3 Methods to Represent IoT Network

While IoT networks become very sophisticated, visual analytics tools become highly demanded. These tools enable developers and users to inspect and manipulate the networks' structure as well as to detect problems and invent optimizations. State-of-the-art solutions for monitoring IoT networks unstructured graphs [15] or 3D models of rooms and objects where IoT devices are located [16].

However, it's not always easy enough to analyze unstructured graph or full 3D environment. Sometimes more informative is a concise structured representation. This is why we propose graphs of circular structure [24] to represent IoT device networks (see Sect. 7).

3.4 Scientific Visualization Tools

Previously, we analyzed state of the art of scientific visualization software including capabilities of different popular stand-alone systems like TecPlot, Origin, EasyPlot, IRIS Explorer, Surfer, Grapher, Voxler, Hesperus, ParaView, Avizo, etc. and scientific visualization libraries and frameworks like OpenDX, VTK, VizIt, ScientificVR, etc. [21]. These software solutions provide high-quality visualization, a lot of different tools and useful functions, but have some drawbacks, which may be crucial in some particular cases:

1. Standardization of input. Almost all popular SVS and libraries require input data in particular standard formats and have no high-level tools for integration with arbitrary third-party data sources.
2. Inability of feedback. Usually there are no means to set up control over the data source from the visualization system and the user can just view the data but cannot steer the process of data generation.
3. Complexity of extending. Most of the SVS and libraries can be extended with the new graphical capabilities by source code changing only. Extending and tuning the SVS by plugins requires programming skills and is complicated for the beginners.
4. Lack of portability. Popular visualization systems are implemented either for desktop computers or mobile devices, not for both.

To tackle the above challenges, we propose the ontology-driven SVS SciVi [22] (see Sect. 4). Besides programmers, there are two types of SciVi users: ontology engineers and casuals. The main goal of ontology engineers is to extend the SciVi knowledge base and thereby provide new capabilities for casuals. We demonstrated how we extended SciVi to create IoT-based exhibition of *Dimetrodon grandis*. The casual users in this case are IoT device markers.

3.5 Modern Reconstruction of *Dimetrodon Grandis*

IoT-based solutions have big potential not only for Smart Systems like Smart Home, but also for interactive exhibitions and installations suitable for museums, scientific art shows, etc. To demonstrate this idea we created interactive exhibition of *Dimetrodon grandis* Romer and Price, 1940, early Permian synapsid lived more than 290 million years ago.

According to the current paleontological knowledge, dimetrodon had a sail on its back with a tight network of blood vessels. This sail served to effectively heat the body by the sunrays. To demonstrate this concept in the interactive way we created animated 3D model of dimetrodon using Blender 3D. We took into account the latest reconstruction research results published by Hartman [12], including sail shape, back curvature and high walk pose.

We uploaded this model to SVS SciVi and created IoT device that detects light direction of real light sources and visualizes how dimetrodon rotates its sail to the light rays (see Sect. 6).

4   Key Concepts of SVS SciVi

The detailed description of SVS SciVi including its architecture and key features ensuring efficient and high-quality rendering on both desktop computers and mobile devices can be found in [22]. Its essential part is the knowledge base containing 3 ontologies:

1. $\overline{L}$ that describes input/output (I/O) statements of programming languages. According to this ontology the regex-based parser is automatically generated, which extracts the related structures of I/O data from the solver's source code. This mechanism is used to automate the process of integration of SciVi with third-party solvers.
2. $\overline{F}$ that describes semantic filters used to optional preprocessing the data before visualization. For example, the described filters can sort the data, cluster them, reduce their amount according given criteria, perform mathematical transformations, etc.
3. $\overline{U}$ that describes supported visual objects and graphical scenes. For example, 2D charts and 3D models are available.

Developer or knowledge engineer can add new filters, graphical objects and scenes to SciVi by extending the ontologies $\overline{F}$ and $\overline{U}$ without core's source code modification.

To define the internal SciVi rendering pipeline we use the data flow diagrams [13]. We developed the high-level graphical editor, which enables the easy way to design data flow diagrams and thereby to describe the data retrieving, transformation and rendering. This editor provides a palette of available filters, graphical objects and scenes. The palette is automatically built according to their descriptions in the ontologies $\overline{F}$ and $\overline{U}$. User can add new diagram nodes from this palette and connect their I/O sockets defining the flow of data. Starting from the data source node, user can define the sequence of filters, connect them with visual objects and finally compose the graphical scenes.

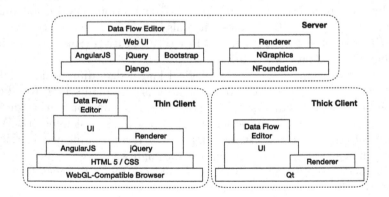

Fig. 1. Stack of software used in SciVi server, thin and thick client

SVS SciVi uses a layered architecture to achieve needed abstraction level from the platform it runs on. The stack of software used in SciVi is shown in the Fig. 1. Thin client is written in JavaScript, thick client's logic is almost entirely implemented in C++ and server is based mainly on C++ and Python; its Web interface is written in JavaScript. Server and thin client share the common code of data flow editor based on AngularJS framework. Thick client has its own data flow editor code to make it more efficient using native drawing API. NFoundation and NGraphics libraries are written in C++ (product of Perm IT-company Nulana Ltd., one of the paper's authors is affiliated with). It provides abstraction layer from the operating system and OpenGL/Direct3D low-level rendering API to enable server-side rendering if needed.

The renderers of client and server are highly configurable thanks to ontology knowledge base, which includes the corresponding links to original and third-party rendering libraries (for example, PixiJS, D3.js and Three.js in the thin client, Qt charts and Assimp in the thick client, etc.).

5   Embedded Scientific Visualization Tools

The aim of this work is to provide self-service solutions for calibration and monitoring of IoT devices by means of embedded scientific visualization tools. These tools make it possible to implement "in situ visualization" [19] for IoT devices. SciVi is capable to connect to arbitrary data source including different electronic devices. The device maker has to set up the SciVi server as intermediate software between the IoT devices and the visualization client (desktop computer, mobile device or browser). This approach is flexible enough, but sometimes it must be simplified for the sake of efficiency. For example, in the museum with interactive stands, the visitor can use his/her mobile device to handle these stands and get corresponding visualization. For this purpose, it's necessary to connect to the interactive stand via browser over WiFi or some similar HTTP-compatible technology and get the data displayed without any additional software. In the other case, when some IoT device is used, it's necessary to calibrate this device and to visualize the data it produces for monitoring purposes. In the last case the direct connection between mobile and IoT devices is preferable.

To achieve this, we propose original tools for automated firmware generation for the IoT device taking into account its specifications. Firmware incorporates both the program code of device logic (called "embedded host"), and the program code of visualization Web-server (called "embedded server"). The thin client is responsible for rendering. The embedded server enables thin client connections, obtains the data from embedded host, transmits them to the client and receives the control commands including the calibrating. The client performs scene rendering and provides the calibration graphical user interface. The "traditional" SciVi assumes that the visualization server is more powerful than the client and specific data processing including some rendering steps can be performed on the server side. But in the case of IoT device firmware the contrary is assumed: the client device should perform all the processing and visualization, because the server platform normally has limitation both in clock frequency and in memory. This firmware is generated by the SciVi server and can include as many visualization routines, as the IoT device memory volume enables.

As mentioned above, previous version of SciVi contained three ontologies in its knowledge base: $\overline{L}$, $\overline{F}$ and $\overline{U}$. To provide the automated generation, we propose to extend the SciVi knowledge base with the ontology $\overline{C}$. This ontology describes different electronic components such as controllers, chips and sensors as well as associated firmware code.

For example, in the Fig. 2 the fragment of ontology $\overline{C}$ describing analog-to-digital converter (ADC) of ESP8266 controller is shown. This popular WiFi-compatible controller is widely used for IoT purposes [4]. The ontology $\overline{C}$ is used in the similar way as ontologies $\overline{F}$ and $\overline{U}$: it supports the data flow diagram editor's functioning and is intended to provide the code fragments necessary for firmware generation. All the four ontologies in SciVi knowledge base have the common part that is a description of supported data types, so they all may be used together at the same time.

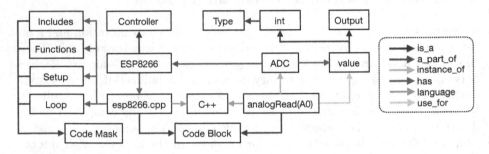

Fig. 2. Fragment of electronic components ontology from the SciVi knowledge base (Color figure online)

The ontologies are represented in standard OWL format. Short code snippets (one-line expressions) are stored directly in the ontology, for example, the call of ADC "analogRead(A0)" in Fig. 2. Larger code blocks are saved in separated files, for example, the firmware template "esp8266.cpp". Code blocks can have masks like "Includes", "Functions", "Setup" and "Loop" of "esp8266.cpp", which are filled automatically by related code during firmware generation. All of these code fragments are stored in the code repository. $\overline{F}$, $\overline{U}$ and $\overline{C}$ ontologies play the role of its semantic index, while the data flow diagram defines the interconnections between the different entities described by these ontologies.

The firmware generator is a part of SciVi server. It is written in Python and executed on the basis of Django, see Fig. 1. Its input is data flow diagram and the type of controller. The generator traverses the data flow diagram and generates the firmware code for chosen controller using the related code fragments according to those parts of ontologies, which are referenced from the data flow diagram nodes. Normally C++-based embedded host and embedded server are created as well as JavaScript-based client. The client is then transmitted to the user via HTTP and communicating with the server via WebSocket. In case of

ESP8266 (see Fig. 2) the *.ino file is generated (so-called "sketch") which can be uploaded to the ESP8266 with the help of Arduino IDE.

6   Evaluation

As a feature-reach use-case to evaluate the proposed approach we demonstrate the creation of a light direction sensor based on ESP8266 controller. This sensor needs feedback for calibration. It detects the average direction to an external light source and uses it to direct the light on the virtual scene. The sensor consists of 3 photo resistors VT90N2 placed at the vertices of an equilateral triangle. Minimal resistance of VT90N2 is reached when the light direction is collinear with the normal n of its surface. The surfaces of resistors are oriented to be 45° to the ground. Thereby the normal vectors n_1, n_2, n_3 of the resistors' surfaces build the basis of the vector space. In this space the direction from the sensor to the light source can be expressed as $l = u_1 n_1 + u_2 n_2 + u_3 n_3$, where u_1, u_2, u_3 are the quotients proportional to the voltage on the corresponding photo resistors. Data flow diagram of the light direction sensor is shown in the Fig. 3.

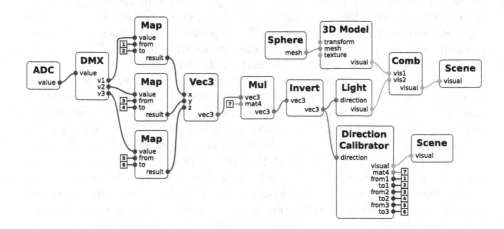

Fig. 3. Data flow diagram for light direction sensor

The ESP8266 controller has only one 10-bit ADC channel depicted on the diagram by "ADC" node with single output. This is why logical demultiplexor (DMX) is used to separate signals from the photo resistors. It corresponds to the analog multiplexor 74HC4051 in the device schematics. The theoretical range of the values obtained from ADC is [0; 1023], however in practice the voltage measured on the resistors does not accurately match that range having some "padding" from the lower and upper boundary. To compensate this, cutting should be performed. The nodes called "Map" cut off their input values according to the "from" and "to" inputs and map them to [0; 1]. The cutting values should be calibrated as they depend on the photo resistors and on the ambient lighting conditions.

The mapped values are then assembled into 3-dimensional vector using node "Vec3", which is multiplied by the 4×4 matrix using node "Mul" to match the virtual scene's basis and the actual orientation of the sensor. To perform multiplication, vector is extended by $w = 1$ and then trimmed back to 3 components. The matrix used as input for the "Mul" node contains rotation and should be calibrated.

The direction of the vector assembled is inverted by the node "Invert" to get the light direction. The result is used to direct the virtual light source depicted with the node "Light", which is then added to the graphical scene. 3D model with sphere as a mesh is added to reflect the light.

To enable device calibration there is special graphical object "Calibrator", which takes the light direction as input and produces corresponding visual object as output for related graphical scene. Calibrator renders coordinate axes and explicitly visualizes the vector of light direction as an arrow in the scene space. It also enables user to rotate the coordinate system and therefore change the rotation matrix for the basis, as well as provides graphical interface to change the ranges for 3 mappings of values obtained from ADC. The output of the calibrator is connected to the "Mul" and "Map" nodes, building the *cycle* in the data flow diagram. While traditional data flow diagrams are acyclic, we need to support feedback to enable calibration. To keep the diagram clean and readable (as well as planar in terms of graph theory) we indicate feedback links with the special numbered markers (see Fig. 3) and not by arcs.

The two "Scene" nodes represent two different graphical scenes, which can be accessed by different URLs determined in the nodes' settings. Switching between these two scenes, user can calibrate the device and view the actual lighting simulation. However, this means the calibration values should be stored when calibrator is shown and reused when the 3D model is rendered. To achieve this, we departed from the traditional data flow principal of "freedom from side-effects" [13] and implemented feedback via global variables. While this breaks a traditional data flow concept, it ensures more flexibility and enables easy and readable representation of calibration actions. We still call the result diagram "data flow", because it still represents the path of data through the preprocessing and rendering pipeline. With current enhancements the pipeline has global mutable state, which can be changed by the nodes in runtime enabling the calibration capabilities.

We used the developed device in the interdisciplinary educational project organized by the Museum of Permian Antiquities. The project is designed mainly for middle and senior schoolchildren. Its idea is to create an interactive exhibition of *Dimetrodon grandis* mentioned in Sect. 3.5.

During the educational lesson the attending schoolchildren assemble the light direction sensor based on ESP8266 controller and create the logic of its firmware as a data flow diagram in SciVi. The idea is to tie the angular position of dimetrodon 3D model to the light direction. Next, SciVi generates the firmware code and the attendees calibrate the device they created. As a result, the rendered dimetrodon automatically moves its body to keep the sail nearly perpendicular to the light direction. The aim of this educational project is to present the modern paleontological knowledge to the schoolchildren in a game form as well as to show the alloy of paleontology, biology, physics, robotics and computer science.

We used skeletal animation supported by Three.js for scientifically accurate rendering of the dimetrodon. To ensure flexibility and low latency of data transmission the communication between client and embedded server based on HTTP and WebSocket is used.

7   Graph-Based Visualization of IoT Network

Perm Regional Museum has many branches including historical and paleontological ones, which are territorially distributed. Going further with the idea of IoT-based interactive exhibitions we plan to build the common environment across different branches. The result network may have complex topology establishing connections not only inside single museum branch over local network, but also between different branches over the Internet. In this case the visual analysis of the network would be needed.

We propose new clear and concise visual model named SciVi::CGraph that accelerates a common understanding of the huge amount of data obtained from distributed IoT networks as well as networks structure. SciVi::CGraph is based on the traditional circle graph [1]. Compared to circle graph SciVi::CGraph has multi-level adaptable ring scale around the graph. This scale enables to demonstrate the hierarchical grouping of data, which is adequate for multidimensional data representation. We have used SciVi::CGraph as a visual model in a real-world project to explore the Machine Learning results of social network processing within a remit of the project titled "Socio-Cognitive Modeling of Social Networks Users Verbal and Non-Verbal Behavior Based on Machine Learning and Geoinformation Technologies". The research results of this project have proved that suggested model is very useful for visual analytics goals and enables to evaluate different data processing algorithms. The reported study is supported by Ministry of Education and Science of the Russian Federation, State Assignment No. 34.1505.2017/PCh (Research Project of Perm State University, 2017–2019).

In a context of designing a Smart Museum [5] SciVi::CGraph can be used to visualize the results of IoT networks monitoring including museum visitors activity monitoring. In this case the suggested model shows the data with respect of the distributed IoT network structure. The devices are visualized taking into account their location, so neighbor devices are grouped together in the graph. Figure 4 demonstrates the distributed IoT network structure. The connections are represented by quadratic parabolas. The traffic volume is mapped to the thicknesses of the graph arcs. The kind of devices such as sensor, display, actuator, etc. is mapped to the color of graph nodes. The power consumption of devices is shown by the histogram drawn as nodes' background. The location hierarchy (halls inside buildings) is represented by the ring scale around the graph. Support of this kind of visualization in SVS SciVi required the expansion of the ontology $\overline{U}$.

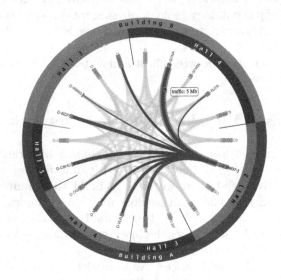

Fig. 4. SciVi::CGraph representation of distributed IoT network structure (Color figure online)

8 Conclusion

In this paper we describe the new version of adaptive SVS SciVi (v3.0) enriched with the high-level features enabling firmware generation for IoT devices. In the context of SVS, IoT devices are treated as solvers generating data to be visualized. The new features as all the previous extensions are added to SciVi in a uniform way by means of ontology-based engineering methods. For this, we extended the SciVi ontological knowledge base with the ontology of electronic components that describes different controllers, sensors and chips and related program resources needed to generate the firmware. This ontology together with ontologies of semantic filters, visual objects and graphical scenes allows the device makers to build data flow diagrams, which describe internal logic of IoT device behavior as well as the calibration and monitoring algorithms.

Currently the calibration is implemented via feedback functionality. The user can tune the device manually according personal needs by sending related control commands while observing the visual representation of device data. But in general the knowledge-driven approach to semantic filtering enables to define automatic calibration algorithms, for example, drift compensation function. To do this within SciVi it is enough to add to ontology knowledge base the corresponding semantic filter that will be automatically applied to raw data obtained from the device.

Upgrade of SciVi knowledge base allows this SVS to play a new role as visual environment for IoT device programming. The paper highlights the testing of the SciVi 3.0 new features by an example of creating the *Dimetrodon grandis* interactive exhibition.

In the future, we plan to build more complex Smart Museum exhibitions using the interconnected IoT devices. To be able to visually inspect distributed IoT networks we propose the new kind of concise visual representation based on circular graph. Also we plan to enrich the IoT ecosystem with augmented reality (AR) capabilities, for example, to generate ontology-based AR-assistant that helps assembling complex IoT devices or networks.

References

1. Ageev, A.: A triangle-free circle graph with chromatic number 5. Discret. Math. **152**, 295–298 (1996). https://doi.org/10.1016/0012-365X(95)00349-2
2. Allan, A.: XOD-a new visual programming language for Arduino. Hackster.io (2017). https://blog.hackster.io/xod-a-new-visual-programming-language-for-arduino-7bc911cdb27. Accessed 31 Mar 2018
3. Ayele, G.: Semantic description of IoT security for smart grid. Master's thesis. University of Agder (2017)
4. Brown, E.: Linux and open source hardware for IoT. Linux.com (2016). https://www.linux.com/news/linux-and-open-source-hardware-iot. Accessed 31 Mar 2018
5. Chianese, A., Piccialli, F.: Designing a smart museum: when cultural heritage joins IoT. In: 2014 Eighth International Conference on Next Generation Mobile Apps, Services and Technologies, pp. 300–306 (2014). https://doi.org/10.1109/NGMAST.2014.21
6. Chuprina, S., Nasraoui, O.: Using ontology-based adaptable scientific visualization and cognitive graphics tools to transform traditional information systems into intelligent systems. Sci. Vis. **8**(1), 23–44 (2016)
7. Doshi, H.S., Shah, M.S., Shaikh, U.S.A.: Internet of Things (IoT): integration of Blynk for domestic usability. Vishwakarma J. Eng. Res. **1**(4), 149–157 (2017)
8. El Kaed, C., Ponnouradjane, A.: A model driven approach accelerating ontology-based IoT applications development. In: CEUR Workshop (2017). http://ceur-ws.org/Vol-2063/sisiot-paper4.pdf. Accessed 31 Mar 2018
9. Gruber, T.R.: A translation approach to portable ontology specifications. Knowl. Acquis. **5**(2), 199–220 (1993). https://doi.org/10.1006/knac.1993.1008
10. Gyrard, A., Serrano, M., Atemezing, G.A.: Semantic web methodologies, best practices and ontology engineering applied to Internet of Things. In: 2015 IEEE 2nd World Forum on Internet of Things (WF-IoT) (2015). https://doi.org/10.1109/WF-IoT.2015.7389090
11. Hachem, S., Teixeira, T., Issarny, V.: Ontologies for the internet of things. In: 8th Middleware Doctoral Symposium (MDS 2011) (2011). https://doi.org/10.1145/2093190.2093193
12. Hartman, S.: Taking a 21st century look at Dimetrodon. Scott Hartman's Skeletal Drawing.com (2016). http://www.skeletaldrawing.com/home/21stcenturydimetrodon. Accessed 31 Mar 2018
13. Lee, B., Hurson, A.: Issues in dataflow computing. Adv. Comput. **37**, 285–333 (1993). https://doi.org/10.1016/S0065-2458(08)60407-6

14. NEXCOM: IoT Development Tool Selection Guide (2016). http://ebook.nexcom. com/Catalog/2016_IoT_Development_Tool_Selection_Guide/IoT_Development_ Tool_Selection_Guide_opf_files/pdfs/IoT_Development_Tool_Selection_Guide.pdf. Accessed 31 Mar 2018
15. nuPSYS: nuGEN™ 3D visualization of IoT networks. nuPSYS (2017). http:// www.nupsys.com/nugen.html. Accessed 31 Mar 2018
16. Puri, D.: Coping with IoT data overload? Try 3D visualization. NetworkWorld (2016). https://www.networkworld.com/article/3140712/internet-of-things/coping-with-iot-data-overload-try-3d-visualization.html. Accessed 31 Mar 2018
17. Rahul: 100 IoT open source development tools and resources. Internet of Things Wiki (2016). https://internetofthingswiki.com/100-iot-open-source-development-tools-and-resources/422/. Accessed 31 Mar 2018
18. Reas, C., Fry, B., Maeda, J.: Processing: A Programming Handbook for Visual Designers and Artists. The MIT Press, Cambridge (2007)
19. Rivi, M., Calori, L., Muscianisi, G., Slavnic, V.: In-situ visualization: state-of-the-art and some use cases. In: PRACE (2011). http://www.prace-ri.eu/IMG/pdf/In-situ_Visualization_State-of-the-art_and_Some_Use_Cases-2.pdf. Accessed 31 Mar 2018
20. Rose, K., Eldridge, S., Chapin, L.: The internet of things: an overview. Technical report. The Internet Society (ISOC) (2015). https://www.internetsociety.org/resources/doc/2015/iot-overview. Accessed 31 Mar 2018
21. Ryabinin, K.: Methods and means for the development of adaptive multiplatform systems to visualize scientific experiments. Ph.D. thesis, Perm State University (2014)
22. Ryabinin, K., Chuprina, S.: Development of ontology-based multiplatform adaptive scientific visualization system. J. Comput.Sci. **10**, 370–381 (2015). https://doi.org/10.1016/j.jocs.2015.03.003
23. Ryabinin, K., Chuprina, S.: Tackle lightweight hardware robotic devices data monitoring problems by means of scientific visualization systems. In: 27th International Conference on Computer Graphics and Vision GraphiCon 2017, pp. 142–146 (2017)
24. Ryabinin, K., Baranov, D., Belousov, K.: Integration of scientific visualization toolset SciVi with information system semograph. In: 27th International Conference on Computer Graphics and Vision GraphiCon 2017, pp. 138–141 (2017)
25. Serrano, M., et al.: IoT semantic interoperability: research challenges, best practices, recommendations and next steps. Technical report, European Research Cluster on The Internet of Things (2015). http://www.internet-of-things-research.eu/pdf/IERC_Position_Paper_IoT_Semantic_Interoperability_Final.pdf. Accessed 31 Mar 2018
26. Seydoux, N., Drira, K., Hernandez, N., Monteil, T.: IoT-O a core-domain IoT ontology to represent connected devices networks. In: Blomqvist, E., Ciancarini, P., Poggi, F., Vitali, F. (eds.) Knowledge Engineering and Knowledge Management, vol. 10024, pp. 561–576. Springer, Cham (2016). https://doi.org/10.1007/978-3-319-49004-5_36
27. Texas Instruments Inc.: The top 6 challenges facing IoT - and how we are overcoming them. TI E2E™ Community (2016). http://e2e.ti.com/blogs_/b/thinkinnovate/archive/2016/02/02/the-top-6-challenges-facing-iot-and-how-we-are-overcoming-them. Accessed 31 Mar 2018
28. Tractica: Consumer robotics. Technical report. Tractica (2017). https://www.tractica.com/research/consumer-robotics/. Accessed 31 Mar 2018
29. W3C: IoT-lite ontology. W3C (2015). https://www.w3.org/Submission/iot-lite/. Accessed 31 Mar 2018

Gated Convolutional LSTM for Speech Commands Recognition

Dong Wang$^{(\boxtimes)}$ ⓘ, Shaohe Lv, Xiaodong Wang, and Xinye Lin

Science and Technology on Parallel and Distributed Laboratoratory,
National University of Defense Technology, Changsha, China
{wangdong08,shaohelv,xdwang}@nudt.edu.cn, lxytcmn@gmail.com

Abstract. As the mobile device gaining increasing popularity, Acoustic Speech Recognition on it is becoming a leading application. Unfortunately, the limited battery and computational resources on a mobile device highly restrict the potential of Speech Recognition systems, most of which have to resort to a remote server for better performance. To improve the performance of local Speech Recognition, we propose *C-1-G-2-Blstm*. This model shares Convolutional Neural Network's ability of learning local feature and Recurrent Neural Network's ability of learning sequence data's long dependence. Furthermore, by adopting the Gated Convolutional Neural Network instead of a traditional CNN, we manage to greatly improve the model's capacity. Our tests demonstrate that *C-1-G-2-Blstm* can achieve a high accuracy at 90.6% on the Google Speech Commands data set, which is 6.4% higher than the state-of-art methods.

Keywords: Acoustic Speech Recognition · Localize
Gated Convolutional Neural Network · Long Short Time Memory

1 Introduction

With the fast advancement of intelligent devices such as robots and smart phones, Acoustic Speech Recognition is becoming more and more popular in human-machine interaction. Speech assistants such as Google Now, Apple Siri, Microsoft Cortana are widely used around the world. To recognize the human speech accurately, most of these systems use a Client-Server (C/S) structure, where the speech recognition models with complex structure and high computing cost are put on cloud servers. The speech data is usually first collected on the mobile devices, then sent to the remote server. After the speech is processed and recognized, the result is then sent back to the mobile devices. Systems using this C/S can achieve good performance, but faces the following limitations. First, they depend heavily on a stable Internet connection, without which the system

This work was supported by National Natural Science Foundation of China No. 61472434, Science and Technology on Parallel and Distributed Laboratoratory Foundation No. 9140C810109150C81002, National University of Defense Technology.

can't work. Second, sending data to a remote server introduces risks of privacy leak [3]. To circumvent these limitations, a speech recognition system that works completely locally is much in demand.

In practice, a few local speech recognition systems are already in deployment. For example, "Google Now" uses a local system to recognize a simple "OK Google" command to wake up the main service. However, due to the limitation of hardware resources, mobile devices can only run relatively simple models, which have limited recognition capabilities. Therefore, most current local speech recognition systems only serve as a wake-up watchdog for more powerful online speech recognition services.

In order to improve the accuracy of local speech recognition systems, we design a deep neural network model based on Gated CNN (Convolutional Neural Network) and RNN (Recurrent Neural Network). The model combines CNN's ability of learning local features and RNN's ability of learning the long-distance dependence features of sequential data. Our experiments show that the model achieves a high accuracy of 90.6% on the Google Speech commands dataset, outperforming the state-of-art work by 6.2%.

Our contribution is two-fold.

- First, we design an efficient model which combines CNN and RNN. Compared with the existing CNN + RNN work [2, 23], our model uses fewer layers and a simpler neural network structure while achieving much higher recognition accuracy.
- Our model adopts the Gated CNN network structure. Compared with conventional CNN, Gated CNN uses self-attention-like operations and more nonlinear transformations, which effectively enhance the model's ability of selecting important features.

2   Related Work

CNN is originally designed for image identification, classification, etc. Since LeCun successfully trained a multi-layer net using CNN in LeNet [10], Deep Nerual Nets based on CNN achieve great success in image related tasks [6,9,15,16]. By adopting the local receptive field, weight sharing, sub-sampling and other technologies, CNN is very robust with the translation and transformation in the data. It also has a strong ability to learn data's local patterns. These features make CNN a great tool in speech processing and natural language processing as well.

As a structure for handling time-sequence data, RNN focuses too much on the last input signals, and suffers from gradient explosion and the vanishing problem. As a result, RNN usually does not work well at its early stage. The proposal of Long-Short Time Memory (LSTM) [8] provides a good solution for these problems and greatly improves RNN's ability of learning long distance dependence. Benefited from LSTM, Gated Recurrent Unit (GRU) [4] and other structures, RNN has achieved a great breakthrough in natural language processing, translation and speech recognition.

In recent years, lots of works are using neural net to fulfill the speech processing task. Google Now [3] uses a fully connected Deep Neural Network (DNN) model to recognize the wake-up command "ok google". Compared with the Key-Word/Filter Hidden Markov Model, which is commonly used in existing Keyword Spotting system, this DNN model achieves 39% performance improvement. However, fully connected DNN ignores the structural patterns of the input data. No matter in what order is the input data organized, the fully connected DNN model will reach the same performance in the end, this will cause problems for speech recognition as the context of speech heavily relies on the speech data's structural feature in both the time and frequency domain. Besides, fully connected DNN methods cannot handle the translation invariance in the data. Different speakers or speaking styles can cause the formats translating in frequency domain, hence can hardly be processed with a fully connected DNN. Although theoretically full connected DNN can be trained with translation invariance, it requires lots of training data [14].

CNN's success in image domain demonstrates its ability to fix the disadvantages of fully connected DNN's. Inspired by this, CNN is more and more used in speech recognition [1,5,7,19,22]. [14] designs a CNN-based neural model, which achieves better recognition results than [3] while reducing the model's scale. [11] uses the CNN neural model and transfer learning, combined with Dilated Kernels for Multi-scale Inputs [21] to recognize speech commands. It builds a 121-layer neural net, pre-trains it on the UrbanSound8K dataset and achieves an accuracy of 84.35% on the Google Speech Commands dataset [20]. On the same data set, [17] designs a 15-layer deep residual net [6] combined with Dilated Kernels for Multi-scale Inputs. In the task of recognizing 12 commands selected from all 30 in Google Speech Commands, the model achieves an accuracy of 95.8%.

Although CNN outperforms fully connected DNN greatly in terms of recognition performance, it also has some disadvantages. The features learned by CNN are just local. Its scope is limited by the filter's shape and CNN's layer number, hence the features cannot cover the entire speech on either the time or frequency domain. To make the features cover a larger scope, the model has to be much deeper. Relatively, RNN shows much better performance in learning long distance dependence of sequential data. [2] proposes a CRNN neural model with 32 CNN layers and 1 RNN layer. Combining CNN's ability of learning local features and RNN's ability of learning long distance dependence, the CRNN neural model achieves an accuracy of 97.7% for detecting the occurrence of "TalkType". To solve the task of translating speech to text, [23] designs a 15-layer neural model based on ConvLSTM (one kind of LSTM which merges CNN inside) and CNN, in combination with many other technologies such as network-in-network, batch normalization, and residual connection. The model achieves a word error rate of 10.5% on the WSJ ASR dataset. However, all these models combining CNN and RNN have the problem of being too deep and complex.

Based on these work and aimed at improving the accuracy of local speech commands recognition, we propose a Gated Convolutional Recurrent Neural Network model. This model combines the advantages of Gated CNN and RNN

networks and ultimately achieves a recognition accuracy of 90.6% on the Google
Speech Commands dataset.

3   Model Design

Figure 1 shows the basic structure of the proposed model, referred to as *C-1-
G-2-Blstm*. The main part of the model is a multi-layer Gated CNN network
connected with a bi-directional RNN network.

The model outputs the probabilities of the input speech being each command. For each speech, the input data firstly passes through a conventional
two-dimensional convolution to increase feature maps, and then passes through
multi-layer Gated CNN to extract local features on different scope scales. After
local feature extraction, the model uses a bi-directional RNN to learn long distance dependence and obtains feature vector of the input speech. Finally, according to the feature vector, the model gives the prediction.

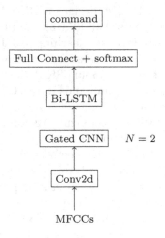

Fig. 1. Model structure

3.1   Speech Preprocessing

For every speech fragment, its corresponding input to the model is the Mel-
Frequency Cepstrum Coefficient (MFCC). In our test, we extract the MFCC
with a frame window of 128 ms, a frame offset of 31.25 ms, and 20 filters. Finally,
for each speech fragment, we get t MFCC frames with $f = 20$ dimensions, where
t depends on the speech's duration.

3.2   CNN Net

CNN has shown a huge advantage in learning the data's local feature. Its successful application in image field inspired us that CNN can also be used to learn speech's time-local feature.

A nice feature of CNN is: as the number of CNN layer increases, the upper layer can have a larger receptive field, thereby extracting the feature of a larger local scope. Therefore, multi-layer CNN networks can help to analyze the speech's features at different scales.

The input of the CNN part is the MFCC frames x, where $x \in \mathbb{R}^{1 \times t \times f}$. Most of the existing work treat MFCC as a two-dimension feature map with shape $t \times f$. Instead, in this paper we treat MFCC as f feature maps with dimension of $1 \times t$. This better corresponds to MFCC's physical meaning: different frequencies are different features. $F \in \mathbb{R}^{m \times n \times h \times r}$ denotes the kernel of two-dimensional convolution, where m and n denote the kernel's height and width, h denotes the number of input feature maps, and r denotes the number of output feature maps.

Conv2d. The first layer in our CNN part is a conventional 2-dimension convolution. In this layer the parameters are: $m = 1, h = t$ and $r > f$. Using these parameters has the following effects. First, with a $m \times n$ convolution in time domain, this layer can learn feature in local time. Second, $h = f$ makes different frequencies treated as different feature map. Third, by set $r > f$, this layer can recombine frequencies and produce more feature maps.

Gated CNN. The second and third CNN layer use Gated Convolution to further learn the local feature of the speech.

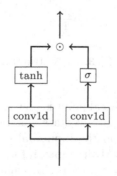

Fig. 2. Gated CNN

Gated convolutional layer is proposed in [12], its structure is shown in Fig. 2. Equation (1) gives the definition of Gated Convolution, which is inspired by the multiplication gate in LSTM.

$$y = \tanh(F_f * x) \odot \sigma(F_g * x) \tag{1}$$

In (1), $*$ is the convolution operation, σ is the sigmoid operation, $\odot$ denotes multiplication between corresponding elements, and F_f, F_g are the convolution kernels of two convolutions respectively.

Compared with conventional CNN, Gated Convolution introduces more non-linear operations and multiplication, which can improve the model's learning and expressing capacity. In addition, Self-Attention [18] is also obtained by multiplying the corresponding elements of tanh and σ.

3.3   RNN Net

CNN network can learn local features in different time periods. However, as time-series signal, speech's characteristics and contents are heavily related to its time order. The same local features appear at different time may have different meanings. This time-related feature can not be learned through CNN or full connected layer.

The successful application of RNN in natural language processing demonstrates its advantages in learning sequence features and long-range dependencies. Some work [1,5] have recently applied RNN in speech recognition with a large vocabulary. In order to characterize the timing feature of the speech, we connect an Bi-directional LSTM network after CNN net. Figure 3 shows the RNN network diagram.

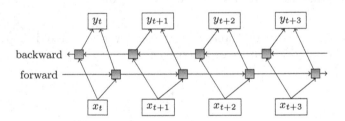

Fig. 3. RNN structure

For the RNN model, the critical point is how to establish the link between the previous information and the current state. As a classic RNN structure, LSTM performs the following steps on the input data. First, calculate the forgotten gate (2), the input gate (3), and the input information (4), second, update the hidden state (5), then the output gate (6), and finally calculate the current step's output according to the output gate and the hidden state (7).

$$f_t = \sigma(W_f \cdot [h_{t-1}, x_t] + b_f) \tag{2}$$

$$i_t = \sigma(W_i \cdot [h_{t-1}, x_t] + b_i) \tag{3}$$

$$\widetilde{C}_t = \tanh(W_c \cdot [h_{t-1}, x_t] + b_c) \tag{4}$$

$$C_t = f_t \odot C_{t-1} + i_t \odot \tilde{C}_t \tag{5}$$

$$o_t = \sigma(W_o \cdot [h_{t-1}, x_t] + b_o) \tag{6}$$

$$h_t = o_t \odot \tanh(C_t) \tag{7}$$

4   Experiments and Analysis

4.1   Dataset

In this paper we use the Google Speech Commands dataset. This dataset was released by Google in August 2017. It includes 65,000 speech data, covering thousands of people reading 30 commands, as well as some background noises. Most of these speech audios are mono, and last for a second, with a sampling rate of 16 KHz, sampling resolution of 16bit. The division of training, validation and test set is shown in Table 1.

Table 1. Statistics of Google Speech Commands

Set	Train	Valid	Test
Scale	51,088	6,798	6,835

4.2   Experiment Settings

To analyze the model from different aspects such as CNN network structure, network depth, the combination of CNN and RNN, and compare it with existing work, we design a variety of models with different structures and conduct extensive experiments. These models are as follows.

- C-p-G-q-Blstm/FullConnect: The model consists of p conventional 2-dimension CNN, q Gated CNN and a bidirectional LSTM (or fully connected layer). By adjusting the values of p, q, and choosing Blstm or FullConnect, we build a variety of different models for speech commands recognition.
- *Transfer Learning Network* [11]: This model pre-trains a 121-layer net on the UrbanSound8K dataset, and then transfers to recognize Google Speech Commands dataset.

In our experiments, each model is trained for specified epochs (it is found that most models can converge to their best performance in 100 epochs) on the training set, then select the best-performing model for evaluation. In order to accurately evaluate the model's performance and eliminate the influence of random factors, the experiment of each model is repeated 10 times. The average of these 10 results is taken as the final evaluation criterion.

For the model *Transfer Learning Network*, we use the result in [11] instead of reproducing it ourselves.

4.3   Experiment Results

Impact of Gated CNN's Depth. To explore the impact of Gated CNN's depth on speech recognition results, by using different number of Gated CNN layers (which means setting different value for q) in model C-p-G-q-$Blstm$, we get model C-1-G-2-$Blstm$, C-1-G-5-$Blstm$, C-1-G-7-$Blstm$, C-1-G-9-$Blstm$, C-1-G-10-$Blstm$, C-1-G-20-$Blstm$, C-1-G-50-$Blstm$. Table 2 gives the final recognition accuracy of these models.

Table 2. The impact of Gated CNN's depth

Model	Valid accuracy (%)	Test accuracy (%)
C-1-G-2-$Blstm$	**90.9**	**90.6**
C-1-G-5-$Blstm$	90.4	90.0
C-1-G-7-$Blstm$	89.7	89.5
C-1-G-9-$Blstm$	88.7	88.2
C-1-G-10-$Blstm$	88.2	87.9
C-1-G-20-$Blstm$	Diverge	Diverge
C-1-G-50-$Blstm$	Diverge	Diverge

Valid Accuracy and Test Accuracy represent the best model's recognition accuracy on the validation set and test set. Experiment results in Table 2 show that, for the Google Speech Commands dataset, deeper Gated CNN network does not necessarily have a better recognition performance. We can see that as the number of Gated CNN layer increases, the model's recognition performance firstly increases and then decreases, and when it reaches a certain number, the model does not converge.

This phenomenon may be caused by the limited amount of the data. A net with too many layers is too large and have too many parameters, which make it difficult to train the net effectively, so it can not achieve good results, or even fails to converge.

Experiment results show that the model C-1-G-2-$Blstm$ with 2-layer Gated CNN achieves the best performance. In the follow-up experiments, this paper will use the model C-1-G-2-$Blstm$ as the evaluation benchmark.

Impact of Gated Convolution. To analyze Gated CNN's help for speech commands recognition, we replace the Gated CNN in model C-1-G-2-$Blstm$, C-1-G-5-$Blstm$, C-1-G-7-$Blstm$ with conventional CNN, getting models C-3-G-0-$Blstm$, C-6-G-0-$Blstm$, C-8-G-0-$Blstm$. Table 3 gives the comparison between the results of models before and after the replacement. From the results we can conclude that compared with the conventional CNN, Gated CNN can efficiently improve the model's prediction accuracy.

Table 3. The impact of Gated CNN

Model	Valid accuracy (%)	Test accuracy (%)
C-1-G-2-Blstm	**90.9**	**90.6**
C-3-G-0-Blstm	87.2	87.2
C-1-G-5-Blstm	**90.4**	**90.0**
C-6-G-0-Blstm	86.9	86.7
C-1-G-7-Blstm	**89.7**	**89.5**
C-8-G-0-Blstm	83.5	83.2

Impact of CNN and RNN. To evaluate whether the combination of CNN and RNN could perform better than just CNN or just RNN, based on the model *C-1-G-2-Blstm*, we design another two models:

- *C-0-G-0-Blstm*: delete the CNN structure in *C-1-G-2-Blstm*, just keep the RNN structure.
- *C-1-G-2-FullConnect*: keep the CNN structure in *C-1-G-2-Blstm*, but replace the RNN structure with full connected layer.

Table 4 gives these models' experiment results. From the table we can see that, compared with the model *C-1-G-2-Blstm* which combines CNN and RNN, just using CNN or RNN results in a drastical decrease in recognition accuracy. Therefore, we can get the conclusion that combining the advantage of CNN and RNN is greatly helpful for speech command recognition.

Table 4. Comparison of CNN and RNN's impact

Model	Valid accuracy (%)	Test accuracy (%)
C-1-G-2-Blstm	**90.9**	**90.6**
C-0-G-0-Blstm	62.5	61.6
C-1-G-2-FullConnect	81.3	81.1

Comparison with Existing Works. In this paper we design two experiments to compare with Transfer Learning Network [11], which is the state-of-art work. Firstly, we compare the *C-1-G-2-Blstm* and Transfer Learning Network's recognition accuracy on all 30 commands in Google Speech Commands dataset. Results are shown in the second column of Table 5. Secondly, we re-train a new *C-1-G-2-Blstm* on the 20 commands selected in [11], and compare it with Transfer Learning Network. Results are shown in the third column of Table 5. From the results we can see that *C-1-G-2-Blstm* greatly outperforms Transfer Learning Network, both on all 30 commands and on the selected 20 commands.

Table 5. Comparison between *C-1-G-2-Blstm* and Transfer Learning Network

Model	Test accuracy_30 (%)	Test accuracy_20 (%)
C-1-G-2-Blstm	**90.6**	**90.6**
Transfer learning	84.4	82.1

Recognition Performance on Every Single Command. Table 6 gives *C-1-G-2-Blstm*'s recognition accuracy on every command. The accuracy decreases from left up to right down in turn. The command "happy" has the highest recognition accuracy of 97.2%, while the command "no" has the lowest recognition accuracy of 84.1%.

Table 6. Recognition accuracy of every command

Comm.[a]	Acc.[b] (%)	Comm.	Acc. (%)	Comm.	Acc. (%)
Happy	**97.2**	Five	92.6	Bed	90.3
Sheila	96.2	Two	92.4	One	90.3
Six	94.7	Off	92.3	Wow	90.2
House	94.7	Marvin	91.4	Dog	89.4
Nine	94.2	Up	91.2	Bird	89.0
Seven	94.1	Stop	91.1	Three	88.0
Cat	94.0	Right	91.1	Go	86.9
Eight	93.8	Four	90.9	Tree	85.5
Left	93.6	On	90.7	Down	85.3
Yes	93.4	Zero	90.4	No	84.1

[a]is abbreviation for "command".
[b]is abbreviation for "accuracy".

After analyzing all the 30 commands we can find that the command "happy" is special and different from other commands in pronunciation, so it's recognition accuracy is the highest. There are 7 commands whose recognition accuracy is below 90%: "dog", "bird", "three", "go", "tree", "down", "no". These commands are easy to be confused with the others. For example, "bird" is similar with "bed" in pronunciation. Main faults during recognizing these seven commands are given in Table 7.

For these 7 commands, we select everyone's most likely wrong recognition and fault probability. The first row in Table 7 gives the groundtruth label, the first column gives the model's recognized label, the values represent the probability.

Take the second column as an example. It shows the distribution of fault recognition for command "no". From this column we can see that when mistakingly recognized, "no" is mistaken for "go" with a probability of 40%, and

Table 7. Main faults in recognition

	No	Go	Down	Tree	Three	Bird	Dog
No	-	**39.4**	**45.9**	-	-	-	21.1
Go	**40.0**	-	**24.3**	-	3.1	5.9	**15.8**
Down	**20.0**	15.2	-	-	-	5.9	**36.8**
Tree	-	-	-	-	**53.1**	-	-
Eight	-	3.0	-	7.1	**12.5**	-	-
Right	-	3.0	-	-	-	**35.3**	-
Bed	5.0	-	5.4-	-	-	**11.8**	-
Three	-	-	2.7	**78.6**	-	-	5.3
Two	-	12.1	2.7	**14.3**	6.2	-	-

mistaken for "down" with a probability of 20%. In fact, "no", "go" and "down" do have similarities in pronunciation.

From Table 7 we can conclude that for those commands with low recognition accuracy, it's mainly because they are similar with some other commands in pronunciation, making it more difficult to distinguish them. This phenomenon shows us a new direction for future work: developing methods to distinguish similar speech commands.

4.4 Model FootPrint

Most models that combine CNN and RNN have a problem of being too deep and complex. For example, [2] proposes a CRNN neural model with 32 CNN layers and 1 RNN layer, [23] designs a 15-layer neural model that contains 8 CNN layers and 7 ConvLSTM (one kind of LSTM which merges CNN inside) layers. Comparing with these work, our *C-1-G-2-Blstm* only uses 3 CNN layers and 1 LSTM layers, greatly reducing the model's complexity. Parameters and multiplications used for the *C-1-G-2-Blstm* is shown in Table 8.

Table 8. Parameters and multiplications used for the *C-1-G-2-Blstm*

Layer	m	n	h	r	Par.	Mult.
Conv2d	1	5	20	64	6.25K	200K
Gated-Conv2d	1	5	64	64	40K	1282K
Gated-Conv2d	1	5	64	64	40K	1282K
Bi-LSTM	1	64	-	-	64.5K	2060K
FC	128	30	-	-	3.78K	3.75K

In our experiments, every training epoch takes 15 s, while every testing epoch takes 0.9 s. Considering that the test set contains 6,835 samples, *C-1-G-2-Blstm* can recognize about 7,000 commands per second.

Based on our *C-1-G-2-Blstm* we build an apk for android cellphones. To build the apk file, we first use TensorFlow's tool to freeze our computing graph into a pb file, which is only 911 kb. Then we build an android apk which use the frozen graph to perform speech commands recognition, the apk is only 22 M.

5   Summary and Future Works

For the task of speech command recognition on mobile device, this paper designs a model *C-1-G-2-Blstm* based on Gated CNN and bidirectional LSTM. This model uses CNN to learn the speech's local features, RNN to learn sequence long-distance dependence features, and Gated CNN to improve the model' capacity. Compared with existing work based on CNN and RNN, our model uses fewer layers and simpler net structure. Finally *C-1-G-2-Blstm* achieves an accuracy of 90.6% on the Google Speech Commands dataset, outperforming the existing state-of-art work by 6.4%.

One of our future work is to further improve the model's recognition performance. [13] points out that the preprocessing methods of speech data, the usage of batch normalization and other technologies such as dilated convolution will affect the model's performance. We are going to conduct experiments on more datasets to evaluate these factors' impact. On the other hand, because speech recognition especially wakeup-word recognition is seriously limited by local hardware resources, it is also a very important development direction to explore how to minimize the model size and computational complexity while ensuring the recognition accuracy.

Acknowledgment. This work is supported by the National Natural Science Foundation of China No. 61472434, Science and Technology on Parallel and Distributed Laboratoratory Foundation No. 9140C810109150C81002.

References

1. Amodei, D., Ananthanarayanan, S., Anubhai, R., Bai, J., Battenberg, E., Case, C., Casper, J., Catanzaro, B., Cheng, Q., Chen, G., et al.: Deep speech 2: end-to-end speech recognition in English and mandarin. In: International Conference on Machine Learning, pp. 173–182 (2016)
2. Arik, S.O., Kliegl, M., Child, R., Hestness, J., Gibiansky, A., Fougner, C., Prenger, R., Coates, A.: Convolutional recurrent neural networks for small-footprint keyword spotting. arXiv preprint arXiv:1703.05390 (2017)
3. Chen, G., Parada, C., Heigold, G.: Small-footprint keyword spotting using deep neural networks. In: 2014 IEEE International Conference on Acoustics, Speech and Signal Processing (ICASSP), pp. 4087–4091. IEEE (2014)
4. Cho, K., Van Merriënboer, B., Gulcehre, C., Bahdanau, D., Bougares, F., Schwenk, H., Bengio, Y.: Learning phrase representations using RNN encoder-decoder for statistical machine translation. arXiv preprint arXiv:1406.1078 (2014)

5. Hannun, A., Case, C., Casper, J., Catanzaro, B., Diamos, G., Elsen, E., Prenger, R., Satheesh, S., Sengupta, S., Coates, A., et al.: Deep speech: scaling up end-to-end speech recognition. arXiv preprint arXiv:1412.5567 (2014)
6. He, K., Zhang, X., Ren, S., Sun, J.: Deep residual learning for image recognition. In: Proceedings of the IEEE Conference on Computer Vision and Pattern Recognition, pp. 770–778 (2016)
7. Hershey, S., Chaudhuri, S., Ellis, D.P., Gemmeke, J.F., Jansen, A., Moore, R.C., Plakal, M., Platt, D., Saurous, R.A., Seybold, B., et al.: CNN architectures for large-scale audio classification. In: 2017 IEEE International Conference on Acoustics, Speech and Signal Processing (ICASSP), pp. 131–135. IEEE (2017)
8. Hochreiter, S., Schmidhuber, J.: Long short-term memory. Neural Comput. 9(8), 1735–1780 (1997)
9. Krizhevsky, A., Sutskever, I., Hinton, G.E.: Imagenet classification with deep convolutional neural networks. In: Advances in Neural Information Processing Systems, pp. 1097–1105 (2012)
10. LeCun, Y., Bottou, L., Bengio, Y., Haffner, P.: Gradient-based learning applied to document recognition. Proc. IEEE 86(11), 2278–2324 (1998)
11. McMahan, B., Rao, D.: Listening to the world improves speech command recognition. arXiv preprint arXiv:1710.08377 (2017)
12. van den Oord, A., Kalchbrenner, N., Espeholt, L., Vinyals, O., Graves, A., et al.: Conditional image generation with PixelCNN decoders. In: Advances in Neural Information Processing Systems, pp. 4790–4798 (2016)
13. Sainath, T.N., Kingsbury, B., Mohamed, A.r., Dahl, G.E., Saon, G., Soltau, H., Beran, T., Aravkin, A.Y., Ramabhadran, B.: Improvements to deep convolutional neural networks for LVCSR. In: 2013 IEEE Workshop on Automatic Speech Recognition and Understanding (ASRU), pp. 315–320. IEEE (2013)
14. Sainath, T.N., Parada, C.: Convolutional neural networks for small-footprint keyword spotting. In: Sixteenth Annual Conference of the International Speech Communication Association (2015)
15. Simonyan, K., Zisserman, A.: Very deep convolutional networks for large-scale image recognition. arXiv preprint arXiv:1409.1556 (2014)
16. Szegedy, C., Liu, W., Jia, Y., Sermanet, P., Reed, S., Anguelov, D., Erhan, D., Vanhoucke, V., Rabinovich, A.: Going deeper with convolutions. In: Proceedings of the IEEE Conference on Computer Vision and Pattern Recognition, pp. 1–9 (2015)
17. Tang, R., Lin, J.: Deep residual learning for small-footprint keyword spotting. arXiv preprint arXiv:1710.10361 (2017)
18. Vaswani, A., Shazeer, N., Parmar, N., Uszkoreit, J., Jones, L., Gomez, A.N., Kaiser, L., Polosukhin, I.: Attention is All You Need. arXiv e-prints, June 2017
19. Wang, Y., Getreuer, P., Hughes, T., Lyon, R.F., Saurous, R.A.: Trainable frontend for robust and far-field keyword spotting. In: 2017 IEEE International Conference on Acoustics, Speech and Signal Processing (ICASSP), pp. 5670–5674. IEEE (2017)
20. Warden, P.: Launching the speech commands dataset. Google Research Blog (2017)
21. Yu, F., Koltun, V.: Multi-scale context aggregation by dilated convolutions. arXiv preprint arXiv:1511.07122 (2015)
22. Zhang, Y., Pezeshki, M., Brakel, P., Zhang, S., Bengio, C.L.Y., Courville, A.: Towards end-to-end speech recognition with deep convolutional neural networks. arXiv preprint arXiv:1701.02720 (2017)
23. Zhang, Y., Chan, W., Jaitly, N.: Very deep convolutional networks for end-to-end speech recognition. In: 2017 IEEE International Conference on Acoustics, Speech and Signal Processing (ICASSP), pp. 4845–4849. IEEE (2017)

Enabling Machine Learning on Resource Constrained Devices by Source Code Generation of the Learned Models

Tomasz Szydlo$^{(\boxtimes)}$, Joanna Sendorek, and Robert Brzoza-Woch

Department of Computer Science, AGH University of Science and Technology,
Krakow, Poland
tomasz.szydlo@agh.edu.pl

Abstract. Due to the development of IoT solutions, we can observe the constantly growing number of these devices in almost every aspect of our lives. The machine learning may improve increase their intelligence and smartness. Unfortunately, the highly regarded programming libraries consume to much resources to be ported to the embedded processors. Thus, in the paper the concept of source code generation of machine learning models is presented as well as the generation algorithms for commonly used machine learning methods. The concept has been proven in the use cases.

Keywords: IoT · Edge computing · Machine learning

1 Introduction

Due to the development of IoT solutions, we can observe the constantly growing number of network enabled devices in almost every aspect of our lives. It includes smart homes, factories, cars, devices and others. They are sources of large amount of data that can be analyzed in order to discover the relations between them. As a result, they can provide functionalities better suited to the needs, predict failures and increase their reliability.

The data generated by the devices can be used by machine learning algorithms to learn and then make predictions. For example, the historical information of engine behaviors may lead to the machine learning models that can be used to predict in advance failures of other engines and be used to plan appropriate repairing actions. Such an approach is possible because of the virtually unlimited resources in the computational clouds to store and process the data from large number of devices.

Such a concept is extremely important in the industry which is facing the revolution termed Industry 4.0. The main concept is focused on including cyber-physical systems, IoT and cognitive systems in the manufacturing. In the so-called smart factories, every aspect of the manufacturing process will be monitored in real-time and then gathered information will be used by the cooperating systems and humans to work coherently. At the same time, the machine

© Springer International Publishing AG, part of Springer Nature 2018
Y. Shi et al. (Eds.): ICCS 2018, LNCS 10861, pp. 682–694, 2018.
https://doi.org/10.1007/978-3-319-93701-4_54

learning algorithms may gain the quality of the final products and decrease the production costs.

One of the important aspects in the industrial IoT is the response time of the systems. For example, in the factory automation, motion control and tactile Internet the acceptable latency is less then 10 ms [8]. It means that the IoT systems using machine learning algorithms in the cloud for that kind of applications are not sufficient due to the fact that Internet routing to the worldwide datacenters introduces significant delays [12].

One of the solutions to circumvent that drawback is to move machine learning algorithms to the edge of the network [10] e.g. to the data center located in the factory and learn only on the local data. As a result, the latency introduced by the communication protocol would be significantly smaller because limited to the local networks, but the gained knowledge would be incomplete. The promising improvement would be to perform machine learning in the cloud environments on a large volume of data and then send learned models to the edge datacenters in order to make predictions locally e.g. in the factories. That approach would increase the accuracy of the predictions due to the variety of sources that data came from in the learning process.

Nevertheless, even with that approach, the devices have to be constantly connected to the local computer network in order to use the machine learning models. Thus, in the research we are moving machine learning models to the embedded devices itself. In our concept, instead of implementing machine learning libraries for embedded devices that can read and interpret the learned models, they are converted to the source code that can be compiled in the device firmware. This enables possibility to embed the these models into embedded processors that may have sporadic access to the network.

The concept presented in the paper can be used to design e.g. smart tools in which machine learning models are used to prevent their damages by modifying internal characteristics according to the usage. Such devices during charging could synchronize itself with a cloud by sending the historical usage logs from their memory and download new firmware with updated machine learning models. The process can be automated using mechanisms presented in the paper.

The scientific contribution of the paper is (i) the concept of source code generation of machine learning models (ii) the generation algorithms for commonly used machine learning methods and finally (iii) practical verification of the method.

Organization of the paper is as follows. Section 2 describes the related work in the field of machine learning for constrained devices. Section 3 discuses concept of the proposed method and the algorithms for commonly used ML algorithms. Section 4 describes the evaluation, while Sect. 5 concludes the paper.

2   Related Work

At the time of writing, numerous machine learning programming libraries are available on the market. They offer a number of algorithms to enable learning with and without supervision. They can be divided into dedicated applications for individual computing nodes (for example Weka, SMILE, scikit-learn, LibSVM) and for high performance computers (cluster/cloud computing e.g. Spark, FlinkML, TensorFlow, AlchemyAPI, PredictionIO). Many large companies offer services which rely on machine learning in public cloud infrastructures. The most popular services of this type are BigML, Amazon Machine Learning, Google Prediction, IBM Watson and Microsoft Azure Machine Learning and the dedicated for IoT such as ThingWorx. These solutions analyze data mostly in the cloud and role of IoT devices comes down to software agents providing data for analysis. Solutions categorized as Big Data Machine Learning and dedicated for cloud computing are a fast-growing branch of machine learning [2].

In the domain of resource-constrained systems we can find many implementations of ML algorithms on mobile and embedded devices that cooperate with the cloud computing. The work of Liu et al. [7] describes an approach to image recognition in which the process is split into two layers: local edge layer constructed with mobile devices and remote server (cloud) layer. In [6] the authors present a software accelerator that enhances deep learning execution on heterogeneous hardware, including mobile devices. In the edge, i.e. on a mobile devices, an acquired image is preprocessed and a segmentation is performed. Then the image is classified on a remote server running pre-trained convolutional neural network (CNN). In [9] the authors propose the utilization of Support Vector Machine (SVM) running on networked mobile devices to detect malware. A more general survey on employing networked mobile devices for edge computing is presented in [11].

There are also implementation of algorithms related to machine learning domain on extremely resource-constrained devices with a few kB of RAM. In [4,5] authors develop extremely efficient machine learning algorithms that can learn on such devices. The problem presented in the paper addresses the same group of devices but is not related to the performing learning process on them but is related to the usage of the models learned elsewhere and used on the devices. It enables possibility to design systems that can perform machine learning in the clouds on a large volume of data and then use the results in the resource-constrained devices.

3 Concept of the Method

In the IoT domain there are several hardware architectures and sets of peripherals in the processors used in the devices [1]. Generally, they can be classified into two categories - application processors that can run Linux and the embedded ones that can run real-time operating systems such as FreeRTOS or be programmed directly on the bare-metal.

On the devices with application processors such as RaspberryPi, the tuned versions of machine learning libraries such as `Tensorflow` or `scikit-learn` can be executed due to the availability of Java, Python and other programming languages. This means that machine learning models can be directly copied between the cloud environment and the device only if the same libraries are used in both places.

The other approach assumes that the models can be moved between various ML libraries. For that purpose, description languages such PMML [3] has been developed. For example, models can be learned in the cloud using Big Data tools then after export/import operation used by the libraries ported to the embedded devices.

The problem is more complex with the second group of embedded devices such as Arduino with resources constrained embedded microcontrollers (MCUs). In this case, porting the high-level and general purpose machine learning libraries is not possible. In this situation, the implementation of description languages such as aforementioned PMML may consume significant device resources. Thus, the authors propose the approach in which source code of the estimator that expresses the learned model is generated and then compiled into the device firmware. The presented concept of the machine learning model source code generation requires three steps to be performed:

1. analysis of the machine-learning algorithm and the way how it can be expressed in the source code,
2. analysis on how to get details of machine-learning model from the ones generated by the particular software or library,
3. analysis on how the final code can be optimized for the target embedded architecture regarding its resource constraints.

In the next subsections, the source code generation algorithms for the commonly used machine learning methods for the classification problem are presented. Additionally the technical details on how to generate the source code based on the popular `scikit-learn` library is discussed. We have also analyzed how the final code should be generated for AVR and ARM embedded processors.

3.1   Bayes Networks Generator

Naive Bayes algorithm is the method which applies probability theorem to the machine learning problems, treating input features and output classes as events. The problem of classification - assigning class for the given input features - is reduced to finding output class event which has highest conditional probability, assuming that input features event has occurred. To calculate the conditional probability, Bayes theorem is applied. Therefore, definition for classification problem can be written as:

$$\operatorname*{argmax}_{y}(P(y|x_1 \dots x_N)) \stackrel{Bayes\ th.}{=} \operatorname*{argmax}_{y} \frac{P(y)P(x_1 \dots x_N|y)}{P(x_1 \dots x_n)}, \tag{1}$$

where:

- $x_1 \dots x_N$ - input features;
- N - number of input features;

- $P(x_1 \ldots x_N)$ - constant probability of input feature event which is the same regardless of output class;
- y - element of output classes events.

In order to calculate right side of Eq. (1), two assumptions are made:

1. Input features are pair-wise independent of each other which allows to calculate probability $P(x_1 \ldots x_N|y)$.
2. The probability distribution of $P(x_i|y)$ is normal distribution $\mathcal{N}(\theta, \sigma)$.

After applying both of the assumptions to the Eq. (1) and natural logarithm function to the density function of normal distribution, problem of classifying the set of features can be written as:

$$\operatorname*{argmax}_{y}\left(logP(y) + \sum_{i=1}^{N}\left[-\frac{1}{2}log2\pi\sigma_{y,i} - \frac{(x_i - \theta_{y,i})^2}{2\sigma_{y,i}} \right] \right), \qquad (2)$$

where:

- M - number of output classes;
- σ, θ - matrices of size $M \times N$ calculated during the learning phase - those relate to parameters of normal distribution;
- $P(y)$ - prior probability for class y calculated as the proportionate part of a class occurrences in the training set.

The necessity of calculating natural logarithm, the only part of equation requiring math module in C, can be eliminated by introducing third matrix - σ_{log} containing element-wise logarithm function applied to matrix $2\pi\sigma$.

Therefore, formula (2) can be reduced to:

$$\operatorname*{argmax}_{y}\left(logP(y) - \frac{1}{2}\sum_{i=1}^{N}\left[\sigma_{log_{y,i}} + \frac{(x_i - \theta_{y,i})^2}{\sigma_{y,i}} \right] \right), \qquad (3)$$

which equation will be the base for construction of program evaluating Bayes model for new set of input features. Implementation of such evaluator in C in presented on listing 1.1.

Listing 1.1. Naive Bayes model evaluation in C.

```
double  sigma [M][N]  = <learned values>;
double  theta [M][N]  = <learned values>;
double  log_sigma [M][N]  = <learned values>;
double  prior [M]  = <calculated values>;

double  temp_sum;
double  class_est [10];

for (int  i = 0;  i < M;  i++){
    temp_sum = 0;
```

```
for (int j = 0; j < N; j++){
    temp_sum += log_sigma[i][j];
    temp_sum += ((x[j] - theta[i][j]) * (x[j] -
        theta[i][j])) / (sigma[i][j]);
}

class_est[i] = prior[i] - 0.5 * temp_sum;
}

return get_max_index(class_est);
```

It can be observed that the evaluator code remains the same as to the structure, regardless of specific learned Naive Bayes model. The program has a structure with declaration part, where matrices σ, θ and σ_{log} are defined, and instruction part which implements formula (3). In case of specific trained model only matrices values has to be set, altogether with M and N constants. Therefore, generation process for naive Bayes algorithm may be reduced to using evaluator template and filling it accordingly with trained values. The other approach to generation will be presented in Sects. 3.2 and 3.3, where not only data declarations but whole program structure relies on trained model.

In scikit-learn, class `sklearn.naive_bayes.GaussianNB` implements aforementioned classifier. Trained instance of model stores values of matrices σ and θ in fields `sigma_` and `theta_` respectively and values of prior probabilities for classes in array `class_prior_`. In result, demanded values for `theta` and `sigma` can be retrieved directly from trained model and values for `prior` and `log_sigma` can be calculated.

3.2 Decision Trees Generator

Decision Tree classifier is based on the algorithm which recursively tries to split training dataset based on the value of one chosen input feature.

Figure 1 presents structure of example decision tree. Each node represents one training data split which corresponds to different condition on chosen feature value. The split condition is created in such a way as to minimize *gini index* in the child nodes. Gini index is calculated as presented on Eq. (4) and describes how well are output classes distributed through the dataset.

$$gini_{index} = 1 - \sum_{i=1}^{M} p_i^2, \tag{4}$$

where:

- M - number of output classes;
- p_i - fraction of representatives of class i in the whole dataset.

Construction of tree is being conducted in learning phase of algorithm, based on training set. Once the tree is constructed, the classification of the new input

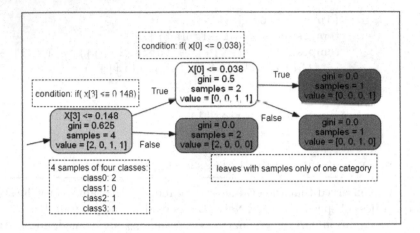

Fig. 1. Example decision tree structure.

sample is done by traversing the tree from top to bottom, evaluating conditions in each node and choosing appropriate child of the node until leaf is reached. Such a structure of trained model is equivalent to a set of hierarchical condition instructions and can be unambiguously conversed to such a structure.

In scikit-learn library, tree structure of trained classifier is held in **tree_** property of the classifier object and consists of commonly used pointer representation. Each node has an unique index used to reference its properties in properties arrays:

- **children_left** - array of left children indexes - index -1 means that there is no left child;
- **children_right** - array of right children indexes - index -1 means that there is no right child;
- **feature** - array of input features on which splitting is conducted;
- **threshold** - array of values on which splitting condition is based;
- **classes** - array of arrays holding count for each output class on given data subset.

Listing 1.2 presents pseudocode of algorithm which generates hierarchy of condition clauses based on trained classifier. The tree structure is processed recursively by pre-order traversal, using aforementioned properties arrays. Visiting each node, appropriate *if-else* clause is created which represents one data split.

Listing 1.2. Tree code generation algorithm.

```
generate_statements(tree):

  recurse(node, depth):
```

```
if node is not leaf:
  indent = get indent for depth
  feature = tree.feature[node]
  threshold = tree.threshold[node]
  return (
      'indent' +
      'if clause' for given feature and threshold +
      recurse(tree.children_left[node], depth + 1) +
      'ending if clause' +
      opening of 'else clause' +
      recurse(tree.children_right[node], depth + 1) +
      closing of 'else clause' )
  else:
    result = 'most numerous class for leaf'
    return 'indent' + result

return recurse(0, 1)
```

3.3 Neural Networks Generator

For the purpose of the authors research and proving concept presented in the article, one class of neural network algorithms has been examined - multilayer perceptron (MLP) which is one of the less complicated neural network methods. MLP aim is to learn the function $f : \mathrm{IR}^N \to \mathrm{IR}^M$, where N is number of input features and M is the number of output classes. The learning process of neural network is out of scope of this paper, but understanding the model evaluation process - execution of function f used in example - is essential to explain code generation for MLP.

Equation (5) presents schema for function f execution. It consists of $H + 1$ consecutive layer transformations, where H is the number of hidden layers and is the parameter of method, determined before training phase. Ith layer transformation consists of the following steps:

1. linear transformation based on previous layer result multiplication by coef[i] matrix;
2. addition of vector itc[i] to the result of previous step;
3. application of the activation function which introduces nonlinearity to the method.

Initial vector for the first transformation is the vector of input features. Activation function for each layer apart from last one - for all hidden layers - is *ReLU* function defined as in Eq. (7). Last layer is activated by application of *softmax* function which enables interpreting last hidden layer result as the probability distribution over set of output classes. Classified output class is the one under index of maximum element in last transformation result vector. In the schema described, elements learned during training phase are lists coef and itc holding parameters for steps 1 and 2 of the layer transformation.

$$
\begin{bmatrix} x_0 \\ x_1 \\ \vdots \\ x_N \end{bmatrix}^T \underbrace{coef[0]}_{N \times p_0} + \underbrace{itc[0]}_{1 \times p_0} \xrightarrow[\text{act.}]{\text{ReLU}} \cdots \quad \begin{bmatrix} a_0 \\ a_1 \\ \vdots \\ a_{H-2} \end{bmatrix}^T \underbrace{coef[H-1]}_{p_{H-2} \times p_{H-1}} + \underbrace{itc[H-1]}_{1 \times p_{H-1}} \xrightarrow[\text{act.}]{\text{ReLU}}
$$

H transformations for each hidden layer

$$
\begin{bmatrix} b_0 \\ b_1 \\ \vdots \\ b_N \end{bmatrix}^T \underbrace{coef[H]}_{p_{H-1} \times M} + \underbrace{itc[H]}_{1 \times M} \xrightarrow[\text{activation}]{\text{softmax}} \begin{bmatrix} y_0 \\ y_1 \\ \vdots \\ y_M \end{bmatrix}^T \xrightarrow[k]{\text{argmax}} y_k
$$

$$(5)$$

- H - number of hidden layers (indexed as $0 \ldots H - 1$)
- $coef$ - matrix of coefficients used to transform layers to different sizes
- itc - intercepts matrix
- y_k - result of classification

$$
softmax(v)_i = \frac{e^{v_i}}{\sum_{j=0}^{K-1} e^{v_j}} \qquad for\ i = 0, \cdots, K - 1; \qquad (6)
$$

where: K - size of vector v

$$
ReLU(x) = max(0, x) \qquad (7)
$$

From the description above it follows that model evaluation code for trained classifier could be implemented as a sequence of matrix operations on consecutive layers. Code for generation algorithm is presented on listing 1.3.

Listing 1.3. Multiple layer network evaluator generation.

```
generate appropriate headers
for i in layer_count - 1:
        generate coef matrix for layer i

for each hidden layer:
    generate layer transformation:
            1. declaration for new result vector
            2. loop of matrix multiplication
            3. generate vectors addition sequence
        generate ReLU activation on result vector

generate layer transformation

generate softmax activation on result vector

generate loop for max index search
```

3.4   Source Code Optimization for Embedded Processors

Resource constrained embedded microcontrollers (MCUs) may be equipped with different microprocessor cores and peripheral sets. From a software engineer point of view, the main difficulties in programming such MCUs are low computing power and small amount of available memories: both operating and for executable firmware storage. In typical MCUs, the non-volatile flash memory is much larger in storage size then the operating memory, because the latter one generates a higher production cost per storage unit.

The computational performance of resource-constrained embedded platforms is generally low when compared to general-purpose application units. There are only a few methods to increase the performance. For example, depending on a software developers skills, the code can be manually optimized or partially implemented in a low level language. That option may be difficult to implement in automated code generating software and the resulting code may not be easily portable between different MCU architectures. A relatively easy way of controlling a balance between code size and execution speed is to find a correct optimization level. GNU C compilers (GCC) offer various standard optimization levels. Below we list the selected ones.

- With $O0$ the optimization is disabled,
- With $O1$ the compiler tries to reduce the execution time and the output code size.
- With $O2$ the compiler optimizes the code as much as possible without introducing a trade-off between the execution time and the output code size.
- With $O3$ the compiler optimizes as in $O2$ with a set of additional flags.
- The Os is referred to as optimization for size. It makes the compiler optimize the code similarly to $O2$ but without increasing the output code size.

Usually embedded microcontrollers may run a relatively simple scheduler or a real-time operating system (RTOS), but do not run an application operating system. In those cases, the memory management relies partly on a software developer. As an example, the AVR 8-bit MCU family has the Harvard architecture in which program and data address spaces are separate. This makes it less convenient to declare read-only variables stored in the microcontrollers program memory. Therefore, the code generator should consider the target MCU architecture. For example, when writing and compiling code for AVR MCUs, a variable with the *const* modifier will be placed in the operating memory. In the case of generating code for previously trained models, we often need a large number of constant values. Storing them in operating memory may quickly cause a shortage of that resource. To store read-only data in the program memory and to retrieve their values the software developer must use a special-purpose macros which work as additional declaration modifiers or access functions, e.g. *PROGMEM* or *pgm_read_float_near*. That problem is non-existent in newer and more advanced microcontrollers which implement a single and unified address space. Those units do not need additional modifiers for objects in code to store and retrieve them to and from the MCU non-volatile memory. Usually, thanks to their more modern design, they are also equipped with more resources than 8-bit AVR.

4 Evaluation

In order to evaluate described code generation methods proposed in the paper, authors have prepared use case demonstrating how trained model could be used for classification on embedded device. The biggest the training set, the more complex and time consuming learning phase is and therefore the advantage of separating it from evaluation phase is the most evident.

For the evaluation purposes, two databases has been used. First one is the mnist database of handwritten digits[1] has been chosen. In order to retrieve dataset fetch_mldata function from scikit-learn library has been used. Dataset fetched this way consists of *70 000* samples, each being vector of length *784* representing one handwritten digit picture. Each picture has dimension of 28 × 28 pixels arranged in row-major order. After choosing and loading described dataset, an instance of each classifier from Sect. 3 has been created and trained on the randomly chosen ninety percent of dataset. For each of them, source code has been generated extracting model evaluation which has been used to classify handwritten digits on touch screen attached to devices. For MLP classifier one hidden layer with 15 neurons has been established.

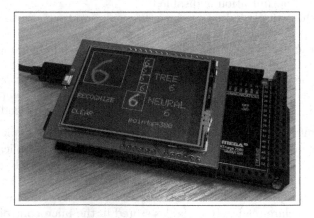

Fig. 2. Digit recognition application for Arduino that uses generated source code of the machine learning models for MNIST dataset

As an additional dataset, for comparison purpose, the iris dataset has been chosen which is much smaller than mnist one. The set contains of 150 samples divided into three categories representing variations of iris flowers: setosa, virginica and versicolor. Input features of samples consists of five parameters of iris flowers. Dataset has been divided into training and testing set similarly to mnist - ninety percent assigned for the training and ten percent assigned for the training. The exact same set of classifiers with parameters have been used for this dataset as for the mnist.

---

[1] http://yann.lecun.com/exdb/mnist/ (access for 23 Feb 2018).

Table 1 contains the size of pickled models from `scikit-library` for selected classifiers. It is worth to notice, that to use that models, the appropriate Python libraries are necessary thus the overall memory requirements are much larger.

The source code generators for machine learning models presented in the paper has been implemented in Python[2]. Based on the aforementioned models learned for the selected databases appropriate source codes were generated. Finally, the concept has been verified on two embedded platforms. First one, depicted in Fig. 2 is based on Arduino Mega with ATmega2560 (8 kB RAM, 256 kB flash) microcontroller and a simple touch screen display. The second platform was STM32F4 Discovery board with ARM STM32F429 (256 kB RAM, 512 kB flash) microcontroller. Table 1 contains the size of compiled source-code for the learned models. For the Arduino platform, the Bayes model for mnist database was too large to feet into the memory, thus was not evaluated. For the other cases, the size of the memory footprint of the compiled classifiers was small enough to fit in the microcontrollers memory.

Table 1. Size of the serialized scikit-learn model and the compiled source-code of the classifier for the AVR and ARM processors

Dataset	Method		Size of models in bytes					Score
		Scikit − learn	AVR	ARM				
				O0	O1	O3	Os	
iris	Bayes	771	2298	2352	2004	3440	2028	1.00
	MLP	12247	2360	4768	4004	5184	3936	0.933
	Tree (float)	2501	272	592	512	16	480	0.933
mnist	Bayes	126164	—	190712	189980	190872	189956	0.556
	MLP	292984	52000	54088	52444	54992	52280	0.919
	Tree	Float	1051335	166476	158592	130336	132816	133200	0.874
		Integer	1051335	75776	72832	53264	55920	54768	

5 Summary

In the paper we have presented the idea of how the machine learning models can be executed on the embedded devices with constrained resources. This allows developers for example to embed sophisticated failure prediction ML models in the home appliances such as toothbrushes, electric drills, kitchen mixers and others increasing their smartness.

The concept presented in the paper can be extended. We are currently working on two problems. First one is related to the mechanisms of how to combine incremental learning in the cloud from IoT sensors with automatic deployment of the learned models to the devices located in the edge environments. The second

---

[2] https://github.com/tszydlo/FogML.

one is related to the development of the generator tools for Big Data ML such as TensorFlow or Apache Flink. The latter one would give a greater applicability and usefulness of the presented method.

Acknowledgment. The research presented in this paper was supported by the National Centre for Research and Development (NCBIR) under Grant No. LIDER/15/0144 /L-7/15/NCBR/2016.

References

1. Al-Fuqaha, A., Guizani, M., Mohammadi, M., Aledhari, M., Ayyash, M.: Internet of things: a survey on enabling technologies, protocols, and applications. IEEE Commun. Surv. Tutor. **17**(4), 2347–2376 (2015)
2. Al-Jarrah, O.Y., Yoo, P.D., Muhaidat, S., Karagiannidis, G.K., Taha, K.: Efficient machine learning for big data: a review. Big Data Res. **2**(3), 87–93 (2015). Big Data, Analytics, and High-Performance Computing
3. Grossman, R.L., Bailey, S., Ramu, A., Malhi, B., Hallstrom, P., Pulleyn, I., Qin, X.: The management and mining of multiple predictive models using the predictive modeling markup language. Inf. Softw. Technol. **41**(9), 589–595 (1999)
4. Gupta, C., Suggala, A.S., Goyal, A., Simhadri, H.V., Paranjape, B., Kumar, A., Goyal, S., Udupa, R., Varma, M., Jain, P.: ProtoNN: compressed and accurate kNN for resource-scarce devices. In: International Conference on Machine Learning, pp. 1331–1340 (2017)
5. Kumar, A., Goyal, S., Varma, M.: Resource-efficient machine learning in 2 KB RAM for the internet of things. In: International Conference on Machine Learning, pp. 1935–1944 (2017)
6. Lane, N.D., Bhattacharya, S., Georgiev, P., Forlivesi, C., Kawsar, F.: Accelerated deep learning inference for embedded and wearable devices using DeepX. In: Proceedings of the 14th Annual International Conference on Mobile Systems, Applications, and Services Companion, p. 109. ACM (2016)
7. Liu, C., Cao, Y., Luo, Y., Chen, G., Vokkarane, V., Ma, Y., Chen, S., Hou, P.: A new deep learning-based food recognition system for dietary assessment on an edge computing service infrastructure. IEEE Trans. Serv. Comput. (2017)
8. Schulz, P., Matthe, M., Klessig, H., Simsek, M., Fettweis, G., Ansari, J., Ali Ashraf, S., Almeroth, B., Voigt, J., Riedel, I., Puschmann, A., Mitschele-Thiel, A., Müller, M., Elste, T., Windisch, M.: Latency critical IoT applications in 5G: perspective on the design of radio interface and network architecture. IEEE Commun. Mag. **55**(2), 70–78 (2017)
9. Shamili, A.S., Bauckhage, C., Alpcan, T.: Malware detection on mobile devices using distributed machine learning. In: 2010 20th International Conference on Pattern Recognition (ICPR), pp. 4348–4351. IEEE (2010)
10. Szydlo, T., Brzoza-Woch, R., Sendorek, J., Windak, M., Gniady, C.: Flow-based programming for IoT leveraging fog computing. In: 2017 IEEE 26th International Conference on Enabling Technologies: Infrastructure for Collaborative Enterprises (WETICE), pp. 74–79, June 2017
11. Tran, T.X., Hosseini, M.P., Pompili, D.: Mobile edge computing: recent efforts and five key research directions. MMTC Commun.-Front. **12**(4), 29–34 (2017)
12. Yi, S., Li, C., Li, Q.: A survey of fog computing: concepts, applications and issues. In: Proceedings of the 2015 Workshop on Mobile Big Data, pp. 37–42. ACM (2015)

Track of Data-Driven Computational Sciences

Fast Retrieval of Weather Analogues in a Multi-petabytes Archive Using Wavelet-Based Fingerprints

Baudouin Raoult[1]([⊠]), Giuseppe Di Fatta[2], Florian Pappenberger[1], and Bryan Lawrence[2,3,4]

[1] European Centre for Medium-Range Weather Forecasts, Reading, UK
{baudouin.raoult,florian.pappenberger}@ecmwf.int
[2] Department of Computer Science, University of Reading, Reading, UK
G.DiFatta@reading.ac.uk, bryan.lawrence@ncas.ac.uk
[3] Department of Meteorology, University of Reading, Reading, UK
[4] National Centre for Atmospheric Science, Reading, UK

Abstract. Very large climate data repositories provide a consistent view of weather conditions over long time periods. In some applications and studies, given a current weather pattern (e.g. today's weather), it is useful to identify similar ones (weather analogues) in the past. Looking for similar patterns in an archive using a brute force approach requires data to be retrieved from the archive and then compared to the query, using a chosen similarity measure. Such operation would be very long and costly. In this work, a wavelet-based fingerprinting scheme is proposed to index all weather patterns from the archive. The scheme allows to answer queries by computing the fingerprint of the query pattern, then comparing them to the index of all fingerprints more efficiently, in order to then retrieve only the corresponding selected data from the archive. The experimental analysis is carried out on the ECMWF's ERA-Interim reanalyses data representing the global state of the atmosphere over several decades. Results shows that 32 bits fingerprints are sufficient to represent meteorological fields over a 1700 km × 1700 km region and allow the quasi instantaneous retrieval of weather analogues.

Keywords: Climate data repositories
Weather analogues · Information retrieval

1 Introduction

Weather analogues is the term used by meteorologists to referrer to similar weather situations. Usually an analogue for a given location or area and forecast lead time is defined as a past prediction, from the same model, that has similar values for selected features of the current model forecast. Before computer simulations were available, weather analogues were the main tool available to forecasters, which is still a usage today [1]. Analogues can be useful on smaller

© Springer International Publishing AG, part of Springer Nature 2018
Y. Shi et al. (Eds.): ICCS 2018, LNCS 10861, pp. 697–710, 2018.
https://doi.org/10.1007/978-3-319-93701-4_55

scale ($\approx$900 km in radius, [2]) as it is otherwise impossible to identify similar patterns in the past given a limited temporal record e.g. at hemispheric scale, similar states the atmosphere would only be observed every 10^{30} years [3]. Usually the maximum record length available is restricted to under 100 years. Weather analogues have many usages. They are used for downscaling model outputs [4], to assess risks of severe weather [5] or managing weather impacts on railway networks [6].

Analogues require comparison of fields and looking for similar patterns in an archive using a brute force approach requires data to be retrieved from the archive and the compared to the query, using a chosen similarity measure. Such operation would be very long and costly on large archive systems as data will typically have to be recalled a tape system.

The aim of this research is to consider an algorithm to index all weather patterns from the archive using a fingerprinting scheme. Queries would be done by computing the fingerprint of the query pattern, then comparing them to the index of all fingerprints, in order to then retrieve the corresponding data from the archive. The main user requirements of such system are:

- the system should be queryable: given a user provided query, the system should return the most similar weather situation from the archive;
- the system should be fast: replies should be perceived by users as "instantaneous", allowing interactive use;
- newly archived data should be added to the index, without the need to retune/retrain the system.

Wavelet fingerprinting has been successfully used to retrieve images [7] and sounds [8]. The objectives of this paper are therefore to introduce an efficient wavelet fingerprinting system for the retrieval of weather analogues. Efficiency here means that the computation of fingerprint is fast, that the resulting fingerprint is small, that fingerprints can be compared quickly and that they can be stored in an efficient data structure. The fingerprinting method has to be accurate as possible, i.e. that returns the "closest" matching weather according to some agreed similarity measure.

2   Related Work

As the world is generating more and more data, efficient information retrieval has become a major challenge, and is therefore a very active field of research. Information is not only limited to text, but also comprises images, movies and sound. There are many methods available to implement such systems [9,10].

The retrieval system proposed in this work is based on wavelets [11,12], which are expected to capture well the wave-like nature of the weather phenomenon. Wavelets are traditionally use for imagery [13–15], in particular compression [16–20] and image retrieval [7,21,22]. Wavelets have also been used to retrieve medical images [23,24], proteins [25], power management [26–28], time-series analysis [29,30] and image similarity [22,23].

This work builds on the results presented by [7,8], which use wavelets-based algorithms for multi-resolution image querying and audio fingerprinting respectively.

3 The ECMWF Data Archive

The European Centre for Medium-Range Weather Forecasts (ECMWF) has been collecting meteorological information since 1980 and its archive has recently reach over 260 petabytes of primary data. ECMWF's archive is referred to as the Meteorological Archiving and Retrieval System (MARS) [31,32]. This archive provides datasets that covers several decades at hourly temporal resolutions. Because of the size of the archive, most of the data is held on tape, therefore only solutions that do not require access to the data are considered.

The MARS archive contains fields, that are the typical output of numerical weather prediction systems. These are usually gridded data, either global or regional. The grids are sets of regularly distributed points (e.g. one grid point every 5 km) over a given area. Model outputs are collections of fields, one for each variable represented, for a given time and horizontal layer: at large scales (greater than 10 km), the interactions between the different layers of the atmosphere are small compared to the effects of large structures and can be ignored. This is why traditionally meteorologists tend to consider fields are being 2D, their vertical coordinate being an attribute of the field, as is time. Fields are therefore a collection of floating point values geographically distributed according to a mesh (called grid). Most of the grids are regularly spaced.

This research will make use of a particular subset of fields so called reanalysis data: a reanalysis is a process by which the same data assimilation system is run on past observations (e.g. over one hundred years), and produces a consistent dataset representing the state of the atmosphere over long periods. This is used for studies linked to climate change [33,34]. These datasets are very well structured and can be easily processed. The data used in this work are selected from the ERA-Interim dataset [35,36], a reanalysis covering the period 1979 to 2014, at 0 UTC (13,149 fields per variable).

Meteorological fields are multidimensional fields, with grid points regularly distributed on the surfaces following the shape Earth: at the surface or at set levels (usually isobaric surface). The fields also vary in time. Although these fields are 4D, they are archived as 2D slices (latitude/longitude), so that users can access long time series of a given surface, or a stack of levels. Fields represent one variable (temperature, pressure, precipitations, etc.), with the value of the variable provided at each grid points.

In the case of regular grids, in which grid points can be organised in a 2D matrix (Fig. 1a), one can see the that this fields can easily be considered as a greyscale image (Fig. 1c, assuming values are normalised to the interval 0–255), although they are traditionally plotted using contours (Fig. 1b).

Four surface variables are selected: 2 m temperature, mean sea level surface pressure (or MSL pressure), 10 m wind speed and total precipitations accumulated over 6 h.

The initial work presented here is limited to a square grid 0.5°×0.5° (≈55 km × 55 km) on the domain 60°N 14°W 44.5°N 1.5°E that covers the British Isles (≈1700 km×1700 km, see Fig. 1), which agrees with the radius of 900 Km presented in [2]. The size of the domain will capture synoptic scales weather patterns.

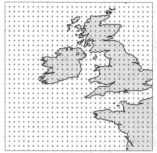 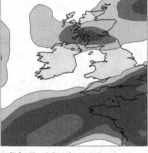 

(a) Geographical distribution of the grid points. (b) Field of total precipitations over 6 hours. (c) Same field plotted over a gray map.

Fig. 1. Nature of the meteorological field used in this research. In the middle panel, the total precipitation field is plotted using the traditional methods: contouring and shading (isoline are spaced logarithmically from 0.4 mm to 100 mm.

4   Definition of a Fingerprinting Scheme

4.1   Fingerprinting

The method proposed is to define the fingerprint F of a meteorological field f as:

$$F(f) = \langle s, r \rangle$$

where:

- s is a bit vector, representing the shape of f, and
- r is a reference value, capturing the intensity of the field f.

The fingerprinting method proposed is as follows:

1. the meteorological field is considered as a 2D grayscale image;
2. a reference value is selected (for example the mean, or the median of the field);
3. the field is compressed using wavelet compression;
4. the reference value is used as a threshold to convert the compressed image into a bitmap;
5. the bits that make the bitmap are extracted and form the shape part of the fingerprint.

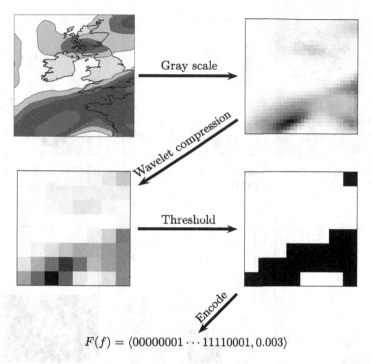

$$F(f) = \langle 00000001 \cdots 11110001, 0.003 \rangle$$

Fig. 2. Algorithm: field fingerprints are computed using wavelet compression and thresholding. In this example, 0.003 is the average value of the field.

The first step is only described here to stress that the algorithm expects the actual values of the field as input, and not a graphical representation (fields are not images). In the case of this research, fields are already available in a binary form, so the first step is not necessary. The method is illustrated in Fig. 2. In that example, the fingerprint is a tuple consisting of a 64 bits vector and a floating-point value. In a modern computer, this would use 128 bits of memory.

4.2 Wavelet Compression

A Discrete Wavelet Transform (DWT) decomposes a signal into approximation and details coefficients; the approximation is a smoothing of the signal, and capture large scale features, while details represent smaller variations around the approximation. The original signal can we reconstructed from all coefficients. Wavelet compression is performed by selecting the approximation coefficient of a given stage of the DWT and discarding the detail coefficients.

We will define the compression factor C as the level of the DWT. As C increases, the number values in the compressed field is divided by 4 (Fig. 3).

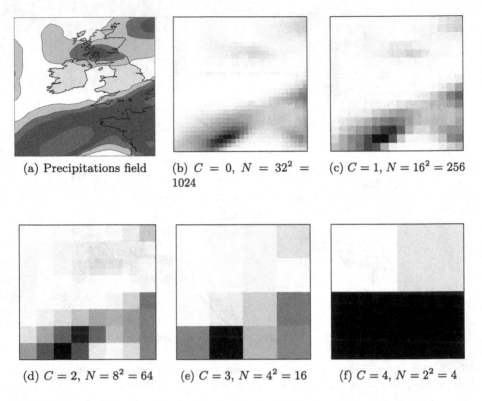

(a) Precipitations field   (b) $C = 0$, $N = 32^2 =$ (c) $C = 1$, $N = 16^2 = 256$
                              1024

(d) $C = 2$, $N = 8^2 = 64$ (e) $C = 3$, $N = 4^2 = 16$ (f) $C = 4$, $N = 2^2 = 4$

Fig. 3. Grey scale images showing the result of wavelet compression of a field of precipitations. C is the compression factor, N is the number of data values remaining after compression.

4.3   Query

Looking up for analogues is done by solving the nearest neighbour problem in a database of fingerprints. In that study, the fingerprints are held in a simple array structure in memory, are they are small enough, and the lookup is implemented as a linear scan. The performance of this setup is sufficient for interactive use. More elaborate data structures and algorithm will be considered at a later stage.

To querying the database for analogues, the user needs to present a meteorological field over a similar area and with the same number of grid points as our current setup. This could be for example today's weather, extracted from the latest analysis from a NWP centre. The fingerprint of the query field is computed and is compared to existing fingerprint. Fingerprints are considered close if the Hamming distance [37] of their bit vectors are close, and their reference values are also close.

4.4   Formal Definition

The problem we are trying to address can be formalised as:

Let v be a meteorological variable (e.g. surface pressure, wind speed...).

Let $\mathcal{A}_v$ be the set of all meteorological fields in the archive for this variable. Assuming that all the fields are defined over the same grid (same geographical coverage, same resolution), $\mathcal{A}_v$ can be considered a subset of $\mathbb{R}^n$, with n being the number of grid points.

Let D be a distance function between the elements of A_v (typically the $L2$-norm).

Let F be the set of fingerprints.

Let δ be a distance function between the elements of F.

We are looking for a mapping $F_v \colon \mathcal{A}_v \mapsto \mathcal{F}$ such that:

$$\forall f_1, f_2, f_3 \in \mathcal{A}_v, D(f_1, f_2) \leq D(f_1, f_3) \tag{1}$$
$$\iff \delta(F_v(f_1), F_v(f_2)) \leq \delta(F_v(f_1), F_v(f_3)).$$

Intuitively, this means that F_v "preserves distances", e.g. if fields are close according to the distance D, their fingerprints must also be close according to the distance δ. Similarly, fields that are far apart must have fingerprints that are far apart. A study of distance preserving embeddings is available from [38].

The aim of this work is to find a mapping that mostly satisfy relation (1), i.e. a mapping for which the relation is true for most elements of $\mathcal{A}_v$.

Traditionally, distance between meteorological fields is computed using the root mean square deviation (RMSD), which is equivalent to the $L2$-norm. Other distances such as Pearson correlation coefficient (PCC) are also used. [39] show the limitations of such metrics. In this study, we will use the $L2$-norm when comparing field, as it is the most commonly used metric in meteorology.

4.5   Validation of the Mapping

As we are considering various fingerprinting schemes, we will compare how "effective" they are. We define the effectiveness of a mapping is a measure of number of elements of $\mathcal{A}_v$ for which relation (1) hold.

A scheme is perfectly effective if for every query q, we always find the field which is closest to q according to the distance D. This can also be stated as: if m be the best match when querying the system with q, the scheme is perfectly effective if there are no field closer to q than m according to the distance D. Conversely, the more fields are closer to q than m, the less effective the method. So, to measure the effectiveness of the fingerprinting scheme, we count how many fields are closer to q than m. Instead of generating dummy query fields, we use every fields from the archive to query a set composed of all other fields.

Using the definitions from Sect. 4.4, for each field q in $\mathcal{A}_v$, let $\mathcal{A}_v^q = \mathcal{A}_v \backslash \{q\}$ be the dataset that excludes this field.

Let m be the best match when querying $\mathcal{A}_v^q$ with q.

Let $\xi_D(q)$ be the query error, defined as the number of fields that are closer to q than m according to a distance D, normalised by the total number of field in $\mathcal{A}_v$:

$$\xi_D(q) = \frac{|\{f \in \mathcal{A}_v^q \mid D(f,q) < D(m,q)\}|}{|\mathcal{A}_v^q|} .$$

$\xi_D(q) = 0$ if the result of querying $\mathcal{A}_v^q$ with q returns the closest field to q according to the distance D, and $\xi_D(q) = 1$ if the resulting field is the furthest away according to D.

We consider the scheme to be validated if $\xi_D(q)$ is negligibly small (e.g. less that 0.05, i.e. 5%) for a large number of values of q (e.g. 80%). This means that for 80% of the queries, less than 5% of all the fields in the dataset will considered a better match than the closest field according to D.

4.6   Choice of the Compression Factor C

In order to select a value for the compression factor C, we compute $\xi_{L2}(q)$ for every field q of the dataset. We then consider the percentage of fields of the dataset for which the $\xi_{L2}(q)$ is below a given value.

Figure 4 shows, for two representative meteorological variables, the sorted distribution of the values ξ_{L2} against the queries, for various values of the compression factor C. Figure 4b shows that for $C = 3$ and for 80% of the queries, less than 4% of the fields are actually closer than the best match. Plotting such graphs for all selected meteorological variables shows that the best results are obtained with the compression factor $C = 3$. This can be explained as follows:

For $C = 1$ and $C = 2$, the compressed field retain a lot of detail and the resulting fingerprints retain many dimensions, and we are affected by the curse of dimensionality.

For $C = 4$, too much information is lost, and dissimilar fields are more likely to have similar fingerprints, thus increasing the probability of mismatching results.

We can see that for total precipitations (Fig. 4a), the results are not as good as for the surface air pressure. This is because this field is not as smooth and continuous, and is by nature not easily captured by the multi-resolution aspect of wavelets.

The value $C = 3$ provides enough information reduction so that generated fingerprints are small, while having a high effectiveness so that matching of fingerprints will provide good results.

4.7   Similarity Measure Between Fingerprints

In Sect. 4.1, we define the fingerprint of f as $F(f) = \langle s, r \rangle$ where:

- s i a bit vector representing the shape of f, and
- r is a reference value, capturing the intensity of the field f.

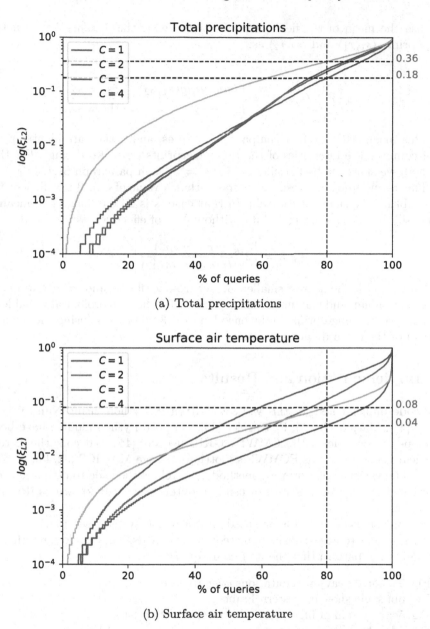

(a) Total precipitations

(b) Surface air temperature

Fig. 4. Choice of the compression factor C. The plots shown are sorted distributions of ξ_{L2} for various values of C. For *Total precipitation*, we see that for $C = 4$, the value of ξ_{L2} at 80% is 0.36. This means that for 20% of the queries, there are more than 36% of all the fields in the dataset that are considered a better match than the closest field according to $L2$. For $C = 3$, this value drops to 18%. For *Surface air temperature*, we can see that the results are much better, and that for $C = 4$, the value at 80% is 0.08 (8%) and for $C = 3$, the value at 80% is 0.04 (4%). In both cases, $C = 3$ gives the best results.

We use the mean of the field for r. We then define the distance between the fingerprints $\langle s_1, r_1 \rangle$ and $\langle s_2, r_2 \rangle$ as:

$$\delta(\langle s_1, r_1 \rangle, \langle s_2, r_2 \rangle) = \begin{cases} hamming(s_1, s_2) & if s_1 \neq s_2, \\ |r_1 - r_2| & \text{otherwise.} \end{cases}$$

This means that we first compare the shapes, and if they are identical, we then compare the intensities of the two fingerprints (lexical ordering). For this method, we show the best results are for $C = 3$, as in paragraph Sect. 4.6.

This is an interesting result as it shows that a value of $C = 3$ is sufficient for s to capture the shape of the field. In that case, s is 16 bits long. The mean r can easily be encoded using 16 bits, without loss of effectiveness:

$$r_{16bits} = \left\lfloor 2^{16} \frac{(r - min_v)}{(max_v - min_v)} \right\rfloor.$$

Where $\lfloor x \rfloor$ is the nearest smaller integer from x (floor), and min_v and max_v are the minimum and maximum values possible for the meteorological variable v. In this case, the fingerprint can be encoded over 32 bits. Tests using the median instead of the mean do not give better results.

5   Implementation and Results

The code implemented for this work is written in Python, using NumPy [40], SciPy [41], Matplotlib [42], PyWavelet [43]. Bespoke Python module have been developed to interface with ECMWF's GRIB decoder [44], to decode the meteorological fields, as well as ECMWF's plotting package MAGICS [32,45], to plot maps. The various fingerprinting methods, as well as the code to estimate their effectiveness. Experiments are run using Jupyter, previously known as iPython notebook [46].

Several artificial patterns are used to query the system (see Fig. 5). These patterns do not represent realistic meteorological fields. They could nevertheless be the kind of pattern that the user could query:

- Fig. 5a: some heavy precipitations over Ireland only.
- Fig. 5b: some snow in western France.
- Fig. 5c: a system of high pressure over the British Isles.
- Fig. 5d: a heat wave over the south east of England and France.

In each case, the system will return a field from the archive that matches the query provided.

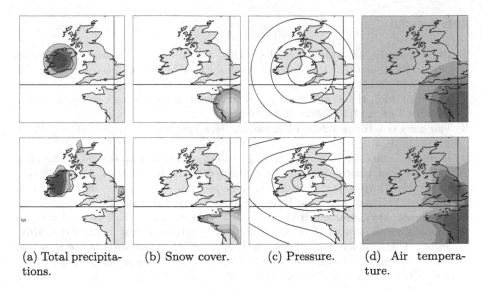

(a) Total precipita-   (b) Snow cover.   (c) Pressure.   (d) Air tempera-
tions.   ture.

Fig. 5. Using artificial fields as queries (first row), and the corresponding best matches (second row).

6   Conclusion and Future Work

In this work the first wavelet base retrieval system for weather analogue has been introduced. Results shows that 32 bits fingerprints are sufficient to represent meteorological fields over a 1700 km × s1700 km region, and that distances between fingerprints provide a realistic proxy to the distance between fields. The small size of the fingerprint means that they can be stored in memory, leading to very short lookup time, fast enough to allow for interactive queries.

As part of our future work, will be considering a method that allows users to describe type of weathers in an interactive fashion. Users will be provided with a tool to "draw" the field they are looking. The pattern drawn will be used as a query to the system, and similar fields will be returned. One of the main challenge of this method will be to ensure that the user's input is realistic from a meteorological point of view.

During our initial research, we have been focussing on weather patterns over the British Isles. As part of the future work, we will consider extending the system to the whole globe.

Weather situations are really similar if all of the parameters (temperature, pressure, wind, etc.) are also similar. We will study how the fingerprinting scheme implemented so far can be extended so that it takes into account several parameters and what are the implication on the index and the matching algorithms.

References

1. Delle Monache, L., Eckel, F.A., Rife, D.L., Nagarajan, B., Searight, K.: Probabilistic Weather Prediction with an Analog Ensemble. Mon. Wea. Rev. **141**(10), 3498–3516 (2013)
2. Van den Dool, H.: A new look at weather forecasting through analogues. Mon. Weather Rev. **117**(10), 2230–2247 (1989)
3. Van den Dool, H.: Searching for analogues, how long must we wait? Tellus A **46**(3), 314–324 (1993)
4. Zorita, E., von Storch, H.: The analog method as a simple statistical downscaling technique: comparison with more complicated methods, pp. 1–16, August 1999
5. Evans, M., Murphy, R.: A historical-analog-based severe weather checklist for central New York and northeast Pennsylvania, pp. 1–8, February 2013
6. Sanderson, M.G., Hanlon, H.M., Palin, E.J., Quinn, A.D., Clark, R.T.: Analogues for the railway network of Great Britain. Meteorol. Appl. **23**(4), 731–741 (2016)
7. Jacobs, C.E., Finkelstein, A., Salesin, D.H.: Fast multiresolution image querying. In: Proceedings of the 22nd Annual Conference on Computer Graphics and Interactive Techniques, pp. 277–286. ACM (1995)
8. Baluja, S., Covell, M.: Waveprint: efficient wavelet-based audio fingerprinting. Pattern Recogn. **41**(11), 3467–3480 (2008)
9. Orio, N.: Music Retrieval: A Tutorial and Review. Now Publishers Inc., Boston (2006)
10. Veltkamp, R., Burkhardt, H., Kriegel, H.P.: State-of-the-Art in Content-Based Image and Video Retrieval. Springer Science & Business Media, Dordrecht (2013). https://doi.org/10.1007/978-94-015-9664-0
11. Daubechies, I.: Orthonormal bases of compactly supported wavelets. Commun. Pure Appl. Math. **41**(7), 909–996 (1988)
12. Walker, J.S.: A primer on wavelets and their scientific applications, pp. 1–156, June 2005
13. Stollnitz, E.J., DeRose, T.D., Salesin, D.H.: Wavelets for computer graphics: a primer part 1, pp. 1–8 (1995)
14. Stollnitz, E.J., DeRose, T.D., Salesin, D.H.: Wavelets for computer graphics: a primer part 2, pp. 1–9 (1995)
15. Stollnitz, E.J., DeRose, T., Salesin, D.H.: Wavelets for Computer Graphics - Theory and Applications. Morgan Kaufmann, San Francisco (1996)
16. Balan, V., Condea, C.: Wavelets and Image Compression. Telecommunication Standardization Sector of ITU, Leden (2003)
17. Porwik, P., Lisowska, A.: The Haar-wavelet transform in digital image processing: its status and achievements. Mach. Graph. Vision **13**(1/2), 79–98 (2004)
18. Shapiro, J.M.: Embedded image coding using zerotrees of wavelet coefficients. IEEE Trans. Signal Process. **41**(12), 3445–3462 (1993)
19. Walker, J.S., Nguyen, T.Q.: Wavelet-based image compression. In: Rao, K.R. et al.: The Transform and Data Compression Handbook. CRC Press LLC, Boca Raton (2001)
20. Zeng, L., Jansen, C., Unser, M., Hunziker, P.: Extension of wavelet compression algorithms to 3D and 4D image data: exploitation of data coherence in higher dimensions allows very high compression ratios, pp. 1–7, October 2011
21. Patrikalakis, N.M.: Wavelet based similarity measurement algorithm for seafloor morphology. Massachusetts Institute of Technology (2006)

22. Regentova, E., Latifi, S., Deng, S.: A wavelet-based technique for image similarity estimation. In: ITCC-00, pp. 207–212. IEEE (2000)
23. Pauly, O., Padoy, N., Poppert, H., Esposito, L., Navab, N.: Wavelet energy map: a robust support for multi-modal registration of medical images. In: IEEE Conference on Computer Vision and Pattern Recognition, CVPR 2009, pp. 2184–2191. IEEE (2009)
24. Traina, A.J.M., Castañón, C.A.B., Traina, Jr., C.: MultiWaveMed: a system for medical image retrieval through wavelets transformations. In: IEEE Computer Society, June 2003
25. Marsolo, K., Parthasarathy, S., Ramamohanarao, K.: Structure-based querying of proteins using wavelets. In: Proceedings of the 15th ACM International Conference on Information and Knowledge Management, pp. 24–33. ACM (2006)
26. Cattani, C., Ciancio, A.: Wavelet clustering in time series analysis. Balkan J. Geom. Appl. **10**(2), 33 (2005)
27. Kocaman, Ç., Özdemir, M.: Comparison of statistical methods and wavelet energy coefficients for determining two common PQ disturbances: sag and swell. In: International Conference on Electrical and Electronics Engineering, ELECO 2009, pp. I-80–I-84. IEEE (2009)
28. Phuc, N.H., Khanh, T.Q., Bon, N.N.: Discrete wavelets transform technique application in identification of power quality disturbances (2005)
29. Gomez-Glez, J.F.: Wavelet methods for time series analysis, pp. 1–45, February 2009
30. Popivanov, I., Miller, R.J.: Similarity search over time-series data using wavelets. In: 18th International Conference on Data Engineering, Proceedings, pp. 212–221. IEEE (2002)
31. Raoult, B.: Architecture of the new MARS server. In: Sixth Workshop on Meteorological Operational Systems, ECMWF, 17–21 November 1997, Shinfield Park, Reading, pp. 90–100 (1997)
32. Woods, A.: Archives and graphics: towards MARS, MAGICS and Metview. In: The European Approach, Medium-Range Weather Prediction, pp. 183–193 (2006)
33. Frauenfeld, O.W., Zhang, T., Serreze, M.C.: Climate change and variability using European Centre for Medium-Range Weather Forecasts reanalysis (ERA-40) temperatures on the Tibetan Plateau. J. Geophys. Res. Atmos. (1984–2012) **110**(D2) (2005)
34. Santer, B.D., Wigley, T.M., Simmons, A.J., Kållberg, P.W., Kelly, G.A., Uppala, S.M., Ammann, C., Boyle, J.S., Brüggemann, W., Doutriaux, C.: Identification of anthropogenic climate change using a second-generation reanalysis. J. Geophys. Res. Atmos. (1984–2012) **109**(D21) (2004)
35. Dee, D., Uppala, S., Simmons, A., Berrisford, P., Poli, P., Kobayashi, S., Andrae, U., Balmaseda, M., Balsamo, G., Bauer, P.: The ERA-Interim reanalysis: configuration and performance of the data assimilation system. Q. J. Royal Meteorol. Soc. **137**(656), 553–597 (2011)
36. Dee, D., Balmaseda, M., Balsamo, G., Engelen, R., Simmons, A., Thépaut, J.N.: Toward a consistent reanalysis of the climate system. Bull. Am. Meteorol. Soc. **95**(8), 1235–1248 (2014)
37. Sixta, S.: Hamming cube and other stuff, pp. 1–18, May 2014
38. Indyk, P., Naor, A.: Nearest-neighbor-preserving embeddings. ACM Trans. Algorithms (TALG) **3**(3), 31 (2007)
39. Mo, R., Ye, C., Whitfield, P.H.: Application potential of four nontraditional similarity metrics in hydrometeorology. J. Hydrometeorology **15**(5), 1862–1880 (2015)

40. Van Der Walt, S., Colbert, S.C., Varoquaux, G.: The NumPy array: a structure for efficient numerical computation. Comput. Sci. Eng. **13**(2), 22–30 (2011)
41. Jones, E., Oliphant, T., Peterson, P.: SciPy: open source scientific tools for Python (2014)
42. Hunter, J.D.: Matplotlib: a 2D graphics environment. Comput. Sci. Eng. **9**(3), 90–95 (2007)
43. Wasilewski, F.: PyWavelets: discrete wavelet transform in python (2010)
44. Fucile, E., Codorean, C.: GRIB API. A database driven decoding library. In: Twelfth Workshop on Meteorological Operational Systems, ECMWF, 2–6 November 2009, Shinfield Park, Reading, pp. 46–47 (2009)
45. O'Sullivan, P.: MAGICS - the ECMWF graphics package. ECMWF Newslett. (62) (1993)
46. Pérez, F., Granger, B.E.: IPython: a system for interactive scientific computing. Comput. Sci. Eng. **9**(3), 21–29 (2007)

Assimilation of Fire Perimeters and Satellite Detections by Minimization of the Residual in a Fire Spread Model

Angel Farguell Caus[1,2], James Haley[2], Adam K. Kochanski[3],
Ana Cortés Fité[1], and Jan Mandel[2(✉)]

[1] HPCA4SE research group, Computer Architecture and Operating Systems
Department, Universitat Autònoma de Barcelona, 08193 Bellaterra, Spain
{angel.farguell,ana.cortes}@uab.cat
[2] Department of Mathematical and Statistical Sciences,
University of Colorado Denver, 1201 Larimer St., Denver, CO 80204, USA
{angel.farguellcaus,james.haley,jan.mandel}@ucdenver.edu
[3] Department of Atmospheric Sciences, University of Utah,
135 S 1460 East Rm 819 (WBB), Salt Lake City, UT 84112-0110, USA
adam.kochanski@utah.edu

Abstract. Assimilation of data into a fire-spread model is formulated as an optimization problem. The level set equation, which relates the fire arrival time and the rate of spread, is allowed to be satisfied only approximately, and we minimize a norm of the residual. Previous methods based on modification of the fire arrival time either used an additive correction to the fire arrival time, or made a position correction. Unlike additive fire arrival time corrections, the new method respects the dependence of the fire rate of spread on diurnal changes of fuel moisture and on weather changes, and, unlike position corrections, it respects the dependence of the fire spread on fuels and terrain as well. The method is used to interpolate the fire arrival time between two perimeters by imposing the fire arrival time at the perimeters as constraints.

1 Introduction

Every year, millions of hectares of forest are devastated by wildfires. This fact causes dramatic damage to innumerable factors as economy, ecosystem, energy, agriculture, biodiversity, etc. It has been recognized that the recent increase in the fire severity is associated with the strict fire suppression policy, that over last decades has led to significant accumulation of the fuel, which when ignited makes fires difficult to control. In order to reverse this effect, prescribed burns are routinely used as a method of fuel reduction and habitat maintenance [22,28]. The previous strategy of putting out all wildland fires is becoming replaced by a new approach where the fire is considered as a tool in the land management practice, and some of the fires are allowed to burn under appropriate conditions in order to reduce the fuel load and meet the forest management goals.

© Springer International Publishing AG, part of Springer Nature 2018
Y. Shi et al. (Eds.): ICCS 2018, LNCS 10861, pp. 711–723, 2018.
https://doi.org/10.1007/978-3-319-93701-4_56

Fire management decisions regarding both prescribed burns, as well as wildland fires, are very difficult. They require a careful consideration of potential fire effects under changing weather conditions, values at risk, firefighter safety and air quality impacts of wildfire smoke [31]. In order to help in the fire management practice, a wide range of models and tools has been developed. The typical operational models are generally uncoupled. In these models, elevation data (slope) and fuel characteristics are used together with ambient weather conditions or general weather forecast as input to the rate of spread model, which computes the fire propagation neglecting the impact of the fire itself on local weather conditions (see BehavePlus [1], FARSITE [9] or PROMETHEUS [29]). As computational capabilities increase, a new generation of coupled fire-atmosphere models become available for fire managers as management tools. In a coupled fire-atmosphere model, weather conditions are computed in-line with the fire propagation. This means that the state of the atmosphere is modified by the fire so that the fire spread model is driven by the local micrometeorology modified by the fire-released heat and moisture fluxes. CAWFE [6], WRF-SFIRE [15], and FOREFIRE/Meso-NH [8], are examples of such models, coupling CFD-type weather models with semi-empirical fire spread models. This approach is fundamentally similar to so-called physics-based models like FIRETEC [12] and WFDS [19], which also use CFD approach to compute the flow near the fire, but focus on flame-scale processes in order to directly resolve combustion, and heat transfer within the fuel and between the fire and the atmosphere. As the computational cost of running these models is too high to facilitate their use as forecasting tools, this paper focuses on the aforementioned hybrid approach, where the fire and the atmosphere evolve simultaneously affecting each other, but the fire spread is parameterized as a function of the wind speed and fuel properties, rather than resolved based on the detailed energy balance.

This article describes upcoming data assimilation components for the coupled fire-atmosphere model WRF-SFIRE [11,13], which combines a mesoscale numerical weather prediction system, WRF [27], with a surface fire behavior model implemented by a level set method, a fuel moisture model [30], and chemical transport of emissions. The coupling between the models is graphically represented in the diagram in Fig. 1. The fire heat flux modifies the atmospheric state (including local winds), which in turn affects fire progression and the fire heat release. WRF-SFIRE has evolved from CAWFE [3,4]. An earlier version [15] is distributed with the WRF release as WRF-Fire [5], and it was recently improved by including a high-order accurate level-set method [20].

The coupling between fire and atmosphere makes initialization of a fire from satellite detections and/or fire perimeters particularly challenging. In a coupled numerical fire-atmosphere model, the ignition procedure itself affects the atmospheric state (especially local updrafts near the fire line and the near fire winds). Therefore, particular attention is needed during the assimilation process in order to assure that realistic fire-induced atmospheric circulation is established at the time of data assimilation. One possible solution to this problem, assuring consistency between the fire and the atmospheric models, is defining an artificial

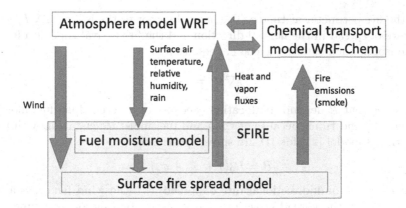

Fig. 1. Diagram of the model coupling in WRF-SFIRE

fire progression history, and using it to replay the fire progression prior to the assimilation time. In this case, the heat release computed from the synthetic fire history is used to spin up the atmospheric model and assure consistency between the assimilated fire and the local micro-meteorology generated by the fire itself.

Fire behavior models run on a mesh given by fuel data availability, typically with about 30 m resolution and aligned with geographic coordinates. The mesh resolution of satellite-based sensors, such as MODIS and VIIRS, however, is typically 375 m–1.1 km in flight-aligned swaths. These sensors provide planet-wide coverage of fire detection several times daily, but data may be missing for various reasons and no detection is possible under clouds; such missing pixels in the swath are marked as not available or as a cloud, and distinct from detections of the surface without fire. Because of the missing data, the statistical uncertainty of detections, the uncertainty in the actual locations of active fire pixels, and the mismatch of scales between the fire model and the satellite sensor, direct initialization of the model from satellite fire detection polygons [7] is of limited value at the fuel map scale. Therefore, the satellite data should be used to steer such models in a statistical sense only.

In this study, we propose a new method of fitting fire arrival time to data, which can be used to generate artificial fire history, which can be used to spin up the atmospheric model for the purpose of starting a simulation from a fire perimeter. In combination with detection data likelihood, the new method can be used also to assimilate satellite fire detection data. This new method, unlike position or additive time corrections, respects the dependence of the fire rate of spread on topography, diurnal changes of fuel moisture, winds, as well as spatial fuel heterogeneity.

2 Fire Spread Model

The state of the fire spread model is the fire arrival time $T(x,y)$ at locations (x,y) in a rectangular simulation domain $\Omega \subset \mathbb{R}^2$. The isoline $T(x,y) = c$ is then the fire perimeter at time c. The normal vector to the isoline is $\nabla T / \|\nabla T\|$. The rate of spread in the normal direction and the fire arrival time at a location on the isoline then satisfy the eikonal equation

$$\|\nabla T\| = \frac{1}{R}. \tag{1}$$

We assume that R depends on location (because of different fuel, fuel moisture, and terrain) and time (because of wind and fuel moisture changing with time). Rothermel's model [24] for 1D fire spread postulates

$$R = R_0(1 + \phi_w + \phi_s), \tag{2}$$

where R_0 is the omnidirectional rate of spread, ϕ_w, the wind factor, is a function of wind in the spread direction, and ϕ_s, the slope factor, is a function of the terrain slope. The 1D model was adapted to the spread over 2D landscape by postulating that the wind factor and the slope factor are functions of the components of the wind vector and the terrain gradient in the normal direction. Thus,

$$R = R\left(x, y, T\left(x, y\right), \nabla T\left(x, y\right)\right). \tag{3}$$

The fire spread model is coupled to an atmospheric model. The fire emits sensible and latent heat fluxes, which change the state of the atmosphere, and the changing atmospheric conditions in turn impact the fire (Fig. 1). Wind affects the fire directly by the wind factor, and temperature, relative humidity and rain affect the fire through changing fuel moisture.

The fire model is implemented on a rectangular mesh by finite differences. For numerical reasons, the gradient in the eikonal equation (1) needs to be implemented by an upwinding-type method [21], which avoids instabilities caused by breaking causality in fire propagation: for the computation of ∇T at a location (x, y), only the values from the directions that the fire is coming from should be used, so the methods switch between one-sided differences depending on how the solution evolves. Sophisticated methods of upwinding type, such as ENO or flux-limiters [23], aim to use more accurate central differences and switch to more stable one-sided upwind differences only as needed. Unfortunately, the switching causes the numerical gradient of T at a mesh node become a nondifferentiable function of the values of T at that point and its neighbors. In addition, we have added a penalty term to prevent the creation of local minima. It was observed in [14] that if, in the level set method, a local minimum appears on the boundary, its value keeps decreasing out of control; we have later found out that this can in fact happen anywhere in the presence of spatially highly variable rate of spread, and we have observed a similar effect here during the minimization process.

3   Fitting the Fire Spread Model to Data

3.1   Minimal Residual Formulation

Consider the situation when the two observed fire perimeters Γ_1 and Γ_2 at times $T_1 < T_2$ are known, and we are interested in the fire progression between the two perimeters. Aside from immediate uses (visualization without jumps, post-fire analysis), such interpolation is useful to start the fire simulation from the larger perimeter Γ_2 at time T_2 by a spin-up of the atmospheric model by the heat fluxes from the interpolated fire arrival time between the fire perimeters; the coupled model can then start from perimeter Γ_2 at time T_2 in a consistent state between the fire and the atmosphere. Interpolation between an ignition point and a perimeter can be handled the same way, with the perimeter Γ_1 consisting of just a single point.

In this situation, we solve the eikonal equation (1) only approximately,

$$\|\nabla T\| \approx \frac{1}{R} \tag{4}$$

imposing the given fire perimeters as constraints,

$$T = T_1 \text{ at } \Gamma_1, \quad T = T_2 \text{ at } \Gamma_2. \tag{5}$$

We formalize (4) as the minimization problem

$$J(T) = \left(\int_\Omega \left| f(\|\nabla T\|_2^2, R^2) \right|^p \right)^{1/p} \to \min_T \text{ subject to (5)}, \tag{6}$$

where $f(x, y)$ is a function such that $f(x, y) = 0$ if and only if $xy = 1$, and Ω is the simulation domain. We mostly use the function $f(x, y) = 1 - xy$ but other functions, such as $f(x, y) = x - 1/y$ have advantages in some situations. There are no boundary conditions imposed on the boundary of Ω.

3.2   Discretization and the Constraint Matrix

The fire simulation domain is discretized by a logically rectangular grid (aligned approximately with longitude and latitude) and perimeters are given as shape files, i.e., collections of points on the perimeter. We express (5) in the form

$$HT = g, \tag{7}$$

where H is a sparse matrix. Since the points in the shape files do not need to lie on the grid, the rows of H are the coefficients of an interpolation from the grid to the points in the shape files, which define the perimeters. We find the coefficients from barycentric interpolation. The rectangles of the grid are split into two triangles each, and, for each triangle, we compute the barycentric coordinates of the points in the shapefile, i.e., the coefficients of the unique linear combination of the vertices of the triangle that equals to the point in the shape file. If all 3 barycentric coordinates are in $[0, 1]$, we conclude that the point is contained in the triangle, the barycentric coordinates are the sought interpolation coefficients, and they form one row of H. For efficiency, most points in the shapefile are excluded up front, based on a comparison of their coordinates with the vertices of the triangle, which is implemented by a fast binary search.

When there is more than one point of the shapefile in any triangle, we condense them into a single constraint, obtained by adding the relevant rows of H. This way, we avoid over constraining the fire arrival time near the perimeter, which should be avoided for the same reason as limiting the number of constraints in mixed finite elements to avoid locking, cf., e.g., [2].

3.3   Numerical Minimization of the Residual

To solve (6) numerically, we use a multiscale descent method similar to multigrid, combining line searches in the direction of changes of the value of T at a single point, and linear combinations of point values as in [18]. We use bilinear coarse grid functions with the coarse mesh step growing by a factor of 2. See Fig. 6(b) for an example of a coarse grid function with distance between nodes 16 mesh steps on the original, finest level. We start from an initial approximate solution that satisfies the constraint $HT = g$ exactly, and project all search directions on the subspace $Hu = 0$, so that the constraint remains satisfied throughout the iterations.

To find a reasonable initial approximation to the fire arrival time, we solve the quadratic minimization problem

$$I\left(T\right) = \frac{1}{2} \int_{\Omega} \left\|(-\triangle)^{\alpha/2} T\right\|^{2} dx dy \rightarrow \min_{T} \text{ subject to (5) and } \frac{\partial T}{\partial \nu} = 0, \quad (8)$$

where ν is the normal direction, $\triangle = \frac{\partial^2}{\partial x^2} + \frac{\partial^2}{\partial y^2}$ is the Laplace operator, and $\alpha > 1$ is generally non-integer. The reason for choosing $\alpha > 1$ is that $\sqrt{I\left(T\right)}$ is the Sobolev $W^{\alpha,2}\left(\Omega\right)$ seminorm and in 2D, the space $W^{\alpha,2}\left(\Omega\right)$ is embedded in continuous functions if and only if $\alpha > 1$. Consequently, $I\left(T\right)$ is not a bound on the value $T\left(x,y\right)$ at any particular point, only averages over some area can be controlled. Numerically, when $\alpha = 1$, minimizing $I\left(T\right)$ with a point constraint, such as an ignition point, results in T taking the shape of a sharp funnel at that point (Fig. 5), which becomes thinner as the mesh is refined. That would be definitely undesirable.

The discrete form of (8) is

$$\frac{1}{2} \langle ST, T \rangle - \langle f, T \rangle \rightarrow \min_{T} \text{ subject to } HT = g, \quad (9)$$

where $S = A^{\alpha}$ with $(-A)$ a discretization of the Laplace operator with Neumann boundary conditions. To solve (9), we first find a feasible solution $u_0 = H'\left(HH'\right)^{-1} g$, so that $Hu_0 = g$, substitute $T = u_0 + v$ to get

$$\frac{1}{2} \langle S\left(u_0 + v\right), u_0 + v \rangle - \langle f, u_0 + v \rangle \rightarrow \min_{T} \text{ subject to } Hv = 0,$$

and augmenting the cost fuction, we get that (9) is equivalent to

$$\frac{1}{2} \langle SPv, Pv \rangle + \frac{\rho}{2} \langle (I - P) v, v \rangle - \langle f_0, v \rangle \rightarrow \min_{T} \text{ subject to } Hv = 0, \quad (10)$$

where $f_0 = f - Su_0$, $P = I - H'(H'H)^{-1}H$ is the orthogonal projection on the nullspace of H, and $\rho > 0$ is an arbitrary regularization parameter. We solve the minimization problem (10) approximately by preconditioned conjugate gradients for the equivalent symmetric positive definite linear system

$$P(SPv - f_0) + \rho(I - P)v = 0. \tag{11}$$

Since S is discretization of the Neumann problem, the preconditioner requires some care. Define Z as the vector that generates the nullspace of S, which consists of the discrete representation of constant functions, and $P_Z = I - Z'(Z'Z)^{-1}Z$ the orthogonal projection on its complement. We use the preconditioner

$$M : r \mapsto PP_Z S^+ P_Z Pr,$$

where S^+ is the inverse of S on the complement of its nullspace, and recover the solution by $T = u_0 + Pv$. The method only requires access to matrix-vector multiplications by S and S^+, which are readily implemented by cosine FFT. We only need to solve (11) to low accuracy to get a reasonable starting point for the nonlinear iterations, but the satisfaction of the constraint $HT = g$ to rounding precision is important.

4 Assimilation of MODIS and VIIRS Fire Detections

Data likelihood is the probability of a specific configuration of fire detection and non-detection pixels given the state of the fire. The probability of MODIS Active Fires detection in a particular sensor pixel as a function of the fraction of the area actively burning and the maximum size of contiguous area burning, was estimated in the validation study [25] using logistic regression. We consider the fraction of the pixel burning and the maximum continuous area burning as a proxy to the fire radiative heat flux in the pixel. The model state is encoded as the fire arrival time at each grid point, and the heat flux can be then computed from the burn model using the fuel properties. Substituting the heat flux into the logistic curve yields a plausible probability of detection for a period starting from the fire arrival time: the probability keeps almost constant while the fire is fresh, and then diminishes.

However, the position uncertainty of the detection is significant, the allowed 3σ-error is listed in VIIRS specifications [26] as 1.5 km, and position errors of such magnitude are indeed occasionally observed. Therefore, the probability of detection at the given coordinates of the center of a sensor pixel in fact depends on the fire over a nearby area, with the contributions of fire model cells weighted by e^{-d^2/σ^2}, where d is the distance of the fire model cell and the nominal center of the sensor pixel, because of the uncertainty where the sensor is actually looking. Assuming that the position errors and the detection errors are independent, we can estimate the contribution of a grid cell to the data likelihood from a combination of the probabilities of detection at the nearby satellite pixels.

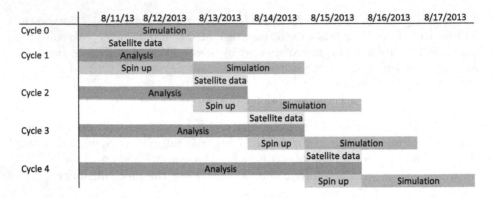

Fig. 2. Data assimilation cycling with atmosphere model spin up. From [17].

Assimilation of data into the fire spread model can be then formulated as an optimization problem to minimize its residual and to maximize the data likelihood. See [10] for further details.

Since the fire model is coupled with an atmosphere model, changing the state of the fire alone makes the state of the coupled model inconsistent. To recover a consistent state, we spin up the atmosphere model from an earlier time, with the modified fire arrival time used instead of the fire arrival time from the fire spread model (Fig. 2). This synthetic fire forcing to the atmospheric model is used to drive atmospheric model [16] and enables establishing fire-induced circulation.

Varying the model state to maximize the data likelihood can also be used to estimate the time and place of ignition as well as other model parameters. The WRF-SFIRE [15] model was run on a mesh of varying GPS coordinates and times and the data likelihoods of the relevant Active Fire detection data is evaluated, allowing the most likely place and time of the fire's ignition to be determined. Figure 3 shows a visualization of the likelihoods of Active Fire detection data for several hundred ignition points at various times. Work is in progress so that an automated process of determining the most likely time and place of ignition can be initiated from collection of satellite data indicating a wildfire has started in a particular geographic region of interest.

5   Computational Experiments

The optimization problem was tested on an idealized case using concentric circles as perimeters in a mesh with 100×100 nodes. The fire spreads equally in all directions from the center of the mesh. The propagation is set at different rates of spread in different sections (Fig. 4(a)). We also set the fire arrival time at the ignition point and compute the fire arrival time on the two perimeters from the given rate of spread, so in this case there exists an exact solution (Fig. 4(b)).

The constraint matrix was constructed by the method described in Sect. 3.2. The initial approximation of the fire arrival time was then found by solving the

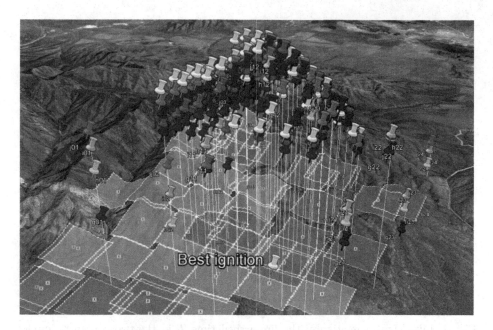

Fig. 3. Estimation of the most likely time and ignition point of a fire by evaluation of MODIS Active Fire data likelihood. The color of the pushpin represents the time of ignition and the height of the pushpin gives the likelihood of ignition at that location. (Color figure online)

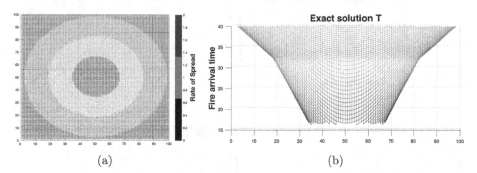

(a)   (b)

Fig. 4. (a) Initial approximation of the fire arrival time T in the two concentric circles perimeter case using different values of α. (b) Exact solution T for the concentric circles problem.

quadratic minimization problem described in Sect. 3.3 with $\alpha = 1.4$. Figure 5 shows the initial approximation of the fire arrival time imposed by the ignition point and the two concentric circles in our particular case and using different values of α from 1 to 1.4. One can see how the unrealistic sharp funnel at the ignition point for $\alpha = 1$ disappears with the increasing value of α.

Then, we run the multigrid method proposed in Sect. 3.3. The coarsening was done by the ratio of 2. The number of sweeps was linearly increasing with the

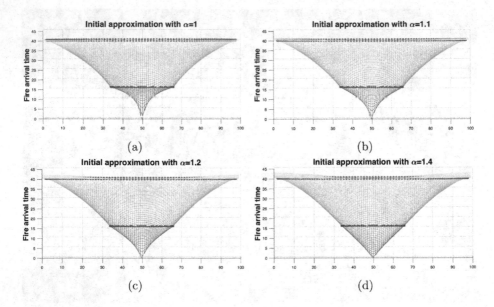

Fig. 5. Initial approximation of the fire arrival time T in the two concentric circles perimeter case using different values of α.

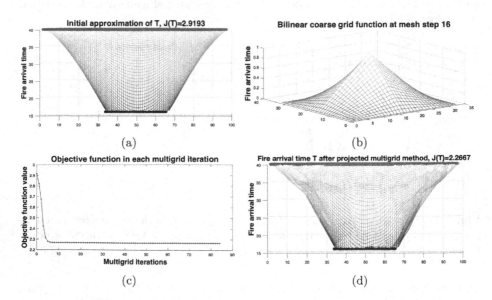

Fig. 6. (a) Initial approximation from the first perimeter at $T_1 = 16$ to the second perimeter at $T_2 = 40$ obtained with $\alpha = 1.4$. (b) Example of a bilinear coarse grid function at mesh step 16. (b) Values of the objective function after each line search iteration of the multigrid experiment. (c) Result of the fire arrival time interpolation after 4 cycles of multigrid experiment.

level. On the coarsest level, the mesh step was 32 and the sweep was done once, the mesh step on the second level was 16 and the sweep was repeated twice, until resolution 1 on the original, finest grid, and sweep repeated 6 times.

Figure 6c shows the decrease in the cost function with the number of line searches on any level. One can observe that the cost function decreased more in the first cycle and at the beginning of iterations on each level.

The final result after 4 cycles of 6 different resolutions (from 32 to 1 decreasing by powers of two) is shown in Fig. 6(d), which is close to the exact solution.

6   Conclusions

We have presented a new method for fitting data by an approximate solution of a fire spread model. The method was illustrated on an idealized example. Application to a real problem are forthcoming.

Acknowledgments. This research was partially supported by grants NSF ICER-1664175 and NASA NNX13AH59G, and MINECO-Spain under contract TIN2014-53234-C2-1-R. High-performance computing support at CHPC at the University of Utah and Cheyenne (doi:10.5065/D6RX99HX) at NCAR CISL, sponsored by the NSF, are gratefully acknowledged.

References

1. Andrews, P.L.: BehavePlus fire modeling system: past, present, and future. In: Paper J2.1, 7th Symposium on Fire and Forest Meteorology (2007). http://ams.confex.com/ams/pdfpapers/126669.pdf. Accessed Sept 2011
2. Brezzi, F., Fortin, M.: Mixed and Hybrid Finite Element Methods. Springer, New York (1991). https://doi.org/10.1007/978-1-4612-3172-1
3. Clark, T.L., Coen, J., Latham, D.: Description of a coupled atmosphere-fire model. Int. J. Wildland Fire **13**, 49–64 (2004). https://doi.org/10.1071/WF03043
4. Coen, J.L.: Simulation of the Big Elk Fire using coupled atmosphere-fire modeling. Int. J. Wildland Fire **14**(1), 49–59 (2005). https://doi.org/10.1071/WF04047
5. Coen, J.L., Cameron, M., Michalakes, J., Patton, E.G., Riggan, P.J., Yedinak, K.: WRF-fire: coupled weather-wildland fire modeling with the weather research and forecasting model. J. Appl. Meteor. Climatol. **52**, 16–38 (2013). https://doi.org/10.1175/JAMC-D-12-023.1
6. Coen, J.L.: Modeling wildland fires: a description of the coupled atmosphere-wildland fire environment model (CAWFE). NCAR Technical note NCAR/TN-500+STR (2013). https://doi.org/10.5065/D6K64G2G
7. Coen, J.L., Schroeder, W.: Use of spatially refined satellite remote sensing fire detection data to initialize and evaluate coupled weather-wildfire growth model simulations. Geophys. Res. Lett. **40**, 1–6 (2013). https://doi.org/10.1002/2013GL057868
8. Filippi, J.B., Bosseur, F., Pialat, X., Santoni, P., Strada, S., Mari, C.: Simulation of coupled fire/atmosphere interaction with the MesoNH-ForeFire models. J. Combust. **2011**, Article ID 540390 (2011). https://doi.org/10.1155/2011/540390

9. Finney, M.A.: FARSITE: fire area simulator - model development and evaluation. Research Paper RMRS-RP-4, Ogden, UT, USDA Forest Service, Rocky Mountain Research Station (1998). https://doi.org/10.2737/RMRS-RP-4. Accessed Dec 2011

10. Haley, J., Farguell Caus, A., Mandel, J., Kochanski, A.K., Schranz, S.: Data likelihood of active fires satellite detection and applications to ignition estimation and data assimilation. In: Viegas, D.X. (ed.) VIII International Conference on Forest Fire Research. University of Coimbra Press (2018, submitted)

11. Kochanski, A.K., Jenkins, M.A., Yedinak, K., Mandel, J., Beezley, J., Lamb, B.: Toward an integrated system for fire, smoke, and air quality simulations. Int. J. Wildland Fire **25**, 534–546 (2016). https://doi.org/10.1071/WF14074

12. Linn, R., Reisner, J., Colman, J.J., Winterkamp, J.: Studying wildfire behavior using FIRETEC. Int. J. Wildland Fire **11**, 233–246 (2002). https://doi.org/10.1071/WF02007

13. Mandel, J., Amram, S., Beezley, J.D., Kelman, G., Kochanski, A.K., Kondratenko, V.Y., Lynn, B.H., Regev, B., Vejmelka, M.: Recent advances and applications of WRF-SFIRE. Nat. Hazards Earth Syst. Sci. **14**(10), 2829–2845 (2014). https://doi.org/10.5194/nhess-14-2829-2014

14. Mandel, J., Beezley, J.D., Coen, J.L., Kim, M.: Data assimilation for wildland fires: ensemble Kalman filters in coupled atmosphere-surface models. IEEE Control Syst. Mag. **29**(3), 47–65 (2009). https://doi.org/10.1109/MCS.2009.932224

15. Mandel, J., Beezley, J.D., Kochanski, A.K.: Coupled atmosphere-wildland fire modeling with WRF 3.3 and SFIRE 2011. Geosci. Model Dev. **4**, 591–610 (2011). https://doi.org/10.5194/gmd-4-591-2011

16. Mandel, J., Beezley, J.D., Kochanski, A.K., Kondratenko, V.Y., Kim, M.: Assimilation of perimeter data and coupling with fuel moisture in a Wildland fire - atmosphere DDDAS. Procedia Comput. Sci. **9**, 1100–1109 (2012). https://doi.org/10.1016/j.procs.2012.04.119. Proceedings of ICCS 2012

17. Mandel, J., Fournier, A., Haley, J.D., Jenkins, M.A., Kochanski, A.K., Schranz, S., Vejmelka, M., Yen, T.Y.: Assimilation of MODIS and VIIRS satellite active fires detection in a coupled atmosphere-fire spread model. In: Poster, 5th Annual International Symposium on Data Assimilation, 18–22 July 2016, University of Reading, UK (2016). http://www.isda2016.net/abstracts/posters/MandelAssimilationof.html. Accessed Dec 2016

18. McCormick, S.F., Ruge, J.W.: Unigrid for multigrid simulation. Math. Comput. **41**(163), 43–62 (1983). https://doi.org/10.2307/2007765

19. Mell, W., Jenkins, M.A., Gould, J., Cheney, P.: A physics-based approach to modelling grassland fires. Intl. J. Wildland Fire **16**, 1–22 (2007). https://doi.org/10.1071/WF06002

20. Muñoz-Esparza, D., Kosović, B., Jiménez, P.A., Coen, J.L.: An accurate fire-spread algorithm in the weather research and forecasting model using the level-set method. J. Adv. Model. Earth Syst. (2018). https://doi.org/10.1002/2017MS001108

21. Osher, S., Fedkiw, R.: Level Set Methods and Dynamic Implicit Surfaces. Springer, New York (2003). https://doi.org/10.1007/b98879

22. Outcalt, K.W., Wade, D.D.: Fuels management reduces tree mortality from wildfires in southeastern United States. South. J. Appl. For. **28**(1), 28–34 (2004)

23. Rehm, R.G., McDermott, R.J.: Fire-front propagation using the level set method. NIST Technical Note 1611, March 2009. https://nvlpubs.nist.gov/nistpubs/Legacy/TN/nbstechnicalnote1611.pdf

24. Rothermel, R.C.: A mathematical model for predicting fire spread in wildland fires. USDA Forest Service Research Paper INT-115 (1972). https://www.fs.fed.us/rm/pubs_int/int_rp115.pdf. Accessed Mar 2018

25. Schroeder, W., Prins, E., Giglio, L., Csiszar, I., Schmidt, C., Morisette, J., Morton, D.: Validation of GOES and MODIS active fire detection products using ASTER and ETM+data. Remote Sens. Environ. **112**(5), 2711–2726 (2008). https://doi.org/10.1016/j.rse.2008.01.005

26. Sei, A.: VIIRS active fires: fire mask algorithm theoretical basis document (2011). https://www.star.nesdis.noaa.gov/jpss/documents/ATBD/D0001-M01-S01-021_JPSS_ATBD_VIIRS-Active-Fires.pdf. Accessed 17 Nov 2013

27. Skamarock, W.C., Klemp, J.B., Dudhia, J., Gill, D.O., Barker, D.M., Duda, M.G., Huang, X.Y., Wang, W., Powers, J.G.: A description of the advanced research WRF version 3. NCAR Technical Note 475 (2008). https://doi.org/10.5065/D68S4MVH. Accessed December 2011

28. Stephens, S.L., Ruth, L.W.: Federal forest-fire policy in the United States. Ecol. Appl. **15**(2), 532–542 (2005). https://doi.org/10.1890/04-0545

29. Tymstra, C., Bryce, R., Wotton, B., Taylor, S., Armitage, O.: Development and structure of Prometheus: the Canadian Wildland fire growth simulation model. Information Report NOR-X-147, Northern Forestry Centre, Canadian Forest Service (2010). http://publications.gc.ca/collections/collection_2010/nrcan/Fo133-1-417-eng.pdf. Accessed March 2018

30. Vejmelka, M., Kochanski, A.K., Mandel, J.: Data assimilation of dead fuel moisture observations from remote automatic weather stations. Int. J. Wildland Fire **25**, 558–568 (2016). https://doi.org/10.1071/WF14085

31. Yoder, J., Engle, D., Fuhlendorf, S.: Liability, incentives, and prescribed fire for ecosystem management. Front. Ecol. Environ. **2**, 361–366 (2004). https://doi.org/10.1890/1540-9295(2004)002[0361:LIAPFF]2.0.CO;2

Analyzing Complex Models Using Data and Statistics

Abani K. Patra[1,3]([✉]), Andrea Bevilacqua[2], and Ali Akhavan Safei[3]

[1] Computational Data Science and Engineering, University at Buffalo,
Buffalo, NY 14260, USA
`abani@buffalo.edu`
[2] Earth Sciences Department, University at Buffalo, Buffalo, NY 14260, USA
[3] Department of Mechanical and Aerospace Engineering, University at Buffalo,
Buffalo, NY 14260, USA

Abstract. Complex systems (e.g., volcanoes, debris flows, climate) commonly have many models advocated by different modelers and incorporating different modeling assumptions. Limited and sparse data on the modeled phenomena does not permit a clean discrimination among models for fitness of purpose, and, heuristic choices are usually made, especially for critical predictions of behavior that has not been experienced. We advocate here for characterizing models and the modeling assumptions they represent using a statistical approach over the full range of applicability of the models. Such a characterization may then be used to decide the appropriateness of a model for use, and, perhaps as needed weighted compositions of models for better predictive power. We use the example of dense granular representations of natural mass flows in volcanic debris avalanches, to illustrate our approach.

Keywords: Model analysis · Statistical analysis

1 Introduction

This paper presents a systematic approach to the study of models of complex systems.

1.1 What Is a Model?

A simple though not necessarily comprehensive definition of a model is that:

A model is a representation of a postulated relationship among inputs and outputs of a system usually informed by observation and a hypothesis that best explains them.

The definition captures two of the most important characteristics

- models depend on a *hypothesis*, and,
- models use the *data from observation* to validate and refine the hypothesis.

Supported by NSF/ACI 1339765.

Errors and uncertainty in the data and limitations in the hypothesis (usually a tractable and computable mathematical construct articulating beliefs like proportionality, linearity, etc.) are immediate challenges that must be overcome to construct useful and credible models.

1.2   Who Needs Them and Why Are There so Many of Them?

A model is most useful in predicting the behavior of a system for unobserved inputs and interpretability or explainability of the system's behavior. Since, models require a hypotheses implies that the model is a formulation of a belief about the data. The immediate consequence of this that the model may be very poor about such prediction even when sufficient care is taken to use all the available data and information since the *subjectivity of the belief* can never be completely eliminated. Secondly, the data at hand may not provide enough information about the system to characterize its behavior at the desired prediction. What makes this problem even more acute is that we are often interested in modeling outcomes that are not observed and perhaps sometimes not observable.

The consequence of this lack of knowledge and limited data is the multiplicity of beliefs about the complex system being modeled and a profusion of models based on different modeling assumptions and data use. These competing models lead to much debate among scientists. Principles like "Occam's razor" and Bayesian statistics [2] provide some guidance but simple robust approaches that allow the testing of models for fitness need to be developed. We present in this paper a simple data driven approach to discriminate among models and the modeling assumptions implicit in each model, given a range of phenomena to be studied. We illustrate the approach by work on granular flow models of large mass flows.

1.3   Models and Assumptions

An assumption is a simple intuitive concept. An assumption is any atomic postulate about relationships among quantities under study, e.g., a linear stress strain relationship $\sigma = E\epsilon$ or neglecting some quantities in comparison to larger quantities $\theta \approx \sin(\theta)$ for small θ. Models are compositions of many such assumptions. The study of models is thus implicitly a study of these assumptions and their composability and applicability in a particular context. Sometimes a good model contains a useless assumption that may be removed, sometimes a good assumption should be implemented inside a different model - these are usually subjective choices, not data driven. Moreover, the correct assumptions may change through time, making *model choice* more difficult.

The rest of the paper will define our approach and a simple illustration using 3 models for large scale mass flows incorporated in our large scale mass flow simulation framework TITAN2D [5]. The availability of 3 distinct models for similar phenomena in the same tool provides us the ability to directly compare inputs, outputs and internal variables in all the 3 models.

1.4   Analysis of Modeling Assumptions and Models

Let us define $\big(M(A), P_{M(A)}\big)$, where A is a set of assumptions, $M(A)$ is the model which combines those assumptions, and P_M is a probability distribution in the parameter space of M. For the sake of simplicity we assume P_M to be uniformly distributed on selected parameter ranges. While the support of P_M can be restricted to a single value by solving an inverse problem for the optimal reconstruction of a particular flow, this is not possible if we are interested in the general predictive capabilities of the model, where we are interested in the outcomes over a whole range.

Stage 1: Parameter Ranges. In this study, we always assume $P_M \sim \bigotimes_{i=1}^{N_M}$ $Unif(a_{i,M}, b_{i,M})$, where N_M is the number of parameters of M. These parameter ranges will be chosen using information gathered from the literature about the physical meaning of those values together with a preliminary testing for physical consistency of model outcomes and range of inputs/outputs of interest.

Stage 2: Simulations and Data Gathering. The simulation algorithms can be represented as (Fig. 1):

Model Evaluation (Simulator)

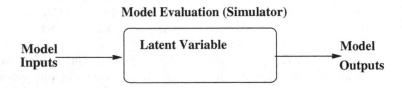

Fig. 1. Models and variables

The *model inputs* are the parameters of M, The *latent variables* include quantities in the model evaluation that are ascribable to specific assumptions A_i. These are usually not observed as outputs from the model. For example in momentum balances of complex flow calculations these could be values of different source terms, dissipation terms and inertia terms. Finally, the *model outputs* include explicit outcomes, e.g., for flow calculations these could be flow height, lateral extent, area, velocity, acceleration, and derived quantities such as Froude number Fr. In general, for each quantity of interest (QoI), we use a Monte Carlo simulation, sampling the input variables and obtaining a family of graphs plotting their expectation, and their 5th and 95th percentiles. Our sampling technique of the input variables is based on the Latin Hypercube Sampling (LHS) idea, and in particular, on the improved space-filling properties of the orthogonal array-based Latin Hypercubes.

Stage 3: Results Analysis. These and other statistics can now be compared to determine the need for different modeling assumptions and the relative merits of different models. Thus, analysis of the data gathered over the entire range of flows for the state variables and outcomes leads to a quantitative basis for accepting or rejecting particular assumptions or models for specific outcomes.

2   Modeling of Mass Flows

Dense large scale granular avalanches are a complex class of flows with physics that has often been poorly captured by models that are computationally tractable. Sparsity of actual flow data (usually only a posteriori deposit information is available), and large uncertainty in the mechanisms of initiation and flow propagation, make the modeling task challenging, and a subject of much continuing interest. Models that appear to represent the physics well in certain flows, may turn out to be poorly behaved in others, due to intrinsic mathematical or numerical issues. Nevertheless, given the large implications on life and property, many models with different modeling assumptions have been proposed.

2.1   Three Models

Modeling in this case proceeds by first assuming that the laws of mass and momentum conservation hold for properly defined system boundaries. The scale of these flows, very long and wide with small depth led to the first most generally accepted assumption, shallowness [13]. This allows an integration through the depth to obtain simpler and more computationally tractable equations. This is the next of many assumptions that have to be made. Both of these are fundamental assumptions which can be tested in the procedure we established above. Since, there is a general consensus and much evidence in the literature of the validity of these assumptions we defer analysis of these to future work. The depth-averaged Saint-Venant equations that result are:

$$\frac{\partial h}{\partial t} + \frac{\partial}{\partial x}(h\bar{u}) + \frac{\partial}{\partial y}(h\bar{v}) = 0$$

$$\frac{\partial}{\partial t}(h\bar{u}) + \frac{\partial}{\partial x}\left(h\bar{u}^2 + \frac{1}{2}kg_zh^2\right) + \frac{\partial}{\partial y}(h\bar{u}\bar{v}) = S_x \qquad (1)$$

$$\frac{\partial}{\partial t}(h\bar{v}) + \frac{\partial}{\partial x}(h\bar{u}\bar{v}) + \frac{\partial}{\partial y}\left(h\bar{v}^2 + \frac{1}{2}kg_zh^2\right) = S_y$$

Here the Cartesian coordinate system is aligned such that z is normal to the surface; h is the flow height in the z direction; $h\bar{u}$ and $h\bar{v}$ are respectively the components of momentum in the x and y directions; and k is the coefficient which relates the lateral stress components, $\bar{\sigma}_{xx}$ and $\bar{\sigma}_{yy}$, to the normal stress component, $\bar{\sigma}_{zz}$. The definition of this coefficient depends on the constitutive model of the flowing material we choose. Note that $\frac{1}{2}kg_zh^2$ is the contribution of hydrostatic pressure to the momentum fluxes. S_x and S_y are the sum local stresses: they include the gravitational driving forces, the basal friction force resisting to the motion of the material, and additional forces specific of rheology assumptions.

The final class of assumptions are the assumptions on the rheology of the flows – in particular in this context assumptions used to model different dissipation mechanisms embedded in S_x, S_y that lead to a plethora of models with much controversy on the most suitable model.

Mohr-Coulomb (MC). Based on the long history of studies in soil mechanics [7], the Mohr-Coulomb (MC) rheology model was developed and used to represent the behavior of geophysical mass flows [13].

Shear and normal stress are assumed to obey Coulomb friction equation, both within the flow and at its boundaries. In other words,

$$\tau = \sigma \tan \phi, \tag{2}$$

where τ and σ are respectively the shear and normal stresses on failure surfaces, and ϕ is a friction angle. This relationship does not depend on the flow speed.

We can summarize the MC rheology assumptions as:

- *Basal Friction* based on a constant friction angle.
- *Internal Friction* based on a constant friction angle.
- *Earth pressure coefficient* formula depends on the Mohr circle.
- The velocity based *curvature effects* are included into the equations.

Under the assumption of symmetry of the stress tensor with respect to the z axis, the earth pressure coefficient $k = k_{ap}$ can take on only one of three values $\{0, \pm 1\}$. The material yield criterion is represented by the two straight lines at angles $\pm \phi$ (the internal friction angle) relative to horizontal direction. Similarly, the normal and shear stress at the bed are represented by the line $\tau = -\sigma \tan(\delta)$ where δ is the bed friction angle.

MC Equations. As a result, we can write down the source terms of the Eq. (1):

$$S_x = g_x h - \frac{\bar{u}}{\|\bar{u}\|} \left[h \left(g_z + \frac{\bar{u}^2}{r_x} \right) \tan(\phi_{bed}) \right] - h k_{ap} \, \text{sgn} \left(\frac{\partial \bar{u}}{\partial y} \right) \frac{\partial (g_z h)}{\partial y} \sin(\phi_{int})$$

$$S_y = g_y h - \frac{\bar{v}}{\|\bar{u}\|} \left[h \left(g_z + \frac{\bar{v}^2}{r_y} \right) \tan(\phi_{bed}) \right] - h k_{ap} \, \text{sgn} \left(\frac{\partial \bar{v}}{\partial x} \right) \frac{\partial (g_z h)}{\partial x} \sin(\phi_{int}) \tag{3}$$

Where, $\bar{u} = (\bar{u}, \bar{v})$, is the depth-averaged velocity vector, r_x and r_y denote the radii of curvature of the local basal surface. The inverse of the radii of curvature is usually approximated with the partial derivatives of the basal slope, e.g., $1/r_x = \partial \theta_x / \partial x$, where θ_x is the local bed slope.

Pouliquen-Forterre (PF). The scaling properties for granular flows down rough inclined planes led to a new formulation of the basal friction stress as a function of the flow depth and velocity [6]. PF rheology assumptions can be summarized as:

- *Basal Friction* is based on an interpolation of two different friction angles, based on the flow regime and depth.

- *Internal Friction* is neglected.
- *Earth pressure coefficient* is equal to one.
- Normal stress is modified by a *hydrostatic pressure force* related to the flow height gradient.
- Velocity based *curvature effects* are included into the equations.

Two critical slope inclination angles are defined as functions of the flow thickness, namely $\phi_{start}(h)$ and $\phi_{stop}(h)$. The function $\phi_{stop}(h)$ gives the slope angle at which a steady uniform flow leaves a deposit of thickness h, while $\phi_{start}(h)$ is the angle at which a layer of thickness h is mobilized. They define two different basal friction coefficients.

$$\mu_{start}(h) = \tan(\phi_{start}(h)) \qquad (4)$$
$$\mu_{stop}(h) = \tan(\phi_{stop}(h)) \qquad (5)$$

An empirical friction law $\mu_b(\|\underset{\sim}{\mathbf{u}}\|, h)$ is then defined in the whole range of velocity and thickness.

PF Equations. The depth-averaged Eq. (1) source terms thus take the following form:

$$S_x = g_x h - \frac{\bar{u}}{\|\underset{\sim}{\mathbf{u}}\|} \left[h \left(g_z + \frac{\bar{u}^2}{r_x} \right) \mu_b(\|\underset{\sim}{\mathbf{u}}\|, h) \right] + g_z h \frac{\partial h}{\partial x}$$
$$S_y = g_y h - \frac{\bar{v}}{\|\underset{\sim}{\mathbf{u}}\|} \left[h \left(g_z + \frac{\bar{v}^2}{r_y} \right) \mu_b(\|\underset{\sim}{\mathbf{u}}\|, h) \right] + g_z h \frac{\partial h}{\partial y} \qquad (6)$$

Voellmy-Salm (VS). The theoretical analysis of dense snow avalanches led to the VS rheology model [9,15]. The following relation between shear and normal stresses holds:

$$\tau = \mu\sigma + \frac{\rho\|\mathbf{g}\|}{\xi} \|\underset{\sim}{\mathbf{u}}\|^2, \qquad (7)$$

where, σ denotes the normal stress at the bottom of the fluid layer and $\mathbf{g} = (g_x, g_y, g_z)$ represents the gravity vector. The VS rheology adds a velocity dependent *turbulent* friction to the traditional velocity independent basal friction term which is proportional to the normal stress at the flow bottom. The two parameters of the model are the bed friction coefficient μ and the turbulent friction coefficient ξ.

We can summarize VS rheology assumptions as:

- *Basal Friction* is based on a constant coefficient, similarly to the MC rheology.
- *Internal Friction* is neglected.
- *Earth pressure coefficient* is equal to one.
- Additional *turbulent friction* is based on the local velocity by a quadratic expression.
- Velocity based *curvature effects* are included into the equations, following an alternative formulation.

The effect of the topographic local curvatures is again taken into account by adding the terms containing the local radii of curvature r_x and r_y. In this case the formula is considering the modulus of velocity instead than the scalar component [3].

VS Equations. Therefore, the final source terms take the following form:

$$S_x = g_x h - \frac{\bar{u}}{\|\underset{\sim}{\bar{u}}\|} \left[h \left(g_z + \frac{\|\underset{\sim}{\bar{u}}\|^2}{r_x} \right) \mu + \frac{\|\underset{\sim}{g}\|}{\xi} \|\underset{\sim}{\bar{u}}\|^2 \right],$$

$$S_y = g_y h - \frac{\bar{v}}{\|\underset{\sim}{\bar{u}}\|} \left[h \left(g_z + \frac{\|\underset{\sim}{\bar{u}}\|^2}{r_y} \right) \mu + \frac{\|\underset{\sim}{g}\|}{\xi} \|\underset{\sim}{\bar{u}}\|^2 \right]. \tag{8}$$

Latent Variables. For analysis of modeling assumptions we need to record and classify the results of different modeling assumptions. These terms are explored in detail in the next sections.

$$RHS_1 = [g_x h, g_y h], \tag{9}$$

it is the gravitational force term, it has the same formulation in all models. The formula of **basal friction force** RHS_2 depends on the model:

$$RHS_2 = - h g_z \tan(\phi_{bed}) \left[\frac{\bar{u}}{\|\underset{\sim}{\bar{u}}\|}, \frac{\bar{v}}{\|\underset{\sim}{\bar{u}}\|} \right], \text{ in MC model.}$$

$$RHS_2 = - h g_z \, \mu_b(\|\underset{\sim}{\bar{u}}\|, h) \left[\frac{\bar{u}}{\|\underset{\sim}{\bar{u}}\|}, \frac{\bar{v}}{\|\underset{\sim}{\bar{u}}\|} \right], \text{ in PF model.} \tag{10}$$

$$RHS_2 = - h g_z \mu \left[\frac{\bar{u}}{\|\underset{\sim}{\bar{u}}\|}, \frac{\bar{v}}{\|\underset{\sim}{\bar{u}}\|} \right], \text{ in VS model.}$$

The formula of the force related to the **topography curvature**, RHS_3, also depends on the model:

$$RHS_3 = - h \tan(\phi_{bed}) \left[\frac{\bar{u}^3}{r_x \|\underset{\sim}{\bar{u}}\|}, \frac{\bar{v}^3}{r_y \|\underset{\sim}{\bar{u}}\|} \right], \text{ in MC model.}$$

$$RHS_3 = - h \, \mu_b(\|\underset{\sim}{\bar{u}}\|, h) \left[\frac{\bar{u}^3}{r_x \|\underset{\sim}{\bar{u}}\|}, \frac{\bar{v}^3}{r_y \|\underset{\sim}{\bar{u}}\|} \right], \text{ in PF model.} \tag{11}$$

$$RHS_3 = - h \mu \left[\frac{\bar{u}\|\underset{\sim}{\bar{u}}\|}{r_x}, \frac{\bar{v}\|\underset{\sim}{\bar{u}}\|}{r_y} \right], \text{ in VS model.}$$

All the three models have an additional force term, having a different formula and meaning in the three models:

$$RHS_4 = -hk_{ap}\sin(\phi_{int}) \left[\text{sgn}(\frac{\partial \bar{u}}{\partial y})\frac{\partial(g_z h)}{\partial y}, \; \text{sgn}(\frac{\partial \bar{v}}{\partial x})\frac{\partial(g_z h)}{\partial x} \right], \text{ in MC model.}$$

$$RHS_4 = g_z h \left[\frac{\partial h}{\partial x}, \frac{\partial h}{\partial y} \right], \text{ in PF model.} \qquad (12)$$

$$RHS_4 = -\frac{\|\underset{\sim}{g}\|}{\xi}\|\underset{\sim}{\bar{u}}\|^2 \left[\frac{\bar{u}}{\|\underset{\sim}{\bar{u}}\|}, \frac{\bar{v}}{\|\underset{\sim}{\bar{u}}\|} \right], \text{ in VS model.}$$

These latent variables can be analyzed locally and globally for discriminating among the different modeling assumption.

2.2   Monte Carlo Process and Statistical Analysis

For our study, the flow range is defined by establishing boundaries for inputs like flow volume and rheology coefficients. Optionally, these could include also flow initiation site and geometry, and the digital elevation map. The Latin Hypercube Sampling is performed over $[0, 1]^3$ for the MC and VS input parameters, and $[0, 1]^4$ for PF input parameters. Those dimensionless samples are linearly mapped to fill the required intervals.

Following the simulations, we generate data for each sample run and each outcome and latent variable $f(\mathbf{x}, t)$ calculated as a function of time on the elements of the computational grid. This analysis generates tremendous volume of data which must then be analyzed using statistical methods for summative impact. The latent variables in this case are the mass and force terms in the conservation laws defined above.

We devise many statistical measures for analyzing the data. For instance, let $(F_i(x, t))_{i=1,...,4}$ be an array of force components, where $x \in \mathbf{R}^2$ is a spatial location, and $t \in T$ is a time instant. The degree of contribution of those force terms can be significantly variable in space and time, and we define the *dominance factors* $(p_j)_{j=1,...,k}$, i.e., the probability of each F_j to be the dominant force at (x, t). Those probabilities provide insight into the dominance of a particular source or dissipation (identified with a particular modeling assumption) term on the model dynamics.

2.3   Overview of the Case Studies

The first case study assumes very simple boundary conditions, and corresponds to an experiment fully described in [16]. It is a classical flow down an inclined plane set-up, including a change in slope to an horizontal plane (Fig. 2 Left). Four locations are selected among the center line of the flow to accomplish local testing. These are: the initial pile location $L_1 = (-0.7, 0)$ m, the middle of the inclined plane $L_2 = (-0.35, 0)$ m, the change in slope $L_3 = (0, 0)$ m, the middle of the flat plane $L_4 = (0.15, 0)$ m.

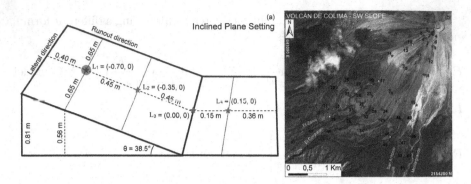

Fig. 2. [Left] inclined plane description, including local samples sites (red stars). Pile location is marked by a blue dot. [Right] (a) Volcán de Colima (México) overview, including 51 numbered local sample sites (stars) and four labeled major ravines channeling the flow. Pile location is marked by a blue dot. Reported coordinates are in UTM zone 13N. Background is a satellite photo. Six points that are adopted as preferred locations are highlighted in yellow. (Color figure online)

The second case study is a block and ash flow down the slope of Volcán de Colima (MX) - an andesitic stratovolcano that rises to 3,860 m above sea level, situated in the western portion of the Trans-Mexican Volcanic Belt (Fig. 2 Right). The modeling of pyroclastic flows generated by explosive eruptions and lava dome collapses of Volcán de Colima is a well studied problem [4, 10–12, 14]. The volcano has been already used as a case study in several studies involving the Titan2D code [8]. We select 51 locations along the flow inundated area to observe model outputs with six of them as preferred locations being representative of different flow regimes.

3   Sample Results

Figure 3 shows the flow height, $h(L, t)$, at the points $(L_i)_{i=1,...,4}$, for the three rheology models. Parameter ranges – outcome of Stage 1 analysis – come from literature and past work in our laboratory. Plot 3 clearly shows the differences in the statistics of the flow outcomes induced by the different choices of rheology at different locations in the plane. Availability of data allows us to subject the data to tests of reasonability both for the means and extremal values. Given a particular type of flow and collected data we can clearly distinguish model skill in capturing not only that flow but also possible flows. Past work [16] allows us to conclude that MC rheology is adequate for modeling simple dry granular flows.

While, the above analysis is interesting in helping us accept or reject particular models a lot of insight can be obtained by examining the behavior of latent variables. Figure 4 shows the spatial average of speed and Froude Number, for the three rheology models for flows at Volcan Colima. Ranges of parameters etc.

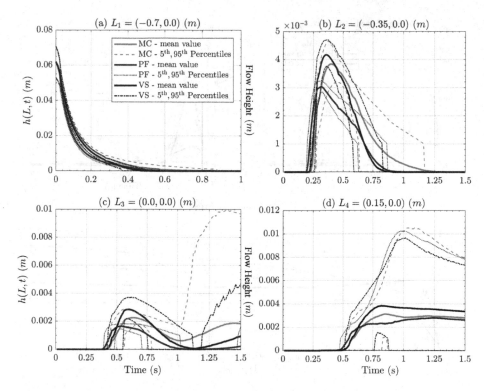

Fig. 3. Records of flow height at four spatial locations of interest. Bold line is mean value, dashed/dotted lines are 5th and 95th percentile bounds. Different rheology models are displayed with different colors. Plots are at different scale, for simplification. (Color figure online)

are obtained from our past work at this site [1]. It also shows the inundated area of flow, as a function of time. Similar analysis of model suitability can be conducted here given recorded deposits. In past work [5], we have tuned MC rheology to match deposits for known block and ash flows but *a priori* predictive ability was limited by inability to tune without knowledge of flow character.

The plots 5a, b, c and 5d, e, f are related to point L_8 and L_{10}, respectively. They are significantly similar. $\boldsymbol{RHS_1}$ related to the gravitational force is the dominant force with a very high chance, $P_1 > 90\%$. In MC and PF there is a small probability, i.e., $P_3 = 5\%$–30% at most, of $\boldsymbol{RHS_3}$ related to topographic curvature effects being the dominant force for a short amount of time, i.e. ~ 5 s. This occurs in the middle of the time interval in which the flow is almost surely inundating the points being observed. In VS it is observed a $P_4 = 5\%$ chance of $\boldsymbol{RHS_4}$ related to the turbulent dissipation being dominant, for a few seconds, anticipating the minimum of no-flow probability. Plots 5g, h, i, are related to point L_{17}, and the plots are split in two sub-frames, following different temporal

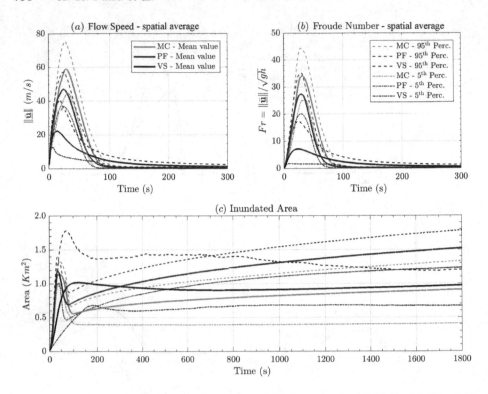

Fig. 4. Comparison between spatial averages of (*a*) flow speed, and (*b*) Froude Number, in addition to the (*c*) inundated area, as a function of time.

scales. In all the models, $\boldsymbol{RHS_2}$ is the most probable dominant force, and its dominance factor has a bell-shaped profile, similar to the complementary of no-flow probability. In all the models, $\boldsymbol{RHS_1}$ has a small chance of being the dominant force. In MC, this is more significant, at most $P_1 = 30\%$, for ~20 s after the flow arrival, and has again about $P_1 = \%2$ chance to be dominant in $[100, 7200]$ s. In PF, the chance is $P_1 = 15\%$ at most, and has two maxima, one short lasting at about 55 s, and the second in $[100, 500]$ s. Also in VS, the chance is at most $P_1 = 15\%$, reached at $[300, 500]$ s, but its profile is unimodal in time, and becomes lower than $P_1 = 2\%$ after 2000 s. In MC and PF, $\boldsymbol{RHS_3}$ has a chance of $P_3 = 10\%$ of being the dominant force, for a short amount of time $[30, 50]$ s and $[40, 50]$ s, respectively. Figure 5 show the Dominance Factors $(P_i)_{i=1,\dots,4}$, for the three rheology models and focusing on the RHS terms moduli, at the three selected points L_8, L_{10}, and L_{17}, closer than 1 Km to the initial pile (in horizontal projection).

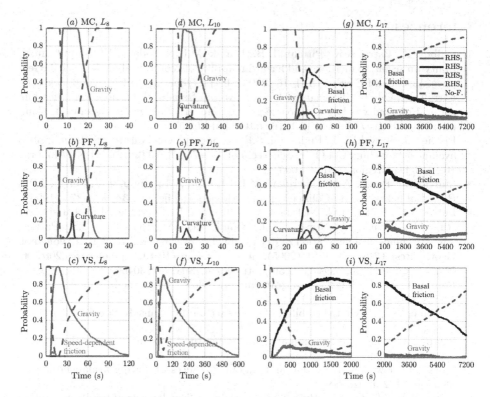

Fig. 5. Records of dominance probabilities of **RHS** force moduli, at three spatial locations of interest, in the first km of runout. Bold line is mean value, dashed/dotted lines are 5th and 95th percentile bounds. No-flow probability is also displayed. (Color figure online)

4   Conclusions

In this study, we have introduced a simple, robust statistically driven method for analyzing complex models. We have used 3 different models arising from different rheology assumptions. The data shows unambiguously the performance of the models across a wide range of possible flow regimes and topographies. We analyze local and global quantities and latent variables. The analysis of latent variables is particularly illustrative of the impact of modeling assumption. Knowledge of which assumptions dominate, and, by how much, at the level of assumptions will allow us to construct efficient models for desired inputs. Such model composition is the subject of ongoing and future work.

References

1. Dalbey, K., Patra, A.K., Pitman, E.B., Bursik, M.I., Sheridan, M.F.: Input uncertainty propagation methods and hazard mapping of geophysical mass flows. J. Geophys. Res.: Solid Earth **113**, 1–16 (2008). https://doi.org/10.1029/2006JB004471
2. Farrell, K., Oden, J.T., Faghihi, D.: A Bayesian framework for adaptive selection, calibration, and validation of coarse-grained models of atomistic systems. J. Comput. Phys. https://doi.org/10.1016/J.JCP.2015.03.071
3. Fischer, J., Kowalski, J., Pudasaini, S.P.: Topographic curvature effects in applied avalanche modeling. Cold Reg. Sci. Technol. **74–75**, 21–30 (2012). https://doi.org/10.1016/j.coldregions.2012.01.005
4. Martin Del Pozzo, A.M., Sheridan, M.F., Barrera, M., Hubp, J.L., Selem, L.V.: Potential hazards from Colima Volcano, Mexico. Geofis. Int. **34**, 363–376 (1995)
5. Patra, A.K., Bauer, A.C., Nichita, C.C., Pitman, E.B., Sheridan, M.F., Bursik, M., Rupp, B., Webber, A., Stinton, A.J., Namikawa, L.M., Renschler, C.S.: Parallel adaptive numerical simulation of dry avalanches over natural terrain. J. Volcanol. Geoth. Res. **139**(1–2), 1–21 (2005). https://doi.org/10.1016/j.jvolgeores.2004.06.014. http://linkinghub.elsevier.com/retrieve/pii/S0377027304002288
6. Pouliquen, O.: Scaling laws in granular flows down rough inclined planes. Phys. Fluids **11**(3), 542–548 (1999)
7. Rankine, W.J.M.: On the stability of loose earth. Phil. Trans. R. Soc. Lond. **147**(2), 9–27 (1857)
8. Rupp, B.: An analysis of granular flows over natural terrain. Master's thesis, University at Buffalo (2004)
9. Salm, B.: Flow, flow transition and runout distances of flowing avalanches. Ann. Glaciol. **18**, 221–226 (1993)
10. Saucedo, R., Macías, J.L., Bursik, M.: Pyroclastic flow deposits of the 1991 eruption of Volcán de Colima, Mexico. Bull. Volcanol. **66**(4), 291–306 (2004). https://doi.org/10.1007/s00445-003-0311-0
11. Saucedo, R., Macías, J., Bursik, M., Mora, J., Gavilanes, J., Cortes, A.: Emplacement of pyroclastic flows during the 1998–1999 eruption of Volcán de Colima, México. J. Volcanol. Geoth. Res. **117**(1), 129–153 (2002). https://doi.org/10.1016/S0377-0273(02)00241-X. http://www.sciencedirect.com/science/article/pii/S037702730200241X
12. Saucedo, R., Macías, J., Sheridan, M., Bursik, M., Komorowski, J.: Modeling of pyroclastic flows of Colima Volcano, Mexico: implications for hazard assessment. J. Volcanol. Geoth. Res. **139**(1), 103–115 (2005). https://doi.org/10.1016/j.jvolgeores.2004.06.019. http://www.sciencedirect.com/science/article/pii/S0377027304002343, modeling and Simulation of Geophysical Mass Flows
13. Savage, S.B., Hutter, K.: The motion of a finite mass of granular material down a rough incline. J. Fluid Mech. **199**, 177 (1989). https://doi.org/10.1017/S0022112089000340. http://journals.cambridge.org/article_S0022112089000340
14. Sheridan, M.F., Macías, J.L.: Estimation of risk probability for gravity-driven pyroclastic flows at Volcan Colima, Mexico. J. Volcanol. Geoth. Res. **66**(1), 251–256 (1995). https://doi.org/10.1016/0377-0273(94)00058-O. http://www.sciencedirect.com/science/article/pii/037702739400058O, models of Magnetic Processes and Volcanic Eruptions
15. Voellmy, A.: Über die Zerstörungskraft von Lawinen. Schweiz Bauzeitung **73**, 159–165, 212–217, 246–249, 280–285 (1955)
16. Webb, A.: Granular flow experiments to validate numerical flow model, TITAN2D. Master's thesis, University at Buffalo (2004)

Research on Technology Foresight Method Based on Intelligent Convergence in Open Network Environment

Zhao Minghui, Zhang Lingling[✉], Zhang Libin, and Wang Feng

University of Chinese Academy of Sciences, Beijing 100190, China
Zhaominghui1993@foxmail.com, zhangll@ucas.ac.cn

Abstract. With the development of technology, the technology foresight becomes more and more important. Delphi method as the core method of technology foresight is increasingly questioned. This paper propose a new technology foresight method based on intelligent convergence in open network environment. We put a large number of scientific and technological innovation topics into the open network technology community. Through the supervision and guidance to stimulate the discussion of expert groups, a lot of interactive information can be generated. Based on the accurate topic delivery, effective topic monitoring, reasonable topic guiding, comprehensive topic recovering, and interactive data mining, we get the technology foresight result and further look for the expert or team engaged in relevant research.

Keywords: Technology foresight · Intelligent convergence
Open network environment

1 Introduction

After 40 years of reform and opening up, China has entered a new historical stage of relying on scientific and technological progress to promote economic and social development. Economic and social development has relied more and more on scientific and technological innovation than ever before [1]. The report of the 19th NPC pointed out that innovation is the first impetus to development and a strategic support for building a modern economic system. More than 10 times mentioned science and technology, more than 50 times emphasized innovation [2].

Technical foresight is a systematic study of the future development of science, technology, economy and society, and the selection of strategic research fields and new generic technologies with the greatest economic and social benefits [3]. As a new tool for strategic analysis and integration, technology foresight creates a new mechanism that is more conducive to the formulation of long-term planning [4]. Technology foresight is an important means of support for strengthening macro-science and technology management capabilities, raising the level of science and technology strategic planning and optimizing the allocation of science and technology resources [5]. With the development of technology, the importance of technology foresight becomes more and more

© Springer International Publishing AG, part of Springer Nature 2018
Y. Shi et al. (Eds.): ICCS 2018, LNCS 10861, pp. 737–747, 2018.
https://doi.org/10.1007/978-3-319-93701-4_58

obvious. More and more countries, regions and organizations attach importance to it and form a global wave. The major developed countries such as the United States, Japan, the United Kingdom and Germany have stepped up their foresight research work on the trend of science and technology development. Some developing countries have also carried out technical foresight research. China has always attached great importance to the macro-strategy study of science and technology and actively carried out technical foresight and key national technology selection tasks, such as the Chinese Academy of Science in the next 20 years in terms of technology foresight research, the Beijing technology foresight action plan and the Shanghai science and technology priority field technology foresight work research plan [6].

The outcome of technology foresight activities depends much on the selection and use of the method. The notable feature of the Delphi method forecaster approach is its increased investment, long duration, and difficult outcome assessment [7], which is increasingly questioned as the scientific and validity of the core technology foresight approach [8, 9]. The development of technology foresight methods and the improvement of research quality are the frontiers and focuses of research in the field of technology foresight. Technology foresight research methods and models are still under continuous development. It is of great theoretical and practical value to carry out the research on methodology of technology foresight in this context.

2   Literature Review

Professor Ben Martin of the University of Sussex first proposed the concept of technology foresight in 1995 as a systematic study of the development of science and technology in the long term so as to determine the most economically and socially important areas of strategic research and major generic technologies [10]. The APEC and OECD also have similar definitions of technological foresight. Technology foresight studies key technologies and common technologies that maximize economic and social benefits based on systematic trends in science, technology, economy and society [11]. The definition of technical foresight in China is slightly biased. In the 2003 China Technology Foresight Report, technological foresight is a systematic study of science, technology, economy and social development in the longer term. Its goal is to identify areas of strategic research and to choose Technological group that has the greatest contribution to economic and social benefits [12]. In general, scholars at home and abroad have basically reached a consensus on the definition of technical foresight and content interpretation.

There are many kinds of technical foresight methods [13, 14], and the foreseeable methods of this dissertation are divided into exploratory predictions, normative predictions, exploratory and normative combinations [15]. Exploratory predictions predict the future of technology based on past and present knowledge. Exploratory foresight is more applicable to situations in which a new technology is predicted to evolve along a deterministic curve, which is thought to describe the inevitable future and almost impossible to influence or change future developments through planning [16]. Normative foresight first assesses future goals, needs, tasks, etc., and then dates back to the present, assuming that the situation to be assessed is reached, pointing out the ways in which these goals can be achieved. Normative foresight provides a reference for allocating the resources needed for the realization of technology [13].

Exploratory predictive methods such as growth curves, TFDEA, bibliometrics, patent analysis, social network analysis, data mining, etc.; normative predictive methods such as morphological analysis, analytic hierarchy process, etc.; exploratory And normative portfolio foresight, such as Delphi method, scenario analysis, cross impact analysis, technology roadmap and so on [17].

Delphi method is the core technology foreseen method [18], mostly using many rounds of expert interviews conducted large-scale consulting survey, the final expert opinion reached consensus to achieve the technical foresight. As technology evolves, large-scale expert surveys have been implemented and are used in a wide variety of applications. For example, in the key technologies and the identification of influencing factors: Some scholars use quantitative Delphi method in many rounds of expert surveys using questionnaires to collect expert opinion [19, 20]. Halal adopts online surveys and statistical methods to improve the efficiency and results of the delphi method [21]. Jun et al. provide patent analysis results to expert-assisted decision-making [22]. Such as science and technology strategy and policy making: Some scholars cluster the questionnaire feedback results [23]. The results of questionnaire analysis are used to support the development strategy and policy formulation of a certain technology, and the key influencing factors of technological development are screened [24]. Rohrbeck builds a network of experts based on interviews with experts and analyzes industry support technologies to advise on technology management in the enterprise [25]. Chen et al. Combined expert survey data with literature and patent data to describe the industry's technology trends using logical growth curve models and formulate patented technology development strategies accordingly [26]. Such as future technology demand forecast: Celiktas screened participants using bibliometrics and provided SWOT results to participants, then conducted an on-line questionnaire using the Delphi method to predict the technical needs for the future energy needs of Turkish countries [27]. Ivlev sets standards for assessment in terms of education, academic achievement and work experience, and provides a screening method for the Delphi method panel system [28].

3   Technology Foresight Method Based on Intelligent Convergence in Open Network Environment

Intelligent convergence in an open network environment will be an important way of predicting the technology, and may even be a disruptive way. Technology foresight are characterized by such characteristics as "crossover, destructiveness, permeability." The open network environment is characterized by "cross-border, openness and community penetration" hotbed". Examples include monitoring, analyzing, calculating and refining scientific and technological innovation topics through Facebook and Twitter social media.

We put a large number of scientific and technological innovation topics into the open network technology community. Through the supervision and guidance to stimulate the discussion of expert groups, we get a lot of interactive information including comments, likes and other interactive activities. Based on the interactive environment of human-human and human-machine, stimulating the emergence of experts' wisdom, putting accurate delivery on innovation topics, effectively monitoring, reasonably guiding, comprehensively recovering, and interactive data mining, we get the result forecasted and find Innovative topic-related research to solve the problem. Specific content as shown below (Fig. 1).

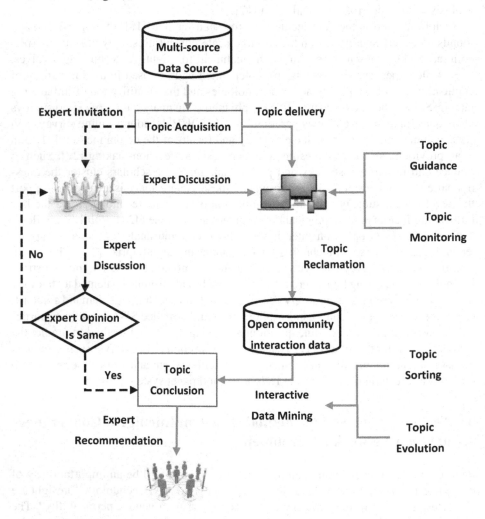

Fig. 1. Technology foresight frame based on intelligent convergence in open network environment

The research has the following innovations: (1) Propose a new method of technology foresight framework based on intelligent convergence in open network environment. Topic Acquisition - Topic Delivery - Topic Monitoring - Topic Guidance - Topic Reclamation - Interactive Data Mining - Topic Conclusion - Expert Testimonials. (2) The combination of qualitative and quantitative, which taking into account the subjective analysis and objective data. (3) The method of data mining for expert wisdom mining. (4) Not only technical foresight, but also problem solving, recommending experts and teams engaged in relevant research. (5) Make full use of open network environment for expert discussions with wide coverage, high participation and high feasibility. (6) Excavation of experts in an open network environment makes the process of technology foresight more automated and intelligent. (7) Based on the discussion of the original science and technology topic, explore the new topic of drift evolution.

4   Critical Technology Joints of Technology Foresight Method Based on Intelligent Convergence in Open Network Environment

The wisdom of science and technology groups under the open network environment will be an important way to produce innovative ideas, and may even be subversive. The group - wise analysis of this study will move from traditional artificial mode to artificial intelligence. The traditional intelligence analysis process relies on the experienced expert team, mainly adopts the mode of "presupposition logic framework + computer assistant processing + artificial judgment", this project will adopt the mode of "big data processing frame + computer depth learning + artificial assistant", which will be a kind of work mode based on artificial intelligence. The scientific and technological prediction based on literature and published scientific and technological information has very significant innovation, and is an important guarantee of this research. For example, the intelligence research institute like IARPA has implemented projects such as ace, fuse, forest, etc. Automatic discovery of scientific frontier and emerging technology from the mass of literature and invite science and technology experts to predict the trend of development to achieve Intelligent convergence.

Based on the large number of scientific and technological topics generated by the wisdom mining of scientific and technological groups, and put into the network technology community, through the guidance to stimulate the experts' speeches, discussions, comments, likes and other interactive behavior, will produce a large amount of interactive information. Based on this interactive information and related data, using the combination of data mining, expert mining, intelligent knowledge management and integrated research hall, thinking science and system science and other theories and methods, further digs out the group wisdom, and obtains the real basic, forward - looking, innovative and subversive science and technology topics.

4.1   Intelligent Delivery of Innovative Topic Based on Semantic Computing

The research content mainly includes the core expert portrait and the important organization portrait, the science and technology community portrait construction, the innovation idea topic and the science and technology community intelligence match, the innovation idea topic and the expert intelligence match (Fig. 2).

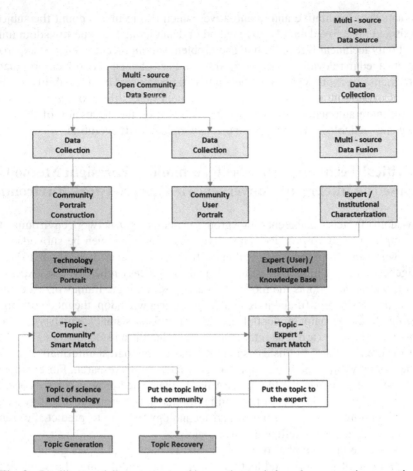

Fig. 2. Intelligence delivery process of innovative topic based on semantic computing

4.2   Intelligent Recycling of Innovative Topics Based on Topic Relevance

Put the topic of innovation into the relevant tech community, and invite relevant experts or users to participate in the discussion. The main research content of intelligent recycling of innovative topics based on topic relevance is how to recycle these discussions on innovative ideas periodically. Specifically, (1) weak relevance topic reply filtering. The two main difficulties in the intelligent recycling of innovative topics under open network environment are the dynamic evolution of topics and the sparsity of training samples. Direct use of recycled comments can lead to a bias in subsequent guidance, so a weak correlation topic comment needs to be filtered in the recovery process. (2) topic summary. There are too many redundant information in the science and technology community, the topic summary aims to extract a few sentences from the innovative topic and its comments for concise topic expression.

4.3 Intelligent Guidance of Innovative Topic Based on Information Recommendation

After the generation and delivery, based on the large data of literature information, real-time analysis and calculation of the topic background knowledge, topic perspective related background knowledge and the background knowledge of interactive information, and then recommend the relevant knowledge and information materials, to carry on the continuous guidance of the topic. The research scheme is shown in the following Fig. 3.

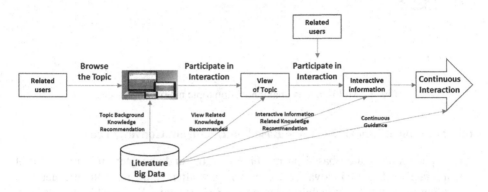

Fig. 3. Intelligent guidance of innovative topic based on information recommendation

4.4 Multi-dimensional Innovation Topic Monitoring and Targeted Guidance

In the whole system structure of this project, the overall effect of the topic is optimized through the topic monitoring module and topic guidance module. The monitoring module and the guide module separately undertake the role of topic launch effect evaluation and topic launch effect evaluation. Specifically, the information flow source of the guidance module includes the multi-dimensional evaluation of topic monitoring and the reasoning of public support knowledge map.

The main research content of topic monitoring includes: topic monitoring: focus tracking, monitoring review information, and monitoring the user login and interactive data in the community, identify the interaction of the problem solving. The main research content of topic guidance includes two parts: module activation and guidance action decision. The guiding action decision-making part is divided into five aspects: sensitive information block, topic answer correction, active topic active activation, topic answer depth guidance and topic answer multiple perspectives (Fig. 4).

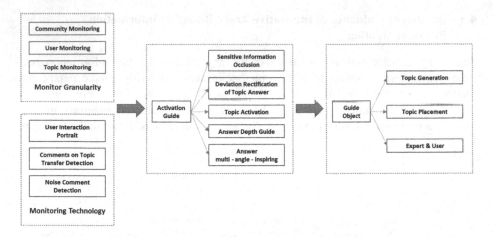

Fig. 4. Multi-dimensional innovation topic monitoring process

4.5 Solution of Innovative Topic Based on Intelligent Convergence

(1) Topic - regeneration based on machine learning and short text mining: A lot of interactive data of innovative topics will get after being put into the network community which is mainly composed of short texts. We use depth learning, parallel/distributed computing method, short text clustering to generate the topic.
(2) Sorting important topics based on expert experience: Users in the network community are a group of people with different cultural and professional backgrounds. How to evaluate their professional level and give scientific weight, which has an important impact on the ranking of the topics.
(3) Expert recommendation based on graph mining, expert mining, intelligent knowledge management and other technologies: Through the complete characterization of experts and establishment of scientific research social network find the high-level experts or teams who can undertake the topic research.

5 Empirical Study of Topic Sorting

This paper first constructs a scoring matrix to sort the topics. The abscissa is n topics in the same field (such as the advanced material field), and the ordinate is m users participating in the review. For example, if user i has commented on topic j, we will perform sentiment analysis on the comment and give a positive or negative score. This score needs to be multiplied with the weight of the commenting user to obtain a weighted score. In this way, a sparse matrix of n * m is formed. The sparse matrix is further calculated and the n topics are sorted. The final score is calculated as follows:

$$final\ score = comment\ score * expert\ weight$$

5.1 Calculation of Comment Score

Sentiment analysis is performed on the user i's comment on the topic j. This article uses crawler technology to crawl AI-related topics from Zhihu communities. Based on Chinese HowNet's Chinese emotional lexicon, the number of positive and negative emotional words matched is respectively obtained. The two tentative weights are both 0.5, final comment score is calculated as follows:

final comment Score = the number of positive words ∗ 0.5 − the number of negative words ∗ 0.5

5.2 Calculation of Expert Weight

According to the pre-set expert user index system, using the specific scoring rules and weights, the expert weights are calculated as follows (Fig. 5):

	user_ID	achieve	recog	page	include	resid	dipl	univ	fans	like	tha	sav	edi	score
0	闲吟客	0.0	0.0	0.0	1.0	0	PhD	加州理工学院 (California Institute of Technology)	2317.0	5205.0	1024.0	1888.0	90.0	5.0
1	韩迪	0.0	1.0	2.0	1.0	北京	博士	清华大学	61585.0	458078.0	64728.0	92080.0	566.0	5.0
2	吴辰晔	0.0	0.0	3.0	0.0	上海	0	清华大学	4735.0	4099.0	418.0	704.0	9.0	5.0
3	何之源	0.0	0.0	0.0	0.0	0	0	0	5248.0	0.0	0.0	0.0	0.0	1.4
4	Since	0.0	0.0	0.0	0.0	上海	硕士	上海交通大学	943.0	2231.0	439.0	831.0	51.0	1.3
5	暮暮迷了路	0.0	0.0	0.0	0.0	0	0	0	1685.0	10771.0	1172.0	723.0	90.0	1.9
6	李炎亮	0.0	0.0	0.0	0.0	陕西	0	0	6.0	4.0	0.0	6.0	2.0	1.0
7	耿锐	0.0	0.0	1.0	0.0	悉尼 (Sydney)	硕士	悉尼大学 (University of Sydney)	1649.0	2670.0	517.0	1317.0	0.0	5.0
8	jackxy	0.0	0.0	0.0	0.0	0	0	0	8.0	61.0	13.0	24.0	9.0	1.1
9	杨熠	0.0	0.0	0.0	0.0	0	0	北京邮电大学(BUPT)	13.0	5.0	2.0	6.0	15.0	1.0
10	zzzz	0.0	0.0	0.0	0.0	0	0	0	3.0	3.0	0.0	1.0	0.0	1.0

Fig. 5. Example of expert weight calculation result

The score of the comment is multiplied with the weight of the expert to get the score of the topic. According to the score, the degree of importance of the topic can be selected. Based on the thesaurus is a traditional sentiment analysis method, the next step we can use machine learning and other methods of supervised learning, and choose a method with higher accuracy.

6 Conclusion

The traditional method of technology foresight has the disadvantages of high cost, low accuracy and deviation of result. The technology foresight method based on intelligent convergence in open network environment combines the qualitative method with quantitative method and has obvious advantages in accuracy and objectivity. Based on the literature and published information, we get potential innovative topics. Then based on human - human, human - machine interaction environment, we discover innovative topic results and related important experts with the method of accurate topic delivery, effective topic monitoring, reasonable topic guidance, comprehensive topic recovery, and interactive data mining.

References

1. 穆荣平. 中国未来 20 年技术预见, (7) (2006). Mu, R.: Technology foresight of China in the next 20 years, (7) (2006)
2. 习近平. 中国共产党第十九次全国代表大会报告. 人民日报 (2017). Xi, J.: Report of the Ninth National Congress of the Communist Party of China. People's Daily (2017)
3. Martin, B.R.: Matching social needs and technological capabilities: research foresight and the implications for social sciences. Paper Presented at the OECD Workshop on Social Sciences and Innovation. United Nations University, Tokyo (2000)
4. 薛军, 杨耀武. 论技术预见及其在制定中长期科技规划中的作用. 软科学 19(1), 53–55 (2005). Xue J., Yang, Y.: On technology foresight and its role in formulating mid- and long-term S&T planning. Soft Sci. 19(1), 53–55 (2005)
5. 杨耀武. 技术预见:科技管理新的战略工具. 科技进步与对策 20(6), 19–21 (2003). Yang, Y.: Technology foresight: a new strategic tool for science and technology management. Sci. Technol. Prog. Policy 20(6), 19–21 (2003)
6. 杨幽红, 冯爱明. 我国技术预见研究现状分析. 科技管理研究 30(20), 218–221 (2010). Yang, Y., Feng, A.: Analysis of present situation of China's technology foresight research. Sci. Technol. Manag. Res. 30(20), 218–221 (2010)
7. Murry Jr., J.W., Hammons, J.O.: Delphi: a versatile methodology for conducting qualitative research. Rev. High. Educ. 18(4), 423–436 (1995)
8. Shin, T.: Delphi study at the multi-country level: gains and limitations. In: The Proceedings of International Conference on Technology Foresight: The Approach to and Potential For New Technology Foresight. National Institute of Science and Technology Policy, Japan (2001). www.nistep.go.jp/achiev/ftx/eng/mat077e/html/mat0771e.html
9. Tichy, G.: The over-optimism among experts in assessment and foresight. Technol. Forecast. Soc. Change 71(4), 341–363 (2004)
10. Martin, B.R.: Foresight in science and technology. Technol. Anal. Strateg. Manag. 7(2), 139–168 (1995)
11. 李万. APEC, UNIDO, OECD 与技术预见. 世界科学 (8), 40–41 (2002). Li, W.: APEC, UNIDO, OECD and technology foresight. World Sci. (8), 40–41 (2002)
12. 技术预测与国家关键技术选择研究组. 中国技术前瞻报告 2003. 中国科技论坛 (2), 53 (2004). Technology Forecasting and National Key Technology Selection Research Group: China technology preview report 2003. China Sci. Technol. Forum (2), 53 (2004)
13. Jantsch, E.: Technological Forecasting in Perspective: A Framework for Technological Forecasting, Its Technique and Organisation; A Description of Activities and an Annotated Bibliography. Organisation for Economic Co-operation and Development, Paris (1967)
14. Vanston, J.H.: Technology forecasting: a practical tool for rationalizing the R&D process. NTQ (New Telecom Q.) 4(1), 57–62 (1996)
15. Technology Futures Analysis Methods Working Group: Technology futures analysis: toward integration of the field and new methods. Technol. Forecast. Soc. Change 71(3), 287–303 (2004)
16. Roberts, E.B.: Exploratory and normative technological forecasting: a critical appraisal. Technol. Forecast. 1(2), 113–127 (1969)

17. 周源,刘怀兰,廖岭等. 基于主题模型的技术预见定量方法综述. 科技管理研究 **37**(11), 185–196 (2017). Zhou, Y., Liu, H., Liao, L., et al.: A quantitative review of quantitative methods based on topic models. Sci. Technol. Manag. Res. **37**(11), 185–196 (2017)
18. Grupp, H., Linstone, H.A.: National technology foresight activities around the globe: resurrection and new paradigms. Technol. Forecast. Soc. Change **60**(98), 85–94 (1999)
19. Borch, K., Rasmussen, B.: Commercial use of GM crop technology: identifying the drivers using life cycle methodology in a technology foresight framework. Technol. Forecast. Soc. Change **69**(8), 765–780 (2002)
20. Celiktas, M.S., Kocar, G.: Foresight analysis of wind power in Turkey. Int. J. Energy Res. **36**(6), 737–748 (2012)
21. Halal, W.E.: Forecasting the technology revolution: results and learnings from the TechCast project. Technol. Forecast. Soc. Change **80**(8), 1635–1643 (2013)
22. Jun, S., Lee, S.J., Ryu, J.B., et al.: A novel method of IP R&D using patent analysis and expert survey. Queen Mary J. Intellect. Prop. **5**(4), 474–494 (2015)
23. Rikkonen, P., Tapio, P.: Future prospects of alternative agro-based bioenergy use in Finland —Constructing scenarios with quantitative and qualitative Delphi data. Technol. Forecast. Soc. Change **76**(7), 978–990 (2009)
24. Ramasubramanian, V., Kumar, A., Prabhu, K.V., et al.: Forecasting technological needs and prioritizing factors in agriculture from a plant breeding and genetics domain perspective: a review. Indian J. Agric. Sci. **84**(3), 311–316 (2014)
25. Rohrbeck, R.: Harnessing a network of experts for competitive advantage: technology scouting in the ICT industry. R&D Manag. **40**(2), 169–180 (2010)
26. Chen, Y.H., Chen, C.Y., Lee, S.C.: Technology forecasting and patent strategy of hydrogen energy and fuel cell technologies. Fuel Energy Abstr. **36**(12), 6957–6969 (2011)
27. Celiktas, M.S., Kocar, G.: Hydrogen is not an utopia for Turkey. Int. J. Hydrog. Energy **35**(1), 9–18 (2010)
28. Ivlev, I., Kneppo, P., Barták, M.: Method for selecting expert groups and determining the importance of experts' judgments for the purpose of managerial decision-making tasks in health system. E A M Ekonomie A Manag. **18**(2), 57–72 (2015)

Prediction of Blasting Vibration Intensity by Improved PSO-SVR on Apache Spark Cluster

Yunlan Wang[✉], Jing Wang, Xingshe Zhou, Tianhai Zhao,
and Jianhua Gu

School of Computer Science, Center for High Performance Computing,
Northwestern Polytechnical University, Xi'an, Shaanxi, China
wangyl@nwpu.edu.cn

Abstract. In order to predict blasting vibration intensity accurately, support vector machine regression (SVR) was adopted to predict blasting vibration velocity, vibration frequency and vibration duration. The mutation operation of genetic algorithm (GA) is used to avoid the local optimal solution of particle swarm optimization (PSO). The improved PSO algorithm is used to search for the best parameters of SVR model. In the experiments, the improved PSO-SVR algorithm was realized on the Apache Spark platform. The execution time and prediction accuracy of the sadovski method, the traditional SVR algorithm, the neural network (NN) algorithm and the improved PSO-SVR algorithm were compared. The results show that the improved PSO-SVR algorithm on Spark is feasible and efficient, and the SVR model can predict the blasting vibration intensity more accurately than other methods.

Keywords: Blasting vibration intensity · Prediction algorithm
PSO-SVR · Spark · Big data

1 Introduction

In the blasting project, predicting the blasting vibration intensity accurately plays an important role in controlling the impact of blasting vibration. The blasting vibration intensity can be estimated by blasting vibration velocity, which is widely used around the world. In practice, sadovski formula is used to calculate blasting vibration velocity [1]. However, the method is not accurate because of the complex environment and many unknown factors in blasting. In order to predict velocity more accurately, Lv et al. used the non-linear regression method to calculate the parameters of the sadovski formula [2]. Shi et al. proposed to use the SVR model to predict velocity and compared SVR with the neural network (NN) method and sadovski method. The results showed that SVR turned out to be a better prediction method [3]. However, the parameters of SVR are empirically set. So it is unreliable to determine the blasting vibration velocity by the traditional SVR method.

Supported by Shaanxi science and technology innovation project plan. NO. 2016KTZDGY04-04.

Y. Shi et al. (Eds.): ICCS 2018, LNCS 10861, pp. 748–759, 2018.
https://doi.org/10.1007/978-3-319-93701-4_59

With the further study of blasting vibration, it has been found that blasting vibration frequency plays an important role in the destruction of buildings. When the vibration frequency is close to the inherent frequency of the building, resonance phenomenon may occur and the building can be easily destroyed. In addition, the vibration duration is an important attribute of blasting vibration intensity [4]. Therefore, we use vibration velocity, frequency and duration to predict the blasting vibration intensity, which is better to guide engineering blasting activities. Many scholars used NN that has three nodes in output layer to predict the above three variables simultaneously, and experiments showed that the relative error of NN was lower than other methods [5, 6, 7, 8]. However, NN method is easy to get the local minimum, and the key parameters, such as hidden layer nodes and learning rate, need to be manually set. Especially when there are abnormal points in the blasting data, the over-fitting feature will reduce the accuracy and the stability of NN model.

The work of this paper is as follows: (1) we combine genetic algorithm (GA) to adjust move direction of particles in PSO, and adopt the appropriate fitness function and encoding method; (2) we use improved PSO to search for the best parameters of SVR model, and use the best SVR model to predict the blasting vibration velocity, frequency and duration; (3) based on the blasting vibration data, we complete the improved PSO-SVR algorithm on the Apache Spark computing cluster, and compare prediction accuracy and time performance with other blasting vibration prediction methods. The results show that the improved PSO-SVR algorithm is more accurate, and it is feasible to predict blasting vibration intensity. Meanwhile, the algorithm is more efficient on the Spark cluster than on single node.

2 Improved PSO-SVR Algorithm

We use three algorithms which include support vector machine regression (SVR), particle swarm optimization (PSO) and genetic algorithm (GA). The SVR is used to predict the blasting vibration intensity, PSO is used to optimize the parameters of SVR, and GA is used to improve the PSO.

2.1 Support Vector Machine Regression

Support vector machine regression (SVR) is used to solve the non-linear regression problem. SVR has the following characteristics compared with other methods: (1) a few data can determine the optimal space, so it is not easy to be over-fitted; (2) the abnormal points of training data result in limited impact on the optimal space, thus the SVR model is stable. However, the prediction accuracy depends on the parameters of SVR model, including penalty parameter, insensitive loss coefficient, kernel function and kernel parameter.

(1) Penalty parameter: The penalty parameter is used to present the interval error and decide the complexity of the SVR model that is controlled by the number of support vectors. Small penalty parameter means that there is a relatively large interval, thus the resulting model is relatively simple.

(2) Insensitive loss coefficient: The insensitive loss coefficient is used to measure the interval error of each data sample. It also controls the complexity of the model. The larger the parameter is, the fewer the number of support vectors obtained and the simpler the SVR model is.

(3) Kernel function: The original feature space maps to the new feature space through the kernel function. Different kernel functions can get different SVR models with different regression functions, so the change of kernel functions will make a big difference in the prediction result of the SVR model [9]. Vol. N. explained the RBF is a better choice for the data without prior knowledge, since blasting vibration data lack of prior knowledge and distribution information [10]. The RBF is shown in formula (1).

$$K(x_i, x_j) = \exp\left(-\gamma \times \left\| x_i - x_j \right\|^2\right) \tag{1}$$

(4) Kernel parameter: The kernel parameter is related to the distribution characteristics of data. Xiao et al. showed that the performance of the SVR models may vary greatly depending on the different kernel parameters [11]. And Üstün et al. proved that when the value range is $\gamma = [0.01, 0.2]$, the predicted result of SVR model is well [12].

In summary, the selection of penalty parameter, insensitive loss coefficient, kernel function and kernel parameter largely determine the quality of the SVR model, and these parameters are related to specific data. Therefore, PSO algorithm is used to optimize parameters of SVR model, and make the prediction error of SVR model smallest. Thus the SVR model based on the blasting vibration data is more accurate.

2.2 Particle Swarm Optimization Algorithm

Particle swarm optimization (PSO) was proposed by Dr. Eberhart and Kennedy in 1995 [13], which was used to simulate foraging behavior of birds. In the description of PSO, each bird is treated as a particle, and each particle represents a potential solution in its own position. In each iteration, the particle adjusts the position and velocity according to the optimal position of the individual, the global optimum position and the position of the previous moment. The algorithm stops its iteration until it reaches to the predetermined termination condition.

We define particle's position at the moment t as Xi(t). The i particle's position is shown in formula (2).

$$X_i(t+1) = X_i(t) + V_i(t+1) \tag{2}$$

$X_i(t)$ represents multidimensional vector, and the number of dimensions depends on the number of parameters to be optimized. Velocity $V_i(t+1)$ is shown in formula (3).

$$V_i(t+1) = \omega V_i(t) + c_1 r_1(t)[pbest - X_i(t)] + c_2 r_2(t)[gbest - X_i(t)] \tag{3}$$

$V_i(t+1)$ can be initialized to 0 or a random value within a given range, ω is the inertia weight that describes the particle's ability to retain its inertia. c_1 and c_2 are learning factors which is usually equal to 2, $r_1(t)$ and $r_2(t)$ are random values between 0 and 1. Besides, *pbest* represents the best location of a particle and *gbest* represents the best position of all the particles.

$$p = \{C, \delta, \gamma\} \tag{4}$$

These parameters can be initialized based on their approximate value range. For example, Üstün et al. gave the range $C = [1, 10^8]$, $\delta = [0, 0.2]$ and $\gamma = [0.01, 0.2]$ [12]. The encoding method makes PSO algorithm be able to optimize multiple parameters simultaneously.

In this paper, the blasting data samples are divided into two parts, one part as training data and another one as test data. The prediction error of the test data can characterize the generalization ability of the SVR model. Therefore, we use the root mean square error (RMSE) function as fitness function to evaluate the quality of particles. The RMSE is shown in formula (5).

$$\text{RMSE} = \sqrt{\frac{1}{n} \sum_{i=1}^{n} (y_i - pre_i)} \tag{5}$$

In above equation, y_i represents the measured value, pre_i represents the predicted value of the SVR model and n is the number of test data samples. The smaller the RMSE is, the better the fitness is.

2.3 Application of Genetic Algorithm in PSO

The traditional PSO has the possibility of falling into the local optimal solution. The genetic algorithm (GA) can expand the search space through cross operation and mutation operation, and search for the optimal solution to avoid falling into the local optimum. In this paper, we introduce the mutation operation of GA into PSO, the mutation operation is performed on the particle with poor fitness so that the particle can jump out of current search space.

In the algorithm, particles with poor fitness can be defined as follows. For each iteration, when the RMSE of a particle exceeds average RMSE, it can be set as a poor particle, then we change the parameters of the poor particles. At least one parameter should be changed, which is randomly selected. If the fitness value of the changed particle is worse, it is discarded to restore the original position.

2.4 The Steps of Improved PSO-SVR Algorithm

We use the improved PSO to search for the best parameters of SVR model, then predict blasting vibration intensity with the best SVR model. The steps are as follows:

(1) Initialization: Initialize the particle swarm randomly, including population size, initial position and velocity, inertia weight, learn factors and other parameters.

(2) Computing fitness value: Compute the fitness value of every particle using the RMSE of the SVR model.

(3) Update *pbest* and *gbest*: For each particle, if the current fitness value is better than previous values of this particle, it would be taken as *pbest*. And *pbest* is compared with the best position of other particles, if it is better, then use it as *gbest*.

(4) Mutation operation: Select the poor particles to carry out mutation operation, and discard the mutation operation if the fitness value of the particle is worse.

(5) Change particle's position: The velocity and position of the particles are updated according to formula (2) and formula (3).

(6) Terminate the iteration: If any of the following termination conditions is met:
   a. the maximum number of iterations is reached;
   b. the resulting solution converges;
   c. the desired result is achieved.
   the process of the parameters optimization is terminated; otherwise return (2).

3 Parallel Design of Improved PSO-SVR on Spark Cluster

Spark is a computing engine designed for large-scale data processing, developed by AMP Labs at the UC Berkeley [14]. Master-slave architecture is adopted by it. In spark, the master node is responsible for scheduling tasks, called driver node and the slave node is used to execute the programs, called executor node. They run as separate processes and communicate with each other. Compared to Hadoop, the intermediate results of Spark can be stored in memory, which improves the efficiency of data accessing, so it is suitable for big data mining tasks.

In the case of large population size or large scale data, it will take long time to run PSO algorithm, and sometimes can not get the satisfied results. The improved PSO-SVR algorithm is parallelized on the Spark cluster. As shown in Fig. 1, the main steps of improved PSO-SVR on the Spark cluster are as follows:

(1) Initialization of the Spark: Python is used to implement the algorithm and spark-submit script of Spark is used to run the program. The SparkConf object is imported to configure application and SparkContext object is created to access Spark cluster.

(2) Data preprocessing: Firstly, the original blasting data is abstracted to resilient distributed dataset (RDD). Secondly, we deal with RDD, including removing duplicate data, filtering data, conversing data and so on, then store the new RDD to Hadoop Distributed File System (HDFS). If necessary, we should cache the data to memory using cache() or persist() method of RDD. After data preprocessing, the quality of blasting data are improved significantly.

(3) Train SVR model on data partitions: Before applying a specific algorithm, the data needs to be reasonably partitioned, and the number of RDD partitions should at least be equivalent to the number of CPU cores in the cluster, only in this way we can achieve full parallelism. Then we execute the improved PSO-SVR algorithm on each data partition to obtain multiple SVR models, and finally reserve the

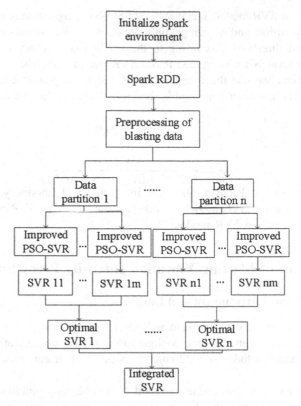

Fig. 1. The improved PSO-SVR algorithm on Spark

optimal SVR model. The process of training SVR model on data partitions is as follows.

- Initialization: For each data partition, multiple swarm of PSO are randomly initialized, including population size, initialing position and velocity and other parameters.
- Tasks distribution: Driver node requires resources from the cluster manager and distributes tasks to the executor nodes, then every work node executes algorithm task.
- PSO optimization: In each iteration of PSO, the particles move according to the position and velocity updating equation, and then carry on mutation operation according to the fitness values of particles.
- Terminate or not: If the termination condition is satisfied, the training process is ended, and the driver node redistributes the new task to the executor nodes.
- Terminate tasks: If all the tasks are completed, the driver node will terminate the executor nodes and release resources through the cluster manager.
- Return the best SVR: We get multiple SVR models from one data partition and return the best SVR model.

(4) Integration of SVR model: The improved PSO-SVR algorithm is implemented on each data partition, and we can get multiple optimal SVR models which meets the user-defined threshold. According to the prediction accuracy of SVR models, these SVR models are integrated into a SVR model using the weighted average method. Then we use the integrated SVR model to predict blasting vibration intensity. The integration method is shown in formulas (6) and (7).

$$y^* = \sum_{i=1}^{n} \omega_i y_i \tag{6}$$

$$\omega_i = \frac{ACC_i}{ACC_1 + ACC_2 + \ldots + ACC_n} \tag{7}$$

y^* represents the predicted result of the integrated SVR model, y_i represents the predicted value of every SVR model. ω_i indicates the weight of SVR model, which is related to the accuracy of SVR model.

4   Experiment of Blasting Vibration Intensity Prediction

4.1   Experimental Environment and Data

In the experiment, Spark runs on Hadoop YARN cluster manager. The Spark cluster has four cluster nodes with the same configuration, and the configuration is shown in Table 1. Each node includes two 12-core processors, so it can execute 24 jobs in parallel.

The experiment is based on one thousand of real blasting vibration data samples that provided by remote vibration measurement system developed by Shaanxi China-Blast Safety Web Technology Co., Ltd. Nine attributes of the blasting data is chosen, including the maximum charge per delay, total charge, horizontal distance, dilution time, etc. The properties predicted include blasting vibration velocity, frequency and duration. The blasting data is divided into two parts equally, one part is the training data and the other part is test data.

Table 1. Configuration of single node on Spark

Software and hardware	Configuration
CPU	Intel (R) Xeon (R) CPU E5-2650 v4 @ 2.20 GHz
Memory	128 GB
Network card	Gigabit
System disk	480G SSD
Other hard disk	5991.5 GB
Operation system	RedHat Enterprise Linux 6.3 x86_64
Hadoop version	Hadoop-2.7.4
Spark version	Spark-2.1.0

4.2 Comparison of Prediction Accuracy

We use four different methods to predict blasting vibration velocity, frequency and duration, including improved PSO-SVR, NN, traditional SVR and Sadovski method. The parameters of SVR models are showed in Table 2, including the empirical parameters of the traditional SVR model and optimized parameters of the improved PSO-SVR model for velocity, frequency and duration.

Table 2. The parameters of different SVR models

Model	Attribute	Parameters of SVR			
		C	δ	K	γ
Traditional SVR	Velocity	100	0.100	RBF	0.111
	Frequency	100	0.100	RBF	0.111
	Duration	100	0.100	RBF	0.111
Improved SVR	Velocity	24.795	0.101	RBF	0.016
	Frequency	74.716	0.056	RBF	0.007
	Duration	92.640	0.060	RBF	0.004

As shown in Table 2, the parameters of the traditional SVR model has the same empirical values for velocity, frequency and duration. The improved PSO-SVR method results in different parameters for them. The predicted results are shown in Figs. 2, 3 and 4. On the abscissa of every figure, thirty samples of test data are selected to show the predicted results.

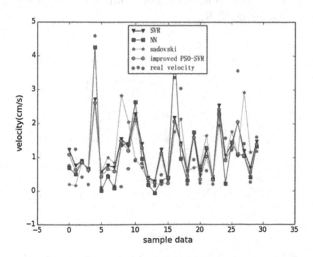

Fig. 2. The predicted results of blasting vibration velocity

As shown in Fig. 2, the scatter points show the real values of blasting vibration velocity, and the four polylines show the predicted values of four methods, including

NN, traditional SVR model, the sadovski method and the improved PSO-SVR method proposed in this paper. According to the figure, the velocity's variation trend of the four methods are similar, and the values predicted by NN and improved PSO-SVR method are much closer to the real values.

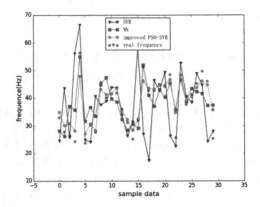

Fig. 3. The predicted results of blasting vibration frequency

As shown in Fig. 3, we use three methods to predict the blasting vibration frequency, including NN method, the traditional SVR method and the improved PSO-SVR method. It can be seen from the figure that the traditional SVR method has a large error between the predicted values and the real values, which is likely because the parameters of the SVR model is unreasonable, while the other two methods are much more precise than traditional SVR.

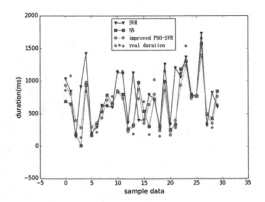

Fig. 4. The predicted results of blasting vibration duration

As shown in Fig. 4, there are three methods to predict blasting vibration duration, including the NN, the traditional SVR and the improved PSO-SVR. From the figure, we can see that the variation trend of NN method and improved PSO-SVR method are almost the same as the real values, while the prediction error of SVR method is relatively large.

From the above experimental results, it can be roughly seen that all of the four methods can predict the blasting vibration intensity. In order to evaluate the accuracy of different methods in detail, the relative error of the test data is used. The smaller the relative error is, the higher the prediction accuracy is. The relative error of different methods are shown in Table 3.

Table 3. Relative error of different methods (%)

Method	Blasting vibration intensity		
	Velocity	Frequency	Duration
Sadovski	41.7	–	–
SVR	20.3	22.1	24.6
NN	30.2	12.8	11.7
Improved PSO-SVR	19.4	8.4	11.5

Table 3 shows the relative errors of the four methods. For the prediction of blasting vibration velocity, the relative errors of SVR and the improved PSO-SVR are much lower than the other two methods. Besides, it can also be seen that the performance of sadovski formula is not good in velocity prediction. For the prediction of frequency and duration, NN and improved PSO-SVR are better than SVR, which means the parameters of SVR need to be determined by blasting data, rather than empirical value. In summary, the improved PSO-SVR algorithm has less error and better prediction ability than other algorithms in the prediction of blasting vibration intensity.

4.3   The Comparison of Running Time on Spark Cluster and Single Node

We achieve the improved PSO-SVR algorithm on the Spark cluster that consist of four nodes. We use ten thousand original blasting data and observe the difference in running time between single node and the Spark cluster.

As shown in Fig. 5, taking the blasting vibration velocity prediction as an example, we compare the running time of the improved PSO-SVR on single node with the Spark cluster of four nodes. When the amount of data is small, the running time on single node is shorter than that on the Spark cluster. The reason is that the initialization, resource allocation, data transmission and nodes communication on Spark cluster. With the data increases, the running time on the Spark cluster is less than single node and their ratio is close to 1/3, thus we infer that the ratio can approach 1/4 when the data is very large. Since there is enough memory at single node, the running time is not affected by memory. But the running time is related to the size of the data and the number of processors. Therefore, the running time on single node linearly increases with the data increases. However, the running time on the Spark cluster tends to increase slowly because there are four nodes to execute tasks in parallel.

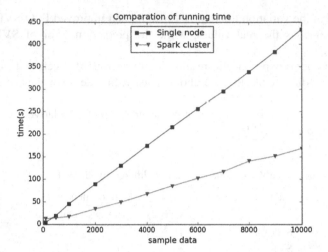

Fig. 5. The running time on single node and Spark cluster

5 Conclusion

Based on the real blasting data, the improved PSO algorithm is adopted to search for the best parameters of the SVR model, and the blasting vibration velocity, frequency and duration is predicted by the optimized SVR model. Results show that the relative prediction error of the improved PSO-SVR method is lower than the other methods. The experiment results also show that the parallel PSO-SVR algorithm on Spark cluster is more efficient than on single node.

However, there are still some problems to be studied in the future. For example, the selection of parameters in the PSO algorithm need to be optimized, and the kernel function of SVR model can be combined with the blasting data and specific application. Since the data is usually stored in multiple data sources such as HDFS and Oracle database, we will study how to access diversity data more quickly from Spark platform.

References

1. Jinxi, Z.: Applicability research of Sadov's vibration formula in analyzing of tunnel blasting vibration velocity. Fujian Constr. Sci. Technol. **5**, 68–70 (2011)
2. Lv, T., Shi, Y.-Q., Huang, C., Li, H., Xia, X., Zhou, Q.-C., Li, J.: Study on attenuation parameters of blasting vibration by nonlinear regression analysis. Geomechanics **28**(9), 1871–1878 (2007)
3. Shi, X., Dong, K., Qiu, X., Chen, X.: Analysis of the PPV prediction of blasting vibration based on support vector machine regression. Blasting **15**(3), 28–30 (2009)
4. Chen, S., Wei, H., Qian, Q.: The study on effect of structure vibration response by blast vibration duration. In: National Coal Blasting Symposium (2008)
5. Badrakh-Yeruul, T., Xia, A., Zhang, J., Wang, T.: Application of neural network based on genetic algorithm in prediction of blasting vibration. Blasting **3**, 140–144 (2014)

6. Xiuzhi, Z., Jianguang, X., Shouru, C.: Study of time and frequency analysis of blasting vibration signal and the prediction of blasting vibration characteristic parameters and damage. Vibr. Shock **28**(7), 73–76 (2009)
7. Wang, J., Huang, Y., Zhou, J.: BP neural network prediction for blasting vibration in open-pit coal mine (3), 322–328 (2016)
8. Mohamadnejad, M., Gholami, R., Ataei, M.: Comparison of intelligence science techniques and empirical methods for prediction of blasting vibrations. Tunn. Undergr. Space Technol. **28**, 238–244 (2012)
9. Qingjie, L., Guiming, C., Xiaofang, L., Qing, Y.: Genetic algorithm based SVM parameter composition optimization. Comput. Appl. Softw. **29**(4), 94–96 (2012)
10. Vol. N.: Learning With Kernels: Support Vector Machines, Regularization, Optimization, and Beyond/Learning Kernel Classifiers (2003). (J. Am. Stat. Assoc. **98**, 489–490)
11. Xiao, J., Yu, L., Bai, Y.: Survey of the selection of kernels and hyper-parameters in support vector regression. J. Southwest Jiaotong Univ. **43**(3), 297–303 (2008)
12. Üstün, B., Melssen, W.J., Oudenhuijzen, M., et al.: Determination of optimal support vector regression parameters by genetic algorithms and simplex optimization. Anal. Chim. Acta **544**(1), 292–305 (2005)
13. Eberhart, R., Kennedy, J.: A new optimizer using particle swarm theory (1995)
14. Karau, H.: Learning Spark - Lightning-Fast Big Data Analysis. Oreilly & Associates Inc., Newton (2015)

Bisections-Weighted-by-Element-Size-and-Order Algorithm to Optimize Direct Solver Performance on 3D hp-adaptive Grids

H. AbouEisha[1], V. M. Calo[2,3,4], K. Jopek[5], M. Moshkov[1], A. Paszyńska[6], and M. Paszyński[5(✉)]

[1] King Abdullah University of Science and Technology, Thuwal, Saudi Arabia
mikhail.moshkov@kaust.edu.sa
[2] Chair in Computational Geoscience, Applied Geology Department,
Western Australian School of Mines, Faculty of Science and Engineering,
Curtin University, Perth, WA, Australia
victor.calo@curtin.edu.au
[3] Mineral Resources, Commonwealth Scientific and Industrial Research Organization
(CSIRO), Kensington, WA 6152, Australia
[4] Curtin Institute for Computation, Curtin University, Perth, WA 6845, Australia
[5] Faculty of Computer Science, Electronics and Telecommunications,
AGH University of Science and Technology, al. Mickiewicza 30,
30-059 Krakow, Poland
paszynsk@agh.edu.pl
[6] Faculty of Physics, Astronomy and Applied Computer Science,
Jagiellonian University, Łojasiewicza 11, 30-348 Krakow, Poland
anna.paszynska@uj.edu.pl
http://home.agh.edu.pl/paszynsk

Abstract. The hp-adaptive Finite Element Method (hp-FEM) generates a sequence of adaptive grids with different polynomial orders of approximation and element sizes. The hp-FEM delivers exponential convergence of the numerical error with respect to the mesh size. In this paper, we propose a heuristic algorithm to construct element partition trees. The trees can be transformed directly into the orderings, which control the execution of the multi-frontal direct solvers during the hp refined finite element method. In particular, the orderings determine the number of floating point operations performed by the solver. Thus, the quality of the orderings obtained from the element partition trees is important for good performance of the solver. Our heuristic algorithm has been implemented in 3D and tested on a sequence of hp-refined meshes. We compare the quality of the orderings found by the heuristic algorithm to those generated by alternative state-of-the-art algorithms. We show 50% reduction in flops number and execution time.

The work was supported by National Science Centre, Poland grant no. DEC-2015/17/B/ST6/01867.

Keywords: *hp* adaptive finite element method · Ordering
Nested-dissections · Multi-frontal direct solvers · Heuristic algorithms

1 Introduction

The finite element method [19] is a widely used approach finding an approximate solution of partial differential equations (PDEs) specified along with boundary conditions and a solution domain. A mesh with hexahedral elements is created to cover the domain and to approximate the solution over it. Then the weak form of the PDE is discretized using polynomial basis functions spread over the mesh. The *hp*-adaptive Finite Element Method (*hp*-FEM) is the most sophisticated version of FEM [9]. It generates a sequence of refined grids, providing exponential convergence of the numerical error with respect to the mesh size. The *hp*-FEM algorithm uses the coarse and the fine meshes in each iteration to compute the relative error and to guide the adaptive refinement process. Selected finite elements are broken into smaller elements. This procedure is called the *h*-refinement. Also, the polynomial orders of approximation are updated on selected edges, faces, and interiors. This procedure is called the *p*-refinement. In selected cases, both *h* and *p* refinements are performed, and this process is called the *hp*-refinement.

The *hp*-FEM is used to solve difficult PDEs, e.g. with local jumps in material data, with boundary layers, strong gradients, generating local singularities, requiring elongated adaptive elements, or utilization of elements with several orders of magnitude difference in dimension. For such kind of meshes iterative solvers deliver convergence problems.

This paper is devoted to the optimization of the element partition trees controlling the LU factorization of systems of linear equations resulting from the *hp*-FEM discretizations over three-dimensional meshes with hexahedral elements. In this paper we focus on a class of *hp* adaptive grids, which has many applications in different areas of computational science and several possible implementations [6–9,21,22,26–28]. The LU factorization for the case of *hp*-adaptive finite element method is performed using multi-frontal direct solvers, such as e.g. MUMPS solver [2–4]. This is because the matrices resulting from the discretization over the computational meshes are sparse, and smart factorization will generate a low number of additional non-zero entries (so-called fill-in) [17,18]. The problem of finding the optimal permutation of the sparse matrix which minimizes the fill-in (the number of new non-zero entries created during the factorization) is NP-complete [29]. In this paper, we propose a heuristic algorithm that works for arbitrary *hp*-adaptive gird, with finite elements of different size and with a different distribution of polynomial orders of approximation spread over finite element edge, faces, and possibly interiors. The algorithm performs recursive weighted partitions of the graph representing the computational mesh and uses these partitions to generate an ordering, which minimizes the fill-in in a quasi-optimal way. The partitions are defined by so-called element partition tree, which can be transformed directly into the ordering.

In this paper we focus on the optimization of the sequential in-core multi-frontal solver [11–13], although the orderings obtained from our element partition trees can be possibly utilized to speed up shared-memory [14–16] or distributed-memory [2–4] implementations as well. This will be the topic of our future work.

The heuristic algorithm proposed in this paper is based on the insights we gained in [1], where we proposed a dynamic programming algorithm to search for quasi-optimal element partition trees. These quasi-optimal trees obtained in [1] are too expensive to generate, and they cannot be used in practice, but rather guide our heuristic methods. From the insights garnered from this optimization process, we have proposed a heuristic algorithm that generates quasi-optimal element partition trees for arbitrary h-refined grids in 2D and 3D. In this paper, we generalize the idea presented in [1] to the class of hp-adaptive grids. The heuristic algorithm uses multilevel recursive bisections with weights assigned to element edges, faces, and interiors. Our heuristic algorithm has been implemented and tested in three-dimensional case. It generates mesh partitions for arbitrary hp-refined meshes, by issuing recursive calls to $METIS\_WPartGraphRecursive$. That is, we use the multilevel recursive bisection implemented in METIS [20] available through the MUMPS interface [2–4], to find a balanced partition of a weighted graph. We construct the element partition tree by recursive calls of the graph bisection algorithm. Our algorithm for the construction of the element partition tree and the corresponding ordering differs from the orderings used by the METIS library (nested dissection) as follows. First, we use a smaller graph, built from the computational mesh, with vertices representing the finite elements and edges representing the adjacency between elements. Second, we weight the vertices of the graph by the volume of finite elements multiplied by the polynomial orders of approximations in the center of the element. Third, we weight the edges of the graph by the polynomial orders of approximations over element faces.

Previously [23, 24], we have proposed bottom-up approaches for constructing element partition trees for h-adaptive grids. Herein, we propose an alternative algorithm, bisections-weighted-by-element-size-and-order, to construct element partition trees using a top-down approach, for hp-adaptive grids. The element size in our algorithm is a proxy for refinement level of the element. The order is related to the polynomial degrees used on finite element edges, faces and interiors.

The plan of the paper is the following. We first define the computational mesh and basis functions which illustrate how these computational grids are transformed into systems of linear equations using the finite element method. Then, we describe the idea of a new heuristic algorithm which uses bisections weighted by elements sizes and polynomial orders of approximation. We show how the ordering can be generated from our element partition tree. The next section includes numerical tests which compare the number of floating point operations and wall-clock time resulting from the execution of the multi-frontal direct solver algorithm on the alternative orderings under analysis.

2 Meshes, Matrices and Orderings for the hp-adaptive Finite Element Methods

We introduce a class of computational meshes that results from the application of an adaptive finite element method [9]. For our analysis, we start from a three-dimensional boundary-value elliptic partial differential equation problem in its weak (variational) form given by (1): Find $u \in V$ such that

$$b\,(u,v) = l\,(v) \quad \forall v \in V \tag{1}$$

where $b\,(u,v)$ and $l\,(v)$ are some problem-dependent bilinear and linear functionals, and

$$V = \{v : \int_{\Omega} \|v\|^2 + \|\nabla v\|^2 dx < \infty, tr\,(v) = 0 \text{ on } \Gamma_D\} \tag{2}$$

is a Sobolev space over an open set Ω called the domain, and Γ_D is the part of the boundary of Ω where Dirichlet boundary conditions are defined.

For a given domain Ω the hp-FEM constructs a finite dimensional subspace $V_{hp} \subset V$ with a finite dimensional polynomial basis given by $\{e^i_{hp}\}_{i=1,\ldots,N_{hp}}$. The subspace V_{hp} is constructed by partitioning the domain Ω into three-dimensional finite elements, with vertices, edges, faces, and interiors, as well as shape functions defined over these objects.

Namely, we introduce one-dimensional shape-functions

$$\hat{\chi}_1(\xi) = 1 - \xi; \quad \hat{\chi}_2(\xi) = \xi; \quad \hat{\chi}_l(\xi) = (1 - \xi)\xi(2\xi - 1)^{l-3}, l = 4,\ldots,p+1 \tag{3}$$

where p is the polynomial order of approximation, and we utilize them to define the three-dimensional hexahedral finite element $\{(\xi_1, \xi_2, \xi_3) : \xi_i \in [0,1], i = 1,3\}$. We define eight shape functions over the eight vertices of the element:

$$\hat{\phi}_1(\xi_1,\xi_2,\xi_3) = \hat{\chi}_1(\xi_1)\hat{\chi}_1(\xi_2)\hat{\chi}_1(\xi_3) \quad \hat{\phi}_2(\xi_1,\xi_2,\xi_3) = \hat{\chi}_2(\xi_1)\hat{\chi}_1(\xi_2)\hat{\chi}_1(\xi_3)$$
$$\hat{\phi}_3(\xi_1,\xi_2,\xi_3) = \hat{\chi}_2(\xi_1)\hat{\chi}_2(\xi_2)\hat{\chi}_1(\xi_3) \quad \hat{\phi}_4(\xi_1,\xi_2,\xi_3) = \hat{\chi}_1(\xi_1)\hat{\chi}_2(\xi_2)\hat{\chi}_1(\xi_3)$$
$$\hat{\phi}_5(\xi_1,\xi_2,\xi_3) = \hat{\chi}_1(\xi_1)\hat{\chi}_1(\xi_2)\hat{\chi}_2(\xi_3) \quad \hat{\phi}_6(\xi_1,\xi_2,\xi_3) = \hat{\chi}_2(\xi_1)\hat{\chi}_1(\xi_2)\hat{\chi}_2(\xi_3)$$
$$\hat{\phi}_7(\xi_1,\xi_2,\xi_3) = \hat{\chi}_2(\xi_1)\hat{\chi}_2(\xi_2)\hat{\chi}_2(\xi_3) \quad \hat{\phi}_8(\xi_1,\xi_2,\xi_3) = \hat{\chi}_1(\xi_1)\hat{\chi}_2(\xi_2)\hat{\chi}_2(\xi_3) \tag{4}$$

$j = 1,\ldots, p_i - 1$ shape functions over each of the twelve edges of the element

$$\hat{\phi}_{9,j}(\xi_1,\xi_2,\xi_3) = \hat{\chi}_{2+j}(\xi_1)\hat{\chi}_1(\xi_2)\hat{\chi}_1(\xi_3) \quad \hat{\phi}_{10,j}(\xi_1,\xi_2,\xi_3) = \hat{\chi}_2(\xi_1)\hat{\chi}_{2+j}(\xi_2)\hat{\chi}_1(\xi_3)$$
$$\hat{\phi}_{11,j}(\xi_1,\xi_2,\xi_3) = \hat{\chi}_{2+j}(\xi_1)\hat{\chi}_2(\xi_2)\hat{\chi}_1(\xi_3) \quad \hat{\phi}_{12,j}(\xi_1,\xi_2,\xi_3) = \hat{\chi}_1(\xi_1)\hat{\chi}_{2+j}(\xi_2)\hat{\chi}_1(\xi_3)$$
$$\hat{\phi}_{13,j}(\xi_1,\xi_2,\xi_3) = \hat{\chi}_{2+j}(\xi_1)\hat{\chi}_1(\xi_2)\hat{\chi}_2(\xi_3) \quad \hat{\phi}_{14,j}(\xi_1,\xi_2,\xi_3) = \hat{\chi}_2(\xi_1)\hat{\chi}_{2+j}(\xi_2)\hat{\chi}_2(\xi_3)$$
$$\hat{\phi}_{15,j}(\xi_1,\xi_2,\xi_3) = \hat{\chi}_{2+j}(\xi_1)\hat{\chi}_2(\xi_2)\hat{\chi}_2(\xi_3) \quad \hat{\phi}_{16,j}(\xi_1,\xi_2,\xi_3) = \hat{\chi}_1(\xi_1)\hat{\chi}_{2+j}(\xi_2)\hat{\chi}_2(\xi_3)$$
$$\hat{\phi}_{17,j}(\xi_1,\xi_2,\xi_3) = \hat{\chi}_1(\xi_1)\hat{\chi}_1(\xi_2)\hat{\chi}_{2+j}(\xi_3) \quad \hat{\phi}_{18,j}(\xi_1,\xi_2,\xi_3) = \hat{\chi}_2(\xi_1)\hat{\chi}_1(\xi_2)\hat{\chi}_{2+j}(\xi_3)$$
$$\hat{\phi}_{19,j}(\xi_1,\xi_2,\xi_3) = \hat{\chi}_2(\xi_1)\hat{\chi}_2(\xi_2)\hat{\chi}_{2+j}(\xi_3) \quad \hat{\phi}_{20,j}(\xi_1,\xi_2,\xi_3) = \hat{\chi}_1(\xi_1)\hat{\chi}_2(\xi_2)\hat{\chi}_{2+j}(\xi_3)$$
$$\tag{5}$$

where p_i is the polynomial order of approximation utilized over the i-th edge. We also define $(p_{ih} - 1) \times (p_{iv} - 1)$ shape functions for $j = 1, \ldots, p_{ih} - 1$ and $k = 1, \ldots, p_{iv} - 1$, over each of six faces of the element

$$\hat{\phi}_2 1(\xi_1, \xi_2, \xi_3) = \hat{\chi}_{2+j}(\xi_1)\hat{\chi}_{2+k}(\xi_2)\hat{\chi}_1(\xi_3) \quad \hat{\phi}_2 2(\xi_1, \xi_2, \xi_3) = \hat{\chi}_{2+j}(\xi_1)\hat{\chi}_{2+k}(\xi_2)\hat{\chi}_2(\xi_3)$$

$$\hat{\psi}_2 3(\zeta_1, \zeta_2, \xi_3) = \hat{\chi}_{2+j}(\xi_1)\hat{\chi}_1(\xi_2)\hat{\chi}_{2+k}(\xi_3) \quad \hat{\phi}_2 4(\xi_1, \xi_2, \xi_3) = \hat{\chi}_2(\xi_1)\hat{\chi}_{2+j}(\xi_2)\hat{\chi}_{2+k}(\xi_3)$$

$$\hat{\phi}_2 5(\xi_1, \xi_2, \xi_3) = \hat{\chi}_{2+j}(\xi_1)\hat{\chi}_2(\xi_2)\hat{\chi}_{2+k}(\xi_3) \quad \hat{\phi}_2 6(\xi_1, \xi_2, \xi_3) = \hat{\chi}_1(\xi_1)\hat{\chi}_{2+j}(\xi_2)\hat{\chi}_{2+k}(\xi_3)$$

$$(6)$$

where p_{ih}, p_{iv} are the polynomial orders of approximations in two directions in the i-th face local coordinates system. Finally, we define $(p_x-1) \times (p_y-1) \times (p_z-1)$ basis functions over an element interior

$$\hat{\phi}_{27,ij}(\xi_1, \xi_2) = \hat{\chi}_{2+i}(\xi_1)\hat{\chi}_{2+j}(\xi_2)\hat{\chi}_{2+k}(\xi_3) \tag{7}$$

where (p_x, p_y, p_z) are the polynomial orders of approximation in three directions, respectively, utilized over an element interior. The shape functions from the adjacent elements that correspond to identical vertices, edges, or faces, they are merged to form global basis functions.

The support interactions of the basis functions defined over the mesh determine the sparsity pattern for the global matrix.

In the example presented in Fig. 1 there are first order polynomial basis functions associated with element vertices, second order polynomials associated with element edges, and second order polynomials in both directions, associated with element interiors. For more details we refer to [9].

We illustrate these concepts with two-dimensional example. Figure 1 presents an exemplary two-dimensional mesh consisting of rectangular finite elements with vertices, edges and interiors, as well as shape functions defined over vertices, edges and interiors of rectangular finite elements of the mesh.

The interactions of supports of basis functions defined over the mesh define the sparsity pattern for the global matrix. In other words, i-th row and j-th column of the matrix is non-zero, if supports of i-th and j-th basis functions overlap. For example, for the $p = 1$ case the global matrix looks like it is presented in Fig. 2. In this case, only vertex functions are present. For $p = 2$, all the basis functions are interacting, and this corresponds to the case presented in Fig. 3.

Traditional sparse matrix solvers construct the ordering based on the sparsity pattern of the global matrix. This is illustrated in the top path in Fig. 4. The sparse matrix is submitted to an ordering generator, e.g., the nested-dissections [20] or the AMD [5] algorithms from the METIS library. The ordering is utilized later to permute the sparse matrix, which results in less non-zero entries generated during the factorization, and lower computational cost of the factorization procedure. In the meantime, the elimination tree is constructed internally by the sparse solver, which guides the elimination procedure[1].

---

[1] In [25] the name elimination tree was also used for the element partition tree.

The alternative approach is discussed in this paper. We construct the element partition tree based on the structure of the computational mesh, using the weighted bisections algorithm. The element partition tree is then browsed in post-order, to obtain the ordering, which defines how to permute the sparse matrix. This is illustrated on the bottom path presented in Fig. 4. For a detailed description on how to construct ordering based on an element partition tree, we refer to Chap. 8 of the book [25].

The sparsity pattern of the matrix rather not depend on the elliptic PDE being solved over the mesh. It strongly depends on the basis functions and the topology of the computational mesh.

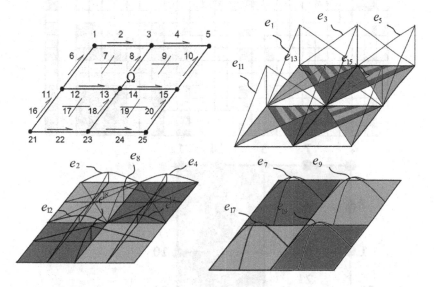

Fig. 1. Examplary four element mesh and basis functions spread over the mesh

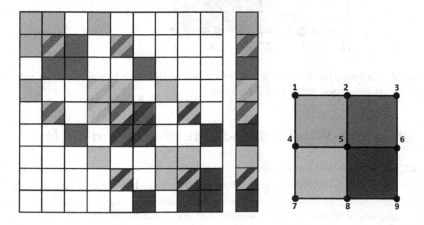

Fig. 2. Matrix resulting from four element mesh with $p = 1$ vertex basis functions.

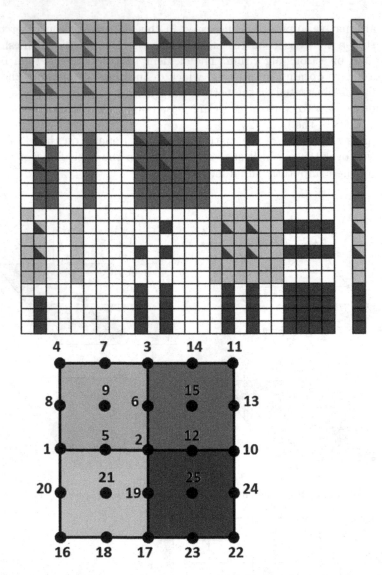

Fig. 3. Matrix resulting from four element mesh with $p = 2$ basis functions related to element vertices, edges, faces and interios.

3 Bisections-Weighted-by-Element-Size-and-Order

The algorithm of bisections-weighted-by-element-size-and-order creates an initial undirected graph G for finite element mesh. Each node of the graph corresponds to one finite element from the mesh. An edge in the graph G exists if the corresponding finite elements have a common face. Additionally, each node of the graph G has an attribute *size* that is defined as follows. For the regular meshes,

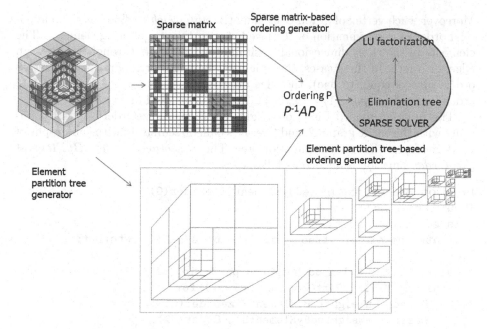

Fig. 4. The construction of the ordering based on sparsity pattern of the matrix, and based on the element partition tree.

GRAPH: VERTICES = ELEMENTS
      WEIGHT   = SCALED ELEMENT SIZE * ORDER OF APPROXIMATION
      EDGES   = ADJACENCY RELATION
      WEIGHT   = ORDER OF APPROXIMATION

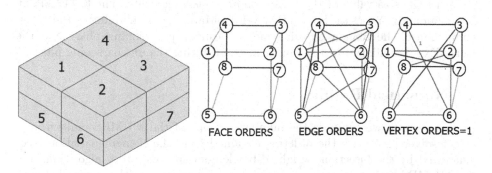

Fig. 5. The exemplary three-dimensional mesh and its weighted graph representation.

as considered in this paper, the size of an element is defined as the volume of the element times the order of the element. For general three-dimensional grids, the volume attribute is defined as the function of a refinement level of an element:

$$volume = 2^{(3*(max\_refinement\_level - refinement\_level))}(p_x - 1)(p_y - 1)(p_z - 1) \quad (8)$$

Moreover, each vertex of graph G has an attribute *weight* defined as the polynomial order of approximation of the face between two neighboring elements. The elements in the three-dimensional mesh may be neighbors through a vertex, an edge, or a face. In these cases, the weight of the edge corresponds to the vertex order (always equal to one), the edge order (defined as $p_{edge} - 1$) or the face order (defined as $(p_{ih} - 1) \times (p_{iv} - 1)$. This is illustrated in Fig. 5.

The function named BisectionWeightedByElementSizeOrder() is called initially with the entire graph G, and later it is called recursively with sub-graphs of G. It generates the element partition tree. The $BisectionWeightedByElement$ $SizeOrder$ function is defined as follows:

```
function BisectionWeightedByElementSizeOrder(G)
If number of nodes in G
   is equal to 1 then
   create one element tree t with the node v ∈ G; return t;
else
   Calculate the balanced weighted partition of G into G1 and G2;
   //calling METIS WPartGraphRecursive() for G
   t1 = BisectionWeightedByElementSizeOrder(G1);
   t2 = BisectionWeightedByElementSizeOrder(G2);
   create new root node t with left child t1 and right child t2
   return t
endif
```

Once the algorithm generates the element partition tree, we extract the ordering and call a sequential solver. Herein, we use METIS_WPartGraphRecursive [20] function to find a balanced partition of a graph, where weights on vertices are equal to the size value of the corresponding mesh elements. The METIS_WPart GraphRecursive uses the Sorted Heavy-EdgeMatching method during the coarsening phase, the Region Growing method during partitioning phase and the Early-Exit Boundary FM refinement method during the un-coarsening phase.

4   Numerical Results

In this section, we compare the number of flops of the MUMPS multi-frontal direct solver [2–4] with the ordering obtained from the element partition trees generated by the bisections-weighted-by-element-size-and-order algorithm, and the MUMPS with automatic selection of the ordering algorithm, compiled with $icntl(7) = 7$. The MUMPS solver chooses either nested-dissection [20] or approximate minimum degree algorithm [5] for this kind of problem, depending on the properties of the sparse matrix. We focus on the model Fichera problem [9,10]: Find u temperature scalar field such that $\nabla u = 0$ on Ω being 7/8 of the cube, with zero Dirichlet b.c. on the internal 1/8 boundary, and Neumann b.c. on the external boundary, computed from the manufactured solution. This model problem has strong singularities at the central point, and along the three internal edges, thus the intensive refinements are required.

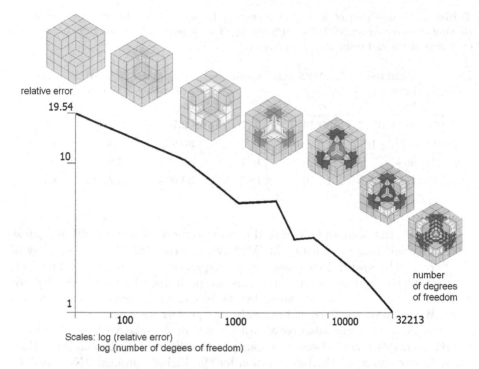

Fig. 6. Exponential convergence of the numerical error with respect to the mesh size for the model Fichera problem, obtained on the generated sequence of coarse grids. The corresponding fine grids are not presented here.

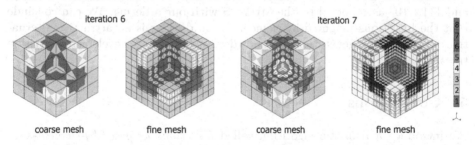

Fig. 7. Coarse and fine meshes of hp-FEM code for the Fichera problem. Various polynomial orders of approximation on element edges, faces and interiors are denoted by different colors. (Color figure online)

The hp-FEM code generates a sequence of hp-refined grids delivering exponential convergence of the numerical error with respect to the mesh size, as presented in Fig. 6. The comparison of flops and wall time concerns the last two grids, the coarse, and the corresponding fine grids, generated by the hp-FEM algorithm, with various polynomial orders of approximation, and element sizes, as presented in Fig. 7. It is summarized in Table 1.

Table 1. Comparison of flops and execution times between bisection-weighted-by-element-size-and-order, with MUMPS equipped with automatic generation of ordering on different three-dimensional adaptive grids.

N	Weighted bisections flops	MUMPS flops	Ratio flops	Weighted bisections time [s]	MUMPS time [s]	Ratio time [s]
3,958	$119 * 10^6$	$140 * 10^6$	1.17	2.7 s	4.52 s	1.67
32,213	$4,797 * 10^6$	$9,469 * 10^6$	1.90	36.02 s	43.21 s	1.19
94,221	$56 * 10^9$	$111 * 10^9$	1.97	14.49 s	28.29 s	1.95
139,425	$132 * 10^9$	$254 * 10^9$	1.92	33.06 s	67.94 s	2.05

To verify the flops and the wall-time performance of our algorithm against alternative ordering provided by MUMPS, we use the PERM IN input array of the library. The hp-FEM code generates a sequence of optimal grids. The decisions about the optimal mesh refinements are performed by using the reference solution on the fine grids, obtained by the global hp-refinement of the coarse grids. We compare the flops and the wall time-performance on the last two iterations performed by the adaptive algorithm, where the relative error, defined as the H1 norm difference between the coarse and the fine mesh solutions is less than 1.0%. In particular, on the last iteration for the Fichera problem (N = 139,425) MUMPS with its default orderings used 67.94 s while with our ordering it used 33.06 s. The number of floating point operations required to perform the factorizations was $254 * 10^9$ as reported by the MUMPS with automatic ordering, and $111 * 10^9$ as reported by the MUMPS with our ordering. We can conclude that the bisections-weighted-by-element-size-and-order is an attractive alternative algorithm for generation of the ordering based on the element partition trees.

5   Conclusions

We introduce a heuristic algorithm called *bisections-weighted-by-element-size-and-order* that utilizes a top-down approach to construct element partition trees. We compare the trees generated by our algorithm against the alternative state-of-the-art ordering algorithms, on a three-dimensional hp-refined grids used to solve the model Fichera problem. We conclude that our ordering algorithm can deliver up to 50% improvement against the state-of-the-art orderings used by MUMPS both in floating-point operations counts as well as wall time.

References

1. AbouEisha, H., Calo, V.M., Jopek, K., Moshkov, M., Paszyńska, A., Paszyński, M., Skotniczny, M.: Element partition trees for two- and three-dimensional h-refined meshes and their use to optimize direct solver performance. Dyn. Program. Int. J. Appl. Math. Comput. Sci. (2017, accepted)
2. Amestoy, P.R., Duff, I.S.: Multifrontal parallel distributed symmetric and unsymmetric solvers. Comput. Methods Appl. Mech. Eng. **184**, 501–520 (2000). https://doi.org/10.1016/S0045-7825(99)00242-X
3. Amestoy, P.R., Duff, I.S., Koster, J., L'Excellent, J.-Y.: A fully asynchronous multifrontal solver using distributed dynamic scheduling. SIAM J. Matrix Anal. Appl. **1**(23), 15–41 (2001). https://doi.org/10.1137/S0895479899358194
4. Amestoy, P.R., Guermouche, A., L'Excellent, J.-Y., Pralet, S.: Hybrid scheduling for the parallel solution of linear systems. Comput. Methods Appl. Mech. Eng. **2**(32), 136–156 (2011). https://doi.org/10.1016/j.parco.2005.07.004
5. Amestoy, P.R., Davis, T.A., Du, I.S.: An approximate minimum degree ordering algorithm. SIAM J. Matrix Anal. Appl. **17**(4), 886–905 (1996). https://doi.org/10.1137/S0895479894278952
6. Babuśka, I., Rheinboldt, W.C.: Error estimates for adaptive finite element computations. SIAM J. Num. Anal. **15**, 736–754 (1978). https://doi.org/10.1137/0715049
7. Babuska, I., Guo, B.Q.: The h, p and hp version of the finite element method: basis theory and applications. Adv. Eng. Softw. **15**(3–4), 159–174 (1992). https://doi.org/10.1016/0965-9978(92)90097-Y
8. Becker, R., Kapp, J., Rannacher, R.: Adaptive finite element methods for optimal control of partial differential equations: basic concept. SIAM J. Control Optim. **39**, 113–132 (2000). https://doi.org/10.1137/S0363012999351097
9. Demkowicz, L., Kurtz, J., Pardo, D., Paszyński, M., Rachowicz, W., Zdunek, A.: Computing with hp Adaptive Finite Element Method. Part II. Frontiers: Three Dimensional Elliptic and Maxwell Problems with Applications. Chapmann & Hall, CRC Press, Boca Raton, London, New York (2007)
10. Demkowicz, L., Pardo, D., Rachowicz, W.: Fully automatic hp-adaptivity in three-dimensions. Comput. Methods Appl. Mech. Eng. **196**(37–40), 4816–4842 (2006). https://doi.org/10.1023/A:1015192312705
11. Duff, I.S., Erisman, A.M., Reid, J.K.: Direct Methods for Sparse Matrices. Oxford University Press Inc., New York (1986)
12. Duff, I.S., Reid, J.K.: The multifrontal solution of indefinite sparse symmetric linear. ACM Trans. Math. Softw. **9**(3), 302–325 (1983). https://doi.org/10.1145/356044.356047
13. Duff, I.S., Reid, K.: The multifrontal solution of unsymmetric sets of linear systems. SIAM J. Sci. Comput. **5**, 633–641 (1984). https://doi.org/10.1137/0905045
14. Fiałko, S.: A block sparse shared-memory multifrontal finite element solver for problems of structural mechanics. Comput. Assist. Mech. Eng. Sci. **16**, 117–131 (2009)
15. Fiałko, S.: The block subtracture multifrontal method for solution of large finite element equation sets. Tech. Trans. 1-NP **8**, 175–188 (2009)
16. Fiałko, S.: PARFES: a method for solving finite element linear equations on multicore computers. Adv. Eng. Softw. **40**(12), 1256–1265 (2010). https://doi.org/10.1016/j.advengsoft.2010.09.002
17. George, A.: An automatic nested dissection algorithm for irregular finite element problems. SIAM J. Num. Anal. **15**, 1053–1069 (1978). https://doi.org/10.1137/0715069

18. Gilbert, J.R., Tarjan, R.E.: The analysis of a nested dissection algorithm. Numer. Math. **50**(4), 377–404 (1986/87). https://doi.org/10.1007/BF01396660
19. Hughes, T.J.R.: The Finite Element Method. Linear Statics and Dynamics Finite Element Analysis. Prentice-Hall, Englewood Cliffs (1987)
20. Karypis, G., Kumar, V.: A fast and high quality multilevel scheme for partitioning irregular graphs. SIAM J. Sci. Comput. **20**(1), 359–392 (1998). https://doi.org/10.1137/S1064827595287997
21. Melenk, J.M.: hp-Finite Element Methods for Singular Perturbations. Springer, Heidelberg (2002). https://doi.org/10.1007/b84212
22. Niemi, A., Babuśka, I., Pitkaranta, J., Demkowicz, L.: Finite element analysis of the Girkmann problem using the modern hp-version and the classical h-version. Eng. Comput. **28**, 123–134 (2012). https://doi.org/10.1007/s00366-011-0223-0
23. Paszyńska, A.: Volume and neighbors algorithm for finding elimination trees for three dimensional h-adaptive grids. Comput. Math. Appl. **68**(10), 1467–1478 (2014). https://doi.org/10.1016/j.camwa.2014.09.012
24. Paszyńska, A., Paszyński, M., Jopek, K., Woźniak, M., Goik, D., Gurgul, P., AbouEisha, H., Moshkov, M., Calo, V.M., Lenharth, A., Nguyen, D., Pingali, K.: Quasi-optimal elimination trees for 2D grids with singularities. Sci. Program. **2015**, 1–18, Article ID 303024 (2015). https://doi.org/10.1155/2015/303024
25. Paszyński, M.: Fast Solvers for Mesh-Based Computations. Taylor and Francis/CRC Press, Boca Raton, London, New York (2016)
26. Schwab, C.: p and hp Finite Element Methods: Theory and Applications in Solid and Fluid Mechanics. Clarendon Press, Oxford (1998)
27. Solin, P., Segeth, K., Dolezel, I.: Higher-Order Finite Element Methods. Chapman & Hall/CRC Press, Boca Raton, London, New York (2003)
28. Szymczak, A., Paszyńska, A., Paszyński, M., Pardo, D.: Preventing deadlock during anisotropic 2D mesh adaptation in hp-adaptive FEM. J. Comput. Sci. **4**(3), 170–179 (2013). https://doi.org/10.1016/j.jocs.2011.09.001
29. Yannakakis, M.: Computing the minimum fill-in is NP-complete. SIAM J. Algebraic Discret. Methods **2**, 77–79 (1981). https://doi.org/10.1137/0602010

Establishing EDI for a Clinical Trial of a Treatment for Chikungunya

Cynthia Dickerson, Mark Ensor, and Robert A. Lodder[(⊠)]

University of Kentucky, Lexington, KY 40506, USA
Lodder@uky.edu

Abstract. Ellagic acid (EA) is a polyphenolic compound with antiviral activity against chikungunya, a rapidly spreading new tropical disease transmitted to humans by mosquitoes and now affecting millions worldwide. The most common symptoms of chikungunya virus infection are fever and joint pain. Other manifestations of infection can include encephalitis and an arthritic joint swelling with pain that may persist for months or years after the initial infection. The disease has recently spread to the U.S.A., with locally-transmitted cases of chikungunya virus reported in Florida. There is no approved vaccine to prevent or medicine to treat chikungunya virus infections. In this study, the Estimated Daily Intake (EDI) of EA from the food supply established using the National Health and Nutrition Examination Survey (NHANES) is used to set a maximum dose of an EA formulation for a high priority clinical trial.

Keywords: Tropical disease · NHANES · Drug development

1 Introduction

1.1 Compound

Ellagic acid (EA) is a polyphenolic compound with health benefits including antioxidant, anti-inflammatory, anti-proliferative, athero-protective, anti-hepatotoxic and anti-viral properties [1, 2]. EA is found in many plant extracts, fruits and nuts, usually in the form of hydrolyzable ellagitannins that are complex esters of EA with glucose. Natural sources high in ellagitannins include a variety of plant extracts including green tea, nuts such as walnuts, pecans and almonds, and fruits, particularly berries, such as blackberries, raspberries and strawberries, as well as grapes and pomegranates.

1.2 Chikungunya

Chikungunya virus is transmitted to humans by mosquitoes. Typical symptoms of chikungunya virus infection are fever and joint pain. Other manifestations may include headache, encephalitis, muscle pain, rash, and an arthritis-like joint swelling with pain that may persist for months or years after the initial infection. The word 'chikungunya' is thought to be derived from its description in the Makonde language, meaning "that which bends up" the deformed posture of people with the severe joint pain and arthritic

© Springer International Publishing AG, part of Springer Nature 2018
Y. Shi et al. (Eds.): ICCS 2018, LNCS 10861, pp. 773–782, 2018.
https://doi.org/10.1007/978-3-319-93701-4_61

symptoms associated with this disease (Chikungunya-Wikipedia, https://en.wikipedia.org/wiki/Chikungunya). There is no vaccine to prevent or medicine to treat chikungunya virus infections.

Millions of people worldwide suffer from chikungunya infections. The disease spreads quickly once it is established in an area. Outbreaks of chikungunya have occurred in countries in Africa, Asia, Europe, and the Indian and Pacific Oceans. Before 2006, chikungunya virus disease was only rarely pinpointed in U.S. travelers. In 2006–2013, studies found a mean of 28 people per year in the United States with positive tests for recent chikungunya infection. All of these people were travelers visiting or returning to the United States from affected areas in Asia, Africa, or the Indian Ocean.

In late 2013, the first local transmission of chikungunya virus in the Americas was identified on the island of St. Martin, and since then all of the other Caribbean countries and territories. (Local transmission means that mosquitoes in the area have been infected with the virus and are spreading it to people.)

Beginning in 2014, chikungunya virus disease cases were reported among U.S. travelers returning from affected areas in the Americas and local transmission was identified in Florida, Puerto Rico, and the U.S. Virgin Islands. In 2014, there were 11 locally-transmitted cases of chikungunya virus in the U.S. All were reported in Florida. There were 2,781 travel-associated cases reported in the U.S. The first locally acquired cases of chikungunya were reported in Florida on July 17, 2014. These cases represent the first time that mosquitoes in the continental United States are thought to have spread the virus to non-travelers. Unfortunately, this new disease seems certain to spread quickly. Data Driven Computational Science (DDCS) offers ways to accelerate drug development in response to the spread of this disease.

EA has been shown to be an inhibitor of chikungunya virus replication in high throughput screening of small molecules for chikungunya [3]. In screening a natural products library of 502 compounds from Enzo Life Sciences, EA at 10 μM produced 99.6% inhibition of chikungunya in an in vitro assay.

1.3   Metabolism

Ellagitannins are broken down in the intestine to eventually release EA. The bioavailability of ellagitannins and EA have been shown to be low in both humans and in animal models, likely because the compounds are hydrophobic and they because are metabolized by gut microorganisms [4–7]. The amount of ellagitannins and EA reaching the systemic circulation and peripheral tissues after ingestion is small to none [6]. It is established that ellagitannins are not absorbed while there is high variability in EA and EA metabolites found in human plasma after ingestion of standardized amounts of ellagitannins and EA [8–10]. These studies indicate that small amounts of EA are absorbed and detectable in plasma with a C_{max} of approximately 100 nM (using standardized doses) and a T_{max} of 1 h [8, 9]. EA is metabolized to glucuronides and methyl-glucuronide derivatives in the plasma. The most common metabolite found in urine and plasma is EA dimethyl ether glucuronide [11].

It appears that the majority of ingested ellagitannins and EA are metabolized by the gut microbiota into a variety of urolithins. Urolithins are dibenzopyran-6-one derivatives that are produced from EA through the loss of one of the two lactones present in EA and then by successive removal of hydroxyl groups. Urolithin D is produced first, followed sequentially by urolithin C, urolithin A, and urolithin B. Urolithins appear in the circulatory system almost exclusively as glucuronide, sulfate and methylated forms as a result of phase II metabolism after absorption in the colon and passage through the liver [12]. While the amount of EA in the circulation is in the nanomolar range, urolithins and their glucuronide and sulfate conjugates circulate at concentrations in the range of 0.2–20 µM [13]. In light of the much larger concentrations of urolithins in the circulation compared to EA, it is must be considered that the reported in vivo health effects of ellagitannin and EA may be largely due to the gut-produced urolithins. Growing evidence, mostly in vitro, supports the idea that urolithins have many of the same effects as EA in vitro. Various studies have shown evidence of anti-inflammatory [14–16], anticarcinogenic [17–20], anti-glycative [21], possibly antioxidant [5, 22], and antimicrobial [23] effects of urolithins.

There is variation in how people metabolize EA into the various urolithins [24–26]. This is not surprising in light of the known differences between individuals in intestinal microbiotic composition. Tomás-Barberán [25] evaluated the urinary urolithin profiles of healthy volunteers after consuming walnuts and pomegranate extracts. They found that, consistent with previous findings, that urolithin A was the main metabolite produced in humans. However, they noted that the subjects could be divided into three groups based on their urinary profiles of urolithins. One group excreted only urolithin A metabolites while a second group excreted urolithin A and isourolithin A in addition to urolithin B. The third group had undetectable levels of urolithins in their urine. These results suggest that people will benefit differently from eating ellagitannin rich foods.

1.4 Use of EDI

Knowledge of the Estimated Daily Intake (EDI) can permit pharmacokinetic and formulation studies to be conducted without prior expensive and time-consuming toxicology studies, especially when the molecule is naturally present in the food supply (see Fig. 1). A subject's dietary level of the compound would normally vary around the EDI. A subject is brought in to the drug evaluation unit, and after the usual ICH E6 procedures and informed consent, is "washed out" of any of the compound might be present from previous food consumption. Typically, washout is accomplished by maintaining the subject on a diet containing none of the compound to be investigated for a period of five or more half-lives. The subject then receives a dose of the compound and blood samples are collected for pharmacokinetic or other analysis. The concentration of the dose is calculated to keep the subject's exposure below the EDI. For this reason, it is important to establish the EDI before the clinical trial is designed and executed. After sufficient samples have been collected, the subject is released and the trial is complete for that subject. The subject then returns to a normal diet and levels increase again to levels similar to those before the study.

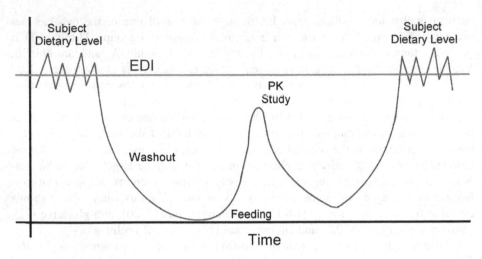

Fig. 1. A pharmacokinetic study can be conducted below the EDI of EA. (Color figure online)

2   Assessment of EA Use

An assessment of the consumption of EA (EA) by the U.S. population resulting from the approved uses of EA was conducted. Estimates for the intake of EA were based on the approved food uses and maximum use level in conjunction with food consumption data included in the National Center for Health Statistics' (NCHS) 2009–2010, 2011–2012, and 2013–2014 National Health and Nutrition Examination Surveys (NHANES) [27–29]. Calculations for the mean and 90th percentile intakes were performed for representative approved food uses of EA combined. The intakes were reported for these seven population groups:

1. infants, age 0 to 1 year
2. toddlers, age 1 to 2 years
3. children, ages 2 to 5 years
4. children, ages 6 to 12 years
5. teenagers, ages 13 to 19 years
6. adults, ages 20 years and up
7. total population (all age groups combined, excluding ages 0–2 years).

3   Food Consumption Survey Data

3.1   Survey Description

The most recent National Health and Nutrition Examination Surveys (NHANES) for the years 2013–2014 are available for public use. NHANES are conducted as a continuous, annual survey, and are released in 2-year cycles. In each cycle, approximately 10,000 people across the U.S. complete the health examination component of the survey. Any combination of consecutive years of data collection is a nationally representative sample of the U.S. population. It is well established that the length of a dietary survey affects the estimated consumption of individual users and that short-term surveys, such as the typical 1-day dietary survey, overestimate consumption over longer time periods [30]. Because two 24-h dietary recalls administered on 2 non-consecutive days (Day 1 and Day 2) are available from the NHANES 2003–2004 and 2013–2014 surveys, these data were used to generate estimates for the current intake analysis.

The NHANES provide the most appropriate data for evaluating food-use and food-consumption patterns in the United States, containing 2 years of data on individuals selected via stratified multistage probability sample of civilian non-institutionalized population of the U.S. NHANES survey data were collected from individuals and households via 24-h dietary recalls administered on 2 non-consecutive days (Day 1 and Day 2) throughout all 4 seasons of the year. Day 1 data were collected in-person in the Mobile Examination Center (MEC), and Day 2 data were collected by telephone in the following 3 to 10 days, on different days of the week, to achieve the desired degree of statistical independence. The data were collected by first selecting Primary Sampling Units (PSUs), which were counties throughout the U.S. Small counties were combined to attain a minimum population size. These PSUs were segmented and households were chosen within each segment. One or more participants within a household were interviewed. Fifteen PSUs are visited each year. For example, in the 2009–2010 NHANES, there were 13,272 persons selected; of these 10,253 were considered respondents to the MEC examination and data collection. 9754 of the MEC respondents provided complete dietary intakes for Day 1 and of those providing the Day 1 data, 8,405 provided complete dietary intakes for Day 2. The release data does not necessarily include all the questions asked in a section. Data items may have been removed due to confidentiality, quality, or other considerations. For this reason, it is possible that a dataset does not completely match all the questions asked in a questionnaire section. Each data file has been edited to include only those sample persons eligible for that particular section or component, so the numbers vary.

In addition to collecting information on the types and quantities of foods being consumed, the NHANES surveys collected socioeconomic, physiological, and demographic information from individual participants in the survey, such as sex, age, height and weight, and other variables useful in characterizing consumption. The inclusion of this information allows for further assessment of food intake based on consumption by specific population groups of interest within the total population.

Sample weights were incorporated with NHANES surveys to compensate for the potential under-representation of intakes from specific population groups as a result of sample variability due to survey design, differential non-response rates, or other factors, such as deficiencies in the sampling frame [28, 29].

3.2   Methods

Consumption data from individual dietary records, detailing food items ingested by each survey participant, were collated by computer in Matlab and used to generate estimates for the intake of EA by the U.S. population. Estimates for the daily intake of

EA represent projected 2-day averages for each individual from Day 1 and Day 2 of NHANES data; these average amounts comprised the distribution from which mean and percentile intake estimates were produced. Mean and percentile estimates were generated incorporating sample weights in order to provide representative intakes for the entire U.S. population. "All-user" intake refers to the estimated intake of EA by those individuals consuming food products containing EA. Individuals were considered users if they consumed 1 or more food products containing EA on either Day 1 or Day 2 of the survey.

3.3   Food Data

Food codes representative of each approved use were chosen from the Food and Nutrition Database for Dietary Studies (FNDDS) for the corresponding biennial NHANES survey. In FNDDS, the primary (usually generic) description of a given food is assigned a unique 8-digit food code [28, 29].

3.4   Food Survey Results

The estimated "all-user" total intakes of EA from all approved food uses of EA in the U.S. by population group is summarized in Figs. 2, 3, 4 and 5.

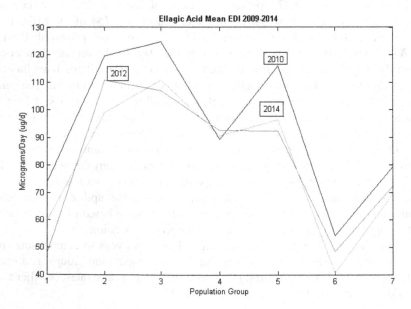

Fig. 2. Children consume more EA on average than adults. Baby foods are often made from ingredients high in EA. The blue line shows data from the 2009–2010 NHANES, the red line data from the 2011–2012 NHANES, and the green line data from the 2013–2014 NHANES. (Color figure online)

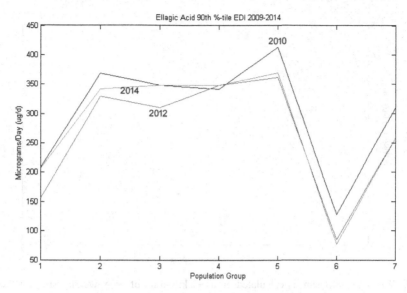

Fig. 3. Teenagers contribute the highest peak in the 90th percentile consumers of EA. The blue line shows data from the 2009–2010 NHANES, the red line data from the 2011–2012 NHANES, and the green line data from the 2013–2014 NHANES. (Color figure online)

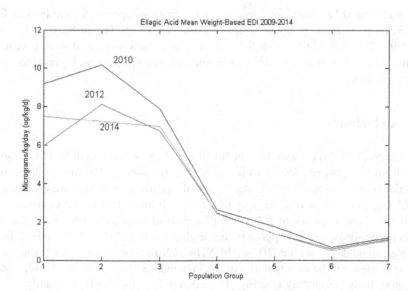

Fig. 4. When EA exposure is calculated on a per kilogram of body weight basis, toddlers aged 1 to 2 years are exposed to the most EA on average. The blue line shows data from the 2009–2010 NHANES, the red line data from the 2011–2012 NHANES, and the green line data from the 2013–2014 NHANES. (Color figure online)

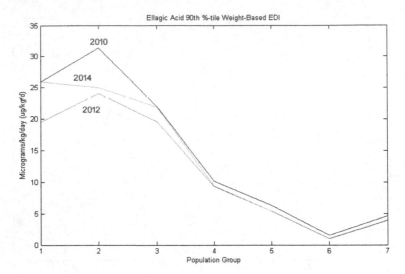

Fig. 5. When EA exposure is calculated on a per kilogram of body weight basis for the 90th percentile consumers, toddlers aged 1 to 2 years are again exposed to the most EA. The blue line shows data from the 2009–2010 NHANES, the red line data from the 2011–2012 NHANES, and the green line data from the 2013–2014 NHANES. (Color figure online)

The estimated "all-user" total intakes of EA from all approved food uses of EA in the U.S. by population group are graphed using NHANES data in Figs. 2, 3, 4 and 5 for 2009–2010, 2011–2012, and 2013–2014. The figures show that over 6 years, the consumption of EA has been fairly constant and that children and teenagers are the major consumers.

4   Conclusions

In summary, 28.3% of the total U.S. population of 2+ years was identified as consumers of EA from the approved food uses in the 2013–2014 survey. The mean intakes of EA by all EA consumers age 2+ ("all-user") from all approved food uses were estimated to be 69.58 µg/person/day or 1.05 µg/kg body weight/day. The heavy consumer (90th percentile all-user) intakes of EA from all approved food-uses were estimated to be 258.33 µg/person/day or 3.89 µg/kg body weight/day. The EDI (red line in Fig. 1) is set at 70 µg/person/day from the 2013-2014 NHANES for consumers ages 2 and up. The next experiment will be an actual trial of EA in human subjects at the EDI with a dose of 3.89 µg/kg body weight/day (see Fig. 1), as determined by this DDCS study.

5   Support

The project described was supported in part by the National Center for Research Resources and the National Center for Advancing Translational Sciences, National Institutes of Health, through Grant UL1TR001998. The content is solely the responsibility of the authors and does not necessarily represent the official views of the NIH. This project was also supported by NSF ACI-1053575 allocation number BIO170011.

References

1. Park, S., Kang, Y.: Dietary ellagic acid suppresses atherosclerotic lesion formation and vascular inflammation in apoE-deficient mice. FASEB J. **27**(1), 861-23 (2013)
2. García-Niño, R.W., Zazueta, C.: Ellagic acid: pharmacological activities and molecular mechanisms involved in liver protection. Pharmacol. Res. **97**, 84–103 (2015)
3. Kaur, P., Thiruchelvan, M., Lee, R.C.H., Chen, H., Chen, K.C., Ng, M.L., Chu, J.J.H.: Inhibition of chikungunya virus replication by harringtonine, a novel antiviral that suppresses viral protein expression. Antimicrob. Agents Chemother. **57**(1), 155–167 (2013)
4. Cerdá, B., et al.: Identification of urolithin A as a metabolite produced by human colon microflora from ellagic acid and related compounds. J. Agric. Food Chem. **53**(14), 5571–5576 (2005)
5. Cerdá, B., et al.: The potent in vitro antioxidant ellagitannins from pomegranate juice are metabolised into bioavailable but poor antioxidant hydroxy–6H–dibenzopyran–6–one derivatives by the colonic microflora of healthy humans. Eur. J. Nutr. **43**(4), 205–220 (2004)
6. Cerdá, B., Tomás-Barberán, F.A., Espín, J.C.: Metabolism of antioxidant and chemopreventive ellagitannins from strawberries, raspberries, walnuts, and oak-aged wine in humans: identification of biomarkers and individual variability. J. Agric. Food Chem. **53**(2), 227–235 (2005)
7. Espín, J.C., et al.: Iberian pig as a model to clarify obscure points in the bioavailability and metabolism of ellagitannins in humans. J. Agric. Food Chem. **55**(25), 10476–10485 (2007)
8. Mertens-Talcott, S.U., et al.: Absorption, metabolism, and antioxidant effects of pomegranate (Punica granatum L.) polyphenols after ingestion of a standardized extract in healthy human volunteers. J. Agric. Food Chem. **54**(23), 8956–8961 (2006)
9. Seeram, N.P., Lee, R., Heber, D.: Bioavailability of ellagic acid in human plasma after consumption of ellagitannins from pomegranate (Punica granatum L.) juice. Clin. Chim. Acta **348**(1), 63–68 (2004)
10. Seeram, N.P., et al.: Pomegranate juice ellagitannin metabolites are present in human plasma and some persist in urine for up to 48 hours. J. Nutr. **136**(10), 2481–2485 (2006)
11. Tomás-Barberan, F.A., Espín, J.C., García-Conesa, M.T.: Bioavailability and metabolism of ellagic acid and ellagitannins. Chem. Biol. Ellagitannins **7**, 293–297 (2009)
12. González-Barrio, R., et al.: UV and MS identification of urolithins and nasutins, the bioavailable metabolites of ellagitannins and ellagic acid in different mammals. J. Agric. Food Chem. **59**(4), 1152–1162 (2011)
13. Espín, J.C., et al.: Biological significance of urolithins, the gut microbial ellagic acid-derived metabolites: the evidence so far. Evid. Based Complement. Altern. Med. **2013**, 1–15 (2013)
14. Larrosa, M., et al.: Anti-inflammatory properties of a pomegranate extract and its metabolite urolithin-A in a colitis rat model and the effect of colon inflammation on phenolic metabolism. J. Nutr. Biochem. **21**(8), 717–725 (2010)
15. Ishimoto, H., et al.: In vivo anti-inflammatory and antioxidant properties of ellagitannin metabolite urolithin A. Bioorg. Med. Chem. Lett. **21**(19), 5901–5904 (2011)
16. Piwowarski, J.P., et al.: Role of human gut microbiota metabolism in the anti-inflammatory effect of traditionally used ellagitannin-rich plant materials. J. Ethnopharmacol. **155**(1), 801–809 (2014)

17. Adams, L.S., et al.: Pomegranate ellagitannin–derived compounds exhibit antiproliferative and antiaromatase activity in breast cancer cells in vitro. Cancer Prevent. Res. 3(1), 108–113 (2010)

18. Seeram, N.P., et al.: In vitro antiproliferative, apoptotic and antioxidant activities of punicalagin, ellagic acid and a total pomegranate tannin extract are enhanced in combination with other polyphenols as found in pomegranate juice. J. Nutr. Biochem. 16(6), 360–367 (2005)

19. Seeram, N.P., Aronson, W.J., Zhang, Y., Henning, S.M., Moro, A., Lee, R.P., Sartippour, M., Harris, D.M., Rettig, M., Suchard, M.A., Pantuck, A.J.: Pomegranate ellagitannin-derived metabolites inhibit prostate cancer growth and localize to the mouse prostate gland. J. Agric. Food Chem. 55(19), 7732–7737 (2007)

20. Larrosa, M., et al.: Urolithins, ellagic acid-derived metabolites produced by human colonic microflora, exhibit estrogenic and antiestrogenic activities. J. Agric. Food Chem. 54(5), 1611–1620 (2006)

21. Liu, W., et al.: Pomegranate phenolics inhibit formation of advanced glycation endproducts by scavenging reactive carbonyl species. Food Funct. 5(11), 2996–3004 (2014)

22. Bialonska, D., et al.: Urolithins, intestinal microbial metabolites of pomegranate ellagitannins, exhibit potent antioxidant activity in a cell-based assay. J. Agric. Food Chem. 57(21), 10181–10186 (2009)

23. Giménez-Bastida, J.A., et al.: Urolithins, ellagitannin metabolites produced by colon microbiota, inhibit quorum sensing in Yersinia enterocolitica: phenotypic response and associated molecular changes. Food Chem. 132(3), 1465–1474 (2012)

24. González-Barrio, R., et al.: Bioavailability of anthocyanins and ellagitannins following consumption of raspberries by healthy humans and subjects with an ileostomy. J. Agric. Food Chem. 58(7), 3933–3939 (2010)

25. Tomás-Barberán, F.A., et al.: Ellagic acid metabolism by human gut microbiota: consistent observation of three urolithin phenotypes in intervention trials, independent of food source, age, and health status. J. Agric. Food Chem. 62(28), 6535–6538 (2014)

26. Truchado, P., et al.: Strawberry processing does not affect the production and urinary excretion of urolithins, ellagic acid metabolites, in humans. J. Agric. Food Chem. 60(23), 5749–5754 (2011)

27. CDC 2006: Analytical and Reporting Guidelines: The National Health and Nutrition Examination Survey (NHANES). National Center for Health Statistics, Centers for Disease Control and Prevention, Hyattsville, Maryland. http://www.cdc.gov/nchs/data/nhanes/nhanes_03_04/nhanes_analytic_guidelines_dec_2005.pdf

28. USDA 2012: What We Eat In America (WWEIA), NHANES: overview. http://www.ars.usda.gov/Services/docs.htm?docid=13793#release. Accessed 29 Jan 2018

29. Bodner-Montville, J., Ahuja, J.K.C., Ingwersen, L.A., Haggerty, E.S., Enns, C.W., Perloff, B.P.: USDA food and nutrient database for dietary studies: released on the web. J. Food Compos. Anal. 19(Suppl. 1), S100–S107 (2006)

30. Hayes, A.W., Kruger, C.L. (eds.): Hayes' Principles and Methods of Toxicology, 6th edn, p. 631. CRC Press, Boca Raton (2014)

Static Analysis and Symbolic Execution for Deadlock Detection in MPI Programs

Craig C. Douglas[1](⊠) and Krishanthan Krishnamoorthy[2]

[1] School of Energy Resources and Department of Mathematics,
University of Wyoming, 1000 E. University Avenue, Laramie, WY 82071-3036, USA
craig.c.douglas@gmail.com
[2] Computer Science Department, University of Wyoming, 1000 E. University
Avenue, Laramie, WY 82071-3315, USA
krishuwyo@gmail.com

Abstract. Parallel computing using MPI has become ubiquitous on multi-node computing clusters. A common problem while developing parallel codes is determining whether or not a deadlock condition can exist. Ideally we do not want to have to run a large number of examples to find deadlock conditions through trial and error procedures. In this paper we describe a methodology using both static analysis and symbolic execution of a MPI program to make a determination when it is possible. We note that using static analysis by itself is insufficient for realistic cases. Symbolic execution has the possibility of creating a nearly infinite number of logic branches to investigate. We provide a mechanism to limit the number of branches to something computable. We also provide examples and pointers to software necessary to test MPI programs.

1 Introduction

While impossible to determine when an arbitrary parallel program halts or goes into deadlock, which is equivalent to the halting problem [18], there are many real world codes in which a determination of deadlock or non-deadlock is possible [12]. This paper only applies when a determination can be made for parallel programs using MPI [8] though it could be extended to similar communications systems.

Software model checking provides an algorithmic analysis of programs and a fundamental framework to construct a program model [11]. A binary decision diagram (BDD) [3] is one of the ways to construct the model and investigate the state of the program. A BDD is a decision tree that is used to produce output based on a calculation from Boolean inputs [3]. Even though the BDD and model checking techniques are excellent, if the program system has a very large number of states, then it will be difficult to travel all feasible paths. According to Biere et al. [4], the symbolic model checking with boolean encoding can handle large program states faster than other approaches. We use the symbolic model checking technique to model a MPI program and simulate its execution

© Springer International Publishing AG, part of Springer Nature 2018
Y. Shi et al. (Eds.): ICCS 2018, LNCS 10861, pp. 783–796, 2018.
https://doi.org/10.1007/978-3-319-93701-4_62

while analyzing the states of the program. By using a symbolic model we create constraints to find feasible paths to follow the execution of the routines or to detect deadlock. We use the Satisfiability Modulo Theories (SMT) [2] method and symbolic execution in order to travel through the path in our symbolic model.

Consider a trivial example program for two processes. Each process uses MPI_Send to send a message to the other process. Each process uses MPI_Recv to receive the message from the other process. Each process then ends with $MPI\_Finalize$. This program obviously does not deadlock.

Our process removes unnecessary code in order to analyze it. We are left with as little as possible in addition to the MPI calls. Table 1 represents the remaining code. Table 2 represents the steps that the symbolic execution takes in order to determine that this example does not deadlock.

Table 1. Sample non-deadlock MPI routines

Process 0	Process 1
$MPI\_Send[1]$	$MPI\_Send[0]$
$MPI\_Recv[1]$	$MPI\_Recv[0]$
$MPI\_Finalize$	$MPI\_Finalize$

Table 2. Non-deadlock MPI routines with possible execution steps and index

Process 0	Process 1
Step 1–$MPI\_Send[1]$	Step 3–$MPI\_Send[0]$
Step 2, Step 6–$MPI\_Recv[1]$	Step 4–$MPI\_Recv[0]$
Step 7–$MPI\_Finalize$	Step 5–$MPI\_Finalize$

The remainder of the paper is organized as follows. In Sect. 2 we discuss background issues and similar, related research. In Sect. 3 we discuss the computational process used to extract the relevant part of a MPI code and how the symbolic execution operates. In Sect. 4 we define the symbolic model and how symbolic execution works. In Sect. 5 we show an interesting example. In Sect. 6 we provide conclusions and discuss future research.

2   Background and Related Research

Initially, we focused not only detect deadlock on but also looked for a solution to prevent executing deadlocked MPI code. When a user executes a MPI program, it is very difficult to identify the process that cause deadlock due to the missing matching MPI_Send for a MPI_Recv in the source code. Our deadlock prevention system should not change user data in the code because that can produce wrong output. However, if necessary, we can change the order of the MPI Routine without affecting the final results. Therefore, we started to focus on a different direction for our research and we have conducted many research studies in MPI deadlock and prevention mechanism areas. Since most of the MPI deadlock detection research have only focused on dynamic analysis of MPI program, that technique does not lead to deadlock prevention concepts.

In [10] an idea is proposed to find MPI deadlock using a graph based approach. This research idea is primarily based on the Wait-for graph, which helps to detect deadlock in operating systems and relational database systems. Wait-for graph considers each process as a node and keeps track of processes when a MPI program executes [14]. If MPI_Recv causes deadlock on a process, it locks and holds the resources to the process. Suppose more than a single process is waiting for resources, then there is a possibility of a deadlock. The above method still requires the MPI program to execute in real time. In addition, possible overhead and performance drops can happen in the deadlock detection mechanism if there are lot of MPI Routines available in a MPI source code. Furthermore, the method cannot help prevent deadlock before it happens during the execution. However, the proposed method can be useful if we use it before the MPI program executes.

Based on our research, we can choose either static or dynamic analysis in order to accomplish our research goal. In the remainder of this section we discuss both methods. We choose static analysis over dynamic analysis after conducting several research studies. Also, static analysis provides deadlock detection and can prevent execution of MPI program before a deadlock occurs.

We can analyze a software program in two ways: by static and dynamic analysis. Dynamic analysis is a very common method in software testing. To be effective dynamic analysis requires that the program produce output during the execution.

A model checking system basically is a finite-state automation that can formally verify the concurrent systems and binary decision diagrams [6]. Also, a model checking system is automatic, which means it can verify a program with a high level representation of the user specified model and can check whether the program satisfies the model. Otherwise, the system provides a counterexample if the formula is not satisfied. In addition, model checking can be used in two ways: through dynamic and static analysis.

Dynamic model checking is widely used in race condition and deadlock detection. Wang et al. discussed finding race conditions in multi threaded programs [19]. Also, this research study shows better algorithms to reduce the unnecessary interleaving of thread execution with the model checking and code instrumentation. Gupta et al. explained that there is a significant performance impact on instrumenting functions, which increases the size of the functions instrumented in the source code [9].

As a result, researchers have introduced a framework to accomplish the code instrumentation in better ways and that can reduce overhead while injecting functions into the source code. So, if we can introduce a similar technology in our research, then the code instrumentation can be very helpful for deadlock avoidance. In addition, the implementation introduces possible ways to inject functions into the source code without changing the context of the MPI program.

Symbolic model checking is used to verify a program in an extremely large scale such that 10^{120} states can be verified, which enables us to perform program analysis through boolean encoding and symbolic behavioral states [5]. Due to this research study our research ideas moved towards the static model checking method. Even though static model checking is suitable for our research, King et al. [16] showed that model checking suffers from the well known state-space explosion problem. This research study introduces a better framework that works with symbolic execution [13], which helps to automate the test case generation and solve the state-space explosion problem efficiently.

3 Computational Process

To do the program analysis using a symbolic model, first we parse the MPI code and extract the information about all of the MPI routines using an Abstract Syntax Tree (AST) [1] that the Rose Compiler [17] generates. We extract the variables and functions from the MPI codes. Then we generate the formulas for our deadlock detection main program. Our main program creates a Yices [20] script in a file that is used by the Yices SMT program.

The main program determines the final result from the output of the Symbolic Execution in Yices. We implemented a validation mechanism that verifies the input file and determines if it has valid MPI function calls so that the Symbolic Execution does not fail due to improper arguments. Then we build formulas for Yices based on the MPI functions.

We currently can analyze a MPI program for a very limited number of MPI functions. The code is extensible in the sense that we can add functions and logic formulas for additional MPI functions, which is part of the future work listed in Sect. 6. When the symbolic model is completed we run it using Yices.

An issue is how long should the Symbolic Execution run in order to find a result from the Yices SMT solver. We specify a last value as symbolic value so the Symbolic Execution only runs until the last value is reached. Determining the specific last value without loss of performance and creating a path explosion problem is a somewhat difficult.

We have introduced a bound variable B (last value) as the maximum integer available when numbering formulas. The formulas are created dynamically and we check the deadlock condition. If we do not have a deadlock conclusion, then we create a formula again with a fresh copy.

4 Symbolic Model and Execution

4.1 The Model

During the extraction process, each MPI function is checked for erroneous parameters. Consider Table 1. It uses a state-space exploration technique. A *state* includes a process scheduling, current step of a MPI routine, index, and path condition.

The path condition is a component that specifies the order of a MPI routine. In Table 2 at Step 2 when $MPI\_Receive$ executes we change the execution to process 1 and choose Step 3. The path condition is essential in our constraints and is maintained in all steps.

We can show the above *state* components in symbols, such as

process scheduling $(p) \wedge$ current step $(j) \wedge$ index $(i) \wedge$ path condition

The *state* is maintained as we execute each MPI routine in the code and we check the logic condition at each step.

We define a token tk for the path condition implementation, which takes a MPI routine for each index of an execution. The token also has the transition implied by the MPI routines to indicate a ready to execute condition for a particular process and index.

We define the variables in a *state* with symbolic values, e.g.,

$$p(process) = <p_0, p_1, \ldots, p_n>, \quad i(index) = <i_0, i_1, \ldots, i_n>,$$
$$\text{and } j(step) = <j_1, j_2, j_3, \ldots, j_n>.$$

For Table 2, $j_i = i$, $i = 1, \cdots, n = 7$.

The process p takes values according to the feasible path condition in the symbolic model, but index i has consistent values that represent the symbolic variable of the current step. Thus, index i is used when creating a fresh formula with a copy of the current step. We continuously create and execute the current step until the symbolic model satisfies the constraints.

If the symbolic model cannot satisfy the constraints for the current step, e.g., at Step n, MPI_Recev cannot find matching MPI_Send at any index i, then that leads to deadlock for the current process. We do not execute the next step until we execute the current step successfully. We create fresh formulas for the current step as necessary for each index i.

$$token[process][index] = transition(MPIRoutines)$$

is denoted by

$$tk_p[i] = \tau_{transition(p)}.$$

The symbolic model must find a feasible path based on the path conditions and MPI routines (cf. Table 2).

We add a buffer to our model that stores the MPI_Send variable required by the $MPI\_Receive$ routine that may execute later in the code. We denote the buffer implementation as follows:

$$buffer[destinationprocess][channel][index] = full \mid empty, \text{ or}$$
$$buf^c_{p'}[i] = full \mid empty.$$

The channel specifies uniqueness of individual routines in each process and prevents overwriting the buffer. The channel implementation is similar to MPI's virtual communication channels, which allows *buffer* to keep storing routines for a respective channel so *MPI_Send* and *MPI_Receive* can communicate over the channel.

In Table 2 at step 1 when we execute the *MPI_Send* routine from process 0 we add a constant value that fills the buffer with the destination process (e.g., set $buf_1^1 = 1$). The constant value indicates that the buffer is full. Since our symbolic execution checks the program states in sequential order, it is important to keep track of which process is eligible to run at the current step, e.g., in Table 2 at step 3, the program jumps to process 1 because at the current step process 0 is not eligible to continue further execution.

We require a scheduling mechanism in the symbolic model that takes the eligible process value p for each i, denoted as $s[i] = p$. Consider Table 2. Then

$$\text{Step } i: s[i] = 0, \text{ for } i = 0, 1, 6, 7 \text{ and}$$
$$\text{Step } j: s[j] = 1, \text{ for } j = 3, 4, 5.$$

Without a scheduling implementation it is difficult to add the correct MPI routine to *token* and is impossible to travel through the feasible paths in the symbolic model. It is one of the important components in the constraints to make decisions so that the symbolic execution runs correctly. In order to schedule the process we need to make sure that the token has a MPI routine and the current step is eligible to execute (e.g., if the current routine is a *MPI_Receive* we need to check if *buffer* has the value from the matching *MPI_Send* before we execute the current step).

4.2   MPI Logic Formulas

We can derive formulas for *MPI_Send* and *MPI_Receive*. For *MPI_Send*,

$$tk_p[i] = \tau_{send(p)} \wedge buf_{p'}^c[i] \neq full) \Longrightarrow$$
$$update(s[i] = p) \wedge update(buf_p^c[i+1] = full) \wedge update(buf_{p'}^c[i+2] = empty).$$

This formula means that at the current index, if the token has a *MPI_Send* routine and the buffer is not full, then we schedule the process p and update the *buffer* with the next index ($i = i + 1$). Also, we update the *buffer* index ($i = i+2$) with the empty value so we prevent overwriting *buffer*. The symbolic execution runs correctly.

For *MPI_Receive*,

$$tk_p[i] = \tau_{recev(p)} \wedge buf_p[i] \neq empty \Longrightarrow$$
$$(update(s[i] = p)) \vee ((p < p_{max}) \longrightarrow (p = p + 1) \vee (p = 0)).$$

This formula means that at the current index, if the token has a *MPI_Receive* routine and the buffer is not full, then we schedule the current process p. In order to update to the next process we check whether the current process is the last available process (represented by *p_max* and is 1 in Table 1) or not. If the current process itself is the last one, then we update the next process with 0. Otherwise, we update with next available process.

4.3 Symbolic Execution

Symbolic execution [13] is a program analysis technique that utilizes the symbolic values instead of the absolute values of a program. For all program inputs, symbolic analysis represents the values of program variables as symbolic expressions of those inputs. As the program executes, at each step the state of the program executes symbolically and it includes the symbolic values of program variables at that point. By using the symbolic execution we simulate the program. We use the path constraints and the program counter on the symbolic values to simulate the execution of a program.

While the symbolic execution is one of the better approach simulating a program, it is also difficult to apply to parallel programming methods. For instance, tracking the PC and execution steps in a process is a difficult task and requires sophisticated approaches other than just the conventional symbolic approach. Here we propose a different symbolic approach by introducing several constraints to better resolve the symbolic analysis.

4.4 Symbolic Encoding

We present an encoding approach that converts the symbolic model into Satisfiability Modulo Theories (SMT) formulas [20]. We include scheduling constraints (S_i), transition constraints (T_i), finalize constraints (F_i), and deadlock constraints (D_i):

$$S_i \wedge T_i \wedge F_i \wedge D_i \tag{1}$$

or

$$S_i \wedge T_i \wedge F_i \rightarrow \neg D_i \tag{2}$$

We check all constraints in each execution step. Note that (1) is equivalent to checking the satisfiability for (2). We use Yices as our SMT solver [7] to solve (2). If each formula is satisfiable, then the solution gives trace output that leads to the conclusion. Based on the trace output we can draw a conclusion on whether the given MPI routines are under deadlock condition or not. For example, if all the constraints become true then the deadlock constraints become false, so the given MPI code has no deadlock. Alternately, if any of the constraints become false, then the deadlock constraint is true and we add a value to the deadlock buffer.

Our program shows detailed information about deadlock that will occur in a MPI program. The constraints are the tools for us to solve the formula which is generated by our program.

4.5 Symbolic Variables

In the symbolic analysis, we check deadlock conditions up to a predefined step bound value B. For each step $i < B$, we add a fresh copy for each variable. That is, $var[i]$ denotes the copy of i at the step. For example, $buff_p^c[i]$ holds values for each step as

$$buf_p^c[0], \ buff_p^c[1], \ buff_p^c[2], \ \cdots, \ buff_p^c[B]$$

and each has a value of $full \mid empty$.

Yices may take additional index i values to solve the formula, which depends on number of MPI routines available and what order those MPI routines are written in the source code. For example, if a MPI source code consists of five MPI routines, then our program may create 12 entries of the formulas with index $i = 11$, but it depends what order the MPI_Send and $MPI\_Receive$ routines are written in the code. If $MPI\_Receive$ appears before the MPI_Send in all the processes then Yices solves the formula and concludes with deadlock with the minimum number of index i value. In that case, the index i value will be equal to the number process available in the code. However, in order to reduce the path explosion, we have optimized the constraints. Therefore, we can reduce the utilization of index i values and prevent solving the same formula over and over with different index i values. If our program finds either deadlock or non deadlock of a MPI code, then we halt the symbolic execution.

Token Variables. The *token* (tk) is used to store a MPI routine in each execution step. During the transition a MPI routine τ in process p and index i has a token, denoted by $tk_p[i] = \tau$. At any step, a single transition per process has a *token*. When τ is executed, then the token moves to next MPI routine. Define $succ(\tau)$ to be the successor of next transition of τ.

Buffer Implementation. Unlike typical programming languages, we cannot store a value in a Yices program. We use the index i, which is used to create a fresh copy of a variable in Yices. We have fresh copy of $buffer$ with current process p for use to store a value. In our symbolic execution $buffer$ is used to store only $full$ or $empty$. We use specific values to represent the $full$ and $empty$ values in Yices depending on the context.

In our symbolic analysis we have six kinds of buffers:

1. Scheduling Buffer
2. Schedule Success Buffer
3. Transition Buffer
4. Transfer Buffer
5. Receive Block Buffer
6. Deadlock Buffer.

We use the *Scheduling Buffer* to store the execution step. We ensure that the current step can be scheduled or that it is necessary to move on to the next process. This situation arises when a $MPI\_Receive$ routine is executed. If $MPI\_Receive$ does not find a matching MPI_Send, then we skip the execution in the current process and move to the next process. Otherwise, we fill the

Scheduling Buffer. We use the *Transfer Buffer* to store each transfer that occurred from one process to another when we do not schedule the current process. Hence, we keep a record of the number of the transfer that happened for each *MPI_Receive* in a process, which helps us to find deadlock in the *Deadlock Constraint*.

The *Scheduling Buffer* avoids conflicts between the MPI routines and stores values for a specific channel and execution index. We fill the *Schedule Success Buffer* when a process is selected to execute. We use *Schedule Success Buffer* to indicate the execution of the current process in *Deadlock Constraint*. If the current *MPI_Receive* does not find a matching *MPI_Send* after some execution and the current *Schedule Success Buffer* is empty, then we use *Schedule Success Buffer* and *Receive Block Buffer* in order to identify a potential deadlock in the code. In this case, *Transfer Buffer* is the number of transfers we made for the current *MPI_Receive* when we attempted to find a matching *MPI_Send*.

If the number of transfers exceeds the number of processes available in the MPI code, then we assume that the current *MPI_Receive* will never find a matching *MPI_Send*. Therefore, we update the *Receive Block Buffer* in *Transfer Buffer Constraint*. As a result, *Schedule Success Buffer* and *Receive Block Buffer* both satisfy the *Deadlock Constraint* formula and becomes *true*. Finally, we update the *Deadlock Buffer* and conclude there is a deadlock in the code.

The *Transition Buffer* is used to store the value or tag of the MPI routine that will identify the matching *MPI_Send* or *MPI_Receive*. For example, in Table 2, if step 1 is permitted to execute, then the *Transition Buffer* acquires a value from *MPI_Send* (or a tag) and the value should be the same for the matching *MPI_Receive* in the destination process. The *MPI_Receive* and *Deadlock Buffers* are tied together. Table 3 shows a deadlock situation in step 2 if the *MPI_Receive* cannot find a matching *MPI_Send*. Then the *Transfer Buffer Constraint* adds the current step into the *Receive Block Buffer*, which occurs in step 4. We perform this operation by using the *Transfer Buffer* and we introduce a constraint to check whether *Transfer Buffer* is *full* or *empty*.

Finally, our program concludes as a deadlock if the *Deadlock Buffer* includes one or more *MPI_Receive* routines. If even one *MPI_Receive* is in the *Deadlock Buffer*, then some *MPI_Receive* could not find a matching *MPI_Send*. So the execution will not continue at least for the blocking *MPI_Send* and *MPI_Receive* as in real MPI execution and will be considered as a potential deadlock in the code (Table 4).

The formulas for both *MPI_Send* and *MPI| − Receive* are quite complex. In [15] are tables that break down the conditions to simple expressions, based on tables, that can be followed to determine correctness.

4.6   MPI Logic Reformulations

The MPI formulas from Sect. 4.2 are reformulated in this section for what they are with the details of this section.

Table 3. Deadlocked MPI routines with possible execution steps

Process 0	Process 1
Step 1–MPI_Send[1]	Step 3, Step 5–MPI_Receive[0]
Step 2, Step 4–MPI_Receive[1]	$MPI\_Receive[0]$
$MPI\_Finalize$	$MPI\_Finalize$

Table 4. Another deadlocked MPI routines with possible execution steps

Process 0	Process 1
Step 1, Step 3–MPI_Receive[0]	Step 2, Step 4–MPI_Receive[0]
MPI_Send[1]	$MPI\_Send[0]$
$MPI\_Finalize$	$MPI\_Finalize$

The main job of the *Scheduling Constraint* is to generate formulas that are responsible for process scheduling. In real MPI execution, each process will execute the MPI routines that belong to the process. Since execution is simulated sequentially, we determine that the current process is eligible to schedule before we execute MPI routines. If the scheduling formula does not execute, then further execution will not take place.

We introduce a program counter (PC) in the MPI constraints. It is used to keep track of duplicate executions of the same MPI routine. In Table 2 after Step 5 and before Step 6, Yices can execute the MPI_Send routine, but it ignores the execution because MPI_Send is already executed successfully in step 1 so we can prevent solving the formula twice and move on to the next step. Therefore, in Table 2 we directly evaluate formulas for $MPI\_Receive$ in Step 6, which helps to minimize the usage of index i and can potentially reduce overhead in our symbolic execution.

The updated formula for MPI_Send is

$$\sum_{k=0}^{k=N} (PC_p[k] \neq full \wedge \exists k \in i) \longrightarrow (tk_p[i] = \tau_{send(p')} \wedge$$
$$buf_{p'}^c[i] \neq full) \longrightarrow update(s[i] = p) \wedge$$
$$update(schedule\_success\_buf_p[i] = full) \wedge$$
$$update(buf_{p'}^c[i+1] = full) \wedge update(buf_{p'}^c[i+2] = empty) \vee$$
$$(update(buf_{p'}^c[i+1] = empty)) \wedge \delta(\{i, \tau, j\}).$$

The updated formula for $MPI\_Receive$ is

$$\sum_{k=0}^{k=N} (PC_p[k] \neq full \wedge \exists k \in i) \longrightarrow (tk_p[i] = \tau_{receive(p)} \wedge \sum_{l=0}^{l=N} buf_p[l] \neq empty)$$
$$\longrightarrow (update(s[i] = p) \wedge update(schedule\_success\_buf_p[i] = full)) \vee (((p < p_{max})$$
$$\longrightarrow (update(p_{i+1} = p + 1)) \vee (update(p_{i+1} = 0))) \wedge update(tk_{p+1}[i+1] =$$
$$succ(\tau)) \wedge update(transfer\_buf_p[i][j_{i+1}] = full)) \wedge \exists l \in i \wedge \delta(\{p, i, \tau, j\}).$$

5 Experiments

All experiments were run on a computer with an Intel Core i7 7700K running at up to 4.20 GHz, 16 GB of DRAM, and a 500 GB solid state drive. We used a virtual environment of a VMware workstation player installed under Windows 10 as the host operating system with Ubuntu 16.04 as the guest operating system.

In Table 5 we show experiments taken from deadlocked MPI code. The MPI codes used in our experiments were based on ones the Internet and we also created some complex MPI codes. The codes all fall into deadlock, though not in an obvious manner.

Table 5. Experiments for deadlocked MPI codes

MPI Routines	Time taken for 10 experiments (secs.)									
	1	2	3	4	5	6	7	8	9	10
4	3.049	3.082	3.035	3.306	3.366	3.401	3.339	3.346	3.380	3.301
8	3.361	3.390	3.364	3.330	3.385	3.440	3.279	4.283	3.391	3.437
8	4.575	4.285	4.198	4.745	4.094	4.156	5.117	5.077	4.062	4.076
12	4.102	4.911	4.159	4.024	5.022	4.233	4.201	4.248	4.145	5.363
24	4.007	3.937	3.979	4.078	3.950	4.039	4.064	4.007	4.127	3.945
24	4.186	4.261	4.203	4.223	4.149	4.274	4.357	4.272	4.199	4.330
48	5.127	5.017	5.030	5.107	5.099	5.031	5.155	4.948	5.042	5.085
64	5.761	5.577	5.724	5.804	5.788	5.605	5.715	5.967	5.677	5.854

MPI Routines	Procs.	Average Time
4	2	3.2605
8	2	3.4660
8	3	4.4385
12	3	4.4408
24	3	4.0133
24	4	4.2454
48	5	5.0641
64	6	5.7472

In some contexts we added several processes instead of including many MPI routines in a few processes. We used 2 and 3 processes for 8 MPI routines. Similarly, we used 3 and 4 processes for 24 MPI routines. We tested with different processes to evaluate the time difference between the number of processes. The results show some differences since the symbolic execution may consume more time as the number of processes increase in the MPI code. We observe that when 24 MPI routines are executed the average time for the execution is less than the previous results. The reason for this difference could be among 24 MPI routines the orphan $MPI\_Receive$ is situated in nearly the best case scenario in the MPI code.

According to the Table 5 for the deadlock detection, the best case scenario would be an orphan *MPI_Receive* executed in the first step in process 0. If an orphan *MPI_Receive* executes at the last step in the final process, then it is the worst cast scenario. The average experiment time in Table 5 is the time the main program took to accomplish all of the tasks, which includes parsing the MPI codes, generating the AST using the ROSE compiler, extracting information from the AST and ROSE compiler, generating Yices codes, running symbolic execution in Yices, analyzing Yices output, and generating the conclusion from results.

Table 6 shows the experiment results for a non-deadlock MPI code. Time consumption for the 24 MPI routines case is higher when compared to Table 5. Since the MPI code is not under deadlock, Yices must run symbolic execution until it finds the last MPI routine in the final process. Hence, Yices consumes more time than running symbolic execution in a similar deadlocked MPI code.

Table 6. Experiments for non-deadlock MPI code

MPI Routines	Time taken for 10 experiments (secs.)									
	1	2	3	4	5	6	7	8	9	10
4	4.88	3.72	3.69	3.58	3.60	3.46	3.71	3.64	3.76	3.60
8	4.17	4.23	4.13	4.11	4.25	4.17	4.15	4.32	5.06	4.19
8	3.65	3.63	4.00	3.67	3.41	3.81	3.56	3.64	3.52	3.48
12	6.79	6.86	6.77	7.20	6.69	6.55	6.70	6.78	6.94	6.76
24	70.39	69.62	69.20	71.32	75.42	72.58	73.40	72.33	71.07	70.14
24	83.94	83.75	77.97	79.6	77.60	79.44	76.72	77.06	77.61	76.86
48	73.02	74.16	75.56	73.76	80.34	77.53	80.91	73.80	74.38	76.53
64	105.11	130.01	105.70	103.30	103.29	107.56	106.71	103.97	104.34	103.64

MPI Routines	Procs.	Average Time
4	2	3.76
8	2	4.28
8	3	3.64
12	3	6.80
24	3	71.55
24	4	79.06
48	5	76.00
64	6	107.36

6   Conclusions and Future Work

We have proposed a novel approach to find deadlock in simple MPI codes using static analysis and symbolic execution. We chose static analysis over dynamic analysis because it helps to verify a program of extremely large scale plus we can find deadlock in MPI programs without numerous executions of the code. Static analysis allows analysis of MPI codes by using static model checking techniques. To perform the static model checking we construct a symbolic model that is the basic element for building the constraints and formulas. Symbolic Execution runs the formulas that we create from constraints in the Yices SMT solver.

Also, in this research we delivered a deadlock detection program that can find deadlock in MPI codes that include only basic MPI communicative routines, e.g., MPI_Send and $MPI\_Receive$. Future research will enable many more MPI routines, such as $MPI\_Barrier$, MPI_Isend, $MPI\_Ireceive$, etc. into our deadlock detection mechanism.

Acknowledgments. This research was supported in part by grants DMS-1722692, ACI-1541392, and ACI-1440610 from the National Science Foundation.

References

1. Aho, A.V., Ullman, J.D.: Principles of Compiler Design. Addison-Wesley, Boston (1977)
2. Barrett, C., Sebastiani, R., Seshia, S., Tinelli, C.: Satisfiability modulo theories. In: Frontiers in Artificial Intelligence and Applications, vol. 185, pp. 825–885. IOS Press (2009)
3. Becker, B., Drechsler, R.: Binary Decision Diagrams: Theory and Implementation. Springer, Heidelberg (1998). https://doi.org/10.1007/978-1-4757-2892-7
4. Biere, A., Cimatti, A., Clarke, E., Zhu, Y.: Symbolic model checking without BDDs. In: Cleaveland, W.R. (ed.) TACAS 1999. LNCS, vol. 1579, pp. 193–207. Springer, Heidelberg (1999). https://doi.org/10.1007/3-540-49059-0_14
5. Chou, C.N., Ho, Y.S., Hsieh, C., Huang, C.Y.: Symbolic model checking on systemc designs. In: DAC Design Automation Conference 2012, pp. 327–333. IEEE Press (2012)
6. Clarke, E.M., Grumberg, O., Long, D.E.: Model checking and abstraction. ACM Trans. Program. Lang. Syst. **16**, 1512–1542 (1994)
7. Elwakil, M., Yang, Z., Wang, L., Chen, Q.: Message race detection for web services by an SMT-based analysis. In: Xie, B., Branke, J., Sadjadi, S.M., Zhang, D., Zhou, X. (eds.) ATC 2010. LNCS, vol. 6407, pp. 182–194. Springer, Heidelberg (2010). https://doi.org/10.1007/978-3-642-16576-4_13
8. Gropp, W., Lusk, E.: Using MPI: Portable Parallel Programming with the Message-Passing Interface. Scientific and Engineering Computation, 3rd edn. MIT Press, Cambridge (2014)
9. Gupta, S., Pratap, P., Saran, H., Arun-Kumar, S.: Dynamic code instrumentation to detect and recover from return address corruption. In: Proceedings of the 2006 International Workshop on Dynamic Systems Analysis, WODA 2006, pp. 65–72. ACM, New York (2006)
10. Hilbrich, T., de Supinski, B.R., Schulz, M., Mueller, M.S.: A graph based approach for MPI deadlock detection. In: Proceedings of the 23rd International Conference on Supercomputing, ICS 2009, pp. 296–305. ACM, New York (2009)
11. Jhala, R., Majumdar, R.: Software model checking. ACM Comput. Surv. **41**, Article ID 21 (2009)
12. Jiang, B.: Deadlock detection is really cheap. ACM SIGMOD Rec. **17**, 2–13 (1988)

13. King, J.C.: A new approach to program testing. In: Hackl, C.E. (ed.) IBM 1974. LNCS, vol. 23, pp. 278–290. Springer, Heidelberg (1975). https://doi.org/10.1007/3-540-07131-8_30

14. Kitsuregawa, K.M., Tanaka, H.: Database Machines and Knowledge Base Machines. Springer, New York (1988). https://doi.org/10.1007/978-1-4613-1679-4

15. Krishnamoorthy, K.: Detect Deadlock in MPI programs using static analysis and symbolic execution. Master's thesis, University of Wyoming, Computer Science Department, Laramie, WY (2017)

16. Khurshid, S., Păsăreanu, C.S., Visser, W.: Generalized symbolic execution for model checking and testing. In: Garavel, H., Hatcliff, J. (eds.) TACAS 2003. LNCS, vol. 2619, pp. 553–568. Springer, Heidelberg (2003). https://doi.org/10.1007/3-540-36577-X_40

17. rosecompiler.org: ROSE compiler. http://www.rosecompiler.org/. Accessed 3 Mar 2018

18. Turing, A.: On computable numbers, with an application to the entscheidungsproblem. Proc. Lond. Math. Soc. **42**, 230–265 (1937)

19. Wang, C., Yang, Y., Gupta, A., Gopalakrishnan, G.: Dynamic model checking with property driven pruning to detect race conditions. In: Cha, S.S., Choi, J.-Y., Kim, M., Lee, I., Viswanathan, M. (eds.) ATVA 2008. LNCS, vol. 5311, pp. 126–140. Springer, Heidelberg (2008). https://doi.org/10.1007/978-3-540-88387-6_11

20. yices.csl.sri.com: The Yices SMT solver.http://yices.csl.sri.com/. Accessed 3 Mar 2018

Track of Mathematical-Methods-and-Algorithms for Extreme Scale

Reproducible Roulette Wheel Sampling for Message Passing Environments

Balazs Nemeth[1(✉)], Tom Haber[1,2], Jori Liesenborgs[1], and Wim Lamotte[1]

[1] Expertise Centre for Digital Media, Wetenschapspark 2,
3590 Diepenbeek, Belgium
{balazs.nemeth,tom.haber,jori.liesenborgs,wim.lamotte}@uhasselt.be
[2] Exascience Lab, Imec, Kapeldreef 75, 3001 Leuven, Belgium

Abstract. Roulette Wheel Sampling, sometimes referred to as Fitness Proportionate Selection, is a method to sample from a set of objects each with an associated weight. This paper introduces a distributed version of the method designed for message passing environments. Theoretical bounds are derived to show that the presented method has better scalability than naive approaches. This is verified empirically on a test cluster, where improved speedup is measured. In all tested configurations, the presented method performs better than naive approaches. Through a renumbering step, communication volume is minimized. This step also ensures reproducibility regardless of the underlying architecture.

Keywords: Genetic algorithms · Roulette wheel selection
Sequential Monte Carlo · HPC · Message passing

1 Introduction

Given a set of n objects with associated weights w_i, the goal of Roulette Wheel Sampling (RWS) is to sample objects where the probability of each object j is given by a normalized weight, $\tilde{w}_j = w_j / \sum_i^n w_i$. In genetic algorithms, objects are individuals and their weight is determined by its fitness [4]. After individuals have been selected for survival, they are either mutated or recombined to form the next generation. RWS is used in the resampling step of Sequential Monte Carlo methods [1,7], where objects are weighted particles. Hereafter, this paper refers to objects in general.

The resampling step is commonly implemented in one of two ways. The first approach, referred to as the cumulative sum approach, is to generate $u \sim \mathcal{U}(0,1)$, and to select the last j for which $u \leq \sum_{i=0}^{j} \tilde{w}_i$. Computing the cumulative sum takes $\mathcal{O}(n)$ time and finding an object takes $\mathcal{O}(\log n)$. The second approach is the alias method [10]. Constructing an alias table takes $\mathcal{O}(n)$ time and taking a sample takes $\mathcal{O}(1)$ time. This results in a lower execution time, but, as Sect. 2 details, the cumulative approach is a better fit for parallelization.

This paper relies on parallel random generation techniques [8]. Since RWS is typically executed multiple times, each object is provided with a unique random

© Springer International Publishing AG, part of Springer Nature 2018
Y. Shi et al. (Eds.): ICCS 2018, LNCS 10861, pp. 799–805, 2018.
https://doi.org/10.1007/978-3-319-93701-4_63

generator from which a random number sequence can be generated in parallel. However, if such techniques are not available, any pseudo random number generator (RNG) that can either jump in its sequence or a pre-generated sequence can be used instead.

Reproducibility is a desirable property of any scientific computing code. For this reason, only methods that output the same samples are considered. This means that the results are reproducible not only for a given parallel configuration if executed repeatedly, but also if the number of processors, p, is changed.

The remainder of this paper is structured as follows. Section 2 describes how to parallelize RWS in a reproducible fashion. Experimental results are shown in Sect. 3. Section 4 lists related work. Section 5 concludes the paper and proposes future work.

2   Reproducible RWS

Given a sequence of weights, $(w_1, \ldots, w_n)$, the output of RWS is a sequence $S_1 = (s_1, \ldots, s_n)$ where s_i is the index of the object that has been selected. Let $S_2 = (s'_1, \ldots, s'_n)$ denote the output sequence of the cumulative sum approach applied to another sequence of weights, constructed by replacing the subsequence $w_j, \ldots, w_{j+k}$ by its sum. The sequence S_1 can be transformed into S_2 as follows. First, if $s_i < j$, then $s'_i = s_i$. Second, if $s_i \in [j, j+k]$, then $s'_i = j$. Finally, if $s_i > j + k$, then $s'_i = s_i - k$. In other words, the cumulative sum approach is only affected partially if weights are aggregated as shown by Fig. 1. Parts of the output sequence that correspond to non-aggregated weights are recoverable.

Let S_3 and S_4 be output sequences of applying the alias method to the same two sequences of weights. Sadly, there is no clear relationship between the elements of S_3 and S_4. The algorithm first calculates the average weight, w_a. Next, the entries of two tables are built by repeatedly combining two weights w_i and w_j for which $w_i < w_a \le w_j$, to form entries of the two tables. Weight w_j is replaced by $w_j - w_a + w_i$ and w_i is removed. The process is repeated until all weights have been removed. With small changes to weights, the entries in this table can change drastically making the alias method unstable. Therefore, this paper focuses on parallelization of the cumulative sum approach, but the alias method is mentioned here since it has the best sequential performance and forms the baseline for comparison in the performance results shown in Sect. 3.

2.1   Naive Approaches to Parallelization

This paper considers only static load balancing, where each of p processors is assigned an equal share of n objects. Collecting all weights at a single processor to perform RWS leads to a centralized approach where the master processor quickly become the bottleneck, and more communication is required as n grows. Therefore, this approach is not considered further.

Let $w_{k,j}$ denote the weights of objects assigned to processor p_k. One straightforward approach to parallelization is to fix the assignment of objects to processors. First, each processor p_k shares all its local weights $w_{k,j}$ through an

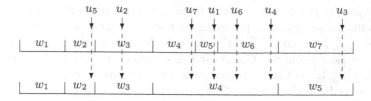

Fig. 1. Effect of replacing the subsequence w_4, w_5, w_6 by their sum. Given the same sequence of random numbers $(u_1, \ldots, u_7)$, where $u_i \sim \mathcal{U}(0, \sum_{i=1}^{7} w_i)$, the sequence at the top is $S_1 = (5, \mathbf{3}, \mathbf{7}, 6, \mathbf{2}, 6, 4)$ and the sequence at the bottom is $S_2 = (4, \mathbf{3}, \mathbf{5}, 4, \mathbf{2}, 4, 4)$. Bold indices are not effected or can be reconstructed.

all-to-all broadcast requiring $\mathcal{O}(n)$ time [5]. Next, since all weights are available, each processor builds the alias table in $\mathcal{O}(n)$ time and generates n/p samples in $\mathcal{O}(n/p)$ time. Each processor requests objects that it needs to initialize all its local output objects. Processors exchange objects by sending objects to their owner. The expected communication volume is $\mathcal{O}(n - n/p)$.

Alternatively, to save bandwidth, processors can also share the sum of their local weights, $W_k = \sum_{j=0}^{n/p} w_{k,j}$, in $\mathcal{O}(p)$ time. It might seem that the alias method could be used in this case as well. However, since the alias table would be built using the weights W_k, a different table would be built depending on p. If the parallel environment changes, the output of the sampling process will change as well, which precludes reproducible results. Instead, once all aggregate weights W_k are available, two cumulative sums are calculated in $\mathcal{O}(n/p + p)$ time and n samples are taken through a nested binary search in $\mathcal{O}(n \log(p) + (n/p) \log(n/p))$ time. Here, the first binary search is over the cumulative sum of W_k. If an object resides on p_k, a second binary search is performed over the cumulative sum of local weights, $w_{k,j}$. A single random number is used for both searches. Again, each object is sent to the processor to which it was assigned.

Three factors limit performance in both of these parallelizations. First, an all-to-all broadcast to share W_k causes communication volume to grow linearly in p. If $w_{k,j}$ are shared, communication volume also grows linearly in n. Second, each processor can communicate with every other processor when objects are exchanged. Third, the total expected communication volume to exchange objects, $\mathcal{O}(n - n/p)$, grows as either n or p increases.

2.2 Distributed Approach

The fundamental issue with the two approaches described above is that objects are assigned to processors and that this assignment is fixed. Instead, if objects are allowed to "move" in a way that minimizes communication required for exchanges, and reproducibility is maintained, efficiency can be improved.

Observe that each W_k will be distributed normally around $\sum_{i=0}^{p} W_i/p$ as n increases since all processors are treated equally. Hence the number of selected objects per processor is expected to be equal. The goal of the method presented in this paper is to exploit this fact to minimize communication. As noted earlier, the cumulative approach is parallelized. For this, each processor p_k needs to know only $\sum_{i=0}^{k-1} W_i$ and $\sum_{i=0}^{p} W_i$ since this determines the offset of its weights $w_{k,j}$ in the global context. Computing this prefix sum takes $\mathcal{O}(p)$ time [2]. In addition, $\sum_{i=0}^{p} W_i$ is needed to normalize the weights, which can be computed with an all-reduce which takes $\mathcal{O}(\log(p))$ time [5]. Next, a cumulative sum of weights $w_{k,j}$ is built locally. A single binary search suffices since a selection of objects owned by any of the processes $p_1, \ldots, p_{k-1}$ is detected directly. Finally, objects are renumbered in such a way that their identifier is independent of p.

Algorithm 1 summarizes these steps. Processor p_k draws u_i from the random generator of object i to determine where the selection is located. The total number of samples, q, for which the selected object is located at the processors $p_0, \ldots, p_{k-1}$ can be tracked since the prefix sum is available at processor p_k. Next, each processor maintains a count table of length n/p to track the number of times each local object is selected. Selections falling on processors $p_{k+1}, \ldots, p_p$, are ignored. After all n samples have been generated, the count table is traversed in $\mathcal{O}(n/p)$ time and objects are created with identifiers starting from q. The identifiers determine which processor owns the object. This renumbering step can be seen as moving objects around without communication.

Algorithm 1. Distributed RWS on processor p_k

Data: Objects $(o_1, \ldots, o_{n/p})$, associated weights $(w_{k,1}, \ldots, w_{k,n/p})$
Result: New objects $(o'_1, \ldots, o'_{n/p})$
$W_k = \sum_{j=0}^{n/p} w_{k,j}$, $W_{\text{total}} = \text{allReduce}(W_k, +)$, $W_{\text{below}} = \text{prefixSum}(W_k)$
countTable $= [0, \ldots, 0]$, $q = 0$
for $i = 1 \ldots n$ **do**
    $u_i \sim \mathcal{U}(0, W_{\text{total}})$
    if $u < W_{\text{below}}$ **then**
        $q = q + 1$
    else if $W_{\text{below}} < u < W_{\text{below}} + W_k$ **then**
        $s = \text{cumSumSearch}(u - W_{\text{below}}, (w_{k,1}, \ldots, w_{k,n/p}))$
        countTable$[s] = $ countTable$[s] + 1$
end
for $i = 1 \ldots n/p$ **do**
    for $j = 1 \ldots$ countTable$[i]$ **do**
        create new object from o_i with identifier q
        $q = q + 1$
    end
end
rebalanceObjects()   ▷ Typically, few objects moved

Sums of local weights W_k will be distributed around $\sum_{i=0}^{p} W_i/p$. Hence, approximately the same number of objects will be selected from each processor and only deviations need to be corrected. This minimizes communication volume. Whenever two processors communicate, one processor will receive objects and the other processor will transmit objects, but never both. This is easy to see by dividing the processors into two groups: $p_1, \ldots, p_k$ and $p_{k+1}, \ldots, p_p$. If the first group has less than $k \times n/p$ objects, objects will be transmitted from the second group to the first. The opposite case is also possible. A useful consequence of the numbering scheme is that, in many cases, rebalancing can be achieved by transferring objects between neighboring processors p_k and p_{k+1}. Compared to the naive approaches from Sect. 2.1 where objects can travel in both directions and tend to travel between any pairs of processors, the presented renumbering scheme reduces network contention. Finally, since identifiers are determined from a global context, they do not depend on the number of processors. This makes the presented method reproducible across different parallel architectures.

3   Results

To evaluate performance in practice, a Message Passing Interface (MPI) implementation of Algorithm 1 is compared with the naive approaches described in Sect. 2.1. Results for the parallel alias method have been omitted since they almost coincide with the results for the naive cumulative approach. Random weights are used during each step. Execution time is averaged over 10 runs, each with a different RNG seed. Figure 2 shows speedup as the number of nodes, p, is increased. The number of objects, n, increases from 2^{14} to 2^{17} vertically. The object size increases from 1 byte to 2048 bytes horizontally.

The test cluster consists of 16 node interconnected with infiniband. Each node has two Intel X5660 processors, running at 2.80 GHz, for a total of 12 cores. Speedup, $S = T_s/T_p$, with respect to the fastest sequential algorithm is studied. Here, T_s is the sequential execution time of the alias method, and T_p is the execution time of the parallel versions with p processes, one for each system in the cluster. Each process consists of 12 threads which map to 12 cores.

First, while it is not clearly visible, both naive methods perform better on a single node than on multiple nodes. The added overhead caused by communication causes performance to degrade.

Second, in the distributed version, only aggregate information is exchanged, while information *per object* is exchanged in the naive versions. With more objects, the communication overhead during the steps leading up to the rebalancing phase for the distributed version will remain minimal. Comparing figures from top to bottom for a fixed object size shows that scalability improves with more objects. For example, with 2^{14} objects of 1 byte each, all approaches show poor scalability. Note that even in this case, the distributed version still outperforms the naive versions. Moving from 2^{14} objects to 2^{17} objects increases the speedup from 2.6x to 10x with 16 nodes.

Third, communication volume in the rebalancing phase is kept to a minimum in the distributed version. Hence, compared to the sequential execution time of the alias method, speedup increases as overhead in the rebalancing phase is kept to a minimum. Comparing results from left to right confirms this behavior. For example, with 2^{15} objects of 1 byte each, speedup is limited to 4x, but with objects of 1024 bytes, this limit increases to 10x.

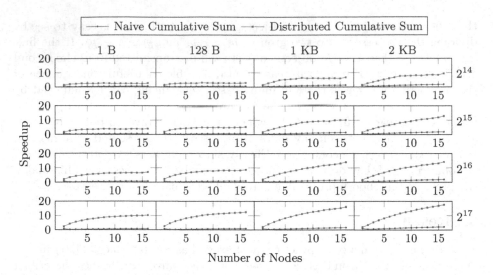

Fig. 2. Performance comparison of the parallel naive approaches described in Sect. 2.1 with the method presented in Sect. 2.2. Horizontally, object size increases from 1 byte to 2048 bytes. Vertically, the number of objects increases from 2^{14} to 2^{17}.

4 Related Work

Parallel genetic algorithms have been extensively studied in the past [3]. A single population can be managed by a master in a master-slave architecture. Again, since the master processor executes RWS, it can become the performance bottleneck. Alternatively, multiple populations can be evolved in parallel on multiple systems with occasional migrations between populations. While this improves utilization of the underlying parallel system, the output will depend on the number of processors. In contrast, the parallelization presented in Sect. 2.2 is only one step of genetic algorithms. It does not impact mathematical properties of the algorithm in which it is used.

Lipowski and Lipowska [6] use rejection sampling to sample from a set of weights w_i. Although the authors do not discuss parallelization, the downside of their method is that its computational complexity is determined by the expected number of attempts before acceptance. This is given by $\max\{w_i\}/\sum_{i=0}^{n} w_i$ which depends on the distribution of weights. Using their method in a message passing environment, either all weights are shared, or repeated communication to share weights is required for each attempt. In contrast, the run time of the parallelization from Sect. 2.2 is independent of the distribution of the weights.

5 Conclusion and Future Work

While the results show that speedup starts to converge, the presented method outperforms the naive approaches. The biggest improvements are expected for use cases with large objects. In all of the tested configurations, the distributed version performs the best and is therefore the preferred approach.

This work uses static load balancing where each processor is assigned an equal number of objects n/p. In practice, RWS is executed iteratively after objects have been updated. Typically, the time required to update objects is imbalanced between consecutive calls to the RWS subroutine. For this reason, future work will focus on dynamic load balancing techniques like work stealing [9]. Instead of restoring balance after each iteration, objects will be stolen from neighboring processors, p_{k-1} and p_{k+1}, if those processors are lagging behind.

The loop over all n objects to generate random numbers on each processor causes speedup to converge as p increases. This part of the presented method can be interpreted as being executed sequentially. It is possible to partition the loop over all processors and have each processor maintain p count tables. However, the reduction in execution time is outweighed by the additional communication volume required to share all weights and count tables. Preliminary testing has shown that, as long as p is small, such partitioning is beneficial. Hence, future work will explore exchanging weights in sets of a few processors to *partially* parallelize the loop over all objects.

Acknowledgments. Part of the work presented in this paper was funded by Johnson & Johnson.

References

1. de Freitas, N., Gordon, N., Doucet, A. (eds.): Sequential Monte Carlo Methods in Practice. Springer, Heidelberg (2001). https://doi.org/10.1007/978-1-4757-3437-9
2. Blelloch, G.E.: Prefix sums and their applications. Technical report. Synthesis of Parallel Algorithms (1990)
3. Cant-Paz, E.: A survey of parallel genetic algorithms. Calculateurs Paralleles et Reseaux Syst. Repartis **10**(2), 141–171 (1998)
4. Goldberg, D.E.: Genetic Algorithms. Pearson Education India, Noida (2006)
5. Kumar, V.: Introduction to Parallel Computing, 2nd edn. Addison-Wesley Longman Publishing Co., Inc., Boston (2002)
6. Lipowski, A., Lipowska, D.: Roulette-wheel selection via stochastic acceptance. Phys. A Stat. Mech. Appl. **391**(6), 2193–2196 (2012)
7. Moral, P.D., Jasra, A., Law, K.J.H., Zhou, Y.: Multilevel Sequential Monte Carlo samplers for normalizing constants. ACM Trans. Model. Comput. Simul. **27**(3), 20:1–20:22 (2017)
8. Salmon, J.K., Moraes, M.A., Dror, R.O., Shaw, D.E.: Parallel random numbers: as easy as 1, 2, 3. In: Proceedings of 2011 International Conference for High Performance Computing, Networking, Storage and Analysis, SC 2011, pp. 16:1–16:12. ACM, New York (2011)
9. Li, S., Hu, J., Cheng, X., Zhao, C.: Asynchronous work stealing on distributed memory systems, pp. 198–202. IEEE, February 2013
10. Vose, M.D.: A linear algorithm for generating random numbers with a given distribution. IEEE Trans. Softw. Eng. **17**(9), 972–975 (1991)

Speedup of Bicubic Spline Interpolation

Viliam Kačala[✉] and Csaba Török[✉]

P. J. Šafárik University in Košice, Jesenná 5, 040 01 Košice, Slovakia
viliam.kacala@student.upjs.sk, csaba.torok@upjs.sk

Abstract. The paper seeks to introduce a new algorithm for computation of interpolating spline surfaces over non-uniform grids with C^2 class continuity, generalizing a recently proposed approach for uniform grids originally based on a special approximation property between biquartic and bicubic polynomials. The algorithm breaks down the classical de Boor's computational task to systems of equations with reduced size and simple remainder explicit formulas. It is shown that the original algorithm and the new one are numerically equivalent and the latter is up to 50% faster than the classic approach.

Keywords: Bicubic spline · Hermite spline · Spline interpolation Speedup · Tridiagonal systems

1 Introduction

Spline interpolation belongs to the common challenges of numerical mathematics due to its application in many fields of computer science such as graphics, CAD applications or data modelling, therefore designing fast algorithms for their computation is an essential task. The paper is devoted to effective computation of bicubic spline derivatives using tridiagonal systems to construct interpolating spline surfaces. The presented *reduced* algorithm for computation of spline derivatives over non-uniform grids at the adjacent segment is based on the recently published approach for uniform spline surfaces [4–6], and it is faster than the de Boor's algorithm [2].

The structure of this article is as follows. Section 2 is devoted to a problem statement. Section 3 briefly reminds some aspects of de Boor's algorithm for computation of spline derivatives. To be self contained, de Boor's algorithm is provided in Appendix and will be further referred to as the *full* algorithm. Section 4 presents the new *reduced* algorithm and the proof of its numerical equality to the full algorithm. The fifth section analyses some details for optimal implementation of both algorithms and provides measurements of actual speed increase of the new approach.

2 Problem Statement

This section defines inputs for the spline surface and requirements, based on which it can be constructed.

© Springer International Publishing AG, part of Springer Nature 2018
Y. Shi et al. (Eds.): ICCS 2018, LNCS 10861, pp. 806–818, 2018.
https://doi.org/10.1007/978-3-319-93701-4_64

For integers $I, J > 1$ consider a non-uniform grid

$$[x_0, x_1, \ldots, x_{I-1}] \times [y_0, y_1, \ldots, y_{J-1}], \tag{1}$$

where

$$\begin{aligned} x_{i-1} < x_i, \quad i = 1, 2, \ldots, I - 1, \\ y_{j-1} < y_j, \quad j = 1, 2, \ldots, J - 1. \end{aligned} \tag{2}$$

According to [2], a spline surface is defined by given values

$$z_{i,j}, \quad i = 0, 1, \ldots, I - 1, \quad j = 0, 1, \ldots, J - 1 \tag{3}$$

at the grid-points, and given first directional derivatives

$$d_{i,j}^x, \quad i = 0, I - 1, \quad j = 0, 1, \ldots, J - 1 \tag{4}$$

at the boundary verticals,

$$d_{i,j}^y, \quad i = 0, 1, \ldots, I - 1, \quad j = 0, J - 1 \tag{5}$$

at the boundary horizontals and cross derivatives

$$d_{i,j}^{x,y}, \quad i = 0, I - 1, \quad j = 0, J - 1 \tag{6}$$

at the four corners of the grid.

The task is to define a quadruple $[z_{i,j}, d_{i,j}^x, d_{i,j}^y, d_{i,j}^{x,y}]$ at every grid-point $[x_i, y_j]$, based on which a bicubic clamped spline surface S of class C^2 can be constructed with properties

$$S(x_i, y_j) = z_{i,j}, \qquad \frac{\partial S(x_i, y_j)}{\partial y} = d_{i,j}^y,$$
$$\frac{\partial S(x_i, y_j)}{\partial x} = d_{i,j}^x, \qquad \frac{\partial^2 S(x_i, y_j)}{\partial x \partial y} = d_{i,j}^{x,y}.$$

For $I = J = 3$ the input situation is illustrated in Fig. 1 below where bold marked values represents (3)–(6) while the remaining non-bold values represent the unknown derivatives to compute.

3   Full Algorithm

The section provides a brief summary of the full algorithm designed by de Boor for computing the unknown first order derivatives that are necessary to compute a C^2 class spline surface over the input grid.

For the sake of readability and simplicity of the model equations and algorithms we introduce the following notation.

Notation 1. *For $k \in \mathbb{N}^0$ and $n \in \mathbb{N}^+$ let $\{h_k\}_{k=0}^n$ be an ordered list of real numbers. Then the value $\widehat{h}_k$ is defined as*

$$\widehat{h}_k = h_{k+1} - h_k, \tag{7}$$

where $h_k \in \{x_k, y_k\}$.

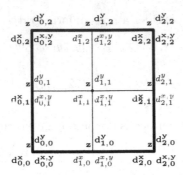

Fig. 1. Input situation for $I, J = 2$.

The full algorithm is based on a model Eq. (8) that contains indices $k = 0, 1, 2$ and parameters d_k, p_k and h_k. This model equation is used to construct different types of equation systems with corresponding indices and parameters.

Let us explain how a model equation can be used to compute first order derivatives with respect to x in the simplest case of a jth row over a 3×3 sized input grid (1) with given values (3)–(6). The input situation is graphically displayed in Fig. 1. To calculate the single unknown $d_{1,j}^x$, substitute the values (h_0, h_1, h_2) with (x_0, x_1, x_2), (p_0, p_1, p_2) with $(z_{0,j}, z_{1,j}, z_{2,j})$ and (d_0, d_1, d_2) with $(d_{0,j}^x, d_{1,j}^x, d_{2,j}^x)$ in (3), (4). Then $d_1 = d_{1,j}^x$ can be calculated using the following model equation, where D stands for derivatives and P for right-hand side parameters,

$$D_{\text{full}}(d_0, d_1, d_2, \widehat{h}_0, \widehat{h}_1) = P_{\text{full}}(p_0, p_1, p_2, \widehat{h}_0, \widehat{h}_1), \tag{8}$$

where

$$D_{\text{full}}(d_0, d_1, d_2, \widehat{h}_0, \widehat{h}_1) = \widehat{h}_0 \cdot d_2 + 2(\widehat{h}_1 + \widehat{h}_0) \cdot d_1 + \widehat{h}_1 \cdot d_0, \tag{9}$$

and

$$P_{\text{full}}(p_0, p_1, p_2, \widehat{h}_0, \widehat{h}_1) = 3 \left(\frac{\widehat{h}_0}{\widehat{h}_1} \cdot p_2 + \frac{\widehat{h}_1^2 - \widehat{h}_0^2}{\widehat{h}_1 \widehat{h}_0} \cdot p_1 - \frac{\widehat{h}_1}{\widehat{h}_0} \cdot p_0 \right). \tag{10}$$

The final algorithm for all rows and columns of any size can be found in Appendix.

4   Reduced Algorithm

The reduced algorithm for uniform splines is originally proposed by this article's second author, see also [6,8]. The model equation was obtained thanks to a special approximation property between biquartic and bicubic polynomials. The resulting algorithm is similar to the de Boor's approach, however the systems of equations are half the size and compute only half of the unknown derivates, while the remaining unknowns are computed using simple remainder formulas.

In the reduced algorithm for uniform grids the total number of arithmetic operations is equal or larger than in the full algorithm. However the algorithm is still faster than the full one thanks to two facts Firstly, it contains fewer costly floating point divisions. The second reason is that the form of the reduced equations and rest formulas is more favourable to some aspects of modern CPU architectures, namely the instruction level parallelism and system of the relatively small fast hardware caches as described in [4].

The way used to derive the new model equations can be easily generalized from uniform to non-uniform grids, however in latter case the equations are more complex and even contain more arithmetic operations than the full equations. Thus it was not clear whether the non-uniform reduced equations would be more efficient. The numerical experiments showed that the instruction level parallelism features of modern CPUs are able to mitigate the higher complexity of reduced equations and therefore imply slightly lower execution time also for non-uniform grids.

The reduced algorithm is based on two different model equations, a main and an auxiliary one, and on an explicit formula. Let us explain how the main model equation can be used to compute derivatives for the simplest case of a jth row over a 5×5 sized grid. By analogy to the previous section, substitute the values $(h_0, \ldots, h_4)$ with $(x_0, \ldots, x_4)$, $(p_0, \ldots, p_4)$ with $(z_{0,j}, \ldots, z_{4,j})$ and $(d_0, \ldots, d_4)$ with $(d_{0,j}^x, \ldots, d_{4,j}^x)$. For the row j of size 5 there are three unknown values d_1, d_2 and d_3. First, calculate $d_2 = d_{2,j}^x$ using the following model equation

$$D_{\text{red}}(d_0, d_2, d_4, \widehat{h}_0, \ldots, \widehat{h}_3) = P_{\text{full}}(p_0, \ldots, p_4, \widehat{h}_0, \ldots, \widehat{h}_3), \qquad (11)$$

where

$$D_{\text{red}}(d_0, d_2, d_4, \widehat{h}_0, \ldots, \widehat{h}_3) = (\widehat{h}_1 + \widehat{h}_0) \cdot d4$$
$$+ \frac{1}{\widehat{h}_2 \widehat{h}_1}(\widehat{h}_3 \widehat{h}_1(\widehat{h}_1 + \widehat{h}_0) + (\widehat{h}_3 + \widehat{h}_2)(\widehat{h}_2 \widehat{h}_0 - 4(\widehat{h}_1 + \widehat{h}_0)(\widehat{h}_2 + \widehat{h}_1))) \cdot d2 \qquad (12)$$
$$+ (\widehat{h}_3 + \widehat{h}_2) \cdot d0,$$

and

$$P_{\text{red}}(p_0, \ldots, p_4, \widehat{h}_0, \ldots, \widehat{h}_3) = 3 \left(\frac{(\widehat{h}_3 + \widehat{h}_2)\widehat{h}_2}{\widehat{h}_1} \left(\frac{(\widehat{h}_1 + \widehat{h}_0)^2 \cdot p_1 - \widehat{h}_1^2 \cdot p_0}{\widehat{h}_0} + \widehat{h}_0 \cdot p_2 \right) \right.$$
$$\left. + \frac{\widehat{h}_1 + \widehat{h}_0}{\widehat{h}_2} \left(\frac{\widehat{h}_1(\widehat{h}_2^2 \cdot p_4 - (\widehat{h}_3 + \widehat{h}_2)^3 \cdot p_3)}{\widehat{h}_3} - \frac{2(\widehat{h}_3 + \widehat{h}_2)(\widehat{h}_2^2 - \widehat{h}_1^2) + \widehat{h}_3 \widehat{h}_1^2}{\widehat{h}_1} \cdot p_2 \right) \right).$$
$$\tag{13}$$

Then the unknown d_1 can be calculated from

$$d_1 = R_{\text{red}}(p_0, p_1, p_2, d_0, d_2, \widehat{h}_0, \widehat{h}_1), \qquad (14)$$

where

$$R_{\text{red}}(p_0, p_1, p_2, d_0, d_2, \widehat{h}_0, \widehat{h}_1) =$$
$$= \frac{-1}{2(\widehat{h}_1 + \widehat{h}_0)\widehat{h}_1 \widehat{h}_0}(3(\widehat{h}_1^2 p_0 + (\widehat{h}_0^2 - \widehat{h}_1^2)p_1 - \widehat{h}_0^2 p_2)\widehat{h}_1 \widehat{h}_0(\widehat{h}_1 d_0 + \widehat{h}_0 d_2)). \qquad (15)$$

Relation (14) will be referred to as the explicit *rest formula* and it is also used
to compute the unknown value $d_3 = R_{red}(p_2, p_3, p_4, d_2, d_4, \widehat{h}_2, \widehat{h}_3)$ with different
indices of the right-hand side parameters.

In case the j-th row contains only four nodes, the model Eq. (11) should be
replaced with the *auxiliary model equation* for even-sized input rows or columns

$$D_{red}^A(d_0, d_2, d_3, \widehat{h}_0, \ldots, \widehat{h}_2) = P_{red}^A(p_0, \ldots, p_3, \widehat{h}_0, \ldots, \widehat{h}_2), \qquad (16)$$

where

$$\begin{aligned}
&D_{red}^A(d_0, d_2, d_3, \widehat{h}_0, \ldots, \widehat{h}_2) \\
&= -2(\widehat{h}_1 + \widehat{h}_0) \cdot d_3 + \frac{\widehat{h}_2 \widehat{h}_0 - 4(\widehat{h}_2 + \widehat{h}_1)(\widehat{h}_1 + \widehat{h}_0)}{\widehat{h}_1} \cdot d_2 + \widehat{h}_2 \widehat{h}_0 \cdot d_0,
\end{aligned} \qquad (17)$$

and

$$\begin{aligned}
P_{red}^A(p_0, \ldots, p_3, \widehat{h}_0, \ldots, \widehat{h}_2) &= 3 \left(\frac{\widehat{h}_2}{\widehat{h}_0} \left(\frac{(\widehat{h}_1 + \widehat{h}_0)^2}{\widehat{h}_1^2} \cdot p_1 - p_0 \right) \right. \\
&\left. + \frac{1}{\widehat{h}_2} \left(-2(\widehat{h}_1 + \widehat{h}_0) \cdot p_3 + \frac{\widehat{h}_0 \widehat{h}_2^2 + 2(\widehat{h}_1 + \widehat{h}_0)(\widehat{h}_1^1 - \widehat{h}_2^2)}{\widehat{h}_1^2} \cdot p_2 \right) \right).
\end{aligned} \qquad (18)$$

Thus the reduced algorithm comprises the equation system constructed from
two model Eqs. (11), (16) to compute even-indexed derivatives and the rest formula (14) to compute the odd-indexed derivatives.

The reduced algorithm for arbitrary sized input grid also consists of four
main steps, similarly to the full algorithm, each evaluating equation systems
constructed from the main (11) and auxiliary (16) model equations, and it is
summarized by the lemma below.

Lemma 1 (Reduced algorithm). *Let the grid parameters $I, J > 2$ and the
x, y, z values and d derivatives be given by (1)–(6). Then the values*

$$\begin{aligned}
d_{i,j}^x, \quad & i = 1, \ldots, I - 2, \quad j = 0, \ldots, J - 1, \\
d_{i,j}^y, \quad & i = 0, \ldots, I - 1, \quad j = 1, \ldots, J - 2, \\
d_{i,j}^{x,y}, \quad & i = 0, \ldots, I - 1, \quad j = 0, \ldots, J - 1
\end{aligned} \qquad (19)$$

*are uniquely determined by the following $\frac{3I+2J+5}{2}$ linear systems of altogether
$\frac{5IJ-I-J-23}{4}$ equations and $\frac{7IJ-7I-7J+7}{4}$ rest formulas:
for each $j = 0, 1, \ldots, J - 2$,*

solve_system(

$$\begin{aligned}
&D_{red}(d_{i-2,j}^x, d_{i,j}, d_{i+2,j}, \widehat{x}_{i-2}, \ldots, \widehat{x}_{i+1}) = P_{red}(z_{i-2,j}, \ldots, z_{i+2,j}, \\
&\widehat{x}_{i-2}, \ldots, \widehat{x}_{i+1}), \text{ where } i \in \{2, 4, \ldots, I - 3\}
\end{aligned} \qquad (20)$$

),

for each $i = 1, 3, \ldots, I - 2$ and $j = 1, 3, \ldots, J - 2$,

$$d_{i,j}^x = R_{red}(\widehat{x}_{i-1}, \widehat{x}_i, z_{i-1,j}, z_{i,j}, z_{i+1,j}, d_{i-1,j}^x, d_{i+1,j}^x), \tag{21}$$

for each $i = 0, 1, \ldots, I - 1$,

> *solve_system(*
> $D_{red}(\widehat{y}_{j-2}, \ldots, \widehat{y}_{j+1}, d_{i,j-2}^y, d_{i,j}^y, d_{i,j+2}) = P_{red}(\widehat{y}_{j-2}, \ldots, \widehat{y}_{j+1},$
> $z_{i,j-2}, \ldots, z_{i,j-2}),$ *where $j \in \{2, 4, \ldots, I - 2\}$*
> *),*

$$\tag{22}$$

for each $j = 1, 3, \ldots, J - 2$ and $i = 1, 3, \ldots, I - 2$,

$$d_{i,j}^y = R_{red}(\widehat{y}_{j-1}, \widehat{y}_j, z_{i,j-1}, z_{i,j}, z_{i,j+1}, d_{i,j-1}^y, d_{i,j+1}^x), \tag{23}$$

for each $j = 0, J - 1$,

> *solve_system(*
> $D_{red}(\widehat{x}_{i-2}, \ldots, \widehat{x}_{i+1}, d_{i-2,j}^{x,y}, x, y_{i,j}, x, y_{i+2,j}) = P_{red}(\widehat{x}_{i-2}, \ldots, \widehat{x}_{i+1},$
> $d_{i-2,j}^x, \ldots, d_{i+2,j}^x),$ *where $i \in \{2, 4, \ldots, I - 3\}$*
> *),*

$$\tag{24}$$

for each $i = 1, 3, \ldots, I - 2$ and $j = 1, 3, \ldots, J - 2$,

$$d_{i,j}^{x,y} = R_{red}(\widehat{x}_{i-1}, \widehat{x}_i, d_{i-1,j}^x, d_{i,j}^x, d_{i+1,j}^x, d_{i-1,j}^{x,y}, d_{i+1,j}^{x,y}), \tag{25}$$

for each $i = 0, 1, \ldots, I - 1$,

> *solve_system(*
> $D_{red}(\widehat{y}_{j-2}, \ldots, \widehat{y}_{j+1}, d_{i,j-2}^{x,y}, d_{i,j}^{x,y}, d_{i,j+2}) = P_{red}(\widehat{y}_{j-2}, \ldots, \widehat{y}_{j+1},$
> $d_{i,j-2}^y, \ldots, d_{i,j-2}^y),$ *where $j \in \{2, 4, \ldots, I - 2\}$*
> *),*

$$\tag{26}$$

for each $j = 1, 3, \ldots, J - 2$ and $i = 1, 3, \ldots, I - 2$,

$$d_{i,j}^y = R_{red}(\widehat{y}_{j-1}, \widehat{y}_j, d_{i,j-1}^y, d_{i,j}^y, d_{i,j+1}^y, d_{i,j-1}^{x,y}, d_{i,j+1}^{x,y}), \tag{27}$$

If I is odd, then the last model equation in steps (20) and (24) needs to be accordingly replaced by auxiliary model Eq. (16). Analogically, if J is odd, the same applies to steps (22) and (26).

Before the actual proof we should note that the reduced algorithm is intended as a faster drop-in replacement for the classic full algorithm. Therefore it should be equivalent to the full algorithm as well as to reach lower execution time to be worth of actual implementation.

Proof. To prove the equivalence of the reduced and the full algorithm we have to show that the former implies the latter.

Consider values and derivatives from (1)–(6) for $I, J = 5$. For the sake of simplicity consider only the jth row of the grid and substitute values $(h_0, \ldots, h_4)$ with $(x_0, \ldots, x_4)$, $(p_0, \ldots, p_4)$ with $(z_{0,j}, \ldots, z_{4,j})$ and $(d_0, \ldots, d_4)$ with $(d_{0,j}^x, \ldots, d_{4,j}^x)$

The unknowns $d_1 = d_{1,j}^x, \ldots, d_3 = d_{3,j}^x$ can be computed by solving the full tridiagonal system (30) of size 3. We have to show that the reduced system (20) with corresponding rest formula (21) is equivalent to the full system of size 3. One can easily notice that (20) consists of only one equation and (21) consists of two rest formulas.

The rest formula with $k = 1, 3$

$$d_k = R_{\text{red}}(p_{k-1}, p_k, p_{k+1}, d_{k-1}, d_{k+1}, \widehat{h}_{k-1}, \widehat{h}_k)$$

can be easily modified into

$$D_{\text{full}}(d_{k-1}, d_k, d_{k+1}, \widehat{h}_{k-1}, \widehat{h}_k) = P_{\text{full}}(p_{k-1}, p_k, p_{k+1}, \widehat{h}_{k-1}, \widehat{h}_k),$$

thus giving us the first and the last equations of the full equation system of size 3. The second equation of the full equation system of size 3 can be obtained from the reduced model Eq. (11). From rest formulas

$$d_1 = R_{\text{red}}(p_0, p_1, p_2, d_0, d_2, \widehat{h}_0, \widehat{h}_1),$$
$$d_3 = R_{\text{red}}(p_2, p_3, p_4, d_2, d_4, \widehat{h}_2, \widehat{h}_3)$$

we express

$$d_0 = R_{\text{red}}^*(p_0, p_1, p_2, d_1, d_2, \widehat{h}_0, \widehat{h}_1),$$
$$d_4 = R_{\text{red}}^{**}(p_2, p_3, p_4, d_2, d_3, \widehat{h}_2, \widehat{h}_3).$$

Then substitute $R_{\text{red}}^*(p_0, p_1, p_2, d_1, d_2, \widehat{h}_0, \widehat{h}_1)$ and $R_{\text{red}}^{**}(p_2, p_3, p_4, d_2, d_3, \widehat{h}_2, \widehat{h}_3)$ for d_0 and d_4 in the reduced model equation

$$D_{\text{red}}(d_0, d_2, d_4, \widehat{h}_0, \ldots, \widehat{h}_3) = P_{\text{full}}(p_0, \ldots, p_4, \widehat{h}_0, \ldots, \widehat{h}_3),$$

thus we get the second equation of the full system.

Analogically, this proof of equivalence can be extended for any number of rows or columns as well as for the case of even sized grid dimensions I and J that use the auxiliary model Eq. (16). □

5   Speed Comparison

The reduced algorithm is numerically equivalent to the full one, however there is still a question of its computational effectiveness.

First of all, let's discuss the implementation details of both algorithms and propose some low level and rather easy optimizations that significantly decrease the execution time. These optimizations positively affect both algorithms, but the reduced one is influenced to a greater extent. Although, it must be mentioned that the reduced algorithm is faster even without the optimization.

5.1   Implementation Details

The base task of both algorithms is computation of the tridiagonal system of equations described in (30), (31), (32) and (33) for the full algorithm and (20), (22), (24) and (26) for the reduced algorithm. It can be easily proved that the reduced systems are diagonally dominant, therefore our reference implementation uses the LU factorization as the basis for both full and reduced algorithms.

There are several options to optimize the equations and formulas used in both algorithms. One option is to modify the model equations to lessen the number of slow division operations, since the double precision floating point division is 3–5 times slower than multiplication, see the CPU instructions documentation [3,9,10]. This will measurably decrease the evaluation time of both algorithms.

Another, more effective optimization is memoization. Consider the full equation system from (30). The equations can be expressed in the form of

$$l_2 \cdot d_2 + l_1 \cdot d_1 + l_0 \cdot d_0 = r_2 \cdot p_2 + r_1 \cdot p_1 + r_0 \cdot p_0 \tag{28}$$

where l_{i-1}, l_i, l_{i+1}, r_{i-1}, r_i and r_{i+1} depend on $\widehat{x}_{i-i}$ and/or $\widehat{x}_i$. Since most of the $\widehat{x}$ values are used more than once in the equation system, these can be precomputed to simplify the equations and to reduce the number of calculations. Analogically, such optimization can be performed for each of the full equation systems and, of course, for each of the reduced equation systems and rest formulas as well, where such simplification will be more beneficial as the model expressions for reduced algorithm (11), (16) and (14) are more complex than those in the full algorithm (8). In our implementation for benchmarking of both algorithms, we consider only optimized equations.

Computational Complexity. We should give some words about importance of the suggested optimization. For I, J being dimensions of an input grid, the total arithmetic operation count of the full algorithm is asymptotically $63IJ$ of which $12IJ$ are divisions. For the reduced algorithm the count is $129IJ$ where the number of divisions is the same. These numbers of operations takes into account the model equations and a LU factorization of equation systems.

Given these numbers it may be questionable if the reduced algorithm is actually faster than the full one. However thanks to the pipelined superscalar nature of the modern CPU architectures and general availability of auto-optimizing compilers, the reduced algorithm is still approximately 15% faster than the full one depending on the size of grid.

For implementations with optimized form of expressions and memoization, the asymptotic number of operations is $33IJ$ of which $3IJ$ are divisions for the full algorithm. For the reduced algorithm the count is significantly lessened to $30IJ$ where the number of divisions is only $1.5IJ$. While the optimized full algorithm is only slightly faster than the unoptimized one, in case of the reduced algorithm the improvements are more noticeable. Comparing such implementations, the reduced algorithm is up to 50% faster than the optimized full algorithm. More detailed comparison of the optimized implementations is in following Subsect. 5.2.

Memory Requirements. For the sake of completness a word about memory requirements and data structures used to store input grid and helper computation buffers should be given.

To store the input grid one needs $I + J$ space to store x and y coordinates of the total $I \cdot J$ grid nodes, and additional $4IJ$ space to store the z, d^x, d^y and d^{xy} values for each node, thus giving us overall $4IJ \mid I \mid J$ space requirement just to store the input values.

Needs of the full and reduced algorithms are quite low considering the size of the input grid. The full tridiagonal systems of Eqs. (30)–(33) needs $5 \cdot max(I, J)$ space to store the lower, main and upper diagonals, right-hand side and an auxiliary buffer vector for the LU factorization. If the memoization technique described above is used, then there is a need for another $3I + 3J$ auxiliary vectors for precomputed right-hand side attributes, thus the total memory requirement for the computationally optimized implementation is $5 \cdot max(I, J) + 3(I + J)$ of space.

The reduced algorithm needs $\frac{5}{2} \cdot max(I, J)$ of space for the non-memoized implementation. Using a memoization optimization the reduced algorithm requires additional $\frac{5}{2}(I + J)$ to store precomputed right-hand side attributes of the equation systems and rest formulas, thus giving us $\frac{5}{2} \cdot (max(I, J) + I + J)$ space needed to store computational data, that is less than the space requirement of the full algorithm.

Mention must be made that the speedup for uniform grid was achieved without special care for memoization that here play a significant role.

Data Structures. Consider the input situation (1)–(6) from Sect. 2. Since the input grid may contain tens of thousands or more nodes the most effective representation of the input grid is a jagged array structure for each of the $z_{i,j}$, $d^x_{i,j}$, $d^y_{i,j}$ and $d^{xy}_{i,j}$ values. Each tridiagonal system from either of the two algorithms always depends on one row of the jagged array, thus during equation system evaluation the entire subarrays of the jagged structure can be effectively cached, supposed that the I or J dimension is not very large, see Table 1. Notice that the iterations have interchanged indices i, j in (30), (20) and (21) compared to the iteration in (31), (33), (22), (23), (26) and (27). For optimal performance an effective implementation should setup the jagged arrays in accordance with how we want to iterate the data [7].

5.2 Measured Speedup

Now it is time to compare optimal implementations of both algorithms taking into account the proposed optimizations in the previous subsection.

For this purpose a benchmark was implemented in C++17 and compiled with a 64 bit GCC 7.2.0 using -*Ofast* optimization level and individual native code generation for each tested CPU using -*march=native* setting. Testing environments comprised several computers with various recent CPUs where each system had 8–32 GB of RAM and Windows 10 operating system installed. The tests were conducted on freshly booted PCs after 5 min of idle time without running any non-essential services or processes like browsers, database engines, etc.

The tested data set comprised the grid $[x_0, x_1, \ldots, x_I] \times [y_0, y_1, \ldots, y_J]$ where $x_0 = -20$, $x_I = 20$, $y_0 = -20$, $y_J = 20$ and values $z_{i,j}$, $d_{i,j}^x$, $d_{i,j}^y$, $d_{i,j}^{x,y}$, see (3)–(6), are given from function $sin\sqrt{x^2 + y^2}$ at each grid-point. Concrete grid dimensions I and J are specified in Tables 1 and 2. The speedup values were gained averaging 5000 measurements of each algorithm.

Table 1 represents measurements on five different CPUs and consists of seven columns. The first column contains the tested CPUs ordered by their release date. Columns two through four contain measured execution times in microseconds for both algorithms and their speed ratios for grid dimension 100×100, while the last three columns analogically consist of times and ratios for grid dimension 1000×1000.

Table 1. Multiple CPU comparison of full and reduced algorithms tested on two datasets. Times are in microseconds.

CPU	$I, J = 100$			$I, J = 1000$		
	Full	Reduced	Speedup	Full	Reduced	Speedup
Intel E8200	619	413	1.50	77540	67188	1.15
AMD A6 3650M	934	657	1.42	173472	145371	1.19
Intel i3 2350M	839	553	1.52	114329	95740	1.19
Intel i7 6700K	267	173	1.54	35123	25828	1.36
AMD X4 845	495	319	1.55	92248	76139	1.21

Table 2, unlike the former table, represents measurements on different sized grids. For the sake of readability the table contains measurements from single CPU.

Let us summarize the measured performance improvement of the reduced algorithm in comparison with the full one. According to Tables 1 and 2 the measured decrease of execution time for small grids of size smaller than 500×500 is approximately 50% while for the datasets of size 1000×1000 or larger the average speedup drops to 30%. A noteworthy fact is, that the measured speed ratio between the full and reduced algorithms is in line for grids with dimensions in the order of hundreds where the total number of spline nodes will be in the order of tens of thousands. In other words the individual rows or columns of the grid should fit in the CPUs' L1 cache. In case of a sufficiently large grid, the caching will be less effective resulting in a much costlier read latency eventually mitigating the speed-up of the reduced algorithm. At some point, for very large datasets, the algorithms will be memory bound and therefore performing similarly.

Table 2. Multiple dataset comparison of full and reduced algorithms tested on i7 6700K. Times are in microseconds.

CPU	Full	Reduced	Speedup
$I, J = 50$	70	45	1.56
$I, J = 100$	267	173	1.54
$I, J = 200$	1117	736	1.52
$I, J = 500$	7680	54645	1.41
$I, J = 1000$	35123	25828	1.36
$I, J = 1500$	89337	69083	1.29
$I, J = 2000$	178875	144083	1.24

6   Discussion

Let us discuss the new algorithm from the numerical and experimental point of view. The reduced algorithm works with two model equations and a simple formula, see (11), (16) and (14). The reduced tridiagonal equation systems (20), (22), (24), (26) created from model Eqs. (11), (16) contain only two times less equations than the corresponding full systems. In addition, the reduced systems are diagonally dominant and therefore, from the theoretical point of view, computationally stable [1], similarly to the full systems. The other half of the unknowns are computed from simple explicit formulas, see (21), (23), (25), (27), and therefore do not present any issue. The maximal numerical difference between the full and reduced system solutions during our experimental calculations in our C++ implementation was shown to be in the order of 10^{-16}. As this computational error is precision-wise the edge of FP64 numbers of the IEEE 754 standard we can conclude that the proposed reduced method yields numerically accurate results in a shorter time.

7   Conclusion

The paper introduced a new algorithm to compute the unknown derivatives used for bicubic spline surfaces of class C^2. The algorithm reduces the size of the equation systems by half and computes the remaining unknown derivatives using simple explicit formulas. A substantial decrease of execution time of derivatives at grid-points has been achieved with lower memory space requirements at the cost of a slightly more complex implementation. Since the algorithm consist of many independent systems of linear equations, it can be also effectively parallelized for both CPU and GPU architectures.

Acknowledgements. This work was partially supported by projects Technicom ITMS 26220220182 and APVV-15-0091 Effective algorithms, automata and data structures.

Appendix

To be self-contained, we provide de Boor's classic algorithm [2] in a slightly modified form for easy comparison with the reduced algorithm.

Lemma 2 (Full algorithm). *Let the grid parameters $I, J > 1$ and the x, y, z values and d derivatives be given by (1)–(6). Then values*

$$
\begin{aligned}
d_{i,j}^{x}, &\quad i = 1, \ldots, I - 2, \quad j = 0, \ldots, J - 1, \\
d_{i,j}^{y}, &\quad i = 0, \ldots, I - 1, \quad j = 1, \ldots, J - 2, \\
d_{i,j}^{x,y}, &\quad i = 0, \ldots, I - 1, \quad j = 0, \ldots, J - 1
\end{aligned}
\tag{29}
$$

are uniquely determined by the following $2I + J + 2$ linear systems of altogether $3IJ - 2I - 2J - 4$ equations:
for each $j = 0, \ldots, J - 1$,

$$
solve\_system(
$$
$$
D_{full}(d_{i-1,j}^{x}, d_{i,j}^{x}, d_{i+1,j}^{x}, \widehat{x}_{i-1}, \widehat{x}_i) = P_{full}(z_{i-1,j}, z_{i,j}, z_{i+1,j}, \widehat{x}_{i-1}, \widehat{x}_i),
$$
$$
where\ i \in \{1, \ldots, I - 2\}
\tag{30}
$$
$$
),
$$

for each $i = 0, \ldots, I - 1$,

$$
solve\_system(
$$
$$
D_{full}(d_{i,j-1}^{y}, d_{i,j}^{y}, d_{i,j+1}^{y}, \widehat{y}_{j-1}, \widehat{y}_j) = P_{full}(z_{i,j-1}, z_{i,j}, z_{i,j+1}, \widehat{y}_{j-1}, \widehat{y}_j),
$$
$$
where\ j \in \{1, \ldots, J - 2\}
\tag{31}
$$
$$
),
$$

for each $j = 0, J - 1$,

$$
solve\_system(
$$
$$
D_{full}(d_{i-1,j}^{x,y}, d_{i,j}^{x,y}, d_{i+1,j}^{x,y}, \widehat{x}_{i-1}, \widehat{x}_i) = P_{full}(d_{i-1,j}^{y}, d_{i,j}^{y}, d_{i+1,j}^{y}, \widehat{x}_{i-1}, \widehat{x}_i),
$$
$$
where\ i \in \{1, \ldots, I - 2\}
\tag{32}
$$
$$
),
$$

for each $i = 0, \ldots, I - 1$,

$$
solve\_system(
$$
$$
D_{full}(d_{i,j-1}^{x,y}, d_{i,j}^{x,y}, d_{i,j+1}^{y}, \widehat{y}_{j-1}, \widehat{y}_j) = P_{full}(d_{i,j-1}^{x}, d_{i,j}^{x}, d_{i,j+1}^{x}, \widehat{y}_{j-1}, \widehat{y}_j),
$$
$$
where\ j \in \{1, \ldots, J - 2\}
\tag{33}
$$
$$
),
$$

References

1. Björck, A.: Numerical Methods in Matrix Computations. Springer, Heidelberg (2015). https://doi.org/10.1007/978-3-319-05089-8
2. de Boor, C.: Bicubic spline interpolation. J. Math. Phys. **41**(3), 212–218 (1962)
3. Intel 64 and IA-32 Architectures Optimization Reference Manual. Intel Corp., C-5-C-16 (2016). http://www.intel.com/content/dam/www/public/us/en/documents/manuals/64-ia-32-architectures-optimization-manual.pdf
4. Kačala, V., Miňo, L.: Speeding up the computation of uniform bicubic spline surfaces. Com. Sci. Res. Not. **2701**, 73–80 (2017)
5. Kačala, V., Miňo, L., Török, Cs.: Enhanced speedup of uniform bicubic spline surfaces. ITAT 2018, to appear
6. Miňo, L., Török, Cs.: Fast algorithm for spline surfaces. Communication of the Joint Institute for Nuclear Research, Dubna, Russia, E11–2015-77, pp. 1–19 (2015)
7. Patterson, J.R.C.: Modern Microprocessors - A 90-Minute Guide!, Lighterra (2015)
8. Török, Cs.: On reduction of equations' number for cubic splines. Matematicheskoe modelirovanie, **26**(11) (2014)
9. Software Optimization Guide for AMD Family 10h and 12h Processors. Advanced Micro Devices Inc., pp. 265–279 (2011). http://support.amd.com/TechDocs/40546.pdf
10. Software Optimization Guide for AMD Family 15h Processors. Advanced Micro Devices Inc., pp. 265–279 (2014). http://support.amd.com/TechDocs/40546.pdf

Track of Multiscale Modelling and Simulation

Multiscale Modelling and Simulation, 15th International Workshop

Derek Groen[1], Valeria Krzhizhanovskaya[2,3], Alfons Hoekstra[2],
Bartosz Bosak[4], and Lin Gan[5]

[1] Brunel University London, Kingston Lane, London UB8 3PH, UK
Derek.Groen@brunel.ac.uk
[2] University of Amsterdam, Amsterdam, The Netherlands
[3] ITMO University, Saint Petersburg, Russia
[4] Poznan Supercomputing and Networking Center, Poznan, Poland
[5] Tsinghua University, Beijing, China

Abstract. Multiscale Modelling and Simulation (MMS) is a computational approach which relies on multiple models, to be coupled and combined for the purpose of solving a complex scientific problem. Each of these models operates on its own space and time scale, and bridging the scale separation between models in a reliable, robust and accurate manner is one of the main challenges today. The challenges engenders much more than scale bridging alone, as code deployment, error quantification, scientific analysis and performance optimization are key aspects to establishing viable scientific cases for multiscale computing. The aim of the MMS workshop, of which this is the 15th edition, is to encourage and consolidate the progress in this multidisciplinary research field, both in the areas of the scientific applications and the underlying infrastructures that enable these applications. In this preface, we summarize the scope of the workshop and highlight key aspects of this year's submissions.

Keywords: Multiscale simulation · Parallel computing
Multiscale computing · Multiscale modelling

Introduction to the Workshop

Modelling and simulation of multiscale systems constitutes a grand challenge in computational science, and is widely applied in fields ranging from the physical sciences and engineering to the life science and the socio-economic domain. Most of the real-life systems encompass interactions within and between a wide range of space and time scales, and/or on many separate levels of organization. They require the development of sophisticated models and computational techniques to accurately simulate the diversity and complexity of multiscale problems, and to effectively capture the wide range of relevant phenomena within these simulations.

Additionally, these multiscale models frequently need large scale computing capabilities, solid uncertainty quantification, as well as dedicated software and services that enable the exploitation of existing and evolving computational ecosystems. Through this workshop we aim to provide a forum for multiscale application developers, framework developers and experts from the distributed infrastructure communities. In doing so we aim to identify and discuss challenges in, and possible solutions for, modelling and simulating multiscale systems, as well as their execution on advanced computational resources and their validation against experimental data.

The series of workshops devoted to multiscale modelling and simulation is organized annually from 2002 [1, 2], and this edition constitutes the 15th occasion that we hold this workshop. The discussed topics cover a range of application domains as well as cross-disciplinary research on multiscale simulation.

The workshop will contain the presentations about theoretical, general concepts of the multiscale computing and those focused on specific use-cases and describing real-life applications of multiscale modelling and simulation.

The first session contains four presentations, geared towards applied mathematics and engineering applications. Vidal-Ferrandiz et al. will present a range of optimization efforts in the context of multiscale modelling of neutron transport, while Olmo-Juan et al. will discuss the modelling of noise propagation in a pressurized water nuclear reactor. Wei Ze et al. will discuss the multi-scale homogenization of pre-treatment rapid and slow filtration processes, both from a computational and an experimental perspective, while Carreno will conclude the session with proposed solutions for the lambda modes problem using block iterative eigensolvers.

The second session contains three presentation, with a focus on medicine and humanity more widely. Garbey et al. will present a flexible hybrid agent-based, particle and partial differential equations method, applied to analyze vascular adaptation in the body. Madrahimov et al., will present results from large-scale network simulations to enable the systematic identification and evaluation of antiviral drugs. Lastly, Groen will present a prototype multiscale migration simulation, which is able to execute in parallel and can be flexibly coupled to microscale models.

Given the nature of the workshop, we look forward to lively discussions as communities from different disciplines will have the opportunity meet and to exchange ideas on general-purpose approaches from different angles. We hope that workshop will help participants to get familiar with the latest multiscale modelling, simulation and computing advances from other fields, and provide new inspiration for their own efforts.

With representation from leading institutions across the globe, the 15th edition of Multiscale Modelling and Simulation Workshop is indeed at the forefront of computational science.

Acknowledgements. We are grateful to all the members of the Programme Committee for their help and support in reviewing the submissions of this year's workshop. This includes D. Coster, W. Funika, Y. Gorbachev, V. Jancauskas, J. Jaroš, Dr Jingheng, P. Koumoutsakos, S. MacLachlan, R. Melnik, L. Mountrakis, T. Piontek, S. Portegies Zwart, A. Revell, F. X. Roux, K. Rycerz, U. Schiller, J. Suter and S. Zasada.

References

1. Groen, D., Bosak, B., Krzhizhanovskaya, V., Hoekstra, A., Koumoutsakos, P.: Multiscale modelling and simulation, 14th international workshop. Procedia Comput. Sci. **108**, 1811–1812 (2017). International Conference on Computational Science, ICCS 2017, 12–14 June 2017, Zurich, Switzerland
2. Krzhizhanovskaya, V., Groen, D., Bozak, B., Hoekstra, A.: Multiscale modelling and simulation workshop: 12 years of inspiration. Procedia Comput. Sci. **51**, 1082–1087 (2015)

Optimized Eigenvalue Solvers
for the Neutron Transport Equation

Antoni Vidal-Ferràndiz[1][(✉)] ⓘ, Sebastián González-Pintor[2] ⓘ,
Damián Ginestar[3] ⓘ, Amanda Carreño[1] ⓘ, and Gumersindo Verdú[1] ⓘ

[1] Instituto Universitario de Seguridad Industrial, Radiofísica y Medioambiental,
Universitat Politècnica de València, València, Spain
anvifer2@upv.es, {amcarsan,gverdu}@iqn.upv.es
[2] Zenuity, Lindholmspiren 2, 41756 Göteborg, Sweden
segonpin@gmail.com
[3] Instituto Universitario de Matemática Multidisciplinar,
Universitat Politècnica de València, València, Spain
dginesta@mat.upv.es

Abstract. A discrete ordinates method has been developed to approximate the neutron transport equation for the computation of the lambda modes of a given configuration of a nuclear reactor core. This method is based on discrete ordinates method for the angular discretization, resulting in a very large and sparse algebraic generalized eigenvalue problem. The computation of the dominant eigenvalue of this problem and its corresponding eigenfunction has been done with a matrix-free implementation using both, the power iteration method and the Krylov-Schur method. The performance of these methods has been compared solving different benchmark problems with different dominant ratios.

Keywords: Neutron transport · Discrete ordinates · Eigenvalues

1 Introduction

Neutron transport simulations of nuclear systems are an important goal to ensure the efficient and safe operation of nuclear reactors. The steady-state neutron transport equation [4] predicts the quantity of neutrons in every region of the reactor and thus, the number of fissions and nuclear reactions. The neutron transport equation for three-dimensional problems is an equation defined in a support space of dimension 7, and this makes that high-fidelity simulations using this equation can only be done using super computers.

Different approximations have been successfully used for deterministic neutron transport. They eliminate the energy dependence of the equations by means of the a multi-group approximation and use a special treatment to eliminate the dependence on the direction of flight of the incident neutrons. The angular discretization of the neutron transport equation chosen in this work has been the Discrete Ordinates method (S_N), which is a collocation method based on a

© Springer International Publishing AG, part of Springer Nature 2018
Y. Shi et al. (Eds.): ICCS 2018, LNCS 10861, pp. 823–832, 2018.
https://doi.org/10.1007/978-3-319-93701-4_65

quadrature set of points for the unit sphere, [4], obtaining equations depending only on the spatial variables. A high-order discontinuous Galerkin finite element method has been used for the spatial discretization. Finally, a large algebraic generalized eigenvalue problem with rank deficient matrices must be solved.

The eigenvalue problem arising from the different approximations to the deterministic neutron transport equations is classically solved with the power iteration method. However, Krylov methods are becoming increasingly popular. These methods permit to solve the eigenvalue problem faster when the power iteration convergence decreases due to high dominance ratios. They also permit to compute more eigenvalues than the largest one. We study the advantage of using a Krylov subspace method such as the Krylov-Schur method for these generalized eigenproblems, compared to the use of simpler solvers as the power iteration method.

The rest of the paper is organized as follows. Section 2 describes the angular discretization method employed. Then, Sect. 3 briefly reviews the power iteration method and the Krylov-Schur methodology to solve the resulting algebraic eigenvalue problem. In Sect. 4 some numerical results are given for one-dimensional problems in order to check which is the optimal quadrature order in the S_N method and the performance of the eigenvalue solvers. Lastly, the main conclusions of the work are summarized in Sect. 5.

2   The Discrete Ordinates Method

The energy multigroup neutron transport equation, which describes the neutron position and energy, can be written as

$$\mathcal{L}_g \psi_g = \sum_{g'=1}^{G} \left(\mathcal{S}_{g,g'} + \frac{1}{\lambda} \chi_g \mathcal{F}_{g'} \right) \psi_{g'}, \qquad g = 1, \ldots, G \qquad (1)$$

where ψ_g is the angular neutron flux of energy group g. $\mathcal{L}_g$ is the transport operator, $\mathcal{S}_{g,g'}$ is the scattering operator and $\mathcal{F}_{g'}$ is the fission source operator. They are defined as

$$\mathcal{L}_g \psi_g = \Omega \cdot \nabla \psi_g + \Sigma_{t,g} \psi_g, \qquad (2)$$

$$\mathcal{S}_{g,g'} \psi_{g'} = \int_{(4\pi)} \Sigma_{s,gg'} \psi_{g'} \mathrm{d}\Omega', \qquad (3)$$

$$\mathcal{F}_{g'} \psi_{g'} = \frac{1}{4\pi} \nu_{g'} \Sigma_{f,g'} \int_{(4\pi)} \psi_{g'} \mathrm{d}\Omega', \qquad (4)$$

where $\Sigma_{t,g}$, $\Sigma_{s,gg'}$ and $\Sigma_{f,g'}$ are the total, scattering and fission cross sections. ν_g is the average number of neutrons produced per fission. Finally, Ω is the unitary solid angle.

This equation is discretized in the angular variable by means of a collocation method on a set of quadrature points of the unit sphere, $\{\Omega_n\}_{n=1}^{N'}$ with their respective weights $\{\omega_n\}_{n=1}^{N'}$. This method is referred as the *Discrete Ordinates* method, S_N [4].

At this point, the scattering cross section is expanded into a series of Legendre polynomials as

$$\Sigma_{s,\,gg'}(\mathbf{r},\,\Omega' \cdot \Omega) = \sum_{l=0}^{L} \frac{l+1}{4\pi} \Sigma_{s,\,gg',\,l}(\mathbf{r}) P_l(\Omega' \cdot \Omega) \tag{5}$$

where the expansion is usually truncated at $L = 0$, assuming isotropic scattering.

The addition theorem of the spherical harmonics gives an expression for $P_l(\Omega' \cdot \Omega)$ as a function of Y_l^m and Y_l^{m*}. Making use of this expression an the orthogonality properties of the spherical harmonics, the scattering source (3) becomes

$$\mathcal{S}_{g,g'}\psi_{g'} = \sum_{l=0}^{L} \Sigma_{s,\,gg',\,l} \sum_{m=-l}^{l} Y_l^m \phi_{g',\,ml} \tag{6}$$

where $\phi_{g',\,ml}$ is the flux moment. The scattering source term calculation is performed projecting it in the spherical harmonics basis. So the projector moment-to-direction operator is expressed as follows

$$\psi(\mathbf{r},\,\Omega) = \mathcal{M}\phi(\mathbf{r}) = \sum_{l=0}^{L} \sum_{m=-l}^{l} Y_l^m(\Omega)\phi_{ml}(\mathbf{r}) \tag{7}$$

and the direction-to-moment operator is

$$\phi_{ml}(\mathbf{r}) = \mathcal{D}\psi(\mathbf{r},\,\Omega) = \int_{(4\pi)} d\Omega\, Y_l^{m*}(\Omega)\psi(\mathbf{r},\,\Omega) \tag{8}$$

where generally $\mathcal{L} \neq \mathcal{M}^{-1}$.

Using the angular discrete ordinates quadrature set the discrete ordinates equation is written as

$$\mathcal{L}_{g,n}\psi_{g,n} = \mathcal{M}_n \sum_{g'=1}^{G} \mathcal{S}_{g,g'}\mathcal{D}\psi_{g'} + \frac{\chi_g}{\lambda} \sum_{g'=1}^{G} \mathcal{F}_{g'}\phi_{g'}^0, \tag{9}$$

$$g = 1,\,\ldots,\,G, \qquad n = 1,\,\ldots,\,N',$$

where

$$\psi_{g,n}(\mathbf{r}) = \psi(\mathbf{r},\,\Omega_n) \tag{10}$$

and the transport and fission operators are redefined by

$$\mathcal{L}_{g,m}\psi_{g,n} = \Omega \cdot \nabla\psi_{g,n} + \Sigma_{t,g}\psi_{g,n}\,,$$

$$\mathcal{F}_{g'}\psi_{g'} = \frac{1}{4\pi}\nu_{g'}\Sigma_{f,g'}\psi_{g'}d\Omega'\,,$$

The angular discretization to the boundary conditions is applied in a straight-forward way, because it we can be applied for the specific set of directions used.

3 Eigenvalue Calculation

The following algebraic generalized eigenvalue problem is obtained from Eq. (9).

$$\mathbf{L}\Psi = \mathbf{MSD}\Psi + \frac{1}{\lambda}\mathbf{XFD}\Psi \tag{11}$$

where each matrix is the result of the energetic, angular and spatial discretization of neutron transport operators. Equation (11) can be arranged into an ordinary eigenvalue problem of the form

$$\mathbf{A}\Phi = \lambda\Phi, \tag{12}$$

where $\mathbf{A} = \mathbf{DH}^{-1}\mathbf{XF}$, $\mathbf{H} = \mathbf{L} - \mathbf{MSD}$ and $\Phi = \mathbf{D}\Psi$. In particular, the solution of the system involving $\mathbf{H}$ is performed as $\mathbf{H}^{-1}v = (\mathbf{I} - \mathbf{L}^{-1}\mathbf{MSD})^{-1}\mathbf{L}^{-1}v$, which greatly reduces the number of iterations needed to solve the system, where $\mathbf{L}^{-1}$ is the most costly operation known as the *transport sweep*.

It must be said that all the matrices involved in this computation are large and sparse. They can have more than hundreds of millions of rows and columns. Then, we cannot explicitly compute the inverse of any of these matrices. Moreover all of these matrices are computed on the fly using a matrix-free scheme [3].

To solve the ordinary eigenvalue problem (12) only the multiplication by the matrix $\mathbf{A}$ is available. Each multiplication is usually called an outer iteration and the total number of outer iterations is defined as O.

The matrices $\mathbf{L}$, $\mathbf{M}$ and $\mathbf{D}$ are block diagonal where each block corresponds to the transport equation for a particular energy group. If a problem does no have up-scattering, the $\mathbf{S}$ is block lower triangular. In that case, the action of the operator $\mathbf{H}$ on a vector is calculated by block forward substitution for each group from high to low energy in a sequence. Each forward substitution requires solving the spatially discretized S_N equations for a single energy group, which is called the source problem [7]. This source problem is usually solved by using an iterative method. The iterations used to solve each source problem are called inner iterations, and the total number of inner iterations used to solve the source problems for every energy group and for every outer iteration is denoted by I. It is worth to notice that each inner iteration performs exactly one transport sweep, so we can expect the computational time to be proportional to the number of transport sweeps, and thus, proportional to the number of inner iterations I.

3.1 Power Iteration Method

The power iteration method to solve the eigenvalue problem (12) reads as the iterative procedure

$$\Phi^{i+1} = \frac{1}{\lambda^{(i)}}\mathbf{A}\Phi^i, \tag{13}$$

where the fundamental eigenvalue is updated at each iteration according to the Rayleigh quotient

$$\lambda^{(i+1)} = \lambda^{(i)}\frac{\Phi^{(i)T}XF\Phi^{(i+1)}}{\Phi^{(i)T}XF\Phi^{(i)}}, \tag{14}$$

where $\Phi^{(i)} = D\Psi^{(i)}$. It has been observed that using Rayleigh quotient for the eigenvalue can usually improve the efficiency of the power iteration method by providing a better estimate (earlier) of the eigenvalue.

Power iteration will converge to the eigenvalue of largest magnitude, k_{eff}. If more than one eigenvalue is requested a deflation technique should be used. In other words, it can be computed one harmonic at a time while decontaminating the subspace of the computed eigenvalue. However, the deflation technique has a very slow convergence. The convergence rate is determined by the dominance ratio $\delta = |\lambda_2|/|\lambda_1|$, where λ_2 is the next largest eigenvalue in magnitude [7]. Convergence of the power iteration method slows as $\delta \to 1.0$.

3.2   Krylov-Schur Method

The Krylov-Schur method is an Arnoldi method which uses an implicit restart based on a Krylov-Schur decomposition [6]. This technique permits to solve more than one eigenvalue without an excessive extra computational cost. In this work, the Krylov-Schur method algorithm has been implemented using the eigenvalue problem library SLEPc [1]. The Arnoldi method is based on the creation of a Krylov subspace of dimension m,

$$\mathcal{K}_m(A, \Phi^{(0)}) = \text{span}\{\Phi^{(0)}, \mathbf{A}\Phi^{(0)}, \dots, \mathbf{A}^{m-1}\Phi^{(0)}\}. \tag{15}$$

If V_m is a basis of the Krylov subspace of dimension m the method is based on the Krylov decomposition of order m,

$$AV_m = V_m B_m + v_{m+1} b*_{m+1}, \tag{16}$$

in which matrix B_m is not restricted to be an upper Hessenberg matrix and b_{m+1} is an arbitrary vector.

Krylov decompositions are invariant under (orthogonal) similarity transformations, so that

$$AV_m Q = V_m Q(Q^T B_m Q) + v_{m+1} b_{m+1}^T Q,$$

with $Q^T Q = I$, is also a Krylov decomposition. In particular, one can choose Q in such way that $S_m = Q^T B_m Q$ is in a (real) Schur form, that is, upper (quasi-)triangular with the eigenvalues in the 1×1 or 2×2 diagonal blocks. This particular class of relation, called Krylov-Schur decomposition, can be written in block form as

$$A\left(\tilde{V}_1 \; \tilde{V}_2\right) = \left(\tilde{V}_1 \; \tilde{V}_2\right) \begin{pmatrix} S_{11} & S_{12} \\ 0 & S_{22} \end{pmatrix} + v_{m+1} \left(\tilde{b}_1^T \; \tilde{b}_2^T\right),$$

and has the nice feature that it can be truncated, resulting into a smaller Krylov-Schur decomposition,

$$A\tilde{V}_1 = \tilde{V}_1 S_{11} + v_{m+1} \tilde{b}_1^T,$$

that can be extended again to order m.

4 Numerical Results

4.1 Seven-Region Heterogeneous Slab

A seven-region one-dimensional slab is solved in order to show the capability of the discrete ordinate method to approximate accurately the neutron transport equation. Figure 1 shows the geometry definition of this problem and Table 1 displays the one energy group cross sections. This benchmark was defined and solved using the Green's Function Method (GFM) in [2].

Table 2 shows a comparison for different quadrature orders of the discrete ordinates method of the first 4 eigenvalues of the 1D heterogenoeus slab problem and their error. The eigenvalue error is defined in pcm $\Delta\lambda = 10^5 |\lambda - \lambda_{\mathrm{ref}}|$ where λ_{ref} is the reference eigenvalue extracted from [2].

Figure 2 shows the neutron flux distribution for the fundamental eigenvalue using S_4, S_{16} and S_{64}. In Fig. 3, we can observe an exponential convergence of all the eigenvalues with the quadrature order, N, in the discrete ordinates method.

Reflector	Fuel	Reflector	Fuel	Reflector	Fuel	Reflector
2.7 cm	2.4 cm	2.7 cm	2.4 cm	2.7 cm	2.4 cm	2.7 cm

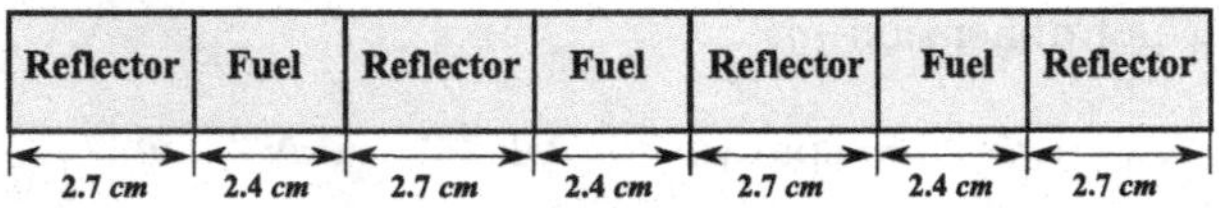

Fig. 1. Geometry of the seven region heterogeneous slab.

Table 1. Eigenvalues results for the 1D heterogeneous slab.

Material	$\nu\Sigma_f(\mathrm{cm}^{-1})$	$\Sigma_s\,(\mathrm{cm}^{-1})$	$\Sigma_t\,(\mathrm{cm}^{-1})$
Fuel	0.178	0.334	0.416667
Reflector	0.000	0.334	0.370370

Table 2. Eigenvalues results for the 1D heterogeneous slab.

	k_{eff}	Δk_{eff}	λ_2	$\Delta\lambda_2$	λ_3	$\Delta\lambda_3$	λ_4	$\Delta\lambda_4$
S_4	1.15885	1476	0.74012	1841	0.53128	2049	0.16603	4602
S_{16}	1.17319	42	0.75808	45	0.55139	38	0.21053	152
S_{64}	1.17359	2	0.75850	3	0.55175	2	0.21200	5
GFM	1.17361		0.75853		0.55177		0.21205	

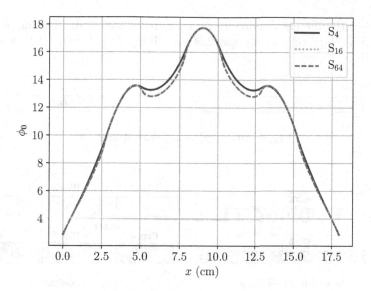

Fig. 2. Scalar neutron flux solution for the fundamental eigenvalue.

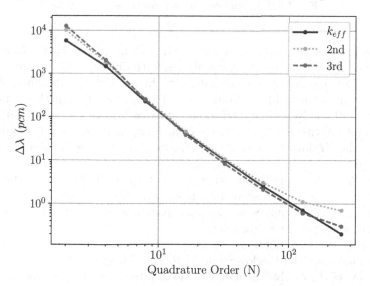

Fig. 3. Eigenvalue errors for the 1D heterogeneous slab.

4.2   MOX Fuel Slab

The second numerical example studied corresponds to a one-dimensional mixed oxide (MOX) problem, derived from the C5G7 benchmark [5]. The MOX fuel geometry is defined in Fig. 4. The assemblies definition and the materials of each assembly are described in Fig. 5a and b. Seven group cross section data are given in reference [5]. In this work, up-scattering has been neglected and different problems with different dominance ratios, δ, have been defined changing the pin size from 1.26 cm to 1.50 cm and 2.00 cm giving $\delta = 0.895$, 0.945 and 0.975, respectively.

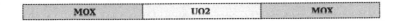

Fig. 4. MOX fuel benchmark definition.

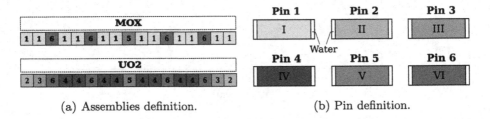

(a) Assemblies definition.   (b) Pin definition.

Fig. 5. MOX fuel benchmark materials definition

Table 3 shows the number of outer, O, and inner iterations, I, using the eigenvalue solvers for the different problems with different dominance ratio that have been defined. It can be seen that for problems with a high dominance ratio Krylov-Schur method can be from 1.5 to 6 times faster than the usual power iteration method. Note that high dominance ratios are needed to outperform power iteration with Krylov-Schur method. Also, for these high dominance ratio problems the Krylov subspace dimension, m, must be high to achieve a better performance.

Figure 6 displays the linear dependence of the CPU time with the number of inner iterations, as expected. In other words, the algorithm spends most of the computational resources in the inner iterations, due to the application of a transport sweep per inner iteration.

It is important to mention here that neglecting the upscattering makes the problem easier for the Krylov-Schur method. This is due to the fact that the product by H^{-1} is only calculated approximately, and the Arnoldi method is more sensible to the error in this approximation than the power iteration. The reason is that the system has to be solved accurately in order to have a Krylov basis, which is essential for the convergence of the Krylov method to the right solution, while solving this system in an approximate manner requires more iterations of the Power Iteration method, but does not affect its final accuracy. Neglecting the up-scattering we solve the system using just one block Gauss-Seidel iteration because of the block lower triangular structure of H, thus neglecting this effect that will be considered in future works.

Table 3. Performance results in the MOX Fuel Slab

δ	Method	m	O	I	Time (s)
0.895	Power iteration	-	31	2410	14.0
	Krylov-Schur	3	25	3771	22.5
	Krylov-Schur	5	14	2129	11.9
	Krylov-Schur	10	10	1509	9.1
0.945	Power iteration	-	100	7447	44.8
	Krylov-Schur	3	31	4542	36.8
	Krylov-Schur	5	17	2484	14.0
	Krylov-Schur	10	20	2914	16.7
0.975	Power iteration	-	191	14264	85.0
	Krylov-Schur	3	53	7876	52.2
	Krylov-Schur	5	23	3364	19.3
	Krylov-Schur	10	17	2484	14.0

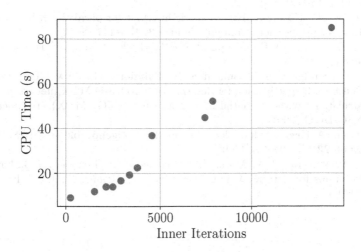

Fig. 6. Dependence of CPU time with the number of inner iterations

5   Conclusions

In this work, a S_N method has been presented to solve the eigenvalue problem associated to the steady-state neutron transport equation. The generalized algebraic eigenvalue problem resulting from the energy, angles and spatial discretization is sparse and large. Then, it was implemented using a matrix-free methodology. Two eigenvalue solvers have been considered, the usual power iteration method and the Krylov-Schur method and the performance of both methods have been evaluated solving different problems with different dominance ratios. From the obtained results in can be concluded that only for problems with high dominance ratios, $\delta > 0.85$, without up-scattering it is worth to use the Krylov subspace method. Also, this method is a good alternative if more than one eigenvalue must be computed. Otherwise it is better to use the simpler power iteration method to compute the dominant eigenvalue and its corresponding eigenfunction for a reactor core.

Acknowledgements. The work has been partially supported by the Ministerio de Economía y Competitividad under projects ENE2017-89029-P and MTM2014-58159-P, the Generalitat Valenciana under PROMETEO II/2014/008 and the Universitat Politècnica de València under FPI-2013.

References

1. Hernandez, V., Roman, J.E., Vidal, V.: SLEPc: a scalable and flexible toolkit for the solution of eigenvalue problems. ACM Trans. Math. Softw. **31**(3), 351–362 (2005)
2. Kornreich, D.E., Parsons, D.K.: The green's function method for effective multiplication benchmark calculations in multi-region slab geometry. Ann. Nucl. Energy **31**(13), 1477–1494 (2004)
3. Kronbichler, M., Kormann, K.: A generic interface for parallel cell-based finite element operator application. Comput. Fluids **63**, 135–147 (2012)
4. Lewis, E.E., Miller, W.F.: Computational Methods of Neutron Transport. Wiley, New York (1984)
5. Lewis, E.E., Smith, M.A., Tsoulfanidis, N., Palmiotti, G., Taiwo, T.A., Blomquist, R.N.: Benchmark specification for deterministic 2-D/3-D MOX fuel assembly transport calculations without spatial homogenization (C5G7 MOX). Technical report, NEA/NSC/DOC (2001)
6. Stewart, G.: A Krylov-Schur algorithm for large eigenproblems. SIAM J. Matrix Anal. Appl. **23**(3), 601–614 (2002)
7. Warsa, J.S., Wareing, T.A., Morel, J.E., McGhee, J.M., Lehoucq, R.B.: Krylov subspace iterations for deterministic k-eigenvalue calculations. Nucl. Sci. Eng. **147**(1), 26–42 (2004)

Multiscale Homogenization of Pre-treatment Rapid and Slow Filtration Processes with Experimental and Computational Validations

Alvin Wei Ze Chew[1] and Adrian Wing-Keung Law[1,2($\boxtimes$)]

[1] School of Civil and Environmental Engineering,
Nanyang Technological University, N1-01c-98,
50 Nanyang Avenue, Singapore 639798, Singapore
cwklaw@ntu.edu.sg
[2] Environmental Process Modelling Centre (EPMC),
Nanyang Environment and Water Research Institute (NEWRI),
1 Cleantech Loop, CleanTech One, #06-08, Singapore 637141, Singapore

Abstract. In this paper, we summarize on an approach which couples the multiscale method with the homogenization theory to model the pre-treatment depth filtration process in desalination facilities. By first coupling the fluid and solute problems, we systematically derive the homogenized equations for the effective filtration process while introducing appropriate boundary conditions to account for the deposition process occurring on the spheres' boundaries. Validation of the predicted results from the homogenized model is achieved by comparing with our own experimentally-derived values from a lab-scale depth filter. Importantly, we identify a need to include a computational approach to resolve for the non-linear concentration parameter within the defined periodic cell at higher orders of reaction. The computational values can then be introduced back into the respective homogenized equations for further predictions which are to be compared with the obtained experimental values. This proposed hybrid methodology is currently in progress.

Keywords: Homogenization theory · Multi-scale perturbation
Porous media filtration · Computational and analytical modelling

1 Introduction

For seawater reverse osmosis (SWRO) desalination, pre-treatment of the seawater source is typically carried out to remove turbidity and natural organic matter to mitigate excessive fouling of the RO modules downstream. The most common pre-treatment technology in medium- and large-scale desalination plants today is rapid granular filtration based on single or dual-media (Voutchkov 2017). The optimised goal of the pre-treatment step is to maximise the productivity of filtered effluent into the downstream RO membranes facility before the maintenance of the granular filter.

© Springer International Publishing AG, part of Springer Nature 2018
Y. Shi et al. (Eds.): ICCS 2018, LNCS 10861, pp. 833–845, 2018.
https://doi.org/10.1007/978-3-319-93701-4_66

Generally, filters' maintenance is resource-expensive and requires proper management to minimize logistical problems. For depth filters, maintenance is achieved via backwashing by mechanically pumping filtered or brine water reversely through the filter, which expands the granular media and flushes away the unwanted materials strained inside. Currently, the standard practice calls for backwashing at a fixed interval typically once every 24 to 48 h (Hand et al. 2005, Voutchkov 2017), without a full diagnosis of the degree of clogging occurring inside the operating filter a priori. Thus, backwashing is either carried out unnecessarily since the filter can still operate effectively for an extended period, or unexpectedly due to elevated turbidity levels in the intake source during stormy seasons which results in either exceedance in effluent turbidity or maximum allowable head loss within the filter before the scheduled maintenance.

Advanced computational methods have facilitated our understanding of the movement of emulated turbidity particles in an idealised pore-structure representation of the filter. In OpenFOAM (The OpenFOAM Foundation), which is an Open-Source Computational Fluid Dynamics (CFD) software, their Eulerian-Lagrangian (EL) approach uses the track-to-face algorithm to simulate the Lagrangian particle movement from one computational grid to the other. The algorithm requires that the size of the Lagrangian particle to be smaller than the smallest length of the computational grid. Hence, for very small Lagrangian particles of $O(10^{-7}m)$, the number of grids in each axial flow direction exceeds $O(10^3)$, resulting in billions of grids for a full three-dimensional (3D) problem which is computationally very expensive.

Theoretical analysis offers another alternative by coupling the homogenization upscaling approach with the multi-scale perturbation technique to reduce the complexity of the macroscopic problem. This approach minimizes the empiricism involved in the model formulation with two key assumptions: (a) a near- or fully-periodic prescribed microstructure, and (b) sufficiently small dimensionless parameters to relate the macroscale and microscale variations. In the following, we describe several important contributions from the literature which adopt this approach to model the remediation process in porous media systems in general.

Mei et al. (1996) derived the homogenized Darcy's Law for saturated porous media by considering the flow past a periodic array of rigid media, followed by the numerical computation of the hydraulic conductivity inside the microscale cell. Mei (1992), Mei et al. (1996) and Mei and Vernescu (2012b) also rigorously derived the convection dispersion equation and solved for the dispersion of a passive solute in the seepage flow through a spatially periodic domain. Bouddour et al. (1996) derived the characteristic models for four varying flow phenomena within the microscale domain to analyse the formation damage in the macroscopic porous media due to erosion and deposition of solid particles. A similar approach was also adopted by Royer et al. (2002) to investigate the transport of contaminants in fractured porous media under varying local Peclet (Pe) numbers, based on the assumption that both convection and molecular diffusion were of equal importance within the microscale domain. Ray et al. (2012) analysed the transport of colloids and investigated the variation to the microstructure during the attachment and detachment of colloidal particles in a two-dimensional (2D) saturated porous media structure by coupling the surface reaction rate and Nernst-

Planck equations. Most recently, Dalwadi et al. (2015) first demonstrated the effectiveness of a decreasing porosity gradient to maximise a filter's trapping capability. They later consider the changes to the microscale media properties to quantify the filter blockage (Dalwadi et al. 2016). The theoretical novelty of these models is notable as they enable one to predict the filter's initial porosity value which attains homogeneous clogging. However, their theoretical analysis has not yet been extended to actual industrial conditions of pre-treatment depth filters.

In this study, we extend on the homogenization theory by Mei and Vernescu (2012a, b) to model the macroscale filter's clogging condition as particles deposition onto the boundaries of the microscale spheres. Our engineering model aims to analytically predict the normalized pressure gradient behavior acting upon the filter by considering the known operating conditions. Subsequently, an experimental study was performed with a lab scale depth filter setup to pre-treat seawater influents under varying conditions. We then compare the derived experimental results with the model predictions for validating the proposed engineering model.

In the following, we first describe the full flow and particle transport equations in Sect. 2 and the adopted homogenization procedures in Sect. 3. In Sect. 4, we present the details of our adopted experimental study. Section 5 compares the experimental and predicted values obtained from the engineering model. The computational methodology to resolve the non-linear multiscale analysis is then discussed in Sect. 6. Finally, we conclude with an overview of our completed works in Sect. 7.

2 Model Formulation

2.1 Model's General Description

The macroscale granular filter is first modelled as an idealized network of non-overlapping three-dimensional rigid ideal spheres which either follows the simple cubic (SC) arrangement (see Fig. 1). The figure is illustrated in its two-dimensional cross-sectional form due to the inherent symmetry of the adopted spheres. However, the analysis remains strictly three-dimensional.

The SC configuration is suitable to encapsulate the clean bed porosity (θ_0) range of 0.5–0.7 for GAC operating filters (Hand et al. 2005; Voutchkov 2012; Voutchkov 2017) as its ultimate contact scenario, whereby each sphere touches one another, results in 0.476 for θ_0. The length of each SC periodic cell (l_{SC}) in Fig. 1 is computed as follows.

$$l_{SC} = \sqrt[3]{\frac{\frac{\pi}{6} d_{c,0}^3}{1 - \theta_0}} \tag{2.1}$$

where $d_{c,0}$ is the effective size of each ideal sphere.

Within each SC periodic cell in Fig. 1, the fluid motion in the available pore space is governed by the incompressible steady-state Stokes equation at low Reynolds number in (2.2) and mass continuity equation in (2.3).

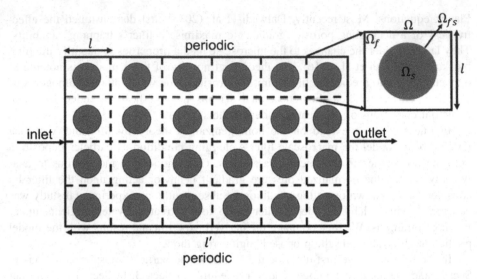

Fig. 1. Cross-sectional (2D) representation of macroscale filter with rigid ideal spheres packed in simple-cubic (SC) arrangement to represent filter grains

$$0 = -\frac{1}{\rho}\frac{\partial p^*}{\partial x_i^*} + \frac{\mu}{\rho}\nabla^2 u_i^*, \quad x \subset \Omega_f(t^*) \tag{2.2}$$

$$\frac{\partial u_i^*}{\partial x_i^*} = 0, \quad x \subset \Omega_f(t^*) \tag{2.3}$$

where x^* is the position vector, u^* the velocity vector, μ the fluid dynamic viscosity, p^* the fluid pressure, and ρ the fluid density.

The transport of solute (turbidity particles or NOM materials), via advection and diffusion, within $\Omega_f(t^*)$ of each SC periodic cell is described in (2.4). We define the concentration of solute, c^* as mass of solute per unit volume of fluid.

$$\frac{\partial c^*}{\partial t^*} + \frac{\partial(c^* u_i^*)}{\partial x_i^*} = D_p^*\nabla^2 c^*, x \subset \Omega_f(t^*) \tag{2.4}$$

where D_p^* the unknown particle diffusivity responsible for the depth filter's removal mechanisms (rapid effective filtration, adsorption), and t^* is time.

We introduce a unique boundary condition in (2.5) to account for the concentration of solute undergoing a n order reaction rate on the fluid-solid interface due to the assumed particle diffusion mechanism.

$$-\frac{\frac{\partial S^*}{\partial x_i^*}}{|\nabla S|} \cdot \left(D_p^*\frac{\partial c^*}{\partial x_i^*}\right) = k_{fs}(c^*)^n, \quad x \subset \Omega_{fs}(t^*) \tag{2.5}$$

where S is the boundary of the sphere, $\frac{\frac{\partial S^*}{\partial x^*_i}}{|\nabla S|}$ the outward normal vector acting on the microscale sphere, k_{fs} the reaction rate occurring on the fluid-solid interface (Ω_{fs}), and $n(\geq 0)$ the order of reaction occurring. It is important to highlight that an increasing n value will violate the linearity of the PDE problem in (2.5), hence we will only analyse the n values of 1 and 2 (assumed to be weakly non-linear) in this study as our first approach.

2.2 Normalization

We then adopt the following scaling variables to normalize (2.2, 2.3, 2.4 and 2.5):
(i) $c^* = c_{0,tss}c$, (ii) $t^* = Tt$, (iii) $u^*_i = Uu_i$, (iv) $x^*_i = lx_i$, (v) $p^* = Pp$, and
(vi)$D^*_p = D_pD$, whereby T, U, P and D_m are the respective scales for the time, velocity, pressure and diffusion parameters, and $c_{0,tss}$ represents the influent's total suspended solids concentration. Three unique macroscopic time scales (T) are also adhered in our analysis: (a) convection time scale (T_c) in (2.6), (b) reaction time scale (T_R) in (2.7), and (c) macroscopic diffusion time scale (T_D) in (2.8).

$$T_c = \frac{l'}{U} \tag{2.6}$$

$$T_R = \frac{l'}{k_{fs}c^{n-1}_{eqm}} \tag{2.7}$$

$$T_D = \frac{(l')^2}{D_p} \tag{2.8}$$

where l' is the characteristic length of the macroscale filter, and k_{fs} adopts the dimensions of $[M^{1-a}L^{3a-2}T^{-1}]$ for generality. The dimensionless microscale Reynolds number (Re), Peclet number (Pe) and Damköhler $(D_{a,l})$ number are also defined in (2.9), (2.10) and (2.11) respectively.

$$Re = \frac{\rho Ul}{\mu} \tag{2.9}$$

$$Pe = \frac{Ul}{D_m} \tag{2.10}$$

$$D_{a,l'} = \frac{T_D}{T_R} = \frac{k_{fs}c^{n-1}_{eqm}l}{\varepsilon D_p} = \frac{D_{a,l}}{\varepsilon} \tag{2.11}$$

where $D_{a,l'}$ the macroscale Damköhler number.

Finally, we note that a small length scale (ε) which is defined as $\frac{l}{l'}$ is adopted for the subsequent homogenization procedures. A dominant balance is defined between the macroscale pressure gradient acting upon the depth filter and the viscous flow resistance around the microscale sphere which enables us to derive the homogenized effective Darcy's Law equation subsequently.

3 Homogenization Procedures

We adopt the multiple-scale coordinates of x and $x' = \varepsilon x$ whereby x is the fast variable defined within the periodic cell, and x' is the slow variable spanning across the macroscopic domain (Mei and Vernescu 2012a, b). The perturbation expansions for the fluid parameters (which are all cell-periodic) can be expressed as follows.

$$H = H^{(0)} + \varepsilon H^{(1)} + \varepsilon^2 H^{(2)} + \dots \tag{3.1}$$

where H can be p, c and u_i.

We then introduce the following spatial derivative to perform the multiple-scale expansions.

$$\frac{\partial}{\partial x_i} \rightarrow \frac{\partial}{\partial x_i} + \varepsilon \frac{\partial}{\partial x_i'} \tag{3.2}$$

To demonstrate the homogenization procedure, we succinctly perform the analysis by adopting the time scale of T_c for rapid filtration conditions. The final dimensionless forms of (2.2, 2.3, 2.4 and 2.5) are then shown in (3.3a, 3.3b, 3.3c and 3.3d) respectively after the appropriate normalization procedures. We note that the extension to slow filtration conditions is achieved by changing the time scale to either T_D or T_R while the homogenization procedures remain unchanged.

$$0 = -\frac{\partial p}{\partial x_i} + \varepsilon \nabla^2 u_i, x \subset \Omega_f(t) \tag{3.3a}$$

$$\frac{\partial u_i}{\partial x_i} = 0, \quad x \subset \Omega_f(t) \tag{3.3b}$$

$$\varepsilon \frac{\partial c}{\partial t} + \frac{\partial(c u_i)}{\partial x_i} = Pe^{-1} D \nabla^2 c, x \subset \Omega_f(t) \tag{3.3c}$$

$$-\frac{\frac{\partial S}{\partial x_i}}{|\nabla S|} \cdot \left(D \frac{\partial c}{\partial x_i} \right) = \varepsilon D_{a,l'} c^n, x \subset \Omega_{fs}(t) \tag{3.3d}$$

To demonstrate our novelty, we confine our homogenization analysis to the solute transport problem (3.3c and 3.3d) while noting that the analysis for the flow problem (3.3a and 3.3b) can be understood from previous multiscale works (Mei et al. 1996; Mei and Vernescu 2012a, b; Dalwadi et al. 2015 and Dalwadi et al. 2016) whereby the homogenized dimensionless Darcy's law can be derived systematically.

3.1 Solute Problem Analysis

By using (3.2), the multi-scale expansion forms (3.3c and 3.3d) are as follows.

$$\varepsilon \frac{\partial}{\partial t}\left(c^{(0)} + \varepsilon c^{(1)} + \ldots\right) + \left(\frac{\partial}{\partial x_i} + \varepsilon \frac{\partial}{\partial x_i'}\right)\left(u_i^{(0)} + \varepsilon u_i^{(1)} + \ldots\right)\left(c^{(0)} + \varepsilon c^{(1)} + \ldots\right)$$

$$= Pe^{-1}D\left(\frac{\partial}{\partial x_j} + \varepsilon \frac{\partial}{\partial x_j'}\right)\left(\frac{\partial}{\partial x_j} + \varepsilon \frac{\partial}{\partial x_j'}\right)\left(c^{(0)} + \varepsilon c^{(1)} + \ldots\right),$$

$$x \subset \Omega_f(t)$$

$$(3.4a)$$

$$-\frac{\frac{\partial S}{\partial x_i}}{|\nabla S|} \cdot \left(D\left(\frac{\partial}{\partial x_i} + \varepsilon \frac{\partial}{\partial x_i'}\right)\left(c^{(0)} + \varepsilon c^{(1)} + \ldots\right)\right) = \varepsilon D_{a,l'}\left(c^{(0)} + \varepsilon c^{(1)} + \ldots\right)^n, \quad (3.4b)$$

$$x \subset \Omega_{fs}(t)$$

At the leading order of ε^0, $c^{(0)}$ is also determined to be independent of the microscale variations. At the next order of ε^1, we systematically derive the following for (3.4a) and (3.4b) respectively.

$$\theta \frac{\partial c^{(0)}}{\partial t} + \tilde{u}_i^{(0)} \frac{\partial c^{(0)}}{\partial x_i'} = -Pe^{-1}D_{a,l'}C_R c^{(0)^n}, x \subset \Omega_f(t) \quad (3.5)$$

subject to the boundary condition of (3.6).

$$-\frac{\frac{\partial S}{\partial x_i}}{|\nabla S|} \cdot \left(D \frac{\partial c^{(1)}}{\partial x_i} + D \frac{\partial c^{(0)}}{\partial x_i'}\right) = D_{a,l'}c^{(0)^n}, x \subset \Omega_{fs}(t) \quad (3.6)$$

where C_R is a proposed dimensionless effective reaction rate which depends on the pore-geometry $\frac{|\Omega_s|}{|\Omega_f|}$ within the periodic cell whereby $|\Omega_s| = \frac{2}{3}\pi d_{c,0}^3$ which represents the volume of the spheres inside the SC periodic cell, and $|\Omega_f|$ represents the volume of fluid within the SC periodic cell.

We then consider the solution for the cell problem of $c^{(1)}$ in the following form (Auriault and Adler 1995, Equation 40).

$$c^{(1)} = \chi_i \frac{\partial c^{(0)}}{\partial x_i'} + \hat{c}^{(1)} \quad (3.7)$$

where χ_i is the microscale periodic vector field of spatial dimensions, and $\hat{c}^{(1)}$ is an integration constant which is independent of the microscale variations. The microscale variation of $c^{(1)}$ from (3.8) is then expressed as follows.

$$\frac{\partial c^{(1)}}{\partial x_i} = \frac{\partial \chi_k}{\partial x_k} \frac{\partial c^{(0)}}{\partial x_i'} + \chi_i \nabla \cdot \nabla' c^{(0)} \quad (3.8)$$

Substituting (3.8) back into (3.6) results in the following modified form.

$$-\frac{\frac{\partial S}{\partial x_i}}{|\nabla S|} \cdot \left(D\left(\frac{\partial \chi_k}{\partial x_k}\frac{\partial c^{(0)}}{\partial x_i'} + \chi_i \nabla \cdot \nabla' c^{(0)}\right) + D\frac{\partial c^{(0)}}{\partial x_i'}\right) = D_{a,l'}c^{(0)^n}, x \subset \Omega_{fs}(t) \quad (3.9)$$

At the next order of ε^2, we obtain the following.

$$\theta\frac{\partial c^{(1)}}{\partial t} + \tilde{u}_i^{(0)}\frac{\partial c^{(1)}}{\partial x_i} + \tilde{u}_i^{(1)}\frac{\partial c^{(0)}}{\partial x_i'}$$

$$= Pe^{-1}\frac{\partial}{\partial x_i'}\left(D\left(\frac{\partial \chi_k}{\partial x_k}\frac{\partial c^{(0)}}{\partial x_i'} + \chi_i \nabla \cdot \nabla' c^{(0)}\right) + D\frac{\partial c^{(0)}}{\partial x_i'}\right) \quad (3.10)$$

$$- nPe^{-1}D_{a,l'}C_R c^{(0)n-1}c^{(1)}, x \subset \Omega_f$$

subject to the following boundary condition.

$$-\frac{\frac{\partial S}{\partial x_i}}{|\nabla S|} \cdot \left(D\frac{\partial c^{(2)}}{\partial x_i} + D\frac{\partial c^{(1)}}{\partial x_i'}\right) = nD_{a,l'}c^{(0)^{n-1}}c^{(1)}, x \subset \Omega_{fs}(t) \quad (3.11)$$

We consider the perturbation expansion of the temporal derivative of $\tilde{c}$ within the SC microscale cell as follows.

$$\frac{\partial \tilde{c}}{\partial t} = \frac{\partial \tilde{c}^{(0)}}{\partial t} + \varepsilon\frac{\partial \tilde{c}^{(1)}}{\partial t} + O(\varepsilon^2) \quad (3.12)$$

To further modify (3.12), we adhere to the respective representations of (3.5) and (3.10) to derive the following.

$$\frac{\partial \tilde{c}}{\partial t} = -\tilde{u}_i^{(0)}\frac{\partial c^{(0)}}{\partial x_i'} - \varepsilon\tilde{u}_i^{(1)}\frac{\partial c^{(0)}}{\partial x_i'} - \varepsilon\tilde{u}_i^{(0)}\frac{\partial c^{(1)}}{\partial x_i'} - Pe^{-1}D_{a,l'}C_R c^{(0)^n}$$

$$+ \varepsilon Pe^{-1}\frac{\partial}{\partial x_i'}\left(D\left(\frac{\partial \chi_k}{\partial x_k}\frac{\partial c^{(0)}}{\partial x_i'} + \chi_i \nabla \cdot \nabla' c^{(0)}\right) + D\frac{\partial c^{(0)}}{\partial x_i'}\right) \quad (3.13)$$

$$- \varepsilon nPe^{-1}D_{a,l'}C_R c^{(0)^{n-1}}c^{(1)} + O(\varepsilon^2), \quad x \subset \Omega_f$$

By assuming $\nabla' c^{(0)} \approx \nabla' c$ and the following relationships of (3.14) and (3.15), we obtain (3.16) from (3.13).

$$\tilde{u}_i\frac{\partial c}{\partial x_i} = \tilde{u}_i^{(0)}\frac{\partial c^{(0)}}{\partial x_i'} + \varepsilon\tilde{u}_i^{(0)}\frac{\partial c^{(1)}}{\partial x_i'} + \varepsilon\tilde{u}_i^{(1)}\frac{\partial c^{(0)}}{\partial x_i'} + O(\varepsilon^2) \quad (3.14)$$

$$c^n = c^{(0)n} + \varepsilon n c^{(0)^{n-1}}c^{(1)} + O(\varepsilon^2) \quad (3.15)$$

$$\frac{\partial \bar{c}}{\partial t} = -\tilde{u}_i \frac{\partial c}{\partial x_i} - Pe^{-1} D_{a,l'} C_R c^n$$
$$+ \varepsilon Pe^{-1} \frac{\partial}{\partial x_i} \left(D\left(\frac{\partial \chi_k}{\partial x_k} \frac{\partial c}{\partial x_i} + \chi_i \nabla \cdot \nabla' c\right) + D\frac{\partial c}{\partial x_i}\right) + O(\varepsilon^2), x \subset \Omega_f \tag{3.16}$$

(3.16) represents the macroscopic effective advection-dispersion-reaction equation which is accurate up to $O(\varepsilon^2)$. We again note that our analysis is confined to the n values of 1 or 2 as our first approach which will be discussed further in the subsequent sections.

4 Experimental Design

We perform a series of rapid filtration experiments for model validations. Figure 2 illustrates the simplified version of our filter setups and the general operational mode to remove both turbidity particles and NOMs materials from the intake seawater source. At regular intervals, samples are collected from both filters to measure turbidity, total suspended solids (TSS) and dissolved organic carbon (DOC) concentrations. Likewise, the pressure gradient measurements of between p_1 and p_2, and between p_3 and p_4 are also taken at designated intervals. The biological slow filtration experiments are currently underway, while we have completed a set of rapid filtration experiments for model validations. Readers are referred to Table 1 for the summary of adopted conditions for the rapid filtration experiments conducted by far.

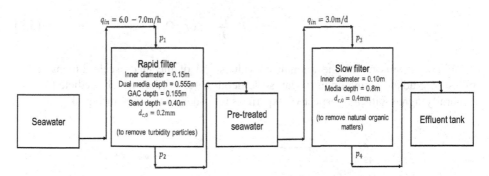

Fig. 2. Schematic representation of hybrid rapid and slow granular filters to remove both turbidity particles and natural organic matters from intake seawater

Table 1. Summary of experimental conditions adopted for pre-treatment rapid filtration

Exp no.	q_{in} (m/h)	$c_{0,tur}$ (NTU)	$c_{0,tss}$ (mg/L)	d_p (μm)	Duration (mins)
1	8.00	6.63	16.6	83.3	90
2	7.40	2.95	7.38	26.0	90
3	8.15	2.72	6.80	507	90

5 Model Validations

We first modify (3.16) into (5.1) by adopting the following assumptions: (i) quasi-steady-state condition for the discharge concentration from the 0.155 m GAC media depth deployed (see Fig. 3), (ii) unidirectional flow within the depth filter, (iii) homogeneous clogging inside the filter, (iv) spatial averaging theorem coupled with periodicity boundary conditions, (v) $n = 1$ for rapid effective filtration, (vi) $Pe^{-1} \sim O(\varepsilon)$ which ensures a dominant balance between advection and the regarded particle diffusion at the macroscale, and (vii) $D_{a,l'} \sim O(\varepsilon^{-1})$.

$$0 = -\tilde{u}_3 \frac{\partial c}{\partial x_3'} - C_R c + \varepsilon^2 \frac{\partial}{\partial x_i'} \left(D \frac{\partial c}{\partial x_i'} \right) + O(\varepsilon^2), x \subset \Omega_f \qquad (5.1)$$

By comparing the respective terms of $O(1)$ of (5.1), we obtain the final solution of (5.2) while including an unknown calibration factor in C_1 to account for the random packing of media grains in the actual depth filter.

$$\tilde{u}_3 = C_1 \frac{C_R x_3'}{\ln\left(\frac{c_{0,tss}}{c}\right)}, x \subset \Omega_f \qquad (5.2)$$

We then adhere to the dimensionless homogenized Darcy's Law equation in the following with respect to the derived form of (5.2).

$$C_1 \frac{C_R x_3'}{\ln\left(\frac{c_{0,tss}}{c}\right)} = -K \frac{\partial p^{(0)}}{\partial x_3'}, x \subset \Omega_f \qquad (5.3)$$

Finally, we compute the normalized values (β) of the macroscale dimensionless pressure gradient acting upon the lab-scale depth filter in (5.4) which predicted values generally agree with the respective experimentally-derived values in Fig. 4.

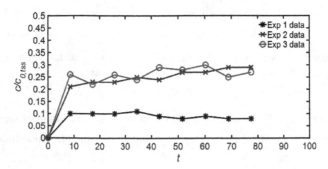

Fig. 3. Transient variations of $\frac{c}{c_0}$ at 0.155 m GAC media depth

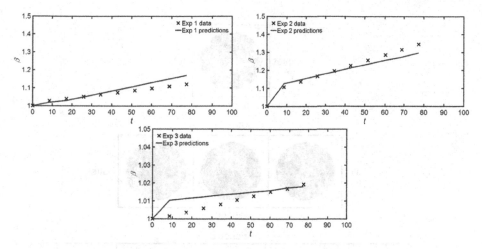

Fig. 4. Comparison between predicted and experimental values of β for Exp 1 to 3

$$\beta = \frac{\left(\frac{\partial p^{(0)}}{\partial x_3}\right)_t}{\left(\frac{\partial p^{(0)}}{\partial x_3}\right)_0}, x \subset \Omega_f \tag{5.4}$$

With respect to Fig. 4, we believe that the agreement will further improve with a higher GAC media depth due to a smaller resultant value in ε.

6 Computational Methodology

In this section, we succinctly describe on our computational methodology to resolve for the non-linear microscale problem of c^n for n greater than 2. Computationally, it is not possible to resolve for a numerical domain having fully periodic flow conditions which is required for the periodic cell problem in Fig. 1. Hence, we propose to adopt the configurations in Fig. 5a, b and c by defining the inlet and outlet zones to the numerical domain as shown. Errors are expected to be incurred due to the imposed boundaries and these errors can gradually be reduced as the length of the domain increases (Fig. 5b and c) to approach the true ε value. However, emulating the full unidirectional depth of the macroscale filter under periodic flow conditions is computationally expensive. Hence, we hypothesize that there exists a ε' value, but is more than the true ε value, which ensures that the error function is sufficiently small for subsequent predictions.

We perform the simulation runs in OpenFOAM AWS (The OpenFOAM Foundation) which enables us to harness on a large number of computer processes if necessary. Our general methodology is as follows.

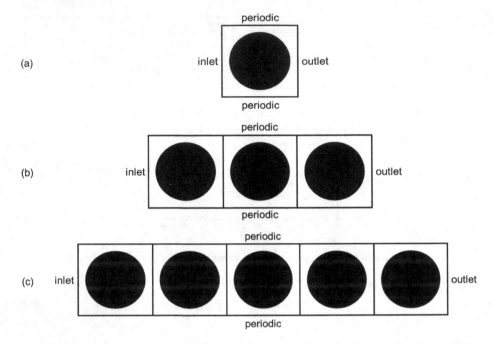

Fig. 5. Simplified representation of numerical domains in OpenFOAM to resolve the non-linear microscale problem of c^n: (a) $\varepsilon' \approx 1.00$, (b) $\varepsilon' \approx 0.333$, (c) $\varepsilon' \approx 0.200$.

i. Introducing the homogenized effective solute transport equations (related to c^n) into the incompressible fluid flow solver (*icoFoam*) for coupling the fluid-solute problems

ii. Introducing a unique boundary condition to account for the solute interactions occurring on the microscale spheres' boundaries

iii. Develop the basic cell geometry of either SC or FCC of varying lengths using CAD program and the *snappyHexMesh* utility in OpenFOAM

iv. Perform the simulation runs while varying the number of computational grids for each analysed domain to check on grid convergence

v. Total simulation runtime for each analysed domain depends on the velocity scale and ε'

vi. Time step of simulation run is varied to check on temporal convergence

vii. Predicted spatial gradient of c^n will be introduced back into the homogenized effective equation to perform the subsequent predictions for the normalized pressure gradient and be compared with the respective experimental values

7   Conclusion

In this study, the multiscale perturbation analysis is coupled with the homogenization theory to model the clogging behaviour of pre-treatment filters in desalination facilities. We have validated our linear homogenization analysis for pre-treatment rapid filtration by comparing the predicted values from the derived effective homogenized equation with our experimentally-derived values for the normalized pressure gradient acting upon the lab-scale filter under varying conditions. To extend the analysis to non-linear perturbation analysis, a computational methodology is required to resolve the micro-scale concentration parameter at higher orders which is difficult to do so analytically. This extension component is currently underway. Finally, extension of the model to slow filtration process can be achieved by changing the time scale to either that of reaction time or diffusion time, while retaining the same homogenization procedures to derive the effective homogenized equations for analysis.

Acknowledgements. The lab-scale rapid pressure filter setup employed in this study is funded by Singapore-MIT Alliance for Research and Technology (SMART) while the lab-scale slow pressure filter setup is funded by the internal core funding from the Nanyang Environment and Water Research Institute (NEWRI), Nanyang Technological University (NTU), Singapore. The first author is also grateful to NTU for the 4-year Nanyang President Graduate Scholarship (NPGS) for his PhD study.

References

Auriault, J.L., Adler, P.M.: Taylor dispersion in porous media: analysis by multiple scale expansions. Adv. Water Resour. **18**(4), 217–226 (1995)

Bouddour, A., Auriault, J.L., Mhamdi-Alaoui, M.: Erosion and deposition of solid particles in porous media: homogenization analysis of a formation damage. Transp. Porous Media **25**(2), 121–146 (1996)

Dalwadi, M.P., Griffiths, I.M., Bruna, M.: Understanding how porosity gradients can make a better filter using homogenization theory. Proc. R. Soc. A Math. Phys. Eng. Sci. **471**(2182) (2015). http://rspa.royalsocietypublishing.org/content/471/2182/20150464

Dalwadi, M., Bruna, M., Griffiths, I.: A multiscale method to calculate filter blockage. J. Fluid Mech. **809**, 264–289 (2016)

Mei, C.C.: Method of homogenization applied to dispersion in porous media. Transp. Porous Media **9**(3), 261–274 (1992)

Mei, C.C., Auriault, J.L., Ng, C.O.: Some applications of the homogenization theory. In: Hutchinson, J.W., Wu, T.Y. (eds.) Advances in Applied Mechanics, vol. 32, pp. 277–348. Elsevier, Amsterdam (1996)

Mei, C.C., Vernescu, B.: Seepage in rigid porous media. In: Homogenization Methods for Multiscale Mechanics, pp. 85–134 (2012a)

Mei, C.C., Vernescu, B.: Dispersion in periodic media or flows. In: Homogenization Methods for Multiscale Mechanics, pp. 135–178 (2012b)

Hand, D.W., Tchobanoglous, G., Crittenden, J.C., Howe, K., Trussell, R.R.: MWH's Water Treatment: Principles and Design, pp. 727–818. Wiley, Hoboken (2005). Chapter 11

Ray, N., van Noorden, T., Frank, F., Knabner, P.: Multiscale modeling of colloid and fluid dynamics in porous media including an evolving microstructure. Transp. Porous Media **95**(3), 669–696 (2012)

Royer, P., Auriault, J.-L., Lewandowska, J., Serres, C.: Continuum modelling of contaminant transport in fractured porous media. Transp. Porous Media **49**(3), 333–359 (2002)

The OpenFOAM Foundation. http://www.OpenFOAM.org/

Voutchkov, N.: Desalination Engineering: Planning and Design, chap. 8, pp. 285–310. McGraw-Hill Professional, New York (2012)

Voutchkov, N.: Granular media filtration. In: Pretreatment for Reverse Osmosis Desalination, pp. 153–186. Elsevier, Amsterdam (2017)

The Solution of the Lambda Modes Problem Using Block Iterative Eigensolvers

A. Carreño[1](✉), A. Vidal-Ferràndiz[1], D. Ginestar[2], and G. Verdú[1]

[1] Instituto Universitario de Seguridad Industrial, Radiofísica y Medioambiental, Universitat Politècnica de València, València, Spain
{amcarsan,gverdu}@iqn.upv.es, anvifer2@upv.es
[2] Instituto Universitario de Matemática Multidisciplinar, Universitat Politècnica de València, València, Spain
dginesta@mat.upv.es

Abstract. High efficient methods are required for the computation of several lambda modes associated with the neutron diffusion equation. Multiple iterative eigenvalue solvers have been used to solve this problem. In this work, three different block methods are studied to solve this problem. The first method is a procedure based on the modified block Newton method. The second one is a procedure based on subspace iteration and accelerated with Chebyshev polynomials. Finally, a block inverse-free Krylov subspace method is analyzed with different preconditioners. Two benchmark problems are studied illustrating the convergence properties and the effectiveness of the methods proposed.

Keywords: Neutron diffusion equation · Eigenvalue problem
Lambda modes · Block method

1 Introduction

The neutron transport equation models the behaviour of a nuclear reactor over the reactor domain [14]. However, due to the complexity of this equation, the energy of the neutrons is discretized into two energy groups and the flux is assumed to be isotropic leading to an approximation of the neutron transport equation known as, the two energy groups neutron diffusion equation [14].

The reactor criticality can be forced by dividing the neutron production rate in the neutron diffusion equation by λ obtaining a steady state equation expressed as a generalized eigenvalue problem, known as the λ-modes problem,

$$\mathcal{L}\phi = \frac{1}{\lambda}\mathcal{M}\phi, \tag{1}$$

where

$$\mathcal{L} = \begin{pmatrix} -\boldsymbol{\nabla}(D_1\boldsymbol{\nabla}) + \Sigma_{a_1} + \Sigma_{12} & 0 \\ -\Sigma_{12} & -\boldsymbol{\nabla}(D_2\boldsymbol{\nabla}) + \Sigma_{a_2} \end{pmatrix},$$

© Springer International Publishing AG, part of Springer Nature 2018
Y. Shi et al. (Eds.): ICCS 2018, LNCS 10861, pp. 846–855, 2018.
https://doi.org/10.1007/978-3-319-93701-4_67

is the neutron loss operator and

$$\mathcal{M} = \begin{pmatrix} \nu\Sigma_{f1} & \nu\Sigma_{f2} \\ 0 & 0 \end{pmatrix}, \qquad \phi = \begin{pmatrix} \phi_1 \\ \phi_2 \end{pmatrix}$$

are the neutron production operator and the neutron flux. The rest of coefficient, called macroscopic cross sections, are dependent on the spatial coordinate. The diffusion cross sections are D_1 (for the first energy group) and D_2 (for the second one); Σ_{a1} and Σ_{a2} denote the absorption cross sections; Σ_{12}, the scattering coefficient from group 1 to group 2. The fission cross sections are Σ_{f1} and Σ_{f2}, for the first and second group, respectively. And ν is the average number of neutron produced per fission.

The eigenvalue (mode) with the largest magnitude shows the criticality of the reactor and its corresponding eigenvector describes the steady state neutron distribution in the core. The next sub-critical modes and their associated eigenfunctions are useful to develop modal methods to integrate the transient neutron diffusion equation.

For the spatial discretization of the λ-modes problem, a high order continuous Galerkin Finite Element Method (FEM) is used, transforming the problem (1) into an algebraic generalized eigenvalue problem

$$Mx = \lambda Lx, \tag{2}$$

where these matrices are not necessarily symmetric (see more details in [17]). However, with several general conditions, it has been proved, that the dominant eigenvalues of this equation are real positive numbers [8].

Different methods have been successfully used to solve this algebraic generalized eigenvalue problem such as the Krylov-Schur method, the classical Arnoldi method, the Implicit Restarted Arnoldi method and the Jacobi-Davidson method [15–17]. However, if we want to compute several eigenvalues and they are very clustered, these methods might have problems to find all the eigenvalues. In practical situations of reactor analysis, the dominance ratios corresponding to the dominant eigenvalues are often near unity. By this reason, block methods, which approximate a set of eigenvalues simultaneously are an alternative since their rate of convergence depends only on the spacing of the group of desired eigenvalues from the rest of the spectrum. In this work, three different block methods are studied and compared with the Krylov-Schur method.

The rest of the paper has been structured in the following way. In Sect. 2, the block iterative methods are presented. In Sect. 3, numerical results to study the performance of the method for two three dimensional benchmark problems are presented. In the last Section, the main conclusions of the paper are collected.

2 Block Iterative Methods

This section describes the block methods to obtain the dominant eigenvalues and their associated eigenvectors of a generalized eigenvalue problem of the form

$$MX = LX\Lambda, \tag{3}$$

where $X \in \mathbb{R}^{n \times q}$ has the eigenvectors in their columns and $\Lambda \in \mathbb{R}^{q \times q}$ has the dominant eigenvalues in its diagonal, n denotes the degrees of freedom in the spatial discretization with the finite element method for the Eq. (1) and q is the number of desired eigenvalues.

2.1   Modified Block Newton Method

The original modified block Newton method was proposed by Lösche in [10] for ordinary eigenproblems. This section briefly reviews an extension of this method given by the authors in [4] for generalized eigenvalue problems.

To apply this method to the problem (3), we assume that the eigenvectors can be expressed as

$$X = ZS, \tag{4}$$

where $Z^T Z = I_q$. Then, problem (3) can be rewritten as

$$MX = LX\Lambda \Rightarrow MZS = LZS\Lambda \Rightarrow MZ = LZS\Lambda S^{-1} \Rightarrow MZ = LZK. \tag{5}$$

If we add the biorthogonality condition $W^T Z = I_q$ in order to determine the problem, with W is a matrix of rank q, it is obtained the following system

$$F(Z, \Lambda) := \begin{pmatrix} MZ - LZK \\ W^T Z - I_q \end{pmatrix} = \begin{pmatrix} 0 \\ 0 \end{pmatrix}. \tag{6}$$

Applying a Newton's iteration to the problem (6), a new approximation arises from the previous iteration as,

$$Z^{(k+1)} = Z^{(k)} - \Delta Z^{(k)}, \qquad K^{(k+1)} = K^{(k)} - \Delta K^{(k)}, \tag{7}$$

where $\Delta Z^{(k)}$ and $\Delta K^{(k)}$ are solutions of the system that is obtained when the Eq. (7) is substituted into (6) and it is truncated at the first terms.

The matrix $K^{(k)}$ is not necessarily a diagonal matrix, as a consequence the system is coupled. To avoid this problem, the modified generalized block Newton method (MGBNM) applies previously two steps. The initial step is to apply the modified Gram-Schmidt process to orthogonalize the matrix $Z^{(k)}$. The second step consist on use the Rayleigh-Ritz projection method for the generalized eigenvalue problem [12]. More details of the method can be found in [4].

2.2   Block Inverse-Free Block Preconditioned Krylov Subspace Method

The block inverse-free preconditioned Arnoldi method (BIFPAM) was originally presented and analyzed for L and M symmetric matrices and $L > 0$ (see [7,11]). Nevertheless, this methodology works efficiently to compute the λ-modes.

We start with the problem for one eigenvalue

$$Mx = \lambda Lx, \tag{8}$$

and an initial approximation (λ_0, x_0). We aim at improving this approximation through the Rayleigh-Ritz orthogonal projecting on the m-order Krylov subspace

$$K_m(M - \lambda_0 L, x_0) := \text{span}\{x_0, (M - \lambda_0 L)x_0, (M - \lambda_0 L)^2 x_0, \ldots, (M - \lambda_k L)^m x_0\}.$$

Arnoldi method is used to construct the basis K_m. The projection can be carried out as

$$Z^T M Z U = Z^T L Z U \Lambda, \tag{9}$$

where Z is a basis of $K_m(M - \lambda_0 L, x_0)$ and then computing the dominant eigenvalue $\Lambda_{1,1}$ and its eigenvector u_1 to obtain the value of $\lambda_1 = \Lambda_{1,1}$ and its eigenvector $x_1 = Z u_1$. In the same way, we compute the eigenvalues and eigenvectors in the following iterations.

If we are interested on computing q eigenvalues of problem (2), we can accelerate the convergence by using the subspace $\mathcal{K}_m$ with

$$\mathcal{K}_m := \bigcup_{i=1}^{q} K_m^i(M - \lambda_{k,i} L, x_{k,i}),$$

where $\lambda_{k,i}$ denotes the i-th eigenvalue computed in the k-th iteration and $x_{k,i}$ its associated eigenvector. Thus, this method can be dealt with through an iteration with a block of vectors that allows computing several eigenvalues simultaneously.

Furthermore, the BIFAM will be accelerated with an equivalent transformation of the original problem by means of a preconditioner. With an approximate eigenpair $(\lambda_{i,k}, x_{i,k})$, we consider for some matrices $P_{i,k}$, $Q_{i,k}$ the transformed eigenvalue problem

$$(P_{i,k}^{-1} M Q_{i,k}^{-1})x = \lambda(P_{i,k}^{-1} L Q_{i,k}^{-1})x \Leftrightarrow \hat{M}_{i,k} x = \lambda \hat{L}_{i,k} x, \tag{10}$$

which has the same eigenvalues as the original problem. Applying one step of the block inverse-free Krylov method to the problem (10), the convergence behaviour will be determined by the spectrum of

$$\hat{C}_{i,k} := \hat{M}_{i,k} - \lambda_{i,k} \hat{L}_{i,k} = P_{i,k}^{-1}(M - \lambda_{i,k} L) Q_{i,k}^{-1}. \tag{11}$$

Different preconditioning transformations can be constructed using different factorizations of the matrix $M - \lambda_{i,k} L$. The main goal must be to choose suitably $P_{i,k}$ and $Q_{i,k}$ to obtain a favorable distribution of the eigenvalues of matrix $\hat{C}_{i,k}$.

In this paper, we have considered the classical incomplete LU factorization with level 0 of fill (ILU(0)). We also use constants $P_{i,k} = P_{1,1}$ and $Q_{i,k} = Q_{1,1}$ obtained from a preconditioner for $M - \lambda_{1,1} L$, where $\lambda_{1,1}$ is a first approximation of the first eigenvalue.

2.3   Chebyshev Filtered Subspace Iteration Method

Subspace iteration with a Chebyshev polynomial filter (CHEFSI) is a well known algorithm in the literature [12, 18]. In this paper, we have studied a version proposed by Berjafa et al. in [5] that iterates over the polynomial filter and the Rayleigh quotient with block structure. This algorithm is implemented for ordinary eigenvalue problems, so the original problem (3) is reformulated as

$$AX = X\Lambda \text{ with } A = L^{-1}M. \tag{12}$$

The goal of this method is to build an invariant subspace for several eigenvectors using multiplication in block. This subspace is diagonalized using previously a polynomial filter in these vectors to improve the competitiveness of the method.

The basic idea for computing the first dominant eigenvalue is the following: Using the notation introduced in Sect. 2, it is known that any vector z can be expanded in the eigenbasis as

$$z = \sum_{i=1}^{n} \gamma_i x_i.$$

Applying a polynomial filter $p(x)$ of degree m to A through a matrix-vector product leads to

$$p_m(A)z = p_m(A)\sum_{i=1}^{n}\gamma_i x_i = \sum_{i=1}^{n} p_m(\lambda_i)\gamma_i x_i,$$

where it is assumed that $\gamma_1 \neq 0$, which is almost always true in practice if z is a random vector.

If we want to compute x_1 as fast as possible, then a suitable polynomial would be a $p(x)$ such that $p(\lambda_1)$ dominates $p(\lambda_j)$, when $j \neq 1$. That it means, the filter must separate the desired eigenvalue from the unwanted ones, so that after normalization $p(A)z$ will be mostly parallel to x_1. This leads us to seek a polynomial which takes small values on the discrete set $R = \{\lambda_2, \ldots, \lambda_n\}$, such that $p_m(\lambda_1) = 1$. However, it is not possible to compute this polynomial with the unacknowledged of all eigenvalues of A. The alternative is use a continuous domain in the complex plane containing R but excluding λ_1 instead of the discrete min-max polynomial. In practice, the continuous domain is restricted to an ellipse E containing the unwanted eigenvalues and then theoretically it can be shown that the best min-max polynomial is the polynomial

$$p_m(\lambda) = \frac{C_m((\lambda - c))/e}{C_m((\lambda_1 - c))/e},$$

where C_m is the Chebyshev polynomial of degree m, c is the center of the ellipse E and e is the distance between the center and the focus of E (see more details in [12]).

In our case, where the eigenvalues are positive real numbers, the ellipse E is restricted to an interval $[\alpha, \beta]$, where $\alpha, \beta > 0$. These values are computed following the algorithms proposed in [18].

3   Numerical Results

The competitiveness of the block methods has been tested on two three dimensional problems: the 3D IAEA reactor [13] and the 3D NEACRP reactor [6]. For the spatial discretization of the λ-modes problem, we have used Lagrange polynomials of degree 3 in the finite element method.

In the numerical results, the global residual error has been used, defined as

$$\text{res} = \max_{i=1,\dots,q} \|Lx_i - \lambda_i M x_i\|^2,$$

where λ_i is the i-th eigenvalue and x_i its associated unitary eigenvector.

As the block methods need an initial approximation of a set of eigenvectors, a multilevel initialization proposed in [3] with two meshes is used to obtain this approximation.

The solutions of linear systems needed to apply the MGBN method and the CHEFSI method have been computed with the GMRES method preconditioned with ILU and a reordering using the Cuthill-McKee method. The dimension of the Krylov subspace for the BIFPAM has been set equal to 8. The degree of the Chebyshev polynomial has been 10.

The methods have been implemented in C++ based on data structures provided by the library Deal.ii [2], PETSc [1] using the definition of the cited papers. For make the computations, we have used a computer that has been an Intel® Core™ i7-4790 @3.60GHz × 8 processor with 32 Gb of RAM running on Ubuntu 16.04 LTS.

3.1   3D IAEA Reactor

The 3D IAEA benchmark reactor is a classical two-group neutron diffusion problem [13]. It has 4579 different assemblies and the coarse mesh used to obtain the initial guess has 1040 cells. The algebraic eigenvalue problems have 263552 and 62558 degrees of freedom, for the fine and the coarse mesh, respectively.

To compare the block methods, the number of iterations for the BIFPAM, the MGBNM and the CHEFSI method and the residual errors are represented in Fig. 1(a) in the computation of four eigenvalues. These eigenvalues are 1.02914, 1.01739, 1.01739 and 1.01526. In this Figure, we observe similar slopes in the convergence histories for the BIFPAM and the CHEFSI method and moreover, they are smaller than the convergence history for the MGBNM since this is a second-order method. The computational times (CPU time) and the residual errors (res) obtained for each method are shown in Fig. 1(b). In this Figure, in contrast to the previous one, it is observed that the most efficient method in time is the BIFPAM although its CPU times are similar to the CPU times obtained for the MGBNM. This means that in spite of the number of iterations needed to converge the BIFPAM is larger than the MGBNM, the CPU time in each iteration is much smaller than the needed to compute one iteration of the MGBNM. It is due to the BIFPAM does not need to solve linear systems.

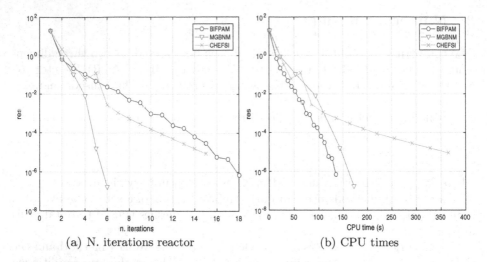

(a) N. iterations reactor

(b) CPU times

Fig. 1. Residual error (res) for the computation of 4 eigenvalues in the IAEA reactor.

3.2   3D NEACRP Reactor

The NEACRP benchmark [6] is also chosen to compare the block methodology proposed. The reactor core has a radial dimension of 21.606 cm × 21.606 cm per cell. Axially the reactor is divided into 18 layers with height (from bottom to top): 30.0 cm, 7.7 cm, 11.0 cm, 15.0 cm, 30.0 cm (10 layers), 12.8 cm (2 layers), 8.0 cm and 30.0 cm. The boundary condition is zero flux in the outer reflector surface. The fine mesh and the coarse mesh considered have 3978 and 1308 cells, respectively. Using polynomials of degree three the fine mesh has 230120 degrees of freedom. The coarse mesh used to initialize the block methods has 7844 degrees of freedom.

Figure 2(a) shows the convergence histories of the BIFPAM, the MGBNM and the CHEFSI method in terms of the number of iterations in the computation of four eigenvalues. The eigenvalues obtained have been 1.00200, 0.988620, 0.985406 and 0.985406. That it means the spectrum for this problem is very clustered. In this Figure, we observe the similar behaviour between the BIF-PAM and the CHEFSI method being these two methods slower in convergence than the MBNM. Figure 2(b) displays the CPU time and the residual errors obtained for each method. In this Figure, we observe that the quickest method is the BIFPAM by the same reason given in the previous. So, the most efficient block method studied is the BIFPAM.

Finally, these block methods are compared with the Krylov-Schur method implemented in the library SLEPc [9] for the NEACRP reactor. This method is a non-block method, but it is a very competitive method to solve eigenvalue problems. The dimension of the Krylov subspace used in the Krylov-Schur method has been $15 + q$ that is the default value of the library. This method is implemented in the library using a locking strategy, so the history block convergence cannot

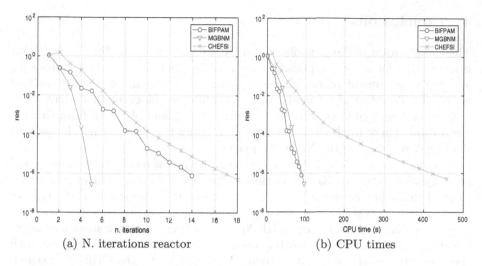

(a) N. iterations reactor   (b) CPU times

Fig. 2. Residual error (res) for the computation of 4 eigenvalues in the NEACRP reactor.

be displayed and compared with the block method presented in this work. The total computational times obtained for a different number of eigenvalues are displayed in Table 1 to compare the block methods with the Krylov-Schur method. The total CPU time of the block methods includes the time needed to compute the initial guess. The tolerance set for all methods has been res $= 10^{-6}$. In this Table, we observe that the BIFPAM and MGBNM methods compute the eigenvalues faster than the Krylov-Schur method from a number of eigenvalues equal to 4, being the fastest the MGBNM. This is also observed when we compute one eigenvalue. For 2 and 3 eigenvalues the CPU times obtained with the Krylov-Schur method are smaller than the CHEFSI method and the BIFPAM, while these values are larger than for the MGBNM. In these cases, it is necessary to use higher subspace dimension than 8 for the BIFPAM to obtain better results. For all cases, it is observed that the CHEFSI method does not improve the times obtained with the other block methods and the Krylov-Schur method.

Table 1. Computational times (s) obtained for the NEACRP reactor using the Krylov-Schur method, the BIFPAM, the MGBNM and the CHEFSI method for different number of eigenvalues

n. eigs (q)	Krylov-Schur	BIFPAM	MGBNM	CHEFSI
1	98	65	76	249
2	134	174	108	390
3	135	207	132	390
4	214	153	149	510
5	237	213	185	630

4   Conclusions

The computation of the λ-modes associated with the neutron diffusion equation is interesting for several applications such as the study of the reactor criticality and the development of modal methods. A high order finite element method is used to discretize the λ-modes problem. Different block methods have been studied and compared to solve the algebraical problem obtained from the discretization. These methods have been tested using two 3D benchmark reactors: the IAEA reactor and the NEACRP reactor.

The main conclusion of this work is that the use of block methods is a good strategy alternative to Krylov methods when we are interested in computing a set of dominant eigenvalues. However, the efficiency depends on the type of method. For generalized eigenvalues problems, the BIFPAM, that does not need to solve linear systems, or the MGBNM, that converges with a short number of iterations, are good choices that improve the computational times obtained with the competitive Krylov-Schur method. With respect to the CHEFSI method, due to their implementation for ordinary eigenvalue problems, it needs to solve many linear systems that makes the method inefficient. In future works, a generalization of this method for generalized eigenvalue problems will be studied.

Acknowledgements. This work has been partially supported by Spanish Ministerio de Economía y Competitividad under projects ENE2017-89029-P, MTM2017-85669-P and BES-2015-072901.

References

1. Balay, S., Abhyankar, S., Adams, M., Brune, P., Buschelman, K., Dalcin, L., Gropp, W., Smith, B., Karpeyev, D., Kaushik, D., et al.: PETSc users manual revision 3.7. Technical report, Argonne National Lab (ANL), Argonne, IL, USA (2016)
2. Bangerth, W., Hartmann, R., Kanschat, G.: deal.II - a general purpose object oriented finite element library. ACM Trans. Math. Softw. **33**(4), 24/1–24/27 (2007)
3. Carreño, A., Vidal-Ferrandiz, A., Ginestar, D., Verdú, G.: Multilevel method to compute the lambda modes of the neutron diffusion equation. Appl. Math. Nonlinear Sci. **2**(1), 225–236 (2017)
4. Carreño, A., Vidal-Ferrandiz, A., Ginestar, D., Verdú, G.: Spatial modes for the neutron diffusion equation and their computation. Ann. Nucl. Energy **110**(Supplement C), 1010–1022 (2017)
5. Di Napoli, E., Berljafa, M.: Block iterative eigensolvers for sequences of correlated eigenvalue problems. Comput. Phys. Commun. **184**(11), 2478–2488 (2013)
6. Finnemann, H., Galati, A.: NEACRP 3-D LWR core transient benchmark, final specification (1991)
7. Golub, G., Ye, Q.: An inverse free preconditioned Krylov subspace method for symmetric generalized eigenvalue problems. SIAM J. Sci. Comput. **24**(1), 312–334 (2002)
8. Henry, A.F.: Nuclear Reactor Analysis, vol. 4. MIT press, Cambridge (1975)
9. Hernandez, V., Roman, J.E., Vidal, V.: SLEPc: a scalable and flexible toolkit for the solution of eigenvalue problems. ACM Trans. Math. Softw. **31**(3), 351–362 (2005)

10. Lösche, R., Schwetlick, R., Timmermann, G.: A modified block Newton iteration for approximating an invariant subspace of a symmetric matrix. Linear Algebra Appl. **275**, 381–400 (1998)
11. Quillen, P., Ye, Q.: A block inverse-free preconditioned Krylov subspace method for symmetric generalized eigenvalue problems. J. Comput. Appl. Math. **233**(5), 1298–1313 (2010)
12. Saad, Y.: Numerical Methods for Large Eigenvalue Problems. SIAM, Philadelphia (1992)
13. American Nuclear Society: Argonne Code Center: Benchmark Problem Book. Technical report, ANL-7416, June 1977
14. Stacey, W.M.: Nuclear Reactor Physics. Wiley, Hoboken (2007)
15. Verdú, G., Ginestar, D., Miró, R., Vidal, V.: Using the Jacobi-Davidson method to obtain the dominant Lambda modes of a nuclear power reactor. Ann. Nucl. Energy **32**(11), 1274 1296 (2005)
16. Verdú, G., Miró, R., Ginestar, D., Vidal, V.: The implicit restarted Arnoldi method, an efficient alternative to solve the neutron diffusion equation. Ann. Nucl. Energy **26**(7), 579–593 (1999)
17. Vidal-Ferrandiz, A., Fayez, R., Ginestar, D., Verdú, G.: Solution of the lambda modes problem of a nuclear power reactor using an h-p finite element method. Ann. Nucl. Energy **72**, 338–349 (2014)
18. Zhou, Y., Saad, Y., Tiago, M.L., Chelikowsky, J.R.: Self-consistent-field calculations using Chebyshev-filtered subspace iteration. J. Comput. Phys. **219**(1), 172–184 (2006)

A Versatile Hybrid Agent-Based, Particle and Partial Differential Equations Method to Analyze Vascular Adaptation

Marc Garbey[1,2,3]($\boxtimes$), Stefano Casarin[1,3], and Scott Berceli[4,5]

[1] Houston Methodist Research Institute, Houston, TX, USA
garbeymarc@gmail.com
[2] Department of Surgery, Houston Methodist Hospital, Houston, TX, USA
[3] LaSIE, UMR CNRS 7356, University of La Rochelle, La Rochelle, France
[4] Department of Surgery, University of Florida, Gainesville, FL, USA
[5] Malcom Randall VAMC, Gainesville, FL, USA

Abstract. Failure of peripheral endovascular interventions occurs at the intersection of vascular biology, biomechanics, and clinical decision making. It is our hypothesis that most of the endovascular treatments share the same driving mechanisms during post-surgical follow-up, and accordingly, a deep understanding of them is mandatory in order to improve the current surgical outcome. This work presents a versatile model of vascular adaptation post vein graft bypass intervention to treat arterial occlusions. The goal is to improve the computational models developed so far by effectively modeling the cell-cell and cell-membrane interactions that are recognized to be pivotal elements for the re-organization of the graft's structure. A numerical method is here designed to combine the best features of an Agent-Based Model and a Partial Differential Equations model in order to get as close as possible to the physiological reality while keeping the implementation both simple and general.

Keywords: Vascular adaptation · Particle model
Immersed Boundary Method · PDE model

1 Introduction and Motivation

The insurgence of an arterial localized occlusion, known as Peripheral Arterial Occlusive Disease (PAOD), is one of the potential causes of tissue necrosis and organ failure and it represents one of the main causes of mortality and morbidity in the Western Society [1,3].

In order to restore the physiological circulation, the most performed technique consists into bypassing the occlusion with an autologous vein graft. Benefits and limitations of this procedure are driven by fundamental mecano-biology

NIH UO1 HL119178-01.

processes that take place immediately after the surgical intervention and that fall under the common field of vascular adaptation.

Today the rate of failures of Vein Graft Bypass (VGBs) as treatment for PAODs remains unacceptably high [4], being the graft itself often subjected to the post-surgical re-occlusive phenomenon known as restenosis. It is our belief that the causes of such failures need to be searched for within the multiscale and multifactorial nature of the adaptation that the graft faces in the post-surgical follow-up in response to the environmental conditions variations, a process commonly known as vascular adaptation.

Figure 1 offers a detailed description of the cited nature of adaptation, where sub-sequent and interconnected variations at genetic, cellular and tissue level concur to create a highly interdependent system driven by several feedback loops.

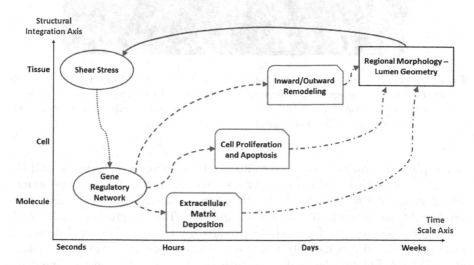

Fig. 1. Multiscale description of vascular adaptation: dynamic interplay between physical forces and gene network that regulates early graft remodeling [7].

The goal of this work is to address the modeling and simulation of the vascular adaptation from a multiscale perspective, by providing a virtual experimental framework to be used to test new clinical hypotheses and to better rank the many factors that promote restenosis. In addition, our hypothesis is that an accurate implementation of the potential forces governing cellular motility during wall re-arrangement is mandatory to obtain a model close enough to the physiological reality. From a qualitative observation of histological evidences, a sample of which is shown in Fig. 2, local distribution of cells across the wall is relatively uniform and we supported that this feature provides some interesting guidances on what the dominant biological mechanism of cellular motility might be.

This study is based on the extensive work carried out by our group on vascular adaptation [5,7] and it represents a big step toward a more accurate replication

Fig. 2. Staining image of a portion of graft's wall: the blue dots identify the cells' nuclei, the stack of images were obtained via confocal microscopy and post-processed in order to correct the artifacts due to the different depths of cells with respect to the plan of visualization. (Color figure online)

of the physiological reality thanks to its ability of taking in account pivotal biological events such as cellular motility and cell-cell, cell-membrane interactions, which in reverse were very difficult to represent with a discrete Agent-Based Model (ABM) implemented on a fixed grid [5]. The adaptation is here replicated on a 2D cross section, a choice justified by the fact that cited data from histology used to qualitatively validate the model are available in the format of a 2D slice. Finally, the model has been cross-validated against a Dynamical System (DS) [11] and the ABM [5] previously cited, a never-trivial feature for a computational model, as it allows to choose the best model to be used according to the purpose of the analysis performed.

2   Methods

In order to replicate the anatomy of the graft, the computational model is organized in 4 sub-domains shown in Fig. 3 that are lumen, tunica intima and media, and external surrounding tissue, where intima and media are separated by the Internal Elastic Lamina (IEL).

The numerical model can be decomposed in three sub-sections respectively corresponding to a software module working on different scales - see Table 1:

– **Mechanical Model (MM):** it locally computes the value of mechanical quantities of interest, such as flow velocity, shear stress, strain energy, *et cetera*.

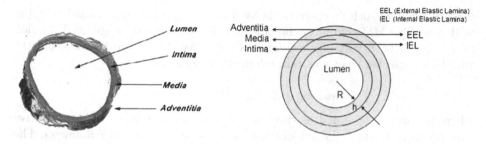

Fig. 3. Morphological structure of a vein graft: between the intima and the media is the Internal Elastic Lamina (IEL) and the External Elastic Lamina (EEL) is between the media and the adventitia [2].

- **Tissue Plasticity (TP):** it defines the driving cellular events, mainly cellular mitosis/apoptosis and matrix deposition/degradation, as stochastic laws driven by constant coefficients.
- **Tissue Remodeling (TR):** it computes the re-organization of the graft structure driven by cellular migration.

Table 1. Multiscale nature of the hybrid model

Space scale versus time scale	Second	Hour	Day
10^{-4} m		TR	TP
10^{-3} m	MM	TR	
10^{-2} m	MM		

The MM is described by a Partial Differential Equations (PDEs) of continuous mechanics [8], TP with an ABM regulating the cells behavior [5,6], and TR by particles moving in a highly viscous incompressible media, which cells motion is computed on the base of a continuum space. The most challenging part is the definition of the forces that drive the cellular motility toward the re-organization of the graft in a way both biologically accurate but also mathematically simple in order to be able to easily calibrate the formula on experimental data for validation purposes. As anticipated in the Introduction, the cornerstone of our model is its multiscale nature and so the numerical discretization and the algorithm implemented for each module will encompass multiple scales both in time and in space detailed in Table 1.

2.1   Mechanical Model (MM)

The blood flow in the lumen is described as a steady incompressible flow that remains constant independently from the inward/outward nature of the remodeling and, accordingly, the standard set of equations of a flow through a pipe was used to simulate such flow across the vein assuming a non-slip condition at the wall [8,9]. The MM computes the flow and the shear stress at the wall, labeled as τ_{wall}, and both variables are updated at every step if the lumen geometry variation is greater than a certain tolerance, in formula:

$$distance(\partial\Omega^{new}_{lumen}, \partial\Omega^{old}_{lumen}) > tol,$$

where distance is intended as the Euclidean distance between two consecutive time points on the same lumen location and $tol \approx 10^{-4}$ m, i.e. a cell diameter. The deformation of the wall can be described both with a thick cylinder approximation, easily computable with a Matlab code [10], or by a Neo-Hookean hyperelastic model, computable by using a finite element technique with FEBio software [9]. The description of the tissue mechanical properties is the one adopted in previous works by our group [5,7,11], and accordingly, being the wall displacement negligible, the strain energy (σ) becomes the main element influencing cellular metabolism within the media. Finally cellular division is driven by the diffusion of a generic Growth Factor (GF) across the wall, which sees in the shear stress its driving force. Denoting it with $G(\tau)$, the GF diffusion is defined as:

$$\frac{\partial G}{\partial t} = c\,\Delta G \ in \ \Omega, \ G_{|\partial\Omega_{lumen}} = F(\tau_{wall}), \ \frac{\partial G}{\partial n}\,|\partial\Omega = 0, \tag{1}$$

where c is the diffusion coefficient.

2.2   Tissue Plasticity (TP)

Cellular and ExtraCellular Matrix (ECM) activity is described with an ABM-based implementation [12], mostly relying on a cellular automata principle governed by stochastic laws, such as each cellular event is associated to a density of probability. We refer to [5,6] for a detailed description of the algorithm, and for completeness, Table 2 provides an axiomatic description of the rules that drive the ABM.

The stochastic model describes how the cellular events depend on the local concentration of the associated GF (1), triggered by shear stress within intima and strain energy within media, creating in this way the bridge between continuum mechanics and TP. Early restenosis is mostly attributable to Intimal Hyperplasia (IH), i.e. an un-controlled growth of the intima toward the lumen, for which a reduction of shear stress stimulates specific GFs to switch their status from quiescent to active. The latter promotes cellular migration toward the intima with subsequent proliferation and deposition of ECM.

To simulate the switching from a normal condition to a perturbed one, representing the response of the system to an environmental conditions variation, the key is to define a so-called basic solution, where the system is stable and regulated by standard conditions that ensure a fair balance both for cellular mitosis/apoptosis and for ECM synthesis/degradation. Intuitively, the basic solution represents a "healthy" vein at time of implant and the perturbed model will evolve driven by mechanical forces in order to recover the perturbation applied

Table 2. Axiomatic description of the set of rules of the ABM

Rule	Variable	Function
$p_{division} = p_{apoptosis} = \alpha_1$	SMC	SMC equilbrium in basic solution
$p_{degradation} = p_{production} = \alpha_2$	ECM	ECM balance in basic solution
$A(t) = \exp{-\frac{t-T}{\delta T}}$; $T = \alpha_3$, $\delta T = \alpha_4$	All	Factor all probability laws by macrophage activity
T and δT	Macrophage	Time of maximum macrophage activity and relaxation time
$p^I_{division} = \alpha_1 A(t)(1 + \alpha_5 \frac{G(\Delta\tau)}{\bar\tau})$	SMC	Probability of SMC division in intima
$p^I_{apoptosis} = \alpha_1 A(t)$	SMC	Probability of SMC apoptosis in intima
$p^I_{production} = \alpha_2 A(t)(1 + \alpha_6 \frac{\Delta\sigma}{\bar\sigma})$	ECM	Probability of ECM production in media
$p^I_{degradation} = \alpha_2 A(t)$	ECM	Probability of ECM degradation in media
$p_{migration} = \alpha_7 A(t)(1 + \alpha_8 \frac{G(\Delta\tau)}{\bar\tau})$	SMC	Probability of SMC migration from intima to media

and to reach back the equilibrium. To simulate the restenosis process, a perturbation of shear stress will be applied in order to promote IH.

2.3   Tissue Remodeling (TR)

The biggest novelty of the model consists into the abandonment of a fixed grid-based structure, used so far [5], in favor of a continuous mechanic description. Accordingly, Smooth Muscular Cells (SMCs) are now described as discs of radius R_{SMC} crawling in a highly viscous flow, and not anymore like dynamic state variables allocated on a static hexagonal grid. As per biological evidences, SMCs can synthetize or degrade ECM, in addition to undergoing mitosis/apoptosis. This generates a source and a sink term respectively in the mass balance that will be used to determine the energy of the structure. The adaptation consists into the response of the structure to an energy unbalance, which sees the reorganization of the system driven by cellular motility in order to recover toward a condition of equilibrium. Remembering that each layer of the graft is bounded by an elastic membrane, the considerations highlighted naturally suggest the use of an Immersed Boundary Method (IBM) [13] in order to simulate the remodeling of the structure, which is so articulated in three phases: (i) an IBM algorithm to take in account SMCs activity and membranes adjustment; (ii) an SMCs motion algorithm; (iii) an inward/outward remodeling algorithm.

IBM Algorithm. A time-split numerical implementation drives the tissue remodeling, meaning that while the TP model is run with a time step of 1 h, the IBM algorithm is run with a variable time step δt that corresponds to the relaxation time of the media with respect to cell division and motility: the larger δt the more cylindrical the graft will end to be. The spatial resolution with step h is linked to the Cartesian nature of the grid and it is chosen to be of the order of a SMC radius. Since the media is described as a highly viscous fluid, we compute the variables V and P, respectively velocity and pressure of the fluid. The IBM algorithm is applied to a square domain $\omega = (0,1)^2 \in \mathbb{R}^2$ in which the vein graft section is embedded. The wall and lumen boundaries of the vein graft and interfaces separating intima from media, see Fig. 3, are described by immersed elastic boundaries: let us denote $\Gamma \in \Omega$ a generic immersed elastic boundary with curvilinear dimension one. X is the Lagrangian position vector of Γ, expressed in the 2-dimensional Cartesian referential. The Lagrangian vector f is the local elastic force density along Γ, also expressed in the Cartesian referential. f is projected onto Ω to get the Eulerian vector field F, that corresponds to the fluid force applied by the immersed elastic boundaries.

If $s \in (0,1)^m$ is the curvilinear coordinate of any points along Γ, and $t \in [0, t_{max}]$ is the time variable, the different mapping can be summarized as it follows:

$$V : (x,t) \in \Omega \times [0, t_{max}] \longrightarrow \mathbb{R}^2$$
$$P : (x,t) \in \Omega \times [0, t_{max}] \longrightarrow \mathbb{R}$$
$$X : (s,t) \in (0,1)^m \times [0, t_{max}] \longrightarrow \Omega$$
$$f : (s,t) \in (0,1)^m \times [0, t_{max}] \longrightarrow \mathbb{R}^2$$
$$F(x,t) \in \Omega \times [0, t_{max}] \longrightarrow \mathbb{R}^2$$

One of the cornerstones of the IBM method is the formulation of the fluid-elasitc interface interaction, which model is unified into a set of coupled Partial Differential Equations (PDEs). To build that, the incompressible Navier-Stokes system writes:

$$\rho \left[\frac{\partial V}{\partial t} + (V \cdot \nabla)V \right] = -\nabla P + \mu \Delta V + F \tag{2}$$

$$\nabla \cdot V = 0 \tag{3}$$

The IBM algorithm requires the extrapolation of the Lagrangian vector f into the Eulerian vector field F from the right end side of (2). For this purpose a distribution of Dirac delta functions δ, is used, such as:

$$F(x,t) = \int_\Gamma f(s,t)\delta(x - X(s,t))\, ds = \begin{cases} f(s,t), & \text{if } x = X(s,t) \\ 0, & \text{otherwise} \end{cases} \tag{4}$$

Its dynamic is regulated with a linear elastic model implemented by using the Hooke law of elasticity, for which the tension of the IB is linear function of the strain energy. The local elastic force density assumes its final form that writes

$$f(s,t) = \sigma \frac{\partial^2 X(s,t)}{\partial s^2}. \tag{5}$$

The IBM algorithm offers dozens of potential possibilities of implementation: the rationale should always be to pursue the right compromise between stability of the scheme and accuracy. Because the fluid is highly viscous, a standard projection scheme for the Navier Stokes equations discretized with finite differences on a staggered grid was used. The momentum equation was discretized with central second order finite differences for the diffusion term and with a method of characteristic for the convective term.

SMC Motility. The second phase of tissue remodeling consists into the computation of SMCs motility. The algorithm to compute the trajectory can be divided in two consecutive steps.

First, SMCs move passively in the matrix by following the media on the base of the local velocity field with the same numerical scheme applied to the discrete point of the immersed boundary, and second, SMCs move also actively driven by multiple potential driving forces, listed below:

- SMCs interact each others. A description of such interactions based on an analogous of the Lennard-Jones potential looks like a smart choice to define an initial framework. Under this hypothesis, during mitosis the two cells may spearate and remain at a distance of about their diameter. This makes the two Lennard-Jones potential coefficients to be cellular size-dependent.
- Further motion of SMCs depends on the gradient of molecules density that are the solution of a reaction-convection diffusion system. Accordingly a generic GF has been introduced with (1) in order to describe the chemotaxis that is originated by the cited gradient.
- Cell motility has a random component that participates to their diffusion through the tissue.
- SMCs may infiltrate area free of cells to preserve the tissue integrity. This motion corresponds to a mechanical homeostasis and it maintains a local balance between SMC and ECM distribution to keep the matrix healthy [14, 15].

The trajectory of a SMC can be so described by tracking its position along time with the following relation:

$$\dot{X} = V_S + V_E + V_G + V_R, \tag{6}$$

where X is the location of the single SMC.

In (6), V_S sums up the repulsive forces between particles. The amplitude of this force decays with the distance and, in first approximation, one can assume a linear decay toward zero in n_S units expressed in cell diameter. Consequently, cell-cell interaction is only possible between elements belonging to the same subdomain, i.e. intima or media, and also interaction is not possible between cells separated by a distance larger than $2\,n_s\,R_{SMC}$, where n_s has been chosen to be of the order of few units.

V_E sums up the attractive forces between the particles that decay linearly as for the cell interaction but in n_e units and become zero above a distance of $2\,n_e\,R_{SMC}$. n_s and n_e have a great influence on the result of the simulation and a deep analysis of them will be useful to address some open problems of the vein graft's biology.

V_G is proportional to the gradient of G that is the generic GF that activates SMC proliferation.

Finally, V_R is a random vector that mimics the noisy character of cell motility. Its intoduction is justified by the assumption that a cell can not move more than a radial unit within the time step δt of the IBM algorithm.

The strong feature of the method here proposed is that it allows us to implement all these elements that are known to play a key role at biological level and to also test several combinations of them. However, compared to our previous ABM [5], the number of unknown parameters used to describe the new cellular motility module grows proportionally with the level of closeness of the model to the physiological reality, and accordingly, a non-linear stability analysis will be needed to find the trade-off between complexity and accuracy as already done in [6].

Inward - Outward Membrane Motion Adjustment. An *ad hoc* adjustment is needed in order to prevent the structure to always promote outward remodeling, seen the incompressibility of the lumen medium. The hypothesis is so that the tissue accommodates to the transmural pressure that is a combination of blood pressure and external pressure from the surrounding tissue toward a state that gives less mechanical stress on cells. This adjustment is still driven by an energy minimization logic, for which at each cycle, the mechanical energy of the wall is computed with the MM and the sign of a sink/source term is decided in accordance with the sign of the derivative that minimizes said energy. Finally, in order to improve the model, we need to consider (i) that macrophages in the wall can be treated with the same framework but of course by adjusting the related parameters; (ii) that the IEL has a certain porosity allowing SMCs to pass through and (iii) that the volume of a "daughter" cell can increase in time.

3   Plan of Simulations

As previously mentioned, a basic solution needs to be retrieved in order to serve as baseline point for the vascular adaptation simulation. The setup to retrieve it and the rationale for the representation of the results are the same already used in [6], and the same is valid for IH, which was then simulated by studying both its early phase (1 day follow up) and its late phase (1 month). After all, a comparison between the two phases is important in order to distinguish the different impact of the several aims of SMCs motility.

Finally, a cross validation between the presented model and a DS developed by our group [11] has been performed on a 4 months follow-up as also done for the original ABM [5] with the motivations highlighted in the Introduction.

In order to perform the cross validation, the DS has been setup with a 50% decrease in shear stress from the baseline value to foster the hyperplasia with initial graft (R), lumen (r), and IEL (re) respectively equal to R = 0.2915, re = 0.2810, and r = 0.2387, all expressed in mm. It is finally important to recall how, in order to calibrate the DS on the new PDE model, the distance between the two models' output, temporal intimal area dynamic in this case, has been minimized by using a Genetic Algorithm (GA).

4   Results

Figure 4(a) shows the generation of the basic solution. Each red dot corresponds to a SMC, while the green circle individuates the IEL. It is important to recall how our modeling effort has been driven by the pursuit of a graft's cross section that shows a uniform distribution of cells across the wall also free from isolated cells occurrence. Already the replication of the initial condition represents a good approximation of the graft's histology. The analysis of the early stage of hyperplasia offers a nice overview of how the accuracy of the model grows along with the number of forces driving SMCs motion implemented. Here SMCs in intima and media are respectively individuated by a red and a black circle, while the IEL lamina is still shown in light green.

Figure 4(b) reports a first example of early stage of IH, where the random motion is the only component driving the adaptation of the strucures. As it is clear from the figure, a uniform distribution of SMCs is not reached in the intima as instead retrievable from a comparison with histology and this is mainly caused by the motion restriction that affects SMCs because of the reduced initial thickness of the intima. By adding the repulsive cell-cell interaction, the distribution of SMCs gets more uniform, as appreciable in Fig. 4(c), even though the formation of clusters that will eventually be trapped in pockets of the lumen wall and there confined by the membrane's tension is still clearly visible. Also important to point out is the tendency that some areas of ECM with no SMCs have to

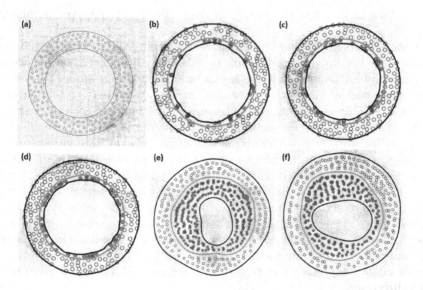

Fig. 4. Cross Section of the vein graft reported in (a) basic solution, i.e. healthy vein condition; early stage of hyperplasia progressively adding up (b) random motion, (c) cell-cell repulsion, and (d) matrix invasion forces; late phase of hyperplasia encroaching the lumen affected by (e) vertical and (f) horizontal stretching of the lumen itself. (Color figure online)

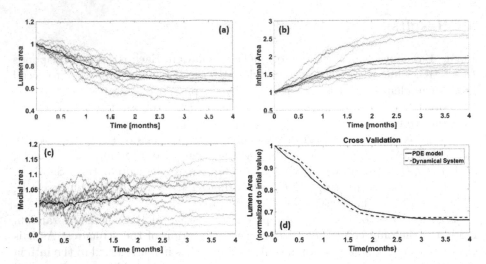

Fig. 5. Intimal Hyperplasia - long term follow-up: temporal dynamic of (a) lumen area, (b) intimal area, and (c) medial area are represented on a 4 months follow-up. Each plot is normalized on the initial value and the output evaluated by taking the average trend (black bold line) out of 10 independent simulation (color lines). Finally, as cross validation in (d), the Dynamical System is calibrated on the mean output of the PDE model (solid line) against the mean output of the DS (dashed line). (Color figure online)

form, taking in this way the model far from the reality observed at histology level.

A more uniform distribution is reached by adding the matrix invasion term as shown in Fig. 4(d), corroborating in this way the belief that an accurate description of SMCs motion is the key in order to obtain a model close enough to the physiological reality. As side consideration, accordingly to the purpose of this work, SMCs proliferation within the media has not been activated, and so it was to be expected a regular uniform distribution of cell within the media layer.

Figure 4(e) and (f) report the result of two independent simulations run with a follow-up of 4 months in order to study the late phase of IH. It is interesting to see how the SMCs distribution retains its asymmetric character, either in a vertical or in a horizontal direction, even though it is not clear if this is justified at histological level or not. If necessary, to promote radial symmetry, a potential solution will be to suppose that SMCs motility has a preferred motion in the direction orthogonal to the radius in order to align the cell arrangement with the dominant radial strain energy. Coupled to it, an increase in the relaxation time dt might be another way to further incentivize SMCs distribution toward radial direction.

Finally, in order to cross-validate the DS and the PDE model, the first step was to reproduce the qualitative patterns of IH with this latter, the results of which can be appreciated in Fig. 5, where the temporal dynamic of lumen area (a), intimal area (b), and medial area (c) are represented. It is useful to remark how, in every panel, each independent simulation is marked with a different color and the average trend, in bold black line, serves as representative one. Finally, the result of the calibration, taking as output the temporal dynamic of lumen area, is reported in Fig. 5(d), showing a high level of accuracy with a percentile error lower than 2%.

5   Conclusion

In the current work, a model of vascular adaptation has been implemented as a generalization of a previous ABM developed by our group. With the new approach we abated the limitation imposed by the use of a fixed grid by using a technique that relies almost entirely on PDEs and differential equation to compute the plasticity of the wall and the motility of the cells. As appreciated in the Results section, the key point to obtain an accurate model consists into the right definition of the forces that drive SMCs motion and of course in their effective implementation. After all, one of the power of the model is exactly its ability to test different hypothesis at computational level in a short time and in an effective way. Two evidences can be learn from our model. First, to consider the invasion of the matrix operated by SMCs is pivotal to maintain mechanical homeostasis [15] and consequently to reproduce experimental data accurately. Second, the definition of the distance threshold that operates the different cell-cell interaction forces are as much important. The obvious next step is the extension of the model toward the third dimension along with an extensive study of data from histology in order to better reconstruct the initial structure of the vein. Finally, the recent work published by Browning et al. [16], based on prostate cancer cell lines, gives an excellent example of what should come next in this vascular adaptation study. Further validation of the model with quantitative metrics on density map of cell migration an spatially accurate proliferation and apoptosis rate is underway and will require extensive post-processing of our experimental data set.

References

1. Go, A.S., American Heart Association Statistics Committee and Stroke Statistics Subcommittee, et al.: Heart disease and stroke statistics - 2014 update: a report from the American Heart Association. Circulation **129**(3), e228–e292 (2014)
2. Jiang, Z., et al.: A novel vein graft model: adaptation to differential flow environments. Am. J. Physiol. - Heart Circ. Physiol. **286**(1), H240–H245 (2004)
3. Roger, V.L., et al.: Heart disease and stroke statistics - 2012 update: a report from the American Heart Association. Circulation **125**(1), e2–e220 (2012)
4. Harskamp, R.E., et al.: Saphenous vein graft failure and clinical outcomes: toward a surro-gate end point in patients following coronary artery bypass surgery. Am. Heart J. **165**, 639–643 (2013)
5. Garbey, M., et al.: Vascular adaptation: pattern formation and cross validation between an agent based model and a dynamical system. J. Theoret. Biol. **429**, 149–163 (2017)

6. Garbey, M., et al.: A multiscale computational framework to understand vascular adaptation. J. Comput. Sci. **8**, 32–47 (2015)
7. Casarin, S., et al.: Linking gene dynamics to vascular hyperplasia - toward a predictive model of vein graft adaptation. PLoS ONE **12**(11), e0187606 (2017)
8. White, F.T.: Viscous Fluid Flow. McGraw-Hill Series in Mechanical Engineering, 2nd edn. McGraw-Hill, New York City (1991)
9. Maas, S.A., et al.: FEBio: finite elements for biomechanics. J. Biomech. Eng. **134**(1), 011005 (2012)
10. Zhao, W., et al.: On thick-walled cylinder under internal pressure. J. Press. Vessel Technol. **125**, 267–273 (2003)
11. Garbey, M., et al.: A multiscale, dynamical system that describes vein graft adaptation and failure. J. Theoret. Biol. **335**, 209–220 (2013)
12. Deutsch, A., et al.: Cellular Automaton Modeling of Biological Pattern Formation. Birkhuser, Boston (2005)
13. Peskin, C.S.: The immersed boundary method. Acta Numer. **11**, 479–517 (2002)
14. Quaranta, V.: Cell migration through extracellular matrix: membrane-type metalloprotein-ases make the way. J. Cell Biol. **149**, 1167–1170 (2000)
15. Humphrey, J.D., et al.: Mechanotransduction and extracellular matrix homeostasis. Nat. Rev. Mol. Cell Biol. **15**(12), 802–812 (2014)
16. Browning, A.P., et al.: Inferring parameters for a lattice-free model of cell migration and proliferation using experimental data. J. Theoret. Biol. **437**, 251–260 (2018)

Development of a Multiscale Simulation Approach for Forced Migration

Derek Groen[(✉)]

Brunel University London, Kingston Lane, London UB8 3PH, UK
Derek.Groen@brunel.ac.uk
http://people.brunel.ac.uk/~csstddg/

Abstract. In this work I reflect on the development of a multiscale simulation approach for forced migration, and present two prototypes which extend the existing Flee agent-based modelling code. These include one extension for parallelizing Flee and one for multiscale coupling. I provide an overview of both extensions and present performance and scalability results of these implementations in a desktop environment.

Keywords: Multiscale simulation · Refugee movements
Agent-based modelling · Parallel computing · Multiscale computing

1 Introduction

In recent years, more and more people have been forcibly displaced from their homes [1], with the number spiraling to over 65 million in 2017. The causes of these displacements are wide-ranging, and can include armed conflict, environmental disasters, or severe economic circumstances [2]. Computational models have been used extensively to study forced migration (e.g., [3,4]), and in particular agent-based modelling has been increasingly applied to provide insights into these processes [5–7]. These insights are important because they could be used to aid the allocation of humanitarian resources or to estimate the effects of policy decisions such as border closures [8].

We have previously presented a simulation development approach to predict the destinations of refugees moving away from armed conflict [9]. The simulations developed using this approach rely on the publicly available Flee agent-based modelling code (www.github.com/djgroen/flee-release), and have been shown to predict 75% of the refugee destinations correctly in three recent conflicts in Africa [9].

An important limitation of our existing approach is the inability to predict *how many* refugees emerge from a given conflict event at a given location. In a preliminary study, we approached this problem from a data science perspective with limited success [10], and as a result we are now exploring the use of simulation. As part of this broader effort, I have adapted the Flee code to enable (a) the parallel execution for superior performance, and (b) the coupling to additional

© Springer International Publishing AG, part of Springer Nature 2018
Y. Shi et al. (Eds.): ICCS 2018, LNCS 10861, pp. 869–875, 2018.
https://doi.org/10.1007/978-3-319-93701-4_69

models. The latter aspect is essential as it allows us to connect simulations of smaller scale population movements, e.g. of people escaping a city of conflict, with simulations of larger scale population movements, e.g. refugee movements nationwide.

In this work, I present the established prototypes to enable parallel, multi-scale simulations of forced migration in this context. In Sect. 2 I discuss the effort on parallelizing Flee, and in Sect. 3 the effort on creating a coupling interface for multiscale modelling. In Sect. 4 I present some preliminary performance results, and in Sect. 5 I reflect on the current progress and its wider implications.

2   Prototype I: A Parallelized Flee

As a first step, I have implemented a parallelized prototype version of the Flee kernel, which is described in detail by Suleimenova et al. [9]. The Flee code is a fairly basic agent-based modelling kernel written in Python 3, and our parallel version relies on the MPI4Py module. In this prototype version, I prioritized simplicity over scalability, and seek to investigate how far I can scale the code, while retaining a simple code base. Overall, the whole parallel implementation is contained within a single file (pflee.py) which extends the base Flee classes and contains less than 300 lines of code at time of writing.

2.1   Parallelization Approach

Within this Flee prototype I chose to parallelize by distributing the agents across processes in equal amounts, regardless of their location. The base function to accomplish this is very simplistic:

```
def addAgent(self, location):
    self.total_agents += 1
    if self.total_agents % self.mpi.size == self.mpi.rank:
        self.agents.append(Person(location))
```

Here, the total number or processes is given by self.mpi.size, and the rank of the current process by self.mpi.rank. I can instantly identify on which process a given agent resides, by using the agent index in conjunction with the "% self.mpi.size" operator.

Compared to existing spatial decomposition approaches (e.g., as used in RePast HPC [11]), our approach has the advantage that both tracking the agents and balancing the computational load is more straightforward. However, it has major disadvantages in that it currently does not support directly interacting agents (agents only interact indirectly through modifying location properties). Adding such interactions would require additional collective communications in the simulation. In the case of Flee, this limitation is not an issue, but it can become a bottleneck for codes with more extensive agent rule sets. Additionally, a limitation of this approach is that the location graph needs to be duplicated across each process, which can become a memory bottleneck for extremely large location graphs.

2.2 Parallel Evolution of the System

The evolve() algorithm, which propagates the system by one time step is structured as follows (functions specific to the parallel implementation are italicized):

1. Update location scores (which determine the attractiveness of locations to
   agents).
2. Evolve all agents on local process.
3. *Aggregate Agent totals across processes.*
4. Complete the travel, for agents that have not done so already.
5. *Aggregate Agent totals across processes.*
6. Increment simulated time counter.

One requires two *MPI_AllGather()* operations per iteration loop. Our existing
refugee simulations currently require 300–1000 iterations per simulation, which
would result in 600–2000 AllGather operations. As these operations require all
processes to synchronize, I would expect them to become a bottleneck at very
large core counts.

3 Prototype II: A Multiscale Flee Model

As a second step, I have implemented a multiscale prototype version of the Flee
kernel. In this prototype version, I again prioritized simplicity over scalability.
Overall, our multiscale implementation is contained within a single file (cou-
pling.py) which accompanies the base flee classes (serial or parallel, depending
on the user preference). The multiscale implementation contains less than 200
lines of code at time of writing.

In the multiscale application, individual locations in the location graph are
registered as *coupled locations*. Any agents arriving at these locations in the
microscale model will then be passed on to the macroscale model using the
coupling interface. The coupling interval is set to 1:1 for purposes of the performance tests performed here (to ease the comparison with single scale performance results), but it is possible to perform multiple iterations in the microscale
submodel for each iteration in the macroscale submodel by changing the coupling interval value. This would then result not only in different spatial scales,
but also differing time scales. In the prototype implementation, the coupling
is performed using file transfers, where at each time step both models write
their agents to file and read the files of the other model for incoming agents.
As a result, two-way coupling is possible, and both models are run concurrently
during the simulation.

In our implementation, the coupling interface is set up as follows:

```
c = coupling.CouplingInterface(e)
c.setCouplingFilenames("in","out")
if(submodel_id > 0):
    c.setCouplingFilenames("out","in")
```

And the coupled locations are registered using a c.addCoupledLocation(), which is called once for each location to be coupled. During the main execution loop, after all other computations have been performed, the coupling activities are initiated using the function c.Couple(t), where t is the current simulated time in days.

4   Tests and Results

In this section I present results from two sets of performance tests, one to determine the speedup of the parallel implementation, and one to test the speedup of the multiscale implementation. All tests were performed on a desktop machine with an Intel i5-4590 processor with 4 physical cores and no hyper-threading technology.

For our tests, I used a simplified location graph, presented in Fig. 1. Note that the size of the location graph only has a limited effect on the computational cost overall, as agents are only aware of locations that are directly connected to their current location.

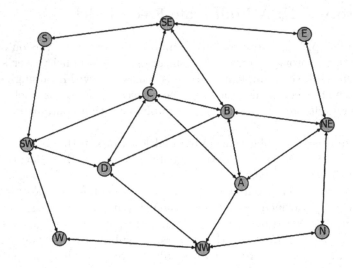

Fig. 1. Location graph of the microscale agent-based model. The location graph of the macroscale agent-based model has a similar level of complexity. This graph was visualized automatically using the Python-based **networkx** package.

4.1   Parallel Performance Tests

In these tests I run a single instance of Flee on the desktop using 1, 2 or 4 processes. I measured the time to completion for the whole simulation using 10000 agents, 100000 agents and one million agents, and present the corresponding results in Table 1. Based on these measurements, Flee is able to obtain a speedup between 2.53 and 3.44 for $p = 4$, depending on the problem size. This indicates that the chosen method of parallelization delivers a quicker time to completion, despite its simplistic nature. However, it is likely that the slow single-core performance of Python codes result in apparent better scaling performance when such codes are parallelized. Consequently, I would expect the obtained speedup to be somewhat lower if this exact strategy were to be applied to a C or Fortran-based implementation of Flee. Given the low temporal density of communications per time step (time steps complete in >0.13 s wall-clock time in our run, during which only two communications take place), it is unlikely that the scalability would be significantly reduced if these tests were to be performed across two interconnected nodes.

Table 1. Scalability results from the Flee prototype. All runs were performed for 10 time steps (production runs typically require 300–1000 time steps). Runs using 8 processes on 4 physical cores did not deliver any additional speedup.

Agents # of	Processes (p) # of	Time to completion [s]	Speedup
10000	1	3.325	1.0
10000	2	1.770	1.88
10000	4	1.315	2.53
100000	1	29.26	1.0
100000	2	14.63	2.0
100000	4	8.896	3.29
1000000	1	277.1	1.0
1000000	2	142.7	1.94
1000000	4	80.58	3.44

4.2 Multiscale Performance Tests

In these tests I run two coupled instances of Flee on the desktop using 1, 2 or 4 processes each. Runs using 4 processes each feature 2 processes per physical core. I measured the time to completion for the whole simulation using 10000 agents, 100000 agents and one million agents, which were inserted in the microscale simulation, but gradually migrated to the macroscale simulation using the coupling interface.

I present the results from the multiscale performance tests in Table 2. Here the multiscale simulations scale up excellently from $1 + 1$ to $2 + 2$ processes, given that the model contains at least 100000 agents. Further speedup can be obtained by mapping 8 processes $(4 + 4)$ to the 4 physical cores (i.e. 2 threads per core), leading to a speedup of 2.9 for coupled models with 1000000 agents in total. This additional scaling is surprising because the cores do not support hyper-threading themselves, but could indicate that individual processes can frequently run at high efficiency even when less than 100% of the CPU capacity is available.

Table 2. Multiscale performance results using two Flee prototype instances. All runs were performed for 10 time steps (production runs typically require 300–1000 time steps). Note: runs using $4 + 4$ processes were performed using only 4 physical cores.

Agents # of	Processes (p) # of	Time to completion [s]	Speedup
10000	$1 + 1$	4.016	1.0
10000	$2 + 2$	2.436	1.65
10000	$4 + 4^*$	2.241	1.79
100000	$1 + 1$	31.08	1.0
100000	$2 + 2$	16.17	1.92
100000	$4 + 4^*$	14.07	2.21
1000000	$1 + 1$	326.7	1.0
1000000	$2 + 2$	161.4	2.02
1000000	$4 + 4^*$	112.8	2.90

Given that both the single scale and multiscale simulations have the same number of agents in the system, it is clear that the multiscale coupling introduces additional overhead. This is because multiscale simulations rely on two Flee instances to execute, and because file synchronization (reading and writing to the local file system) is performed at every time step between the instances. It is possible to estimate the total multiscale overhead by comparing the fastest single scale simulation for each problem size with the fastest multiscale simulation for each problem size. In doing so, I find that the overhead is smaller for larger problem sizes, ranging from 70% (2.241 vs 1.315) for simulations with 10000 agents to 40% (112.8 vs 80.58) for those with 100000 agents.

5   Discussion

In this work I have presented two prototype extensions to the Flee code, to enable respectively parallel execution and multiscale coupling. The parallel implementation delivers reasonable speedup when using a single node, but is likely to require further effort in order to make Flee scale efficiently on larger clusters and supercomputers. However, uncertainty quantification and sensitivity analysis are essential in agent-based models, and even basic production runs require 100 s of instances to cover the essential areas for sensitivity analysis. As such, even a modestly effective parallel implementation can enable a range of Flee replicas to efficiently use large computational resources. The multiscale coupling interface enables users to combine two Flee simulations (and theoretically more than two), using one to resolve small scale population movements, and one to resolve large scale movements. Through the use of a plain text file format (.csv), it also becomes possible to couple Flee to other models. However, this implementation is still in its infancy, as the coupling overhead is relatively large (40–70%) and the range of coupling methods very limited (file exchange only). Indeed, the aim now will be to integrate the Flee coupling with more mature coupling software such as MUSCLE2 [12], to enable more flexible and scalable multiscale simulations, using supercomputers and other large computational resources.

A last observation is in regards to the development time required to create these extensions. Using MPI4Py, I found that both the parallel implementation and the coupling interface took very little time to implement. In total, I spent less than 40 person hours of development effort.

Acknowledgements. I am grateful to Robin Richardson from UCL for his comments on the draft of this manuscript. This work was performed within the wider context of the EU H2020 project "Computing Patterns for High Performance Multiscale Computing" (ComPat, grant no. 671564).

References

1. UNHCR: Figures at a glance. United Nations High Commissioner for Refugees (2017). http://www.unhcr.org/uk/figures-at-a-glance.html
2. Moore, W.H., Shellman, S.M.: Whither will they go? A global study of refugees destinations, 1965–1995. Int. Stud. Q. **51**(4), 811–834 (2007)
3. Willekens, F.: Migration flows: measurement, analysis and modeling. In: White, M.J. (ed.) International Handbook of Migration and Population Distribution. IHP, vol. 6, pp. 225–241. Springer, Dordrecht (2016). https://doi.org/10.1007/978-94-017-7282-2_11
4. Shellman, S.M., Stewart, B.M.: Predicting risk factors associated with forced migration: an early warning model of Haitian flight. Civ. Wars **9**(2), 174–199 (2007)
5. Kniveton, D., Smith, C., Wood, S.: Agent-based model simulations of future changes in migration flows for Burkina Faso. Global Environ. Change **21**, 34–40 (2011)
6. Johnson, R.T., Lampe, T.A., Seichter, S.: Calibration of an agent-based simulation model depicting a refugee camp scenario. In: Proceedings of the 2009 Winter Simulation Conference (WSC), pp. 1778–1786 (2009)
7. Sokolowski, J.A., Banks, C.M.: A methodology for environment and agent development to model population displacement. In: Proceedings of the 2014 Symposium on Agent Directed Simulation (2014)
8. Groen, D.: Simulating refugee movements: where would you go? Proc. Comput. Sci. **80**, 2251–2255 (2016)
9. Suleimenova, D., Bell, D., Groen, D.: A generalized simulation development approach for predicting refugee destinations. Sci. Rep. **7**, 13377 (2017)
10. Chan, N.T., Suleimenova, D., Bell, D., Groen, D.: Modelling refugees escaping violent events: a feasibility study from an input data perspective. In: Proceedings of the Operational Research Society Simulation Workshop (SW18) (2018). (in press)
11. Collier, N., North, M.: Repast HPC: a platform for large-scale agentbased modeling. Large-Scale Comput. Tech. Complex Syst. Simul. 81–110 (2011)
12. Borgdorff, J., Mamonski, M., Bosak, B., Kurowski, K., Belgacem, M.B., Chopard, B., Groen, D., Coveney, P., Hoekstra, A.: Distributed multiscale computing with muscle 2, the multiscale coupling library and environment. J. Comput. Sci. **5**(5), 719–731 (2014)

Author Index